Focus on NURSING PHARMACOLOGY

Amy M. Karch, RN, MS
Assistant Professor of Clinical Nursing
University of Rochester School of Nursing
Rochester, New York

Lippincott
Philadelphia • New York • Baltimore

Acquisitions Editor: Margaret Zuccarini
Assistant Editor: Helen Kogut
Senior Project Editor: Tom Gibbons
Senior Production Manager: Helen Ewan
Production Coordinator: Nannette Winski
Design Coordinator: Brett MacNaughton
Indexer: Michael Ferreira

The author and the publisher have endeavored to ensure that Web sites listed in the text were active prior to publication. However, due to the Internet's evolving nature, Web addresses may have changed or sites may have ceased to exist since publication.

Library of Congress Cataloging-in-Publication Data

Karch, Amy Morrison, 1949-
Focus on nursing pharmacology / Amy M. Karch.
p. ; cm.
Includes bibliographical references and index.
ISBN 0-7817-1835-X (alk. paper)
1. Pharmacology. 2. Nursing. I. Title
[DNLM: 1. Pharmaceutical Preparations—Nurses' Instruction. 2. Drug Therapy—Nurses' Instruction. 3. Pharmacology—Nurses' Instruction. QV 4 K183f 2000]
RM300 .K37 2000
615.1—dc21

99-046440

Care has been taken to confirm the accuracy of the information presented and to describe generally accepted practices. However, the authors, editors, and publisher are not responsible for errors or omissions or for any consequences from application of the information in this book and make no warranty, express or implied, with respect to the contents of the publication.

The authors, editors and publisher have exerted every effort to ensure that drug selection and dosage set forth in this text are in accordance with current recommendations and practice at the time of publication. However, in view of ongoing research, changes in government regulations, and the constant flow of information relating to drug therapy and drug reactions, the reader is urged to check the package insert for each drug for any change in indications and dosage and for added warnings and precautions. This is particularly important when the recommended agent is a new or infrequently employed drug.

Some drugs and medical devices presented in this publication have Food and Drug Administration (FDA) clearance for limited use in restricted research settings. It is the responsibility of the health care provider to ascertain the FDA status of each drug or device planned for use in their clinical practice.

9 8 7 6 5 4 3 2 1

Dedicated to my best friend and soulmate,
my husband Fred,
for all of his support, encouragement,
constructive criticism, patient teaching, and love.

Reviewers

Jean Krajicek Bartek, PhD, ARNP
Associate Professor
University of Nebraska Medical Colleges of Nursing and Medicine
Omaha, Nebraska

Barbara F. Bell, RN, MSEd, MSN
Professor of Nursing
New Mexico Junior College
Hobbs, New Mexico

Joyce S. Billue, EdD, RN, CS, RNP
Associate Professor
Community Nursing Medical College of Georgia
Augusta, Georgia

Patricia A. Dickman, BA, RN
Nursing Instructor
BM Spurr School of Practical Nursing
Glen Dale, West Virginia

Margaret H. Doherty, RN, MS, CCRN
Instructor, Department of Nursing
Sonoma State University
Rohnert Park, California

Mary Fenimore, AAS, BS, MA, EdD
Professor of Nursing
Pasco-Hernando Community College
New Port Richey, Florida

Kathryn J. Gaspard, PhD
Senior Lecturer
University of Wisconsin—Milwaukee
School of Nursing
Milwaukee, Wisconsin

Pauline M. Green, PhD, RN
Associate Professor
Howard University Division of Nursing
Washington, District of Columbia

Ruth N. Grendell, DNSc, RN
Professor of Nursing
Point Loma Nazarene University
San Diego, California

Mary Rebecca Harry, RN, BSN, MEd
Nursing Instructor
Crowder College
Neosho, Missouri

Mervin R. Helmuth, RN, MN
Associate Professor of Nursing
Goshen College
Goshen, Indiana

Juliette Kruse, RN, MS
Clinical Instructor
San Francisco State University
San Francisco, California

Carol Ann Barnett Lammon, RN, BSN, MSN
Assistant Professor of Nursing
University of Alabama
Tuscaloosa, Alabama

Renee Lewis, MS, RN, CCRN
Professor of Nursing Science
Rose State College
Midwest City, Oklahoma

Wanda K. Mohr, PhD, RNC
Assistant Professor
University of Pennsylvania
School of Nursing
Philadelphia, Pennsylvania

Dorothy M. Obester, PhD, RN, MSN, BSNE
Professor of Nursing
St. Francis College
Loretto, Pennsylvania

Sally P. Scavone, RN, BSN, MS
Associate Professor
Erie Community College/City Campus
Buffalo, New York

Cynthia V. Sommer, PhD, MT (ASCP)
Associate Professor
Department of Biological Sciences
University of Wisconsin—Milwaukee
Milwaukee, Wisconsin

Patricia A. Stockert, RN, MS
Associate Professor
Saint Francis Medical Center College of Nursing
Peoria, Illinois

Eva Streetz, RN, BSN, MSN
Instructor
Long Beach City College
Long Beach, California

Preface

Pharmacology is a difficult course to teach in a standard nursing curriculum, whether it is a diploma, associate, baccalaureate, or graduate program. Teachers are difficult to find, and time and money often dictate that the invaluable content of such a course is incorporated into other courses. As a result, the content is often lost. At the same time, changes in medical care delivery—more outpatient and home care, shorter hospital stays, and more self-care—have resulted in additional legal and professional responsibilities for nurses, making them more responsible for the safe and effective delivery of drug therapy. Pharmacology should not be such a formidable obstacle in nursing curriculum. The study of drug therapy incorporates physiology, pathophysiology, chemistry, and nursing fundamentals—subjects that are already taught in most schools. A textbook that approaches pharmacology as an understandable, teachable, and learnable subject would greatly facilitate the incorporation of this subject into nursing curricula. Yet many nursing pharmacology texts are large and burdensome, mainly because they have needed to cover not only the basic pharmacology but also the particulars included in each area considered.

The concept for this text is based on the availability of annually published nursing drug guides, which cover all the information that a nursing student or nurse should need to know about each individual drug and which then can serve as the ideal companion to a basic nursing pharmacology text. By removing the laborious information on each drug and referring students to the nursing drug guide (which could then be used directly in patient care and care planning), the nursing pharmacology text becomes a succinct, practical book that allows students to learn the concepts involved in the study of pharmacology without overwhelming them with thousands of specific drug details.

With this goal in mind, *Focus on Nursing Pharmacology* provides a concise, user-friendly, and uncluttered text with a study guide package for the modern student. This difficult subject is presented in a streamlined, understandable, teachable, and learnable manner. Because this book is designed to be used in conjunction with a handbook of current drug information, it avoids clutter by focusing on "need-to-understand" content and by directing the student to refer to a nursing drug guide for specific, current, and up-to-date drug details.

The text reviews and integrates previously learned knowledge of physiology, chemistry, and nursing fundamentals into chapters focused on helping students conceptualize what is important to know about each group of drugs. Line art and tabular information summarize pertinent concepts, thereby facilitating student learning. Special features further focus student learning on clinical application, critical thinking, and patient teaching. In addition, a CD-ROM containing more than 700 drug monographs is included with the text, providing a "comfortable" source of specific drug detail when the student is ready to assimilate that detail. Finally, more than 130 pages of study guide activities are included within this unique, all-in-one educational resource for teaching and learning nursing pharmacology.

ORGANIZATION

The organization of *Focus on Nursing Pharmacology* is based on the "simple to complex" approach, much like the syllabus for a basic nursing pharmacology course. Because students learn best "from the bottom up," Part 1 begins with an overview of basic nursing pharmacology. Building upon this foundation, Part 2 introduces the teaching of drug classes, starting with the chemotherapeutic agents—both antimicrobial and antineoplastic drugs. Because the effectiveness of these drugs depends on their interference with the most basic element of body physiology—the cell—students can easily understand the pharmacology of this class. Mastering the pharmacotherapeutic effects of this drug class helps establish a firm grasp of the basic principles taught in Part 1. Once the easiest pharmacological concepts are understood, the student is prepared to move on to the more challenging physiologic and pharmacologic concepts.

In Part 3, the immune system drugs are taught because recent knowledge about the immune system has made it the cornerstone of modern therapy. All of the immune system drugs act in ways that the immune system would itself if it were able. Recent immunological research has contributed to much greater understanding of this system, making it important to position information about drugs affecting this system close to the beginning of the text, instead of at the end as has been customary.

Parts 4 and 5 of the text address drugs that affect the nervous system, the basic functioning system of the body. Following the nervous system, and closely related to it, is the endocrine system and associated drug classes in Part 6. The sequence of these parts introduces students to the concept of control, teaches them about the interrelatedness of these two systems, and prepares them for understanding many aspects of shared physiological function and the inevitable linking of the two systems into one: the neuroendocrine system.

Parts 7, 8, and 9 discuss drugs affecting the reproductive, cardiovascular, and renal systems, respectively. The sequencing of cardiovascular and renal drugs is logical because most of the augmenting cardiovascular drugs (such as diuretics) affect the renal system. Part 10 covers respiratory system drugs, which provide the link between the left and right ventricles of the heart. Part 11 addresses drugs acting on the gastrointestinal system. The GI system stands on its own; it does not share any actions or interactions with any other system.

TEXT FEATURES

The features in *Focus on Nursing Pharmacology* are designed to skillfully support the text discussion, encouraging the student to look at the whole patient and to focus on the essence of information that is important to learn about each drug class, thereby enhancing the student's learning potential.

TERMS

- **Chapter pedagogy** includes a drug list, chapter outline, key term list, chapter introduction, bulleted chapter summary, and bibliography to guide student learning, focusing on the seminal information presented in each chapter. In the Nursing Considerations section, italics highlight the rationale for each nursing intervention. In the chapter drug list, a **P** appears next to each drug that is considered to be the prototype for its specific class. A glossary at the end of the text defines all key terms.
- **In-text drug summary tables** clearly identify the drugs within a class, highlighting them by generic and brand names and usual indications. A **P** appears next to each drug that is considered to be the prototype for its specific class in these tables.

DATA LINK **Data Link icons** direct the student to the generic drug name that can be used to quickly access more detailed drug monograph information in the nursing drug guide.

WWW.WEB LINKS **Web link icons** alert the student to electronic sources of drug information and drug therapy for specific diseases.

- **Nursing Challenges** teach the student the salient and sometimes life-preserving nursing interventions for a specific drug or drug therapy.
- **Cultural/Gender/Life-Span Considerations** encourage the student to consider the patient as a unique individual with a special set of characteristics that not only can influence variations in drug effectiveness, but also can impact the patient's perspective on drug therapy.
- **Nursing Care Guides** present general guidelines related to the nursing management of drug therapy for a particular class of drugs.
- **Patient Teaching Checklists** provide a basic framework for creating a customized patient education plan.
- **Case Studies** illustrate clinical application of drugs, drug effects, and patient variations for a specific drug.
- A **Student Study Guide** is included at the end of the text, providing an immediate opportunity to apply the principles learned in each chapter. The combined text and study guide package offers ample opportunity for study and review for every student using this text.

DATA LINK A **CD-Rom** presents more than 700 drug monographs for easy reference to drug details needed for quality patient care. It also allows the student to formulate a customized patient teaching plan for any of the 700 drugs. In addition, it contains information on Canadian drug names and laws; appendix-like information on vitamins, parenterals, and other drugs; and the answer key for the student Study Guide questions.

ANCILLARY PACKAGE

For Students

- Student Study Guide—is organized chapter by chapter to match the text and provides creative interactive learning experiences to enhance the 'real' learning your students will enjoy when using this text and study guide package. Many activities involve learning to use drug information resources available on the Web and so work to expand the power of your students to access and critique the availability and quality of drug information on the Web.

DATA LINK CD-ROM—provides full access to more than 750 drug monographs and more than 8000 drugs contained in the unique appendices. Students can simply click the mouse to instantly create a customized client teaching printout for any drug monograph. This exciting electronic feature is an invaluable aid that will provide customized teaching materials and support the teaching experiences for your students.

For Faculty

- Instructor's Manual—provides tips and guidance helpful in preparing for class and implementing the contents of this creative new text package. Gleaned from many years of teaching nursing pharmacology, these tips will prove helpful in spicing up your class presentation, help to stimulate interactive learning experiences for your students, and work together with the text, study guide, and CD-ROM to fully enhance the learning potential of your students. Overhead transparency masters provide clear copies of the many illustrations unique to this text.
- Test Bank—available on disk, this testbank of more than 750 completely new NCLEX-style test items is available in ASCII format and capable of full manipulation in your own word-processing software. This feature provides the opportunity for adding, changing, and rearranging test items to meet your specific teaching and testing needs.

For Faculty and Students

- PharmPhax—semi-annual newsletter mailed *free* to faculty who adopt this text for distribution to each student enrolled in the class. PharmPhax offers constantly updated drug information to ensure the most current drug information possible. The newsletter includes Web addresses to access electronic sources of new drug information.

TO THE STUDENT USING THIS TEXT

As you begin your study of pharmacology, don't be overwhelmed or confused by all of the details. The study of drugs fits perfectly into your study of the human body—anatomy, physiology, chemistry, nutrition, psychology, and sociology. Approach the study of pharmacology from the perspective of putting all of the pieces together; this can be not only fun but challenging! Work to understand the concepts and all of the details will fall into place, be easy to remember, and apply to the clinical situation. This understanding will help you in creating the picture of the whole patient as you are learning to provide comprehensive nursing care. This text is designed to help you accomplish all of this in a simple and concise manner. Good luck!

Amy M. Karch, RN, MS

Acknowledgments

I would like to thank the various people who have worked so hard to make this book a reality: the many students and colleagues who have, for so long, pushed for a pharmacology book that was straightforward and user-friendly; my acquisitions editor at Lippincott Williams & Wilkins, Margaret Zuccarini, who had the vision and the drive to see this project through and who has become a mentor and a friend; my developmental editor Rose Foltz, who has a wonderful way with words and could truly test the waters for meaning and clarity and who loves flowers and spring; Helen Kogut, our editorial assistant, who somehow manages to keep everything in order and flowing smoothly; Gretchen Metzger, the last part of the ideal publishing team, who worked her magic and then moved on to follow her own dream; my wonderful husband, Fred Karch, who not only tolerated moods, deadlines, lack of sleep, and endless questions, but who also salvaged a hard drive when the world seemed the bleakest; Tim, Jyoti, Mark, Janelle, Cortney, and Kathryn, who continue to thrive and grow and have become the wonderful, supportive people in my life; and Cider, who doesn't move so well anymore but still manages a friendly wagging tail and an understanding lick when it is needed most.

Contents

CD-ROM Contents

PART

1

Introduction to Nursing Pharmacology

CHAPTER 1

Introduction to Drugs

CHAPTER OUTLINE

INTRODUCTION
PHARMACOLOGY
SOURCES AND EVALUATION OF DRUGS
Sources of Drugs
- *PLANTS*
- *ANIMAL PRODUCTS*
- *INORGANIC COMPOUNDS*
- *SYNTHETIC SOURCES*

Drug Evaluation
- *PHASES OF DRUG DEVELOPMENT*
- *FDA APPROVAL*
- *CONTINUAL EVALUATION*

LEGAL REGULATION OF DRUGS
Pregnancy Categories
Controlled Substances
GENERIC DRUGS
ORPHAN DRUGS
OVER-THE-COUNTER DRUGS
SOURCES OF DRUG INFORMATION
Package Inserts
Reference Books
Journals
Internet Information
CHAPTER SUMMARY
BIBLIOGRAPHY

KEY TERMS

adverse effects
brand name
chemical name
drugs
Food and Drug Administration (FDA)
generic drugs
generic name
genetic engineering
orphan drugs
over-the-counter (OTC) drugs
pharmacology
pharmacotherapeutics
phase I study
phase II study
phase III study
phase IV study
preclinical trials
teratogenic

INTRODUCTION

The human body works through a complicated series of chemical reactions and processes. ***Drugs*** are chemicals that are introduced into the body to cause some sort of change. When drugs are administered, the body begins a sequence of processes designed to handle the new chemicals. These processes, which involve breaking down and eliminating the drugs, in turn affect the body's complex series of chemical reactions.

Understanding how drugs act on the body to cause changes and applying that knowledge in the clinical setting are important aspects of nursing practice, for many reasons. For instance, patients today often follow complicated drug regimens and receive potentially toxic drugs. Many also manage their own care at home. The nurse is in a unique position regarding drug therapy because nursing responsibilities include the following:

- Administering drugs
- Assessing drug effects
- Intervening to make the drug regimen more tolerable
- Providing patient teaching about drugs and the drug regimen

Knowing how drugs work makes these tasks easier to handle, thus enhancing drug therapy.

This text is designed to provide the pharmacological basis for understanding drug therapy. The physiology of a body system and the related actions of many drugs on that system are presented in a way to allow clear understanding of how drugs work and what to anticipate when giving a particular type of drug. Thousands of drugs are available for use, and it is impossible to memorize all of the individual differences of drugs in a class.

This text addresses general drug information. The nurse can refer to the companion *Lippincott's Nursing Drug Guide (LNDG),* or to another drug guide, to obtain the specific details required for safe and effective drug administration. Within this text are references to pertinent monographs for drugs listed in a given class or chapter. The drug monographs in *LNDG* follow a format similar to the one used in this text, thus allowing the nurse to easily use *LNDG* to incorporate what is learned about pharmacology into actual clinical practice.

A nursing care guide in each text chapter serves as a model for developing nursing care guides for any drugs being administered (Table 1-1). The various sections of each drug monograph in *LNDG* also can be used to develop other care guides or teaching plans (Figure 1-1). The nurse can use this text as a resource for the basic concepts of pharmacology, and *LNDG* (or another nursing drug guide) as an easy-to-use reference in the clinical setting.

PHARMACOLOGY

Pharmacology is the study of the biological effects of chemicals. In clinical practice, health care providers focus on how chemicals act on living organisms. Nurses deal with ***pharmacotherapeutics,*** or clinical pharmacology, the branch of pharmacology involving drugs used to treat, prevent, or diagnose disease. Clinical pharmacology addresses two key concerns: the drug's effects on the body, and the body's response to the drug.

Because a drug can have many effects, the nurse must know which ones may occur when a particular drug is administered. Some drug effects are therapeutic, or helpful. But others are undesirable or potentially dangerous. These negative effects are called ***adverse effects.*** (See Chapter 3, Toxic Effects of Drugs, for a detailed discussion of adverse effects.)

SOURCES AND EVALUATION OF DRUGS

Drugs are available from varied sources, both natural and synthetic. The drugs listed in this book and in the companion *LNDG* have been through rigorous testing and are approved for sale to the public, either with or without a prescription from a health care provider.

Sources of Drugs

Chemicals that might prove useful as drugs can come from many natural sources, such as plants, animals, or inorganic compounds, or they may be developed synthetically. To become a drug, a chemical must have a demonstrated therapeutic value or efficacy without severe toxicity or damaging properties.

PLANTS

Plants or plant parts have been used as medicines since prehistoric times. Even today, plants are an important source of chemicals that are developed into drugs. For example, digitalis products used to treat cardiac disorders and various opiates used for sedation are still derived from plants. Table 1-2 provides examples of drugs derived from plant sources.

Drugs also may be processed using a synthetic version of the active chemical found in the plant. An example of this type of drug is dronabinol (*Marinol*), which contains the active ingredient delta-9-tetra-

TABLE 1-1

SAMPLE NURSING CARE GUIDE FROM *LIPPINCOTT'S NURSING DRUG GUIDE* FOR A PATIENT ON AN NSAID

Assessment	Nursing Diagnosis	Implementation	Evaluation
History (contraindications/cautions) Ulcerative GI disease Peptic ulcer Renal dysfunction Hepatic dysfunction Pregnancy Lactation Known allergies to: other NSAIDs, aspirin	Potential sensory-perceptual alteration secondary to CNS effects Potential alteration in comfort related to GI upset, headache Potential ineffective gas exchange related to possible hypersensitivity reaction	Safe and appropriate administration of the drug Provision of safety and comfort measures: Drug given with meals Alleviation of GI upset, headache Safety provisions if dizziness or visual disturbances occur	Monitor for therapeutic effects of the drug: decrease in the signs and symptoms of inflammation Monitor for adverse effects of drug: GI upset Liver function changes CNS effects CHF
Medication History (possible drug–drug interactions) Sulfonamides Hydantoin Probenecid Oral anticoagulants Oral hypoglycemics Physical Assessment (screen for contraindications, establish a baseline for effects and adverse effects) CNS: affect, reflexes, peripheral sensation CV: BP, P, peripheral perfusion, auscultation GI: bowel sounds, liver evaluation, stool guaiac Skin: Lesions Blood tests: CBC, liver and renal function tests	Knowledge deficit regarding drug therapy	Patient teaching regarding: Drug Side effects to anticipate Warnings Reactions to report Support and encouragement to cope with disease, therapy, and side effects Provision of emergency and life-support measures in cases of acute hypersensitivity	Renal or urinary tract dysfunction Blood dyscrasias Visual changes Rash Asthma Anaphylactic reactions Evaluate effectiveness of patient teaching program: patient can state name of drug, dose of drug, use of drug, adverse effects to expect, reactions to report Evaluate effectiveness of comfort and safety measures Monitor for drug–drug interactions if patient is on an interacting drug Evaluate effectiveness of life-support measures if needed

(Karch, A.M. [2000]. *2000 Lippincott's nursing drug guide*. Philadelphia: Lippincott Williams & Wilkins.)

hydrocannabinol found in marijuana. It helps prevent nausea and vomiting in cancer patients but does not have all of the adverse effects that occur when the marijuana leaf is smoked.

Sometimes a drug effect occurs from ingestion of plant-derived food. For instance, the body converts natural licorice to a false aldosterone, resulting in fluid retention and hypokalemia or low serum potassium levels if large amounts of licorice are eaten. However, people seldom think of licorice as a drug.

Finally, plants have become the main component of the growing alternative therapy movement. Table 1-3 provides information on alternative and complementary therapies.

ANIMAL PRODUCTS

Animal products are used to replace human chemicals that are not produced because of disease or genetic problems. Until recently, insulin for treating diabetes was obtained exclusively from cow and pig pancreas tissue. Now ***genetic engineering***—the process of altering DNA—permitted scientists to produce human insulin by altering *Escherichia coli* bacteria, making insulin a better product without some of the impurities that come with animal products.

Thyroid drugs and growth hormone preparations also may be obtained from animal thyroid and hypothalamus tissues. But many of these preparations are now created synthetically and are considered to be purer and safer to use than preparations derived from animals.

INORGANIC COMPOUNDS

Salts of various elements can have therapeutic effects in the human body. Aluminum, fluoride, iron and even gold are used to treat various conditions. The

Generic name — **anagrelide hydrochloride**

Pronunciation guide — *(an agh' rah lide)*

Brand name — Agrylin

FDA pregnancy category — **Pregnancy Category C**

Therapeutic drug class — **Drug classes**
Platelet reducing agent

Action of drug on the body — **Therapeutic actions**
Reduces platelet production by decreasing megakaryocyte hypermaturation; inhibits cyclic AMP and ADP collagen-induced platelet aggregation. At therapeutic doses has no affect on WBC counts or coagulation parameters; may affect RBC parameters.

Uses for the drug
Evaluation points—resolution or stabilization of those conditions

Indications
- Treatment of essential thrombocytopenia to reduce elevated platelet count and the risk of thrombosis

Conditions limiting use of drug
Assessment points—history of these conditions, physical assessment indicating these conditions

Contraindications/cautions
- Use caution in the presence of renal or hepatic disorders, pregnancy, lactation, known heart disease, thrombocytopenia.

Forms and dosages available for use

Recommended dose of drug for adults, pediatrics, etc.

Dosage
Available Forms: Capsules—0.5, 1 mg
ADULT: Initially 0.5 mg PO qid or 1 mg PO bid. After 1 wk, reevaluate and adjust the dosage as needed; do not increase by more than 0.5 mg/d each week. Maximum dose 10 mg/d or 2.5 mg as a single dose.
PEDIATRIC: Safety and efficacy not established.

Action of body on the drug—*points for assessment* (hepatic function), cautions, and contraindications

Pharmacokinetics

Route	Onset	Peak
Oral	Rapid	1 h

Metabolism: Hepatic metabolism; $T_{1/2}$: 3 d
Distribution: Crosses placenta; may pass into breast milk
Excretion: Urine

Effects of drug on the body—not therapeutic but can be expected
Assessment points—baselines for these systems
Nursing diagnosis—potential alterations resulting from these effects
Evaluation—presence/absence of these effects

Adverse effects
- GI: *Diarrhea, nausea, vomiting, abdominal pain,* flatulence, dyspepsia, anorexia, pancreatitis, ulcer, CVA
- **Hematological:** *Thrombocytopenia*
- **CNS:** Dizziness, headaches, asthenia, paresthesias
- **CV:** CHF, tachycardia, MI, complete heart block, atrial fibrillation, hypertension, *palpitations*
- **Other:** Rash, purpura

Clinically important drug-food interactions — Anticipated interactions
Assessment points—history of use of these drugs, physical response
Evaluation—changes from anticipated therapeutic response related to drug interactions

- Reduced availability of anagrelide if taken with food

Nursing Considerations

Assessment — Points to establish baselines, determine factors contraindicating drug use or requiring caution

- ***History:*** Allergy to anagrelide, thrombocytopenia, hemostatic disorders, bleeding ulcer, intracranial bleeding, severe liver disease, lactation, renal disorders, pregnancy, known heart disease
- ***Physical:*** Skin color, lesions; orientation; bowel sounds, normal output; CBC, liver and renal function tests

Implementation — Nursing actions, in chronologic order, for safe and effective drug therapy

- Perform platelet counts q 2 d during the first week of therapy and at least weekly thereafter; if thrombocytopenia occurs, decrease dosage of drug and arrange for supportive therapy.
- Advise patient to use barrier contraceptives while receiving this drug; it may harm the fetus.
- Monitor patient for any sign of excessive bleeding—bruises, dark stools, etc.—and monitor bleeding times.

Drug-specific teaching points — Teaching points to include on patient teaching program
Nursing diagnosis—knowledge deficit regarding drug therapy
Evaluation—points patient should be able to repeat

- Take drug on an empty stomach.
- Be aware that it may take longer than normal to stop bleeding while on this drug; avoid contact sports, use electric razors, etc.; apply pressure for extended periods to bleeding sites.
- Avoid pregnancy while on this drug; it could harm the fetus. Use barrier contraceptives.
- Know that upset stomach, nausea, diarrhea, loss of appetite (small, frequent meals may help) may occur.
- Notify any dentist or surgeon that you are on this drug before invasive procedures.
- Report fever, chills, sore throat, skin rash, bruising, bleeding, dark stools or urine, palpitations, chest pain.

FIGURE 1-1. Types of information available in each drug monograph in *Lippincott's Nursing Drug Guide.*

TABLE 1-2

DRUGS DERIVED FROM PLANTS

Plant	Product
Riccinus communis	seed oil castor oil (*Neolide*)
Digitalis purpurea Foxglove plant	leaves dried leaves digitalis leaf
Papaver somniferum Poppy plant	unripe capsule juice opium (*Paregoric*) morphine (*Roxanol*) codeine papaverine (*Pavabid*)

effects of these elements usually have been discovered accidentally when a cause–effect relationship is observed. Table 1-4 shows examples of some elements used for their therapeutic benefit.

SYNTHETIC SOURCES

Today, many drugs are developed synthetically after chemicals in plants, animals or the environment have been screened for signs of therapeutic activity. As noted above, scientists use genetic engineering to alter bacteria to produce chemicals that are therapeutic and effective. Other technical advances allow scientists to alter a chemical with proven therapeutic effectiveness to make it better. Sometimes, a small change in a chemical's structure can make that chemical more useful as a drug—more potent, more stable, less toxic. These technological advances have led to the development of groups of similar drugs, all of which are derived from an original prototype, but each of which has slightly different properties, making a particular drug more desirable in a specific situation. For example, the cephalosporins are a group of antibiotics derived from the same chemical structure. Alterations in the chemical rings or attachments to that structure make it possible for some of these drugs to be absorbed orally, while others must be given parenterally. Some of these drugs cause severe toxic effects like renal toxicity, whereas others do not.

Drug Evaluation

When a chemical that might have therapeutic value is identified, it must undergo a series of scientific tests to evaluate its actual therapeutic and toxic effects. This process is tightly controlled by the ***Food and Drug Administration (FDA),*** an agency of the United States Department of Health and Human Services that regulates the development and sale of drugs. FDA-regulated tests are designed to assure the safety and reliability of any drug approved in this country. For every 100,000 chemicals that are identified as being potential drugs, estimates are that only about 5 end up being marketed.

PHASES OF DRUG DEVELOPMENT

Before receiving final FDA approval to be marketed to the public, drugs must pass through several stages of development. These include preclinical trials and phase I, II, and III studies.

Preclinical Trials

In ***preclinical trials,*** chemicals that may have therapeutic value are tested on laboratory animals for two main purposes:

1. To determine whether they have the presumed effects in living tissue.
2. To evaluate any adverse effects.

Animal testing is important because unique biological differences can cause very different reactions to the chemical. These differences can be found only in living organisms, so computer-generated models alone are often inadequate.

At the end of the preclinical trials, some chemicals will be discarded for the following reasons:

- The chemical lacks therapeutic activity when used with living animals.
- The chemical is too toxic to living animals to be worth the risk of developing into drugs.
- The chemical is highly ***teratogenic*** (cause adverse effects to the fetus).
- The safety margins are so small that the chemical would not be useful in the clinical setting.

Some chemicals, however, will be found to have therapeutic effects and reasonable safety margins. This means that the chemicals are therapeutic at doses that are reasonably different from doses that cause toxic effects. Such chemicals will pass the preclinical trials and advance to phase I studies.

Phase I Studies

Phase I studies use human volunteers to test the drugs. These studies are more tightly controlled than preclinical trials and are performed by specially trained clinical investigators. The volunteers are fully informed of possible risks and may be paid for their participation.

Generally, the volunteers are healthy, young men. Women are not good candidates for phase I studies because the chemicals may exert unknown effects on a woman's ova. Because women are born with all of the ova they are ever going to have, there is too much

TABLE 1-3

ALTERNATIVE AND COMPLEMENTARY THERAPIES

Many natural substances are used by the public for self-treatment of many complaints. These substances, derived from folklore or various cultures, often have ingredients that have been identified and have known therapeutic activities. Some of these substances have unknown mechanisms of action, but over the years have been reliably used to relieve specific symptoms. There is an element of the placebo effect in using some of these substances. The power of believing that something will work and that there is some control over the problem is often very beneficial in achieving relief from pain or suffering. Some of these substances may contain yet unidentified ingredients, which, when discovered, may prove very useful in the modern field of pharmacology. Because these products are not regulated or monitored, there is always a possibility of toxic effects. Some of these products may contain ingredients that interact with prescription drugs. A history of the use of these alternative therapies may explain unexpected reactives to some drugs.

Substance	Reported Use
alfalfa	Topical: healing ointment, relief of arthritis pain Oral: arthritis treatment, strength giving
aloe leaves	Topical: treatment of burns, healing of wounds Oral: treatment of chronic constipation
anise	Oral: relief of dry cough, treatment of flatulence
apple	Oral: control of blood glucose, constipation
arnica gel	Topical: relieves pain from muscle or soft tissue injury
bilberry	Oral: treatment of diabetes; cardiovascular problems; lowers cholesterol and triglycerides; treatment of diabetic retinopathy
birch bark	Topical: treatment of infected wounds, cuts Oral: as tea for relief of stomach ache
blackberry	Oral: as a tea for generalized healing; treatment of diabetes
burdock	Oral: treatment of diabetes; atropine-like side effects, uterine stimulant
camomile	Topical: treatment of wounds, ulcer, conjunctivitis Oral: treatment of migraines, gastric cramps, relief of anxiety
catnip leaves	Oral: treatment of bronchitis, diarrhea
cayenne pepper	Topical: treatment of burns, wounds, relief of toothache pain
celery	Oral: lowers blood glucose, acts as a diuretic; may cause potassium depletion
chicken soup	Oral: breaks up respiratory secretions, bronchodilator, relieves anxiety
chicory	Oral: treatment of digestive tract problems, gout; stimulates bile secretions
comfrey	Topical: treatment of wounds, cuts, ulcers Oral: gargle for tonsillitis
coriander	Oral: weight loss, lowers blood glucose
dandelion root	Oral: treatment of liver and kidney problems; decreases lactation (after delivery or with weaning); lowers blood glucose
DHEA	Oral: slows aging, improves vigor—"Fountain of Youth"; androgenic side effects
Di huang	Oral: treatment of diabetes mellitus
dried root bark of lycium Chinese mill	Oral: lowers cholesterol, lowers blood glucose
echinacea	Oral: treatment of colds, flu; stimulates the immune system, attacks viruses
elder bark and/or flowers	Topical: gargle for tonsillitis, pharyngitis Oral: treatment of fever, chills
ephedra	Oral: increases energy, relieves fatigue; *warning:* associated with serious complications, withdrawn in some states
ergot	Oral: treatment of migraine headaches, treatment of menstrual problems, hemorrhage
eucalyptus	Topical: treatment of wounds Oral: decreases respiratory secretions, suppresses cough
fennel	Oral: treatment of colic, gout, flatulence; enhances lactation
fenugreek	Oral: lowers cholesterol levels; reduces blood glucose; aids in healing
fish oil	Oral: treatment of coronary diseases, arthritis, colitis, depression, aggression, attention deficit disorder
garlic	Oral: treatment of colds, diuretic; prevention of coronary artery disease, intestinal antiseptic; lowers blood glucose, anticoagulant
ginger	Oral: treatment of nausea, motion sickness, postoperative nausea (may increase risk of miscarriage)
ginkobe	Oral: increases cerebral blood flow, improves concentration and memory
ginseng	Oral: aphrodisiac, mood elevator, tonic; antihypertensive; decreases cholesterol levels; lowers blood glucose
goldenrod leaves	Oral: treatment of renal disease, rheumatism, sore throat, eczema
goldenseal	Oral: lowers blood glucose, aids healing

(continued)

TABLE 1-3

ALTERNATIVE AND COMPLEMENTARY THERAPIES (Continued)

Substance	Reported Use
guayusa	Oral: lowers blood glucose; weight loss
hop	Oral: sedative; aids healing; alters blood glucose
horehound	Oral: expectorant; treatment of respiratory problems, GI disorders
Java plum	Oral: treatment of diabetes mellitus
juniper berries	Oral: increases appetite, aids digestion, diuretic, urinary tract disinfectant; lowers blood glucose
kava	Oral: treatment of nervous anxiety, stress, restlessness; tranquilizer
kudzu	Oral: reduces cravings for alcohol; being researched for use with alcoholics
ledum tincture	Topical: treatment of insect bites, puncture wounds; dissolves some blood clots and bruises
licorice	Oral: prevents thirst, soothes coughs; treats "incurable" chronic fatigue syndrome
mandrake root	Oral: treatment of fertility problems
marigold leaves/flowers	Oral: relief of muscle tension, increases wound healing
melatonin	Oral: relief of jet lag, treatment of insomnia
milk thistle	Oral: treatment of hepatitis, cirrhosis, fatty liver due to alcohol or drugs
mistletoe leaves	Oral: weight loss; relief of signs and symptoms of diabetes
momordica charantia (Karela)	Oral: blocks intestinal absorption of glucose; lowers blood glucose; weight loss
nightshade leaves/roots	Oral: stimulates circulatory system; treatment of eye disorders
parsley seeds/leaves	Oral: treatment of jaundice, asthma, menstrual difficulties, conjunctivitis
peppermint leaves	Oral: treatment of nervousness, insomnia, dizziness, cramps, coughs Topical: rubbed on forehead to relieve tension headaches
raspberry	Oral: healing of minor wounds; control and treatment of diabetes
rosemary	Topical: relief of rheumatism, sprains, wounds, bruises, eczema Oral: gastric stimulation, relief of flatulence, stimulation of bile release, relief of colic
rue extract	Topical: relief of pain associated with sprains, groin pulls, whiplash
saffron	Oral: treatment of menstrual problems, abortifacient
sage	Oral: lowers blood pressure; lowers blood glucose
sarsaparilla	Oral: treatment of skin disorders, rheumatism
saw palmetto	Oral: treatment of benign prostatic hyperplasia
St. John's wort	Oral: treatment of depression Topical: treatment of puncture wounds, insect bites, crushed fingers or toes
sweet violet flowers	Oral: treatment of respiratory disorders, emetic
tarragon	Oral: weight loss; prevents cancer; lowers blood glucose
thyme	Topical: liniment, treatment of wounds, gargle Oral: antidiarrhetic, relief of bronchitis and laryngitis
valerian	Oral: sedative/hypnotic; reduces anxiety, relaxes muscles
white willow bark	Oral: treatment of fevers
xuan seng	Oral: lowers blood glucose; slows heart rate; treatment of congestive heart failure

(Karch, A.M. [2000]. *2000 Lippincott's nursing drug guide.* Philadelphia: Lippincott Williams & Wilkins.)

TABLE 1-4

EXAMPLES OF ELEMENTS USED FOR THEIR THERAPEUTIC EFFECTS

Element	Therapeutic Use
Aluminum	Antacid to decrease gastric acidity Management of hyperphosphatemia Prevention of the formation of phosphate urinary stones
Fluoride	Prevention of dental cavities Prevention of osteoporosis
Gold	Treatment of rheumatoid arthritis
Iron	Treatment of iron deficiency anemia

risk involved in taking a drug that might destroy or alter the ova. Men, however, produce sperm daily, so there is less potential for complete destruction or alteration of the sperm.

Some chemicals are therapeutic in other animals but have no effects in humans. Investigators in phase I studies scrutinize the drugs being tested for effects in humans. They also look for adverse effects and toxicity. At the end of phase I studies, many chemicals are dropped from the process for the following reasons:

- They lack therapeutic effect in humans.
- They cause unacceptable adverse effects.
- They are highly teratogenic.
- They are too toxic.

Interestingly, some chemicals move to the next stage of testing despite undesirable effects. For example, the hypertensive drug minoxidil (*Loniten*) effectively treats malignant hypertension, but causes unusual hair growth on the palms and other body areas. However, because it was so much more effective at the time of its development than any other antihypertensive drug, it proceeded to phase II studies. (Now, its hair-growing effect has been channeled for therapeutic use into various hair-growth preparations such as *Rogaine*.)

Phase II Studies

Phase II studies allow clinical investigators to try the drug with patients who have the disease that the drug is meant to treat. Patients are told about the possible benefits of the drug and are invited to participate in the study. Those who consent to participate are fully informed about possible risks and are followed very closely, often at no charge to them, to evaluate the drug effects. Usually, phase II studies are performed at various sites across the country—in hospitals, clinics, doctor's offices—and are monitored by representatives of the pharmaceutical company studying the drug.

At the end of phase II studies, a drug may be removed from further investigation for the following reasons:

- It is less effective than anticipated.
- It is too toxic when used with patients.
- It produces unacceptable adverse effects.
- It has a low benefit-to-risk ratio, meaning that the therapeutic benefit it provides does not outweigh the risk of potential adverse effects that it causes.
- It is no more effective than other drugs already on the market, making the cost of continued research and production less attractive to the drug company.

A drug that continues to show promise as a therapeutic agent receives additional scrutiny in phase III studies.

Phase III Studies

Phase III studies involve using the drug in a vast clinical market. Prescribers are informed of all the known reactions to the drug and precautions required for its safe use. Prescribers follow patients very closely, monitoring them for any adverse effects. Sometimes, prescribers may ask patients to keep journals in which to record any symptoms experienced. Prescribers then evaluate the reported effects to determine if they are caused by the disease or the drug. This information is collected by the drug company that is developing the drug and shared with the FDA. When the drug is used widely, totally unexpected responses may occur. A drug that produces unacceptable adverse effects or unforeseen reactions is usually removed from further study by the drug company. In some cases, the FDA may have to request that a drug be removed from the market.

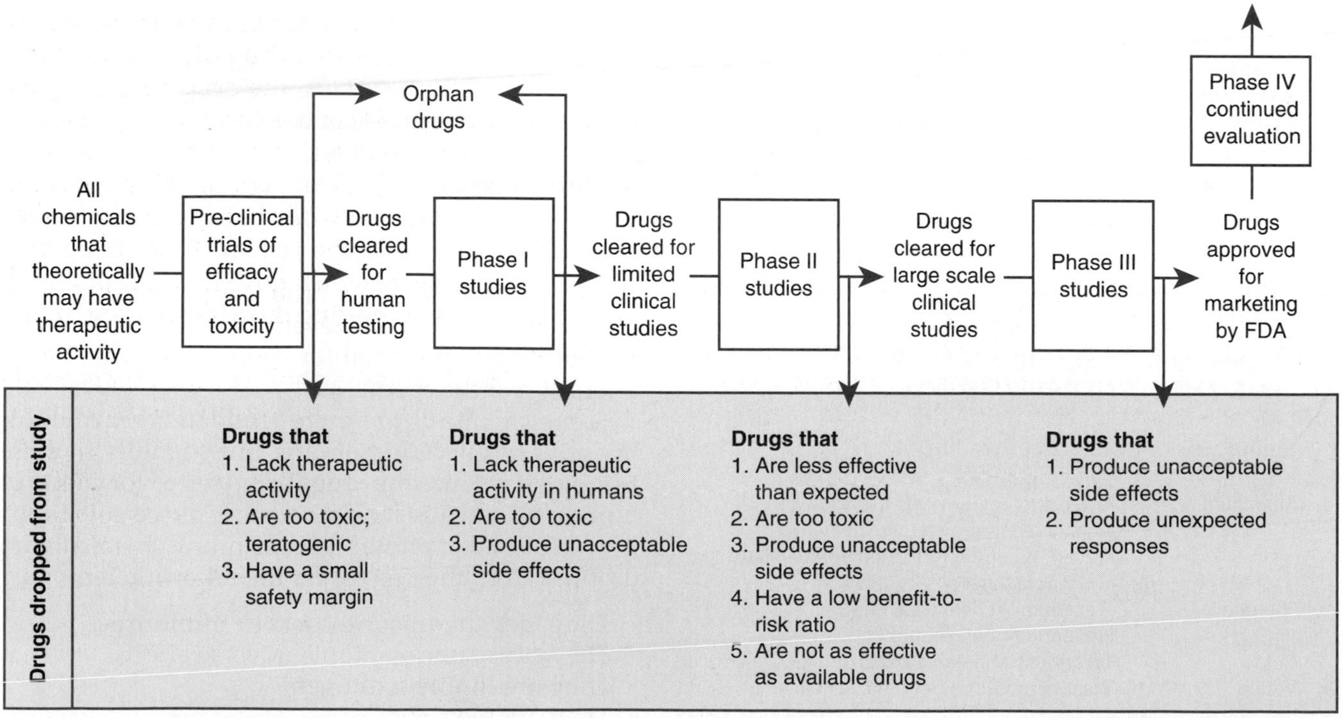

FIGURE 1-2. Phases of drug development.

FDA APPROVAL

Drugs that finish phase III studies are evaluated by the FDA, which relies on committees of experts familiar with the specialty area in which the drugs will be used. Only those drugs that receive FDA committee approval may be marketed. Figure 1-2 recaps the various phases of drug development discussed.

It is estimated that the entire drug development and approval process can take 5 to 6 years, resulting in the so-called "drug lag" in the United States. In some instances, a drug that is available in another country may not be available here for years. The FDA regards public safety as primary in drug approval, so the process remains strict. However, the process may be accelerated in certain instances involving treatment of deadly diseases. For example, some drugs (including delavirdine [*Rescriptor*] and efavirenz [*Sustiva*]) that were thought to offer a benefit to patients with acquired immune deficiency syndrome (AIDS), a potentially fatal immune disorder, were pushed through because of the progressive nature of AIDS and the lack of a cure. All literature associated with these drugs indicates that long-term effects and other information about the drug may not yet be known.

Besides the drug lag issue, there also are concerns about the high costs of drug approval. In 1996, the estimated cost of taking a chemical from discovery to marketing as a drug was about $40 to $50 million. Because of this kind of financial investment, pharmaceutical companies are unwilling to risk approval of a drug that might cause serious problems and prompt lawsuits.

CONTINUAL EVALUATION

An approved drug is given a ***brand name*** or trade name by the pharmaceutical company that developed it. The ***generic name*** of a drug is the original designation that the drug is given when the drug company applies for the approval process. ***Chemical names*** are names that reflect the chemical structure of a drug. Some drugs are known by all three names. It can be confusing to study drugs when so many different names are used for the same compound. In this text, the generic and chemical names always appear in straight print, and the brand names of drugs always appear in italics (for example, *Rogaine*). See Box 1-1 for examples of such drug names.

After a drug is approved for marketing, it enters a phase of continual evaluation or ***phase IV study.*** Prescribers are obligated to report to the FDA any untoward or unexpected adverse effects associated with drugs they are using, and the FDA continually evaluates this information. Some drugs cause unexpected effects that are not seen until wide distribution occurs. Sometimes, those effects are therapeutic. For example, patients taking the antiparkinsonism drug amantadine (*Symmetrel*) were found to have fewer cases of influenza than other patients, leading to the discovery that amantadine is an effective antiviral agent.

Other times, those unexpected effects are dangerous. In 1998, the antihypertensive drug mibefradil (*Posicor*) was pulled from the market not long after its release because patients taking it were found to have more cardiac morbidity. In 1997, the diet drug dexfenfluramine (*Redux*) was removed from the market only months after its release because patients developed serious heart problems. These problems were not seen in any of the premarket studies.

LEGAL REGULATION OF DRUGS

The FDA regulates the development and sale of drugs. Local laws further regulate the distribution and administration of drugs. In most cases, the strictest law is the one that prevails. Nurses should become familiar with the rules and regulations in the area in which they practice. These regulations may vary from state to state, and may even vary within states.

Over the years, the FDA has become more powerful, usually in response to a drug disaster affecting many people. In the 1930s, the drug *Elixir of Sulfanilamide* was distributed in a vehicle of ethylene glycol that had never been tested in humans. It turned out that ethylene glycol is toxic to humans, and hundreds of people died while many others became very ill. This led the to the Federal Food, Drug and Cosmetic Act of 1938, which gave the FDA power to enforce standards for testing drug toxicity and monitoring labeling.

In the 1960s, the drug thalidomide (*Thalidomid*) was used as a sleeping aid by pregnant women, resulting in the birth of many babies with limb deformities. The public outcry resulted in the Kefauver-

BOX 1-1

EXAMPLES OF GENERIC, CHEMICAL AND BRAND NAMES OF DRUGS

levothyroxine sodium	←	**generic name**	→	colfosceril palmitate
L-thyroxine, T_4	←	**chemical name**	→	dipalmitoylphosphatidylcholine
Eltroxin, Levothroid, Synthroid	←	**brand names**	→	*Exosurf Neonatal*

TABLE 1-5

FEDERAL LEGISLATION AFFECTING THE CLINICAL USE OF DRUGS

Year Enacted	Law	Impact
1906	Pure Food and Drug Act	Prevented the marketing of adulterated drugs; required labeling to eliminate false or misleading claims
1938	Federal Food, Drug and Cosmetic Act of 1938	Mandated tests for drug toxicity and provided means for recall of drugs; established procedures for introducing new drugs; gave FDA the power of enforcement
1951	Durham-Humphrey Amendment	Tightened control of certain drugs; specified drugs to be labeled "may not be distributed without a prescription"
1962	Kefauver-Harris Act	Tightened control over the quality of drugs; gave FDA regulatory power over the procedure of drug investigations; stated that efficacy as well as safety of drugs had to be established
1970	Controlled Substances Act	Defined drug abuse and classified drugs as to their potential for abuse; provided strict controls over the distribution, storage, and use of these drugs
1983	Orphan Drug Act	Provided incentives for the development of orphan drugs for treatment of rare diseases

BOX 1-2

FDA PREGNANCY CATEGORIES

The Food and Drug Administration has established five categories to indicate the potential for a systemically absorbed drug to cause birth defects. The key differentiation among the categories rests upon the degree (reliability) of documentation and the risk-benefit ratio.

Category A: Adequate studies in pregnant women have not demonstrated a risk to the fetus in the first trimester of pregnancy, and there is no evidence of risk in later trimesters.

Category B: Animal studies have not demonstrated a risk to the fetus but there are no adequate studies in pregnant women. *or* Animal studies have shown an adverse effect, but adequate studies in pregnant women have not demonstrated a risk to the fetus during the first trimester of pregnancy, and there is no evidence of risk in later trimesters.

Category C: Animal studies have shown an adverse effect on the fetus but there are no adequate studies in humans; the benefits from the use of the drug in pregnant women may be acceptable despite its potential risks. *or* There are no animal reproduction studies and no adequate studies in humans.

Category D: There is evidence of human fetal risk, but the potential benefits from the use of the drug in pregnant women may be acceptable despite its potential risks.

Category X: Studies in animals or humans demonstrate fetal abnormalities or adverse reaction; reports indicate evidence of fetal risk. The risk of use in a pregnant woman clearly outweighs any possible benefit.

Regardless of the designated Pregnancy Category or presumed safety, *no* drug should be administered during pregnancy unless it is clearly needed.

Harris Act of 1962, which gave the FDA regulatory control over the testing and evaluating of drugs, and set standards for the efficacy and safety of drugs.

Other laws have given the FDA control over monitoring potentially addictive drugs and for monitoring, to some extent, the sale of drugs available without prescriptions.

Table 1-5 provides a summary of these laws.

Pregnancy Categories

As part of the standards for testing and safety, the FDA requires that each new drug be assigned to a pregnancy category (Box 1-2). The categories indicate a drug's potential or actual teratogenic effects, or adverse effects on the fetus, thus offering guidelines for use of a particular drug in pregnancy. Research into the development of the human fetus, especially the nervous system, has led many health care providers to recommend that no drug be used during pregnancy because of potential effects on the developing fetus. In cases in which a drug is needed, it is recommended that the drug of choice be one in which the benefit outweighs the potential risk.

Controlled Substances

The Controlled Substances Act of 1970 also has established categories for the ranking of the abuse potential of various drugs. This same act gave control over the coding of drugs and the enforcement of these codes to the FDA and the Drug Enforcement Agency (DEA), a part of the Department of Justice. The FDA studies the drugs and determines their abuse potential, while the DEA enforces their control. Drugs with abuse potential are called controlled substances. Box 1-3 contains descriptions of each category, or schedule.

The prescription, distribution, storage and use of these drugs is closely monitored by the DEA in an at-

> **BOX 1-3**
>
> ### DEA SCHEDULES OF CONTROLLED SUBSTANCES
>
> The Controlled Substances Act of 1970 regulates the manufacturing, distribution, and dispensing of drugs which are known to have abuse potential. The Drug Enforcement Agency (DEA) is responsible for the enforcement of these regulations. The controlled drugs are divided into five DEA schedules based on their potential for abuse and physical and psychological dependence.
>
> **Schedule I *(C-I)*:** High abuse potential and no accepted medical use (heroin, marijuana, LSD)
>
> **Schedule II *(C-II)*:** High abuse potential with severe dependence liability (narcotics, amphetamines, and barbiturates)
>
> **Schedule III *(C-III)*:** Less abuse potential than Schedule II drugs and moderate dependence liability (nonbarbiturate sedatives, nonamphetamine stimulants, limited amounts of certain narcotics)
>
> **Schedule IV *(C-IV)*:** Less abuse potential than Schedule III and limited dependence liability (some sedatives, antianxiety agents, and nonnarcotic analgesics)
>
> **Schedule V *(C-V)*:** Limited abuse potential. Primarily small amounts of narcotics (codeine) used as antitussives or antidiarrheals. Under federal law, limited quantities of certain Schedule V drugs may be purchased without a prescription directly from a pharmacist. The purchaser must be at least 18 years of age and must furnish suitable identification. All such transactions must be recorded by the dispensing pharmacist.
>
> Prescribing physicians and dispensing pharmacists must be registered with the DEA, which also provides forms for the transfer of Schedule I and II substances and establishes criteria for the inventory and prescribing of controlled substances. State and local laws are often more stringent than federal law. In any given situation, the more stringent law applies.

tempt to decrease substance abuse of prescribed medications. Each prescriber has a DEA number, which allows the DEA to monitor prescription patterns and possible abuse. A nurse should be familiar not only with the DEA guidelines for controlled substances, but also the local policies and procedures, which might be even more rigorous.

GENERIC DRUGS

When a drug receives approval for marketing from the FDA, the drug formula is given a time-limited patent, much like an invention is patented. When the patent runs out on a brand name drug (and the length of time that patent is good depends on the type of chemical), the drug can be produced by other manufacturers. ***Generic drugs*** are chemicals that are produced by companies that just manufacture drugs. These companies do not have the research, advertising or, sometimes, the quality control departments that pharmaceutical companies have, allowing them to produce the generic drugs more cheaply.

In the past, some quality-control problems have been found with generic products. For example, the binders used in a generic drug may not be the same as those used in the brand name product, so the way the body breaks down and uses the drugs may differ. Thus, the bioavailability of the drug is different from that of the brand name product.

Many states require that a drug be dispensed in the generic form if one is available. This requirement helps keep down the cost of drugs and health care. Some prescribers, however, request that a drug be "dispensed as written" or DAW—that is, that the brand name product be used. By doing this, the prescriber ensures the quality control and bioavailability expected with that drug. These elements may be most important in drugs that have narrow safety margins, such as digoxin (*Lanoxin*), a heart drug, and warfarin (*Coumadin*), an anticoagulant. The initial cost may be higher, but some prescribers feel that in the long run, the cost to the patient will be less.

ORPHAN DRUGS

Orphan drugs are drugs that have been discovered, but which are not financially viable and therefore have not been "adopted" by any drug company. Orphan drugs may be useful in treating a rare disease, or may have potentially dangerous adverse effects. Orphan drugs are often abandoned following preclinical trials or phase I studies. The Orphan Drug Act of 1983 provided tremendous financial incentives to drug companies to adopt these drugs and develop them. This incentive will help the drug company put the drug through the rest of the testing process, even though the market for the drug in the long run may be very small (as, for instance, in the case of a rare neurological disease that only affects a small number of people). Some drugs in this book and in the companion *LNDG* have orphan drug uses.

OVER-THE-COUNTER DRUGS

Over-the-counter (OTC) drugs are products that are available without prescriptions for self-treatment of a variety of complaints. Some of these drugs were approved as prescription drugs but were found to be very safe and useful for patients without the need of a prescription. Some of these drugs were not rigorously screened and tested by the current drug evaluation protocols because they were developed and marketed before the current laws were put into effect.

Many of these drugs were "grandfathered" into use because they had been used for so long. The FDA is currently testing the effectiveness of many of these products and, in time, will evaluate all of them.

Though OTC drugs have been found to be safe when "taken as directed," there are several problems related to OTC drugs that nurses should consider:

- Taking these drugs may mask the signs and symptoms of underlying disease, making diagnosis difficult.
- Taking these drugs with prescription medications may result in drug interactions and can interfere with drug therapy.
- Not taking these drugs as directed may result in serious overdoses.

Patients may not consider OTC drugs to be medications, and so do not report their use. Nurses should always include specific questions about OTC drug use when taking a drug history and provide information in all drug teaching protocols about avoiding OTC use while on prescription drugs.

SOURCES OF DRUG INFORMATION

Pharmacology and drug therapy changes so quickly that it is important to have access to sources of information about drug doses, therapeutic and adverse effects and nursing-related implications. Text books provide valuable background and basic information to help in the understanding of pharmacology, but in clinical practice, it is important to have access to up-to-the minute information. There are several sources of drug information readily available.

Package Inserts

All drugs come with a package insert prepared by the manufacturer following strict FDA regulations. The

BOX 1-4

INTERNET INFORMATION

Ways to get started and to evaluate sites with drug information on the Internet.

Good Places to Begin (Search Tools and Places to Browse)

Alta Vista
http://www.altavista.digital.com
Cliniweb
http://www.ohsu.edu/cliniweb
Hardin Meta Directory of Internet Health Sources
http://www.lib.uiowa.edu/hardin/md/index.html
MetaCrawler
http://www.metacrawler.com
Yahoo Search
http://www.yahoo.com

Learning More About the Internet

Learn the Net
http://learnthenet.com
To Find an ISP
http://www.thelist.com
Evaluating Web sites
http://www.science.widener.edu/~withers/webeval.htm
http://www.mitretek.org/hiti/showcase/documents/criteria.html

Government Sites

Agency for Health Care Policy and Research
http://www.ahcpr.gov
CancerNet (National Cancer Institute)
http://wwwicic.nci.nih.gov
Centers for Disease Control
http://www.cdc.gov
Drug Formulary
http://www.intmed.mcw.edu/drug.html
Food and Drug Administration
http://www.fda.gov
Healthfinder
http://www.healthfinder.gov
National Institutes of Health
http://www.nih.gov
National Institutes of Safety and Health
http://www.cdc.gov/niosh.homepage.html
National Library of Medicine
http://www.nlm.nih.gov
Office of Disease Prevention and Health Promotion
http://www.hhs.gov/PPIP/

Nursing and Health Care Sites

American Diabetes Association
http://www.diabetes.org
American Nurses Association
http://www.ana.org
Cumulative Index to Nursing and Allied Health Literature
http://www.cinahl.com
International Council of Nurses
http://www.icn.ch/
Joint Commission on Accreditation of Healthcare Organizations
http://www.jcaho.org
Journal of the American Medical Association
http://www.ama-assn.org/journals/standing/jama/jamahome.htm
Lippincott's NursingCenter
http://www.nursingcenter.com
Mayo Health Oasis
http://www.mayohealth.org
Medscape
http://www.medscape.com
Merck & Co. (search the Merck Manual)
http://www.merck.com
New England Journal of Medicine
http://www.nejm.org
Nurse Practitioner Web page
http://www.cyberportal.net/npweb/index.html
RxList
http://www.rxlist.com

package insert contain all of the chemical and study information that led to the drug's approval. Package inserts sometimes are difficult to understand.

Reference Books

The *Physician's Drug Reference* or *PDR* is a compilation of the package insert information from drugs used in this country, along with some drug advertising. This information is cross-referenced. The book may be difficult to use.

Drug Facts and Comparisons provides a wide range of drug information, including comparisons of drug costs, patient information sections and preparation and administration guidelines. This book is organized by drug class and can be more user-friendly than the PDR.

AMA Drug Evaluations contains detailed monographs in an unbiased format including many new drugs and drugs still in the research stage.

Lippincott's Nursing Drug Guide has drug monographs organized alphabetically and includes nursing implications and patient teaching points.

Journals

Medical Letter is a monthly review of new drugs, drug classes, and specific treatment protocols. *American Journal of Nursing* offers information on new drugs, drug errors and nursing implications.

Internet Information

Box 1-4 lists some informative Internet sites for obtaining drug information, patient information or therapeutic information related to specific disease states.

CHAPTER SUMMARY

- Drugs are chemicals that are introduced into the body to bring about some sort of change.
- Drugs can come from many sources: plants, animals, elements, synthetic preparations.
- The Food and Drug Administration (FDA) regulates the development and marketing of drugs to assure safety and efficacy.
- Preclinical trials involve testing potential drugs on laboratory animals to determine their potential therapeutic effects and adverse effects.
- Phase I studies test potential drugs on healthy, human subjects.
- Phase II studies test potential drugs on patients who have the disease the drugs are designed to treat.
- Phase III studies test drugs in the clinical setting to determine any unanticipated effects or lack of effectiveness.
- FDA pregnancy categories indicate the potential or actual teratogenic effects of a drug.
- DEA controlled substances categories indicate the abuse potential and associated regulations of a drug.
- Generic drugs are sold under their chemical names, not brand names; they may be cheaper but not necessarily as safe as brand name drugs.
- Orphan drugs are chemicals that have been discovered to have some therapeutic effect, but which are not financially advantageous to develop into drugs.
- OTC drugs are available without prescription for the self-treatment of various complaints.

BIBLIOGRAPHY

Anderson, P. O. (1998). *Handbook of critical drug data* (8th ed.). Hamilton, IL: Drug Intelligence.

Cardinale, V. (1998). Consumers looking for more answers, clearer directions. *Drug Topics Supplement, 142*(11), 23a.

Drug facts and comparisons. (1999). St. Louis: Facts and Comparisons.

Fitzgerald, M. (1994). Pharmacological highlights: Principles of pharmacokinetics. *Journal of the American Academy of Nursing Practice, 6*(12), 581.

Food and Drug Administration. (1994). FDA Launches MEDWATCH program. Monitoring adverse drug reactions. *NP News, 2,* 1, 4.

Hardman, J. G., Limbird, L. E., Molinoff, P. B., Ruddon, R. W., & Gilman, A. G. (Eds.). (1996). *Goodman and Gilman's the pharmacological basis of therapeutics* (9th ed.). New York: McGraw-Hill.

The Medical Letter on Drugs and Therapeutics. (1999). New Rochelle, NY: Medical Letter.

CHAPTER 2

Drugs and the Body

CHAPTER OUTLINE

KEY TERMS

absorption
biotransformation
chemotherapeutic agents
critical concentration
distribution
excretion
first-pass effect
half-life
pharmacodynamics
pharmacokinetics
placebo effect
receptor sites
selective toxicity

INTRODUCTION

To understand what happens when a drug is administered, the nurse must understand ***pharmacodynamics,*** or how the drug affects the body, and ***pharmacokinetics,*** or how the body acts on the drug. These processes form the basis for the guidelines that have been established regarding drug administration, for example, why certain agents are given intramuscularly (IM) and not intravenously (IV), why some drugs are taken with food and others are not, the usual dose to use, and so on. Knowing the basic principles of pharmacodynamics and pharmacokinetics will help the nurse to anticipate therapeutic and adverse drug effects and to intervene in ways that assure the most effective drug regimen for the patient.

PHARMACODYNAMICS

Pharmacodynamics is the science dealing with interactions between the chemical components of living systems and the foreign chemicals, including drugs, that enter those systems. All living organisms function by a series of complicated, continual chemical reactions. So when a new chemical enters the system, multiple changes in and interferences with cell functioning may occur. To avoid such problems, drug development works to provide the most effective and least toxic chemicals for therapeutic use.

DRUG ACTIONS

Drugs usually work in one of four ways:

1. To replace or act as substitutes for missing chemicals.
2. To increase or stimulate certain cellular activities.
3. To depress or slow cellular activities.
4. To interfere with the functioning of foreign cells, such as invading microorganisms or neoplasms. (Drugs that act in this way are called ***chemotherapeutic agents.***)

There are several possible ways that drugs can achieve these results, which are described below.

Receptor Sites

Many drugs are thought to act at specific areas on cell membranes called ***receptor sites.*** The receptor sites react with certain chemicals to cause an effect within the cell. In many situations, nearby enzymes break down the reacting chemicals and open up the receptor site for further stimulation.

To better understand this process, think of how a key works in a lock. The specific chemical (the key) approaches a cell membrane and finds a perfect fit (the lock) at a receptor site (Figure 2-1). The interaction between the chemical and the receptor site affects enzyme systems within the cell. The activated enzyme systems then produce certain effects, such as increased or decreased cellular activity, changes in cell membrane permeability, or alterations in cellular metabolism.

Some drugs interact directly with receptor sites to cause the same activity that natural chemicals would cause at that site. These drugs are called agonists (see Figure 2-1). For example, insulin reacts with specific insulin receptor sites to change cell membrane permeability, thus promoting the movement of glucose into the cell.

Other drugs act to prevent the breakdown of natural chemicals that are stimulating the receptor site. For example, monoamine oxidase (MAO) inhibitors block the breakdown of norepinephrine by the enzyme MAO. (Normally, MAO breaks down norepinephrine, removes it from the receptor site, and recycles the components to form new norepinephrine.) The blocking action of MAO inhibitors allows norepinephrine to stay on the receptor site, stimulating the cell longer and leading to prolonged norepinephrine effects. Those effects can be therapeutic (e.g., relieve depression) or adverse (e.g., increase heart rate and blood pressure).

Selective serotonin reuptake inhibitors (SSRIs) work similarly to MAO inhibitors in that they also exert a blocking action. Specifically, they block removal of serotonin from receptor sites. This action leads to prolonged stimulation of brain cells, which is thought to provide relief from depression.

Some drugs react with receptor sites to block normal stimulation, producing no effect. For example, curare (a drug used on the tips of spears in the Amazon to paralyze prey and cause death) occupies receptor sites for acetylcholine, which is necessary for muscle contraction and movement. Curare prevents muscle stimulation, causing paralysis. Curare is said to be a competitive antagonist of acetylcholine (see Figure 2-1).

Still other drugs may react with specific receptor sites on a cell and by reacting there, prevent the reaction of another chemical with a different receptor site on that cell. Such drugs would be called noncompetitive antagonists (see Figure 2-1).

In the case of certain drugs, the actual mechanisms of action are unknown. But speculation exists that many drugs use the receptor site mechanism to bring about their effects.

Drug–Enzyme Interactions

Drugs also can cause chemical reactions by interfering with the enzyme systems that act as catalysts for various chemical reactions. Enzyme systems work in

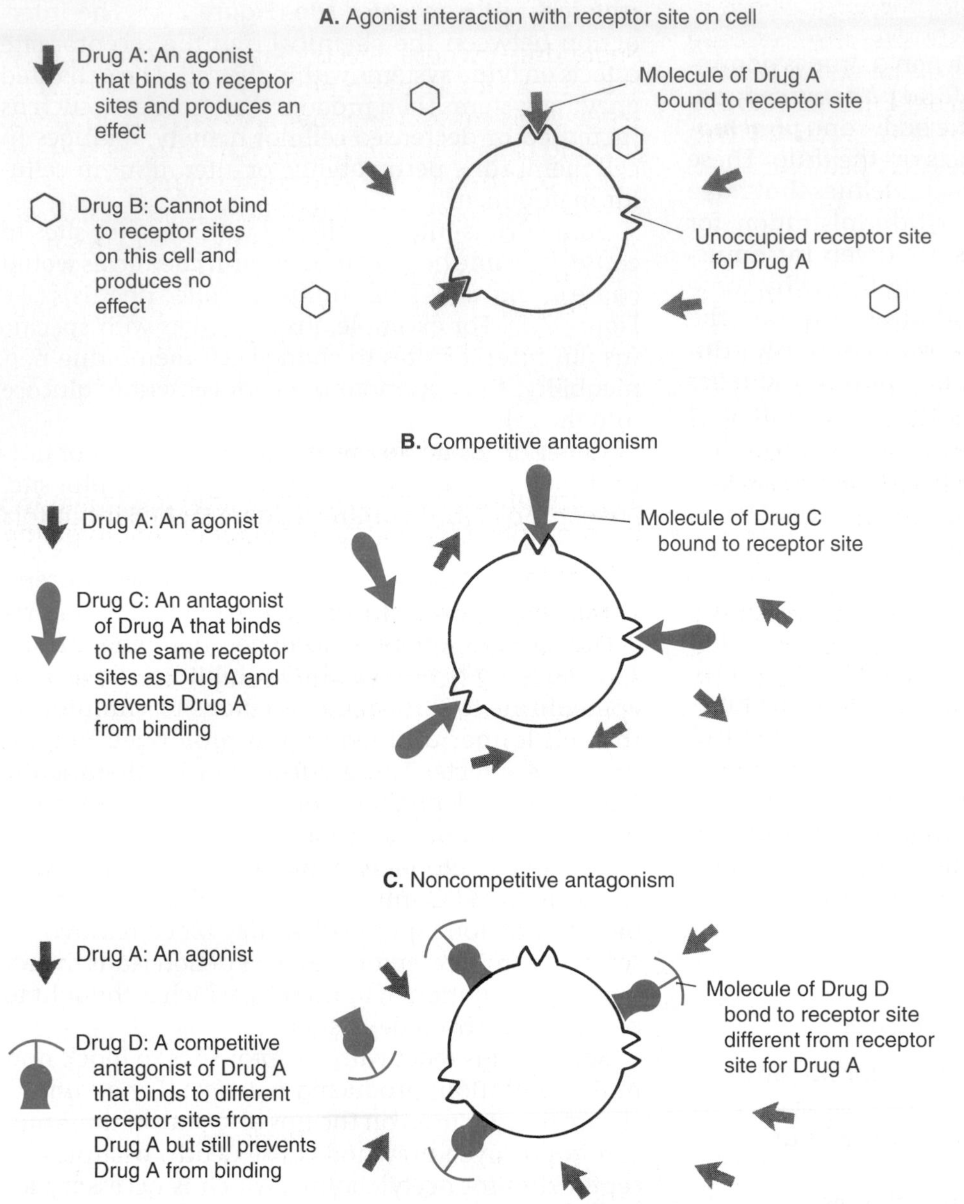
A. Agonist interaction with receptor site on cell
Drug A: An agonist that binds to receptor sites and produces an effect
Drug B: Cannot bind to receptor sites on this cell and produces no effect
Molecule of Drug A bound to receptor site
Unoccupied receptor site for Drug A
B. Competitive antagonism
Drug A: An agonist
Drug C: An antagonist of Drug A that binds to the same receptor sites as Drug A and prevents Drug A from binding
Molecule of Drug C bound to receptor site
C. Noncompetitive antagonism
Drug A: An agonist
Drug D: A competitive antagonist of Drug A that binds to different receptor sites from Drug A but still prevents Drug A from binding
Molecule of Drug D bond to receptor site different from receptor site for Drug A

FIGURE 2-1. Receptor theory of drug action. (*A*) Agonist interaction with receptor site on cell: molecules of drug A react with specific receptor sites on cells of effector organs and change the cell's activity. (*B*) Competitive antagonism: drug A and drug C have an affinity for the same receptor sites and compete for these sites; drug C has a greater affinity, occupies more of the sites, and antagonizes drug A. (*C*) Noncompetitive antagonism: drug D reacts with a receptor site that is different from the receptor site for drug A, but still somehow prevents drug A from binding with its receptor sites. Drugs that act by inhibiting enzymes can be pictured as acting similarly to the receptor site antagonists illustrated in *B* and *C*, above. Enzyme inhibitors block the binding of molecules of normal substrate to active sites on the enzyme.

a cascade effect, with one enzyme activating another and eventually causing a cellular reaction. When just one step in one of the many enzyme systems is blocked, normal cell function is disrupted. Acetazolamide (*Diamox*) is a diuretic that blocks the enzyme carbonic anhydrase, which will subsequently alter the hydrogen ion and water exchange system in the kidney as well as the eye.

Selective Toxicity

Ideally, all chemotherapeutic agents would act only on enzyme systems that are essential for the life of a pathogen or neoplastic cell, and not affect healthy cells. The ability of a drug to attack only those systems found in foreign cells is known as ***selective toxicity.*** Penicillin, an antibiotic used to treat bacterial infections, has selective toxicity. It affects an enzyme system unique to bacteria, causing bacterial cell death without disrupting normal cell functioning.

Unfortunately, most other chemotherapeutic agents also destroy normal human cells, causing many of the adverse effects associated with antipathogen and antineoplastic chemotherapy. Cells that reproduce or are replaced rapidly (e.g., bone marrow cells, gastrointestinal cells, hair follicles) are more easily affected by these agents. Consequently, the goal of many chemotherapeutic drug regimens is to deliver a dose that will be toxic to the invading cells, yet cause the least amount of toxicity to the host.

PHARMACOKINETICS

Pharmacokinetics involves the study of ***absorption, distribution,*** metabolism or ***biotransformation,*** and ***excretion*** of drugs. (These processes are discussed in detail below.) In clinical practice, pharmacokinetic considerations include the onset of drug action, drug half life, timing of the peak effect, duration of drug effects, metabolism or biotransformation of the drug, and the site of excretion. Figure 2-2 outlines these processes, which are described below.

Critical Concentration

After a drug is administered, its molecules first must be absorbed into the body, then make their way to the reactive tissues. If a drug is going to work properly on these reactive tissues, thus having a therapeutic effect, it has to reach a high enough concentration in the body. The amount of a drug needed to cause a therapeutic effect is called the ***critical concentration.***

Drug evaluation studies determine the critical concentration required to cause the desired therapeutic effect. The recommended dosage of a drug is based on the amount that needs to be given to eventually reach the critical concentration. Too much of a drug will produce toxic effects, while too little will not produce the desired therapeutic effects.

LOADING DOSE

Some drugs whose effects may be needed quickly, but which would take a prolonged period of time to reach a critical concentration, have a recommended loading dose. Digoxin (*Lanoxin*), a drug used to increase the strength of heart contractions, and many of the xanthine bronchodilators (aminophylline, theophylline, and others) used to treat asthma attacks are often started with a loading dose to reach the critical concentration. The critical concentration then is maintained at the recommended dosing schedule.

Dynamic Equilibrium

The actual concentration that a drug reaches in the body results from a dynamic equilibrium involving several factors:

- Absorption from the site of entry
- Distribution to the active site
- Biotransformation (metabolism) in the liver
- Excretion from the body

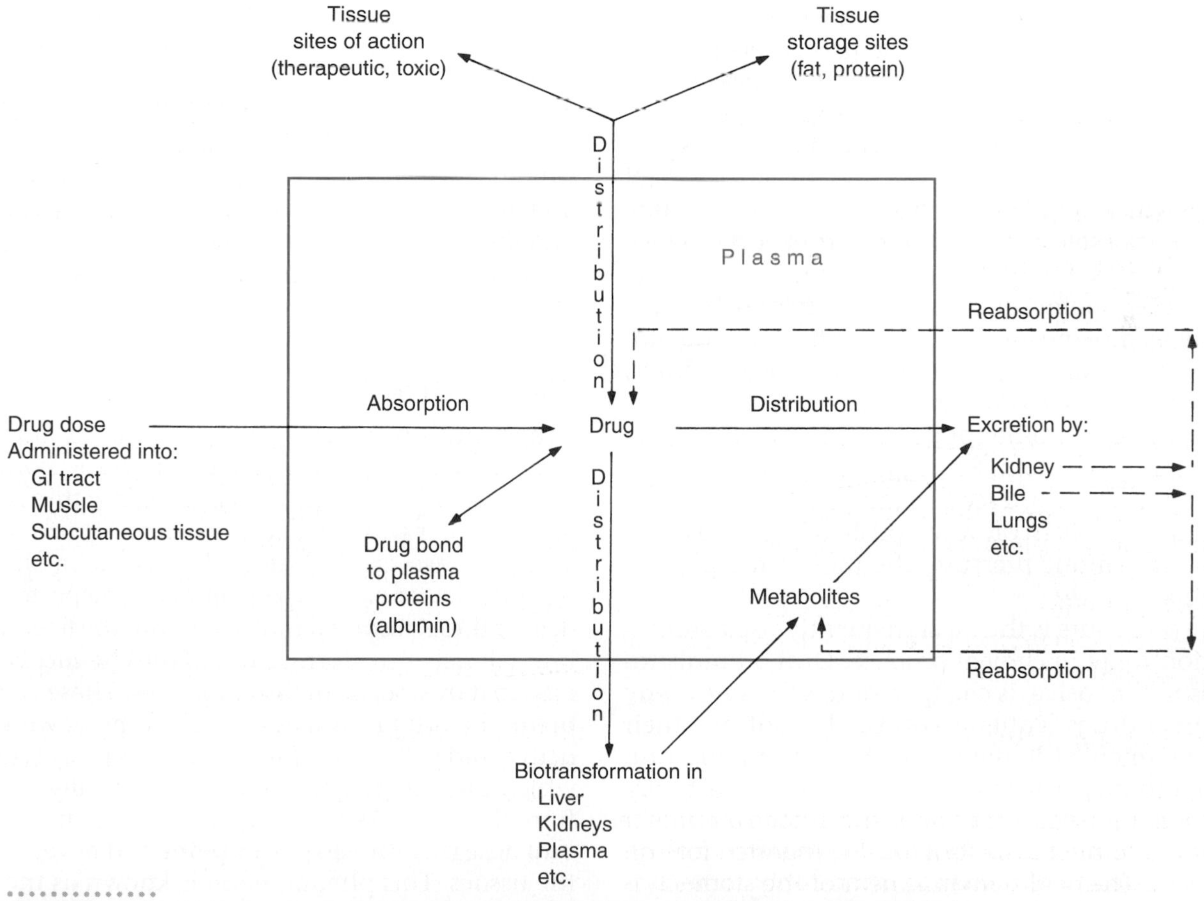

FIGURE 2-2. The processes by which a drug is handled in the body. *Dashed lines* indicate that some portion of a drug and its metabolites may be reabsorbed from the excretory organs. The dynamic equilibrium of drug pharmacokinetics is shown.

These factors are key elements in determining the amount of drug needed (dose) and the frequency of the dose repetition (scheduling) required to reach the critical concentration for the desired length of time. When administering a drug, the nurse needs to consider the phases of pharmacokinetics to try to make the drug regimen as effective as possible.

Absorption

In order to reach reactive tissues, a drug must first make its way into the circulating fluids of the body. ***Absorption*** refers to what happens to a drug from the time it is introduced to the body until it reaches the circulating fluids and tissues. Drugs can be absorbed from many different areas in the body: through the gastrointestinal (GI) tract either orally or rectally, through mucous membranes, through the skin, through the lung, and through muscle or subcutaneous tissues (see Figure 2-2).

Drugs can be absorbed into cells through various processes, which include passive diffusion, active transport, and filtration. Passive diffusion is the major process through which drugs are absorbed into the body. Passive diffusion occurs across a concentration gradient. When there is more drug on one side of a cell membrane, the drug will move to the area of lower concentration. This process does not require any cellular energy and it occurs more quickly if the drug molecule is small, is soluble in water and in lipids (cell membranes are made of lipids and proteins; see Chapter 5 for details), and has no electrical charge which could repel it from the cell membrane.

Unlike passive diffusion, active transport is a process that uses energy to actively move a molecule across a cell membrane. The molecule may be large or may be moving against a concentration gradient. This process is not very important in absorbing drugs, but is often used in drug excretion in the kidney.

Filtration is another process the body commonly uses in drug excretion. Filtration involves movement through pores in the cell membrane down a concentration gradient or, when pushed by hydrostatic, blood, or osmotic pressure, the pull of the plasma proteins.

The oral route is the most frequently used administration route in clinical practice. Oral administration is not invasive, is cheaper, and is the safest way to deliver drugs. Patients can easily continue their drug regimen at home when they are taking oral medications.

Oral administration subjects the drug to a number of barriers aimed at destroying the ingested foreign chemical. The acidic environment of the stomach is one of the first barriers to foreign chemicals. The acid breaks down many compounds and inactivates others. This fact is taken into account by pharmaceutical companies when preparing capsules or tablets of drugs. The binders that are used often are designed to break down in a certain acidity and release the active drug to be absorbed.

When food is present, stomach acidity is higher and the stomach empties more slowly, thus exposing the drug to the acidic environment for longer periods of time. Certain foods that increase stomach acidity, such as milk products, alcohol, and protein, will also speed the breakdown of many drugs. Other foods may chemically bind drugs or block their absorption. To decrease the effects of this acid barrier and the direct effects of certain foods, oral drugs ideally should be given 1 hour before or 2 hours after a meal.

Some drugs that cannot survive in sufficient quantity when given orally need to be injected directly into the body. Drugs that are injected intravenously (IV) reach their full strength at the time of injection, avoiding initial breakdown. These drugs are more apt to cause toxic effects because the margin for error in dosage is much smaller. Drugs that are injected intramuscularly (IM) are absorbed directly into the capillaries in the muscle and sent into circulation. This takes time, as the drug needs to be picked up by the capillary and taken into the veins. Because males have more vascular muscles than females, IM injections in males reach a peak level faster than in females. Subcutaneous (SC) injections deposit the drug just under the skin where it is slowly absorbed into circulation. Timing of absorption varies with SC injection, depending on the fat content of the injection site and the state of local circulation.

Table 2-1 outlines the various factors that affect drug absorption.

FIRST-PASS EFFECT

Drugs that are taken orally are usually absorbed from the small intestine directly into the portal venous system, the blood vessels that flow through the liver on their way back to the heart. Aspirin and alcohol are two drugs that are known to be absorbed from the lower end of the stomach. The portal veins deliver these absorbed molecules into the liver, which immediately transforms most of the chemicals delivered to it by a series of liver enzymes. These enzymes break the drug into metabolites, some of which are active and will cause effects in the body and some of which are deactivated and can be readily excreted from the body. As a result, a large percentage of the oral dose is destroyed at this point and never reaches the tissues. This phenomenon is known as the ***first-pass effect.*** The recommended dose for oral drugs can be considerably higher than the recommended

TABLE 2-1

FACTORS AFFECTING ABSORPTION OF DRUGS

Route	Factors Affecting Absorption
IV	None: direct entry into the venous system
IM	Perfusion or blood flow to the muscle Fat content of the muscle Temperature of the muscle: cold will vasoconstrict and decrease absorption
SC	Perfusion or blood flow to the tissue Fat content of the tissue Temperature of the tissue: cold will vasoconstrict and decrease absorption
PO (oral)	Acidity of stomach Length of time in stomach Blood flow to GI tract Presence of interacting foods or drugs
PR (rectal)	Perfusion or blood flow to the rectum Lesions in the rectum Length of time retained for absorption
Mucous membranes (sublingual, buccal)	Perfusion or blood flow to the area Integrity of the mucous membranes Presence of food or smoking Length of time drug retained in area
Topical (skin)	Perfusion or blood flow to area Integrity of skin
Inhalation	Perfusion or blood flow to the area Integrity of lung lining Ability to administer drug properly

dose for parenteral drugs, taking the first-pass effect into account.

Injected drugs and drugs absorbed from sites other than the GI tract undergo a similar biotransformation when they pass through the liver. Some of the active drug already will have had a chance to reach the reactive tissues before reaching the liver, making the injected drug more effective at a lower dose than the oral equivalent.

Distribution

The portion of the drug that gets through the first-pass effect is delivered to circulation for transport throughout the body. ***Distribution*** involves the movement of a drug to the body's tissues (see Figure 2-2). Much like absorption, factors that can affect distribution include the drug's lipid solubility and ionization, and the perfusion of the reactive tissue.

For example, tissue perfusion is a factor in treating a diabetic patient who has a lower leg infection and needs antibiotics to destroy the bacteria in the area. In this case, systemic drugs may not be effective because part of the disease process involves changes in vasculature and decreased blood flow to some areas, particularly the lower limbs. If there is not adequate blood flow to the area, little antibiotic can be delivered to the tissues and little antibiotic effect will be seen.

In the same way, patients who are in a cold environment may experience vasoconstriction in the extremities, preventing blood flow to those areas. Thus, they would be unable to deliver drugs to those areas and would receive little therapeutic effect from drugs intended to react with those tissues.

Many drugs are bound to proteins and are not lipid soluble. These drugs cannot be distributed to the central nervous system because of the effective blood–brain barrier (see below), which is highly selective in allowing lipid soluble substances to pass into the nervous system.

PROTEIN BINDING

Most drugs are bound to some extent to proteins in the blood to be carried in circulation. This protein–drug complex is relatively large and cannot enter into capillaries and then into tissues to react. The drug must be freed from the protein binding site at the tissues.

Some drugs are tightly bound and are released very slowly. These drugs have a very long duration of action because they are not freed to be broken down or excreted, and so are very slowly released into the reactive tissue. Some drugs are loosely bound. These drugs tend to act quickly and to be excreted quickly. Some drugs may compete with each other for protein binding sites and alter the effectiveness or toxicity of a drug when the two drugs are given together.

BLOOD–BRAIN BARRIER

The blood–brain barrier is a protective system of cellular activity that keeps many things (foreign invaders, poisons) away from the central nervous system (CNS). Drugs that are highly lipid soluble are more likely to pass through the blood–brain barrier and reach the CNS. Drugs that are not lipid soluble are not able to pass the blood–brain barrier. This can be of clinical significance when trying to treat a brain infection with antibiotics. Nearly all antibiotics are nonlipid soluble and will not cross the blood–brain barrier. Effective antibiotic treatment can only occur when the infection is bad enough to alter the blood–brain barrier and allow antibiotics to cross.

Although many drugs can cause adverse CNS effects, this is often due to indirect drug effects, and not the actual reaction of the drug with CNS tissue. For example, alterations in glucose levels and electrolyte changes can interfere with nerve functioning and produce CNS effects.

PLACENTA/BREAST MILK

Many drugs readily pass through the placenta and affect the developing fetus in pregnant women. As stated earlier, it is best not to administer any drugs to pregnant women because of the possible risk to the fetus. Drugs should be given only when the benefit clearly outweighs any risk.

Many other drugs are secreted into breast milk, thus having the potential to affect the neonate. Because of this possibility, the nurse must always check the ability of a drug to pass into breast milk when giving a drug to a nursing mother.

Biotransformation (Metabolism)

The body is well prepared to deal with myriad foreign chemicals. Enzymes in the liver, in many cells, in the lining of the gastrointestinal tract, and even circulating in the body detoxify foreign chemicals to protect the fragile homeostasis that keeps the body functioning (see Figure 2-2). Almost all of the chemical reactions that the body uses to convert drugs and other chemicals into nontoxic substances are based on a few processes that work to make the chemical less active and more easily excreted from the body.

LIVER ENZYME SYSTEMS

The liver is the single most important site of drug metabolism or biotransformation, the process by which drugs are changed into new, less active chemicals. Think of the liver as a sewage treatment plant. Everything that is absorbed from the gastrointestinal tract first enters the liver to be "treated." The liver detoxifies many chemicals and uses others to produce needed enzymes and structures.

The hepatic cells' intracellular structures are lined with enzymes, which are packed together in what is called the hepatic microsomal system. Because orally administered drugs enter the liver first, the enzyme systems immediately work on the absorbed drug to biotransform it. As explained above, this is the first-pass effect and it is responsible for neutralizing most of the drugs that are taken.

The presence of a chemical that is metabolized by a particular enzyme system often increases the activity of that enzyme system. This process is referred to as enzyme induction. Only a few basic enzyme systems are responsible for metabolizing most of the chemicals that pass through the liver. Consequently, increased activity in that enzyme system speeds the metabolism of the drug that caused the enzyme induction as well as any other drug that is metabolized using that same enzyme system. This explains why some drugs cannot be taken together effectively, since the presence of one drug speeds the metabolism of other drugs, preventing them from reaching their therapeutic levels. It also explains why liver disease is often a contraindication to certain drug use and is frequently a reason to use caution with certain drugs. If the liver is not functioning effectively, the drug is not metabolized as it should be and toxic levels can develop rather quickly.

Excretion

Excretion is the removal of a drug from the body. The skin, saliva, the lungs, bile, and feces are some of the routes used to excrete drugs. The kidneys, however, play the most important role in drug excretion (see Figure 2-2). Drugs that have been made water soluble in the liver are often readily excreted from the kidney by glomerular filtration, the passage of water and water soluble components from the plasma into the renal tubule.

Other drugs are secreted or reabsorbed through the renal tubule by active transport systems. The acidity of the urine can play an important part in the excretions. The active transport systems that move the drug into the tubule often do so by exchanging it for acid or bicarbonate molecules. This is an important concept to remember when trying to clear a drug rapidly from the system or trying to understand why a drug is being given at the usual dose but is reaching toxic levels in the system. The patient's kidney functioning and urine acidity are important things to consider before administering a drug. Kidney dysfunction can lead to toxic levels of a drug in the body because the drug cannot be excreted.

Figure 2-3 outlines the pharmacokinetic processes that are undergone by a drug administered orally.

HALF-LIFE

The ***half-life*** of a drug is the time it takes for the amount of drug in the body to decrease to one-half of the peak level it previously achieved. For instance, if a patient takes 20 mg of a drug with a half-life of 2 hours, 10 mg of the drug will remain 2 hours after administration. Two hours later, 5 mg will be left (one-half of the previous level); in 2 more hours, only 2.5 mg will remain. This information is important in determining the appropriate timing for a drug dose.

The half-life is determined by a balance of all of the factors working on that drug: absorption, distribution, biotransformation, and excretion. The absorption rate, the speed of biotransformation, the distrib-

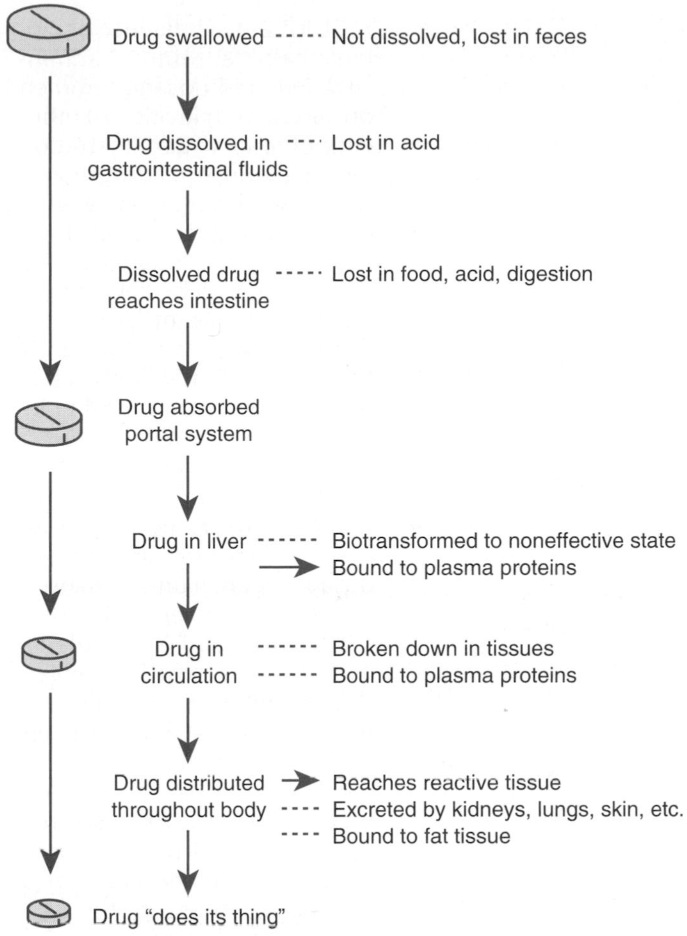

FIGURE 2-3. Pharmacokinetics affect the amount of a drug reaching reactive tissues. Very little of an oral dose of a drug actually reaches reactive sites.

ution to the tissues, and how fast a drug is excreted are all taken into consideration when determining the half-life of the drug. The half-life that is indicated in any drug monograph is the half-life for a healthy person. Using this information, the half-life of a drug for a patient with kidney or liver dysfunction (which could prolong the biotransformation and the time for excretion of a drug) can be estimated and changes made in the dosage schedule by the prescriber.

The timing of drug administration is important to achieve the most effective drug therapy. Nurses can use their knowledge of drug half-life to explain the importance of following a schedule of drug administration in the hospital or at home. Figure 2-4 shows the effects of drug administration on the critical concentration.

FACTORS INFLUENCING DRUG EFFECTS

When administering a drug to a patient, the nurse must be aware that the human factor has a tremendous influence on what actually happens to a drug when it enters the body. No two people react in exactly the same way to any given drug. Even though textbooks and drug guides explain the pharmacodynamics and pharmacokinetics of a drug, the nurse needs to remember that that information usually is based on studies of healthy, adult males. Things may be very different in the clinical setting. Consequently, before administering any drug, the nurse must consider a number of factors. These are discussed in detail below and summarized in Box 2-1.

Weight

The recommended dosage of a drug is based on drug evaluation studies and is targeted at a 150-pound person. People who are much heavier than that may require larger doses to get a therapeutic effect from a drug because they have increased tissues to perfuse and increased receptor sites in some reactive tissue. People who are much lighter than the norm may require smaller doses of a drug. Toxic effects may occur at the recommended dosage if the person is very small.

Age

Age is a factor primarily in children and older adults. Children metabolize many drugs differently than adults and have immature systems for handling drugs. While many drugs come with recommended pediatric dosages, others can be converted to pediatric dosages using one of several conversion formulas (Box 2-2).

Older adults undergo many physical changes that are a part of the aging process. Their bodies may respond very differently in all aspects of pharmacokinetics—less effective absorption, less efficient distribution because of fewer plasma proteins and less efficient perfusion, altered biotransformation or metabolism of the drug because of liver changes with age, and less effective excretion due to less efficient kidneys. Many drugs now come with recommended geriatric dosages. Other drugs may need decreased dosages in the elderly.

When administering drugs to a patient at either end of the age spectrum, the nurse should monitor closely for desired effects. If the effects are not what would normally be expected, a dosage adjustment should be considered.

Gender

Physiological differences between men and women can influence a drug's effect. When giving IM injections, for example, it is important to remember that males have more vascular muscles, so the effects of the drug will be seen sooner than with females.

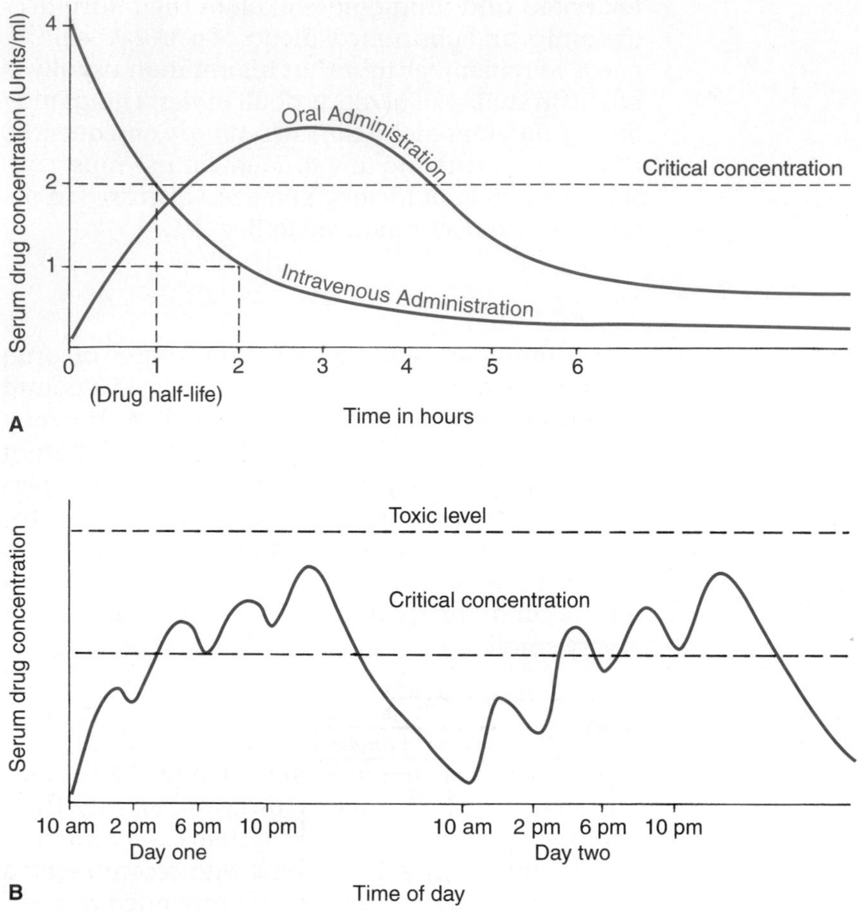

FIGURE 2-4. Influence of biologic half-life, route of administration, and dosage regimen on serum drug levels. (*A*) Influence of route of administration on time course of drug levels following a single dose of a drug. The dashed lines indicate how the biologic half-life of the drug may be determined from the curve of drug concentration after an IV dose. At time zero, immediately after the injection, there were 4 units of drug in each milliliter of serum. The drug concentration fell to half this amount, 2 units/ml, after 1 hour, the drug's biologic half-life. (*B*) Influence of dosage regimen on serum drug levels (drug given qid, 10-2-6-10). The drug accumulates as successive doses are given throughout each day; the drug is being given at a rate greater than the patient's body can eliminate it. This dosage regimen has been chosen so that the patient will have a therapeutic level of the drug for a significant portion of the day, yet never have a toxic level of the drug.

BOX 2-1 ***FACTORS AFFECTING THE BODY'S RESPONSE TO A DRUG***

- Weight
- Age
- Gender
- Physiological factors—diurnal rhythm, electrolyte balance, acid–base balance, hydration
- Pathological factors—disease, hepatic dysfunction, renal dysfunction, GI dysfunction, vascular disorders, low blood pressure
- Genetic factors
- Immunological factors—allergy
- Psychological factors—placebo effect, health beliefs, compliance
- Environmental factors—temperature, light, noise
- Drug tolerance
- Cumulation effects

Females have more fat cells than males, so drugs that deposit in fat may be slowly released and cause effects for a prolonged period of time. For example, gas anesthetics have an affinity for depositing in fat and may cause drowsiness and sedation sometimes weeks after surgery.

Of course, women who are given any drug should always be questioned about the possibility of pregnancy. The use of drugs in pregnant women is not recommended unless the benefit clearly outweighs the potential risk to the fetus.

Physiological Factors

Physiological differences such as diurnal rhythm of the nervous and endocrine systems, acid–base balance, hydration, and electrolyte balance can affect the way that a drug works on the body and the way

BOX 2-2

FORMULAE FOR CALCULATING DOSAGES

Pediatric Dosages

Children often require different doses of drugs than adults because children's bodies often handle drugs very differently from adults' bodies. The "standard" drug dosages listed in package inserts and references such as the PDR refer to the adult dosage. In some cases, a pediatric dosage is suggested, but in many cases it will need to be calculated based on the child's age, weight, or body surface. The following are some standard formulae for calculating the pediatric dose.

Fried's Rule

$$\text{infant's dose } (< 1 \text{ y}) = \frac{\text{infant's age (in mo)}}{150 \text{ mo}} \times \text{average adult dose}$$

Young's Rule

$$\text{child's dose } (1-12 \text{ y}) = \frac{\text{child's age (in yrs)}}{\text{child's age (in yrs)} + 12} \times \text{average adult dose}$$

Clark's Rule

$$\text{child's dose} = \frac{\text{weight of child (lb)}}{150 \text{ lb}} \times \text{average adult dose}$$

Surface Area Rule

$$\text{child's dose} = \frac{\text{surface area of child (in square meters)}}{1.73} \times \text{average adult dose}$$

The surface area of a child is determined using a nomogram which determines surface area based on height and weight measurements.

Pediatric dosage calculations should be checked by two persons. Many institutions have procedures for double checking the dosage calculation of those drugs (eg, digoxin) used most frequently in the pediatric area.

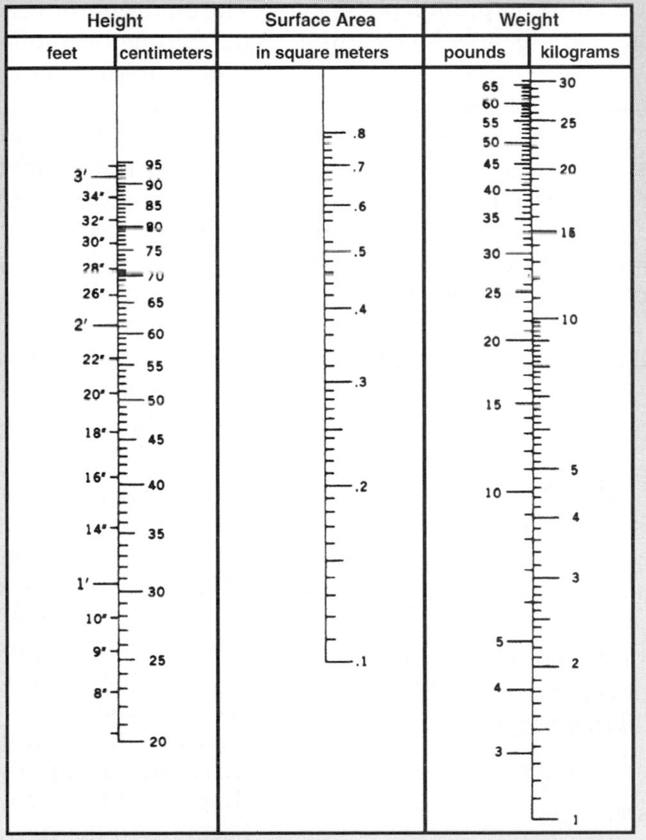

Nomogram for estimating surface area of infants and young children. To determine the surface area of the patient, draw a straight line between the point representing the height on the left vertical scale and the point representing the weight on the right vertical scale. The point at which this line intersects the middle vertical scale represents the patient's surface area in square meters.

that the body handles a drug. If a drug does not produce the desired effect, review the patient's acid–base and electrolyte profile and the timing of the drug.

Pathological Factors

Drugs are usually used to treat disease or pathology. However, the disease that the drug is intended to treat can change the functioning of the chemical reactions within the body and thus change the response to the drug.

Other pathological conditions can change the basic pharmacokinetics of a drug. For example, GI disorders can affect the absorption of many oral drugs. Vascular diseases and low blood pressure alter the distribution of a drug, preventing it from being delivered to the reactive tissue and making it nontherapeutic. Liver or kidney diseases affect the way that a drug is biotransformed and excreted and can lead to toxic reactions when the usual dose is given.

Genetic Factors

Genetic differences can sometimes explain a patient's varied response to a drug. Some people lack certain enzyme systems necessary for metabolizing a drug, while others have overactive enzyme systems and break down drugs very quickly. Still others have differing metabolisms or slightly different enzymatic makeup which alter their chemical reactions and the effects of a given drug. Predictable differences in the pharmacokinetics and pharmacodynamic effects of drugs can be anticipated with people of particular cultural backgrounds because of genetic makeup. These differences will be highlighted throughout this book.

Immunological Factors

People can develop an allergy to a drug. After exposure to its proteins, a person can develop antibodies to a drug. With future exposure to that drug, that person may experience a full-blown allergic reaction. Sensitivity to a drug can range from dermatological effects to anaphylaxis, shock, and death. (Drug allergies are discussed in detail in Chapter 3.)

Psychological Factors

The patient's attitude about a drug has been shown to have a real effect on how that drug works. A drug is more likely to be effective if the patient thinks it will work than when the patient believes it will not work. This is called the ***placebo effect.***

The patient's personality influences compliance to the drug regimen. Some people who feel that they can influence their health actively seek health care and willingly follow a prescribed regimen. These people usually trust the medical system and feel that their efforts will be positive. Other people do not trust the medical system and may feel that they have no control over their own health and may be unwilling to comply with any prescribed therapy. Knowing a patient's health-seeking history and feelings about health care are important in planning an educational program that will work for that particular patient. It is also important to know this information when arranging for necessary follow-up and evaluations.

As the caregiver most often involved in drug administration, the nurse is in a position to influence the patient's attitude about drug effectiveness. Frequently, the nurse's positive attitude, combined with additional comfort measures, can improve the patient's response to a medication.

Environmental Factors

The environment can affect the success of drug therapy. Some drug effects are helped by a quiet, cool, nonstimulating environment. For example, sedating drugs are given to help people to relax or to decrease tension. Cutting down on external stimuli to decrease tension and stimulation will help the drug to be more effective. Other drug effects may be influenced by temperature. For example, antihypertensives that are regulated during cold, winter months may become too effective in warmer environments, when natural vasodilation to release heat tends to lower the blood pressure. If a patient's response to a medication is not as expected, the nurse might look for changes in environmental conditions.

Tolerance

Some drugs are tolerated by the body over time. This may be because of increased biotransformation of the drug, increased resistance to its effects, or other pharmacokinetic factors. Drugs that are tolerated no longer cause the same reaction and need to be taken in increasingly larger doses to achieve a therapeutic effect. An example of this type of drug is morphine, an opiate used for pain relief. The longer that morphine is taken, the more tolerant the body becomes to the drug, so larger and larger doses are needed to relieve pain. Clinically, this situation can be avoided by giving the drug in smaller doses or in combination with other drugs that may also relieve pain. Cross-tolerance, or resistance to drugs within the same class, may also occur in some situations.

Cumulation

When a drug is taken in successive doses at intervals that are shorter than recommended, or when the body is not able to eliminate a drug properly, the drug can accumulate in the body, leading to toxic levels and adverse effects. This can be avoided by following the drug regimen precisely. In reality, with many people managing their own drug regimens at home, strict compliance to a drug regimen seldom occurs. Some people will take all of their medication first thing in the morning, so they won't forget to take the pills later in the day. Others will realize that they forgot a dose and take two to make up for it. Many interruptions of everyday life can interfere with strict adherence to a drug regimen. When a drug is causing serious adverse effects, review the drug regimen with the patient to find out how the drug is being taken, then educate the patient appropriately.

Drug–Drug Interactions

When two or more drugs are taken together, there is a possibility that these drugs will interact with each other to cause unanticipated effects in the body. Usually this is an increase or decrease in the desired therapeutic effect of one or all of the drugs, or an increase in adverse effects.

Clinically significant drug–drug interactions occur with drugs that have small margins of safety. That means that if there is very little difference between a therapeutic dose and a toxic dose of the drug, interference with the drug's pharmacokinetics or pharmacodynamics can produce serious problems. For example, drug–drug interactions can occur in the following situations:

- At the site of absorption: One drug prevents or accelerates absorption of the other drug. For example, the antibiotic tetracycline is not absorbed from the GI tract if calcium or calcium products are present in the stomach.
- During distribution: One drug competes for the protein binding site of another drug, so the second drug cannot be transported to the reactive tissue. For example, aspirin will compete with the drug methotrexate (*Rheumatrex*) for protein binding sites. Because aspirin is more competitive, the result is increased release of methotrexate and increased toxicity to the tissues.
- During biotransformation: One drug stimulates or blocks the metabolism of the other drug. Warfarin (*Coumadin*), an oral anticoagulant, is biotransformed more quickly if barbiturates, rifampin, and many other drugs are given at the same time. Because the warfarin is biotransformed more quickly, higher doses will be needed to achieve the desired effect.
- During excretion: One drug competes for excretion with the other drug, leading to accumulation and toxic effects of one of the drugs. Digoxin (*Lanoxin*) and quinidine (*Quinaglute*) are both excreted from the same sites in the kidney. If given together, the quinidine is more competitive for these sites and is excreted, whereas digoxin levels increase because it cannot be excreted.
- At the site of action: One drug may be an antagonist of the other drug, or may cause effects opposite of the other drug, leading to no therapeutic effect. This is seen when an antihypertensive drug is taken with an allergy drug that also increases blood pressure. The effects on blood pressure are negated, and there is a loss of the antihypertensive effectiveness of the drug.

Whenever two or more drugs are being given together, the nurse should first consult a drug guide for a listing of clinically significant drug–drug interactions. Sometimes problems can be avoided by spacing the drugs apart or adjusting dosages. Check the monograph of any drug that is being given to monitor for clinically important drug–drug interactions.

Drug–Food Interactions

Certain foods can interact with drugs in much the same way that drugs can interact with each other. For the most part, this interaction occurs when the drug and the food are in direct contact in the stomach. Some foods increase acid production, speeding the breakdown of the drug molecule and preventing absorption and distribution of the drug. Some foods chemically react with certain drugs and prevent their absorption into the body. The antibiotic tetracycline cannot be taken with iron products for this reason. Tetracycline also binds with calcium to some extent and should not be taken with foods or other drugs containing calcium.

As stated earlier, oral drugs are best taken on an empty stomach. If the patient cannot tolerate the drug on an empty stomach, the food selected to be taken with the drug should be something that is known not to interact. Drug monographs list important drug–food interactions and give guidelines to avoid problems and optimize the drug's therapeutic effects.

Drug–Laboratory Test Interactions

As explained previously, the body works using a series of chemical reactions. Because of this, administration of a particular drug may alter tests that are done on various chemical levels or reactions as part of a diagnostic study. This drug–laboratory test interaction is a result of the drug being given, and not necessarily a result of a change in the body's responses or actions. It is important to keep these interactions in mind when evaluating a patient's diagnostic tests. If one test result is off and it does not fit in with the clinical picture or other test results, consider the possibility of a drug–laboratory test interference. For example, dalteparin (*Fragmin*), a low molecular weight heparin used to prevent deep vein thrombosis after abdominal surgery, may cause increased ACT and ALT levels (liver enzymes) with no injury to liver cells or hepatitis.

ACHIEVING THE OPTIMAL THERAPEUTIC EFFECT

As overwhelming as all of this information may seem, most patients can follow a drug regimen to achieve optimum therapeutic effects without serious adverse effects. Avoiding problems is the best way to treat adverse or ineffective drug effects. The nurse should incorporate basic history and physical assessment factors into any care plan, so obvious problems can be spotted and handled promptly. When giving a drug that just does not do what it is expected to do, the nurse should further examine the factors that are known to influence drug effects (see Box 1-1). Frequently, the drug regimen can be modified to deal with that influence. Rarely is it necessary to completely stop a needed drug regimen because of adverse or intolerable effects. The nurse is the caregiver in the best position to assess problems early, intervene appropriately, and prevent serious problems from occurring.

CHAPTER SUMMARY

- Pharmacodynamics is the study of the way that drugs affect the body.
- Most drugs work by replacing natural chemicals, by stimulating normal cell activity, or by depressing normal cell activity.
- Chemotherapeutic agents work to interfere with normal cell functioning causing cell death. The most desirable chemotherapeutic agents are those with selective toxicity to foreign cells and foreign cell activities.
- Drugs frequently act at specific receptor sites on cell membranes to stimulate enzyme systems within the cell and to alter the cell's activities.
- Pharmacokinetics is the study of the way the body deals with drugs and includes absorption, distribution, biotransformation, and excretion of the drug.
- The goal of established dosing schedules is to achieve a critical concentration of the drug in the body. This critical concentration is the amount of the drug necessary to achieve the drug's therapeutic effects.
- Arriving at a critical concentration involves the dynamic equilibrium between drug absorption, distribution, metabolism or biotransformation, and excretion.
- Absorption involves moving a drug into the body for circulation. Oral drugs are absorbed from the small intestine and undergo many changes and are affected by many things in the process. IV drugs are injected directly into circulation and do not need additional absorption.
- Drugs are distributed to various tissues throughout the body depending on their solubility and ionization. Most drugs are bound to plasma proteins for transport to reactive tissues.
- Drugs are metabolized or biotransformed into less toxic chemicals by various enzyme systems in the body. The liver is the primary site of drug metabolism or biotransformation.
- The first-pass effect is the breakdown of oral drugs in the liver immediately after absorption. Drugs given by other routes often reach reactive tissues before passing through the liver for biotransformation.
- Drug excretion is removal of the drug from the body. This occurs mainly through the kidneys.
- The half-life of a drug is the amount of time it takes for an amount of drug in the body to decrease to one-half of the peak level it previously achieved. The half-life is affected by all aspects of pharmacokinetics. Knowing the half-life of a drug will help to predict dosing schedules and duration of effects.
- The actual effects of a drug are determined by the pharmacokinetics, the pharmacodynamics, and many human factors that will change the drug's effectiveness.
- To provide the safest, most effective drug therapy, the nurse must consider all of the interacting aspects that influence drug concentration and effectiveness.

BIBLIOGRAPHY

Batt, A. M. et al. (1994). Drug metabolizing enzymes related to laboratory medicine: Cytochrome P-450 and UDP glucuronosyltransferases. *Clinica Chimica Acta, 226*, 171–190.

DeMaagd, G. (1995). High-risk drugs in the elderly population. *Geriatric Nursing, 16*(5), 198–207.

Edwards, J. (1997). Guarding against adverse drug events. *American Journal of Nursing, 97*(5), 26–31.

Hardman, J. G., Limbird, L. E., Molinoff, P. B., Ruddon, R. W., & Gilman, A. G. (Eds.). (1996). *Goodman and Gilman's the pharmacological basis of therapeutics* (9th ed.). New York: McGraw-Hill.

Kelly, J. (1995). Pharmacodynamics and drug therapy. *Professional Nursing, 10*(12), 792–796.

O'Mahoney, M. S. & Woodhouse, K. W. (1994). Age, environmental factors and drug metabolism. *Pharmacology and Therapeutics, 61,* 279–287.

Pirmohamed, M. et al. (1996). The role of active metabolites in drug toxicity. *Drug Safety, 11,* 114–144.

The Medical Letter on Drugs and Therapeutics. (1999). New Rochelle, NY: Medical Letter.

Wetterberg, L. (1994). Light and biological rhythms. *Journal of Internal Medicine, 235,* 5–19.

Wissmann, J. (1996). Strategies for teaching critical thinking in pharmacology. *Nurse Educator, 21,* 42–46

CHAPTER 3

Toxic Effects of Drugs

CHAPTER OUTLINE

KEY TERMS

blood dyscrasia
dermatological reactions
drug allergy
hypersensitivity
poisoning
stomatitis
superinfections

INTRODUCTION

All drugs are potentially dangerous. Even though chemicals are carefully screened and tested on animals and in people before they are released as drugs, drug products often cause unexpected or unacceptable reactions when they are given. Drugs are chemicals, and the human body operates by a vast series of chemical reactions. Consequently, many effects can be seen when just one chemical factor is altered. Today's potent and amazing drugs can cause a great variety of reactions, many of which are more severe than ever seen before.

ADVERSE EFFECTS

As noted previously, adverse effects are undesired effects that may be unpleasant or even dangerous. They can occur for many reasons, including the following:

- The drug may have other effects on the body besides the therapeutic effect.
- The patient may be sensitive to the drug being given.
- The drug's action on the body can cause other responses that are undesirable or unpleasant.
- The patient may be taking too much or too little of the drug, leading to adverse effects.

The nurse, as the caregiver who most frequently administers medications, must be constantly alert for signs of drug reactions of different types. Patients and their families need to be taught what to look for when patients are taking drugs at home. Some adverse effects can be countered with specific comfort measures or precautions. Knowing that these effects may occur and what actions can be taken to prevent or cope with them may be the critical factor in helping the patient to comply with drug therapy.

Adverse drug effects can be of several types: primary actions, secondary actions, and hypersensitivity.

Primary Actions

One of the most common occurrences in drug therapy is the development of adverse effects from simple overdosage. In such cases, the patient suffers from effects that are merely an extension of the desired effect. For example, an anticoagulant may act so effectively that the patient experiences excessive and spontaneous bleeding. This type of adverse effect can be avoided by monitoring the patient carefully and adjusting the prescribed dose to fit that particular patient's needs.

In the same way, a patient taking an antihypertensive drug may become dizzy, weak, or faint when taking the "recommended dose," but will be able to adjust to the drug therapy with a reduced dose. These effects may be caused by individual response to the drug, high or low weight, age, or underlying pathology that alters the effects of the drug.

Secondary Actions

Drugs can produce a wide variety of effects in addition to the desired pharmacological effect. Sometimes the drug dose can be adjusted so that the desired effect can be achieved without producing undesired secondary reactions. But sometimes this is not possible, and the adverse effects are almost inevitable. In such cases, the patient needs to be informed that these effects may occur and counseled in ways to cope with the undesired effects. For example, many antihistamines are very effective in drying up secretions and helping breathing, but they also cause drowsiness. The patient taking antihistamines needs to know that driving a car or operating dangerous machinery could pose a serious problem because of the drowsiness, and so should be avoided.

Hypersensitivity

Some patients are excessively responsive to either the primary or the secondary effects of a drug. This is known as ***hypersensitivity,*** and it may result from a pathological or underlying condition. As noted previously, many drugs are excreted through the kidneys. If a patient has kidney problems, for example, the drug may not be excreted and may accumulate in the body, causing toxic effects.

Hypersensitivity also could occur if the patient has an underlying condition that makes the drug effects especially unpleasant or dangerous. For example, a patient with an enlarged prostate who takes an anticholinergic drug may develop urinary retention or even bladder paralysis when the drug's effects block the urinary sphincters. This patient would need to be taught to empty the bladder before taking the drug. A reduced dosage also may be required to avoid these potentially serious effects on the urinary system.

DRUG ALLERGY

A ***drug allergy*** occurs when the body forms antibodies to a particular drug, causing an immune response when the person is reexposed to the drug. A patient cannot be allergic to a drug that has never been taken, although patients can have cross allergies within the same drug class. Many people state that they have a drug allergy because of the effects of a drug. For example, one patient stated that she was allergic to the diuretic furosemide (*Lasix*). Upon further questioning, the nurse discovered that the patient was "allergic" to the drug because it made her urinate frequently—the desired drug effect, but one that the patient thought was a reaction to the drug. Patients who state that they have a drug "allergy" should be further questioned as to the nature of the allergy. Many patients do not receive needed treatment because the response to the drug is not understood.

Drug allergies fall into four main classifications: anaphylactic, cytotoxic, serum sickness, and delayed reactions (Table 3-1). The nurse, as the primary caregiver involved in administering drugs, must constantly assess for potential drug allergies and be prepared to intervene appropriately.

DRUG-INDUCED TISSUE AND ORGAN DAMAGE

Drugs can act directly or indirectly to cause many types of adverse effects in various tissues, structures, and organs (Figure 3-1). These drug effects account for many of the cautions that are noted before drug administration begins. The possible occurrence of these effects also accounts for the fact that the use of some drugs is contraindicated in patients with a particular history or underlying pathology. The specific contraindications and cautions for the administration of a particular drug are noted with each drug type discussed in this book and in the individual monographs in your nursing drug guide. These effects occur frequently enough that the nurse should be aware of the presentation of the drug-induced damage and appropriate interventions that should be used if they occur.

Dermatological Reactions

Dermatological reactions are adverse reactions involving the skin. These can range from a simple rash to potentially fatal exfoliative dermatitis. Many adverse reactions involve the skin because many drugs can deposit there or cause direct irritation to the tissue. Procainamide (*Pronestyl*), a drug used to treat cardiac arrhythmias, causes a characteristic skin rash in many patients using the drug.

TABLE 3-1

TYPES OF DRUG ALLERGIES

Allergy Type	Assessment	Interventions
Anaphylactic reaction This allergy involves an antibody that reacts with specific sites in the body to cause the release of chemicals, including histamine, that produce immediate reactions (mucous membrane swelling and constricting bronchi) that can lead to respiratory distress and even respiratory arrest.	Hives, rash, difficulty breathing, increased BP, dilated pupils, diaphoresis, "panic" feeling, increased heart rate, respiratory arrest	Administer epinephrine, 0.3 ml of a 1:1000 solution, SC for adults or 0.01 mg/kg of 1:1000 SC for pediatric patients. Massage the site to speed absorption rate. Repeat the dose every 15–20 minutes, as appropriate. Notify the prescriber and/or primary caregiver and discontinue the drug. Be aware that prevention is the best treatment. Counsel patient with known allergies to wear a Medic-Alert identification and, if appropriate, to carry an emergency epinephrine kit.
Cytotoxic reaction This allergy involves antibodies that circulate in the blood and attack antigens (the drug) on cell sites, causing death of that cell. This reaction is not immediate but may be seen over a few days.	CBC showing damage to blood-forming cells (decreased Hct, decreased WBC, decreased platelets); liver function tests showing elevated liver enzymes; renal function test showing decreased renal function	Notify the prescriber and/or primary caregiver and discontinue the drug. Support the patient to prevent infection and conserve energy until the allergic response is over.
Serum-sickness reaction This allergy involves antibodies that circulate in the blood and cause damage to various tissues by depositing in blood vessels. This reaction may occur up to a week or more after exposure to the drug.	Itchy rash, high fever, swollen lymph nodes, swollen and painful joints, edema of the face and limbs	Notify the prescriber and/or primary caregiver and discontinue the drug. Provide comfort measures to help the patient cope with the signs and symptoms (cool environment, skin care, positioning, ice to joints, administer antipyretics or anti-inflammatory agents, as appropriate).
Delayed allergic reaction This reaction occurs several hours after exposure and involves antibodies that are bound to specific white cells.	Rash, hives, swollen joints (similar to the reaction to poison ivy)	Notify the prescriber and/or primary caregiver and discontinue drug. Provide skin care and comfort measures that may include antihistamines or topical corticosteroids.

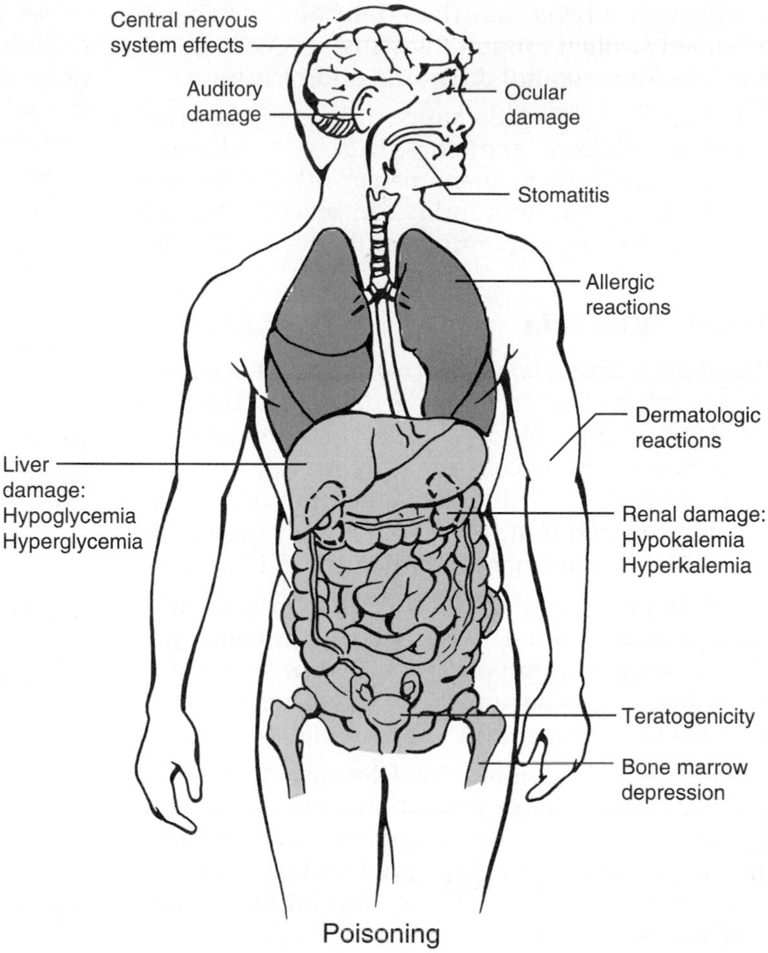

FIGURE 3-1. Variety of adverse effects associated with drug use.

Assessment. Hives, rashes, lesions. Severe reactions may include exfoliative dermatitis, which is characterized by rash and scaling, fever, enlarged lymph nodes, and enlarged liver; and the potentially fatal erythema multiforme exudativum (Stevens-Johnson syndrome), which is characterized by dark red papules appearing on the extremities with no pain or itching; often these appear in rings or disk-shaped patches.

Interventions. In mild cases, or where the benefit of the drug outweighs the discomfort of skin lesion, provide frequent skin care; instruct the patient to avoid rubbing, tight or rough clothing, and harsh soaps or perfumed lotions; administer antihistamines, as appropriate. In severe cases, discontinue the drug and notify prescriber and/or primary caregiver. Be aware that in addition to the above interventions, topical corticosteroids, antihistamines, and emollients are frequently used.

Stomatitis

Stomatitis, or inflammation of the mucous membranes, can occur because of a direct toxic reaction to the drug, or because the drug deposits in the end capillaries in the mucous membranes, leading to inflammation. Fluorouracil (*Adrucil*), an antineoplastic agent, causes mouth sores or stomatitis in most of the patients who take it.

Assessment. Swollen gums, inflamed gums (gingivitis), swollen and red tongue (glossitis), difficulty swallowing, bad breath, pain in the mouth and throat.

Interventions. Provide frequent mouth care with a nonirritating solution. Offer nutrition evaluation and development of a tolerated diet usually involving frequent meals. If necessary, arrange for a dental consultation. Note that antifungal agents and/or local anesthetics are sometimes used.

Superinfections

One of the body's protective mechanisms is the wide variety of bacteria that live within or on the surface of the body. This bacterial growth is called the normal flora. The normal flora protect the body from invasion by other bacteria, viruses, fungi, and so on. Several kinds of drugs (especially antibiotics) destroy the normal flora, leading to the development of ***superinfections.***

ASSESSMENT. Fever, diarrhea, black-hairy tongue, inflamed swollen tongue (glossitis), mucous membrane lesions, vaginal discharge and/or itching.

INTERVENTIONS. Provide supportive measures (frequent mouth care, skin care, access to bathroom facilities, small and frequent meals). Administer antifungal therapy as appropriate. In severe cases, discontinue the drug responsible for the superinfection.

Blood Dyscrasia

Blood dyscrasia is bone marrow suppression caused by drug effects. This occurs when drugs that can cause cell death (antineoplastics, antibiotics) are used. Because bone marrow cells multiply rapidly, they are said to be rapidly turning over. Since they go through cell division and multiply so often, they are highly susceptible to any agent that disrupts cell function.

ASSESSMENT. Fever, chills, sore throat, weakness, back pain, dark urine, decreased Hct (anemia), low platelet count (thrombocytopenia), low WBC count (leukopenia), a reduction of all cellular elements of the CBC (pancytopenia).

INTERVENTIONS. Monitor blood counts. Provide supportive measures (rest, protection from exposure to infections, protection from injury, avoidance of activities that might result in injury or bleeding). In severe cases, discontinue the drug or stop administration until the bone marrow recovers to a safe level.

Toxicity

LIVER INJURY

As explained, oral drugs are absorbed and passed directly into the liver in the first-pass effect. This exposes the liver cells to the full impact of the drug before it is broken down for circulation throughout the body. Most drugs are metabolized in the liver, so any metabolites that are irritating or toxic will also affect liver integrity.

ASSESSMENT. Fever, malaise, nausea, vomiting, jaundice, change in color of urine or stools, abdominal pain or colic, elevated liver enzymes (AST [SGOT], ALT [SGPT]) alterations in bilirubin levels, changes in clotting factors (PTT changes).

INTERVENTIONS. Discontinue the drug and notify the prescriber and/or primary caregiver. Offer supportive measures (small, frequent meals, skin care, cool environment, rest periods).

RENAL INJURY

The glomerulus in the kidney has a very small capillary network that filters the blood into the renal tubule. Some drug molecules are just the right size to get plugged into the capillary network, causing acute inflammation and severe renal problems. Some drugs are excreted from the kidney unchanged; these drugs have the potential to directly irritate the renal tubule and alter normal absorption and secretion processes. Gentamicin (*Garamycin*), a potent antibiotic, is frequently associated with renal toxicity.

ASSESSMENT. Elevated BUN, elevated creatinine levels, decreased Hct, electrolyte imbalances, fatigue, malaise, edema, irritability, skin rash.

INTERVENTIONS. Notify the prescriber and/or primary caregiver and discontinue the drug as needed. Offer supportive measures (positioning, diet and fluid restrictions, skin care, electrolyte therapy, rest periods, controlled environment). In severe cases, be aware that dialysis may be required for survival.

POISONING

Poisoning occurs when an overdose of a drug damages multiple body systems, leading to the potential for fatal reactions. Assessment parameters vary with the particular drug. Treatment of drug poisoning also varies, depending on the drug. Throughout this book, specific antidotes or treatments to poisoning will be identified, if known. Emergency measures and life support often are needed in severe cases.

Alterations in Glucose Metabolism

HYPOGLYCEMIA

Some drugs affect metabolism and the use of glucose, causing low serum blood glucose levels, or hypoglycemia. Glipizide (*Glucotrol*) and glyburide (*DiaBeta*) are antidiabetic agents whose desired action is a lower blood glucose, but which can lower blood glucose too far, causing hypoglycemia.

ASSESSMENT. Fatigue; drowsiness; hunger; anxiety; headache; cold/clammy skin; shaking and lack of coordination (tremulousness); increased heart rate; increased blood pressure; numbness and tingling of the mouth, tongue, and/or lips; confusion; rapid and shallow respirations. In severe cases, seizures and/or coma may occur.

INTERVENTIONS. Restore glucose, intravenously (IV) or orally if possible. Provide supportive measures (skin care, environmental control of light and temperature, rest). Institute safety measures to prevent injury or falls. Offer reassurance to help the patient cope with the experience.

HYPERGLYCEMIA

Some drugs stimulate the breakdown of glycogen or alter metabolism in such a way as to cause high serum glucose levels, or hyperglycemia. Ephedrine (generic), a drug used as a bronchodilator and antiasthma drug as well as to relieve nasal congestion, can break down stored glycogen and cause an elevation of blood glucose by its effects on the sympathetic nervous system.

ASSESSMENT. Fatigue, increased urination (polyuria), increased thirst (polydipsia), deep respirations (Kussmaul's respirations), restlessness, increased hunger (polyphagia), nausea, hot or flushed skin, fruity odor to breath.

INTERVENTIONS. Administer insulin therapy to decrease blood glucose as appropriate. Provide support to help the patient deal with signs and symptoms (access to bathroom facilities, controlled environment, reassurance, mouth care).

Electrolyte Imbalances

HYPOKALEMIA

Some drugs affecting the kidney can cause low serum potassium levels (hypokalemia) by altering the renal exchange system. For example, loop diuretics function by causing the loss of potassium as well as sodium and water. Potassium is essential for the normal functioning of nerves and muscles.

ASSESSMENT. Serum potassium (K+) less than 3.5 mEq/L, weakness, numbness and tingling in the extremities, muscle cramps, nausea, vomiting, diarrhea, decreased bowel sounds, irregular pulse, weak pulses, orthostatic hypotension, disorientation. In severe cases paralytic ileus (absent bowel sounds, abdominal distention, acute abdomen) may occur.

INTERVENTIONS. Replace serum potassium and carefully monitor serum levels and patient response. Provide supportive therapy (safety precautions to prevent injury or falls, orient patient, comfort measures for pain and discomfort).

HYPERKALEMIA

Some drugs that affect the kidney, such as the potassium-sparing diuretics, can lead to potassium retention and a resultant increase in serum potassium levels (hyperkalemia). Other drugs that cause cell death or injury, such as many antineoplastic agents, also can cause the cells to release potassium, leading to hyperkalemia.

ASSESSMENT. Serum potassium level over 5.0 mEq/L, weakness, muscle cramps, diarrhea, numbness and tingling, slow heart rate, low blood pressure, decreased urine output, difficulty breathing.

INTERVENTIONS. Institute measures to decrease serum potassium, including use of sodium polystyrene sulfonate. Offer supportive measures to cope with discomfort. Institute safety measures to prevent injury or falls. Monitor cardiac effects and be prepared for cardiac emergency. In severe cases, be aware that dialysis may be needed.

Sensory Effects

OCULAR TOXICITY

The blood vessels in the retina are very tiny and called "end arteries." That is, they stop and do not interconnect with other arteries feeding the same cells. Some drugs are deposited into these tiny arteries, causing inflammation and tissue damage. Chloroquine (*Aralen*), a drug used to treat some rheumatoid diseases, can cause retinal damage and even blindness.

ASSESSMENT. Blurring of vision, color vision changes, corneal damage, blindness.

INTERVENTIONS. Monitor the patient's vision carefully when on known ocular toxic drugs. Consult with the prescriber and/or primary caregiver and discontinue the drug as appropriate. Provide supportive measures, especially if vision loss is not reversible. Monitor lighting and exposure to sunlight.

AUDITORY DAMAGE

Tiny vessels and nerves in the eighth cranial nerve are easily irritated and damaged by certain drugs. The macrolide antibiotics can cause severe auditory nerve damage. Aspirin, one of the most commonly used drugs, is often linked to auditory ringing and eighth cranial nerve effects.

ASSESSMENT. Dizziness, ringing in the ears (tinnitus), loss of balance, loss of hearing.

INTERVENTIONS. Monitor the patient's perceptual losses or changes. Provide protective measures to prevent falling or injury. Consult with the prescriber to decrease dose or discontinue drug. Provide supportive measures to cope with drug effects.

Neurological Effects

GENERAL CNS EFFECTS

Though the brain is fairly well protected from many drug effects by the blood–brain barrier, some drugs do affect neurological functioning, either directly or by altering electrolyte or glucose levels. Beta blockers, used to treat hypertension, angina, and many other conditions, can cause feelings of anxiety, insomnia, and nightmares.

ASSESSMENT. Confusion, delirium, insomnia, drowsiness, hyperreflexia or hyporeflexia, bizarre dreams, hallucinations.

INTERVENTIONS. Provide safety measures to prevent injury. Caution the patient to avoid dangerous situations such as driving a car or operating dangerous machinery. Orient the patient and provide support. Consult with the prescriber to decrease drug dose or discontinue drug.

ATROPINE-LIKE (CHOLINERGIC) EFFECTS

Some drugs mimic the effects of the parasympathetic nervous system by directly or indirectly stimulating cholinergic receptors. Donepezil (*Aricept*), a drug used to treat Alzheimer's disease, causes many cholinergic effects. Many cold remedies and antihistamines also cause cholinergic effects.

ASSESSMENT. Dry mouth, altered taste perception, dysphagia, heartburn, constipation, bloating, paralytic ileus, urinary hesitancy and retention, impotence, blurred vision, cycloplegia, photophobia, headache, mental confusion, nasal congestion, palpitations, decreased sweating, dry skin.

INTERVENTIONS. Provide sugarless lozenges, mouth care to help mouth dryness. Arrange for bowel program as appropriate. Have the patient void before taking the drug to aid voiding. Provide safety measures if vision changes occur. Arrange for medication for headache, nasal congestion as appropriate. Advise the patient to avoid hot environments and to take protective measures to prevent falling and dehydration if exposed to heat due to decreased sweating.

PARKINSON-LIKE SYNDROME

Drugs that directly or indirectly affect dopamine levels in the brain can cause a syndrome that resembles Parkinson's disease. Many of the antipsychotic or neuroleptic drugs can cause this effect. In most cases, the effects will go away when the drug is withdrawn.

ASSESSMENT. Lack of activity, akinesia, muscular tremors, drooling, changes in gait, rigidity, extreme restlessness or "jitters" (akathisia), spasms (dyskinesia).

INTERVENTIONS. Discontinue the drug, if necessary. Know that treatment with anticholinergics or antiparkinson drugs may be recommended if the benefit outweighs the discomfort of adverse effects. Provide small, frequent meals if swallowing becomes difficult. Provide safety measures if ambulation becomes a problem.

NEUROLEPTIC MALIGNANT SYNDROME (NMS)

General anesthetics and other drugs that have direct CNS effects can cause a generalized syndrome that includes high fever.

ASSESSMENT. Extrapyramidal symptoms, hyperthermia, autonomic disturbances, fever.

INTERVENTIONS. Discontinue the drug, if necessary. Know that treatment with anticholinergics or antiparkinson drugs may be required. Provide supportive care to lower body temperature. Institute safety precautions as needed.

Teratogenicity

Many drugs that reach the developing fetus or embryo can cause death or congenital defects. The exact effects of a drug on the fetus may not be known. In some cases, a predictable syndrome occurs when a drug is given to a pregnant woman. In any situation, a pregnant woman who is given a drug needs to be advised of the possible effects on the baby. Before administering a drug to a pregnant patient, the actual benefits should be weighed against the potential risks. All pregnant women should be advised not to self-medicate during the pregnancy.

INTERVENTIONS. Provide emotional and physical support for dealing with fetal death or birth defects.

Box 3-1 summarizes all of the adverse effects that have been described throughout this chapter.

BOX 3-1

SUMMARY OF ADVERSE DRUG EFFECTS

- Extension of primary action
- Occurrence of secondary action
- Allergic reactions
  - Anaphylactic reactions
  - Cytotoxic reactions
  - Serum-sickness reactions
  - Delayed allergic reactions
- Tissue and organ damage
  - Dermatologic reactions
  - Stomatitis
  - Superinfections
  - Blood dyscrasia
  - Toxicity
    - Liver injury
    - Renal injury
    - Poisoning
  - Alterations in glucose metabolism
    - Hypoglycemia
    - Hyperglycemia
  - Electrolyte imbalances
    - Hypokalemia
    - Hyperkalemia
  - Sensory effects
    - Ocular toxicity
    - Auditory damage
  - Neurological effects
    - General CNS effects
    - Atropine-like (cholinergic) effects
    - Parkinson-like syndrome
    - Neuroleptic malignant syndrome (NMS)
  - Teratogenicity

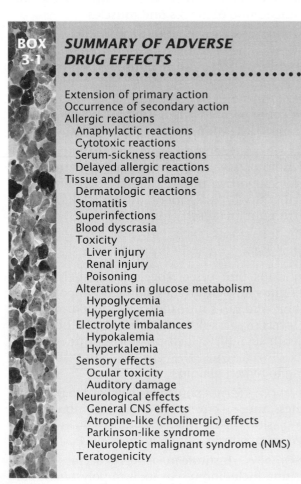

CHAPTER SUMMARY

- No drug does only what is desired of it. All drugs have adverse effects associated with them.
- Adverse drug effects can range from allergic reactions to tissue and cellular damage. The nurse, as the health care provider most associated with drug administration, needs to assess each situation for potential adverse effects and intervene appropriately to minimize those effects.
- Adverse effects can be extensions of the primary action of a drug or secondary effects that are not necessarily desirable, but unavoidable.
- Allergic reactions can occur when a person makes antibodies to a drug or drug protein. When a person is exposed to that drug another time, an immune response may occur. Allergic reactions can be of various types. The exact response should be noted to avoid future confusion in patient care.
- Tissue damage can include skin problems, mucous membrane inflammation, blood dyscrasia, superinfections, liver toxicity, hypoglycemia or hyperglycemia, renal toxicity, electrolyte disturbances, various CNS problems (ocular, auditory toxicity, neuroleptic malignant syndrome, Parkinson-like syndrome, atropine-like effects), teratogenicity, and overdose poisoning.

BIBLIOGRAPHY

Barditch-Crovo, P. (1995). Adverse reactions to therapy for HIV infections. *Emergency Medical Clinics of North America, 13,* 133–146.

Brody, T. M. et al. (1994). *Human pharmacology: Molecular to clinical* (2nd ed.). St. Louis: C.V. Mosby.

Drug Facts & Comparisons. (1999). St. Louis: Facts & Comparisons.

Food and Drug Administration. (1994). FDA Launches MEDWATCH program; Monitoring adverse drug reactions. *NP News, 2,* 1, 4.

Hardman, J. G., Limbird, L. E., Molinoff, P. B., Ruddon, R. W., & Gilman, A. G. (Eds.). (1996). *Goodman and Gilman's the pharmacological basis of therapeutics* (9th ed.). New York: McGraw-Hill.

The Medical Letter on Drugs and Therapeutics. (1999). New Rochelle, NY: Medical Letter.

CHAPTER

4

Nursing Management

CHAPTER OUTLINE

INTRODUCTION
NURSING: ART AND SCIENCE
THE NURSING PROCESS
Assessment
PAST HISTORY
PHYSICAL ASSESSMENT
Nursing Diagnosis
Interventions
PROPER DRUG ADMINISTRATION
COMFORT MEASURES
PATIENT/FAMILY EDUCATION
Evaluation
CHAPTER SUMMARY
BIBLIOGRAPHY

KEY TERMS

assessment
nursing
nursing diagnosis
nursing process

INTRODUCTION

The delivery of medical care today is in a constant state of change, and sometimes crisis. The population is aging, resulting in more chronic disease and more complex care issues. The population also is transient, resulting in unstable support systems and fewer at-home care providers and helpers. At the same time, medicine is undergoing a technological boom—CT scans, NMRIs, experimental drugs, and so on. Patients are being discharged earlier from acute care facilities, or are not being admitted at all for procedures that used to be treated in-hospital with follow-up support and monitoring provided. Patients also are becoming more responsible for their own care and for following complicated medical regimens at home.

NURSING: ART AND SCIENCE

Nursing is a unique and complex science as well as a nurturing and caring art. In the traditional sense, nursing has been viewed as ministering and soothing the sick. In the current state of medical changes, nursing also has become increasingly technical and scientific. Nurses have had to assume increasing responsibilities that involve not only nurturing and caring, but also assessing, diagnosing, and intervening with patients to treat, to prevent, and to educate in order to help patients cope with various health states.

The nurse deals with the whole person: the physical, emotional, intellectual, social, and spiritual aspects. The nurse needs to consider how a person responds to treatment, disease, and the change in lifestyle that may be required. The nurse is the key health care provider who is in the position to assess the whole patient, to administer therapy as well as medications, to teach the patient how to best cope with the therapy to assure the best outcomes, and to evaluate the effectiveness of the therapy. Being able to do this requires a broad knowledge base in the basic sciences (anatomy, physiology, nutrition, chemistry, pharmacology), the social sciences (sociology, psychology), education, and many other disciplines.

THE NURSING PROCESS

Though all nursing theorists do not completely agree on the process that defines the practice of nursing, most theorists do include certain key elements in the ***nursing process.*** These elements are the basic components of the decision-making or problem-solving process:

- ***Assessment*** (gathering information)
- ***Nursing diagnosis*** (analyzing the information gathered to arrive at some conclusions)
- Interventions (actions undertaken to meet the patient's needs, such as administration, education, and comfort measures)
- Evaluation (determining the effects of the interventions that were performed)

In general, the nursing process provides an effective method for handling all of the scientific and technical information as well as the unique emotional, social, and physical factors that each patient brings to a given situation. With respect to drug therapy, using the nursing process ensures that the patient receives the best, most efficient, scientifically based holistic care. Box 4-1 outlines the steps of the nursing process, which are discussed in detail below.

Assessment

The first step of the nursing process is the systematic, organized collection of data about the patient. Because the nurse is responsible for holistic care, these

BOX 4-1

THE STEPS OF THE NURSING PROCESS

Nursing Process

↓

Assessment

Past history
- Chronic conditions
- Drug use
- Allergies
- Level of education
- Level of understanding of disease and therapy
- Social supports
- Financial supports
- Pattern of health care

Physical assessment
- Weight
- Age
- Physical parameters related to the disease state or known drug effects

↓

Nursing Diagnosis

↓

Interventions

Proper drug administration
- Drug
- Storage
- Route
- Dosage
- Preparation
- Timing
- Recording

Comfort measures
- Placebo effect
- Managing side effects
- Lifestyle adjustments

Patient/family education

↓

Evaluation

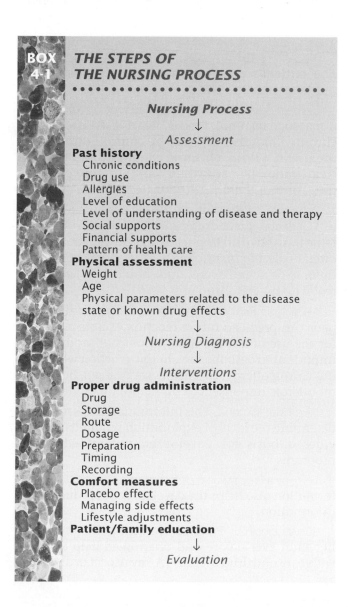

data must include information about physical, intellectual, emotional, social, and environmental factors. These data provide the nurse with the facts needed to plan educational and discharge programs, arrange for appropriate consultations, and monitor physical response to treatment or to disease.

In clinical practice, the process of assessment never ends. The patient is not in a steady state, but is in a dynamic state, adjusting to physical, emotional, and environmental influences. Each nurse develops a unique approach to the organization of the assessment, an approach that is functional and useful in the clinical setting and that makes sense to that nurse and that clinical situation.

Drug therapy is a complex and important part of health care, and the principles of drug therapy need to be incorporated into every patient assessment plan. The particular information that is needed varies with each drug, but the concepts involved are similar. Two key areas that need to be assessed are history (of past illnesses and the current problem) and physical status.

PAST HISTORY

The patient's past experiences and illnesses can influence a drug's effect.

CHRONIC CONDITIONS. The presence of certain conditions (such as renal disease, heart disease, diabetes, chronic lung disease) may be contraindications to the use of a drug. Or these conditions may require that caution be used when administering a certain drug, or that the drug dosage be adjusted.

DRUG USE. Prescription drugs, over-the-counter (OTC) drugs, street drugs, alcohol, nicotine, and caffeine may have an impact on a drug's effect. Patients often neglect to mention OTC drugs, not considering them to be actual drugs, and should be asked specifically about OTC drug use.

ALLERGIES. Past exposure to a drug or other allergens can predict a future reaction or note a caution for the use of a drug, food, or animal product. It is important to describe the allergic reaction when noting a drug allergy. In some cases, the reaction is not an allergic response, but an actual drug effect.

LEVEL OF EDUCATION. This information helps the nurse determine the level of explanation required and provides a basis for developing patient education programs.

LEVEL OF UNDERSTANDING OF DISEASE AND THERAPY. This information also helps the development of educational information.

SOCIAL SUPPORTS. Patients are being discharged earlier than ever before and often need help at home with care and drug therapy. A key aspect of discharge planning involves determining what support, if any, is available to the patient at home. In many situations, it will also involve referral to appropriate community resources.

FINANCIAL SUPPORTS. The high cost of health care in general, and of medications in particular, needs to be considered when initiating drug therapy. Because of financial constraints, a patient may not follow through with the prescribed drug regimen. In such cases, the nurse may refer the patient to appropriate resources that may offer financial assistance.

PATTERN OF HEALTH CARE. Knowing how a patient seeks health care gives the nurse valuable information to include in the educational plan. Does this patient routinely seek follow-up care or wait for emergency situations? Does the patient tend to self-treat many complaints, or is every problem brought to a health care provider?

PHYSICAL ASSESSMENT

WEIGHT. A patient's weight helps determine whether the recommended drug dosage is appropriate. Because the recommended dosage typically is based on a 150-pound adult male, patients who are much lighter or much heavier will need a dosage adjustment.

AGE. Patients at the extremes of the age spectrum—children and older adults—often require dosage adjustments based on the functional level of the liver and kidneys and the responsiveness of other organs.

PHYSICAL PARAMETERS RELATED TO THE DISEASE STATE OR KNOWN DRUG EFFECTS. Assessing these factors before drug therapy begins provides a baseline level to which future assessments can be compared to determine the effects of drug therapy. The specific parameters that need to be assessed depend on the disease process being treated and on the expected therapeutic and adverse effects of the drug therapy. For example, if a patient is being treated for chronic pulmonary disease, the respiratory status and reserve will need to be assessed, especially if a drug is being given that has known effects on the respiratory tract. In contrast, a thorough respiratory evaluation would not be warranted in a patient with no known pulmonary disease who is taking a drug with no known effects on the respiratory system. Because the nurse has the greatest direct and continual contact with the patient, the nurse has the best opportunity to detect minute changes that ultimately determine the course of drug therapy: therapeutic success or discontinuation because of adverse or unacceptable responses.

NOTE: Refer to the monographs in the companion *Lippincott's Nursing Drug Guide,* or review the monographs in the particular drug guide being used, for the specific parameters that need to be assessed in relation to the particular drug being discussed. This assessment provides not only the baseline information needed before giving that drug, but also the data required to evaluate the effects of that drug on the patient. This information should supplement the overall nursing assessment of the patient, which includes social, intellectual, financial, environmental, and other physical data.

Nursing Diagnosis

Once data have been collected, the nurse must organize and analyze that information to arrive at a nursing diagnosis. A nursing diagnosis is simply a statement of the patient's status from a nursing perspective. This statement directs appropriate nursing interventions. A nursing diagnosis shows actual or potential alteration in patient function based on the assessment of the clinical situation. Because drug therapy is only a small part of the overall patient situation, nursing diagnoses that are related to drug therapy must be incorporated into a total picture of the patient.

In the nursing considerations sections of this book, the nursing diagnoses listed are those that reflect potential alteration of function based only on the particular drug's actions (i.e., therapeutic and adverse effects). No consideration is given to environmental or disease-related problems. These diagnoses, culled from the North American Nursing Diagnosis Association (NANDA) list of accepted nursing diagnoses, are only a part of the overall nursing diagnoses related to the patient's situation.

NOTE: For a complete listing of NANDA-accepted nursing diagnoses, refer to the companion *Lippincott's Nursing Drug Guide,* Appendix V, or review the particular nursing drug guide being used.

Interventions

The assessment and diagnosis of the patient situation will direct specific nursing interventions. There are three types of interventions that are frequently involved in drug therapy: drug administration, provision of comfort measures, and patient/family education.

PROPER DRUG ADMINISTRATION

There are seven points to consider in the safe and effective administration of a drug, as follows:

1. *Drug:* Know that it is standard nursing practice to ensure that the drug being administered is the correct dose and the correct drug, and that it is being given at the correct time and to the correct patient.
2. *Storage:* Be aware that some drugs require specific storage environments (e.g., refrigeration, protection from light).
3. *Route:* Determine the best route of administration; this is often established by the formulation of the drug. Nurses can often have an impact in modifying the route to arrive at the most efficient, comfortable route for the patient based on the patient's specific situation. When establishing the prescribed route, check the proper method of administering a drug by that route.
4. *Dosage:* Calculate drug dosage appropriately, either based on the available drug form, patient body weight or surface area, or kidney function.
5. *Preparation:* Know the specific preparation required before administering any drug. For example, oral drugs may need to be shaken or crushed. Parenteral drugs may need to be reconstituted or diluted with specific solutions. Topical drugs may require specific handling, such as the use of gloves during administration, or shaving of a body area before application.
6. *Timing:* Recognize that the administration of one drug may require coordination with the administration of other drugs, foods, or physical parameters. As the caregiver most frequently involved in administering drugs, the nurse must be aware of and juggle all of these factors, as well as educate the patient to do this on his or her own.
7. *Recording:* After assessing the patient, making the appropriate nursing diagnoses, and delivering the correct drug, by the correct route, in the correct dose, at the correct time, document that information in accordance with the local requirements for recording medication administration.

COMFORT MEASURES

Nursing is in the unique position to help the patient cope with the effects of drug therapy.

PLACEBO EFFECT. The anticipation that a drug will be helpful (placebo effect) has been proven to have tremendous impact on actual success of drug therapy. So the nurse's attitude and support can be a critical part of drug therapy; a back rub, a kind word, and a positive approach may be as beneficial as the drug itself.

MANAGING ADVERSE EFFECTS. These interventions can be directed at decreasing the impact of the anticipated adverse effects of the drug and promoting patient safety. Such interventions include environmental control (temperature, light), safety measures (avoiding driving, avoiding the sun, using side rails), and physical comfort (skin care, laxatives, frequent meals).

LIFESTYLE ADJUSTMENT. Some drug effects will require that a patient change his or her lifestyle to cope effectively. For example, patients taking diuretics may have to rearrange the day to be near toilet facilities when the drug works. Patients taking MAO inhibitors have to adjust their diet to prevent serious drug effects from the interaction of certain foods. In some cases the change in lifestyle that is needed can have a tremendous impact on the patient and affect coping and compliance with any medical regimen.

NOTE: Special points regarding drug administration and related comfort measures are noted with each drug class discussed in this book. Refer to the individual drug monographs in the companion *Lippincott's Nursing Drug Guide,* or in the particular drug guide being used, for more detailed interventions regarding a specific drug.

PATIENT/FAMILY EDUCATION

With patients becoming increasingly responsible for their own care, it is essential that they have all of the information necessary to assure safe and effective drug therapy at home. In fact, many states now require that patients be given written information. Key elements that need to be included in any drug education program are as follows:

1. *Name, dose, and action of drug:* Many patients see more than one health care provider, so knowing this information is crucial to ensuring safe and effective drug therapy and avoiding drug–drug interactions.
2. *Timing of administration:* Teach patients when to take the drug with respect to frequency, other drugs, and meals.
3. *Special storage and preparation instructions:* Some drugs require particular handling; inform patients how to carry out these requirements.
4. *Specific OTC drugs to avoid:* Many patients do not consider OTC drugs to be actual drugs and may inadvertently take them along with their prescribed medications, causing unwanted or even dangerous drug–drug interactions. Prevent these situations by explaining which drugs to avoid.
5. *Special comfort or safety measures:* Teach patients how to cope with anticipated adverse effects to ease anxiety and avoid noncompliance with drug therapy. Also educate patients about the importance of follow-up tests or evaluation.
6. *Safety measures:* Instruct all patients to keep drugs out of the reach of children. Remind all patients to inform *any* health care provider they see about the drugs or drugs they are taking; this can prevent drug–drug interactions and misdiagnoses based on drug effects.
7. *Specific points about drug toxicity:* Give patients a list of warning signs of drug toxicity. Advise patients to notify their health care provider if any of these effects occur.
8. *Specific warnings about drug discontinuation:* Some drugs with a small margin of safety and drugs with particular systemic effects cannot be stopped abruptly without dangerous effects. Alert patients taking these drugs to this problem and encourage them to call their health care provider immediately if they cannot take their medication for any reason (e.g., illness, financial constraints).

NOTE: Refer to the companion *Lippincott's Nursing Drug Guide,* Appendix T, for a basic patient teaching guide that can be used in conjunction with the drug-specific teaching points found in each drug monograph, or review the particular nursing drug guide being used.

Evaluation

Evaluation is part of the continual process of patient care that leads to changes in assessment, diagnosis, and intervention. The patient is continually evaluated for therapeutic response, the occurrence of drug adverse effects, and the occurrence of drug–drug, drug–food or drug–laboratory test interactions. The efficacy of the nursing interventions and the education program must be evaluated. In some situations, the nurse will evaluate the patient simply by reapplying the beginning steps of the nursing process and analyzing for change (Figure 4-1). In some cases of drug therapy, particular therapeutic drug levels also need to be evaluated.

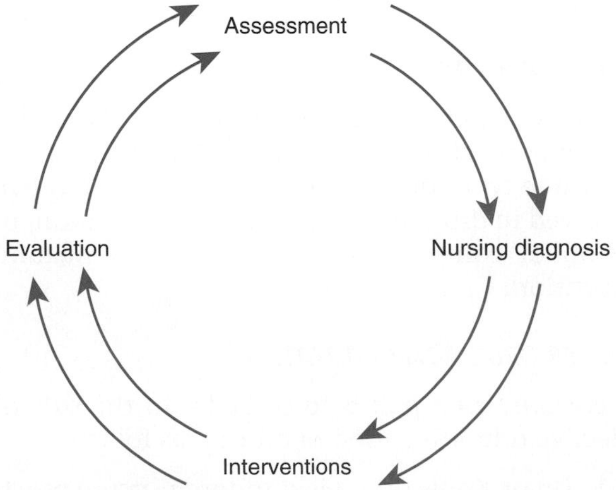

FIGURE 4-1. The continual, dynamic nature of the nursing process.

CHAPTER SUMMARY

- Nursing is a complex art and science that provides for the nurturing and care of the sick as well as prevention and education services.
- The nursing process is a problem-solving process involving assessment, nursing diagnoses, interventions, and evaluation. It is an ongoing, dynamic process that provides safe and efficient care.
- Nursing assessment must include information on history of past illnesses and current complaint as well as physical examination to provide a data base of baseline information to assure safe administration of a drug and to evaluate the drug's effectiveness and adverse effects.
- Nursing diagnoses use the data gathered during the assessment to determine actual or potential problems that will require specific nursing interventions.
- Nursing interventions should include proper administration of a drug; comfort measures to help the patient cope with the drug effects; patient and family education regarding the drug effects, ways to avoid adverse effects, warning signs to report, and any other specifics regarding that drug that will facilitate patient compliance.
- Evaluation is a continual process that assesses the situation and leads to new diagnoses or interventions as the patient reacts to the drug therapy.
- A nursing care guide and patient education materials can be prepared for each drug being given using information about a drug's therapeutic effects, adverse effects, and special considerations.

BIBLIOGRAPHY

Bates, B. (1994). *A guide to physical examination and history taking* (6th ed.). Philadelphia: Lippincott Williams & Wilkins.

Buchanan, L. M. (1994). Therapeutic nursing intervention knowledge development and outcome measures for advanced practice. *Nursing and Health Care, 15*(4).

Carpenito, L. J. (1995). *Nursing care plans and documentation* (2nd ed.). Philadelphia: Lippincott.

Carpenito, L. J. (1995). *Nursing diagnosis: Application in clinical practice* (6th ed.). Philadelphia: Lippincott.

Cohen, M. (1994). Medication errors . . . misprinted doses. FDA Precautions. *Nursing, 94*(3), 14.

McCloskey, J. & Bulechek, G. (Eds.). (1996). *Nursing interventions classification* (2nd ed.). St. Louis: C.V. Mosby.

Redman, B. (1997). *The practice of patient education* (8th ed.). St. Louis: Mosby–Year Book.

PART

2

Chemotherapeutic Agents

CHAPTER

5

Introduction to Cell Physiology

CHAPTER OUTLINE

KEY TERMS

cell cycle
cell membrane
cytoplasm
diffusion
endocytosis
exocytosis
histocompatibility antigens
lipoprotein
lysosomes
mitochondria
nucleus
organelles
osmosis
ribosomes

INTRODUCTION

Chemotherapeutic drugs are agents that affect cells by either altering cellular function or disrupting cellular integrity, causing cell death, or preventing cellular reproduction, eventually leading to cell death. To understand the actions and the adverse effects caused by chemotherapeutic agents, it is important to understand the basic functioning of the cell.

Chemotherapeutic drugs are used to destroy both organisms that invade the body (bacteria, viruses, parasites, protozoa, fungi, and so on) and abnormal cells within the body (neoplasms or cancers). By keeping in mind the various properties of the cell and cell processes, nurses may help determine interventions that increase therapeutic effectiveness of a drug and limit the undesired adverse effects.

THE CELL

The cell is the basic structural unit of the body. The cells that make up living organisms, which are arranged into tissues and organs, all have the same basic structure. Each cell has a ***nucleus,*** a ***cell membrane,*** and ***cytoplasm,*** which contains a variety of ***organelles*** (Figure 5-1).

Cell Nucleus

The nucleus of a cell contains all of the genetic material that is necessary for cell reproduction and for regulation of cellular production of proteins. Each cell is "programmed" by the genes for the production of specific proteins that allow the cell to carry out its function, maintain cell homeostasis or stability, and promote cellular division. The nucleus is encapsulated in its own membrane and remains distinct from the rest of the cytoplasm. A small spherical mass, called the nucleolus, is located within the nucleus. Within this mass are dense fibers and proteins that will eventually become the ***ribosomes,*** the sites of protein synthesis within the cell.

The nucleus also contains genes, or sequences of DNA, that control basic cell functions and allow for cell division. Genes are responsible for the formation of messenger RNA and transcription RNA, which are involved in the production of the proteins unique to the cell. The DNA necessary for cell division is found on long strains called chromatin. These structures line up and enlarge during the process of cell division.

Cell Membrane

The cell is surrounded by a thin barrier called the cell membrane, which separates the intracellular fluid from the extracellular fluid. The membrane is

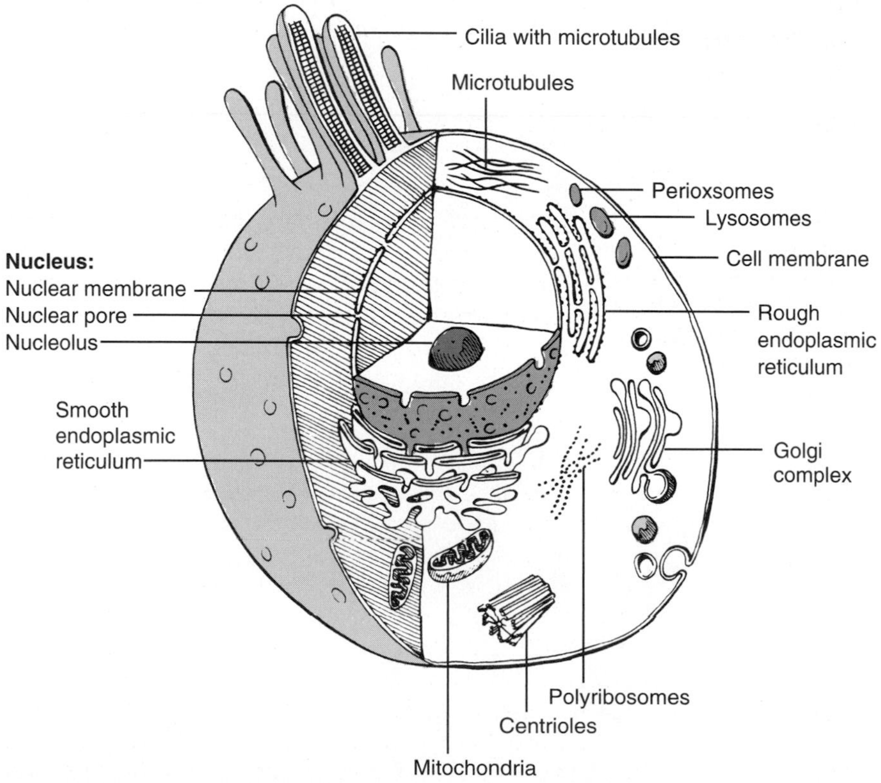

FIGURE 5-1. General structure of a cell and the location of its organelles.

essential for maintaining the cellular integrity and is equipped with many mechanisms for maintaining cell homeostasis.

LIPOPROTEINS

The cell membrane, which consists of lipids and proteins, is a ***lipoprotein*** structure. The two components are arranged in a freely moving double layer. The membrane is largely lipids—phospholipids, glycolipids, and cholesterol. The phospholipids, which are bipolar in nature, line up with their polar regions pointing toward the interior or the exterior of the cell and their nonpolar regions lying within the cell membrane. The polar region mixes well with water, and the nonpolar region repels water. This property allows the membrane to act as a barrier, keeping the cytoplasm within the cell and regulating what can enter the cell (Figure 5-2). The freely moving nature of the membrane allows it to adjust to the changing shape of the cell.

Receptor Sites

Embedded in the lipoprotein membrane are a series of peripheral proteins with several functions. As discussed in Chapter 2, one type of protein located on the cell membrane is known as a receptor site. This protein reacts with specific chemicals outside the cell to stimulate a reaction within a cell. For example, the receptor site for insulin reacts with the hormone insulin to cause the activation of ATP within the cell. This reaction will alter the cell permeability to glucose. Receptor sites are very important in the functioning of neurons, muscle cells, endocrine glands, and so on, and they play a very important role in clinical pharmacology.

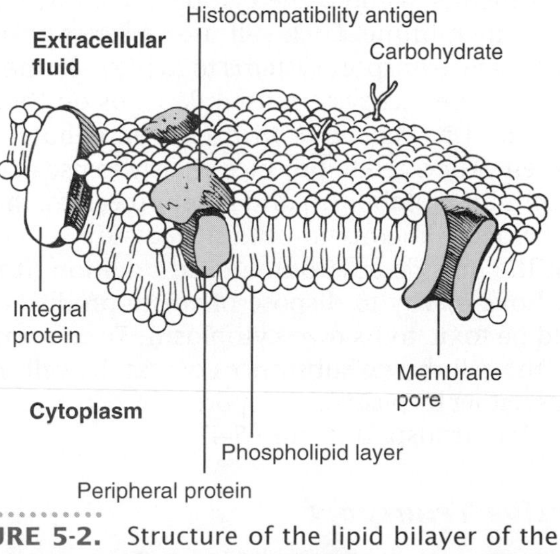

FIGURE 5-2. Structure of the lipid bilayer of the cell membrane. (Bullock, B. L. [2000]. *Focus on pathophysiology.* Philadelphia: Lippincott Williams & Wilkins.)

Identifying Markers

Other surface proteins become surface antigens, or genetically determined identifying markers. These proteins provide the ***histocompatibility antigens*** or human leukocyte antigens (HLA) that the body uses to identify a cell as a self-cell, or a cell belonging to that individual. The body's immune system recognizes these proteins and acts to protect self-cells and to destroy non–self-cells. When an organ is transplanted from one person to another, a great effort is made to match as many histocompatibility antigens as possible to reduce the chance that the "new" body will reject the transplanted organ.

Histocompatibility antigens can be changed in several ways: by cell injury, with viral invasion of a cell, with age, and so on. When the markers are altered, the body's immune system reacts to the change and can ignore it, allowing neoplasms to grow and develop. The immune system may also attack the cell, leading to many of the problems associated with autoimmune disorders and chronic inflammatory conditions.

CHANNELS

Channels or pores within the cell membrane are made by proteins in the cell wall that allow the passage of small substances in or out of the cell. Specific channels have been identified for sodium, potassium, calcium, chloride, bicarbonate, and water, and other channels may also exist. Some drugs are designed to affect certain channels specifically. For example, calcium channel blockers prevent the movement of calcium into a cell through calcium channels.

Cytoplasm

The cell cytoplasm lies within the cell membranes. This complex area, which contains many ***organelles,*** or structures with specific functions, is the site of activities of cellular metabolism and special cellular functions. The organelles within the cytoplasm include the ***mitochondria,*** the endoplasmic reticulum, free ribosomes, the Golgi apparatus, and the ***lysosomes.***

MITOCHONDRIA

The mitochondria are rod-shaped power plants within each cell that produce energy in the form of ATP, which allows the cell to function. Mitochondria are plentiful in very active cells such as muscle cells and are relatively scarce in inactive cells such as bone cells. Mitochondria, which can reproduce when a cell is very active, are always very abundant in cells that consume energy. For example, cardiac muscle cells, which must work continually to keep the heart contracting, contain a great number of mitochondria.

Milk-producing cells in breast tissue, which are normally quite dormant, contain very few mitochondria. If a woman is lactating, however, the mitochondria will become more abundant to meet the demands of the milk-producing cells. The mitochondria can take carbohydrates, fats, and proteins from the cytoplasm and make ATP using the Krebs cycle, which depends on oxygen. Cells use the ATP to maintain homeostasis, produce proteins, and carry out specific functions. If oxygen is not available, lactic acid builds up as a by-product of the cellular respiration. Lactic acid leaves the cell to be transported to the liver for conversion to glycogen and carbon dioxide.

ENDOPLASMIC RETICULUM

Much of the cytoplasm of a cell is made up of a fine network of channels known as cisternae, which are interconnected channels that form what is called the endoplasmic reticulum. The undulating surface of the endoplasmic reticulum provides a large surface for chemical reactions within the cell. Many granules that contain enzymes and ribosomes, which produce protein, are scattered over the surface of the endoplasmic reticulum. Production of proteins, nonproteins, hormones, and other substances takes place here. The breakdown of many toxic substances may also occur in these channels.

FREE RIBOSOMES

Other ribosomes that are not bound to the surface of the endoplasmic reticulum exist throughout the cytoplasm. These free-floating ribosomes produce proteins that are important to the structure of the cell and some of the enzymes that are necessary for cellular activity.

GOLGI APPARATUS

The Golgi apparatus is a series of flattened sacs that may be part of the endoplasmic reticulum. These structures prepare hormones or other substances for secretion by processing them and packaging them in vesicles to be moved to the cell membrane for excretion from the cell. In addition, the Golgi apparatus may also produce lysosomes and store other synthesized proteins and enzymes until they are needed.

LYSOSOMES

Lysosomes are membrane-covered organelles that contain specific digestive enzymes, which can break down protein, nucleic acid, carbohydrates, and lipids. These organelles form a membrane around any substance that needs to be digested and secrete the digestive enzymes directly into the isolated area, protecting the rest of the cytoplasm from injury. The lysosomes are responsible for digesting worn or damaged sections of a cell, which they accomplish by encapsulating the area and self-digesting it. If a cell dies and the membrane ruptures, the release of lysosomes causes the cell to self-destruct.

This phenomenon can be seen with old lettuce in the refrigerator. The side of the lettuce that has been "lying down" for a prolonged period of time becomes brown and wet as the lettuce cells die and self-digest when their lysosomes are released. If the lettuce is not used, the released lysosomes begin to digest any healthy lettuce that remains, with the eventual destruction of the entire head of lettuce. Lysosomes are important in ecology. Dead trees, animals, and other organisms self-digest and disappear.

CELL PROPERTIES

Cells have certain properties that allow them to survive. ***Endocytosis*** involves incorporation of material into the cell. Pinocytosis, a form of endocytosis, refers to the engulfing of specific substances that have reacted with a receptor site on the cell membrane. This process allows cells to absorb nutrients, enzymes, and other materials. Phagocytosis is a similar process, but it allows the cell, usually a neutrophil or macrophage, to engulf a bacterium or a foreign protein and destroy it within the cell by secreting digestive enzymes into the area. ***Exocytosis*** is the opposite of endocytosis. This property allows a cell to move a substance to the cell membrane and then secrete the substance outside the cell. Hormones, neurotransmitters, enzymes, and so on that are produced within a cell are excreted into the body using this process (Figure 5-3).

Homeostasis

The main goal of a cell is to maintain homeostasis, which means keeping the cytoplasm stable within the cell membrane. Each cell uses a series of active and passive transport systems to achieve homeostasis, and the exact system used depends on the type of cell and its reactions with the immediate environment. For a cell to produce energy to use to carry out cellular metabolism and other processes, the cell must have a means to obtain necessary elements from the outside environment. In addition, it must also have a way to dispose of waste products that could be toxic to its own cytoplasm. To accomplish this, the cell moves substances across the cell membrane, either by passive transport or by active (energy-requiring) transport (Figure 5-4).

Passive Transport

Passive transport occurs without the expenditure of energy and can occur across any semipermeable membrane. There are essentially three types of pas-

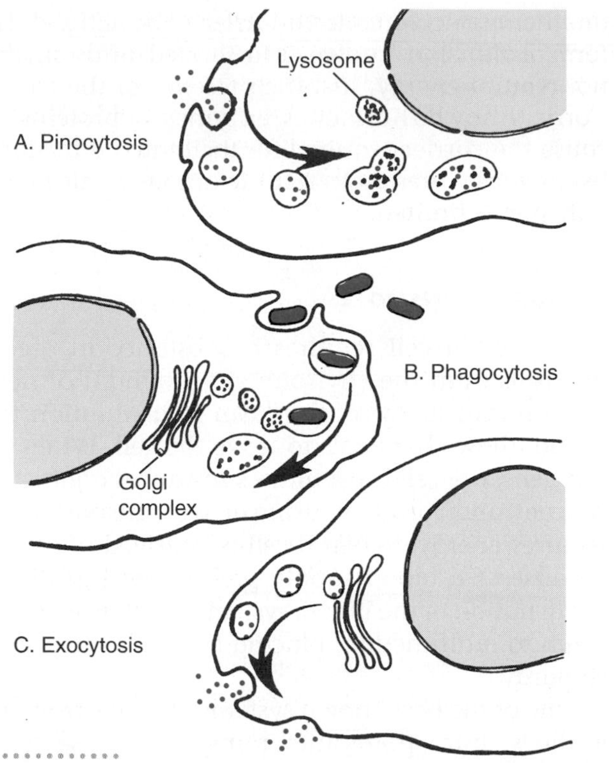

FIGURE 5-3. Schematic representation of endocytosis and exocytosis. Pinocytosis (*A*) is the movement of nutrients and needed substances through specific receptors on the cell surface. Phagocytosis (*B*) involves the destruction of engulfed proteins or bacteria. Exocytosis (*C*) is the movement of substances (waste products, hormones, neurotransmitters) out of the cell.

sive transport: ***diffusion, osmosis,*** and facilitated diffusion.

DIFFUSION

Diffusion is the movement of a substance from a region of higher concentration to a region of lower concentration. The difference in the concentration of a substance in the two regions is called the concentration gradient, and the greater the concentration gradient, the faster the substance usually moves. Movement into and out of a cell is regulated by the cell membrane. Some substances move through the channels or pores in the cell membrane. Small substances and materials with no ionic charge move most freely through the channels. Substances with a negative charge move more freely than substances with a positive charge. Substances that move into and out of a cell by diffusion include sodium, potassium, calcium, carbonate, oxygen, bicarbonate, and water.

When a cell is very active and utilizing energy and oxygen, the concentration of oxygen within the cell decreases. However, the concentration of oxygen outside the cell remains relatively high, so the oxygen moves across the concentration gradient to supply needed oxygen to the inside of the cell. Cells use this process to maintain homeostasis during many activities occurring in the life of the cell.

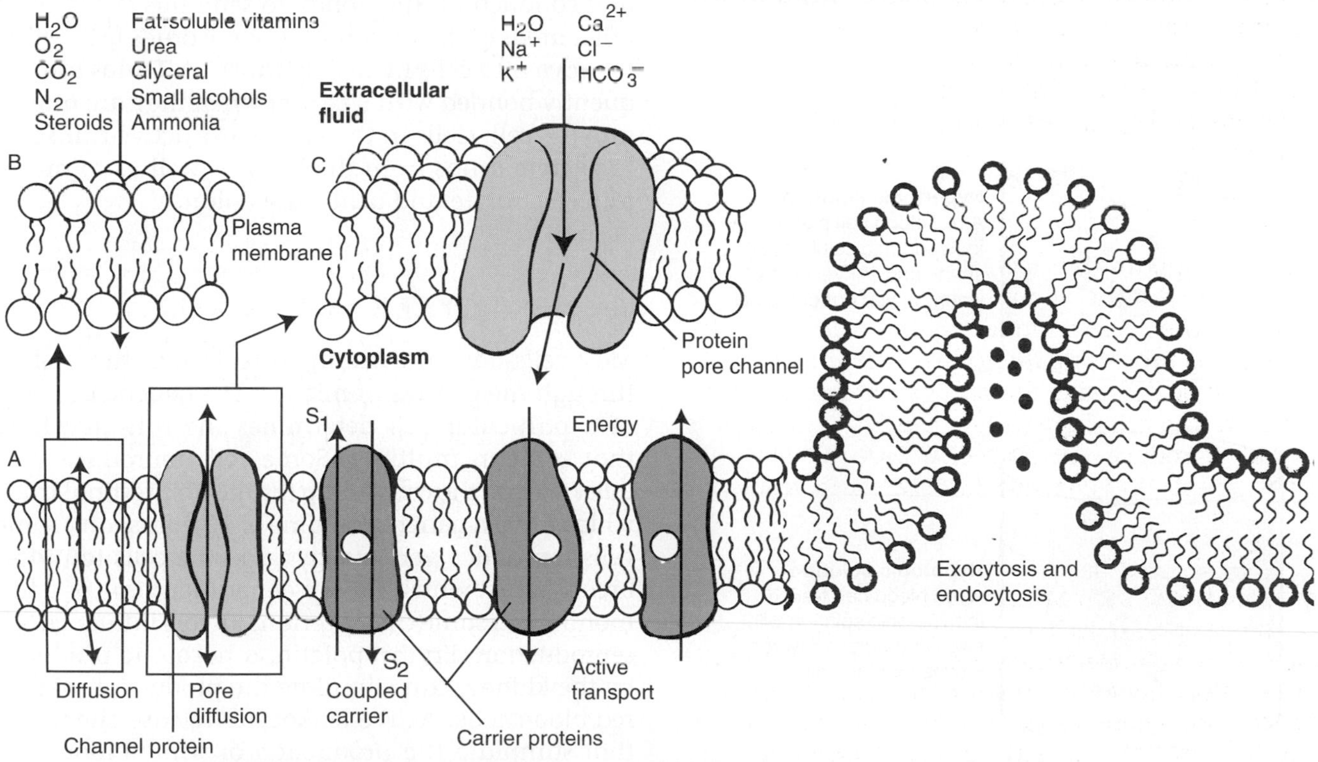

FIGURE 5-4. (*A*) Schematic representation of transport across the cell membrane, including (*B*) *diffusion* through a cell membrane and (*C*) *pore diffusion* through a protein channel.

OSMOSIS

Osmosis, a special form of diffusion, is the movement of water across a semipermeable membrane from an area that is low in diffused solutes to one that is high in diffused solutes. The water is attempting to equalize the dilution of the solutes. The movement of water across a cell membrane by diffusion from an area of high concentration to an area of low concentration creates pressure on the cell membrane. This pressure is called osmotic pressure. The greater the concentration of solutes in the solution to which the water is flowing, the higher the osmotic pressure.

A fluid that contains the same concentration of solutes as human plasma is an isotonic solution. A fluid that contains a higher concentration of solutes than human plasma is a hypertonic solution, and it draws water from cells. A fluid that contains a lower concentration of solutes than human plasma is hypotonic, and it loses water to cells. For example, if a human red blood cell, which has a cytoplasm that is isotonic with human plasma, is placed into a hypertonic solution, it shrinks and shrivels because the water inside the cell diffuses out of the cell into the solution. If the same cell is placed into a hypotonic solution, the cell swells and bursts because the water moves from the solution into the cell (Figure 5-5).

FACILITATED DIFFUSION

Sometimes a substance cannot move freely on its own in or out of a cell. This substance may attach to another molecule, called a carrier, to be diffused. This form of diffusion, known as facilitated diffusion, does not require energy, just the presence of the carrier. Carriers may be hormones, enzymes, or proteins. Because the carrier required for facilitated diffusion is usually only present in a finite amount, this type of diffusion is limited.

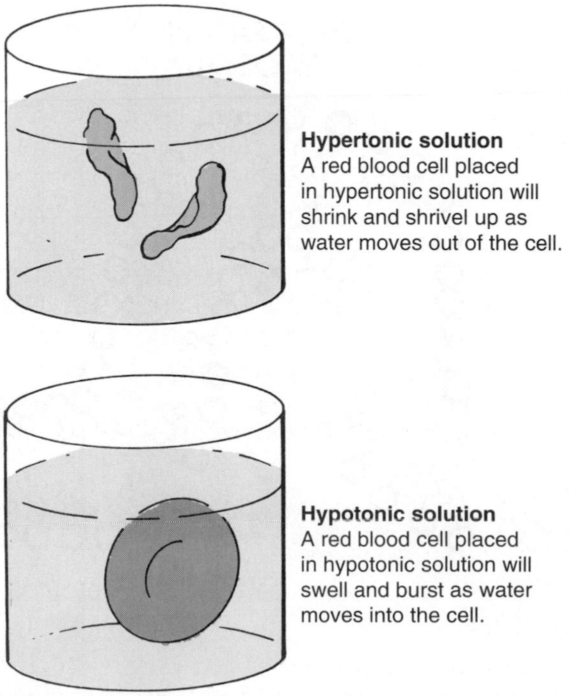

Hypertonic solution
A red blood cell placed in hypertonic solution will shrink and shrivel up as water moves out of the cell.
Hypotonic solution
A red blood cell placed in hypotonic solution will swell and burst as water moves into the cell.

FIGURE 5-5. Red blood cell response to hypertonic and hypotonic solutions.

Active Transport

Sometimes a cell requires a substance in greater amounts than the environment around it or needs to maintain its own cytoplasm in a situation that would allow chemicals to leave the cell. When this happens, the cell must move substances against the concentration gradient using active transport, which requires energy. When a cell is deprived of oxygen because of a blood supply problem or insufficient oxygenation of the blood, systems of active transport begin to malfunction, placing the cell's integrity in jeopardy.

One of the best known systems of active transport is the sodium–potassium pump. Cells use active transport to maintain a cytoplasm with higher levels of potassium and lower levels of sodium than the extracellular fluid. This allows the cell to maintain an electrical charge on the cell membrane, which gives many cells the electrical properties of excitation, or the ability to generate a movement of electrons, and conduction, the ability to send this stimulus to other areas of the membrane. Some drugs use energy to move into cells by active transport. Drugs are frequently bonded with a carrier when they are moved into the cell. Cells in the kidney use active transport to excrete drugs from the body as well as to maintain electrolyte and acid–base balance.

CELL CYCLE

Most cells have the ability to reproduce themselves through the process of mitosis. The genetic makeup of a particular cell determines the rate at which that cell can multiply. Some cells reproduce very quickly (e.g., the cells lining the gastrointestinal tract, which have a generation time of 72 hours) and some cells reproduce very slowly (e.g., the cells found in breast tissue, which have a generation time of a few months). In some cases, certain factors influence cell reproduction. Erythropoietin, a hormone produced by the kidney, can stimulate the production of new red blood cells. Active leukocytes release chemicals that stimulate the production of white blood cells when the body needs new ones. Regardless of the rate of reproduction, each cell has approximately the same life cycle. The life cycle of a cell is called the ***cell cycle*** and consists of four active phases and a resting phase (Figure 5-6).

G_0 Phase

During the G_0 phase, or resting phase, the cell is stable. It is not making any proteins associated with cell division and is basically dormant. Cells in the G_0 phase cause a problem in the treatment of some cancers. Cancer chemotherapy usually works on active, dividing cells, leaving resting cells fairly untouched. When the resting cells are stimulated to become active and regenerate, the cancer can return, which is why cancer chemotherapeutic regimens are complicated and extended over time and why a 5-year cancer-free period is usually the basic guide for considering a cancer to be cured.

G_1 Phase

When a cell is stimulated to emerge from its resting phase, it enters what is called the G_1 phase, which ranges from the time from stimulation of cell reproduction until the formation of DNA. During this period, the cell synthesizes the substances that are needed for DNA formation. The cell is actively collecting materials to make these substances and producing the building blocks for DNA.

S Phase

The next phase, called the S phase, involves the actual synthesis of DNA, which is an energy-consuming activity. The cell remains in this phase until the amount of cellular DNA has doubled.

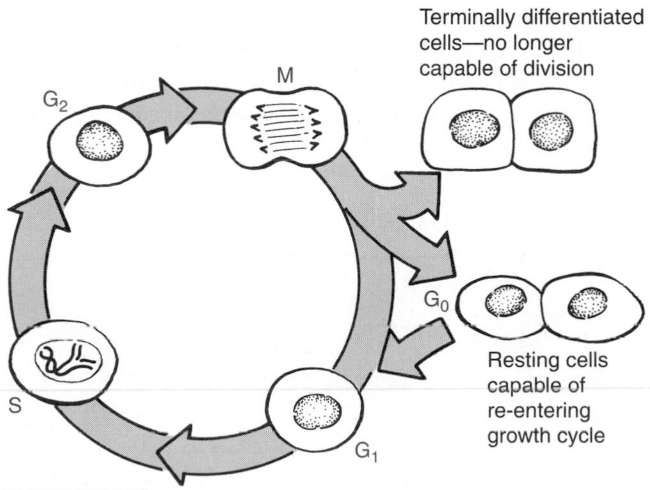

FIGURE 5-6. Diagram of the cell cycle, with G_0, G_1, S, G_2, and M phases. (Bullock, B. L. [2000]. *Focus on pathophysiology*. Philadelphia: Lippincott Williams & Wilkins.

G_2 Phase

When the cellular DNA has doubled in preparation for replication, the G_2 phase begins. During this phase, the cell produces all the substances that are required for the manufacture of the mitotic spindles.

M Phase

When the cell has produced all the substances necessary for the formation of a new cell, or daughter cell, the cell undergoes cell division or mitosis. This occurs during the M phase of the cell cycle. During this phase, the cell splits to form two identical daughter cells, a process called mitosis.

WWW.WEB LINKS

Students may want to consult the following Internet sources:

Information on cells, properties, membranes:
http://library.advanced.org/35641

Information on cell physiology, theories of cell formation, ongoing cellular research:
http://www.historyoftheuniverse.com/cell.html

Information on cell structure, properties, division:
http://tqd.advanced.org/12413/index.html

CLINICAL SIGNIFICANCE OF CELL PHYSIOLOGY

Understanding the basic structure and function of the cell may help in understanding the therapeutic and toxic effects of the various classes of chemotherapeutic agents. Drugs may alter the cell membrane, causing the cell to rupture and die. Or they may deprive the cell of certain nutrients, altering the proteins that the cell produces, and interfering with normal cell functioning and cell division. It is important to remember that the vast majority of chemotherapeutic agents do not possess complete selective toxicity, so these drugs affect normal cells of patients to some extent.

CHAPTER SUMMARY

- The cell is the basic structural unit of all living organisms.
- The cell is composed of a nucleus, which contains genetic material and controls the production of proteins by the cell; a cytoplasm, which contains various organelles important to cell function; and

the cell membrane, which separates the inside of the cell from the outside environment.

- The cell membrane functions as a fluid barrier made of lipids and proteins. The arrangement of the lipoprotein membrane controls what enters and leaves the cell.
- Proteins on the cell membrane surface can act either as receptor sites for specific substances or as histocompatibility markers that identify the cell as a self-cell.
- Channels or pores in the cell membrane allow for easier movement of specific substances needed by the cell for normal functioning.
- Mitochondria are rod-shaped organelles that produce energy in the form of ATP for use by cells.
- Ribosomes are sites of protein production within the cell cytoplasm. The specific proteins produced by a cell are determined by the genetic material within the cell nucleus.
- The Golgi apparatus packages particular substances for removal from the cell (e.g., neurotransmitters, hormones).
- Lysosomes are packets of digestive enzymes located in the cell cytoplasm. These enzymes are responsible for destroying injured or nonfunctioning parts of the cell and for cellular disintegration when the cell dies.
- Endocytosis is the process of moving substances into a cell by extending the cell membrane around the substance and engulfing it. Pinocytosis refers to the engulfing of necessary materials, and phagocytosis refers to the engulfing and destroying of bacteria or other proteins by white blood cells.
- Exocytosis is the process of removing substances from a cell by moving them toward the cell membrane and changing the cell membrane to allow the passage of the substance out of the cell.
- Cells maintain homeostasis by regulating the movement of solutes and water into and out of the cell.
- Diffusion, which does not require energy, is the movement of solutes from a region of high concentration to a region of lower concentration across a concentration gradient.
- Osmosis, which, like diffusion, does not require energy, is the movement of water from an area low in solutes to an area high in solutes. Osmosis exerts a pressure against the cell membrane called osmotic pressure.
- Active transport, an energy-requiring process, is the movement of particular substances against a concentration gradient. Active transport is important in maintaining cell homeostasis.
- Cells replicate at differing rates depending on the genetic programming of the cell. All cells go through a life cycle consisting of the following phases: G_0, the resting phase; G_1, which involves the production of proteins for DNA synthesis; S, which involves the synthesis of DNA; G_2, which involves the manufacture of the materials needed for mitotic spindle production; and M, the mitotic phase, in which the cell splits to form two identical daughter cells.
- Chemotherapeutic drugs act on cells to cause cell death or alteration. All properties of the drugs that affect cells should be considered when giving a chemotherapeutic agent.

BIBLIOGRAPHY

Bullock, B. S. (2000). *Focus on pathophysiology*. Philadelphia: Lippincott Williams & Wilkins.

Fox, S. (1991). *Perspectives on human biology*. Dubuque, IA: Wm. C. Brown Publishers.

Ganong, W. (1999). *Review of medical physiology* (19th ed.). Norwalk, CT: Appleton & Lange.

Guyton, A. & Hall, J. (1996). *Textbook of medical physiology*. Philadelphia: W.B. Saunders.

Hardman, J. G., Limbird, L. E., Molinoff, P. B., Ruddon, R. W., & Gilman, A. G. (Eds.). (1996). *Goodman and Gilman's the pharmacological basis of therapeutics* (9th ed.). New York: McGraw Hill.

CHAPTER 6

Anti-Infective Agents

bacitracin
chloramphenicol
meropenem
polymyxin B
spectinomycin
vancomycin

CHAPTER OUTLINE

KEY TERMS

culture
prophylaxis
resistance
sensitivity testing
spectrum

INTRODUCTION

Anti-infectives are drugs that are designed to act selectively on foreign organisms that have invaded and infected the body of a human host. Ideally, these drugs would be toxic to the infecting organisms only, and have no effect on the host cells. In other words, these agents would possess selective toxicity, or the ability to affect certain proteins or enzyme systems that are used by bacteria but not by human cells. Although human cells are different from the cells of the invading organisms, they are somewhat similar, and no anti-infective drug has been developed yet that does not affect the host.

This chapter focuses on the principles involved in the use of anti-infective therapy. Following chapters discuss specific agents that are used to treat particular infections: antibiotics, which are used to treat bacterial infections; antivirals; antifungals; antiprotozoals, which are used to treat infections caused by specific protozoa, including malaria; anthelmintics, which are used to treat infections caused by worms; and antineoplastics, which are used to treat cancers, diseases caused by abnormal cells.

ANTI-INFECTIVE THERAPY

For centuries, people used various naturally occurring chemicals in an effort to treat disease. Often this was a random act that proved useful. For instance, the ancient Chinese found that applying moldy soybean curds to boils and infected wounds helped prevent infection or hastened cure. Their finding was, perhaps, a precursor to the penicillins used today.

The use of drugs to treat systemic infections is a relatively new concept. The first drugs used to treat systemic infections were developed in the 1920s. Paul Ehrlich was the first scientist to work on developing a synthetic chemical that would be effective only against infection-causing cells, not human cells. His research led the way for the scientific investigation into anti-infective agents. In the late 1920s, scientists discovered penicillin in a mold sample; in 1935, the sulfonamides were introduced. Since then, the number of anti-infectives available for use has grown tremendously. However, many of the organisms that these drugs were designed to treat are rapidly learning to repel the effects of anti-infectives, so much work remains to deal with these emergent strains.

Mechanisms of Action

Anti-infectives may act on the cells of the invading organisms in several different ways. The goal is interference with the normal function of the invading organism to prevent it from reproducing and to cause cell death without affecting host cells. Various mechanisms of action are briefly described here. The specific mechanism of action for each drug class is discussed in the next few chapters.

- Some anti-infectives interfere with biosynthesis of the bacterial cell wall. Because bacterial cells have a slightly different composition than human cells, this is an effective way to destroy the bacteria without interfering with the host (Box 6-1). The penicillins work in this way.
- Some anti-infectives prevent the cells of the invading organism from using substances essential to their growth and development, leading to an inability to divide and eventually to cell death. The sulfonamides, the antimycobacterial drugs, and trimethoprim work in this way.
- Many anti-infectives interfere with the steps involved in protein synthesis, a necessary function to maintain the cell and allow for cell division. The aminoglycosides, the macrolides, and chloramphenicol work in this way.
- Other anti-infectives alter the permeability of the cell membrane to allow essential cellular components to leak out, causing cell death. Some antibiotics, antifungals, and antiprotozoal drugs work in this manner (Figure 6-1).

Anti-Infective Activity

The anti-infectives that are used today vary in their effectiveness against different invading organisms, that is, they have different ***spectrums*** of activity.

Some are so selective in their action that they are effective against only a few microorganisms with a very specific metabolic pathway or enzyme. These drugs are said to have a narrow spectrum of activity (Box 6-2).

BOX 6-1

ANTI-INFECTIVE MECHANISM: INTERFERENCE WITH CELL WALL SYNTHESIS

Bacitracin (*Baci-IM, AK-Tracin, Baciguent*) is an antibiotic that interferes with the cell wall synthesis of susceptible staphylococcal bacteria. Adverse effects include nephrotoxicity and superinfection. Because of the development of resistant strains and more potent antibiotics, bacitracin is now indicated only for the treatment of respiratory infections in infants caused by susceptible staphylococci, treatment of eye infections, prevention of infections in minor skin wounds, and treatment of minor skin infections caused by susceptible strains of staphylococci. Bacitracin is available in IM, ophthalmic, and topical preparations.

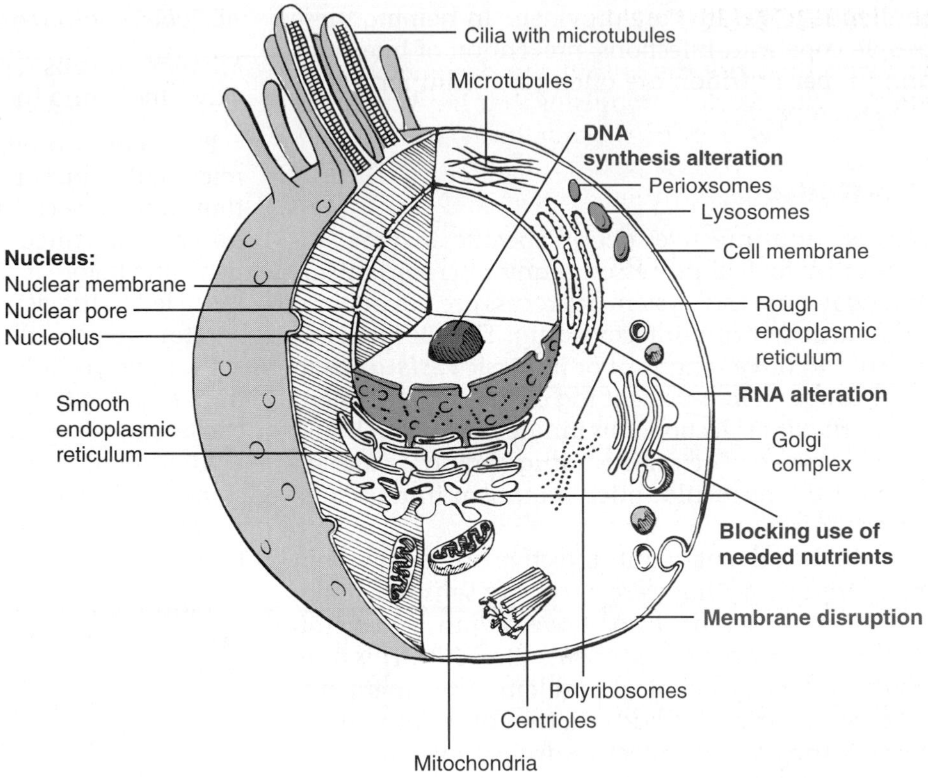

FIGURE 6-1. Anti-infectives can affect cells by disrupting the cell membrane, interfering with DNA synthesis, altering RNA, or blocking the use of essential nutrients.

Other drugs interfere with biochemical reactions in many different kinds of microorganisms, making them useful in the treatment of a wide variety of infections. Such drugs are said to have a broad spectrum of activity. Some anti-infectives are so active against the infective microorganisms that they actually cause the death of the cells they affect. These drugs are said to be bactericidal. Some anti-infectives are not as aggressive against invading organisms, and they interfere with the ability of the cells to reproduce or divide. These drugs are said to be bacteriostatic. Several drugs are both bactericidal and bacteriostatic, often depending on the concentration of the drug that is present. Many of the adverse effects noted with the use of anti-infectives are associated with the aggressive properties of the drugs and their effect on the cells of the host as well as those of the pathogen.

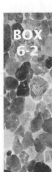

BOX 6-2

NARROW SPECTRUM ANTIBIOTIC

Spectinomycin (*Trobicin*) is an example of an antibiotic with very specific effects. This drug interferes with protein synthesis, leading to cell death, only in susceptible strains of *Neisseria gonorrhoeae*. Spectinomycin is not known to be effective against any other bacteria, and its use is limited to treatment of specific gonococcal infections. The drug is given as one IM injection.

Human Immune Response

The goal of anti-infective therapy is reduction of the population of the invading organism to a point where the human immune response can take care of the infection. For a drug to be aggressive enough to eliminate all traces of any invading pathogen, it may be toxic to the host as well. The immune response (see Chapter 13) involves a complex interaction between chemical mediators, leukocytes, lymphocytes, antibodies, and locally released enzymes and chemicals. When this response is completely functional, and all of the necessary proteins, cells, and chemicals are being produced by the body, it can isolate and eliminate foreign proteins, including bacteria, fungi, viruses, and so on. However, when people are immune compromised for any reason (e.g., malnutrition, age, AIDS, use of immune suppressant drugs), the immune system may be incapable of dealing effectively with the invading organisms. It is difficult to treat any infections in these patients for two reasons: (1) anti-infective drugs cannot totally eliminate the pathogen without causing severe toxicity in the host, and (2) these patients do not have the immune response in place to deal with even a few invading organisms. These patients present a real challenge to health care providers. In helping these people cope with infections, prevention of infections and proper nutrition are often just as important as drug therapy.

Resistance

Because anti-infectives act on specific enzyme systems or biological processes, many microorganisms that do not use that system or process are not affected by a particular anti-infective drug. These organisms are said to have a natural or intrinsic ***resistance*** to these drugs. When prescribing a drug for treatment of a particular infection, this innate resistance should be anticipated. The selected drug should be known to affect the particular microorganism that is causing the infection.

Since the advent of anti-infective drugs, however, microorganisms that were once very sensitive to the effects of particular drugs have begun to develop acquired resistance to the agents (Box 6-3). This may result in a serious clinical problem. The emergence of resistant strains of bacteria and other organisms poses a threat: anti-infective drugs may no longer control potentially life-threatening diseases, and uncontrollable epidemics may occur.

BOX 6-3

BACTERIAL RESISTANCE TO AN ANTI-INFECTIVE DRUG

Vancomycin (*Vancocin, Vancoled*) is an antibiotic that interferes with cell wall synthesis in susceptible bacteria. It was developed as a result of a need for a drug that could be used both in patients who are intolerant to or allergic to penicillin and/or cephalosporins and in the treatment of patients with staphylococcal infections that no longer respond to penicillin or cephalosporins.

This anti-infective drug can be used orally or IV to treat life-threatening infections when less toxic drugs cannot be used. It is used orally as prophylaxis against bacterial endocarditis in patients who cannot take penicillins or cephalosporins and to treat staphylococcal infections in people who do not respond to either of these groups of drugs.

Because vancomycin may be highly toxic, it is reserved for very special situations. It can cause renal failure, ototoxicity, superinfections, and a condition known as "red man syndrome," which is characterized by sudden and severe hypotension, fever, chills, paresthesias, and erythema or redness of the neck and back. When it is the only antibiotic that is effective against a specific bacteria, however, the benefits outweigh the risks.

ACQUIRING RESISTANCE

Microorganisms develop resistance in a number of ways, including the following:

- Producing an enzyme that deactivates the antimicrobial drug. For example, some strains of bacteria that were once controlled by penicillin now produce an enzyme called penicillinase, which inactivates penicillin before it can affect the bacteria. This occurrence led to the development of new drugs that were resistant to penicillinase.
- Changing cellular permeability to prevent the drug from entering the cell or altering transport systems to exclude the drug from active transport into the cell.
- Altering binding sites on the membranes or ribosomes that then no longer accept the drug.
- Producing a chemical that acts as an antagonist to the drug.

Most commonly, the development of resistance depends on the degree to which the drug acts to eliminate the invading microorganisms that are most sensitive to its effects. The remaining cells may be somewhat resistant to the effects of the drug, and over time, these cells form the majority in the population. These cells differ from the general population of the species because of slight variations in their biochemical processes or biochemicals. The drug does not cause a mutation of these cells; it simply allows the somewhat different cells to become the majority or dominant group after the elimination of the sensitive cells. Other microbes may develop resistance through actual genetic mutation. A mutant cell survives the effects of an antibiotic and divides, forming a new colony of resistant microbes with a genetic composition that provides resistance to the anti-infective agent.

PREVENTING RESISTANCE

Because the emergence of resistant strains of microbes is a serious public health problem that continues to grow, health care providers must work together to prevent the emergence of resistant pathogens. Exposure to an antimicrobial agent leads to the development of resistance, so it is important to limit the use of antimicrobial agents to the treatment of specific pathogens known to be sensitive to the drug being used.

Drug dosage is important in preventing the development of resistance. Doses should be high enough, and the duration of drug therapy should be long enough to eradicate even slightly resistant microorganisms. The recommended dosage for a specific anti-infective agent takes this issue into account. Around-the-clock dosing eliminates the peaks and valleys in drug concentration and helps maintain a constant therapeutic level to prevent the emergence of resistant microbes during times of low concentration. The duration of drug use is also important. This is critical to ensure that the microbes are completely, not partially, eliminated and not given the chance to grow and develop resistant strains.

It has proved to be difficult to convince people who are taking anti-infective drugs that the timing of dosing and the length of time they take the drug is important. Many people stop taking the drugs once they start to feel better and then keep the remainder of a prescription to treat themselves sometime in the future when they do not feel well. This practice favors the emergence of resistant strains.

Health care providers should also be cautious about the indiscriminate use of anti-infectives. Antibiotics are not effective in the treatment of viral infections or illnesses such as the common cold. However, many patients demand prescriptions for these drugs when they visit practitioners because they are convinced that they need to take something to feel better. Health care providers who prescribe anti-infectives without knowing the causative organism and which drugs might be appropriate are promoting the emergence of resistant strains of microbes. With many serious illnesses, including pneumonias, where the causative organism is suspected, antibiotic therapy may be started as soon as a culture is taken and before the results are known. Health care providers also tend to try newly introduced, more powerful drugs when a more established drug may be just as effective. Using a powerful drug in this way leads to the rapid emergence of resistant strains to that drug, perhaps limiting its potential usefulness when it might be truly necessary.

TREATMENT OF SYSTEMIC INFECTIONS

Many infections that once led to lengthy, organ-damaging, or even fatal illnesses are now managed quickly and efficiently with the use of systemic anti-infective agents. Before the introduction of penicillin to treat strep infections, many people developed rheumatic fever with serious cardiac complications. Today rheumatic fever and the resultant cardiac valve defects are seldom seen. Several factors should be considered before beginning one of these chemotherapeutic regimens to ensure that the patient obtains the greatest benefit possible with the fewest adverse effects. These factors include identification of the correct pathogen and selection of a drug that is most likely to (1) cause the least complications for that particular patient, and (2) be most effective against the pathogen involved.

Identification of the Pathogen

Identification of the infecting pathogen is through a ***culture*** of the infected area. Bacterial cultures are performed in a laboratory, where a swab of infected tissue is allowed to grow on an agar plate. Staining techniques and microscopic examination are used to identify the offending bacterium. When investigators search for parasitic sources of infection, stool can be examined for ova and parasites. Microscopic examination of other samples is also used for detecting fungal and protozoal infections. The correct identification of the organism causing the infection is an important first step in determining what anti-infective drug should be used.

Sensitivity of the Pathogen

In many situations, health care providers use a broad-spectrum anti-infective agent that has been shown likely to be most effective in treating an infection with certain presenting signs and symptoms. In other cases of severe infections, a broad-spectrum antibiotic is started after a culture is taken but before the exact causative organism has been identified. Again, experience influences selection of the drug, based on the presenting signs and symptoms. In many cases, it is necessary to perform ***sensitivity testing*** on the cultured microbes. Sensitivity testing shows which drugs are capable of controlling the particular microorganism. This testing is especially important with microorganisms having known resistant strains. In these cases, culture and sensitivity testing identify the causal pathogen and the most appropriate drug for treating the infection.

Combination Therapy

In some situations, a combination of two or more types of drugs effectively treats infections. When the offending pathogen is known, combination drugs may be effective in interfering with its cellular structure in different areas or developmental phases. Combination therapy may be used for several reasons:

- The health care provider may use a smaller dosage of each drug, leading to fewer adverse effects but still having a therapeutic impact on the pathogen.
- Some drugs are synergistic, which means that they are more powerful when given in combination.
- Many microbial infections are caused by more than one organism, and each pathogen may react to a different anti-infective agent.
- Sometimes, the combined effects of the different drugs delay the emergence of resistant strains. This is important in the treatment of tuberculosis, a mycobacterial infection; in malaria, a protozoal infection;

and in some bacterial infections. However, resistant strains seem to be more likely to emerge when fixed combinations are used over time, at least in some cases. Individualizing the combination seems to be more effective in destroying the pathogen without allowing time for the emergence of strains that are resistant to the drugs.

ADVERSE REACTIONS TO ANTI-INFECTIVE THERAPY

Because anti-infective agents affect cells, it is always possible that the host cells will also be damaged (Box 6-4). No anti-infective agent has been developed that is completely free of adverse effects. The most commonly encountered adverse effects associated with the use of anti-infective agents include direct toxic effects on the kidney, gastrointestinal (GI) tract, and nervous system. Hypersensitivity reactions and superinfections also occur.

Kidney Damage

Kidney damage occurs most frequently with drugs that are metabolized by the kidney and then eliminated in the urine. Such drugs, which have a direct toxic effect on the fragile cells in the kidney, can cause conditions ranging from renal dysfunction to full-blown renal failure. When patients are taking these drugs (e.g., aminoglycosides), they should be monitored closely for any sign of renal dysfunction. To prevent any accumulation of the drug in the kidney, they should also be well hydrated throughout the course of the drug therapy.

BOX 6-4 SERIOUS ADVERSE EFFECTS OF ANTIBIOTIC TREATMENT

Chloramphenicol (*Chloromycetin*), an older antibiotic, prevents bacterial cell division in susceptible bacteria. Because of the potential toxic effects of this drug, its use is limited to serious infections for which no other antibiotic is effective. Chloramphenicol produces a "gray syndrome" in neonates and premature babies, which is characterized by abdominal distention, pallid cyanosis, vasomotor collapse, irregular respirations, and even death. In addition, the drug may cause bone marrow depression, including aplastic anemia that can result in death. These effects are seen even with the use of the ophthalmic and otic forms of the drug. Although the use of chloramphenicol is severely limited, it has stayed on the market because it is used to treat serious infections caused by bacteria that are not sensitive to any other antibiotic. It is available in oral, IV, ophthalmic, and otic forms.

GI Toxicity

GI toxicity is very common with many of the anti-infectives. Many of these agents have direct toxic effects on the cells lining the GI tract, causing nausea, vomiting, stomach upset, or diarrhea, and such effects are sometimes severe (Box 6-5). There is also some evidence that the death of the microorganisms releases chemicals and toxins into the body, which can stimulate the chemoreceptor trigger zone (CTZ) in the medulla and induce nausea and vomiting.

In addition, some anti-infectives are toxic to the liver. These drugs may cause hepatitis and even liver failure. When patients are taking drugs known to be toxic to the liver (e.g., many of the cephalosporins), they should be monitored closely and the drug stopped at any sign of liver dysfunction.

Neurotoxicity

Some anti-infectives can damage or interfere with the function of nerve tissue, usually in areas where drugs tend to accumulate in high concentrations (Box 6-6). For example, the aminoglycoside antibiotics collect in the eighth cranial nerve and may cause dizziness, vertigo, and loss of hearing. Chloroquine, which is used to treat malaria and some other rheumatoid disorders, may accumulate in the retina and optic nerve and cause blindness. Other anti-infectives may cause dizziness, drowsiness, lethargy, changes in reflexes, and even hallucinations when they irritate specific nerve tissues.

Hypersensitivity Reactions

Allergic or hypersensitivity reactions reportedly occur with many antimicrobial agents. Most of these agents, which are protein bound for transfer through the cardiovascular system, are able to induce anti-

BOX 6-5 SEVERE GI TOXICITY RESULTING FROM ANTI-INFECTIVE TREATMENT

Meropenem (*Merrem IV*), an IV antibiotic, inhibits the synthesis of bacterial cell walls in susceptible bacteria. It is used to treat intra-abdominal infections and some cases of meningitis caused by susceptible bacteria. Meropenem almost always causes very uncomfortable GI effects; in fact, use of this drug has been associated with potentially fatal pseudomembranous colitis. It also results in headache, dizziness, rash, and superinfections. Because of its toxic effects on GI cells, it is used only in those infections with proven sensitivity to meropenem and reduced sensitivity to less toxic antibiotics.

BOX 6-6

NERVE DAMAGE CAUSED BY AN ANTI-INFECTIVE AGENT

Polymyxin B (generic), an older antibiotic, uses a surfactant-like reaction to enter the bacterial cell membrane and disrupt it, leading to cell death in susceptible gram-negative bacteria. This drug is available for IM, IV, or intrathecal use, as well as an ophthalmic agent for the treatment of infections caused by susceptible bacteria. Because of the actions of polymyxin B on cell membranes, however, it can be toxic to the human host, leading to nephrotoxicity, neurotoxicity (facial flushing, dizziness, ataxia, paresthesias, and drowsiness), and drug fever and rashes. Therefore, it is reserved for use in acute situations when the invading bacteria has been proven to be sensitive to this particular agent and less sensitive to other, less toxic antibiotics.

body formation in susceptible people. With the next exposure to the drug, immediate or delayed allergic responses may occur. Some of these drugs have demonstrated cross-sensitivity (e.g., penicillins and cephalosporins), and care must be taken to obtain a complete patient history before administering one of these drugs. It is important to determine what the allergic reaction was and when the patient experienced it (e.g., after first use of drug, after years of use). Some patients report having a drug allergy, but closer investigation indicates that their reaction actually constitutes an anticipated effect or known adverse effect to a drug. Proper interpretation of this information is important in allowing treatment of a patient with a drug that is very effective against a known pathogen to which the patient reported a supposed allergic reaction.

Superinfections

One offshoot of the use of anti-infectives, especially broad-spectrum anti-infectives, is destruction of the normal flora. By destroying the normal flora, opportunistic pathogens that were kept in check by the "normal" bacteria have the opportunity to invade tissues and cause infections. These opportunistic infections are called superinfections. Common superinfections include vaginal or GI yeast infections, which are associated with antibiotic therapy, and infections caused by *Proteus* and *Pseudomonas* throughout the body, which are a result of broad-spectrum antibiotic use. If patients receive drugs that are known to induce superinfections, they should be monitored closely and the appropriate treatment for the superinfection started as soon as possible.

PROPHYLAXIS

Sometimes it is clinically useful to use anti-infectives as a means of ***prophylaxis,*** to prevent infections before they occur. For example, when patients anticipate traveling to an area where malaria is endemic, they begin taking antimalarial drugs before the journey and periodically during the trip. Patients who are undergoing GI or genitourinary surgery, which might introduce bacteria from those areas into the system, often have antibiotics ordered immediately following the surgery and periodically after surgery, as appropriate, to prevent infection from occurring in the first place. Patients with known cardiac valve disease, valve replacements, and other conditions are especially prone to the development of subacute bacterioendocarditis because of the vulnerability of their heart valves. These patients use prophylactic antibiotic therapy as a precaution when undergoing invasive procedures, including dental work. Refer to the American Heart Association's recommended schedule for this prophylaxis.

CHAPTER SUMMARY

- Anti-infectives are drugs that are designed to act on foreign organisms that have invaded and infected the human host with selective toxicity, which means they affect biological systems or structures that are found in the invading organisms but not in the host.
- The goal of anti-infective therapy is interference with normal function of invading organisms to prevent them from reproducing and promotion of cell death without negatively affecting the host cells. The infection should be eradicated with the least toxicity to the host and least likelihood for development of resistance.
- Anti-infectives can work by altering the cell membrane of the pathogen, by interfering with protein synthesis, or by interfering with the ability of the pathogen to obtain needed nutrients.
- Anti-infectives also work to kill invading organisms or to prevent them from reproducing to deplete the size of the invasion to one that can be dealt with by the human immune system.
- Pathogens can develop resistance to the effects of anti-infectives over time when (1) mutant organisms that do not respond to the anti-infective become the majority of the pathogen population, or (2) when the pathogen develops enzymes to block the anti-infectives or alternate routes to obtain nutrients or maintain their cell membrane.
- An important aspect of clinical care involving anti-infective agents is preventing or delaying the

development of resistance. This can be done by ensuring that the particular anti-infective agent is the drug of choice for this specific pathogen and that it is given in high enough doses for sufficiently long periods to rid the body of the pathogen.

- Culture and sensitivity testing of a suspected infection ensures that the correct drug is being used to treat the infection effectively. Culture and sensitivity testing should be performed before an anti-infective is prescribed.
- Anti-infectives can have several adverse effects on the human host, including renal toxicity, multiple GI effects, neurotoxicity, hypersensitivity reactions, and superinfection.
- Some anti-infectives are used as a means of prophylaxis when patients expect to be in situations that will expose them to a known pathogen (e.g., traveling to an area where malaria is endemic, having oral or invasive GI surgery when a person is susceptible to subacute bacterioendocarditis).

Bibliography

Bullock, B. L. (2000). *Focus on pathophysiology.* Philadelphia: Lippincott Williams & Wilkins.

Drug Facts & Comparisons. (1999). St. Louis: Facts & Comparisons.

Drug Facts: www.pharminfo.com/drugdb

Hardman, J. G., Limbird, L. E., Molinoff, P. B., Ruddon, R. W., & Gilman, A. G. (Eds.). (1996). *Goodman and Gilman's the pharmacological basis of therapeutics* (9th ed.). New York: McGraw Hill.

Karch, A. M. (1999). *2000 Lippincott's nursing drug guide.* Philadelphia: Lippincott Williams & Wilkins.

Porth, C. M. (1994). *Pathophysiology: Concepts of altered health states* (4th ed.). Philadelphia: Lippincott.

The Medical Letter on Drugs and Therapeutics. (1999). New Rochelle, NY: Medical Letter.

CHAPTER 7

Antibiotics

Aminoglycosides
- amikacin
- P gentamicin
- kanamycin
- neomycin
- netilmicin
- tobramycin

Cephalosporins
- P cefaclor
- cefadroxil
- cefazolin
- cefdinir
- cefepime
- cefixime
- cefmetazole
- cefonicid
- cefoperazone
- cefotaxime
- cefotetan
- cefoxitin
- cefpodoxime
- cefprozil
- ceftazidime
- ceftibuten
- ceftizoxime
- ceftriaxone
- cefuroxime
- cephalexin
- cephapirin
- cephradine
- loracarbef

Fluoroquinolones
- P ciprofloxacin
- enoxacin
- grepafloxacin
- levofloxacin
- lomefloxacin
- norfloxacin
- ofloxacin
- sparfloxacin
- trovafloxacin

Macrolides
- azithromycin
- clarithromycin
- dirithromycin
- P erythromycin

Lincosamides
- P clindamycin
- lincomycin

Monobactam antibiotics
- aztreonam

Penicillins and penicillinase-resistant antibiotics
- Penicillins
  - P amoxicillin
  - ampicillin
  - bacampicillin
  - carbenicillin
  - mezlocillin
  - penicillin G benzathine
  - penicillin G potassium
  - penicillin G procaine
  - penicillin V
  - piperacillin
  - ticarcillin
- Penicillinase-resistant antibiotics
  - P cloxacillin
  - dicloxacillin
  - nafcillin
  - oxacillin

Sulfonamides
- sulfadiazine
- P sulfamethizole
- sulfamethoxazole
- sulfasalazine
- sulfisoxazole

Tetracyclines
- demeclocycline
- doxycycline
- minocycline
- oxytetracycline
- P tetracycline

Antimycobacterial antibiotics
- Antituberculosis drugs
  - capreomycin
  - cycloserine
  - ethambutol
  - ethionamide
  - P isoniazid
  - pyrazinamide
  - rifabutin
  - rifampin
  - rifapentine
- Leprostatic drugs
  - clofazimine
  - P dapsone

CHAPTER OUTLINE

KEY TERMS

aerobic
anaerobic
antibiotic
bactericidal
bacteriostatic
gram-negative
gram-positive
synergistic

INTRODUCTION

Antibiotics are chemicals that inhibit specific bacteria. Those substances that prevent the growth of bacteria are said to be ***bacteriostatic,*** and those that kill bacteria directly are said to be ***bactericidal.*** Several antibiotics are both bactericidal and bacteriostatic, depending on the concentration of the particular drug. Antibiotics are used to treat a wide variety of systemic and topical infections. Many new infections appear each year, and researchers are challenged to develop new antibiotics to deal with each new threat. Antibiotics are made in three ways: by living microorganisms; by synthetic manufacture; and, in some cases, through genetic engineering. Discussed in this chapter are the major classes of antibiotics: aminoglycosides, cephalosporins, fluoroquinolones, lincosamides, macrolides, monobactams, penicillins and penicillinase-resistant drugs, sulfonamides, tetracyclines, and the disease-specific antimycobacterials and leprostatic drugs.

BACTERIA AND ANTIBIOTICS

Bacteria can invade the human body through many routes: respiratory, gastrointestinal (GI), skin, and so on. Once bacteria invade the body, the body becomes the host for the bacteria, supplying needed nutrients and enzymes that the bacteria need for reproduction. Unchallenged, the invading bacteria can multiply and send out other bacteria to further invade tissue. The human immune response is activated when bacteria invade. Many of the signs and symptoms of an infection are related to the immune response to the invader as the body tries to rid itself of the foreign cells. Fever, lethargy, slow-wave sleep induction, and the classic signs of inflammation (i.e., redness, swelling, heat, and pain) all indicate that the body is responding to an invader.

The goal of antibiotic therapy is to decrease the population of the invading bacterium to a point at which the human immune system can effectively deal with the invader. To determine which antibiotic would effectively treat a specific infection, the causative organism must be identified. Culture and sensitivity testing is performed to identify the invading bacterium by growing it in the laboratory and then determining the antibiotic to which that particular bacterium is most sensitive (i.e., responds to best). Antibiotics have been developed to interfere with specific proteins or enzyme systems, so they are effective against only bacteria that use certain proteins or types of enzymes. ***Gram-positive*** bacteria accept a positive stain during testing and are frequently associated with infections of the respiratory tract and soft tissues. In contrast, ***gram-negative*** bacteria accept a negative stain and are frequently associated with infections of the genitourinary (GU) or GI tract. ***Aerobic*** bacteria depend on oxygen for survival, whereas ***anaerobic*** bacteria do not use oxygen (e.g., those bacteria associated with gangrene).

When culture and sensitivity testing is not possible, either because the source of the infection is not identifiable or because the patient is too sick to wait for treatment, clinicians attempt to administer a drug with a broad spectrum of activity, or a wide range of effects. Antibiotics that interfere with a biochemical reaction common to many organisms are known as broad-spectrum antibiotics. These drugs are often given at the beginning of treatment until the exact organism and sensitivity can be established. Because these antibiotics have such a wide range of effects, they are frequently associated with adverse effects. Human cells have many of the same properties as bacterial cells and can be affected in much the same way, so damage may occur to the human cells as well as the bacterial cells.

In choosing an antibiotic, clinicians also look for a drug with selective toxicity, or the ability to strike foreign cells with little or no effect on human cells. There is no perfect antibiotic that has no effect on the human host, and this factor should be considered in antibiotic selection. Because various antibiotics have anticipated adverse effects, certain drugs may be contraindicated in patients who are immune compromised, have severe GI disease, are debilitated, and so forth. The antibiotic of choice is one that affects the causative organism and leads to the fewest adverse effects for the patient involved.

In some cases, antibiotics are given in combination. These antibiotics are ***synergistic,*** or work together to increase their effectiveness. Using synergistic antibiotics allows the clinician to use a lower dose of each antibiotic to achieve the desired effect.

Another use of a combination means that a lower dose of one antibiotic can be used, which helps reduce the adverse effects of a particular drug and makes it more useful in certain clinical situations. Or one drug may "help" another become more effective (Box 7-1)

In some situations, antibiotics are used as a means of prophylaxis, or prevention of potential infection. Patients who will soon be in a situation that commonly results in a specific infection (i.e., patients undergoing GI surgical procedures which may introduce GI bacteria into the bloodstream or peritoneum) may be given antibiotics before they are exposed to the bacteria. Usually large, one-time doses of antibiotic are given to destroy any bacteria that enter the host immediately and prevent a serious infection.

RESISTANCE

Bacteria have survived for hundreds of years because they are able to adapt to their environment. They do this by altering their cell wall or enzyme systems to become resistant to unfavorable conditions or situations. Many species of bacteria have developed resistance to certain antibiotics. For example, bacteria that were once very sensitive to penicillin have developed an enzyme called penicillinase, which effectively inactivates many of the penicillin-type drugs. New drugs had to be developed to treat infections involving these once-controlled bacteria effectively. Because these drugs are resistant to penicillinase, they can no longer be inactivated by the bacteria. Other new drugs are in development and testing (Box 7-2).

The longer an antibiotic has been in use, the greater the chance of the development of a resistant strain. Efforts to control the emergence of resistant strains involve intense education programs that advocate the use of antibiotics only when necessary and effective, not for treating viral infections such as the common cold.

In addition, the use of antibiotics may result in the development of superinfections or overgrowth of resistant pathogens such as bacteria, fungi, or yeasts because antibiotics (particularly broad-spectrum agents) destroy bacteria in the flora that normally work to keep these opportunistic invaders in check. When "normal" bacteria are destroyed or greatly reduced in number, there is nothing to prevent the invaders from occupying the host. In most cases the superinfection is an irritating adverse effect (e.g., vaginal yeast infections, candidiasis, diarrhea). But in some cases, the superinfection may be more severe than the original infection being treated. Treating the superinfection leads to new adverse effects and the potential for different superinfections, with the development of a vicious cycle of treatment and resistance.

BOX 7-1 COMBINATION DRUGS TO FIGHT RESISTANT BACTERIA

Clavulanic acid protects certain antibiotics from breakdown by bacterial beta-lactamase enzymes, which are enzymes developed by the bacteria to protect them from the effects of antibiotics. A combination of amoxicillin and clavulanic acid (*Augmentin*) is a commonly used drug that allows the amoxicillin to remain effective against certain strains of resistant bacteria. The theory behind the combination of ticarcillin and clavulanic acid (*Timentin*) is similar. Sulbactam is another drug that increases the effectiveness of antibiotics against certain resistant bacteria. When combined with ampicillin in the drug *Unasyn*, sulbactam inhibits many bacterial penicillinase enzymes, broadening the spectrum of the ampicillin. In this combination, sulbactam is also slightly antibacterial.

BOX 7-2 NEW ANTIBIOTIC DRUG CLASS INVESTIGATED

A new class of antibiotics called streptogramins, which is being investigated in clinical settings, became available for emergency use in February 1996. Two drugs in this new class, quinupristin and dalfoprostin, are available in a combination form called *Synercid*. When used together, they work synergistically, and they have been effective in treating vancomycin-resistant enterococci, resistant *Staphylococcus aureus*, and resistant *S. epidermidis*. The drug also seems to be active against penicillin-resistant pneumococcus. This class of drugs is just one of many classes being investigated to deal with the increasing problem of resistant bacteria.

AMINOGLYCOSIDES

The aminoglycosides are a group of powerful antibiotics that are used to treat serious infections caused by gram-negative aerobic bacilli. Because most of these drugs have potentially serious adverse effects, newer, less toxic drugs have replaced aminoglycosides in less serious infections.

Amikacin (*Amikin, Amikacin*) is available for short-term intramuscular (IM) or intravenous (IV) use for serious gram-negative infections. The potential for nephrotoxicity and ototoxicity with amikacin is very high, so the drug is used only as long as absolutely necessary.

NURSING CHALLENGE

Proper Use of Antibiotics

As part of their patient education plans, nurses should include information about the risks and dangers of antibiotic abuse by incorporating some of the following points:

- Explain clearly that a particular antibiotic is effective against only certain bacteria and that a culture needs to be taken to identify that bacteria.
- Explain that bacteria can develop resistant strains that will not be affected by antibiotics in the future, so using antibiotics now may make them less effective in situations in which they are really necessary.
- Ensure that patients understand the importance of taking the full course of medication as prescribed, even if they feel better. Stopping an antibiotic midway through a regimen often leads to the development of resistant bacteria. Many people also will save unused medications to self-treat future infections, or to share with other family members.
- Tell patients that allergies may develop with repeated exposures to certain antibiotics. In addition, explain to patients that saving antibiotics to take later, when they think they need them again, may lead to earlier development of an allergy and will negate important tests that attempt to identify the bacteria that may be making them sick.
- Offer other medications such as antihistamines and decongestants to patients who request antibiotics; this may satisfy their need for something to take. Explaining that viral infections do not respond to antibiotics may offer little consolation for patients who are suffering from a cold or the flu.

The publicity that many emergent, resistant strains of bacteria have received in recent years may help to get the message across to patients about the need to take the full course of an antibiotic and to use antibiotics only when they are the appropriate drug of choice.

Gentamicin (*Garamycin*) is available in many forms: ophthalmic, topical, IV, intrathecal, impregnated beads on surgical wire, and liposomal injection. It covers a wide variety of infections, including *Pseudomonas* and once-rare infections seen in patients with AIDS.

Kanamycin (*Kantrex*), which is available in parenteral and oral forms, is also used to treat hepatic coma when ammonia-producing bacteria in the GI tract cause serious illness and as an adjunctive therapy to decrease GI bacterial flora. Kanamycin should not be used for more than 7 to 10 days because of the potential toxic effects of the drug.

Neomycin (*Mycifradin*) is a slightly milder aminoglycoside that is used to suppress GI bacteria preoperatively, to treat hepatic coma, and as a topical agent to treat skin wounds and infections.

Netilmicin (*Netromycin*) is reserved for short-term IV or IM treatment of very serious infections.

Tobramycin (*Nebcin, Tobrex*) is used for short-term IM or IV treatment of very serious infections. This drug is also available in an ophthalmic form for treatment of ocular infections caused by susceptible bacteria.

THERAPEUTIC ACTIONS AND INDICATIONS

The aminoglycosides are bactericidal; they inhibit protein synthesis in susceptible strains of gram-negative bacteria, leading to loss of functional integrity of the bacterial cell membrane, which causes cell death (Figure 7-1). These drugs are used to treat serious infections caused by susceptible strains of gram-negative bacteria, including *Pseudomonas aeruginosa, Escherichia coli, Proteus* species, the *Klebsiella-Enterobacter-Serratia* group, *Citrobacter* species, and *Staphylococcus* species such as *S. aureus.* Aminoglycosides are indicated for the treatment of serious infections susceptible to penicillin when penicillin is contraindicated, and they can be used in severe infections before culture and sensitivity tests have been completed.

CONTRAINDICATIONS/CAUTIONS

Aminoglycosides are contraindicated in the following conditions: known allergy to any aminoglycosides; renal or hepatic disease that could be exacerbated by toxic aminoglycoside effects and that could interfere with drug metabolism and excretion, leading to more toxicity; preexisting hearing loss, which could be intensified by toxic drug effects on the auditory nerve; active infection with herpes or mycobacterial infections that could be worsened by the effects of an aminoglycoside on normal defense mechanisms; myasthenia gravis and parkinsonism, which are often exacerbated by the effects of a particular aminoglycoside on the nervous system; and lactation, because aminoglycosides are excreted in breast milk and could cause potentially serious effects in the baby. Caution should be used during pregnancy; aminoglycosides are only used in the treatment of severe infections, and the benefits of the drug should be carefully weighed against potential adverse effects on the fetus.

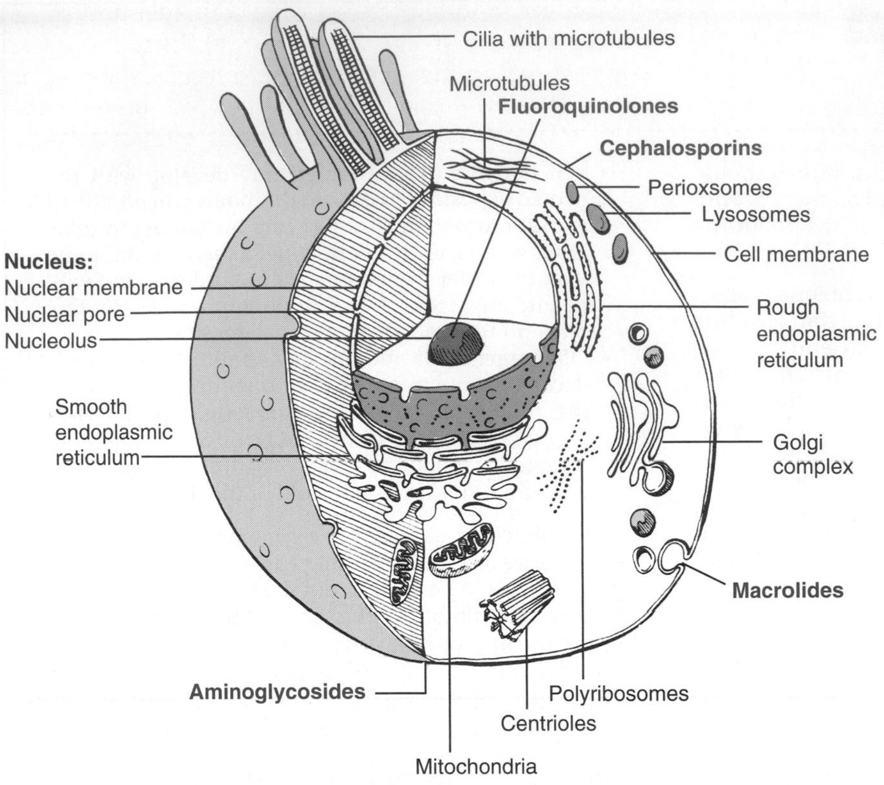

FIGURE 7-1. Sites of cellular action of aminoglycosides, cephalosporins, fluoroquinolones, and macrolides. Aminoglycosides disrupt the cell membrane. Cephalosporins cause bacteria to build weak cell walls when dividing. Fluoroquinolones interfere with DNA enzymes necessary for growth and reproduction. Macrolides change protein function by binding to the cell membrane to cause cell death or prevent cell division.

ADVERSE EFFECTS

Many serious adverse effects are associated with the use of aminoglycosides, which limit their usefulness. Central nervous system (CNS) effects include ototoxicity to irreversible deafness; vestibular paralysis resulting from drug effects on the auditory nerve; confusion; depression; disorientation; and numbness, tingling, and weakness related to drug effects on other nerves. Renal toxicity, which may progress to renal failure, is caused by direct drug toxicity in the glomerulus. Depressed bone marrow resulting from direct drug effects on the rapidly dividing cells in the bone marrow may occur, leading to immune suppression and resultant superinfections, fever, and so on. GI effects include nausea, vomiting, diarrhea, weight loss, stomatitis, and hepatic toxicity. These effects are a result of direct GI irritation, loss of bacteria of the normal flora with resultant superinfections, and toxic effects in the mucous membranes and liver as the drug is metabolized. Cardiac effects can include palpitations, hypotension, and hypertension. Hypersensitivity reactions include purpura, rash, urticaria, and exfoliative dermatitis.

CLINICALLY IMPORTANT DRUG–DRUG INTERACTIONS

If aminoglycosides are taken in combination or with potent diuretics, the incidence of ototoxicity, nephrotoxicity, and neurotoxicity increases. This combination should be avoided if at all possible. If these antibiotics are given with anesthetics, nondepolarizing neuromuscular blockers, succinylcholine, and citrate anticoagulated blood, increased neuromuscular blockade and paralysis is possible. If a patient who has been receiving an aminoglycoside requires surgery, the fact that the aminoglycoside has been given should be indicated prominently on the chart. Following surgery, the patient will require extended monitoring and support. In addition, most aminoglycosides have a synergistic bactericidal effect when given in combination with penicillins, cephalosporins, carbenicillin, and ticarcillin. This synergism is used therapeutically to increase the effectiveness of treatment in certain conditions.

DATA LINK

Data link to the following aminoglycosides in your nursing drug guide:

AMINOGLYCOSIDES

Name	Brand Name	Usual indications
amikacin	*Amikin, Amikacin*	Treatment of serious gram-negative infections
P gentamicin	*Garamycin*	Treatment of *Pseudomonas* infections and wide variety of gram-negative infections
kanamycin	*Kantrex*	Treatment of hepatic coma to decrease GI normal flora

neomycin	*Mycifradin*	Suppression of GI normal flora preoperatively; treatment of hepatic coma; topical treatment of skin wounds
netilmicin	*Netromycin*	Short term IV treatment of very serious infections
tobramycin	*Nebcin, Tobrex*	Short term IV or IM treatment of serious infections; ocular infections caused by susceptible bacteria

NURSING CONSIDERATIONS
for patients receiving aminoglycosides

Assessment

HISTORY. Screen for the following: known allergy to any aminoglycoside (obtain specific information about the allergic reaction and the times it has occurred); history of renal or hepatic disease; preexisting hearing loss; active infection with herpes, vaccinia, varicella, or fungal or mycobacterial infections; myasthenia gravis; parkinsonism; infant botulism; and current pregnancy or lactation status.

PHYSICAL ASSESSMENT. Physical assessment should be performed to establish baseline data for assessing the effectiveness of the drug and the occurrence of any adverse effects associated with drug therapy. Perform culture and sensitivity tests at the site of infection. Conduct orientation and reflex assessment as well as auditory testing to evaluate any CNS effects of the drug. Assess vital signs: respiratory rate; adventitious sounds to monitor for signs of infection or hypersensitivity reactions; temperature to assess for signs and symptoms of infection; blood pressure to monitor for cardiovascular effects of the drug. Renal and hepatic function tests should be done to determine baseline function of these organs and assess for the need to adjust dosage.

Nursing Diagnoses

Patients who receive aminoglycosides may have the following nursing diagnoses related to drug therapy:

- Pain related to GI, CNS effects of drug
- Sensory–perceptual alteration related to CNS effects
- Potential for infection related to bone marrow suppression
- Fluid volume excess related to nephrotoxicity
- Knowledge deficit regarding drug therapy

Implementation

- Check culture and sensitivity reports *to ensure that this is the drug of choice for this patient.*
- Ensure that the patient receives the full course of the aminoglycoside as prescribed, divided around the clock *to increase effectiveness and decrease the risk of development of resistant strains.*
- Monitor the site of infection and presenting signs and symptoms (e.g., fever, lethargy) throughout the course of drug therapy. *Failure to resolve these signs and symptoms may indicate the need to reculture the site. Arrange to continue drug therapy for at least 2 days after the resolution of all signs and symptoms.*
- Monitor the patient regularly for signs of nephrotoxicity, neurotoxicity, and bone marrow suppression *to effectively arrange for discontinuation of drug or decreased dosage, as appropriate, if any of these toxicities occur.*
- Provide safety measures *to protect the patient if CNS effects occur.*
- Provide small, frequent meals as tolerated, frequent mouth care, and ice chips or sugarless candy to suck *to provide relief and maintain nutrition if stomatitis and sore mouth are problems,* and adequate fluids *to replace fluid lost with diarrhea.*
- Ensure that the patient is hydrated at all times during drug therapy *to minimize renal toxicity from drug exposure.*
- Ensure that the patient is instructed about the appropriate dosage regimen and possible adverse effects *to enhance patient knowledge about drug therapy and to promote compliance.*

The patient should:

Take safety precautions such as changing position slowly and avoiding driving and hazardous tasks, if CNS effects occur.

Try to drink a lot of fluids and to maintain nutrition (very important) even though nausea, vomiting, and diarrhea may occur.

Avoid exposure to other infections (e.g., crowded areas, people with known infectious diseases).

Report difficulty breathing, severe headache, loss of hearing or ringing in the ears, or changes in urine output to their health care provider.

Evaluation

- Monitor patient response to the drug (resolution of bacterial infection).
- Monitor for adverse effects (orientation and affect, hearing changes, bone marrow suppression, renal toxicity, hepatic dysfunction, GI effects).
- Evaluate the effectiveness of the teaching plan (patient can name drug, dosage, possible adverse effects to watch for, and specific measures to help avoid adverse effects).
- Monitor the effectiveness of comfort and safety measures and compliance with the regimen.

CEPHALOSPORINS

The cephalosporins were first introduced in the 1960s. These drugs are similar to the penicillins in structure and in activity. Over time, four generations of cephalosporins have been introduced, each group with its own spectrum of activity, which is described as follows.

First-generation cephalosporins are largely effective against the same gram-positive bacteria that are affected by penicillin G as well as the gram-negative bacteria *Proteus mirabilis, Escherichia coli,* and *Klebsiella pneumoniae.* (PEcK is an easy way to remember which drugs are susceptible to the first-generation cephalosporins.)

Second-generation cephalosporins are effective against those strains as well as *Haemophilus influenzae, Enterobacter aerogenes,* and *Neisseria* species. (Remember HENPeCK.) The second-generation drugs are less effective against gram-positive bacteria.

Third-generation cephalosporins are relatively weak against gram-positive bacteria, but are more potent against the gram-negative bacilli as well as *Serratia marcescens.* (Remember HENPeCKS.)

Fourth-generation cephalosporins are just now being developed. The first drug of this group, cefepime (*Maxipime*), is active against gram-negative and gram-positive organisms, including cephalosporin-resistant staphylococcus and *Pseudomonas aeruginosa.*

Table 7-1 lists the various cephalosporins and special notes about their use.

THERAPEUTIC ACTIONS AND INDICATIONS

The cephalosporins are both bactericidal and bacteriostatic, depending on the dose used and the specific drug involved. In susceptible bacteria, these agents basically interfere with the cell–wall-building ability of bacteria when they divide. That is, they prevent the bacteria from biosynthesizing the framework of their cell wall. The bacteria with weakened cell walls swell and burst as a result of the osmotic pressure within the cell (see Figure 7-1).

Cephalosporins are indicated for the treatment of infections caused by susceptible bacteria. Selection of an antibiotic from this class depends on the sensitivity of the involved organism, the route of choice, and sometimes the cost involved. It is important to reserve the use of cephalosporins for appropriate situations, because cephalosporin-resistant bacteria are appearing in increasing numbers. Before beginning therapy, a culture and sensitivity test should always be performed to evaluate the causative organism and appropriate sensitivity to the antibiotic being used (see Table 7-1).

CONTRAINDICATIONS/CAUTIONS

These drugs should not be used in patients with known allergies to cephalosporins or penicillins because a cross-sensitivity often occurs. In addition, caution must be used in patients with renal failure that may interfere with the excretion of the drug, leading to toxic levels, as well as in pregnant and lactating women because of potential effects on the fetus or infant.

ADVERSE EFFECTS

The most common adverse effects of the cephalosporins involve the GI tract and include nausea, vomiting, diarrhea, anorexia, abdominal pain, and flatulence (common). Pseudomembranous colitis, a potentially dangerous disorder, has also been reported with some aminoglycosides. A particular drug should be discontinued immediately at any sign of violent, bloody diarrhea or abdominal pain.

CNS symptoms include headache, dizziness, lethargy, and paresthesias. Nephrotoxicity is also associated with the use of cephalosporins, most particularly in patients who have a predisposing renal insufficiency. Other adverse effects include superinfections, which frequently occur because of the death of protective bacteria of the normal flora. The patient receiving parenteral cephalosporins should also be monitored for the possibility of phlebitis (IV) or local abscess at the site of IM injection.

CLINICALLY IMPORTANT DRUG–DRUG INTERACTIONS

The concurrent administration of cephalosporins with aminoglycosides leads to an increased risk of nephrotoxicity. Patients who receive this combination should be monitored frequently, including evaluation of serum BUN and creatinine levels. Patients who receive oral anticoagulants in addition to cephalosporins may experience increased bleeding and should receive teaching instructions to monitor for blood loss (e.g., bleeding gums, easy bruising) to be aware that the dose of the oral anticoagulant may need to be reduced. When alcohol is consumed while receiving cephalosporins, many patients experience a disulfiram-like reaction, which may occur up to 72 hours after the drug is discontinued. Patients should be warned about this possible reaction and urged to refrain from the use of alcohol for 72 hours after the drug is stopped.

DATA LINK

Data link to the cephalosporins in your nursing drug guide (see Table 7-1).

NURSING CONSIDERATIONS
for patients receiving cephalosporins

Assessment

HISTORY. Screen for the following: known allergy to any cephalosporin, penicillin, or any other allergens

TABLE 7-1

CEPHALOSPORINS

Name	Brand Name(s)	Route(s) of Administration	Usual Indication
FIRST-GENERATION CEPHALOSPORINS			
cefadroxil	*Duricef*	Oral	Indicated for UTIs, pharyngitis, and tonsillitis caused by group A β-hemolytic streptococci, skin infections
cefazolin	*Kefzol, Zolicef*	IV, IM	Respiratory tract, skin, GU, biliary tract, bone, joint, and myocardial infections as well as sepsis
cephalexin	*Keflex, Bioflex*	Oral	Respiratory, skin, bone, and GU infections; used for otitis media in children
cephapirin	*Cefadyl*	IV, IM	Respiratory tract, skin, GU, biliary tract, bone, joint, and myocardial infections as well as sepsis and osteomyelitis
cephradine	*Velosef*	Oral, IV, IM	Respiratory tract, skin, GU, biliary tract, bone, joint, and myocardial infections as well as sepsis and osteomyelitis; useful in situations where switch from parenteral to oral route is expected (i.e., preoperative prophylaxis followed by oral postoperative prophylaxis)
SECOND-GENERATION CEPHALOSPORINS			
P **cefaclor**	*Ceclor*	Oral	Respiratory tract infections, skin infections, UTIs, otitis media; must be taken every 8–12 hours around the clock
cefmetazole	*Zefazone*	IV	Used for severe infections; preoperative prophylaxis for cesarean section, abdominal or vaginal surgery, biliary, or colorectal surgery
cefonicid	*Monocid*	IV, IM	Used for severe infections; preoperative prophylaxis for cesarean section, abdominal or vaginal surgery, biliary or colorectal surgery
cefotetan	*Cefotan*	IV, IM	Used for severe infections; preoperative prophylaxis for cesarean section, abdominal or vaginal surgery, biliary or colorectal surgery
cefoxitin	*Mefoxin*	IV, IM	Used for severe infections; preoperative prophylaxis for cesarean section, abdominal or vaginal surgery, biliary or colorectal surgery; more effective in gynecologic infections and intra-abdominal infections than some other agents
cefprozil	*Cefzil*	Oral	Pharyngitis, tonsillitis, otitis media, sinusitis, secondary bronchial infections, and skin infections; should be taken every 12 hours for 10 days
cefuroxime	*Ceftin, Zinacef*	Oral, IV, IM	Wide range of infections, as listed for other second-generation drugs; also used to treat Lyme disease and preferred in situations involving an anticipated switch from parenteral to oral drug use
loracarbef	*Lorabid*	Oral	Pharyngitis, tonsillitis, otitis media, sinusitis, UTIs, secondary bronchial infections, and skin infections; should be taken every 12 hours for 7–14 days
THIRD-GENERATION CEPHALOSPORINS			
cefdinir	*Omnicef*	Oral	Respiratory infections, otitis media, sinusitis, laryngitis, bronchitis, skin infections; suspension available for children
cefixime	*Suprax*	Oral	Uncomplicated UTIs, respiratory infections, otitis media, uncomplicated gonorrhea; may be given as a single, daily dose, making compliance easier
cefoperazone	*Cefobid*	IV, IM	Moderate to severe skin, urinary tract, and respiratory tract infections; pelvic inflammatory disease; intra-abdominal infections; peritonitis; septicemia
cefotaxime	*Claforan*	IV, IM	Moderate to severe skin, urinary tract, and respiratory tract infections; pelvic inflammatory disease; intra-abdominal infections; peritonitis; septicemia; bone infections; CNS infections; preoperative prophylaxis
cefpodoxime	*Vantin*	Oral	Respiratory infections, UTIs, gonorrhea, skin infections, and otitis media; given every 12 hours for 7–14 days
ceftazidime	*Ceptaz, Tazicef*	IV, IM	Moderate to severe skin, urinary tract, and respiratory tract infections; intra-abdominal infections; septicemia; bone infections; CNS infections
ceftibuten	*Cedax*	Oral	Pharyngitis, tonsillitis, exacerbations of bronchitis, otitis media; once-a-day dosing increases compliance available as suspension for children
ceftizoxime	*Cefizox*	IV, IM	Respiratory, gynecologic, pelvic inflammatory, intra-abdominal, skin, and bone and joint infections; also used for sepsis and meningitis

(continued)

TABLE 7-1

CEPHALOSPORINS (Continued)

Name	Brand Name(s)	Route(s) of Administration	Usual Indication
ceftriaxone	*Rocephin*	IV, IM	Moderate to severe skin, urinary tract, and respiratory tract infections; pelvic inflammatory disease; intra-abdominal infections; peritonitis; septicemia; bone infections; CNS infections; preoperative prophylaxis; unlabeled use for treatment of Lyme disease
FOURTH-GENERATION CEPHALOSPORIN			
cefepime	*Maxipime*	IV, IM	Moderate to severe skin, urinary tract, and respiratory tract infections; must be injected for 10 days for greatest effectiveness

because cross-sensitivity often occurs (obtain specific information about the allergic reaction and the times it has occurred); history of renal disease, which could exacerbate nephrotoxicity related to the cephalosporin; and current pregnancy or lactation status.

PHYSICAL ASSESSMENT. Physical assessment should be performed to establish baseline data for assessing the effectiveness of the drug and the occurrence of any adverse effects associated with drug therapy. Perform culture and sensitivity tests at the site of infection. Examine skin for any rash or lesions to provide a baseline for possible adverse effects. Note respiratory status, including rate, depth, and adventitious sounds to provide a baseline. Check renal function tests, including BUN and creatinine clearance, to assess the status of renal functioning to determine any needed alteration in dosage. Examine injection sites to provide a baseline for determining adverse reactions or abscess formation.

Nursing Diagnoses

Patients receiving a cephalosporin may have the following nursing diagnoses related to drug therapy:

- Pain related to GI, CNS effects of drug
- Potential for infection related to repeated injections
- Fluid volume deficit and nutritional imbalance related to diarrhea
- Knowledge deficit regarding drug therapy

Implementation

- Check culture and sensitivity reports *to ensure that this is the drug of choice for this patient.*
- Monitor renal function tests prior to and periodically during therapy *to arrange for appropriate dosage reduction as needed.*
- Ensure that the patient receives the full course of the cephalosporin as prescribed, divided around the clock *to increase effectiveness and to decrease the risk of development of resistant strains.*
- Monitor the site of infection and presenting signs and symptoms (e.g., fever, lethargy) throughout the course of drug therapy. *Failure to resolve these signs and symptoms may indicate the need to reculture the site. Arrange to continue drug therapy for at least 2 days after the resolution of all signs and symptoms.*
- Provide small, frequent meals as tolerated, frequent mouth care, and ice chips or sugarless candy to suck if stomatitis and sore mouth are problems *to relieve discomfort and provide nutrition* and adequate fluids *to replace fluid lost with diarrhea.*
- Monitor patient for any signs of superinfections *to arrange for treatment of superinfections if they do occur.*
- Monitor injection sites regularly *to provide warm compresses and gentle massage to injection sites if painful or swollen; if signs of phlebitis occur, remove IV line and reinsert in a different vein.*
- Provide safety measures, including adequate lighting, use of siderails, and assistance with ambulation *to protect patient if CNS effects occur.*
- Ensure that the patient is instructed about the appropriate dosage scheduling regimen and about possible side effects *to enhance patient knowledge about drug therapy and to promote compliance.*

The patient should:

Take safety precautions including changing position slowly and avoiding driving and hazardous tasks, if CNS effects occur.

Try to drink a lot of fluids and to maintain nutrition (very important) even though nausea, vomiting, and diarrhea may occur.

Report difficulty breathing, severe headache, severe diarrhea, dizziness, or weakness to a health care provider.

Avoid alcoholic beverages while receiving cephalosporins and for at least 72 hours after completing the drug, because serious side effects could occur.

Evaluation

- Monitor patient response to the drug (resolution of bacterial infection).
- Monitor for adverse effects (orientation and affect; renal toxicity; hepatic dysfunction; GI effects; local irritation, including phlebitis at injection and IV sites).
- Evaluate the effectiveness of the teaching plan (patient can name drug, dosage, possible adverse effects to expect, and specific measures to help avoid adverse effects).
- Monitor the effectiveness of comfort and safety measures and compliance with the regimen.

FLUOROQUINOLONES

The fluoroquinolones are a relatively new class of antibiotics with a broad spectrum of activity. These drugs, which are all made synthetically, are associated with relatively mild adverse reactions. The most widely used fluoroquinolone is ciprofloxacin (*Cipro*), which is effective against a wide spectrum of gram-negative bacteria. It is available in injectable, oral, and topical forms. Other fluoroquinolones include the following agents:

- Enoxacin (*Penetrex*) is an oral agent used for the treatment of urinary tract infections and selected sexually transmitted diseases.
- Grepafloxacin (*Raxar*) is an oral agent that has proven very effective in treating community-acquired pneumonia and chronic bronchitis as well as various urinary tract infections caused by susceptible bacteria.
- Levofloxacin (*Levaquin*), which is available in oral and IV forms, may be used to treat respiratory, urinary tract, skin, and sinus infections caused by susceptible gram-negative bacteria. Because of its parenteral availability it may be preferred for severe infections or when oral drugs cannot be used.
- Lomefloxacin (*Maxaquin*) is an oral drug that can be used to treat lower respiratory tract infections as well as many urinary tract infections. It is the drug of choice for preoperative and postoperative prophylaxis to prevent urinary tract infections following transurethral procedures or transrectal prostate biopsies.
- Norfloxacin (*Noroxin*) is recommended only for the treatment of various urinary tract infections caused by susceptible gram-negative bacteria.
- Ofloxacin (*Floxin, Ocuflox*) can be given IV or orally to treat respiratory, skin, and urinary tract infections as well as pelvic inflammatory disease. In addition, this drug is available as an ophthalmic agent for the treatment of ocular infections caused by susceptible bacteria.
- Sparfloxacin (*Zagam*) is an oral agent used to treat community-acquired pneumonia and acute bronchitis caused by susceptible bacteria.
- Trovafloxacin and alatrofloxacin (*Trovan, Trovan IV*), which are available in IV and oral forms, may be used to treat a wide spectrum of infections caused by susceptible gram-negative bacteria, including respiratory, intra-abdominal, urinary tract, gynecologic, and skin. Strains that have become resistant to the very frequently used ciprofloxacin may still be sensitive to this newer fluoroquinolone.

THERAPEUTIC ACTIONS AND INDICATIONS

The fluoroquinolones enter the bacterial cell by passive diffusion through channels in the cell membrane. Once inside, they interfere with the action of DNA enzymes necessary for the growth and reproduction of the bacteria (see Figure 7-1). This leads to cell death because the bacterial DNA is damaged and the cell cannot be maintained. At the moment, the fluoroquinolones have the advantage of a unique way of disrupting bacterial activity. There is little cross-resistance with other forms of antibiotics. However, the misuse of these drugs in the short time the class has been used has led to the existence of resistant strains of bacteria. Because so many resistant strains are emerging, infected tissue should always be cultured to determine the exact bacterial cause and sensitivity.

The fluoroquinolones are indicated for the treatment of infections caused by susceptible strains of gram-negative bacteria including *E. coli, Proteus mirabilis, K. pneumoniae, Enterobacter cloacae, Proteus vulgaris, Proteus rettgeri, Morganella morgani, Moraxella catarrhalis, H. influenzae, Pseudomonas aeruginosa, Citrobacter freundii, S. aureus, S. epidermis,* some *N. gonorrhoeae,* and group D streptococci. These infections frequently include urinary tract, respiratory tract, and skin infections.

CONTRAINDICATIONS/CAUTIONS

Fluoroquinolones are contraindicated in patients with any known allergy to any fluoroquinolone and in pregnant or lactating women, because the drugs have unknown effects on fetuses and infants. Caution should be used in the presence of renal dysfunction, which could interfere with the excretion of the drug; and seizures, which could be exacerbated by the drug effects on cell membrane channels.

ADVERSE EFFECTS

Several adverse effects are associated with the use of fluoroquinolones. The most common conditions are headache, dizziness, insomnia, and depression, related to possible effects on the CNS membranes. GI effects include nausea, vomiting, diarrhea, and dry mouth related to direct drug effect on the GI tract and possibly to stimulation of the chemoreceptor trigger zone (CTZ) in the central nervous system. Immunologic effects include bone marrow depression, which may be related to drug effects on the cells of the bone marrow that rapidly turn over. Other adverse effects include fever, rash, and photosensitivity, a potentially serious adverse effect that can cause severe skin reactions. Patients should be advised to avoid sun and ultraviolet light exposure and use protective clothing and sunscreens.

CLINICALLY IMPORTANT DRUG–DRUG INTERACTIONS

When fluoroquinolones are taken concurrently with iron salts, sulcrafate, mineral supplements, or antacids, the therapeutic effect of the fluoroquinolone is decreased. If this drug combination is necessary, administration of the two agents should be separated by at least 4 hours. When fluoroquinolones are taken with drugs that increase QT_c intervals or cause torsades de pointes (quinidine, procainamide, amiodarone, sotalol, bepridil, erythromycin, terfenadine, astemizole, cisapride, pentamidine, tricyclics, phenothiazines), severe-to-fatal cardiac reactions are possible. These combinations should be avoided, but if they must be used, patients should be hospitalized, with continual cardiac monitoring. In combination with theophylline, fluoroquinolones lead to occurrence of increased theophylline levels because the two drugs use similar metabolic pathways. The theophylline dose should be decreased by one-half, and serum levels should be monitored carefully. In addition, when fluoroquinolones are combined with NSAIDs, an increased risk of CNS stimulation is possible. If this combination is used, patient should be monitored closely, especially those who have any history of seizures or CNS problems.

DATA LINK

Data link to the following fluoroquinolones in your nursing drug guide:

FLUOROQUINOLONES

Name	Brand Name	Usual Indications
P ciprofloxacin	*Cipro*	Treatment of infections caused by a wide spectrum of gram-negative bacteria
enoxacin	*Penetrex*	Treatment of urinary tract infections and sexually transmitted diseases
grepafloxacin	*Raxar*	Treatment of community acquired pneumonia, chronic bronchitis, urinary tract infections
levofloxacin	*Levaquin*	Treatment of respiratory, urinary tract, skin and sinus infections caused by susceptible gram-negative bacteria
lomefloxacin	*Maxaquin*	Treatment of lower respiratory tract and urinary tract infections; preoperative and postoperative prophylaxis for transurethral prostate biopsies
norfloxacin	*Noroxin*	Treatment of urinary tract infections
ofloxacin	*Floxin, Ocuflox*	Treatment of respiratory, skin, and urinary tract infections; pelvic inflammatory disease; ocular infections
sparfloxacin	*Zagam*	Treatment of community acquired pneumonia and chronic bronchitis
trovafloxacin alatrofloxacin	*Trovan* *Trovan IV*	Treatment of a wide spectrum of gram-negative infections, including strains that may be resistant to ciprofloxacin

NURSING CONSIDERATIONS
for patients receiving fluoroquinolones

Assessment

HISTORY. Screen for the following: known allergy to any fluoroquinolone (obtain specific information about the allergic reaction and the times it has occurred); history of renal disease that could interfere with excretion of the drug; current pregnancy or lactation status because of potential adverse effects on the fetus or infant.

PHYSICAL ASSESSMENT. Physical assessment should be performed to establish baseline data for assessing the effectiveness of the drug and the occurrence of any adverse effects associated with drug therapy. Perform culture and sensitivity tests at the site of infection. Examine the skin for any rash or lesions to provide a baseline for possible adverse effects. Conduct assessment of orientation, affect, and reflexes to establish a baseline for any CNS effects of the drug. Perform renal function tests, including BUN and creatinine clearance, to evaluate the status of renal functioning to assess necessary changes in dosage.

Nursing Diagnoses

The patient receiving a fluoroquinolone may have the following nursing diagnoses related to drug therapy:

- Pain related to GI, CNS, skin effects of drug
- Fluid volume deficit and nutritional imbalance related to GI effects
- Knowledge deficit regarding drug therapy

Implementation

- Check culture and sensitivity reports *to ensure that this is the drug of choice for this patient.*

• Monitor renal function tests prior to therapy *to appropriately arrange for dosage reduction if necessary.*
• Ensure that the patient receives the full course of the fluoroquinolone as prescribed *to eradicate the infection and to help prevent the emergence of resistant strains.*
• Monitor the site of infection and presenting signs and symptoms (e.g., fever, lethargy, urinary tract signs and symptoms) throughout the course of drug therapy. *Failure to resolve these signs and symptoms may indicate the need to reculture the site. Arrange to continue drug therapy for at least 2 days after the resolution of all signs and symptoms.*
• Provide small, frequent meals as tolerated, frequent mouth care, and ice chips or sugarless candy to suck if dry mouth is a problem *to relieve discomfort and provide nutrition;* provide adequate fluids *to replace fluid lost with diarrhea.*
• Provide safety measures, including adequate lighting, use of siderails, assistance with ambulation *to protect patient if CNS effects occur.*
• Ensure that the patient receives instructions about the appropriate dosage scheduling regimen and possible adverse effects *to enhance patient knowledge about drug therapy and to promote compliance.*

The patient should:

Take safety precautions including changing position slowly and avoiding driving and hazardous tasks if CNS effects occur.
Try to drink a lot of fluids and to maintain nutrition (very important), although nausea, vomiting, and diarrhea may occur.
Avoid ultraviolet light and sun exposure, using protective clothing and sunscreens.
Report difficulty breathing, severe headache, severe diarrhea, severe skin rash, fainting spells, and heart palpitations to a health care provider.

Evaluation

• Monitor patient response to the drug (resolution of bacterial infection).
• Monitor for adverse effects (orientation and affect, GI effects, photosensitivity).
• Evaluate the effectiveness of the teaching plan (patient can name drug, dosage, possible adverse effects to expect, and specific measures to help avoid adverse effects).
• Monitor the effectiveness of comfort and safety measures and compliance with the regimen.

MACROLIDES

The macrolides are antibiotics that interfere with protein synthesis in susceptible bacteria. Erythromycin (*E-Mycin, ERYC,* and others), the first macrolide to be developed, proved to be a good alternative for patients who were allergic to penicillins. It is the drug of choice for treating Legionnaire's disease, infections caused by *Corynebacterium diphtheriae, Ureaplasma,* syphilis, mycoplasmal pneumonias, and chlamydial infections.

Azithromycin (*Zithromax*) is used for treating mild-to-moderate respiratory infections and urethritis in adults and is effective in treating otitis media and pharyngitis/tonsillitis in children. Clarithromycin (*Biaxin*) is an expensive oral agent that has been shown to be effective in treating several respiratory, skin, sinus, and maxillary infections. In addition, it is effective against mycobacteria. Dirithromycin (*Dynabac*) is effective in treating susceptible upper and lower respiratory tract infections, skin infections, and pharyngitis/tonsillitis. It also has the advantage of once-a-day dosing, which increases compliance in many cases.

THERAPEUTIC ACTIONS AND INDICATIONS

The macrolides, which may be bactericidal or bacteriostatic, exert their effect by binding to the bacterial cell membrane and causing a change in protein function (see Figure 7-1). This action can prevent the cell from dividing or cause cell death depending on the sensitivity of the bacteria and the concentration of the drug.

Macrolides are indicated for the treatment of the following conditions: acute infections caused by susceptible strains of *Streptococcus pneumoniae, Mycoplasm pneumoniae, Listeria monocytogenes,* and *Legionella pneumophila;* infections caused by group A beta-hemolytic streptococcus; pelvic inflammatory disease caused by *N. gonorrhoeae;* upper respiratory infections (URIs) caused by *H. influenzae* (with sulfonamides); infections caused by *Corynebacterium diphtheriae* and *C. minutissimum* (with antitoxin); intestinal amebiasis; and infections caused by *Chlamydia trachomatis.* In addition, macrolides may be used as prophylaxis for endocarditis before dental procedures in patients with valvular heart disease who are allergic to penicillin. Topical macrolides are indicated for the treatment of ocular infections caused by susceptible organisms and acne vulgaris, and they may also be used prophylactically against infection in minor skin abrasions and the treatment of skin infections caused by sensitive organisms.

CONTRAINDICATIONS/CAUTIONS

Macrolides are contraindicated in the presence of known allergy to any macrolide, because cross-sensitivity occurs. Ocular preparations are contraindicated in the presence of viral, fungal, or mycobacterial infections of the eye that can be exacerbated by loss of bacteria of the normal flora. Caution should be used in patients with hepatic dysfunction that could alter the metabolism of the drug; in lactating women, because macrolides secreted in breast milk can cause diarrhea and superinfections in the infant; and in pregnant women because of potential adverse effects on the developing fetus.

ADVERSE EFFECTS

Relatively few adverse effects are associated with the macrolides. The most frequent ones, which involve the direct effects of the drug on the GI tract, are often uncomfortable enough to limit the use of the drug in some patients. These include abdominal cramping, anorexia, diarrhea, vomiting, and pseudomembranous colitis. Other effects include neurological symptoms such as confusion, abnormal thinking, and uncontrollable emotions, which could be related to drug effects on the CNS membranes; hypersensitivity reactions ranging from rash to anaphylaxis; and superinfections related to the loss of normal flora.

CLINICALLY IMPORTANT DRUG–DRUG INTERACTIONS

Increased serum levels of digoxin occur when digoxin is taken concurrently with macrolides. Patients who receive both drugs should have their digoxin levels monitored and dosage adjusted during and after treatment with the macrolide. In addition, when oral anticoagulants, theophyllines, carbamazepine, and corticosteroids are administered concurrently with macrolides, the effects of these drugs reportedly increase as a result of metabolic changes in the liver. Patients who take any of these combinations may require reduced dosage of the particular drug and careful monitoring. When cycloserine is taken with macrolides, increased serum levels of cycloserine have occurred, with the resultant risk of renal toxicity. This combination should be avoided if at all possible. Because the combination of macrolides and astemizole may lead to potentially fatal cardiac arrhythmias, this combination should also be avoided.

CLINICALLY IMPORTANT DRUG–FOOD INTERACTIONS

The presence of food in the stomach decreases the absorption of oral macrolides. Thus, the antibiotic should be given on an empty stomach, 1 hour before or at least 2 to 3 hours after meals. It should be taken with a full glass of water.

DATA LINK

Data link to the following macrolides in your nursing drug guide:

MACROLIDES

Name	Brand Name	Usual Indication
azithromycin	*Zithromax*	Treatment of mild-to-moderate respiratory infections and urethritis in adults and otitis media and pharyngitis/tonsillitis in children
clarithromycin	*Biaxin*	Treatment of various respiratory, skin, sinus, and maxillary infections, effective against mycobacteria
dirithromycin	*Dynabac*	Treatment of respiratory tract and skin infections
P erythromycin	*E-Mycin, Eryc,* and others	Treatment of infections in people allergic to penicillin, Legionnaires' disease, infections caused by *Corynebacterium diphtheriae, Ureaplasma*, syphilis, mycoplasmal pneunomias; chlamydial infections

NURSING CONSIDERATIONS
for patients receiving macrolides

Assessment

HISTORY. Screen for the following: known allergy to any macrolide (obtain specific information about the allergic reaction and the times it has occurred); history of liver disease that could interfere with metabolism of the drug; and current pregnancy or lactation status because of potential adverse effects on the fetus or infant.

PHYSICAL ASSESSMENT. Physical assessment should be performed to establish baseline data for assessing the effectiveness of the drug and the occurrence of any adverse effects associated with drug therapy. Perform culture and sensitivity tests at the site of infection. Examine the skin for any rash or lesions to provide a baseline for possible adverse effects. Monitor temperature to detect infection. Conduct assessment of orientation, affect, and reflexes to establish a baseline for any CNS effects of the drug. Assess liver function tests to evaluate the status of renal functioning to determine any needed alteration in dosage.

Nursing Diagnoses

The patient receiving a macrolide may have the following nursing diagnoses related to drug therapy:

- Pain related to GI, CNS effects of drug
- Potential for infection related to superinfections
- Knowledge deficit regarding drug therapy

Implementation

- Check culture and sensitivity reports *to ensure that this is the drug of choice for this patient.*
- Monitor hepatic function tests prior therapy; arrange *to reduce dosage as needed.*
- Ensure that the patient receives the full course of the macrolide as prescribed *to eradicate the infection and to help prevent the emergence of resistant strains.*
- Monitor the site of infection and presenting signs and symptoms (e.g., fever, lethargy, urinary tract signs and symptoms) throughout the course of drug therapy. *Failure to resolve these signs and symptoms may indicate the need to reculture the site. Arrange to continue drug therapy for at least 2 days after the resolution of all signs and symptoms.*
- Provide small, frequent meals as tolerated *to assure adequate nutrition with GI upset;* frequent mouth care and ice chips or sugarless candy to suck if dry mouth is a problem *to provide relieve of discomfort;* and adequate fluids *to replace fluid lost with diarrhea.*
- Ensure ready access to bathroom facilities *to alleviate problems with diarrhea.*
- Provide safety measures *to protect patient if CNS effects occur.*
- Arrange appropriate treatment of superinfections as needed *to decrease severity of infection and complications.*
- Ensure patient instruction about the appropriate dosage regimen and possible adverse effects *to enhance patient knowledge about drug therapy and to promote compliance.*

The patient should:

Take safety precautions, including changing position slowly and avoiding driving and hazardous tasks if CNS effects occur.

Try to drink a lot of fluids and to maintain nutrition (very important) even though nausea, vomiting, and diarrhea may occur.

Report difficulty breathing, severe headache, severe diarrhea, severe skin rash, and mouth or vaginal sores to a health care provider.

Evaluation

- Monitor patient response to the drug (resolution of bacterial infection).
- Monitor for adverse effects (orientation and affect, GI effects, superinfections).
- Evaluate the effectiveness of the teaching plan (patient can name the drug, dosage, possible adverse effects to expect, and specific measures to help avoid adverse effects.)
- Monitor the effectiveness of comfort and safety measures and compliance with the regimen.

LINCOSAMIDES

The lincosamides are similar to the macrolides but more toxic. The lincosamides react at nearly the same site in bacterial protein synthesis and are effective against the same strains of bacteria (Figure 7-2).

Clindamycin (*Cleocin*) is reserved for use in the treatment of severe infections caused by the same strains of bacteria that are susceptible to macrolides. GI reactions, which are often severe, limit the usefulness of clindamycin. Severe pseudomembranous colitis has occurred as a result of treatment. However, for a serious infection caused by a susceptible bacterium, clindamycin may be the drug of choice. It is available in parenteral as well as in topical and vaginal forms for the treatment of local infections.

Lincomycin (*Lincocin*) is indicated for the treatment of severe infections when penicillin cannot be given and when other, less toxic antibiotics such as the macrolides cannot be used. Severe GI reactions, including fatal pseudomembranous colitis, have occurred with the use of this drug. Some other toxic effects that limit the usefulness of this drug are pain, skin infections, and bone marrow depression. Nursing care of patients on these drugs is the same as for the patients on macrolides with additional precautions. These include carefully monitoring GI activity and fluid balance and stopping the drug at the first sign of severe or bloody diarrhea.

DATA LINK

Data link to the following lincosamides in your nursing drug guide:

LINCOSAMIDES

Name	Brand Name	Usual Indication
P clindamycin	*Cleocin*	Treatment of severe infections when penicillin or other less toxic antibiotics cannot be used
lincomycin	*Lincocin*	Treatment of severe infections when penicillin or other less toxic antibiotics cannot be used

MONOBACTAM ANTIBIOTICS

The only monobactam antibiotic currently available for use is aztreonam (*Azactam*). Among the antibiotics, its structure is unique for antibiotics, and little cross-resistance occurs. Aztreonam is effective against gram-negative enterobacteria and has no effect on gram-positive or anaerobic bacteria. The drug is a safe alternative for treatment of infections caused by susceptible bacteria in patients who may be allergic to penicillins or cephalosporins.

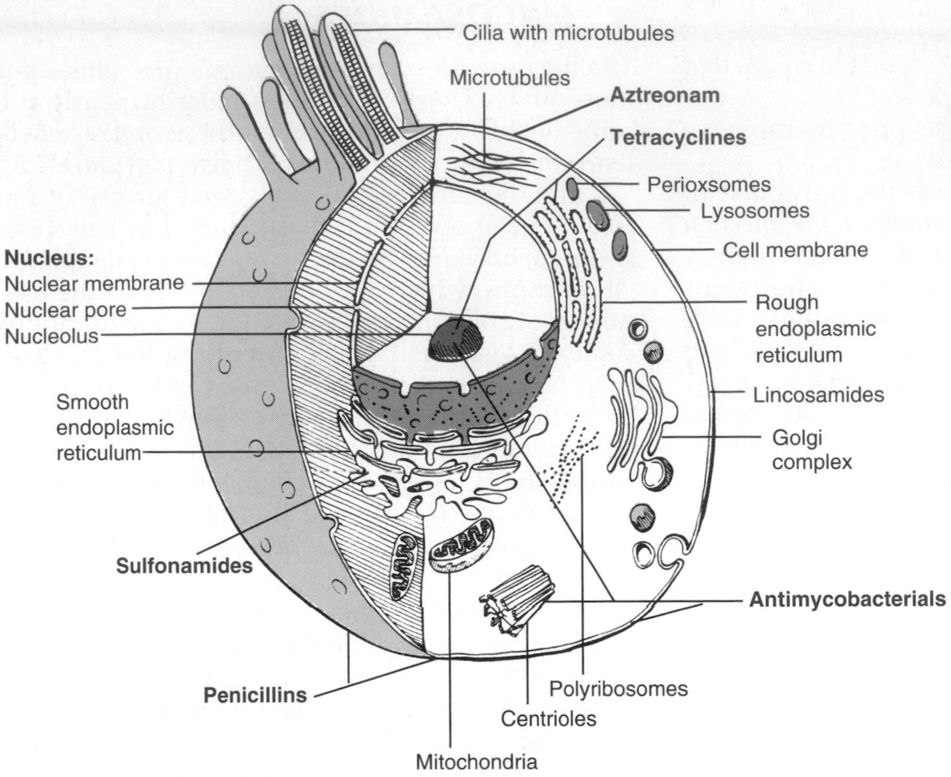

FIGURE 7-2. Sites of cellular action of lincosamides, aztreonam, penicillins, sulfonamides, tetracyclines, and antimycobacterial drugs. Lincosamides change protein function and prevent cell division or cause cell death. Aztreonam alters cell membranes to allow leakage of intracellular substances and causes cell death. Penicillins prevent bacteria from building their cells during division. Sulfonamides inhibit folic acid synthesis for RNA and DNA production. Tetracyclines inhibit protein synthesis and thus prevent reproduction. Antimycobacterial drugs affect mycobacteria in three ways to: (1) affect the mycolic coat of the bacteria, (2) alter DNA and RNA, and (3) prevent cell division.

THERAPEUTIC ACTIONS AND INDICATIONS

Aztreonam disrupts bacterial cell wall synthesis, leading to leakage of cellular contents and cell death in susceptible bacteria (see Figure 7-2). The drug is indicated for the treatment of urinary tract, skin, intra-abdominal, and gynecologic infections as well as septicemia caused by susceptible bacteria including *E. coli, Enterobacter, Serratia, Proteus, Salmonella, Providencia, Pseudomonas, Citrobacter, Haemophilus, Neisseria,* and *Klebsiella.* Aztreonam is available for IV and IM use only.

CONTRAINDICATIONS/CAUTIONS

Aztreonam is contraindicated with any known allergy to aztreonam. Caution should be used in patients with a history of acute allergic reaction to penicillins or cephalosporins because of the possibility of cross-reactivity, in those with renal or hepatic dysfunction that could interfere with the metabolism and excretion of the drug, and pregnant and lactating women because of potential adverse effects on the neonate.

ADVERSE EFFECTS

The adverse effects associated with the use of aztreonam are relatively mild. Local GI effects include nausea, GI upset, vomiting, and diarrhea. Hepatic enzyme elevations related to direct drug effects on the liver may also occur. Other effects include inflammation, phlebitis, and discomfort at injection sites as well as the potential for allergic response, including anaphylaxis.

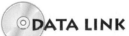

DATA LINK

Data link to the following monobactam antibiotic in your nursing drug guide:

MONOBACTAM ANTIBIOTIC

Name	Brand Name	Usual Indication
aztreonam	*Azactam*	Treatment of gram-negative enterobacteria, often as an alternate to penicillin

NURSING CONSIDERATIONS
for patients receiving aztreonam

Assessment

HISTORY. Screen for the following: known allergy to aztreonam (obtain specific information about the allergic reaction and the times it has occurred); history of acute allergic reactions to penicillins or cephalosporins; history of liver or kidney disease that could interfere with metabolism and excretion of the drug; and current pregnancy or lactation status because of potential adverse effects on the fetus or infant.

PHYSICAL ASSESSMENT. Physical assessment should be performed to establish baseline data for assessing the effectiveness of the drug and the occurrence of any adverse effects associated with drug therapy. Perform culture and sensitivity tests at the site of infection. Monitor temperature to detect infection. Abdominal examination should be performed and liver and kidney function tests should be done to check the status of liver and renal functioning to determine any needed alteration in dosage.

Nursing Diagnoses

The patient receiving aztreonam may have the following nursing diagnoses related to drug therapy:

- Pain related to GI and local effects of drug
- Knowledge deficit regarding drug therapy

Implementation

- Check culture and sensitivity reports *to ensure that this is the drug of choice for this patient.*
- Monitor hepatic and renal function tests prior to therapy *to arrange to reduce dosage as needed.*
- Ensure that the patient receives the full course of aztreonam as prescribed *to eradicate the infection and to help prevent the emergence of resistant strains.*
- Monitor the site of infection and presenting signs and symptoms (e.g., fever, lethargy) throughout the course of drug therapy. *Failure to resolve these signs and symptoms may indicate the need to reculture the site. Arrange to continue drug therapy for at least 2 days after the resolution of all signs and symptoms.*
- Provide small, frequent meals as tolerated, frequent mouth care, and ice chips or sugarless candy to suck if dry mouth is a problem *to relieve discomfort and assure nutrition;* provide adequate fluids *to replace fluid lost with diarrhea.*
- Ensure ready access to bathroom facilities *to alleviate problems associated with diarrhea.*
- Ensure that the patient is instructed about the route of administration and possible side effects *to enhance patient knowledge about drug therapy and to promote compliance.* The drug can only be given IV or IM, so patient will not be responsible for administration of the drug.

The patient should:

Try to drink a lot of fluids and to maintain nutrition (very important), even though nausea, vomiting, and diarrhea may occur.

Report difficulty breathing, severe diarrhea, or mouth or vaginal sores to a health care provider.

Evaluation

- Monitor patient response to the drug (resolution of bacterial infection).
- Monitor for adverse effects (orientation and affect, GI effects, local inflammation).
- Evaluate the effectiveness of the teaching plan (patient can name the drug, dosage, possible adverse effects to expect, and specific measures to help avoid adverse effects).
- Monitor the effectiveness of comfort and safety measures and compliance with the regimen.

PENICILLINS AND PENICILLINASE-RESISTANT ANTIBIOTICS

Penicillin was the first antibiotic introduced for clinical use. Sir Alexander Fleming used *Penicillium* molds to produce the original penicillin in the 1920s. Subsequent versions of penicillin have been developed to decrease the adverse effects of the drug and to modify it to act on resistant bacteria.

With the prolonged use of penicillin, more and more bacterial species have synthesized the enzyme penicillinase to counteract the effects of penicillin. Researchers developed a subsequent group of drugs with a resistance to penicillinase, which allowed them to remain effective against bacteria that are now resistant to the penicillins. Table 7-2 lists the various penicillins and penicillinase-resistant antibiotics and special notes about their use. The actual drug chosen depends on the sensitivity of the bacteria causing the infection, the desired route available, and personal experience of the clinician with the particular agent. Culture and sensitivity tests should always be performed to ensure that the causative organism is sensitive to the penicillin being selected for use. With the emergence of many resistant strains of bacteria, this becomes increasingly important.

THERAPEUTIC ACTIONS AND INDICATIONS

The penicillins and penicillinase-resistant antibiotics produce bactericidal effects by interfering with the ability of susceptible bacteria to build their cell walls when they are dividing (see Figure 7-2). These drugs prevent the bacteria from biosynthesizing the framework of the cell wall, and the bacteria with weakened cell walls swell and then burst from the osmotic pressure within the cell. Because human cells do not use the biochemical process that the bacteria use to form the cell wall, this effect is a selective toxicity.

The penicillins are indicated for the treatment of streptococcal infections, including pharyngitis, tonsillitis, scarlet fever, and endocarditis; pneumococcal infections; staphylococcal infections; fusospirochetal infections; rat-bite fever; diphtheria; anthrax; syphilis; and uncomplicated gonococcal infections.

TABLE 7-2
PENICILLINS

Name	Brand Names	Route(s) of Administration	Usual Indications
PENICILLINS			
penicillin G			
benzathine	*Bicillin, Permapen*	IM	Usually used as a single dose IM injection
potassium	*Pfizerpen*	IM, IV	Treatment of severe infections; used for several days in some cases
procaine	*Crysticillin-AS*	IM	Treatment of moderately severe infections daily for 8–12 days
penicillin V	*Beepen K, Betapen*	Oral	Used for prophylaxis for bacterial endocarditis; Lyme disease, UTIs, and other susceptible infections
EXTENDED SPECTRUM PENICILLINS			
ampicillin	*D-Amp, Omnipen*	Oral, IM, IV	Broad spectrum of activity; useful form if switch from parenteral to oral is anticipated; monitor for nephritis
P amoxicillin	*Amoxil, Trimox,* etc.	Oral	Broad spectrum of uses for adults and children.
bacampicillin	*Spectrobid*	Oral	Upper and lower respiratory tract infections; soft tissue infections and severe infections with less susceptible organisms; monitor for potential pseudomembranous colitis
carbenicillin	*Geocillin*	Oral	Treatment of UTIs in adults; not used in children
mezlocillin	*Mezlin*	IM, IV	Treatment of severe infections and broad range of susceptible infections; four to six injections per day may make this undesirable in some patients
piperacillin	*Pipracil*	IM, IV	Treatment of severe infections and for postoperative prophylaxis; need for four to six injections per day or IV infusion limits use in some patients
ticarcillin	*Ticar*	IM, IV	Severe infections caused by susceptible bacteria
PENICILLASE-RESISTANT ANTIBIOTICS			
P cloxacillin	*Cloxapen, Tegapen*	Oral	Infections due to pencillinase-producing staphylococci; must be taken around the clock for 10 days
dicloxacillin	*Dyapen, Dycill*	Oral	Infections due to pencillinase-producing staphylococci; must be taken around the clock for 10 days
nafcillin	*Nafcil, Nallpen*	Oral, IM, IV	Infections due to pencillinase-producing staphylococci as well as group A hemolytic streptococci, plus *S. viridans;* drug of choice if switch to oral form is anticipated
oxacillin	*Bactocill, Prostaphilin*	Oral, IM, IV	Infections due to pencillinase-producing staphylococci; streptococci; drug of choice if switch to oral form is anticipated

At high doses, these drug are also used to treat meningococcal meningitis.

CONTRAINDICATIONS/CAUTIONS

These drugs are contraindicated in the presence of known allergies to penicillin, cephalosporins, or other allergens. Penicillin sensitivity tests are available if the patient's history of allergy is unclear and a penicillin is the drug of choice. Caution should be exercised in the presence of renal disease (lowered doses will be necessary as excretion will be reduced) and pregnancy and lactation (diarrhea and superinfections may occur in the infant).

ADVERSE EFFECTS

The major adverse effects of penicillin therapy involve the GI tract. Common adverse effects include nausea, vomiting, diarrhea, abdominal pain, glossitis, stomatitis, gastritis, sore mouth, and furry tongue. These effects are primarily related to the loss of bacteria from the normal flora and the subsequent opportunistic infections that occur. Superinfections, including yeast infections, are also very common and are again associated with the loss of bacteria from the normal flora. Pain and inflammation at the injection site can occur with injectable forms of the drugs. Hypersensitivity reactions may include rash, fever, wheezing, and, with repeated exposure, anaphylaxis that can progress to anaphylactic shock and death.

CLINICALLY IMPORTANT DRUG–DRUG INTERACTIONS

If penicillins and penicillinase-resistant antibiotics are taken concurrently with tetracyclines, a decrease in the effectiveness of the penicillins results. This combination should be avoided if at all possible, or penicillin dosages will need to be raised, which could increase the occurrence of adverse effects. In addition, when the parenteral forms of penicillins and penicillinase-resistant drugs are administered in combination with any of the parenteral aminoglycosides, inactivation of the aminoglycosides occurs. These combinations should also be avoided.

DATA LINK

Data link to the penicillins and penicillinase-resistant antibiotics in your nursing drug guide (see Table 7-2).

NURSING CONSIDERATIONS
for patients receiving penicillins and penicillinase-resistant antibiotics

Assessment

HISTORY. Screen for the following: known allergy to any cephalosporins, penicillins, or other allergens because cross-sensitivity often occurs (obtain specific information about the allergic reaction and the times it has occurred); history of renal disease that could interfere with excretion of the drug; and current pregnancy or lactation status.

PHYSICAL ASSESSMENT. Physical assessment should be performed to establish baseline data for evaluating the effectiveness of the drug and the occurrence of any adverse effects associated with drug therapy. Perform culture and sensitivity tests at the site of infection. Examine the skin and mucous membranes for any rash or lesions to provide a baseline for possible adverse effects. Note respiratory status to provide a baseline for the occurrence of hypersensitivity reactions. Examine the abdomen, to monitor for adverse effects. Evaluate renal function tests, including BUN and creatinine clearance, to assess the status of renal functioning to determine any needed alteration in dosage. Examine injection sites to provide a baseline for determining adverse reactions or abscess formation.

Nursing Diagnoses

The patient receiving a penicillin may have the following nursing diagnoses related to drug therapy:

- Pain related to GI effects of drug
- Alteration in nutrition related to multiple GI effects of the drug, superinfections
- Knowledge deficit regarding drug therapy

Implementation

- Check culture and sensitivity reports *to ensure that this is the drug of choice for this patient.*
- Monitor renal function tests prior to and periodically during therapy *to arrange for dosage reduction as needed.*
- Ensure that the patient receives the full course of the penicillin as prescribed, divided around the clock *to increase effectiveness.*
- Explain storage requirements for suspensions and the importance of completing the prescription even if signs and symptoms have disappeared *to increase effectiveness of the drug and decrease the risk of the development of resistant strains.*
- Monitor the site of infection and presenting signs and symptoms (e.g., fever, lethargy) throughout the course of drug therapy. *Failure to resolve these signs and symptoms may indicate the need to reculture the site. Arrange to continue drug therapy for at least 2 days after the resolution of all signs and symptoms.*
- Provide small, frequent meals as tolerated, frequent mouth care, and ice chips or sugarless candy to suck if stomatitis and sore mouth are problems *to relieve discomfort and assure nutrition,* and adequate fluids *to replace fluid lost with diarrhea.*
- Monitor the patient for any signs of superinfections and *arrange for treatment of superinfections if they do occur.*
- Monitor injection sites regularly *to provide warm compresses and gentle massage to injection sites if painful or swollen;* if signs of phlebitis occur, *remove the IV line and reinsert it in a different vein.*
- Ensure patient instruction about the appropriate dosage regimen and possible adverse effects *to enhance patient knowledge about drug therapy and to promote compliance.*

The patient should:

Try to drink a lot of fluids and to maintain nutrition (very important) even though nausea, vomiting, and diarrhea may occur.

Report difficulty breathing, severe headache, severe diarrhea, dizziness, weakness, mouth sores, and vaginal itching or sores to a health care provider.

(See Patient Teaching Checklist: Antibiotics/Penicillins.)

Evaluation

- Monitor patient response to the drug (resolution of bacterial infection).
- Monitor for adverse effects (GI effects; local irritation, phlebitis at injection and IV sites; superinfections).
- Evaluate the effectiveness of the teaching plan (patient can name the drug, dosage, possible adverse effects to expect, and specific measures to help avoid adverse effects).

PATIENT TEACHING CHECKLIST

Antibiotics/Penicillins

Create customized patient teaching materials for a specific antibiotic/penicillin from your CD-ROM. Your patient teaching should stress the following points for drugs within this class:

The penicillins are used to help destroy specific bacteria that are causing infections in the body. They are effective against only certain bacteria; they are not effective against viruses, cold germs, or other bacteria. To clear up a bacterial infection, the penicillins have to act on the bacteria over a period of time, so it is very important to complete the full course of this penicillin to avoid recurrence of the infection.

The drug should be taken on an empty stomach with a full glass of water; one hour before meals or 2 to 3 hours after meals is best. Do not use fruit juice, soft drinks, or milk to take your drug, because these foods may interfere with its effectiveness. (This does not apply with bacampicillin, amoxicillin, or penicillin V.)

Common effects of these drugs include stomach upset, diarrhea, changes in taste, and change in the color of the tongue. Small, frequent meals may help. It is important to try to maintain your nutrition. These effects should go away when the drug is stopped.

Report any of the following to your health care provider: hives, rash, fever, difficulty breathing, severe diarrhea.

Tell any doctor, nurse, or other health care provider that you are taking this drug.

Keep this drug and all medications out of the reach of children.

Do not share this drug with other people, and do not use this medication to self-treat other infections.

It is very important that you complete the full course of your prescription, even if you feel better.

This Teaching Checklist reflects general patient teaching guidelines. It is not meant to be a substitute for drug-specific teaching information, which is available in nursing drug guides.

- Monitor the effectiveness of comfort and safety measures and compliance with the regimen (see Nursing Care Guide: Antibiotics/Penicillins).

SULFONAMIDES

The sulfonamides, or sulfa drugs, are drugs that inhibit folic acid synthesis. Folic acid is necessary for the synthesis of purine and pyrimidines that are precursors of RNA and DNA. For cells to grow and reproduce, they require folic acid. Humans, who cannot synthesize folic acid, depend on the folate found in the diet to obtain this essential substance. Bacteria are impermeable to folic acid and must synthesize it inside the cell.

Because of the emergence of resistant bacterial strains and the development of newer antibiotics, the sulfa drugs are not used much any more. However, they remain an inexpensive and effective treatment for urinary tract infections and trachoma, especially in developing countries and when cost is an issue.

Sulfadiazine is an oral agent with broad use in infections caused by susceptible bacteria. Sulfamethizole (*Thiosulfil Forte*) is reserved for the treatment of urinary tract infections caused by susceptible bacteria. Sulfamethoxazole (*Gantanol*), which is used the same way as sulfadiazine, is the drug of choice for severe infections and for the treatment of meningococcal meningitis caused by susceptible bacteria.

Sulfisoxazole is used for a broad spectrum of infections caused by susceptible bacteria. This drug is also recommended by the Centers for Disease Control and Prevention for the treatment of sexually transmitted diseases and has the unlabeled use of prophylaxis for recurrent otitis media.

Sulfasalazine (*Azulfidine*) is a sulfapyridine that is carried by aminosalicylic acids (aspirin) that release the aminosalicylic acid in the colon. Sulfasalazine is used in the treatment of ulcerative colitis and Crohn's disease because of the direct anti-inflammatory effect of the aspirin. In a delayed-release form, this sulfa drug is also used to treat rheumatoid arthritis in patients who are not responsive to other treatments.

Co-trimoxazole (*Septra, Bactrim*) is a combination drug that contains sulfamethoxazole and trimethoprim, another antibacterial drug. This combination has proven to be very effective in treating otitis media, bronchitis, urinary tract infections, and pneumonitis caused by *Pneumocystis carinii,* which is becoming a serious problem in immune compromised patients (e.g., those with AIDS).

NURSING CARE GUIDE
Antibiotics/Penicillins

Assessment	Nursing Diagnoses	Implementation	Evaluation
HISTORY			
Allergies to any of these drugs or other antibiotics; renal or liver dysfunction; pregnancy and lactation; other drugs administered	Pain related to GI effects, superinfections	Check culture and sensitivity tests prior to giving drug.	Evaluate drug effects: resolution of bacterial infection.
	Knowledge deficit regarding drug therapy	Monitor renal function and arrange to reduce dose as necessary.	Monitor for adverse effects: GI effects, superinfections, liver changes.
		Ensure that patient receives the full course of treatment; space dosage around the clock; administer oral drug on an empty stomach.	
	Alteration in nutrition related to GI effects	Provide small, frequent meals and monitor nutritional status.	Monitor for drug–drug interactions as indicated for each drug.
		Monitor for superinfections and arrange treatment as indicated.	Evaluate effectiveness of patient teaching program.
		Provide support and reassurance for dealing with drug effects and discomfort.	Evaluate effectiveness of comfort and safety measures.
		Provide patient teaching regarding drug name, dosage, adverse effects, precautions, and warning signs to report.	
PHYSICAL EXAMINATION			
General: temperature, culture site of infection, affect			
Skin: color, lesions, texture			
Local: infection sites			
GI: abdominal, liver evaluation			
Hematologic: CBC and differential; renal and hepatic function tests			

THERAPEUTIC ACTIONS AND INDICATIONS

The sulfonamides competitively block PABA (para-aminobenzoic acid) to prevent the synthesis of folic acid in susceptible bacteria that synthesize their own folates for the production of RNA and DNA (see Figure 7-2). This includes gram-negative and gram-positive bacteria such as *Chlamydia trachomatis; Nocardia;* and some strains of *H. influenzae, E. coli,* and *P. mirabilis.* These drugs are used for the treatment of trachoma (a leading cause of blindness), nocardiosis (which causes pneumonias and brain abscesses and inflammation), urinary tract infections, and sexually transmitted diseases.

CONTRAINDICATIONS/CAUTIONS

The sulfonamides are contraindicated with any known allergy to any sulfonamide; to sulfonylureas or thiazide diuretics, because cross-sensitivities occur; during pregnancy, because the drugs can cause birth defects as well as kernicterus; and during lactation, because of a risk of kernicterus, diarrhea, and rash in the infant. Caution should be used in patients with renal disease or a history of kidney stones because of the possibility of increased toxic effects of the drugs.

ADVERSE EFFECTS

Adverse effects associated with sulfonamides include GI effects such as nausea, vomiting, diarrhea, abdominal pain, anorexia, stomatitis, and hepatic injury, which are all related to direct irritation of the GI tract and the death of normal bacteria. Renal effects are related to the filtration of the drug in the glomerulus and include crystalluria, hematuria, and proteinuria, which can progress to a nephrotic syndrome and possible toxic nephrosis. CNS effects include headache, dizziness, vertigo, ataxia, convulsions, and depression (possibly related to drug effects on the nerves). Bone marrow depression related to drug effects on the cells in the bone marrow that turn over rapidly may occur. Dermatologic effects include photosensitivity and rash related to direct effects on the dermal cells. A wide range of hypersensitivity reactions may also occur.

CLINICALLY IMPORTANT DRUG–DRUG INTERACTIONS

If sulfonamides are taken with tolbutamide, tolazamide, glyburide, glipizide, acetohexamide, or chlorpropamide, the risk of hypoglycemia increases. If this combination is needed, the patient should be monitored and a dosage adjustment of the antidiabetic agent should be made. An increase in dosage will then be needed when the sulfonamide is stopped.

When sulfonamides are taken in combination with cyclosporine, the risk of nephrotoxicity rises. If this combination is essential, the patient should be monitored closely and the sulfonamide stopped at any sign of renal dysfunction.

DATA LINK

Data link to the following sulfonamide antibiotics in your nursing drug guide:

SULFONAMIDE ANTIBIOTICS

Name	Brand Name	Usual Indication
sulfadiazine	generic	Treatment of broad spectrum of infections
P sulfamethizole	*Thiosulfil Forte*	Treatment of urinary tract infections
sulfamethoxazole	*Gantanol*	Treatment of severe infections including meningococcal meningitis
sulfisoxazole	generic	Treatment of wide range of infections including various sexually transmitted diseases
sulfasalazine	*Azulfidine*	Treatment of ulcerative colitis and Crohn's disease
cotrimoxazole	*Septra, Bactrim*	Treatment of otitis media, bronchitis, urinary tract infections, and pneumonitis caused by *Pneumocystis carinii*

NURSING CONSIDERATIONS
for patients receiving sulfonamides

Assessment

HISTORY. Screen for the following: known allergy to any sulfonamides, sulfonylureas, or thiazide diuretics, because cross-sensitivity often results (obtain specific information about the allergic reaction and the times it has occurred); history of renal disease that could interfere with excretion of the drug and lead to increased toxicity; and current pregnancy or lactation status.

PHYSICAL ASSESSMENT. Physical assessment should be performed to establish baseline data for assessing the effectiveness of the drug and the occurrence of any adverse effects associated with drug therapy. Perform culture and sensitivity tests at the site of infection. Examine skin and mucous membranes for any rash or lesions to provide a baseline for possible adverse effects. Note respiratory status to provide a baseline for the occurrence of hypersensitivity reactions. Conduct assessment of orientation, affect, and reflexes to monitor for adverse drug effects and examination of abdomen to monitor for adverse effects. Monitor renal function tests, including BUN and creatinine clearance, to evaluate the status of renal functioning to determine any needed alteration in dosage. CBC should be performed to establish a baseline to monitor for adverse effects.

Nursing Diagnoses

The patient receiving a sulfonamide may have the following nursing diagnoses related to drug therapy:

- Pain related to GI, CNS, skin effects of drug
- Sensory–perceptual alteration related to CNS effects
- Alteration in nutrition related to multiple GI effects of the drug
- Knowledge deficit regarding drug therapy

Implementation

- Check culture and sensitivity reports *to ensure that this is the drug of choice for this patient, and repeat cultures if response is not as anticipated.*
- Monitor renal function tests prior to and periodically during therapy *to arrange for a dosage reduction as necessary.*
- Ensure that the patient receives the full course of the sulfonamide as prescribed *to increase therapeutic effects and decrease risk of development of resistant strains.*
- Administer the oral drug on an empty stomach 1 hour before or 2 hours after meals with a full glass of water *to assure adequate absorption of the drug.*
- Discontinue the drug immediately if hypersensitivity reactions occur *to prevent potentially fatal reactions.*
- Provide small, frequent meals as tolerated, frequent mouth care, and ice chips or sugarless candy to suck if stomatitis and sore mouth are problems *to relieve discomfort and assure nutrition,* and adequate fluids *to replace fluid lost with diarrhea.*
- Monitor CBC and urinalysis prior to and periodically during therapy *to check for adverse effects.*
- Ensure patient instruction in the appropriate dosage regimen and the proper way to take the drug (on an empty stomach with a full glass of water), and possible adverse effects, *to enhance patient knowledge about drug therapy and to promote compliance.*

The patient should:

Avoid driving or operating dangerous machinery, because dizziness, lethargy, and ataxia may occur.

Try to drink a lot of fluids and to maintain nutrition (very important), even though nausea, vomiting, and diarrhea may occur.

Report difficulty breathing, rash, ringing in the ears, fever, sore throat, and blood in the urine to a health care provider.

Evaluation

- Monitor patient response to the drug (resolution of bacterial infection).
- Monitor for adverse effects (GI effects, CNS effects, rash, and crystalluria).
- Evaluate the effectiveness of the teaching plan (patient can name the drug, dosage, possible adverse effects to expect, and specific measures to help avoid adverse effects).
- Monitor the effectiveness of comfort and safety measures and compliance with the regimen.

TETRACYCLINES

The tetracyclines were developed as semisynthetic antibiotics based on the structure of a common soil mold. They work by inhibiting protein synthesis in susceptible bacteria. They are composed of four rings, which is how they got their name. Researchers have developed newer tetracyclines to increase absorption and tissue penetration. Widespread resistance to the tetracyclines has limited their use in recent years.

Tetracycline (*Sumycin, Panmycin,* and others) is available in oral and topical forms for the treatment of a wide variety of infections, including acne vulgaris and minor skin infections caused by susceptible organisms. When penicillin is contraindicated, tetracycline is often used. Tetracycline is also available as an ophthalmic agent to treat superficial ocular lesions due to susceptible microorganisms and as a prophylactic agent for ophthalmia neonatorum caused by *N. gonorrhoeae* and *C. trachomatis.*

Demeclocycline (*Declomycin*) is available in oral form for the treatment of a wide variety of infections. Like tetracycline, it is also often utilized when penicillin is contraindicated.

Doxycycline (*Doryx, Doxy-Caps,* and others) is available for oral and IV use. Used for a wide variety of infections, this drug is recommended in the treatment of traveler's diarrhea and some sexually transmitted diseases.

Minocycline (*Minocin*) is also available in IV and oral forms. It is used to treat severe infections caused by susceptible bacteria. In addition, minocycline is the drug of choice in the treatment of meningococcal carriers (not the disease itself) and various uncomplicated GU and gynecologic infections.

Oxytetracycline (*Terramycin*) is available for oral, IM, and IV use. It is used to treat a wide variety of infections caused by susceptible bacteria as well as infections when penicillin is contraindicated. Oxytetracycline is also used as an adjunct therapy in the treatment of acute intestinal amebiasis.

THERAPEUTIC ACTIONS AND INDICATIONS

The tetracyclines inhibit protein synthesis in susceptible bacteria, leading to the inability of the bacteria to multiply (see Figure 7-2). Because the affected protein is similar to a protein found in human cells, these drugs can be toxic to humans at high concentrations. Tetracyclines, which are effective against a wide range of bacteria, are indicated in the treatment of infections caused by rickettsiae, *Mycoplasma pneumoniae, Borrelia recurrentis,*

Haemophilus influenzae, H. ducreyi, Pasteurella pestis, P. tularensis, Bartonella bacilliformis, Bacteroides, Vibrio comma, V. fetus, Brucella, E. coli, Enterobacter aerogenes, Shigella, Acinetobacter calcoaceticus, Klebsiella, Diplococcus pneumoniae, and *Staphylococcus aureus;* agents that cause psittacosis, ornithosis, lymphogranuloma venereum, and granuloma inguinale; when penicillin is contraindicated in susceptible infections; and for the treatment of acne and uncomplicated GU infections caused by *Chlamydia trachomatis.* Some of the tetracyclines are also used as adjuncts in the treatment of some protozoal infections.

CONTRAINDICATIONS/CAUTIONS

Tetracyclines are contraindicated in the presence of known allergy to tetracyclines or to tartrazine (i.e., in specific oral preparations that contain tartrazine) and during pregnancy and lactation because of effects on the bones and teeth. Tetracyclines should be used with caution in children under 8 years of age because of potential damage to the bones and teeth, and in patients with hepatic and renal dysfunction, because the drug is concentrated in the bile and excreted in the urine. The ophthalmic preparation is contraindicated in the presence of fungal, mycobacterial, or viral ocular infections because of the risk of exacerbation of the infection with death of bacteria of the normal flora.

ADVERSE EFFECTS

The major adverse effects of tetracycline therapy involve direct irritation of the GI tract and include nausea, vomiting, diarrhea, abdominal pain, glossitis, and dysphagia. Fatal hepatotoxicity related to the drug's irritating effect on the liver has also been reported. Skeletal effects involve damage to the teeth and bones. Because tetracyclines have an affinity for teeth and bones, they accumulate there, leading to weakening of the bone or tooth structure as well as staining and pitting of the teeth and bones. Dermatologic effects include photosensitivity and rash. Superinfections, including yeast infections, occur when bacteria of the normal flora are destroyed. Local effects such as pain and stinging with topical or ocular application are fairly common. Less frequent are hematologic effects, such as hemolytic anemia and bone marrow depression secondary to the drug effects on the cells of the bone marrow that turn over rapidly. Hypersensitivity reactions reportedly range from urticaria to anaphylaxis, including intracranial hypertension.

CLINICALLY IMPORTANT DRUG–DRUG INTERACTIONS

When penicillin G and tetracyclines are taken concurrently, the effectiveness of penicillin G decreases. If this combination is used, the dose of the penicillin should be increased. When oral contraceptives are taken with tetracyclines, decreased effectiveness of the contraceptives is possible. Patients who take oral contraceptives should be advised to use an additional form of birth control while receiving the tetracycline. When methoxyflurane is combined with tetracycline, the risk of nephrotoxicity increases. If at all possible, this combination should be avoided. In addition, digoxin toxicity rises when tetracyclines are taken concurrently. Digoxin levels should be monitored and dosage adjusted appropriately during treatment and after the tetracycline is discontinued. Finally, decreased absorption of tetracyclines results from oral combinations with calcium salts, magnesium salts, zinc salts, aluminum salts, bismuth salts, iron, urinary alkalinizers, and charcoal.

CLINICALLY IMPORTANT DRUG–FOOD INTERACTIONS

Because oral tetracyclines are not absorbed effectively if taken with food or dairy products, tetracyclines should be given on an empty stomach 1 hour before or 2 to 3 hours after any meal or other medication.

DATA LINK

Data link to the following tetracyclines in your nursing drug guide:

TETRACYCLINES

Name	Brand Name	Usual Indication
demeclocyline	*Declomycin*	Treatment of a wide variety of infections when penicillin cannot be used
doxycycline	*Doryx, Doxy-Caps*	Treatment of a wide variety of infections including traveler's diarrhea and sexually transmitted diseases
minocycline	*Minocin*	Treatment of meningococcal carriers and various uncomplicated GU and gynecologic infections
oxytetracycline	*Terramycin*	Treatment of a variety of infections caused by susceptible bacteria when penicillin is contraindicated; adjunct therapy in the treatment of acute intestinal amebiasis
P tetracycline	*Sumycin, Panmycin*	Treatment of a wide variety of infections, including acne vulgaris, minor skin infections caused by susceptible organisms; as ophthalmic agent to treat superficial ocular lesions due to susceptible microorganisms; prophylactic agent for ophthalmia neonatorum caused by *N. gonorrhoeae* and *C. trachomatis*

CASE STUDY

Antibiotics and Oral Contraceptive Use

PRESENTATION

G. S., a 27-year-old married woman, began graduate school with plans to start a family in 2 years after completion of her program. She has successfully used low-dose birth control pills for 4 years and had planned to continue this method of birth control. A few weeks into the fall semester, she developed severe sinusitis that cultured out a strain of *Klebsiella* that was sensitive to tetracycline. She received treatment with a standard 5-day course of the antibiotic, and at the end of the 5 days, the sinusitis has resolved.

In mid-January, G. S. presented to the student health clinic with a number of complaints, which turned out to be caused by pregnancy. Uterine size was consistent with a 12-week gestation. She denied any lapse in birth control pill use.

CRITICAL THINKING QUESTIONS

What most likely led to this pregnancy? How do tetracyclines and some other antibiotics and oral contraceptives interact? What are the possible ramifications of continuing to take oral contraceptives during a pregnancy? What nursing interventions are appropriate at this time? What options are available and what plans for nursing interventions should be made at this first visit? Think about the possibility of birth defects, about the stage in her life, and the issues that G. S. is trying to cope with. Also think about the nature of her personality and the problems that she may face with an unplanned pregnancy and potential problems with the fetus.

DISCUSSION

Several antibiotics, including tetracycline, are known to lead to the failure of oral contraceptives as evidenced by breakthrough bleeding and unplanned pregnancy. Although the exact way in which these drugs interact is incompletely understood, it is thought that the antibiotics destroy certain bacteria in the normal flora of the GI tract. These bacteria are necessary for the breakdown and eventual absorption of the female hormones contained in the contraceptives.

The 5 days of antibiotic treatment together with the time necessary for rebuilding the normal flora was enough time for the hypothalamus to lose the negative feedback signal provided by the contraceptives to prevent ovulation and preparation of the uterus. Without sensing the hormone levels, the hypothalamus released gonadotropic-releasing hormone, which led to the release of follicle-stimulating hormone, luteinizing hormone, and subsequent ovulation.

G. S., a compulsive, organized woman, may be overwhelmed by the emotional and physical stress of this unplanned pregnancy. She may investigate the possibility of birth defects while taking oral contraceptives during pregnancy and discover that cardiac and sexual organ and accessory organ deformities can occur. Because she may wish to undergo further studies to determine fetal abnormalities, she should be referred to an obstetrician and possibly a genetic counselor.

G. S. will need a great deal of support and understanding during the next few days and weeks. Just having someone to talk to may be beneficial. She should receive help in understanding the reason for the birth control failure and be encouraged to read all of the literature that comes with oral contraceptives as well as patient teaching information that should have been given out with the antibiotic. Whether she decides to terminate the pregnancy or carry it to term, she will need continued medical management and emotional support. All of the health care professionals who are involved with her care should use this as an example of the importance of clear, concise patient teaching in the administration of drug therapy.

NURSING CONSIDERATIONS
for patients receiving tetracyclines

Assessment

HISTORY. Screen for the following: known allergy to any tetracyclines or tartrazine in certain oral preparations because cross-sensitivity often occurs (obtain specific information about the allergic reaction and the times it has occurred); history of renal or hepatic disease which could interfere with metabolism and excretion of the drug and lead to increased toxicity; current pregnancy or lactation status; and age. Because of the adverse effects on the bones and teeth, tetracyclines are not recommended for children under the age of 8 years.

PHYSICAL ASSESSMENT. Physical assessment should be performed to establish baseline data for assessing the effectiveness of the drug and the occurrence of any adverse effects associated with drug therapy. Perform culture and sensitivity tests at the site of infection. Conduct examination of the skin for any rash or lesions to provide a baseline for possible adverse effects. Note respiratory status to provide a baseline for the occurrence of hypersensitivity reactions. Evaluate renal and liver function tests, including BUN and creatinine clearance, to assess the status of renal and liver functioning to determine any needed alteration in dosage.

Nursing Diagnoses

The patient receiving a tetracycline may have the following nursing diagnoses related to drug therapy:

- Diarrhea related to drug effects
- Alteration in nutrition related to GI effects, alteration in taste, superinfections.
- Alteration in skin integrity related to rash and photosensitivity
- Knowledge deficit regarding drug therapy

Implementation

- Check culture and sensitivity reports *to ensure that this is the drug of choice for this patient and repeat cultures if response is not as anticipated.*
- Monitor renal and liver function tests prior to and periodically during therapy *to arrange for a dosage reduction as needed.*
- Ensure that the patient receives the full course of the tetracycline as prescribed. Administer the oral drug on an empty stomach 1 hour before or 2 hours after meals with a full glass of water. Do not administer with any antacids or salts. *These actions will increase effectiveness and decrease development of resistant strains.*
- Discontinue the drug immediately if hypersensitivity reactions occur *to avoid the possibility of severe reactions.*
- Provide small, frequent meals as tolerated, frequent mouth care, and ice chips or sugarless candy to suck if stomatitis and sore mouth are problems *to relieve discomfort and assure nutrition;* provide adequate fluids *to replace fluid lost with diarrhea.*
- Monitor for signs of superinfections *to arrange for treatment as appropriate.*
- Protect the patient from exposure to the sun with protective clothing and sunscreen as appropriate if skin rash occurs *to prevent severe photosensitivity reactions.*
- Ensure that the patient receives instructions about the appropriate dosage scheduling regimen, how to take the oral drug, and possible side effects *to enhance patient knowledge about drug therapy and to promote compliance.*

The patient should:

Try to drink a lot of fluids and to maintain nutrition (very important) even though nausea, vomiting, and diarrhea may occur.

Use barrier contraceptives because oral contraceptives may not be effective while using a tetracycline.

Know that superinfections may occur. Appropriate treatment can be arranged through the health care provider.

Use sunscreens and protective clothing if sensitivity to the sun occurs.

Report difficulty breathing, rash, itching, watery diarrhea, cramps, and changes in color of urine or stool to the health care provider.

Evaluation

- Monitor patient response to the drug (resolution of bacterial infection).
- Monitor for adverse effects (GI effects, rash, and superinfections).
- Evaluate the effectiveness of the teaching plan (patient can name the drug, dosage, possible adverse effects to expect, and specific measures to help avoid adverse effects).
- Monitor the effectiveness of comfort and safety measures and compliance with the regimen.

ANTIMYCOBACTERIAL ANTIBIOTICS

Mycobacteria, the group of bacteria that contain the pathogens that cause tuberculosis and leprosy, are classified on the basis of their ability to hold a stain even in the presence of a destaining agent such as acid. Because of this property, they are called "acid-fast" bacteria. The mycobacteria have an outer coat of mycolic acid that protects them from many disinfectants and allows them to survive for long periods of time in the environment. These slow-growing bacteria may need to be treated for several years before they can be eradicated.

Mycobacteria cause serious infectious diseases. The bacterium *Mycobacterium tuberculosis* causes tuberculosis, the leading cause of death due to infectious disease in the world. For several years, the disease was thought to be under control, but with the increasing number of immune compromised people and the emergence of resistant bacterial strains, tuberculosis is once again on the rise. *Mycobacterium leprae* causes leprosy, or Hansen's disease, which is characterized by disfiguring skin lesions and destruction in the respiratory tract. Leprosy is also a worldwide health problem and is infectious when the mycobacteria invade the skin and respiratory tract of susceptible individuals. *Mycobacterium avium-intracellulare,* which causes mycobacterium-avium complex (MAC), is seen in patients with AIDS or in other patients who are severely immune compromised. Rifabutin (*Mycobutin*), which was developed as an antituberculous drug, is most effective against *M. avium-intracellulare.*

Antituberculous Drugs

Tuberculosis can lead to serious damage in the lungs, the GU tract, bones, and the meninges. Because *M. tuberculosis* is so slow growing, the treatment must be continued for 6 months to 2 years.

The first-line drugs for treating tuberculosis are as follows:

- Isoniazid (*Nydrazid,* [INH]), which affects the mycolic acid coating of the bacterium
- Rifampin (*Rifadin, Rimactane*), which alters DNA and RNA activity in the bacterium
- Ethionamide (*Trecator S.C.*), which prevents cell division
- Rifapentine (*Priftin*), which alters DNA and RNA activity, causing cell death

These drugs are used in combinations of two or more drugs until bacterial conversion occurs or maximum improvement is seen.

If the patient is not able to take one or more of these drugs, or if the disease continues to progress because of the emergence of a resistant strain, the second-line drugs can be used:

- Ethambutol (*Myambutol*), which inhibits cellular metabolism
- Pyrazinamide (generic), which is both bactericidal and bacteriostatic

These drugs are used in combination with at least one other antituberculous drug.

If therapeutic success is still not achieved, a third-line combination of two antituberculous drugs can be tried:

- Capreomycin (*Capastat*), whose mechanism of action is not known
- Cycloserine (*Seromycin),* which inhibits cell wall synthesis and leads to cell death.

Using the drugs in combination helps to decrease the emergence of resistant strains and to affect the bacteria at various phases during their long, slow life cycle.

Leprostatic Drugs

Antibiotics used to treat leprosy include dapsone (generic) and clofazimine (*Lamprene*). Dapsone has been the mainstay of leprosy treatment for many years, although resistant strains are emerging. Similar to the sulfonamides, dapsone inhibits folate synthesis in susceptible bacteria. In addition to its use in leprosy, dapsone is used to treat *P. carinii* pneumonia in AIDS patients and for a variety of infections caused by susceptible bacteria, as well as for brown recluse spider bites.

Clofazimine, which binds to bacterial DNA sites and causes cell death, has been useful in the treatment of dapsone-resistant leprosy. The drug is used as part of initial leprosy treatment in combination with dapsone to prevent the development of resistant strains.

Recently, the hypnotic drug thalidomide has been approved for use for a condition that occurs after treatment for leprosy (Box 7-3).

THERAPEUTIC ACTIONS AND INDICATIONS

Most of the antimycobacterial agents act on the DNA of the bacteria, leading to a lack of bacteria growth and eventually bacterial death (see Figure 7-2). Isoniazid specifically affects the mycolic acid coat around the bacteria. Although many of the antimycobacterial agents are effective against other species of susceptible bacteria, their primary indications are treatment of tuberculosis or leprosy (as previously indicated). The antituberculous drugs are always used in combination to affect the bacteria at various stages and to help to decrease the emergence of resistant strains.

BOX 7-3

THALIDOMIDE APPROVED FOR NEW USE

In the 1950s, the drug thalidomide became internationally known because it caused serious fetal abnormalities (e.g., lack of limbs, defective limbs) in many women who received the drug during pregnancy. This outrage led to the recall of thalidomide in the United States and the establishment of more stringent standards for drug testing and labeling. In 1998, the U.S. Food and Drug Administration (FDA) approved the use of this controversial drug for the treatment of erythema nodosum leprosum, which is a painful inflammatory condition related to an immune reaction to dead bacteria following treatment for leprosy. To use this drug, a woman must have a negative pregnancy test, receive instruction in the use of birth control, and sign a release stating that she understands the risks associated with the drug. These limits on the use of a drug were the first such restrictions ever ordered by the FDA.

CONTRAINDICATIONS/CAUTIONS

Antimycobacterial drugs are contraindicated in the presence of any known allergy to these agents; with severe renal or hepatic failure that could interfere with the metabolism or excretion of the drug; with severe CNS dysfunction that could be exacerbated by the actions of the drugs; and in pregnancy because of possible adverse effects on the fetus. If an antituberculous regimen is necessary during pregnancy, the combination of isoniazid, ethambutol, and rifampin is considered the safest.

ADVERSE EFFECTS

CNS effects such as neuritis, dizziness, headache, malaise, drowsiness, and hallucinations are often reported. These effects are related to direct effects of the drugs on neurons. These drugs also are irritating to the GI tract, causing nausea, vomiting, anorexia, stomach upset, and abdominal pain. Rifampin, rifabutin, and rifapentine cause discoloration of body fluids from urine to sweat and tears. Patients should be alerted to the fact that orange-tinged urine, sweat, and tears may stain clothing and often permanently stain contact lenses. This can be frightening if the patient is not alerted to the possibility that this will happen. As with other antibiotics, there is always a possibility of hypersensitivity reactions and the patient should be monitored on a regular basis.

CLINICALLY IMPORTANT DRUG–DRUG INTERACTIONS

When rifampin and isoniazid are used in combination, the possibility of toxic liver reactions is increased. Patients should be monitored closely. Increased metabolism and decreased drug effectiveness occur as a result of administration of quinidine, metoprolol, propranolol, corticosteroids, oral contraceptives, oral anticoagulants, oral antidiabetic agents, digoxin, theophylline, methadone, phenytoin, verapamil, cyclosporine, and ketoconazole in combination with rifampin or rifabutin. Patients who are taking these drug combinations should be monitored closely and dosage adjustments made as needed.

DATA LINK

Data link to the following antimycobacterial drugs in your nursing drug guide:

ANTIMYCOBACTERIAL DRUGS

Name	Brand Name	Usual Indication
ANTITUBERCULOUS DRUGS		
capreomycin	*Capastat*	Second-line drug for treatment of *Mycobacterium tuberculosis*
cycloserine	*Seromycin*	Second-line drug for treatment of *Mycobacterium tuberculosis*
ethambutol	*Myambutol*	Second-line drug for treatment of *Mycobacterium tuberculosis*
ethionamide	*Trecator S.C.*	First-line drug for treatment of *Mycobacterium tuberculosis*
P isoniazid	*Nydrazid, INH*	First-line drug for treatment of *Mycobacterium tuberculosis*
pyrazinamide	generic	Second-line drug for treatment of *Mycobacterium tuberculosis*
rifabutin	*Mycobutin*	Treatment of *M. avium-intracellulare* (MAC) in patients with advanced HIV infection
rifampin	*Rifadin, Rimactane*	First-line drug for treatment of *Mycobacterium tuberculosis*
rifapentine	*Priftin*	First-line drug for treatment of *Mycobacterium tuberculosis*
LEPROSTATIC DRUGS		
P dapsone	generic	Treatment of leprosy, *P. carinii* pneumonia in AIDS patients, variety of infections caused by susceptible bacteria; brown recluse spider bites
clofazimine	*Lamprene*	Treatment of dapsone-resistant leprosy

NURSING CONSIDERATIONS
for patients receiving antimycobacterial antibiotics

Assessment

HISTORY. Screen for the following: known allergy to any antimycobacterial drug (obtain specific information about the allergic reaction and the times it has occurred); history of renal or hepatic disease that could interfere with metabolism and excretion of the drug and lead to increased toxicity; history of CNS dysfunction, including seizure disorders and neuritis that could be exacerbated by adverse drug effects; and current pregnancy status.

PHYSICAL ASSESSMENT. Physical assessment should be performed to establish baseline data for assessing the effectiveness of the drug and the occurrence of any adverse effects associated with drug therapy. Perform culture and sensitivity tests to establish the sensitivity of the organism being treated. Examine skin for any rash or lesions to provide a baseline for possible adverse effects. Evaluate CNS for orientation, affect, and reflexes to establish a baseline and to monitor for adverse effects. Note respiratory status to provide a baseline for the occurrence of hypersensitivity reactions. Evaluate renal and liver function tests, including BUN and creatinine clearance, to assess the status of renal and liver functioning to determine any needed alteration in dosage.

Nursing Diagnoses

The patient receiving an antimycobacterial drug may have the following nursing diagnoses related to drug therapy:

- Alteration in nutrition related to GI effects
- Sensory–perceptual alteration related to CNS effects of the drug
- Pain related to GI, CNS effects of drug
- Knowledge deficit regarding drug therapy

Implementation

- Check culture and sensitivity reports *to ensure that this is the drug of choice for this patient and repeat cultures if response is not as anticipated.*
- Monitor renal and liver function tests prior to and periodically during therapy *to arrange for dosage reduction as needed.*
- Ensure that the patient receives the full course of the drugs *to improve effectiveness and decrease the risk of development of resistant strains.* These drugs are taken for years and often in combination. Periodic medical evaluation and reteaching is often essential *to ensure compliance.*
- Discontinue the drug immediately if hypersensitivity reactions occur *to avert potentially serious reactions.*
- Provide small, frequent meals as tolerated, frequent mouth care, and adequate fluids *to relieve discomfort and assure nutrition;* and monitor nutrition if GI effects become a problem.
- Ensure that the patient is instructed about the appropriate dosage regimen, use of drug combinations, and possible adverse effects *to enhance patient knowledge about drug therapy and to promote compliance.*

The patient should:

Try to drink a lot of fluids and to maintain nutrition (very important) even though nausea, vomiting, and diarrhea may occur.

Use barrier contraceptives and understand that oral contraceptives may not be effective while using antimycobacterial drugs.

Understand that a normal effect of some of these drugs is to stain body fluids orange and that if this occurs, the fluids may stain clothing and tears may stain contact lenses.

Report difficulty breathing, hallucinations, numbness and tingling, worsening of condition, fever and chills, or changes in color of urine or stool to a health care provider.

Evaluation

- Monitor patient response to the drug (resolution of mycobacterial infection).
- Monitor for adverse effects (GI effects, CNS changes, and hypersensitivity reactions).
- Evaluate the effectiveness of the teaching plan (patient can name the drug, dosage, possible adverse effects to expect, and specific measures to help avoid adverse effects).
- Monitor the effectiveness of comfort and safety measures and compliance with the regimen.

WWW.WEB LINKS

Health care providers and patients may want to consult the following Internet sources:

Information on aminoglycosides:
http://www.cop.ufl.edu/centers/dis/ODA.htm

Information on cephalosporins:
http://www.fhsu.edu/nursing/otitis/c-chart.html

Information on penicillins:
http://www.healthanswers.com/database/USP_di/easy2read/AN-0988126.html

Information on tuberculosis:
http://www.lupingroup.com/index1.htm

Information on resources for patients with tuberculosis:
http://www.cpmc.columbia.edu/resources/tbcpp/

Information on leprosy:
http://www.leprosy.org/pt/PTINFO/leprosy.htm

Information on infectious disease, disease prevention, recommendations for treatment and treatment schedules—Centers for Disease Control and Prevention:
http://www.cdc.gov

CHAPTER SUMMARY

- Antibiotics work by disrupting protein or enzyme systems within a bacterium, causing cell death (bactericidal) or preventing multiplication (bacteriostatic).
- The proteins or enzyme systems affected by antibiotics are more likely to be found or used in bacteria than in human cells.
- The goal of antibiotic therapy is to reduce the number of invading bacteria so that the normal immune system can deal with the infection.
- The primary therapeutic use of each antibiotic is determined by the bacterial species that are sensitive to that drug, the clinical condition of the patient receiving the drug, and the benefit-to-risk ratio for the patient.

- The longer an antibiotic has been available, the more likely that mutant bacterial strains that are resistant to the mechanisms of antibiotic activity will have developed.
- The most common adverse effects to antibiotics involve the GI tract (nausea, vomiting, diarrhea, anorexia, abdominal pain) and superinfections (invasion of the body by normally occurring microorganisms that are usually kept in check by the normal flora).
- It is very important to use antibiotics cautiously, to complete the full course of an antibiotic prescription, and to avoid saving antibiotics for self-medication in the future to prevent or contain the growing threat of resistant strains.
- A patient/family teaching program should address these issues: the proper administration procedure for the drug; the importance of completing the full course of the drug therapy, even if the patient feels better; avoidance of saving the drug for later self-medication; and the importance of keeping a record of any reactions to antibiotics.

BIBLIOGRAPHY

Bullock, B. L. (2000). *Focus on pathophysiology*. Philadelphia: Lippincott Williams & Wilkins.

The choice of antibacterial drugs. (1996). *Medical Letter on Drugs and Therapeutics, 38*(971).

Hardman, J. G., Limbird, L. E., Molinoff, P. B., Ruddon, R. W., & Gilman, A. G. (Eds.). (1996). *Goodman and Gilman's the pharmacological basis of therapeutics* (9th ed.). New York: McGraw Hill.

Karch, A. M. (1999). *2000 Lippincott's nursing drug guide*. Philadelphia: Lippincott Williams & Wilkins.

Malseed, R. (1995). *Textbook of pharmacology and nursing care*. Philadelphia: Lippincott-Raven.

McEvoy, B. R. (Ed.). (1998). *Facts and comparisons 1996*. St. Louis: Lippincott.

Professional's guide to patient drug facts. (1998). St. Louis: Facts and Comparisons.

CHAPTER
8

Antiviral Agents

Agents for influenza A and respiratory viruses
- amantadine
- ribavirin
- **P** rimantadine

Agents for herpes and CMV
- **P** acyclovir
- cidofovir
- famciclovir
- foscarnet
- ganciclovir
- valacyclovir

Agents for HIV and AIDS
- Reverse transcriptase inhibitors
  - abacavir
  - delavirdine
  - efavirenz
  - **P** lamivudine
  - nevirapine
- Protease inhibitors
  - **P** indinavir
  - nelfinavir
  - ritonavir
  - saquinavir
- Nucleosides
  - didanosine
  - **P** zalcitabine
- Antiretrovirus agents
  - stavudine
  - **P** zidovudine

Locally active antiviral agents
- **P** idoxuridine
- imiquimod
- fomivirsen
- penciclovir
- trifluridine
- vidarabine

CHAPTER OUTLINE

KEY TERMS

acquired immunodeficiency syndrome (AIDS)
AIDS-related complex (ARC)
cytomegalovirus (CMV)
helper T cell
herpes
human immunodeficiency virus (HIV)
influenza A
interferons
nucleosides
protease inhibitors
reverse transcriptase inhibitors
virus

INTRODUCTION

Viruses cause a variety of conditions, ranging from warts to the common cold and "flu" to diseases such as chickenpox and measles. A single virus particle is composed of a piece of DNA or RNA inside a protein coat. To carry on any metabolic processes, including replication, a virus must enter a cell. Once a virus has injected its DNA or RNA into its host cell, that cell is altered—that is, it is "programmed" to control the metabolic processes that the virus needs to survive. The virus, including the protein coat, replicates in the host cell (Figure 8-1). When the host cell can no longer carry out its own metabolic functions because of the viral invader, the host cell dies and releases the new viruses into the body to invade other cells.

Because a virus is contained inside of a human cell while it is in the body, it has proved difficult to develop effective drugs that destroy the virus without harming the human host. ***Interferons*** (Chapter 13) are released by the host in response to viral invasion of a cell and prevent the replication of that particular virus. Some interferons that affect particular viruses are now available through genetic engineering programs. Other drugs that are now used in treating viral infections have been effective against a limited number of viruses. Viruses that respond to some antiviral therapy include *influenza A* and some respiratory viruses, ***herpes, cytomegalovirus (CMV), human immunodeficiency virus (HIV)*** that causes ***acquired immunodeficiency syndrome (AIDS)***, and some viruses that cause warts and some eye infections.

AGENTS FOR INFLUENZA A AND RESPIRATORY VIRUSES

Influenza A and other respiratory viruses, including influenza B and respiratory syncytial virus (RSV), invade the respiratory tract and cause the signs and symptoms of respiratory "flu." Amantadine (*Symmetrel*) was first used to treat Parkinson's disease. However, patients who took amantadine did not get influenza during flu season, and this drug is used in the treatment as well as prevention of respiratory viral infections. Ribavirin (*Virazole*) is effective against influenza A, RSV, and herpes viruses. This agent has been used in the treatment of children with RSV and has been tested for use in several other viral conditions. Rimantadine (*Flumadine*), a synthetic agent, is used to prevent influenza A infections.

THERAPEUTIC ACTIONS AND INDICATIONS

Although the exact mechanism of action of drugs that combat respiratory viruses is not known, it is

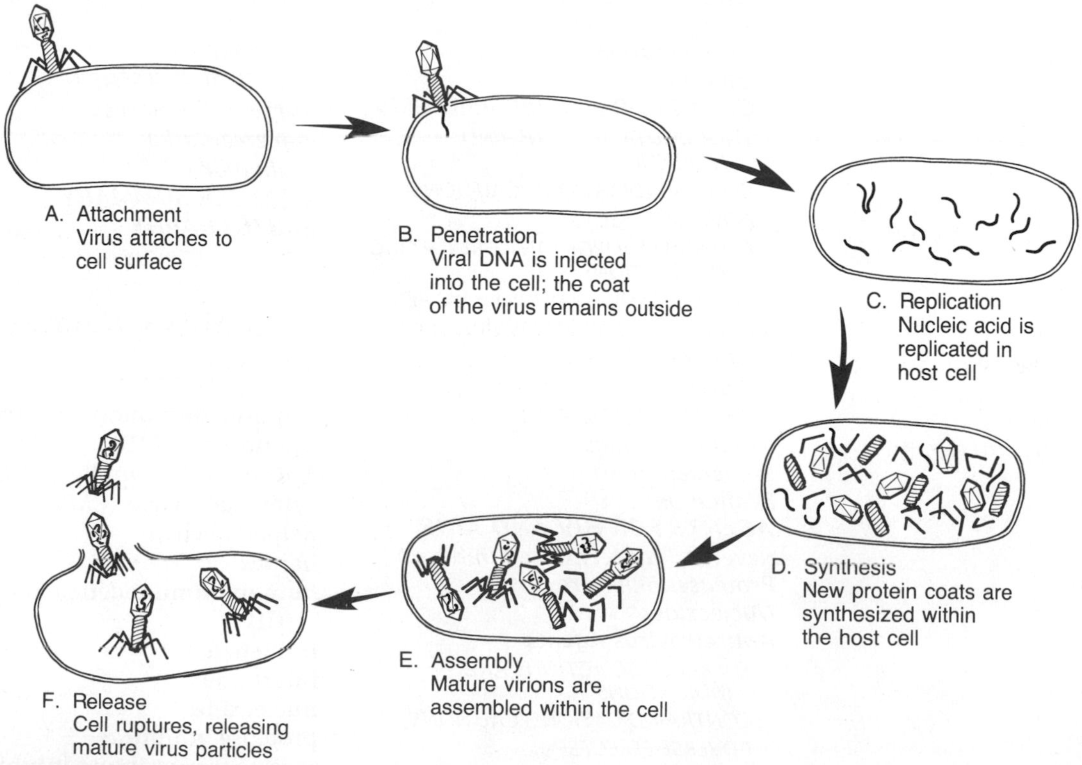
A. Attachment
Virus attaches to cell surface
B. Penetration
Viral DNA is injected into the cell; the coat of the virus remains outside
C. Replication
Nucleic acid is replicated in host cell
D. Synthesis
New protein coats are synthesized within the host cell
E. Assembly
Mature virions are assembled within the cell
F. Release
Cell ruptures, releasing mature virus particles

FIGURE 8-1. The stages in the replication cycle of a virus. (Bullock, B. L. [2000]. *Focus on pathophysiology*. Philadelphia: Lippincott Williams & Wilkins.)

believed that these agents may prevent the shedding of the viral protein coat and the entry of the virus into the cell (Figure 8-2). This action prevents viral replication, causing viral death. These antiviral drugs are indicated for preventing influenza A infection, which is especially important in health care workers or other high-risk individuals, and reducing the severity of infection if it occurs.

CONTRAINDICATIONS/CAUTIONS

Caution should be used when giving these antiviral agents to patients with a known allergy; to pregnant or lactating women; and to patients with renal or liver disease, which could alter the drug metabolism and excretion.

ADVERSE EFFECTS

Use of these antiviral agents is frequently associated with various adverse effects that may be related to possible effects on dopamine levels in the brain, which include the following: lightheadedness, dizziness, and insomnia; nausea; orthostatic hypotension; and urinary retention.

CLINICALLY IMPORTANT DRUG–DRUG INTERACTIONS

Patients who receive amantadine or rimantadine may experience increased atropine-like effects if either of these drugs is given with anticholinergic drugs.

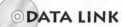

DATA LINK

Data link to the following agents for influenza A and respiratory viruses in your nursing drug guide:

INFLUENZA A AND RESPIRATORY VIRUS DRUGS

Name	Brand Name	Usual Indications
amantadine	*Symmetrel*	Treatment of Parkinson's disease; treatment and prevention of respiratory virus infections
ribavirin	*Virazole*	Treatment of influenza A, RSV, and herpes virus infections
P rimantadine	*Flumadine*	Prevention of influenza A infections

NURSING CONSIDERATIONS
for patients receiving influenza A and respiratory virus drugs

Assessment

HISTORY. Patients who receive respiratory antiviral agents should be assessed for any of the following conditions that are either contraindications to the use of these drugs or precautionary measures: known history of allergy to antivirals; history of liver or renal dysfunction that might interfere with drug metabolism and excretion; and current pregnancy or lactation status.

PHYSICAL ASSESSMENT. Physical assessment should be performed to establish baseline data for evaluating

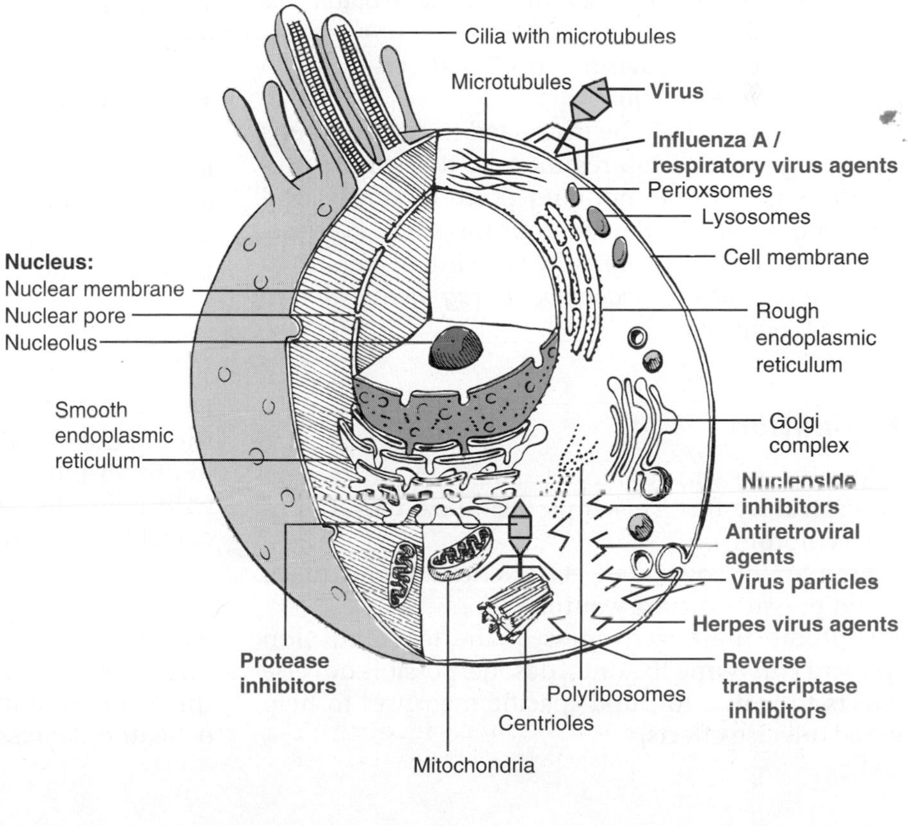

FIGURE 8-2. Agents for influenza A and respiratory viruses prevent shedding of the protein coat and entry of virus into the cell. Herpes virus agents alter viral DNA production. Agents that attempt to control HIV and AIDS work in the following ways: nucleosides interfere with HIV replication by blocking protein synthesis; reverse transcriptase inhibitors block the transfer of information that allows viral replication; protease inhibitors block protease within the virus, leading to immature, noninfective virus particles; and antiretroviral agents prevent viral replication.

the effectiveness of the drug and the occurrence of any adverse effects associated with drug therapy. Include screening for orientation and reflexes to evaluate any central nervous system (CNS) effects of the drug; vital signs (respiratory rate, adventitious sounds, temperature) to assess for signs and symptoms of the viral infections; blood pressure to monitor for orthostatic hypotension; urinary output to monitor genitourinary (GU) effects of the drug; and renal and hepatic function tests to determine baseline function of these organs.

Nursing Diagnoses

The patient receiving a respiratory antiviral drug may have the following nursing diagnoses related to drug therapy:

- Pain related to gastrointestinal (GI), CNS, GU effects of drug
- Sensory–perceptual alteration related to CNS effects
- Knowledge deficit regarding drug therapy

Implementation

- Start drug regimen as soon after exposure to the virus as possible *to achieve best effectiveness and decrease risks of complications of viral infection.*
- Administer influenza A vaccine prior to the flu season if at all possible *to prevent the disease and decrease the risk of complications.*
- Administer the full course of the drug *to obtain the full beneficial effects.*
- Provide safety provisions if CNS effects occur *to protect patient from injury.*
- The patient should be instructed in the appropriate dosage scheduling regimen; to take safety precautions including changing position slowly and avoiding driving and hazardous tasks if CNS effects occur; and to report difficulty walking or talking *to enhance patient knowledge about drug therapy and to promote compliance.*

Evaluation

- Monitor patient response to the drug (prevention of respiratory flu-like symptoms; alleviation of flu-like symptoms).
- Monitor for adverse effects (orientation and affect, blood pressure, urinary output).
- Evaluate the effectiveness of the teaching plan (patient can name the drug, dosage, possible adverse effects to watch for, and specific measures to help avoid adverse effects).
- Monitor the effectiveness of comfort and safety measures and compliance with the regimen.

AGENTS FOR HERPES AND CMV

Herpes viruses account for a broad range of conditions, including cold sores, encephalitis, shingles, and genital infections. *CMV,* although slightly different from the herpes virus, can affect the eye, respiratory tract, and liver and reacts to many of the same drugs. A number of antiviral drugs are used to combat these infections. Acyclovir (*Zovirax*) is specific for herpes virus infections. Cidofovir (*Vistide*), a new drug, is used to treat CMV retinitis. Famciclovir (*Famvir*) is most effective in treating herpes infections. Foscarnet (*Foscavir*), which is available in intravenous (IV) form only, is usually reserved for treatment of CMV and herpes simplex infections in immune compromised patients. Ganciclovir (*Cytovene*), which is available in IV and oral forms, is used for long-term treatment of CMV infections. Valacyclovir (*Valtrex*) is an oral agent used for the treatment of herpes zoster and genital herpes.

THERAPEUTIC ACTIONS AND INDICATIONS

Drugs that combat herpes and CMV inhibit viral DNA replication by competing with viral substrates to form shorter, noneffective DNA chains (see Figure 8-2). This action not only prevents replication of the virus, but it has little effect on the host cells of humans, because their DNA uses different substrates. These antiviral agents are indicated for the treatment of the DNA viruses herpes simplex, herpes zoster, and CMV. Research has shown that they are very effective in immune compromised individuals such as patients with AIDS, those taking immune suppressants, and those with multiple infections.

CONTRAINDICATIONS/CAUTIONS

Drugs indicated for treatment of herpes and CMV should not be used in patients with known allergies to antiviral agents; during pregnancy or lactation; with renal disease, which could interfere with the excretion of the drug; and with severe CNS disorders.

ADVERSE EFFECTS

The adverse effects most commonly associated with these antivirals include nausea and vomiting, headache and depression, and rash and hair loss. Rash, inflammation, and burning often occurs at sites of IV injection and topical application. Renal dysfunction and renal failure also have been reported.

CLINICALLY IMPORTANT DRUG–DRUG INTERACTIONS

The risk of nephrotoxicity increases when agents indicated for the treatment of herpes and CMV are used in combination with other nephrotoxic drugs. The risk of drowsiness also rises when these antiviral agents are taken with zidovudine, an antiretroviral agent.

DATA LINK

Data link to the following agents for herpes virus and CMV in your nursing drug guide:

AGENTS FOR HERPES VIRUS AND CMV

Name	Brand Name	Usual Indications
P acyclovir	*Zovirax*	Treatment of herpes virus infections
cidofovir	*Vistide*	Treatment of CMV retinitis
famciclovir	*Famvir*	Treatment of herpes virus infections
foscarnet	*Foscavir*	Treatment of CMV and herpes simplex infections in immune compromised patients
ganciclovir	*Cytovene*	Long-term treatment of CMV infections
valacyclovir	*Valtrex*	Treatment of herpes zoster and genital herpes

NURSING CONSIDERATIONS
for patients receiving agents for herpes virus and CMV

Assessment

HISTORY. Patients receiving DNA active antiviral agents should be assessed for the following conditions: any history of allergy to antivirals; renal dysfunction that might interfere with the metabolism and excretion of the drug; severe CNS disorders that could be aggravated; and pregnancy or lactation, which are cautions or contraindications to the use of these drugs.

PHYSICAL ASSESSMENT. Physical assessment should be performed to establish baseline data for assessing the effectiveness of the DNA active antiviral drug and the occurrence of any adverse effects associated with drug therapy. Assess orientation and reflexes to evaluate any CNS effects of the drug. Examine skin—color, temperature, and lesions—to monitor the effectiveness of the drug. Evaluate renal function tests to determine baseline function of the kidneys.

Nursing Diagnoses

The patient receiving a DNA active antiviral agent may have the following nursing diagnoses related to drug therapy:

- Pain related to GI, CNS, local effects of drug
- Sensory–perceptual alteration related to CNS effects
- Knowledge deficit regarding drug therapy

Implementation

- Ensure good hydration *to decrease the toxic effects on the kidneys.*
- Administer the drug as soon as possible after the diagnosis has been made *to improve effectiveness of the antiviral activity.*
- Ensure that the patient takes the complete course of the drug regimen *to improve effectiveness and decrease the risk of the emergence of resistant viruses.*
- Wear protective gloves when applying the drug topically *to decrease risk of exposure to the drug and inadvertent absorption.*
- Provide safety precautions if CNS effects occur (e.g., use of side rails, appropriate lighting, orientation, assistance) *to protect patient from injury.*
- Warn the patient that GI upset, nausea, and vomiting can occur *to prevent undue anxiety and increase awareness of the importance of nutrition.*
- Monitor renal function tests periodically during treatment *to detect and respond to renal toxicity as early as possible.*
- Provide the patient instruction about the drug *to enhance patient knowledge about drug therapy and to promote compliance.*

The patient should:

Avoid sexual intercourse if genital herpes is being treated because these drugs do not cure the disease.

Wear protective gloves when applying topical agents.

Avoid driving and hazardous tasks if dizziness and drowsiness occur.

Evaluation

- Monitor patient response to the drug (alleviation of signs and symptoms of herpes or CMV infection).
- Monitor for adverse effects (orientation and affect, GI upset, and renal function).
- Evaluate the effectiveness of the teaching plan (patient can name the drug, dosage, possible adverse effects to watch for, and specific measures to help avoid adverse effects).

• Monitor the effectiveness of comfort and safety measures and compliance with the regimen.

AGENTS FOR HIV AND AIDS

The ***human immunodeficiency virus (HIV)*** attacks the ***helper T cells*** within the immune system. This virus enters the helper T cells and multiples within the cells. When the cell ruptures, it sends many new viruses to attack other helper T cells. The end result is that the immune system loses an important monitor that propels the immune reaction into full force when the body is invaded.

Loss of T-cell function causes AIDS or ***AIDS-related complex (ARC),*** diseases that are characterized by the emergence of a variety of opportunistic infections and cancers that occur when the immune system is depressed and unable to function properly. The HIV mutates over time, presenting a slightly different configuration with each new generation. Treatment of AIDS and ARC has been difficult for two reasons: (1) the length of time the virus can remain dormant within the T cells (i.e., from months to years), and (2) adverse effects of many potent drugs, which may include further depression of the immune system. At present, a combination of several different antiviral drugs is used to attack the virus at various points in its life cycle to achieve maximum effectiveness with the least amount of toxicity. The types of antiviral agents that are used to treat HIV infections are the reverse transcriptase inhibitors, the protease inhibitors, the nucleosides, and antiretroviral agents.

Reverse Transcriptase Inhibitors

The ***reverse transcriptase inhibitors*** bind directly to HIV reverse transcriptase, which blocks both RNA and DNA-dependent DNA polymerase activities. They prevent the transfer of information that would allow the virus to replicate and survive. Abacavir (*Ziagen*) is used in combination therapy for adults and children. Delaviridine (*Rescriptor*) must be used in combination therapy regimens because resistant strains develop rapidly when it is used alone. Efavirenz (*Sustiva*), a relatively new drug, is used for the treatment of adults and children. Lamivudine (*Epivir*) is recommended specifically for use with zidovudine. Nevirapine (*Viramune*) is recommended for use in adults only.

Protease Inhibitors

The ***protease inhibitors*** block protease activity within the HIV virus. Protease is essential for the maturation of infectious virus, and without it, an HIV particle is immature and noninfective. The protease inhibitors that are available for use include indinavir (*Crixivan*), which is available for treatment of

NURSING CHALLENGE

Public Education About AIDS

When AIDS was first diagnosed in the early 1980s, it was found in a certain population in New York City. The people in this group tended to be homosexuals, intravenous drug users, and debilitated with poor hygiene and nutrition habits. Originally, a number of health care practitioners thought that the disease was a syndrome of opportunistic infections that occurred in a population that had repeated exposures to infections that naturally depleted the immune system. It wasn't until several years later that the human immunodeficiency virus (HIV) was identified. Since then, it has been discovered that HIV infection is rampant in many African countries. The infection also has spread throughout the United States in populations that are not homosexual, not intravenous drug users, and who have good nutrition and hygiene habits. As health care practitioners have learned, HIV is not particular about the body it invades. And once introduced into a body, it infects T cells and causes HIV infection.

When a patient is diagnosed with HIV infection, the nurse faces a tremendous challenge for patient education and support. The patient and any significant others should be counseled about the risks of transmission—and be reassured about ways that it is not transmitted. They will need to learn about drug protocols, T cell levels, adverse drug effects, and anticipated progress of the disease. They also will need consistent support and a phone number to call with questions at any time. Many communities have AIDS support groups and other resources that can prove very helpful; the nurse can direct the patient to these resources as appropriate.

The combination of drugs that are being used today and the constant development of more drugs make the disease less of a death sentence than it was in the past. Many people live for a long period of time with HIV infections. Currently, an AIDS vaccine is being studied and offers hope for preventing this disease in the future.

Public education is key for promoting the acceptance and support of the patient with HIV infection or the patient with AIDS, who needs a great deal of support and assistance. Nurses can be role models for dealing with HIV patients and provide informal public education when the opportunity presents.

adults; nelfinavir (*Viracept*), which must be given in combination with other drugs and can be used in the treatment of children; ritonavir (*Norvir*), which can be used alone and is available for use in treating adults and children; and saquinavir (*Fortovase, Invirase*), which is used in combination regimens for the treatment of adults.

Nucleosides

Nucleosides interfere with HIV replication by inhibiting cell protein synthesis, leading to viral death. The nucleosides include didanosine (*Videx*), which is used to treat advanced infections in adults and children and zalcitabine (*Hivid*), which is used in combination with zidovudine to treat advanced cases of HIV.

Antiretrovirus Agents

Antiretrovirus agents act to prevent replication in various retroviruses, including HIV. Their action is related to their conversion to triphosphates in the body. Zidovudine (*AZT, Retrovir*) is one of the first drugs found to be effective in the treatment of AIDS. It is used to treat symptomatic disease in adults and children and to prevent maternal transmission of HIV. Stavudine (*Zerit*) is reserved for patients who have become resistant or intolerant to other therapy. It is not recommended for use in children and has been associated with severe bone marrow depression and anemia.

THERAPEUTIC ACTIONS AND INDICATIONS

The antiviral agents used to treat HIV and AIDS operate at various points in the life cycle of the HIV virus and result in its death or inactivation (see Figure 8-2). Used in combination, these drugs can affect more viral particles and reduce the number of mutant viruses that are formed and spread to noninfected cells. They are indicated for the treatment of patients with documented AIDS or ARC with decreased numbers of T cells and evidence of increased opportunistic infections.

CONTRAINDICATIONS/CAUTIONS

Because these drugs are used in the treatment of a potentially fatal disease with no known cure, there are no true contraindications to their use. Zidovudine is the drug of choice during pregnancy to block maternal transmission of the virus. Caution should be used with known allergies to any of these drugs and with hepatic or renal dysfunction, which could lead to increased drug levels and toxicity, and with pregnancy and lactation because of potential adverse effects on the neonate.

ADVERSE EFFECTS

The adverse effects reported with the use of these drugs are often not distinguishable from the effects of the ongoing disease process. Adverse effects that are most often reported include the CNS effects of headache, dizziness, and myalgia; GI upset, including nausea, vomiting, and diarrhea; hepatic toxicity related to direct drug effects on the liver; fever and flu-like symptoms; rash (which is potentially fatal in some patients); and bone marrow depression, including agranulocytosis and anemia.

CLINICALLY IMPORTANT DRUG–DRUG INTERACTIONS

If nelfinavir is combined with astemizole, cisapride, rifampin, triazolam, or midazolam, severe toxic effects and life-threatening arrhythmias may potentially occur, and these combinations should be avoided. Indinavir and nevirapine interact to cause severe toxicity. Thus, if these two drugs are given in combination, the dosage should be adjusted and the patient monitored closely. When oral contraceptives are taken in combination with several of these antiviral agents, episodes of ineffective contraception have been reported. Affected patients should be advised to use barrier contraceptives.

DATA LINK

Data link to the following agents for HIV and AIDS in your nursing drug guide:

HIV AND AIDS DRUGS

Name	Brand Name	Usual Indications
REVERSE TRANSCRIPTASE INHIBITORS		
abacavir	*Ziagen*	Combination therapy for the treatment of adults and children with HIV
delaviridine	*Rescriptor*	Part of combination therapy regimens for HIV
efavirenz	*Sustiva*	Treatment of adults and children with HIV
P lamivudine	*Epivir*	With zidovudine for the treatment of adults and children with HIV
nevirapine	*Viramune*	Treatment of adults with HIV
PROTEASE INHIBITORS		
P indinavir	*Crixivan*	Treatment of adults with HIV
nelfinavir	*Viracept*	Combination therapy for the treatment of adults and children with HIV
ritonavir	*Norvir*	Monotherapy for the treatment of adults and children
saquinavir	*Fortovase, Invirase*	Treatment of adults with HIV as part of combination therapy

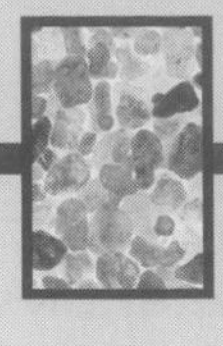

CASE STUDY

Antiviral Agents for HIV/AIDS

PATIENT SCENARIO

H. P. is a 34-year-old attorney who was diagnosed with AIDS, having a positive HIV test 3 years ago. Although his T cell count had been stabilized with treatment with zidovudine, it recently dropped remarkably. He presented with numerous opportunistic infections and Kaposi's sarcoma. H. P. admitted that he had been under tremendous stress at work and at home in the past few weeks. He began taking a combination regimen of lamivudine, zidovudine, ritonavir, and zalcitabine.

CRITICAL THINKING QUESTIONS

What are the important nursing implications in this case? What role would stress play in the progress of this disease? What specific issues should be discussed? What other clinical implications should be considered?

DISCUSSION

Combination therapy with antivirals has been found to be effective in decreasing some of the morbidity and mortality associated with HIV and AIDS. However, this treatment does not cure the disease. H. P. needs to understand that opportunistic infections can still occur and that regular medical help should be sought. H. P. also needs to understand that these drugs do not decrease the risk of transmitting HIV by sexual contact or through blood contamination and should be encouraged to take appropriate precautions.

It is important to make a dosing schedule for H. P. or even prepare a weekly drug box to ensure that all of the medications are taken as indicated. H. P. should also receive interventions to help him decrease his stress; activation of the sympathetic nervous system during periods of stress is known to depress the immune system. Further depression of his immune system could accelerate the development of opportunistic infections and decrease the effectiveness of his antiviral drugs. Measures that could be used to decrease stress should be discussed and tried with H. P.

Discussion of adverse effects that H. P. may experience is important. H. P. may experience GI upset and discomfort while taking all of these anti-HIV/AIDS medications. Small, frequent meals may help alleviate the discomfort. It is important that every effort be made to maintain H. P.'s nutritional state, and a nutritional consultation may be necessary if GI effects are severe. H. P. may also experience dizziness, fatigue, and confusion, which may cause more problems for him at work and may require changes in his work load. Because some of the prescribed drugs need to be taken around the clock, provisions may be needed to allow H. P. to take his drugs on time throughout the day. For example, H. P. may need to wear an alarm wrist watch, establish planned breaks in his schedule at dosing times, or devise other ways to allow him to follow his drug regimen without interfering with his work schedule. The adverse effects and inconvenience of these many drugs may add to the stress that H. P. is experiencing. It is important that a health care provider work consistently with him to help him to manage his disease and treatment as effectively as possible.

NUCLEOSIDES		
didanosine	*Videx*	Treatment of advanced infections in adults and children with HIV
P zalcitabine	*Hivid*	Treatment of advanced infections in adults and children with HIV, as part of combination therapy
ANTIRETROVIRAL AGENTS		
stavudine	*Zerit*	Treatment of adults who have become resistant to or intolerant of other therapy
P zidovudine	*AZT, Retrovir*	Treatment of symptomatic HIV in adults and children; prevention of maternal transmission of HIV

NURSING CONSIDERATIONS
for patients receiving agents for HIV and AIDS

Assessment

HISTORY. Screen for the following: any history of allergy to antivirals; renal or hepatic dysfunction that might interfere with the metabolism and excretion of the drug; and pregnancy or lactation, which can be cautions to the use of these drugs.

PHYSICAL ASSESSMENT. Physical assessment should be performed to establish baseline data for assessing the effectiveness of the drug and the occurrence of any adverse effects associated with drug therapy. Perform assessment of orientation and reflex to evaluate any CNS effects of the drug. Examine the skin—color, temperature, and lesions—to monitor the effectiveness of the drug. Check temperature to monitor for infections. Evaluate hepatic and renal function tests to determine baseline function of the kidneys and liver. Check CBC with differential to monitor bone marrow activity and T-cell numbers to indicate effectiveness of the drugs.

Nursing Diagnoses

The patient receiving drugs for HIV and AIDS may have the following nursing diagnoses related to drug therapy:

- Pain related to GI, CNS, dermatologic effects of drug

• Sensory–perceptual alteration related to CNS effects
• Alteration in nutrition, less than body requirements, related to GI effects of the drugs
• Knowledge deficit regarding drug therapy

Implementation

• Monitor renal and hepatic function prior to and periodically during therapy *to detect renal or hepatic function changes and arrange to reduce dosage or provide treatment as needed.*
• Ensure that the patient takes the complete course of the drug regimen and takes all drugs included in a particular combination *to improve effectiveness of the drug and decrease the risk of emergence of resistant viral strains.*
• Administer drug around the clock if indicated *to provide the critical concentration needed to be effective.* Monitor nutritional status if GI effects are severe *to take appropriate action to maintain nutrition.*
• Stop drug if severe rash occurs, especially if accompanied by blisters, fever, and so forth, *to avert potentially serious reactions.*
• Provide safety precautions if CNS effects occur (e.g., the use of side rails, appropriate lighting, orientation, assistance) *to protect patient from injury.*
• Teach the patient *to enhance patient knowledge about drug therapy and to promote compliance.* Include teaching points that because these drugs do not cure the disease, appropriate precautions should still be taken to prevent transmission.

The patient should:

Have regular medical care.
Have periodic blood tests, which are necessary to monitor the effectiveness and toxicity of the drug.
Realize that GI upset, nausea, and vomiting may occur but that effort must be taken to maintain adequate nutrition.
Avoid driving and hazardous tasks if dizziness and drowsiness occur.
Report extreme fatigue, severe headache, difficulty breathing, and severe rash to a health care provider. (See Patient Teaching Checklist: Antiviral Agents for HIV/AIDS.)

Evaluation

• Monitor patient response to the drug (alleviation of signs and symptoms of AIDS or ARC and maintenance of T-cell levels).
• Monitor for adverse effects (orientation and affect, GI upset, renal and hepatic function, skin, and levels of blood components).
• Evaluate the effectiveness of the teaching plan (patient can name the drug, dosage, possible adverse effects to watch for, and specific measures to help avoid adverse effects).
• Monitor the effectiveness of comfort and safety measures and compliance with the regimen (see Nursing Care Guide: Antiviral Agents for HIV/AIDS).

WWW.WEB LINKS

Health care providers and patients may want to consult the following Internet sources:

Information on AIDS and HIV research, treatments, resources:
http://www.infoweb.org

Information on drug protocols, new HIV research:
http://www.cdc.gov

Information on up-to-date AIDS clinical trials:
http://www.critpath.org/trials.htm

Health information for professionals and consumers:
http://www.aegis.com

LOCALLY ACTIVE ANTIVIRAL AGENTS

Some antiviral agents are given locally to treat local viral infections. These agents include the following:

• Idoxuridine (*Herplex*), which is applied directly to the eye and is used to treat herpes simplex keratitis
• Imiquimod (*Aldara*), which is applied locally for the treatment of genital and perianal warts
• Penciclovir (*Denavir*), which is applied locally for the treatment of herpes labialis (cold sores) on the face and lips (not to be applied to mucous membranes)
• Fomivirsen (*Vitravene*), which is injected into the eye to treat CMV retinitis in patients with AIDS
• Trifluridine (*Viroptic*), which is applied locally to treat herpes simplex infections in the eye
• Vidarabine (*Vira-A*), used locally to treat herpes simplex infections of the eye that are not responsive to idoxuridine

THERAPEUTIC ACTIONS AND INDICATIONS

These antiviral agents act on viruses by interfering with normal viral replication and metabolic pro-

PATIENT TEACHING CHECKLIST

Antiviral Agents for HIV/AIDS

Create customized patient teaching materials for a specific antiviral agent from your CD-ROM. Your patient teaching should stress the following points for drugs within this class:

An antiviral works in combination with other antivirals to stop the replication of HIV, to control AIDS, and to maintain the functioning of your immune system.

These drugs are not a cure for HIV, AIDS, or ARC. Opportunistic infections may occur, and regular medical follow-up should be sought to deal with the disease.

These drugs do not reduce the risk of transmission of HIV to others by sexual contact or by blood contamination; use appropriate precautions.

Common effects of these drugs include:

- Dizziness, weakness, and loss of feeling—Change positions slowly. If you feel drowsy, avoid driving and dangerous activities.
- Headache, fever, muscle aches—Analgesics may be ordered to alleviate this discomfort. Consult with your health care provider.
- Nausea, loss of appetite, change in taste—Small, frequent meals may help. It is important to try to maintain your nutrition. Consult your health care provider if this becomes a severe problem.

Report any of the following to your health care provider: excessive fatigue, lethargy, severe headache, difficulty breathing, or skin rash.

Avoid over-the-counter medications. If you feel that you need one of these, check with your health care provider first.

Regular medical evaluations, including blood tests, are needed to monitor the effects of these drugs on your body and to adjust dosages as needed.

Tell any doctor, nurse, or other health care provider that you are taking these drugs.

Keep this drug and all medications out of the reach of children. Do not share these drugs with other people.

This Teaching Checklist reflects general patient teaching guidelines. It is not meant to be a substitute for drug-specific teaching information, which is available in nursing drug guides.

cesses. As noted above, they are indicated for specific, local viral infections.

CONTRAINDICATIONS/CAUTIONS

Locally active antiviral drugs are not absorbed systemically, but caution should be used with known allergic reactions to any topical drugs.

ADVERSE EFFECTS

Because these drugs are not absorbed systemically, the adverse effects most commonly reported are local burning, stinging, and discomfort. These usually occur at the time of administration and pass with time.

DATA LINK

Data link to the following locally active antiviral agents in your nursing drug guide:

LOCALLY ACTIVE ANTIVIRAL AGENTS

Name	Brand Name	Usual Indications
fomivirsen	*Vitravene*	Ophthalmic injection to treat CMV retinitis in patients with AIDS
P idoxuridine	*Herplex*	Ophthalmic agent used to treat herpes simplex keratitis (drug of choice)
imiquimod	*Aldara*	Local treatment of genital and perianal warts
penciclovir	*Denavir*	Local treatment of herpes labialis (cold sores) on the face and lips

NURSING CARE GUIDE
Antiviral Agents for HIV/AIDS

Assessment	Nursing Diagnoses	Implementation	Evaluation
HISTORY			
Allergies to any of these drugs; bone marrow depression; renal or liver dysfunction; pregnancy and lactation	Pain related to GI, skin, CNS effects	Monitor CBC and differential prior to and every 2 weeks during therapy.	Evaluate drug effects: relief of signs and symptoms of AIDS, ARC; stabilization of T cell levels.
	Sensory, perceptual alterations related to CNS effects	Provide comfort and implement safety measures: assistance, temperature control, lighting control, mouth care, back rubs.	Monitor for adverse effects: GI alterations, dizziness, confusion, headache, fever.
	Alteration in nutrition, more than body requirements related to GI effects	Provide small, frequent meals and monitor nutritional status.	Monitor for drug–drug interactions as indicated for each drug.
	Knowledge deficit regarding drug therapy	Monitor for opportunistic infections and arrange treatment as indicated.	Evaluate effectiveness of patient teaching plan.
		Provide support and reassurance for dealing with drug effects and discomfort.	Evaluate effectiveness of comfort and safety measures.
		Provide patient teaching regarding drug name, dosage, adverse effects, warnings, precautions, and signs to report.	
PHYSICAL EXAMINATION			
Skin: color, lesions, texture			
CNS: affect, reflexes, *orientation*			
GI: abdominal, liver evaluation			
Hematologic: CBC and differential, renal and hepatic function tests			

trifluridine	*Viroptic*	Ophthalmic ointment to treat herpes simplex infections in the eye
vidarabine	*Vira-A*	Ophthalmic agent to treat herpes simplex infections of the eye not responsive to idoxuridine

NURSING CONSIDERATIONS
for patients receiving locally active antiviral agents

Assessment

HISTORY. Patients receiving locally active antiviral agents should be assessed for any history of allergy to antivirals.

PHYSICAL ASSESSMENT. Physical assessment should be performed to establish baseline data for evaluating the effectiveness of the drug and the occurrence of any adverse effects associated with drug therapy, including inflammation at the site of infection.

Nursing Diagnoses

The patient receiving locally active antiviral drugs may have the following nursing diagnoses related to drug therapy:

- Pain related to local effects of drug
- Knowledge deficit regarding drug therapy

Implementation

- Ensure proper administration of the drug *to improve effectiveness and decrease risk of adverse effects.*
- Stop drug if severe local reaction occurs or open lesions occur near the site of administration *to prevent systemic absorption.*
- Teach the patient about the drug being used *to enhance patient knowledge about drug therapy and to promote compliance.* Include teaching points that although these drugs do not cure the disease, they should alleviate discomfort and prevent damage to healthy tissues. Encourage the patient to report severe local reaction or discomfort.

Evaluation

- Monitor patient response to the drug (alleviation of signs and symptoms of viral infection).
- Monitor for adverse effects (local irritation and discomfort).
- Evaluate the effectiveness of the teaching plan (patient can name the drug, dosage, proper administration technique, and the adverse effects to watch for and report to a health care provider).
- Monitor the effectiveness of comfort and safety measures and compliance with the regimen.

CHAPTER SUMMARY

- Viruses are particles of DNA or RNA surrounded by a protein coat that survive by injecting their own DNA or RNA into a healthy cell and taking over its functioning.
- Because viruses are contained within human cells, it has been difficult to develop drugs that are effective antivirals and that do not destroy human cells. Antiviral agents are available that are effective against only a few types of viruses.
- Influenza A and respiratory viruses cause the signs and symptoms of the common cold or "flu." The drugs that are available to prevent the replication of these viruses are used for prophylaxis against these diseases during peak seasons.
- Herpes and CMV are DNA viruses that cause a multitude of problems, including cold sores, encephalitis, infections of the eye and liver, and genital herpes.
- Helper T cells are essential for maintaining a vigilant, effective immune system. When these cells are decreased in number or effectiveness, opportunistic infections occur. AIDS and ARC are sets of opportunistic infections that occur when the immune system is depressed.
- HIV, which specifically attacks helper T cells, may remain dormant in T cells for long periods of time and has been known to mutate easily.
- Antivirals that are effective against HIV and AIDS include reverse transcriptase inhibitors, protease inhibitors, nucleosides, and antiretroviral drugs, all of which affect the way the virus communicates, replicates, or matures within the cell. These drugs are given in combination to most effectively destroy the HIV virus and prevent mutation.
- Some antivirals are available only for the local treatment of viral infections, including warts and eye infections. These drugs are not absorbed systemically.

BIBLIOGRAPHY

Bullock, B. L. (2000). *Focus on pathophysiology.* Philadelphia: Lippincott Williams & Wilkins.

Centers for Disease Control and Prevention. (1997). USPHS/IDSA guidelines for the prevention of opportunistic infections in persons infected with HIV. U.S. Department of Health and Human Services. *MMWR, 46* (No. RR 12).

Guberski, R. D. (1997). Treatment of AIDS in adults: An update. *American Journal for Nurse Practitioners, 1*(1), 22–26.

Hardman, J. G., Limbird, L. E., Molinoff, P. B., Ruddon, R. W., & Gilman, A. G. (Eds.). (1996). *Goodman and Gilman's the pharmacological basis of therapeutics* (9th ed.). New York: McGraw Hill.

Karch, A. M. (2000). *2000 Lippincott's nursing drug guide.* Philadelphia: Lippincott Williams & Wilkins.

Malseed, R. (1995). *Textbook of pharmacology and nursing care.* Philadelphia: Lippincott-Raven.

McEvoy, B. R. (Ed.). (1999). *Facts and comparisons 1999.* St. Louis: Facts and Comparisons.

Professional's guide to patient drug facts. (1999). St. Louis: Facts and Comparisons.

CHAPTER 9

Antifungal Agents

Systemic antifungals
- amphotericin B
- fluconazole
- flucytosine
- itraconazole
- ketoconazole
- **P** miconazole
- nystatin

Topical antifungals
- butenafine
- butoconazole
- **P** clotrimazole
- econazole
- gentian violet
- naftifine
- oxiconazole
- terbinafine
- tolnaftate

CHAPTER OUTLINE

KEY TERMS

Candida
ergosterol
fungus
mycosis
tinea

INTRODUCTION

Fungal infections in humans range from conditions such as the annoying "athlete's foot" to potentially fatal systemic infections. An infection caused by a ***fungus*** is called a ***mycosis.*** A fungus differs from a bacteria in that the fungus has a rigid cell wall that is made up of chitin and various polysaccharides and a cell membrane that contains ***ergosterol.*** The composition of the protective layers of the fungal cell makes the organism resistant to antibiotics. Conversely, because of their cellular makeup, bacteria are resistant to antifungal drugs.

The incidence of fungal infections has increased with the rising number of immune compromised individuals—patients with AIDS and AIDS-related complex, those taking immunosuppressant drugs, those who have undergone transplant surgery or cancer treatment, and members of the increasingly large elderly population—who are no longer able to protect themselves from the many fungi that are found throughout the environment. For example, ***Candida,*** a fungus that is normally found on mucous membranes, can cause yeast infections or "thrush" of the gastrointestinal (GI) tract and vagina in immunosuppressed patients.

SYSTEMIC ANTIFUNGALS

The drugs used to treat systemic fungal infections can be toxic to the host and are not used indiscriminately. It is important to get a culture of the fungus causing the infection to assure that the right drug is being used so that the patient is not put at risk from the toxic adverse effects associated with these drugs.

Amphotericin B (*Fungizone, Abelcet, Amphotec, AmBisome*), available in intravenous (IV) form, is a very potent drug with many unpleasant side effects that can cause renal failure. This drug is indicated for advanced and progressive systemic fungal infections, including aspergillosis, leishmaniasis, cryptococcosis, blastomycosis, moniliasis, coccidioidomycosis, histoplasmosis, and mucormycosis. Amphotericin B can also be used topically to treat resistant *Candida* infections. Because of the many adverse effects associated this agent, it is reserved for use in progressive, potentially fatal infections.

Flucytosine (*Ancoban*), available in an oral form, is a less toxic drug that is used for the treatment of systemic infections caused by *Candida* and *Cryptococcus.*

Nystatin (*Mycostatin, Nilstat, Nystex*) is used orally for the treatment of intestinal candidiasis. In addition, it is available in a number of topical preparations—oral suspension; troche; and vaginal suppository, cream, and ointment—for the treatment of local candidiasis, vaginal candidiasis, and cutaneous and mucocutaneous infections caused by *Candida* species.

A group of other agents called azoles are newer drugs that are used to treat systemic fungal infections. Although they are less toxic than amphotericin B, they may also be less effective in very severe and progressive infections. The azoles include the following drugs:

- Ketoconazole (*Nizoral*) is used orally to treat many of the same mycoses as amphotericin B. It works by blocking the activity of a steroid in the fungal wall and has the side effect of blocking the activity of human steroids, including testosterone and cortisol. Because of this action, ketoconazole is not the drug of choice in patients with endocrine or fertility problems. This agent is used topically as a shampoo to reduce the scaling associated with dandruff and as a cream to treat topical mycoses.
- Fluconazole (*Diflucan*) is available in oral and IV preparations, so a patient who is seriously ill can be treated with the IV form and then switched to the oral form as his or her condition improves. Fluconazole, which is not associated with the endocrine problems seen with ketoconazole, is used to treat candidiasis, cryptococcal meningitis, other systemic fungal infections. This drug has been used successfully as a prophylactic method for reducing the incidence of candidiasis in bone marrow transplant recipients.
- Itraconazole (*Sporanox*) is an oral agent used for the treatment of assorted systemic mycoses. This drug, which has been associated with hepatic failure, should not be used in patients with hepatic failure and should be used with caution in cases of hepatic impairment.
- Miconazole (*Monistat*) is available for IV use in the treatment of severe systemic mycoses and in several topical forms (vaginal suppository, cream, powder, and spray) for therapy of local, topical mycoses, including bladder and vaginal infections and athlete's foot. Fewer adverse effects are associated with this drug than with amphotericin B or ketoconazole. It can be used in patients with hepatic and renal dysfunction.

THERAPEUTIC ACTIONS AND INDICATIONS

All of the systemic antifungal drugs function to alter the cell permeability of the fungus, leading to cell death and prevention of replication (Figure 9-1). Some agents, including amphotericin B, nystatin, fluconazole, itraconazole, and miconazole, bind to the ergosterol to open pores in the cell membrane. In contrast, ketoconazole impairs the synthesis of the ergosterol, allowing increased cell permeability and leakage of cellular components, leading to cell death. These agents are indicated for the treatment of systemic infections caused by susceptible fungi.

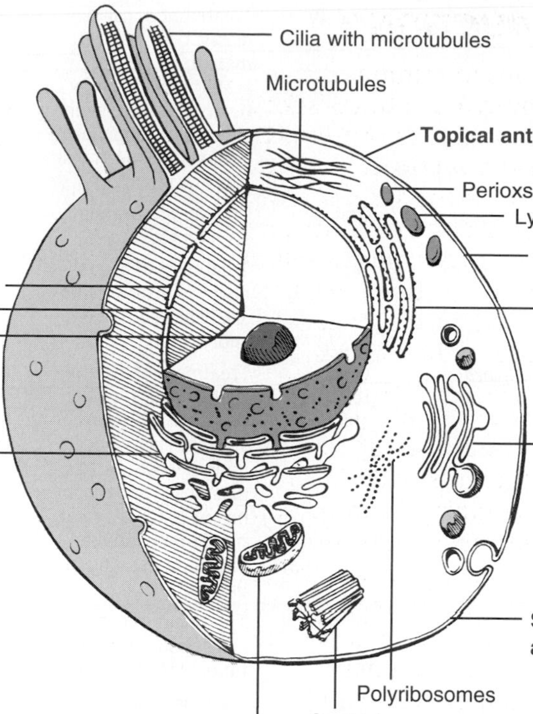

FIGURE 9-1. Sites of action of antifungal agents. The systemic antifungals (amphotericin B, fluconazole, flucytosine, itraconazole, ketoconazole, miconazole, nystatin) alter fungal cell permeability, leading to prevention of replication and cell death. The topical antifungals (butenafine, butoconazole, clotrimazole, econazole, gentian violet, naftifine, oxiconazole, terbinafine, and tolnaftate) alter cell permeability, leading to prevention of replication and cell death.

CONTRAINDICATIONS/CAUTIONS

Caution should be used when these systemic antifungal agents are administered to anyone with a known allergy; during pregnancy and lactation (use should be reserved for life-threatening infections); and with renal or liver disease, which could either alter drug metabolism and excretion or undergo further changes as a result of the actions of the drug.

ADVERSE EFFECTS

Adverse effects frequently encountered with the use of these antifungal agents include central nervous system (CNS) effects such as headache, dizziness, fever, shaking, chills, and malaise. GI effects include nausea, vomiting, dyspepsia, and anorexia. Hepatic dysfunction, which is seen more often with itraconazole, is associated with the toxic effects of the drug on the liver. Dermatologic effects such as rash and pruritus associated with local irritation may occur. Renal dysfunction, which is more often seen with amphotericin B, is probably related to the drug effects on cell membranes.

CLINICALLY IMPORTANT DRUG–DRUG INTERACTIONS

Patients who receive amphotericin B should take neither other nephrotoxic drugs nor corticosteroids unless absolutely necessary, because of the increased risk of severe renal toxicity. The azole family of antifungal drugs can cause increased serum levels of the following agents: cyclosporine, digoxin, oral hypoglycemics, warfarin, oral anticoagulants, and phenytoin. Toxicity may occur because the azoles reduce the metabolic activity needed for metabolism of these drugs. If these combinations cannot be avoided, patients should be closely monitored and dosage adjustments made. Because the azoles have also been associated with potentially severe cardiovascular events when taken with lovastatin, simvastatin, astemizole, cisapride, triazolam, and midazolam, these combinations with azoles should be avoided.

DATA LINK

Data link to the following systemic antifungal agents in your nursing drug guide:

SYSTEMIC ANTIFUNGALS

Name	Brand Name	Routes	Usual Indications
amphotericin B	*Fungizone, Abelcet*	IV, topical	Treatment of aspergillosis, leishmaniasis, cryptococcosis, blastomycosis, moniliasis, coccidioidomycosis, histoplasmosis, and mucormycosis; topical treatment of resistant candida

fluconazole	*Diflucan*	Oral, IV	Treatment of candidiasis, cryptococcal meningitis, other systemic fungal infections; reducing the incidence of candidiasis in bone marrow transplant recipients
flucytosine	*Ancoban*	Oral	Treatment of candidiasis, cryptococcosis
itraconazole	*Sporanox*	Oral	Treatment of blastomycosis, histoplasmosis, aspergillosis, onychomycosis
ketoconazole	*Nizoral*	Oral, topical, shampoo	Treatment of aspergilleishmaniasis, cryptococcosis, blastomycosis, moniliasis, coccidioidomycosis, histoplasmosis, and mucormycosis; topical treatment of mycoses, to reduce the scaling of dandruff
P miconazole	*Monistat*	IV, topical	Treatment of candidiasis, serious systemic fungal infections
nystatin	*Mycostatin, Nilstat Nystex*	Oral, topical	Treatment of candidiasis

NURSING CONSIDERATIONS
for patients receiving systemic antifungals

Assessment

HISTORY. Screen for the following: history of allergy to antifungals; history of liver or renal dysfunction that might interfere with metabolism and excretion of the drug; and pregnancy or lactation, which are cautions or contraindications to the use of these drugs.

PHYSICAL ASSESSMENT. Physical assessment should be performed to establish baseline data for assessing the effectiveness of the drug and the occurrence of any adverse effects associated with drug therapy. Perform a culture of the infected area to make an accurate determination of the type and responsiveness of fungus. Assess orientation and reflexes to evaluate any CNS effects of the drug. Examine the skin for color and lesions to check for dermatologic effects of the drug. Evaluate renal and hepatic function tests to determine baseline function of these organs to assess possible toxicity during drug therapy.

Nursing Diagnoses

The patient receiving a systemic antifungal drug may have the following nursing diagnoses related to drug therapy:

- Pain related to GI, CNS, local effects of drug
- Sensory–perceptual alteration related to CNS effects
- Knowledge deficit regarding drug therapy

Implementation

- Arrange for appropriate culture and sensitivity tests before beginning therapy *to ensure that the appropriate drug is being used.* Treatment can begin before tests results are known *because of the seriousness of the systemic infections.*
- Administer the full course of the drug *to get the full beneficial effects,* which may be as long as 6 months for some chronic infections.
- Monitor IV sites *to ensure that phlebitis does not occur.* Treat appropriately and restart IV at another site if phlebitis occurs.
- Monitor renal and hepatic function prior to and periodically during treatment *to arrange to stop drug if signs of organ failure occur.*
- Provide comfort and safety provisions if CNS effects occur (e.g., siderails and assistance with ambulation for dizziness and weakness, analgesics for headache, antipyretics for fever and chills, temperature regulation for fever) *to protect the patient from injury.*
- Provide small, frequent, nutritious meals if GI upset is severe. Monitor nutritional status, and arrange a dietary consult as needed *to ensure nutritional status.* GI upset may be decreased by taking an oral drug with food.
- Provide patient instruction *to enhance patient knowledge about drug therapy and to promote compliance.*

The patient should:

Follow the appropriate dosage regimen.

Take safety precautions, including changing position slowly and avoiding driving and hazardous tasks if CNS effects occur.

Take an oral drug with meals and try small, frequent meals if GI upset is a problem.

Report sore throat, unusual bruising and bleeding, and yellowing of the eyes or skin, all of which could indicate hepatic toxicity; severe nausea and vomiting, which could interfere with nutritional state and slow recovery; and severe local irritation with local application, which could indicate a sensitivity reaction and worsening of the infection, to a health care provider.

(See Patient Teaching Checklist: Antifungal Agents.)

Evaluation

- Monitor patient response to the drug (resolution of fungal infection).
- Monitor for adverse effects (orientation and affect, nutritional state, skin color and lesions, renal and hepatic function).
- Evaluate the effectiveness of the teaching plan (patient can name the drug, dosage, possible adverse

PATIENT TEACHING CHECKLIST

Antifungal Agents

Create customized patient teaching materials for a specific antifungal agent from your CD-ROM. Your patient teaching should stress the following points for drugs within this class: An antifungal drug works to destroy the fungi that have invaded the body. Because of the way that antifungal drugs work, they may need to be taken over a long period of time. It is very important to take all of the prescribed medication.

Common adverse effects of this drug include:

- Headache and weakness—Change positions slowly. An analgesic may be ordered to help alleviate the headache. If you feel drowsy, avoid driving or dangerous activities.
- Stomach upset, nausea, and vomiting—Small, frequent meals may help. Take the drug with food if appropriate, as this may decrease the GI upset associated with these drugs. (Note: Ketoconazole must be taken on an empty stomach at least 2 hours before a meal, antacids, milk products, or any other drugs.) Try to maintain adequate nutrition.

Report any of the following to your health care provider: severe vomiting, abdominal pain, fever or chills, yellowing of the skin or eyes, dark urine or pale stools, or skin rash.

Avoid over-the-counter medications. If you feel that you need one of these, check with your health care provider first.

Take the full course of your prescription. Never use this drug to self-treat any other infection or give it to any other person.

Tell any doctor, nurse, or other health care provider that you are taking this drug.

Keep this drug and all medications out of the reach of children.

This Teaching Checklist reflects general patient teaching guidelines. It is not meant to be a substitute for drug-specific teaching information, which is available in nursing drug guides.

effects to watch for, and specific measures to help avoid adverse effects).

• Monitor the effectiveness of comfort and safety measures and compliance with the regimen (see Nursing Care Guide: Antifungal Agents).

TOPICAL ANTIFUNGALS

Some antifungal drugs are available only in topical forms for treating a variety of skin and mucous membrane-related mycoses. Fungi that cause these infections are called dermatophytes. These diseases include a variety of ***tinea*** infections, which are often referred to as ringworm, although the causal organism is a fungus, not a worm. Types of tinea include athlete's foot (tinea pedis), jock itch (tinea cruris), and yeast infections of the mouth and vagina often caused by *Candida*. Because the antifungal drugs reserved for use as topical agents are often too toxic for systemic administration, care should always be taken when using them near open or draining wounds that might permit systemic absorption.

A number of topical antifungal drugs are available for use. Gentian violet, a very old agent, is of limited usefulness because it stains skin and clothing. In addition, it is very toxic when absorbed, so it cannot be used near active lesions. Butenafine (*Mentax*), which is applied only once a day for 4 weeks, is used for tinea infections. Butoconazole (*Femstat*), an over-the-counter (OTC) cream, is used in the treatment of vaginal *Candida* infections. Clotrimazole (*Lotrimin, Mycelex*), another OTC preparation, is used for treating oral and vaginal *Candida* infections and as a cream or lotion for treating tinea infections. Econazole (*Spectazole*) is used for treating tinea infections. This drug can cause intense, local burning and irritation, and it should be discontinued if these conditions become severe. Naftifine (*Naftin*) is a very powerful local antifungal that should not be used longer than 4 weeks. Oxiconazole (*Oxistat*) can be used for up to 1 month and applied once daily or twice daily as needed. Terbinafine (*Lamisil*) can be used for 1 to 4 weeks and applied twice daily. This drug should be stopped when the fungal condition appears to be improved or if local irritation and pain become too great. Tolnaftate (*Tinactin, Aftate*), an OTC drug, is very effective in the treatment of athlete's foot.

NURSING CARE GUIDE
Antifungal Agents

Assessment	Nursing Diagnoses	Implementation	Evaluation
HISTORY			
Allergies to any of these drugs, renal or liver dysfunction, pregnancy and lactation	Pain related to GI, local, CNS effects	Culture infection prior to beginning therapy.	Evaluate drug effects: relief of signs and symptoms of fungal infection.
	Sensory, perceptual alterations related to CNS effects	Provide comfort and implement safety measures: assistance and siderails, temperature control, lighting control, mouth care, skin care.	Monitor for adverse effects: GI alterations, dizziness, confusion, headache, fever, renal, hepatic dysfunction, local pain, discomfort.
	Alteration in nutrition, less than body requirements related to GI effects	Provide small, frequent meals and monitor nutritional status.	Monitor for drug–drug interactions as indicated for each drug.
	Knowledge deficit regarding drug therapy	Provide support and reassurance for dealing with drug effects and discomfort.	Evaluate effectiveness of patient teaching program.
		Provide patient teaching regarding drug name, dosage, adverse effects, precautions, and warning signs to report.	Evaluate effectiveness of comfort and safety measures.
PHYSICAL EXAMINATION			
Local: culture of infected site			
Skin: color, lesions, texture			
GU: urinary output			
GI: abdominal, liver evaluation			
Hematologic: renal and hepatic function tests			

WWW.WEB LINKS

Health care providers and patients may want to consult the following Internet sources:

Information on drug protocols, fungal research:
http://www.cdc.gov

Information on candidiasis infections for patients and professionals:
http://orion.einet.edu

Information about athlete's foot infections:
http://www.athletesfoot.com/

Information about systemic fungal infections, including incidence, diagnosis, and treatments:
http://www.ohsu.edu/cliniweb/c1

Health information for professionals and consumers:
http://www.critpath.org/aric/dirt/05-06

THERAPEUTIC ACTIONS AND INDICATIONS

The topical antifungal drugs work to alter the cell permeability of the fungus, causing prevention of replication and fungal death (see Figure 9-1). They are indicated only for the local treatment of mycoses, including *Candida,* tinea infections, and so on.

CASE STUDY

Poor Nutrition and Opportunistic Infections

PRESENTATION

P. P., a 19-year-old woman and aspiring model, complains of abdominal pain, difficulty swallowing, and a very sore throat. The strict diets she has followed for long periods of time have sometimes amounted to a starvation regimen. In the past 18 months, she has received treatment for a variety of bacterial infections (e.g., pneumonia, cystitis) with a series of antibiotics.

P. P. appears to be a very thin, extremely pale young woman who looks older than her stated age. Her mouth is moist, and small, white colonies that extend down the pharynx cover the mucosa. A vaginal examination reveals similar colonies. Cultures are performed, and it is determined that she has mucocutaneous candidiasis. She is started on ketoconazole (*Nizoral*) and asked to return in 10 days for follow-up.

CRITICAL THINKING QUESTIONS

What are the effects of a variety of antibiotics on the normal flora? Think about the possible cause of the mycosis. What happens to the immune system and the skin and mucous membranes when a person's nutritional status becomes insufficient? How is P. P.'s chosen profession affecting her health? What are the possible ramifications of suggesting that P. P. change her profession or her lifestyle? What are the important nursing implications for P. P.? Think about how the nurse can work with P. P. to ensure some compliance with therapy and a return to a healthy state.

DISCUSSION

Because of P. P.'s appearance, a complete physical examination should be performed before drug therapy is initiated. It is necessary to know baseline functioning to evaluate any underlying problems that may exist. Poor nutrition and total starvation result in characteristic deficiencies that predispose individuals to opportunistic infections and prevent their bodies from protecting themselves adequately through inflammatory and immune responses. In this case, the fact that liver changes often occur with poor nutrition is particularly important; such hepatic dysfunction may cause deficient drug metabolism and lead to toxicity.

An intensive program of teaching and support should be started for P. P., who should have an opportunity to vent her feelings and fears. She needs help accepting her diagnosis and adapting to the drug therapy and nutritional changes that are necessary for the effective treatment of this infection. She should understand the possible causes of her infection (poor nutrition and the loss of normal flora secondary to antibiotic therapy); the specifics of her drug therapy, including timing and administration; and adverse effects and warning signs that should be reported. P. P. should be monitored closely for adverse effects and followed regularly while taking the ketoconazole. Nutritional counseling or referral to a dietitian for thorough nutritional teaching may prove beneficial.

The actual resolution of the fungal infection may only occur after a combination of prolonged drug and nutritional therapy. Because the required therapy will affect P. P.'s lifestyle tremendously, she will need a great deal of support and encouragement to make the necessary changes to maintain compliance. A health care provider, such as a nurse whom P. P. trusts and with whom she can regularly discuss her concerns may be an essential element in helping eradicate the fungal infection.

Because these agents are very toxic, they are not intended for systemic use, and they are not indicated for use in open lesions or wounds because of the increased risk of systemic absorption.

CONTRAINDICATIONS/CAUTIONS

Because these drugs are not absorbed systemically, contraindications are limited to known allergy to any of these drugs.

ADVERSE EFFECTS

When these drugs are applied locally as a cream, lotion, or spray, local effects include irritation, burning, rash, and swelling. When taken as a suppository or troche, adverse effects include nausea, vomiting, and hepatic dysfunction (related to absorption of some of the drug by the GI tract) or urinary frequency, burning, and change in sexual activity (related to local absorption in the vagina).

CLINICALLY IMPORTANT DRUG–DRUG INTERACTIONS

Because these drugs are not generally absorbed systemically, there are no reported drug–drug interactions.

DATA LINK

Data link to the following topical antifungal agents in your nursing drug guide:

TOPICAL ANTIFUNGALS

Name	Brand Name	Usual Indications
gentian violet	generic	Treatment of topical mycosis
butenafine	*Mentax*	Treatment of tinea infections
butoconazole	*Femstat*	OTC—treatment of vaginal *Candida* infections
P clotrimazole	*Lotrimin, Mycelex*	OTC—treatment of oral and vaginal *Candida* infections; tinea infections
econazole	*Spectazole*	Treatment of tinea infections
naftifine	*Naftin*	Short term (up to 4 weeks) treatment of severe topical mycosis
oxiconazole	*Oxistat*	Short term (up to 4 weeks) treatment of topical mycosis
terbinafine	*Lamisil*	Short term (1–4 weeks) treatment of topical mycosis
tolnaftate	*Tinactin, Aftate*	OTC—treatment of athlete's foot

NURSING CONSIDERATIONS
for patients using topical antifungals

Assessment

HISTORY. Patients who receive a topical antifungal agent should be assessed for any known allergy to any topical antifungal agent.

PHYSICAL ASSESSMENT. Physical assessment should be performed to establish baseline data for assessment of the effectiveness of the drug and the occurrence of any adverse effects associated with drug therapy. Perform culture and sensitivity testing of the affected area to determine the causative fungus and appropriate medication. Conduct local evaluation (color, temperature, lesions, and so on) to monitor the effectiveness of the drug and to monitor for local adverse effects to the drug.

Nursing Diagnoses

The patient receiving a topical antifungal drug may have the following nursing diagnoses related to drug therapy:

- Pain related to local effects of drug
- Knowledge deficit regarding drug therapy

Implementation

- Culture the affected area before beginning therapy *to establish causative fungus.*
- Ensure that the patient takes the complete course of the drug regimen *to achieve maximal results.*
- Ensure that the patient is using the correct method of administration depending on the route *to improve effectiveness and decrease risk of adverse effects:*
  - Troches should be dissolved slowly in the mouth.
  - Vaginal suppositories, creams, and tablets should be inserted high into the vagina with the patient remaining recumbent for at least 10 to 15 minutes after insertion.
  - Topical creams and lotions should be rubbed into the affected area after it has been cleansed with soap and water.
- Stop the drug if a severe rash occurs, especially if accompanied by blisters, or if local irritation and pain are very severe. *This may indicate a sensitivity to the drug or worsening of the condition being treated.*
- Provide patient instruction *to enhance patient knowledge about drug therapy and to promote compliance.*

The patient should:

Know the correct method of drug administration.

Know the length of time necessary to treat the infection adequately.

When treating athlete's foot, clean, dry socks are important in helping eradicate the infection.

Occlusive dressings should be avoided, because of the risk of increasing systemic absorption. Drugs should not be placed near open wounds or active lesions because these agents are not intended to be absorbed systemically.

Severe local irritation or burning or worsening of the infection should be reported to a health care provider (refer to the Patient Teaching Checklist: Antifungals).

Evaluation

- Monitor patient response to the drug (alleviation of signs and symptoms of the fungal infection).
- Monitor for adverse effects: rash, local irritation, and burning.
- Evaluate the effectiveness of the teaching plan (patient can name the drug, dosage, possible adverse effects to watch for, and specific measures to help avoid adverse effects).
- Monitor the effectiveness of comfort and safety measures and compliance with the regimen (refer to the Nursing Care Guide: Antifungals).

CHAPTER SUMMARY

- A fungus is a cellular organism with a hard cell wall that contains chitin and polysaccharides and a cell membrane that contains ergosterols.
- Any infection with a fungus is called a mycosis. Systemic fungal infections, which can be life-

threatening, are increasing with the rise in the number of immune compromised patients.

- Systemic antifungals alter the cell permeability, leading to the leaking of cellular components. This causes prevention of cell replication and cell death.
- Because systemic antifungals can be very toxic, patients should be monitored closely while receiving these drugs. Adverse effects may include hepatic and renal failure.
- Local fungal infections include vaginal and oral yeast infections (*Candida*) and a variety of tinea infections, including athlete's foot and jock itch.
- Topical antifungals are agents that are too toxic to be used systemically but are effective in the treatment of local fungal infections.
- Proper administration of topical antifungals improves their effectiveness. They should not be used near open wounds or lesions.
- Topical antifungals can cause serious local irritation, burning, and pain. These drug should be stopped if these conditions occur.

Bibliography

Bullock, B. L. (2000). *Focus on pathophysiology*. Philadelphia: Lippincott Williams & Wilkins.

Hardman, J. G., Limbird, L. E., Molinoff, P. B., Ruddon, R. W., & Gilman, A. G. (Eds.). (1996). *Goodman and Gilman's the pharmacological basis of therapeutics* (9th ed.). New York: McGraw Hill.

Karch, A. M. (2000). *2000 Lippincott's nursing drug guide.* Philadelphia: Lippincott Williams & Wilkins.

Malseed, R. (1995). *Textbook of pharmacology and nursing care.* Philadelphia: Lippincott-Raven.

McEvoy, B. R. (Ed.). (1999). *Facts and comparisons 1999.* St. Louis: Facts and Comparisons.

Professional's guide to patient drug facts. (1999). St. Louis: Facts and Comparisons.

CHAPTER 10

Antiprotozoal Agents

Antimalarials

- **P** chloroquine
- halofantrine
- hydroxychloroquine
- mefloquine
- primaquine
- pyrimethamine
- quinine

Other antiprotozoals

- atovaquone
- **P** metronidazole
- pentamidine

CHAPTER OUTLINE

INTRODUCTION
MALARIA
Life Cycle of Plasmodium
ANTIMALARIALS
THERAPEUTIC ACTIONS AND INDICATIONS
CONTRAINDICATIONS/CAUTIONS
ADVERSE EFFECTS
CLINICALLY IMPORTANT DRUG–DRUG INTERACTIONS
NURSING CONSIDERATIONS for patients receiving antimalarial agents
Assessment
HISTORY
PHYSICAL ASSESSMENT
Nursing Diagnoses
Implementation
Evaluation
OTHER PROTOZOAL INFECTIONS
Amebiasis
Leishmaniasis
Trypanosomiasis
Trichomoniasis
Giardiasis
Pneumocystis carinii *Pneumonia (PCP)*
OTHER ANTIPROTOZOAL AGENTS
THERAPEUTIC ACTIONS AND INDICATIONS
CONTRAINDICATIONS/CAUTIONS
ADVERSE EFFECTS
NURSING CONSIDERATIONS for patients receiving antiprotozoal drugs
Assessment
HISTORY
PHYSICAL ASSESSMENT
Nursing Diagnoses
Implementation
Evaluation
CHAPTER SUMMARY
BIBLIOGRAPHY

KEY TERMS

amebiasis
Anopheles **mosquito**
cinchonism
giardiasis
leishmaniasis
malaria
Plasmodium
Pneumocystis carinii **pneumonia (PCP)**
protozoa
trichomoniasis
trophozoite
trypanosomiasis

INTRODUCTION

Infections caused by ***protozoa*** are very common in several parts of the world. In tropical areas, where these types of illnesses are most prevalent, many people suffer multiple infestations at the same time. These infections are relatively rare in the United States, but with people traveling throughout the world in increasing numbers, it is not unusual to find an individual who returns home from a trip to Africa, Asia, or South America with fully developed protozoal infections. Protozoa thrive in tropical climates but they may also survive and reproduce in any area where people live in very crowded and unsanitary conditions. This chapter focuses on protozoal infections that are caused by insect bites (***malaria, trypanosomiasis,*** and ***leishmaniasis***), as well as protozoal infections that are caused by ingestion or contact with the causal organism (***amebiasis, giardiasis,*** and ***trichomoniasis***).

MALARIA

Malaria is a parasitic disease that has killed hundreds of millions of people and even changed the course of history. The course of several African battles and the building of the Panama Canal have been altered by outbreaks of malaria. Even with the introduction of drugs for the treatment of this disease, it remains endemic in many parts of the world. Malaria is spread via the bite of an ***Anopheles mosquito,*** which harbors the protozoal parasite and carries it to humans. This is the only known method of disease transmission.

Four protozoal parasites have been identified as causes of malaria:

- *Plasmodium falciparum* is considered to be the most dangerous type of protozoan. Infection with this protozoan results in an acute, rapidly fulminating disease with high fever, severe hypotension, swelling and reddening of the limbs, loss of red blood cells, and even death.
- *Plasmodium vivax* causes a milder form of the disease, seldom resulting in death.
- *Plasmodium malariae* is endemic in many tropical countries and causes very mild signs and symptoms in the population. It can cause more acute disease in travelers to the area.
- *Plasmodium ovale,* which is rarely seen, seems to be in the process of being eradicated.

Part of the problem with malaria control is that the female mosquito, which is responsible for transmitting the disease, has developed a resistance to the insecticides designed to eradicate the mosquito. Widespread efforts at mosquito control were successful for a long period of time, with fewer cases of malaria seen each year. As the insecticide-resistant mosquitoes continue to flourish, however, the incidence of malaria is again increasing. In addition, the protozoa that cause malaria have developed strains resistant to the usual antimalarial drugs. This combination of factors has led to a worldwide public health challenge.

Life Cycle of Plasmodium

The parasites that cause human malaria spend part of their life in the *Anopheles* mosquito and part of their life in the human host (Figure 10-1). When a mosquito bites an individual who is infected with malaria, it sucks blood infested with gametocytes, which are male and female forms of the ***plasmodium.*** These gametocytes mate in the stomach of the mosquito and produce a zygote that goes through several phases before forming sporozoites (spore animals) that make their way to the mosquito's salivary glands. The next person who is bitten by that mosquito is injected with thousands of these sporozoites. These animals travel through the bloodstream, where they quickly become lodged in the human liver and other tissues and invade the cells.

In these cells, these organisms undergo asexual cell division and reproduction. Over the next week to 10 days, these primary tissue schizonts grow and multiply within their invaded cells. Merozoites are formed from the primary schizonts, and these burst from the invaded cells which rupture from overexpansion. These merozoites enter the circulation and invade red blood cells, in which they continue to divide until the blood cells also burst, sending more merozoites into the circulation to invade more red blood cells.

Eventually, there are a large number of merozoites in the body and many ruptured and invaded red blood cells. At this point, the acute malarial attack occurs. The rupture of the red blood cells causes chills and fever related to the pyrogenic effects of the protozoa and the toxic effects of the red blood cell components on the system. This cycle of chills and fever usually occurs about every 72 hours.

With *P. vivax* and *P. malariae* malaria, this cycle may continue for a long period of time. Many of the tissue schizonts lay dormant and eventually find their way to the liver, where they multiply and then invade more red blood cells and again cause the acute cycle. This may occur for years in an untreated patient.

With *P. falciparum* malaria, there are no extrahepatic sites for the schizonts. If the patient survives an acute attack, no prolonged periods of relapses occur. The first attack of this type of malaria can

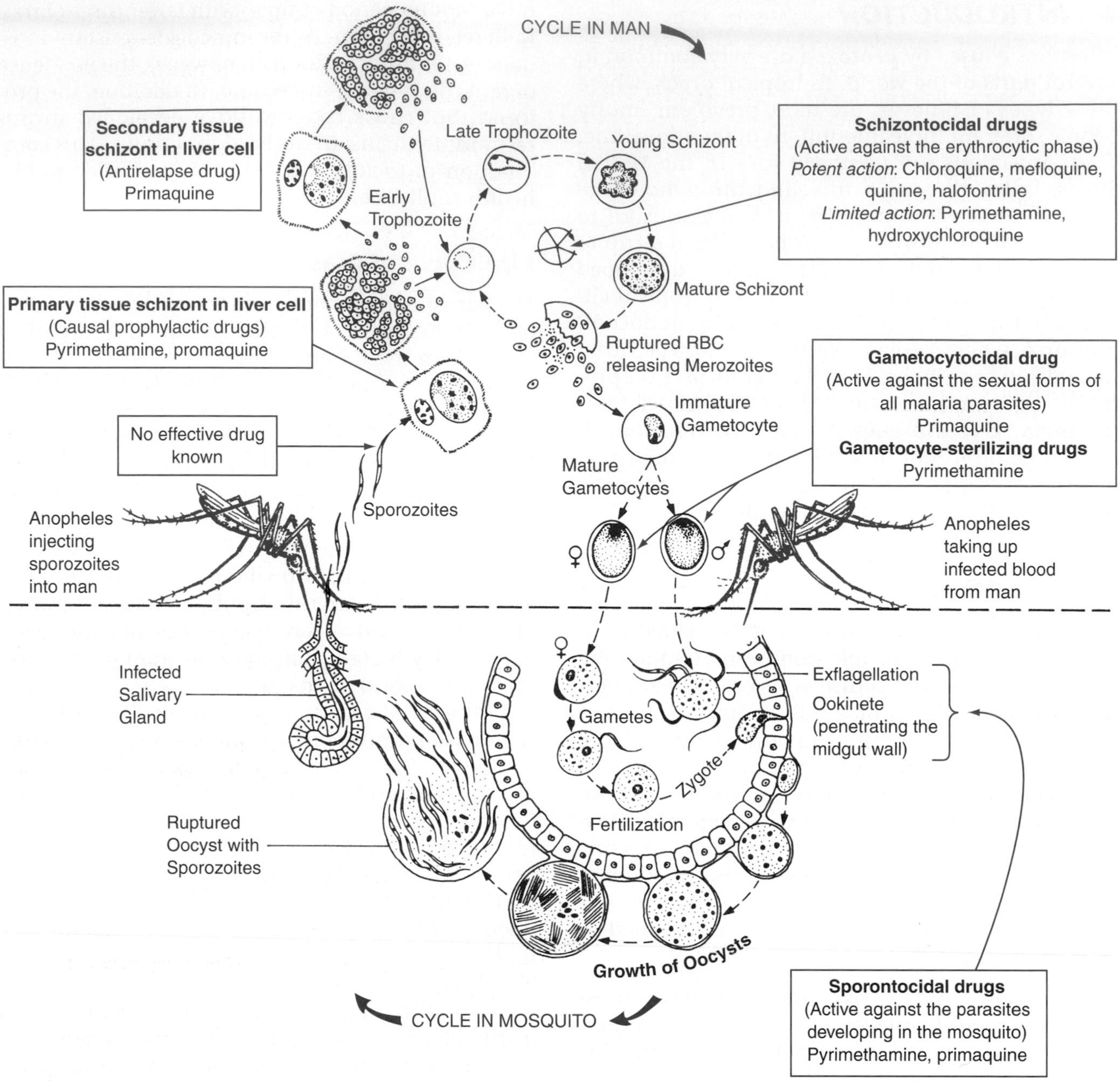

FIGURE 10-1. Types of antimalarial drugs in relation to the stages in the life cycle of *Plasmodium.*

destroy so many red blood cells that the patient's capillaries become clogged, and the circulation to vital organs is interrupted, leading to death.

ANTIMALARIALS

Antimalarial drugs are usually given in combination form to attack the plasmodium at various stages of its life cycle. Using this approach, it is possible to prevent the acute malarial reaction in individuals who have been infected by the parasite.

Quinine, the first drug found to be effective in the treatment of malaria, is now reserved for use in chloroquine-resistant infections in combination with other agents. Quinine affects the DNA synthesis of the plasmodium, leading to an inability to reproduce effectively. The drug may lead to severe diarrhea and a condition called ***cinchonism*** (nausea, vomiting, tinnitus, and vertigo), which makes it less desirable than newer, less toxic drugs.

Chloroquine (*Aralen*) is currently the mainstay of antimalarial therapy. This drug enters human red blood cells and changes the metabolic pathways necessary for the reproduction of the plasmodium. In addition, this agent is directly toxic to parasites that absorb it because it is acidic, and it decreases the ability of the parasite to synthesize DNA, leading to a blockage of reproduction. Chloroquine sometimes has serious adverse effects such as hepatic toxicity, permanent eye damage, and blindness.

Hydroxychloroquine (*Plaquenil*) inhibits parasite reproduction, and by blocking the synthesis of protein production, it can cause the death of the plasmodium. This drug is used in combination therapy, usually with primaquine, for greatest effectiveness.

Mefloquine (*Lariam*) increases the acidity of plasmodial food vacuoles, causing cell rupture and death. In combination therapy, mefloquine is used in malarial prevention as well as treatment.

Primaquine, another very old drug for treating malaria, similar to quinine, disrupts the mitochondria of the plasmodium. It also causes death of gametocytes and exoerythrocytic forms and prevents other forms from reproducing. Because of this action, it is especially useful in preventing relapses of *P. vivax* and *P. malariae* infections.

Pyrimethamine (*Daraprim*) is used in combination with more rapidly acting agents to suppress malaria by blocking the use of folic acid in protein synthesis by the plasmodium, eventually leading to inability to reproduce and cell death.

Halofantrine (*Halfan*), the newest antimalarial agent, is effective in the erythrocyte stage of the disease and causes the death of the plasmodium. Apparently, it has no effect on the sporozoite or gametocyte phases or the hepatic stage of the disease, so it is most effective when used in combination with other antimalarials.

THERAPEUTIC ACTIONS AND INDICATIONS

Research has demonstrated that the antimalarial agents are effective in interrupting plasmodial reproduction of protein synthesis in the red blood cell stage of the life cycle as well as in the hepatic and gametocyte stages in some cases (Figure 10-2). Chemotherapeutic agents, which do not appear to affect the sporozoites, are used in the prophylaxis and treatment of acute attacks of malaria caused by susceptible strains of *Plasmodium.*

CONTRAINDICATIONS/CAUTIONS

Contraindications to the use of antimalarials are the presence of any known allergy to any of these drugs; cases of liver disease or alcoholism, because of (1) the parasitic invasion of the liver, and (2) the need for the hepatic metabolism to avoid reaching toxic levels; and lactation because the drugs can enter breast milk and could be toxic to the infant. Caution

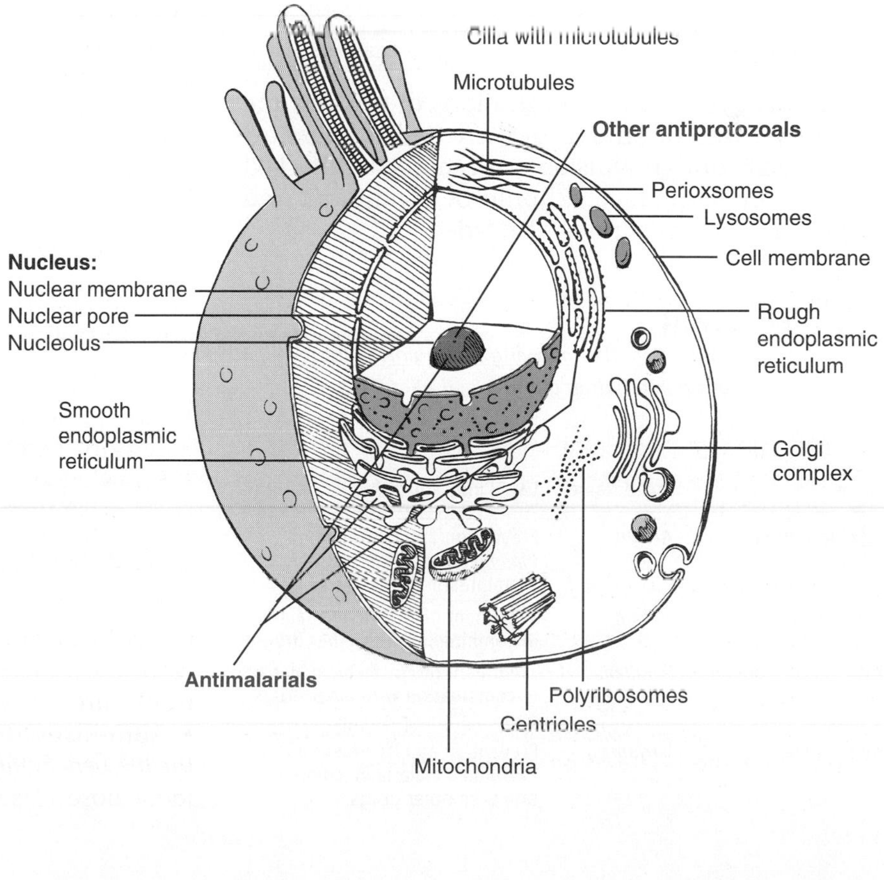

FIGURE 10-2. Sites of action of antimalarials and other antiprotozoals. Antimalarials block protein synthesis and cause cell death. Other antiprotozoals block DNA synthesis, prevent cell reproduction, and lead to cell death.

should be used with retinal disease or damage because many of these drugs can affect vision and the retina, and the likelihood of problems increases if the retina is already damaged; with psoriasis or porphyria because of skin damage; and with damage to mucous membranes that can occur as a result of the effects of the drug on proteins and protein synthesis.

ADVERSE EFFECTS

A number of adverse effects are encountered with the use of these antimalarial agents. Headache, dizziness, fever, shaking, chills, and malaise are associated with central nervous system (CNS) effects of the drugs and immune reaction to the release of the mitozoites. Nausea, vomiting, dyspepsia, and anorexia are associated with direct drug effects on the gastrointestinal (GI) tract and effects on CNS control of vomiting related to cell death and protein changes. Hepatic dysfunction is associated with the toxic effects of the drug on the liver and the effects of the disease on the liver. Dermatologic effects include rash, pruritus, and loss of hair associated with changes in protein synthesis. Visual changes, including possible blindness related to retinal damage from the drug, and ototoxicity related to additional nerve damage may occur. Cinchonism (nausea, vomiting, tinnitus, and vertigo) is more commonly seen with high levels of quinine and is related to drug effects in the CNS. This effect can be seen with any quinine-related drug if toxic levels occur.

CLINICALLY IMPORTANT DRUG–DRUG INTERACTIONS

The patient receiving combinations of the quinine derivatives and quinine is at increased risk for cardiac toxicity and convulsions and should be checked very closely. Drug levels should be monitored and dosage adjustments made as needed.

DATA LINK

Data link to the following antimalarial drugs in your nursing drug guide:

ANTIMALARIALS

Name	Brand Name	Usual Indications
P chloroquine	*Aralen*	Prevention and treatment of *Plasmodia* malaria; treatment of extraintestinal amebiasis
halofantrine	*Halfan*	Treatment of *Plasmodia* malaria in combination with other drugs
hydroxychloroquine	*Plaquenil*	Treatment of *Plasmodia* malaria in combination with other drugs, particularly primaquine
mefloquine	*Lariam*	Prevention and treatment of *Plasmodia* malaria in combination with other drugs
primaquine	generic	Prevention of relapses of *P. vivax* and *P. malariae* infections; radical cure of *vivax* malaria
pyrimethamine	*Daraprim*	Prevention of *Plasmodia* malaria, in combination with other agents to suppress transmission; treatment of toxoplasmosis
quinine	generic	Treatment of chloroquine-resistant *Plasmodia* infections

NURSING CONSIDERATIONS
for patients receiving antimalarial agents

Assessment

HISTORY. Screen for the following: history of allergy to any of the antimalarials; liver dysfunction or alcoholism that might interfere with the metabolism and excretion of the drug; porphyria or psoriasis, which could be exacerbated by the drug effects; retinal disease that could increase the visual disturbances associated with these drugs; and lactation, because these drugs could enter the breast milk and be toxic to the infant.

PHYSICAL ASSESSMENT. Physical assessment should be performed to establish baseline data for assessment of the effectiveness of the drug and the occurrence of any adverse effects associated with drug therapy. Assess CNS (reflexes and muscle strength). Perform retinal examination and auditory and ophthalmic screening to detect cautions for drug use and to evaluate changes that occur as a result of drug therapy. Obtain liver evaluation and liver function tests to determine appropriateness of therapy and to monitor for toxicity. Perform blood culture to determine which *Plasmodium* is causing the disease. Conduct examination of the skin (lesions, color, temperature, and texture) to monitor for adverse effects.

Nursing Diagnoses

The patient receiving an antimalarial drug may have the following nursing diagnoses related to drug therapy:

- Pain related to GI, CNS, skin effects of drug
- Sensory–perceptual alteration related to CNS effects
- Knowledge deficit regarding drug therapy

Implementation

- Arrange for appropriate culture and sensitivity tests before beginning therapy *to assure proper drug for susceptible Plasmodia.* Treatment may begin before tests results are known.
- Administer the complete course of the drug *to get the full beneficial effects.* Mark a calendar for prophylactic doses. Use combination therapy as indicated.

- Monitor hepatic function and ophthalmologic examination prior to and periodically during treatment *to effectively arrange to stop drug if signs of failure or deteriorating vision occur.*
- Provide comfort and safety measures if CNS effects occur such as siderails and assistance with ambulation with dizziness and weakness *to prevent patient injury.* Provide oral hygiene and ready access to bathroom facilities as needed *to cope with GI effects.*
- Provide small, frequent, nutritious meals if GI upset is severe *to ensure adequate nutrition.* Monitor nutritional status and arrange a dietary consult as needed. Taking the drug with food may also decrease GI upset.
- Ensure that the patient is instructed concerning the appropriate dosage regimen *to enhance patient knowledge about drug therapy and to promote compliance.*

The patient should:

Take safety precautions including changing position slowly and avoiding driving and hazardous tasks if CNS effects occur.

Take the drug with meals and try small, frequent meals if GI upset is a problem.

Report blurring of vision that may indicate retinal damage; loss of hearing or ringing in the ears, which could indicate CNS toxicity; and fever or worsening of condition, which could indicate a resistant strain or noneffective therapy.

Evaluation

- Monitor patient response to the drug (resolution of malaria or prevention of malaria).
- Monitor for adverse effects (orientation and affect, nutritional state, skin color and lesions, hepatic function, and visual and auditory changes).
- Evaluate the effectiveness of the teaching plan (patient can name the drug, dosage, possible adverse effects to watch for, and specific measures to help avoid adverse effects).
- Monitor the effectiveness of comfort and safety measures and compliance with the regimen.

WWW.WEB LINKS

Health care providers and patients may want to consult the following Internet sources:

Information on malaria, including information for travelers:
http://www.cdc.gov/travel/malinfo.htm

Information on malaria incidence, treatment, prevention, support:
http://www.hawaii.gov/doh/resource/comm_dis/cddmalar.htm

Information on trypanosomiasis:
http://www.thirdworldtraveler.com/Disease/sleeping_sickness.html

Information about giardiasis, support, treatment, prevention, teaching:
http://www.vdh.state.va.us/epi/giarf.htm

Information about amebiasis—prevention, incidence, treatments:
http://www.aomc.org/ComDiseases/Amebiasis.html

Information about leishmaniasis, including traveler's information, treatment:
http://www.ohsu.edu/cliniweb/c3

CULTURAL CONSIDERATIONS

Potential for Hemolytic Crisis

Patients with G-6-PD deficiency (which is more likely to occur in Greeks, Italians, and other people of Mediterranean descent) may experience a hemolytic crisis if taking the following antimalarial agents: chloroquine, primaquine, and quinine. Patients of Greek, Italian, or Mediterranean ancestry should be questioned about potential G-6-PD deficiency history. If no history is known, they should be tested before any of these drugs are prescribed. If testing is not possible and the drugs are needed, the patient should be monitored very closely and informed about the potential need for hospitalization and emergency services.

OTHER PROTOZOAL INFECTIONS

Other protozoal infections that are encountered in clinical practice include amebiasis, leishmaniasis, trypanosomiasis, trichomoniasis, and giardiasis. These infections, which are caused by single-celled protozoa, are usually associated with unsanitary, crowded conditions and use of poor hygienic practices. Patients traveling to some other countries may encounter these infections, which also appear increasingly in the United States.

Amebiasis

Amebiasis, an intestinal infection caused by *Entamoeba histolytica,* is often known as amebic dysentery. *E. histolytica* has a two-stage life cycle (Figure 10-3). The organism exists in two stages: (1) a cystic, dormant stage in which the protozoan can live for long periods of time outside of the body or in the human intestine, and (2) a ***trophozoite*** stage in the ideal environment—the human large intestine.

NURSING CHALLENGE

World Travel and the Spread of Pathogens

Nowadays, people are traveling to more exotic areas of the world than ever before. Because of this, people are being exposed to more pathogens than ever before—and they also are potentially spreading pathogens to different areas of the world. Pathogens that are endemic in one area of the world, causing mild disease, can be quite devastating in a population that has not previously been exposed to that pathogen.

World health agencies and governments have established guidelines for prophylaxis and treatment of such diseases for travelers. People who are planning to travel out of the country should contact their local Health Department or the Centers for Disease Control and Prevention (CDC), http://www.cdc/gov/travel, for the latest information on what prophylactic measures are required in the area that they plan to visit, and to learn about potential health hazards in that area. The information is updated frequently and should be consulted regularly.

Patients who have been traveling to other areas of the world and who present with any illness should be questioned about where they traveled, what precautions (including prophylactic measures) were taken, and when they first experienced any signs and symptoms of illness. The CDC can be consulted for the diagnosis and treatment guidelines for any tropical disease unfamiliar to a health care provider, as well as what precautions should be used in caring for such patients.

The disease is transmitted while the protozoan is in the cystic stage in fecal matter, from which it can enter water and the ground. It can be passed to other humans who drink this water or eat food that has been grown in this ground. The cysts are swallowed and pass, unaffected by gastric acid, into the intestine. Some of these cysts are passed in fecal matter, and some of them become trophozoites that grow and reproduce. The trophozoites migrate into the colon mucosa, where they penetrate into the intestinal wall, forming erosions. These forms of *Entamoeba* release a chemical that dissolves mucosal cells, and eventually they eat away tissue until they reach the vascular system, which carries them throughout the body. The trophozoites lodge in the liver, lungs, heart, brain, and so on.

Early signs of amebiasis include mild to fulminate diarrhea. In the worst cases, if the protozoan is able to invade extraintestinal tissue, it can dissolve this tissue and eventually cause the death of the host. Some individuals can become carriers of the disease without overt signs and symptoms. These people seem to be resistant to the intestinal invasion but pass the cysts on in the stool.

Leishmaniasis

Leishmaniasis is a disease caused by a protozoan passed from sand flies to humans. The sand fly injects an asexual form of this flagellated protozoan, called a promastigote, into the human where it is rapidly attacked and digested by human macrophages. Inside the macrophages, the promastigote divides, forming many new forms called amastigotes, which keep dividing and kill the macrophage, releasing the amastigotes into the system to be devoured by more macrophages. Thus, a cyclic pattern of infection is established. These amastigotes can cause serious lesions in the skin, the viscera, or the mucous membranes of the host.

Trypanosomiasis

Trypanosomiasis is infection with *Trypanosoma*. Two such parasitic protozoa cause very serious and often fatal diseases in humans.

African sleeping sickness, which is caused by *Trypanosoma brucei gambiense,* is transmitted by the tsetse fly. After the pathogenic organism lives and grows in human blood, it then eventually invades the CNS, leading to an acute inflammation that results in lethargy, prolonged sleep, and even death.

Chagas' disease, which is caused by *Trypanosoma cruzi,* is nearly endemic in many South American countries. This protozoan results in a severe cardiomyopathy that accounts for numerous deaths and disabilities in certain regions.

Trichomoniasis

Trichomoniasis, which is caused by another flagellated protozoan, *Trichomonas vaginalis,* is a common cause of vaginitis. This infection is usually spread during sexual intercourse by males who have no signs and symptoms of infection. In females, this protozoan causes reddened, inflamed vaginal mucosa; itching; burning; and a yellowish-green discharge.

Giardiasis

Giardiasis, which is caused by *Giardia lamblia,* is the most commonly diagnosed intestinal parasite in the United States. This protozoan forms cysts, which

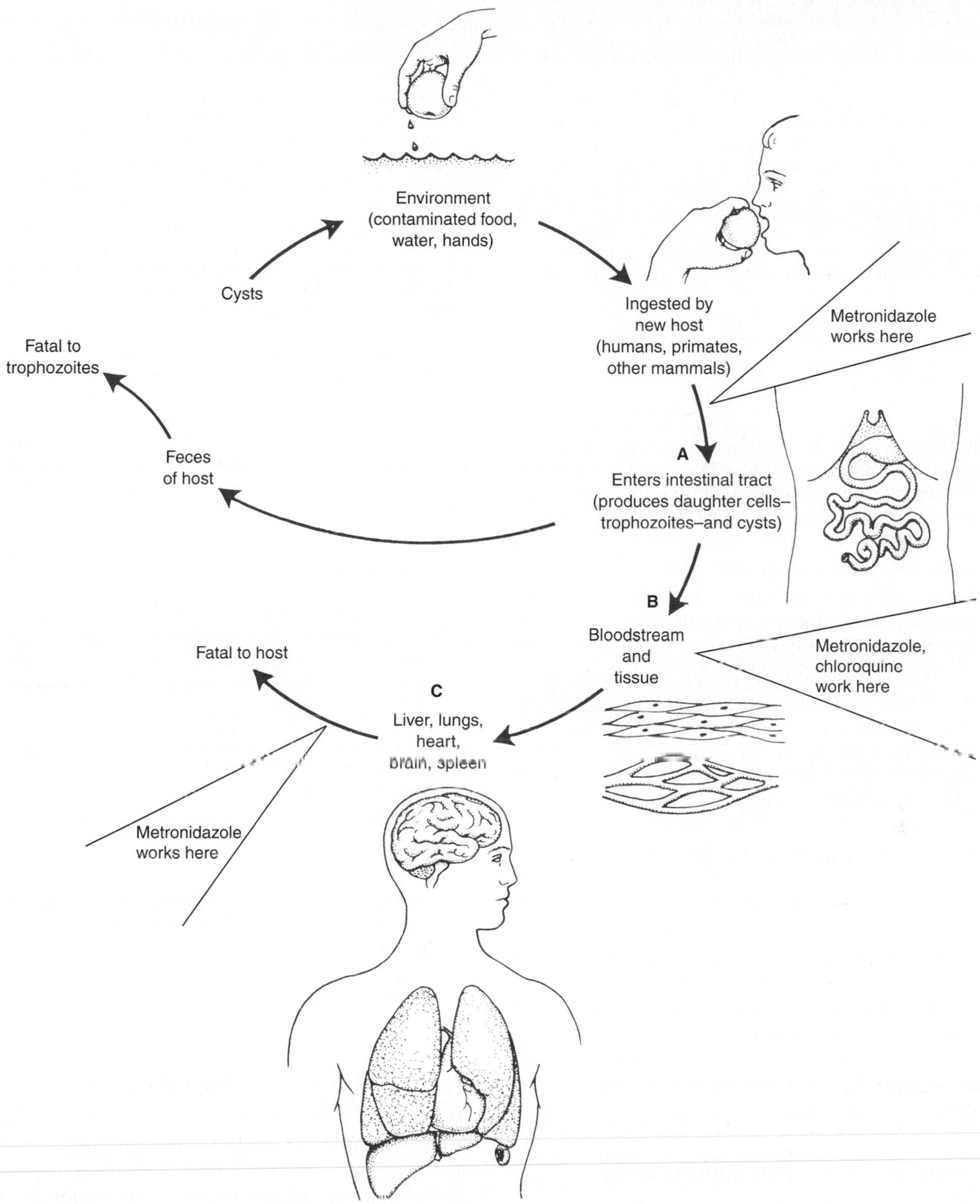

FIGURE 10-3. Life cycle of *Entamoeba histolytica* and the sites of action of metronidazole and chloroquine, which are used to treat amebiasis.

CASE STUDY

Coping with Amebiasis

PRESENTATION

J. C., a 20-year-old male college student, reported to the university health center complaining of severe diarrhea, abdominal pain, and most recently, blood in his stool. He had a mild fever and appeared to be dehydrated and very tired. The young man, who denied travel outside of the country, reported eating most of his meals at the local beer joint where he worked in the kitchen each night making pizza.

A stool sample for ova and parasites (O & P) was obtained, and a diagnosis of amebiasis was made. J. C. was placed on metronidazole. A public health referral was sent to find the source of the infection, which was the kitchen of the beer joint where J. C. worked. The kitchen was shut down until all of the food, utensils, and environment passed state health inspection. Although a potential epidemic was averted (only three other cases of amebiasis were reported), the action of the public health officials added a new stress to this student's life. He was unemployed for several months.

CRITICAL THINKING QUESTIONS

What are the important nursing implications for J. C.? Think about the usual nutritional state of a college student who eats most of his meals in a pizza place. What are the implications for recovery when a patient is malnourished and then has a disease which causes severe diarrhea, dehydration, and potential malnourishment? Consider how difficult it will be for J. C. to be a full-time student while trying to cope with the signs and symptoms of his disease as well as the adverse effects associated with his drug therapy and the need to maintain adequate nutrition to allow some healing and recovery. What potential problems could the added stress of being out of work have for J. C.? Consider the physiological impact of stress as well as the psychological problems of trying to cope with one more stressor.

DISCUSSION

J. C. needs a great deal of reassurance and an explanation of his disease. He learns that oral hygiene and small, frequent meals will help alleviate some of his discomfort until the metronidazole can control the amebiasis, that good hygiene and strict hand washing when the disease is active will help to prevent transmission; and that he should watch for the occurrence of specific adverse drug effects such as a possible severe reaction to alcohol (he was advised to avoid alcoholic beverages while on this drug), GI upset and a strange metallic taste (the importance of good nutrition to promote healing of the GI tract was stressed), dizziness or lightheadedness, and superinfections.

J. C. was scheduled for a follow-up examination for stool O&P and nutritional status. Metronidazole was continued until the stool sample came back negative. He needed and received a great deal of support and encouragement because he was far from home, and the disease and the drug effects were sometimes difficult to cope with. The effects of stress—decreasing blood flow to the GI tract, for example—can make it more difficult for J. C. to recover from this disease. Support and encouragement were major factors in his eventual recovery. He was given a telephone number to call if he needed information or support and a complete set of written instructions regarding the disease and the drug therapy.

survive outside the body and allow transmission through contaminated water or food, and trophozoites, which break out of the cysts in the upper small intestine and eventually cause signs and symptoms. Diarrhea, rotten egg–smelling stool, and pale and mucous-filled stool are commonly seen. Some patients experience epigastric distress, weight loss, and malnourishment as a result of the invasion of the mucosa.

Pneumocystis Carinii *Pneumonia (PCP)*

Pneumocystis carinii is an endemic protozoan that does not usually cause illness in humans. When a human becomes immune suppressed, because of AIDS or AIDS-related complex, the use of immune suppressant drugs, or advanced age, this parasite is able to invade the lung, leading to severe inflammation and the condition known as ***Pneumocystis carinii pneumonia (PCP).*** This disease is the most common opportunistic infection in patients with AIDS.

OTHER ANTIPROTOZOAL AGENTS

Drugs that are available for the treatment of these various protozoan infections include many of the malarial drugs; chloroquine is effective against extraintestinal amebiasis and pyrimethamine is also effective in treating toxoplasmosis. Other antiprotozoals include the following agents:

- Atovaquone (*Mepron*), which is especially active against PCP

• Metronidazole (*Flagyl, MetroGel, Noritate*), which is used to treat amebiasis, trichomoniasis, and giardiasis
• Pentamidine (*Pentam 300, Nebupent*), which is used as an inhalation agent and a systemic agent in the treatment of PCP and as a systemic drug in the treatment of trypanosomiasis and leishmaniasis

THERAPEUTIC ACTIONS AND INDICATIONS

These antiprotozoal agents act to inhibit DNA synthesis in susceptible protozoa, leading to the inability to reproduce and cell death (see Figure 10-2). These drugs are indicated for the treatment of infections caused by susceptible protozoa.

CONTRAINDICATIONS/CAUTIONS

Contraindications include the presence of any known allergy or hypersensitivity to any of these drugs; and pregnancy, because drug effects on developing fetal DNA and proteins can cause fetal abnormalities and even death. Caution should be used in the presence of CNS disease because of possible exacerbation when the drug affects the CNS; hepatic disease, because of possible exacerbation when hepatic drug effects occur; candidiasis, because of the risk of superinfections; and lactation, because these drugs may pass into breast milk and could have severe adverse effects on the infant.

ADVERSE EFFECTS

Adverse effects that can be seen with these antiprotozoal agents include such CNS effects as headache, dizziness, ataxia, loss of coordination, and peripheral neuropathy related to drug effects on the neurons. GI effects include nausea, vomiting, diarrhea, unpleasant taste, and cramps and changes in liver function. Superinfections also can occur when the normal flora is disrupted.

DATA LINK

Data link to the following antiprotozoal drugs in your nursing drug guide:

ANTIPROTOZOAL DRUGS

Name	Brand Name	Usual Indications
atovaquone	*Mepron*	Treatment of PCP
P metronidazole	*Flagyl, MetroGel, Noritate*	Treatment of amebiasis, trichomoniasis, giardiasis
pentamidine	*Pentam 300, Nebupen*	As inhalation treatment of PCP, as systemic agent in the treatment of trypanosomiasis and leishmaniasis

NURSING CONSIDERATIONS for patients receiving antiprotozoal drugs

Assessment

HISTORY. Screen for the following: history of allergy to any of the antiprotozoals; liver dysfunction that might interfere with the metabolism and excretion of the drug or be exacerbated by the drug; pregnancy, which is a contraindication, and lactation, because these drugs could enter the breast milk and be toxic to the infant; CNS disease that could be exacerbated by the drug; and candidiasis that could become severe as a result of the effects of these drugs on the normal flora.

PHYSICAL ASSESSMENT. Physical assessment should be performed to establish baseline data for determination of the effectiveness of the drug and the occurrence of any adverse effects associated with drug therapy. Conduct an examination of the CNS to check reflexes and muscle strength to detect cautions for drug use and to evaluate changes that occur as a result of drug therapy. Evaluate liver and liver function tests to determine appropriateness of therapy and to monitor for toxicity. Obtain cultures to determine the exact protozoa causing the disease. Examine the skin and mucous membranes to check for lesions, color, temperature, and texture to monitor for adverse effects and superinfections.

Nursing Diagnoses

The patient receiving an antiprotozoal drug may have the following nursing diagnoses related to drug therapy:

• Pain related to GI, CNS effects of drug
• Alteration in nutrition, less than body requirements, related to severe GI effects of drug
• Sensory–perceptual alteration related to CNS effects
• Knowledge deficit regarding drug therapy

Implementation

• Arrange for appropriate culture and sensitivity tests before beginning therapy *to assure proper drug for susceptible organisms.* Treatment may begin before tests results are known.
• Administer the complete course of the drug *to get the full beneficial effects.* Use combination therapy as indicated.
• Monitor hepatic function prior to and periodically during treatment *to arrange to effectively stop the drug if signs of failure or worsening liver function occur.*
• Provide comfort and safety measures if CNS effects occur, such as siderails and assistance with ambula-

PATIENT TEACHING CHECKLIST

Antiprotozoal Agents

Create customized patient teaching materials for a specific antiprotozoal agent from your CD-ROM. Your patient teaching should stress the following points for drugs within this class: An antiprotozoal drug acts to destroy certain protozoa that have invaded your body. Because it affects specific phases of the protozoal life cycle, it must be taken over a period of time to be effective. It is very important to take all the drug that has been ordered for you.

This drug frequently causes stomach upset. If it causes you to have nausea, heartburn, or vomiting, take the drug with meals or a light snack.

Common effects of this drug include:

- Nausea, vomiting, and loss of appetite—Take the drug with food and have small, frequent meals.
- Superinfections of the mouth, vagina, and skin—These go away when the course of the drug has been taken. If they become uncomfortable, notify your health care provider for an appropriate solution.
- Dry mouth, strange metallic taste (metronidazole)—Frequent mouth care and sucking sugarless lozenges may help. This effect will also go away when the course of the drug is finished.
- Intolerance to alcohol (nausea, vomiting, flushing, headache, and stomach pain)—Avoid alcoholic beverages or products containing alcohol while on this drug.

Report any of the following to your health care provider: sore throat, fever, or chills; skin rash or redness; severe GI upset; and unusual fatigue, clumsiness, or weakness.

Take the full course of your prescription. Never use this drug to self-treat any other infection or give it to any other person.

Tell any doctor, nurse, or other health care provider that you are taking this drug.

Keep this drug and all medications out of the reach of children.

This Teaching Checklist reflects general patient teaching guidelines. It is not meant to be a substitute for drug-specific teaching information, which is available in nursing drug guides.

tion with dizziness and weakness, *to prevent injury to the patient.* Provide oral hygiene and ready access to bathroom facilities as needed *to cope with GI effects.*

- Arrange for treatment of superinfections as appropriate *to prevent severe infections.*
- Provide small, frequent, nutritious meals if GI upset is severe *to ensure proper nutrition.* Monitor nutritional status and arrange a dietary consult as needed. Taking the drug with food may also decrease GI upset.
- Ensure that the patient should be instructed in the appropriate dosage regimen *to enhance patient knowledge about drug therapy and to promote compliance.*

The patient should:

Take safety precautions including changing position slowly and avoiding driving and hazardous tasks if CNS effects occur.

Take the drug with meals and try small, frequent meals if GI upset is a problem.

Report severe GI problems and interference with nutrition; fever and chills that may indicate the presence of a superinfection; and dizziness, unusual fatigue, or weakness that may indicate CNS effects (see Patient Teaching Checklist: Antiprotozoal Agents).

Evaluation

- Monitor patient response to the drug (resolution of infection and negative cultures for parasite).
- Monitor for adverse effects (orientation and affect, nutritional state, skin color and lesions, hepatic function, and occurrence of superinfections).
- Evaluate the effectiveness of the teaching plan (patient can name the drug, dosage, possible adverse effects to watch for, and specific measures to help avoid adverse effects).
- Monitor the effectiveness of comfort and safety measures and compliance with the regimen (see Nursing Care Guide: Antiprotozoal Agents).

NURSING CARE GUIDE
Antiprotozoal Agents

Assessment	Nursing Diagnoses	Implementation	Evaluation
HISTORY			
Allergies to any of these drugs, renal or liver dysfunction, pregnancy and lactation	Pain related to GI, superinfection effects	Culture infection prior to beginning therapy.	Evaluate drug effects: resolution of protozoal infection.
	Sensory, perceptual alterations related to CNS effects	Provide comfort and safety measures: oral hygiene, safety precautions, treatment of superinfections, maintenance of nutrition.	Monitor for adverse effects: GI alterations, dizziness, confusion, CNS changes, vision loss, renal, hepatic function, superinfections.
	Alteration in nutrition, less than body requirements related to GI effects	Provide small, frequent meals and monitor nutritional status.	Monitor for drug–drug interactions as indicated for each drug.
	Knowledge deficit regarding drug therapy	Provide support and reassurance for dealing with drug effects and discomfort.	Evaluate effectiveness of patient teaching program.
		Provide patient teaching regarding drug name, dosage, adverse effects, precautions, and warning signs to report and hygiene measures to observe.	Evaluate effectiveness of comfort and safety measures.
PHYSICAL EXAMINATION			
Local: culture of infection			
CNS: orientation, affect, vision, reflexes			
Skin: color, lesions, texture			
Respiratory: respiration rate, adventitious sounds			
GI: abdominal, liver evaluation			
Hematologic: renal and hepatic function tests			

CHAPTER SUMMARY

- A protozoa is a parasitic cellular organism. Its life cycle includes a parasitic phase inside human tissues or cells.
- Malaria, which occurs in many tropical parts of the world, has been spreading in recent years because of resistance to insecticides occurring in the *Anopheles* mosquito.
- Malaria is caused by *Plasmodium* protozoa, which must go through a cycle in the *Anopheles* mosquito before being passed to humans by the mosquito bite. Once in humans, the protozoa invades red blood cells.
- The characteristic cyclic chills and fever of malaria occur when red blood cells burst, releasing more protozoa into the bloodstream.
- Malaria is treated using a combination of drugs that attack the protozoan at various stages in its life cycle.
- Amebiasis is caused by the protozoan *Entamoeba histolytica,* which invades human intestinal tissue after being passed to humans through unsanitary food or water.
- Leishmaniasis, a protozoan-caused disease, can result in serious lesions in the mucosa, viscera, and skin.

- Trypanosomiasis, which is caused by infection with a *Trypanosoma* parasite, may assume two forms. African sleeping sickness leads to inflammation of the CNS, and Chagas' disease results in serious cardiomyopathy.
- Trichomoniasis is caused by *Trichomonas vaginalis.* This common cause of vaginitis results in no signs or symptoms in males but serious vaginal inflammation in females.
- Giardiasis, which is caused by *Giardia lamblia,* is the most commonly diagnosed intestinal parasite in the United States. This disease may lead to serious malnutrition when the pathogen invades intestinal mucosa.
- *Pneumocystis carinii* is an endemic protozoan that does not usually cause illness in humans unless humans become immune suppressed. *Pneumocystis carinii* pneumonia is the most common opportunistic infection seen in AIDS patients.
- Patients receiving antiprotozoal agents should be monitored regularly to detect any serious adverse effects, including loss of vision, liver toxicity, and so on.

Bibliography

Andrews, M., & Boyle, J. (1999). *Transcultural concepts in nursing care.* Philadelphia: Lippincott Williams & Wilkins.

Bullock, B. L. (2000). *Focus on pathophysiology.* Philadelphia: Lippincott Williams & Wilkins.

Hardman, J. G., Limbird, L. E., Molinoff, P. B., Ruddon, R. W., & Gilman, A. G. (Eds.). (1996). *Goodman and Gilman's the pharmacological basis of therapeutics* (9th ed.). New York: McGraw Hill.

Karch, A. M. (2000). *2000 Lippincott's nursing drug guide.* Philadelphia: Lippincott Williams & Wilkins.

Malseed, R. (1995). *Textbook of pharmacology and nursing care.* Philadelphia: Lippincott-Raven Publishers.

McEvoy, B. R. (Ed.). (1999). *Facts and comparisons 1999.* St. Louis: Facts and Comparisons.

Professional's guide to patient drug facts. (1999). St. Louis: Facts and Comparisons.

CHAPTER 11

Anthelmintic Agents

albendazole
ivermectin
P mebendazole
oxamniquine
praziquantel
pyrantel
thiabendazole

CHAPTER OUTLINE

INTRODUCTION
INTESTINE-INVADING WORMS
Nematodes
PINWORMS
WHIPWORMS
THREADWORMS
ROUNDWORMS
HOOKWORMS
Platyhelminths: Cestodes
TISSUE-INVADING WORM INFECTIONS
Trichinosis
Filariasis
Schistosomiasis
ANTHELMINTICS
THERAPEUTIC ACTIONS AND INDICATIONS
CONTRAINDICATIONS/CAUTIONS
ADVERSE EFFECTS
CLINICALLY IMPORTANT DRUG–DRUG INTERACTIONS
NURSING CONSIDERATIONS for patients receiving anthelmintics
Assessment
HISTORY
PHYSICAL ASSESSMENT
Nursing Diagnoses
Implementation
Evaluation
CHAPTER SUMMARY
BIBLIOGRAPHY

KEY TERMS

cestode
helminth
nematode
pinworm
roundworm
schistosomiasis
threadworm
trichinosis
whipworm

INTRODUCTION

About one billion people have worms in their gastrointestinal (GI) tract or other tissues, which makes helminthic infections among the most common of all diseases. These infestations are very common in tropical areas, but are also often found in other regions, including countries such as the United States and Canada. With so many people traveling in many parts of the world, it is not uncommon for a traveler to pick up a helminthic infection in another country and inadvertently bring it home, where the worms are able to infect other individuals. The ***helminths*** that most commonly infect humans are of two types: the ***nematodes*** or ***roundworms,*** and the platyhelminths or flatworms.

INTESTINE-INVADING WORMS

Many of the worms that infect humans live only in the intestinal tract. Proper diagnosis of a helminthic infection requires a stool examination for ova and parasites. Treatment of a helminthic infection entails the use of an anthelmintic drug. Another important part of therapy for helminthic infections involves the prevention of reinfection or spreading of existing infection. Measures such as thorough hand washing after using the toilet; frequent laundering of bed linens and underwear in very hot, chlorine-treated water; disinfection of toilets and bathroom areas after each use; and good personal hygiene to wash away ova are important to the effectiveness of drug therapy and prevention of the spread of the disease.

Nematodes

Nematodes, or roundworms, include the very commonly encountered ***pinworms, whipworms, threadworms,*** *Ascaris,* and hookworms. These worms cause diseases that range from mild to potentially deadly.

PINWORMS

Pinworms, which stay in the intestine, cause little discomfort except for perianal itching or occasional vaginal itching. Infection with pinworms is the most common helminthic infection among school-age children.

WHIPWORMS

Whipworms attach themselves to the wall of the colon, and when large numbers of them are in the intestine, they cause colic and bloody diarrhea. In severe cases, worm infestation may result in a prolapse of the intestinal wall and a blood–loss-related anemia.

THREADWORMS

Threadworms are more pervasive than most of the other helminths. After burrowing into the wall of the

---

NURSING CHALLENGE

Pinworm Infections

Infestations with worms can be a frightening and traumatic experience for most people. Seeing the worm can be an especially difficult experience. Some worm infestations are not that uncommon in this country, especially infestation with pinworms. Pinworms can spread very rapidly among children in schools, summer camps, and other institutions. Once the infestation starts, careful hygiene measures and drug therapy are required to eradicate the disease. After the diagnosis has been made and appropriate drug therapy started, proper hygiene measures will be essential. Some suggested hygiene measures that might help to control the infection include the following:

- Keep the child's nails cut short and hands well scrubbed, because reinfection results from the worm's eggs being carried back to the mouth after becoming lodged under the fingernails after scratching the pruritic perianal area.
- Give the child a shower in the morning to wash away any ova deposited in the anal area during the night.
- Change and launder undergarments, bed linens, and pajamas every day.
- Disinfect toilet seats daily and the floors of bathrooms and bedrooms periodically.
- Encourage the child to use vigorous hand washing after using the toilet.

In some areas of the country, parents are asked to check for worm ova by pressing sticky tape against the anal area in the morning before bathing. The sticky tape is then pressed against a slide that can be taken or sent to a clinical laboratory for evaluation. It may take 5 to 6 weeks to get a clear reading with this testing. Some health care providers feel that the psychological trauma involved in doing this type of follow-up, especially with a school-age child, makes this task too onerous to ask parents to do. Instead, many feel that the ease of treating this relatively harmless disease makes it more prudent to continue to treat as prescribed and to forgo the follow-up testing.

It is important to assure patients and families that these types of infections do not necessarily reflect negatively on their hygiene or lifestyle. It will take a coordinated effort between medical personnel, families, and patients to get control of pinworm infestations.

small intestine, female worms lay eggs, which hatch into larvae that invade many body tissues, including the lungs, liver, and heart. In very severe cases, death may occur from pneumonia or from lung or liver abscesses that result from larval invasion.

ROUNDWORMS

Worldwide, *Ascaris* infection is the most prevalent helminthic infection, which may occur wherever sanitation is poor. Although many individuals have no idea that they have this infestation unless they see a worm in their stool, some people may become quite ill.

Initially, the individual ingests fertilized worm eggs, which hatch in the small intestine and then make their way to the lungs, where they may cause cough, fever, and other signs of a pulmonary infiltrate. The larvae then migrate back to the intestine where they grow to adult size (i.e., about as long and as big around as an earthworm), and they can cause abdominal distention and pain. In the most severe cases, intestinal obstruction by masses of worms may occur.

HOOKWORMS

Hookworms attach themselves to the small intestine of infected individuals and suck blood from the walls of the intestine. This damages the intestinal wall and can cause severe anemia with lethargy, weakness, and fatigue. Malabsorption problems may occur as the small intestinal mucosa is altered. Treatment for anemia and fluid and electrolyte disturbances is an important part of the therapy for this infection.

Platyhelminths: Cestodes

The platyhelminths are flatworms that include the ***cestodes,*** or tapeworms, that live in the human intestine and flukes, or schistosomes, that invade other tissues as part of their life cycle. Cestodes are segmented flatworms with a head, or scolex, and a variable number of segments that grow from the head, which sometimes form worms that are several yards long. Individuals with a tapeworm may experience some abdominal discomfort and distention as well as weight loss, because the worm eats the ingested nutrients. Many affected patients require a great deal of psychological support when they excrete parts of the tapeworm or when the worm comes out the mouth or nose, which may occur occasionally.

TISSUE-INVADING WORM INFECTIONS

Some of the worms that invade the body exist outside of the intestinal tract and may seriously damage the tissues they invade. Because of their location within healthy tissue, they can also be more difficult to treat.

Trichinosis

Trichinosis is the disease caused by ingestion of the encysted larvae of the roundworm *Trichinella spiralis* in undercooked pork. The larvae of this worm, which is deposited in the intestinal mucosa, passes into the bloodstream and is carried throughout the body. They can penetrate skeletal muscle and can cause an inflammatory reaction in cardiac muscle and the brain. Fatal pneumonia, heart failure, and encephalitis may occur.

The best treatment for this trichinosis is prevention. Because the larvae are ingested by humans in undercooked pork, freezing meats, monitoring the food eaten by pigs, and instructing people in the proper cooking of pork can be most beneficial.

Filariasis

Filariasis refers to infection of the blood and tissues of healthy individuals by worm embryos, which are injected by biting insects. These threadlike embryos, or filariae, can overwhelm the lymphatic system and cause massive inflammatory reactions. This may lead to severe swelling of the hands, feet, legs, arms, scrotum, or breast—a condition called elephantiasis.

Schistosomiasis

Schistosomiasis (Figure 11-1) is an infection by a fluke that is carried by a snail. This disease is a common problem in parts of Africa, Asia, and certain South American and Caribbean countries that have climates and snails conducive to the life cycle of *Schistosoma.*

A description of the life cycle of *Schistosoma* follows. The eggs, which are excreted in the urine and feces of infected individuals, hatch in freshwater into a form that infects a certain snail. Larvae, known as cercariae, develop in the snail, which sheds the cercariae back into the freshwater pond or lake. People become infected when they come in contact with the infested water. The larvae attach to the skin and quickly burrow into the bloodstream and lymphatics. After they move into the lungs and later the liver, they mature into adult worms that mate and migrate to the intestines and urinary bladder. The female worms then lay large numbers of eggs, which are expelled in the feces and urine, and the cycle begins again.

Signs and symptoms of infection with this helminth may be a pruritic rash where the larva attaches to the skin, which is often called swimmer's itch. About 1 or 2 months later, affected individuals may suffer several weeks of fever, chills, headache, and other symptoms. Chronic or severe infestation may

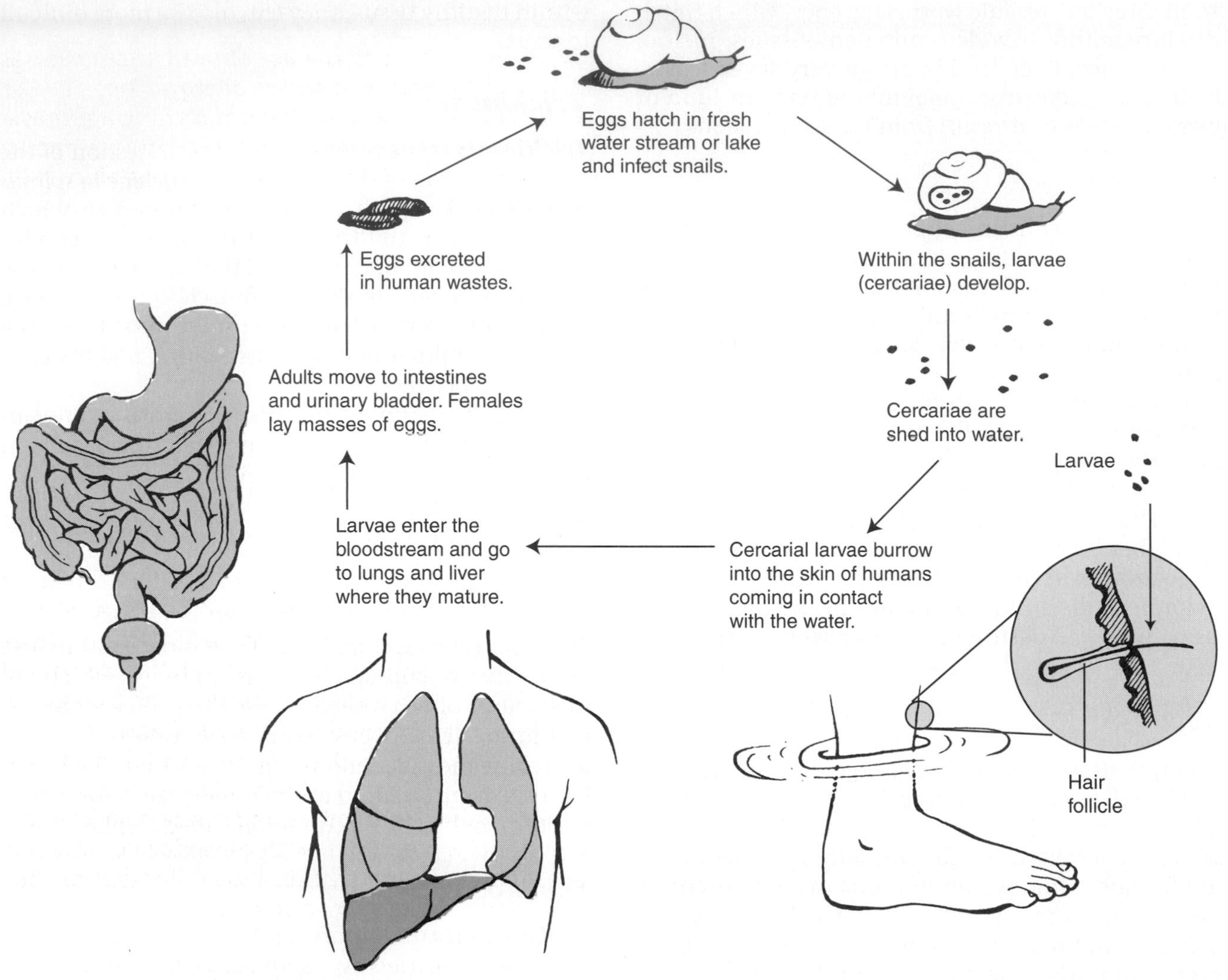
Eggs hatch in fresh
water stream or lake
and infect snails.
Within the snails, larvae
(cercariae) develop.
Cercariae are
shed into water.
Larvae
Cercarial larvae burrow
into the skin of humans
coming in contact
with the water.
Hair
follicle
Larvae enter the
bloodstream and go
to lungs and liver
where they mature.
Adults move to intestines
and urinary bladder. Females
lay masses of eggs.
Eggs excreted
in human wastes.

FIGURE 11-1. Life cycle of *Schistosoma.*

lead to abdominal pain and diarrhea as well as blocking of blood flow to areas of the liver, lungs, and central nervous system (CNS). These blockages can lead to liver and spleen enlargement as well as signs of CNS and cardiac ischemia.

ANTHELMINTICS

The anthelmintic drugs act on metabolic pathways that are present in the invading worm, but are absent or significantly different in the human host. Mebendazole (*Vermox*), probably the most commonly used of all of the anthelmintics, is effective against pinworms, roundworms, whipworms, and hookworms. It is available in the form of a chewable tablet, and a typical 3-day course can be repeated in 3 weeks if needed. Because mebendazole is rarely absorbed systemically, it has few adverse effects. It should not be used during pregnancy because of possible fetal harm.

Pyrantel (*Antiminth, Pin-Rid,* and others) is an oral drug that is effective against pinworms and roundworms. Because this agent is given as a single dose, it may be preferred for patients who may have trouble remembering to take medications or follow drug regimens. Adverse effects associated with pyrantel include possibly uncomfortable GI side effects and diarrhea.

Thiabendazole (*Mintezol*) may also be used in the treatment of roundworm, hookworm, and whipworm infections, but it is not the drug of choice if one of the other drugs can be used because it is not as effective as these other agents and may cause more uncomfortable adverse effects. However, this agent is the drug of choice for therapy of threadworm infections, and it can be used to alleviate the signs and symptoms of invasive trichinosis.

CULTURAL CONSIDERATIONS

Travelers and Helminths

People who come from or travel to areas of the world where schistosomiasis is endemic should always be assessed for the possibility of infection with such a disease when seen for health care. Areas of the world in which this disease is endemic are mainly tropical settings, such as Puerto Rico, islands of the West Indies, Africa, parts of South America, the Philippines, China, Japan, and Southeast Asia. People traveling to these areas should be warned about wading, swimming, or bathing in fresh-water streams, ponds, or lakes. For example, swimming in the Nile is a popular attraction on Egyptian vacation tours; however, this activity may result in a lasting (unhappy) memory when the traveler returns home and is diagnosed with schistosomiasis. The nurse can suggest to patients who are planning a visit to one of these areas that they contact the Centers for Disease Control and Prevention (CDC) for health and safety guidelines, as well as things to watch for when returning home. The CDC can be reached on-line at http://www.cdc.gov/travel

Oxamniquine (*Vansil*), an oral drug, is useful in the treatment of all stages of schistosomal infection with *Schistosoma mansoni.*

Albendazole (*Albenza*) is effective against active lesions caused by pork tapeworm and cystic disease of the liver, lungs, and peritoneum caused by dog tapeworm. A very powerful drug, albendazole has serious adverse effects, including renal failure and bone marrow depression. It should only be used when the causative worm has been identified.

Ivermectin (*Stromectol*) is effective against the nematode that causes onchocerciasis, or river blindness, which is found in tropical areas of Africa, Mexico, and South America. The drug is also used to treat threadworm disease or strongyloidiasis. Ivermectin should never be taken during pregnancy, because it can cause serious fetal harm.

Praziquantel (*Biltricide*) is very effective in the treatment of a wide number of schistosomiases or flukes. This drug, which is taken in a series of three doses at 4- to 6-hour intervals, has relatively few adverse effects.

THERAPEUTIC ACTIONS AND INDICATIONS

Anthelmintics are indicated for the treatment of infections by certain susceptible worms and are not interchangeable. Anthelmintics interfere with metabolic processes in particular worms, as noted above (Figure 11-2).

CONTRAINDICATIONS/CAUTIONS

Contraindications to the use of anthelmintic drugs include the presence of known allergy to any of these drugs; lactation, because the drugs can enter breast milk and could be toxic to the infant; and pregnancy (in most cases), because of reported associated fetal abnormalities or death. Caution should be used with renal or hepatic disease that interferes with the metabolism or excretion of drugs that are absorbed systemically and in cases of severe diarrhea and malnourishment, which could alter the effects of the drug on the intestine and any preexisting helminths.

ADVERSE EFFECTS

Adverse effects frequently encountered with the use of these anthelmintic agents are related to their absorption or direct action in the intestine. Mebendazole and pyrantel are not generally absorbed systemically and may cause abdominal discomfort, diarrhea, or pain. Anthelmintics that are absorbed systemically may cause the following effects: headache and dizziness; fever, shaking, chills, and malaise associated with an immune reaction to the death of the worms; and rash, pruritus, and loss of hair. Changes in protein synthesis by the liver to Stevens-Johnson syndrome is associated with thiabendazole use (this may be fatal). Also, renal failure and severe bone marrow depression is associated with albendazole, which is quite toxic to some human tissue. Patients on this drug should be monitored carefully.

CLINICALLY IMPORTANT DRUG–DRUG INTERACTIONS

Combinations of theophylline and thiabendazole may lead to increased theophylline levels, and patients who take both these drugs may require frequent monitoring and dosage reduction. The effects of albendazole, which are already severe, may increase if the drug is combined with dexamethasone, praziquantel, or cimetidine. These combinations should be avoided if at all possible, and if they are necessary, patients should be monitored closely for occurrence of adverse effects.

DATA LINK

Data link to the following anthelmintics in your nursing drug guide:

ANTHELMINTICS

Name	Brand Name	Usual Indications
albendazole	*Albenza*	Treatment of active lesions caused by pork tapeworm and cystic disease of the liver, lungs, and peritoneum caused by dog tapeworm.

CASE STUDY

Anthelmintics

PRESENTATION

V. Y., a 33-year-old Vietnamese man, underwent a complete physical examination in preparation for a training job in custodial work at a local hospital. He was a refugee who came to the United States 6 months ago as part of a church-sponsored resettlement program. In the course of the examination, it was found that he had a history of chronic diarrhea, hepatomegaly, pulmonary rales, and splenomegaly. Further tests indicated that he had chronic schistosomiasis. Because of V. Y.'s limited use of the English language, he was hospitalized so that his disease, which was unfamiliar to most of the associated health care providers, could be monitored. He was treated with praziquantel.

CRITICAL THINKING QUESTIONS

What are the important nursing implications for V. Y.? Think about the serious limitations that are placed on medical care, particularly patient teaching, when the patient and the health care workers do not speak the same language. What innovative techniques could be used to teach this patient about the disease, the drugs, and the hygiene measures that are important for him to follow? Are the other patients or workers in the hospital exposed to any health risks? What sort of educational program should be developed to teach them about this disease and to allay any fears or anxieties they may have? What special interventions are needed to explain the drug therapy and any adverse effects or warning signs that V. Y. should be watching for?

DISCUSSION

A language barrier can be a real handicap in the health care system. In many cases, pictures can assist communication. For example, the need for nutritious foods is conveyed by using appropriate pictures of foods that should be eaten. Frequent reinforcement is necessary, because the patient has no way of letting you know that he really understands the message that you are trying to convey. The patient is prepared for discharge through careful patient teaching that may involve pictures, calendars, and clocks so that he is given every opportunity to comply with his medical regimen.

In addition, the nursing staff should contact the local health department to determine whether the local sewer system can properly handle contaminated wastes. In this case, the staff learned from the Centers for Disease Control and Prevention (CDC) that the snail intermediate host does not live in this country, so the hazards posed by this waste are small and normal disposal of the wastes should be appropriate.

V. Y. is also observed for signs of adverse effects, although praziquantel is a relatively mild drug. Drug fever, abdominal pain, or dizziness may occur. If dizziness occurs, safety precautions, such as assistance with ambulation, use of side rails, and adequate lighting, will need to be taken without alarming the patient.

ivermectin	*Stromectol*	Treatment of threadworm disease or strongyloidiasis; onchocersiasis or river blindness
P mebendazole	*Vermox*	Treatment of diseases caused by pinworms, roundworms, whipworms, and hookworms
oxamniquine	*Vansil*	Treatment of all stages of schistosomal infection with *Schistosoma mansoni*
praziquantel	*Biltricide*	Treatment of a wide number of schistosomiases or flukes
pyrantel	*Antiminth, Pin-Rid*	Treatment of diseases caused by pinworms and roundworms
thiabendazole	*Mintezol*	Treatment of diseases caused by roundworms, hookworms, and whipworms

NURSING CONSIDERATIONS
for patients receiving anthelmintics

Assessment

HISTORY. Screen for the following: history of allergy to any of the anthelmintics; hepatic or renal dysfunction that might interfere with the metabolism and excretion of the drug; pregnancy, which is a contraindication to the use of some of these agents because of reported effects on the fetus; lactation, because these drugs could enter the breast milk and be toxic to the infant.

PHYSICAL ASSESSMENT. Physical assessment should be performed to establish baseline data for determining the effectiveness of the drug and the occurrence of any adverse effects associated with drug therapy. Obtain a culture of stool for ova and parasites to determine the infecting worm and establish appropriate treatment. Examine reflexes and muscle strength to evaluate changes that occur as a result of drug therapy. Conduct hepatic evaluation, including liver function tests, to determine appropriateness of therapy and to monitor for toxicity. Check renal function tests to determine appropriateness of therapy and to monitor for toxicity. Examine skin (lesions, color, temperature, texture) to

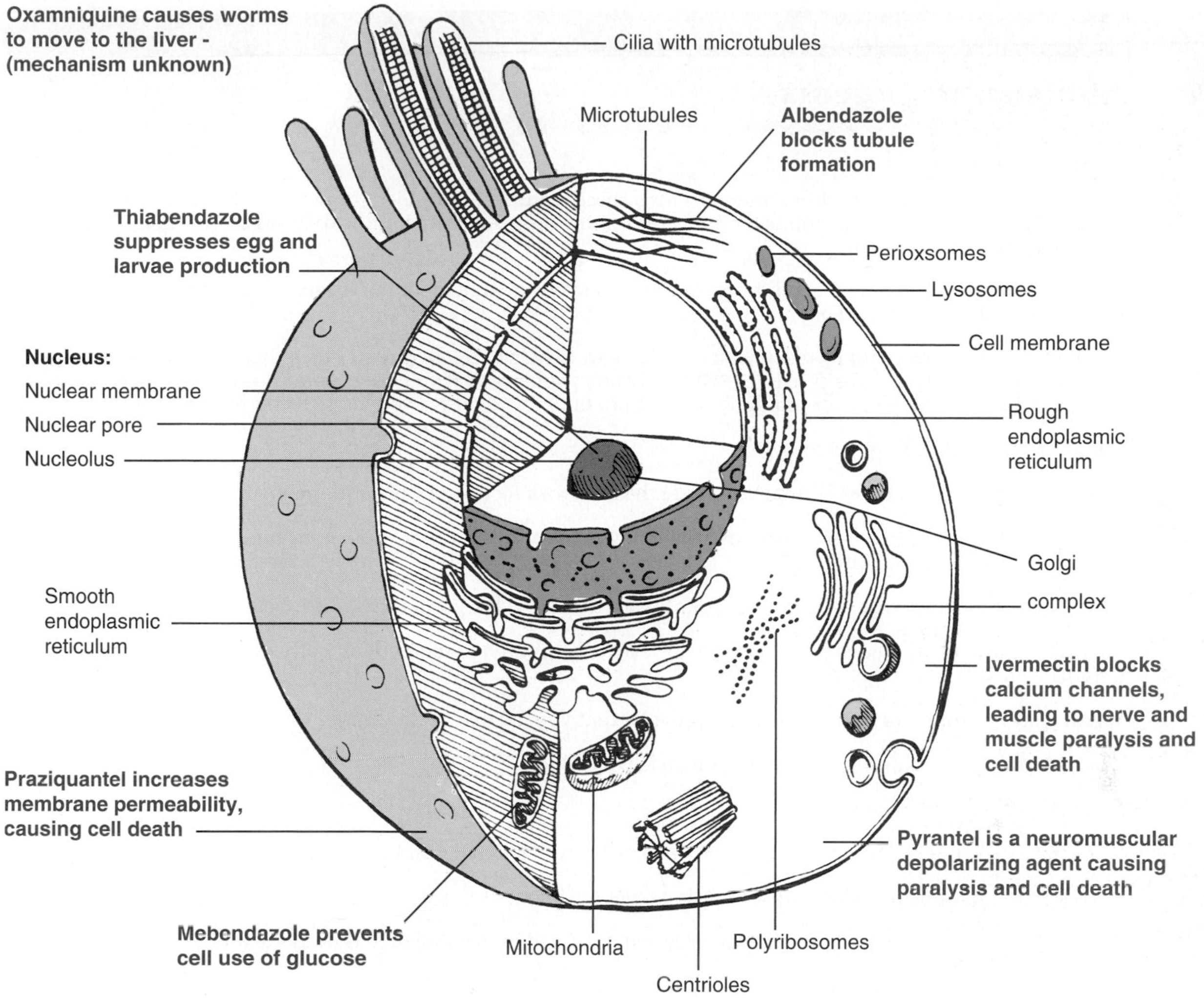
Oxamniquine causes worms to move to the liver - (mechanism unknown)
Cilia with microtubules
Microtubules
Albendazole blocks tubule formation
Thiabendazole suppresses egg and larvae production
Perioxsomes
Lysosomes
Cell membrane
Nucleus:
Nuclear membrane
Nuclear pore
Nucleolus
Rough endoplasmic reticulum
Golgi
complex
Smooth endoplasmic reticulum
Ivermectin blocks calcium channels, leading to nerve and muscle paralysis and cell death
Praziquantel increases membrane permeability, causing cell death
Pyrantel is a neuromuscular depolarizing agent causing paralysis and cell death
Mebendazole prevents cell use of glucose
Mitochondria
Polyribosomes
Centrioles

FIGURE 11-2. General structure of a cell, showing the sites of action of the anthelmintic agents. Mebendazole interferes with the ability to use glucose, leading to an inability to reproduce and cell death. Albendazole blocks tubule formation, resulting in cell death. Oxamniquine causes male worms to move to the liver, where they are trapped, and female worms to stop laying eggs; the exact mechanism is unknown. Ivermectin blocks calcium channels, leading to nerve and muscle paralysis and cell death. Pyrantel is a neuromuscular polarizing agent that causes paralysis and cell death. Thiabendazole both suppresses egg and larva production and blocks a helminth-specific enzyme that promotes the development of eggs and larvae. Praziquantel increases membrane permeability, leading to a loss of intracellular calcium and muscular paralysis; it may also result in disintegration of the integument.

monitor for adverse effects and abdomen to evaluate any baseline changes related to the infection and to monitor for improvement and the possibility of adverse effects.

Nursing Diagnoses

The patient receiving an anthelmintic drug may have the following nursing diagnoses related to drug therapy:

- Pain related to GI, CNS, skin effects of drug
- Alteration in self concept related to diagnosis and treatment
- Knowledge deficit regarding drug therapy

Implementation

- Arrange for appropriate culture and sensitivity tests before beginning therapy *to ensure that the appropriate drug is being used.*

PATIENT TEACHING CHECKLIST

Anthelmintic Agents

Create customized patient teaching materials for a specific anthelmintic agent from your CD-ROM. Your patient teaching should stress the following points for drugs within this class: An anthelmintic destroys certain helminths, or worms, that have invaded your body.

It is important that you take the full course of the drug to ensure that all of the worms, in all phases of their life cycle, have disappeared from your body.

You may take this drug with meals or with a light snack to help decrease any stomach upset that you may experience. If you have chewable tablets, be sure to chew them before swallowing. If you have regular tablets, swallow them whole and avoid holding them in your mouth for any length of time, because a very unpleasant taste may occur.

Common effects of this drug include:

- Nausea, vomiting, and loss of appetite—Take the drug with food, and eat small, frequent meals.
- Dizziness and drowsiness—If this occurs, avoid driving a car or operating dangerous machinery. Change positions slowly to avoid falling or injury.

Report any of the following conditions to your health care provider: fever, chills, rash, headache, weakness, or tremors.

Take all the drug(s) that have been prescribed. Never use this drug to self-treat any other infection or give it to any other person.

Tell any doctor, nurse, or other health care provider that you are taking this drug.

Keep this drug and all medications out of the reach of children.

For intestinal worm infections

Some measures that help prevent worm reinfection or spread to other family members include the following:

- Vigorous hand washing with soap after using toilet facilities.
- Showering in the morning to wash away any ova deposited in the anal area during the night.
- Changing and laundering undergarments, bed linens, and pajamas daily.
- Disinfecting toilets and toilet seats daily and bathroom and bedroom floors periodically.

This Teaching Checklist reflects general patient teaching guidelines. It is not meant to be a substitute for drug-specific teaching information, which is available in nursing drug guides.

- Administer the complete course of the drug *to obtain the full beneficial effects.* Ensure that chewable tablets are chewed. The drug may be taken with food if necessary, and high-fat meals that might interfere with drug effectiveness should be avoided.
- Monitor hepatic and renal function prior to and periodically during treatment *to arrange to stop administration of albendazole if signs of failure occur.*
- Provide comfort and safety measures including siderails and assistance with ambulation if CNS effects occur, such as dizziness and weakness, *to protect patient from injury.* Provide oral hygiene and ready access to bathroom facilities as needed *to cope with GI effects.*
- Provide small, frequent, nutritious meals if GI upset is severe *to ensure adequate nutrition.* Monitor nutritional status and arrange a dietary consult as needed. Taking the drug with food may also decrease GI upset.
- Ensure that the patient is instructed about the appropriate dosage regimen and other measured *to enhance patient knowledge about drug therapy and to promote compliance.*

The patient should:

Take safety precautions, including changing position slowly and avoiding driving and hazardous tasks if CNS effects occur.

Take the drug with meals and try small, frequent meals if GI upset is a problem.

Note the importance of strict hand washing and hygiene measures, including daily laundering of underwear and bed linens, daily disinfection of toilet facilities, and periodic disinfection of bathroom floors.

NURSING CARE GUIDE
Anthelmintic Agents

Assessment	Nursing Diagnoses	Implementation	Evaluation
HISTORY Allergies to any of these drugs, renal or liver dysfunction, pregnancy or lactation	Pain related to GI, CNS effects	Culture for ova and parasites prior to beginning therapy.	Evaluate drug effects: resolution of helminth infection.
	Sensory, perceptual alterations related to CNS effects	Provide comfort and safety measures: antipruritics for anal rash, small, frequent meals, safety precautions, hygiene measures, maintenance of nutrition.	Monitor for adverse effects: GI alterations, CNS changes, dizziness and confusion, renal and hepatic function.
	Knowledge deficit regarding drug therapy	Monitor nutritional status as needed.	Monitor for drug–drug interactions as indicated for each drug.
		Provide support and reassurance to deal with drug effects, discomfort, and diagnosis.	Evaluate effectiveness of patient teaching program.
		Provide patient teaching regarding drug name, dosage regimen, adverse effects and precautions to report, and hygiene measures to observe.	Evaluate effectiveness of comfort and safety measures.
PHYSICAL EXAMINATION Local: culture of infection CNS: orientation, affect Skin: color, lesions, texture GI: abdominal and liver evaluation, including hepatic function tests GU: renal function tests			

Report fever, severe diarrhea, or aggravation of condition, which could indicate a resistant strain or noneffective therapy, to a health care provider (see Patient Teaching Checklist: Anthelmintic Agents).

Evaluation

- Monitor patient response to the drug (resolution of helminth infestation and improvement in signs and symptoms).
- Monitor for adverse effects (orientation and effect, nutritional state, skin color and lesions, hepatic and renal function, and abdominal discomfort and pain).
- Evaluate the effectiveness of the teaching plan (patient can name the drug, dosage, possible adverse effects to watch for, and specific measures to help avoid adverse effects).
- Monitor the effectiveness of comfort and safety measures and compliance with the regimen (see Nursing Care Guide: Anthelmintic Agents).

WWW.WEB LINKS

Health care providers and patients may want to consult the following Internet sources:

Information on pinworms:
http://www.aafp.org/patientinfo/pinworms.html

Information on preventing and dealing with pinworm infections:

http://www.rockwoodclinic.com/abc.htm

Information on schistosomiasis—incidence, precautions, treatments:

http://www.who.int/ctd/html/schisto.html

Information about other intestinal parasites:

http://www.cdfound.to.it/html/intpar1.html

Information for travelers about potential helminth infestations, precautions, treatments, warning signs:

http://www.cdc.gov/travel

CHAPTER SUMMARY

- Helminths are worms that cause disease by invading the human body. Helminths that affect humans include nematodes (round-shaped worms) such as pinworms, hookworms, threadworms, whipworms, and roundworms.
- Pinworms are the most frequent helminth infection in the United States, and roundworms or *Ascaris* are the most frequent cause of helminth infections throughout the world.
- Platyhelminths (flatworms) include tapeworms and flukes.
- Some helminths invade body tissues and can seriously damage lymphatic tissue, lungs, CNS, heart, liver, and so on. These include trichinosis-causing tapeworms found in undercooked pork; filariae, which occur when threadlike worm embryos clog up vascular spaces; and schistosomiasis-causing flukes, which can invade the liver, lungs, CNS, and so on. Schistosomiasis is a common problem in many tropical areas in which the snail that is necessary in the life cycle of the fluke lives.
- Anthelmintic drugs affect metabolic processes that are either different in worms than in human hosts or are not found in humans. These agents all cause death of the worm by interfering with normal functioning.
- Prevention is a very important part of the treatment of helminths. Thorough hand washing; laundering of bed linens, pajamas, and underwear to destroy ova that are shed during the night; and disinfection of toilet facilities daily (at least) and bathroom floors periodically help stop spread of these disease. In addition, proper sanitation and hygiene in food preparation and storage is also essential for reducing the incidence of these infestations.
- Patient teaching is important for decreasing the stress and anxiety that may occur when individuals are diagnosed with a worm infestation.

BIBLIOGRAPHY

Andrews, M. & Boyle, J. (1999). *Transcultural concepts in nursing care.* Philadelphia: Lippincott Williams & Wilkins.

Bullock, B. L. (2000). *Focus on pathophysiology.* Philadelphia: Lippincott Williams & Wilkins.

Gilman, A. G., Rall, T. W., Nies, A. S., & and Taylor, P. (Eds.). (1997). *Goodman and Gilman's the pharmacological basis of therapeutics* (9th ed.). New York: McGraw Hill.

Karch, A. M. (1999). *2000 Lippincott's nursing drug guide.* Philadelphia: Lippincott Williams & Wilkins.

Malseed, R. (1995). *Textbook of pharmacology and nursing care.* Philadelphia: Lippincott-Raven Publishers.

McEvoy, B. R. (Ed.). (1999). *Facts and comparisons 1999.* St. Louis: Facts and Comparisons.

Professional's guide to patient drug facts. (1999). St. Louis: Facts and Comparisons.

CHAPTER 12

Antineoplastic Agents

Alkylating agents
- busulfan
- carboplatin
- carmustine
- P chlorambucil
- cisplatin
- cyclophosphamide
- ifosfamide
- lomustine
- mechlorethamine
- melphalan
- streptozocin
- thiotepa

Antimetabolites
- cytarabine
- floxuridine
- fludarabine
- fluorouracil
- mercaptopurine
- P methotrexate
- thioguanine

Antineoplastic antibiotics
- bleomycin
- dactinomycin
- daunorubicin
- P doxorubicin
- idarubicin
- mitomycin
- mitoxantrone
- pentostatin
- plicamycin

Mitotic inhibitors
- etoposide
- teniposide
- vinblastine
- P vincristine
- vinorelbine

Hormones and hormone modulators
- anastrazole
- estramustine
- letrozole
- P tamoxifen
- testolactone
- toremifene

Miscellaneous antineoplastic agents
- altretamine
- asparaginase
- cladribine
- dacarbazine
- docetaxel
- gemcitabine
- hydroxyurea
- irinotecan
- mitotane
- paclitaxel
- pegasparagase
- porfimer
- procarbazine
- topotecan
- tretinoin

Antineoplastic adjunctive therapy
- amifostine
- dexrazoxane
- leucovorin
- mesna

CHAPTER OUTLINE

KEY TERMS

alopecia
anaplasia
antineoplastic drug
autonomy
bone marrow suppression
carcinoma
metastasis
neoplasm
sarcoma

INTRODUCTION

One branch of chemotherapy involves drugs developed to act on and kill or alter human cells—the ***antineoplastic drugs,*** which are designed to fight ***neoplasms*** or cancers. When chemotherapy is mentioned, most people think of cancer treatment. Antineoplastic drugs alter human cells in a variety of ways, and it is hoped that they have a greater impact on the abnormal cells that make up the neoplasm or cancer. This area of pharmacology, which has grown tremendously in recent years, now includes many drugs that act on or are part of the immune system; these substances fight the cancerous cells using components of the immune system instead of destroying cells directly (Chapter 13). This chapter discusses the classic antineoplastic approach and those drugs that are used in cancer chemotherapy.

NEOPLASMS

Cancer is a disease that can strike a person at any age. It remains second only to coronary disease as the leading cause of death in the United States. Treatment of cancer can be a long and debilitating experience that leads to many disabilities in adults.

All cancers start with a single cell that is genetically different from the other cells in the surrounding tissue. This cell divides, passing along its abnormalities to daughter cells, eventually producing a tumor or neoplasm that has characteristics quite different from the original tissue. The cancerous cells exhibit ***anaplasia,*** a loss of cellular differentiation and organization, which leads to a loss of their ability to function normally. They also exhibit ***autonomy,*** growing without the usual homeostatic restrictions that regulate cell growth and control, which allows the cells to form a tumor.

Over time, these neoplastic cells grow uncontrollably, invading and damaging healthy tissue in the area and even undergoing ***metastasis,*** or traveling from the place of origin to develop new tumors in other areas of the body where conditions are favorable for cell growth (Figure 12-1). The abnormal cells release enzymes that generate blood vessels in the area to supply both oxygen and nutrients to the cells, thus contributing to their growth. Overall, the cancerous cells rob the host cells of energy and nutrients and block normal lymph and vascular vessels as the result of pressure and intrusion on normal cells, leading to a loss of normal cellular function.

The body's immune system can damage some neoplastic cells. T cells, which recognize the abnormal cells and destroy them; antibodies, which form in response to parts of the abnormal cell protein; interferons; and tissue necrosis factor all play a role in the body's attempt to eliminate the abnormal cells before they become uncontrollable and threaten the life of the host. Once the neoplasm has grown and enlarged, it may overwhelm the immune system, which is no longer able to manage the problem.

Causes of Cancer

What causes the cells to mutate and become genetically different is not clearly understood. In some cases, a genetic predisposition to such a mutation can be found. Breast cancer, for example, seems to have a definite genetic link. In other cases, viral infection, constant irritation and cell turnover, and even stress have been blamed for the ensuing cancer. Stress reactions suppress the activities of the immune system

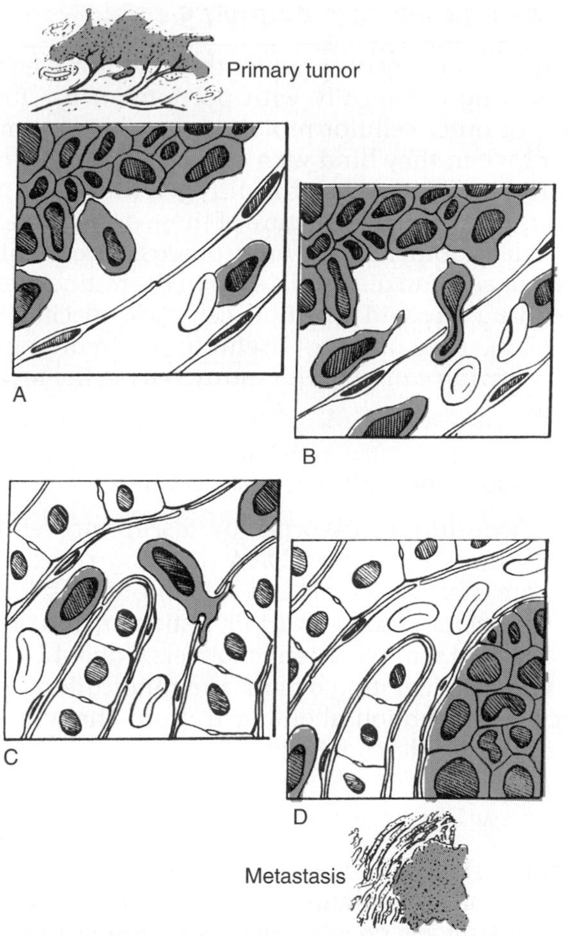

FIGURE 12-1. Metastasis of cancer cells. (*A*) Growth of primary tumor and invasion of the surrounding tissues. (*B*) Movement of tumor cells into the endothelium and basement membrane of the surrounding capillary. (*C*) Shed tumor cells in lungs, brain, liver become trapped and penetrate the capillary wall to establish themselves in this new environment. (*D*) Proliferation at the new site, which requires a conducive environment with blood supply and nutrition.

(Chapter 27), so if a cell is mutating while a person is under prolonged stress, research indicates that the cell has a better chance of growing into a neoplasm than when the person's immune system is fully active. Pipe smokers are at increased risk for developing tongue and mouth cancers because the heat and chemicals in the pipe are constantly destroying normal cells, which must be replaced rapidly, increasing the chances for the development of a mutant cell. People living in areas with carcinogenic or cancer-causing chemicals in the air, water, or even the ground are at increased risk of developing mutant cells as a reaction to these toxic chemicals. Cancer clusters are often identified in such high-risk areas. Most likely, a mosaic of factors coming together in one person leads to development of the neoplasm.

Types of Cancer

Cancers can be divided into two groups: (1) solid tumors, and (2) hematologic malignancies such as the leukemias and lymphomas, which occur in the blood-forming organs. Solid tumors may originate in any body organ and may be further divided into ***carcinomas,*** or tumors that originate in epithelial cells, and ***sarcomas,***or tumors that originate in the mesenchyma and are made up of embryonic connective tissue cells. Examples of carcinomas include granular cell tumors of the breast, bronchogenic tumors arising in cells lining the bronchial tubes, and squamous and basal tumors of the skin. Sarcomas include osteogenic tumors, which form in the primitive cells of the bone, and rhabdomyosarcomas, which occur in striated muscles.

ANTINEOPLASTIC DRUGS

Antineoplastic drugs can work by affecting cell survival or boosting the immune system in its efforts to combat the abnormal cells. Chapter 15 discusses the immune agents that are used to combat cancer. This chapter focuses on those drugs that affect cell survival. The antineoplastic drugs that are commonly used today include the alkylating agents, antimetabolites, antineoplastic antibiotics, mitotic inhibitors, hormones and hormone modulators, and a group of antineoplastic agents that cannot be classified elsewhere.

As discussed in Chapter 5, all cells progress through a cell cycle. Different types of cells progress at different rates. Rapidly multiplying cells, or cells that replace themselves quickly, include those that line the gastrointestinal (GI) tract and those in hair follicles, skin, and bone marrow. These cells complete the cell cycle every few days. Cells that proceed very slowly through the cell cycle include those in the breasts, testicles, and ovaries. Some cells take weeks, months, or even years to complete the cycle.

Cancer cells tend to move through the cell cycle at about the same rate as their cells of origin, and malignant cells that remain in a dormant phase for long periods of time are difficult to destroy. These cells can emerge long after cancer treatment has finished—after weeks, months, or years—to begin their division and growth cycle all over again. For this reason, antineoplastic agents are often given in sequence over periods of time, in the hope that the drugs will affect the cancer cells as they emerge from dormancy or move into a new phase of the cell cycle.

The adverse effects of cancer chemotherapy are often unpleasant and debilitating, and it is essential that patients understand the importance of returning every few weeks to go through the chemotherapy, with its adverse effects, over and over again. Most cancer patients are not considered to be "cured" until they have been cancer-free for a period of 5 years because of the possibility of cancer cells emerging from dormancy and causing new tumors or problems. No cells have yet been identified that can remain dormant for longer than 5 years, so the chances of the emergence of one after that time are very slim.

The goal of cancer therapy, much like that of anti-infective therapy, is to limit the offending cells enough so that the immune system can control them without causing too much toxicity to the host. However, this is a particularly difficult task when using antineoplastic drugs, because these agents are not specific to mutant cells but affect human cells, too. In most cases, antineoplastic drugs primarily affect rapidly multiplying human cells, which have many cells in many phases of the cell cycle (e.g., those in the hair follicles, GI tract, bone marrow). Some of these drugs also influence fertility as a result of toxic effects on ova and sperm production. In addition, these agents are usually selective for rapidly growing cells, so they are dangerous during pregnancy. Because of the possible occurrence of serious fetal effects, pregnancy is a contraindication to the use of antineoplastic drugs.

Cancer treatment is aimed at destroying cancer cells by using several methods: surgery to remove them, stimulation of the immune system to destroy them, radiation therapy to destroy the cells, or drug therapy to kill the cells during various phases of the cell cycle. To do this effectively, without too much damage to the host, combination therapy is often most successful. Surgery, followed by radiation and/or chemotherapy, is very effective with some cancers. A collection of chemotherapeutic agents that work at different phases of the cell cycle is frequently most effective in treating many cancers. Your nursing drug guide presents the most frequently used combinations of chemotherapeutic agents and the types of cancer against which they are most effective.

Many antineoplastic drugs often result in another adverse effect, cancer itself, because they cause cell death, leading to the need for cell growth and the increased risk of mutant cell development. In addition, they jeopardize the immune system by causing ***bone marrow suppression,*** inhibiting the blood-forming components of the bone marrow and interfering with the body's normal protective actions against abnormal cells. Other specific adverse effects may occur with particular drugs, but the patient's hematologic profile will always need to be assessed for toxic effects.

A cancerous mass may be so large that no therapy can arrest its growth without killing the host. In such cases, cancer chemotherapeutic agents are used as palliative therapy to shrink the size of the tumor and alleviate some of the signs and symptoms of the cancer, decreasing pain and increasing function. Here the goal of drug therapy is not to cure the disease but to try to improve the quality of life in a situation where there is no cure.

ALKYLATING AGENTS

The alkylating agents produce their cytotoxic effects by reacting chemically with portions of the RNA, DNA, or other cellular proteins, and they are most potent when they bind with cellular DNA. The oldest drugs in this class are the nitrogen mustards, and modifications of the structure of these drugs have led to the development of the nitrosoureas. Because alkylating agents can affect cells even in the resting phase, these drugs are said to be non–cell-cycle-specific (Figure 12-2). They are most useful in the treatment of slow-growing cancers, with many cells in the resting phase.

THERAPEUTIC ACTIONS AND INDICATIONS

The alkylating agents work by disrupting cellular mechanisms that affect DNA, causing cell death. They are effective against various lymphomas; leukemias; myelomas; some ovarian, testicular, and breast cancers; and some pancreatic cancers. Table 12-1 lists the various alkylating agents, their indications, and specific information about each drug. These agents are not used interchangeably.

CONTRAINDICATIONS/CAUTIONS

Caution should be used when giving alkylating agents to any individual with a known allergy to any of the alkylating agents; during pregnancy or lactation when these drugs are contraindicated because of potential severe effects on the neonate; with bone marrow suppression, which is often the index for redosing and dosing levels; or with suppressed renal or hepatic function, which may interfere with the metabolism or excretion of these drugs and often indicates a need to change the dosage.

ADVERSE EFFECTS

Adverse effects frequently encountered with the use of these alkylating agents are listed below. Table 12-1 indicates the most common adverse effects for each agent. Amifostine (*Ethyol*) and mesna (*Mesnex*) are cytoprotective (cell-protecting) drugs that may be given to limit certain effects of cisplatin and ifosfamid, respectively (Box 12-1).

Hematologic effects include bone marrow suppression, with leukopenia, thrombocytopenia, anemia, and pancytopenia secondary to the effects of the drugs on the rapidly multiplying cells of the bone marrow. GI effects include nausea, vomiting, anorexia, diarrhea, and mucous membrane deterioration, all of which are related to the drugs' effects on the rapidly multiplying cells of the GI tract. Hepatic toxicity and renal toxicity may occur, depending on the exact mechanism of action. ***Alopecia,*** or hair loss, related to effects on the hair follicles, may also occur.

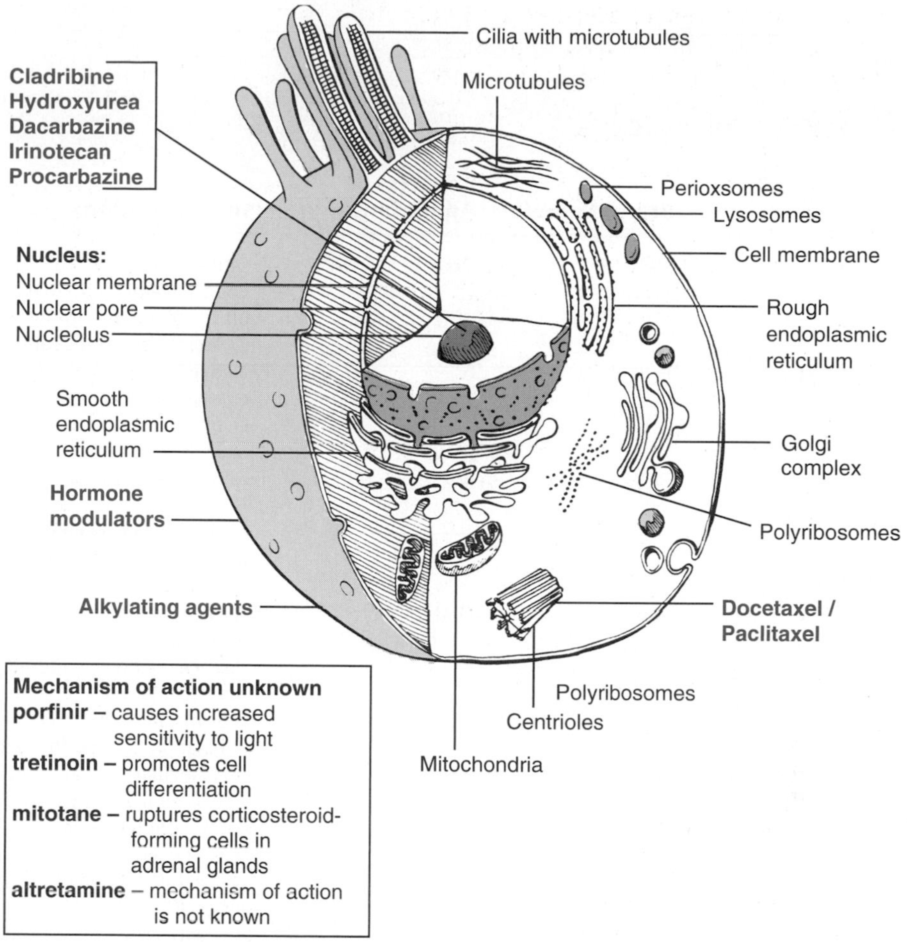

FIGURE 12-2. Sites of action of non—cell cycle–specific antineoplastic agents. Hormone modulators react with specific receptor sites to block cell growth and activity. Docetaxel and paclitaxel inhibit microtubular reorganization. Cladribine and hydroxyurea block DNA synthesis; dacarbazine blocks DNA and RNA synthesis; irinotecan disrupts DNA strands; procarbizine inhibits DNA, RNA, and protein synthesis.

CLINICALLY IMPORTANT DRUG–DRUG INTERACTIONS

Alkylating agents that are known to cause hepatic or renal toxicity should be used cautiously with any other drugs that have similar effects. In addition, drugs that are toxic to the liver may adversely affect drugs that are metabolized in the liver or that act in the liver (e.g., oral anticoagulants). Specific drug–drug interactions for each agent are listed in your nursing drug guide.

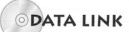

DATA LINK

Data link to the alkylating agents in your nursing drug guide (see Table 12-1).

NURSING CONSIDERATIONS for patients receiving alkylating agents

Assessment

HISTORY. Screen for the following: history of allergy to any of the alkylating agents; bone marrow suppression; renal or hepatic dysfunction; and pregnancy or lactation.

PHYSICAL ASSESSMENT. Physical assessment should be performed to establish baseline data for determining the effectiveness of the drug and the occurrence of any adverse effects associated with drug therapy. Include screening for orientation and reflexes to evaluate any central nervous system (CNS) effects; respiratory rate and adventitious sounds to monitor the disease and to evaluate for respiratory or hypersensitivity effects; pulse, rhythm, and auscultation to monitor for systemic or cardiovascular effects; and bowel sounds and mucous membrane status to monitor for GI effects. Evaluate the following laboratory tests: CBC with differential, and renal and liver function tests to monitor for dosage adjustment as needed and to evaluate toxic drug effects.

Nursing Diagnoses

The patient receiving an alkylating agent may have the following nursing diagnoses related to drug therapy:

- Pain related to GI, CNS, skin effects of drug
- Alteration in self-concept related to alopecia, skin effects, impaired fertility

TABLE 12-1

ALKYLATING AGENTS

Name	Brand Name(s)	Route(s) of Administration	Usual Indications	Special Notes
busulfan	*Myleran*	Oral	Treatment of chronic myelogenous leukemia; not effective in blastic phase or without the Philadelphia chromosome	Dosing monitored by effects on bone marrow; always push fluids to decrease toxic renal effects; alopecia is common
carboplatin	*Paraplatin*	IV	Palliative treatment of returning ovarian cancer after prior chemotherapy; may be useful in several other cancers	Dosage and timing determined by bone marrow response; alopecia is common
carmustine	*BiCNU, Gliadel*	IV	Treatment of brain tumors, Hodgkin's disease, and multiple myelomas; available in implantable wafer form for treatment of glioblastoma	Dosage determined by bone marrow toxicity, usually not repeated for 6 weeks; often used in combination therapy
P chlorambucil	*Leukeran*	Oral	Treatment of lymphomas and leukemias including Hodgkin's disease; being considered for the treatment of rheumatoid arthritis and other conditions	Toxic to liver and bone marrow; dosing based on bone marrow response
cisplatin	*Platinol-AQ*	IV	Combination therapy for metastatic testicular or ovarian tumors, advanced bladder cancers	Neurotoxic, nephrotoxic, and can cause serious hypersensitivity reactions
cyclophosphamide	*Cytoxan, Neosar*	Oral, IV	Treatment of lymphoma, myelomas, leukemias, and other cancers in combination with other drugs	Hemorrhagic cystitis is a potentially fatal side effect; alopecia is common
ifosfamide	*Ifex*	IV	Combination therapy as a third-line agent in treating germ cell testicular cancers; being tested for treatment of other cancers	Alopecia is common
lomustine	*CeeNu*	Oral	Palliative combination therapy for Hodgkin's disease and primary and metastatic brain tumors	Immune suppression and GI effects are common
mechlorethamine	*Mustargen*	IV	Nitrogen mustard; palliative treatment in Hodgkin's disease, leukemia, bronchial carcinoma, and other cancers; injected for treatment of effusions secondary to cancer metastases	GI toxicity, bone marrow suppression, and impaired fertility are common
melphalan	*Alkeran*	Oral, IV	Nitrogen mustard; palliative treatment for multiple myeloma, ovarian cancers	Oral route is preferred; pulmonary fibrosis, bone marrow suppression, and alopecia are common
streptozocin	*Zanosar*	IV	Treatment of metastatic islet cell carcinoma of the pancreas	GI and renal toxicity are common; causes infertility; wear rubber gloves to avoid drug contact with the skin—if contact occurs, wash thoroughly with soap and water
thiotepa	*Thioplex*	IV	Treatment of adenocarcinoma of the breast and uterus, and papillary carcinoma of the bladder; available intrathecally to treat effusion	Infertility, rash, GI toxicity, dizziness, headache, and bone marrow suppression are common

BOX 12-1

DRUGS THAT PROTECT CELLS FROM ALKYLATING AGENTS

- Amifostine (*Ethyol*) is a cytoprotective (cell-protecting) drug that preserves healthy cells from the toxic effects of cisplatin. It is thought to react to the specific acidity and vascularity of nontumor cells to protect them, and it may also act as a scavenger of free radicals that may be released by cells that have been exposed to cisplatin. Amifostine is given IV within 30 minutes of starting cisplatin therapy; timing is very important to its effectiveness. Now approved for use to prevent the renal toxicity associated with the use of cisplatin in patients with advanced ovarian cancer, amifostine is under investigation as an agent to protect lung fibroblasts from the effects of paclitaxel. Because amifostine is associated with severe nausea and vomiting, concurrent administration of an antiemetic is recommended. It also can cause hypotension, and patients should be monitored closely for this condition.
- Mesna (*Mesnex*) is a cytoprotective agent that is used to reduce the incidence of both ifosfamide-caused hemorrhagic cystitis and cyclophosphamide-induced hemorrhagic cystitis. Mesna, which is known to react chemically with urotoxic metabolites of ifosfamide, is given IV at the time of the ifosfamide injection and 4 and 8 hours afterward. Because it has been associated with nausea and vomiting, an antiemetic may be useful.

- Fear, anxiety related to diagnosis and treatment
- Knowledge deficit regarding drug therapy

Implementation

- Arrange for blood tests prior to, periodically during, and for at least 3 weeks after therapy *to monitor bone marrow function. Discontinue the drug or reduce the dose as needed.*
- Administer medication according to scheduled protocol and in combination with other drugs as indicated *to improve effectiveness.*
- Ensure that the patient is well hydrated *to decrease risk of renal toxicity.*
- Provide small, frequent meals; frequent mouth care; and dietary consult as *appropriate to maintain nutrition when GI effects are severe.* Antiemetics may be helpful in some cases.
- Arrange for proper head covering at extremes of temperature if alopecia occurs; a wig, scarf, or hat is *important for maintaining body temperature.* If alopecia is an anticipated effect of drug therapy, advise the patient to obtain a wig or head covering before the condition occurs *to promote self-esteem and a positive body image.*
- Provide patient teaching *to enhance patient knowledge about drug therapy and to promote compliance* regarding:

  The appropriate dosage regimen, including dates to return for further doses.

  The importance of covering the head at extremes of temperature. If alopecia is an anticipated effect of drug therapy, advise the patient to obtain a wig or head covering before the condition occurs to promote self-esteem and a positive body image.

  The need to try to maintain nutrition if GI effects are severe.

  The need to plan appropriate rest periods because fatigue and weakness are common effects of the drugs.

  The possibility of impaired fertility; the patient may wish to consult a health care provider.

  The importance of not taking the drugs during pregnancy and using barrier contraceptives (see Patient Teaching Checklist: Antineoplastic Agents).

Evaluation

- Monitor patient response to the drug (alleviation of cancer being treated, palliation of signs and symptoms of cancer).
- Monitor for adverse effects (bone marrow suppression, GI toxicity, neurotoxicity, alopecia, renal or hepatic dysfunction).
- Evaluate the effectiveness of the teaching plan (patient can name the drug, dosage, possible adverse effects to watch for, and specific measures to help avoid adverse effects). (See Nursing Care Guide: Antineoplastic Agents.)

ANTIMETABOLITES

Antimetabolites are drugs that have a similar chemical structure to various natural metabolites that are necessary for the growth and division of rapidly growing neoplastic cells and normal cells. Antimetabolites replace those needed metabolites and prevent normal cellular function. The use of these drugs has been somewhat limited because of the ability of neoplastic cells to develop a resistance to these agents rather rapidly. For this reason, these drugs are usually used as part of a combination therapy.

THERAPEUTIC ACTIONS AND INDICATIONS

The antimetabolites inhibit DNA production in cells that depend on certain natural metabolites to produce their DNA. Many of these agents inhibit

PATIENT TEACHING CHECKLIST

Antineoplastic Agents

Create customized patient teaching materials for a specific antineoplastic agent from your CD-ROM. Your patient teaching should stress the following points for drugs within this class: Antineoplastic agents work to destroy cells at various phases of their life cycle. These drugs are prescribed to kill cancer cells that are growing in the body. Because these drugs also affect normal cells, they sometimes cause many adverse effects.

Common adverse effects of this drug include:

- Nausea and vomiting—Antiemetic drugs and sedatives may help. Your health care provider will be with you to help if these effects occur.
- Loss of appetite—It is very important to keep up your strength. Tell people if there is something that you would be interested in eating—*anything* that appeals to you. Alert someone if you feel hungry, regardless of the time of day.
- Loss of hair—Your hair will grow back, although its color or consistency may be different from what it was originally. It may help to purchase a wig before you lose your hair so that you can match appearance if you would like to. Hats and scarves may also be worn. It is very important to keep your head covered in extremes of temperature and to protect yourself from the sun, the heat, and the cold. Because much of the body's heat can be lost through the head, not protecting yourself could cause serious problems.
- Mouth sores—Frequent mouth care is very helpful. Try to avoid very hot or spicy foods.
- Fatigue, malaise—Frequent rest periods and careful planning of your day's activities can be very helpful.
- Bleeding—You may bruise more easily than you normally do, and your gums may bleed while you are brushing your teeth. Special care should be taken when shaving or brushing your teeth. Avoid activities that might cause an injury and medications that contain aspirin.
- Susceptibility to infection—Avoid people with infections or colds and avoid crowded, public places. In some cases, the people who are caring for you may wear gowns and masks to protect you from their germs.

Report any of the following to your health care provider: bruising and bleeding, fever, chills, sore throat, difficulty breathing, flank pain, and swelling in your ankles or fingers.

Take the full course of your prescription. It is very important to take the complete regimen that has been ordered for you. Cancer cells grow at different rates and go through rest periods when they are not susceptible to the drugs, and the disease must be attacked over time to eradicate the problem.

Tell any doctor, nurse, or other health care provider that you are taking this drug.

Try to maintain a balanced diet while you are taking this drug. Drink 10 to 12 glasses of water each day during the drug therapy.

Use a barrier contraceptive while you are taking this drug. These drugs can cause serious effects to a developing fetus, and precautions must be taken to avoid pregnancy. If you think that you are pregnant, consult your health care provider immediately.

You need to have periodic blood tests and examinations while you are taking this drug. These tests help guard against serious adverse effects and may be needed to determine the next dose of your drug.

This Teaching Checklist reflects general patient teaching guidelines. It is not meant to be a substitute for drug-specific teaching information, which is available in nursing drug guides.

thymidylate synthetase, DNA polymerase, or folic acid reductase, all of which are needed for DNA synthesis. They are most effective in rapidly dividing cells, where they prevent cell replication, leading to cell death (Figure 12-3). The antimetabolites are indicated for the treatment of various leukemias, including some GI and basal cell cancers. Table 12-2 lists the antimetabolites, their indications, and specific information about each drug. Methotrexate is also indicated for the treatment of rheumatoid arthritis and psoriasis.

CONTRAINDICATIONS/CAUTIONS

Caution should be used when administering antimetabolites to any individual with a known allergy to any of the antimetabolites; during pregnancy and lactation, when these drugs are contraindicated because of potential severe effects on the neonate; with bone marrow suppression, which is often the index for redosing and dosing levels; with renal or hepatic dysfunction, which might interfere with the metabolism or excretion of these drugs and often indicates

NURSING CARE GUIDE
Antineoplastic Agents

Assessment	Nursing Diagnoses	Implementation	Evaluation
HISTORY Allergies to any of these drugs, renal or hepatic dysfunction, pregnancy or lactation, bone marrow suppression, GI ulceration	Pain related to GI, CNS, skin effects Alteration in nutrition related to GI effects Alteration in self-concept related to diagnosis, therapy, adverse effects Knowledge deficit regarding drug therapy	Ensure safe administration of the drug. Provide comfort and safety measures: mouth and skin care, rest periods, safety precautions, antiemetics as needed, maintenance of nutrition, head covering. Provide support and reassurance to deal with drug effects, discomfort, and diagnosis. Provide patient teaching regarding drug name, dosage, adverse effects, precautions to take, signs and symptoms to report, and comfort measures to observe.	Evaluate drug effects: resolution of cancer. Monitor for adverse effects: GI toxicity, bone marrow suppression, CNS changes, renal and hepatic damage, alopecia, extravasation of drug. Monitor for drug–drug interactions as indicated for each drug. Evaluate effectiveness of patient teaching program. Evaluate effectiveness of comfort and safety measures.
PHYSICAL EXAMINATION Local: evaluation of injection site CNS: orientation, affect, reflexes Skin: color, lesions, texture GI: abdominal, liver evaluation Laboratory tests: CBC with differential; renal and hepatic function tests			

a need to change the dosage; and with known GI ulcerations or ulcerative diseases that might be exacerbated by the effects of these drugs.

ADVERSE EFFECTS

Adverse effects frequently encountered with the use of the antimetabolites are listed below. To counteract the effects of treatment with one antimetabolite, methotrexate, the drug leucovorin is sometimes given (Box 12-2).

Hematologic effects include bone marrow suppression, with leukopenia, thrombocytopenia, anemia, and pancytopenia secondary to the effects of the drugs on the rapidly multiplying cells of the bone marrow. Toxic GI effects include nausea, vomiting, anorexia, diarrhea, and mucous membrane deterioration, all of which are related to drug effects on the rapidly multiplying cells of the GI tract. CNS effects include headache, drowsiness, aphasia, fatigue, malaise, and dizziness. Patients should be advised to take precautions if these conditions occur. Like alkylating agents, effects of the antimetabolites may include possible hepatic toxicity or renal toxicity depending on the exact mechanism of action. Alopecia may also occur.

CLINICALLY IMPORTANT DRUG–DRUG INTERACTIONS

Antimetabolites that are known to cause hepatic or renal toxicity should be used with care with any other drugs known to have the same effect. In addi-

NURSING CHALLENGE

Antiemetics and Cancer Chemotherapy

Antineoplastic drugs can directly stimulate the chemoreceptor trigger zone (CTZ) in the medulla to induce nausea and vomiting. These drugs also cause cell death, which releases many toxins into the system—and which in turn stimulate the CTZ. Because patients expect nausea and vomiting with the administration of antineoplastic agents, the higher, cortical centers of the brain can stimulate the CTZ to induce vomiting at just the thought of the chemotherapy.

A variety of antiemetic agents have been used in the course of antineoplastic therapy. Sometimes a combination of drugs is most helpful. It should also be remembered that an accepting environment, plenty of comfort measures (environmental control, mouth care, ice chips, and so on), and support for the patient can help decrease the discomfort associated with the emetic effects of these drugs. Antihistamines to decrease secretions and corticosteroids to relieve inflammation are useful as adjunctive therapies.

Drugs that are known to help in treating antineoplastic-chemotherapy-induced nausea and vomiting include the agents listed below.

- Dronabinol (*Marinol*) is a synthetic derivative of delta-9-tetrahydrocannabinol, the active ingredient in marijuana; this is not usually a first-line drug because of associated CNS effects.
- Ondansetron (*Zofran*) and granisetron (*Kytril*) block serotonin receptors in the CTZ and are among the most effective antiemetics, especially if combined with a corticosteroid such as dexamethasone.
- Alprazolam (*Xanax*) and lorazepam (*Ativan*), which are benzodiazepines, seem to be effective in directly blocking the CTZ to relieve nausea and vomiting caused by cancer chemotherapy; they are especially effective when combined with a corticosteroid.
- Haloperidol (*Haldol*) is a dopaminergic blocker that also is believed to have direct CTZ effects.
- Metoclopramide (*Reglan*) calms the activity of the GI tract; it is especially effective if combined with a corticosteroid, an antihistamine, and a centrally acting blocker such as haloperidol or lorazepam.
- Prochlorperazine (*Compazine*) is a phenothiazine that has been found to have strong antiemetic action in the CNS; it can be given by a variety of routes.

Nausea and vomiting are unavoidable aspects of many chemotherapeutic regimens. However, treating the patient as the chemotherapy begins, using combination regimens, and providing plenty of supportive and comforting nursing care can help to alleviate some of the distress associated with these adverse effects.

tion, drugs that are toxic to the liver may adversely affect drugs that are metabolized in the liver or that act in the liver (e.g., oral anticoagulants). Specific drug–drug interactions for each agent are listed in your nursing drug guide.

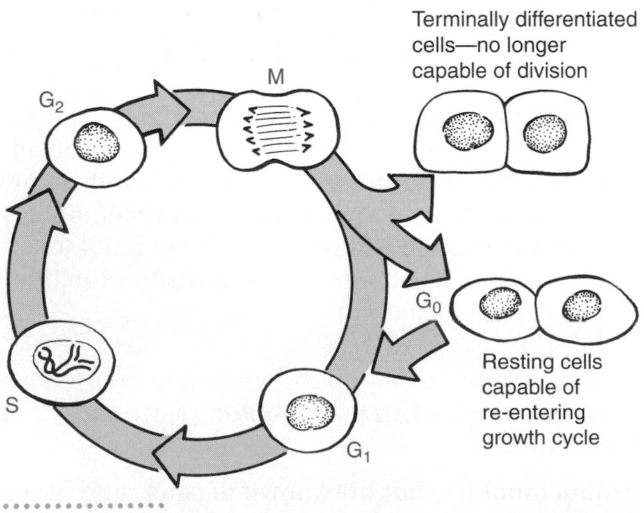

FIGURE 12-3. Sites of action of cell cycle–specific antineoplastic agents.

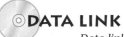

DATA LINK

Data link to the antimetabolites in your nursing drug guide (see Table 12-2).

NURSING CONSIDERATIONS for patients receiving antimetabolites

Assessment

HISTORY. Screen for the following: history of allergy to the specific antimetabolite; bone marrow suppression; renal or hepatic dysfunction; pregnancy or lactation; and GI ulcerative disease.

PHYSICAL ASSESSMENT. Physical assessment should be performed to establish baseline data for determining the effectiveness of the drug and the occurrence of any adverse effects associated with drug therapy. Include screening for orientation and reflexes to evaluate any CNS effects; respiratory rate and adventitious sounds to monitor the disease and to evaluate for respiratory or hypersensitivity effects; pulse, rhythm, and auscultation to monitor for systemic or cardiovascular effects; and bowel sounds and mucous membrane status to monitor for GI effects. Evaluate the following laboratory tests: CBC

TABLE 12-2

ANTIMETABOLITES

Name	Brand Name(s)	Route(s) of Administration	Usual Indications	Special Notes
cytarabine	*Ara-C, Cytosar-U*	IV, SC	Treatment of meningeal and myolocytic leukemias; used in combination with other agents	GI toxicity and cytarabine syndrome (fever, myalgia, bone pain, chest pain, rash, conjunctivitis, and malaise) are common—this syndrome sometimes responds to corticosteroids; alopecia may occur
floxuridine	*FUDR*	Continuous arterial infusion	Palliative management of GI adenocarcinoma metastatic to the liver in patients who are not candidates for surgery	Administer by intra-arterial line only; bone suppression, GI toxicity, neurotoxicity, and alopecia are common
fludarabine	*Fludara*	IV	Treatment of chronic lymphocytic leukemia; unresponsive B cell CLL with no progress with at least one other treatment	CNS toxicity can be severe; GI toxicity, respiratory complications, renal failure, and a tumor lysis syndrome are common
fluorouracil	*Adrucil, Efudex, Fluoroplex*	IV, topical	Palliative treatment of various GI cancers; topical treatment of basal cell carcinoma and actinic and solar keratoses	GI toxicity, bone marrow suppression, alopecia, and skin rash are common; avoid occlusive dressings with topical forms; wash hands thoroughly after coming in contact with drug
mercaptopurine	*Purinethol*	Oral	Remission induction and maintenance therapy in acute leukemias	Bone marrow toxicity and GI toxicity are common; hyperuricemia is a true concern—ensure that the patient is well hydrated during therapy
P methotrexate	*Folex, Rheumatrex*	Oral, IV	Treatment of leukemias, psoriasis, and rheumatoid arthritis	Hypersensitivity reactions can be severe; liver toxicity and GI complications are common; monitor for bone marrow suppression and increased susceptibility to infections; dose pack available for the oral treatment of psoriasis and rheumatoid arthritis
thioguanine	generic	Oral	Remission induction and maintenance of acute leukemias alone or in combination therapy	Bone marrow suppression, GI toxicity, miscarriage, and birth defects have been reported; monitor bone marrow status to determine dosage and redosing; ensure that the patient is well hydrated during therapy to minimize hyperuricemia—patient may respond to allopurinol and urine alkalinization

BOX 12-2

A DRUG THAT PROTECTS AGAINST AN ANTIMETABOLITE

Leucovorin (*Wellcovorin*) is an active form of folic acid that is used to "rescue" normal cells from the adverse effects of methotrexate therapy in the treatment of osteosarcoma. This drug is also used to treat folic acid deficient conditions such as sprue, nutritional deficiency, pregnancy, and lactation. Leucovorin is given orally or IV at the time of methotrexate therapy, and for the next 72 hours. Use of this drug has been associated with pain at the injection site.

with differential and renal and liver function tests to monitor for dosage adjustment as needed and to evaluate toxic drug effects.

Nursing Diagnoses

The patient receiving an antimetabolite may have the following nursing diagnoses related to drug therapy:

- Pain related to GI, CNS, skin effects of drug
- Alteration in self-concept related to alopecia, skin effects, impaired fertility

- Fear, anxiety related to diagnosis and treatment
- Knowledge deficit regarding drug therapy

Implementation

- Arrange for blood tests to monitor bone marrow function prior to, periodically during, and for at least 3 weeks after therapy *to arrange to discontinue the drug or reduce the dose as needed.*
- Administer medication according to scheduled protocol and in combination with other drugs as indicated *to improve effectiveness of drug therapy.*
- Ensure that the patient is well hydrated *to decrease risk of renal toxicity.*
- Provide small, frequent meals; frequent mouth care; and dietary consult as appropriate *to maintain nutrition when GI effects are severe.* Antiemetics may be helpful in some cases.
- Arrange for proper head covering at extremes of temperature if alopecia occurs; a wig, scarf, or hat *is important for maintaining body temperature.* If alopecia is an anticipated effect of drug therapy, advise the patient to obtain a wig or head covering before the condition occurs *to promote self-esteem and a positive body image.*
- Provide patient teaching *to enhance patient knowledge about drug therapy and to promote compliance* regarding:

  The appropriate dosage regimen, including dates to return for further doses.

  The need to try to maintain nutrition if GI effects are severe.

  The importance of covering the head at extremes of temperature if alopecia is anticipated.

  The need to plan appropriate rest periods because fatigue and weakness are common effects of the drugs.

  Possible dizziness, headache, and drowsiness; if these occur, the patient should avoid driving or using dangerous equipment.

  The possibility of impaired fertility; the patient may wish to consult a health care provider.

  The importance of not taking the drugs during pregnancy and using barrier contraceptives (refer to Patient Teaching Checklist: Antineoplastic Agents).

Evaluation

- Monitor patient response to the drug (alleviation of cancer being treated, palliation of signs and symptoms of cancer, palliation of rheumatoid arthritis, psoriasis).
- Monitor for adverse effects (bone marrow suppression, GI toxicity, neurotoxicity, alopecia, renal or hepatic dysfunction).
- Evaluate the effectiveness of the teaching plan (patient can name the drug, dosage, possible adverse effects to watch for, and specific measures to help avoid adverse effects).
- Monitor the effectiveness of comfort and safety measures and compliance with the regimen. (Refer to Nursing Care Guide: Antineoplastic Agents.)

ANTINEOPLASTIC ANTIBIOTICS

Antineoplastic antibiotics are selective not only for bacterial cells; they are also toxic to human cells. Because these drugs tend to be more toxic to cells that are multiplying rapidly, they are useful in the treatment of certain cancers. These cell-cycle-specific drugs interfere with cellular DNA, disrupting it and causing cell death (see Figure 12-3). Some antineoplastic antibiotics break up DNA links, and others prevent DNA synthesis. Like other antineoplastics, the main adverse effects of these drugs are seen in cells that multiply rapidly: cells in the bone marrow, GI tract, and skin.

THERAPEUTIC ACTIONS AND INDICATIONS

The antineoplastic antibiotics are cytotoxic and interfere with DNA synthesis. Table 12-3 lists the various antineoplastic antibiotics, their indications, and specific information about each drug. Their potentially serious adverse effects may limit their usefulness in patients with preexisting diseases or who are debilitated and more susceptible to these effects.

CONTRAINDICATIONS/CAUTIONS

Caution should be used when giving antineoplastic antibiotics to an individual with a known allergy to the antibiotic or related antibiotics and during pregnancy and lactation, when these drugs are contraindicated because of potential severe effects on the neonate. Care should also be taken in patients with the following conditions: bone marrow suppression, which is often the index for redosing and dosing levels; suppressed renal or hepatic function, which might interfere with the metabolism or excretion of these drugs and often indicates a need to change the dosage; known GI ulcerations or ulcerative diseases, which may be exacerbated by the effects of these drugs; pulmonary problems with bleomycin, mitomycin, or pentostatin; cardiac problems with idarubicin and mitoxantrone; and bleeding disorders with plicamycin, which is specifically toxic to these systems.

CASE STUDY

Antineoplastic Therapy and Breast Cancer

PRESENTATION

A 34-year-old white woman, B. P. is a school teacher with two young daughters. She noted a slightly painful lump under her arm when showering. About 2 weeks later, she found a mass in her right breast. Initial patient assessment found that she had no other underlying medical problems, no allergies, and took no medications. Her family history was most indicative: many of the women in her family—her mother, two grandmothers, three aunts, two older sisters, and one younger sister—died of breast cancer when they were in their early 30s. All data from the initial examination, including an evaluation of the lump in the upper outer quadrant of her breast and the presence of a fixed axillary node, were recorded as baseline for further drug therapy and treatment. B. P. underwent a radical mastectomy with biopsy report for grade IV infiltrating ductal carcinoma (28 of 35 lymph nodes were positive for tumor) and then radiation therapy. Then she began a 1-year course of cytoxan, methotrexate, and 5-FU (CMF).

CRITICAL THINKING QUESTIONS

What are the important nursing implications for B. P.? Think about the outlook for B. P., based on her biopsy results and her family history.

What are the effects of high levels of stress on the immune system and the body's ability to fight cancer?

What impact will this disease have on B. P.'s job and her family? Think about the adverse drug effects that can be anticipated. How can good patient teaching help B. P. to anticipate and cope with these many changes and unpleasant effects?

What future concerns should be addressed or at least approached at this point in the treatment of B. P.'s disease? What are the implications for her two daughters? How may a coordinated health team work to help the daughters cope with their mother's disease as well as the prospects for their future?

DISCUSSION

The extent of B. P.'s disease, as evidenced by the biopsy results, does not signify a very hopeful prognosis. In this case, the overall nursing care plan should take not only the acute needs related to surgery and drug therapy but also future needs related to potential debilitation, and even the prospect of death, into account. Immediate needs include comfort and teaching measures to help B. P. deal with the mastectomy and recovery from the surgery. She should be given an opportunity to vent her feelings and thoughts in a protected environment. Efforts should be made to help her to organize her life and plans around her radiation therapy and chemotherapy.

The adverse effects associated with the antineoplastic agents she will be given should be explained and possible ways to cope should be discussed. These effects include the following:

- Alopecia—B. P. should be reassured that her hair will grow back, but she will need to cover her head in extremes of temperature. Purchasing a wig before the hair loss begins may be a good alternative to trying to remember later what her hair was like.
- Nausea and vomiting—These effects will most often occur immediately after the drugs are given. Antiemetics may be ordered, but they are frequently not very effective.
- Bone marrow suppression—This will make B. P. more susceptible to disease, which could be a problem for a teacher and a mother with young children. Ways to avoid contact and infection as well as warning signs to report immediately should be discussed.

Because the antineoplastic therapy will be a long-term regimen, it might help to prepare a calendar of drug dates for use in planning other activities and events. All of B. P.'s treatment should be incorporated into a team approach that helps B. P. and her family deal with the impact of this disease and its therapy, as well as with the potential risk to her daughters. B. P.'s daughters are in a very high risk group for this disease, so the importance of frequent examinations as they grow up needs to be stressed. In some areas of the country, health care providers are encouraging prophylactic mastectomies for women in this very high risk group.

ADVERSE EFFECTS

Adverse effects frequently encountered with the use of these antibiotics include bone marrow suppression, with leukopenia, thrombocytopenia, anemia, and pancytopenia secondary to the effects of the drugs on the rapidly multiplying cells of the bone marrow. Toxic GI effects include nausea, vomiting, anorexia, diarrhea, and mucous membrane deterioration, all of which are related to drug effects on the rapidly multiplying cells of the GI tract. Like the alkylating agents and antimetabolites, effects of antineoplastic antibiotics may include renal or hepatic toxicity, depending on the exact mechanism of action. Alopecia may also occur. Specific drugs are toxic to the heart and lungs; Box 12-3 discusses a

TABLE 12-3

ANTINEOPLASTIC ANTIBIOTICS

Name	Brand Name	Route(s) of Administration	Usual Indications	Special Notes
bleomycin	*Blenoxane*	SC, IV, IM	Palliative treatment of squamous cell carcinomas, testicular cancers, and lymphomas; used to treat malignant pleural effusion	GI toxicity, severe skin reactions, and hypersensitivity reactions may occur; pulmonary fibrosis can be a serious problem—baseline and periodic chest x-rays and pulmonary function tests are necessary
dactinomycin	*Cosmegan*	IV	Part of combination drug regimen in the treatment of a variety of sarcomas and carcinomas; potentiates the effects of radiation therapy	Bone marrow suppression and GI toxicity, which may be severe, limit the dose; effects may not appear for 1 to 2 weeks; local extravasation can cause necrosis and should be treated with injectable corticosteroids, ice to the area, and restart of the IV in a different vein
daunorubicin	*DaunXome*	IV	First-line treatment of advanced HIV infection and associated Kaposi's sarcoma	Complete alopecia is common, and GI toxicity and bone suppression may also occur, severe necrosis may occur at sites of local extravasation—immediate treatment with corticosteroids, normal saline, and ice may help; if ulcerations occur, a plastic surgeon should be called
P doxorubicin	*Adriamycin*	IV	Treatment of a number of leukemias and cancers; used to induce regression; available in a liposomal form for the treatment of AIDS-associated Kaposi's sarcoma	Complete alopecia is common: GI toxicity and bone suppression may occur; severe necrosis may occur at sites of local extravasation—immediate treatment with corticosteroids, normal saline, and ice may help; if ulcerations occur, a plastic surgeon should be called; toxicity is dose-related—an accurate record of each dose received is important in determining dosage
idarubicin	*Idamycin*	IV	Combination therapy for treatment of acute myeloid leukemia in adults	May cause severe bone marrow suppression, which regulates dosage; associated with cardiac toxicity, which can be severe; GI toxicity and local necrosis with extravasation are also common; severe necrosis may occur at sites of local extravasation—immediate treatment with corticosteroids, normal saline, and ice may help; if ulcerations occur, a plastic surgeon should be called; it is essential to monitor heart and bone marrow function to protect the patient from potentially fatal adverse effects
mitomycin	*Mutamycin*	IV	Treatment of disseminated adenocarcinoma of the stomach and pancreas	Severe pulmonary toxicity, alopecia, injection site and GI toxicity occur
mitoxantrone	*Novantrone*	IV	Part of combination therapy in the treatment of adult leukemias; treatment of bone pain in advanced prostatic cancer	Severe bone marrow suppression may occur and limits dosage; alopecia, GI toxicity, and congestive heart failure often occur; avoid direct skin contact with the drug—use gloves and goggles; monitor bone marrow activity and cardiac activity to adjust dosage or discontinue drug as needed
pentostatin	*Nipent*	IV	Treatment of adult patients with alpha interferon-resistant hairy cell leukemia	Fatal pulmonary toxicity has occurred with the use of this drug; GI toxicity, headache, rash, sepsis, and fever are common; monitor respiratory and bone marrow status and arrange to adjust dosage as appropriate; wear protective clothing and goggles when handling this drug

TABLE 12-3

ANTINEOPLASTIC ANTIBIOTICS (Continued)

Name	Brand Name	Route(s) of Administration	Usual Indications	Special Notes
plicamycin	*Mithracin*	IV	Treatment of malignant testicular tumor not amenable to surgery or radiation therapy; treatment of hypercalcemia and hypercalciuria not responsive to other treatments in patients with advanced neoplasms	GI toxicity, local cellulitis, fever, and pain are common; hemorrhagic syndrome with epistaxis to severe bleeding and death has occurred; monitor bleeding times and adjust dosage as needed; monitor injection sites for cellulitis and arrange appropriate treatment

cardioprotective drug that interferes with the effects of doxorubicin. Plicamycin has been associated with a hemorrhagic syndrome (see Table 12-3).

CLINICALLY IMPORTANT DRUG–DRUG INTERACTIONS

Antimetabolites that are known to cause hepatic or renal toxicity should be used with care with any other drugs known to have the same effect. Drugs that result in toxicity to the heart or lungs should be used with caution with any other drugs that produce that particular toxicity. Specific drug–drug interactions for each agent are listed in your nursing drug guide.

DATA LINK

Data link to the antineoplastic antibiotics agents in your nursing drug guide (see Table 12-3).

BOX 12-3

CARDIOPROTECTIVE ANTINEOPLASTIC DRUG

Dexrazoxane (*Zinecard*), a powerful intracellular chelating agent, is a cardioprotective drug that interferes with the cardiotoxic effects of doxorubicin. The associated adverse effects are difficult to differentiate from those attributable to doxorubicin. This agent is approved for use to prevent the cardiomyopathy associated with doxorubicin in doses of over 300 mg/m^2 in women with metastatic breast cancer. Dexrazoxane is given IV in a dosage proportional to the doxorubicin dose 30 minutes before the doxorubicin is administered.

NURSING CONSIDERATIONS for patients receiving antineoplastic antibiotic agents

Assessment

HISTORY. Screen for the following: history of allergy to the antibiotic in use; bone marrow suppression; renal or hepatic dysfunction; respiratory or cardiac disease; pregnancy or lactation; and GI ulcerative disease.

PHYSICAL ASSESSMENT. Physical assessment should be performed to establish baseline data for determining the effectiveness of the drug and the occurrence of any adverse effects associated with drug therapy. Include screening for orientation and reflexes to evaluate any CNS effects; respiratory rate and adventitious sounds to monitor the disease and evaluate for respiratory or hypersensitivity effects; pulse, rhythm, auscultation, and baseline ECG to monitor for systemic or cardiovascular effects; and bowel sounds and mucous membrane status to monitor for GI effects. Evaluate the following laboratory tests: CBC with differential and renal and liver function tests to monitor for dosage adjustment as needed and to evaluate toxic drug effects. Clotting times should be obtained for patients receiving plicamycin.

Nursing Diagnoses

The patient receiving an antineoplastic antibiotic may have the following nursing diagnoses related to drug therapy:

- Pain related to GI, CNS, local effects of drug
- Alteration in self-concept related to alopecia, skin effects

- Fear, anxiety related to diagnosis and treatment
- Knowledge deficit regarding drug therapy

Implementation

- Arrange for blood tests to monitor bone marrow function prior to, periodically during, and for at least 3 weeks after therapy *to arrange to discontinue the drug or reduce the dose as needed.* Monitor cardiac and respiratory function as well as clotting times as appropriate for the drug being used.
- Administer medication according to scheduled protocol and in combination with other drugs as indicated *to improve effectiveness of drug therapy.*
- Ensure that the patient is well hydrated *to decrease risk of renal toxicity.*
- Provide small, frequent meals; frequent mouth care; and dietary consult as appropriate *to maintain nutrition when GI effects are severe.* Antiemetics may be helpful in some cases.
- Arrange for proper head covering at extremes of temperature if alopecia occurs; a wig, scarf, or hat is *important for maintaining body temperature.* If alopecia is an anticipated effect of drug therapy, advise the patient to obtain a wig or head covering before the condition occurs *to promote self-esteem and a positive body image.*

Provide patient teaching *to enhance patient knowledge about drug therapy and to promote compliance* regarding:

The appropriate dosage regimen, including dates to return for further doses.

The need to try to maintain nutrition if GI effects are severe.

The importance of covering the head at extremes of temperature if alopecia is anticipated.

The need to plan appropriate rest periods because fatigue and weakness are common effects of the drugs.

Possible dizziness, headache, and drowsiness; if these occur, the patient should avoid driving or using dangerous equipment.

The possibility of impaired fertility; the patient may wish to consult a health care provider.

The importance of not taking the drugs during pregnancy and using barrier contraceptives (refer to Patient Teaching Guide: Antineoplastic Agents).

Evaluation

- Monitor patient response to the drug (alleviation of cancer being treated and palliation of signs and symptoms of cancer).
- Monitor for adverse effects (bone marrow suppression, GI toxicity, neurotoxicity, alopecia, renal or hepatic dysfunction, and cardiac or respiratory dysfunction).
- Evaluate the effectiveness of the teaching plan (patient can name the drug, dosage, possible adverse effects to watch for, and specific measures to help avoid adverse effects). (Refer to Nursing Care Guide: Antineoplastic Agents.)

WWW.WEB LINKS

Health care providers and patients may want to consult the following Internet sources:

Information on cancer, including research, protocols, and new information, maintained by the National Cancer Institute of the National Institutes of Health:
http://cancernet.nci.nih.gov

Information on cancer care and general patient education:
http://cancerguide.org

Information on numerous cancer connections, support groups, treatment, resources:
http://www.cancer.org

Information about on-line resources related to all types of cancer:
http://www.acor.org

Educational materials for patients and health care providers:
http://www.oncolink.upenn.edu

Information about the Oncology Nurses Society:
http://www.ons.org

MITOTIC INHIBITORS

Mitotic inhibitors are drugs that kill cells as the process of mitosis begins (see Figure 12-3). These cell-cycle-specific agents inhibit DNA synthesis. Like other antineoplastics, the main adverse effects with the mitotic inhibitors occur with cells that rapidly multiply: those in the bone marrow, GI tract, and skin.

THERAPEUTIC ACTIONS AND INDICATIONS

The mitotic inhibitors interfere with the ability of a cell to divide, block, or alter DNA synthesis, thus causing cell death. These drugs are used for the treatment of a variety of tumors and leukemias. Table 12-4 lists the mitotic inhibitors, their indications, and specific

TABLE 12-4
MITOTIC INHIBITORS

Name	Brand Name(s)	Route(s) of Administration	Usual Indications	Special Notes
etoposide	*Toposar, VePesid*	Oral, IV	Part of combination therapy in treatment of refractory testicular tumor and small cell lung carcinoma	Fatigue, GI toxicity, bone marrow suppression, and alopecia are common; monitor bone marrow function to adjust dosage; rapid fall in BP can occur during IV infusion, so monitor patient carefully; avoid direct skin contact with the drug—use protective clothing and goggles
teniposide	*Vumon*	IV	Combination treatment for induction therapy in childhood acute lymphoblastic leukemia	GI toxicity, CNS effects, bone marrow suppression, and alopecia are common; monitor bone marrow function to adjust dosage; avoid direct skin contact with the drug—use protective clothing and goggles; rapid fall in BP can occur during IV infusion, so monitor patient carefully
vinblastine	*Velban*	IV	Palliative treatment of various lymphomas and sarcomas; treatment of advanced Hodgkin's disease and alone or as part of combination therapy for treatment of advanced testicular germ cell cancers	GI toxicity, CNS effects, and total loss of hair are common; antiemetics may help; avoid contact with drug and monitor injection sites for reactions
P vincristine	*Oncovin, Vincasar*	IV	Treatment of acute leukemia and various lymphomas and sarcomas	Extensive CNS effects, GI toxicity, local irritation at injection site, and hair loss are common; SIADH also been reported; monitor urine output and arrange for fluid restriction and diuretics as needed
vinorelbine	*Navelbine*	IV	First-line treatment of unresectable advanced small cell lung cancer; stage IV non-small cell lung cancer and stage III non-small cell lung cancer with cisplatin	GI and CNS toxicity are common; total loss of hair, local reaction at injection site, and bone marrow suppression also occur; prepare a calendar with return dates for the series of injections; avoid extravasation, and arrange for hyaluronidase infusion if it occurs; antiemetics may be helpful

information about each drug. They are not interchangeable, and each drug has a specific use.

CONTRAINDICATIONS/CAUTIONS

Caution should be used when giving these drugs to anyone with a known allergy to the drug or related drugs and during pregnancy and lactation when these drugs are contraindicated because of potential severe effects on the neonate. Care should also be taken in patients with the following conditions: bone marrow suppression, which is often the index for redosing and dosing levels; renal or hepatic dysfunction, which could interfere with the metabolism or excretion of these drugs and often indicates a need to change the dosage; and known GI ulcerations or ulcerative diseases, which may be exacerbated by the effects of these drugs.

ADVERSE EFFECTS

Adverse effects frequently encountered with the use of mitotic inhibitors include bone marrow suppression, with leukopenia, thrombocytopenia, anemia, and pancytopenia secondary to the effects of the drugs on the rapidly multiplying cells of the bone marrow. GI effects include nausea, vomiting, anorexia, diarrhea, and mucous membrane deterioration. Like the other antineoplastic agents, effects of the mitotic inhibitors may include possible hepatic or renal toxicity, depending on the exact mechanism of action. Alopecia may also occur. These drugs also cause necrosis and cellulitis if extravasation occurs, so injection sites should be regularly monitored and appropriate action taken as needed if extravasation should occur.

CLINICALLY IMPORTANT DRUG–DRUG INTERACTIONS

Mitotic inhibitors that are known to be toxic to the liver or the CNS should be used with care with any other drugs known to have the same adverse effect. Specific drug–drug interactions for each agent are listed in your nursing drug guide.

DATA LINK

Data link to the mitotic inhibitors in your nursing drug guide (see Table 12-4).

NURSING CONSIDERATIONS
for patients receiving mitotic inhibitors

Assessment

HISTORY. Screen for the following: history of allergy to the drug used (or related drugs); bone marrow suppression; renal or hepatic dysfunction; pregnancy or lactation; and GI ulcerative disease.

PHYSICAL ASSESSMENT. Physical assessment should be performed to establish baseline data for determining the effectiveness of the drug and the occurrence of any adverse effects associated with drug therapy. Include screening for orientation and reflexes to evaluate any CNS effects; skin, to evaluate for lesions as well as hair and hair distribution to monitor for adverse effects; respiratory rate and adventitious sounds to monitor the disease and to evaluate for respiratory or hypersensitivity effects; and bowel sounds and mucous membrane status to monitor for GI effects. Evaluate the following laboratory tests: CBC with differential and renal and liver function tests to monitor for dosage adjustment as needed and to evaluate toxic drug effects. Regular evaluation of injection sites should be performed to check for signs of extravasation or inflammation.

Nursing Diagnoses

The patient receiving a mitotic inhibitor may have the following nursing diagnoses related to drug therapy:

- Pain related to GI, CNS, local effects of drug
- Alteration in self-concept related to alopecia, skin effects
- Fear, anxiety related to diagnosis and treatment
- Knowledge deficit regarding drug therapy

Implementation

- Arrange for blood tests to monitor bone marrow function prior to, periodically during, and for at least 3 weeks after therapy *to arrange to discontinue the drug or reduce the dose as needed.*
- Avoid direct skin or eye contact with the drug. *Wear protective clothing and goggles while preparing and administering the drug to prevent toxic reaction to the drug.*
- Administer medication according to scheduled protocol and in combination with other drugs as indicated *to improve effectiveness of drug therapy.*
- Ensure that the patient is well hydrated *to decrease risk of renal toxicity.*
- Monitor injection sites *to arrange appropriate treatment for extravasation, local inflammation, or cellulitis.*
- Provide small, frequent meals; frequent mouth care; and dietary consult as appropriate *to maintain nutrition* when GI effects are severe. Antiemetics may be helpful in some cases.
- Arrange for proper head covering at extremes of temperature if alopecia or epilation occurs; a wig, scarf, or hat is important *for maintaining body temperature.* If alopecia is an anticipated effect of drug therapy, advise the patient to obtain a wig or head covering before the condition occurs *to promote self-esteem and a positive body image.*
- Provide patient teaching *to enhance patient knowledge about drug therapy and to promote compliance* regarding:

  The appropriate dosage regimen, including dates to return for further doses.

  The need to try to maintain nutrition if GI effects are severe.

  The importance of covering the head at extremes of temperature if alopecia is anticipated.

  The need to plan appropriate rest periods because fatigue and weakness are common effects of the drugs.

  Possible dizziness, headache, and drowsiness; if these occur, the patient should avoid driving or using dangerous equipment.

  The possibility of impaired fertility; the patient may wish to consult a health care provider.

  The importance of not taking the drugs during pregnancy and using barrier contraceptives (refer to Patient Teaching Checklist: Antineoplastic Agents).

Evaluation

- Monitor patient response to the drug (alleviation of cancer being treated and palliation of signs and symptoms of cancer).
- Monitor for adverse effects (bone marrow suppression, GI toxicity, neurotoxicity, alopecia, renal or hepatic dysfunction, and local reactions at the injection site).
- Evaluate the effectiveness of the teaching plan (patient can name the drug, dosage, possible adverse effects to watch for, and specific measures to help avoid adverse effects). (Refer to Nursing Care Guide: Antineoplastic Agents.)

HORMONES AND HORMONE MODULATORS

Some cancers, particularly those involving the breast tissue, ovaries, and uterus, are sensitive to estrogen stimulation. Estrogen receptor sites on the tumor react with circulating estrogen, and this reaction stimulates the tumor cells to grow and divide. Several antineoplastic agents are used to block or interfere with these receptor sites to prevent the growth of the cancer and in some situations to actually cause cell death.

THERAPEUTIC ACTIONS AND INDICATIONS

The hormones and hormone modulators used as antineoplastics are receptor-site-specific or hormone-specific to block the stimulation of growing cancer cells that are sensitive to the presence of that hormone (see Figure 12-2). These drugs are indicated for the treatment of breast cancer in postmenopausal women or women without ovarian function. Table 12-5 lists the hormones and hormone modulators, their uses, and specific information about each drug. Note that estramustine is indicated for the treatment of advanced prostatic cancer sensitive to hormone manipulation.

CONTRAINDICATIONS/CAUTIONS

Caution should be used when giving hormones and hormone modulators to anyone with a known allergy to any of these drugs; during pregnancy, when blocking of estrogen effects can lead to fetal death and serious problems for the mother; and during lactation, when these drugs are contraindicated because of potential severe effects on the neonate. Care should also be taken in patients with bone marrow suppression, which is often the index for redosing and dosing levels, and renal or hepatic dysfunction, which could interfere with the metabolism or excretion of these drugs and often indicates a need to change the dosage. Hypercalcemia is a contraindication to the use of toremifene, which is known to increase calcium levels.

ADVERSE EFFECTS

Adverse effects frequently encountered with the use of these drugs involve the effects that are seen when estrogen is blocked or inhibited. Menopause-associated effects include hot flashes, vaginal spotting, vaginal dryness, moodiness, and depression. Other effects include bone marrow suppression and GI toxicity, including hepatic dysfunction. Hypercalcemia is also encountered as the calcium is pulled out of the bones without estrogen activity to promote calcium deposition.

CLINICALLY IMPORTANT DRUG–DRUG INTERACTIONS

If hormones and hormone modulators are taken with oral anticoagulants, there is often an increased risk of bleeding. Care should also be taken with any drugs that might increase serum lipid levels.

DATA LINK

Data link to the hormones and hormone modulators in your nursing drug guide (see Table 12-5).

NURSING CONSIDERATIONS
for patients receiving hormones and hormone modulators

Assessment

HISTORY. Screen for the following: history of allergy to the drug in use or any related drugs; bone marrow suppression; renal or hepatic dysfunction; pregnancy or lactation; hypercalcemia; and hypercholesterolemia.

PHYSICAL ASSESSMENT. Physical assessment should be performed to establish baseline data for determining the effectiveness of the drug and the occurrence of any adverse effects associated with drug therapy. Include screening for orientation and reflexes to evaluate any CNS effects; skin, to evaluate for lesions, hair, and hair distribution to monitor for adverse drug effects; blood pressure, pulse, and perfusion to evaluate the status of the cardiovascular system and monitor for adverse drug effects; and bowel sounds and mucous membrane status to monitor for GI effects. Evaluate the following laboratory tests: CBC with differential and renal and liver function tests to monitor for dosage adjustment as needed and to evaluate toxic drug effects.

TABLE 12-5

HORMONES AND HORMONE MODULATORS

Name	Brand Name	Route of Administration	Actions	Usual Indications	Special Notes
anastrazole	*Arimidex*	Oral	Antiestrogen drug that blocks estradiol production without effects on adrenal hormones	Treatment of advanced breast cancer in postmenopausal women following tamoxifen therapy	GI effects and signs and symptoms of menopause (hot flashes, mood swings, edema, and vaginal dryness and itching) and bone pain and back pain treatable with analgesics may occur; monitor lipid levels in patients at risk for high cholesterol
estramustine	*Emcyt*	Oral	Binding to estrogen steroid receptors, causing alkalinization of the cell and cell death	Palliative treatment of metastatic and progressive prostate cancer	GI toxicity, rash, bone marrow suppression, breast tenderness, and cardiovascular toxicity are common; 30 to 90 days of therapy may be required before effects are seen; monitor cardiovascular, hepatic, and bone marrow function throughout therapy
letrozole	*Femare*	Oral	Prevention of conversion of precursors to estrogens in all tissues	Treatment of advanced breast cancer in postmenopausal women with disease following antiestrogen therapy	GI toxicity, bone marrow depression, alopecia, hot flashes, and CNS depression are common; discontinue drug at any sign that the cancer is progressing
P tamoxifen	*Nolvadex*	Oral	Antiestrogen that competes with estrogen for receptor sites in target tissues	Used in combination therapy with surgery to treat breast cancer; treatment of advanced breast cancer in men and women; first drug approved for the prevention of breast cancer in women at high risk for breast cancer	Signs and symptoms of menopause, CNS depression, bone marrow suppression, and GI toxicity are common; possible change in visual acuity and corneal opacities and retinopathy, so pretherapy and periodic ophthalmic examinations are indicated
testolactone	*Teslac*	Oral	Synthetic androgen; antineoplastic effects in postmenopausal women with breast cancer, which are not clearly understood, are thought to be a competitive reaction for estrogen receptor sites	Used to treat breast cancer in postmenopausal women and in premenopausal women in whom ovarian function has been terminated	GI effects and hypercalcemia are common; virilization (hirsutism, deepening of voice, clitoral enlargement, facial hair growth, and altered libido) is often an unacceptable reaction that limits drug use in some women; monitoring of serum calcium is important during the course of the therapy
toremifene	*Fareston*	Oral	Binding to estrogen receptors and prevention of growth of breast cancer cells	Treatment of advanced breast cancer in women with estrogen receptor-positive disease	Signs and symptoms of menopause, CNS depression, and GI toxicity are common

Nursing Diagnoses

The patient receiving a hormone or hormone modulator may have the following nursing diagnoses related to drug therapy:

- Pain related to GI, CNS, menopausal effects of drug
- Alteration in self concept related to antiestrogen effects, virilization
- Fear, anxiety related to diagnosis and treatment
- Knowledge deficit regarding drug therapy

Implementation

- Arrange for blood tests to monitor bone marrow function prior to and periodically during therapy *to discontinue the drug or reduce the dose as needed.*
- Provide small, frequent meals; frequent mouth care; and dietary consult as appropriate *to maintain nutrition* when GI effects are severe.
- Provide comfort measures *to help the patient cope with menopausal signs and symptoms* such as hygiene measures, temperature control, and stress reduction.
- Reduce the dosage if these effects become severe or intolerable.
- Advise the patient of the need to use contraceptive measures while taking these drugs *to avert serious fetal harm which could result;* the use of barrier contraceptives is recommended.
- Provide patient teaching *to enhance patient knowledge about drug therapy and to promote compliance* regarding:

    The appropriate dosage regimen, including dates to return for further doses.
    Maintenance of nutrition even if GI effects are severe.
    Not taking these drugs during pregnancy and using barrier contraceptives.
    Staying in a cool environment.
    Practicing good hygiene and skin care and using stress reduction to cope with menopausal effects (refer to Patient Teaching Checklist: Antineoplastic Agents).

Evaluation

- Monitor patient response to the drug (alleviation of cancer being treated and palliation of signs and symptoms of cancer being treated).
- Monitor for adverse effects (bone marrow suppression, GI toxicity, menopausal signs and symptoms, hypercalcemia, and cardiovascular effects).
- Evaluate the effectiveness of the teaching plan (patient can name the drug, dosage, possible adverse effects to watch for, and specific measures to help avoid adverse effects). (Refer to Nursing Care Guide: Antineoplastic Agents.)

MISCELLANEOUS ANTINEOPLASTIC AGENTS

Many other agents that do not fit into one of the previously discussed groups are used as antineoplastics to cause cell death. These drugs are used for treating a wide variety of cancers. Table 12-6 lists the unclassified antineoplastic drugs, their indications, and anticipated adverse effects. Specific information about each drug may be obtained in your nursing drug guide. (See Figure 12-2 for sites of action of the miscellaneous antineoplastic agents.)

DATA LINK

Data link to the miscellaneous antineoplastic agents in your nursing drug guide (see Table 12-6).

CULTURAL CONSIDERATIONS ••••

Alternative Therapies and Cancer

The diagnosis of cancer and the sometimes devastating effects of cancer treatment often drive patients to seek out alternative therapies, either as adjuncts to traditional cancer therapy, or sometimes instead of traditional therapy. Because Asian Americans and Pacific islanders often see drug therapy and other cancer therapies as part of the yin/yang belief system, they may turn to a variety of herbal therapies to balance their systems.

The nurse should be aware of some potential interactions that may occur when alternative therapies are used:

- Echinacea—May be hepatotoxic; increases the risk of hepatotoxicity when taken with antineoplastics that are hepatotoxic
- Gincko—Inhibits blood clotting, which can cause problems following surgery or with bleeding neoplasms
- Saw palmetto—May increase the effects of various estrogen hormones and hormone modulators; advise patients taking such drugs to avoid this herb
- St. John's Wort—Can greatly increase photosensitivity, which can cause problems with patients who have received radiation therapy or are taking drugs that cause other dermatologic effects

If a patient has an unexpected reaction to a drug being used, ask about the use of alternative therapies. Many of these agents are untested and interactions and adverse effects are not well documented.

TABLE 12-6

MISCELLANEOUS ANTINEOPLASTICS

Name	Brand Name	Route(s) of Administration	Actions	Usual Indications	Special Notes
altretamine	*Hexalen*	Oral	Cytotoxicity, with mechanism of action unknown	Single agent used in the palliative treatment of persistent or recurrent ovarian cancer	Severe bone marrow suppression, peripheral sensory neuropathy, and severe GI toxicity may limit the use of this drug; allowing a 14-day rest may alleviate the adverse effects sufficiently to allow redosing
asparaginase	*Elspar*	IM, IV	Enzyme that hydrolyzes the amino acid asparagine that is needed by malignant cells for protein synthesis; inhibits cell proliferation; most effective in G_1 phase of the cell cycle	Part of combination therapy to induce remission in children with acute lymphocytic leukemia	Severe bone marrow suppression, renal toxicity, and fatal hyperthermia may occur; hypersensitivity reactions are common—patients should be tested and desensitized, if necessary, before using the drug
cladribine	*Leustatin*	IV	Blockage of DNA synthesis and repair causing cell death in active and resting lymphocytes and monocytes	Indicated for the treatment of hairy cell leukemia	Severe bone marrow suppression and subsequent increased susceptibility to infection, neurotoxicity, and respiratory complications may occur; must be continuously infused over 7 days; avoid exposure of skin or eyes to the drug—wear protective clothing and goggles when handling the drug
dacarbazine	*DTIC-Dome*	IV	Inhibition of DNA and RNA synthesis, causing cell death; cell cycle-nonspecific	Treatment of metastatic malignant melanoma and as second-line therapy in combination with other drugs for the treatment of Hodgkin's disease	Bone marrow suppression, GI toxicity, and severe photosensitivity are common; extravasation can cause tissue necrosis or cellulitis—use extreme care and monitor injection sites regularly
docetaxel	*Taxotere*	IV	Inhibition of the microtubular reorganization is essential for dividing cells, leading to cell death in rapidly dividing cells	Treatment of patients with locally advanced or metastatic breast cancer after treatment with conventional drugs	Severe bone marrow suppression, which limits dosage of the drug, and fluid retention, which may precipitate cardiac problems occur; premedicate with corticosteroids to decrease fluid retention; use care when handling the drug (protective clothing and goggles are recommended)
gemcitabine	*Gemzar*	IV	S phase cell cycle-specific; causes cell death by disrupting DNA and RNA synthesis	First-line treatment of locally advanced or metastatic adenocarcinoma of the pancreas in patients who have received 5-FU	Severe bone marrow suppression, GI toxicity, pain, and alopecia may occur
hydroxyurea	*Hydrea*	Oral	Inhibition of enzymes essential for the synthesis of DNA, causing cell death	Treatment of melanoma, ovarian cancer, and chronic myelocytic leukemia, in combination for primary squamous cell cancers of the head and neck; used in the treatment of sickle cell anemia	Bone marrow suppression, headache, rash, GI toxicity, and renal dysfunction may occur; encourage patient to drink 10–12 glasses of water a day while taking this drug

irinotecan	*Camptosar*	IV	Disruption of DNA strands during DNA synthesis, causing cell death	Treatment of metastatic colon or rectal cancer after treatment with 5-FU	Severe bone marrow suppression, which regulates dose of the drug, may occur, GI toxicity, dyspnea, and alopecia also result
mitotane	*Lysoderm*	Oral	Cytotoxicity to corticosteroid-forming cells of the adrenal gland	Treatment of inoperable adrenal cortical carcinoma	GI toxicity and CNS toxicity with vision and behavioral changes may occur, adrenal insufficiency—monitor for adrenal insufficiency and arrange for replacement therapy as indicated
paclitaxel	*Taxol*	IV	Inhibition of normal dynamic reorganization of micro-tubules, leading to cell death	Treatment of ovarian cancer, breast cancer, and AIDS-related Kaposi's sarcoma	Severe bone marrow suppression, which regulates the dose of the drug, may result—this may lead to the occurrence of opportunistic infections; GI toxicity, cardiovascular depression, and alopecia; avoid direct contact with the drug—wear protective clothing and goggles
pegasparagase	*Oncaspar*	IM, IV	Enzyme that hydrolyzes the amino acid asparagine, which is needed by malignant cells for protein synthesis; inhibition of cell proliferation, most effective in G_1 phase of the cell cycle	Treatment of acute lymphocytic leukemia in patients who are hypersensitive to asparaginase	Potentially fatal hyperthermia, bone marrow suppression, renal toxicity, and pancreatitis may occur; monitor patient regularly and arrange decreased dosage as appropriate if toxic effects result
porfimer	*Photofrin*	IV	Photosensitizing agent	Used with laser light to decrease tumor size in patients with obstructive esophageal cancers who are not responsive to laser treatment alone	Has been associated with pleural effusion and fistula and GI and cardiac toxicity; must be given in conjunction with scheduled laser treatment, with at least 30 days between treatments; protect patient from exposure to light with protective clothing for 30 days following treatment (sunscreens are not effective); avoid direct contact with the drug—protective clothing and goggles are suggested
procarbazine	*Matulane*	Oral	Inhibition of DNA, RNA, and protein synthesis, leading to cell death	Used in combination for treatment of stage III and IV Hodgkin's disease	Bone marrow toxicity, GI toxicity, and skin lesions limit use in some patients; severity of adverse effects regulates the dose of the drug
topotecan	*Hycamtin*	IV	Damage to DNA strand, causing cell death during cell division	Treatment of patients with metastatic ovarian cancer after failure of other agents	Severe bone marrow suppression, which regulates the dose of the drug, may occur, total alopecia GI toxicity, and CNS effects may also limit the use of the drug; analgesics may be helpful
tretinoin	*Vesanoid*	Oral	Promotion of cell differentiation and the repopulation of the bone marrow with normal cells in patients with acute promyelocytic leukemia (APL)	Used to induce remission in APL	Can cause severe respiratory and cardiac toxicity, including MI and cardiac arrest; GI toxicity, pseudotumor cerebri (papilledema, headache, nausea, vomiting, and visual changes); skin rash; and fragility may limit use in some patients; discontinue drug at first sign of toxic effects, and use for induction of remission only (then other chemotherapeutic agents should be used)

CHAPTER SUMMARY

- Cancers arise from a single abnormal cell that multiplies and grows.
- Cancers can be diseases of the blood and lymph tissue or the growth of tumors arising from epithelial cells (carcinomas) or mesenchymal cells and connective tissue (sarcomas).
- Cancer cells lose their normal function (anaplasia), develop characteristics that allow them to grow in an uninhibited way (autonomy), and have the ability to travel to other sites in the body that are conducive to their growth (metastasis).
- Antineoplastic drugs affect both normal cells and cancer cells by disrupting cell function and division at various points in the cell cycle.
- Most cancer drugs are most effective against cells that multiply rapidly, that is, proceed through the cell cycle quickly. These cells include most neoplasms, bone marrow cells, cells in the GI tract, and cells in the skin or hair follicles.
- The goal of cancer chemotherapy is to decrease the size of the neoplasm so that the human immune system can deal with it.
- Antineoplastic drugs are often given in combination so that they can affect cells in various stages of the cell cycle and affect cells that are emerging from rest or moving to a phase of the cycle that is disrupted by these drugs.
- Adverse effects associated with antineoplastic therapy include effects caused by damage to the rapidly multiplying cells such as bone marrow suppression, which may limit the drug use; GI toxicity, with nausea, vomiting, mouth sores, and diarrhea; and alopecia, or hair loss.
- Chemotherapeutic agents should not be used during pregnancy or lactation because they may result in potentially serious adverse effects on the rapidly multiplying cells of the neonate.

BIBLIOGRAPHY

Bullock, B. L. (2000). *Focus on pathophysiology*. Philadelphia: Lippincott Williams & Wilkins.

Gilman, A. G., Rall, T. W., Nies, A. S., & Taylor, P. (Eds.). (1997). *Goodman and Gilman's the pharmacological basis of therapeutics* (9th ed.). New York: McGraw Hill.

Karch, A. M. (2000). *2000 Lippincott's nursing drug guide*. Philadelphia: Lippincott Williams & Wilkins.

Malseed, R. (1995). *Textbook of pharmacology and nursing care*. Philadelphia: Lippincott-Raven Publishers.

McEvoy, B. R. (Ed.). (1999). *Facts and comparisons 1999*. St. Louis: Facts and Comparisons.

Professional's guide to patient drug facts. (1999). St. Louis: Facts and Comparisons.

PART 3

Drugs Acting on the Immune System

CHAPTER 13

Introduction to the Immune Response and Inflammation

CHAPTER OUTLINE

KEY TERMS

antibodies
antigen
arachidonic acid
B cells
calor
chemotaxis
complement
dolor
Hageman factor
interferons
interleukins
kinin system
leukocytes
lymphocytes
macrophages
phagocytes
phagocytosis
pyrogen
rubor
T cells
tumor

INTRODUCTION

The body has many defense systems in place to keep it intact and to protect it from external stressors. These stressors can include bacteria, viruses, other foreign pathogens or non–self-cells, trauma, and exposure to extremes of environmental conditions. The same defense systems that protect the body also help to repair it following cellular trauma or damage. Understanding the basic mechanisms involved in these defense systems helps to explain the actions of the drugs that affect the immune system and inflammation.

BODY DEFENSES

The body's defenses include barrier defenses, cellular defenses, the inflammatory response, and the immune response. These are discussed in detail below.

Barrier Defenses

Certain anatomical barriers exist to prevent the entry of foreign pathogens and to serve as important lines of defense in protecting the body.

SKIN

The skin is the first line of defense. The skin acts as a physical barrier to protect the internal tissues and organs of the body. Glands in the skin secrete chemicals that destroy or repel many pathogens. The skin sloughs off daily, making it difficult for any pathogen to colonize on the skin. Finally, an array of normal flora bacteria live on the skin and destroy many disease-causing pathogens.

MUCOUS MEMBRANES

Mucous membranes line the areas of the body that are exposed to external influences, but do not have the benefit of skin protection. These body areas include the respiratory tract, which is exposed to air; the gastrointestinal (GI) tract, which is exposed to anything ingested by mouth; and the genitourinary (GU) tract. Like the skin, the mucous membrane is a physical barrier to invasion. It also secretes a sticky mucus, which traps invaders and inactivates them for later destruction and removal by the body. The mucus works much like fly-paper at trapping flies.

In the respiratory tract, the mucous membrane is lined with tiny, hair-like processes called cilia. The cilia sweep any captured pathogens or foreign materials upward toward the mouth either to be swallowed or to cause irritation to the area and be removed by a cough or a sneeze.

In the GI tract, the mucous membrane serves as a protective coating, preventing erosion of GI cells by the acidic environment of the stomach, the digestive enzymes of the small intestine, and the waste products that accumulate in the large intestine. The mucous membrane also secretes mucous that serves as a lubricant throughout the GI tract to facilitate movement of the food bolus and waste products.

In the GU tract, the mucous membrane provides direct protection against injury and trauma and traps any pathogens in the area for destruction by the body.

GASTRIC ACID

The stomach secretes acid in response to many stimuli. The acidity of the stomach not only aids digestion, but also destroys many would-be pathogens that are either ingested or swallowed following removal from the respiratory tract.

MAJOR HISTOCOMPATIBILITY COMPLEX (MHC)

The body's last barrier defense is the ability to identify cells as self-cells, not foreign cells. All of the cells and tissues of each person are marked for identification as part of that individual's genetic code. No two people have exactly the same code. In humans, the genetic identification code is carried on a chromosome and is called the major histocompatibility complex (MHC). The MHC produces several proteins called histocompatibility antigens or human leukocyte antigens (HLA) that are found on the cell membrane and allow the body to recognize cells as being self-cells. Cells that do not have these proteins are identified as foreign and are destroyed by the body.

Cellular Defenses

Any foreign pathogen that manages to get past the barrier defenses will encounter the human immune system or mononuclear phagocyte system (MPS). Previously called the reticuloendothelial system, the MPS is composed of the thymus gland, the lymphatic tissue, leukocytes, lymphocytes, and numerous chemical mediators.

MYELOCYTES

Stem cells in the bone marrow produce two types of white blood cells or ***leukocytes:*** lymphocytes and myelocytes. The ***lymphocytes*** are the key components of the immune system and consist of T cells, B cells, and natural killer cells (see "The immune response," below). The myelocytes can develop into a number of different cell types that are important in both the basic inflammatory response and in the immune response. Myelocytes include neutrophils, basophils, eosinophils, and monocytes or macrophages (Figure 13-1).

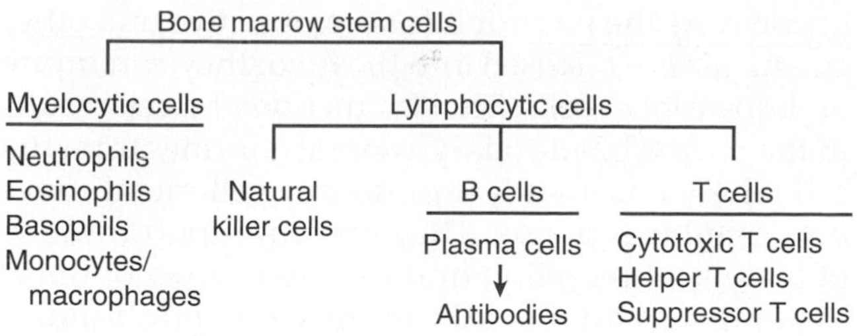

FIGURE 13-1. Types of white blood cells, or leukocytes, produced by the body.

Neutrophils

Neutrophils are polymorphonuclear leukocytes that are capable of diapedesis (movement outside of the bloodstream) and ***phagocytosis*** (engulfing and digesting foreign material). When the body is injured or invaded by a pathogen, neutrophils are rapidly produced and move to the site of the insult to attack the foreign substance. Because neutrophils are able to engulf and digest foreign material, they are called ***phagocytes.*** Phagocytes are able to identify non-self-cells using the MHC and can engulf these cells or mark them for destruction by active T cells.

Basophils

Basophils are myelocytic leukocytes that are not capable of phagocytosis. They are full of chemical substances important for initiating and maintaining an immune or inflammatory response. These substances include histamine, heparin, and chemicals used in the inflammatory response.

Eosinophils

Eosinophils are circulating myelocytic leukocytes whose exact function is not understood. They are often found at the site of allergic reactions and may be responsible for removing the proteins and active components of the immune reaction from the site of an allergic response.

Monocytes/Macrophages

Monocytes or mononuclear phagocytes are also called ***macrophages.*** They are mature leukocytes that are capable of phagocytizing an ***antigen*** (foreign protein). They also can process antigens to present them to active lymphocytes for destruction. Macrophages can be circulating phagocytes or fixed in specific tissues, such as the Kupffer cells in the liver, the cells in the alveoli of the respiratory tract, and the microglia in the central nervous system (CNS), GI, circulatory, and lymph tissues. These cells are active phagocytes and can release chemicals necessary to elicit a strong inflammatory reaction. Macrophages help remove foreign material from the body, including pathogens, debris from dead cells, and necrotic tissue from injury sites, so the body can heal. These cells respond to chemical mediators (released by other cells that are active in the inflammatory and immune responses) to increase the intensity or response and to facilitate the body's reaction (Figure 13-2).

MAST CELLS

Mast cells are fixed basophils that do not circulate, but are found in the respiratory and GI tracts and in the skin. They release many of the chemical mediators of the inflammatory and immune responses when they are stimulated by local irritation.

TISSUE AND GLAND CONNECTIONS

Lymphoid tissue that plays an important part in the cellular defense system includes the following: lymph nodes, spleen, thymus gland (a bipolar gland located in the middle of the chest, which becomes smaller with age), bone marrow, and lymphoid tissue throughout the respiratory and GI tracts. The bone marrow and the thymus gland are important for the creation of the cellular components of the MPS and also have a role in their differentiation and regulation. The lymph nodes and lymphoid tissue store concentrated populations of leukocytes and lymphocytes in positions that facilitate their surveillance for and destruction of foreign proteins. Other cells travel through the cardiovascular and lymph systems to search for foreign proteins or to reach the sites of injury or pathogen invasion.

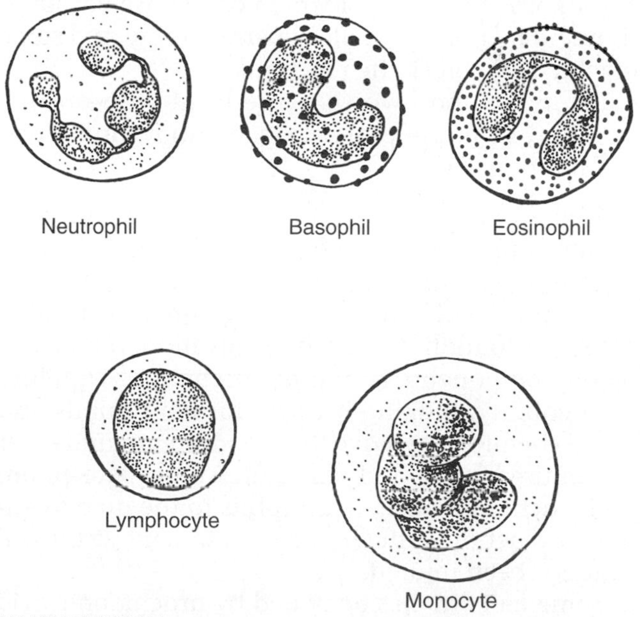

FIGURE 13-2. Appearance of different types of leukocytes. (Bullock, B. L. [2000]. *Focus on pathophysiology.* Philadelphia: Lippincott Williams & Wilkins.)

The Inflammatory Response

The inflammatory response is the local reaction of the body to invasion or injury. Any insult to the body that injures cells or tissues sets into action a series of events and chemical reactions.

Cell injury causes the activation of a chemical in the plasma called Factor XII or ***Hageman factor.*** Hageman factor is responsible for activating at least three systems in the body: the ***kinin system,*** which will be discussed here; the clotting cascade, which starts blood clotting; and the plasminogen system, which starts the dissolution of blood clots. These last two systems will be discussed in Part 8, Drugs Acting on the Cardiovascular System.

Hageman factor activates kallikrein, a substance found in the local tissues, which causes the precursor substance kininogen to be converted to bradykinin and other kinins. Bradykinin was the first kinin identified and the one that is best understood. Bradykinin causes local vasodilation to bring more blood to the injured area and to allow white blood cells to escape into the tissues. It also stimulates nerve endings to cause pain, which alerts the body to the injury.

Bradykinin also causes the release of arachidonic acid from the cell membrane. ***Arachidonic acid*** is known to cause the release of other substances called autocoids. These substances act like local hormones, being released from cells, causing an effect in the immediate area and then being broken down. These autocoids include the following:

- Prostaglandins, some of which augment the inflammatory reaction and some of which block it
- Leukotrienes, some of which can cause vasodilation and increased capillary permeability and some of which can block the reactions
- Thromboxanes, which cause local vasoconstriction and facilitate platelet aggregation and blood coagulation.

While this series of Hageman-factor-initiated events is proceeding, another locally mediated response is occurring. Injury to a cell membrane will cause the local release of histamine. Histamine causes vasodilation, which brings more blood and blood components to the area; changes capillary permeability, making it easier for neutrophils and blood chemicals to leave the blood stream and enter the injured area; and stimulates pain perception. These activities bring neutrophils to the area to engulf and get rid of the invader, or to remove the cell that has been injured.

Some leukotrienes activated by arachidonic acid have a property called ***chemotaxis.*** Chemotaxis is the ability to attract neutrophils and stimulate them and other macrophages in the area to be very aggressive. As the neutrophils become active and other chemicals are released into the area, they can injure or destroy local cells. The destruction of a cell results in the release of various lysosomal enzymes from the cell. These enzymes lyse or destroy cell membranes and cellular proteins. They are an important part of biological recycling and the breakdown of once-living tissues after death. In the case of an inflammatory reaction, they can cause local cellular breakdown and further inflammation, which can develop into a vicious cycle leading to cell death.

Many inflammatory diseases, such as rheumatoid arthritis and systemic lupus erythematosus, are examples of these uncontrolled cycles. The prostaglandins and leukotrienes are important to the inflammatory response because they act to moderate the reaction, thus preventing this destructive cycle from happening on a regular basis. Many of the drugs used to affect the inflammatory and immune systems modify or interfere with these inflammatory reactions.

CLINICAL PRESENTATION

Activation of the inflammatory response produces a characteristic clinical picture. The Latin words ***calor*** (heat), ***tumor*** (swelling), ***rubor*** (redness), and ***dolor*** (pain) describe a typical inflammatory reaction. Calor or heat occurs because of the increased blood flow to the area. Tumor or swelling occurs because of the fluid leaking into the tissues as a result of the change in capillary permeability. Rubor or redness is related again to the increase in blood flow caused by the vasodilation. Dolor or pain comes from the activation of pain fibers by histamine and the kinin system. These signs and symptoms occur anytime a cell is injured (Figure 13-3).

For example, scratch the top of your hand and wait for about a minute. The direct line of the scratch will be red (rubor) and raised (tumor). If you feel it gently, it will be warmer than the surrounding area (calor). You should also experience a burning sensation or discomfort at the site of the scratch (dolor). Invasion of the lungs by a bacteria can produce pneumonia. If the lungs could be examined closely, they would also show the signs and symptoms of inflammation. They would be very red from increased blood flow; fluid would start to leak out of the capillaries, which can often be heard as rales; the patient would complain of chest discomfort; and the increased blood flow to the area of infection would make it appear hot, or very active on a scan. No matter what the cause of the insult, the body's local response is the same.

Once the inflammatory response is underway and neutrophils become active, engulfing and digesting

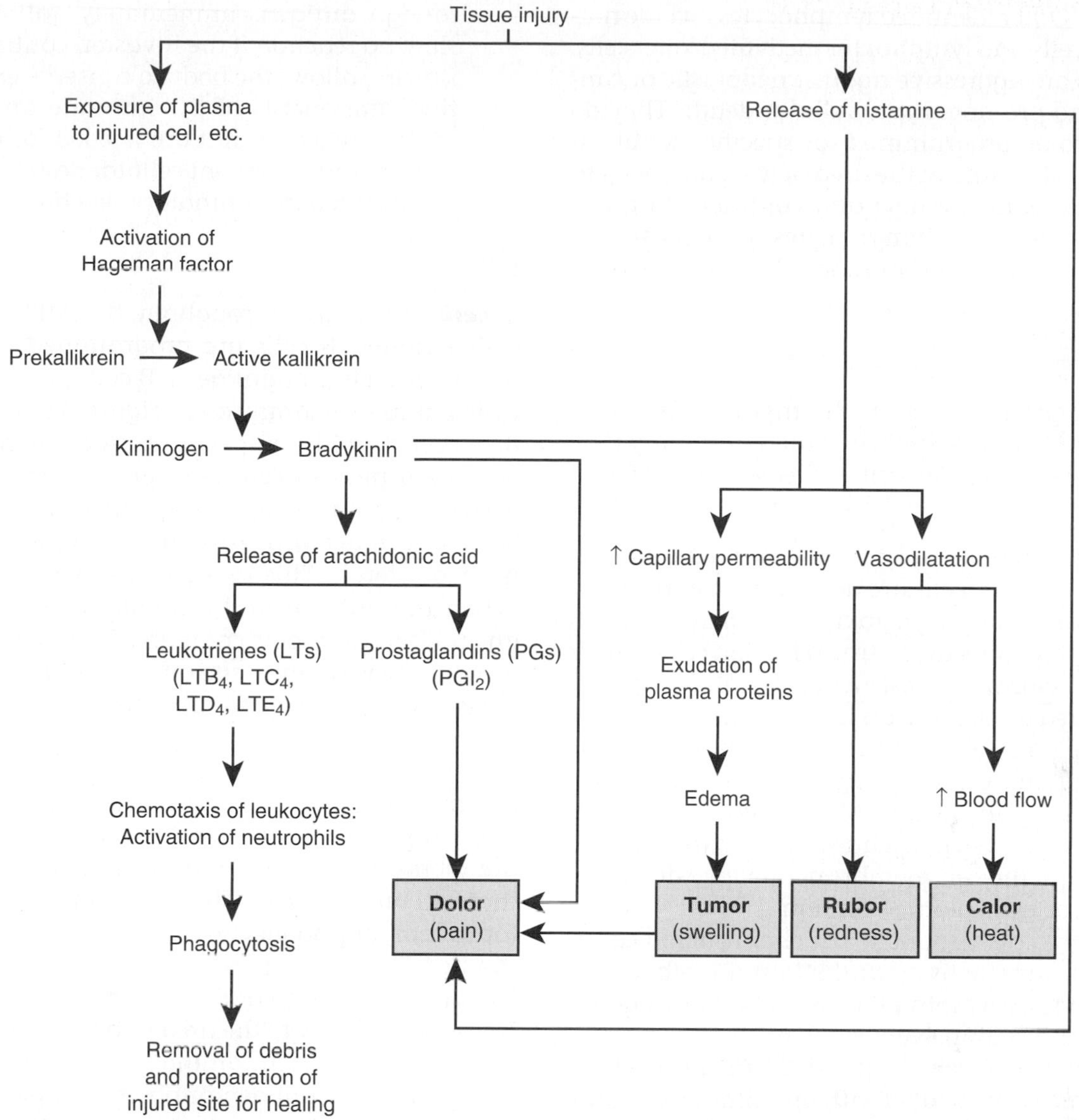

FIGURE 13-3. The inflammatory response in relation to the four cardinal signs of inflammation.

the injured cell or the invader, they release a chemical which is a natural ***pyrogen,*** or fever-causing substance. This pyrogen resets specific neurons in the hypothalamus to maintain a higher body temperature, seen clinically as a fever. The higher temperature acts as a catalyst to many of the body's chemical reactions, making the inflammatory and immune responses more effective. Treating fevers remains a controversial subject because lowering a fever decreases the efficiency of the immune and inflammatory responses.

The leukotrienes (activated through the kinin system) affect the brain to induce slow-wave sleep, which is thought to be important for saving energy to fight the invader. They also cause myalgia and arthralgia (muscle and joint pain)—common signs and symptoms of various inflammatory diseases—which also cause reduced activity and save energy. All of these chemical responses make up the total clinical picture of an inflammatory reaction.

The Immune Response

More specific invasion can stimulate a more specific response through the immune system. The lymphocytes produced in the bone marrow by the stem cells can develop into T lymphocytes (so named because they migrate from the bone marrow to the thymus gland for activation and maturation) or B lymphocytes (so named because they are activated in the bursa of Fabricius in the chicken, though the specific point of activation in humans has not been identified). Other identified lymphocytes include natural killer cells and lymphokine-activated killer cells. These cells are aggressive against neoplastic or cancer cells and promote rapid cellular death. They do not seem to be programmed for specific identification of cells. Research in the area of lymphocyte identification is relatively new and continues to grow. There may be other lymphocytes with particular roles in the immune response that have not yet been identified.

T CELLS

T cells are programmed in the thymus gland and provide what is called cell-mediated immunity (Figure 13-4). T cells develop into at least three different cell types.

1. *Effector or cytotoxic T cells* are found around the body. These T cells are aggressive against non–self-cells, releasing cytokines, or chemicals, that can either directly destroy a foreign cell or mark it for aggressive destruction by phagocytes in the area by eliciting an inflammatory response. These non–self-cells have different membrane identifying antigens, not the antigens established by the person's MHC. These can be cells that have been invaded by a virus, which changes the cell membrane, neoplastic cancer cells, or transplanted foreign cells.
2. *Helper T cells* respond to the chemical indicators of immune activity and stimulate other lymphocytes, including B cells, to be more aggressive and responsive.
3. *Suppressor T cells* respond to rising levels of chemicals associated with an immune response to suppress or slow the reaction. The balance of these two cells—the helper and suppressor T cells—allows for rapid response to body injury or invasion by pathogens, which may destroy foreign antigens immediately, followed by a slowing reaction if the invasion continues. This slowing allows the body to conserve energy and the components of the immune and inflammatory reaction that are needed for basic protection and to prevent cellular destruction from a continued inflammatory reaction.

B CELLS

B cells are found throughout the MPS in groups called clones. B cells are programmed to identify specific proteins, or antigens. B cells provide what is called humoral immunity (Figure 13-5). When a B cell reacts with its specific antigen, it changes to become a plasma cell. Plasma cells produce ***antibodies,*** or immunoglobulins, which circulate in the body and react with this specific antigen when it is encountered. This is a direct chemical reaction. When the antigen and antibody react, they form an antigen-antibody complex. This new structure reveals a new receptor site on the antibody that activates a series of plasma proteins in the body called ***complement.***

Complement proteins react in a cascade fashion to form a ring around the antigen-antibody complex. The complement can destroy the antigen by altering the membrane to allow an osmotic inflow of fluid that will burst the cell. They also induce chemotaxis (attraction of phagocytic cells to the area), increase the activity of phagocytes, and release histamine. Histamine release causes vasodilation, which increases blood flow to the area and brings in all of the components of the inflammatory reaction to destroy the antigen. The antigen-antibody-complement complex will precipitate out of the circulatory system and deposit in various sites, including end arteries in joints, the eye, the kidney, and the skin. The signs and symptoms of the inflammatory response can

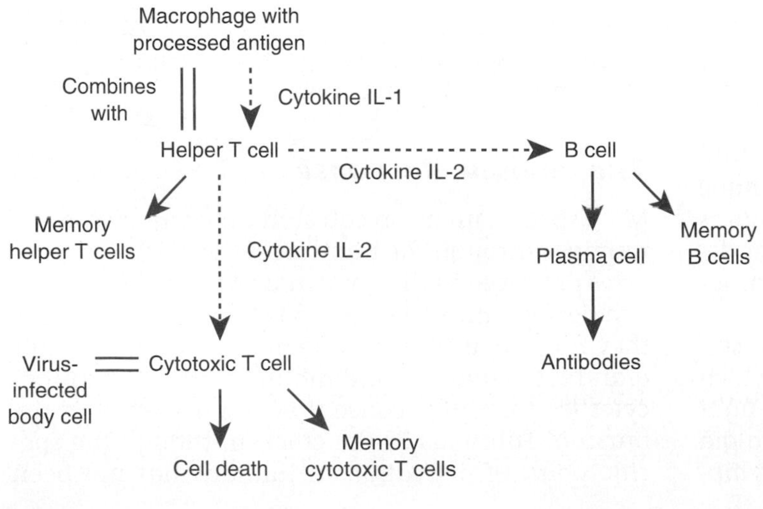

FIGURE 13-4. The cell-mediated immune response. Activation of a T cell by a "nonself" cell results in responses that destroy the foreign cell.

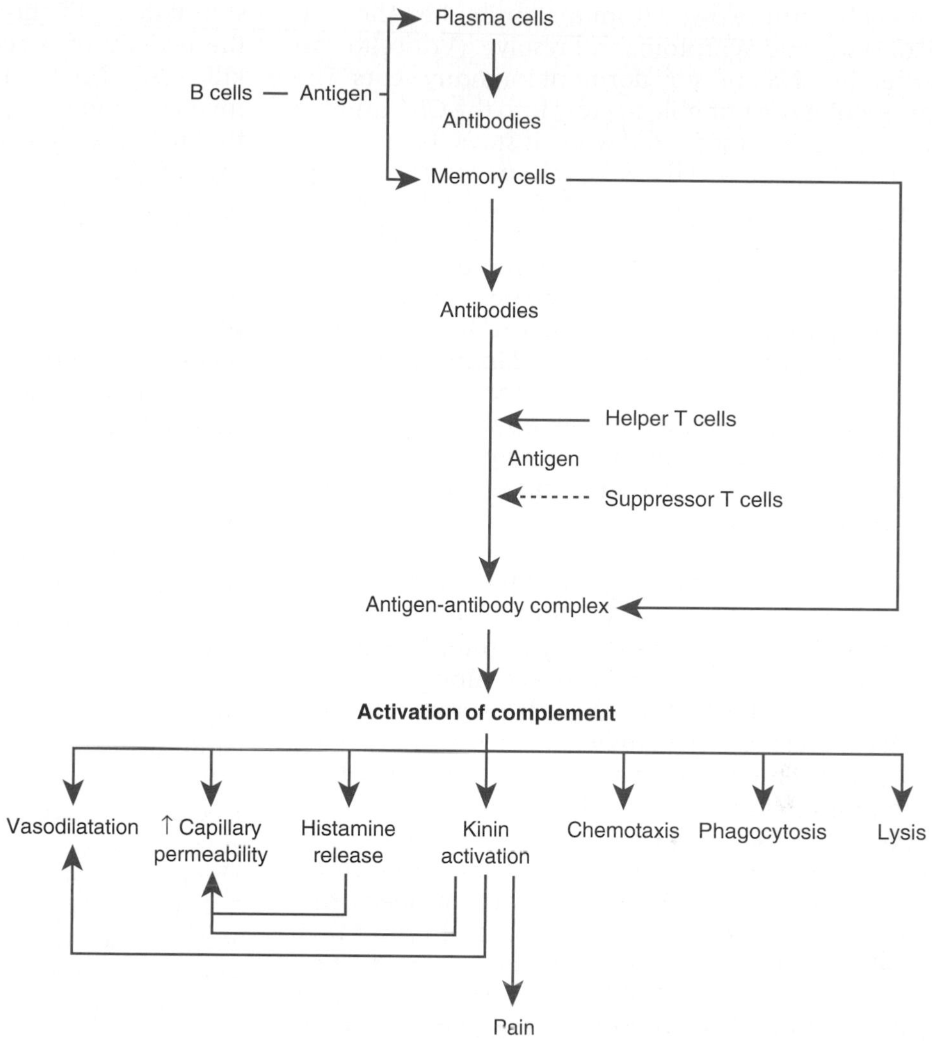

FIGURE 13-5. The humoral immune response.

be seen where the antigen-antibody complexes are deposited. Chicken pox eruptions are an example of an antigen-antibody-complement complex that deposits in the skin and causes a local inflammatory reaction.

The initial formation of antibodies, or primary response, takes several days. Once activated, the B cells form memory cells that will form antibodies for immediate release in the future if the antigen is encountered. The antibodies are released in the form of immunoglobulins. Five different types of immunoglobulins have been identified. The first immunoglobulin that is released is called IgM and it contains the antibodies produced at the first exposure to the antigen. IgG is another form of immunoglobulin and it contains antibodies made by the memory cells which circulate and enter the tissue; most of the immunoglobulin found in the serum is IgG. IgA is found in tears, saliva, sweat, mucous, and bile. It is secreted by plasma cells in the GI and respiratory tracts and in epithelial cells. These antibodies react with specific pathogens that are encountered in exposed areas of the body. IgE is present in small amounts and seems to be related to allergic responses and to activation of mast cells. IgD is another identified immunoglobulin whose role has not been determined.

This process of antibody formation, called acquired or active immunity, is a lifelong reaction. For example, a person exposed to chicken pox will have a mild respiratory reaction when the virus (varicella) first enters the respiratory tract. There will then be a 2- to 3-week incubation period as the body is forming IgM antibodies and preparing to attack any chicken pox virus that appears. The chicken pox virus enters a cell and multiplies. The cell will eventually rupture and eject more viruses into the system. When this happens, the body is ready to respond with the immediate release of antibodies and a full-scale antigen-antibody response seen throughout the body. Fever, myalgia, arthralgia, and skin lesions are all part of the immune response to the virus. Once all of the invading chicken pox viruses have been destroyed, or have entered the CNS to safely hibernate away from the antibodies, the clinical signs and symptoms will resolve. (Varicella can enter the CNS and stay dormant for many years. The antibodies are not able to cross into the CNS and the virus remains unaffected while it stays there.)

The B memory cells will continue to make a supply of immunoglobulin, IgM, for use with any future exposure to the chicken pox virus. That exposure usually does not evolve into a clinical case because the viruses are destroyed immediately upon entering the body and do not have a chance to multiply. Older patients with weakened immune systems, people who are immunosuppressed, or individuals who have depleted their immune system fighting an infection are at risk for developing shingles if they have had chicken pox earlier in their lives. The dormant virus, which has aged and changed somewhat, is able to leave the CNS along a nerve root because the immunosuppressed body is slow to respond. The antibodies will eventually respond to the varicella and the signs and symptoms of shingles will occur as the virus is attacked along the nerve root. Figure 13-6 outlines this entire process.

B clones cluster in areas where they are most likely to encounter the specific antigen that they have been programmed to recognize. For example, pathogens or antigens that are introduced into the body via the respiratory tract will meet up with the B cells in the tonsils and upper respiratory tract; antigens that enter the body through the GI tract will meet their B cells situated in the esophagus and GI tract. Theorists believe that the B cells are programmed genetically and are formed by the time of birth. Clones of B cells contain similar cells. The introduction of an antigen to which there are no pre-programmed B cells could result in widespread disease, because the body would have no way of responding. A big concern of space travel has always been the introduction of a completely new antigen to the earth, explaining the long periods of decontamination after rocks or debris are brought back to earth. Germ warfare research is ongoing in some countries to develop an antigen that has not been seen before and to which people would have no response.

OTHER MEDIATORS

Several other factors also play an important role in the immune reaction. ***Interferons*** are chemicals that are secreted by cells that have been invaded by viruses and possibly by other stimuli. The interferons prevent viral replication and also suppress malignant cell replication and tumor growth.

Interleukins are chemicals secreted by active leukocytes to influence other leukocytes. Interleukin 1 stimulates T and B cells to initiate an immune response. Interleukin 2 is released from active T cells to stimulate production of more T cells and to increase the activity of B cells, cytotoxic cells, and natural killer cells. Interleukins also cause fever, arthralgia, myalgia, and slow-wave sleep induction—all things that help the body to conserve energy to use in fighting off the invader. Several other factors released by lymphocytes and basophils have been identified. These include interleukins such as B cell growth factor, macrophage-activating factor, macrophage-inhibiting factor, platelet-activating factor, eosinophil chemotactic factor, and neutrophil chemotactic factor. The thymus gland also releases a number of hormones that aid in the maturation of T cells and that circulate in the body to stimulate and communicate with T cells. Thymosin, a thymus hormone that has been replicated, is important in the maturation of T cells and cell-mediated immunity. Research is ongoing on the use of thymosin in certain leukemias and melanomas to stimulate the immune response.

Tumor necrosis factor (TNF), a cytokine, is a chemical released by macrophages that inhibits tumor growth and can actually cause tumor regression. It also works with other chemicals to make the inflammatory and immune responses more aggressive and efficient. Research is ongoing to determine the therapeutic effectiveness of TNF. TNF receptor sites are now available for injection into patients with acute rheumatoid arthritis. These receptors sites react with TNF released by the macrophages in this inflammatory disease. All of these chemicals act as communication factors within the immune system, allowing the coordination of the immune response.

Interrelationships of the Immune and Inflammatory Responses

The immune and inflammatory responses work together to protect the body and to maintain a level of homeostasis within the body. Helper T cells stimulate the activity of B cells and effector T cells. Suppressor T cells monitor the chemical activity in the body and act to suppress B cell and T cell activity when the foreign antigen is under control. Both the B cells and T cells ultimately depend on an effective inflammatory reaction to achieve the end goal of destruction of the foreign protein or cell (Figure 13-7).

PATHOPHYSIOLOGY INVOLVING THE IMMUNE SYSTEM

Several conditions can arise that cause problems involving the immune system. Many of these conditions are treated by drugs that stimulate or suppress the immune system. These conditions include

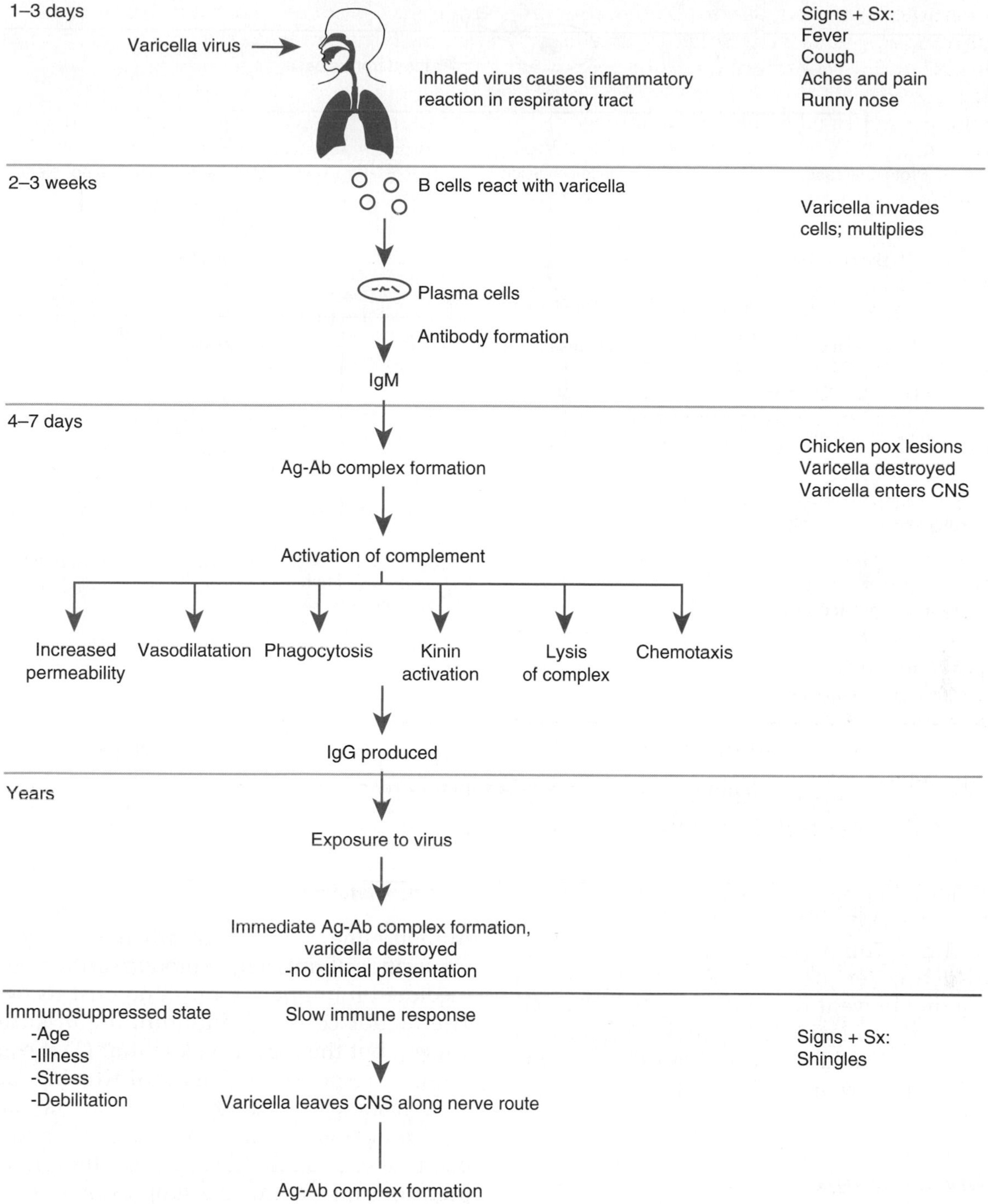

FIGURE 13-6. Process of response to varicella exposure in humans.

neoplasm, viral invasion, autoimmune disease, and transplant rejection.

Neoplasms

Neoplasms occur when mutant cells escape the normal surveillance of the immune system and begin to grow and multiply. This can happen in many ways. For example, aging causes a decreased efficiency of the immune system, allowing some cells to escape. Location of the mutant cells can present a problem for getting the lymphocytes to an area to respond. Mutant cells in breast tissue, for example, are not well perfused with blood and may escape detection until they are quite abundant in number. "Sneaking through" of a cell can occur. Sometimes cells are able

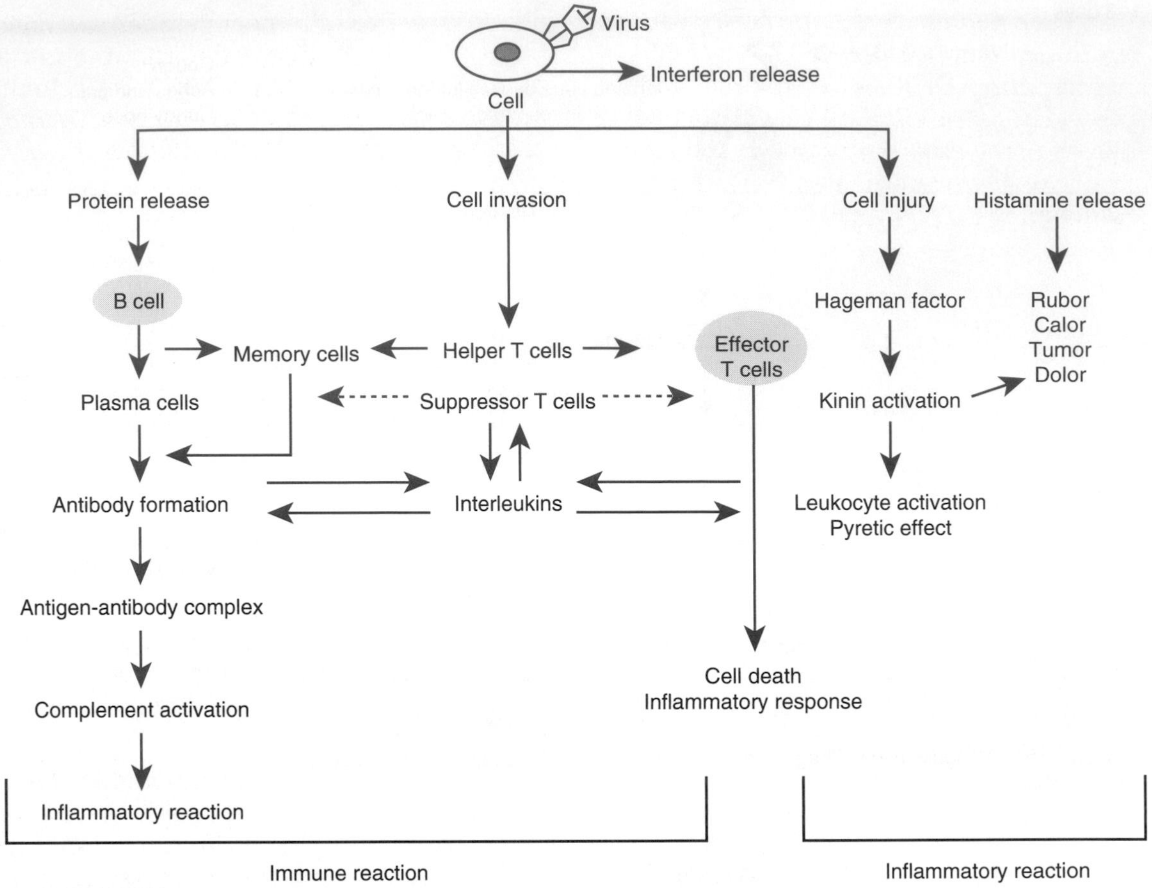

FIGURE 13-7. Interrelationship of immune inflammatory reactions.

to avoid detection by the T cells until the growing mass of cells is so large that the immune system cannot deal with it. Tumors can produce blocking antibodies which cover the antigen receptor sites on the tumor and prevent recognition by the cytotoxic T cells. A weakly antigenic tumor may develop. Such a tumor elicits a mild response from the immune system and somehow tricks the T cells into allowing it to survive.

Viral Invasion of Cells

Viruses are parasites that can only survive by invading a host cell which provides the nourishment necessary for viral replication. Invasion of a cell alters the cell membrane and the antigenic presentation of the cell, the MHC. This change can activate cellular immunity or can be so subtle that the immune system's response to the cell is mild or absent. In some cases the response activates a cellular immune reaction to normal cells similar to the one that was invaded. This is one theory for the development of autoimmune disease.

Autoimmune Disease

Autoimmune disease occurs when the body responds to specific self-antigens to produce antibodies or cell-mediated immune responses against its own cells. The actual cause of autoimmune disease is not known, but theories speculate that (1) it could be a result of response to a cell that was invaded by a virus, leading to antibody production to similar cells; (2) production of auto-antibodies is a normal process that goes on all the time, and that in a state of immunosuppression, the suppressor T cells do not suppress auto-antibody production; and (3) there is a genetic predisposition to develop autoantibodies.

Transplant Rejection

With the growing field of organ transplant, more is being learned about the body's reaction to foreign cells introduced to the body. Effort is always made to match a donor's HLA molecules as closely as possible to the recipient's histocompatibility leukocyte antigens. The more closely the foreign cells can be matched, the less aggressive the immune reaction will be. Self-transplant, or autotransplant, results in no immune response. All other transplants produce an immune reaction. The effector T cells are activated by the presence of the foreign cells and cytokines are released to stimulate an immune and inflammatory reaction and destroy the foreign cells.

WWW.WEB LINKS

Health care providers and patients may want to consult the following Internet sources:

Detailed review of the immune system:
http://www.keratin.com/am/amindex.shtml

Fun travel through the virtual immune system:
http://www.thebody.com/step/immune.html

CHAPTER SUMMARY

- The body has several defense mechanisms in place to protect it from injury or foreign invasion: the skin, mucous membranes, normal flora, gastric acid, and the inflammatory and immune responses.
- The inflammatory response is a general response to any cell injury.
- The inflammatory response involves activation of Hageman factor to stimulate the kinin system and release of histamine from injured cells to generate local inflammatory responses.
- The response to the inflammatory stimuli involves local vasodilation, increased capillary permeability, and the stimulation of pain fibers. These reactions alert the person to the injury and bring an increased blood flow to the area.
- The clinical presentation of an inflammatory reaction is heat, redness, swelling, and pain (calor, rubor, tumor, and dolor).
- The immune response provides a specific reaction to foreign cells or proteins.
- Several types of T cells exist: effector or cytotoxic T cells, helper T cells, and suppressor T cells. Effector or cytotoxic T cells immediately destroy foreign cells. Helper T cells stimulate the immune and inflammatory reactions. Suppressor T cells dampen the immune and inflammatory responses to conserve energy and prevent cellular damage.
- B cells are programmed to recognize specific proteins or foreign antigens. Once in contact with a protein, the B cells produce antibodies (immunoglobulins) which will react with that protein.
- Reaction of an antibody with the specific receptor site on the protein activates the complement cascade of proteins and lyses the associated protein or precipitates an aggressive inflammatory reaction around it.
- Other chemicals are involved in the communication between parts of the immune system and with local response to invasion. Any of these chemicals have the potential to alter the immune response.
- The T cells, B cells, and inflammatory reaction work together to protect the body from invasion, limit the response to that invasion, and return the body to a state of homeostasis.
- Patient problems that occur within the immune system include the development of neoplasms, viral invasion of cells triggering immune responses, autoimmune disease, and transplant rejection.

BIBLIOGRAPHY

Bullock, B. L. (2000). *Focus on pathophysiology.* Philadelphia: Lippincott Williams & Wilkins.

Ganong, W. (1999). *Review of medical physiology* (18th ed.). Norwalk, CT: Appleton & Lange.

Guyton, A. & Hall, J. (1996). *Textbook of medical physiology.* Philadelphia: W.B. Saunders.

Hardman, J. G., Limbird, L. E., Molinoff, P. B., Ruddon, R. W., & Gilman, A. G. (Eds.). (1996). *Goodman and Gilman's the pharmacological basis of therapeutics* (9th ed.). New York: McGraw Hill.

Karch, A. M. (2000). *2000 Lippincott's nursing drug guide.* Philadelphia: Lippincott Williams & Wilkins.

Peakman, M. & Vergani, D. (1997). *Basic and clinical immunology.* New York: Churchill-Livingstone.

Stites, D. P., Terr, A. I., & Parslow, T. G. (Eds.). (1997). *Medical immunology* (9th ed.). Stamford, CT: Appleton & Lange.

CHAPTER 14

Anti-Inflammatory Agents

Salicylates
- **P** aspirin
- choline magnesium trisalicylate
- choline salicylate
- mesalamine
- olsalazine
- salsalate
- sodium thiosalicylate

Nonsteroidal anti-inflammatory drugs (NSAIDs)
- diclofenac
- diflunisal
- etodolac
- fenoprofen
- flurbiprofen
- **P** ibuprofen
- indomethacin
- ketoprofen
- ketorolac
- meclofenamate
- mefenamic acid
- nabumetone
- naproxen
- oxaprozin
- piroxicam
- sulindac
- tolmetin

Other related drugs
- **P** acetaminophen
- auranofin
- **P** aurothioglucose
- etanercept
- gold sodium thiomalate
- hylan G-F 20
- leflunomide
- penicillamine
- sodium hyaluronate

CHAPTER OUTLINE

KEY TERMS

analgesic
anti-inflammatory
antipyretic
chrysotherapy
nonsteroidal anti-inflammatory drugs (NSAIDs)
salicylates

INTRODUCTION

The inflammatory response is designed to protect the body from injury and pathogens. It employs a variety of potent chemical mediators to produce the reaction that helps to destroy pathogens and promote healing. As the body reacts to these chemicals, it produces some signs and symptoms of disease, such as swelling, pain, fever, aches, and pains. Occasionally, the inflammatory response becomes a chronic condition and can actually result in body damage, leading to increased inflammatory reactions. ***Anti-inflammatory*** agents generally block or alter the chemical reactions associated with the inflammatory response to stop one or more of the signs and symptoms of inflammation.

ANTI-INFLAMMATORY AGENTS

Several different types of drugs are used as anti-inflammatory agents. Corticosteroids (discussed in Chapter 34) are used systemically to block the inflammatory and immune systems. Blocking these important protective processes may produce many adverse effects, including decreased resistance to infection and neoplasms. Corticosteroids also are used topically to produce a local anti-inflammatory effect without as many adverse effects. Antihistamines (discussed in Chapter 52) are used to block the release of histamine in the initiation of the inflammatory response. In this chapter, discussion of anti-inflammatory agents focuses on salicylates, nonsteroidal anti-inflammatory drugs (NSAIDs), and other related drugs.

Salicylates are popular anti-inflammatory agents, not only because of their ability to block the inflammatory response, but also because of their ***antipyretic*** (fever blocking) and ***analgesic*** (pain blocking) properties. They are generally available without prescription and are relatively nontoxic when used as directed.

Nonsteroidal anti-inflammatory drugs (NSAIDs) are some of the most widely used drugs in the United States. They provide strong anti-inflammatory and analgesic effects, yet do not have the same adverse effects associated with the corticosteroids.

Acetaminophen also is a widely used agent. It has antipyretic and analgesic properties, but does not have the anti-inflammatory effects of the salicylates or the NSAIDs.

Because many of these anti-inflammatory drugs are available over-the-counter (OTC), there is potential for abuse and overdosing. In addition, patients may take these drugs and block the signs and symptoms of a present illness, thus causing the potential for misdiagnosis of a problem. Patients also may combine these drugs and unknowingly produce toxic levels. All of these drugs have adverse effects that can be dangerous if toxic levels are reached.

In 1999, a new class of anti-inflammatory agents called COX-2 inhibitors was introduced. These are discussed in Box 14-1.

SALICYLATES

Salicylates are some of the oldest anti-inflammatory drugs used. They were extracted from willow bark, poplar trees, and other plants by ancient peoples to treat fever, pain, and what we now call inflammation. The synthetic salicylates include the following:

Aspirin (*Bayer, Empirin* and others): one of the most widely used drugs for treating inflammatory conditions; is available OTC.

BOX 14-1

COX-2 INHIBITORS

In 1999, the first of a new class of anti-inflammatory drugs—called COX-2 inhibitors—was introduced. Traditional NSAIDs work to block the enzymes cyclooxygenase-1 (COX-1) and cyclooxygenase-2 (COX-2), which block the formation of prostaglandins. COX-1 is present in all tissues and seems to be involved in many body functions, including blood clotting, protecting the stomach lining, and maintaining sodium and water balance in the kidney. COX-1 turns arachidonic acid into prostaglandins as needed in a variety of tissues. COX-2 is active at sites of trauma or injury when more prostaglandins are needed.

Traditional NSAIDs block both COX-1, necessary for many body functions, and COX-2, which responds to trauma and injury. The adverse effects associated with the NSAIDs are related to the blocking of both of these enzymes and changes in the functions that they influence—GI integrity, blood clotting, and sodium and water balance. The COX-2 inhibitors are designed to only affect COX-2 activity, the enzyme that becomes active in response to trauma and injury. They do not interfere with COX-1, which is needed for normal functioning of these systems. Consequently, these drugs should not have the associated adverse effects seen when both COX-1 and COX-2 are inhibited.

Celecoxib (*Celebrex*) was the first drug of this class approved for the acute and long-term treatment of signs and symptoms of rheumatoid arthritis and osteoarthritis. It is not approved for any other use because of the lack of long-term studies to determine its safety and efficacy. The adverse effects seen with this drug include headache, dizziness, insomnia, and rash. Bone marrow depression may also occur. As with many of the anti-inflammatory drugs, there is a risk of severe to fatal anaphylactic reactions when used.

Choline magnesium trisalicylate (*Trilisate*): used for mild pain and fevers and to treat arthritis.

Choline salicylate (*Arthropan*): used to treat mild pain and fevers as well as arthritis; available only as an OTC drug.

Mesalamine (*Pentasa* and others): a unique compound that releases aspirin in the large intestine for a direct anti-inflammatory effect in ulcerative colitis or other large intestine inflammation.

Olsalazine (*Dipentum*): a drug that is converted to mesalamine in the colon and has the same direct anti-inflammatory effects.

Salsalate (*Argesic* and others): used to treat pain, fever, and inflammation.

Sodium thiosalicylate (*Rexolate*): used mainly for episodes of acute gout and muscular pain, and to treat rheumatic fever.

A person who does not respond to one salicylate may respond to a different one.

THERAPEUTIC ACTIONS AND INDICATIONS

Salicylates inhibit the synthesis of prostaglandin, an important mediator of the inflammatory reaction (Figure 14-1). The antipyretic effect of salicylates may be related to the blocking of a prostaglandin mediator of pyrogens (chemicals that cause an increase in body temperature and that are released by active white blood cells) at the thermoregulatory center of the hypothalamus. At low levels, aspirin also affects platelet aggregation by inhibiting the synthesis of thromboxane A, a potent vasoconstrictor that normally increases platelet aggregation and blood clot formation. At higher levels, aspirin inhibits the synthesis of prostacyclin, a vasodilator that inhibits platelet aggregation.

Salicylates are indicated for the treatment of mild to moderate pain, fever, and numerous inflammatory conditions, including rheumatoid arthritis and osteoarthritis. Aspirin at low doses is indicated for the prevention of transient ischemic attack (TIA) and stroke in males with a history of emboli. It also is indicated to reduce the risk of death and myocardial infarction (MI) in patients with a history of MI or unstable angina.

CONTRAINDICATIONS/CAUTIONS

The use of salicylates is contraindicated in the presence of known allergy to salicylates, other NSAIDs (more common with a history of nasal polyps,

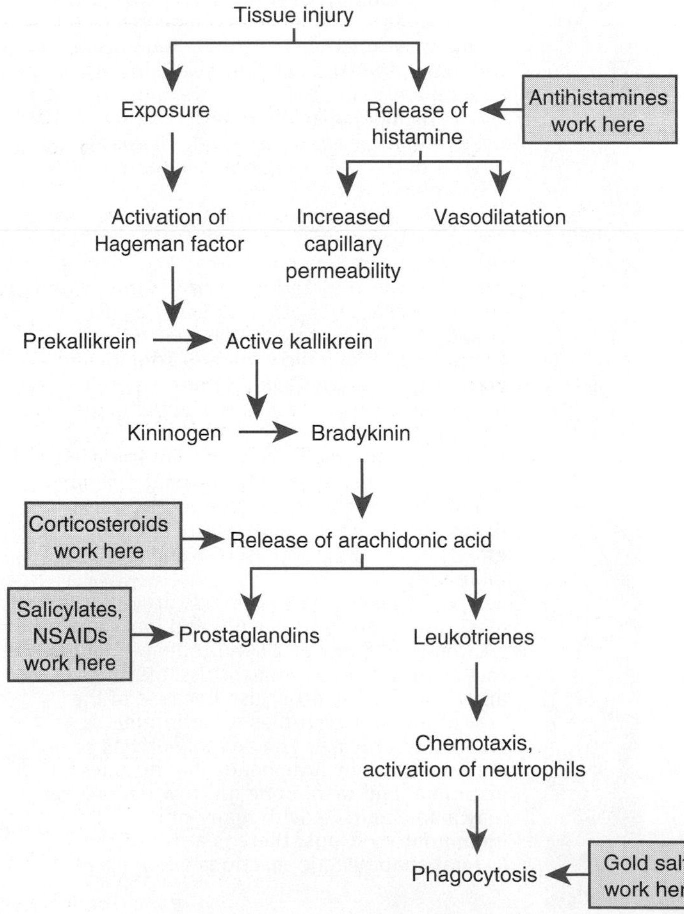

FIGURE 14-1. Sites of action of anti-inflammatory agents.

NURSING CHALLENGE

Rheumatoid Arthritis

Rheumatoid arthritis is a chronic, systemic disease that affects people of all ages. It is considered to be an autoimmune disease. Patients with rheumatoid arthritis have high levels of rheumatoid factor (RF), an antibody to immunoglobulin (IgG). RF interacts with circulating IgG to form immune complexes, which tend to deposit in the synovial fluid of joints as well as in the eye and other small vessels. The formation of the immune complex activates complement and precipitates an inflammatory reaction. During the immune reaction, lysosomal enzymes are released that destroy the tissues surrounding the joint. This destruction of normal tissue causes a further inflammatory reaction, and a cycle of destruction and inflammation ensues. Over time, the joint becomes severely damaged and the synovial space fills with scar tissue.

The patient with rheumatoid arthritis is in chronic pain, related to the release of the chemicals involved in the inflammatory process and the pressure of the swelling tissues in the joint capsule. At this time there is no cure for rheumatoid arthritis. Treatment is aimed at relieving the signs and symptoms of inflammation and delaying the progressive damage to the joints. The patient with this disease will progressively lose the use of the joint, which affects mobility as well as the ability to carry on the activities of daily living. Depression is not an uncommon side effect to this disease.

Specific nursing interventions can help to alleviate some of the signs and symptoms of rheumatoid arthritis and help the patient to cope with the disease. These interventions include physical therapy; range of motion exercises; application of hot and cold packs to the joints; weight-bearing exercises; spacing activities throughout the day to make the most of energy and movement reserves; and assistance devices for normal daily activities (e.g., big handles on utensils and pens to help patients do things for themselves when they cannot grasp small handles). Thorough teaching about drug regimens can also help prevent adverse effects and increase compliance.

Patients may have to progress through a series of drugs as various agents lose their effectiveness. Aspirin, NSAIDs, gold therapy, and more potent anti-arthritis drugs may all be used at one time or another. The patient with rheumatoid arthritis will profit from a relationship with a consistent, reliable health care provider who listens, offers support, and has knowledge of new drugs and treatments to improve the quality of life. Many community support and information groups are available as resources to patients—and to health care providers who work with these patients. For a listing of available resources in your area, contact the Arthritis Foundation: http://www.arthritis.org.

asthma, or chronic urticaria), or tartrazine (a dye that has a cross-sensitivity with aspirin); bleeding abnormalities (because of the changes in platelet aggregation associated with these drugs); impaired renal function; chicken pox or influenza (risk of Reye's syndrome in children and teenagers); surgery or other invasive procedures scheduled within a week (because of the risk of increased bleeding); and during pregnancy (increased risk of fetal malformation and maternal bleeding problems at delivery) and lactation (because of the potential risk to the infant).

ADVERSE EFFECTS

The adverse effects associated with the use of salicylates may be the result of direct drug effects on the stomach (nausea, dyspepsia, heartburn, epigastric discomfort) and clotting systems (blood loss, bleeding abnormalities). Salicylism can occur with high levels of aspirin; dizziness, ringing in the ears, difficulty hearing, nausea, vomiting, diarrhea, mental confusion, and lassitude can occur. Acute salicylate toxicity may occur at 20- to 25-g doses in adults or 4-g doses in children. Signs of salicylate toxicity include respiratory alkalosis; hyperpnea; tachypnea; hemorrhage; excitement; confusion; pulmonary edema; convulsions; tetany; metabolic acidosis; fever; coma; and cardiovascular, renal, and respiratory collapse.

CLINICALLY IMPORTANT DRUG–DRUG INTERACTIONS

The salicylates interact with many other drugs, primarily because of alterations in absorption, effects on the liver, or extension of the therapeutic effects of the salicylate and/or the interacting drug. The list of interacting drugs in each drug monograph should be consulted and the prescriber consulted before adding or removing a salicylate from any drug regimen.

DATA LINK

Data link to the following salicylates in your nursing drug guide:

SALICYLATES

Name	Brand Name	Usual Indications
P aspirin	*Bayer, Empirin,* others	Treatment of fever, pain, inflammatory conditions; at low dose to prevent the risk of death and MI in patients with history of MI, prevention of TIAs in males

choline magnesium trisalicylate	*Trilisate*	Relief of mild pain, fevers; treatment of arthritis
choline salicylate	*Arthropan*	Relief of mild pain, fevers; treatment of arthritis
mesalamine	*Pentasa*, others	Treatment of ulcerative colitis and other inflammatory bowel disease
olsalazine	*Dipentum*	Treatment of ulcerative colitis and other inflammatory bowel disease
salsalate	*Argesic*, others	Treatment of pain, fever, inflammation
sodium thiosalicylate	*Rexolate*	Relief of gout, muscular pain; treatment of rheumatic fever

NURSING CONSIDERATIONS
for patients receiving salicylates

Assessment

HISTORY. Screen for any known allergies to any salicylates, NSAIDs, or tartrazine; pregnancy or lactation; renal disease; bleeding disorders; chicken pox; influenza; and pregnancy or lactation.

PHYSICAL ASSESSMENT. Include screening for baseline status before beginning therapy and for any potential adverse effects: the presence of any skin lesions; temperature; orientation, reflexes, eighth cranial nerve function, and affect; pulse, blood pressure, perfusion; respirations, adventitious sounds; liver evaluation; bowel sounds; and CBC, liver and renal function tests, urinalysis, stool guaiac, and clotting times.

Nursing Diagnoses

The patient receiving salicylates may have the following nursing diagnoses related to drug therapy:

- Pain related to central nervous system (CNS) and gastrointestinal (GI) effects
- Ineffective breathing patterns if toxic effects occur
- Sensory–perceptual alteration if toxic effects occur
- Knowledge deficit regarding drug therapy

Implementation

- Administer with food if GI upset is severe; *provide small, frequent meals to alleviate GI effects.*
- Administer drug as indicated; monitor dosage *to avoid toxic levels.*
- Monitor for severe reactions *to avoid problems and provide emergency procedures* (gastric lavage, induction of vomiting, charcoal) if they occur.
- Arrange for supportive care and comfort measures (rest, environmental control) *to decrease temperature or alleviate inflammation.*
- Assure that the patient is well hydrated during therapy *to decrease the risk of toxicity developing.*
- Provide thorough patient teaching, including measures to avoid adverse effects and warning signs of problems as well as proper administration *to increase knowledge about drug therapy and to increase compliance with drug regimen.*
- Offer support and encouragement *to deal with the drug regimen.*

Evaluation

- Monitor patient response to the drug (improvement in condition being treated, relief of signs and symptoms of inflammation).
- Monitor for adverse effects (GI upset, CNS changes, bleeding).
- Evaluate effectiveness of teaching plan (patient can name drug, dosage, adverse effects to watch for, specific measures to avoid adverse effects).
- Monitor effectiveness of comfort measures and compliance to regimen.

NONSTEROIDAL ANTI-INFLAMMATORY DRUGS (NSAIDS)

The nonsteroidal anti-inflammatory drugs are a relatively new drug class that has become one of the most commonly used types in the United States. This group of drugs includes the following agents:

Propionic acids

Fenoprofen (*Nalfon*): used to treat pain and manage arthritis.

Flurbiprofen (*Ansaid*): used for long-term management of arthritis and as a topical preparation for managing pain after eye surgery.

Ibuprofen (*Motrin, Advil,* and others): used as an OTC pain medication and for long-term management of arthritis pain and dysmenorrhea; the most widely used of the NSAIDs.

Ketoprofen (*Orudis*): available for short-term management of pain and as a topical agent to relieve ocular itching due to seasonal rhinitis.

Naproxen (*Naprosyn*): available for OTC pain relief and to treat arthritis and dysmenorrhea.

Oxaprozin (*Daypro*): very successfully used to manage arthritis.

Acetic acids

Diclofenac (*Voltaren*): used to treat acute and long-term pain associated with inflammatory conditions.

Etodalac (*Lodine*): widely used for arthritis pain.

Indomethacin (*Indocin*): available in oral, topical, and rectal preparations for the relief of moderate to severe pain associated with inflammatory conditions and in intravenous form to promote closure of the patent ductus arteriosus in premature infants.

Ketorolac (*Torodal*): used for short-term management of pain and topically to relieve ocular itching.
Nabumetone (*Relafen*): used to treat acute and chronic arthritis pain.
Sulindac (*Clinoril*): used for long-and short-term treatment of the signs and symptoms of various inflammatory conditions.
Tolmetin (*Tolectin*): used to treat acute attacks of rheumatoid arthritis and juvenile arthritis.

Fenamates

Meclofenamate (generic): used to treat dysmenorrhea, mild pain, and arthritis.
Mefenamic acid (*Ponstel*): used only for short-term treatment of pain.
Piroxicam (*Feldene*): used to treat acute and chronic arthritis.
Diflunisal (*Dolobid*): used for moderate pain and for the treatment of arthritis.

The choice of NSAID depends on personal experience and the patient's response to the drug. A patient may have little response to one NSAID and fantastic response to another. It may take several trials to determine the drug of choice for any particular patient.

THERAPEUTIC ACTIONS AND INDICATIONS

The anti-inflammatory, analgesic, and antipyretic effects of the NSAIDs are largely related to inhibition of prostaglandin synthesis (see Figure 14-1). The NSAIDs block two enzymes known as cyclooxygenase-1 (COX-1) and cyclooxygenase-2 (COX-2) to stop turning arachidonic acid into prostaglandins (see Box 14-1). By interfering with this part of the inflammatory reaction, NSAIDs block inflammation before all of the signs and symptoms can develop. They also block various other functions of the prostaglandins including protection of the stomach lining, regulation of blood clotting, and water and salt balance in the kidney. The exact mechanism of action is not fully understood.

The NSAIDs are indicated for the relief of the signs and symptoms of rheumatoid arthritis and osteoarthritis; for the relief of mild to moderate pain; for the treatment of primary dysmenorrhea; and for fever reduction.

CONTRAINDICATIONS/CAUTIONS

The NSAIDs are contraindicated in the presence of allergy to any NSAID or salicylate; with cardiovascular dysfunction or hypertension because of the varying effects of the prostaglandins; with peptic ulcer or known GI bleeding because of the potential to exacerbate the GI bleeding; and during pregnancy and lactation because of potential effects on the neonate. Caution should be used with renal or hepatic dysfunction, which could alter the metabolism and excretion of these drugs.

ADVERSE EFFECTS

Patients receiving NSAIDs often experience nausea, dyspepsia, GI pain, constipation, diarrhea, or flatulence caused by direct GI effects of the drug. The potential for GI bleeding is often a cause of discontinuation of the drug. Headache, dizziness, somnolence, and fatigue also occur frequently and could be related to prostaglandin activity in the CNS. Bleeding, platelet inhibition, and even bone marrow depression have been reported with chronic use and are probably related to blocking of prostaglandin activity. Rash and mouth sores may occur; and anaphylactoid reactions to fatal anaphylactic shock have been reported in cases of severe hypersensitivity.

CLINICALLY IMPORTANT DRUG–DRUG INTERACTIONS

There is often a decreased diuretic effect when these drugs are taken with loop diuretics; there is a potential for decreased antihypertensive effect of beta blockers if these drugs are combined; and there have been reports of lithium toxicity, especially when combined with ibuprofen. Patients who receive these combinations should be monitored closely and appropriate dosage adjustments made by the prescriber.

DATA LINK

Data link to the following NSAIDs in your nursing drug guide:

NSAIDS

Name	Brand Name	Usual Indications
diclofenac	*Voltaren*	Treatment of acute and chronic pain associated with inflammatory conditions
diflunisal	*Dolobid*	Treatment of moderate pain, arthritis
etodolac	*Lodine*	Treatment of arthritis pain
fenoprofen	*Nalfon*	Treatment of pain, arthritis
flurbiprofen	*Ansaid*	Long-term management of arthritis; topically to manage pain after eye surgery
P ibuprofen	*Motrin, Advil, others*	Treatment of pain, arthritis, dysmenorrhea
indomethacin	*Indocin*	Relief of moderate to severe pain in PO, topical, and PR forms; closure of PDA in premature infants, given IV
ketoprofen	*Orudis*	Short-term management of pain; topically to relieve ocular itching
ketorolac	*Torodal*	Short-term management of pain; topically to relieve ocular itching
meclofenamate	generic	Treatment of dysmenorrhea, mild pain, arthritis

mefenamic acid	*Ponstel*	Short-term treatment of pain
nabumetone	*Relafen*	Treatment of acute and chronic arthritis pain
naproxen	*Naprosyn*	Treatment of pain, arthritis, dysmenorrhea
oxaprozin	*Daypro*	Treatment of arthritis
piroxicam	*Feldene*	Treatment of acute and chronic arthritis
sulindac	*Clinoril*	Treatment of various inflammatory conditions
tolmetin	*Tolectin*	Treatment of acute flares of rheumatoid and juvenile arthritis

NURSING CONSIDERATIONS
for patients receiving NSAIDs

Assessment

HISTORY. Screen for any known allergies to any salicylates, NSAIDs, or tartrazine; pregnancy or lactation; hepatic or renal disease; cardiovascular dysfunction, hypertension; and GI bleeding or peptic ulcer.

PHYSICAL ASSESSMENT. Include screening for baseline status before beginning therapy and for any potential adverse effects: the presence of any skin lesions; temperature; orientation, reflexes, and affect; pulse, blood pressure, perfusion; respirations, adventitious sounds; liver evaluation; bowel sounds; and CBC, liver and renal function tests, urinalysis, stool guaiac, and serum electrolytes.

Nursing Diagnoses, Implementation, and Evaluation

Refer to the nursing consideration sections for the salicylates. (See Nursing Care Guide and Patient Teaching Checklist for NSAIDs.)

WWW.WEB LINKS

Health care providers and patients may want to consult the following Internet sources for additional information:

Information on arthritis—disease, treatments, research:
http://www.arthritis.org/

Guide to finding additional information, support groups:
http://www.interaccess.com/ihpnet/health.html

Information on drug research and development, warnings, information:
http://www.fda.gov/fdahomepage.html

OTHER RELATED DRUGS

Other drugs that are used to treat inflammatory conditions include acetaminophen (*Tylenol*), gold compounds, and other anti-arthritic drugs. Acetaminophen is used to treat moderate to mild pain and fever and often is used in place of the NSAIDs or salicylates. The gold compounds are used to prevent and suppress arthritis in selected patients with rheumatoid arthritis. The other anti-arthritic drugs are specifically used to block the inflammatory process and tissue damage associated with rheumatoid arthritis.

Acetaminophen

THERAPEUTIC ACTIONS AND INDICATIONS

Acetaminophen acts directly on the thermoregulatory cells in the hypothalamus to cause sweating and vasodilation; this in turns causes the release of heat and lowers fever. The mechanism of action related to the analgesic effects of acetaminophen has not been identified.

Acetaminophen is indicated for the treatment of pain and fever associated with a variety of conditions, including influenza; for the prophylaxis of children receiving DPT immunizations (since aspirin may mask Reye's syndrome in children); and for the relief of musculoskeletal pain associated with arthritis.

CONTRAINDICATIONS/CAUTIONS

Acetaminophen is contraindicated in the presence of allergy to acetaminophen. It should be used cautiously in the presence of pregnancy and lactation (because of potential effects on the neonate) and in the presence of hepatic dysfunction or chronic alcoholism (because of associated toxic effects on the liver).

ADVERSE EFFECTS

Adverse effects associated with acetaminophen use include headache, hemolytic anemia, renal dysfunction, skin rash, and fever. Hepatotoxicity is a potentially fatal adverse effect that is usually associated with chronic use and overdose and is related to direct toxic effects on the liver.

CLINICALLY IMPORTANT DRUG–DRUG INTERACTIONS

There is an increased risk of bleeding with oral anticoagulants because of effects on the liver; of toxicity with chronic ethanol ingestion because of toxic effects on the liver; and of hepatotoxicity if combined with barbiturates, carbamazepine, hydantoins, rifampin, and sulfinpyrazone. These combinations should be avoided, but if they cannot, appropriate dosage

NURSING CARE GUIDE
NSAIDs

Assessment	Nursing Diagnoses	Implementation	Evaluation
HISTORY			
Allergies to any NSAID or aspirin, pregnancy, lactation, renal or hepatic impairment, ulcerative GI disease, peptic ulcer, hearing impairment, blood dyscrasias	Pain related to GI effects, headache Sensory–perceptual alteration related to CNS effects Ineffective gas exchange secondary to hypersensitivity reactions Knowledge deficit regarding drug therapy	Assure proper administration of the drug. Administer with food if GI upset occurs. Provide supportive and comfort measures to deal with adverse effects: small, frequent meals, safety measures if CNS effects occur, measures for headache, bowel training as needed. Provide patient teaching regarding drug name, dosage, side effects, precautions, and warnings to report. Provide life support and emergency measures in cases of hypersensitivity.	Evaluate drug effects: decrease in signs and symptoms of inflammation. Monitor for adverse effects: CNS changes, rash, GI upset, CHF, liver dysfunction, asthma, anaphylaxis. Monitor for drug–drug interactions as indicated for each drug. Evaluate effectiveness of patient teaching program. Evaluate effectiveness of comfort/safety measures. Evaluate effectiveness of life support and emergency measures if appropriate.
PHYSICAL EXAMINATION			
Neurological: orientation, reflexes, affect Skin: color, lesions CV: P, cardiac auscultation, BP, perfusion GI: liver evaluation, bowel sounds Lab tests: CBC, liver and renal function tests			

adjustment should be made and the patient should be monitored closely.

Gold Compounds

Some patients with rheumatic inflammatory conditions do not respond to the usual anti-inflammatory therapies and their conditions worsen despite weeks or months of standard pharmacological treatment. Some of these patients will respond to treatment with gold salt, also known as ***chrysotherapy.*** The gold salts that are currently available for use include the following: auranofin (*Ridaura*), an oral agent used for long-term therapy; aurothioglucose (*Solganal*), an injected drug that is recommended for treatment early in the disease before too much tissue damage has been done; and gold sodium thiomalate (*Aurolate*), an injected drug much like aurothioglucose.

THERAPEUTIC ACTIONS AND INDICATIONS

Gold salts are absorbed by macrophages, which results in inhibition of phagocytosis (see Figure 14-1). By blocking phagocytosis, the release of lysosomal enzymes is inhibited and tissue destruction is decreased. This action allows gold salts to suppress and prevent some arthritis and synovitis. Gold salts are indicated to treat selected cases of rheumatoid and juvenile rheumatoid arthritis in patients who have been unresponsive to standard therapy. These drugs do not repair damage; they prevent further damage and so are most effective if used early in the disease.

PATIENT TEACHING CHECKLIST

NSAIDs

Create customized patient teaching materials for a specific NSAID from your CD-ROM. Your patient teaching should stress the following points for drugs within this class: Nonsteroidal anti-inflammatory drugs, or NSAIDs work in the body to decrease inflammation and to relieve the signs and symptoms of inflammation, such as pain, swelling, heat, tenderness, and redness.

Some of the following adverse effects may occur:

- Nausea, vomiting, abdominal discomfort—Taking the drug with food or eating small, frequent meals may help. If these effects persist, consult with your health care provider.
- Diarrhea, constipation—These effects may decrease over time; assure ready access to bathroom facilities and consult with your health care provider for possible treatment.
- Drowsiness, dizziness, blurred vision—Avoid driving or performing tasks that require alertness if you experience any of these problems.
- Headache—If this becomes a problem, consult with your health care provider. Do not self-treat with aspirin or other analgesics.

Tell any health care provider who is taking care of you that you are taking this drug.

Avoid the use of over-the-counter preparations while you are on this drug. If you feel that you need one of these drugs, consult with your health care provider for the most appropriate choice.

Report any of the following to your health care provider: sore throat, fever, rash, itching, weight gain or swelling in the ankles or fingers, changes in vision, black or tarry stools.

Keep this drug and all medications out of the reach of children.

This Teaching Checklist reflects general patient teaching guidelines. It is not meant to be a substitute for drug-specific teaching information, which is available in nursing drug guides.

CONTRAINDICATIONS/CAUTIONS

Gold salts can be quite toxic and are contraindicated in the presence of any known allergy to gold, severe diabetes, congestive heart failure, severe debilitation, renal or hepatic impairment, hypertension, blood dyscrasias, recent radiation treatment, history of toxic levels of heavy metals, and pregnancy and lactation.

ADVERSE EFFECTS

A variety of adverse effects are common with the use of gold salts and are probably related to their deposition in the tissues and effects at that local level: stomatitis, glossitis, gingivitis, pharyngitis, laryngitis, colitis, diarrhea, and other GI inflammation; gold bronchitis and interstitial pneumonitis; bone marrow depression; vaginitis, nephrotic syndrome; dermatitis, pruritus, exfoliative dermatitis; and allergic reactions ranging from flushing, fainting, and dizziness to anaphylactic shock.

CLINICALLY IMPORTANT DRUG–DRUG INTERACTIONS

These drugs should not be combined with penicillamine, antimalarials, cytotoxic drugs, or immunosuppressive agents other than low-dose corticosteroids because of the potential for severe toxicity.

Other Anti-Arthritis Drugs

Five new drugs were made available in 1998 to relieve the pain and suffering of patients with acute rheumatoid arthritis who were no longer responsive to conventional therapy. These include etanercept (*Enbrel*), hylan G-F 20 (*Synvisc*), leflunomide (*Arava*), penicillamine (*Depen*), and sodium hyaluronate (*Hyalgan*). Etanercept is used subcutaneously (SC), alone or with methotrexate. Hylan G-F 20 is derived from chicken combs that contain high levels of hylans with elastic and viscous properties. It is injected into the knees of arthritis patients in a series of three injections.

Leflunomide is an oral drug associated with severe hepatic toxicity. Penicillamine is a chelating agent used to remove copper that lowers IgM rheumatoid factor levels. Sodium hyaluronate contains high levels of hylans to lubricate joints. It is injected into the knee of arthritis patients in a series of five injections.

CULTURAL CONSIDERATIONS ••••

Sensitivity to Anti-Inflammatory Drugs

African Americans have a documented decreased sensitivity to the pain-relieving effects of many of the anti-inflammatory drugs. They do, however, have an increased risk of developing GI adverse effects to these drugs, including acetaminophen. This should be taken into consideration when using these drugs as analgesics. Increased dosages may be needed to achieve a pain-blocking effect, but the increased dosage will put these patients at an even greater risk for developing the adverse GI effects associated with these drugs. These patients should be monitored closely, and efforts should be made to decrease pain using nondrug measures such as positioning, environmental control, physical therapy, warm soaks, and so on. If African American patients are placed on anti-inflammatory drugs, they should be educated about the signs and symptoms of GI bleeding and what to report. They also should be monitored regularly for any adverse reactions to these drugs.

THERAPEUTIC ACTIONS AND INDICATIONS

Etanercept contains genetically engineered tumor necrosis factor receptors derived from Chinese hamster ovary cells. These receptors react with free-floating tumor necrosis factor released by active leukocytes in autoimmune inflammatory disease to prevent the damage caused by tumor necrosis factor. It is indicated for SC use in the reduction of the signs and symptoms of active rheumatoid arthritis.

Leflunomide directly inhibits an enzyme which is active in the autoimmune process that leads to rheumatoid arthritis, preventing the signs and symptoms of inflammation and blocking the structural damage this inflammation can cause. Leflunomide is indicated for the treatment of active rheumatoid arthritis to relieve symptoms and to slow the progression of the disease.

Penicillamine lowers the IgM rheumatoid factor levels in patients with acute rheumatoid arthritis, relieving the signs and symptoms of inflammation, though it may take 2 to 3 months of therapy before a response is noted.

Hylan G-F 20 and sodium hyaluronate are both hyaluronic acid derivatives that have elastic and viscous properties. As noted above, these drugs are injected directly into the joints of patients with severe rheumatoid arthritis of the knee. They seem to cushion and lubricate the joint and relieve the pain associated with degenerative arthritis.

CONTRAINDICATIONS/CAUTIONS

These drugs are contraindicated in the presence of allergy to the drugs or to the animal products from which they were derived (Chinese hamster products in etanercept; chicken products in hylan G-F 20 and sodium hyaluronate); with pregnancy and lactation, because of the potential for adverse effects on the neonate; with acute infections, because of the blocking of normal inflammatory pathways; and with liver or renal impairment, which could be exacerbated by these drugs.

ADVERSE EFFECTS

A variety of adverse effects are common with the use of these drugs including local irritation at injection sites (etanercept, hylan G-F 20, and sodium hyaluronate), pain with injection, and increased risk of infection. Leflunomide is associated with potentially fatal hepatic toxicity and rashes. Penicillamine is associated with a potentially fatal myasthenic syndrome, bone marrow depression, and assorted hypersensitivity reactions.

CLINICALLY IMPORTANT DRUG–DRUG INTERACTIONS

Hylan G-F 20 and sodium hyaluronate should not be injected at the same time as local anesthetics. Because leflunomide can cause severe liver dysfunction if combined with other hepatotoxic drugs, this combination should be avoided. There is decreased absorption of penicillamine if taken with iron salts or antacids; if these are given together, they should be separated by at least 2 hours.

DATA LINK

Data link to these anti-inflammatory and anti-arthritis drugs in your nursing drug guide:

ANTIINFLAMMATORY AND ANTI-ARTHRITIS AGENTS

Name	Brand Name	Usual Indications
P acetaminophen	*Tylenol*	Relief of pain, fever in a variety of situations
auranofin	*Ridaura*	Long-term therapy for rheumatic disorders
P aurothioglucose	*Solganal*	Injected drug for early treatment of rheumatic disorders
etanercept	*Enbrel*	Reduction of signs and symptoms of severe rheumatoid arthritis in patients unresponsive to other therapy
gold sodium thiomalate	*Aurolate*	Injected drug for early treatment of rheumatic disorders
hylan G-F 20	*Synvisc*	Relief of pain in the knees of arthritis patients unresponsive to conventional treatment

CASE STUDY

Aspirin and Rheumatoid Arthritis

PRESENTATION

G. T. is an 82-year-old male on a fixed income with a 14-year history of rheumatoid arthritis. He is seen in the clinic for evaluation of his arthritis and to address his complaint that the drugs are not doing any good. On examination, it was found that G. T.'s range of motion, physical examination of joints, and overall presentation had not changed since his last visit. G. T. stated that he had been taking aspirin, as prescribed, for his arthritis. But he had read that aspirin can cause severe stomach problems, so he had switched to *Ecotrin* (an aspirin and antacid combination). This drug was much more expensive than he could handle on his fixed income, so he had started taking the drug only once every three days.

CRITICAL THINKING QUESTIONS

Think about the pathophysiology of rheumatoid arthritis and how the drugs ordered act on the inflammatory process. How can the nurse best explain the disease and the drug regimen to this patient? What could be contributing to G.T.'s perception that his condition has worsened ? What nursing interventions would be appropriate to help G. T. cope with his disease and his need for medication?

DISCUSSION

G. T. should be offered encouragement and support to deal with his progressive disease and the drug regimen required. The fact that his physical examination has not changed but he perceives that the disease is worse may reflect other underlying problems that are making it more difficult for him to cope with chronic pain and limitations. The nurse should explore his social situation, any changes in his living situation, or support services. A physical examination should be done to determine whether other physical problems have emerged that could be adding to his sense that things are getting worse. The actions of aspirin on the arthritic process should be reviewed in basic terms, with emphasis on the importance of preventing further damage and maintaining high enough levels of aspirin to control the arthritis signs and symptoms. Pictures of the process involved in rheumatoid arthritis may help; the simpler the better in most cases.

G. T. also should be taught that all aspirin is the same, so it is acceptable to buy the cheapest generic aspirin. He can check the expiration date to make sure that the drug is fresh and still therapeutic, or that it does not smell like vinegar. The expensive combination product that G. T. has been using has not been proven to be any more effective at helping arthritis or at decreasing adverse effects than generic aspirin.

If G. T. has been having GI complaints with the aspirin, he can be encouraged to take the drug with food and to have small, frequent meals to keep stomach acid levels at a more steady state. If G. T. has not been having any GI complaints, he should be asked to report any immediately. The importance of the placebo effect cannot be overlooked with this patient. Many patients actually state that they feel better when they are using well-recognized, brand-name products. With support and encouragement, G. T. can be helped to follow his prescribed drug regimen and delay further damage from his arthritis.

leflunomide	*Arava*	Treatment of active rheumatoid arthritis, to relieve signs and symptoms and slow progression of disease
penicillamine	*Depen*	Treatment of severe, active rheumatoid arthritis in patients unresponsive to conventional therapy
sodium hyaluronate	*Hyalgan*	Relief of pain in the knees of arthritis patients unresponsive to conventional treatment

NURSING CONSIDERATIONS
for patients receiving other related drugs

Nursing considerations for patients receiving the drugs listed above are similar to those for patients receiving other anti-inflammatory drugs. Details related to each individual drug can be found in the specific drug monograph in your nursing drug guide.

CHAPTER SUMMARY

- The inflammatory response, important for protecting the body from injury and invasion, produces many of the signs and symptoms associated with disease, including fever, aches and pains, and lethargy.
- Chronic or excessive activity by the inflammatory response can lead to the release of lysosomal enzymes and tissue destruction.
- Anti-inflammatory drugs block various chemicals associated with the inflammatory reaction. Anti-inflammatory drugs also may have antipyretic (anti-fever) and analgesic (anti-pain) activities.
- Salicylates block prostaglandin activity. NSAIDs block prostaglandin synthesis. Acetaminophen causes vasodilation and heat release, lowering fever and working to relieve pain. Gold salts prevent macrophage phagocytosis, lysosomal release, and tissue

damage. Etanercept contains tumor necrosis factor receptors to deactivate tumor necrosis factor and slow progression of autoimmune diseases. Leflunomide deactivates an enzyme active in autoimmune disease. Penicillamine is a chelating agent that lowers levels of IgM rheumatoid factor in acute rheumatoid arthritis. Hylan G-F 20 and hyaluronate are viscous and elastic hyaluronic acid derivatives that lubricate arthritic knees and stop some of the pain of inflammation.

- Salicylates can cause acidosis and eighth cranial nerve damage. NSAIDs are most associated with GI irritation and bleeding. Acetaminophen can cause serious liver toxicity. The gold salts cause many systemic inflammatory reactions. Other anti-arthritis drugs are associated with local injection site irritation and increased susceptibility to infection. Leflunomide is associated with severe hepatic toxicity.

- Many anti-inflammatory drugs are available OTC and care must be taken to prevent abuse or overuse of these drugs. Many combination products contain the same ingredient and overdose can easily occur.

Bibliography

Agrawal, N. M., & Aziz, K. (1998). Prevention of gastrointestinal complications with nonsteroidal antiinflammatory drugs. *Journal of Rheumatology Supplement, 51,* 17–20.

Bullock, B. L. (2000). *Focus on pathophysiology.* Philadelphia: Lippincott Williams & Wilkins.

Cash, J. M., & Wilder, R. L. (1995). Refractory rheumatoid arthritis: Therapeutic options. *Rheumatic Diseases Clinics North America, 21* (1), 1–18.

Hardman, J. G., Limbird, L. E., Molinoff, P. B., Ruddon, R. W., & Gilman, A. G. (Eds.). (1996). *Goodman and Gilman's the pharmacological basis of therapeutics* (9th ed.). New York: McGraw Hill.

Karch, A. M. (2000). *2000 Lippincott's nursing drug guide.* Philadelphia: Lippincott Williams & Wilkins.

Lancaster, C. (1995). Effective nonsteroidal antiinflammatory drugs devoid of gastrointestinal side effects: Do they really exist? *Digestive Diseases and Sciences, 13* (Suppl 1), 40–47.

McEvoy, B. R. (Ed.). (1999). *Drug Facts & Comparisons.* St. Louis: Facts & Comparison.

The Medical Letter on Drugs and Therapeutics. (1999). New Rochelle, NY: Medical Letter.

CHAPTER 15

Immune Modulators

Immune stimulants

Interferons

- interferon alfa-2a
- **P** interferon alfa-2b
- interferon alfacon-1
- interferon alfa-n3
- interferon beta-1a
- interferon beta-1b
- interferon gamma-1b

Interleukins

- **P** aldesleukin
- oprelvekin

T/B cell modulator

- **P** levamisole

Immune suppressants

T/B cell suppressors

- azathioprine
- **P** cyclosporine
- glatiramer acetate
- mycophenolate
- tacrolimus

Monoclonal antibodies

- basiliximab
- daclizumab
- infliximab
- **P** muromonab-CD3
- palivizumab
- rituximab
- trastuzumab

CHAPTER OUTLINE

KEY TERMS

immune stimulant
immune suppressant
monoclonal antibodies
recombinant DNA technology

INTRODUCTION

As the name implies, immune modulators are used to modify the actions of the immune system. ***Immune stimulants*** are used to energize the immune system when it is exhausted from fighting prolonged invasion or needs help fighting a specific pathogen or cancer cell. ***Immune suppressants*** are used to block the normal effects of the immune system in cases of organ transplant (in which non–self-cells are transplanted into the body and destroyed by the immune reaction) and in autoimmune disorders (in which the body's defenses recognize self-cells as foreign and work to destroy them).

The knowledge base about the actions and components of the immune system is growing and changing daily. As new discoveries are made and interactions understood, new applications will be found for modulating the immune system in a variety of disorders.

IMMUNE STIMULANTS

Immune stimulants include the interferons, which are released from cells in response to viral invasion; the interleukins, synthetic compounds much like the interleukins that communicate between lymphocytes, which stimulate cellular immunity and inhibit tumor growth; and a T/B cell modulator called levamisole (*Ergamisol*), which restores immune function and also stimulates immune system activity (Figure 15-1).

The Interferons

Interferons are naturally produced and released by human cells that have been invaded by viruses. They may also be released from cells in response to other stimuli. A number of interferons are available for use today. Several are produced by ***recombinant DNA technology;*** these include interferon alfa-2a (*Roferon-A*), interferon alfa-2b (*Intron-A*), interferon alfacon-1 (*Infergen*), and interferon beta-1b (*Betaseron*). Interferon alfa-n3 (*Alferon N*) is produced by harvesting human leukocytes and is injected directly into warts. Interferon beta-1a (*Avonex*) is produced from Chinese hamster ovary cells. Interferon gamma-1b (*Actimmune*) is produced by *Escherichia coli* bacteria. The interferon of choice depends on the particular indication.

THERAPEUTIC ACTIONS AND INDICATIONS

Interferons act to prevent virus particles from replicating inside other cells. They also stimulate interferon receptor sites on non-invaded cells to stimulate the production of anti-viral proteins, which will prevent viruses from entering the cell. In addition, interferons have been found to inhibit tumor growth and replication. Interestingly, interferon gamma-1b also acts like an interleukin, stimulating phagocytes to be more aggressive.

Interferons are indicated for treating selected leukemias (alfa-2a, alfa-2b); multiple sclerosis (beta-1a, beta-1b); intralesional treatment of warts (alfa-n3, alfa-2b); chronic hepatitis C (alfacon-1), chronic hepatitis B or non–A/non–B/C (alfa-2b); AIDS-related Kaposi's sarcoma (alfa-2a, alfa-2b); and severe infections caused by chronic granulomatous disease (gamma-1b). Most of the interferons are being tested for the treatment of various cancers and AIDS-related problems.

CONTRAINDICATIONS/CAUTIONS

The use of interferons is contraindicated in the presence of known allergy to any interferon or product components and during pregnancy and lactation. Caution should be used in the presence of known cardiac disease, myelosuppression, or central nervous system (CNS) dysfunction of any kind.

ADVERSE EFFECTS

The adverse effects associated with the use of interferons are associated with the immune or inflammatory reaction that is being stimulated (e.g., lethargy, myalgia, arthralgia, anorexia, nausea). Other commonly seen adverse effects include headache, dizziness, bone marrow depression, photosensitivity, and liver impairment.

DATA LINK

Data link to the following interferons in your nursing drug guide:

INTERFERONS

Name	Brand Name	Usual Indications
interferon alfa-2a	*Roferon-A*	Treatment of leukemias, Kaposi's sarcoma
P interferon alfa 2b	*Intron A*	Treatment of leukemias, Kaposi's sarcoma, warts, hepatitis B, malignant melanoma
interferon alfacon-1	*Infergen*	Treatment of chronic hepatitis C
interferon alfa-n3	*Alferon N*	Intralesional treatment of warts
interferon beta-1a	*Avonex*	Treatment of multiple sclerosis
interferon beta-1b	*Betaseron*	Treatment of multiple sclerosis
interferon gamma-1b	*Actimmune*	Treatment of serious, chronic granulomatous disease

The Interleukins

Interleukins are chemicals produced by T cells to communicate between leukocytes. Two interleukin-2 preparations are available for use. Interleukin-2

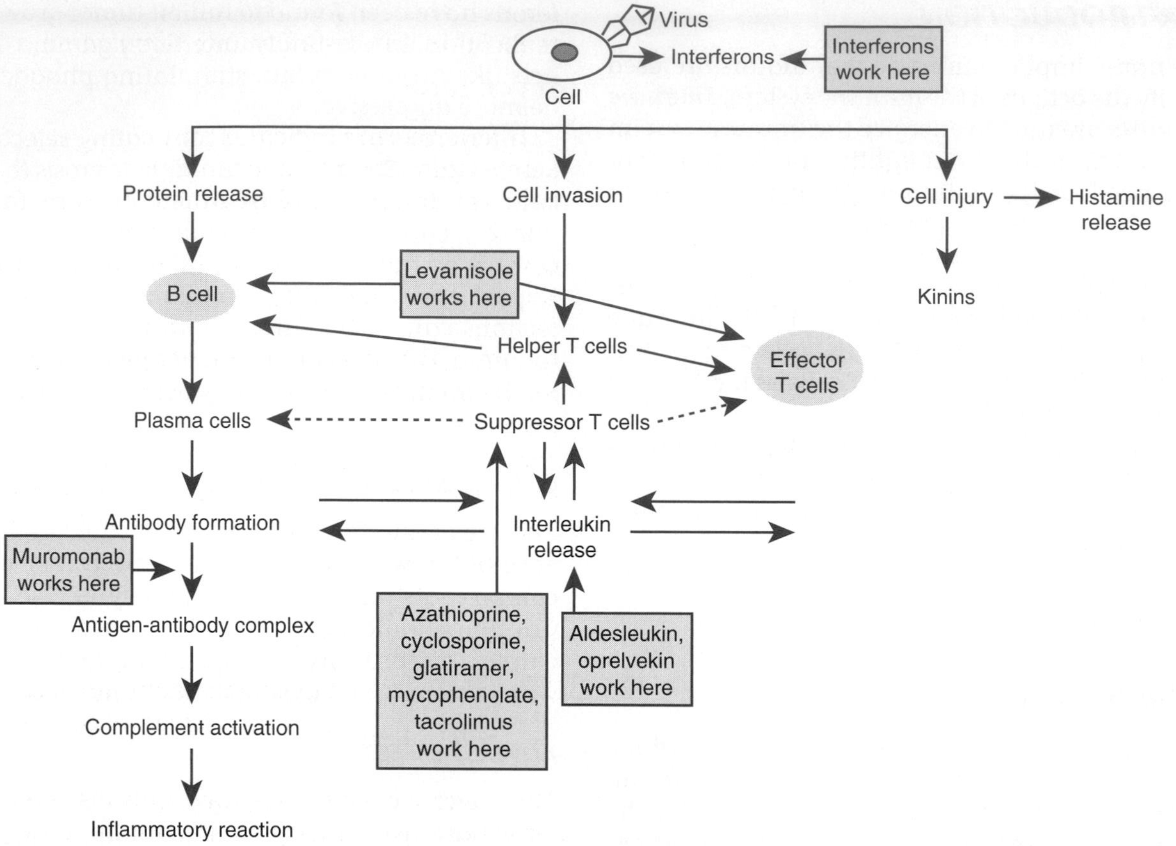

FIGURE 15-1. Sites of action of the immune modulators.

stimulates cellular immunity by increasing the activity of natural killer cells, platelets, and cytokines. Aldesleukin (*Proleukin*) is a human interleukin produced by recombinant DNA technology using *E. coli* bacteria. Oprelvekin (*Neumega*) is a new agent, released in 1998, that is also produced by DNA technology.

THERAPEUTIC ACTIONS AND INDICATIONS

Interleukin-2 is produced by helper T cells to activate cellular immunity and inhibit tumor growth by increasing lymphocyte numbers and their activity. There will be an increase in the number of natural killer cells and lymphocytes, in cytokine activity, and in the number of circulating platelets. Interleukins are indicated for the treatment of specific renal carcinomas (aldesleukin) and for the prevention of severe thrombocytopenia (an abnormal decrease in the number of platelets) following myelosuppressive chemotherapy in select patients (oprelvekin).

CONTRAINDICATIONS/CAUTIONS

Interleukins are contraindicated in the presence of any allergy to an interleukin or *E. coli*-produced product and during pregnancy and lactation. Caution should be used with renal, liver, or cardiovascular impairment.

ADVERSE EFFECTS

The adverse effects associated with the interleukins can be attributed to their effect on the body during inflammation (e.g., lethargy, myalgia, arthralgia, fatigue, fever). Respiratory difficulties, CNS changes, and cardiac arrhythmias also have been reported.

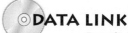

DATA LINK

Data link to the following interleukins in your nursing drug guide:

INTERLEUKINS

Name	Brand Name	Usual Indications
P aldesleukin	*Proleukin*	Treatment of specific renal carcinomas
oprelvekin	*Neumega*	Prevention of severe thrombocytopenia following myelosuppressive chemotherapy

T/B cell modulator

The drug levamisole (*Ergamisol*) is an immune stimulant that restores suppressed immune function in certain situations.

THERAPEUTIC ACTIONS AND INDICATIONS

Levamisole stimulates B cells, which in turn stimulates antibody formation, enhances T cell activity, and increases the activity of both monocytes and macrophages. Levamisole is indicated for the treatment of Dukes stage C colon cancer after surgical resection and in conjunction with fluorouracil therapy. With further research, the indications may be expanded to include other carcinomas.

CONTRAINDICATIONS/CAUTIONS

Levamisole is contraindicated in the presence of any known allergy to levamisole or its components, and in pregnancy and lactation because of possible adverse effects to the neonate.

ADVERSE EFFECTS

The most common adverse effects seen with levamisole are related to immune stimulation (so-called flu-like effects: fatigue, lethargy, myalgia, arthralgia, fever). Other adverse effects that have been reported include gastrointestinal (GI) upset, nausea, taste perversions, and diarrhea; dizziness, headache, and depression; bone marrow depression; dermatitis; and hair loss.

CLINICALLY IMPORTANT DRUG–DRUG INTERACTIONS

There is a possibility of a disulfiram-type reaction if this drug is combined with alcohol. Patients should be cautioned to avoid this combination. There also is a possibility of increased phenytoin levels and toxicity if levamisole is combined with phenytoin. If such a combination cannot be avoided, phenytoin levels should be monitored and appropriate dosage reductions made.

DATA LINK

Data link to the following T/B cell modulator in your nursing drug guide:

T/B CELL MODULATOR

Name	Brand Name	Usual Indication
P levamisole	*Ergamisol*	Treatment of Dukes stage C colon cancer after resection

NURSING CONSIDERATIONS
for patients receiving immune stimulants

Assessment

HISTORY. Screen for any known allergies to any of these drugs or their components; pregnancy or lactation; hepatic, renal, or cardiac disease; bone marrow depression; and CNS disorders, including seizures, to monitor for conditions that would contraindicate or require cautious use of the drug.

PHYSICAL ASSESSMENT. Include screening for baseline status before beginning therapy and for any potential adverse effects: the presence of any skin lesions; weight; temperature; orientation, reflexes; pulse, blood pressure, ECG, rhythm; liver evaluation; CBC, liver and renal function tests; and assessment of condition being treated.

Nursing Diagnoses

The patient receiving immune stimulants may have the following nursing diagnoses related to drug therapy:

- Pain related to CNS, GI, and flu-like effects
- Nutrition, less than body requirements, related to flu-like effects
- Anxiety related to diagnosis and drug therapy
- Knowledge deficit regarding drug therapy

Implementation

- Arrange for laboratory tests prior to and periodically during therapy, including CBC and differential *to monitor for drug effects and adverse effects.*
- Administer drug as indicated; instruct the patient and significant other if injections are required *to assure that the patient will be able to receive the drug if the patient is not able to administer it.*
- Monitor for severe reactions *in order to arrange to discontinue drug immediately if they occur.*
- Arrange for supportive care and comfort measures for flu-like symptoms (e.g, rest, environmental control, acetaminophen). Assure that patient is well hydrated during therapy *to prevent severe adverse effects.*
- Instruct female patients in the use of barrier contraceptives *to avoid pregnancy during therapy, because of the potential for adverse effects on the fetus.*
- Provide thorough patient teaching, including measures to avoid adverse effects, warning signs of problems, and proper administration *to increase knowledge about drug therapy and to increase compliance with drug regimen.*
- Offer support and encouragement *to deal with the diagnosis and the drug regimen.*

Evaluation

- Monitor patient response to the drug (improvement in condition being treated).
- Monitor for adverse effects (flu-like symptoms, GI upset, CNS changes, bone marrow depression).
- Evaluate the effectiveness of the teaching plan (patient can name drug, dosage, adverse effects to watch for, specific measures to avoid adverse effects).
- Monitor the effectiveness of comfort measures and compliance to the regimen.

IMMUNE SUPPRESSANTS

Immune suppressants often are used in conjunction with corticosteroids, which block the inflammatory reaction and decrease initial damage to cells. They are especially beneficial in cases of organ transplant and in autoimmune diseases. The immune suppressants include T/B cell suppressors and ***monoclonal antibodies***—antibodies produced by a single clone of B cells that react with specific antigens.

T/B Cell Suppressors

There are several T/B cell immune suppressors available for use. Only one, cyclosporine (*Sandimmune*), is used to suppress rejection in a variety of transplant scenarios. It also is the most commonly used immune suppressant. Azathioprine (*Imuran*) is used specifically to prevent rejection in renal homotransplants and to treat rheumatoid arthritis (an autoimmune disorder) in select patients. Glatiramer acetate (*Copaxone*) is used specifically to reduce the number of relapses in multiple sclerosis, which are thought to be related to an autoimmune reaction. Mycophenolate (*CellCept*) is an oral drug used with cyclosporine and corticosteroids to prevent organ rejection following renal and heart transplants. Tacrolimus (*Prograf*) is used to prevent liver transplant rejection.

Ongoing drug studies continue to explore the unlabeled use of many of these agents to prevent other transplant rejections.

THERAPEUTIC ACTIONS AND INDICATIONS

The exact mechanism of action of the T/B cell suppressors is not understood. It has been shown that

---

CASE STUDY

Holistic Care for a Transplant Patient

PRESENTATION

After waiting on a transplant list for 4 years, T. B. received a human heart transplant to replace his heart, which had been severely damaged by cardiomyopathy. Before getting the transplant, T. B. was bedridden, on oxygen and near death. The transplant has given T. B. a "new lease on life," and he is determined to do everything possible to stay healthy and improve his activity and lifestyle. Currently, he is being maintained on cyclosporine, mycophenolate, and steroids.

CRITICAL THINKING QUESTIONS

What important teaching facts would help T. B. to achieve his goal? Think about the psychological impact of the heart transplant and the "new lease on life." What activity, dietary, and supportive guidelines should be outlined for T. B? What impact will T. B.'s drug regimen have on his plans? How can all of the aspects of his condition and medical care be coordinated to give T. B. the best possible advantages for the future?

DISCUSSION

T. B.'s medical regimen will include a very complicated combination of rehabilitation, nutrition, drug therapy, and prevention. T. B. should know the risks of transplant rejection and the measures that will be used to prevent it. He also should know the names of his medications and when to take them, the signs and symptoms of rejection to watch for, and what to do if they occur. T. B. must understand the need to prevent exposure to infections and the precautions required, such as avoiding crowded areas and people with known diseases, avoiding injury, and taking steps to maintain cleanliness and avoid infection if an injury occurs.

The medications that T. B. is taking may cause him to experience flu-like symptoms, which can be quite unpleasant. A restful, quiet environment may help to decrease his stress. Acetaminophen may be ordered to help alleviate the fever, aches, and pains.

T. B. also may experience GI upset, nausea, and vomiting related to drug effects. A nutritional consultation may be requested to help T. B. maintain a good nutritional state. Frequent mouth care and small, frequent meals may help. Proper nutrition will help T. B. to recover, heal, and maintain his health.

T. B.'s primary health care provider will need to work with the transplant surgeon, rehabilitation team, nutritionist, and cardiologist to coordinate a total program that will help T. B. to avoid problems and make the most of his transplanted heart.

they do block antibody production by B cells, inhibit suppressor and helper T cells, and modify the release of interleukins and of T cell growth factor (see Figure 15-1).

The T/B cell suppressors are indicated for the prevention and treatment of specific transplant rejections. Azathioprine has been approved for the treatment of rheumatoid arthritis. Many of the T/B cell suppressors are used to treat a variety of autoimmune disorders and other transplant rejections as unlabeled uses for the drugs.

CONTRAINDICATIONS/CAUTIONS

The use of T/B cell suppressors is contraindicated in the presence of any known allergy to the drug or its components and during pregnancy and lactation. Caution should be used with renal or hepatic impairment or in the presence of known neoplasms, which potentially could spread with immune system suppression.

ADVERSE EFFECTS

Patients receiving these drugs are at increased risk for infection and for the development of neoplasms because of the blockage of the immune system. Other potentially dangerous adverse effects include hepatotoxicity, renal toxicity, renal dysfunction, and pulmonary edema. Patients may experience headache, tremors, the development of secondary infections such as acne, GI upset, diarrhea, and hypertension.

CLINICALLY IMPORTANT DRUG–DRUG INTERACTIONS

There is an increased risk of toxicity if these drugs are combined with other drugs that are hepatotoxic or nephrotoxic. Extreme care should be used if such combinations are used. Other reported drug–drug interactions are drug-specific (see your nursing drug guide).

DATA LINK

Data link to the following T/B cell suppressors in your nursing drug guide:

T/B CELL SUPPRESSORS

Name	Brand Name	Usual Indications
azathioprine	*Imuran*	Prevention of rejection in renal homotransplants; treatment of rheumatoid arthritis
cyclosporine	*Sandimmune*	Suppression of rejection in a variety of transplant situations
glatiramer acetate	*Copaxone*	Reduction of the number of relapses in multiple sclerosis
mycophenolate	*CellCept*	Prevention of rejection following renal and heart transplants
tacrolimus	*Prograf*	Prevention of rejection following liver transplant

Monoclonal Antibodies

Antibodies that attach to specific receptor sites are being developed to respond to very specific situations. In 1998, six new monoclonal antibodies were marketed, exemplifying the rapid pace with which these agents are being developed and approved for clinical use.

THERAPEUTIC ACTIONS AND INDICATIONS

Muromonab-CD3 (*Orthoclone OKT3*), the first monoclonal antibody approved for use, is a T–cell-specific antibody that is available as an intravenous (IV) agent. It reacts as an antibody to human T cells, disabling the T cells to act as an immune suppressor (see Figure 15-1). Muromonab is indicated for the treatment of acute allograft rejection in renal transplant patients. It also is indicated for the treatment of steroid-resistant acute allograft rejection in heart and liver transplant patients.

Basiliximab (*Simulect*) and daclizumab (*Zenepax*) are monoclonal antibodies to interleukin-2 receptor sites on activated T-lymphocytes, which react with those sites and block cellular response to allograft transplants. They are approved for use in preventing renal transplant rejection.

Infliximab (*Remicade*) is a monoclonal antibody to tumor necrosis factor. It is used to decrease the signs and symptoms of Crohn's disease in patients who do not respond to conventional therapy.

Palivizumab (*Synagis*) is a monoclonal antibody to the antigenic site on respiratory syncytial virus (RSV), which inactivates that virus. It is used to prevent RSV disease in high-risk children.

Rituximab (*Rituxan*) is a monoclonal antibody to specific sites on activated B lymphocytes and is used in the treatment of follicular B-cell non-Hodgkin's lymphoma.

Trastuzumab (*Herceptin*) is a monoclonal antibody that reacts with human epidermal growth factor receptor 2 (HER2), a genetic defect that is seen in select metastatic breast cancers. It is used in the treatment of metastatic breast cancer in tumors that overexpress HER2.

CONTRAINDICATIONS/CAUTIONS

Monoclonal antibodies are contraindicated in the presence of any known allergy to the drug or to murine products, and in the presence of fluid overload. They should be used cautiously with fever (treat the fever before beginning therapy), previous administration of the monoclonal antibody (serious hypersensitivity reactions can occur with repeat administration), and pregnancy (because of the potential for adverse effects on the fetus).

ADVERSE EFFECTS

The most serious adverse effects associated with the use of monoclonal antibodies are acute pulmonary edema (dyspnea, chest pain, wheezing) associated with severe fluid retention, and cytokine release syndrome (flu-like symptoms than can progress to third spacing of fluids and shock). Other adverse effects that can be anticipated include fever, chills, malaise, myalgia, nausea, diarrhea, vomiting, and increased susceptibility to infection.

CLINICALLY IMPORTANT DRUG–DRUG INTERACTIONS

Use caution and arrange to reduce dosages if monoclonal antibodies are combined with any other immunosuppressant drugs because severe immune suppression with increased infections and neoplasms can occur.

DATA LINK

Data link to the following monoclonal antibodies in your nursing drug guide:

MONOCLONAL ANTIBODIES

Name	Brand Name	Usual Indications
basiliximab	*Simulect*	Prevention of renal transplant rejection
daclizumab	*Zenepax*	Prevention of renal transplant rejection
infliximab	*Remicade*	To decrease the signs and symptoms of Crohn's disease in patients who do not respond to other therapy
P muromonab-CD3	*Orthoklone, OKT3*	Prevention of renal transplant rejection; treatment of steroid-resistant rejection in heart and liver transplants
palivizumab	*Syangis*	Prevention of serious RSV (respiratory syncytial virus) infections in high-risk children
rituximab	*Rituxan*	Treatment of relapsed follicular B-cell non-Hodgkin's lymphoma B lymphocytes
trastuzumab	*Herceptin*	Treatment of metastatic breast cancer with tumors that over-express HER2 (human epidermal growth factor receptor 2)

NURSING CONSIDERATIONS
for patients receiving immune suppressants

HISTORY. Screen for any known allergies to any of these drugs or their components; pregnancy or lactation; renal or hepatic impairment; and history of neoplasm.

PHYSICAL ASSESSMENT. Include screening for baseline status before beginning therapy and for any potential adverse effects: the presence of any skin lesions; weight; temperature; orientation, reflexes; pulse, blood pressure, ECG; liver evaluation; CBC, liver, and renal function tests; and assessment of condition being treated.

GENDER CONSIDERATIONS

Immune Modulators and Pregnancy

Generally, immune modulators are contraindicated for use during pregnancy and lactation, largely because these drugs have been associated with fetal abnormalities, increased maternal and fetal infections, and suppressed immune responses in nursing babies. Female patients should be informed of the risk of using these drugs during pregnancy and receive counseling in the use of barrier contraceptives. (The use of barrier contraceptives is advised because the effects of oral contraceptives may be altered by liver changes or changes in the body's immune response, potentially resulting in unexpected pregnancy.)

If a patient taking immune modulators becomes pregnant or decides that she wants to become pregnant, she should discuss this with her health care provider and review the risks associated with the drug or drugs being taken. The monoclonal antibodies should be used with caution during pregnancy and lactation. Because long-term studies of most of these drugs are not yet available, it may be prudent to advise patients taking these drugs to avoid pregnancy if possible.

Nursing Diagnoses

The patient receiving immune suppressants may have the following nursing diagnoses related to drug therapy:

- Pain related to CNS, GI, and flu-like effects
- Risk for infection related to immune suppression
- Nutrition, less than body requirements, related to nausea and vomiting
- Knowledge deficit regarding drug therapy

Implementation

- Arrange for laboratory tests prior to and periodically during therapy, including CBC, differential, and liver and renal function tests *to monitor for drug effects and adverse effects.*
- Administer the drug as indicated; instruct the patient and significant other if injections are required *to assure proper administration of the drug.*
- Protect the patient from exposure to infections and maintain strict aseptic technique for any invasive procedures *to prevent infections during immunosuppression.*

PATIENT TEACHING CHECKLIST

Immune Suppressants

Create customized patient teaching materials for a specific immune suppressant from your CD-ROM. Your patient teaching should stress the following points for drugs within this class: An immune suppressant is given to depress your body's immune system and prevent rejection of your transplanted tissue.

You should never stop taking your drug without consulting your health care provider. If your prescription is low, or you are unable to take the medication for *any* reason, notify your health care provider.

Some of the following adverse effects may occur:

- Nausea, vomiting—Taking the drug with food and eating small, frequent meals may help.
- Diarrhea—This may not decrease; assure ready access to bathroom facilities.
- Flu-like symptoms—Rest and a cool and peaceful environment may help; acetaminophen may be ordered to help relieve this discomfort.
- Skin rash, mouth sores—Frequent skin and mouth care may ease these effects.

You will have an increased susceptibility to infection because your body's normal defenses will be decreased. You should avoid crowded places or people with known infections. If you notice any signs of illness or infection, notify your health care provider immediately.

This drug should not be taken during pregnancy. Use of a barrier contraceptive is recommended. If you wish to become pregnant, or find that you are pregnant, consult with your health care provider immediately.

Tell any doctor, nurse, or other health care provider that you are taking this drug.

You will need to have periodic blood tests and perhaps biopsies while you are being treated with this drug.

Report any of the following to your health care provider: unusual bleeding or bruising; fever, sore throat, mouth sores; fatigue; any sign of infection; injury.

Keep this drug out of the reach of children. Do not give this medication to anyone else or take any similar medication that has not been prescribed for you.

This Teaching Checklist reflects general patient teaching guidelines. It is not meant to be a substitute for drug-specific teaching information, which is available in nursing drug guides.

- Arrange for supportive care and comfort measures for flu-like symptoms (rest, environmental control, acetaminophen) *to decrease patient discomfort and increase compliance.*
- Monitor nutritional status during therapy; provide small, frequent meals, mouth care, and nutritional consult as necessary *to ensure adequate nutrition.*
- Instruct female patients in the use of barrier contraceptives *to avoid pregnancy during therapy, because of the risk of adverse effects to the fetus.*
- Provide thorough patient teaching, including measures to avoid adverse effects, warning signs of problems, and proper administration (see Patient Teaching Checklist: Immune Suppressants).
- Offer support and encouragement *to deal with the diagnosis and the drug regimen.*

Evaluation

- Monitor patient response to the drug (prevention of transplant rejection; improvement in autoimmune disease or cancer; prevention of RSV disease; improvement in signs and symptoms of Crohn's disease).
- Monitor for adverse effects (flu-like symptoms, GI upset, increased infections, neoplasms, fluid overload).
- Evaluate the effectiveness of the teaching plan (patient can name drug, dosage, adverse effects to watch for, specific measures to avoid adverse effects).
- Monitor the effectiveness of comfort measures and compliance to the regimen (see Nursing Care Guide: Immune Suppressants).

WWW. WEB LINKS

Health care providers and patients may want to consult the following Internet sources:

Information on cancers (including leukemias and Kaposi's sarcoma) and treatments:
http://www.oncolink.upenn.edu

NURSING CARE GUIDE

Immune Suppressants

Assessment	Nursing Diagnoses	Implementation	Evaluation
HISTORY Allergies to any immune suppressant, pregnancy, lactation, renal or hepatic impairment, history of neoplasm	Pain related to CNS, GI, flu-like symptoms Risk for infection, related to immune suppression Nutrition, less than body requirements, related to GI effects Knowledge deficit regarding drug therapy	Arrange for laboratory tests prior to and periodically during therapy. Administer drug as indicated. Protect patient from exposure to infection. Provide supportive and comfort measures to deal with adverse effects. Monitor nutritional status and intervene as needed. Provide patient teaching regarding drug name, dosage, adverse effects and precautions, warning signs to report.	Evaluate drug effects: prevention of transplant rejection; improvement of autoimmune disease. Monitor for adverse effects: infection, flu-like symptoms, GI upset, fluid overload, neoplasm. Monitor for drug–drug interactions as indicated for each drug. Evaluate effectiveness of patient teaching program. Evaluate effectiveness of comfort and safety measures.
PHYSICAL EXAMINATION Neurological: orientation, reflexes, affect General: temperature, weight CV: pulse, cardiac auscultation, BP, edema, ECG GI: liver evaluation Lab tests: CBC, liver and renal function tests, condition being treated			

Information on multiple sclerosis (updates, treatments, contact groups):

http://www.nmss.org/home.html

Information on drug research and drug profiles:

http://www.pharminfo.com/pin_hp.html

Information on drug research and development, new approvals, alerts, and warnings:

http://www.fda.gov/fdahomepage.html

Information about organ transplants:

Listserv@wuvmd.wustl.edu

CHAPTER SUMMARY

- Immune stimulants boost the immune system when it is exhausted from fighting off prolonged invasion or needs help fighting a specific pathogen or cancer cell.
- Immune suppressants are used to depress the immune system when needed to prevent transplant rejection or severe tissue damage associated with autoimmune disease.
- Interferons are naturally released from cells in the response to viral invasion; they are used to treat various cancers and warts.
- Interleukins stimulate cellular immunity and inhibit tumor growth, they are used to treat very specific cancers.
- Adverse effects seen with immune stimulants are related to the immune response (flu-like symptoms including fever, myalgia, lethargy, arthralgia, and fatigue).
- Immune suppressants are used in a variety of specific transplant situations. Research is ongoing to extend the use of various immune suppressants in other situations, including various autoimmune disorders.

- Increased susceptibility to infection and increased risk of neoplasm are potentially dangerous effects associated with the use of immune suppressants. Patients need to be protected from infection, injury, and invasive procedures.

BIBLIOGRAPHY

Bullock, B. L. (2000). *Focus on pathophysiology*. Philadelphia: Lippincott Williams & Wilkins.

Hardman, J. G., Limbird, L. E., Molinoff, P. B., Ruddon, R. W., & Gilman, A. G. (Eds.). (1996). *Goodman and Gilman's the pharmacological basis of therapeutics* (9th ed.). New York: McGraw Hill.

Karch, A. M. (2000). *2000 Lippincott's Nursing Drug Guide.* Philadelphia: Lippincott Williams & Wilkins.

McEvoy, B. R. (Ed.). (1999). *Drug facts and comparisons.* St. Louis: Facts & Comparisons.

The Medical Letter on Drugs and Therapeutics. (1999). New Rochelle, NY: Medical Letter.

CHAPTER 16

Vaccines and Sera

Vaccines
- Bacterial vaccines
  - BCG
  - cholera vaccine
  - **P** haemophilus B conjugated vaccine
  - haemophilus B conjugated vaccine and hepatitis B surface antigen
  - haemophilus B conjugated vaccine with tetanus toxoid
  - meningococcal polysaccharide vaccine
  - plague vaccine
  - pneumococcal vaccine, polyvalent
  - typhoid vaccine
  - Lyme disease
- Toxoids
  - diphtheria and tetanus toxoids, combined, adsorbed
  - **P** diphtheria and tetanus toxoids and acellular pertussis vaccine, absorbed
  - diphtheria and tetanus toxoids and whole cell pertussis vaccine with haemophilus
  - influenza B conjugated vaccine
- Viral vaccines
  - hepatitis A vaccine
  - hepatitis A vaccine, inactivated
  - hepatitis B vaccine
  - influenza virus vaccine
  - Japanese encephalitis vaccine
  - measles virus vaccine
  - **P** measles, mumps, rubella vaccine
  - mumps virus vaccine
  - poliovirus vaccine, live, oral, trivalent
  - poliovirus vaccine, inactivated
  - rabies vaccine
  - rubella virus vaccine
  - yellow fever vaccine
  - varicella virus vaccine

Immune sera
- hepatitis B immune globulin
- **P** immune globulin intramuscular
- immune globulin intravenous
- lymphocyte immune globulin
- rabies immune globulin
- respiratory syncytial virus immune globulin
- RHO immune globulin
- RHO immune globulin IV
- RHO immune globulin, micro-dose
- tetanus immune globulin
- varicella zoster immune globulin

Antitoxins/Antivenins
- **P** antivenin
- Black Widow spider antivenin
- diphtheria antitoxin

CHAPTER OUTLINE

KEY TERMS

active immunity
antitoxins
immune sera
immunization
passive immunity
serum sickness
vaccine

INTRODUCTION

Vaccines, immune sera and ***antitoxins*** are usually referred to as biologicals. They are used to stimulate the production of antibodies, to provide preformed antibodies to facilitate an immune reaction, or to react specifically with the toxins produced by an invading pathogen. Prudent, prophylactic medical care requires the routine administration of certain vaccines to prevent diseases before they occur.

IMMUNITY

Immunity is a state of relative resistance to a disease that develops after exposure to the specific disease-causing agent. People are not born with immunity to diseases, so they must acquire immunity by stimulating B cell clones to form plasma cells, then antibodies.

Active immunity occurs when the body recognizes a foreign protein and begins producing antibodies to react with that specific protein or antigen. After plasma cells are formed to produce antibodies, specific memory cells that produce the same antibodies are created. If the specific foreign protein is introduced into the body again, these memory cells react immediately to release antibodies. This type of immunity is thought to be lifelong.

Passive immunity occurs when preformed antibodies are injected into the system and react with a specific antigen. These antibodies come from animals that have been infected with the disease or humans who have had the disease and have developed antibodies. The circulating antibodies act the same as those produced from plasma cells, recognizing the foreign protein and attaching to it, rendering it harmless. Unlike active immunity, passive immunity is limited. It lasts only as long as the circulating antibodies last, because the body does not produce its own antibodies. In some cases, the host human produces antibodies to the circulating antibodies. This results in ***serum sickness,*** a massive immune reaction. Signs and symptoms of serum sickness include fever, arthritis, flank pain, myalgia, and arthralgia.

IMMUNIZATION

Immunization is the process of artificially stimulating active immunity by exposing the body to weakened or less toxic proteins associated with specific disease-causing organisms. The goal is to cause an immune response without having the patient suffer the full course of a disease. Children routinely are immunized against many infections that were once quite devastating (Figure 16-1). For example, smallpox was one of the first diseases against which children were immunized. Today, it has virtually been wiped out in the world. Diphtheria, pertussis, tetanus, haemophilus B, hepatitis B, chicken pox, polio, measles, mumps, and rubella are all standard immunizations today.

VACCINES

Vaccine comes from the Latin word for smallpox, *vaccinia.* Vaccines are immunizations containing weakened or altered protein antigens that stimulate formation of antibodies against a specific disease (Figure 16-2). They are used to promote active immunity.

Vaccines can be made from chemically inactivated microorganisms or from live, weakened viruses or bacteria. Toxoids are vaccines that are made from the toxins produced by the microorganism. The toxins are altered so that they are no longer poisonous, but still have the recognizable protein antigen that will stimulate antibody production.

The particular vaccine that is used depends on the possible exposure a person will have to a particular disease and the age of the patient. Some vaccines

Immunization	*Birth*	*2 mo*	*4 mo*	*6 mo*	*12–15 mo*	*18 mo*	*4–6 y*	*11–12 y*	*14–16 y*
Hepatitis B	X	X			X				
DPT		X	X	X		X			
Rotavirus		X	X	X					
Tetanus/diphtheria booster							X	X	
H. influenzae b		X	X	X	X				
Measles, mumps, rubella					X		X		
Poliovirus		X	X		X		X		

Suggested by the American Academy of Pediatrics, 1998.

FIGURE 16-1. Recommended immunization schedules for adults and children. (Karch, A. M. [2000]. *2000 Lippincott's nursing drug guide.* Philadelphia: Lippincott Williams & Wilkins.)

CULTURAL CONSIDERATIONS

Pediatric Immunization

It is a well-documented concept that by preventing potentially devastating diseases, society not only can prevent unneeded suffering and even death, but also can save valuable citizens for the future. Pediatric immunization has helped to greatly decrease the incidence of most childhood diseases and has prevented the complications associated with many of these diseases. In the United States, routine immunization is considered standard medical practice.

Ensuring that every child has the opportunity to receive the recommended immunizations has become a political as well as social issue. The cost of preventing a disease that most people have never even seen may be difficult to justify to families who have trouble putting food on the table. Widespread campaigns to provide free immunizations and health screening to all children have tried to address this problem, but have not been totally successful.

In addition, periodic reports of severe or even fatal reactions to standard immunizations alarm many parents about the risks of immunizations. These parents need facts as well as reassurance about modern efforts to prevent and screen for these reactions.

Public education efforts should be directed at providing parents with information about pediatric immunization, and encouraging them to act on that information. Nurses are often in the ideal position to provide this information, either during prenatal visits, while screening for other problems, or even standing in line at a grocery store. It is important for nurses to be well versed on the need for standard immunizations and screening to prevent severe reactions. The Centers for Disease Control and Prevention (http://www.cdc.gov) offers current information and updates for health care providers, while Pedinfo (http://www.uab.edu/pedinfo/index.html) offers information and resources for concerned parents as well as health professionals.

LIFE-SPAN CONSIDERATIONS

Immunization for Adults

There are a number of reasons why adults should receive certain immunizations. For example, adults who are traveling to areas at high risk for particular diseases—and who may not have previously been exposed to those diseases—are advised to be immunized. In addition, older adults and adults with chronic diseases are advised to be immunized yearly with an influenza vaccine, and once with a pneumococcal pneumonia vaccine. These vaccines provide some protection against diseases that can prove dangerous for older people and people with chronic lung, cardiovascular, or endocrine disorders. The influenza vaccine changes yearly, depending on predictions of which flu strain might be emergent in that year. The pneumonia vaccine contains 23 strains and is felt to offer lifetime protection. Tetanus shots also are recommended for adults every 10 years, or with any injury that potentially could precipitate a tetanus infection. Screening for immunizations should be a standard part of adult health care as well as pediatric care.

are only used in children, and some vaccines cannot be used in infancy. Some vaccines require booster doses—doses that are given a few months after the initial dose to further stimulate antibody production. In many cases, antibody titers (levels of the antibody in the serum) can be used to evaluate a person's response to an immunization and determine the need for a booster dose.

THERAPEUTIC ACTIONS AND INDICATIONS

Vaccines stimulate active immunity in people who are at high risk for developing a particular disease. The vaccine needed for a patient will depend on the exposure that person will have to the pathogen. That exposure is usually determined by where the person lives, travel plans, and work or family environment exposures. Vaccines provide lifelong immunity to the disease against which the patient is being immunized.

CONTRAINDICATIONS/CAUTIONS

The use of vaccines is contraindicated in the presence of immune deficiency (the vaccine could cause disease, and the body will not be able to respond as anticipated in an immune deficient state); during pregnancy (because of potential effects on the fetus and the success of the pregnancy); with known allergies to any of the components of the vaccine (refer to each individual vaccine for specifics); or to patients receiving immune globulin or who have received blood or blood products in the last 3 months (a serious immune reaction could occur).

Caution should be used any time a vaccine is given to a child with a history of febrile convulsions or cerebral injury, or in any condition in which a potential fever would be dangerous. Caution also should be used in the presence of any acute infection.

ADVERSE EFFECTS

Adverse effects of vaccines are associated with the immune or inflammatory reaction that is being stim-

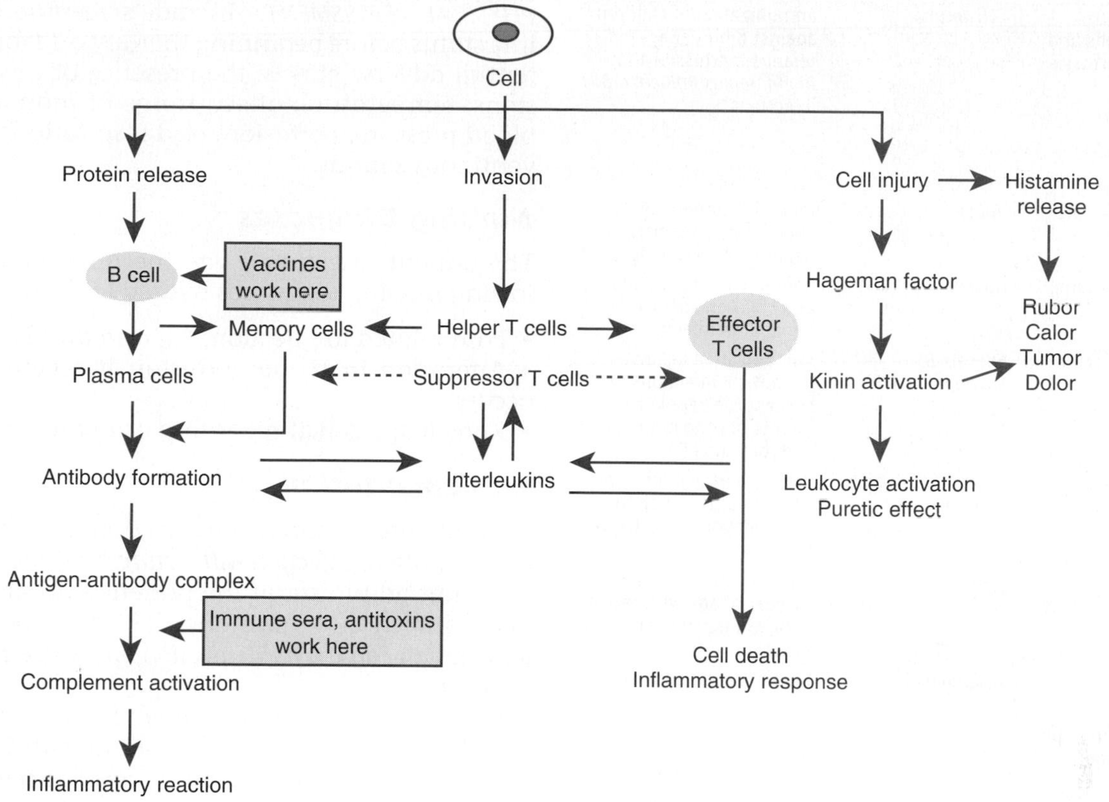

FIGURE 16-2. Sites of action of vaccines, immune sera and antitoxins.

ulated: moderate fever, rash, malaise, chills, fretfulness, drowsiness, anorexia, vomiting, irritability. Pain, redness, swelling, and even nodule formation at the injection site is also common. In rare instances, severe hypersensitivity reactions have been reported.

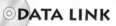

DATA LINK

Data link to the following vaccines in your nursing drug guide:

VACCINES

Name	Brand Name	Usual Indications
BACTERIAL VACCINES		
BCG	*TICE BCG*	Prevention of tuberculosis with high risk of exposure
cholera vaccine	generic	Immunization against cholera for areas high in cholera
P haemophilus B conjugated vaccine	*HibTITER, Pedvax-HIB ProHIBIT*	Immunization of children against *haemophilus B* infections
haemophilus B conjugated vaccine and hepatitis B surface antigen	*Comvax*	Immunization of children against *haemophilus B* and hepatitis B infections
haemophilus B conjugated vaccine with tetanus toxoid	*ActHIB, OmniHib*	Immunization of children against *haemophilus B* and tetanus infections
meningococcal polysaccharide vaccine	*Menomune-A/C/Y/W-135*	Immunization against meningococcal infections in endemic areas
plague vaccine	generic	Immunization of persons at risk for exposure to plague
pneumococcal vaccine, polyvalent	*Pneumovax 23, Pnu-Immune 23*	Immunization against pneumococcal infections
typhoid vaccine	*Vivotif Berna Vaccine*	Immunization against typhoid fever
Lyme disease	*Lymerix*	Immunization against Lyme disease in susceptible persons
TOXOIDS		
diphtheria and tetanus toxoids, combined, adsorbed	*DT, Td*	Immunization of adults and children >7 years of age against diphtheria and tetanus
diphtheria and tetanus toxoids and whole cell pertussis vaccine, absorbed	*Tri-Immunol*	Immunization of children against diphtheria, tetanus, and pertussis
P diphtheria and tetanus toxoids and acellular pertussis vaccine, absorbed	*DtaP*	Immunization of children against diphtheria, tetanus, and pertussis

diphtheria and tetanus toxoids and whole cell pertussis vaccine with *haemophilus influenza* B conjugated vaccine	*Tetramune*	Immunization of children against diphtheria, tetanus, pertussis, and *haemophilus influenza B* infections
VIRAL VACCINES		
hepatitis A vaccine	*Vaqta*	Immunization of adults and children against hepatitis A infections
hepatitis A vaccine, inactivated	*Havrix*	Immunization of adults and children against hepatitis A infections
hepatitis B vaccine	*Energix-B, Recombivax-HB*	Immunization against hepatitis B infections in susceptible people and infants born to mothers with hepatitis B
influenza virus vaccine	*Fluzone, Flu-Shield Fluvirin*	Prophylaxis in adults and children at high risk for complications of influenza infections
Japanese encephalitis vaccine	*JE-Vax*	Immunization of persons >1 year of age who reside in or will travel to endemic areas
measles virus vaccine	*Attenuvax*	Immunization against measles
P measles, mumps, rubella vaccine	*MMR-II*	Immunization against measles, mumps, and rubella in adults and children > 15 months of age
mumps virus vaccine	*Mumpsvax*	Immunization against mumps in persons > 12 months of age
poliovirus vaccine, live, oral, trivalent	*Orimune*	Immunization against polio infections in children through 18 years of age
poliovirus vaccine, inactivated	*IPOL*	Immunization against polio infections in adults and children who cannot take oral polio vaccine
rabies vaccine	*Imvax Rabies*	Preexposure immunization against rabies for high-risk people
rubella virus vaccine	*Meruvax II*	Immunization against rubella in adults and children > 12 months of age
varicella virus vaccine	*Varivax*	Immunization against chicken pox infections in adults and children ≥ 12 months of age
yellow fever vaccine	*YF-Vax*	Immunization of travelers to areas endemic in yellow fever

NURSING CONSIDERATIONS for patients receiving vaccines

Assessment

HISTORY. Screen for any known allergies to any vaccines and the components of the one being used; pregnancy; recent administration of immune globulin or blood products; immune deficiency; and acute infection.

PHYSICAL ASSESSMENT. Include screening for baseline status before beginning therapy and for any potential adverse effects: the presence of any skin lesions; temperature; affect; range of motion; pulse, blood pressure, perfusion; and respirations and adventitious sounds.

Nursing Diagnoses

The patient receiving a vaccine may have the following nursing diagnoses related to drug therapy:

- Pain related to injection, GI, and flu-like effects
- Alteration in tissue perfusion if severe reaction occurs
- Knowledge deficit regarding drug therapy

Implementation

- Do not use to treat acute infection; *a vaccine is only used to prevent infection with future exposures.*
- Do not administer if the patient exhibits signs of acute infection or immune deficiency *because the vaccine can cause a mild infection and exacerbate acute infections.*
- Do not administer if the patient has received blood, blood products, or immune globulin within the last 3 months *because severe immune reaction could occur.*
- Arrange for proper preparation and administration of the vaccine; check on each injection, timing and dosage, *because dosage, preparation, and timing vary with individual vaccines.*
- Maintain emergency equipment on standby, including epinephrine, *in case of severe hypersensitivity reaction.*
- Arrange for supportive care and comfort measures for flu-like symptoms (rest, environmental control, acetaminophen) and for injection discomfort (local heat application, anti-inflammatories, resting arm) *to promote patient comfort.*
- Be aware that children should not receive aspirin to treat the discomforts associated with the immunization. *Aspirin can mask warning signs of Reye's syndrome, a potentially serious disease.*
- Provide thorough patient teaching, including measures to avoid adverse effects; warning signs of problems; and the need to keep a written record of immunizations (see Patient Teaching Checklist: Vaccines), *to increase knowledge about drug therapy and to increase compliance with drug regimen.*
- Provide a written record of the immunization, including the need to return for booster immunizations and timing of the boosters, if necessary, *to increase patient compliance to medical regimens.*

Evaluation

- Monitor patient response to the drug (prevention of disease, appropriate antibody titer levels).
- Monitor for adverse effects (flu-like symptoms; GI upset; local pain, swelling, nodule formation at injection site).

CASE STUDY

Educating a Parent About Vaccines

PRESENTATION

S. D. is a 25-year-old, first-time mother who has brought her 2-month-old daughter to the well-baby clinic for a routine evaluation. The baby was found to be healthy, growing well, and within normal parameters for her age. At the end of the visit, the nurse prepared to give the baby the first of her routine immunizations. S. D. became concerned and expressed fears about paralysis and infant deaths associated with immunizations.

CRITICAL THINKING QUESTIONS

What information should S. D. be given about immunizations? What nursing interventions would be appropriate at this time? Think of ways to explain the importance of immunizations to S. D. while supporting her concerns for the welfare of her baby. How can this experience be incorporated into a teaching plan for S. D. and her baby?

DISCUSSION

S. D. should be reassured before the baby is immunized. The nurse can tell her that in the past, paralysis and infant deaths have been reported, but that efforts continue to make the vaccines pure. Careful monitoring of the child and the child's response to each immunization can help avoid such problems. Assure S. D. that the immunizations will prevent her daughter from contracting many, sometimes deadly, diseases. Praise S. D.'s efforts to research information that might affect her baby and for asking questions that could have an impact on her child and her understanding of her care.

The recommended schedule of immunizations should be given to S. D. so that she is aware of what is planned and how the various vaccines are spaced and combined. She should be encouraged to monitor the baby after each injection for fever, chills, and flu-like reactions When she gets home, she can medicate the baby with acetaminophen to avert many of these symptoms before they happen. (S. D. should be advised not to give the baby aspirin, which could cover up Reye's syndrome, a potentially serious disorder.) S. D. also should be told that the injection site might be sore, swollen, and red, but that this will pass in a couple of days. S. D. can ease the baby's discomfort by applying warm soaks to the area for about 10 to 15 minutes every 2 hours.

S. D. should be encouraged to write down all of the immunizations that the baby has had and to keep this information handy for easy reference. She should also be encouraged to record any adverse effects that occur after each immunization. If reactions are uncomfortable, it is possible to split doses of future immunizations.

The nurse should give S. D. a chance to vent her concerns and fears. First-time parents may be more anxious than experienced ones when dealing with issues involving a new baby. To alleviate S. D.'s anxiety, the nurse should provide a phone number that S. D. can call if the baby seems to be having a severe reaction, or if S. D. wants to discuss any questions or concerns. She should feel that support is available for any concern that she may have. Because this interaction is likely to form the basis for future interactions with S. D., it is important to establish a sense of respect and trust.

- Evaluate the effectiveness of the teaching plan (patient can name drug, dosage, adverse effects to watch for, has written record of immunizations).
- Monitor the effectiveness of comfort measures and compliance to the regimen (see Nursing Care Guide: Vaccines).

WWW.WEB LINKS

Patients traveling to various parts of the world can obtain information on vaccines that are needed and food and travel precautions online at

http://www.travelhealth.com

IMMUNE SERA AND ANTITOXINS

As explained earlier, passive immunity can be achieved by providing preformed antibodies to a specific antigen. These antibodies are found in immune sera, which may contain antibodies to toxins, venins, bacteria, viruses, or even red blood cell antigenic factors. The term ***immune sera*** is usually used to refer to sera that contain antibodies to specific bacteria or viruses. The terms ***antitoxin*** and antivenin are used to refer to immune sera that has antibodies to very specific toxins that might be released by invading pathogens or to venom that might be injected through spider or snake bites.

PATIENT TEACHING CHECKLIST

Vaccines

Create customized patient teaching materials for a specific vaccine from your CD-ROM. Your patient teaching should stress the following points for drugs within this class:

This immunization helps your body to develop antibodies to protect you against ___________ if you should be exposed to the disease.

The injection site might be sore and painful. Heat applied to the area may help this discomfort and speed your recovery.

Adverse effects that you might experience include fever, muscle aches, joint aches, fatigue, and malaise. Aspirin or acetaminophen may help these discomforts; check with your health care provider for the best choice for you. Children should not be given aspirin because it could prevent the recognition of a disease called Reye's syndrome. Rest, small meals, and a quiet environment may also help you to feel better.

The adverse effects should pass within 2 to 3 days. If they become unduly uncomfortable or persist longer than a few days, notify your health care provider.

Booster immunizations are required for many, but not all immunizations. You should receive a booster immunization in ___________ months (if appropriate).

This Teaching Checklist reflects general patient teaching guidelines. It is not meant to be a substitute for drug-specific teaching information, which is available in nursing drug guides.

THERAPEUTIC ACTIONS AND INDICATIONS

Immune sera are used to provide passive immunity to a specific antigen or disease. They also may be used as prophylaxis against specific diseases following exposure in patients who are immune suppressed. In addition, immune sera may be used to lessen the severity of a disease after known or suspected exposure to the disease (see Figure 16-2 for sites of action of immune sera and antitoxins).

CONTRAINDICATIONS/CAUTIONS

Immune sera are contraindicated in the presence of any history of severe reaction to any immune sera or to products similar to the components of the sera. They should be used with caution during pregnancy (because of potential risk to the fetus); with coagulation defects or thrombocytopenia; or with a known history of previous exposure to the immune sera (as increased risk of hypersensitivity reaction occurs with each use).

ADVERSE EFFECTS

Adverse effects can be attributed either to the effect of immune sera on the immune system (rash, nausea, vomiting, chills, fever) or to allergic reactions (chest tightness, falling blood pressure, difficulty breathing). Local reactions are very common (swelling, tenderness, pain, muscle stiffness at the injection site).

DATA LINK

Data link to the following immune sera and antitoxins in your nursing drug guide:

IMMUNE SERA

Name	Brand Name	Usual Indications
hepatitis B immune globulin	*H-BIG, Hyperhep*	Postexposure prophylaxis against hepatitis B
P immune globulin intramuscular	*Gamma Globulin*	Prophylaxis after exposure to hepatitis A, measles, varicella, rubella
immune globulin intravenous	*GamimuneN, Gammagard,* and others	Prophylaxis after exposure to hepatitis A, measles, varicella, rubella; bone marrow transplant; Kawasaki's disease; chronic lymphocytic leukemia; treatment of patients with immunoglobulin deficiency
lymphocyte immune globulin	*Atgam*	Management of allograft rejection in renal transplants, treatment of aplastic anemia
rabies immune globulin	*Hyerab, Imogam*	Protection against rabies in nonimmunized patients exposed to rabies
respiratory syncytial virus immune globulin	*Respigam*	Prevention of RSV infection in children < 24 months of age with bronchopulmonary dysplasia or premature birth

NURSING CARE GUIDE
Vaccines

Assessment	Nursing Diagnoses	Implementation	Evaluation
HISTORY Allergies to the serum base, pregnancy, lactation, acute infection, immunosuppression	Pain related to infection, flu-like symptoms Alteration in tissue perfusion if severe reaction occurs Knowledge deficit regarding drug therapy	Ensure proper preparation and administration of vaccine within appropriate time frame. Provide supportive and comfort measures to deal with adverse effects: antiinflammatory/antipyretic, local heat application, small meals, rest, quiet environment. Provide patient teaching regarding drug name, dosage, adverse effects and precautions, warnings signs to report. Provide emergency life support if needed for acute reaction.	Evaluate drug effects: serum titers reflecting immunization (if appropriate). Monitor for adverse effects: pain, flu-like symptoms, local discomfort. Monitor for drug–drug interactions as indicated for each drug. Evaluate effectiveness of patient teaching program. Evaluate effectiveness of comfort and safety measures. Evaluate effectiveness of emergency measures if needed.
PHYSICAL EXAMINATION General: temperature CV: pulse, cardiac auscultation, BP, edema, perfusion Respiratory: respirations, adventitious sounds Skin: lesions Joints: range of motion			

RHO immune globulin	*Gamulin Rh* and others	Prevention of sensitization to the Rh factor
RHO immune globulin IV	*Win RHO*	Prevention of sensitization to the Rh factor
RHO immune globulin, micro-dose	*HypRho-D Mini-Dose* and others	Prevention of sensitization to the Rh factor
tetanus immune globulin	*Hyper-Tet*	Passive immunization against tetanus at time of injury
varicella zoster immune globulin	*Varicella Zoster Immune*	Passive immunization against varicella zoster in immunosuppressed patients exposed to disease
ANTITOXINS/ANTIVENINS		
P antivenin	generic	Neutralizes the venom of various snakes
Black Widow spider antivenin	*Antivenin*	Treatment of symptoms of Black Widow spider bites
diphtheria antitoxin	generic	Prevention or treatment of diphtheria

NURSING CONSIDERATIONS
for patients receiving immune sera or antitoxins

Assessment

HISTORY. Screen for any known allergies to any of these drugs or their components; pregnancy; previous exposure to the serum being used; thrombocytopenia, coagulation disorders; and immunization history.

PHYSICAL ASSESSMENT. Include screening for baseline status before beginning therapy and for any potential adverse effects: the presence of any skin lesions; temperature; orientation, reflexes; pulse, blood pressure, respirations, and adventitious sounds.

Nursing Diagnoses

The patient receiving immune sera may have the following nursing diagnoses related to drug therapy:

- Pain related to local, GI, and flu-like effects
- Alteration in tissue perfusion related to possible severe reactions
- Knowledge deficit regarding drug therapy

Implementation

- Do not administer to any patient with a history of severe reaction to immune globulins or to the components of the drug being used *because severe immune reactions can occur.*
- Administer the drug as indicated; *preparation varies with each product.*
- Monitor for severe reactions and have emergency equipment ready *in case of severe reaction.*
- Arrange for supportive care and comfort measures for flu-like symptoms (rest, environmental control, acetaminophen) and for the local reaction (heat to injection site, anti-inflammatories) *to promote patient comfort.*
- Provide thorough patient teaching, including measures to avoid adverse effects and warning signs of problems *to improve patient compliance.*
- Provide a written record of immune sera use and encourage the patient or family to keep that information *to ensure proper medical treatment.*

Evaluation

- Monitor the patient's response to the drug (improvement in disease signs and symptoms, prevention of severe disease).
- Monitor for adverse effects (flu-like symptoms, GI upset, local inflammation and pain).
- Evaluate the effectiveness of the teaching plan (patient can name drug, dosage, adverse effects to watch for, specific measures to avoid adverse effects, need to retain written record of injection).
- Monitor the effectiveness of comfort measures and compliance to the regimen.

CHAPTER SUMMARY

- Immunity is a state of relative resistance to a disease that only develops after exposure to the specific disease-causing agent.
- Active immunity occurs when a person is stimulated to make antibodies against specific proteins; memory cells then release antibodies immediately if that protein enters the body again.
- Passive immunity occurs when a person is given preformed antibodies to a specific protein. This offers immediate protection from exposure to the protein, but the protection is limited to the circulating antibodies.
- Immunizations are given to stimulate active immunity in a person who is at high risk for exposure to specific diseases. Immunizations are a standard part of preventive medicine.
- Vaccines contain weakened or partial proteins from specific antigens that stimulate the production of antibodies to that protein, thus providing active immunity.
- Immune sera provide preformed antibodies to specific proteins that a person has been exposed to or is at high risk for exposure.
- Serum sickness, a massive immune reaction, occurs more frequently with immune sera than with vaccines. Patients need to be monitored for any history of hypersensitivity reactions and emergency equipment should be available.
- Patients should be advised to keep a written record of all immunizations or immune sera used. Booster doses may be needed to further stimulate antibody production.

BIBLIOGRAPHY

AMA drug evaluations. (1998). Chicago: American Medical Association.

Bullock, B. L. (2000). *Focus on pathophysiology.* Philadelphia: Lippincott Williams & Wilkins.

Hardman, J. G., Limbird, L. E., Molinoff, P. B., Ruddon, R. W., & Gilman, A. G. (Eds.). (1996). *Goodman and Gilman's the pharmacological basis of therapeutics* (9th ed.). New York: McGraw Hill.

Karch, A. M. (2000). *2000 Lippincott's nursing drug guide.* Philadelphia: Lippincott Williams & Wilkins.

McEvoy, B. R. (Ed.).(1999). *Drug facts & comparisons.* St. Louis: Facts & Comparisons.

The Medical Letter on Drugs and Therapeutics. (1999). New Rochelle, NY: Medical Letter.

PART 4

Drugs Acting on the Central and Peripheral Nervous Systems

CHAPTER 17

Introduction to Nerves and the Nervous System

CHAPTER OUTLINE

KEY TERMS

action potential
afferent
axon
dendrite
depolarization
effector
efferent
engram
forebrain
hindbrain
limbic system
midbrain
neuron
neurotransmitter
repolarization
Schwann cell
soma
synapse

INTRODUCTION

The nervous system is responsible for controlling the functions of the human body, analyzing incoming stimuli, and integrating internal and external responses. The nervous system is composed of the central nervous system (the brain and spinal cord) and the peripheral nervous system. The peripheral nervous system (PNS) is composed of sensory receptors that bring information into the central nervous system (CNS) and motor nerves that carry information away from the CNS to facilitate response to stimuli. The autonomic nervous system, which is discussed in Chapter 27, uses components of the central and peripheral nervous systems to regulate automatic or unconscious responses to stimuli.

The structural unit of the nervous system is the nerve cell, or neuron. The billions of nerve cells that make up the nervous system are organized to allow movement; realization of various sensations; response to internal and external stimuli; and learning, thinking, and emotion. The mechanisms that are involved in all of these processes are not clearly understood. The actions of drugs that are used to affect the functioning of the nerves and the responses that these drugs cause throughout the nervous system provide some of the current theories about the workings of the nervous system.

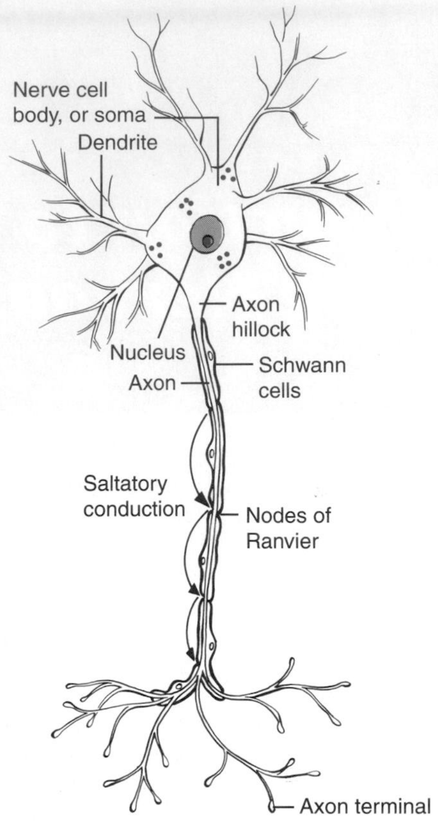

FIGURE 17-1. The neuron, functional unit of the nervous system.

PHYSIOLOGY OF THE NERVOUS SYSTEM

The nervous system operates using electrical impulses and chemical messengers to transmit information throughout the body and to respond to internal and external stimuli. The properties and function of the neuron provide the basis for all nervous system function.

Neurons

As noted above, the ***neuron*** is the structural unit of the nervous system. The human body contains about 14 billion neurons. About 10 billion of these are located in the brain, and the remainder make up the spinal cord and peripheral nervous system.

Neurons have several distinctive cellular features. Each neuron is made up of a cell body, or ***soma,*** which contains the cell nucleus, cytoplasm, and various granules and other particles (Figure 17-1). Short, branch-like projections that cover most of the surface of a neuron are known as ***dendrites.*** These structures, which provide increased surface area for the neuron, bring information into the neuron from other neurons.

One end of the nerve body extends into a long process that does not branch out until the very end of the process. This elongated process is called the nerve ***axon***, and it emerges from the soma at the axon hillock (see Figure 17-1). The axon of a nerve can be extremely tiny or it can extend for several feet. The axon carries information from a nerve to be transmitted to ***effector*** cells—cells in a muscle, a gland, or another nerve. This transmission occurs at the end of the axon where the axon branches out in what is called the axon terminal.

The axons of many nerves are packed closely together in the nervous system and look like cable or fiber tracts. ***Afferent*** fibers are nerve axons that run from peripheral receptors into the CNS. In contrast, ***efferent*** fibers are nerve axons that carry nerve impulses from the CNS to the periphery to stimulate muscles or glands. (An easy way to remember the difference between afferent and efferent: efferent fibers exit from the CNS.)

Neurons are unable to reproduce, so if nerves are destroyed, they are lost. If dendrites and axons are lost, nerves regenerate those structures. For this regeneration to occur, the soma and the axon hillock must remain intact. For a clinical example, consider a person who has closed a car door on his or her finger.

Sensation and movement may be lost or limited for a certain period of time, but because the nerve bodies for most of the nerves in the hand are located in ganglia (groups of nerve bodies) in the wrist, they are able to regenerate the damaged axon or dendrites. Over time, sensation and full movement return.

Research on possible ways to stimulate the reproduction of nerves is under way. Although scientists have used nerve growth factor with fetal cell implants to stimulate some nerve growth, it must still be assumed that nerves are unable to reproduce.

Action Potential

Nerves send messages by conducting electrical impulses called ***action potentials.*** Nerve membranes, which are capable of conducting action potentials along the entire membrane, send messages to nearby neurons or to effector cells that may be located inches to feet away using this electrical communication system. Like all cell membranes, nerve membranes have various channels or pores that control the movement of substances into and out of the cell. Some of these channels allow the movement of sodium, potassium, and calcium. When cells are at rest, their membranes are impermeable to sodium. However, the membranes are permeable to potassium ions.

The sodium–potassium pump that is active in the membranes of neurons is responsible for this property of the membrane. This system pumps sodium ions out of the cell and potassium ions into the cell. At rest, more sodium ions are outside the cell membrane, and more potassium ions are inside. Electrically, the inside of the cell is relatively negative compared with the outside of the membrane, which establishes an electrical potential along the nerve membrane. When nerves are at rest, this is referred to as the resting membrane potential of the nerve.

Stimulation of a neuron causes ***depolarization*** of the nerve, which means that the sodium channels open in response to the stimulus, and sodium ions rush into the cell following the established concentration gradient. If an electrical monitoring device is attached to the nerve at this point, a positive rush of ions is recorded. The electrical charge on the inside of the membrane changes from relatively negative to relatively positive. This sudden reversal of membrane potential is called the action potential (Figure 17-2), which lasts less than a microsecond. Using the sodium–potassium pump, the cell then returns that section of membrane to the resting membrane potential, a process called ***repolarization.*** The action potential generated at one point along a nerve membrane stimulates the generation of an action potential in the adjacent portions of the cell membrane, and the stimulus travels the length of the cell membrane.

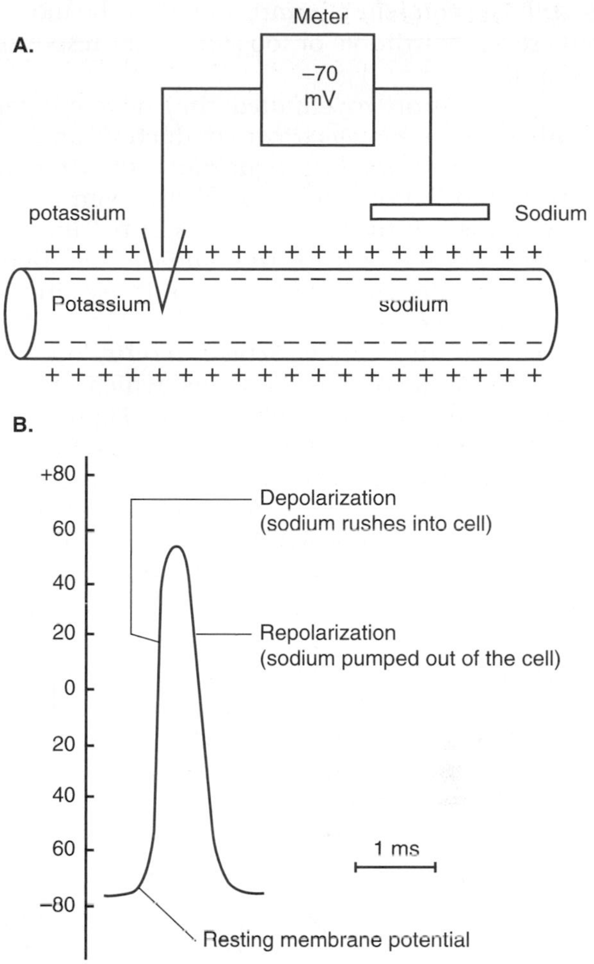

FIGURE 17-2. The action potential. (A) A segment of an axon showing that, at rest, the inside of the membrane is relatively negatively charged and the outside is positively charged. A pair of electrodes placed as shown would record a potential difference of about −70 mV; this is the resting membrane potential. (B) An action potential of about 1 msec that, as shown, would be recorded if the axon shown in A were brought to threshold. At the peak of the action potential, the charge on the membrane reverses polarity.

Nerves can respond to stimuli several hundred times per second, but for a given stimulus to cause an action potential, it must have sufficient strength and must occur when the nerve membrane is able to respond—that is, when it has repolarized. A nerve cannot be stimulated again while it is depolarized. The balance of sodium and potassium across the cell membrane must be reestablished.

Nerves require energy (i.e., oxygen and glucose) and the correct balance of the electrolytes sodium and potassium to maintain normal action potentials and transmit information into and out of the nervous system. If an individual has anoxia or hypoglycemia, the nerves might not be able to maintain the sodium–potassium pump, and he or she may become severely irritable or too stable (not responsive to stimuli).

Long nerves are myelinated: they have a myelin sheath that speeds electrical conduction and protects the nerves from the fatigue that results from frequent formation of action potentials. Even though many of the tightly packed nerves in the brain do not need to travel far to stimulate another nerve, they are myelinated. The effect of this myelination is not understood.

Myelinated nerves have ***Schwann cells,*** located at specific intervals along the axons, which are very resistant to electrical stimulation (see Figure 17-1). The Schwann cells wrap themselves around the axon in jelly-roll fashion. Between the Schwann cells are areas of uncovered nerve membrane called the nodes of Ranvier. So-called "leaping" nerve conduction occurs along these exposed nerve fibers. An action potential excites one section of nerve membrane, and the electrical impulse then "skips" from one node to the next, generating an action potential. Because the membrane is forming fewer action potentials, the speed of conduction is much faster and the nerve is protected from exhaustion or using up energy to form multiple action potentials. This node-to-node mode of conduction is termed saltatory or leaping transmission.

If the Schwann cells become enlarged or swollen and block the nodes of Ranvier, conduction does not occur because the electrical impulse has a limited firing range. A stimulus may simply be "lost" along the nerve, as in the neuromuscular disease multiple sclerosis. Believed to be an autoimmune disorder that attacks Schwann cells and leads to swelling and scarring of these cells, this disease is characterized by a progressive loss of nerve response and muscle function.

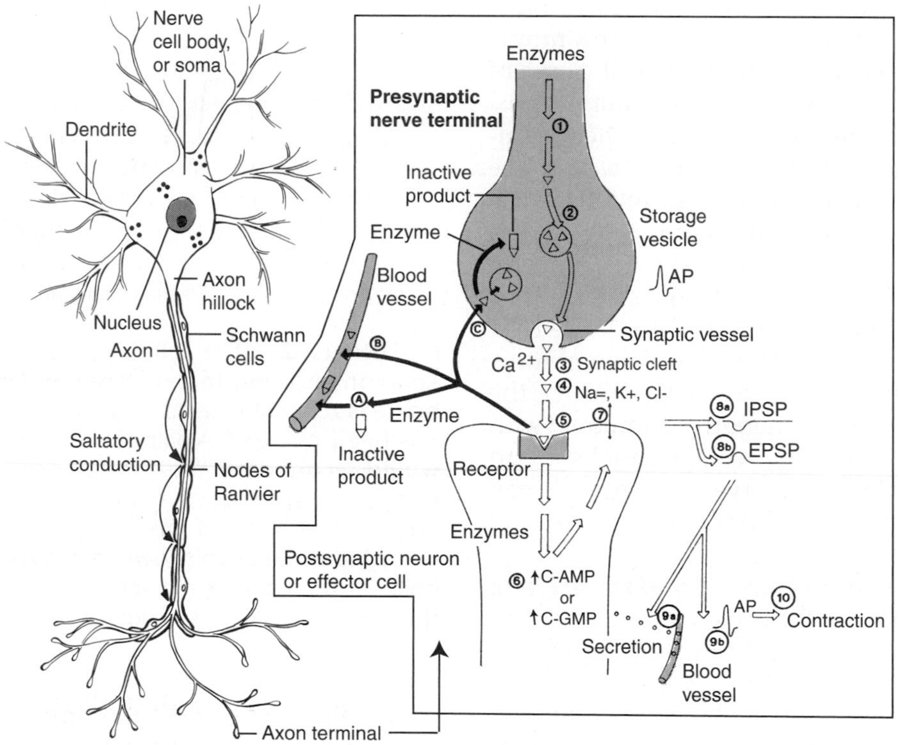

FIGURE 17-3. The sequence of events in synaptic transmission: (1) synthesis of the neurotransmitter; (2) uptake of the neurotransmitter into storage vesicles; (3) release of the neurotransmitter by an action potential in the presynaptic nerve; (4) diffusion of the neurotransmitter across the synaptic cleft; (5) combination of the neurotransmitter with a receptor; (6) a sequence of events leading to activation of second messengers within the postsynaptic nerve; (7) change in permeability of the postsynaptic membrane to one or more ions, causing (8a) an inhibitory postsynaptic potential or (8b) an excitatory postsynaptic potential. Characteristic responses of the postsynaptic cell are as follows: (9a) the gland secretes hormones; (9b) the muscle cells have an action potential; and (10) the muscle contracts. The action of the neurotransmitter is terminated by one or more of the following processes: (A) inactivation by an enzyme; (B) diffusion out of the synaptic cleft and removal by the vascular system; and (C) reuptake into the presynaptic nerve followed by storage in a synaptic vesicle or deactivation by an enzyme.

Nerve Synapse

When the electrical action potential reaches the end of an axon, the electrical impulse comes to a halt. At this point the stimulus no longer travels at the speed of electricity. The transmission of information between nerves and between nerves and glands and muscles is chemical. Nerves communicate with other nerves or effectors at the nerve ***synapse*** (Figure 17-3). The synapse is made up of a presynaptic nerve, the synaptic cleft, and the postsynaptic effector cell. The nerve axon, called the presynaptic nerve, releases a chemical called a ***neurotransmitter*** into the synaptic cleft, and the neurotransmitter reacts with a very specific receptor site on the postsynaptic cell to cause a reaction.

Neurotransmitters

Neurotransmitters stimulate postsynaptic cells either by exciting or inhibiting them. The reaction that occurs when a neurotransmitter stimulates a receptor site depends on the specific neurotransmitter that it releases and the receptor site it activates. A nerve may produce only one type of neurotransmitter, using building blocks such as tyrosine or choline from the extracellular fluid, often absorbed from dietary sources. The neurotransmitter, packaged into vesicles, moves to the terminal membrane of the axon, and when the nerve is stimulated, the vesicles contract and push the neurotransmitter into the synaptic cleft. The calcium channels in the nerve membrane are open during the action potential, and the presence of calcium causes the contraction. When the cell repolarizes, calcium leaves the cell, and the contraction stops. Once released into the synaptic cleft, the neurotransmitter reacts with very specific receptor sites to cause a reaction.

To return the effector cell to a resting state so that it can be stimulated again, if needed, neurotransmitters must be inactivated. Neurotransmitters may be either reabsorbed by the presynaptic nerve in a process called reuptake (i.e., a recycling effort by the nerve to reuse the materials and save resources) or broken down by enzymes in the area (e.g., monoamine oxidase [MAO] breaks down the neurotransmitter norepinephrine; the enzyme acetylcholinesterase breaks down the neurotransmitter acetylcholine). Several neurotransmitters have been identified. As research continues, other neurotransmitters may be discovered, and the actions of known neurotransmitters will be better understood.

The following are selected neurotransmitters:

- Acetylcholine, which communicates between nerves and muscles, is also important as the preganglionic neurotransmitter throughout the autonomic nervous system and as the postganglionic neurotransmitter in the parasympathetic nervous system.
- Norepinephrine and epinephrine are catecholamines, which are released by nerves in the sympathetic branch of the autonomic nervous system. These neurotransmitters also occur in high levels in particular areas of the brain such as the ***limbic system***.
- Dopamine, which is found in high concentrations in certain areas of the brain, is related to coordination of impulses and responses, both motor and intellectual.
- Gamma-aminobutyric acid (GABA), which is found in the brain, inhibits nerve activity and is important in preventing overexcitability or stimulation such as seizure activity.
- Serotonin, which is also found in the limbic system, is important in arousal and sleep as well as in preventing depression and promoting motivation.

Many of the drugs that affect the nervous system involve altering the activity of the nerve synapse. These drugs have several functions, including blocking the reuptake of neurotransmitters so that they are present in the synapse in greater quantities and cause more stimulation of receptor sites; blocking receptor sites so that the neurotransmitter cannot stimulate the receptor site; blocking the enzymes that break down neurotransmitters to cause an increase in neurotransmitter concentration in the synapse; stimulating specific receptor sites when the neurotransmitter is not available; and causing the presynaptic nerve to release greater amounts of the neurotransmitter.

WWW.WEB LINKS

To explore the virtual nervous system, visit these Internet sites:

http://www.InnerBody.com

http://www.vh.org/Providers/textbooks/BrainAnatomy/BrainAnatomy.html

CENTRAL NERVOUS SYSTEM

The CNS consists of the brain and the spinal cord, the two parts of the body that contain the vast majority of nerves. The bones of the vertebrae protect the spinal cord, and the bones of the skull, which are corrugated much like an egg carton and designed to absorb impact, protect the brain (Figure 17-4). In addition, the meninges, which are membranes that cover the nerves in the brain and spine, furnish further protection.

The blood–brain barrier, a functioning boundary, also plays a defensive role. It keeps toxins, proteins, and other large structures out of the brain and prevents their contact with the sensitive and fragile neurons. The blood–brain barrier represents a ther-

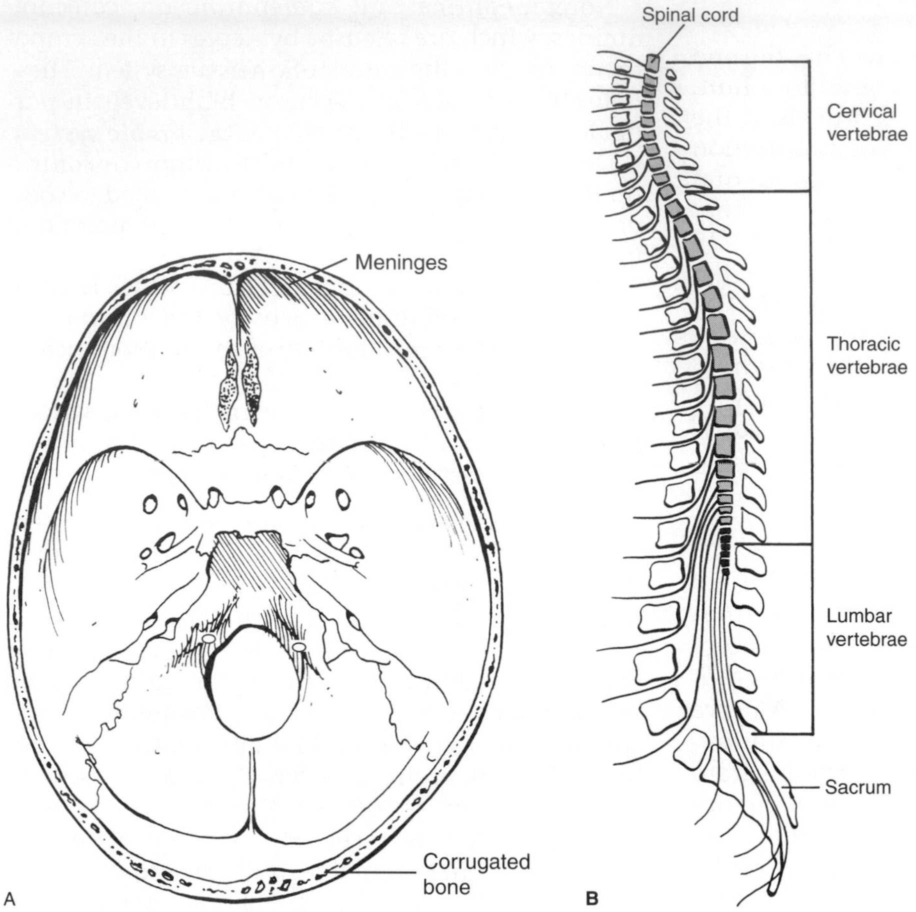

FIGURE 17-4. Bony and membranous protection of (*A*) the brain and (*B*) the spine.

apeutic challenge to drug treatment of brain-related disorders, because a large percentage of drugs are carried bound to plasma proteins and are unable to cross into the brain. When a patient is suffering from a brain infection, antibiotics cannot cross into the brain until the infection is so severe that the blood–brain barrier can no longer function.

The brain has a unique blood supply to protect the neurons from lack of oxygen and glucose. Two arteries, the carotids, branch off the aortic arch and go up into each side of the brain at the front of the head, and two other arteries, the vertebrals, enter the back of the brain to become the basilar arteries. These arteries all deliver blood to a common vessel at the bottom of the brain called the circle of Willis, which distributes the blood to the brain as it is needed (Figure 17-5). The role of the circle of Willis becomes apparent when an individual has an occluded carotid artery. Although the passage of blood through one of the carotid arteries may be negligible, the areas of the brain on that side will still have a full blood supply because of the blood sent to those areas via the circle of Willis.

Anatomy of the Brain

The brain has three major divisions: the ***hindbrain,*** the ***midbrain,*** and the ***forebrain*** (Figure 17-6).

The ***hindbrain,*** which runs from the top of the spinal cord into the midbrain, is the most primitive area of the brain and contains the brainstem, where the pons and medulla oblongata are located. These areas of the brain control basic, vital functions such as the respiratory centers, which control breathing; the cardiovascular centers, which regulate blood pressure; the chemoreceptor trigger zone and emetic zone, which control vomiting; the swallowing center, which coordinates the complex swallowing reflex; and the reticular activating system (RAS), which controls arousal and awareness of stimuli and contains the sleep center. The RAS filters the billions of incoming messages, selecting only the most significant for response. When levels of serotonin become high in the RAS, the system shuts down, and sleep occurs. After the medulla absorbs serotonin from the RAS, when the levels are low enough, consciousness or arousal results.

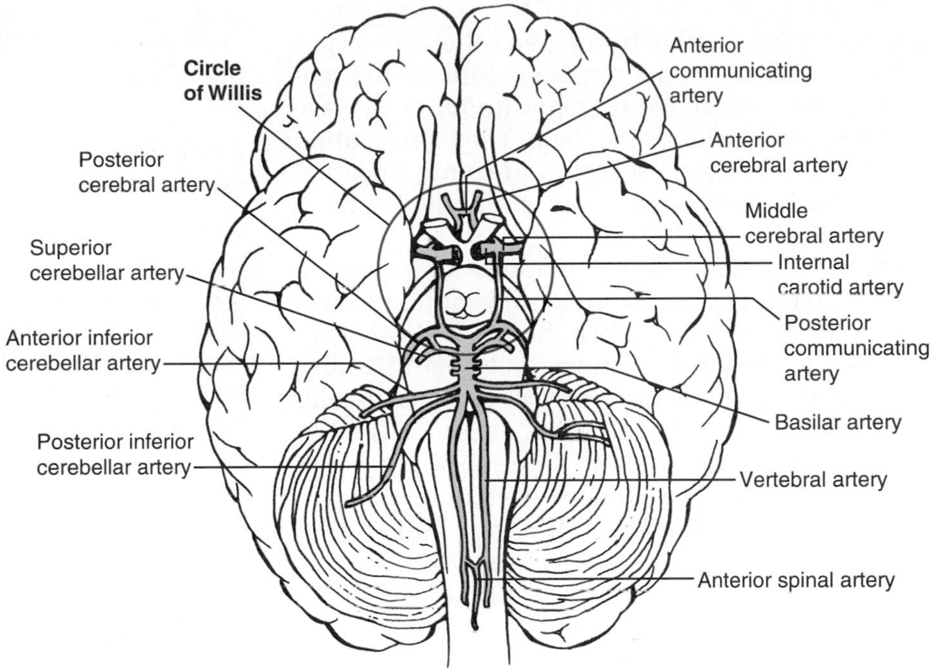

FIGURE 17-5. The protective blood supply of the brain: the carotid, vertebral, and basilar arteries joining to form the circle of Willis. (Bullock, B. L. [2000]. *Focus on pathophysiology.* Philadelphia: Lippincott Williams & Wilkins.)

The cranial nerves, which also emerge from the hindbrain, involve *specific* senses (sight, smell, hearing, balance, taste) and some muscle activity of the head and neck (chewing, eye movement, and so on) (see Figure 17-6). The cerebellum, a part of the brain that looks like a skein of yarn and lies behind the other parts of the hindbrain, coordinates the motor function that regulates posture, balance, and voluntary muscle activity.

The midbrain contains the thalamus, the hypothalamus, and the limbic system (see Figure 17-6). The thalamus sends direct information into the cerebrum to transfer sensations such as cold, heat, pain, touch, and muscle sense. The hypothalamus, which is poorly protected by the blood–brain barrier, acts as a major sensor for activities in the body. Areas of the hypothalamus are responsible for temperature control, water balance, appetite, and fluid balance. In addition, the hypothalamus plays a central role in the endocrine system and the autonomic nervous system.

The limbic system is an area of the brain that contains high levels of three neurotransmitters: epinephrine, norepinephrine, and serotonin. Stimulation of this area, which appears to be responsible for the expression of emotions, may lead to anger, pleasure, motivation, stress, and so on. This part of the brain seems to be largely responsible for the human aspect of brain function. Drug therapy aimed at alleviating emotional disorders such as depression and anxiety often involves attempting to alter the levels of epinephrine, norepinephrine, and serotonin.

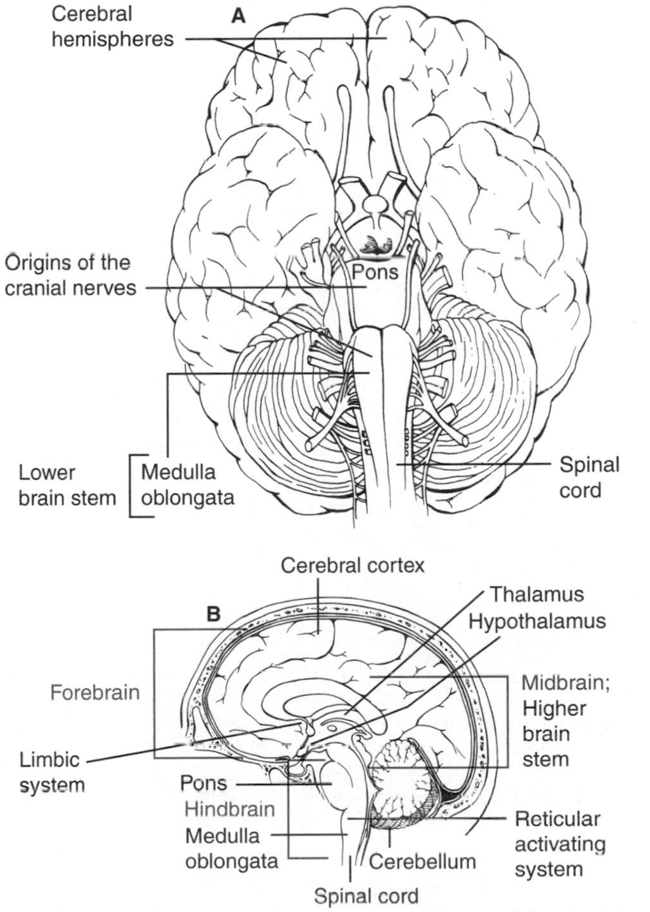

FIGURE 17-6. Anatomy of the brain. (*A*) A view of the underside of the brain. (*B*) The medial or midsagittal view of the brain.

The forebrain is made up of two cerebral hemispheres joined together by an area called the corpus callosum. These two hemispheres contain the sensory neurons, which receive nerve impulses, and the motor neurons, which send them. They also contain areas that coordinate speech and communication and seem to be the area where learning takes place (see Figures 17-6 and 17-7).

Different areas of the brain appear to be responsible for receiving and sending information to specific areas of the body. When the brain is viewed at autopsy, it looks homogenous, but scientists have mapped the general areas that are responsible for sensory response, motor function, and so on (see Figure 17-7). In conjunction with the cerebellum, groups of ganglia or nerve cell bodies called the basal ganglia, located at the bottom of the brain, make up the extrapyramidal motor system. This system coordinates motor activity for unconscious activities such as posture and gait.

Anatomy of the Spinal Cord

The spinal cord is made up of 31 pairs of spinal nerves. Each spinal nerve has two components or roots. These mixed nerve parts include a sensory fiber (called the dorsal root) and a motor fiber (called the ventral root). The spinal sensory fibers bring information into the CNS from the periphery. The motor fibers cause movement or reaction.

Functions of the Central Nervous System

The brain is responsible for coordinating the reactions of individuals to the constantly changing external and internal environment. In all animals, the function of this organ is essentially the same. The human component involving emotions, learning, and conscious response takes the human nervous system beyond a simple reflex system and complicates the responses seen to any stimulus.

SENSORY FUNCTIONS

Millions of sensory impulses are constantly streaming into the CNS from peripheral receptors. Many of these impulses go directly to specific areas of the brain designated to deal with input from particular areas of the body or from the senses. The response that occurs as a result of these stimuli can be altered by efferent neurons that respond to emotions through the limbic system, to learned responses stored in the cerebral cortex, or to autonomic input mediated through the hypothalamus.

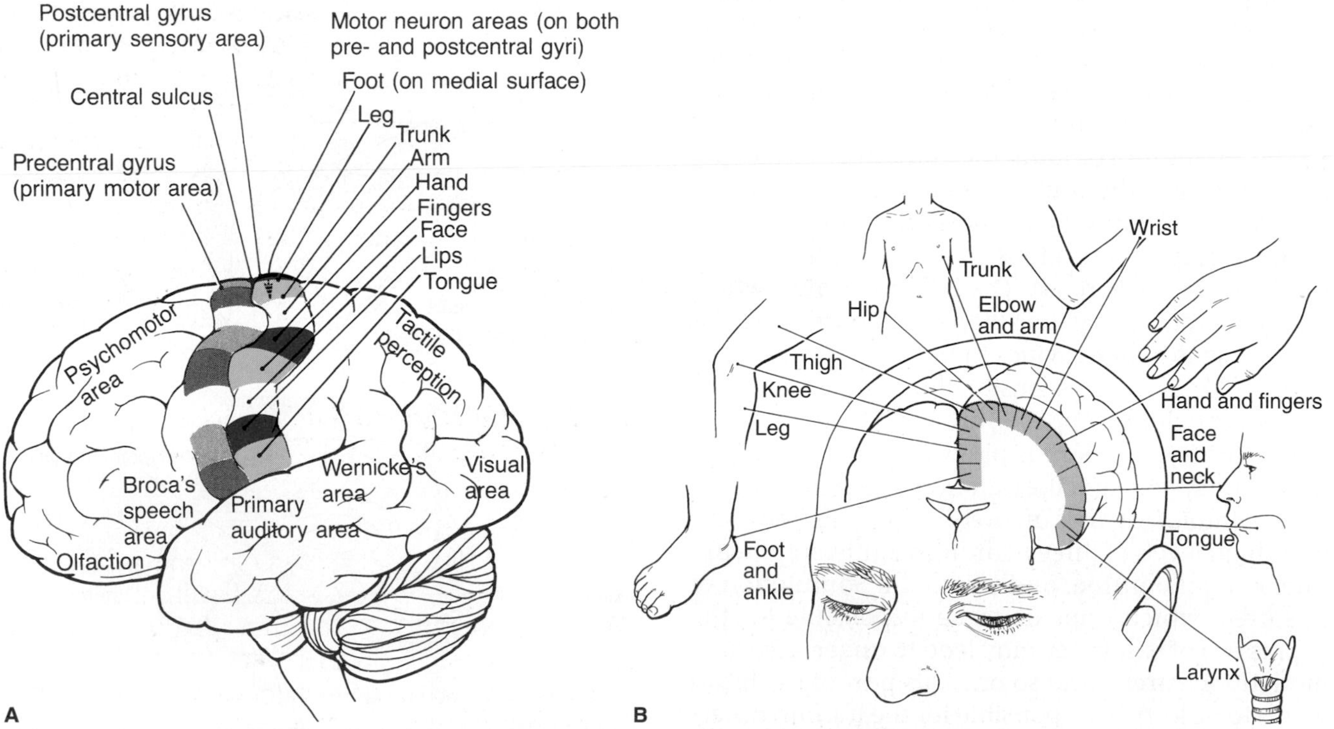

FIGURE 17-7. Functional areas of the brain. (*A*) Topographical organization of functions of control and interpretation in the cerebral cortex. (*B*) Areas of the brain that control specific areas of the body. Size indicates relative distribution of control. (Bullock, B. L. [2000]. *Focus on pathophysiology.* Philadelphia: Lippincott Williams & Wilkins.)

The intricacies of the human brain can change the response to a sensation depending on the situation. People may react differently to the same stimulus. For example, if an individual drops a can on his or her foot, the physiologic response is one of pain and a stimulation of the sympathetic branch of the autonomic nervous system. If the person is alone or in a very comfortable environment (e.g., fixing dinner at home), he or she may scream, swear, or jump around. But if that person is in the company of other people (e.g., a cooking teacher working with a class), he or she may be much more dignified and quiet.

MOTOR FUNCTIONS

The sensory nerves that enter the brain react with related motor nerves to cause a reaction mediated by muscles or glands. The motor impulses that leave the cortex are further regulated or coordinated by the pyramidal system, which coordinates voluntary movement, and the extrapyramidal system, which coordinates unconscious motor activity that regulates control of position and posture. For example, some drugs may interfere with the extrapyramidal system and cause tremors, shuffling gait, and lack of posture and position stability. Motor fibers from the cortex cross to the other side of the spinal cord before emerging to interact with peripheral effectors. In this way, motor stimuli coming from the right side of the brain affect motor activity on the left side of the body. For example, an area of the left cortex may send an impulse down to the spinal cord; this impulse will react with an interneuron, cross to the other side of the spinal cord, and cause a finger on the right hand to twitch.

INTELLECTUAL AND EMOTIONAL FUNCTIONS

The way that the cerebral cortex uses sensory information is not clearly understood, but research has recently demonstrated that the two hemispheres of the brain process information in different ways. The right side of the brain is the more artistic side, concerned with forms and shapes, and the left side is more analytical, concerned with names, numbers, and processes. Why the two hemispheres are different and how they develop differently is not known.

When learning takes place, distinct layers of the cerebral cortex are affected, and an actual membrane change occurs in a neuron to store information in the brain permanently. Learning begins as an electrical circuit called an ***engram,*** a reverberating circuit of action potentials that eventually becomes a long-term, permanent memory in the presence of the proper neurotransmitters and hormones. Scientists do not understand how this happens, but it is known that the nerve requires oxygen, glucose, and sleep to process this engram into a permanent memory. The engram is responsible for short-term memory. When patients have a decreased blood supply to the brain, short-term memory may be lost, and they are not able to remember new things. Unable to remember new things, the brain falls back on long-term, permanent memory for daily functioning. For example, a patient may be introduced to a nurse and have no recollection of the nurse 2 hours later, but may be able to recall the events of several years ago vividly.

Several substances appear to affect learning. Antidiuretic hormone, which is released during reactions to stress, increases learning. In situations in which a person is trying to learn, it may help to feel slightly stressed. Too much stress prevents learning, however. A patient who is a little nervous about upcoming surgery seems to display a better mastery of facts about the surgery and postoperative procedures than either one who is very stressed and scared or one who appears to show no interest and no concerns. Oxytocin also seems to increase actual learning. Because childbirth is the only known time that oxytocin levels increase, the significance of this is not understood. Nurses who work with maternity patients should know that women in labor will very likely remember the smallest details about the whole experience and can use whatever opportunity is made available to do teaching.

In addition, the limbic system appears to play an important role in how a person learns and reacts to stimuli. The emotions associated with a memory as well as with the present have an impact on stimulus response. The placebo effect (a documented effect of the mind on drug therapy; if a person perceives that a drug will be effective, it is much more likely to actually be effective), which uses the actions of the cerebrum and the limbic system, can have a tremendous impact on drug response. Events that are perceived as stressful by some patients may be seen as positive by other patients.

CLINICAL SIGNIFICANCE OF DRUGS THAT ACT ON THE NERVOUS SYSTEM

The features of the human nervous system, including the complexities of the human brain, sometimes make it difficult to predict the exact reaction of a particular patient to a given drug. When a drug is used to affect the nervous system, the occurrence of many systemic effects is always a possibility, because the nervous system affects the entire body. Various chapters in this section address the individual classes of drugs used to treat disorders of the nervous system, including their adverse effects. An understanding of the actions of specific drugs makes it easier to anticipate what therapeutic and adverse effects might occur. In addition, nurses should also consider all of the learned, cultural, and emotional aspects of the patient's situation in an attempt to provide optimal therapeutic benefit and minimal adverse effects.

CHAPTER SUMMARY

- The nervous system, which consists of the central and peripheral nervous systems, is responsible for control of the human body, analysis of stimuli coming into the system, and integration of internal and external responses to stimuli.
- The neuron, the functional unit of the nervous system, consists of a cell body or soma, dendrites that bring information to the nerve, and an axon that takes information away from the nerve.
- Although nerves do not reproduce, they can regenerate injured parts if the soma and axon hillock remain intact.
- Efferent nerves are nerves that take information out of the CNS to effector sites; afferent nerves are sensory nerves that take information into the CNS.
- Nerves transmit information by way of electrical charges called action potentials. An action potential is a sudden change in membrane charge from negative to positive and is caused when stimulation of a nerve opens sodium channels and allows positive sodium ions to flow into the cell.
- The flow of sodium ions into a nerve results in depolarization of the nerve membrane. Immediately, repolarization occurs, and the sodium–potassium pump in the cell membrane pumps out sodium and potassium ions and leaves the inside of the membrane relatively negative to the outside.
- When the transmission of action potentials reaches the axon terminal, it causes the release of chemicals called neurotransmitters, which cross the synaptic cleft to stimulate an effector cell, which can be another nerve, a muscle, or a gland.
- A neurotransmitter must be produced by a nerve (each nerve can produce only one kind); it must be released into the synapse when the nerve is stimulated; it must react with a very specific receptor site to cause a reaction; and it must be immediately broken down or removed from the synapse so that the cell can be ready to be stimulated again.
- Much of the drug therapy in the nervous system involves receptor sites and the release or reuptake and breakdown of neurotransmitters.
- The CNS consists of the brain and spinal cord, which are protected by bone and meninges. To ensure blood flow to the brain if a vessel should become damaged, the brain also has a protective blood supply moderated by the circle of Willis.
- The hindbrain, the most primitive area of the brain, contains the centers that control basic, vital functions. The pons, medulla, and reticular activating system, which regulates arousal and awareness, are all located in the hindbrain. The cerebellum, which helps coordinate motor activity, is found at the back of the hindbrain.
- The midbrain consists of the hypothalamus, thalamus, and the limbic system. The limbic system is responsible for the expression of emotion, and the thalamus and hypothalamus coordinate internal and external responses and direct information into the cerebral cortex.
- The cerebral cortex consists of two hemispheres, which regulate the communication between sensory and motor neurons and are the sites of thinking and learning.
- The mechanisms of learning and processing learned information are not understood. Emotion-related factors influence the human brain, which handles stimuli and responses in complex ways.
- Much remains to be learned about the human brain and how drugs influence it. The actions of many drugs that have known effects on human behavior are not understood.

BIBLIOGRAPHY

Bullock, B. L. (2000). *Focus on pathophysiology*. Philadelphia: Lippincott Williams & Wilkins.

Fox, S. (1991). *Perspectives on human biology*. Dubuque, IA: Wm. C. Brown Publishers.

Ganong, W. (1999). *Review of medical physiology* (19th ed.). Norwalk, CT: Appleton & Lange.

Guyton, A. & Hall, J. (1996). *Textbook of medical physiology*. Philadelphia: W. B. Saunders.

Hardman, J. G., Limbird, L. E., Molinoff, P. B., Ruddon, R. W., & Gilman, A. G. (Eds.). (1996). *Goodman and Gilman's the pharmacological basis of therapeutics* (9th ed.). New York: McGraw Hill.

CHAPTER 18

Anxiolytic and Hypnotic Agents

Benzodiazepines
- alprazolam
- chlordiazepoxide
- clonazepam
- clorazepate
- P diazepam
- estazolam
- flurazepam
- lorazepam
- midazolam
- oxazepam
- quazepam
- temazepam
- triazolam

Barbiturates
- amobarbital
- aprobarbital
- butabarbital
- mephobarbital
- pentobarbital
- P phenobarbital
- secobarbital

Other anxiolytic/hypnotic drugs
- buspirone
- chloral hydrate
- diphenhydramine
- ethchlorvynol
- glutethimide
- paraldehyde
- promethazine
- zolpidem

CHAPTER OUTLINE

KEY TERMS

anxiety
anxiolytic
barbiturate
benzodiazepine
hypnosis
hypnotic
sedation
sedative

INTRODUCTION

The drugs discussed in this chapter are used to alter an individual's responses to the environment. They have been called ***anxiolytics,*** because they can prevent feelings of tension or fear; ***sedatives,*** because they can calm patients and make them unaware of their environment; ***hypnotics,*** because they can cause sleep; and minor tranquilizers, because they can produce a state of tranquility in anxious patients. At one time, one drug would be used at different dosages to yield each of these effects. Further research into how the brain reacts to outside stimuli has resulted in the increased availability of specific agents that produce particular goals and avoid unwanted adverse effects.

STATES AFFECTED BY ANXIOLYTIC/HYPNOTIC DRUGS

Anxiety

Anxiety is a feeling of tension, nervousness, apprehension, or fear that usually involves unpleasant reactions to a stimulus, whether actual or unknown. Anxiety is often accompanied by the signs and symptoms of the sympathetic stress reaction (see Chapter 27), which may include sweating, fast heart rate, rapid breathing, and elevated blood pressure. Mild anxiety, a not uncommon reaction, may serve as a stimulus or motivator in some situations. A person who feels anxious about being alone in a poorly lit parking lot at night may be motivated to take extra safety precautions. When anxiety becomes overwhelming or severe, it can interfere with the activities of daily living and lead to medical problems related to the chronic stimulation of the sympathetic nervous system. A severely anxious person may be afraid to leave the house or to interact with other people. In these cases, treatment is warranted. Anxiolytic drugs are drugs that are used to lyse or break the feeling of anxiety.

Sedation

The loss of awareness and reaction to environmental stimuli is termed ***sedation.*** This condition may be desirable in patients who are restless, nervous, irritable, or overreacting to stimuli. Although sedation is anxiolytic, it may also lead to drowsiness, which frequently occurs with sedation. For example, sedative-induced drowsiness may be a concern with outpatients who need to be alert and responsive in their normal lives. On the other hand, this tiredness may be desirable when treating patients who are about to undergo surgery or other procedures and who are receiving medical support. The choice of an anxiolytic drug depends on the situation in which it will be used, keeping the related adverse effects in mind.

Hypnosis

Extreme sedation results in further central nervous system (CNS) depression and sleep, or ***hypnosis.*** Hypnotics are used to help people fall asleep by causing sedation. Drugs that are effective hypnotics act on the reticular activating system (RAS) and block the brain's response to incoming stimuli. Hypnosis, therefore, is the extreme state of sedation, in which the person no longer senses or reacts to incoming stimuli.

BENZODIAZEPINES

Benzodiazepines, the most frequently used anxiolytic drugs, prevent anxiety without causing much associated sedation. In addition, they are less likely to cause physical dependence than many of the older sedatives/hypnotics that are used to relieve anxiety. Table 18-1 lists the currently available benzodiazepines, including common indications, and specific information about each drug.

THERAPEUTIC ACTIONS AND INDICATIONS

The benzodiazepines act in the limbic system and the RAS to make gamma-aminobutyric acid more effective, causing interference with neuron firing (Figure 18-1). This leads to an anxiolytic effect at doses lower than those required to induce sedation and hypnosis. The exact mechanism of action is not clearly understood.

The benzodiazepines are indicated for the treatment of the following conditions: anxiety disorders, alcohol withdrawal, hyperexcitability and agitation, and preoperative relief of anxiety and tension to aid in balanced anesthesia.

CONTRAINDICATIONS/CAUTIONS

Contraindications to benzodiazepines include the presence of allergy to any benzodiazepine. Other contraindications include psychosis, which could be exacerbated by sedation, and acute narrow-angle glaucoma, shock, coma, or acute alcoholic intoxication, which could all be exacerbated by the depressant effects of these drugs.

In addition, these sedatives/hypnotics are contraindicated in pregnancy, because a predictable syndrome of cleft lip or palate, inguinal hernia, cardiac

TABLE 18-1

BENZODIAZEPINES

Drug	Brand Name	Route(s) of Administration	Onset of Action*	Duration of Action*	Usual Indication(s)	Special Notes
alprazolam	*Xanax*	oral	30 min	4–6 hr	Anxiety, panic attacks	Taper after long-term therapy
chlordiazepoxide	*Librium*	oral, IV, IM	10–15 min	2–3 days	Anxiety, alcohol withdrawal, preoperative anxiolytic	Monitor injection sites
clonazepam	*Klonopin*	oral	varies	weeks	Seizures	(See Chapter 21)
clorazepate	*Tranxene*	oral	rapid	days	Anxiety, alcohol withdrawal, adjunctive therapy for partial seizures	Taper dosage; (see Chapter 21)
P diazepam	*Valium*	oral, rectal, IM, IV	5–60 min	3 hr	Anxiety, alcohol withdrawal, muscle relaxant, antiepileptic, antitetanus, preoperative anxiolytic	Monitor injection sites; drug of choice if route change is anticipated; taper after long-term therapy
estazolam	*ProSom*	oral	45–60 min	2 hr	Hypnotic; treatment of insomnia	Monitor liver and renal function as well as CBC if used long term
flurazepam	*Dalmane*	oral	varies	30–60 min	Hypnotic; treatment of insomnia	Monitor liver and renal function as well as CBC if used long term
lorazepam	*Ativan*	oral, IM, IV	1–30 min	12–24 hr	Anxiety, preanesthetic anxiolytic	Monitor injection sites; reduce dosage of narcotics given with this drug
midazolam	*Versed*	IV	15 min	30–60 min	Anesthesia	Causes respiratory depression, cough, hiccups; monitor respiratory function
oxazepam	*Serax*	oral	slow	2–4 hr	Anxiety, alcohol withdrawal	Preferred for use in elderly patients
quazepam	*Doral*	oral	varies	4–6 hr	Hypnotic; treatment of insomnia	Monitor liver and renal function, CBC if used long term; taper after long-term therapy
temazepam	*Restoril*	oral	varies	4–6 hr	Hypnotic; treatment of insomnia	Taper after long-term therapy
triazolam	*Halcion*	oral	varies	2–4 hr	Hypnotic; treatment of insomnia	Monitor liver and renal function, CBC if used long term; taper after long-term therapy

*Onset of action and duration are important in selecting the correct drug for a particular use.

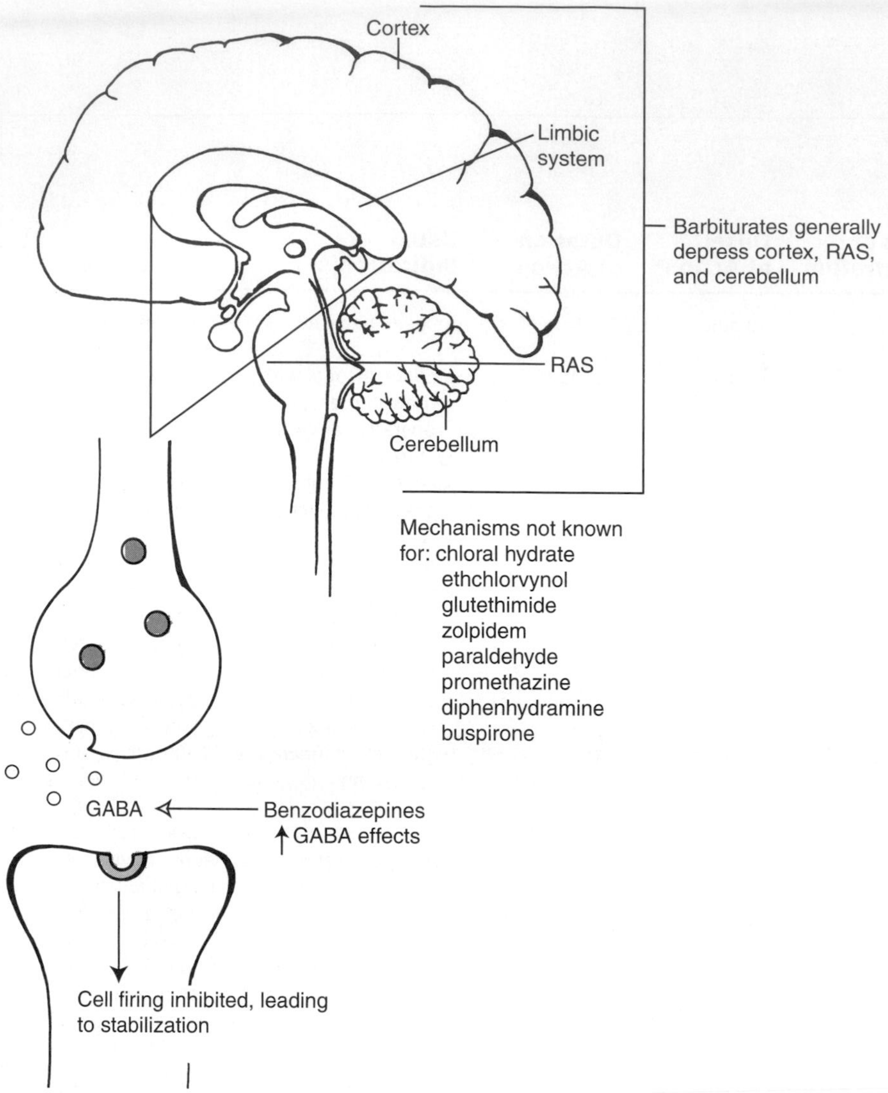

FIGURE 18-1. Sites of action of the benzodiazepines and barbiturates.

defects, microcephaly, or pyloric stenosis occurs when these drugs are taken in the first trimester. Neonatal withdrawal syndrome may also result. Lactation is also a contraindication, because of potential adverse effects on the neonate (e.g., sedation).

Caution should be used with the elderly or debilitated, because of the possibility of unpredictable reactions, and in cases of renal or hepatic dysfunction, which may alter the metabolism and excretion of these drugs, resulting in direct toxicity. Dosage adjustments are usually needed in such patients.

ADVERSE EFFECTS

The adverse effects of benzodiazepines are associated with the impact of these drugs on the central and peripheral nervous systems. Nervous system effects include sedation, drowsiness, depression, lethargy, blurred vision, headaches, apathy, lightheadedness, and confusion. In addition, mild paradoxical excitatory reactions may occur during the first 2 weeks of therapy.

Several other kinds of adverse effects may occur. GI conditions such as dry mouth, constipation, nausea, vomiting, and elevated liver enzymes may result. Hiccups are often associated with the use of midazolam. Cardiovascular problems may include hypotension, hypertension, arrhythmias, palpitations, and respiratory difficulties. Hematologic conditions such as blood dyscrasias and anemia are possible. Genitourinary (GU) effects include urinary retention and hesitancy, loss of libido, and changes in sexual functioning. Because phlebitis, local reactions, and thrombosis may occur at local injection sites, such sites should be monitored.

Abrupt cessation of these drugs may lead to a withdrawal syndrome characterized by nausea, headache, vertigo, malaise, and nightmares.

CASE STUDY
Benzodiazepines

PATIENT SCENARIO

P. P., a 43-year-old mother of three teenage sons, comes to the outpatient department for a routine physical examination. Results are unremarkable except for blood pressure of 145/90 mm Hg, a pulse of 98 beats/min, and apparent tension—she is jittery, avoids eye contact, and sometimes has teary eyes. She says that she is having some difficulty dealing with "life in general."

P. P. then describes her problems. Her sons present many stresses, and her husband is busy with job-related concerns, has little time to deal with home problems, and is demanding when at home. In addition, she is entering early menopause and having trouble coping with the idea of menopause as well as with some of the symptoms. Overall, she feels that she has no outlet for her anger, tension, or stress.

A health care provider, who assures P. P. that this problem is common in women of her age, prescribes the benzodiazepine diazepam (*Valium*) to help her deal with her anxiety.

CRITICAL THINKING QUESTIONS

What sort of crisis intervention would be most appropriate? What nursing interventions should be done at this point? What nondrug interventions might be helpful? What other support systems could be used to help P. P. deal with all that is going on in her life? Think about the overwhelming problems that P. P. has to deal with on a day-to-day basis and how the anxiolytic effects of diazepam might change her approach to these problems. Could they actually get worse? Develop a care plan for the long-term care of P. P.

DISCUSSION

Anxiolytics are useful for controlling the unpleasant signs and symptoms of anxiety. The benzodiazepine prescribed for P. P. may provide some immediate relief, enable her to survive the "crisis" period, and plan changes in her "life in general." However, the associated drowsiness and sedation may make coping with the problems in her life even more difficult. She should know the adverse effects of diazepam, the warning signs to look for, and the health problems to report.

Follow-up evaluation should be scheduled. Further meetings with the same health care provider are important for the long-term solution to P. P.'s anxiety. Her need for the drug therapy should be reevaluated once she is able to discover other support systems and develop other ways of coping. Although anxiolytics may be beneficial initially, they do not solve the problems that are causing the anxiety in the first place. In this case, the causes for the anxiety are specific, and the anxiolytic should only be considered an aid in getting over a crisis period.

Unlike P. P., many patients in severe crisis do not consciously identify the many causes of stress, or stressors. However, P. P. has identified a list of factors that make her life stressful. This facilitates the development of strategies for helping her to cope with her stressors. She may use the following support systems to find ways of coping:

- Referral to a counselor, where the entire family is involved in identification of problems and ways of dealing with them.
- Community supports—clergy, support groups.
- Support groups for women in various stages of life (e.g., entering menopause, mothers of children who are becoming teenagers). Just having the opportunity to discuss problems and explore ways of dealing with them helps many people.
- Hormone replacement therapy to ease her way through menopause. Additional benefits include decreased risk of both heart disease and osteoporosis. Controlling some of the irritating signs and symptoms of menopause may alleviate some of the stress.

CLINICALLY IMPORTANT DRUG–DRUG INTERACTIONS

The risk of CNS depression increases if benzodiazepines are taken with alcohol and other CNS depressants, so such combinations should be avoided. In addition, the therapeutic effects of benzodiazepines increase if they are taken with cimetidine, oral contraceptives, or disulfiram. If any of these drugs are used with benzodiazepines, patients should be monitored and the appropriate dosage adjustments made. Finally, the impact of benzodiazepines may be decreased if given with theophyllines or ranitidine. If either of these drugs is used, dosage adjustment may be necessary.

DATA LINK

Data link to the benzodiazepines, listed in Table 18-1, in your nursing drug guide.

NURSING CONSIDERATIONS
for patients receiving benzodiazepines

Assessment

HISTORY. Screen for the following: any known allergies to benzodiazepines; impaired liver or kidney function, which could alter the metabolism and excretion of a particular drug; any condition that might be exacerbated by the depressant effects of the drugs such as glaucoma, coma, psychoses, shock, and acute alcohol intoxication; and pregnancy and lactation.

PHYSICAL ASSESSMENT. Include screening for baseline status before beginning therapy to check for occurrence of any potential adverse effects. Assess for the following: temperature and weight; skin color and lesions; affect, orientation, reflexes, and vision; pulse, blood pressure, and perfusion; respiratory rate, adventitious sounds, and presence of chronic pulmonary disease; and bowel sounds upon abdominal examination. Laboratory tests should include renal and liver function tests and a CBC.

Nursing Diagnoses

The patient receiving a benzodiazepine may have the following nursing diagnoses related to drug therapy:

- Alteration in thought processes and sensory–perceptual alteration related to CNS effects
- Potential for injury related to CNS effects
- Disturbance in sleep pattern related to CNS effects
- Knowledge deficit regarding drug therapy

Implementation

- Do not administer intra-arterially *because serious arteriospasm and gangrene could occur.* Monitor injection sites carefully for local reactions *to institute treatment as soon as possible.*
- Do not mix IV drugs in solution with any other drugs *to avoid potential drug–drug interactions.*
- Give parenteral forms only if oral forms are not feasible or available, and switch to oral forms as soon as possible, *which are safer and less likely to cause adverse effects.*
- Give IV drugs slowly *because these agents, particularly midazolam, have been associated with hypotension, bradycardia, and cardiac arrest.*
- Arrange to reduce the dosage of narcotic analgesics in patients receiving a benzodiazepine *to decrease potentiated effects and sedation.*
- Maintain patients who receive parenteral benzodiazepines in bed for a period of at least 3 hours. Do not permit ambulatory patients to operate a motor vehicle following an injection *to ensure patient safety.*
- Monitor hepatic and renal function as well as CBC during long-term therapy *to detect dysfunction and to arrange to taper and discontinue drug if dysfunction occurs.*
- Taper dosage gradually after long-term therapy, especially in epileptic patients. *Acute withdrawal could precipitate seizures in these patients. Acute withdrawal may also cause withdrawal syndrome.*
- Provide comfort measures *to help patients tolerate drug effects* such as having them void before dosing, instituting a bowel program as needed, giving food with the drug if gastrointestinal (GI) upset is severe, environmental control (lighting, temperature, stimulation), safety precautions (use of side rails, assistance with ambulation), orientation.
- Provide thorough patient teaching, including drug name, prescribed dosage, measures for avoidance of adverse effects, and warning signs that may indicate possible problems. Instruct patients about the need for periodic monitoring and evaluation *to enhance patient knowledge about drug therapy and to promote compliance* (see Patient Teaching Checklist: Benzodiazepines).
- Offer support and encouragement *to help patient cope with diagnosis and drug regimen.*
- If necessary, use flumazenil (Box 18-1), the benzodiazepine antidote *for treatment of overdose.*

Evaluation

- Monitor patient response to the drug (alleviation of signs and symptoms of anxiety, sleep, sedation).
- Monitor for adverse effects (sedation, hypotension, cardiac arrhythmias, hepatic or renal dysfunction, blood dyscrasias).
- Evaluate effectiveness of teaching plan (patient can give the drug name, dosage, possible adverse effects to watch for, specific measures to help avoid adverse effects, and the importance of continued follow-up).
- Monitor effectiveness of comfort measures and compliance with regimen (see Nursing Care Guide: Benzodiazepines).

BARBITURATES

The ***barbiturates*** were once the sedative/hypnotic drugs of choice. Not only is the likelihood of sedation and other adverse effects greater with these drugs than with newer sedative/hypnotic drugs, but the risk of addiction and dependence is also greater. For these reasons, newer anxiolytic drugs have replaced the barbiturates in most instances. Table 18-2 lists the currently available barbiturates, including common indications, and specific information about each drug.

THERAPEUTIC ACTIONS AND INDICATIONS

The barbiturates are general CNS depressants that inhibit neuronal impulse conduction in the ascending RAS, depress the cerebral cortex, alter cerebellar function, and depress motor output (see Figure 18–1). Thus, they can cause sedation, hypnosis, and anesthesia, and, in extreme cases, coma. In general, barbiturates are indicated for the relief of the signs and symptoms of anxiety, sedation, insomnia, preanesthesia, and seizures. Parenteral forms, which reach

PATIENT TEACHING CHECKLIST

Benzodiazepines

Create customized patient teaching materials for a specific benzodiazepine from your CD-ROM. Your patient teaching should stress the following points for drugs within this class:

Benzodiazepines are used to relieve tension or nervousness. Although the exact way that these drugs work is not completely understood, this group of drugs relaxes muscle spasms, relieves insomnia, and may help manage convulsive disorders.

Common effects of these drugs include:

- Dizziness, drowsiness, nervousness, and insomnia—Avoid driving or performing hazardous or delicate tasks that require concentration if these effects occur.
- Nausea, vomiting, and weight loss—Small, frequent meals may help to relieve the nausea. Monitor your weight loss and if it becomes severe, consult your health care provider. Do not take this drug with antacids.
- Constipation or diarrhea—These reactions also often pass with time. If they do not, consult with your health care provider for appropriate therapy.
- Vision changes, slurred speech, and unsteadiness—These effects may pass with time. Take extra care in your activities for the first few days. If these reactions do not go away after 3 to 4 days, consult your health care provider.

Report any of the following conditions to your health care provider: rash, fever, sore throat, insomnia, depression, clumsiness, and nervousness.

If you are discontinuing this drug, tell your health care provider about the following conditions: trembling, muscle cramps, sweating, irritability, confusion, and seizures.

Tell any doctor, nurse, or other health care provider that you are taking this drug.

Keep this drug and all medications out of the reach of children.

Avoid the use of over-the-counter (OTC) medications while you are taking this drug. If you feel that you need one of these OTC preparations, consult with your health care provider about the best choice. Many OTC drugs may interfere with your benzodiazepine.

Avoid alcohol while you are taking this drug. The alcohol benzodiazepine combination can cause serious problems.

If you have been taking this drug for a prolonged period of time, do not stop taking it suddenly. Your body will need time to adjust to the loss of the drug, and the dosage will need to be reduced gradually to prevent serious problems from developing.

This Teaching Checklist reflects general patient teaching guidelines. It is not meant to be a substitute for drug-specific teaching information, which is available in nursing drug guides.

peak levels faster and have a faster onset of action, may be used for treatment of acute manic reactions and many forms of seizures (see Chapter 21).

CONTRAINDICATIONS/CAUTIONS

Contraindications to barbiturates are the presence of allergy to any barbiturate and a previous history of addiction to sedative/hypnotic drugs, because the barbiturates are more addicting than many other anxiolytics. Other contraindications are latent or manifest porphyria, which may be exacerbated; marked hepatic impairment or nephritis, which may alter the metabolism and excretion of these drugs; and respiratory distress or severe respiratory dysfunction, which could be exacerbated by the CNS depression caused by these drugs. Pregnancy is a contraindication because of potential adverse effects on the fetus.

Caution should be used with barbiturates in patients with acute or chronic pain because barbiturates may cause paradoxical excitement, thus masking other symptoms; with seizure disorders, because abrupt withdrawal of a barbiturate can precipitate status epilepticus; and with chronic hepatic, cardiac, or respiratory diseases, which could be exacerbated by the depressive effects of these drugs. Care should

BOX 18-1

A BENZODIAZEPINE ANTIDOTE

Flumazenil (*Romazicon*), a benzodiazepine antidote, acts by inhibiting the effects of the benzodiazepines at GABA receptors. It is used for three purposes: (1) to treat benzodiazepine overdose, (2) to reverse the sedation caused by benzodiazepines that are used as adjuncts for general anesthesia, and (3) to reverse sedation produced for diagnostic tests or other medical procedures.

Flumazenil, which is available for IV use only, is injected into the tubing of a running IV. The drug has a rapid onset of action that peaks 5 to 10 minutes after administration. Because this drug has a half-life of about 1 hour, it may be necessary to repeat injections of flumazenil in cases in which a long-acting benzodiazepine was used.

Patients who receive flumazenil should be monitored continually, and life-support equipment should be readily available. If a particular patient has been taking a benzodiazepine for a long period of time, administration of flumazenil may precipitate a rapid withdrawal syndrome that necessitates supportive measures. Headache, dizziness, vertigo, nausea, and vomiting may be associated with flumazenil.

be taken with lactating women because of the potential for adverse effects on the infant.

ADVERSE EFFECTS

As previously stated, the adverse effects caused by barbiturates are more severe than those associated with other, newer sedatives/hypnotics. Thus, the barbiturates are no longer considered the mainstay for the treatment of anxiety. In addition, the development of physical tolerance and psychological dependence is more likely with the barbiturates than with other anxiolytics.

The most common adverse effects are related to general CNS depression. CNS effects may include drowsiness, somnolence, lethargy, ataxia, vertigo, a feeling of a "hangover," thinking abnormalities, paradoxical excitement, anxiety, and hallucinations. GI signs and symptoms such as nausea, vomiting, constipation, diarrhea, and epigastric pain may occur. Associated cardiovascular effects may include bradycardia, hypotension (particularly with IV administration), and syncope. Serious hypoventilation may occur, and respiratory depression and laryngospasm may also result, particularly with IV administration. Hypersensitivity reactions, including rash, serum sickness, and sometimes fatal Stevens-Johnson syndrome may also occur.

CLINICALLY IMPORTANT DRUG–DRUG INTERACTIONS

Increased CNS depression results if these agents are taken with other CNS depressants, including alcohol, antihistamines, and other tranquilizers. If other CNS depressants are used, dosage adjustments are necessary. There is often an altered response to phenytoin if combined with barbiturates. Evaluate the patient frequently if this combination cannot be avoided.

If barbiturates are combined with monoamine oxidase (MAO) inhibitors, increased serum levels and effects occur. If the older sedatives/hypnotics are combined with MAO inhibitors, patients should be monitored closely and necessary dosage adjustments made. In addition, because of an enzyme induction effect of the barbiturates in the liver, the following drugs may not be as effective as desired: oral anticoagulants, digoxin, tricyclic antidepressants (TCAs), corticosteroids, oral contraceptives, estrogens, acetaminophen, metronidazole, phenmetrazine, carbamazepine, beta blockers, griseofulvin, phenylbutazones, theophyllines, quinidine, and doxycycline. If these agents are given in combination with barbiturates, patients should be monitored closely; frequent dosage adjustments may be necessary to achieve the desired therapeutic effect.

DATA LINK

Data link to the barbiturates, listed in Table 18-2, in your nursing drug guide.

NURSING CONSIDERATIONS
for patients receiving barbiturates

Assessment

HISTORY. Screen for the following: any known allergies to barbiturates or a history of addiction to sedative/hypnotic drugs; impaired hepatic or renal function that could alter the metabolism and excretion of the drug; cardiac dysfunction or respiratory dysfunction; seizure disorders; acute or chronic pain disorders; and pregnancy or lactation.

PHYSICAL ASSESSMENT. Include screening for baseline status before beginning therapy and the occurrence of any potential adverse effects. Assess the following: temperature and weight; blood pressure and pulse, including perfusion; skin color and lesions; affect, orientation, and reflexes; respiratory rate and adventitious sounds; and upon abdominal examination, bowel sounds.

Nursing Diagnoses

The patient receiving a barbiturate may have the following nursing diagnoses related to drug therapy:

- Alteration in thought processes and sensory–perceptual alteration related to CNS effects

NURSING CARE GUIDE
Benzodiazepines

Assessment	Nursing Diagnoses	Implementation	Evaluation
HISTORY Allergies to any of these drugs; renal or hepatic dysfunction; pregnancy, lactation; glaucoma; coma; shock; acute alcohol intoxication	Alteration in thought processes and sensory perceptual alteration related to CNS effects Potential for injury related to CNS effects Disturbance in sleep patterns related to CNS effects Knowledge deficit regarding drug therapy	Do not administer intra-arterially; monitor injection sites. Provide comfort and safety measures: small meals; in bed for 3 hr after parenteral use; side rails; drug with food if GI upset occurs; bowel program as needed; taper dosage after long-term use; reduce dosage if given with narcotics; lower dose with renal or hepatic impairment. Give IV drugs slowly. Provide support and reassurance to deal with drug effects. Provide patient teaching regarding drug, dosage, adverse effects, what to report, safety precautions.	Evaluate drug effects: Relief of signs and symptoms of anxiety, sedation, sleep. Monitor for adverse effects: sedation, dizziness, insomnia, blood dyscrasias; GI upset; hepatic or renal dysfunction; cardiovascular effects. Monitor for drug–drug interactions as indicated for each drug. Evaluate effectiveness of patient teaching program. Evaluate effectiveness of comfort and safety measures.
PHYSICAL EXAMINATION Cardiovascular: blood pressure, pulse, perfusion CNS: orientation, affect, reflexes, vision Skin: color, lesions, texture Respiratory: respiration, adventitious sounds GI: abdominal examination, bowel sounds Laboratory tests: liver and renal function tests, CBC			

- Potential for injury related to CNS effects
- Impaired gas exchange related to respiratory depression
- Knowledge deficit regarding drug therapy

Implementation

- Do not administer these drugs intra-arterially *because serious arteriospasm and gangrene could occur. Monitor injection sites carefully for local reactions.*
- Do not mix IV drugs in solution with any other drugs *to avoid potential drug–drug interactions.*
- Give parenteral forms only if oral forms are not feasible or available, and switch to oral forms as soon as possible *to avoid serious reactions or adverse effects.*
- Give IV medications slowly *because rapid administration may cause cardiac problems.*
- Provide standby life-support facilities *in case of severe respiratory depression or hypersensitivity reactions.*
- Taper dosage gradually after long-term therapy, especially in epileptic patients. *Acute withdrawal may precipitate seizures or cause withdrawal syndrome in these patients.*
- Provide comfort measures *to help patients tolerate drug effects,* including small, frequent meals; access to

TABLE 18-2

BARBITURATES USED AS ANXIOLYTICS/HYPNOTICS

Drug Name	Brand Name	Route(s) of Administration	Onset of Action*	Duration of Action*	Usual Indication(s)	Special Notes
amobarbital	*Amytal Sodium*	oral, IM, IV	15–60 min	3–8 hr	Sedative/hypnotic; convulsions, manic reactions	Monitor carefully if used IV
aprobarbital	*Alurate*	oral	45–60 min	6–8 hr	Short-term sedation, sleep induction	Taper gradually, may be habit forming
butabarbital	*Butisol*	oral	45–60 min	6–8 hr	Short-term sedative/hypnotic	Taper gradually after long-term use
mephobarbital	*Mebaral*	oral	30–60 min	10–16 hr	Anxiolytic; anti-epileptic	Taper gradually after long-term use
pentobarbital	*Nembutal*	oral, IM, IV	10–15 min	2–4 hr	Sedative/hypnotic, preanesthetic	Taper gradually after long-term use; give IV slowly; monitor injection sites
P phenobarbital	*Luminal*	oral, IM, IV	10–60 min	4–16 hr	Sedative/hypnotic, control of seizures; preanesthetic	Taper gradually after long-term use; give IV slowly; monitor injection sites
secobarbital	*Seconal*	rectal, IM, IV	rapid	1–4 hr	Preanesthetic sedation, convulsive seizures of tetanus	Taper gradually after long-term use; give IV slowly; monitor injection sites

*Onset of action and duration are important in selecting the correct drug for a particular use.

bathroom facilities; bowel program as needed; food with drug if GI upset is severe; and environmental control, safety precautions, orientation, and appropriate skin care as needed.

- Provide thorough patient teaching, including drug name, prescribed dosage, measures for avoidance of adverse effects, and warning signs that may indicate possible problems. Instruct patients about the need for periodic monitoring and evaluation *to enhance patient knowledge about drug therapy and to promote compliance.*
- Offer support and encouragement *to help patient cope* with diagnosis and drug regimen.

CULTURAL CONSIDERATIONS

Effects of Delayed Metabolism of Benzodiazepines

Special care should be taken when anxiolytic/hypnotic drugs are given to African Americans. About 15% to 20% of African Americans are genetically predisposed to delayed metabolism of benzodiazepines. As a result, they may develop high serum levels of these drugs, with increases in sedation and incidence of adverse effects. If an anxiolytic/hypnotic agent is the drug of choice for an African-American individual, the smallest possible dose should be used, and the patient should be monitored very closely during the first week of treatment. Dosage adjustments are necessary to achieve the most effective dose with the fewest adverse effects.

Evaluation

- Monitor patient response to the drug (alleviation of signs and symptoms of anxiety, sleep, sedation, reduction in seizure activity).
- Monitor for adverse effects (sedation, hypotension, cardiac arrhythmias, hepatic or renal dysfunction, skin reactions, dependence).
- Evaluate effectiveness of teaching plan (patient can give the drug name, dosage, possible adverse effects to watch for, specific measures to help avoid adverse effects, and the importance of continued follow-up).
- Monitor effectiveness of comfort measures and compliance with regimen.

WWW.WEB LINKS

Health care providers and patients may want to consult the following Internet sources:

Information on benzodiazepines:
http://www.noah.cuny.edu/illness/mentalhealth/cornell/medications/benzodiaz.html

Information on anxiety and anxiety-related disorders:
http://anxiety.cmhc.com

Information on research, treatment, and support groups related to anxiety and anxiety-related disorders:
http://www.adaa.org

Information on education programs related to anxiety and anxiety-related disorder:
http://www.nimh.nih.gov

Patient-oriented and professional information on issues related to mental health:
http://mhsource.com

OTHER ANXIOLYTIC/ HYPNOTIC DRUGS

There are other drugs that are used to treat anxiety or produce hypnosis that do not fall into either the benzodiazepine or the barbiturate group. See Table 18-3 for a summary of the other anxiolytic/hypnotic drugs. Such medications include the following:

- Paraldehyde (*Paral*), a very old drug, is still used orally and rectally to sedate patients with delirium tremens or psychiatric conditions characterized by extreme excitement.
- Chloral hydrate (*Aquachlora*) is frequently used to produce nocturnal sedation or preoperative sedation. Its mechanism of action is unknown.
- Ethchlorvynol (*Placidyl*), glutethimide (generic) and zolpidem (*Ambien*), which all cause sedation, are used for the short-term treatment of insomnia.
- Antihistamines (promethazine [*Phenergan*], diphenhydramine [*Benadryl*]) can be very sedating in some people and are used as preoperative medications and postoperatively to decrease the need for narcotics.
- Buspirone (*BuSpar*), a new antianxiety agent, has no sedative, anticonvulsant, or muscle-relaxant properties, and its mechanism of action is unknown. However, it reduces the signs and symptoms of anxiety without many of the CNS effects and severe adverse effects associated with other anxiolytic drugs.

TABLE 18-3

OTHER ANXIOLYTIC/HYPNOTIC DRUGS

Drug Name	Brand Name	Route(s) of Administration	Usual Indication(s)	Special Notes
buspirone	*BuSpar*	oral	Anxiety disorders; unlabeled use; signs and symptoms of premenstrual syndrome	May cause dry mouth, headache
chloral hydrate	*Aquachloral*	oral, rectal	Nocturnal sedation, preoperative sedation	Withdraw gradually over 2 weeks in patients maintained for weeks or months
diphenhydramine	*Benadryl*	oral, IM, IV	Sleep aid, motion sickness, allergic rhinitis	Antihistamine, drying effects common
ethchlorvynol	*Placidyl*	oral	Short-term treatment of insomnia (up to 1 week)	Dispense least amount possible to depressed and/or suicidal patients; withdraw gradually if used for prolonged period
glutethimide	Generic	oral	Short-term treatment of insomnia (up to 1 week)	Dispense least amount possible to depressed and/or suicidal patients; withdraw gradually if used for prolonged period
paraldehyde	*Paral*	oral, rectal	Sedation in acute psychiatric excitement and acute alcoholic withdrawal	Dilute before use; use food to improve taste; avoid contact with plastic; keep away from heat or; flame; discard any unused portion
promethazine	*Phenergan*	oral, IM, IV	Decrease in need for post-operative pain relief, pre-operative sedation	Antihistamine; monitor injection sites carefully
zolpidem	*Ambien*	oral	Short-term treatment of insomnia	Dispense least amount possible to depressed and/or suicidal patients; withdraw gradually if used for prolonged period

DATA LINK

Data link to the other anxiolytic/hypnotic drugs, listed in Table 18-3, in your nursing drug guide.

CHAPTER SUMMARY

- Anxiety is a feeling of tension, nervousness, apprehension, or fear. It is usually an unpleasant reaction to an actual or an unknown stimulus. In extreme cases, anxiety may produce physiologic manifestations and may interfere with life.
- Anxiolytics, or minor tranquilizers, are drugs used to treat anxiety by depressing the CNS. When given at higher doses, these drugs may be sedatives or hypnotics.
- Sedatives block the awareness of and reaction to environmental stimuli, resulting in associated CNS depression that may cause drowsiness, lethargy, and other effects. This action can be beneficial when a patient is very excited or afraid.
- Hypnotics further depress the CNS, particularly the RAS, to cause an inhibition of neuronal arousal and sleep induction.
- Benzodiazepines are a group of drugs used as anxiolytics. They react with GABA inhibitory sites to depress the CNS. They can cause drowsiness, lethargy, and other CNS effects.
- Barbiturates are an older class of drugs used as anxiolytics, sedatives, and hypnotics. Because they are associated with potentially serious adverse effects and interact with many other drugs, they are less desirable than the benzodiazepines or other anxiolytics.
- Buspirone, a newer anxiolytic drug, does not cause sedation or muscle relaxation. Because of the absence of CNS effects, it is much preferred in certain circumstances, for instance, when a person must drive, go to work, or maintain alertness.

BIBLIOGRAPHY

Bailey, K. (1998). *Psychotropic drug facts.* Philadelphia: Lippincott-Raven.

Bullock, B. L. (2000). *Focus on pathophysiology.* Philadelphia: Lippincott Williams & Wilkins.

Hardman, J. G., Limbird, L. E., Molinoff, P. B., Ruddon, R. W., & Gilman, A. G. (Eds.). (1996). *Goodman and Gilman's the pharmacological basis of therapeutics* (9th ed.). New York: McGraw Hill.

Karch, A. M. (2000). *2000 Lippincott's nursing drug guide.* Philadelphia: Lippincott Williams & Wilkins.

Malseed, R. (1995). *Textbook of pharmacology and nursing care.* Philadelphia: Lippincott-Raven.

McEvoy, B. R. (Ed.). (1999). *Facts and comparisons 1999.* St. Louis: Facts and Comparisons.

Professional's guide to patient drug facts. (1999). St. Louis: Facts and Comparisons.

CHAPTER 19

Antidepressant Agents

Tricyclic antidepressants
- amitriptyline
- amoxapine
- clomipramine
- desipramine
- doxepin
- P imipramine
- maprotiline
- nortriptyline
- protriptyline
- trimipramine

MAO inhibitors
- isocarboxazid
- P phenelzine
- tranylcypromine

Selective serotonin reuptake inhibitors
- citalopram
- P fluoxetine
- fluvoxamine
- paroxetine
- sertraline

Other antidepressants
- P bupropion
- mirtazapine
- nefazodone
- trazodone
- venlafaxine

CHAPTER OUTLINE

KEY TERMS

affect
biogenic amine
depression
monoamine oxidase (MAO) inhibitor
selective serotonin reuptake inhibitor (SSRI)
tricyclic antidepressant (TCA)
tyramine

INTRODUCTION

When you ask people how they feel, they may say "pretty good" or "not so great." People's responses are usually appropriate to what is happening in their lives, and they describe themselves as being in a good mood or a bad mood. Some days are better than others.

Affect is a term that is used to refer to people's feelings in response to their environment, whether positive and pleasant or negative and unpleasant. All people experience different affective states at various times in their lives. These states of mind, which change in particular situations, usually do not last very long or often involve extremes of happiness or depression. When a person's mood goes far beyond the usual, normal "ups and downs," it is known as an affective disorder.

DEPRESSION AND ANTIDEPRESSANTS

Depression, a very common affective disorder, strikes millions of people every year. In depression, feelings of sadness are much more severe and long-lasting than the suspected precipitating event, and the mood of affected individuals is much more intense. The depression may not even be traceable to a specific event or stressor (i.e., there are no external causes). Patients who are depressed may have little energy, sleep disturbances, a lack of appetite, limited libido, and inability to perform activities of daily living. They may describe overwhelming feelings of sadness, despair, hopelessness, and disorganization.

In many cases, the depression is never diagnosed, and the patient is treated for physical manifestations of the underlying disease such as fatigue, malaise, obesity, anorexia, or even alcoholism and drug dependence. Clinical depression is an actual disorder that can interfere with a person's family life, job, and social interactions. Left untreated, it can produce multiple physical problems that can lead to further depression or in extreme cases, even to suicide.

Biogenic Amine Theory of Depression

Research on the development of the drugs known to be effective in relieving depression led to the formulation of the current hypothesis regarding the cause of depression. Scientists have theorized that depression results from a deficiency of norepinephrine (NE), dopamine, or serotonin (5HT), which are all ***biogenic amines,*** in key areas of the brain. Both NE and 5HT are released throughout the brain by neurons that react with multiple receptors to regulate arousal, alertness, attention, moods, appetite, and sensory processing. Deficiencies of these neurotransmitters may develop for three known reasons. First, monoamine oxidase (MAO) may break them down to be recycled or restored in the neuron. Second, rapid fire of the neurons may lead to their depletion. Third, the number or sensitivity of postsynaptic receptors may increase, thus depleting neurotransmitter levels.

Depression may also occur as a result of other yet unknown causes. This condition may be a syndrome that reflects either activity or the lack of activity in a number of sites in the brain including the arousal center (RAS), the limbic system, and basal ganglia.

Drug Therapy

Today, the use of agents that alter the concentration of neurotransmitters in the brain is the most effective means of treating depression with drugs. The antidepressant drugs used today counteract the effects of neurotransmitter deficiencies in three ways. First, they may inhibit the effects of MAO, leading to increased NE or 5HT in the synaptic cleft. Second, they may block reuptake by the releasing nerve, leading to increased neurotransmitter levels in the synaptic cleft. Third, they may regulate receptor sites and breakdown of neurotransmitters, leading to an accumulation of neurotransmitter in the synaptic cleft.

Antidepressants may be classified into three groups: the ***tricyclic antidepressants,*** the ***MAO inhibitors,*** and the ***selective serotonin reuptake inhibitors.*** Other drugs that are used as antidepressants similarly increase the synaptic cleft concentrations of these neurotransmitters (Figure 19-1).

TRICYCLIC ANTIDEPRESSANTS

The tricyclic antidepressants (TCAs), including the amines, secondary amines, and tetracyclics, all reduce the reuptake of 5HT and norepinephrine into nerves. Because all TCAs are similarly effective, the choice of TCA depends on individual response to the drug and tolerance of adverse effects. A patient who does not respond to one TCA may respond to another drug from this class. Table 19-1 lists the currently available TCAs, including the specific type and occurrence of sedation and other adverse effects.

THERAPEUTIC ACTIONS AND INDICATIONS

The TCAs inhibit the presynaptic reuptake of the neurotransmitters norepinephrine and serotonin, which leads to an accumulation of these neurotransmitters in the synaptic cleft and increased stimulation of the postsynaptic receptors. The exact mechanism

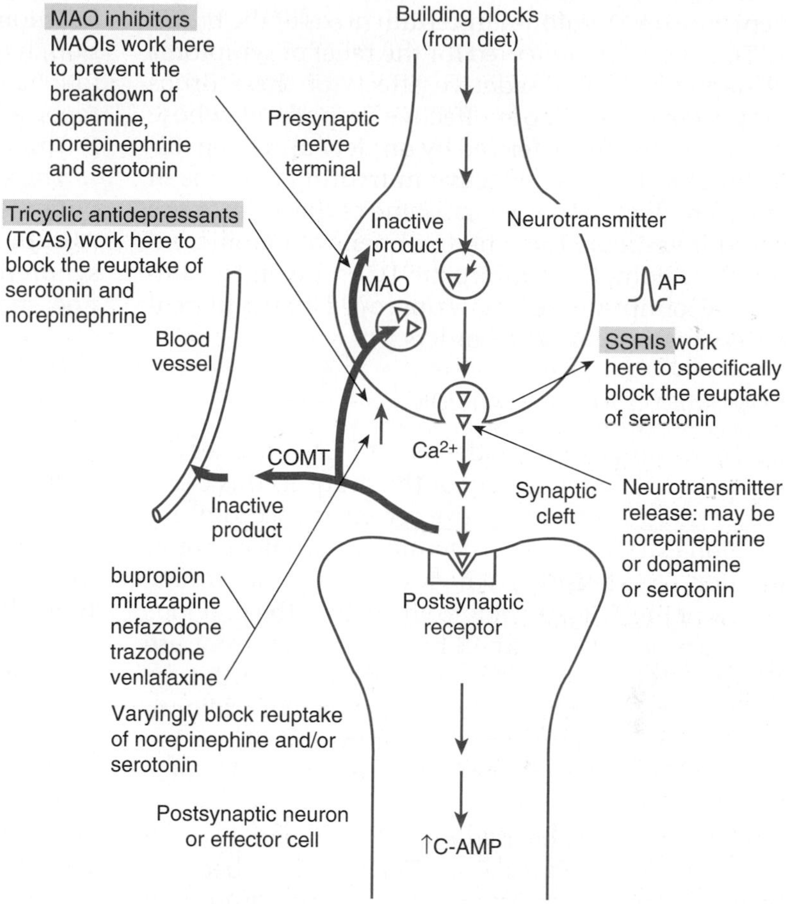

FIGURE 19-1. Sites of action for the antidepressants: MAO inhibitors, tricyclic antidepressants, SSRIs, and other agents.

TABLE 19-1

TRICYCLIC ANTIDEPRESSANTS: ADVERSE EFFECTS MOST FREQUENTLY ASSOCIATED WITH EACH DRUG

			Effects			
Drug	**Brand Name**	**Type**	*Sedation*	*Anticholinergic*	*Hypotension*	*Cardiovascular*
amitriptyline	*Elavil*	amine	++++	++++	++++	+++
amoxapine	*Ascendin*	amine	+	+	++	++
clomipramine	*Anafranil*	amine	+++	+++	+++	+++
desipramine	*Norpramin*	secondary amine	+	+	++	++
doxepin	*Sinequan*	amine	+++	+++	++	++
P imipramine	*Tofranil*	amine	++	++	+++	++
maprotiline	*Ludiomil*	tetracyclic	++	+	++	++
nortriptyline	*Aventyl* *Pamelor*	secondary amine	+	+	+	+
protriptyline	*Vivactil*	secondary amine	+	+++	+	+
trimipramine	*Surmontil*	amine	+++	++	++	++

++++ = marked effects
+++ = moderate effects
++ = mild effects
+ = negligible effects

of action in decreasing depression is not known, but is thought to be due to the accumulation of norepinephrine and serotonin in certain areas of the brain.

The TCAs are indicated for the relief of symptoms of depression. The sedative effects of these drugs may make them more effective in patients whose depression is characterized by anxiety and sleep disturbances. They are effective in treating enuresis in children older than 6 years. Some of these drugs are being investigated for the treatment of chronic, intractable pain. In addition, the TCAs are anticholinergic. Clomipramine is now approved for use to treat obsessive-compulsive disorders.

CONTRAINDICATIONS/CAUTIONS

One contraindication to the use of TCAs includes the presence of allergy to any of the drugs in this class. Other contraindications are recent myocardial infarction (MI) because of potential occurrence of reinfarction or extension of the infarct with the cardiac effects of the drug, myelography within the previous 24 hours or in the next 48 hours, or concurrent use of an MAO inhibitor because of the potential for serious adverse effects or toxic reactions. In addition, pregnancy and lactation are contraindications because of the potential for adverse effects in the fetus and neonate.

Caution should be used with TCAs in patients with preexisting cardiovascular (CV) disorders, because of the cardiac stimulatory effects of the drug, and with any condition that would be exacerbated by the anticholinergic effects (angle closure glaucoma, urinary retention, prostate hypertrophy, gastrointestinal [GI] or genitourinary [GU] surgery). Care should also be taken in psychiatric patients who may exhibit a worsening of psychoses or paranoia and manic-depressive patients who may shift to a manic stage. In addition, caution is necessary in patients with a history of seizures, because the seizure threshold may be decreased secondary to the stimulation of the receptor sites, and in elderly patients. The presence of hepatic or renal disease, which could interfere with the metabolism and excretion of these drugs and lead to toxic levels, also necessitates caution.

ADVERSE EFFECTS

The adverse effects of TCAs are associated with the effects of the drugs on the central nervous system (CNS) and peripheral nervous system. Sedation, sleep disturbances, fatigue, hallucinations, disorientation, visual disturbances, difficulty in concentrating, weakness, ataxia, and tremors may occur.

Use of TCAs may lead to GI anticholinergic effects such as dry mouth, constipation, nausea, vomiting, anorexia, increased salivation, cramps, and diarrhea. Resultant GU effects may include urinary retention and hesitancy, loss of libido, and changes in sexual functioning. CV effects such as orthostatic hypotension, hypertension, arrhythmias, MI, angina, palpitations, and stroke may pose problems. Miscellaneous reported effects include alopecia, weight gain or loss, flushing, chills, and nasal congestion.

These adverse effects may be intolerable to some patients, who then stop taking the particular TCA. Abrupt cessation of all TCAs causes a withdrawal syndrome characterized by nausea, headache, vertigo, malaise, and nightmare.

CLINICALLY IMPORTANT DRUG–DRUG INTERACTIONS

If TCAs are given with cimetidine, fluoxetine, or ranitidine, an increase in TCA levels results, with an increase in both therapeutic and adverse effects, especially anticholinergic conditions. Patients should be monitored closely, and appropriate dosage reductions should be made.

Other drug combinations may also pose problems. The combination of TCAs and oral anticoagulants leads to higher serum levels of the anticoagulants and increased risk of bleeding. Blood tests should be frequent, and appropriate dosage adjustments in the oral anticoagulant should be made. If TCAs are combined with sympathomimetics or clonidine, the risk of arrhythmias and hypertension is increased. This combination should be avoided, especially in patients with underlying CV disease.

The combination of TCAs with MAO inhibitors leads to a risk of a severe hyperpyretic crisis with severe convulsions, hypertensive episodes, and death. This combination should be avoided. Although TCAs and MAO inhibitors have been used together in selected patients who do not respond to a single agent, the risk of severe adverse effects is very high.

DATA LINK

Data link to the tricyclic antidepressants, listed in Table 19-1, in your nursing drug guide.

NURSING CONSIDERATIONS
for patients receiving tricyclic antidepressants

Assessment

HISTORY. Screen for the following: any known allergies to these drugs; impaired liver or kidney function that could alter the metabolism and excretion of the drug; glaucoma; benign prostatic hypertrophy (BPH); cardiac dysfunction; GI obstruction; surgery; recent MI; and pregnancy or lactation. Find out whether the patient has a history of seizure disorders or psychiatric problems or myelography within the past

24 hours or in the next 48 hours, or is taking an MAO inhibitor.

PHYSICAL ASSESSMENT. Include screening for baseline status before beginning therapy and for any potential adverse effects. Assess the following: temperature and weight; skin color and lesions; affect, orientation, and reflexes; vision; blood pressure, including orthostatic blood pressure; pulse and perfusion; respiratory rate and adventitious sounds; and bowel sounds upon abdominal examination. Obtain an ECG as well as renal and liver function tests.

Nursing Diagnoses

The patient receiving a TCA may have the following nursing diagnoses related to drug therapy:

- Pain related to anticholinergic effects, headache, CNS effects
- Alteration in cardiac output related to CV effects
- Alteration in thought processes and sensory–perceptual alteration related to CNS effects
- Potential for injury related to CNS effects
- Knowledge deficit regarding drug therapy

Implementation

- Limit drug access to potentially suicidal patients *because of the potential for overdose.*
- Maintain initial dosage for 4 to 8 weeks *to evaluate the therapeutic effect.*
- Give parenteral forms only if oral forms are not feasible or available; switch to an oral form, *which is less toxic and associated with fewer adverse effects, as soon as possible.*
- Give the major portion of the dose at bedtime if drowsiness and anticholinergic effects are severe, *to decrease risk of patient injury. Elderly patients may not be able to tolerate larger doses.*
- Reduce the dosage if minor adverse effects occur, and discontinue the drug slowly if major or potentially life-threatening adverse effects occur to *ensure patient safety.*
- Provide comfort measures *to help the patient tolerate drug effects.* These may include voiding before dosing, bowel program as needed, taking food with the drug if GI upset is severe, and environmental control (lighting, temperature, stimuli).
- Provide thorough patient teaching, including drug name, prescribed dosage, measures for avoidance of adverse effects, and warning signs that may indicate possible problems. Instruct patients about the need for periodic monitoring and evaluation *to enhance patient knowledge about drug therapy and to promote compliance.*
- Offer support and encouragement *to help patients cope with diagnosis and drug regimen.*

Evaluation

- Monitor patient response to the drug (alleviation of signs and symptoms of depression).
- Monitor for adverse effects (sedation, anticholinergic effects, hypotension, cardiac arrhythmias).
- Evaluate effectiveness of teaching plan (patient can give the drug name, dosage, possible adverse effects to watch for, specific measures to help avoid adverse effects, and importance of continued follow-up).
- Monitor effectiveness of comfort measures and compliance with regimen.

MONOAMINE OXIDASE INHIBITORS

At one time, MAO inhibitors were used more often, but now they are used rarely because they require a specific dietary regimen to prevent toxicity. Safer drugs that are usually just as effective in most people have replaced them. Agents still in use include the following:

- Isocarboxazid (*Marplan*), which once became unavailable because it was no longer used frequently, reappeared in 1998 when researchers found that some patients who did not respond to the newer, safer antidepressants could respond to this drug.
- Phenelzine (*Nardil*) is also reserved for use in patients who do not respond to other antidepressants or who cannot take other antidepressants for some reason.
- Tranylcypromine (*Parnate*) is used for adult outpatients with reactive depression. This agent is also associated with potentially fatal drug–food interactions.

The choice of an MAO inhibitor depends on the prescriber's experience and individual response. A patient who may not respond to one MAO inhibitor may respond to another.

THERAPEUTIC ACTIONS AND INDICATIONS

The MAO inhibitors irreversibly inhibit MAO, an enzyme found in nerves and other tissues, including the liver, which breaks down the biogenic amines norepinephrine, dopamine, and serotonin. This allows these amines to accumulate in the synaptic cleft and in neuronal storage vesicles, causing increased stimulation of the postsynaptic receptors and relief of depression.

The MAO inhibitors are generally indicated for the treatment of the signs and symptoms of depression in patients who cannot tolerate or do not respond to other, safer antidepressants.

CONTRAINDICATIONS/CAUTIONS

Contraindications to the use of MAO inhibitors include allergy to any of these antidepressants; pheochromocytoma, where the sudden increases in norepinephrine levels could result in severe hypertension and CV emergencies; CV disease, including hypertension, coronary artery disease (CAD), angina, and congestive heart failure (CHF), because these could be exacerbated by increased NE levels; and known abnormal CNS vessels or defects, because the potential increase in blood pressure and vasoconstriction associated with higher NE levels could precipitate a stroke. A history of headaches may also be a contraindication.

Other contraindications include renal or hepatic impairment, which could alter the metabolism and excretion of these drugs and lead to toxic levels, and myelography within the past 24 hours or in the next 48 hours, because of the risk of severe reaction to the dye used in myelography.

In addition, caution should be used with psychiatric patients, who could be overstimulated or shift to a manic phase secondary to the stimulation associated with the MAO inhibitors, and in patients with seizure disorders or hyperthyroidism, both of which could be exacerbated by the stimulation of these drugs. Care should also be taken with patients who are soon to undergo elective surgery because of the potential for unexpected effects with NE accumulation during the stress reaction, and with pregnant or breastfeeding women because of potential adverse effects on the fetus and neonate.

ADVERSE EFFECTS

The MAO inhibitors are associated with more adverse effects, more of which are fatal, than most other antidepressants. The effects relate to the accumulation of NE in the synaptic cleft. Dizziness, excitement, nervousness, mania, hyperreflexia, tremors, confusion, insomnia, agitation, and blurred vision may occur.

MAO inhibitors may result in liver toxicity. Other GI effects may include nausea, vomiting, diarrhea or constipation, anorexia, weight gain, dry mouth, and abdominal pain. Urinary retention, dysuria, incontinence, and changes in sexual function may also pose problems. CV effects may include orthostatic hypotension, arrhythmias, palpitations, angina, and the potentially fatal hypertensive crisis. This condition is characterized by occipital headache, palpitations, neck stiffness, nausea, vomiting, sweating, dilated pupils, photophobia, tachycardia, and chest pain. It may progress to intracranial bleeding and fatal stroke.

CLINICALLY IMPORTANT DRUG–DRUG INTERACTIONS

Drug interactions of MAO inhibitors with other antidepressants include hypertensive crisis, coma, and severe convulsions with TCAs, and a potentially life-threatening serotonin syndrome with selective serotonin reuptake inhibitors (SSRIs). A period of 6 weeks should elapse after stopping an SSRI before beginning an MAO inhibitor.

If MAO inhibitors are given with other sympathomimetic drugs (e.g., methyldopa, guanethidine), sympathomimetic effects increase. Combinations with insulin or oral antidiabetic agents result in additive hypoglycemic effects. Patients who receive these combinations must be monitored closely, and appropriate dosage adjustments should be made.

CLINICALLY IMPORTANT DRUG–FOOD INTERACTIONS

Tyramine and other pressor amines that are found in food, which are normally broken down by MAO enzymes in the GI tract, may be absorbed in high concentrations in the presence of MAO inhibitors, causing increased blood pressure. The hypertensive crisis is often associated with eating foods that contain tyramine. In addition, tyramine causes the release of stored NE from nerve terminals, which further contributes to high blood pressure. Patients who take MAO inhibitors should avoid the tyramine-containing foods listed in Table 19-2.

DATA LINK

Data link to the following MAO inhibitors in your nursing drug guide:

MAO INHIBITORS

Name	Brand Name	Usual Indication
isocarboxazid	*Marplan*	Depression not responsive to other agents
P phenelzine	*Nardil*	Depression not responsive to other agents
tranylcypromine	*Parnate*	Adult reactive depression

NURSING CONSIDERATIONS for patients receiving MAO inhibitors

Assessment

HISTORY. Screen for the following: any known allergies to these drugs; impaired liver or kidney function that could alter the metabolism and excretion of the drug; cardiac dysfunction; GI or GU obstruction; surgery, including elective surgery; seizure disorders; psychiatric conditions; and occurrence of myelography within the past 24 hours or in the next 48 hours.

TABLE 19-2

TYRAMINE-CONTAINING FOODS

Foods High in Tyramine	Foods With Moderate Amounts of Tyramine	Foods With Low Amounts of Tyramine
Aged cheeses: cheddar cheese, blue cheese, Swiss cheese, Camembert Aged or fermented meats, fish or poultry: chicken paté, beef liver paté, caviar Brewer's yeast Fava beans Red wines: Chianti, burgundy, sherry, vermouth Smoked or pickled meats, fish or poultry: herring, sausage, corned beef, salami, pepperoni	Meat extracts: consommé, bouillon Pasteurized light and pale beer Avocados	Distilled liquors: vodka, gin, Scotch, rye Cheeses: American, mozzarella, cottage cheese, cream cheese Chocolate Fruits: figs, raisins, grapes, pineapple, oranges Sour cream Soy sauce Yogurt

Find out whether female patients are pregnant or breastfeeding.

PHYSICAL ASSESSMENT. Include screening for baseline status before beginning therapy and for any potential adverse effects. Assess the following: temperature and weight; skin color and lesions; affect, orientation, and reflexes; vision; blood pressure, including orthostatic blood pressure; pulse and perfusion; respiratory rate and adventitious sounds; and bowel sounds upon abdominal examination. Obtain an ECG and renal and liver function tests.

Nursing Diagnoses

The patient receiving an MAO inhibitor may have the following nursing diagnoses related to drug therapy:

- Pain related to sympathomimetic effects, headache, CNS effects
- Alteration in cardiac output related to CV effects
- Alteration in thought processes and sensory–perceptual alteration related to CNS effects
- Potential for injury related to CNS effects
- Knowledge deficit regarding drug therapy

Implementation

- Limit drug access to potentially suicidal patients *to decrease the risk of overdose.*
- Monitor patient for 2 to 4 weeks *to ascertain onset of full therapeutic effect.*
- Monitor BP and orthostatic BP carefully *to arrange for slow increase in dosage as needed for patients who show tendency toward hypotension.*
- Monitor liver function prior to and periodically during therapy *to arrange to discontinue the drug at the first sign of liver toxicity.*
- Discontinue the drug and monitor the patient carefully at any complaint of severe headache *to decrease the risk of severe hypertension and cerebrovascular effects.*
- Maintain phentolamine or other adrenergic blocker on standby *as treatment in case of hypertensive crisis.*
- Provide comfort measures *to help the patient tolerate drug effects.* These include voiding before dosing, instituting a bowel program as needed, taking food with the drug if GI upset is severe, and environmental control (lighting, temperature, decreased stimulation).
- Provide a list of potential drug–food interactions that may cause severe toxicity *to decrease the risk of serious drug–food interaction.* Provide a diet that is low in tyramine-containing foods.
- Provide thorough patient teaching, including drug name, prescribed dosage, measures for avoidance of adverse effects, and warning signs that may indicate possible problems. Instruct patients about the need for periodic monitoring and evaluation *to enhance patient knowledge about drug therapy and to promote compliance.*
- Offer support and encouragement *to help patients cope with the disease and drug regimen.*

Evaluation

- Monitor patient response to the drug (alleviation of signs and symptoms of depression).
- Monitor for adverse effects (sedation, sympathomimetic effects, hypotension, cardiac arrhythmias, GI disturbances, hypertensive crisis).
- Evaluate the effectiveness of the teaching plan (patient can give the drug name, dosage, possible adverse effects to watch for, specific measures to help avoid adverse effects, importance of continued follow-up, and importance of avoiding foods high in tyramine).

- Monitor the effectiveness of comfort measures and compliance with the regimen.

SELECTIVE SEROTONIN REUPTAKE INHIBITORS

The SSRIs, the newest group of antidepressant drugs, specifically block the reuptake of serotonin, with little to no effect on norepinephrine. Because SSRIs do not have the many adverse effects associated with the TCAs and the MAO inhibitors, they are a better choice for many patients. SSRIs include the following agents:

- Fluoxetine (*Prozac*), the first SSRI, has been successfully used to treat depression, obsessive-compulsive disorders, and bulimia. It is being investigated for use in treating other psychiatric disorders.
- Fluvoxamine (*Luvox*), which is under investigation for the treatment of depression, is now indicated only for the treatment of obsessive-compulsive disorder.
- Paroxetine (*Paxil*) is indicated for the treatment of depression, panic disorders, and obsessive-compulsive disorders.
- Sertraline (*Zoloft*) is used to treat depression and obsessive-compulsive disorders.
- Citalopram (*Celexa*), the newest SSRI, is indicated only for the treatment of depression.

With the SSRIs, a period of up to 4 weeks is necessary for realization of the full therapeutic effect. Patients may respond well to one SSRI and show little or no response to another one. The choice of drug depends on the indications and individual response.

THERAPEUTIC ACTIONS AND INDICATIONS

As previously stated, SSRIs more specifically block the reuptake of serotonin, with little effect on NE. This action increases the levels of serotonin in the synaptic cleft and may contribute to the antidepressant and other effects attributed to these drugs.

The SSRIs are indicated for the treatment of depression, obsessive-compulsive disorders, panic attacks, and bulimia. Ongoing investigations are focusing on the use of these antidepressant drugs in the treatment of other psychiatric disorders.

CONTRAINDICATIONS/CAUTIONS

The SSRIs are contraindicated in the presence of allergy to any of these drugs and during pregnancy because of the potential for serious adverse effects on the fetus.

Caution should be used in the following conditions: during lactation because of the potential for adverse effects on the infant; with impaired renal or hepatic function that could alter the metabolism and excretion of the drug, leading to toxic effects; and with diabetes, which could be exacerbated by the stimulating effects of these drugs.

ADVERSE EFFECTS

The adverse effects associated with SSRIs, which are related to the effects of increased serotonin levels, include CNS effects such as headache, drowsiness, dizziness, insomnia, anxiety, tremor, agitation, and seizures. GI effects such as nausea, vomiting, diarrhea, dry mouth, anorexia, constipation, and changes in taste, and GU effects that include painful menstruation, cystitis, sexual dysfunction, urgency, and impotence often may occur. Respiratory changes may include cough, dyspnea, upper respiratory infections,

> **CULTURAL CONSIDERATIONS ••••**
>
> ***The Popularity of Prozac***
>
> A rise in the diagnosis of depression has occurred in the 1990s, with that decade's fast-paced lifestyle, high-stress jobs, explosion of information availability, and rapid change. Many people, who have high expectations of both themselves and others, are often overworked and overstimulated to a point that they become clinically depressed.
>
> There is now a selection of relatively safe and nontoxic drugs that can be used to treat depression—the SSRIs. For several years, the SSRIs remained in the top-selling category of prescription drugs. Fluoxetine (*Prozac*), in particular, has been the subject of numerous talk shows, books, and movies. In many ways, *Prozac* was the "in" drug of the 1990s. This societal phenomenon put pressure on health care providers to prescribe drugs that might not have been appropriate to the patient situation. In some instances, patients just wanted the drug that helped their friends. They may not have been willing to listen to their health care provider or to take the time to be properly diagnosed; they just wanted an SSRI. *Prozac* may not be the solution to everyone's problem, and it is often difficult to explain this to a patient. It also may be hard to get the patient to understand that this drug is not a quick fix, taking 4–6 weeks to achieve full therapeutic effectiveness. Fortunately, the SSRIs have the least adverse effects of the antidepressants, and such fads usually pass in a few years.
>
> It is important to remember the powerful effects of the media on health care–seeking behavior. As more and more drugs are advertised in magazines and on television, patients are becoming aware of options and "cures" that they might like to try. Patient education is a tricky yet important part of any health care intervention and an extremely important aspect of health care in our society.

and pharyngitis. Other reported effects include sweating, rash, fever, and pruritus.

CLINICALLY IMPORTANT DRUG–DRUG INTERACTIONS

Because of the risk of serotonin syndrome if SSRIs are used with MAO inhibitors, this combination should be avoided and at least 2 to 4 weeks allowed between types of drugs if switching from one to the other. In addition, the use of SSRIs with TCAs results in increased therapeutic and toxic effects. If these combinations are used, patients should be monitored closely, and appropriate dosage adjustments should be made.

DATA LINK

Data link to the following SSRIs in your nursing drug guide:

SELECTIVE SEROTONIN REUPTAKE INHIBITORS

Name	Brand Name	Usual Indication
citalopram	*Celexa*	Treatment of depression
P fluoxetine	*Prozac*	Treatment of depression, bulimia, obsessive-compulsive disorders
fluvoxamine	*Luvox*	Treatment of obsessive-compulsive disorders
paroxetine	*Paxil*	Treatment of depression, obsessive-compulsive disorders, panic disorders
sertraline	*Zoloft*	Treatment of depression, obsessive-compulsive disorders

NURSING CONSIDERATIONS
for patients receiving SSRIs

Assessment

HISTORY. Screen for the following: any known allergies to SSRIs; impaired liver or kidney function, which could alter the metabolism and excretion of the drug; and diabetes mellitus. Find out whether female patients are pregnant or breastfeeding.

PHYSICAL ASSESSMENT. Include screening for baseline status before beginning therapy and for any potential adverse effects. Assess for the following: temperature and weight; skin color and lesions; affect, orientation, and reflexes; vision; blood pressure and pulse; respiratory rate and adventitious sounds; and bowel sounds upon abdominal examination. Obtain renal and liver function tests.

Nursing Diagnoses

The patient receiving an SSRI may have the following nursing diagnoses related to drug therapy:

- Pain related to GI, GU, CNS effects
- Alteration in thought processes and sensory–perceptual alteration related to CNS effects
- Alteration in nutrition related to GI effects
- Knowledge deficit regarding drug therapy

Implementation

- Arrange for lower dosage in elderly patients and those with renal or hepatic impairment *because of the potential for severe adverse effects.*
- Monitor patient for up to 4 weeks *to ascertain onset of full therapeutic effect before adjusting dosage.*
- Establish suicide precautions for severely depressed patients, and limit the quantity of the drug dispensed *to decrease the risk of overdose.*
- Administer the drug once a day in the morning *to achieve optimal therapeutic effects.* If the dosage is increased or if the patient is having severe GI effects, the dosage can be divided.
- Suggest that patients use barrier contraceptives *to prevent pregnancy while taking this drug, because serious fetal abnormalities can occur.*
- Provide comfort measures *to help patients tolerate drug effects.* These may include voiding before dosing, instituting a bowel program as needed, taking food with the drug if GI upset is severe, or environmental control (lighting, temperature, stimuli).
- Provide thorough patient teaching, including the drug name, prescribed dosage, measures for avoidance of adverse effects, and warning signs that may indicate possible problems. Instruct patients about the need for periodic monitoring and evaluation *to enhance patient knowledge about drug therapy and to promote compliance* (see Patient Teaching Checklist: Selective Serotonin Reuptake Inhibitors [SSRIs]).
- Offer support and encouragement *to help patients cope with the disease and drug regimen.*

Evaluation

- Monitor patient response to the drug (alleviation of signs and symptoms of depression, obsessive-compulsive disorder, bulimia, panic disorder).
- Monitor for adverse effects (sedation, dizziness, GI upset, respiratory dysfunction, GU problems, skin rash).
- Evaluate effectiveness of teaching plan (patient can give the drug name, dosage, possible adverse effects to watch for, specific measures to help avoid adverse effects, importance of continued follow-up, and importance of avoiding pregnancy).
- Monitor the effectiveness of comfort measures and compliance with the regimen (see Nursing Care Guide: Selective Serotonin Reuptake Inhibitors).

PATIENT TEACHING CHECKLIST

Selective Serotonin Reuptake Inhibitors (SSRIs)

Create customized patient teaching materials for a specific selective serotonin reuptake inhibitor (SSRI) from your CD-ROM. Your patient teaching should stress the following points for drugs within this class:

SSRIs change the concentration of serotonin in specific areas of the brain. This increase in serotonin levels is believed to relieve depression.

The drug should be taken once a day in the morning. If your dosage has been increased or you are having stomach upset, the dose may be divided.

It may take up to 4 weeks before you feel the full effects of this drug. Continue to take the drug every day during that time so that the concentration of the drug in your body eventually reaches effective levels.

Common effects of these drugs include:

- Dizziness, drowsiness, nervousness, and insomnia—If these effects occur, avoid driving or performing hazardous or delicate tasks that require concentration.
- Nausea, vomiting, and weight loss—Small, frequent meals may help. Monitor your weight loss, and if it becomes excessive, consult your health care provider.
- Sexual dysfunction and flu-like symptoms—These effects may be temporary. Consult with your health care provider if these conditions become bothersome.

Report any of the following conditions to your health care provider: rash, mania, seizures, and severe weight loss.

Tell any doctor, nurse, or other health care provider that you are taking this drug.

Keep this drug and all medications out of the reach of children.

Do not take this drug during pregnancy because severe fetal abnormalities could occur. The use of barrier contraceptives is recommended while you are taking this drug. If you think that you are pregnant, or would like to become pregnant, consult with your health care provider.

This Teaching Checklist reflects general patient teaching guidelines. It is not meant to be a substitute for drug-specific teaching information, which is available in nursing drug guides.

OTHER ANTIDEPRESSANTS

Some other effective antidepressants do not fit into one of the three groups that have been discussed in this chapter. These drugs have varying effects on NE, 5HT, and dopamine. Although it is not known how these actions are related to clinical efficacy, these agents may be most effective in treating depression in patients who do not respond to other antidepressants. They may even be used before the MAO inhibitors or TCAs, which have many more adverse effects. Other antidepressants include the following:

- Bupropion (*Wellbutrin, Zyban*), which weakly blocks reuptake of NE, 5HT, and dopamine, is effective in the treatment of depression. At lower doses, this drug is effective in smoking cessation.
- Mirtazapine (*Remeron*) is used to treat depression. How its many anticholinergic effects relate to its antidepressive effects is not known.
- Nefazodone (*Serzone*), which is given twice daily, is effective in the treatment of some depression.
- Trazodone (*Desyrel*), which blocks 5HT and some serotonin precursor reuptake, is effective in some forms of depression but has many CNS effects associated with its use.
- Venlafaxine (*Effexor*) has fewer adverse CNS effects and is known to mildly block reuptake of NE, 5HT, and dopamine. It is very effective in treating some depression and its popularity has increased with the introduction of an extended release form that does away with the multiple dosing per day that is required with the regular form.

WWW.WEB LINKS

Health care providers and patients may want to consult the following Internet sources:

Information on depression including diagnosis, research, treatment:
http://www.depression.com

NURSING CARE GUIDE

Selective Serotonin Reuptake Inhibitors (SSRIs)

Assessment	Nursing Diagnoses	Implementation	Evaluation
HISTORY Allergies to any of these drugs; renal or hepatic dysfunction; pregnancy or lactation; diabetes	Pain related to GI, GU, CNS effects Alteration in thought processes related to CNS effects Alteration in nutrition related to GI effects Knowledge deficit regarding drug therapy	Administer drug in morning; divide doses if high or GI upset. Provide comfort, safety measures: small meals; void before dosing; side rails; pain medication as needed; suggest barrier contraceptive; limit dosage to potentially suicidal patients; lower dose with renal or hepatic impairment. Provide support and reassurance to deal with drug effects (4 week delay in full effectiveness). Provide patient teaching regarding drug, dosage, adverse effects, conditions to report, need to use barrier contraceptives.	Evaluate drug effects: relief of signs and symptoms of depression, obsessive–compulsive disorder, panic disorders. Monitor for adverse effects: sedation, dizziness, insomnia; respiratory dysfunction; GI upset; GU problems; skin rash. Monitor for drug–drug interactions as indicated for each drug. Evaluate effectiveness of patient teaching program. Evaluate effectiveness of comfort and safety measures.
PHYSICAL EXAMINATION Cardiovascular: BP, P CNS: orientation, affect, reflexes, vision Skin: color, lesions; texture Respiratory: respiration, adventitious sounds GI: abdominal examination, bowel sounds Laboratory tests: hepatic and renal function tests			

Information on depression, signs and symptoms, community resources, support groups:
http://depression.cmhc.com

Information on women and depression:
http://www.nimh.nih.gov/depression/women/wom.htm

Information on education programs related to depression, stress, drug therapy and so forth for patients and health professionals:
http://www.teachhealth.com

Patient-oriented and professional information on issues related to mental health:
http://www.nimh.nih.gov

DATA LINK

Data link to the following antidepressants in your nursing drug guide:

OTHER ANTIDEPRESSANTS

Name	Brand Name	Usual Indication
P bupropion	*Wellbutrin, Zyban*	Treatment of depression, smoking cessation
mirtazapine	*Remeron*	Treatment of depression
nefazodone	*Serzone*	Treatment of depression
trazodone	*Desyrel*	Treatment of depression
venlafaxine	*Effexor*	Treatment of depression

CASE STUDY

Use of SSRIs

PATIENT SCENARIO

D. J., a 46-year-old married woman, complains of weight gain, malaise, fatigue, sleeping during the day, loss of interest in daily activities, and bouts of crying for no apparent reason. On examination, she weighs 8 pounds more than the standard weight for her height; all other findings are within normal limits. In conversation with a nurse, D. J. says that in the past 10 months, several events have occurred. She lost both her parents, her only child graduated from high school and went off to college, her nephew died of renal failure, her one sister received a diagnosis of metastatic breast cancer, and she herself lost her job as a day-care provider when the family moved out of town. In addition, a veterinarian diagnosed the family cat of 17 years with terminal leukemia. D.J. was started on fluoxetine (*Prozac*) and given an appointment for a visit with a counselor.

CRITICAL THINKING QUESTIONS

What nursing interventions are appropriate at this time? What sort of crisis intervention would be most appropriate? Balance the benefits of pointing out all of the losses and points of grief that you detect in D. J.'s story with the risks of upsetting her strained coping mechanisms. What can D. J. expect to experience as a result of the SSRI therapy? How can you help D. J. cope during the lengthy period it takes to reach therapeutic effects? What other future interventions should be planned with D. J.?

DISCUSSION

Many patients in severe crisis do not consciously identify the many things that cause stress. They have developed coping mechanisms to help them survive and cope with their day-to-day activities. However, D. J. seems to have reached her limit, and she exhibits many of the signs and symptoms of depression.

It is hoped that the fluoxetine, an SSRI, will enable D. J. to regain her ability to cope and her normal affect. The drug should give her brain a chance to reach a new biochemical balance. Before she begins taking the fluoxetine, she should receive a written sheet listing the pertinent drug information, adverse effects to watch for, warning signs to report, and a telephone number to call in case she has questions later or just needs to talk. The written information is especially important, because she may not remember drug-related discussions or instructions clearly.

Once the SSRI reaches therapeutic levels, which may take as long as 4 weeks, D. J. may start to feel like her "old self" and may be strong enough to finally begin dealing with all her grief. She may recover from her need for the SSRI over time and the medication can be withdrawn.

Because it may take up to 4 weeks for the fluoxetine to produce its full therapeutic effect, the referral of D. J. to a counselor may be the best way to ensure that she can talk to someone who has the time to listen and to help her face her losses and resolve any problems she may be experiencing. If a counselor is not available, it is important to establish a trusting relationship and to give D. J. the time that she needs to work out some of her feelings. It might be possible to refer D. J. to community support groups for dealing with loss and grieving. She also might be able to consult with an employment agency regarding other day-care provider positions that might fit her needs.

CHAPTER SUMMARY

- Affect is a term that is used to refer to the feelings that people experience when they respond emotionally.
- Depression is an affective disorder characterized by overwhelming sadness, despair, and hopelessness that is inappropriate with respect to the event that precipitated the depression. A very common problem, depression is associated with many physical manifestations, and the condition is often misdiagnosed. It could be that depression is caused by a series of events that are not yet understood.
- The biogenic amine theory states that depression is caused by a deficiency of the biogenic amines—norepinephrine, serotonin, and dopamine—in certain key areas of the brain.
- Antidepressant drugs—TCAs, MAO inhibitors, and SSRIs—increase the concentrations of the biogenic amines in the brain.
- Selection of an antidepressant depends on individual drug response and tolerance of associated adverse effects. The adverse effects of TCAs are sedating and anticholinergic; those of MAO inhibitors are CNS-related and sympathomimetic; and those of SSRIs are fewer but do cause CNS changes.
- Other antidepressants with unknown mechanisms of action are also effective in treating depression.

BIBLIOGRAPHY

Bailey, K. (1998). *Psychotropic drug facts.* Philadelphia: Lippincott-Raven.

Bullock, B. L. (2000). *Focus of pathophysiology.* Philadelphia: Lippincott Williams & Wilkins.

Hardman, J. G., Limbird, L. E., Molinoff, P. B., Ruddon, R. W., & Gilman, A. G. (Eds.). (1996). *Goodman and Gilman's the pharmacological basis of therapeutics* (9th ed.). New York: McGraw-Hill.

Karch, A. M. (2000). *2000 Lippincott's nursing drug guide.* Philadelphia: Lippincott Williams & Wilkins.

Malseed, R. (1995). *Textbook of pharmacology and nursing care.* Philadelphia: Lippincott-Raven.

McEvoy, B. R. (Ed.). (1999). *Facts and comparisons 1999.* St. Louis: Facts and Comparisons.

Professional's guide to patient drug facts. (1999). St. Louis: Facts and Comparisons.

CHAPTER 20

Psychotherapeutic Agents

Antipsychotic/neuroleptic drugs
- Typical antipsychotics
  - P chlorpromazine
  - fluphenazine
  - haloperidol
  - loxapine
  - mesoridazine
  - molindone
  - perphenazine
  - pimozide
  - prochlorperazine
  - promazine
  - thioridazine
  - thiothixene
  - trifluoperazine
  - triflupromazine
- Atypical antipsychotics
  - P clozapine
  - olanzapine
  - quetiapine
  - risperidone

Antimanic drug
- lithium

CNS stimulants
- dextroamphetamine
- P methylphenidate
- modafinil
- pemoline

CHAPTER OUTLINE

KEY TERMS

antipsychotic
attention-deficit disorder
major tranquilizer
mania
narcolepsy
neuroleptic
schizophrenia

INTRODUCTION

The drugs discussed in this chapter are used to treat psychoses—perceptual and behavioral disorders. These psychotherapeutic drugs are targeted at thought processes rather than affective states. Although these drugs do not cure any of these disorders, they do help patients function in a more acceptable manner and carry on activities of daily living.

MENTAL DISORDERS AND THEIR CLASSIFICATION

Mental disorders are now thought to be caused by some inherent dysfunction within the brain that leads to abnormal thought processes and responses. Most theories attribute these disorders to some sort of chemical imbalance in specific areas within the brain. Diagnosis of a mental disorder is often based on distinguishing characteristics described in the *Diagnostic and Statistical Manual of Mental Disorders,* 4th edition (DSM-IV). Because no diagnostic laboratory tests are available, patient assessment and response must be carefully evaluated to determine the basis of a particular problem. Selected disorders are discussed below.

Schizophrenia, the most common type of psychosis, can be very debilitating and prevents affected individuals from functioning in society. Characteristics of schizophrenia include hallucinations, paranoia, delusions, speech abnormalities, and affective problems. This disorder, which seems to have a very strong genetic association, may reflect a fundamental biochemical abnormality.

Mania, with its associated bipolar illness (i.e., manic depression), is characterized by periods of extreme overactivity and excitement. Bipolar illness involves extremes of depression followed by hyperactivity and excitement. This condition may reflect a biochemical imbalance followed by overcompensation on the part of neurons and their inability to reestablish stability.

Narcolepsy is characterized by daytime sleepiness and sudden periods of loss of wakefulness. This disorder may reflect problems with the stimulation of the brain by the reticular activating system (RAS) or problems with response to that stimulation.

Attention-deficit disorders involve a variety of conditions characterized by an inability to concentrate on one activity for longer than a few minutes and a state of hyperkinesis. These conditions are usually diagnosed in school-aged children, but can occur in adults.

ANTIPSYCHOTIC/ NEUROLEPTIC DRUGS

The ***antipsychotic*** drugs, which are essentially dopamine receptor blockers, are used to treat disorders that involve thought processes. Because of their associated neurological adverse effects, these medications are also called ***neuroleptic*** agents. At one time, these drugs were known as ***major tranquilizers.*** However, that name is no longer used because the primary action of these drugs is not sedation but a change in neuron stimulation and response (Figure 20-1).

Table 20-1 lists the antipsychotics in use today and gives information about their relative potency and associated adverse effects. Any of these drugs may be effective in a particular patient; the selection of a specific drug depends on the desired potency and patient tolerance of the associated adverse effects. A patient who does not respond to one drug may react successfully to another agent. To determine the best therapeutic regimen for a particular patient, it may be necessary to try more than one drug.

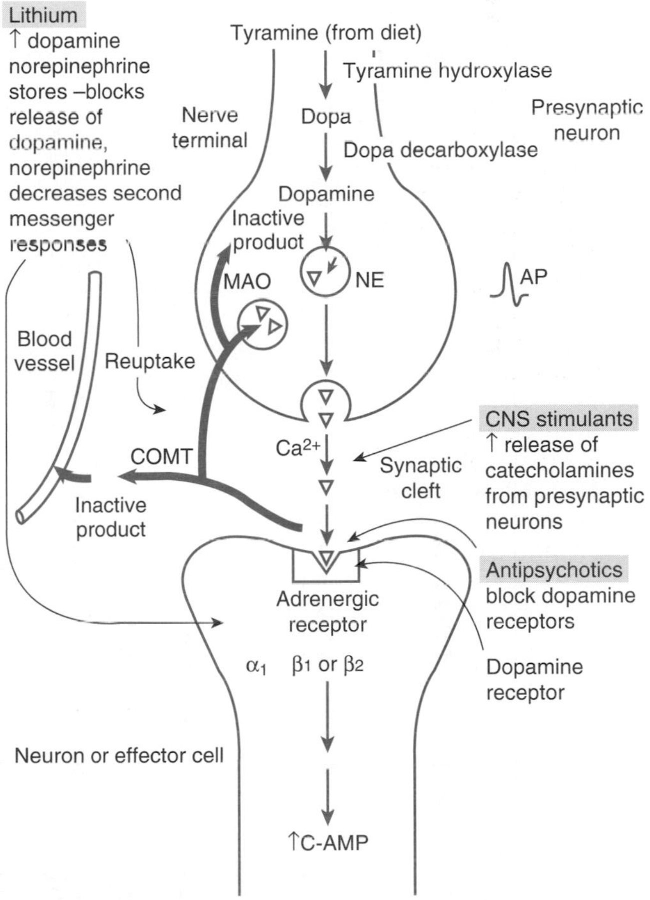

FIGURE 20-1. Sites of action of the drugs used to treat mental disorders: antipsychotics, CNS stimulants, lithium.

TABLE 20-1

ANTIPSYCHOTICS/NEUROLEPTICS

Drug	Brand Name(s)	Potency	Associated Adverse Effects*				Usual Indication(s)
			Sedation	*Anticholinergic*	*Hypotension*	*Extrapyramidal*	
TYPICAL ANTIPSYCHOTICS							
P chlorpromazine	*Thorazine*	low	++++	+++	+++	++	Management of manifestations of psychotic disorders; behavioral problems in children
fluphenazine	*Moditen, Prolixin*	high	+	+	+	++++	Management of manifestations of psychotic disorders, particularly long-term therapy
haloperidol	*Haldol*	high	+	+/–	+	++++	Management of manifestations of psychotic disorders; behavioral problems in children
loxapine	*Loxitane*	medium	+++	++	++	+++	Management of manifestations of psychotic disorders
mesoridazine	*Serentil*	low	++++	++	++	+	Schizophrenia, alcoholism, behavioral problems in mental deficiency and chronic brain syndromes
molindone	*Moban*	medium	+	++	+/–	+	Management of manifestations of psychotic disorders
perphenazine	*Trilafon*	medium	++	+	++	+++	Management of manifestations of psychotic disorders
pimozide	*Orap*	high	+	+	++	+++	Suppression of motor and phonic tics with Tourette's syndrome
prochlorperazine	*Compazine*	low	+	++	+	+++	Management of manifestations of psychotic disorders
promazine	*Prozine, Sparine*	low	+	++	+	+++	Management of manifestations of psychotic disorders
thioridazine	*Mellaril*	low	++++	+++	+++	+	Management of manifestations of psychotic disorders; behavioral problems in children (short-term); psychoses with multiple presentations
thiothixene	*Navine, Sparine*	high	+	+	+	++++	Management of manifestations of psychotic disorders
trifluoperazine	*Stelazine, Sparine*	high	+	+	+	++++	Management of manifestations of psychotic disorders
triflupromazine	*Vesprin, Sparine*	low	+	++	+	+++	Management of manifestations of psychotic disorders
ATYPICAL ANTIPSYCHOTICS							
P clozapine	*Clozaril*	low	++++	++	+++	+/–	Severely ill schizophrenics unresponsive to other therapy
olanzapine	*Zyprexa, Sparine*	high	++++	++	+++	+	Management of manifestations of psychotic disorders
quetiapine	*Seroquel, Sparine*	medium	++++	++	++	+/–	Management of manifestations of psychotic disorders
risperidone	*Risperdal, Sparine*	high	+++	+	++	++	Management of manifestations of psychotic disorders

*Each + indicates increased incidence of that adverse effect.

Antipsychotics can be classified as either typical or atypical. The classic, typical antipsychotics are primarily dopamine receptor blockers that result in several adverse effects associated with dopamine blockade, including hypotension, anticholinergic effects, and extrapyramidal effects. Newer, atypical antipsychotics block both dopamine receptors and serotonin receptors. This action may help alleviate some of the unpleasant neurological effects of the typical antipsychotics.

THERAPEUTIC ACTIONS AND INDICATIONS

It is not understood which of the several actions of antipsychotics corrects the manifestations of schizophrenia. The typical antipsychotic drugs block dopamine receptors, preventing the stimulation of the postsynaptic neurons by dopamine. They also depress the RAS, limiting the stimuli coming into the brain; and they have anticholinergic, antihistamine, and alpha-adrenergic blocking effects, all related to the blocking of the dopamine receptor sites. Atypical antipsychotics block both dopamine receptor and serotonin receptors. This action may help alleviate some of the unpleasant neurological effects and depression associated with the typical antipsychotics.

The antipsychotics are indicated for schizophrenia, as well as for manifestations of other psychotic disorders including hyperactivity, combative behavior, agitation in the elderly, and severe behavioral problems in children (short-term control).

CONTRAINDICATIONS/CAUTIONS

Antipsychotic drugs are contraindicated in the presence of underlying diseases that could be exacerbated by the dopamine-blocking effects of these drugs. They are also contraindicated in the following conditions: central nervous system (CNS) depression, circulatory collapse, Parkinson's disease, coronary disease, severe hypotension, bone marrow suppression, and blood dyscrasias.

Caution should be used in the presence of medical conditions that could be exacerbated by the anticholinergic effects of the drugs such as glaucoma, peptic ulcer, and urinary or intestinal obstruction. In addition, care should be taken in patients with seizure disorders, because the threshold for seizures could be lowered; thyrotoxicosis, because of the possibility of severe neurosensitivity; and active alcoholism because of potentiation of CNS depression.

Other situations that warrant caution include myelography within the last 24 hours or scheduled for the next 48 hours, because severe neuron reaction to the dye can occur, and pregnancy or lactation because of the potential of adverse effects on the fetus or neonate. Because children are more apt to develop dystonia from the drugs, which could confuse the diagnosis of Reye's syndrome, caution should be used with children less than 12 years who have CNS infections or chicken pox. The use of antipsychotics may result in bone marrow suppression, leading to blood dyscrasias, so care should be taken with patients who are immunosuppressed or suffering from cancer.

ADVERSE EFFECTS

The adverse effects associated with the antipsychotic drugs are related to their dopamine-blocking, anticholinergic, antihistamine, and alpha-adrenergic activities. The most common CNS effects are sedation, weakness, tremor, drowsiness, and extrapyramidal effects—pseudoparkinsonism, dystonia, akathisia, tardive dyskinesia, and potentially irreversible neuroleptic malignant syndrome. Anticholinergic effects include dry mouth, nasal congestion, flushing, constipation, urinary retention, sexual impotence, glaucoma, blurred vision, and photophobia. Cardiovascular (CV) effects, which are probably related to the dopamine-blocking effects, include hypotension, orthostatic hypotension, cardiac arrhythmias, congestive heart failure, and pulmonary edema.

Respiratory effects such as laryngospasm, dyspnea, and bronchospasm may also occur. The phenothiazines (chlorpromazine, fluphenazine, prochlorperazine, promethazine, and thioridazine) often turn the urine pink to reddish-brown as a result of their excretion. Although this effect may cause great patient concern, it has no clinical significance. In addition, bone marrow suppression is a possibility with some antipsychotic agents.

CLINICALLY IMPORTANT DRUG–DRUG INTERACTIONS

Because the combination of antipsychotics with beta blockers may lead to an increase in the effect of both drugs, this combination should be avoided if possible. Antipsychotic–alcohol combinations result in an increased risk of CNS depression, and antipsychotic–anticholinergic combinations lead to increased anticholinergic effects, so dosage adjustments are necessary. Patients who take either of these combinations should be monitored closely for adverse effects, and supportive measures should be provided.

DATA LINK

Data link to the antipsychotic/neuroleptic drugs, listed in Table 20-1, in your nursing drug guide.

CASE STUDY

Chronic Schizophrenia and Long-term Therapy with Phenothiazines

PRESENTATION

B. A., a 36-year-old, single, professional woman, was diagnosed with chronic schizophrenia when she was a senior in high school. Her condition has been well controlled with phenothiazines, and she is able to maintain steady employment, live in her own home, and carry on a fairly active social life. At her last evaluation, she appeared to be developing bone marrow suppression and her physician decided to try to taper the drug. As the dosage was being lowered, B. A. became withdrawn and listless, missed several days of work, and canceled most of her social engagements. Afraid of interacting with people, she stayed in bed most of the time. She reported having thoughts of death and paranoid ideation about her neighbors that she was beginning to think might be true.

CRITICAL THINKING QUESTIONS

What nursing interventions are appropriate at this time? What supportive measures might be useful to help B. A. cope with this crisis and allow her to function normally again? What happens to brain chemistry after long-term therapy with phenothiazines? What drug options should be tried? Are there any other options that might be useful?

DISCUSSION

Schizophrenia is not a disorder that can be resolved with proper counseling. B. A., an educated woman with a long history of taking phenothiazines, realizes the necessity of drug therapy to correct the chemical imbalance in her brain. She may need an antipsychotic with a high potency to return her to the level of functioning she had reached before experiencing this setback. Her knowledge of her individual responses can be used to help select an appropriate drug and dosage. Her experiences may also facilitate her care planning and new drug regimen.

B. A. will need support to cope with problems at work from her inability to go in to work, to cope with feelings about not meeting her social obligations, and to find the motivation to get up and become active again. She might do well with behavior modification techniques that give her some control over her activities and allow her to use her knowledge and experience with her own situation to her advantage in forming a new medical regimen. She may need support in explaining her problem to her employer and her social contacts in ways that will avoid the prejudice associated with mental illness and will allow her every opportunity to return to her regular routine as soon as she can.

Because it may take several months to find the drug or drugs that will bring B. A. back to a point of stabilization, it is important to have a consistent, reliable health care team in place to support her through this stabilization period. She should have a reliable contact person to call when she has questions and when she needs support.

NURSING CONSIDERATIONS
for patients receiving antipsychotic/neuroleptic drugs

Assessment

HISTORY. Screen for the following: any known allergies to these drugs, severe CNS depression, circulatory collapse, coronary disease, brain damage, severe hypotension, glaucoma, respiratory depression, urinary or intestinal obstruction, thyrotoxicosis, seizure disorder, bone marrow suppression, pregnancy and lactation, and myelography within the past 24 hours or scheduled in the next 48 hours. In children less than 12 years, screen for CNS infections.

PHYSICAL ASSESSMENT. Include screening for baseline status before beginning therapy and for any potential adverse effects. Assess the following: temperature; skin color and lesions; CNS orientation, affect, reflexes, and bilateral grip strength; bowel sounds and reported output; pulse, auscultation, and blood pressure, including orthostatic blood pressure; respiration rate and adventitious sounds; and urinary output. Obtain liver and renal function tests, thyroid function tests, and CBC.

Nursing Diagnoses

The patient receiving antipsychotics may have the following nursing diagnoses related to drug therapy:

- Impaired physical mobility related to extrapyramidal effects
- Alteration in cardiac output related to hypotensive effects
- Potential for injury related to CNS effects and sedation

- Alteration in urinary elimination related to anticholinergic effects
- Knowledge deficit regarding drug therapy

Implementation

- Do not allow the patient to crush or chew sustained-release capsules, *which will decrease their absorption and effectiveness.*
- If the patient receives parenteral forms, keep the patient recumbent for 30 minutes *to reduce the risk of orthostatic hypotension.*
- Consider warning the patient or the patient's guardians about the risk of development of tardive dyskinesias with continued use *so they are prepared for that neurological change.*
- Monitor CBC *to arrange to discontinue the drug at signs of bone marrow suppression.*
- Arrange for gradual dose reduction after long-term use. *Abrupt withdrawal has been associated with gastritis, nausea, vomiting, dizziness, arrhythmias, and insomnia.*
- Provide positioning of legs and arms *to decrease the discomfort of dyskinesias.*
- Provide sugarless candy and ice chips *to increase secretions* and frequent mouth care *if dry mouth is a problem.*
- Encourage the patient to void before taking a dose *if urinary hesitancy or retention is a problem.*
- Provide safety measures such as side rails and assistance with ambulation if CNS effects or orthostatic hypotension occur *to prevent patient injury.*
- Provide for vision examinations *to determine ocular changes and arrange appropriate dosage change.*
- Provide thorough patient teaching, including drug name, prescribed dosage, measures for avoidance of adverse effects, warning signs that may indicate possible problems, and the need for monitoring and evaluation *to enhance patient knowledge about drug therapy and to promote compliance* (see Patient Teaching Checklist: Antipsychotic/Neuroleptic Drugs). Warn patients that urine may have a pink to reddish-brown color.
- Offer support and encouragement *to help patients cope with their drug regimen.*

Evaluation

- Monitor patient response to the drug (decrease in signs and symptoms of psychotic disorder).
- Monitor for adverse effects (sedation, anticholinergic effects, hypotension, extrapyramidal effects, bone marrow suppression).
- Evaluate effectiveness of teaching plan (patient can give the drug name and dosage, possible adverse effects to watch for, specific measures to prevent adverse effects, and warning signs to report).
- Monitor the effectiveness of comfort measures and compliance with the regimen (see Nursing Care Guide: Antipsychotic/Neuroleptic Drugs).

ANTIMANIC DRUG

Mania, the opposite of depression, occurs in individuals with bipolar disorders—a period of depression followed by a period of mania. The cause of mania is not understood, but it is thought to be an overstimulation of certain neurons in the brain. The mainstay for treatment of mania is lithium.

Lithium salts (*Lithane, Lithotabs*) are taken orally for the management of manic episodes and prevention of future episodes. These very toxic drugs can cause severe CNS, renal, and pulmonary problems that may lead to death. Despite the potential for serious adverse effects, lithium is used with caution, because it is consistently effective in the treatment of mania. The therapeutically effective serum level is 0.5 to 1.2 mEq/L.

THERAPEUTIC ACTIONS AND INDICATIONS

Lithium functions in several ways. It alters sodium transport in nerve and muscle cells; inhibits the release of norepinephrine and dopamine, but not serotonin, from stimulated neurons; increases the intraneuronal stores of norepinephrine and dopamine slightly; and decreases intraneuronal content of second messengers. This last mode of action may allow it to selectively modulate the responsiveness of hyperactive neurons that might contribute to the manic state. Although the biochemical actions of lithium are known, the exact mechanism of action in decreasing the manifestations of mania are not understood.

Lithium is indicated for the treatment of manic episodes of manic-depressive or bipolar illness and for maintenance therapy to prevent or diminish the frequency and intensity of future manic episodes. This agent is currently being investigated for the improvement of neutrophil counts in patients with cancer chemotherapy-induced neutropenia and as prophylaxis of cluster headaches and migraine headaches.

CONTRAINDICATIONS/CAUTIONS

Lithium is contraindicated in the presence of hypersensitivity to lithium or tartrazine (found in *Lithane*). In addition, it is contraindicated in the following conditions: significant renal or cardiac disease that could be exacerbated by the toxic effects of the drug; a history of leukemia; and metabolic disorders, including sodium depletion, dehydration, and diuretic use, because lithium depletes sodium reabsorption and severe hyponatremia may occur. (Hyponatremia leads to lithium retention and toxicity.) Pregnancy

PATIENT TEACHING CHECKLIST

Antipsychotic/Neuroleptic Drugs

Create customized patient teaching materials for a specific antipsychotic/neuroleptic drug from your CD-ROM. Your patient teaching should stress the following points for drugs within this class:

Antipsychotic/neuroleptic drugs affect the activities of certain chemicals in your brain and are used to treat certain mental disorders. Drugs in this group should be taken exactly as prescribed. Because these drugs affect many body systems, it is important that you undergo medical evaluation regularly.

Common effects of these drugs include:

- Dizziness, drowsiness, and fainting—Avoid driving or performing hazardous tasks or delicate tasks that require concentration if these occur. Change position slowly. The dizziness usually passes after 1 to 2 weeks of drug use.
- Pink or reddish urine (with phenothiazines)—These drugs sometimes causes the urine to change color. Do not be alarmed by this change; it does not mean that your urine contains blood.
- Sensitivity to light—Bright light might hurt your eyes and sunlight might burn your skin more easily. Wear sunglasses and protective clothing when you must be out in the sun.
- Constipation—Consult with your health care provider if this becomes a problem.

Report any of the following conditions to your health care provider: sore throat, fever, rash, tremors, weakness, and vision changes.

Tell any doctor, nurse, or other health care provider that you are taking this drug.

Keep this drug and all medications out of the reach of children.

Avoid the use of alcohol or other depressants while you are taking this drug. You also may want to limit your use of caffeine if you have increased tension or insomnia.

Avoid the use of over-the-counter drugs while you are on this drug. Many of them contain ingredients that could interfere with the effectiveness of your drug. If you feel that you need one of these preparations, consult with your health care provider about the most appropriate choice.

Take this drug exactly as prescribed. If you run out of medicine or find that you cannot take your drug for any reason, consult your health care provider. After this drug has been used for a period of time, additional adverse effects may occur if it is suddenly stopped. This drug will need to be tapered over time.

This Teaching Checklist reflects general patient teaching guidelines. It is not meant to be a substitute for drug-specific teaching information, which is available in nursing drug guides.

and lactation are also contraindications because of the potential for adverse effects on the fetus and neonate.

Caution should be used in any condition that could alter sodium levels such as protracted diarrhea or excessive sweating; with suicidal or impulsive patients; and with infection with fever, which could be exacerbated by the toxic effects of the drug.

ADVERSE EFFECTS

The adverse effects associated with lithium are directly related to serum levels of the drug.

- Serum levels of less than 1.5 mEq/L: CNS problems, including lethargy, slurred speech, muscle weakness, and fine tremor; polyuria, which relates to renal toxicity; and beginning of gastric toxicity, with nausea, vomiting, and diarrhea.
- Serum levels of 1.5 to 2.0 mEq/L: intensification of all of the above reactions, with ECG changes.
- Serum levels of 2.0 to 2.5 mEq/L: possible progression of CNS effects to ataxia, clonic movements, hyperreflexia, and seizures; possible CV effects such as severe ECG changes and hypotension; large output of dilute urine secondary to renal toxicity; fatalities secondary to pulmonary toxicity.
- Serum levels above 2.5 mEq/L: complex multiorgan toxicity occurs, with a real risk of death.

CLINICALLY IMPORTANT DRUG–DRUG INTERACTIONS

Some drug–drug combinations should be avoided. A lithium-haloperidol combination may result in an encephalopathic syndrome, consisting of weakness, lethargy, confusion, tremors, extrapyramidal symptoms, leukocytosis, and irreversible brain damage.

NURSING CARE GUIDE
Antipsychotic Neuroleptic Drugs

Assessment	***Nursing Diagnoses***	***Implementation***	***Evaluation***
HISTORY Allergies to any of these drugs; CNS depression; CV disease; pregnancy or lactation; myelography; glaucoma; hypotension; thyrotoxicosis; seizures; CNS infections in children <12.	Impaired physical mobility related to extrapyramidal effects Potential for injury related to CNS effects Alteration in cardiac output related to CV effects Alteration in urinary elimination related to anticholinergic effects Knowledge deficit regarding drug therapy	Give drug in evening; do not allow patient to chew or crush sustained release capsules. Provide comfort and safety measures: void before dosing; side rails; sugarless lozenges, mouth care; safety measures if CNS effects occur; positioning to relieve dyskinesia discomfort; taper dose after long-term therapy. Provide support and reassurance to help patient cope with drug effects. Provide patient teaching regarding drug, dosage, adverse effects, conditions to report, precautions.	Evaluate drug effects: relief of signs and symptoms of psychotic disorders. Monitor for adverse effects: sedation, dizziness, insomnia; anticholinergic effects; extrapyramidal effects; bone marrow depression; skin rash. Monitor for drug–drug interactions as indicated for each drug. Evaluate effectiveness of patient teaching program. Evaluate effectiveness of comfort and safety measures.
PHYSICAL EXAMINATION CV: BP, P, orthostatic BP CNS: orientation, affect, reflexes, vision Skin: color, lesions, texture Respiratory: respiration, adventitious sounds GI: abdominal examination, bowel sounds Laboratory tests: thyroid, liver and renal function tests, CBC			

If lithium is given with carbamazepine, increased CNS toxicity may occur, and a lithium-iodide salt combination results in an increased risk of hypothyroidism. Patients who receive either of these combinations should be monitored carefully. In addition, a thiazide diuretic–lithium combination increases the risk of lithium toxicity because of the loss of sodium and increased retention of lithium. If this combination is used, the dosage of lithium should be decreased and the patient monitored closely.

In the following instances, the serum lithium level should be followed closely and appropriate dosage adjustments made. With the combination of lithium and some urine alkalinizing drugs, including antacids and tromethamine, there is a possibility of decreased effectiveness of lithium. If lithium is combined with indomethacin and some NSAIDs, higher plasma levels of lithium occur.

DATA LINK

Data link to the following antimanic drugs in your nursing drug guide:

ANTIMANIC DRUG

Name	Brand Names	Usual Indications
lithium	*Lithane, Lithotabs*	Treatment of manic episodes of manic-depressive illness; maintenance therapy to prevent or diminish the frequency and intensity of future manic episodes.

NURSING CONSIDERATIONS for patients receiving an antimanic drug

Assessment

HISTORY. Screen for the following: any known allergies to lithium or tartrazine; renal or CV disease; dehydration; sodium depletion, use of diuretics, protracted sweating, or diarrhea; suicidal or impulsive patients with severe depression; pregnancy or lactation; and infection with fever.

PHYSICAL ASSESSMENT. Include screening for baseline status before beginning therapy and for any potential adverse effects. Assess the following: temperature; skin color and lesions; CNS orientation, affect, and reflexes; bowel sounds and reported output; pulse, auscultation, and blood pressure, including orthostatic blood pressure; respiration rate and adventitious sounds; and urinary output. Obtain liver and renal function tests, thyroid function tests, CBC, and baseline ECG.

Nursing Diagnoses

The patient receiving lithium may have the following nursing diagnoses related to drug therapy:

- Pain related to gastrointestinal (GI), CNS, vision effects
- Potential for injury related to CNS effects
- Alteration in urinary elimination related to renal toxic effects
- Alteration in thought processes related to CNS effects
- Knowledge deficit regarding drug therapy

Implementation

- Give the drug cautiously, with daily monitoring of serum lithium levels to patients with significant renal or CV disease, dehydration, or debilitation, as well as those taking diuretics *to monitor for toxic levels and to arrange for appropriate dosage adjustment.*
- Give the drug with food or milk *to alleviate GI irritation if GI upset is severe.*
- Arrange to decrease dose following acute manic episodes. *Lithium tolerance is greatest during acute episodes and decreases when the acute episode is over.*
- Ensure that the patient maintains adequate intake of salt and fluid *to decrease toxicity.*
- Monitor the patient's clinical status closely, especially during the initial stages of therapy *to provide appropriate supportive management as needed.*
- Arrange for small frequent meals, sugarless lozenges to suck, and frequent mouth care *to increase secretions and decrease discomfort as needed.*
- Provide safety measures such as side rails and assistance with ambulation if CNS effects occur *to prevent patient injury.*
- Provide thorough patient teaching, including drug name, prescribed dosage, measures for avoidance of adverse effects, warning signs that may indicate possible problems, and the need to avoid pregnancy while taking lithium *to enhance patient knowledge about drug therapy and to promote compliance.*
- Offer support and encouragement *to help the patient cope with the drug regimen.*

Evaluation

- Monitor patient response to the drug (decreased manifestations and frequency of manic episodes).
- Monitor for adverse effects (CV toxicity, renal toxicity, GI upset, respiratory complications).
- Evaluate the effectiveness of the teaching plan (patient can give the drug name and dosage and describe the possible adverse effects to watch for, specific measures to help avoid adverse effects, warning signs to report, and the need to avoid pregnancy).
- Monitor the effectiveness of comfort measures and compliance with the regimen.

CENTRAL NERVOUS SYSTEM (CNS) STIMULANTS

CNS stimulants are used clinically to treat both attention-deficit disorders and narcolepsy. Paradoxically, these drugs calm hyperkinetic children and help them focus on one activity for a longer period. They also redirect and excite the arousal stimuli from the RAS (see Figures 20-1 and 20-2).

The CNS stimulants that are used to treat attention-deficit disorder and narcolepsy include the following:

- Methylphenidate (*Ritalin*), which is a very commonly used drug for the treatment of attention-deficit disorders and other behavioral syndromes associated with hyperactivity, as well as narcolepsy
- Dextroamphetamine (*Dexedrine*), an oral drug, which is also used as short-term adjunctive therapy for exogenous obesity
- Modafinil (*ProVigil*), a new drug, which is only approved for use in treating narcolepsy. It is not associated with many of the systemic stimulatory effects of some of the other CNS stimulants.
- Pemoline (*Cylert*), which is only approved for use in attention-deficit disorders and other behavioral syndromes associated with hyperactivity. It is not associated with many of the systemic stimulatory effects of amphetamine-type stimulatory drugs.

THERAPEUTIC ACTIONS AND INDICATIONS

The CNS stimulants act as cortical and RAS stimulants, possibly by increasing the release of catecholamines from presynaptic neurons, leading to an increase in stimulation of the postsynaptic neurons.

CULTURAL CONSIDERATIONS

Antipsychotic Drugs

The ways in which patients in certain cultural groups respond to antipsychotic drugs—either physiologically or emotionally—may vary. Therefore, when a pharmacologic regimen is incorporated into overall patient care, health care providers must consider and respect an individual patient's cultural beliefs and needs.

- African Americans respond more rapidly to antipsychotic medications and have a greater risk of developing disfiguring adverse effects, such as tardive dyskinesia. Consequently, these patients should be started off at the lowest possible dose and monitored closely. African Americans also display a higher red blood cell plasma lithium ratio than Caucasians and report more adverse effects from lithium therapy. These patients should be monitored closely because they have a higher potential for lithium toxicity at standard therapeutic ranges.
- Patients in Asian countries, such as India, Turkey, Malaysia, China, Japan, and Indonesia, receive lower doses of neuroleptics and lithium to achieve the same therapeutic response as seen in patients in the United States. This may be due to these individuals' lower body mass as well as metabolic differences, and may have implications for dosing protocols for patients in these ethnic groups who undergo therapy in the United States.
- Arab American patients metabolize antipsychotic medications more slowly than Asian Americans and may require lower doses to achieve the same therapeutic effects as Caucasians.
- Individuals in some cultures use herbs and other folk remedies, and the use of herbs may interfere with the metabolism of Western medications. The nurse should carefully assess for herbal use and be aware of potential interactions.

The paradoxical effect of calming hyperexcitability through CNS stimulation seen in attention-deficit syndrome is believed to be related to an increased stimulation of an immature RAS, leading to the ability to be more selective in response to incoming stimuli.

The CNS stimulants are indicated for the treatment of attention-deficit syndromes, including behavioral syndromes characterized by hyperactivity and distractibility, as well as narcolepsy.

CONTRAINDICATIONS/CAUTIONS

The CNS stimulants are contraindicated in the presence of known allergy to the drug. Other contraindications include the following conditions: marked anxiety, agitation, or tension, or severe fatigue or

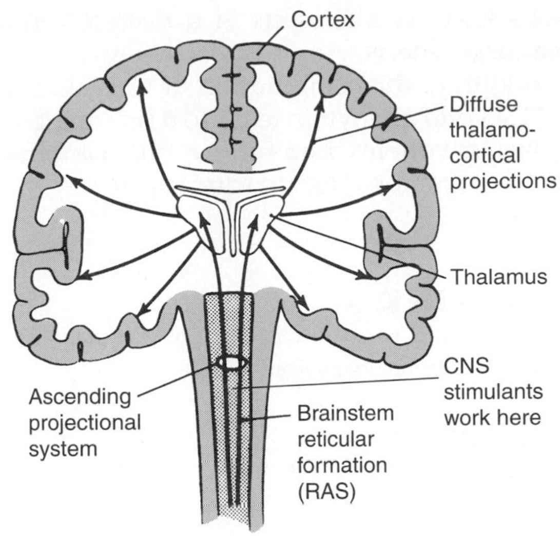

FIGURE 20-2. Site of action of the CNS stimulants in the RAS.

glaucoma, which could be exacerbated by the CNS stimulation caused by these drugs; cardiac disease, which could be aggravated by the stimulatory effects of these drugs; and pregnancy and lactation, because of the potential for adverse effects on the fetus and neonate.

Caution should be used in the presence of a history of seizures, which could be potentiated by the CNS stimulation; with a history of drug dependence, including alcoholism, because these drugs may result in physical and psychological dependence; and with hypertension, which could be exacerbated by the stimulatory effects of these drugs.

ADVERSE EFFECTS

The adverse effects associated with these drugs are related to the CNS stimulation they cause. CNS effects can include nervousness, insomnia, dizziness, headache, blurred vision, and difficulty with accommodation. GI effects such as anorexia, nausea, and weight loss may occur. CV effects can include hypertension, arrhythmias, and angina. Skin rashes are a common reaction to some of these drugs. Physical and psychological dependence may also develop. Because CNS stimulants have this effect, the drugs are controlled substances.

CLINICALLY IMPORTANT DRUG–DRUG INTERACTIONS

The following two combinations of CNS stimulants with other drugs should be avoided if possible: the CNS stimulant–MAO inhibitor combination, which leads to an increased risk of adverse effects and increased toxicity, and the CNS stimulant–guanethidine combination, which results in a decrease in antihypertensive effects.

In addition, the combination of CNS stimulants with TCAs and phenytoin leads to a risk of increased drug levels. Patients who receive this combination should be monitored for toxicity.

DATA LINK

Data link to the following CNS stimulants in your nursing drug guide:

CNS STIMULANTS

Name	Brand Name	Usual Indications
dextroamphetamine	*Dexedrine*	Narcolepsy, attention-deficit disorders, behavioral syndromes, exogenous obesity
P methylphenidate	*Ritalin*	Narcolepsy, attention-deficit disorders, behavioral syndromes
modafinil	*ProVigil*	Narcolepsy
pemoline	*Cylert*	Attention-deficit disorders, behavioral syndromes

NURSING CONSIDERATIONS
for patients receiving CNS stimulants

Assessment

HISTORY. Screen for the following: any known allergies to the drug; glaucoma, anxiety, tension, fatigue, or seizure disorders; cardiac disease and hypertension; pregnancy or lactation; and a history of leukemia and drug dependency, including alcoholism.

PHYSICAL ASSESSMENT. Include screening for baseline status before beginning therapy and for any potential adverse effects. Assess the following: temperature; skin color and lesions; CNS orientation, affect, and reflexes; ophthalmic examination; bowel sounds and reported output; pulse, auscultation, and blood pressure, including orthostatic blood pressure; respiration rate and adventitious sounds; and urinary output. Obtain a CBC.

Nursing Diagnoses

The patient receiving CNS stimulants may have the following nursing diagnoses related to drug therapy:

- Alteration in thought processes related to CNS effects of the drug
- Alteration in cardiac output related to CV effects of the drug
- Risk for injury related to CNS and visual effects of the drug
- Knowledge deficit regarding drug therapy

Implementation

- Ensure proper diagnosis of behavioral syndromes and narcolepsy *because these drugs should not be used until underlying medical causes of the problem are ruled out.*
- Arrange to interrupt the drug periodically in children receiving the drug for behavioral syndromes *to determine whether symptoms recur and therapy should be continued.*
- Arrange to dispense the least amount of drug possible *to minimize the risk of overdose and abuse.*
- Administer the drug before 6 PM *to reduce the incidence of insomnia.*
- Monitor weight, CBC, and ECG *to assure early detection of adverse effects and proper interventions.*
- Consult with the school nurse or counselor *to ensure comprehensive care of school-aged children receiving CNS stimulants.*
- Provide safety measures such as side rails and assistance with ambulation if CNS effects occur, *to prevent patient injury.*
- Provide thorough patient teaching, including drug name, prescribed dosage, measures for avoidance of adverse effects, warning signs that may indicate possible problems, and the need for monitoring and evaluation *to enhance patient knowledge about drug therapy and to promote compliance.* Offer support and encouragement *to help the patient cope with the drug regimen.*

Evaluation

- Monitor patient response to the drug (decrease in manifestations of behavioral syndromes; decrease in daytime sleep and narcolepsy).
- Monitor for adverse effects (CNS stimulation, CV effects, rash, physical or psychological dependence, GI dysfunction).
- Evaluate the effectiveness of the teaching plan (patient can give the drug name and dosage, name possible adverse effects to watch for and specific measures to help avoid adverse effects, and describe the need for follow-up and evaluation).
- Monitor the effectiveness of comfort measures and compliance with the regimen.

WWW.WEB LINKS

Health care providers and patients may want to consult the following Internet sources:

Information on sleep disorders research and treatment:

http://www.uic.edu/depts/cnr/cindex.htm

NURSING CHALLENGE

School Nursing and Ritalin *Administration*

In the past several years, the number of school children who received diagnoses of attention-deficit disorder or minimum brain dysfunction and were placed on methylphenidate (*Ritalin*) has increased dramatically. Because this drug needs to be given two to three times each day, it has become the responsibility of the school nurse to dispense the drug during the day. Some school nurses have reportedly spent between 50% and 70% of their time administering these drugs and completing the necessary paperwork.

Along with the responsibility of administering the drug comes the responsibility of assessing children's response to the drug and coordinating the teacher's and health care providers' input into each individual case, including the incidence of adverse effects and the appropriateness of the drug therapy. The nurse should:

- Ensure that the proper diagnosis is made before supporting the use of the drug.
- Constantly evaluate and work with the primary health care provider to regularly challenge children without the drug to see if the drug is doing what is expected or if the child is maturing and no longer needs the drug therapy.

The school nurse will need to be prepared to be an advocate for the best therapeutic intervention for a particular child. Because long-term methylphenidate therapy is associated with many adverse effects, use of the drug should not be taken lightly.

Information on education programs, research, and other information related to mental illness:
http://www.cmhc.com

Information on mental health resources, support groups, and related information:
http://www.mhsource.com

Information on mental health related issues in the child and adolescent:
http://www.aacp.org

Information about specific diagnoses, treatment, support groups:
http://www.psyche-web.com
http://mentalhelp.net

CHAPTER SUMMARY

- Mental disorders are disorders of thought processes that may be caused by some inherent dysfunction within the brain. Psychoses are thought disorders.
- Schizophrenia, the most common psychosis, is characterized by delusions, hallucinations, and inappropriate responses to stimuli.
- Mania is a state of hyperexcitability, one extreme of bipolar disorder.
- An attention-deficit disorder is a behavioral syndrome characterized by hyperactivity and a short attention span.
- Narcolepsy is a disorder characterized by daytime sleepiness and sudden loss of wakefulness.
- Antipsychotics are dopamine-receptor blockers that are effective in helping people with mental disorders to organize thought patterns and respond appropriately to stimuli.
- Antipsychotics can cause hypotension, anticholinergic effects, sedation, and extrapyramidal effects including parkinsonism, ataxia, and tremors.
- Lithium, a membrane stabilizer, is the only effective antimanic drug. Because it is a very toxic salt, serum levels must be carefully monitored to prevent severe toxicity.
- CNS stimulants, which stimulate cortical levels and the RAS to increase RAS activity, are used to treat attention-deficit disorders and narcolepsy. These drugs improve concentration and the ability to filter and focus incoming stimuli.

BIBLIOGRAPHY

Bailey, K. (1998). *Psychotropic drug facts.* Philadelphia: Lippincott-Raven.

Bullock, B. L. (2000). *Focus on pathophysiology.* Philadelphia: Lippincott Williams & Wilkins.

Hardman, J. G., Limbird, L. E., Molinoff, P. B., Ruddon, R. W., & Gilman, A. G. (Eds.). (1996). *Goodman and Gilman's the pharmacological basis of therapeutics* (9th ed.). New York: McGraw-Hill.

Karch, A. M. (2000). *2000 Lippincott's nursing drug guide.* Philadelphia: Lippincott Williams & Wilkins.

Malseed, R. (1995). *Textbook of pharmacology and nursing care.* Philadelphia: Lippincott-Raven.

McEvoy, B. R. (Ed.). (1999). *Facts and comparisons 1999.* St. Louis: Facts and Comparisons.

Professional's guide to patient drug facts. (1999). St. Louis: Facts and Comparisons.

CHAPTER 21

Antiepileptic Agents

Drugs for treating tonic-clonic (grand mal) seizures
- Hydantoins
  - ethotoin
  - fosphenytoin
  - mephenytoin
  - P phenytoin
- Barbiturates and barbiturate-like drugs
  - phenobarbital
  - primidone
- Benzodiazepines
  - clonazepam
  - clorazepate
  - P diazepam

Drugs for treating absence (petit mal) seizures
- Succinimides
  - P ethosuximide
  - methsuximide
  - phensuximide

Other drugs for absence (petit mal) seizures
- P valproic acid
- zonisamide

Drugs for treating partial (focal) seizures
- P carbamazepine
- gabapentin
- lamotrigine
- tiagabine
- topiramate

CHAPTER OUTLINE

KEY TERMS

absence seizure
antiepileptic
convulsion
epilepsy
focal seizure
generalized seizure
grand mal seizure
petit mal seizure
seizure
status epilepticus
tonic-clonic seizure

INTRODUCTION

Epilepsy, the most prevalent of the neurological disorders, is not a single disease, but a collection of different syndromes. All of these conditions are characterized by the same feature: sudden discharge of excessive electrical energy from nerve cells located within the brain, which leads to a ***seizure.*** In some cases, this release stimulates motor nerves, resulting in ***convulsions,*** with tonic-clonic muscle contractions that have the potential to cause injury, tics, or spasms. Other discharges may stimulate autonomic or sensory nerves and cause very different effects such as a barely perceptible temporary lapse in consciousness or a sympathetic reaction.

The treatment of epilepsy varies widely, depending on the exact problem and its manifestations. The drugs that are used to manage epilepsy are called ***antiepileptics.*** These agents are sometimes referred to as anticonvulsants, but because all types of epilepsy do not involve convulsions, this term is not generally applicable. The drug of choice for any given situation depends on the type of epilepsy and patient tolerance for associated adverse effects (Table 21-1).

NATURE OF EPILEPSY

The form that a particular seizure takes depends on the location of the cells that initiate the electrical discharge and the neural pathways that are stimulated by the initial volley of electrical impulses. For the most part, epilepsy seems to be caused by abnormal neurons that are very sensitive to stimulation or over-respond for some reason. They do not appear to be

TABLE 21-1

TYPES OF SEIZURES AND THE DRUGS USED TO TREAT THEM

	Type of Seizure						
Drug	*Tonic-clonic (grand mal)*	*Absence (petit mal)*	*Myoclonic*	*Febrile*	*Status Epilepticus*	*Simple Partial (focal)*	*Complex Partial (focal)*
BARBITURATES							
phenobarbital	O	—	—	X	O	O	—
primidone	O	—		O	—	O	O
BENZODIAZEPINES							
clonazepam	—	O	X	—	—	—	—
clorazepate	—	—	—	—	—	O	O
diazepam	—	—	—	—	X	—	—
HYDANTOINS							
ethotoin	X	—	—	—	—	—	—
fosphenytoin	—	—	—	—	O	—	—
mephenytoin	O	—	O	—	—	—	—
phenytoin	X	—	—	—	X	X	X
SUCCINIMIDES							
ethosuximide	—	X	—	—	—	—	—
methsuximide	—	O	—	—	—	—	—
phensuximide	—	O	—	—	—	—	—
OTHER DRUGS							
valproic acid	—	O	X	—	—	—	—
zonisamide	—	O	—	—	—	—	—
DRUGS FOR FOCAL SEIZURES							
carbamazepine	X	—	—	—	—	X	X
gabapentin	—	—	—	—	—	O	O
lamotrigine	—	—	—	—	—	O	O
tiagabine	—	O	—	—	—	O	O
topiramate	—	—	—	—	—	O	O

X = primary treatment; a drug of choice
O = adjunctive therapy or used when unresponsive to other treatments
— = not a use

different from other neurons in any other way. Seizures caused by these abnormal cells are called primary seizures because no underlying cause can be identified. In some cases, however, outside factors—head injury, drug overdose, environmental exposure, and so on—may precipitate seizures. Such seizures are often referred to as secondary seizures.

Classification of Seizures

Correct diagnosis of seizure type is very important for determining the correct medication to prevent future seizures while causing the fewest problems and adverse effects. Seizures may be grouped into two main types, and they are further classified within these two categories.

GENERALIZED SEIZURES

Generalized seizures begin in one area of the brain and rapidly spread throughout both hemispheres of the brain. Patients who have a generalized seizure usually experience a loss of consciousness resulting from this massive electrical activity throughout the brain. Generalized seizures are further classified into the following five types:

- ***Tonic-clonic seizures,*** formerly known as a ***grand mal seizures,*** involve dramatic tonic-clonic muscle contractions, loss of consciousness, and a recovery period characterized by confusion and exhaustion.
- ***Absence seizures,*** formerly known as ***petit mal seizures,*** involve abrupt, brief (3–5 seconds) periods of loss of consciousness. Absence seizures occur commonly in children and frequently disappear at puberty.
- Myoclonic seizures involve short, sporadic periods of muscle contractions that last for several minutes. They are relatively rare and are often secondary seizures.
- Febrile seizures are related to very high fevers and usually involve convulsions. Febrile seizures most frequently occur in children and are usually self limiting and do not reappear.
- ***Status epilepticus,*** potentially the most dangerous of seizure conditions, is a state in which seizures rapidly recur again and again.

PARTIAL SEIZURES

Partial seizures, which are also called ***focal seizures,*** involve one area of the brain and do not spread throughout the entire organ. The presenting symptoms depend on exactly where the excessive electrical discharge is occurring in the brain. Partial seizures can be further classified as follows:

- Simple partial seizures occur in a single area of the brain and may involve a single muscle movement or sensory alteration.
- Complex partial seizures involve complex sensory changes such as hallucinations, mental distortion, changes in personality, loss of consciousness, and social inhibitions. Motor changes may include involuntary urination, chewing motions, diarrhea, and so on. The onset of complex partial seizures usually occurs by the late teens.

DRUGS FOR TREATING TONIC-CLONIC (GRAND MAL) SEIZURES

Various drugs are used to treat tonic-clonic (grand mal) seizures. Drugs that are used to treat generalized seizures stabilize the nerve membranes by blocking channels in the cell membrane or altering receptor sites. Because they work generally on the central nervous system (CNS), sedation and other CNS effects often result. In particular, the drugs that are indicated for tonic-clonic seizures—the hydantoins and phenobarbital and primidone—affect the entire brain and reduce the chance of sudden electrical outburst. Associated adverse effects are often related to total brain stabilization (Figure 21-1).

Hydantoins

The hydantoins stabilize nerve membranes and limit the spread of excitability from the initiating focus (see Figure 21-1). Because hydantoins are generally less sedating than many other antiepileptics, they may be the drugs of choice in patients who are not willing to tolerate sedation and drowsiness. They do have significant adverse effects (e.g., severe liver toxicity). In many situations, less toxic drugs (e.g., the benzodiazepines) have replaced them.

The hydantoins include the following agents:

- Phenytoin (*Dilantin*), the prototype hydantoin, is used in the treatment of tonic-clonic seizures and status epilepticus as well as in the prevention and treatment of seizures following neurosurgery. It is available in oral and parenteral forms.
- Ethotoin (*Peganone*) is used to control tonic-clonic and myoclonic seizures.
- Fosphenytoin (*Cerebyx*) is used for short-term control of status epilepticus and to prevent seizures following neurosurgery.
- Mephenytoin (*Mesantoin*) is used for the treatment of tonic-clonic, myoclonic, and partial (focal) seizures in patients who do not respond to less toxic antiepileptic agents. This drug has been associated

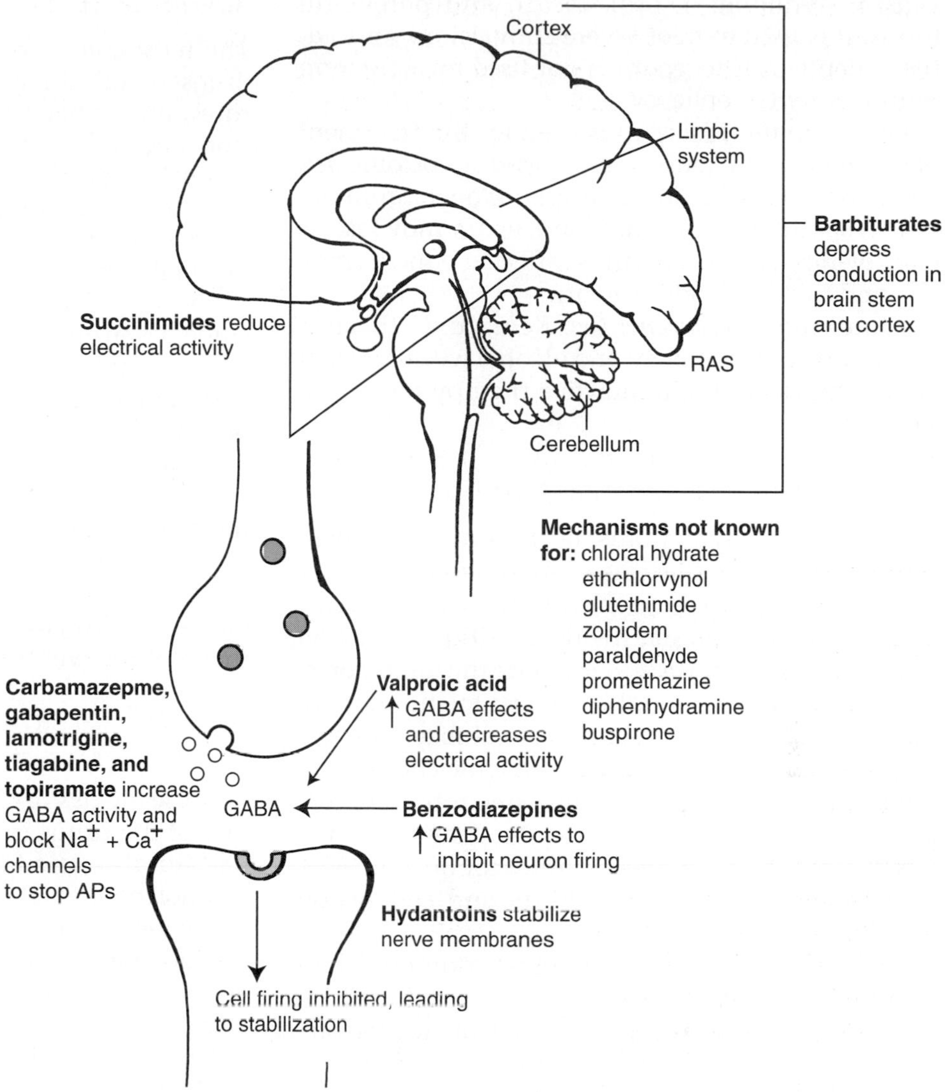

FIGURE 21-1. Sites of action of drugs used to treat various types of epilepsy.

with severe hepatic toxicity, bone marrow suppression, and often unacceptable dermatologic reactions.

Barbiturates and Barbiturate-Like Drugs

Phenobarbital (*Solfoton, Luminal*), which is available in oral and parenteral forms, is used for the emergency control of status epilepticus and acute seizures associated with eclampsia, tetanus, and so on. In addition, it is used orally for the long-term management of tonic-clonic and cortical focal seizures and can be very effective in treatment of simple partial seizures.

Primidone (*Mysoline*), which is structurally very similar to phenobarbital, is an alternate choice in the treatment of tonic-clonic or partial seizures. It tends to have a longer half-life than phenobarbital and is available only in an oral form. Primidone may be combined with other agents in treating seizures that cannot be controlled by any other antiepileptic.

Benzodiazepines

The benzodiazepines may potentiate the effects of gamma aminobutyric acid, an inhibitory neurotransmitter that stabilizes nerve cell membranes. These drugs, which appear to act primarily in the limbic system and the reticular activating system (RAS), also cause muscle relaxation and relieve anxiety without affecting cortical functioning substantially. In general, these drugs have limited toxicity and are well tolerated by most people. (See Chapter 18 for use of benzodiazepines as sedatives and anxiolytics.) The benzodiazepines described below are used as antiepileptics.

Diazepam (*Valium*), the prototype benzodiazepine, is useful in relieving tension, anxiety, and muscle spasm. Available in oral, rectal, and parenteral forms, it is used to treat severe convulsions and status epilepticus. Diazepam is not used for long-term management of epilepsy.

Clonazepam (*Klonopin*) is used for the treatment of absence (petit mal) seizures and myoclonic seizures. Patients who do not respond to succinimides may respond to this drug. Clonazepam may lose its effectiveness within 3 months (affected patients may respond to dosage adjustment).

Clorazepate (*Tranxene, Gen-Xene,* and others) is also indicated for anxiety and alcohol withdrawal. It is sometimes used as adjunctive therapy for partial seizures.

THERAPEUTIC ACTIONS AND INDICATIONS

In general, the hydantoins, barbiturates, and benzodiazepines all stabilize nerve membranes throughout the CNS to decrease excitability and hyperexcitability to stimulation. By decreasing conduction through nerve pathways, they reduce the tonic-clonic, muscular, and emotional responses to stimulation. Both hydantoins and barbiturates stabilize the nerve membrane directly by influencing ionic channels in the cell membrane. Specifically, phenobarbital depresses conduction in the lower brainstem and the cerebral cortex and depresses motor conduction. Benzodiazepines decrease excitability and conduction (see Figure 21-1).

Several drugs in three groups—hydantoins, barbiturates, and benzodiazepines—are indicated for tonic-clonic seizures and status epilepticus, for prevention of seizures that occur following neurosurgery, and for adjunctive therapy for other seizure disorders or sedation and muscle relaxation (varies with drug).

CONTRAINDICATIONS/CAUTIONS

Hydantoins, barbiturates, and benzodiazepines are generally contraindicated in the presence of allergy to any of these drugs. Many of these agents are associated with specific birth defects and should not be used in pregnancy unless the risk of seizures outweighs the potential risk to the fetus. In such cases, they should be given only if the mother has been informed of the potential risks. Other contraindications include lactation, because these drugs cross into breast milk and may cause adverse effects on the neonate, and coma, depression, or psychoses that could be exacerbated by the generalized CNS depression.

Caution should be used with elderly or debilitated patients who may respond adversely to the CNS depression and those patients with impaired renal or liver function that may interfere with drug metabolism and excretion.

ADVERSE EFFECTS

The most common adverse effects associated with drugs in all three groups—hydantoins, barbiturates, and benzodiazepines—relate to CNS depression and its effects on body function: depression, confusion, drowsiness, lethargy, fatigue, constipation, dry mouth, anorexia, cardiac arrhythmias and changes in blood pressure, urinary retention, and loss of libido.

Specific adverse effects with the hydantoins include severe liver toxicity, bone marrow suppression, gingival hyperplasia, and potentially serious dermatologic reactions (e.g., hirsutism, coarsening of facial skin), which are all directly related to cellular toxicity.

In addition, benzodiazepines and phenobarbital may be associated with physical dependence and withdrawal syndrome. Phenobarbital has also been linked to severe dermatologic reactions and development of drug tolerance related to changes in drug metabolism over time.

CLINICALLY IMPORTANT DRUG–DRUG INTERACTIONS

Because the risk of CNS depression is increased when any of the drugs in the three groups—hydantoins, barbiturates, and benzodiazepines—are taken with alcohol, patients should be advised not to drink alcohol while they are taking these agents. In addition, the individual drugs are associated with a wide variety of drug–drug interactions. Therefore, a drug reference should be reviewed carefully before any drug is added or withdrawn from a therapeutic regimen that involves any of these drugs.

DATA LINK

Data link to the following hydantoins, barbiturates, and benzodiazepines in your nursing drug guide:

DRUGS FOR TREATING TONIC-CLONIC (GRAND MAL) SEIZURES

Name	Brand Name(s)	Usual Indication(s)
HYDANTOINS		
ethotoin	*Peganone*	Tonic-clonic (grand mal) and psychomotor seizures
fosphenytoin	*Cerebyx*	Short-term control of status epilepticus, prevention of seizures following neurosurgery
mephenytoin	*Mesantoin*	Tonic-clonic (grand mal), psychomotor, and partial (focal) seizures
P phenytoin	*Dilantin*	Tonic-clonic (grand mal) seizures, status epilepticus prevention, and treatment of seizures following neurosurgery

BARBITURATES AND BARBITURATE-LIKE DRUGS		
phenobarbital	*Solfoton, Luminal*	Sedative/hypnotic, tonic-clonic (grand mal) seizures, status epilepticus, cortical focal seizures, simple partial seizures
primidone	*Mysilon*	Tonic-clonic (grand mal), partial, and refractory seizures
BENZODIAZEPINES		
clonazepam	*Klonopin*	Absence (petit mal) and myoclonic seizures
clorazepate	*Tranxene, Gen-Xene*	Anxiety, alcohol withdrawal, adjunct therapy in the treatment of partial seizures
P diazepam	*Valium*	Relieving tension, anxiety; muscle spasm; short-term treatment of severe convulsions, status epilepticus

NURSING CONSIDERATIONS for patients receiving hydantoins

See Chapter 18 for nursing considerations for patients receiving barbiturates or benzodiazepines.

Assessment

HISTORY. Screen for the following: any known allergies to these drugs; cardiac arrhythmias, hypotension, diabetes, coma, psychoses; pregnancy and lactation; and renal or hepatic dysfunction. Obtain a description of seizures, including onset, aura, duration, and recovery.

PHYSICAL ASSESSMENT. Include screening for baseline status before beginning therapy and for any potential adverse effects. Assess the following: skin color and lesions; temperature; CNS orientation, affect, reflexes, and bilateral grip strength; bowel sounds and reported output; pulse, auscultation, and blood pressure; urinary output; and EEG, if appropriate. Assess liver and renal function tests.

Nursing Diagnoses

The patient receiving hydantoins may have the following nursing diagnoses related to drug therapy:

- Pain related to gastrointestinal (GI), CNS, genitourinary (GU) effects
- Alteration in thought processes related to CNS effects
- Potential for injury related to CNS effects
- Alteration in skin integrity related to dermatologic effects
- Knowledge deficit regarding drug therapy

Implementation

- Discontinue the drug at any sign of hypersensitivity reaction or liver dysfunction, or severe skin rash *to limit reaction and prevent potentially serious reactions.*
- Administer the drug with food *to alleviate GI irritation if GI upset is a problem.*
- Monitor for adverse effects and provide appropriate supportive care as needed *to help the patient cope with these effects.*
- Monitor for drug–drug interactions *to arrange to adjust dosages appropriately if any drug is added to or withdrawn from the drug regimen.*
- Arrange for counseling for women of childbearing age who are taking these drugs. *Because these drugs have the potential to cause serious damage to the fetus, women should understand the risk of birth defects and use barrier contraceptives to avoid pregnancy.*
- Provide thorough patient teaching, including drug name and prescribed dosage, as well as measures for avoidance of adverse effects, warning signs that may indicate possible problems, and the need for monitoring and evaluation *to enhance patient knowledge about drug therapy and to promote compliance* (see Patient Teaching Checklist: Antiepileptic Agents).
- Suggest the wearing or carrying of a Medic-Alert bracelet *to alert emergency workers and healthcare providers about the use of an antiepileptic drug.*
- Offer support and encouragement *to help the patient cope with the drug regimen.*

Evaluation

- Monitor patient response to the drug (decrease in incidence or absence of seizures; serum drug levels within the therapeutic range).
- Monitor for adverse effects (CNS changes, GI depression, urinary retention, arrhythmias, blood pressure changes, liver toxicity, bone marrow suppression, severe dermatologic reactions).
- Evaluate effectiveness of teaching plan (patient can give the drug name and dosage and name possible adverse effects to watch for, and specific measures to prevent adverse effects; patient is aware of the risk of birth defects and the need to carry information about the diagnosis and use of this drug).
- Monitor the effectiveness of comfort measures and compliance with the regimen (see Nursing Care Guide: Antiepileptic Agents [Hydantoins]).

DRUGS FOR TREATING ABSENCE (PETIT MAL) SEIZURES

Absence or petit mal seizures involve a brief, sudden and self-limiting loss of consciousness. The patient may just stare into space or may exhibit rapid blinking, which could last 3 to 5 seconds. Many people may not be aware that a seizure is happening. This type of seizure frequently occurs in children, starting

PATIENT TEACHING CHECKLIST

Antiepileptic Agents

Create customized patient teaching materials for a specific antiepileptic agent from your CD-ROM. Your patient teaching should stress the following points for drugs within this class:

Antiepileptic agents are used to stabilize abnormal cells in the brain that have been firing excessively and causing seizures. The timing of these doses is very important. To be effective, this drug must be taken regularly. Do *not* stop taking this drug suddenly. If for any reason you are unable to continue taking the drug, notify your health care provider at once. This drug must be slowly withdrawn when it is discontinued.

Common effects of these drugs include:

- Fatigue, weakness, and drowsiness—Try to space activities evenly throughout the day and allow rest periods to avoid these effects. Take safety precautions and avoid driving or operating dangerous machinery if these conditions occur.
- Headaches and difficulty sleeping—These usually disappear as your body adjusts to the drug. If they persist and become too uncomfortable, consult with your health care provider.
- GI upset, loss of appetite, and diarrhea or constipation—Taking the drug with food or eating small, frequent meals may help alleviate this problem.

Report any of the following conditions to your health care provider: skin rash, severe nausea and vomiting, impaired coordination, yellowing of the eyes or skin, fever, sore throat, personality changes, and unusual bleeding or bruising.

It is advisable to wear or carry a Medic-Alert warning so that any person who takes care of you in an emergency will know that you are taking this drug.

Tell any doctor, nurse, or other health care provider that you are taking this drug.

Keep this drug and all medications out of the reach of children.

Do not take any other drug, including over-the-counter medications and alcohol, without consulting with your health care provider. Many of these preparations interact with the drug and could cause adverse effects.

If you become pregnant or decide to become pregnant while you are taking this drug, it is important that you discuss the implications with your health care provider. Use of barrier contraceptives is recommended to avoid pregnancy.

Report and record any seizure activity that you have while you are taking this drug.

Take this drug exactly as prescribed. Regular medical follow-up, which may include blood tests, will be necessary to evaluate the effects of this drug on your body.

This Teaching Checklist reflects general patient teaching guidelines. It is not meant to be a substitute for drug-specific teaching information, which is available in nursing drug guides.

around 3 years of age, and usually disappears by puberty.

Succinimides

The drugs that are most frequently used to treat these seizures are different from the drugs used to treat or prevent tonic-clonic seizures. The succinimides and drugs that modulate the inhibitory neurotransmitter GABA are most frequently used. The succinimides include the following agents:

- Ethosuximide (*Zarontin*) is the drug of choice for treating absence seizures. It has relatively few adverse effects compared with many other antiepileptic drugs. Ethosuximide is available for oral use.
- Methsuximide (*Celontin*), another oral drug, is used to treat absence seizures that are resistant to other drugs. It has been associated with bone marrow suppression.
- Phensuximide (*Milontin*) is also used for treatment of absence seizures that are resistant to other agents.

THERAPEUTIC ACTIONS AND INDICATIONS

Although the exact mechanism of action is not understood, the succinimides suppress the abnormal electrical activity in the brain that is associated with absence seizures. The action may be related to activity in inhibitory neural pathways in the brain (see Figure 21-1).

NURSING CARE GUIDE
Antiepileptic Agents (Hydantoins)

Assessment	Nursing Diagnoses	Implementation	Evaluation
HISTORY Allergies to any of these drugs; hypotension; arrhythmias; bone marrow suppression; coma; psychoses; pregnancy and lactation; hepatic or renal dysfunction.	Pain related to GI, CNS, GU effects Potential for injury related to CNS effects Alteration in thought processes related to CNS effects Knowledge deficit regarding drug therapy Alteration in skin integrity related to dermatological effects	Discontinue drug at first sign of liver dysfunction, skin rash. Provide comfort and safety measures: positioning; give with meals; barrier contraceptives; skin care. Provide support and reassurance to cope with diagnosis and drug effects. Provide patient teaching regarding drug, dosage, drug effects, symptoms to report, need to wear medical alert information.	Evaluate drug effects: decrease in incidence and frequency of seizures; serum drug levels within therapeutic range. Monitor for adverse effects: CNS effects (multiple); bone marrow suppression; rash, skin changes; GI effects—nausea, anorexia; arrhythmias. Monitor for drug–drug interactions: increased depression with CNS depressants, alcohol; varies with individual drug. Evaluate effectiveness of patient teaching program. Evaluate effectiveness of comfort and safety measures.
PHYSICAL EXAMINATION CV: BP, P, peripheral perfusion CNS: orientation, affect, reflexes, strength, EEG Skin: color, lesions, texture, temperature GI: abdominal examination, bowel sounds Resp: respiration, adventitious sounds Laboratory tests: renal and liver function tests			

Ethosuximide, phensuximide, and methsuximide are all indicated for the control of absence seizures. Ethosuximide should be tried first, and phensuximide and methsuximide should be reserved for the treatment of such seizures in patients who are refractory to other agents because they are associated with more severe adverse effects.

CONTRAINDICATIONS/CAUTIONS

The succinimides are contraindicated in the presence of allergy to any of these drugs. Caution should be used with succinimides in the following conditions: renal or hepatic disease, which could interfere with the metabolism and excretion of these drugs and lead to toxic levels; pregnancy and lactation because of the potential of adverse effects on the fetus and neonate; and intermittent porphyria, which could be exacerbated by the adverse effects of these drugs.

ADVERSE EFFECTS

Many of the adverse effects associated with the succinimides are related to their depressing effects in the CNS, including depression, drowsiness, fatigue, ataxia, insomnia, headache, and blurred vision. GI

CASE STUDY

Antiepileptic Therapy

PRESENTATION

J. M., an athletic, 18-year-old high school senior, suffered his first seizure during math class. He seemed attentive and alert, and then he suddenly slumped to the floor and suffered a full tonic-clonic (grand mal) seizure. The other students, who were very frightened, did not know what to do. Fortunately, the teacher was familiar with seizures and quickly reacted to protect J. M. from hurting himself and to explain what was happening to the other students.

J. M. received a diagnosis of idiopathic generalized epilepsy with tonic-clonic (grand mal) seizures. The combination of phenytoin and phenobarbital that he began taking made him quite drowsy during the day. These drugs were unable to control the seizures, and he suffered three more seizures in the next month—one at school and two at home. J. M. is now undergoing reevaluation for possible drug adjustment and nursing counseling.

CRITICAL THINKING QUESTIONS

What teaching implications should be considered when meeting with J. M.? Consider his age and the setting of his first seizure. What problems may J. M. encounter in school and in athletics related to the diagnosis and the prescribed medication? Consider measures that may help him avoid some of the unpleasant side effects related to this particular drug therapy. Driving a car may be a central social focus in the life of a high school senior. What problems can be anticipated and confronted before they occur concerning laws that forbid new epileptics from driving? Develop a teaching protocol for J. M.. How will you involve the entire family in the teaching plan?

DISCUSSION

On their first meeting, it is important for the nurse to establish a trusting relationship with J. M. and his family. J. M., who is at a sensitive stage of development, requires a great deal of support and encouragement to cope with the diagnosis of epilepsy and the need for drug therapy. He may need to ventilate his feelings and concerns and discuss how he can reenter school without worrying about having a seizure in class.

Nurses should implement a thorough drug teaching program, including a description of warning signs to watch for that should be reported to a health care professional. J. M. should be encouraged to take the following preventive measures:

- Have frequent oral hygiene to protect the gums.
- Avoid operating dangerous machinery or performing tasks that require alertness while drowsy and confused.
- Pace activities as much as possible to help deal with any fatigue and malaise.
- Take the drug(s) with meals if GI upset is a problem.

This information should be given to both J. M. and to his family in written form for future reference, along with the name of a health care professional and phone number to call with questions or comments. The importance of continuous medication to suppress the seizures should be stressed. The adverse effects of many of these drugs make it difficult for some patients to remain compliant with their drug regimen.

After discussion with J. M., the nurse should meet with his family members, who also need support and encouragement to deal with his diagnosis and its implications. They need to know what seizures are, how the prescribed antiepileptic drugs affect the seizures, what they can do when seizures occur, and complete information about the drug(s) and anticipated drug effects. In addition, it is important to work with family members to try to figure out if any particular thing precipitated the seizures. In other words, was there any warning or aura? This may help with adjustment of drug dosages or avoidance of certain situations or stimuli that precipitate seizures. Family members should be encouraged to report and record any seizure activity that occurs.

Most states do not permit newly diagnosed epileptics to drive when first diagnosed and have varying regulations about the return of the driver's license after a seizure-free interval. If driving makes up a major part of J. M.'s social activities, this news may be even more unacceptable than his diagnosis. J. M. and his family should be counseled and helped to devise other ways of getting places and coping with this restriction. J. M. may be interested in referral to a support group for teens with similar problems where they can share ideas, support, and frustrations.

J. M.'s condition is a chronic one that will require continual drug therapy and evaluation. He will need periodic reteaching and should have the opportunity to ask further questions and to ventilate his feelings. J. M. should be encouraged to wear or carry a Medic-Alert tag so that emergency medical personnel are aware of his diagnosis and the medications he is taking.

depression with nausea, vomiting, anorexia, weight loss, GI pain, and constipation or diarrhea may also occur. Bone marrow suppression, including potentially fatal pancytopenia, and dermatologic reactions such as pruritus, urticaria, alopecia, and Steven-Johnson syndrome may occur as a result of direct chemical irritation of the skin and bone marrow.

CLINICALLY IMPORTANT DRUG–DRUG INTERACTIONS

Use of succinimides with primidone may cause a decrease in serum levels of primidone. Patients should be monitored and appropriate dosage adjustments made if these two agents are used together.

DATA LINK

Data link to the following succinimides in your nursing drug guide:

DRUGS FOR TREATING ABSENCE (PETIT MAL) SEIZURES: SUCCINIMIDES

Name	Brand Name	Usual Indication
P ethosuximide	*Zarontin*	Drug of choice for absence (petit mal) seizures
methsuximide	*Celontin*	Treatment of absence (petit mal) seizures in patients refractory to other agents
phensuximide	*Milontin*	Treatment of absence (petit mal) seizures in patients refractory to other agents

NURSING CONSIDERATIONS
for patients receiving succinimides

Assessment

HISTORY. Screen for the following: any known allergies to these drugs; pregnancy or lactation; renal or hepatic dysfunction; and intermittent porphyria.

PHYSICAL ASSESSMENT. Include screening for baseline status before beginning therapy and any potential adverse effects. Assess the following: temperature; skin color and lesions; CNS orientation, affect, reflexes, and bilateral grip strength; EEG if appropriate; bowel sounds and reported output; pulse, auscultation, and blood pressure; and urinary output. Check liver and renal function tests.

Nursing Diagnoses

The patient receiving succinimides may have the following nursing diagnoses related to drug therapy:

- Pain related to GI, CNS, dermatologic effects
- Alteration in thought processes related to CNS effects
- Potential for infection related to bone marrow suppression
- Alteration in skin integrity related to dermatologic effects
- Knowledge deficit regarding drug therapy

Implementation

- Administer the drug with food *to alleviate GI irritation if GI upset is a problem.*
- Monitor CBC prior to and periodically during therapy *to detect bone marrow suppression early and provide appropriate interventions.*
- Discontinue the drug if skin rash, bone marrow suppression, or unusual depression or personality changes occur *to prevent the development of more serious adverse effects.*
- Discontinue the drug slowly, and never withdraw the drug quickly *because rapid withdrawal may precipitate absence seizures.*
- Arrange for counseling for women of childbearing age who are taking these drugs. *Because these drugs have the potential to cause serious damage to the fetus, women should understand the risk of birth defects and use barrier contraceptives to avoid pregnancy.*
- Evaluate for therapeutic blood levels (40–100 μg/ml).
- Provide thorough patient teaching, including the drug name and prescribed dosage, as well as measures for avoidance of adverse effects, warning signs that may indicate possible problems, and the need for monitoring and evaluation *to enhance patient knowledge about drug therapy and to promote compliance.*
- Suggest the wearing or carrying of a Medic-Alert bracelet *to alert emergency workers and healthcare providers about the use of an antiepileptic drug.*
- Offer support and encouragement *to help the patient cope with the drug regimen.*

Evaluation

- Monitor patient response to the drug (decrease in incidence or absence of seizures; serum drug level within therapeutic range).
- Monitor for adverse effects (CNS changes, GI depression, arrhythmias, blood pressure changes, bone marrow suppression, severe dermatologic reactions).
- Evaluate the effectiveness of the teaching plan (patient can give the drug name and dosage and name possible adverse effects to watch for, and specific measures to prevent adverse effects; patient is aware of the risk of birth defects and the need to carry information about the diagnosis and use of this drug).
- Monitor the effectiveness of comfort measures and compliance with the regimen.

OTHER DRUGS FOR TREATING ABSENCE (PETIT MAL) SEIZURES

Two other drugs used in the treatment of absence seizures do not fit into a specific drug class.

One such drug is valproic acid (*Depakene*), which reduces abnormal electrical activity in the brain and may also increase GABA activity at inhibitory receptors. This agent is the drug of choice in treating myoclonic seizures. Because it is sometimes associated with hepatic toxicity and because other agents may have fewer adverse effects, valproic acid is a second choice drug for the treatment of absence seizures. It

NURSING CHALLENGE

Helping Patients Deal With a Diagnosis of Epilepsy

Epilepsy, with its stigma, is frightening to people who know little about the disease. This condition has long been associated with some sort of brain dysfunction or possession by the devil or evil spirits. In some eras, exorcism was the first choice of treatment for a person with a seizure disorder. A person who receives a diagnosis of epilepsy must deal with this stigma as well as the significance of the diagnosis. What does having epilepsy mean? Individuals who are newly diagnosed with epilepsy must consider restrictions to their independence as well as the prospect of chronic therapy for control of this problem.

In our society, the ability to be readily mobile—drive to appointments, work, or religious obligations—is very important to many people. Most states require physicians to report new diagnoses of epilepsy. In most cases, the driving privileges of affected individuals are revoked, at least temporarily. The conditions for recovering the license vary with the diagnosis and the laws of each state.

The person who is newly diagnosed with epilepsy not only has to cope with the stigma but also the loss of a driver's license. The nurse may be in the best position to help the patient adjust to both of these problems through patient education and referrals to community resources. Thorough patient teaching should include:

- Explanations of old stigmas
- Ways in which people may react to the diagnosis
- Ways patients can educate family, friends, and employers about the realities of the condition and its treatment
- Actions to take if a seizure occurs so that no injuries occur and no panic develops
- Information about the availability of public transportation
- Contact information regarding other community support services

Many communities have epilepsy support groups that have information on valuable resources as well as updated facts about the laws of each area. When patients are first adjusting to epilepsy and its implications, it may help to put them in contact with such organizations. The local chapter of the Epilepsy Foundation of America may be able to offer support groups, lists of resources, and support. Individuals with epilepsy should have several options for getting around without feeling that they are being a burden or an imposition.

is also effective in mania, migraine headaches, and partial seizures.

The other drug, zonisamide (*Zonegran*), is a new agent that inhibits voltage-sensitive sodium and calcium channels, thus stabilizing nerve cell membranes and modulating calcium-dependent presynaptic release of excitatory neurotransmitters. It is used as an adjunct to other drugs for the treatment of absence seizures. When it is discontinued, zonisamide should be tapered over 2 weeks because of a risk of precipitating seizures. Patients who take this drug should be very well hydrated; there is a risk of renal calculi development.

DATA LINK

Data link to the following drugs used for treating absence seizures in your nursing drug guide:

OTHER DRUGS FOR TREATING ABSENCE (PETIT MAL) SEIZURES

Name	Brand Name	Usual Indications
valproic acid	*Depakene*	Absence (petit mal) seizures, mania, migraine headaches, partial (focal) seizures
zonisamide	*Zonegran*	Adjunct for treating absence (petit mal) seizures

DRUGS FOR TREATING PARTIAL (FOCAL) SEIZURES

Focal seizures or partial seizures are so called because they involve only part of the brain and usually originate from one site or focus. The presenting

CULTURAL CONSIDERATIONS

Altered Metabolism of Antiepileptic Drugs

Due to differences in liver enzyme functioning among Arab Americans and Asian Americans, patients in these ethnic groups may not metabolize antiepileptic drugs in the same way as patients in other ethnic groups. They not only may require lower doses to achieve the same therapeutic effects but also frequent dose adjustment. Nurses need to be aware that the therapeutic range for patients in these ethnic groups may differ from standard norms and that these patients may be more apt to show adverse or toxic reactions to antiepileptic drugs at lower doses. As with all medications, the lowest possible dose should be used. Serum drug levels should be closely monitored and titrated carefully and slowly to achieve the maximum benefits with fewest adverse effects.

symptoms will depend on exactly where in the brain the excessive electrical discharge is occurring. Partial seizures can be simple, involving only a single muscle or reaction, or complex, involving a series of reactions or emotional changes.

Drugs used in the treatment of partial seizures include the following:

- Carbamazepine (*Tegretol, Atretol,* and others), which is often the drug of choice for treatment of partial seizures. Chemically related to the tricyclic antidepressants, it has also been used in the treatment of tonic-clonic seizures and trigeminal neuralgia. It has the ability to inhibit polysynaptic responses and to block sodium channels to prevent the formation of repetitive action potentials in the abnormal focus.
- Gabapentin (*Neurontin*), which is used as adjunctive therapy in the treatment of focal seizures.
- Lamotrigine (*Lamictal*), which is also used as adjunctive therapy in the treatment of focal seizures. It may inhibit voltage-sensitive sodium and calcium channels, stabilize nerve cell membranes and modulate calcium-dependent presynaptic release of excitatory neurotransmitters.
- Tiagabine (*Gabitril*), which is a relatively new drug that is used as adjunctive therapy in the treatment of partial seizures. It has been associated with serious skin rash. It binds to GABA reuptake receptors, causing an increase in GABA levels in the brain. Since GABA is an inhibitory neurotransmitter, the result is a stabilizing of nerve membranes and a decrease in excessive activity.
- Topiramate (*Topamax*), another new drug that is used as adjunctive therapy for partial seizures in adults. It has been associated with CNS depression. It may interfere with sodium channels, causing a stabilizing of nerve membranes, and it also may increase GABA activity.

THERAPEUTIC ACTIONS AND INDICATIONS

The drugs used to control partial seizures stabilize nerve membranes in two ways: either directly, by altering sodium and calcium channels, or indirectly, by increasing the activity of GABA, an inhibitory neurotransmitter, thus decreasing excessive activity (see Figure 21-1). Each of these drugs has a slightly different mechanism of action, as noted earlier.

These drugs are indicated for the treatment of partial seizures. Carbamazepine is used as monotherapy, and the four other drugs are used as adjunctive therapy.

CONTRAINDICATIONS/CAUTIONS

Contraindications to the drugs used to control partial seizures include the following conditions: presence of any known allergy to the drug; bone marrow suppression, which could be exacerbated by the drug effects; and severe hepatic dysfunction, which could be exacerbated and could interfere with the metabolism of the drugs.

Caution should be used in the following situations: in pregnancy or lactation because of the potential adverse effects on the fetus or neonate; with renal or hepatic dysfunction, which could alter the metabolism and excretion of the drugs; and with renal stones, which could be exacerbated by the effects of some of these agents.

ADVERSE EFFECTS

The most frequently occurring adverse effects associated with the drugs used for partial seizures relate to the CNS depression that results. The following conditions may occur: drowsiness, fatigue, weakness, confusion, headache, and insomnia; GI depression, with nausea, vomiting, and anorexia; and upper respiratory infections. These antiepileptics can also be directly toxic to the liver and the bone marrow, causing dysfunction. The exact effects of each drug vary.

CLINICALLY IMPORTANT DRUG–DRUG INTERACTIONS

If any of these drugs are taken with other CNS depressants or alcohol, a potential for increased CNS depression exists. Patients should be cautioned to avoid alcohol while taking drugs for partial seizures, or to take extreme precautions if such combinations cannot be avoided. In addition, numerous drug–drug interactions are associated with carbamazepine. A drug reference should be consulted whenever a drug is added to or withdrawn from a carbamazepine-containing regimen. Dosage adjustments may be necessary.

DATA LINK

Data link to the following drugs used for treating partial seizures in your nursing drug guide:

DRUGS FOR TREATING PARTIAL (FOCAL) SEIZURES

Name	Brand Name(s)	Usual Indications
P carbamazepine	(*Tegretol, Atretol*)	Drug of choice for partial (focal) seizures; tonic-clonic (grand mal) seizures, trigeminal neuralgia.
gabapentin	(*Neurontin*)	Adjunct in treating partial seizures
lamotrigine	(*Lamictal*)	Adjunct in treating partial seizures
tiagabine	(*Gabitril*)	Adjunct in treating partial seizures
topiramate	(*Topamax*)	Adjunct in treating partial seizures

NURSING CONSIDERATIONS for patients receiving drugs to treat partial (focal) seizures

Assessment

HISTORY. Screen for the following: any known allergies to these drugs; pregnancy or lactation; bone marrow suppression; hepatic dysfunction; renal dysfunction; and renal stones.

PHYSICAL ASSESSMENT. Include screening for baseline status before beginning therapy and any potential adverse effects. Assess the following: temperature; skin color and lesions; CNS orientation, affect, reflexes, and bilateral grip strength; EEG; pulse and blood pressure; respiration and adventitious sounds; and bowel sounds and reported output. Check liver and renal function tests, urinalysis, and CBC with differential.

Nursing Diagnoses

The patient taking a drug to treat partial seizures may have the following nursing diagnoses related to drug therapy:

- Pain related to GI, CNS effects
- Alteration in thought processes related to CNS effects
- Potential for injury related to CNS, bone marrow effects
- Knowledge deficit regarding drug therapy

Implementation

- Administer the drug with food *to alleviate GI irritation if GI upset is a problem.*
- Monitor CBC prior to and periodically during therapy *to detect and prevent serious bone marrow suppression.*
- Discontinue the drug if skin rash, bone marrow suppression, unusual depression, or personality changes occur *to prevent further serious adverse effects.*
- Discontinue the drug slowly, and never withdraw the drug quickly *because rapid withdrawal may precipitate seizures.*
- Arrange for counseling for women of childbearing age who are taking these drugs. *Because these drugs have the potential to cause serious damage to the fetus, women should understand the risk of birth defects and use barrier contraceptives to avoid pregnancy.*
- Evaluate for therapeutic blood levels of carbamazepine (4–12 µg/ml).
- Provide thorough patient teaching, including drug name and prescribed dosage, as well as measures for avoidance of adverse effects, warning signs that may indicate possible problems, and the need for monitoring and evaluation *to enhance patient knowledge about drug therapy and to promote compliance.*
- Suggest the wearing or carrying of a Medic-Alert bracelet *to alert emergency workers and healthcare providers about the use of an antiepileptic drug.*
- Offer support and encouragement *to help the patient cope with the drug regimen.*

Evaluation

- Monitor patient response to the drug (decrease in incidence or absence of seizures).
- Monitor for adverse effects (CNS changes, GI depression, bone marrow suppression, severe dermatologic reactions, liver toxicity, renal stones).
- Evaluate effectiveness of teaching plan (patient can give the drug name and dosage and name possible adverse effects to watch for, and specific measures to prevent adverse effects; patient is aware of the risk of birth defects and the need to carry information about the diagnosis and use of this drug).

WWW.WEB LINKS

Health care providers and patients may want to consult the following Internet sources:

Information on epilepsy, including support groups, research, treatment:
http://www.efa.org/indexf.htm

Information on education programs, research, and other information related to seizure disorders:
http://www.ninds.nih.gov

Information about epilepsy research, treatment, laws:
http://www.noah.cuny.edu

Information on neurosciences, including current research, theories, and so on:
http://www.neuroscience.miningco.com/index.htm

CHAPTER SUMMARY

- Epilepsy is a collection of different syndromes, all of which have the same characteristic: a sudden discharge of excessive electrical energy from nerve cells located within the brain. This event is called a seizure.
- Seizures can be divided into two groups: generalized and partial (focal).
- Generalized seizures can be further classified as tonic-clonic, or grand mal; absence, or petit mal; myoclonic; febrile; and rapidly recurrent (status epilepticus).

- Partial (focal) seizures can be further classified as simple or complex.
- Drug treatment depends on the type of seizure that the patient has experienced and the toxicity associated with the available agents.
- Drug treatment is directed at stabilizing the overexcited nerve membranes and/or increasing the effectiveness of GABA, an inhibitory neurotransmitter.
- Adverse effects associated with antiepileptics (e.g., insomnia, fatigue, confusion, GI depression, bradycardia) reflect the CNS depression caused by the drugs.
- Patients being treated with an antiepileptic should be advised to wear or carry a Medic-Alert notification to alert emergency medical professionals of their epilepsy and their use of antiepileptics.

Bibliography

Bailey, K. (1998). *Psychotropic drug facts.* Philadelphia: Lippincott-Raven.

Bullock, B. L. (2000). *Focus on pathophysiology*. Philadelphia: Lippincott Williams & Wilkins.

Hardman, J. G., Limbird, L. E., Molinoff, P. B., Ruddon, R. W., & Gilman, A. G. (Eds.). (1996). *Goodman and Gilman's the pharmacological basis of therapeutics* (9th ed.). New York: McGraw-Hill.

Karch, A. M. (2000). *2000 Lippincott nursing drug guide.* Philadelphia: Lippincott Williams & Wilkins.

Malseed, R. (1995). *Textbook of pharmacology and nursing care.* Philadelphia: Lippincott-Raven.

McEvoy, B. R. (Ed.). (1999). *Facts and comparisons 1999.* St. Louis: Facts and Comparisons.

Professional's guide to patient drug facts. (1999). St. Louis: Facts and Comparisons.

CHAPTER 22

Antiparkinsonism Agents

Anticholinergics
- benztropine
- **P** biperiden
- diphenhydramine
- procyclidine
- trihexyphenidyl

Dopaminergics
- amantadine
- bromocriptine
- carbidopa-levodopa
- **P** levodopa
- pergolide
- pramipexole
- ropinirole

Adjunctive agent
- tolcapone

CHAPTER OUTLINE

KEY TERMS

anticholinergic
bradykinesia
corpus striatum
dopaminergic
Parkinson's disease
substantia nigra

INTRODUCTION

In the 1990s, several prominent figures—former heavyweight boxing champion Mohammed Ali, United States Attorney-General Janet Reno, and actor Michael J. Fox—learned that they had ***Parkinson's disease,*** a progressive, chronic neurological disorder. In general, Parkinson's disease may develop in people of any age, but it usually affects those who are past middle age and entering their 60s or even older. Therefore, the occurrence of Parkinson's disease in these leading individuals who are all relatively young people is that much more interesting. The cause of the condition is not known.

At this time, there is no cure for Parkinson's disease. Therapy is aimed at management of signs and symptoms to provide optimal functioning for as long as possible.

PARKINSON'S DISEASE AND PARKINSONISM

Lack of coordination is characteristic of Parkinson's disease or parkinsonism. Rhythmic tremors develop, insidiously at first. In some muscle groups, these tremors lead to rigidity, and in others, weakness. Affected patients may have trouble maintaining position or posture, and they may develop the condition known as ***bradykinesia,*** marked by difficulties performing intentional movements and extreme slowness or sluggishness.

As Parkinson's disease progresses, walking becomes a problem; a shuffling gait is a hallmark of the condition. In addition, patients may drool, and their speech may be slow and slurred. As the cranial nerves are affected, they may develop a mask-like expression. Parkinson's disease does not affect the higher levels of the cerebral cortex, so a very alert and intelligent person may be trapped in a progressively degenerating body.

Causal Theories

Although the cause of Parkinson's disease is not known, it is known that the signs and symptoms of the disease relate to damage to neurons in the basal ganglia of the brain (Figure 22-1). Theories about the cause of the degeneration range from viral infection, blows to the head, brain infection, atherosclerosis, and exposure to certain drugs or environmental factors.

Despite the fact that the actual cause is not known, the mechanism that causes the signs and symptoms of Parkinson's disease is understood. In a part of the brain called the ***substantia nigra,*** a dopamine-rich area, nerve cell bodies begin to degenerate. This process results in a reduction of the number of impulses sent to the ***corpus striatum*** in the basal ganglia. This area of the brain, in conjunction with the substantia nigra, helps maintain muscle tone not related to any particular movement. The corpus striatum is connected to the substantia nigra by a series

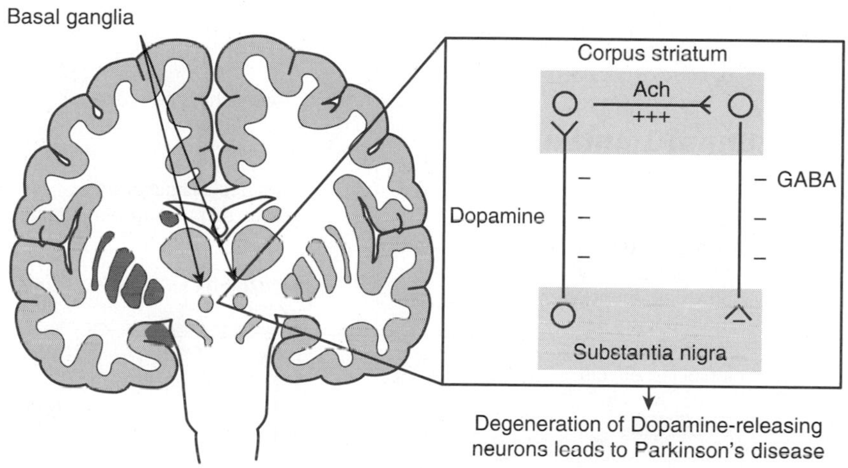

FIGURE 22-1. Schematic representation of the degeneration of neurons that leads to Parkinson's disease. Cells in the corpus striatum send impulses to the substantia nigra using GABA to inhibit activity. In turn, the substantia nigra sends impulses to the corpus striatum using dopamine to inhibit activity. Cortical areas use acetylcholine to stimulate intentional movements.

of neurons that use the inhibitory neurotransmitter GABA (gamma amino butyric acid). The substantia nigra sends nerve impulses back into the corpus stratum using the inhibitory neurotransmitter dopamine. The two areas then mutually inhibit activity in a balanced manner.

Higher neurons from the cerebral cortex secrete acetylcholine in the area of the corpus stratum as an excitatory neurotransmitter to coordinate intentional movements of the body. When there is a decrease in dopamine in the area, it causes a chemical imbalance in this area of the brain that allows the cholinergic, excitatory cells to dominate. This affects the functioning of the basal ganglia and of the cortical and cerebellar components of the extrapyramidal motor system. The extrapyramidal system is one that provides coordination for unconscious muscle movements, including those that control position, posture, and movement. The result of this imbalance in the motor system is apparent as the manifestations of Parkinson's disease (see Figure 22-1).

Drug Therapy

At this time, there is no treatment that arrests the neuron degeneration of Parkinson's disease and the eventual decline in patient function. Surgical procedures involving the basal ganglia are available with varying success at prolonging the degeneration caused by this disease. Drug therapy remains the primary treatment (Figure 22-2).

Today, therapy is aimed at restoring the balance between the declining dopamine levels, which have an inhibitory effect on the neurons in the basal ganglia, and the now-dominant cholinergic neurons, which are excitatory. This may help reduce the signs and symptoms of parkinsonism and restore normal function.

Total management of patient care in individuals with Parkinson's disease presents a challenge. Patients should be encouraged to be as active as possible, to perform exercises to prevent the development of skeletal deformities, and to attend to their own care as long as they can. Both patients and family need instruction about following drug protocols and monitoring adverse effects as well as encouragement and support for coping with the progressive nature of the disease. Because of the degenerative effects of this disease, patients may be depressed and emotional. They may require a great deal of psychological as well as physical support.

ANTICHOLINERGICS

Anticholinergics are drugs that oppose the effects of acetylcholine at receptor sites in the substantia nigra and the corpus striatum, thus helping restore chemical balance in the area. At this time, the anticholinergics used to treat parkinsonism are synthetic drugs that have been developed to have a greater affinity for cholinergic receptor sites in the central

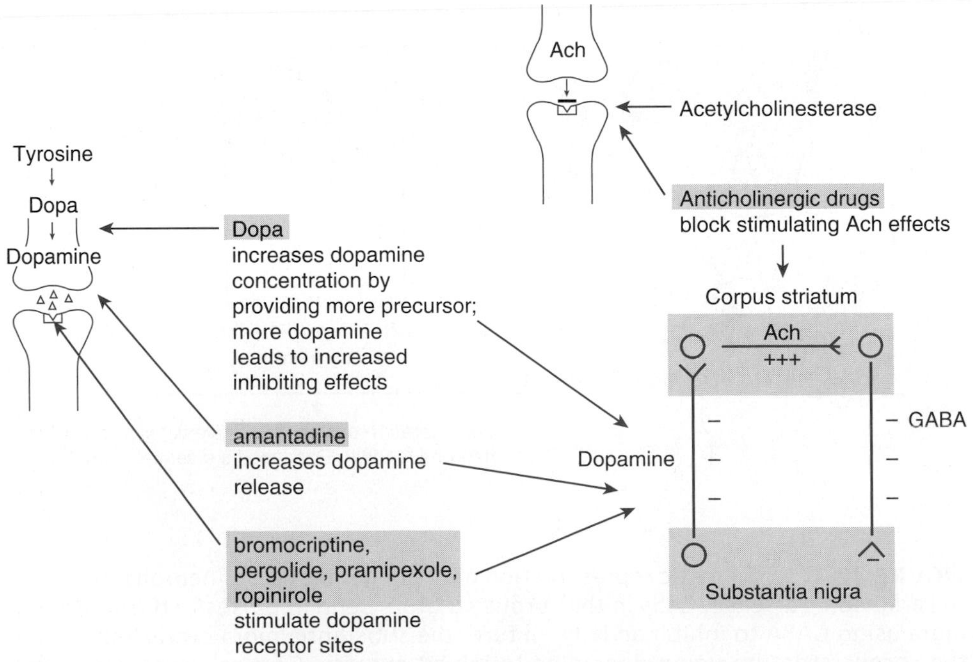

FIGURE 22-2. Sites of action of the drugs used to treat Parkinson's disease.

nervous system (CNS) than those in the peripheral nervous system. However, they still block, to some extent, the cholinergic receptors that are responsible for stimulation of the parasympathetic nervous system's postganglionic effectors and are associated with the adverse effects resulting from this blockage (see Chapter 31), including slowed GI motility and secretions with dry mouth and constipation, urinary retention, blurred vision, and dilated pupils.

Anticholinergics used to treat Parkinson's disease include:

- Benztropine (*Cogentin*), which is available in oral and IM/IV forms. This agent is used to treat parkinsonism and parkinson-like symptoms that occur as a result of drug effects of phenothiazines.
- Biperiden (*Akineton*), which is available in oral and IM forms. This medication is used for the adjunctive treatment of parkinsonism and the drug-induced parkinsonism associated with phenothiazine use.
- Diphenhydramine (*Benadryl*), which is also used for many other purposes, is often used in combination with other agents to treat Parkinson's disease. This agent is indicated for the treatment of parkinsonism, including drug-induced disease, especially in elderly patients who cannot tolerate more potent drugs or in patients at the early stages of disease.
- Procyclidine (*Kemadrin*), which is available only in the oral form. This agent is used for treatment of any parkinsonism. In severe cases, it is combined with other drugs, and it is often the drug of choice in the control of the excessive salivation that occurs with the use of neuroleptic medication.
- Trihexyphenidyl (*Artane*), which is used as adjunct therapy with levodopa. It can be used alone for the control of drug-induced extrapyramidal disorders.

THERAPEUTIC ACTIONS AND INDICATIONS

The anticholinergics block the action of acetylcholine in the CNS to help normalize the acetylcholine–dopamine imbalance. As a result, these drugs reduce the degree of rigidity and, to a lesser extent, the tremors associated with Parkinson's disease. The peripheral anticholinergic effects that sometimes occur with the use of these drugs help alleviate some of the other adverse effects associated with Parkinson's disease, including drooling.

Anticholinergic drugs are indicated for the treatment of parkinsonism, whether idiopathic, atherosclerotic, or postencephalitic, and for the relief of symptoms of extrapyramidal disorders associated with the use of some drugs, including phenothiazines. Although these drugs are not as effective as levodopa in the treatment of advancing cases of the disease, they may be useful as adjunctive therapy and when patients no longer respond to levodopa.

CONTRAINDICATIONS/CAUTIONS

Anticholinergics are contraindicated in the presence of allergy to any of these agents. In addition, they are contraindicated in narrow-angle glaucoma, gastrointestinal (GI) obstruction, genitourinary (GU) obstruction, and prostatic hypertrophy, all of which could be exacerbated by the peripheral anticholinergic effects of these drugs; and in myasthenia gravis, which could be exacerbated by the blocking of acetylcholine receptor sites at neuromuscular synapses.

Caution should be used in the presence of the following conditions: tachycardia and other arrhythmias; hypertension or hypotension, because the blocking of the parasympathetic system may cause a dominance of sympathetic stimulatory activity; hepatic or renal dysfunction, which could interfere with the metabolism and excretion of the drugs and lead to toxic levels; and lactation, because the drugs cross into breast milk and may cause adverse effects in infants. In addition, these agents should be used with caution in individuals who work in hot environments, because reflex sweating may be blocked. These people are at risk for heat prostration.

ADVERSE EFFECTS

The use of anticholinergics for parkinsonism is associated with CNS effects that relate to the blocking of central acetylcholine receptors such as disorientation, confusion, and memory loss. Agitation, nervousness, delirium, dizziness, lightheadedness, and weakness may also occur.

Anticipated peripheral anticholinergic effects include dry mouth, nausea, vomiting, paralytic ileus, and constipation related to the decreased GI secretions and motility. In addition, other adverse effects may occur, including the following: tachycardia, palpitations, and hypotension related to the blocking of the suppressive cardiac effects of the parasympathetic nervous system; urinary retention and hesitancy related to a blocking of bladder muscle activity and sphincter relaxation; blurred vision and photophobia related to pupil dilation and blocking of lens accommodation; and flushing and reduced sweating related to a blocking of the cholinergic sites that stimulate sweating and blood vessel dilation in the skin.

CLINICALLY IMPORTANT DRUG–DRUG INTERACTIONS

When these anticholinergic drugs are used with other drugs that have anticholinergic properties, including the tricyclic antidepressants and the phenothiazines, there is a risk of potentially fatal paralytic ileus and an increased risk of toxic psychoses. If such combinations must be given, patients should be monitored closely. Dosage adjustments should be made, and supportive measures should be taken. In addition, when antipsychotic drugs are combined with anticholinergics, there is a risk for decreased therapeutic effect of the antipsychotics, possibly because of a central antagonism of the two agents.

DATA LINK

Data link to the following anticholinergic antiparkinsonism drugs:

ANTICHOLINERGIC ANTIPARKINSONISM DRUGS

Name	Brand Name	Usual Indications
benztropine	*Cogentin*	Parkinsonism, drug-induced parkinsonism
P biperiden	*Akineton*	Parkinsonism, drug-induced parkinsonism
diphenhydramine	*Benadryl*	Parkinsonism, particularly in the elderly or those with mild forms
procyclidine	*Kemadrin*	Parkinsonism; control of excessive salivation
trihexyphenidyl	*Artane*	Adjunct to levodopa in treating parkinsonism

NURSING CONSIDERATIONS for patients receiving anticholinergic antiparkinsonism drugs

Assessment

HISTORY. Screen for the following: any known allergies to these drugs; GI depression or obstruction; urinary hesitancy or obstruction; benign prostatic hypertrophy (BPH); cardiac arrhythmias or hypotension; glaucoma; myasthenia gravis; lactation; renal or hepatic dysfunction; and exposure to a hot environment.

PHYSICAL ASSESSMENT. Include screening for baseline status before beginning therapy and for any potential adverse effects. Assess the following: temperature; skin color and lesions; CNS orientation, affect, reflexes, bilateral grip strength, and spasticity evaluation; respiration and adventitious sounds; pulse, blood pressure, and cardiac output; bowel sounds and reported output; urinary output, bladder palpation; and liver and renal function tests.

Nursing Diagnoses

The patient taking an anticholinergic antiparkinsonism drug may have the following nursing diagnoses related to drug therapy:

- Pain related to GI, CNS, GU effects
- Alteration in thought processes related to CNS effects
- Potential for injury related to CNS effects
- Knowledge deficit regarding drug therapy

Implementation

- Arrange to decrease dosage or discontinue the drug *if dry mouth becomes so severe that swallowing becomes difficult. Provide sugarless lozenges to suck and frequent mouth care to help with this problem.*
- Give the drug with caution and arrange for a decrease in dosage in hot weather or with exposure to hot environments *because patients are at increased risk for heat prostration.*
- Give the drug with meals if GI upset is a problem, before meals if dry mouth is a problem, and after meals if drooling occurs and the drug causes nausea *to facilitate compliance with drug therapy.*
- Monitor bowel function and institute a bowel program *if constipation is severe.*
- Ensure that the patient voids before taking the drug *if urinary retention is a problem.*
- Establish safety precautions if CNS or vision changes occur *to prevent patient injury.*
- Provide thorough patient teaching about topics such as the drug name and prescribed dosage, measures to help avoid adverse effects, warning signs that may indicate problems, and the need for periodic monitoring and evaluation *to enhance patient knowledge about drug therapy and to promote compliance.*
- Offer support and encouragement *to help the patient cope with the disease and drug regimen.*

Evaluation

- Monitor patient response to the drug (improvement in signs and symptoms of parkinsonism).
- Monitor for adverse effects (CNS changes, urinary retention, GI depression, tachycardia, decreased sweating, flushing).
- Evaluate the effectiveness of the teaching plan (patient can give the drug name and dosage, name possible adverse effects to watch for and specific measures to prevent adverse effects, and discuss the importance of continued follow-up).
- Monitor the effectiveness of comfort measures and compliance with the regimen.

WWW.WEB LINKS

Health care providers and patients may want to consult the following Internet sources:

Information on parkinsonism, ataxia, and related disorders including support groups, research, treatment:
http://www.ataxia.org/

LIFE-SPAN CONSIDERATIONS

Effects of Parkinson's Disease

Although Parkinson's disease may affect individuals of any age, gender, or nationality, the frequency of the disease increases with age. This debilitating condition, which affects more males than females, may be one of many chronic problems associated with aging.

The drugs that are used to manage Parkinson's disease are associated with more adverse effects in older people with long-term problems. Both anticholinergic and dopaminergic drugs aggravate glaucoma, BPH, constipation, cardiac problems, and COPD. Special precautions and frequent follow-up are necessary for older patients with Parkinson's disease, and their drug dosages may need to be adjusted frequently to avoid serious problems. In many cases, other agents are given to counteract the effects of these drugs, and patients then have complicated drug regimens with many associated adverse effects and problems. Consequently, it is essential for these patients to have extensive, written drug teaching protocols.

The eventual dependence and lack of control that accompany Parkinson's disease are devastating to all patients and their families, but may be particularly overwhelming to individuals who value high degrees of autonomy, self-determination, and independence. Although these characteristics are not associated with any particular ethnic group, they are valued more highly among certain cultures than others. For example, Latinos—who traditionally have strong extended family ties—may not have the same problems adjusting to a chronic, debilitating illness in a relative as members of other ethnic groups. It is important for the nurse to assess all families with sensitivity to determine what convictions they hold and plan nursing care accordingly.

Information on education programs, research, other information related to parkinsonism:
http://www.ninds.nih.gov

Information about parkinsonism research, treatment:
http://www.noah.cuny.edu

Information on neurosciences, including current research and theories:
http://www.neuroguide.com

Information on support services and aids for activities of daily living:
http://www.accessunlimited.com/links.html

DOPAMINERGICS

Dopaminergics, drugs that increase the effects of dopamine at receptor sites, have been proven to be even more effective than anticholinergics in the treatment of parkinsonism. Dopamine itself does not cross the blood–brain barrier and other drugs that act like dopamine or increase dopamine concentrations indirectly must be used to increase dopamine levels in the brain. These drugs are effective as long as enough intact neurons remain in the substantia nigra to respond to increased levels of dopamine. When the neural degeneration has progressed beyond a certain point, patients no longer respond to these drugs.

Levodopa (*Dopar*) is the mainstay of treatment for parkinsonism. This precursor of dopamine crosses the blood–brain barrier, where it is converted to dopamine. In this way, it acts like a replacement therapy. Levodopa is almost always given in combination form with carbidopa as a fixed combination drug (*Sinemet*). In this combination form, carbidopa inhibits the enzyme dopa decarboxylase in the periphery, diminishing the metabolism of levodopa in the GI tract and in peripheral tissues and leading to higher levels to cross the blood–brain barrier. Because it decreases the amount of levodopa needed to reach a therapeutic level in the brain, the dosage of levodopa can be decreased, which reduces the incidence of adverse side effects.

Thus, in combination with carbidopa, smaller doses of levodopa are needed to achieve the same therapeutic effect. Carbidopa is not the only agent that is used primarily to improve the effectiveness of levodopa therapy (Box 22-1).

Other dopaminergics that are used in the treatment of parkinsonism include:

- Amantadine (*Symmetrel*), which is an antiviral drug that also seems to increase the release of dopamine. This drug can be effective as long as there is a possibility of more dopamine release.

BOX 22-1 *ADJUNCT TO LEVODOPA THERAPY*

Tolcapone (*Tasmar*) is used with levodopa-carbidopa to further increase plasma levels of levodopa. Tolcapone blocks the enzyme catechol methyltransferase, which is responsible for the breakdown of dopamine. Because this drug has been associated with fulminant and potentially fatal liver damage, it is contraindicated in the presence of liver disease. Tolcapone is reserved for use in later stages of Parkinson's disease when levodopa-carbidopa are losing their effectiveness.

- Bromocriptine (*Parlodel*), which acts as a direct dopamine agonist on dopamine receptor sites in the substantia nigra. Because this drug does not depend on cells in the area to biotransform it or to increase release of already produced dopamine, it may be effective longer than levodopa or amantadine.
- Pergolide (*Permax*), which is used as an adjunct to levodopa-carbidopa therapy. It directly stimulates postsynaptic dopamine receptors in the substantia nigra, an effect that also may lead to inhibition of prolactin secretion and a rise in growth hormone levels.
- Pramipexole (*Mirapex*), which is a newer drug that directly stimulates dopamine receptors in the substantia nigra. It may be effective after levodopa effects have weakened.
- Ropinirole (*Requip*), which is a newer drug that directly stimulates dopamine receptors. It has proven useful both in the early stages as well as in the later stages of Parkinson's disease in conjunction with levodopa, when the effects of levodopa are no longer sufficient to provide symptomatic relief.

THERAPEUTIC ACTIONS AND INDICATIONS

The dopaminergics work by increasing the levels of dopamine in the substantia nigra or directly stimulating the dopamine receptors in that area. This action helps restore the balance between the inhibitory and stimulating neurons. The dopaminergics are indicated for the relief of the signs and symptoms of idiopathic Parkinson's disease. Amantadine, which is also used as an antiviral agent, may also be effective in treating drug-induced Parkinson's disease.

When neurodegeneration has progressed to the extent that the nerves are damaged or gone, these drugs are no longer effective. These drugs control Parkinson's disease only as long as functioning dopamine receptors remain in the substantia nigra.

CONTRAINDICATIONS/CAUTIONS

The dopaminergics are contraindicated in the presence of any known allergy to the drug or drug components. They are also contraindicated in the following conditions: angle-closure glaucoma, which could be exacerbated by these drugs; history or presence of suspicious skin lesions with levodopa, because this drug has been associated with the development of melanoma; and lactation because of potential adverse effects on the baby.

Caution should be used with any condition that could be exacerbated by dopamine receptor stimulation such as the following: cardiovascular disease, including myocardial infarction, arrhythmias, and hypertension; bronchial asthma; history of peptic ulcers; urinary tract obstruction; and psychiatric disorders. Care should also be taken in pregnancy, because these drugs cross the placenta and could adversely affect the fetus, and in renal and hepatic disease, which could interfere with the metabolism and excretion of the drug.

ADVERSE EFFECTS

The adverse effects associated with the dopaminergics usually result from stimulation of dopamine receptors. CNS effects may include anxiety, nervousness, headache, malaise, fatigue, confusion, mental changes, blurred vision, muscle twitching, and ataxia. Peripheral effects may include anorexia, nausea, vomiting, dysphagia, and constipation or diarrhea; cardiac arrhythmias, hypotension, palpitations; bizarre breathing patterns; urinary retention; and flushing, increased sweating, and hot flashes. Bone marrow depression and hepatic dysfunction may also occur.

CLINICALLY IMPORTANT DRUG–DRUG INTERACTIONS

If dopaminergics are combined with monoamine oxidase (MAO) inhibitors, therapeutic effects increase and a risk of hypertensive crisis exists. The MAO inhibitor should be stopped 14 days before beginning therapy with a dopaminergic. The combination of levodopa with vitamin B_6 and with phenytoin may lead to decreased efficacy. Reduced effectiveness may also result if dopaminergics are combined with dopamine antagonists. In addition, patients who take dopaminergics should be cautioned to avoid OTC vitamins; if such medications are used, the patient should be monitored closely, because a decrease in effectiveness can result.

DATA LINK

Data link to the following dopaminergic antiparkinsonism drugs:

DOPAMINERGIC ANTIPARKINSONISM DRUGS

Name	Brand Name	Usual Indications
amantadine	*Symmetrel*	Antiviral; idiopathic and drug-induced parkinsonism
bromocriptine	*Parlodel*	Idiopathic Parkinson's disease; may be beneficial in later stages when response to levodopa decreases
P levodopa	*Dopar*	Idiopathic Parkinson's disease
pergolide	*Permax*	Adjunct with levodopa-carbidopa for idiopathic Parkinson's disease
pramipexole	*Mirapex*	Idiopathic Parkinson's disease
ropinirole	*Requip*	Idiopathic Parkinson's disease in early stages and in later stages combined with levodopa

PATIENT TEACHING CHECKLIST

Levodopa

Create customized patient teaching materials for levodopa from your CD-ROM. Your patient teaching should stress the following points:

Levodopa increases the levels of dopamine in central areas of the brain, helping to reduce the signs and symptoms of Parkinson's disease. Often this drug is combined with carbidopa, which allows the correct levels of levodopa to reach the brain. People who take this drug must have their individual dosage needs adjusted over time.

Common effects of this drug include:

- Fatigue, weakness, and drowsiness—Try to space activities evenly throughout the day and allow rest periods to avoid these sometimes very discouraging side effects. Take safety precautions and avoid driving or operating dangerous machinery if these conditions occur.
- Dizziness, fainting—Change position slowly to avoid dizzy spells.
- Increased sweating, darkening of urine—This is a normal reaction. Avoid very hot environments.
- Headaches, difficulty sleeping—These usually pass as the body adjusts to the drug. If they become too uncomfortable and persist, consult with your health care provider.

Report any of the following conditions to your health care provider: uncontrolled movements of any part of the body; chest pain, palpitations; depression or mood changes; difficulty in voiding; or severe or persistent nausea and vomiting.

Be aware that vitamin B_6 interferes with the effects of levodopa. If you feel that you need a vitamin B_6-containing product, consult with your health care provider about using an agent that does not contain vitamin B_6. In addition, avoid eating large quantities of health foods that contain vitamin B_6 such as grains and brans. If you are taking a levodopa-carbidopa combination, these precautions are not as important.

Tell any doctor, nurse, or other health care provider that you are taking this drug.

Keep this drug and all medications out of the reach of children.

Do not overexert yourself when you begin to feel better. Pace yourself.

Take this drug exactly as prescribed. Be sure to obtain regular medical follow-up, which is necessary to evaluate the effects of this drug.

This Teaching Checklist reflects general patient teaching guidelines. It is not meant to be a substitute for drug-specific teaching information, which is available in nursing drug guides.

NURSING CONSIDERATIONS
for patients receiving dopaminergic antiparkinsonism drugs

Assessment

HISTORY. Screen for the following: any known allergies to these drugs or drug components; GI depression or obstruction; urinary hesitancy or obstruction; cardiac arrhythmias or hypertension; glaucoma; respiratory disease; pregnancy or lactation; and renal or hepatic dysfunction. With levodopa, check for skin lesions or history of melanoma.

PHYSICAL ASSESSMENT. Include screening for baseline status before beginning therapy and for any potential adverse effects. Assess the following: temperature; skin color and lesions; CNS orientation, affect, reflexes, bilateral grip strength, and spasticity evaluation; vision; respiration and adventitious sounds; pulse, blood pressure, and cardiac output; bowel sounds and reported output; and urinary output and bladder palpation. Check liver and renal function tests and CBC with differential.

Nursing Diagnoses

The patient taking a dopaminergic antiparkinsonism drug may have the following nursing diagnoses related to drug therapy:

- Pain related to GI, CNS, GU effects
- Alteration in thought processes related to CNS effects
- Potential for injury related to CNS effects and incidence of orthostatic hypertension
- Knowledge deficit regarding drug therapy

NURSING CARE GUIDE
Levodopa

Assessment	Nursing Diagnoses	Implementation	Evaluation
HISTORY			
Allergies to any of these drugs; COPD; arrhythmias; hypotension; hepatic or renal dysfunction; pregnancy and lactation; psychoses; peptic ulcer; glaucoma.	Pain related to GI, GU, CNS effects Potential for injury related to CNS effects Alteration in thought processes related to CNS effects Knowledge deficit regarding drug therapy	Ensure safe and appropriate administration of drug. Provide comfort and safety measures: positioning, slow changes; orientation; safety measures; pain medication as needed; give drug with food; administer with carbidopa; void before each dose. Provide support and reassurance to deal with disease and drug effects. Provide patient teaching regarding drug, dosage, drug effects, symptoms to report.	Evaluate drug effects: relief of signs and symptoms of Parkinson's disease. Monitor for adverse effects: CNS effects; renal changes; GI effects (constipation); urinary retention; increased sweating, flushing. Monitor for drug–drug interactions: hypertensive crisis with MAO inhibitors; decreased effects with vitamin B_6, or phenytoin. Evaluate effectiveness of patient teaching program. Evaluate effectiveness of comfort and safety measures.
PHYSICAL EXAMINATION			
CV: blood pressure, pulse, peripheral perfusion, ECG CNS: orientation, affect, reflexes, grip strength Renal: output, bladder palpation GI: abdominal examination, bowel sounds Resp: respiration, adventitious sounds Laboratory tests: renal and liver function tests, CBC			

Implementation

• Arrange to decrease dosage of the drug if therapy has been interrupted for any reason *to prevent acute peripheral dopaminergic effects.*

• Evaluate disease progress and signs and symptoms periodically and record *for reference of disease progress and drug response.*

• Give the drug with meals *to alleviate GI irritation if GI upset is a problem.*

• Monitor bowel function and institute a bowel program *if constipation is severe.*

• Ensure that the patient voids before taking the drug *if urinary retention is a problem.*

• Establish safety precautions *if CNS or vision changes occur, to prevent patient injury.*

• Monitor hepatic, renal, and hematologic tests periodically during therapy *to detect early signs of dysfunction to consider reevaluation of drug therapy.*

• Provide support services and comfort measures as needed *to improve patient compliance.*

• Provide thorough patient teaching about topics such as the drug name and prescribed dosage, measures to help avoid adverse effects, warning signs that may indicate problems, and the need for periodic monitoring and evaluation *to enhance patient knowledge about drug therapy and to promote compliance* (see Patient Teaching Checklist: Levodopa).

CASE STUDY

Effects of Vitamin B_6 Intake on Levodopa Levels

PRESENTATION

S. S., a 58-year-old man with well-controlled Parkinson's disease, presents with severe nausea, anorexia, fainting spells, and heart palpitations. He has been maintained on levodopa for the Parkinson's disease, and he claims to have followed his drug regimen religiously.

According to S. S., the only change in his lifestyle has been the addition of several health foods and vitamins. His daughter, who recently returned from her freshman year in college, has begun a new "health" regimen, including natural foods and plenty of supplemental vitamins. She was so enthusiastic about her new approach to life that everyone in the family agreed to give this diet a try.

CRITICAL THINKING QUESTIONS

Based on S. S.'s signs and symptoms, what has probably occurred? In Parkinson's disease, is it possible to differentiate a deterioration of illness from a toxic drug reaction? What nursing implications should be considered when teaching S. S. and his family about the effects of vitamin B_6 on levodopa levels? In what ways can the daughter cope with her role in this crisis? Develop a new care plan for S. S. that involves all family members, including drug teaching.

DISCUSSION

The presenting symptoms reflect an increase in parkinsonism symptoms as well as an increase in peripheral dopamine reactions (palpitations, fainting, anorexia, nausea, and so on). It is necessary to determine whether the problem involves a further degeneration in the neurons in the substantia nigra or the particular medication that S.S. has been taking. Many patients lose their responsiveness to levodopa as the neural degeneration continues.

The explanation of the new lifestyle—full of grains, natural foods, and vitamins—alerted a nurse to the possibility of excessive vitamin B_6 intake. In reviewing the vitamin bottles and some of the food packages supplied by S. S., it seemed that too much vitamin B_6, which speeds the conversion of levodopa to dopamine before it can cross the blood–brain barrier, might well be the problem. The signs and symptoms of parkinsonism recurred.

S. S. should be evaluated regarding the status of his Parkinson's disease and then be restarted on levodopa. The smallest dose possible should be used to begin drug therapy, with slow increases to achieve the maximum benefit with the least side effects. It would be wise to consider combining the drug with carbidopa to prevent some of the patient's recent problems.

In addition, S. S. should receive thorough drug teaching in a written form for future reference, including the need to avoid vitamin B_6. His entire family should be involved in an explanation of what happened and how this situation can be avoided in the future. Because the daughter may feel especially guilty about her role, she should have the opportunity to discuss her feelings and explore the positive impact of healthy food on nutrition and quality of life. This situation can serve as a good teaching example for staff, as well as presenting them with an opportunity to review drug therapy in Parkinson's disease and the risks and benefits of more extreme diets.

- Offer encouragement *to help the patient cope with the disease and drug regimen.*

Evaluation

- Monitor patient response to the drug (improvement in signs and symptoms of parkinsonism).
- Monitor for adverse effects (CNS changes, urinary retention, GI depression, tachycardia, increased sweating, flushing).
- Evaluate the effectiveness of the teaching plan (patient can give the drug name and dosage, name possible adverse effects to watch for and specific measures to prevent adverse effects, and discuss the importance of continued follow-up).
- Monitor the effectiveness of comfort measures and compliance with the regimen (see Nursing Care Guide: Levodopa).

CHAPTER SUMMARY

- Parkinson's disease is a progressive, chronic neurological disorder for which there is no cure.
- Signs and symptoms of Parkinson's disease include tremor, changes in posture and gait, slow and deliberate movements (bradykinesia), and eventually drooling and changes in speech.
- Loss of dopamine-secreting neurons in the substantia nigra is characteristic of Parkinson's disease. Destruction of dopamine-secreting cells leads to an imbalance between excitatory cholinergic cells and inhibitory dopaminergic cells.
- Drug therapy for Parkinson's disease is aimed at restoring the dopamine–acetylcholine balance. The signs and symptoms of the disease can be managed until the degeneration of neurons is so extensive that a therapeutic response no longer occurs.

- Anticholinergic drugs are used to block the excitatory cholinergic receptors and dopaminergic drugs are used to increase dopamine levels or to directly stimulate dopamine receptors.
- Many adverse effects are associated with the drugs used for treating Parkinson's disease, including CNS changes, anticholinergic (atropine-like) effects, and dopamine stimulation in the peripheral nervous system.

Bibliography

Bailey, K. (1998). *Psychotropic drug facts.* Philadelphia: Lippincott-Raven.

Bullock, B. L. (2000). *Focus on pathophysiology.* Philadelphia: Lippincott Williams & Wilkins.

Hardman, J. G., Limbird, L. E., Molinoff, P. B., Ruddon, R. W., & Gilman, A. G. (Eds.). (1996). *Goodman and Gilman's the pharmacological basis of therapeutics* (9th ed.). New York: McGraw-Hill.

Karch, A. M. (2000). *2000 Lippincott's nursing drug guide.* Philadelphia: Lippincott Williams & Wilkins.

Malseed, R. (1995). *Textbook of pharmacology and nursing care.* Philadelphia: Lippincott-Raven.

McEvoy, B. R. (Ed.). (1999). *Facts and comparisons 1999.* St. Louis: Facts and Comparisons.

Professional's guide to patient drug facts. (1999). St. Louis: Facts and Comparisons.

CHAPTER 23

Muscle Relaxants

Centrally acting skeletal muscle relaxants

- **P** baclofen
- carisoprodol
- chlorphenesin
- chlorzoxazone
- cyclobenzaprine
- methocarbamol
- orphenadrine

Direct-acting skeletal muscle relaxant

- **P** dantrolene

CHAPTER OUTLINE

KEY TERMS

basal ganglia
cerebellum
extrapyramidal tract
hypertonia
interneuron
pyramidal tract
spasticity

INTRODUCTION

Many injuries and accidents result in local damage to muscles or the skeletal anchors of muscles. These injuries may lead to muscle spasm and pain, which may be of a long duration and interfere with normal functioning. Damage to central nervous system (CNS) neurons may cause a permanent state of muscle spasticity as a result of loss of nerves that help maintain balance in controlling muscle activity.

Neuron damage, whether temporary or permanent, may be treated with skeletal muscle relaxants. Most skeletal muscle relaxants work in the brain and spinal cord, where they interfere with the cycle of muscle spasm and pain. However, one skeletal muscle relaxant, dantrolene, enters muscle fibers directly.

NERVES AND MOVEMENT

Posture, balance, and movement are the result of a constantly fluctuating sequence of muscle contraction and relaxation. The nerves that regulate these actions are the spinal motor neurons. These neurons are influenced by higher brain level activity in the cerebellum and basal ganglia, which provide coordination of contractions, and the cerebral cortex, which allows conscious thought to regulate movement.

Spinal Reflexes

The spinal reflexes are the simplest nerve pathways that monitor movement and posture (Figure 23-1). Spinal reflexes can be simple, involving an incoming sensory neuron and an outgoing motor neuron, or more complex, involving interneurons that communicate with the related centers in the brain. Simple reflex arcs involve sensory receptors in the periphery and spinal motor nerves. Such reflex arcs, which make up what is known as the spindle gamma loop system, respond to stretch receptors on muscle fibers to cause a muscle fiber contraction that relieves the stretch. In this system, nerves from stretch receptors form a synapse with gamma nerves in the spinal cord, which send an impulse to the stretched muscle fibers to stimulate their contraction. These reflexes are responsible for maintaining muscle tone and keeping an upright position against the pull of gravity. Other spinal reflexes may involve synapses with ***interneurons*** within the spinal cord, which adjust movement and response based on information from higher brain centers and coordinate movement and position.

Brain Control

Many areas within the brain influence the spinal motor nerves. Areas of the brain stem, the ***basal ganglia,*** and the ***cerebellum*** modulate spinal motor nerve activity and help coordinate activity between various muscle groups, thus allowing coordinated movement and control of body muscle motions. Nerve areas within the cerebral cortex allow conscious, or intentional, movement. Nerves within the cortex send signals down the spinal cord, where they cross to the opposite side of the spinal cord before sending out nerve impulses to cause muscle

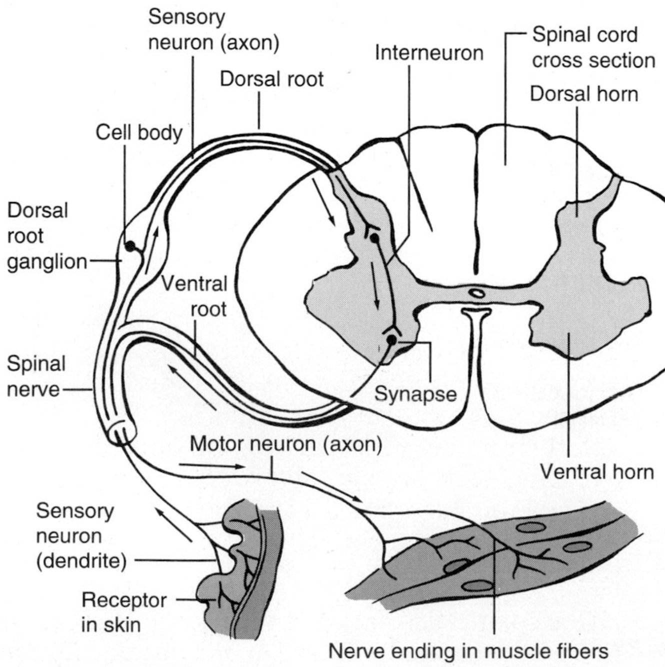

FIGURE 23-1. Reflex arc showing the pathway of impulses.

contraction. In this way, each side of the cortex controls muscle movement on the opposite side of the body.

Different fibers control different types of movements. These fibers that control precise, intentional movement make up the ***pyramidal tract*** within the CNS. The ***extrapyramidal tract*** is composed of cells from the cerebral cortex as well as from several subcortical areas, including the basal ganglia and the cerebellum. This tract modulates or coordinates unconsciously controlled muscle activity, and it allows the body to make automatic adjustments in posture or position and balance. The extrapyramidal tract controls lower level, or crude, movements.

NEUROMUSCULAR ABNORMALITIES

All of the above areas work together to allow for a free flow of impulses into and out of the CNS to coordinate posture, balance, and movement. When injuries, diseases, and toxins affect the normal flow of information into and out of the CNS motor pathways, many clinical signs and symptoms may develop, ranging from simple muscle spasms to ***spasticity,*** or sustained muscle spasm, and paralysis.

Muscle Spasm

Muscle spasms often result from injury to the musculoskeletal system—for example, over-stretching a muscle, wrenching a joint, or tearing a tendon or ligament. These injuries can cause violent and painful involuntary muscle contractions. It is thought that these spasms are caused by the flood of sensory impulses coming to the spinal cord from the injured area. These impulses can be passed through interneurons to spinal motor nerves, which stimulate an intense muscle contraction. The contraction cuts off blood flow to the muscle fibers in the injured area, causing lactic acid to accumulate, resulting in pain. The new flood of sensory impulse caused by the pain may lead to further muscle contraction, and a vicious circle may develop.

Muscle Spasticity

Muscle spasticity is the result of damage to neurons within the CNS rather than injury to peripheral structures. Because the spasticity is caused by nerve damage in the CNS, it is a permanent condition. Spasticity may result from an increase in excitatory influences or a decrease in inhibitory influences within the CNS. The interruption in the balance between all of these higher influences within the CNS may lead to excessive stimulation of muscles, or ***hypertonia,*** in opposing muscle groups at the same time, a condition that may cause contractures and permanent structural changes. This control imbalance also results in a loss of coordinated muscle activity.

For example, the signs and symptoms of cerebral palsy and paraplegia are related to the disruption in the nervous control of the muscles. The exact presentation of any of these chronic neurologic disorders depends on the specific nerve centers and tracts that are damaged and how the control imbalance is manifested.

CENTRALLY ACTING SKELETAL MUSCLE RELAXANTS

The centrally acting skeletal muscle relaxants work in the CNS to interfere with the reflexes that are causing the muscle spasm. Because these drugs lyse or destroy spasm, they are often referred to as spasmolytics. They work in the upper levels of the CNS, so possible depression must be anticipated with their use.

These drugs include:

- Baclofen (*Lioresal*), which is used for the treatment of muscle spasticity associated with neuromuscular diseases such as multiple sclerosis, muscle rigidity, and spinal cord injuries. This agent, which is available in oral and intrathecal forms, can be administered via a delivery pump for the treatment of central spasticity.
- Carisoprodol (*Soma*), which is indicated for the relief of discomfort associated with musculoskeletal pain. It may be safer in older patients or those with renal or hepatic dysfunction.
- Chlorphenesin (*Malate*), which has the same indication as carisoprodol.
- Chlorzoxazone (*Paraflex*), which also has the same indication as carisoprodol.
- Cyclobenzaprine (*Flexeril*), which is recommended for the relief of discomfort associated with painful, acute musculoskeletal conditions. This agent, available only in an oral form, is a newer drug with few adverse effects.
- Methocarbamol (*Robaxin*), which is used to relieve the same conditions as cyclobenzaprine and also to alleviate signs and symptoms of tetanus. It is available only in the parenteral form.
- Orphenadrine (*Banflex, Flexoject*), another parenteral drug, which is available for the relief of acute, painful musculoskeletal conditions. This agent is also being tried for the relief of quinidine-induced leg cramps.

Diazepam (*Valium*), a drug widely used as an anxiety agent (see Chapter 18), may be an effective centrally acting skeletal muscle relaxant. It may be advantageous in situations in which anxiety may precipitate the muscle spasm.

Other measures in addition to the above drugs should be used to alleviate muscle spasm and pain. Such modalities as rest of the affected muscle, heat applications to increase blood flow to the area to remove the pain-causing chemicals, physical therapy to return the muscle to normal tone and activity, and anti-inflammatory agents (including NSAIDs) if the underlying problem is related to injury or inflammation may help.

THERAPEUTIC ACTIONS AND INDICATIONS

Although the exact mechanism of action is not known, it is thought to involve action in the upper or spinal interneurons. The primary indication for the use of centrally acting skeletal muscle agents is the relief of discomfort associated with acute, painful musculoskeletal conditions as an adjunct to rest, physical therapy, and other measures.

CONTRAINDICATIONS/CAUTIONS

Centrally acting skeletal muscle relaxants are contraindicated in the presence of any known allergy to any of these drugs and with skeletal muscle spasms resulting from rheumatic disorders. In addition, baclofen should not be used to treat any spasticity that contributes to locomotion, upright position, or increased function. Blocking this spasticity results in loss of these functions.

All centrally acting skeletal muscle relaxants should be used cautiously in the following circumstances: with a history of epilepsy, because the CNS depression and imbalance caused by these drugs may exacerbate the seizure disorder; with cardiac dysfunction, because muscle function may be depressed; with any condition marked by muscle weakness that the drugs could make much worse; and with hepatic or renal dysfunction, which could interfere with the metabolism and excretion of the drugs, leading to toxic levels. These agents should be used with caution in pregnancy or lactation, because the fetus or neonate may suffer adverse effects.

ADVERSE EFFECTS

The most frequently seen adverse effects associated with these drugs relate to drug-caused CNS depression: drowsiness, fatigue, weakness, confusion, headache, and insomnia. Gastrointestinal (GI) disturbances, which may be linked to CNS depression of the parasympathetic reflexes, include nausea, dry mouth, anorexia, and constipation. In addition, hypotension and arrhythmias may occur, again as a result of depression of normal reflex arcs. Urinary frequency, enuresis, and feelings of urinary urgency reportedly may occur. Chlorzoxazone may discolor the urine, becoming orange to purple-red when metabolized and excreted. Patients should be warned about this effect to prevent any fears of blood in the urine.

CLINICALLY IMPORTANT DRUG–DRUG INTERACTIONS

If any of the centrally acting skeletal muscle relaxants are taken with other CNS depressants or alcohol, CNS depression may increase. Patients should be cautioned to avoid alcohol while taking these muscle relaxants; if this combination cannot be avoided, they should take extreme precautions.

DATA LINK

Data link to the following centrally acting skeletal muscle relaxants in your nursing drug guide:

CENTRALLY ACTING SKELETAL MUSCLE RELAXANTS

Name	Brand Name	Usual Indications
P baclofen	*Lioresal*	Muscle spasticity, spinal cord injuries
carisoprodol	*Soma*	Relief of discomfort of acute musculoskeletal conditions
chlorphenesin	*Malate*	Relief of discomfort of acute musculoskeletal conditions
chlorzoxazone	*Paraflex*	Relief of discomfort of acute musculoskeletal conditions
cyclobenzaprine	*Flexeril*	Relief of discomfort of acute musculoskeletal conditions
methocarbamol	*Robaxin*	Relief of discomfort of acute musculoskeletal conditions; tetanus
orphenadrine	*Banflex*	Relief of discomfort of acute musculoskeletal conditions; quinidine-induced leg cramps

NURSING CONSIDERATIONS
for patients receiving centrally acting skeletal muscle relaxants

Assessment

HISTORY. Screen for the following: any known allergies to these drugs; cardiac depression, epilepsy, muscle weakness, rheumatic disorder; pregnancy and lactation; and renal or hepatic dysfunction.

PHYSICAL ASSESSMENT. Include screening for baseline status before beginning therapy and for any potential adverse effects. Assess the following: temperature; skin color and lesions; CNS orientation, affect, reflexes, bilateral grip strength, and spasticity evaluation; bowel sounds and reported output; and liver and renal function tests.

Nursing Diagnoses

The patient who is receiving a centrally acting skeletal muscle relaxant may have the following nursing diagnoses related to drug therapy:

- Pain related to GI, CNS effects
- Alteration in thought processes related to CNS effects
- Potential for injury related to CNS effects
- Knowledge deficit regarding drug therapy

Implementation

- Discontinue the drug at any sign of hypersensitivity reaction or liver dysfunction *to prevent severe toxicity.*
- If using baclofen, taper drug slowly over 1 to 2 weeks *to prevent the development of psychoses and hallucinations.* Use baclofen cautiously in patients whose spasticity contributes to mobility, posture, or balance *to prevent loss of this function.*
- If the patient is receiving baclofen through a delivery pump, the patient should understand the pump, the reason for frequent monitoring, and how to adjust the dose and the programming of the unit *to enhance patient knowledge and promote compliance.*
- Monitor respiratory status *to evaluate adverse effects and arrange for appropriate dosage adjustment or discontinuation of the drug.*
- Provide thorough patient teaching, including drug name, prescribed dosage, measures for avoidance of adverse effects, warning signs that may indicate possible problems, and the need for monitoring and evaluation *to enhance patient knowledge about drug therapy and to promote compliance.*
- Offer support and encouragement *to help the patient cope with the drug regimen.*

Evaluation

- Monitor patient response to the drug (improvement in muscle spasm and relief of pain; improvement in muscle spasticity).
- Monitor for adverse effects (CNS changes, GI depression, urinary urgency).
- Evaluate the effectiveness of the teaching plan (patient can give the drug name and dosage, name possible adverse effects to watch for and specific measures to prevent adverse effects, and describe, if necessary, proper intrathecal administration).
- Monitor the effectiveness of comfort measures and compliance with the regimen.

WWW.WEB LINKS

Health care providers and patients may want to consult the following Internet sources:

Information on muscle physiology and muscle disorders and diseases:
http://www1.umn.edu/cmmd/cmmd.html

Information on malignant hyperthermia:
http://www.mhaus.org

Information for patients and health care professionals about cerebral palsy research, treatment:
http://www.ucppgmc.com/index.html

Patient information regarding cerebral palsy:
http://www.spinalcord.org

Information on support services and aids for activities of daily living, support groups, and community resources for patients with cerebral palsy:
http://avenue.gen.va.us/Health/HomeHealth/paralysis.html

DIRECT-ACTING SKELETAL MUSCLE RELAXANTS

One drug is currently available for use in treating spasticity that directly affects peripheral muscle contraction. This drug, dantrolene (*Dantrium*), has become important in the management of spasticity associated with neuromuscular diseases such as cerebral palsy, multiple sclerosis, muscular dystrophy, polio, tetanus, quadriplegia, and amyotrophic lateral sclerosis (ALS). This agent is not used for the treatment of muscle spasms associated with musculoskeletal injury or rheumatic disorders.

THERAPEUTIC ACTIONS AND INDICATIONS

Dantrolene acts within skeletal muscle fibers, interfering with the release of calcium from the muscle tubules (Figure 23-2; Box 23-1). This action prevents the fibers from contracting. Dantrolene does not interfere with neuromuscular transmissions, and it does not affect the surface membrane of skeletal muscle.

Dantrolene is indicated for the control of spasticity resulting from upper motor neuron disorders, including spinal cord injury, myasthenia gravis, muscular dystrophy, and cerebral palsy (oral form). Continued long-term use is justified as long as the drug reduces painful and disabling spasticity. Long-term use results in a decrease of the amount and intensity of required nursing care.

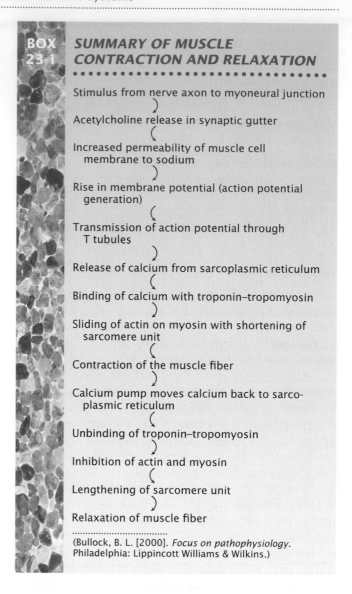

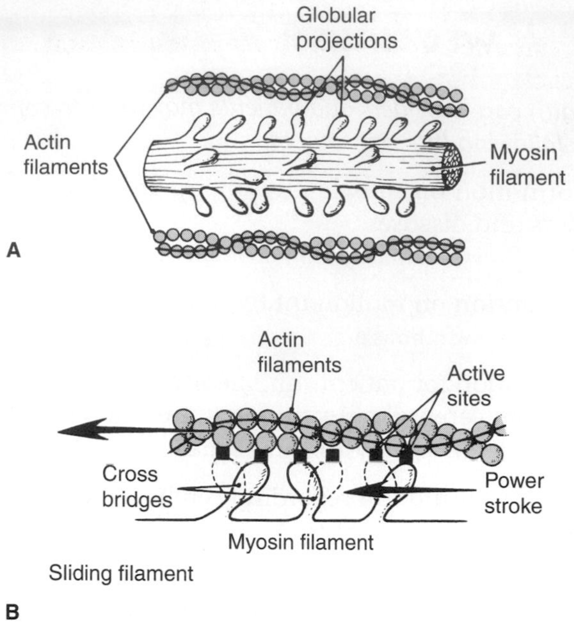

FIGURE 23-2. Sliding filament mechanism of muscle contraction. (*A*) The relationship between the myosin filament and the actin filament projections. (*B*) The bridges formed by the myosin filament move along successive sites on the actin filaments, as outlined in Box 23-1. (Bullock, B. L. [2000]. *Focus on pathophysiology.* Philadelphia: Lippincott Williams & Wilkins.)

BOX 23-1

SUMMARY OF MUSCLE CONTRACTION AND RELAXATION

Stimulus from nerve axon to myoneural junction
↓
Acetylcholine release in synaptic gutter
↓
Increased permeability of muscle cell membrane to sodium
↓
Rise in membrane potential (action potential generation)
↓
Transmission of action potential through T tubules
↓
Release of calcium from sarcoplasmic reticulum
↓
Binding of calcium with troponin–tropomyosin
↓
Sliding of actin on myosin with shortening of sarcomere unit
↓
Contraction of the muscle fiber
↓
Calcium pump moves calcium back to sarcoplasmic reticulum
↓
Unbinding of troponin–tropomyosin
↓
Inhibition of actin and myosin
↓
Lengthening of sarcomere unit
↓
Relaxation of muscle fiber

(Bullock, B. L. [2000]. *Focus on pathophysiology.* Philadelphia: Lippincott Williams & Wilkins.)

Dantrolene is also indicated for the prevention of malignant hyperthermia, a state of intense muscle contraction and resulting hyperpyrexia. Malignant hyperthermia may occur as an adverse reaction to certain neuromuscular junction blockers (this occurs more often with succinylcholine than with other neuromuscular junction blockers [Chapter 26]) that are used to induce paralysis during surgery. Dantrolene is used orally as preoperative prophylaxis in susceptible patients who must undergo anesthesia as well as after acute episodes to prevent recurrence. The agent is also used parenterally to treat malignant hyperthermia crisis.

CONTRAINDICATIONS/CAUTIONS

Dantrolene is contraindicated in the presence of any known allergy to the drug. It is also contraindicated in the following conditions: spasticity that contributes to locomotion, upright position, or increased function, which would be lost if that spasticity was blocked; active hepatic disease, which might interfere with the metabolism of the drug, and because of known liver toxicity; and with lactation, because the drug may cross into breast milk and cause adverse effects in the infant.

Caution should be used in the following circumstances: in females and patients who are more than 35 years of age because of increased risk of potentially fatal hepatocellular disease; in patients with a history of liver disease or previous dysfunction, which could make the liver more susceptible to cellular toxicity; in those with respiratory depression, which could be exacerbated by muscular weakness; and in those with cardiac disease, because cardiac muscle depression may be a risk.

ADVERSE EFFECTS

The most frequently seen adverse effects associated with these drugs relate to drug-caused CNS depression: drowsiness, fatigue, weakness, confusion, headache and insomnia, and visual disturbances. GI disturbances may be linked to direct irritation or to alterations in smooth muscle function due to the drug-induced calcium effects. Such adverse GI effects may include GI irritation, diarrhea, constipation, and abdominal cramps. Dantrolene may also cause direct hepatocellular damage and hepatitis that may be fatal. Urinary frequency, enuresis, and feel-

GENDER/LIFE-SPAN CONSIDERATIONS

Understanding the Risks of Liver Damage With Dantrolene

Dantrolene (*Dantrium*) is associated with potentially fatal hepatocellular injury. When liver damage begins to occur, patients often experience a prodrome, or warning syndrome, which includes anorexia, nausea, and fatigue. The incidence of such hepatic injury is greater in females and patients over 35 years of age.

In females, a combination of dantrolene and estrogen seems to affect the liver, thus posing a greater risk. Women of all ages may be at increased risk, because those entering menopause may be taking hormone replacement therapy to protect them from heart disease and osteoporosis. Patients over 35 years of age are at increasing risk of liver injury because of the changing integrity of the liver cells that comes with age and exposure to toxins over time.

If a particular woman needs dantrolene for relief of spasticity, she should not be taking any estrogens (e.g., birth control pills, hormone replacement therapy), and she should be monitored closely for any sign of liver dysfunction. For safer relief of spasticity in these patients, baclofen may be helpful.

ings of urinary urgency reportedly occur, and crystalline urine with pain or burning on urination may result. In addition, several unusual adverse effects may occur, including acne, abnormal hair growth, rashes, photosensitivity, abnormal sweating, chills, and myalgia.

CLINICALLY IMPORTANT DRUG–DRUG INTERACTIONS

If dantrolene is combined with estrogens, the incidence of hepatocellular toxicity is apparently increased. If possible, this combination should be avoided.

DATA LINK

Data link to the following direct-acting skeletal muscle relaxant in your nursing drug guide:

DIRECT-ACTING SKELETAL MUSCLE RELAXANT

Name	Brand Name	Usual Indications
dantrolene	*Dantrium*	Upper motor neuron-associated muscle spasticity; spinal cord injuries; prevention and management of malignant hyperthermia

NURSING CONSIDERATIONS
for patients receiving a direct-acting skeletal muscle relaxant

Assessment

HISTORY. Screen for the following: any known allergies to these drugs; cardiac depression; epilepsy; muscle weakness; respiratory depression; pregnancy and lactation; and renal or hepatic dysfunction.

PHYSICAL ASSESSMENT. Include screening for baseline status before beginning therapy and for any potential adverse effects. Assess the following: temperature; skin color and lesions; CNS orientation, affect, reflexes, bilateral grip strength, and spasticity; respiration and adventitious sounds; pulse, ECG, and cardiac output; bowel sounds and reported output; and liver and renal function tests.

Nursing Diagnoses

The patient taking a direct-acting skeletal muscle relaxant may have the following nursing diagnoses related to drug therapy:

- Pain related to GI, CNS effects
- Alteration in thought processes related to CNS effects
- Potential for injury related to CNS effects
- Knowledge deficit regarding drug therapy

Implementation

- Discontinue the drug at any sign of liver dysfunction. *Early diagnosis of liver damage may prevent permanent dysfunction. Arrange for the drug to be discontinued if signs of liver damage appear.* A prodrome, with nausea, anorexia, and fatigue, is present in 60% of patients with evidence of hepatic injury.
- Monitor IV sites for potential extravasation *because the drug is alkaline and very irritating to tissues.*
- Institute other supportive measures (e.g., ventilation, anticonvulsants as needed, cooling blankets) for the treatment of malignant hyperthermia *to support patient through the reaction.*
- Periodically discontinue the drug for 2 to 4 days *to monitor therapeutic effectiveness.* A clinical impression of exacerbation of spasticity indicates a positive therapeutic effect and justifies continued use of the drug.
- Establish a therapeutic goal before beginning oral therapy (e.g., to gain or enhance ability to engage in a therapeutic exercise program; to use braces; to accomplish transfer maneuvers) *to promote patient compliance and a sense of success with therapy.*

PATIENT TEACHING CHECKLIST

Direct-Acting Skeletal Muscle Relaxant

Create customized patient teaching materials for a specific direct-acting skeletal muscle relaxant from your CD-ROM. Your patient teaching should stress the following points for drugs within this class:

Direct-acting skeletal muscle relaxants cause muscles that are clinically spastic to relax. Because these drugs could have serious effects on the liver, it is important that you receive regular medical evaluation.

Common effects of these drugs include:

- Fatigue, weakness, and drowsiness—Try to space activities evenly throughout the day and allow rest periods to avoid these sometimes very discouraging side effects. If they become too severe, consult your health care provider.
- Dizziness and fainting—Change position slowly to avoid dizzy spells. If these should occur, you should avoid driving, operating dangerous machinery, or performing delicate tasks.
- Diarrhea—Be sure to be near bathroom facilities if this occurs. This effect usually subsides after a few weeks.

Report any of the following to your health care provider: fever, chills, rash, itching, changes in the color of urine and stool, or yellowish tint to the eyes or skin.

Avoid the use of alcohol or other depressants while you are taking this drug. Serious weakness and muscle depression could occur.

Tell any doctor, nurse, or other health care provider that you are taking these drugs.

Keep this drug and all other medications out of the reach of children.

Take this drug exactly as prescribed. Regular medical follow-up is necessary to evaluate the effects of this drug on your body.

This Teaching Checklist reflects general patient teaching guidelines. It is not meant to be a substitute for drug-specific teaching information, which is available in nursing drug guides.

- Discontinue the drug if diarrhea becomes severe *to prevent dehydration and electrolyte imbalance.* The drug may be restarted at a lower dose.
- Provide thorough patient teaching, including drug name, prescribed dosage, measures for avoidance of adverse effects, warning signs that may indicate possible problems, and the need for monitoring and evaluation *to enhance patient knowledge about drug therapy and to promote compliance* (see Patient Teaching Checklist: Direct-Acting Skeletal Muscle Relaxant).
- Offer support and encouragement *to help the patient cope with the drug regimen.*

Evaluation

- Monitor patient response to the drug (improvement in spasticity, improvement in movement and activities).
- Monitor for adverse effects (CNS changes, diarrhea, liver toxicity, urinary urgency).
- Evaluate the effectiveness of the teaching plan (patient can give the drug name and dosage, name possible adverse effects to watch for and specific measures to prevent adverse effects, and therapeutic goals).
- Monitor the effectiveness of comfort measures and compliance with the regimen (see Nursing Care Guide: Direct-Acting Skeletal Muscle Relaxant).

CHAPTER SUMMARY

- Movement and control of muscles is regulated by spinal reflexes and influences from upper-level central nervous system areas, including the basal ganglia, cerebellum, and cerebral cortex.
- Spinal reflexes can be simple, involving an incoming sensory neuron and an outgoing motor neuron; or more complex, involving interneurons that communicate with the related centers in the brain.
- Upper-level controls of muscle activity include the pyramidal tract in the cerebellum, which regulates coordination of intentional muscle movement, and the extrapyramidal tract in the cerebellum and basal ganglia, which coordinates crude movements related to unconscious muscle activity.

NURSING CARE GUIDE
Direct-Acting Skeletal Muscle Relaxant

Assessment	Nursing Diagnoses	Implementation	Evaluation
HISTORY			
Allergies to any of these drugs, respiratory depression, muscle weakness, hepatic or renal dysfunction, pregnancy and lactation	Pain related to GI, CNS effects Potential for injury related to CNS effects Alteration in thought processes related to CNS effects Knowledge deficit regarding drug therapy	Discontinue drug at first sign of liver dysfunction. Provide comfort and safety measures: positioning, orientation, safety measures, pain medication as needed, monitor for extravasation, institute other measures for treatment of malignant hyperthermia. Provide support and reassurance to deal with spasticity and drug effects. Provide patient teaching concerning drug, dosage, drug effects, symptoms to report.	Evaluate drug effects: relief of spasticity, improvement in function. Monitor for adverse effects: CNS effects (multiple), respiratory depression, rash, skin changes, GI effects (diarrhea, liver toxicity), urinary urgency, weakness. Monitor for drug–drug interactions: increased depression with CNS depressant, alcohol; increased liver toxicity with estrogens. Evaluate effectiveness of patient teaching program. Evaluate effectiveness of comfort and safety measures. Periodically discontinue drug for 2–4 days to evaluate therapeutic effectiveness.
PHYSICAL EXAMINATION			
CV: blood pressure, pulse, peripheral perfusion, ECG CNS: orientation, affect, reflexes, grip strength Skin: color, lesions, texture, temperature GI: abdominal exam, bowel sounds Respiratory: respiration, adventitious sounds Laboratory tests: renal and liver function tests			

- Damage to a muscle or anchoring skeletal structure may result in the arrival of a flood of impulses to the spinal cord. Such overstimulation may lead to a muscle spasm or a state of increased contraction.
- Damage to motor neurons can cause muscle spasticity, with a lack of coordination between muscle groups and loss of coordinated activity, including the ability to perform intentional tasks and maintain posture, position, and locomotion.
- Centrally acting skeletal muscle relaxants are used to relieve the effects of muscle spasm, and dantrolene, a direct-acting skeletal muscle relaxant, is used to control spasticity and prevent malignant hyperthermia.

CASE STUDY

Dantrolene Therapy for a Patient With Cerebral Palsy

PRESENTATION

L. G., a 26-year-old male, was diagnosed with cerebral palsy shortly after birth. He is currently living in a community maintenance home with six other affected individuals under the supervision of two adult care givers. During the past few months, his spasticity has become progressively more severe, making it impossible for him to carry on his activities of daily living without extensive assistance.

After clinical evaluation, his health care team decided to try a course of dantrolene therapy. In a discussion of the risks of hepatic dysfunction, L. G. decided that the potential benefit was much more important to him at this stage in his life than the risks of hepatotoxicity. He received a baseline complete physical examination, including liver enzymes. He started taking the drug, and a clinic staff member scheduled L. G. for a visit by a public health nurse in 4 days.

CRITICAL THINKING QUESTIONS

What basic principles must be included in the nursing care plan for L. G. for the visiting nurses? Think about the importance of including the adult care givers in any teaching or evaluation programs. Consider specific problems that could develop that L. G. would not be able to handle on his own. What therapeutic goals might the nurse set with L. G. and his care givers? How might these be evaluated? What additional drug-related information should be posted in the community home and reviewed with L. G. and his care givers?

DISCUSSION

On the first visit to his home, it is important for the nurse to establish a relationship with L. G. and with his care givers. They should all realize that drug therapy, as well as other measures, are needed to help him attain his full potential and make use of his existing assets. Step-by-step therapeutic goals should be established and written down for future reference. Small, reachable goals such as partially dressing himself, walking to the table for meals, and managing parts of his daily hygiene routine are best at the beginning. Written goals provide a good basis for future evaluation when the drug is stopped for a few days to evaluate its therapeutic effectiveness. It also helps L. G. to see progress and improvement.

In addition, the nurse should perform a complete examination to obtain baseline data. The patient should be asked about any noticeable changes or problems since starting the drug. If improvement appears to have occurred, the dosage may be slowly increased until the optimal level of functioning has been achieved. The nurse is in a position to evaluate this and report it to his primary care giver.

While in the home, the nurse should evaluate resources and limitations in the patient's environment and suggest improvements (e.g., use of leg braces, environmental controls). L. G. and his care givers should receive a drug teaching card, which includes a phone number for expression of questions or concerns, that highlights warning signs of liver disease and findings to report. The nurse should discuss anticipated return dates for liver function testing to ensure that L. G. is able to keep the appointments. The health care team should work closely with the patient to maximize his involvement in his care and to minimize unnecessary problems and confusion. Because the treatment involves a long-term commitment, a good working relationship between all members of the health care team is important in ensuring continuity of care and optimal results.

BIBLIOGRAPHY

Bullock, B. L. (2000). *Focus on pathophysiology*. Philadelphia: Lippincott Williams & Wilkins.

Hardman, J. G., Limbird, L. E., Molinoff, P. B., Ruddon, R. W., & Gilman, A. G. (Eds.). (1996). *Goodman and Gilman's the pharmacological basis of therapeutics* (9th ed.). New York: McGraw-Hill.

Karch, A. M. (2000). *2000 Lippincott's nursing drug guide.* Philadelphia: Lippincott Williams & Wilkins.

Malseed, R. (1995). *Textbook of pharmacology and nursing care.* Philadelphia: Lippincott-Raven.

McEvoy, B. R. (Ed.). (1999). *Facts and comparisons 1999.* St. Louis: Facts and Comparisons.

Professional's guide to patient drug facts. (1999). St. Louis: Facts and Comparisons.

CHAPTER 24

Narcotics and Antimigraine Agents

Narcotics
- Narcotic agonists
  - codeine
  - fentanyl
  - hydrocodone
  - hydromorphone
  - levomethadyl
  - levorphanol
  - meperidine
  - methadone
  - **P** morphine
  - opium
  - oxycodone
  - oxymorphone
  - propoxyphene
  - remifentanil
  - sufentanil
- Narcotic agonists-antagonists
  - buprenorphine
  - butorphanol
  - dezocine
  - nalbuphine
  - **P** pentazocine
- Narcotic antagonists
  - nalmefene
  - **P** naloxone
  - naltrexone

Antimigraine drugs
- Ergot derivatives
  - dihydroergotamine
  - **P** ergotamine
  - methysergide
- Triptans
  - naratriptan
  - rizatriptan
  - **P** sumatriptan
  - zolmitriptan

CHAPTER OUTLINE

KEY TERMS

A fibers
A-delta and C fibers
ergot derivatives
gate control theory
migraine headache
narcotics
narcotic agonists
narcotic agonists-antagonists
narcotic antagonists
opioid receptors
spinothalamic tracts
triptan

INTRODUCTION

Pain, by definition, is a sensory and emotional experience associated with actual or potential tissue damage. The perception of pain is part of the clinical presentation in many disorders and is one of the hardest sensations for patients to cope with during the course of a disease or dysfunction. The drugs involved in the management of severe pain, whether acute or chronic, are discussed in this chapter. These agents all work in the central nervous system (CNS)—the brain and the spinal cord—to alter the way that pain impulses arriving from peripheral nerves are processed. These agents can change the perception and tolerance of pain. Two major types of drugs are considered here: the ***narcotics,*** the opium derivatives that are used to treat many types of pain, and the antimigraine drugs, which are reserved for the treatment of ***migraine headaches,*** a type of severe headache.

PAIN PERCEPTION

Pain occurs whenever tissues are damaged. The injury to cells releases many chemicals, including the kinins and prostaglandins, which stimulate specific sensory nerves (Figure 24–1). Two small-diameter sensory nerves, called the ***A-delta and C fibers,*** respond to stimulation by generating nerve impulses that produce pain sensations. Pain impulses from the skin, subcutaneous tissues, muscles, and deep visceral structures are conducted to the dorsal, or posterior, horn of the spinal cord on these fibers. In the spinal cord, these nerves form synapses with spinal cord nerve that then send impulses to the brain.

In addition, large-diameter sensory nerves enter the dorsal horn of the spinal cord. These so-called ***A fibers*** do not transmit pain impulses; instead, they transmit sensations associated with touch and temperature. The A fibers, which are larger and conduct impulses more rapidly than the smaller fibers, can actually block the ability of the smaller fibers to transmit their signals to the secondary neurons in the spinal cord. The dorsal horn, therefore, can be both excitatory and inhibitory with pain impulses that are transmitted from the periphery.

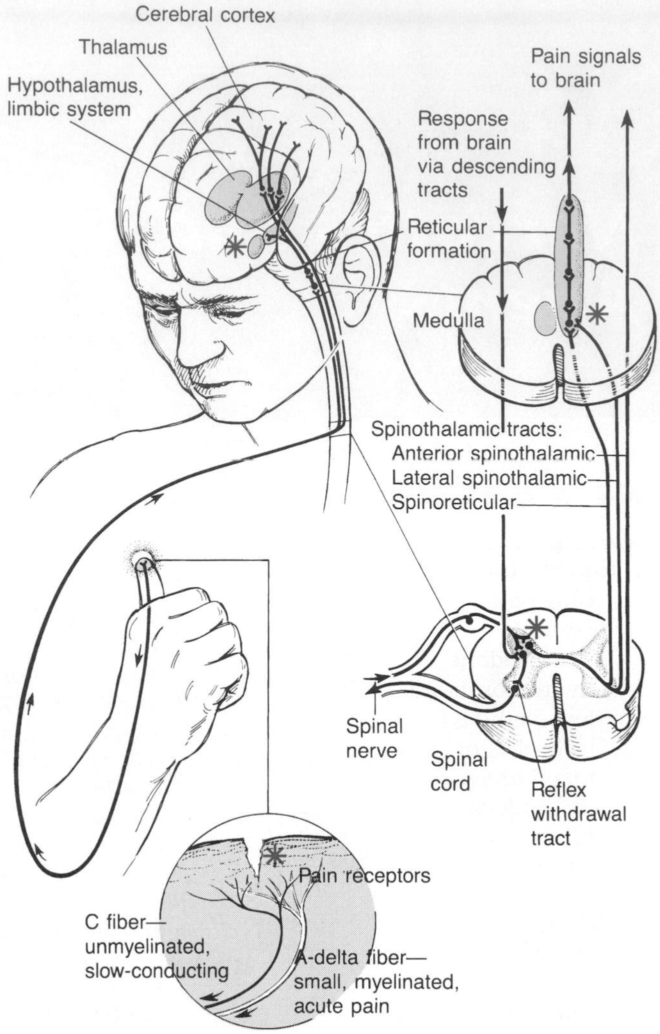

FIGURE 24-1. Neural pathways of pain. (Bullock, B. L. [2000]. *Focus on pathophysiology.* Philadelphia: Lippincott Williams & Wilkins.)

The impulses reaching the dorsal horn are transmitted upward toward the brain by a number of specific ascending nerve pathways. These pathways run from the spinal cord into the thalamus, where they form synapses with various nerve cells that transmit the information to the cerebral cortex, along the ***spinothalamic tracts.*** According to the ***gate control theory,*** the transmission of these impulses can be modulated all along these tracts (Figure 24-2). All along the spinal cord, the interneurons can act as "gates" by blocking the ascending transmission of pain impulses. It is thought that the gates can be closed by stimulation of the larger A fibers and by descending impulses coming down the spinal cord

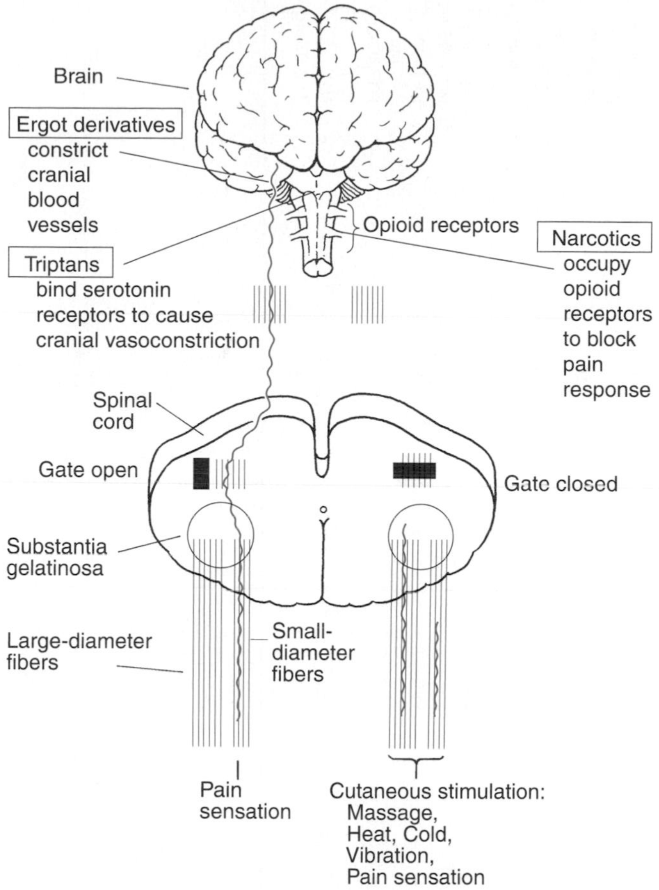

FIGURE 24-2. Gate control theory of pain. Narcotics occupy opioid receptors to block pain response. Ergot derivatives constrict cranial blood vessels, and triptans bind serotonin receptors to cause cranial vasoconstriction.

from higher levels in such areas as the cerebral cortex, the limbic system, and the reticular activating system.

The inhibitory influence of the higher brain centers on the transmission of pain impulses helps explain much of the mystery associated with pain. Several factors, including learned experiences, cultural expectations, individual tolerance, and the placebo effect, can activate the descending inhibitory nerves from the upper central nervous system. Pain management usually involves the use of drugs, but it may also incorporate these other factors. The placebo effect, stress reduction, acupuncture, and back rubs (which stimulate the A fibers) all can play an important role in the effective management of pain.

Narcotics

The narcotics, or opioids, were first derived from the opium plant. Although most narcotics are now synthetically prepared, their chemical structure resembles that of the original plant alkaloids. All drugs in this class are similar in that they occupy specific ***opioid receptors*** in the CNS.

Opioid Receptors

These receptors respond to naturally occurring peptins, the endorphins and the enkephalins. These receptors are found in the CNS, on nerves in the periphery, and on cells in the gastrointestinal (GI) tract. In the brainstem, opioid receptors help control blood pressure, pupil diameter, GI secretions, and the chemoreceptor trigger zone that regulates nausea and vomiting, cough, and respiration. In the spinal cord and thalamus, these receptors help integrate and relate incoming information about pain. In the hypothalamus, they may interrelate the endocrine and neural response to pain. In the limbic system, the receptors incorporate emotional aspects of pain and response to pain. At peripheral nerve sites, the opioids may block the release of neurotransmitters that are related to pain and inflammation.

The different narcotic drugs that are used vary with the type of opioid receptors with which they react. This accounts for a change in pain relief as well as a variation in the side effects that can be anticipated. Four types of opioid receptors have been identified: mu (μ), kappa (κ), beta (β) and sigma (σ). The μ receptors are primarily pain-blocking receptors. Besides analgesia, μ receptors also account for respiratory depression, a feeling of euphoria, decreased GI activity, pupil constriction, and the development of physical dependence. The κ receptors have been associated with some analgesia and with pupil constriction, sedation, and dysphoria. Enkephalins react with β receptors in the periphery to modulate pain transmission. The σ receptors cause pupil dilation and may be responsible for the hallucinations, dysphoria, and psychoses that can occur with narcotic use.

NARCOTIC AGONISTS

The ***narcotic agonists*** are drugs that react with the opioid receptors throughout the body to cause analgesia, sedation, or euphoria. Anticipated effects other than analgesia are mediated by the types of opioid receptors affected by each drug. Because of the potential for the development of physical dependence while taking these drugs, the narcotic agonists are classified as controlled substances. The degree of control is determined by the relative ability of each drug to cause physical dependence. The narcotic agonists that are available are listed in Table 24-1.

THERAPEUTIC ACTIONS AND INDICATIONS

The narcotic agonists act at specific opioid receptor sites in the CNS to produce analgesia, sedation, and

TABLE 24-1

COMPARISON OF NARCOTIC AGONIST ANALGESICS

Drug	Brand Name(s)	Routes	Onset	Duration	Analgesia	Sedation	Depressed Respiration	Constipation	Antitussive	Dependence	Equianalgesic Dose
codeine		oral, IM, IV	10–30 min	4–6 hr	x	x	x	x	xx	x	PO 200 mg IM 120 mg
fentanyl	*Duragesic*	oral, IM, IV, transdermal	7–8 min	1–2 hr	xx	x	—	—	—	?	IM 0.1 mg
hydrocodone	*Hycodan*	oral	10–20 min	4–6 hr	x	—	x	—	xx	x	PO 5–10 mg
hydromorphone	*Dilaudid*	oral, SC, IM	15–30 min	4–5 hr	xx	x	xx	x	xx	xx	PO 7.5 mg IM 1.3–1.5 mg
levomethadyl	*ORLAAM*	oral	slow	72 hr	x	x	x	x	x	x	NA
levorphanol	*Levo-Dromoran*	oral, SC	30–90 min	6–8hr	xx	xx	xx	xx	xx	xx	PO 4 mg IM 2 mg
meperidine	*Demerol*	oral, SC, IM, IV	10–15 min	2–4 hr	xx	x	xx	x	x	xx	PO 300 mg IM 75 mg
methadone	*Dolophine*	oral, SC, IM	10–60 min	4–12 hr	xx	x	xx	xx	xx	x	PO 10–20 mg IM 10 mg
P morphine	*Roxanal, Astomorph*	oral, PR, SC, IM, IV	20–60 min	5–7 hr	xx	xx	xx	xx	xx	xx	PO 30–60 mg IM 10 mg
opium	*Paregoric*	oral	varies	3–7 hr	x	x	x	xx	—	x	NA
oxycodone	*OxyContin*	oral	15–30 min	4–6 hr	xx	xx	xx	xx	xx	xx	PO 30 mg IM 10–15 mg
oxymorphone	*Numorphan*	PR, SC, IM, IV	5–30 min	3–6 hr	xx	—	xx	xx	x	xx	PR 10 mg IM 1 mg
propoxyphene	*Darvon, Darvocet*	oral	varies	2–2.5 hr	x	x	x	—	x	x	PO 130–200 mg
remifentanil	*Utiva*	IV	immediate	5 min	xx	xx	xx	x	x	—	NA
sufentanil	*Sufenta*	IV	immediate	5 min	xx	xx	xx	x	x	—	IM 0.02 mg

a sense of well being. They are used as antitussives and as adjuncts to general anesthesia to produce rapid analgesia, sedation, and respiratory depression. Indications for narcotic agonists include relief of severe acute or chronic pain; preoperative medication; analgesia during anesthesia; and specific individual indications depending on their receptor affinity. Table 24-1 indicates the available routes for each drug, the onset and duration of action, and the degree to which the various opioid effects are stimulated by each drug. If known, the equianalgesic dosage is also given. This is the dose of each drug that would be required to achieve the same level of analgesia as the corresponding dose of the other narcotic agents.

In deciding which narcotic to use in any particular situation, it is important to consider all of these aspects and select the drug that will be most effective in each situation with the least adverse effects for the patient. For instance, if you want an analgesic that is long acting but not too sedating for an outpatient, hydrocodone might be the drug that best fits your objectives (see Table 24-1).

CONTRAINDICATIONS/CAUTIONS

The narcotic agonists are contraindicated in the following conditions: presence of any known allergy to any narcotic agonist; pregnancy, labor, and lactation because of potential adverse effects on the fetus or neonate, including respiratory depression; diarrhea caused by poisons because the depression of GI activity could lead to increased absorption and toxicity; and following biliary surgery or surgical anastomoses because of the adverse effects associated with GI depression and narcotics.

Caution should be used in patients with respiratory dysfunction, which could be exacerbated by the respiratory depression caused by these drugs; recent GI or genitourinary (GU) surgery; acute abdomen or ulcerative colitis, which could become worse with the depressive effects of the narcotics; head injuries, alcoholism, delirium tremens, or cerebral vascular disease, which could be exacerbated by the CNS effects of the drugs; and liver and renal dysfunction, which could alter the metabolism and excretion of the drugs.

ADVERSE EFFECTS

The most frequently seen adverse effects associated with narcotic agonists relate to their effects on various opioid receptors. Respiratory depression with apnea, cardiac arrest, and shock may result from narcotic-caused CNS respiratory depression. Orthostatic hypotension is commonly seen with some narcotics. Such GI effects as nausea, vomiting, constipation, and biliary spasm may occur as a result of CTZ stimulation and negative effects on GI motility. Neurological effects such as lightheadedness, dizziness, psychoses, anxiety, fear, hallucinations, pupil constriction, and impaired mental processes may occur as a result of the stimulation of CNS opioid receptors in the cerebrum, limbic system, and hypothalamus. GU effects, including ureteral spasm, urinary retention, hesitancy, and loss of libido, may be related to direct receptor stimulation or to CNS activation of sympathetic pathways. In addition, sweating and dependence, both physical and psychological, are possible, more so with some agents than with others.

CLINICALLY IMPORTANT DRUG–DRUG INTERACTIONS

When narcotic agonists are given with the barbiturate general anesthetics, and some phenothiazines and MAO inhibitors, the likelihood of respiratory depression, hypotension, and sedation or coma is increased. If these drug combinations cannot be avoided, patients should be monitored closely and appropriate supportive measures taken.

DATA LINK

Data link to the narcotic agonists, which are listed on Table 24-1, in your nursing drug guide.

NURSING CONSIDERATIONS
for patients receiving narcotic agonists

Assessment

HISTORY. Screen for the following: any known allergies to these drugs; pregnancy; respiratory dysfunction, GI, or biliary surgery; psychoses; convulsive disorders; diarrhea caused by toxins; alcoholism or delirium tremens; and renal and hepatic dysfunction.

PHYSICAL ASSESSMENT. Include screening for baseline status before beginning therapy and for any potential adverse effects. Assess the following: CNS orientation, affect, reflexes, pupil size; respiration and adventitious sounds; pulse, blood pressure, and cardiac output; bowel sounds and reported output; bladder palpation, voiding pattern. Check liver and renal function tests, as well as EEG and ECG as appropriate.

Nursing Diagnoses

The patient receiving a narcotic agonist may have the following nursing diagnoses related to drug therapy:

- Pain related to GI, CNS, GU effects
- Sensory–perceptual alteration related to CNS effects

PATIENT TEACHING CHECKLIST

Narcotics

Create customized patient teaching materials for a specific narcotic from your CD-ROM. Your patient teaching should stress the following points for drugs within this class:

A narcotic is used to relieve pain. *Do not hesitate* to take this drug if you feel uncomfortable. It is important to use the drug before the pain becomes severe and thus becomes more difficult to treat.

Common effects of these drugs include:

- Constipation—Your health care provider will suggest an appropriate bowel program to alleviate this common problem.
- Dizziness, drowsiness, and visual changes—If any of these occur, avoid driving, operating dangerous machinery, or performing delicate tasks. If this occurs in the hospital, the side rails on the bed may be put up for your own protection
- Nausea and loss of appetite—Taking the drug with food may help. Lying quietly until these sensations pass may also help alleviate this problem.

Report any of the following to your health care provider: severe nausea or vomiting, skin rash, or shortness of breath or difficulty breathing.

Avoid the use of alcohol, antihistamines, and other over-the-counter drugs while taking this drug. Many of these drugs could interact with this narcotic.

Tell any doctor, nurse, or other health care provider that you are taking this drug.

Keep this drug and all medications out of the reach of children.

Do not take any leftover medication for other disorders, and do not let anyone else take your medication.

Take this drug exactly as prescribed. Regular medical follow-up is necessary to evaluate the effects of this drug on your body.

This Teaching Checklist reflects general patient teaching guidelines. It is not meant to be a substitute for drug-specific teaching information, which is available in nursing drug guides.

- Impaired gas exchange related to respiratory depression
- Alteration in bowel elimination, constipation related to GI effects
- Knowledge deficit regarding drug therapy

Implementation

- Provide a narcotic antagonist and equipment for assisted ventilation on standby during IV administration *to support patient in case severe reaction occurs.*
- Monitor injection sites for irritation and extravasation *in order to provide appropriate supportive care if needed.*
- Monitor timing of analgesic doses. *Prompt administration may provide a more acceptable level of analgesia and lead to quicker resolution of the pain.*
- Use extreme caution when injecting a narcotic into any body area that is chilled or has poor perfusion or shock *because absorption may be delayed. After repeated doses, an excessive amount is absorbed all at once.*
- Use additional measures to relieve pain such as back rubs, stress reduction, hot packs, and ice packs *to increase the effectiveness of the narcotic and reduce pain.*
- Assure patients that the risk of addiction is minimal. *Most patients who receive narcotics for medical reasons do not develop dependency syndromes.*
- Provide thorough patient teaching, including drug name and prescribed dosage, as well as measures for avoidance of adverse effects, warning signs that may indicate possible problems, and the need for monitoring and evaluation *to enhance patient knowledge about drug therapy and to promote compliance* (see Patient Teaching Checklist: Narcotics).
- Offer support and encouragement *to help the patient cope with the drug regimen.*

Evaluation

- Monitor patient response to the drug (relief of pain, cough suppression, sedation).
- Monitor for adverse effects (CNS changes, GI depression, respiratory depression, constipation).
- Evaluate the effectiveness of the teaching plan (patient can give the drug name and dosage and describe possible adverse effects to watch for, specific measures to prevent adverse effects, and warning signs to report).

NURSING CARE GUIDE
Narcotic Agonists

Assessment	Nursing Diagnoses	Implementation	Evaluation
HISTORY Allergies to any of these drugs, respiratory depression, GI or biliary surgery, hepatic or renal dysfunction, pregnancy and lactation, alcoholism, convulsive disorders	Pain related to GI, CNS, GU effects Sensory–perceptual alteration related to CNS effects Impaired gas exchange related to respiratory depression Knowledge deficit regarding drug therapy Alteration in bowel elimination, constipation	Provide a narcotic antagonist, facilities for assisted ventilation during IV administration. Provide comfort and safety measures: orientation, safety measures, accurate timing of doses, monitor for extravasation, use additional measures for pain relief to increase effects. Provide support and reassurance to deal with drug effects, addiction potential. Provide patient teaching about drug, dosage, drug effects, symptoms to report.	Evaluate drug effects: relief of pain, sedation, cough suppression. Monitor for adverse effects: CNS effects (multiple), respiratory depression, rash, skin changes, GI depression, constipation. Monitor drug–drug interactions: increased respiratory depression, sedation, coma with barbiturate anesthetics, MAO inhibitors, phenothiazines. Evaluate effectiveness of patient teaching program. Evaluate effectiveness of comfort and safety measures.
PHYSICAL EXAMINATION CV: blood pressure, pulse, peripheral perfusion, ECG CNS: orientation, affect, reflexes, grip strength Skin: color, lesions, texture, temperature GI: abdominal exam, bowel sounds Respiratory: respiration, adventitious sounds Laboratory tests: renal and liver function tests			

• Monitor the effectiveness of comfort measures and compliance with the regimen (see Nursing Care Guide: Narcotic Agonists).

NARCOTIC AGONISTS-ANTAGONISTS

The ***narcotic agonists-antagonists*** stimulate certain opioid receptors but block other such receptors. These drugs, which have less abuse potential than the pure narcotic agonists, all have about the same analgesic effect as morphine. Like morphine, they may cause sedation, respiratory depression, and constipation. They have also been associated with more psychotic-like reactions, and they may even induce a withdrawal syndrome in patients who been taking narcotics for a long period of time.

Available narcotic agonists-antagonists include:

• Buprenorphine (*Buprenex*), which is recommended for treatment of mild to moderate pain. It is available for use in IM and IV forms.
• Butorphanol (*Stadol, Stadol NS*), which is used as preoperative medication to relieve moderate to severe pain. This drug is formulated in IM or IV preparations, and as a nasal spray. It is effective in treating migraine headaches with fewer peripheral adverse

CASE STUDY

Using Morphine to Relieve Pain

PRESENTATION

L. M., a 25-year-old businessman, was in a serious automobile accident and suffered a fractured pelvis, a fractured left tibia, a fractured right humerus, and multiple contusions and abrasions. For the first 2 days following surgery to reduce the fractures, L. M. was heavily sedated. As healing progressed, he was maintained on IM injections of morphine every 4 hours prn for pain. L. M. requested medication every 2 to 3 hours and became very agitated by the end of the prescribed 4 hours. L. M.'s physician decided to switch him to meperidine given IM every 3 hours for 2 days and then switched to oral dosage in an attempt to wean him from the narcotics.

CRITICAL THINKING QUESTIONS

What basic principles must be included in the nursing care plan for this patient? Think about the difficult position the floor nurse is in when L. M. begins demanding pain relief before the prescribed time limit. What implications will his agitation have on the way that the staff responds to him and on other patients in the area? What other nursing measures could be used to help relieve pain and make the narcotic more effective? What plans could the health team make with L. M. to give him more control over his situation and increase the chances that the pain relief will be effective?

DISCUSSION

In assessing L. M.'s response to drug therapy, it is apparent that the morphine was not providing the desired therapeutic effect. Numerous research studies have shown that, in general, the dosage of narcotics prescribed for acute pain relief provides inadequate analgesic coverage. It could be that the dose of morphine ordered for L. M. is just not sufficient to relieve his pain. This patient has many causes of acute pain and will heal more quickly if the pain is managed better. He has requested more drugs because the dosage is too small or the intervals between doses are too long to effectively relieve his pain. IV morphine could be added to complement his pain management. Other measures may be successful in helping the morphine relieve the pain; back rubs, environmental control to decrease excessive stimuli (e.g., controlling noise, lighting, temperature, and interruptions), and stress reduction may all be useful.

L. M. may be very anxious about his injuries, and the opportunity to ventilate his feelings and concerns may alleviate some of the tension associated with pain. He may fear that if he does not request the medication early, he will not get it by the prescribed time. The nursing staff can work on this concern and figure out a way to assure him that the medication will be delivered. Changing from morphine to meperidine may improve the analgesic effects, partly because of a placebo reaction that may occur when he is told that this drug will be more effective and partly because people respond differently to different narcotics.

The health care team should try to discuss the concerns with L. M., including the concern about physical dependence. L. M. is a businessman and so may respond positively to having some input into his care; he may even offer suggestions on how he could cope better and adjust to his situation. Cortical impulses can close gates as effectively as descending inhibitory pathways, and stimulation of the cortical pathways through patient education and active involvement should be considered an important aspect of pain relief. Because L. M.'s injuries are extensive, a long-term approach should be taken to his care. The sooner that L. M. can be involved, the better the situation will be for everyone involved.

effects than many of the traditional antimigraine drugs.

- Dezocine (*Dalgan*), which is used in IM and IV forms to treat moderate to severe pain, to add balanced anesthesia (preoperatively), and to relieve postpartum pain.
- Nalbuphine (*Nubain*), which is used to treat moderate to severe pain, as an adjunct for general anesthesia, and to relieve pain during labor and delivery. This drug, which is formulated in SC, IM, and IV preparations, should not be used in sulfite-allergic patients.
- Pentazocine (*Talwin*), which is also available in an oral form, making it the preferred drug for patients who will be switched from parenteral to oral forms following surgery or labor. This drug has been abused in combination with tripelennamine (Ts and Blues) because of a hallucinogenic, euphoric effect of the two drugs, with potentially fatal complications.

THERAPEUTIC ACTIONS AND INDICATIONS

The narcotic agonists-antagonists act at specific opioid receptor sites in the CNS to produce analgesia, sedation, euphoria, and hallucinations. In addition, they block opioid receptors that may be stimulated by other narcotics. These drugs have three functions: (1) relief of moderate to severe pain, (2) adjuncts to general anesthesia, and (3) relief of pain during labor and delivery.

CONTRAINDICATIONS/CAUTIONS

Narcotic agonists-antagonists are contraindicated in the presence of any known allergy to any narcotic agonist-antagonist and during pregnancy and lactation because of potential adverse effects on the fetus and neonate, including respiratory depression. (However, these drugs may be used to relieve pain during labor and delivery.)

Caution should be used in cases of physical dependence on a narcotic, because a withdrawal syndrome may be precipitated; the narcotic antagonistic properties can block the analgesic effect and intensify the pain. Narcotic agonists-antagonists may be desirable in relieving chronic pain in patients who are susceptible to narcotic dependence, but extreme care must be used if patients are switched directly from a narcotic agonist to one of these drugs.

Caution should also be exercised in the following conditions: with chronic obstructive pulmonary disease or other respiratory dysfunction, which could be exacerbated by respiratory depression; with acute myocardial infarction (MI), documented coronary artery disease (CAD), or hypertension that could be exacerbated by cardiac stimulatory effects of these drugs; and with renal or hepatic dysfunction that could interfere with the metabolism and excretion of the drug.

Pentazocine also may cause cardiac stimulation including arrhythmias, hypertension, and increased myocardial oxygen consumption, which could lead to angina, MI, or congestive heart failure. Care must be used with patients with known heart disease.

ADVERSE EFFECTS

The most frequently seen adverse effects associated with narcotic agonists-antagonists relate to their effects on various opioid receptors. Respiratory depression with apnea and suppression of the cough reflex is associated with the respiratory depression caused by the narcotics. Nausea, vomiting, constipation, and biliary spasm may occur as a result of CTZ stimulation and the negative effects on GI motility. Lightheadedness, dizziness, psychoses, anxiety, fear, hallucinations, and impaired mental processes may occur as a result of the stimulation of CNS opioid receptors in the cerebrum, limbic system, and hypothalamus. GU effects, including ureteral spasm, urinary retention, hesitancy, and loss of libido, may be related to direct receptor stimulation or to CNS activation of sympathetic pathways. Although sweating and dependence, both physical and psychological, are possible, their occurrence is considered less likely than with narcotic agonists.

CLINICALLY IMPORTANT DRUG–DRUG INTERACTIONS

When narcotic agonists-antagonists, like narcotic agonists, are given with barbiturate general anesthetics, the likelihood of respiratory depression, hypotension, and sedation or coma increases. If this combination cannot be avoided, patients should be monitored closely and appropriate supportive measures taken.

Use of narcotic agonists-antagonists in patients who have previously received narcotics puts these patients at risk. When such a sequence of drugs is used, patients require support and monitoring.

DATA LINK

Data link to the following narcotic agonists-antagonists in your nursing drug guide:

NARCOTIC AGONISTS-ANTAGONISTS

Name	Brand Name	Usual Indications
buprenorphine	*Buprenex*	Mild to moderate pain
butorphanol	*Stadol*	Preoperative medication, moderate to severe pain, migraine headache
dezocine	*Dalgan*	Preoperative medication, moderate to severe pain, postpartum pain
nalbuphine	*Nubain*	Labor and delivery, adjunct to general anesthesia, moderate to severe pain
P pentazocine	*Talwin*	Moderate to severe pain, labor and delivery, postpartum pain, adjunct to general anesthesia

NURSING CONSIDERATIONS for patients receiving narcotic agonists-antagonists

Assessment

HISTORY. Screen for the following: any known allergies to these drugs and to sulfites if using nalbuphine; pregnancy and lactation; respiratory dysfunction; MI or CAD; and renal and hepatic dysfunction.

PHYSICAL ASSESSMENT. Include screening for baseline status before beginning therapy and for any potential adverse effects. Assess the following: CNS orientation, affect, reflexes, and pupil size; respiration and adventitious sounds; pulse, blood pressure, and cardiac output; bowel sounds and reported output; and liver and renal function tests as well as ECG.

Nursing Diagnoses

The patient receiving a narcotic agonist-antagonist may have the following nursing diagnoses related to drug therapy:

- Pain related to GI, CNS effects
- Sensory–perceptual alteration related to CNS effects
- Impaired gas exchange related to respiratory depression
- Knowledge deficit regarding drug therapy

Implementation

- Provide a narcotic antagonist and equipment for assisted ventilation on standby during IV administration *to provide patient support in case of severe reaction.*
- Monitor injection sites for irritation and extravasation *in order to provide appropriate supportive care if needed.*
- Monitor timing of analgesic doses. *Prompt administration may provide a more acceptable level of analgesia and lead to quicker resolution of the pain.*
- Use extreme caution when injecting these drugs into any body area that is chilled or has poor perfusion or shock *because absorption may be delayed and after repeated doses, an excessive amount is absorbed all at once.*
- Use additional measures to relieve pain (e.g., back rubs, stress reduction, hot packs, ice packs) *to increase the effectiveness of the narcotic being given and reduce pain.*
- Institute comfort and safety measures such as side rails, assistance with ambulation *to ensure patient safety;* bowel program as needed to treat constipation; use environmental controls *to decrease stimulation;* and provide small frequent meals *to relieve GI distress if GI upset is severe.*
- Assure patients that the risk of addiction is minimal. *Most patients who receive these drugs for medical reasons do not develop dependency syndromes.*
- Provide thorough patient teaching, including drug name and prescribed dosage, as well as measures for avoidance of adverse effects, warning signs that may indicate possible problems, and the need for monitoring and evaluation *to enhance patient knowledge about drug therapy and to promote compliance* (see Patient Teaching Checklist: Narcotics).
- Offer support and encouragement *to help the patient cope with the drug regimen.*

Evaluation

- Monitor patient response to the drug (relief of pain, sedation).
- Monitor for adverse effects (CNS changes, GI depression, respiratory depression, arrhythmias, hypertension).
- Evaluate the effectiveness of the teaching plan (patient can give the drug name and dosage and describe possible adverse effects to watch for, specific measures to prevent adverse effects, and warning signs to report).
- Monitor the effectiveness of comfort measures and compliance with the regimen.

NARCOTIC ANTAGONISTS

The **narcotic antagonists** are drugs that bind strongly to opioid receptors, but they do not activate the receptors. These agents are useful in blocking unwanted adverse effects associated with narcotics such as respiratory depression, and they play a role in the treatment of narcotic overdose. These drugs do not have an appreciable effect in most people, but individuals who are addicted to narcotics experience the signs and symptoms of withdrawal when rapidly receiving these drugs.

The narcotic antagonists in use today include:

CULTURAL/LIFE-SPAN CONSIDERATIONS

Differences in Responses to Narcotic Therapy

Due to physical and cultural differences among various ethnic groups, patients from certain groups respond differently to particular medications. Nurses should keep in mind that patients in some ethnic groups are genetically predisposed to metabolize medications differently. For example, Arab Americans may not achieve the same pain relief from narcotics as patients in other ethnic groups; their inborn differences in metabolism may require larger doses to achieve therapeutic effects.

Some African-American patients seem to have a decreased sensitivity to the pain-relieving qualities of some narcotics, although the reason for this is unknown. Moreover, increasing the dosage of these medications may not increase the level of pain relief and actually may be toxic. Thus, another class of medication might be used to "boost" the pain-relieving qualities of the narcotic.

Among some immigrant and first-generation Asian Americans, it may not be socially acceptable to show strong emotion, such as that associated with pain. The sensitive nurse will frequently ask such patients if they are comfortable or require additional medication.

Likewise, the nurse should ask elderly patients specifically if they require pain medication. Because many older patients may recall a time when nurses were able to spend more time with patients, they may tend to believe that the nurse will meet their needs.

• Nalmefene (*Revex*), which can be used IV, IM, or SC to reverse the effects of narcotics and to manage known or suspected narcotic overdose.
• Naloxone (*Narcan*) which is used IV, IM, or SC to reverse adverse effects of narcotics and to diagnose suspected acute narcotic overdose.
• Naltrexone (*ReVia*), which is used orally in the management of alcohol or narcotic dependence as part of a comprehensive treatment program.

THERAPEUTIC ACTIONS AND INDICATIONS

The narcotic antagonists block opioid receptors and reverse the effects of opioids, including respiratory depression, sedation, psychomimetic effects, and hypotension. Their effects are seen in people who have been using narcotics or are dependent on narcotics.

These agents are indicated for reversal of the adverse effects of narcotic use, including respiratory depression and sedation, and for treatment of narcotic overdose. Naloxone is used to diagnose narcotic overdose using the naloxone challenge, and naltrexone is used as part of a comprehensive program to treat narcotic and/or alcoholic dependence.

CONTRAINDICATIONS/CAUTIONS

Narcotic antagonists are contraindicated in the presence of any known allergy to any narcotic antagonist. Caution should be used in the following circumstances: during pregnancy and lactation because of potential adverse effects on the fetus and neonate; with narcotic addiction because of the precipitation of a withdrawal syndrome; and with cardiovascular (CV) disease, which could be exacerbated by the reversal of the depressive effects of narcotics.

ADVERSE EFFECTS

The most frequently seen adverse effects associated with these drugs relate to the blocking effects of the opioid receptors. The most common effect is an acute narcotic abstinence syndrome that is characterized by nausea, vomiting, sweating, tachycardia, hypertension, tremulousness, and feelings of anxiety. CNS excitement and reversal of analgesia is especially common postoperatively. CV effects related to the reversal of the opioid depression can include tachycardia, blood pressure changes, arrhythmias, and pulmonary edema.

DATA LINK

Data link to the following narcotic antagonists in your nursing drug guide:

NARCOTIC ANTAGONISTS

Name	Brand Name	Usual Indications
nalmefene	*Revex*	Reversal of opioid effects, management of narcotic overdose
P naloxone	*Narcan*	Diagnosis of narcotic overdose, reversal of opioid effects
naltrexone	*ReVia*	Adjunct treatment of alcohol or narcotic dependence

NURSING CONSIDERATIONS
for patients receiving narcotic antagonists

Assessment

HISTORY. Screen for the following: any known allergies to these drugs; pregnancy and lactation; MI or CAD; and narcotic addiction.

PHYSICAL ASSESSMENT. Include screening for baseline status before beginning therapy and for any potential adverse effects. Assess the following: CNS orientation, affect, reflexes, and pupil size; respiration and adventitious sounds; pulse, blood pressure, and cardiac output; and ECG.

Nursing Diagnoses

The patient receiving a narcotic antagonist may have the following nursing diagnoses related to drug therapy:

• Pain related to withdrawal, CV effects
• Alteration in cardiac output related to CV effects
• Knowledge deficit regarding drug therapy

Implementation

• Maintain open airway and provide artificial ventilation and cardiac massage *as needed to support the patient. Administer vasopressors as needed to manage narcotic overdose.*
• Administer naloxone challenge before giving naltrexone *because of serious risk of acute withdrawal.*
• Monitor patient continually, *adjusting the dosage as needed, during treatment of acute overdose.*
• Provide comfort and safety measures *to help the patient cope with withdrawal syndrome.*
• Ensure that patients receiving naltrexone have been narcotic free for 7 to 10 days *to prevent severe withdrawal syndrome. Check urine opioid levels if there is any question.*
• If the patient is receiving naltrexone as part of a comprehensive narcotic or alcohol withdrawal program, the patient should be advised to wear or carry a Medic-Alert warning *so that medical personnel know how to treat the patient in an emergency.*

- Institute comfort and safety measures such as side rails and assistance with ambulation *to ensure patient safety;* institute bowel program as needed *for treatment of constipation;* use environmental controls *to decrease stimulation;* and provide small frequent meals *to relieve GI irritation* if GI upset is severe.
- Provide thorough patient teaching, including drug name and prescribed dosage, as well as measures for avoidance of adverse effects, warning signs that may indicate possible problems, and the need for monitoring and evaluation *to enhance patient knowledge about drug therapy and to promote compliance* (see Patient Teaching Checklist: Narcotics).
- Offer support and encouragement *to help the patient cope with the drug regimen.*

Evaluation

- Monitor patient response to the drug (reversal of opioid effects).
- Monitor for adverse effects (CV changes, arrhythmias, hypertension).
- Evaluate the effectiveness of the teaching plan (patient can give the drug name and dosage and describe possible adverse effects to watch for, specific measures to prevent adverse effects, and warning signs to report).
- Monitor the effectiveness of comfort measures and compliance with the regimen.

MIGRAINE HEADACHES AND THEIR TREATMENT

The term migraine headache is used to describe several different syndromes, all of which include severe, throbbing headaches on one side of the head. This pain can be so severe that it can cause widespread disturbance, affecting GI and CNS function, including mood and personality changes.

Migraine headaches should be distinguished from cluster headaches and tension headaches. Cluster headaches usually begin during sleep and involve sharp, steady eye pain that lasts 15 to 90 minutes with sweating, flushing, tearing, and nasal congestion. Tension headaches, which usually occur at times of stress, feel like a dull band of pain around the entire head and last from 30 minutes to a week. They are accompanied by anorexia, fatigue, and a mild intolerance to light or sound.

There are at least two types of migraine headaches. Common migraines, which occur without an aura, present with severe, unilateral, pulsating pain that is frequently accompanied by nausea, vomiting, and sensitivity to light and sound. Such migraine headaches are often aggravated by physical activity. Classic migraines are usually preceded by an aura, or a sensation involving sensory or motor disturbances, that usually occurs about a half hour before the pain begins. The pain and adverse effects are the same as those of the common migraine.

It is believed that the underlying cause of migraine headaches is arterial dilation. Headaches accompanied by an aura are associated with a hypoperfusion of the brain during the aura stage, followed by reflex arterial dilation and a hyperperfusion. The underlying cause and continued state of arterial dilation are not clearly understood, but they may be due to the release of bradykinins, serotonin, or a response to other hormones and chemicals.

For many years, the one standard treatment for migraine headaches was acute analgesia, often involving a narcotic, plus control of lighting and sound and the use of ***ergot derivatives.*** In the late 1990s, a new class of drugs, the ***triptans,*** was found to be extremely effective in treating migraine headaches without the adverse effects associated with ergot derivative use.

ERGOT DERIVATIVES

The ergot derivatives cause constriction of cranial blood vessels and decrease the pulsation of cranial arteries. As a result, they reduce the hyperperfusion of the basilar artery vascular bed. Because these agents are associated with many systemic adverse effects, their usefulness is limited in some patients.

Available ergot derivatives include:

- Dihydroergotamine (*Migranol*), which can be used in the IM or IV form, or as a nasal spray, to provide

> **GENDER CONSIDERATIONS**
>
> ***Headache Distribution***
>
> Headaches are distributed in the general population in a definite gender-related pattern. For example:
>
> - Migraine headaches are three times more likely to occur in women than men.
> - Cluster headaches are more likely to occur in men than in women.
> - Tension headaches are more likely to occur in women than in men.
>
> There is some speculation that the female predisposition to migraine headaches may be related to the vascular sensitivity to hormones. Some women can directly plot migraine occurrence to periods of fluctuations in their menstrual cycle. The introduction of the triptan class of antimigraine drugs has been beneficial for many of these women.

rapid relief from migraine headache. This agent is the drug of choice if no other route of administration is possible.

• Ergotamine (generic), the prototype drug in this class, which was the mainstay of migraine headache treatment before the triptans became available. This agent is administered sublingually for rapid absorption. *Cafergot,* the very popular oral form, combines ergotamine with caffeine to increase its absorption from the GI tract.

• Methysergide (*Sansert*), which is not used for acute attacks but to prevent attacks or to decrease the intensity and frequency of attacks. It is an oral drug with a very slow onset and long duration of action.

THERAPEUTIC ACTIONS AND INDICATIONS

The ergot derivatives block alpha adrenergic and serotonin receptor sites in the brain to cause a constriction of cranial vessels, a decrease in cranial artery pulsation, and a decrease in the hyperperfusion of the basil artery bed. These drugs are indicated for the prevention or abortion of migraine or vascular headaches. Methysergide is only indicated for the prevention of vascular headaches.

CONTRAINDICATIONS/CAUTIONS

Ergot derivatives are contraindicated in the following circumstances: in the presence of allergy to ergot preparations; with CAD, hypertension, or peripheral vascular disease, which could be exacerbated by the CV effects of these drugs; with impaired liver or renal function, which could alter the metabolism and excretion of these drugs; and with pregnancy and lactation because of the potential for adverse effects on the fetus and neonate (ergotism [vomiting, diarrhea, seizures] has been reported in affected infants).

Caution should be used in two instances: with pruritus, which could become worse with drug-induced vascular constriction; and with malnutrition, because ergot derivatives stimulate the CTZ and may cause severe GI reactions, possibly worsening malnutrition.

ADVERSE EFFECTS

The adverse effects of ergot derivatives can be related to the drug-induced vascular constriction. CNS effects include numbness, tingling of extremities, and muscle pain; CV effects such as pulselessness, weakness, chest pain, arrhythmias, localized edema and itching, and MI may also occur. In addition, the direct stimulation of the CTZ can cause GI upset, nausea, vomiting, diarrhea. Ergotism, a syndrome associated with the use of these drugs, presents as nausea, vomiting, severe thirst, hypoperfusion, chest pain, blood pressure changes, confusion, drug dependency (with prolonged use), and a drug withdrawal syndrome.

CLINICALLY IMPORTANT DRUG–DRUG INTERACTIONS

If these drugs are combined with beta blockers, the risk of peripheral ischemia and gangrene is increased. This combination should be avoided.

DATA LINK

Data link to the following ergot derivatives in your nursing drug guide:

ERGOT DERIVATIVES

Name	Brand Name	Usual Indications
dihydroergotamine	*Migranol*	Rapid treatment of acute attacks of migraines
P ergotamine	generic	Prevention and abortion of migraine attacks
methysergide	*Sansert*	Prophylaxis of migraines

NURSING CONSIDERATIONS
for patients receiving ergot derivatives

Assessment

HISTORY. Screen for the following: any known allergies to ergot derivatives; pregnancy or lactation; MI, CAD, or hypertension; impaired renal or hepatic function; and pruritus and malnutrition.

PHYSICAL ASSESSMENT. Include screening for baseline status before beginning therapy and for any potential adverse effects. Assess the following: temperature; skin color, and lesions; CNS orientation, affect, and reflexes; respiration and adventitious sounds; pulse, blood pressure, and cardiac output; and ECG and liver and renal function tests.

Nursing Diagnoses

The patient receiving an ergot derivative may have the following nursing diagnoses related to drug therapy:

• Pain related to GI, vasoconstrictive effects
• Alteration in cardiac output related to CV effects
• High risk for injury related to loss of peripheral sensation
• Knowledge deficit regarding drug therapy

Implementation

• Avoid prolonged use or excessive dosage *to prevent severe adverse effects.*
• Arrange for the use of atropine or phenothiazines if nausea and vomiting are severe *as these are the appropriate drugs to relieve nausea and vomiting.*

- Provide comfort and safety measures such as environmental controls and stress reduction *for the prevention of headache and provide additional pain relief as needed.*
- Assess extremities carefully to ensure that no decubitus ulcer or gangrene is present *when using drugs that will cause peripheral vasoconstriction, which could further aggravate these conditions.*
- Provide supportive measures *to ensure patient safety if acute overdose should occur.*
- Provide thorough patient teaching, including drug name and prescribed dosage, as well as measures for avoidance of adverse effects, warning signs that may indicate possible problems, and the need for monitoring and evaluation *to enhance patient knowledge about drug therapy and to promote compliance.*
- Offer support and encouragement *to help the patient cope with the drug regimen.*

Evaluation

- Monitor patient response to the drug (prevention or abortion of migraine headaches).
- Monitor for adverse effects (CV changes, arrhythmias, hypertension, peripheral vasoconstriction).
- Evaluate the effectiveness of the teaching plan (patient can give the drug name and dosage and describe possible adverse effects to watch for, specific measures to prevent adverse effects, and warning signs to report).
- Monitor the effectiveness of comfort measures and compliance with the regimen.

WWW.WEB LINKS

Health care providers and patients may want to consult the following Internet sources:

Information on pain, physiology and management:
http://www.ampainsoc.org

Information on education programs, research, other information related to pain management:
http://www.aapainmanage.org

Information on chronic pain and the use of narcotics:
http://www.mayohealth.org/mayo/9710/htm/morphine.htm

Information on headache pain—research, cause, management:
http://www.healthtouch.com/level/leaflets/ninds/ninds169.htm

Information on migraines—support groups, treatment, research:
http://www.nih.gov/health/chip/ninds/headac

Information for patients and patient families on migraine headaches—understanding them, treatments, support groups:
http://www.geocities.com/HotSprings/Spa/7379/migraine.html

TRIPTANS

The triptans are a new class of drugs that cause cranial vascular constriction and relief of migraine headache pain in many patients. These drugs are not associated with all of the vascular and GI effects of the ergot derivatives. The triptan of choice for a particular patient depends on personal experience and other preexisting medical conditions. A patient may have a poor response to one triptan and respond well to another.

Available triptans include:

- Sumatriptan (*Imitrex*), the first drug of this class, which is used for the treatment of acute migraine attacks. It can be given orally, SC, or by nasal spray; when given SC, it has been proven very effective against cluster headaches.
- Naratriptan (*Amerge*), which is used orally only for the treatment of acute migraines. It has been associated with severe birth defects and is not recommended for patients with severe renal or hepatic dysfunction.
- Rizatriptan (*Maxalt*), which is used orally for the treatment of acute migraine attacks with or without aura. This drug is also available as a fast-dissolving tablet that is placed in the mouth. Because this agent seems to have more angina-related effects, it is not recommended for patients with a history of CAD.
- Zolmitriptan (*Zomig*), which is used orally only for the treatment of acute migraine.

THERAPEUTIC ACTIONS AND INDICATIONS

The triptans bind to selective serotonin receptor sites to cause vasoconstriction of cranial vessels, relieving the signs and symptoms of migraine headache. They are indicated for the treatment of acute migraine and are not used for prevention of migraines.

CONTRAINDICATIONS/CAUTIONS

Triptans are contraindicated with any of the following conditions: allergy to any triptan; pregnancy because of the possibility of severe adverse effects on the fetus; and active CAD, which could be exacerbated by the vessel-constricting effects of these drugs. These drugs should be used with caution in elderly patients because of the possibility of underlying vascular disease; in lactating women because of the possibility of adverse effects on the infant; and with renal or hepatic dysfunction, which could alter the metabolism and excretion of the drug.

ADVERSE EFFECTS

The adverse effects associated with the triptans are related to the vasoconstrictive effects of the drugs. CNS effects may include numbness, tingling, burning sensation, feelings of coldness or strangeness, dizziness, weakness, myalgia, and vertigo. GI effects such as dysphagia and abdominal discomfort may occur. CV effects may be severe and include blood pressure alterations and tightness or pressure in the chest.

CLINICALLY IMPORTANT DRUG–DRUG INTERACTIONS

Combining triptans with ergot-containing drugs results in a risk of prolonged vasoactive reactions. There is a risk of severe adverse effects if these drugs are used within 2 weeks of discontinuation of an MAO inhibitor because of the increased vasoconstrictive effects that occur. If triptans are to be given, it should be clear that the patient has not received an MAO inhibitor in more than 2 weeks.

DATA LINK

Data link to the following triptans in your nursing drug guide:

TRIPTANS

Name	Brand Name	Usual Indications
naratriptan	*Amerge*	Acute migraines
rizatriptan	*Maxalt*	Acute migraines
P sumatriptan	*Imitrex*	Acute migraines, cluster headaches
zolmitriptan	*Zomig*	Acute migraines

NURSING CONSIDERATIONS
for patients receiving triptans

Assessment

HISTORY. Screen for the following: any known allergies to triptans; pregnancy; and MI, CAD, or hypertension.

PHYSICAL ASSESSMENT. Include screening for baseline status before beginning therapy and for any potential adverse effects. Assess the following: temperature; skin color and lesions; CNS orientation, affect, and reflexes; respiration and adventitious sounds; pulse, blood pressure, and cardiac output; ECG and liver and renal function tests.

Nursing Diagnoses

The patient receiving a triptan may have the following nursing diagnoses related to drug therapy:

- Pain related to CV, vasoconstrictive effects
- Alteration in cardiac output related to CV effects
- Sensory–perceptual alteration related to CNS effects
- Knowledge deficit regarding drug therapy

Implementation

- Administer the drug to relieve acute migraines; *these drugs are not used for prevention.*
- Arrange for safety precautions if CNS and visual changes occur *to prevent patient injury.*
- Provide comfort and safety measures such as environmental controls and stress reduction *for the relief of headache.* Provide additional pain relief as needed.
- Monitor the blood pressure of any patient with a history of CAD, and discontinue the drug if any sign of angina or prolonged hypertension occurs *to prevent severe vascular effects.*
- Provide thorough patient teaching, including drug name and prescribed dosage, as well as measures for avoidance of adverse effects, warning signs that may indicate possible problems, and the need for monitoring and evaluation *to enhance patient knowledge about drug therapy and to promote compliance.*
- Offer support and encouragement *to help the patient cope with the drug regimen.*

Evaluation

- Monitor patient response to the drug (relief of acute migraine headaches).
- Monitor for adverse effects (CV changes, arrhythmias, hypertension, CNS changes).
- Evaluate the effectiveness of the teaching plan (patient can give the drug name and dosage and describe possible adverse effects to watch for, specific measures to prevent adverse effects, and warning signs to report).
- Monitor the effectiveness of comfort measures and compliance with the regimen.

CHAPTER SUMMARY

- Pain occurs any time that tissue is injured and various chemicals are released. The pain impulses are carried to the spinal cord by small diameter A-delta and C fibers, which form synapses with interneurons in the dorsal horn of the spinal cord.
- Pain impulses travel from the spine to the cortex via spinothalamic tracts that can be modulated

along the way at specific gates. These gates can be closed to block transmission of pain impulses by descending nerves from the upper CNS, which relate to emotion, culture, placebo effect, and stress; and by large-diameter sensory A fibers that are associated with touch.

- Opioid receptors, which are found throughout various tissues in the body, react with endogenous endorphins and enkephalins to modulate the transmission of pain impulses.

- Narcotics, derived from the opium plant, react with opioid receptors to relieve pain. In addition, they lead to constipation, respiratory depression, sedation, and suppression of the cough reflex, and they stimulate feelings of well-being or euphoria.

- Because narcotics are associated with the development of physical dependence, they are controlled substances.

- The effectiveness and adverse effects associated with specific narcotics are associated with their particular affinity for various types of opioid receptors.

- Narcotic agonists react with opioid receptor sites to stimulate their activity.

- Narcotic agonists-antagonists react with some opioid receptor sites to stimulate activity and block other opioid receptor sites. These drugs are not as addictive as pure narcotic agonists.

- Narcotic antagonists, which work to reverse the effects of narcotics, are used to treat narcotic overdose or to reverse unacceptable adverse effects.

- Migraine headaches are severe, throbbing headaches on one side of the head that may be associated with an aura or warning syndrome. These headaches are thought to be caused by arterial dilation and hyperperfusion of the brain vessels.

- Treatment of migraines may involve either ergot derivatives or triptans. Ergot derivatives cause vasoconstriction and are associated with sometimes severe systemic vasoconstrictive effects, whereas triptans, a new class of selective serotonin receptor blockers, cause CNS vasoconstriction but are not associated with as many adverse systemic effects.

Bibliography

Bullock, B. L. (2000). *Focus on pathophysiology*. Philadelphia: Lippincott Williams & Wilkins.

Hardman, J. G., Limbird, L. E., Molinoff, P. B., Ruddon, R. W., & Gilman, A. G. (Eds.). (1996). *Goodman and Gilman's the pharmacological basis of therapeutics* (9th ed.). New York: McGraw-Hill.

Karch, A. M. (2000). *2000 Lippincott's nursing drug guide*. Philadelphia: Lippincott Williams & Wilkins.

Malseed, R. (1995). *Textbook of pharmacology and nursing care*. Philadelphia: Lippincott-Raven.

McEvoy, B. R. (Ed.). (1999). *Facts and comparisons 1999*. St. Louis: Facts and Comparisons.

Professional's guide to patient drug facts. (1999). St. Louis: Facts and Comparisons.

CHAPTER 25

General and Local Anesthetic Agents

General anesthetics
- Barbiturates
  - methohexital
  - **P** thiopental
- Nonbarbiturate general anesthetics
  - droperidol
  - etomidate
  - ketamine
  - **P** midazolam
  - propofol

Gases
- cyclopropane
- ethylene
- **P** nitrous oxide

Volatile liquids
- desflurane
- enflurane
- **P** halothane
- isoflurane
- methoxyflurane
- sevoflurane

Local anesthetics
- Esters
  - **P** benzocaine
  - butamben
  - chloroprocaine
  - procaine
  - tetracaine
- Amides
  - bupivacaine
  - dibucaine
  - etidocaine
  - **P** lidocaine
  - mepivacaine
  - prilocaine
  - ropivacaine
- Other
  - dyclonine
  - pramoxine

CHAPTER OUTLINE

KEY TERMS

amnesia
analgesia
balanced anesthesia
general anesthetic
induction
local anesthetic
plasma esterase
unconsciousness
volatile liquid

INTRODUCTION

Anesthetics are drugs that are used to cause complete or partial loss of sensation. The anesthetics can be subdivided into general and local anesthetics depending on their site of action.

General anesthetics are central nervous system (CNS) depressants used to produce loss of pain sensation and consciousness. ***Local anesthetics*** are drugs used to cause loss of pain sensation and feeling in a designated area of the body without the systemic effects associated with severe CNS depression. This chapter discusses various general and local anesthetics.

GENERAL ANESTHETICS

When administering general anesthetics, several different drugs are combined to achieve the following goals: ***analgesia,*** loss of pain perception; ***unconsciousness,*** loss of awareness of one's surroundings; and ***amnesia,*** inability to recall what took place. General anesthetics also block the body's reflexes. Blockage of autonomic reflexes prevents response of involuntary reflexes to injury to the body that might compromise a patient's cardiac, respiratory, gastrointestinal (GI), and immune status. Blockage of muscle reflexes prevents jerking movements that might interfere with the success of the surgical procedure.

Risk Factors Associated with General Anesthetics

Use of general anesthetics involves a widespread CNS depression, which is not without risks. Several factors must be taken into consideration before using general anesthesia, which usually involves a series of drugs aimed at achieving the best effect with the fewest side effects. Because of the wide systemic effects of general anesthetics, patients should be evaluated for potential risks. When anesthetic drugs are selected, these factors are kept in mind so that the potential risk to each particular patient is minimized.

CNS factors: presence of any underlying neurological disease (e.g., epilepsy, stroke, myasthenia gravis), which presents a risk for abnormal reaction to the CNS-depressing and muscle-relaxing effects of these drugs.

Cardiovascular factors: presence of underlying vascular disease, coronary artery disease, and hypotension, which put patients at risk for severe reactions to anesthesia, including hypotension and shock, arrhythmias, and ischemia.

Respiratory factors: presence of obstructive pulmonary diseases (e.g., asthma, chronic obstructive pulmonary disease, bronchitis), which can complicate the delivery of gas anesthesia as well as the intubation and mechanical ventilation that must be used in most general anesthesia.

Renal and hepatic function: conditions that interfere with the metabolism and excretion of anesthetics (e.g., acute renal failure, hepatitis) which could result in prolonged anesthesia and the need for continued support during recovery. Toxic reactions to accumulation of abnormally high levels of anesthesia may even occur.

Balanced Anesthesia

With a wide variety of drugs available, the anesthesiologist has the opportunity to try to balance the therapeutic effects needed with the potential for adverse effects by ordering a variety of anesthetic drugs. ***Balanced anesthesia*** is the use of a combination of drugs, each with a specific effect, to achieve analgesia, muscle relaxation, unconsciousness, and amnesia, rather than the use of a single drug.

Balanced anesthesia commonly involves the following agents:

Preoperative medications, which may include the use of anticholinergics that decrease secretions to facilitate intubation and prevent bradycardia associated with neural depression.

Sedative/hypnotics to relax the patient, facilitate amnesia, and decrease sympathetic stimulation.

Antiemetics to decrease the nausea and vomiting associated with GI depression.

Antihistamines to decrease the chance of allergic reaction and to help dry up secretions.

Narcotics to aid analgesia and sedation.

Many of these drugs are given before the anesthetic to facilitate the process, and some are maintained during surgery to aid the anesthetic, allowing therapeutic effects at lower doses. For example, patients may receive a neuromuscular junction (NMJ) blocker and a rapid-acting IV anesthetic to induce anesthesia and then a gas anesthetic to balance it during the procedure and allow easier recovery. Careful selection of appropriate anesthetic agents along with monitoring and support of the patient may help alleviate many problems.

Administration of General Anesthetics

Anesthesia is delivered by a physician or nurse anesthetist trained in the delivery of these potent drugs with equipment for intubation, mechanical ventilation, and full life support. During the delivery of anesthesia, the patient can go through predictable stages, referred to as the depth of anesthesia. These stages are as follows:

Stage 1, the analgesia stage, refers to the loss of pain sensation, with the patient still conscious and able to communicate.

Stage 2, the excitement stage, is a period of excitement and often combative behavior, with many signs of sympathetic stimulation (e.g., tachycardia, increased respirations, blood pressure changes).

Stage 3, surgical anesthesia, involves relaxation of skeletal muscles, return of regular respirations, and progressive loss of eye reflexes and pupil dilation. Surgery can be safely performed in stage 3.

Stage 4, medullary paralysis, is very deep CNS depression with loss of respiratory and vasomotor center stimuli in which death can occur rapidly.

INDUCTION

Induction is the period from the beginning of anesthesia until stage 3, or surgical anesthesia. The danger period for many patients during induction is stage 2 because of the systemic stimulation that occurs. Many times a rapid-acting anesthetic is used to move quickly through this phase and into stage 3. Neuromuscular junction blockers may be used during induction to facilitate intubation, which is necessary to support the patient with mechanical ventilation during anesthesia.

MAINTENANCE

Maintenance is the period from after stage 3 until the surgical procedure is complete. A slower, more predictable anesthetic such as a gas anesthetic may be used to maintain the anesthesia once the patient is in stage 3.

RECOVERY

Recovery is the period from the discontinuation of the anesthetic until the patient has regained consciousness, movement, and the ability to communicate. During recovery, the patient must be continuously monitored to provide life support as needed and to monitor for any adverse effects of the drugs being used.

TYPES OF GENERAL ANESTHETICS

Several different types of drugs are used as general anesthetics. These include barbiturate and nonbarbiturate anesthetics, volatile liquids, and gas anesthetics (Table 25-1).

Barbiturate Anesthetics

The barbiturate anesthetics are intravenous drugs used to induce rapid anesthesia which is then maintained with an inhaled drug. They include the following:

- Thiopental (*Pentothal*) which is probably the most widely used of the intravenous anesthetics. This agent has a very rapid onset of action and ultrashort recovery period. Because it has no analgesic properties, the patient may need additional analgesics after surgery.
- Methohexital (*Brevital*), which has a rapid onset of action and a recovery period that is even more ultrashort. This agent cannot come in contact with silicone (rubber stoppers and disposable syringes often contain silicone) because it will cause an immediate breakdown of the silicone. As a result, it poses special problems, and special precautions must be taken. Like thiopental, methohexital also lacks analgesic properties, and the patient may require postoperative analgesics. Because of its rapid onset, this drug may cause respiratory depression and apnea, so it should not be used until the anesthesiologist and staff are ready and equipped for intubation and respiratory support.

Nonbarbiturate Anesthetics

The other drugs used for IV administration in anesthesia are nonbarbiturates with a wide variety of effects. Such anesthetics include the following:

- Midazolam (*Versed*), which is the prototype nonbarbiturate anesthetic. This agent has a rapid onset but does not reach peak effectiveness for 30 to 60 minutes. It is more likely to cause nausea and vomiting than some of the other anesthetics.
- Droperidol (*Inapsine*), which has a rapid onset of action and an ultrashort recovery period. It should be used with caution in patients with renal or hepatic failure. During the recovery period, this agent may cause hypotension, chills, hallucinations, and drowsiness.
- Etomidate (*Amidate*), which has an ultrashort onset and rapid recovery period. This agent is sometimes used for sedation of patients on ventilators. During the recovery phase, many patients experience myoclonic and tonic movements as well as nausea and vomiting. Etomidate is not recommended for use in children less than 10 years of age.
- Ketamine (*Ketalar*), which has a rapid onset of action and a very slow recovery period (45 min). This agent has been associated with a bizarre state of unconsciousness in which the patient appears to be awake but is unconscious and cannot feel pain. This drug, which causes sympathetic stimulation with

TABLE 25-1

GENERAL ANESTHETICS

Drug	Brand Name	Onset	Recovery	Analgesia	Systems Alert					
					CV	*Resp*	*CNS*	*GI*	*Renal*	*Hepatic*
BARBITURATES										
methohexital	*Brevital*	rapid	ultra, ultrashort	none	–	+++	–	–	–	–
P thiopental	*Pentothal*	rapid	ultrashort	none	–	–	–	–	–	–
NONBARBITURATE ANESTHETICS										
droperidol	*Inapsine*	3–10 min	2–4 h	–	++	–	+	–	+	+
etomidate	*Amidate*	1 min	3–5 min	–	–	–	+	++	–	–
ketamine	*Ketalar*	rapid	45 min	+	++	–	+++	–	–	–
P midazolam	*Versed*	15 min	rapid	+	–	+++	–	++	–	–
propofol	*Diprivan*	rapid	rapid	+	++	+	++	–	–	–
GASES										
cyclopropane	(orange)	1–2 min	rapid	–	–	–	++	++	–	–
ethylene	(red)	rapid	rapid	–	–	–	+	+	–	–
P nitrous oxide	(blue)	1–2 min	rapid	++++	+++	+	+	–	–	–
VOLATILE LIQUIDS										
desflurane	*Suprane*	rapid	rapid	+	–	++++	–	–	–	–
enflurane	*Ethrane*	rapid	rapid	+	+	+	–	–	++	–
P halothane	*Fluothane*	rapid	rapid	+	++	–	–	+	–	+++
isoflurane	generic	rapid	rapid	+	++	+	–	+	–	–
methoxyflurane	*Penthrane*	slow	prolonged	+	+	++	–	–	+	–
sevoflurane	*Ultane*	rapid	rapid	+	–	++	–	–	–	–

Systems alert indicates physiological systems with anticipated adverse effects to these drugs. When drugs are selected, the patient's condition and potential for serious problems with these adverse effects should be considered.
– = no effect; + = mild effect; ++ = moderate effect; +++ = strong effect; ++++ = powerful effect.

increase in blood pressure and heart rate, may be helpful in situations when cardiac depression is dangerous. Ketamine crosses the blood–brain barrier and can cause hallucinations, dreams, and psychotic episodes.

• Propofol (*Diprivan*), which is a very short-acting anesthetic with a rapid onset of action often used for short procedures. It often causes local burning on injection. It can cause bradycardia, hypotension and, in extreme cases, pulmonary edema.

Anesthetic Gases

Like all inhaled anesthetics, anesthetic gases enter the bronchi and alveoli, rapidly pass into the capillary system (because gases flow from areas of higher concentration to areas of lower concentration), and are transported to the heart to be pumped throughout the body. These gases have a very high affinity for fatty tissue, including the lipid membrane of the nerves in the CNS. The gases pass quickly into the brain and cause severe CNS depression. Once the patient is in stage 3 of anesthesia, the anesthetist regulates the amount of gas that is delivered to ensure that it is sufficient to keep the patient unconscious and not enough to cause severe depression. This is done by decreasing the concentration of the gas that is flowing into the bronchi, creating a concentration gradient that results in the movement of gas in the opposite direction—out of the tissues and back to expired air.

Anesthetic gases include the following:

• Nitrous oxide (blue cylinder), which is the prototype anesthetic gas. Although this agent is a very potent analgesic, it is the weakest of the gas anesthetics and the least toxic. It moves so quickly in and out of the body that it can actually increase the volume of closed body compartments such as sinuses. Because nitrous oxide is such a potent analgesic with rapid onset and recovery, it is often used for dental surgery. Nitrous oxide is usually combined with other agents for anesthetic use. It can block the reuptake of oxygen postoperatively and cause hypoxia. Because of this reaction, it is always given in combination with oxygen. Susceptible patients should be monitored for signs of hypoxia, chest pain, and stroke.

• Cyclopropane (orange cylinders), which has a rapid onset of action and rapid recovery. This agent is not a good analgesic, and the patient may experience pain, headache, nausea, vomiting, and delirium during the recovery phase.

• Ethylene (red cylinders), which is less toxic than most of the other gas anesthetics. However, its use can leave the patient with a headache and a very unpleasant taste. This agent has a rapid onset of action and rapid recovery.

Volatile Liquids

Inhaled anesthetics are either gases or ***volatile liquids*** that are unstable at room temperature and release gases. These gases are then inhaled by the patient, so these volatile liquids act like gas anesthetics.

Most of the volatile liquids in use today are halogenated hydrocarbons such as the following:

• Halothane (*Fluothane*), which is the prototype of the volatile liquids. It has a rapid onset of action and rapid recovery. It is associated with vomiting, bradycardia, and hypotension and has an increased risk of causing hepatic toxicity. Halothane is metabolized in the liver to toxic hydrocarbons and bromide; thus, it can contribute to hepatic toxicity. Its recovery syndrome is also characterized by fever, anorexia, nausea, vomiting, and eventual hepatitis, which may progress to fatal hepatic necrosis. Although this syndrome is rare, halothane is not used more frequently than every 3 weeks to reduce patient risk.

• Desflurane (*Suprane*), which has a rapid onset and rapid recovery. This agent is associated with a collection of respiratory reactions, including cough, increased secretions, and laryngospasm. Thus, it should be avoided in patients with respiratory problems or in those with increased sensitivity. In addition, use is not recommended for induction in pediatric patients.

• Enflurane (*Ethrane*), which has a rapid onset and rapid recovery. Because this agent is associated with renal toxicity, cardiac arrhythmias, and respiratory depression, it is not to be used for patients with known cardiac or respiratory disease or with renal dysfunction.

• Isoflurane (generic), which has a rapid onset and recovery. It can cause muscle relaxation. Isoflurane is associated with hypotension, hypercapnia, muscle soreness, and a bad taste in the mouth, but it does not cause cardiac arrhythmias and respiratory irritation like some other volatile liquids.

• Methoxyflurane (*Penthrane*), which has a slow onset of action and results in a prolonged recovery. This agent can cause renal toxicity, respiratory depression, and hypotension. Methoxyflurane is rarely used except during labor and delivery, where it may be used briefly because it does not relax the uterus and allows labor to continue.

• Sevoflurane (*Ulane*), which is the newest of the volatile liquids. This agent has a very rapid onset of action and a very rapid clearance. Because of this, adverse effects are thought to be minimal.

OVERVIEW OF GENERAL ANESTHETICS

THERAPEUTIC ACTIONS AND INDICATIONS

The mechanism of action of the general anesthetics is not understood (Figure 25-1). It is known that depression of the reticular activating system and the cerebral cortex occurs, however. General anesthetics are indicated for producing sedation, hypnosis, anesthesia, amnesia, and unconsciousness to allow performance of painful surgical procedures.

CONTRAINDICATIONS/CAUTIONS

General anesthetics are contraindicated with status asthmaticus because of the difficulty in providing ventilatory support to these patients and the risk of

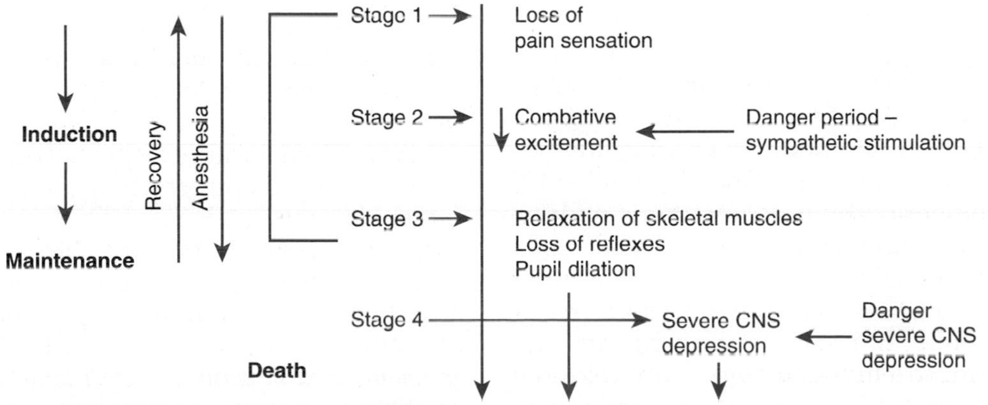

FIGURE 25-1. Stages of general anesthesia.

exacerbation of the problem with CNS depression. These agents are also contraindicated when there is an absence of suitable veins for IV administration, which would be dangerous if life support measures became necessary and IV delivery of life-saving drugs was essential.

Caution should be used in cases of severe cardiovascular disease, hypotension, or shock; conditions in which hypnotic effects may be prolonged or potentiated with increased intracranial pressure; and with myasthenia gravis, all of which could be exacerbated by the depressive effects of these drugs and may require extra support and prolonged monitoring during surgery. Droperidol should be used with caution in patients with renal or hepatic failure.

ADVERSE EFFECTS

The adverse effects associated with general anesthetics are often associated with the depressive effects of these drugs and may include the following conditions: circulatory depression; hypotension; shock; decreased cardiac output; arrhythmias; respiratory depression, including apnea, laryngospasm, bronchospasm, hiccups, and coughing; headache; nausea and vomiting; prolonged somnolence; and in some cases, delirium. The halogenated hydrocarbons may cause malignant hyperthermia, with extreme muscle rigidity, severe hyperpyrexia, acidosis, and in some cases death. If this condition occurs, it is treated with dantrolene. In addition, there is also always a risk of skin breakdown secondary to immobility when patients receive general anesthetics.

CLINICALLY IMPORTANT DRUG–DRUG INTERACTIONS

Several potentially dangerous drug–drug interactions have been reported with the general anesthetics. When ketamine and halothane are used in combination, severe cardiac depression with hypotension and bradycardia may occur. If these agents must be used together, the patient should be monitored closely. Ketamine may also potentiate the muscular blocking of NMJ blockers, and the patient may require prolonged periods of respiratory support. Combinations of barbiturate anesthetics and narcotics may produce apnea more commonly than with other analgesics. The nonbarbiturate anesthetic midazolam is associated with increased toxicity and length of recovery when used in combination with inhaled anesthetics, other CNS depressants, narcotics, propofol, and thiopental. If any of these agents are used in combination, careful balancing of drug doses is necessary.

DATA LINK

Data link to the general anesthetics listed in Table 25-1, in your nursing drug guide.

NURSING CONSIDERATIONS for patients receiving general anesthetics

Assessment

HISTORY. Screen for the following: any known allergies to general anesthetics; impaired liver or kidney function; myasthenia gravis; personal or family history of malignant hyperthermia; and cardiac or respiratory disease.

PHYSICAL ASSESSMENT. Include screening for baseline status before beginning therapy and for any potential adverse effects. Assess the following: temperature and weight; skin color and lesions; affect, orientation, reflexes, pupil size and reaction, and muscle tone and response; pulse, blood pressure, and ECG; respiration and adventitious sounds; bowel sounds and abdominal examination; and renal and liver function tests.

Nursing Diagnoses

The patient receiving a general anesthetic may have the following nursing diagnoses related to drug therapy:

- Impaired gas exchange related to respiratory depression
- Alteration in skin integrity related to immobility
- Alteration in thought processes and sensory–perceptual alteration related to CNS depression
- Knowledge deficit regarding drug therapy

Implementation

- The drug must be administered by trained personnel (usually an anesthesiologist) *because of the potential risks associated with its use.*
- Maintain equipment on standby to maintain airway and provide mechanical ventilation *when patient is not able to maintain respiration because of CNS depression.*
- Monitor temperature *for prompt detection and treatment of malignant hyperthermia. Maintain dantrolene on standby.*
- Monitor pulse, respiration, blood pressure, ECG, and cardiac output continually during administration. In addition, monitor temperature and reflexes. *Dosage adjustment may be needed to alleviate potential problems and maximize overall benefit with the least toxicity.*

• Monitor the patient until the recovery phase is complete and the patient is conscious and able to move and communicate *to assure patient safety.*
• Provide comfort measures *to help the patient tolerate drug effects. Provide pain relief as appropriate, reassurance and support to deal with effects of anesthesia and loss of control, skin care and turning to prevent breakdown, and supportive care for conditions such as hypotension and bronchospasm.*
• Provide thorough patient teaching preoperatively, *realizing that most patients who receive the drug will be unconscious or will be receiving teaching about a particular procedure.*
• Information about the anesthetic (e.g., what to expect, rate of onset, time to recovery) should be incorporated into the teaching plan.
• Offer support and encouragement *to help the patient cope with the procedure and drugs being used.*

Evaluation

• Monitor patient response to the drug (analgesia, loss of consciousness).
• Monitor for adverse effects (respiratory depression, hypotension, bronchospasm, GI slowdown, skin breakdown, malignant hyperthermia).
• Evaluate the effectiveness of the teaching plan (patient can relate anticipated effects of the drug and the recovery process).
• Monitor the effectiveness of comfort measures and compliance with the regimen.

WWW.WEB LINKS

Health care providers and patients may want to consult the following Internet sources:

Information on anesthesia—physiology, research:
http://www.anesthesia.net

Information on regional anesthesia:
http://www.pain.com/reg_ana/default.com

Information for patients about types of anesthesia, research, teaching protocols:
http://www.asahq.org

Information on local anesthetics—types, actions, research, uses:
http://www.anes.ccf.org.8080/pilot/ortho/la_pharm.htm

CULTURAL CONSIDERATIONS ••••

Loss of Control Associated With Anesthesia

Patients in certain ethnic groups may have difficulty with the loss of control that accompanies the use of general or local anesthesia. Therefore, the nurse should be alert for the possibility of increased stress in particular patients. Such individuals may require additional reassurance, frequent monitoring, and the opportunity to participate actively in plans for the procedure and the recovery process.

LOCAL ANESTHETICS

Local anesthetics are drugs that cause a loss of sensation in limited areas of the body. They are used primarily to prevent the patient from feeling pain for varying periods of time after they have been administered in the peripheral nervous system. In increasing concentrations, local anesthetics can also cause the loss of the following sensations (in this sequence): temperature, touch, proprioception (position sense), and skeletal muscle tone. If these other aspects of nerve function are progressively lost, recovery occurs in the reverse order of the loss.

The local anesthetics are very powerful nerve blockers, and it is very important that their effects are limited to a particular area of the body. They should not be absorbed systemically. Systemic absorption could produce toxic effects on the nervous system and the heart (e.g., severe CNS depression, cardiac arrhythmias). Local anesthetics are either esters or amides. The esters are broken down immediately in the plasma by enzymes known as ***plasma esterases***. The amides are metabolized more slowly in the liver, and serum levels of these drugs can increase and lead to toxicity.

Modes of Administration

The way that a local anesthetic is administered helps increase its effectiveness by delivering it directly to the area that is causing or will cause the pain, thus decreasing systemic absorption and related toxic effects (Figure 25-2). There are five types of local anesthetic administration: topical, infiltration, field block, nerve block, and intravenous regional anesthesia.

TOPICAL

Topical anesthesia involves applying a cream, lotion, ointment, or drop of a local anesthetic to traumatized skin to relieve pain. It can also involve applying the lotion, cream, ointment, or drops to the mucous

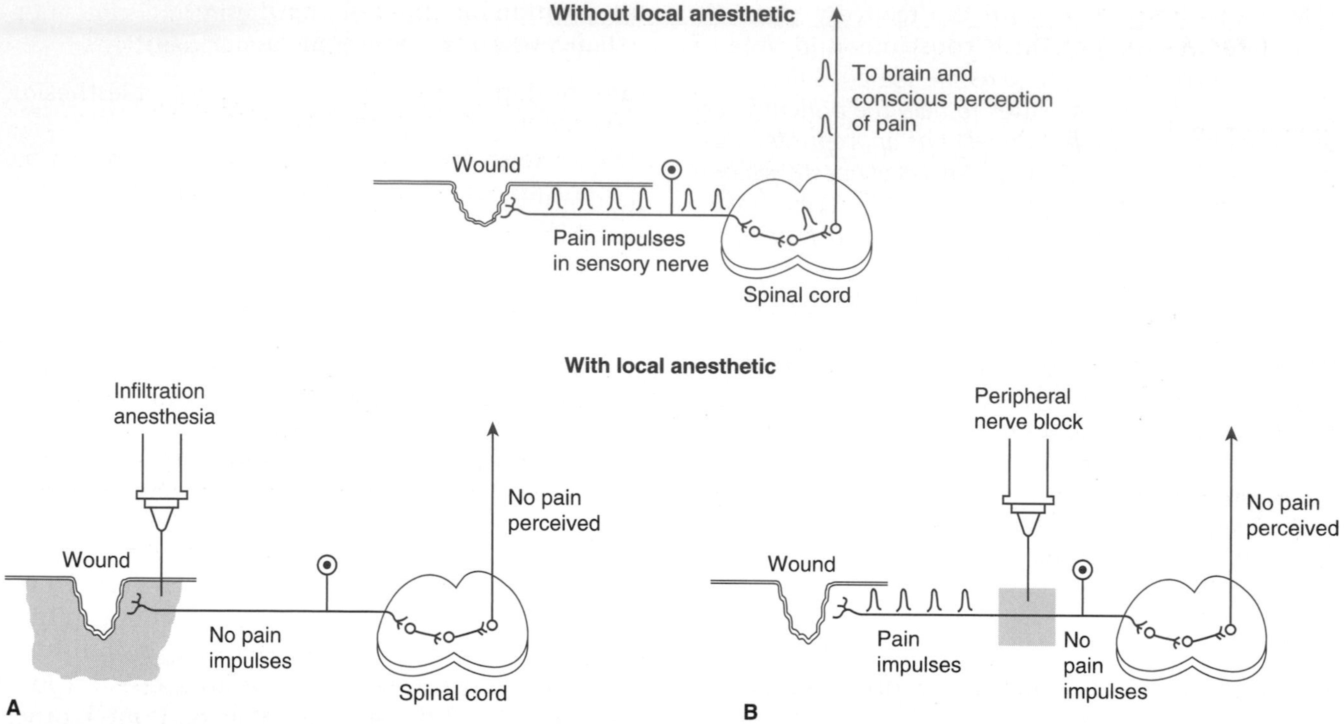

FIGURE 25-2. Mechanism of action of local anesthetics. An injury produces pain impulses (actually action potentials) that are conducted and transmitted in an area of the brain in which pain is perceived. (*A*) Conduction of the pain impulse has been blocked by infiltration anesthesia at the site of the injury. (*B*) A nerve block at some distance from the injury. Local anesthetics block the movement of sodium into the nerve and prevent nerve depolarization, stopping the transmission of the pain impulse.

membranes in the eye, nose, throat, mouth, urethra, anus, or rectum to relieve pain or to anesthetize the area to facilitate a medical procedure. Although systemic absorption is rare with topical application, it may occur if there is damage or breakdown to the tissues in the area.

INFILTRATION

Infiltration anesthesia involves injecting the anesthetic directly into the tissues to be treated (e.g., sutured, drilled, cut). This injection brings the anesthetic into contact with the nerve endings in the area and prevents them from transmitting nerve impulses to the brain.

FIELD BLOCK

Field block anesthesia involves injecting the anesthetic all around the area that will be affected by the operation. This is more intense than infiltration anesthesia because it comes in contact with all the nerve endings surrounding the area. This type of block is often used for tooth extractions.

NERVE BLOCK

Nerve block anesthesia involves injecting the anesthetic at some point along the nerve or nerves that run to and from the region in which the loss of pain sensation or muscle paralysis is desired. These blocks are performed not in the surgical field but at some distance from the field and involve a greater area with potential for more adverse effects. Several types of nerve blocks are possible. A peripheral nerve block blocks the sensory and motor aspects of a particular nerve for relief of pain or for diagnostic purposes, and a central nerve block involves injecting the anesthetic into the roots of the nerves in the spinal cord. Epidural anesthesia entails injection of the drug into the space where the nerves emerge from the spinal cord, and a caudal block involves injection into the sacral canal, below the epidural area.

INTRAVENOUS REGIONAL ANESTHESIA

Intravenous regional anesthesia involves carefully draining all of the blood from an arm or leg, securing a tourniquet to prevent the anesthetic from entering the general circulation, and then injecting the anesthetic into the vein of the arm or leg. This technique is used for very particular surgical procedures.

CHARACTERISTICS OF LOCAL ANESTHETICS

Several agents may be used as local anesthetics. The agent of choice depends on the method of administration, the length of time the area is to be anesthetized, and consideration of potential adverse effects. Table 25-2 lists the available local anesthetics, with the preferred method of administration, time of onset, duration, and any special considerations.

THERAPEUTIC ACTIONS AND INDICATIONS

Local anesthetics work by causing a temporary interruption in the production and conduction of nerve impulses. They affect the permeability of nerve mem-

TABLE 25-2

LOCAL ANESTHETICS

Drug	Brand Name(s)	Onset	Duration	Administration	Special Considerations
ESTERS					
P benzocaine	*Dermoplast, Lanacane, Unguentine*	1 min	30–60 min	Skin, mucous membranes	Avoid tight bandages with skin prep.
butamben	*Butesin Picrate*	slow	30–60 min	Skin, mucous membranes	Note that swallowing may be difficult if used in throat.
chloroprocaine	*Nesacaine*	6–15 min	15–75 min	Nerve block, caudal, epidural	Do not use with subarachnoid administration.
procaine	*Novocain*	2–25 min	15–75 min	Infiltration, peripheral, spinal, dental	Monitor skin condition if immobile; keep supine to avoid headache after spinal.
tetracaine	*Pontocaine*	15–30 min	2–25 hr	Spinal, prolonged spinal, skin	Monitor skin condition if immobile; provide reassurance if prolonged; keep supine to avoid headache after spinal.
AMIDES					
bupivacaine	*Marcaine, Sensorcaine*	5–20 min	2–7 hr	Local, epidural, dental, caudal, subarachnoid, sympathetic, retrobulbar	Do not use Bier Block—deaths have occurred.
dibucaine	*Nupercainal*	<15 min	3–4 hours	Skin, mucous membranes	Monitor for local reactions.
etidocaine	*Duranest HCl*	3–15 min	2–5 hours	Peripheral block, OB, pelvic, abdominal, alveolar block	Monitor skin condition.
P lidocaine	*Dilocaine, Solarcaine, Xylocaine*	5–15 min	30–90 min	Caudal, epidural, spinal, cervical, dental, skin, mucous membrane	Know that this drug is short acting and preferred for short procedures; be aware of danger if absorbed systemically.
mepivacaine	*Carbocaine, Isocaine*	3–15 min	45–90 min	Nerve block, OB, cervical, epidural, dental, local infiltration	Use caution with renal impairment.
prilocaine	*Cilanest*	1–15 min	.5–3 hours	Nerve block, dental	Advise patients not to bite themselves.
ropivacaine	*Naropin*	1–5 min	2–6 hours	Nerve block, epidural, caudal	Avoid rapid infusion; offers good pain management post-op and OB.
OTHER					
dyclonine	*Dyclone*	<10 min	<60 min	Mucous membranes	Know that this drug is used for diagnostic and preps for medical procedures.
pramoxine	*Tronothone, FrameGel, Itch-X*	3–5 min	< 60 min	Skin, mucous membranes	Do not cover with tight bandages.

PATIENT TEACHING CHECKLIST

Local Anesthetics

Create customized patient teaching materials for a specific anesthetic from your CD-ROM. Your patient teaching should stress the following points for drugs within this class:

Procedure:

- What it will feel like (any numbness, tingling, inability to move, pressure, pain, choking?)
- Any anticipated discomfort
- How long the procedure will last
- Concerns that arise during the procedure: report any discomfort and ask any questions as they arise

Recovery:

- How long recovery will take
- Feelings to anticipate: tingling, numbness, pressure, and itching
- Pain that will be felt as the anesthesia wears off
- Measures to reduce pain in the area
- Signs and symptoms to report (pain along a nerve route, palpitations, feeling faint, disorientation)

This Teaching Checklist reflects general patient teaching guidelines. It is not meant to be a substitute for drug-specific teaching information, which is available in nursing drug guides.

branes to sodium ions, which normally infuse into the cell in response to stimulation. By preventing the sodium ions from entering the nerve, they stop the nerve from depolarizing. A particular section of nerve cannot be stimulated, and nerve impulses directed toward that section of the nerve are lost when they reach that area. Local anesthetics are indicated for infiltration anesthesia, peripheral nerve block, spinal anesthesia, and the relief of local pain.

CONTRAINDICATIONS/CAUTIONS

The local anesthetics are contraindicated with any of the following conditions: history of allergy to any one of these agents or to parabens; heart block, which could be greatly exacerbated with systemic absorption; shock, which could alter the local delivery and absorption of these drugs; and decreased plasma esterases, which could result in toxic levels of the ester-type local anesthetics.

ADVERSE EFFECTS

The adverse effects of these drugs may be related to their local blocking of sensation (e.g., skin breakdown, self-injury, biting oneself). Other problematic effects are associated with the route of administration and the amount of drug that is absorbed systemically. These effects are related to the blocking of nerve depolarization throughout the system. Effects that may occur include CNS effects such as headache, restlessness, anxiety, dizziness, tremors, blurred vision, and backache; GI effects such as nausea and vomiting; cardiovascular effects such as peripheral vasodilation, myocardial depression, arrhythmias, and blood pressure changes, all of which may lead to fatal cardiac arrest; and respiratory arrest.

CLINICALLY IMPORTANT DRUG–DRUG INTERACTIONS

When local anesthetics and succinylcholine are given concurrently, increased and prolonged neuromuscular blockade occurs. There is also less risk of systemic absorption and increased local effects if these drugs are combined with epinephrine.

DATA LINK

Data link to the local anesthetics, listed in Table 25-2, in your nursing drug guide.

NURSING CONSIDERATIONS
for patients receiving local anesthetics

Assessment

HISTORY. Screen for the following: any known allergies to these drugs or parabens, impaired liver function, low plasma esterases, heart block, and shock.

PHYSICAL ASSESSMENT. Include screening for baseline status before beginning therapy and for any potential adverse effects. Assess the following: body temperature and weight; skin color and lesions; affect,

NURSING CARE GUIDE

Local Anesthetics

Assessment	Nursing Diagnoses	Implementation	Evaluation
HISTORY Allergies to any of these drugs or to parabens, cardiac disorders, vascular problems, hepatic dysfunction	Sensory–perceptual alteration related to anesthesia Alteration in skin integrity related to immobility Potential for injury related to loss of sensation, mobility Knowledge deficit regarding drug therapy	Administer drug under strict supervision. Provide comfort and safety measures: positioning, skin care, side rails, pain medication as needed, maintain airway, ventilate patient, antidotes on standby. Provide support and reassurance to deal with loss of sensation and mobility. Provide patient teaching about procedure being performed, what to expect. Provide life support as needed.	Evaluate drug effects: loss of sensation, loss of movement. Monitor for adverse effects: cardiovascular effects (BP changes, arrhythmias), respiratory depression, GI upset, CNS alterations, skin breakdown, anxiety, fear. Monitor for drug–drug interactions as indicated for each drug. Evaluate effectiveness of patient teaching program. Evaluate effectiveness of comfort and safety measures. Constantly monitor vital signs and return to normal muscular function and sensation.
PHYSICAL EXAMINATION CV: blood pressure, pulse, peripheral perfusion, ECG CNS: orientation, affect, reflexes, vision Skin: color, lesions, texture, sweating Respiratory: respiration, adventitious sounds Laboratory tests: liver function tests, plasma esterases			

orientation, reflexes, pupil size and reaction, and muscle tone and response; pulse, blood pressure, and ECG; respiration and adventitious sounds; and liver function tests and plasma esterases (if appropriate).

Nursing Diagnoses

The patient receiving a local anesthetic may have the following nursing diagnoses related to drug therapy:

- Sensory–perceptual alteration related to anesthetic effect
- Alteration in skin integrity related to immobility
- Potential for injury related to loss of sensation and mobility
- Knowledge deficit regarding drug therapy

Implementation

- Maintain equipment on standby *to maintain airway and provide mechanical ventilation.*
- Ensure that drugs for managing hypotension, cardiac arrest, and CNS alterations are on standby *in case of severe reaction and toxicity.*

CASE STUDY

Spinal Anesthesia

PRESENTATION

A. M., a 32-year-old male athlete with a prior history of asthma (which could indicate pulmonary dysfunction), was admitted to the hospital for an inguinal hernia repair. At the patient's request, the surgeon elected to use a local anesthetic employing spinal anesthesia. Because the extent of the repair was unknown (A. M. had undergone two previous repairs), etidocaine, a long-acting anesthetic, was selected. He remained alert (BP 120/64, P 62, R 10) and stable throughout the procedure.

Two hours after the conclusion of the procedure, A. M. appeared agitated (BP 154/68, P 88, R 12). Although he did not complain of discomfort, he did state that he still had no feeling and had only limited movement of his legs.

CRITICAL THINKING QUESTIONS

What safety precautions need to be taken? What nursing interventions should be done at this point? How could the patient be reassured? Think about the anxiety level of the patient—an athlete who elected to have local anesthesia may have a problem with control and feel somewhat invincible. Consider the anxiety that loss of mobility and sensation in the legs may cause in a person who makes his living as an athlete. In addition, consider the expected duration of action of etidocaine and the rate of return of function.

DISCUSSION

Etidocaine is a long-acting anesthetic with effects that might persist for several hours. The timing of the drug's effects should be explained to A. M., and he should be monitored for a period of time to determine whether his agitated state and slightly elevated vital signs are a result of anxiety or an unanticipated reaction to the surgery or the drug. Life-support equipment should be on standby in case his condition is a toxic drug reaction or some unanticipated problem following surgery.

The nurse is in the best position to perform the following interventions: explaining the effects of the drug and the anticipated recovery schedule; keeping the patient as flat as possible to decrease the headache usually associated with spinal anesthesia; encouraging the patient to turn from side to side periodically to allow skin care to be performed and to alleviate the risk of pressure sore development; and staying with the patient as much as possible to reassure him, to answer questions, and to encourage him to talk about his feelings and reaction.

If the agitated state is due to a stress reaction, following comfort measures, teaching, and reassurance, it should return to normal. An elevated systolic pressure with a normal diastolic pressure is often an indication of a sympathetic stress response. An athlete is more likely than most people to suffer great anxiety and fear if his legs become numb and he is unable to move them. The teaching and comfort measures may be all that is needed to relieve the anxiety and ensure a good recovery.

- Ensure that patients receiving spinal anesthesia are well hydrated and remain lying down for up to 12 hours after the anesthesia *to minimize headache.*
- Establish safety precautions *to prevent skin breakdown and injury during the time that the patient has a loss of sensation and/or mobility.*
- Provide comfort measures *to help the patient tolerate drug effects.* Provide pain relief as appropriate; reassurance and support *to deal with the effects of anesthesia and loss of control;* skin care and turning *to prevent breakdown;* and supportive care for hypotension.
- Provide thorough patient teaching *to explain what to expect, safety precautions that will be needed, and when to expect return of function* (see Patient Teaching Checklist: Local Anesthetics).
- Offer support and encouragement *to help the patient cope with the procedure and drugs being used.*

Evaluation

- Monitor patient response to the drug (loss of feeling in designated area).
- Monitor for adverse effects (respiratory depression, blood pressure changes, arrhythmias, GI upset, skin breakdown, injury, CNS alterations).
- Evaluate the effectiveness of the teaching plan (patient can relate the anticipated effects of the drug and the recovery process) (see Nursing Care Guide: Local Anesthetics).

CHAPTER SUMMARY

- General anesthetics are drugs used to produce pain relief, analgesia, amnesia, and unconsciousness, and to block muscle reflexes that could interfere with a surgical procedure or put the patient at risk for harm.

- The use of general anesthetics involves a widespread CNS depression that could be harmful, especially in patients with underlying CNS, cardiovascular, or respiratory diseases.
- Anesthesia proceeds through predictable stages from loss of sensation to total CNS depression and death.
- Induction of anesthesia is the time from the beginning of anesthesia administration until the patient reaches surgical anesthesia.
- Balanced anesthesia involves giving a variety of drugs, including anticholinergics, rapid IV anesthetics, inhaled anesthetics, NMJ blockers, and narcotics.
- Patients receiving general anesthetics should be monitored for any adverse effects and to provide reassurance and provide safety precautions until the recovery of sensation, mobility, and ability to communicate.
- Local anesthetics block the depolarization of nerve membrane, preventing the transmission of pain sensations and motor stimuli.
- Local anesthetics are administered so as to deliver the drug directly to the desired area and to prevent systemic absorption, which could lead to serious interruption of nerve impulses and response.
- Ester-type local anesthetics are immediately destroyed by plasma esterases. Amide local anesthetics are destroyed in the liver and have a greater risk of accumulation and systemic toxicity.
- Nursing care of patients receiving anesthetics should include safety precautions to prevent injury and skin breakdown, support and reassurance to deal with the loss of sensation and mobility, and patient teaching regarding what to expect to decrease stress and anxiety.

Bibliography

Bullock, B. L. (2000). *Focus on pathophysiology*. Philadelphia: Lippincott Williams & Wilkins.

Hardman, J. G., Limbird, L. E., Molinoff, P. B., Ruddon, R. W., & Gilman, A. G. (Eds.). (1996). *Goodman and Gilman's the pharmacological basis of therapeutics* (9th ed.). New York: McGraw-Hill.

Karch, A. M. (2000). *2000 Lippincott's nursing drug guide*. Philadelphia: Lippincott Williams & Wilkins.

Malseed, R. (1995). *Textbook of pharmacology and nursing care*. Philadelphia: Lippincott-Raven.

McEvoy, B. R. (Ed.). (1999). *Facts and comparisons 1999*. St. Louis: Facts and Comparisons.

Professional's guide to patient drug facts. (1999). St. Louis: Facts and Comparisons.

CHAPTER 26

Neuromuscular Junction Blocking Agents

Nondepolarizing neuromuscular blockers
- atracurium
- cistatracurium
- doxacurium
- metocurine
- mivacurium
- pancuronium
- pipercuronium
- rocuronium
- P tubocurarine
- vecuronium

Depolarizing neuromuscular blockers
- P succinylcholine

CHAPTER OUTLINE

KEY TERMS

acetylcholine receptor site
depolarizing
malignant hyperthermia
nondepolarizing
paralysis
sarcomere
sliding filament theory

INTRODUCTION

Drugs that affect the neuromuscular junction, the neuromuscular junction (NMJ) blockers, can be divided into two groups. One group, the ***nondepolarizing*** neuromuscular junction blockers, includes those agents that act as antagonists to acetylcholine at the neuromuscular junction and prevent depolarization of muscle cells. The other group, the ***depolarizing*** neuromuscular junction blockers (of which there is one drug), act as an acetylcholine agonist at the junction, causing stimulation of the muscle cell and then preventing it from repolarizing. Both of these types of drugs are used to cause ***paralysis,*** or loss of muscular function, for performance of surgical procedures or facilitation of mechanical ventilation.

THE NEUROMUSCULAR JUNCTION

The NMJ blockers affect the normal functioning of muscles by interfering with the normal processes that occur at the junction of nerve and muscle cell. The functional unit of a muscle is called a ***sarcomere,*** which is made up of light and dark filaments formed by actin and myosin molecules arranged in orderly stacks that give the sarcomere a striated or striped appearance (Figure 26-1). Normal muscle function involves the arrival of a nerve impulse at the motor nerve terminal followed by the release of acetylcholine into the synaptic cleft. At the ***acetylcholine receptor site*** on the effector side of the synapse, the acetylcholine interacts with the nicotinic cholinergic receptors, causing depolarization of the muscle membrane. This depolarization allows the release of calcium ions stored in tubules into the cell. The calcium binds to troponin, a chemical found throughout the sarcomere, and the binding of troponin causes the release of actin and myosin binding sites, allowing them to react with each other.

The actin and myosin molecules react with each other again and again, sliding along the filament and making it shorter. This is a contraction of the muscle fiber according to the ***sliding filament theory.*** As the calcium is removed from the cell during repolarization of the muscle membrane, the troponin is freed and prevents the actin and myosin from reacting with each other. The muscle filament then relaxes or slides back to the resting position. Muscle tone results from a dynamic balance between excitatory and inhibitory impulses to the muscle. Muscle paralysis may occur when acetylcholine cannot react with the cholinergic muscle receptor or when the muscle cells cannot repolarize to allow new stimulation and muscle contraction.

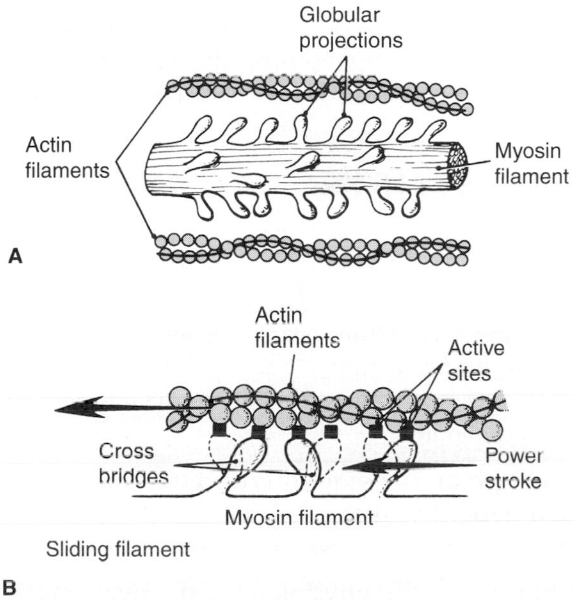

FIGURE 26-1. Sliding filament theory of muscle contraction. (Bullock, B. L. [2000]. *Focus on pathophysiology.* Philadelphia: Lippincott Williams & Wilkins.)

NONDEPOLARIZING NEUROMUSCULAR JUNCTION BLOCKERS

The first nondepolarizing NMJ blocker to be discovered was curare, a poison used on the tips of arrows or spears by primitive hunters to paralyze their game. Animals died when their respiratory muscles became paralyzed. Because the poison was destroyed by the cooking process or gastric acid when eaten (if the meat was eaten raw), it was safe for humans.

Curare was first purified for clinical use as the NMJ blocker tubocurarine. All nondepolarizing NMJ blockers are similar in structure to acetylcholine and occupy the muscular cholinergic receptor site, preventing acetylcholine from reacting with the receptor. These agents do not cause activation of muscle cells, and consequently muscle contraction does not occur. Because they are not broken down by acetylcholinesterase, their effect is more long-lasting than that of acetylcholine. NMJ blockers are used when clinical situations require muscle paralysis.

DEPOLARIZING NEUROMUSCULAR JUNCTION BLOCKER: SUCCINYLCHOLINE

Succinylcholine, a depolarizing NMJ blocker, attaches to the acetylcholine receptor site on the muscle cell, depolarizing the muscle. This depolarization causes stimulation of the muscle and muscle contraction.

Unlike acetylcholine, succinylcholine is not broken down instantly, and the result is a prolonged contraction of the muscle, which cannot be restimulated. Eventually a gradual repolarization occurs as continually stimulated channels in the cell membrane close.

THERAPEUTIC ACTIONS AND INDICATIONS

All of the NMJ blockers are structurally similar to acetylcholine and compete with acetylcholine for muscle acetylcholine receptor sites. They are hydrophilic, instead of lipophilic, so they do not readily cross the blood–brain barrier. The nondepolarizing NMJ blockers act by blocking the ACh receptor so that it cannot be stimulated. Depolarizing NMJ blockers prevent muscle movement by prohibiting the depolarization of the muscle membrane. The depolarizing NMJ blocker succinylcholine (*Anectine, Quelicin*) works by reacting with the ACh receptor and causing a prolonged depolarization, which first causes muscle contraction and then flaccid paralysis. Both effects cause muscles to stop responding to stimuli and paralysis occurs. Clinically, muscle twitching occurs when the drug is first given, followed by flaccid paralysis. Succinylcholine has a rapid onset of action and a short duration of action because it is broken down by cholinesterase in the plasma (Figure 26-2).

These drugs are indicated for any situation in which muscle paralysis is desired. The therapeutic uses of NMJ blocking are as follows:

- To serve as an adjunct to general anesthetics during surgery, when reflex muscle movement could interfere with the surgical procedure or the delivery of gas anesthesia.
- To facilitate mechanical intubation by preventing resistance to passing the endotracheal tube and in situations in which patients "fight" or resist the respirator.
- To facilitate electroconvulsive therapy when intense skeletal muscle contractions as a result of electric shock could cause the patient broken bones or other injury.

Several NMJ blockers are available, with different times of onset and durations of activity. The drug of choice in any given situation is determined by the procedure being performed, including the estimated time involved (Table 26-1).

CONTRAINDICATIONS/CAUTIONS

The NMJ blockers are contraindicated in the following conditions: known allergy to any of these drugs; myasthenia gravis, because blocking the ACh cholinergic receptors aggravates the neuromuscular disease, which results from a destruction of the ACh receptor sites and increases the muscular effects (see Chapter 30); renal or hepatic disease, which could interfere with the metabolism or excretion of these drugs, thus leading to toxic effects; and pregnancy (these drugs are used in cesarean sections, but the dose needs to be decreased to protect the fetus) and lactation because of the potential adverse effects on the fetus and neonate.

Caution should be used in patients with any family or personal history of ***malignant hyperthermia,*** a serious adverse effect associated with these drugs characterized by extreme muscle rigidity, severe hyperpyrexia, acidosis, and death in some cases. Caution should also be used in the following circumstances: pulmonary or cardiovascular dysfunction, which could be made worse by the paralysis of the respiratory muscles and resulting change in perfusion and respiratory function; altered fluid and electrolyte imbalance, which could affect membrane stability and muscular function; and respiratory conditions that could be made worse by the histamine release associated with some of these agents.

In addition, succinylcholine should be used with caution with fractures, because the muscle contractions it causes may lead to additional trauma; with narrow-angle glaucoma or penetrating eye injuries, because intraocular pressure increases; and with paraplegia or spinal cord injuries, which could cause loss of potassium from the overstimulated cells and hyperkalemia. Extreme caution should be taken in the presence of genetic or disease-related conditions causing low plasma cholinesterase levels such as cirrhosis, metabolic disorders, carcinoma, burns, dehydration, malnutrition, hyperpyrexia, thyroid toxicosis, collagen diseases, and exposure to neurotoxic insecticides. Low plasma cholinesterase levels may result in a very prolonged paralysis because succinylcholine is not broken down in the plasma and continues to stimulate the receptor site, leading to a need for prolonged support after the drug is discontinued.

WWW.WEB LINKS

Health care providers and patients may want to consult the following Internet sources:

Information on cholinesterase deficiencies—research, diagnosis, and so on:

http://www.anesthesia.wisc.edu/Topics/Physiology/pseudocholin.html

Information on the diagnosis and treatment of malignant hyperthermia:

http://www.inhaus.org/whatismh.html

Information on the physiology of the neuromuscular junction, effects of blocking the junction:

http://www.ohsu.edu/cliniweb/A11/A11.195.443.780.550.html

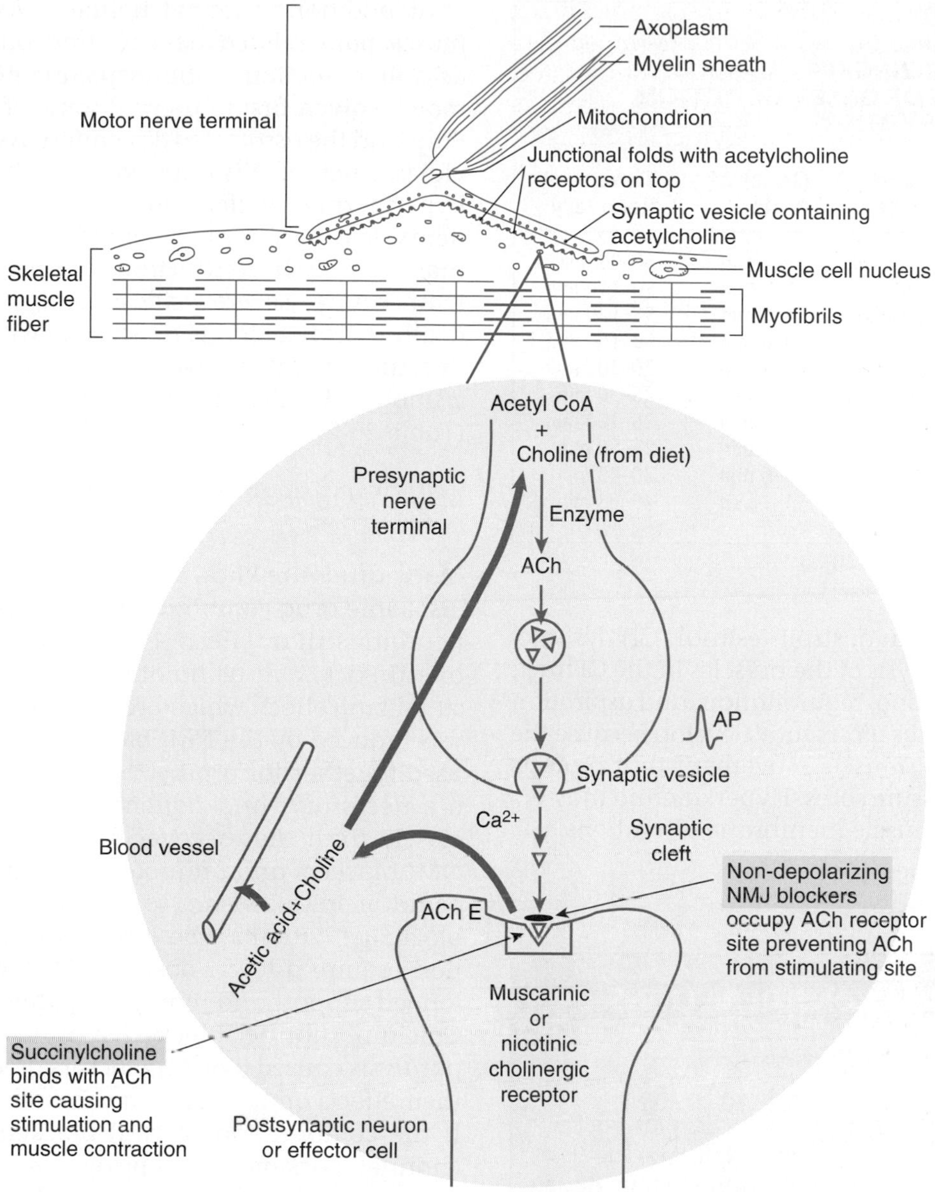

FIGURE 26-2. Sites of action of the NMJ blockers.

Information on paralysis of ventilator patients, particularly the use of pancuronium:

http://www.sccm.org/accm/guidelines/guide_body_p03.htm

Patient guides to general anesthetics, what to expect, how they work:

http://www.asr.net/~PtGuide/general.htm

ADVERSE EFFECTS

The adverse effects related to the use of NMJ blockers are associated with the paralysis of muscles. Profound and prolonged muscle paralysis is always possible, and patients must be supported until they are able to resume voluntary and involuntary muscle movement. When the respiratory muscles are paralyzed, depressed respiration, bronchospasm, and apnea are anticipated adverse effects. NMJ blockers are never used without an anesthesiologist present who can provide artificial respiration and deliver oxygen under positive pressure. Intubation is an anticipated procedure with these drugs.

Histamine release associated with many of the NMJ blockers may cause respiratory obstruction with wheezing and bronchospasm. Hypotension and cardiac arrhythmias may occur in patients who do not adapt to the drugs effectively, use drugs for prolonged periods, have certain underlying conditions, and take certain drugs (vecuronium) that are known to affect cardiovascular receptors. Prolonged drug

TABLE 26-1

NONDEPOLARIZING NMJ BLOCKERS: COMPARISON OF ONSET OF ACTION AND RECOVERY TIMES

Drug	Brand Name	Onset of Action	Time to Recovery
atracurium	*Tracrium*	3–5 min	60–90 min
cistatracurium	*Nimbex*	5–7 min	50–110 min
doxacurium	*Nuromax*	4–9 min	55–120 min
metocurine	*Metubine*	4–6 min	90–160 min
mivacurium	*Mivacron*	2–4 min	20–30 min
pancuronium	*Pavulon*	4 min	25–90 min
pipercuronium	*Arduan*	1–3 min	25–100 min
rocuronium	*Zemuron*	1–2 min	25–50 min
tubocurarine	generic	2–6 min	20–45 min
vecuronium	*Norcuron*	1–3 min	45–65 min

use may also result in gastrointestinal (GI) dysfunction related to paralysis of the muscles in the GI tract; constipation, vomiting, regurgitation, and aspiration may occur. Decubitus ulcers may develop because the patient loses reflex muscle movement that protects the body from pressure sores. Hyperkalemia may occur as a result of muscle membrane alterations.

CULTURAL CONSIDERATIONS

Succinylcholine and Paralysis

Succinylcholine is broken down in the body by cholinesterase, an enzyme found in the plasma. Several conditions may cause the body to produce less of this enzyme, such as cirrhosis, metabolic disorders, carcinoma, burns, dehydration, malnutrition, hyperpyrexia, thyrotoxicosis, collagen diseases, and exposure to neurotoxic insecticides. If plasma cholinesterase levels are low, the serum levels of succinylcholine remain elevated, and the paralysis can last much longer than anticipated. These patients need support and ventilation for long periods after surgery.

There is also a genetic predisposition to low plasma cholinesterase levels. Patients should be asked whether they or any family member has a history of either low plasma cholinesterase levels or prolonged recovery from anesthetics. Alaskan Eskimos belong to such a genetic group, and they are especially likely to suffer prolonged paralysis and inability to breathe for several hours after succinylcholine has been used for surgery. If there is no other drug of choice for these patients, special care must be taken to monitor their response and ensure their breathing for an extended postoperative period.

In addition, succinylcholine is associated with muscle pain, related to the contraction of the muscles as a first reaction. A nondepolarizing NMJ blocker may be given first to prevent some of these contractions and the associated discomfort. Aspirin also alleviates much of this pain postprocedure. Malignant hyperthermia, which may occur in susceptible patients, is a very serious condition characterized by massive muscle contraction, sharply elevated body temperature, severe acidosis and, if uncontrolled, death. This reaction is most likely with succinylcholine, and treatment involves dantrolene (see Chapter 23) to inhibit the muscle effects of the NMJ blocker (Table 26-2).

CLINICALLY IMPORTANT DRUG–DRUG INTERACTIONS

Many drugs are known to react with the NMJ blockers. Some drug combinations result in an increased neuromuscular effect. Halogenated hydrocarbon anesthetics such as halothane cause a membrane stabilizing effect, which greatly enhances the paralysis induced by the NMJ blockers. If these drugs are used together for a procedure, dosage adjustments are necessary, and patients should be monitored closely until they recover fully. A combination of NMJ blockers and aminoglycoside antibiotics (e.g., gentamicin) also leads to increased neuromuscular blockage. Patients who receive this drug combination require a lower dose of NMJ blocker and prolonged support and monitoring after the procedure. Calcium channel blockers may also increase the paralysis caused by NMJ blockers greatly because of their effects on the calcium channels in the muscle. If the combination of NMJ blockers and calcium channel blockers cannot be avoided, the dose of the neuromuscular junction agent should be lowered and the patient monitored closely until complete recovery occurs.

If NMJ blockers are combined with cholinesterase inhibitors, the effectiveness of the NMJ blockers is decreased because of a buildup of acetylcholine in the synaptic cleft. Combination with xanthines (e.g., theophylline, aminophylline) could result in a reversal of the neuromuscular blockage. Patients receiving this combination of drugs should be monitored very closely during the procedure for the potential of early arousal and return of muscle function.

DATA LINK

Data link to the NMJ blockers, listed in Table 26-2, in your nursing drug guide.

TABLE 26-2

NMJ BLOCKERS: NONDEPOLARIZING AND DEPOLARIZING AGENTS

Drug	Brand Name(s)	Usual Indication(s)	Special Considerations	Potential Problems
NONDEPOLARIZING AGENTS				
atracurium	*Tracrium*	Mechanical ventilation Surgical procedures	Long duration of action Do not use before induction of anesthesia Reduce dose in renal failure	Has no effect on pain perception or consciousness Bradycardia more common
cistracurium	*Nimbex*	Surgical procedures Facilitates intubation	Intermediate action	No known effect on pain perception or consciousness Contains benzyl alcohol; avoid use in neonates
doxacurium	*Nuromax*	Surgical procedures Facilitates intubation Mechanical ventilation		No known effect on pain perception or consciousness Contains benzyl alcohol; avoid use with neonates
metocurine	*Metubine*	Surgical procedures Electroshock therapy		Not as likely to cause histamine release as tubocurarine Twice as potent as tubocurarine in children; recovery time is the same as in adults
mivacurium	*Mivacron*	Short surgical procedures Facilitates endotracheal intubation	Rapid recovery	No effect on pain perception or consciousness Dosage may be affected by renal or hepatic impairment
pancuronium	*Pavulon*	Surgical procedures Mechanical ventilation	With long-term use for mechanical ventilation, monitor for prolonged adverse effects	Vagalytic effect, associated with increased heart rate
pipercuronium	*Arduan*	Surgical procedures of ≤ 90 min Facilitates endotracheal intubation		Not as likely as tubocurarine to cause bradycardia Not recommended for long-term use No effect on pain perception or consciousness
rocuronium	*Zemuron*	Preferred for rapid intubation Short outpatient surgical procedures	Rapid onset Use caution with hepatic impairment	No effect on pain perception or consciousness May be associated with pulmonary hypertension
P tubocurarine	generic	Surgical procedures Electroshock therapy Diagnosis of myasthenia gravis when neostigmine or edrophonium are not conclusive		May cause histamine release and increase secretions May cause neuroganglia blockade and hypotension
vecuronium	*Norcuron*	Short surgical procedures Intubation Mechanical ventilation	Monitor with long-term use during ventilation; if response does not occur with first twitch test, discontinue or decrease dosage to prevent overmedication	Contains benzyl alcohol; avoid use in neonates, can cause fatalities in premature infants Excessive dosage and prolonged use may be associated with permanent muscle damage
DEPOLARIZING AGENT				
P succinylcholine	*Anectine, Quelicin*	Surgical procedures Intubation Mechanical ventilation		May cause myalgia secondary to muscle contraction Associated with increased intraocular pressure Increased intragastric pressure may cause vomiting More likely to cause malignant hyperthermia

PATIENT TEACHING CHECKLIST

Neuromuscular Junction Blockers

Create customized patient teaching materials for a specific neuromuscular junction blocker from your CD-ROM. Your patient teaching should stress the following points for drugs within the class:

Before the ________________________________ [surgery, ventilation, intubation (whichever is appropriate)], you will be given a drug to paralyze your muscles called a neuromuscular blocking agent. It is important that your muscles do not move at this time because it could interfere with the procedure.

Common effects of these drugs include **complete paralysis.**

- You will not be able to move or to speak while you are receiving this drug.
- You will not be able to breathe on your own, and you will receive assistance in breathing.
- This drug may not affect your level of consciousness, and it may be very frightening to be unable to communicate with anyone around you. Someone will be with you and will try to anticipate your needs and will explain what is going on at all times.
- This drug may have no effect on your pain perception. Every effort will be made to make sure that you do not experience pain.
- If you receive the drug succinylcholine, you may experience back and throat pain related to muscle contractions that occur. You will be able to take aspirin to relieve this discomfort.
- Recovery of your muscle function may take __________, and someone will be nearby at all times until you have recovered from the paralysis.

This Teaching Checklist reflects general patient teaching guidelines. It is not meant to be a substitute for drug-specific teaching information, which is available in nursing drug guides.

NURSING CONSIDERATIONS
for patients receiving neuromuscular junction blockers

Assessment

HISTORY. Screen for the following: any known allergies to these drugs; impaired liver or kidney function; myasthenia gravis; lactation; pregnancy; impaired cardiac or respiratory function; personal or family history of malignant hyperthermia; and fractures, narrow angle glaucoma, or paraplegia.

PHYSICAL ASSESSMENT. Include screening for baseline status before beginning therapy and for any potential adverse effects. Assess the following: body temperature; skin color and lesions; affect, orientation, reflexes, pupil size and reactivity, and muscle tone and response; pulse, blood pressure, and ECG; respiration and adventitious sounds; bowel sounds and abdominal examination; as well as renal and liver function tests and serum electrolytes.

Nursing Diagnoses

The patient receiving an NMJ blocker may have the following nursing diagnoses related to drug therapy:

- Impaired gas exchange related to depressed respirations
- Alteration in skin integrity related to immobility
- Impaired verbal communication, fear related to paralysis
- Knowledge deficit regarding drug therapy

Implementation

- Administration of the drug should be performed by trained personnel (usually an anesthesiologist) *because of the potential for serious adverse effects and the need for immediate ventilatory support.*
- Have supplies and equipment on standby *to maintain airway and provide mechanical ventilation.*
- Do not mix the drug with any alkaline solutions such as barbiturates *because a precipitate may form.*
- Test patient response and recovery periodically if the drug is being given long-term *to maintain mechanical ventilation. Discontinue the drug if response does not occur or is greatly delayed.*
- Monitor patient temperature *for prompt detection and treatment of malignant hyperthermia.*
- Maintain dantrolene on standby *for treatment of malignant hyperthermia if it should occur.*
- Arrange for a small dose of a nondepolarizing NMJ blocker before using succinylcholine *to reduce adverse effects associated with muscle contraction.*

CASE STUDY

Using Succinylcholine in an Elderly Patient

PRESENTATION

S. N., an 82-year-old white woman in very good health, has been admitted to the hospital for an exploratory laparotomy to evaluate a probable abdominal mass. On admission, health care practitioners learned that she had a history of mild hypertension that was well regulated by diuretic therapy. She received a baseline physical examination and preoperative instruction. On the morning of the surgery, it was noted that the anesthesiologist planned to give her a general anesthetic and succinylcholine to ensure muscle paralysis.

CRITICAL THINKING QUESTIONS

What nursing care plans should be made for S. N.? Consider the patient's age and associated chronic problems that often occur with aging. Also consider the support that she has available and potential physical and emotional support that she might need before and after this procedure. Using an NMJ blocker in the elderly presents some nursing challenges that may not be seen with younger patients. What particular nursing care activities should be considered with S. N.? Because S. N. has been maintained on long-term diuretic therapy, she is at special risk for electrolyte imbalance. What, if any, complications could arise if S. N. has electrolyte disturbances before surgery?

DISCUSSION

Before going into surgery, the preoperative teaching protocol should be reviewed with the patient. S. N. should be advised that she may experience back, neck, and throat pain after the procedure. Assure her that this is normal and that aspirin will be made available to alleviate the discomfort. Review deep breathing and coughing; she may need encouragement to clear secretions from her lungs and ensure full inflation. It is usually easier to do this if it is a familiar activity. S. N.'s serum electrolytes should be evaluated before surgery, because potassium imbalance can cause unexpected effects with succinylcholine. Renal and hepatic function tests should also be performed to ensure that the dosage of the NMJ blocker is not excessive.

During the procedure, S. N.'s cardiac and respiratory status should be monitored carefully for any potential problems, an effect that is more common in people with underlying physical problems. Because of S. N.'s age and potential circulatory problems, she should receive meticulous skin care and turning as soon as the procedure allows this kind of movement. She should be turned frequently during the recovery period and her skin checked for any breakdown. Nursing personnel must be near the patient until she has regained muscle control and the ability to communicate. She should be evaluated for the need for pain medication and position adjustments.

S. N. will require further teaching about her diagnosis and potential treatment. This should wait until she has regained full ability to communicate and is able to respond and participate in any discussion that may be held. At that time, she may require emotional support and encouragement. It may be necessary to contact available family or social service agencies regarding her physical and medical needs.

- Maintain a cholinesterase inhibitor on standby *to overcome excessive neuromuscular blockade caused by nondepolarizing NMJ blockers.*
- Provide a peripheral nerve stimulator on standby *to assess the degree of neuromuscular block, if appropriate.*
- Provide comfort measures *to help the patient tolerate drug effects* such as pain relief as appropriate; reassurance, support, and orientation for conscious patients unable to move or communicate; skin care and turning to prevent skin breakdown; and supportive care *for emergencies such as hypotension and bronchospasm.*
- Monitor patient response closely (blood pressure, temperature, pulse, respiration, reflexes) *and adjust dosage accordingly to ensure the greatest therapeutic effect with minimal risk of toxicity.*
- Incorporate information on this drug into a thorough preoperative patient teaching plan *because most patients who receive the drug will receive teaching about a particular procedure and will be unconscious when the drug is given* (see Patient Teaching Checklist: Neuromuscular Junction Blockers).
- Offer support and encouragement *to help the patient cope with drug effects.*

Evaluation

- Monitor patient response to the drug (adequate muscle paralysis).
- Monitor for adverse effects (respiratory depression, hypotension, bronchospasm, GI slowdown, skin breakdown, fear related to helplessness and inability to communicate).
- Evaluate the effectiveness of the teaching plan (patient can relate anticipated effects of the drug and the recovery process).
- Monitor the effectiveness of comfort measures and compliance with the regimen (see Nursing Care Guide: Neuromuscular Junction Blockers).

NURSING CARE GUIDE
Neuromuscular Junction Blockers

Assessment	*Nursing Diagnoses*	*Implementation*	*Evaluation*
HISTORY Allergies to any of these drugs, COPD, cardiac disorders, myasthenia gravis, pregnancy and lactation, hepatic or renal dysfunction, fractures, glaucoma	Alteration of gas exchange related to impaired gas exchange Alteration in skin integrity related to immobility Knowledge deficit regarding drug therapy Impaired verbal communication, fear related to paralysis and inability to communicate	Administer drug under strict supervision. Provide comfort and safety measures: positioning, skin care, temperature control, pain medication as needed, maintain airway, ventilate patient, antidotes on standby. Provide support and reassurance to deal with paralysis and inability to communicate. Provide patient teaching about procedure being performed, what to expect. Provide life support as needed.	Evaluate drug effects: muscle paralysis. Monitor for adverse effects: CV effects (tachycardia, hypotension, respiratory distress, increased respiratory secretions), GI effects (constipation, nausea), skin breakdown, anxiety, fear. Monitor for drug–drug interactions as indicated for each drug. Evaluate effectiveness of patient teaching program. Evaluate effectiveness of comfort and safety measures. Constantly monitor vital signs and return to normal muscular function.
PHYSICAL EXAMINATION CV: BP, P, peripheral perfusion, ECG CNS: orientation, affect, reflexes, vision Skin: color, lesions, texture, sweating GU: urinary output, bladder tone GI: abdominal exam Resp: R, adventitious sounds			

CHAPTER SUMMARY

- The nerves communicate with muscles at a point called the neuromuscular junction, using acetylcholine as the neurotransmitter.
- NMJ blockers prevent skeletal muscle function.
- Nondepolarizing NMJ blockers prevent acetylcholine from exciting the muscle, and paralysis ensues because the muscle is unable to respond.
- Depolarizing NMJ blockers cause muscle paralysis by acting like acetylcholine and exciting the muscle (depolarization), preventing repolarization and further stimulation of that muscle cell.
- NMJ blockers are primarily used as adjuncts to general anesthesia, to facilitate endotracheal intubation, to facilitate mechanical ventilation, and to prevent injury during electroconvulsive therapy.
- Adverse effects of NMJ blockers such as prolonged paralysis, inability to breathe, weakness, muscle pain and soreness, and effects of immobility are related to muscle function blocking.
- Care of patients receiving NMJ blockers must include support and reassurance, because communication is decreased with paralysis; vigilant maintenance of airways and respiration; prevention of skin breakdown; and monitoring for return of function.

BIBLIOGRAPHY

Bullock, B. L. (2000). *Focus on pathophysiology*. Philadelphia: Lippincott Williams & Wilkins.

Hardman, J. G., Limbird, L. E., Molinoff, P. B., Ruddon, R. W., & Gilman, A. G. (Eds.). (1996). *Goodman and Gilman's the pharmacological basis of therapeutics* (9th ed.). New York: McGraw-Hill.

Karch, A. M. (2000). *2000 Lippincott's nursing drug guide*. Philadelphia: Lippincott Williams & Wilkins.

Malseed, R. (1995). *Textbook of pharmacology and nursing care*. Philadelphia: Lippincott-Raven.

McEvoy, B. R. (Ed.). (1999). *Facts and comparisons 1999*. St. Louis: Facts and Comparisons.

Professional's guide to patient drug facts. (1999). St. Louis: Facts and Comparisons.

PART

5

Drugs Acting on the Autonomic Nervous System

CHAPTER 27

Introduction to the Autonomic Nervous System

CHAPTER OUTLINE

KEY TERMS

acetylcholinesterase
adrenergic receptors
alpha receptor
autonomic nervous system
beta receptor
cholinergic receptor
ganglia
monoamine oxidase (MAO)
muscarinic receptor
nicotinic receptor
parasympathetic nervous system
sympathetic nervous system

INTRODUCTION

The ***autonomic nervous system*** (ANS) is sometimes called the involuntary or visceral nervous system because it mostly functions with little conscious awareness of its activity. Working closely with the endocrine system, the ANS helps to regulate and integrate the body's internal functions within a relatively narrow range of normal, on a minute-to-minute basis. The ANS integrates parts of the central nervous system (CNS) and peripheral nervous system (PNS) to automatically react to changes in the internal and external environment.

GENERAL FUNCTIONS

The main nerve centers for the autonomic nervous system are located in the hypothalamus, the medulla, and the spinal cord. Nerve impulses that arise in peripheral structures are carried to these centers by afferent nerve fibers. These integrating centers in the CNS respond by sending out efferent impulses along the autonomic nerve pathways. These impulses adjust the functioning of various internal organs in ways that keep the body's internal environment constant, or homeostatic.

The ANS works to regulate blood pressure, heart rate, respiration, body temperature, water balance, urinary excretion, and digestive functions, among other things. The minute-to-minute control exerted by this system results from an interrelationship between opposing divisions of the autonomic system: the sympathetic and the parasympathetic divisions (Figure 27-1).

WWW.WEB LINKS

To explore the virtual autonomic nervous system, consult the following Internet sources:

http://www.InnerBody.com

http://www.scuchico.edu/~pmccaff/syllabi/SPPA362/notes-UNIT8.html

DIVISIONS OF THE AUTONOMIC NERVOUS SYSTEM

Throughout the ANS, nerve impulses are carried from the CNS to the outlying organs by way of a two-neuron system. In most PNS activities, the CNS nerve body sends an impulse directly to an effector organ or muscle. The ANS does not send impulses directly to the periphery. Instead, axons from CNS neurons end in ***ganglia,*** or groups of nerve bodies that are packed together, located outside the CNS. These ganglia receive information from the preganglionic neuron that started in the CNS and relay that information along postganglionic neurons. The postganglionic neurons transmit impulses to the neuroeffector cells—muscles, glands, and organs. The ANS is divided into two branches that differ in three basic ways: (1) the location of the originating cells in the CNS, (2) the location of the nerve ganglia, and (3) the preganglionic and postganglionic neurons (Table 27-1).

The Sympathetic Nervous System

The ***sympathetic nervous system*** (SNS) is sometimes referred to as the "fight or flight" system, or the system responsible for preparing the body to respond to stress. Stress can either be internal, such as cell injury or death, or external, which is a perceived or learned reaction to various external situations or stimuli. The SNS acts much like an accelerator, speeding things up for action.

ANATOMY

The SNS is also called the thoracolumbar system because the CNS cells that originate impulses for this system are located in the thoracic and lumbar sections of the spinal cord. These cells send out short preganglionic fibers that synapse or communicate with nerve ganglia located in chains running along the side of the spinal cord. The neurotransmitter that is released by these preganglionic nerves is acetylcholine. The nerve ganglia, in turn, send out long postganglionic fibers that synapse with neuroeffectors, using norepinephrine or epinephrine as the neurotransmitter. One of the sympathetic ganglia, on either side of the spinal cord, will not develop postganglionic axons but will produce norepinephrine and epinephrine, which will be secreted directly into the blood stream. These ganglia have evolved into the adrenal medullas. When the SNS is stimulated, the chromaffin cells of the adrenal medullas secrete epinephrine and norepinephrine directly into the blood stream.

FUNCTIONS

When stimulated, the SNS prepares the body to flee or to turn and fight (Figure 27-2). Cardiovascular activity increases; blood pressure and heart rate increase, as does blood flow to the skeletal muscles. Respiratory efficiency also increases; bronchi are dilated to allow more air to enter with each breath, and the respiratory rate increases. Pupils dilate to permit more light to enter the eye to improve vision

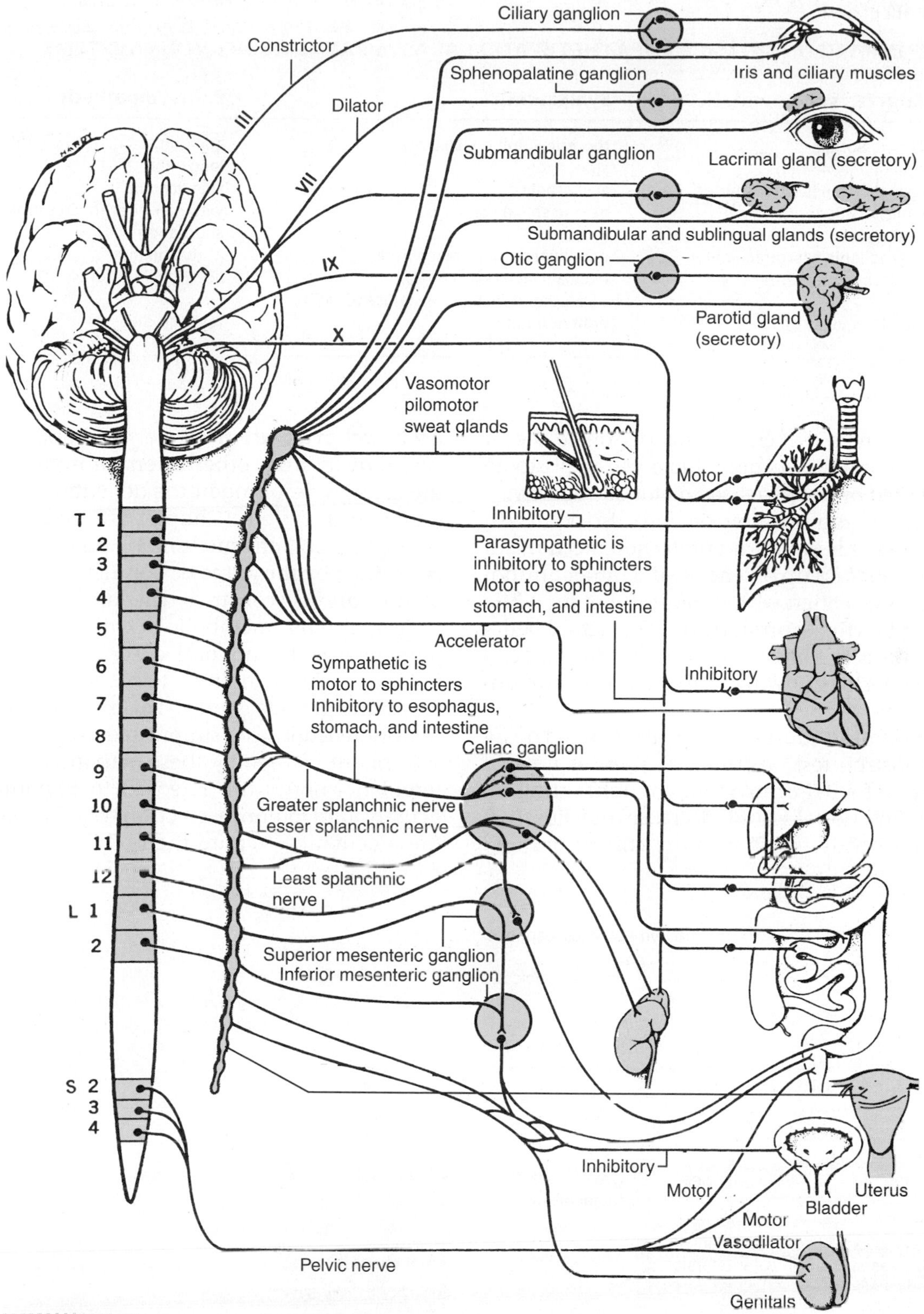

FIGURE 27-1. The autonomic nervous system. The parasympathetic, or craniosacral, division sends long preganglionic fibers that synapse with a second nerve cell in ganglia located close to or within the organs that are then innervated by short postganglionic fibers. The sympathetic, or thoracolumbar, division sends relatively short preganglionic fibers to the chains of paravertebral ganglia and to certain outlying ganglia. The second cell shown sends relatively long postganglionic fibers to the organs that they innervate.

TABLE 27-1

COMPARISON OF THE SYMPATHETIC AND PARASYMPATHETIC NERVOUS SYSTEMS

Characteristic	Sympathetic	Parasympathetic
CNS nerve origin	thoracic, lumbar spinal cord	cranium, sacral spinal cord
Preganglionic neuron	short axon	long axon
Preganglionic neurotransmitter	acetylcholine	acetylcholine
Ganglia location	next to spinal cord	within or near effector organs
Postganglionic neuron	long axon	short axon
Postganglionic neurotransmitter	norephinephrine, epinephrine	acetylcholine
Neurotransmitter terminator	Monoamine oxidase (MAO), catechol-o-methyltransferase (COMT)	acetylcholinesterase
General response	fight or flight	rest and digest

in darkened areas (which helps a person to see in order to fight or flee). Sweating increases, to dissipate heat generated by the increased metabolic activity.

Piloerection (hair standing on end) also occurs. In lower animals, this important protection mechanism makes the fur stand up on end, so if a larger animal attacks, he is often left with a mouthful of fur while the intended victim scurries away. The actual benefit to humans is not known, except that this activity helps to generate heat when the core body temperature is too low.

SNS stimulation causes blood to be diverted away from the gastrointestinal tract, as there is no real need to digest food during a flight or fight situation. Because of this, bowel sounds decrease and digestion slows dramatically; sphincters are constricted and no bowel evacuation can occur. Blood is also diverted away from other internal organs, including the kidneys, resulting in the activation of the renin-angiotensin system (Chapter 40) and a further increase in blood pressure and blood volume as water is retained by the kidneys. Sphincters in the urinary bladder are also constricted, leading to no urination.

Several other metabolic activities occur that prepare the body to fight or flee. For example, glucose is formed in glycogenolysis, to increase blood glucose levels and provide energy. The immune and inflammatory reactions are suppressed, to preserve energy that might be used by these activities. The corticosteroid hormones are released to regulate glucose activity and balance electrolytes. Together, all of these activities prepare the body to flee or to fight

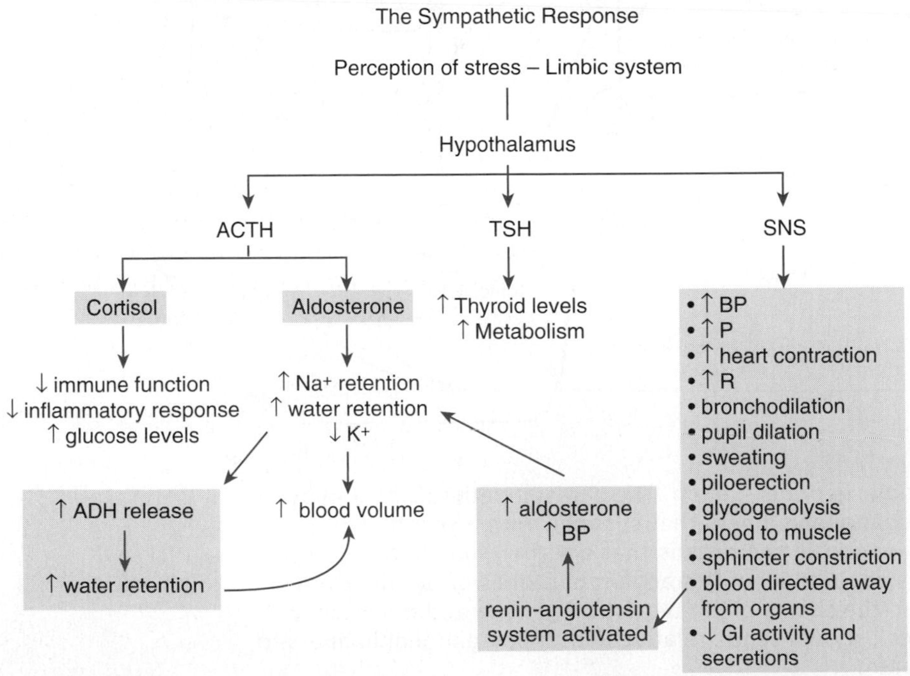

FIGURE 27-2. The "Fight or Flight" response.

more effectively. When overstimulated, they can also lead to system overload and a variety of diseases.

Adrenergic Transmission

Sympathetic postganglionic nerves that synthesize, store, and release norepinephrine are referred to as adrenergic nerves. Adrenergic nerves are also found within the CNS. The chromaffin cells of the adrenal medulla also are adrenergic because they synthesize, store, and release norepinephrine as well as epinephrine.

NOREPINEPHRINE SYNTHESIS AND STORAGE

Norepinephrine belongs to a group of structurally related chemicals called catecholamines. Dopamine and epinephrine are also catecholamines. Norepinephrine is made by the nerve cells using tyrosine, which is obtained in the diet. Dopa is produced by a nerve, using tyrosine from the diet and other chemicals. With the help of the enzyme dopa decarboxylase it is converted to dopamine, which, in turn, is converted to norepinephrine in adrenergic cells. The norepinephrine then is stored in granules or storage vesicles within the cell. These vesicles move down the nerve axon to the terminals of the axon, where they line up along the cell membrane. To be an adrenergic nerve, the nerve must contain all of the enzymes and building blocks necessary to produce norepinephrine (Figure 27-3).

NOREPINEPHRINE RELEASE

When the nerve is stimulated, the action potential travels down the nerve axon and arrives at the axon terminal (see Chapter 17). The action potential then depolarizes the axon membrane. This action allows calcium into the nerve, causing the membrane to contract and the storage vesicles to fuse with the cell membrane, then dump their load of norepinephrine into the synaptic gap or cleft. The norepinephrine travels across the very short gap to very specific adrenergic receptor sites on the effector cell on the other side of the synaptic gap.

ADRENERGIC RECEPTORS

The receptor sites that react with neurotransmitters at adrenergic sites have been classified as ***alpha receptors*** and ***beta receptors;*** further classifications include $alpha_1$, $alpha_2$, $beta_1$, and $beta_2$ receptors. The distinction arises because different drugs that are known to affect the SNS may affect parts of the sympathetic response, but not all of it. It is thought that receptors may respond to different concentrations of norepinephrine or different ratios of norepinephrine and epinephrine. ***Adrenergic receptors*** can be stimulated by the neurotransmitter released from the axon in the immediate vicinity, and further stimulated by circulating norepinephrine and epinephrine secreted directly into the blood stream by the adrenal medulla.

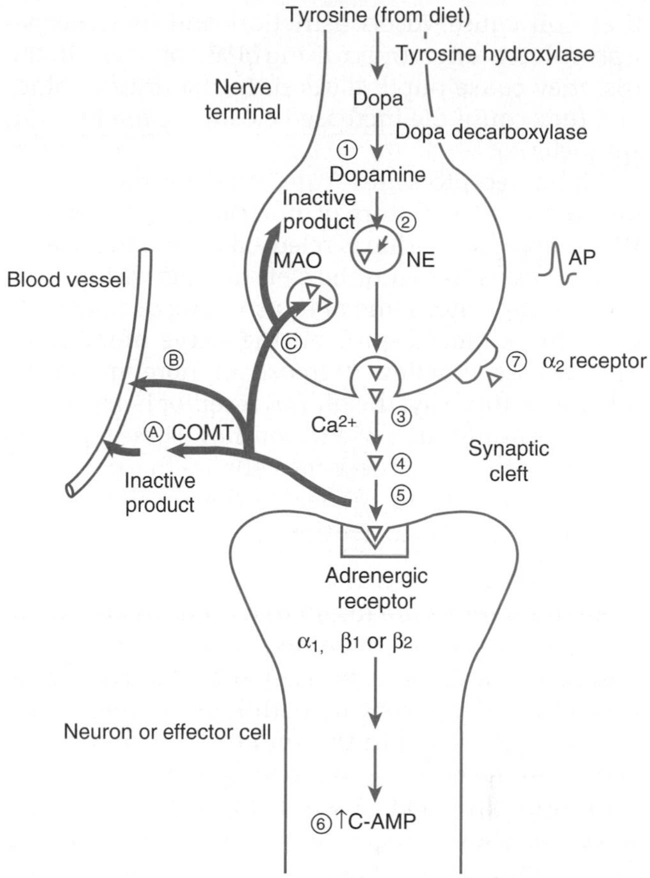

FIGURE 27-3. Sequence of events at an adrenergic synapse. (*1*) Dopamine, a precursor of norepinephrine (NE), is synthesized from tyrosine in several steps. Metyrosine inhibits tyrosine hydroxylase; a drug given with dopa to parkinsonian patients inhibits dopa decarboxylase. (*2*) Dopamine is taken into the storage vesicle and converted to norepinephrine (NE, V). (*3*) Release of neurotransmitter by action potential (AP) in presynaptic nerve. (*4*) Diffusion of neurotransmitter across synaptic cleft. (*5*) Combination of neurotransmitter with receptor. The events resulting from NE occupying receptor sites depend on the nature of the postsynaptic cell. (*6*) Interaction of NE with many β receptors leads to ↑ synthesis of cAMP. (*7*) Change in permeability of postsynaptic membrane to one or more ions. (*A*) An enzyme, COMT, inactives the NE, but the most important way in which the action of NE is terminated is by (*C*), reuptake into the presynaptic neuron where it may be reused or inactivated by another enzyme, MAO. (*B*) The neurotransmitter may also diffuse away from the synaptic cleft.

Alpha Receptors

$Alpha_1$ receptors are found in blood vessels, the iris, and in the urinary bladder. In blood vessels, they can cause vasoconstriction and increase peripheral resistance, thus raising blood pressure. In the iris, they cause pupil dilation. In the urinary bladder, they cause the increased closure of the internal sphincter.

$Alpha_2$ receptors are located on nerve membranes and act as modulators of norepinephrine release. When norepinephrine is released from a nerve ending, it crosses the synaptic cleft to react with its specific receptor site. Some of it also flows back to react with the alpha receptor on the nerve membrane. This causes a reflex decrease in norepinephrine release. In this way, the $alpha_2$ receptor helps to prevent overstimulation of effector sites. These receptors are also found on the beta cells in the pancreas, where they help to moderate the insulin release stimulated by SNS activation.

Beta Receptors

$Beta_1$ receptors are found in cardiac tissue, where they can stimulate increased myocardial activity and increased heart rate. They are also responsible for increased lipolysis in peripheral tissues. $Beta_2$ receptors are found in the smooth muscle in blood vessels, in the bronchi, in the periphery, and in uterine muscle. In blood vessels, $beta_2$ stimulation leads to vasodilation. $Beta_2$ receptors also cause dilation in the bronchi. In the periphery, they can cause increased muscle and liver breakdown of glycogen and increased release of glucagon from the alpha cells of the pancreas. Stimulation of $beta_2$ receptors in the uterus results in relaxed uterine smooth muscle.

TERMINATION OF TRANSMISSION

Once norepinephrine has been released into the synaptic cleft, stimulation of the receptor site is terminated only when any extra norepinephrine, as well as the neurotransmitter that has reacted with the receptor site, is disposed of. Most of the free norepinephrine molecules are taken up by the nerve terminal that released them. This neurotransmitter is then repackaged into vesicles to be released later with nerve stimulation. This is an effective recycling effort by the nerve. Enzymes are also in the area as well as in the liver to metabolize or biotransform any remaining norepinephrine or any norepinephrine that is absorbed into circulation. These enzymes are ***monoamine oxidase (MAO)*** and catechol-o-methyltransferase (COMT).

The Parasympathetic Nervous System

In many areas, the ***parasympathetic nervous system*** works in opposition to the SNS. This allows the autonomic system to maintain a fine control over internal homeostasis. For instance, the SNS increases heart rate, while the parasympathetic system decreases it. Therefore, the ANS can influence heart rate by increasing or decreasing sympathetic activity, as well as by increasing or decreasing parasympathetic activity. This is very much like controlling the speed of a car by moving between the accelerator or the brake or a combination of the two. Whereas the SNS is associated with the stress reaction and expenditure of energy, the parasympathetic system is associated with activities that help the body to store up or conserve energy, a "rest and digest" response (Table 27-2).

ANATOMY

The parasympathetic nervous system is sometimes called the craniosacral system because the CNS neurons that originate parasympathetic impulses are found in the cranium (one of the most important being the vagus or tenth cranial nerve) and the sacral area of the spinal cord (see Figure 27-1). The parasympathetic nervous system has long preganglionic axons that meet in ganglia located close to or within the organ that they are going to affect. The postganglionic axon is very short, going directly to the effector cell. The neurotransmitter used by both the preganglionic and postganglionic neurons is acetylcholine.

FUNCTIONS

Parasympathetic nervous system stimulation results in the following actions:

- Increased motility and secretions in the gastrointestinal tract to promote digestion and absorption of nutrients.
- Decreased heart rate and contractility to conserve energy and provide rest for the heart.
- Constriction of the bronchi with increased secretions.
- Relaxation of the gastrointestinal and urinary bladder sphincters, allowing evacuation of waste products.
- Pupillary constriction, which decreases the light entering the eye and decreases stimulation of the retina.

These activities are aimed at increasing digestion, absorption of nutrients, and building of essential proteins as well as a general conservation of energy.

Cholinergic Transmission

Neurons that use acetylcholine as their neurotransmitter are called cholinergic neurons. There are approximately four basic kinds of cholinergic nerves:

TABLE 27-2

EFFECTS OF AUTONOMIC STIMULATION

Effector Site	Sympathetic Reaction	Receptor	Parasympathetic Reaction
Heart	↑ rate, contractility ↑ A-V conduction	$beta_1$	↓ rate, ↓ A-V conduction
Blood vessels			
Skin, mucous membranes	constriction	$alpha_1$	——
Skeletal muscle	dilation	$beta_2$	——
Bronchial muscle	relaxation (dilation)	$beta_2$	constriction
GI system			
Muscle motility and tone	↓ activity	$beta_2$	↑ activity
Sphincters	contraction	$alpha_1$	relaxation
Secretions	↓ secretions	$beta_2$	↑ activity
Salivary glands	thick secretions	$alpha_1$	copious, watery secretions
Gallbladder	relaxation	?	contraction
Liver	glyconeogenesis	$beta_2$	
Urinary bladder			
Detrusor muscle	relaxation	$beta_2$	contraction
Trigone muscle and sphincter	contraction	$alpha_1$	relaxation
Eye structures			
Iris radial muscle	contraction (pupil dilates)	$alpha_1$	——
Iris sphincter muscle	——		contraction (pupil constricts)
Ciliary muscle	——		contraction (lens accommodates for near vision)
Lacrimal glands	——		↑ secretions
Skin structures			
Sweat glands	↑ in sweating	Sympathetic cholinergic	——
Piloerector muscles	contracted (goosebumps)	$alpha_1$	——
Sex organs			
Male	emission	$alpha_1$	erection (vascular dilation)
Female	uterine relaxation	$beta_2$	——

(—— means no reaction or response)

1. All preganglionic nerves in the autonomic nervous system, both SNS and parasympathetic nervous system
2. Postganglionic nerves of the parasympathetic nervous system and a few SNS nerves, such as those that reenter the spinal cord and cause general body reactions like sweating
3. Motor nerves on skeletal muscles
4. Cholinergic nerves within the CNS

ACETYLCHOLINE SYNTHESIS AND STORAGE

Acetylcholine (ACh) is an ester of acetic acid and an organic alcohol called choline. Cholinergic nerves use choline, obtained in the diet, to produce ACh. The last step in the production of the neurotransmitter involves choline acetyltransferase, an enzyme that is also produced within cholinergic nerves. Just like norepinephrine, the ACh is produced in the nerve and travels to the end of the axons, where it is packaged into vesicles. To be a cholinergic nerve, the nerve must contain all of the enzymes and building blocks necessary to produce acetylcholine.

ACETYLCHOLINE RELEASE

The vesicles full of ACh move to the nerve membrane and when an action potential reaches the nerve terminal, calcium entering the cell causes the membrane to contract and secrete the neurotransmitter into the synaptic cleft. The ACh travels across the synaptic cleft and reacts with very specific ***cholinergic receptor*** sites on the effector cell (Figure 27-4).

ACETYLCHOLINE RECEPTORS

Acetylcholine receptors are found on organs and muscles. They have been classified as ***muscarinic receptors*** and ***nicotinic receptors.*** This classification is based on very early research of the autonomic nervous system that used muscarine (a plant alkaloid from mushrooms) and nicotine (a plant alkaloid found in tobacco plants) to study the actions of the parasympathetic nervous system.

Muscarinic Receptors

As the name implies, muscarinic receptors are receptors that can be stimulated using muscarine.

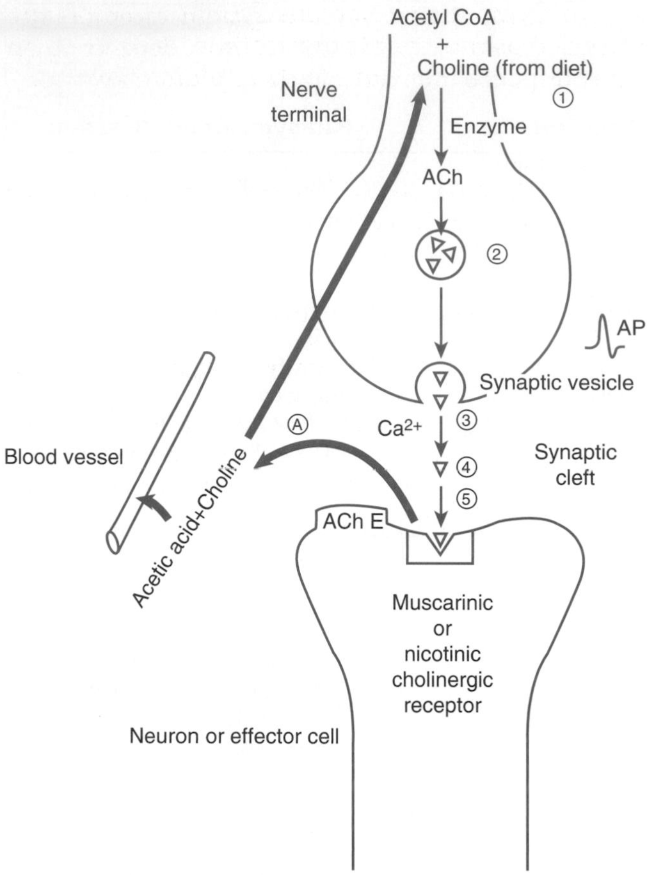

FIGURE 27-4. Sequence of events at a cholinergic synapse. (*1*) Synthesis of acetylcholine (ACh) from choline (a substance in the diet) and a cofactor (the enzyme is choline acetyltransferase. (*2*) Uptake of neurotransmitter into storage (synaptic) vesicle. (*3*) Release of neurotransmitter by action potential (AP) in presynaptic nerve. (*4*) Diffusion of neurotransmitter across synaptic cleft. (*5*) Combination of neurotransmitter with receptor. The events resulting from ACh occupying receptor sites depend on the nature of the postsynaptic cell. ACh excites some cells and inhibits others. (*A*) An enzyme, acetylcholinesterase (AChE) on the postsynaptic cell, inactivates ACh. Some of the products diffuse into the circulation, but most of the choline formed is taken up and reused by the cholinergic neuron.

They are found in visceral effector organs, in sweat glands, and in some vascular smooth muscle. Stimulation of muscarinic receptors causes pupil constriction, increased gastrointestinal motility and secretions (including saliva), increased urinary bladder contraction, and a slowing of the heart rate.

Nicotinic Receptors

Nicotinic receptors are located in the CNS, the adrenal medulla, the autonomic ganglia, and the neuromuscular junction. Stimulation of nicotinic receptors causes muscle contractions, autonomic responses, and release of norepinephrine and epinephrine from the adrenal medulla.

TERMINATION OF TRANSMISSION

Once the effector cell has been stimulated by ACh, it is important to stop the stimulation and to get rid of the ACh. The destruction of the ACh is carried out by the enzyme ***acetylcholinesterase.*** This enzyme reacts with the ACh and forms a chemically inactive compound. The breakdown of the released ACh is accomplished in a thousandth of a second and the receptor is vacated, allowing the effector membrane to repolarize and be ready for the next stimulation.

CHAPTER SUMMARY

- The autonomic nervous system (ANS) works with the endocrine system to regulate internal functioning and maintain homeostasis.
- The autonomic nervous system is divided into two branches, the sympathetic nervous system (SNS) and the parasympathetic nervous system.
- The two branches of the ANS work in opposition to maintain minute-to-minute regulation of the internal environment and to allow rapid response to stress situations.
- The SNS, when stimulated, is responsible for the fight or flight response. It prepares the body for immediate reaction to stressors by increasing metabolism, diverting blood to big muscles, and increasing cardiac and respiratory function.
- The parasympathetic nervous system, when stimulated, acts as a rest and digest response. It increases the digestion, absorption, and metabolism of nutrients and slows metabolism and function to save energy.
- The SNS is composed of CNS cells arising in the thoracic or lumbar area of the spinal cord, short preganglionic axons, ganglia located near the spinal cord, and long postganglionic axons that react with effector cells. The neurotransmitter used by the preganglionic cells is acetylcholine; the neurotransmitter used by the postganglionic cells is norepinephrine.
- One SNS ganglia on either side of the spinal cord does not develop postganglionic axons, but secretes norepinephrine directly into the blood stream to travel throughout the body to react with adrenergic receptor sites. This ganglia evolved into the adrenal medulla.
- The parasympathetic nervous system is composed of CNS cells arising in the cranium and sacral region of the spinal cord, long preganglionic axons that secrete ACh, ganglia located very close to or within the effector tissue, and short postganglionic axons that also secrete ACh.

- Norepinephrine is made by adrenergic nerves using tyrosine from the diet. It is packaged in storage vesicles which align up on the axon membrane and is secreted into the synaptic cleft when the nerve is stimulated. It reacts with specific receptor sites and is then broken down by MAO or COMT to relax the receptor site and recycle the building blocks of norepinephrine.
- ACh is made by choline from the diet and packaged into storage vesicles to be released by the cholinergic nerve into the synaptic cleft. ACh is broken down to an inactive form almost immediately by acetylcholinesterase.
- SNS adrenergic receptors are classified as being $alpha_1$, $alpha_2$, $beta_1$, and $beta_2$ receptors based on the effectors that they stimulate.
- Parasympathetic nervous system receptors are classified as muscarinic or nicotinic, depending on what response they have to these plant alkaloids.

Bibliography

Bullock, B. L. (2000). *Focus on pathophysiology*. Philadelphia: Lippincott Williams & Wilkins.

Fox, S. (1991). *Perspectives on human biology*. Dubuque, IA: Wm. C. Brown.

Ganong, W. (1991). *Review of medical physiology* (15th ed.). Norwalk, CT: Appleton & Lange.

Guyton, A. & Hall, J. (1996). *Textbook of medical physiology*. Philadelphia: W.B. Saunders.

Hardman, J. G., Limbird, L. E., Molinoff, P. B., Ruddon, R. W., & Gilman, A. G. (Eds). (1996). *Goodman and Gilman's the pharmacological basis of therapeutics* (9th ed.). New York: McGraw-Hill.

CHAPTER 28

Adrenergic Agents

Alpha and beta adrenergic agonists
- dobutamine
- **P** dopamine
- ephedrine
- epinephrine
- metaraminol
- norepinephrine

Alpha-specific adrenergic agonists
- clonidine
- **P** phenylephrine

Beta-specific adrenergic agonists
- **P** isoproterenol
- ritodrine

Also see beta adrenergic agonists in Chapter 53:
- albuterol
- bitolterol
- isoetharine
- metaproterenol
- pirbuterol
- salmeterol
- terbutaline

CHAPTER OUTLINE

KEY TERMS

adrenergic agonist
alpha agonist
beta agonist
glycogenolysis
sympathomimetic

INTRODUCTION

Adrenergic agonists are also called **sympathomimetic** drugs because they mimic the effects of the sympathetic nervous system (SNS). The therapeutic and adverse effects associated with these drugs are related to their stimulation of adrenergic receptor sites. The use of adrenergic agonists varies from ophthalmic preparations for dilating pupils to systemic preparations used to support people in shock.

ADRENERGIC AGONISTS

The therapeutic and adverse effects associated with these drugs are related to their stimulation of adrenergic receptors sites (Figure 28-1). That stimulation can be either direct, by occupation of the adrenergic receptor, or indirect, by modulating the release of neurotransmitter from the axon. Some drugs act in both ways.

Alpha and Beta Adrenergic Agonists

Drugs that are generally sympathomimetic (that is, they stimulate all of the adrenergic receptors) are alpha and beta agonists. Some of these drugs are preparations of catecholamines.

Epinephrine (*Adrenalin, Sus-Phrine,* etc.) is a naturally occurring catecholamine that interacts with both alpha and beta adrenergic receptors. It is used therapeutically in the treatment of shock, when increased blood pressure and heart contractility is essential; as one of the primary treatments for bronchospasm, by

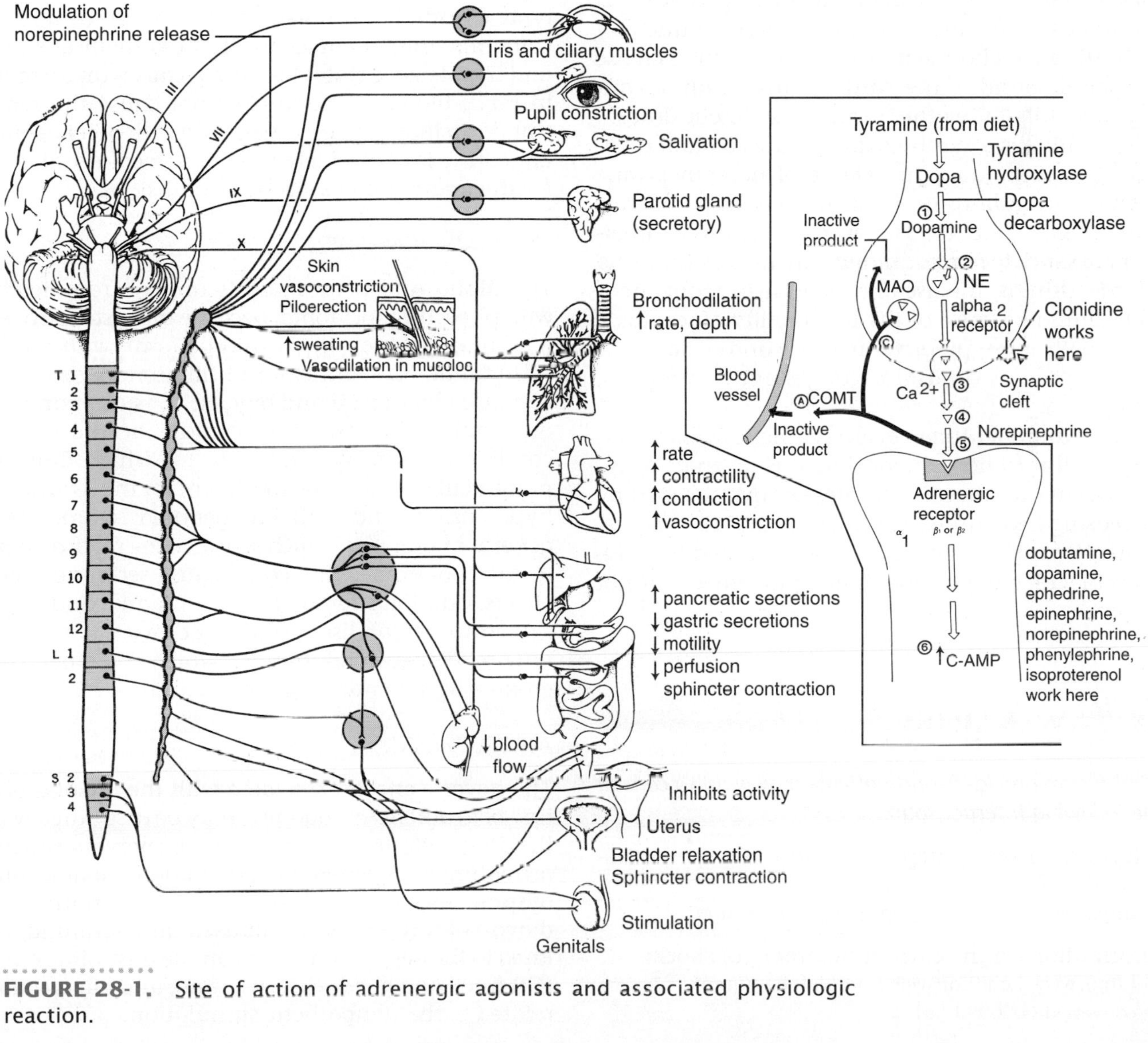

FIGURE 28-1. Site of action of adrenergic agonists and associated physiologic reaction.

direct dilation of the bronchi; as an ophthalmic agent to reduce intraocular pressure in glaucoma and decrease the production of aqueous humor; and to produce a local vasoconstriction that prolongs the effects of local anesthetics.

Norepinephrine (*Levophed*), another naturally occurring catecholamine, is not used as frequently. It is used IV to treat shock or during cardiac arrest to get sympathetic activity, but it has been replaced in recent years by dopamine. Dopamine (*Intropin*) is the sympathomimetic of choice for the treatment of shock. It stimulates the heart and blood pressure but also causes a renal and splanchnic arteriole dilation which increases blood flow to the kidney, preventing the diminished renal blood supply and possible renal shutdown that can occur with epinephrine and norepinephrine.

Dobutamine (*Dobutrex*) is a synthetic catecholamine that has a slight preference for $beta_1$ receptor sites. It is used in the treatment of congestive heart failure, as it can increase myocardial contractility without much change in rate and does not increase oxygen demand of the cardiac muscle, an advantage over all of the other sympathomimetic drugs.

Ephedrine is a synthetically produced plant alkaloid that stimulates the release of norepinephrine from nerve endings and directly acts on adrenergic receptor sites. Once used for everything from the treatment of shock to chronic management of asthma and allergic rhinitis, the use of ephedrine in many areas is declining because of the availability of less toxic drugs with more predictable onset and action. It is heavily used as a nasal decongestant in a topical, nasal form.

Metaraminol (*Aramine*) is a synthetic agent that is very similar to norepinephrine. It is given as a single parenteral injection to prevent hypotension by increasing myocardial contractility and causing peripheral vasoconstriction. Its use is limited to situations in which dopamine or norepinephrine cannot be used.

WWW.WEB LINKS

Health care providers and patients may want to consult the following Internet sources:

Information on epinephrine and basic sympathomimetic effects:
http://www.healthgate.com/preg/topic48.shtml

Information on the current treatment of shock:
http://www.healthanswers.com/database/ami/converted/000039.html

Information on the acute nursing care of patients in shock as well as research articles:
http://www.aacn.org

Information on cardiovascular research, treatments, heart transplants:
http://www.acc.org/login/index.taf

THERAPEUTIC ACTIONS AND INDICATIONS

The effects of the sympathomimetic drugs are mediated by the adrenergic receptors in target organs: heart rate increases with increased myocardial contractility, bronchi dilate and respirations increase in rate and depth, vasoconstriction occurs with increase in blood pressure, intraocular pressure decreases, ***glycogenolysis*** occurs throughout the body, pupils dilate, and sweating can increase (see Figure 28-1). These drugs are indicated for the treatment of hypotensive states or shock, bronchospasm, and some types of asthma. As noted earlier, dopamine has become the drug of choice for the treatment of shock and hypotensive states because it causes an increase in renal blood flow and does not cause the renal shutdown that has been associated with other agents. Ephedrine is also widely used as a local nasal drug for the treatment of seasonal rhinitis.

CONTRAINDICATIONS/CAUTIONS

The alpha and beta agonists are contraindicated with pheochromocytoma, because the systemic overload of catecholamines could be fatal; with tachyarrhythmias or ventricular fibrillation, because the increased heart rate and oxygen consumption usually caused by these drugs could exacerbate these conditions; with hypovolemia, for which fluid replacement would be the treatment for the associated hypotension; and with halogenated hydrocarbon general anesthetics, which sensitize the myocardium to catecholamines and could cause serious cardiac effects. Caution should be used with any kind of peripheral vascular disease (atherosclerosis, Raynaud's disease, diabetic endarteritis), which could be exacerbated by systemic vasoconstriction.

ADVERSE EFFECTS

The adverse effects associated with the use of alpha and beta adrenergic agonists may be associated with the drug's effects on the sympathetic nervous system: arrhythmias, hypertension, palpitations, angina, and dyspnea related to the effects on the heart and cardiovascular (CV) system; nausea and vomiting, related to the depressant effects on the gastrointestinal (GI) tract; and headache, sweating, and piloerection related to the sympathetic stimulation.

CLINICALLY IMPORTANT DRUG–DRUG INTERACTIONS

Increased effects of tricyclic antidepressants and monoamine oxidase (MAO) inhibitors can occur because of increased norepinephrine levels or receptor stimulation that occurs with both drugs. There is an increased risk of hypertension if given with any other drugs that cause hypertension.

DATA LINK

Data link to the following alpha and beta adrenergic agonists in your nursing drug guide:

ALPHA AND BETA ADRENERGIC AGONISTS

Name	Brand Name	Usual Indications
dobutamine	*Dobutrex*	Treatment of CHF
P dopamine	*Intropin*	Treatment of shock
ephedrine	*Kondon's Nasal*	Treatment of signs and symptoms of seasonal rhinitis
epinephrine	*Adrenalin, Susphrine*	Treatment of shock; glaucoma; to prolong effects of regional anesthetic
metaraminol	*Aramine*	Treatment of shock if norepinephrine or dopamine cannot be used
norepinephrine	*Levophed*	Treatment of shock; cardiac arrest

NURSING CONSIDERATIONS
for patients receiving alpha and beta adrenergic agonists

Assessment

HISTORY. Screen for the following: any known allergies to these drugs; pheochromocytoma, tachyarrhythmias or ventricular fibrillation, hypovolemia; general anesthesia with halogenated hydrocarbon anesthetics, which would be contraindications to the use of the drug; and the presence of vascular disease, which would require cautious use of the drug.

PHYSICAL ASSESSMENT. Include screening for baseline status before beginning therapy and for any potential adverse effects: skin color, temperature; pulse, blood pressure, ECG; respiration, adventitious sounds; and urine output and electrolytes.

Nursing Diagnoses

The patient receiving an alpha and beta agonist may have the following nursing diagnoses related to drug therapy:

- Pain related to CV and systemic effects
- Alteration in cardiac output related to CV effects
- Alteration in tissue perfusion related to CV effects
- Knowledge deficit regarding drug therapy

Implementation

- Use extreme caution in calculating and preparing doses of these drugs; *even small errors could have serious effects.* Always dilute drug before use, if not prediluted.
- Monitor patient response closely (blood pressure, ECG, urine output, cardiac output) and adjust dosage accordingly *to ensure most benefit with least amount of toxicity.*
- Maintain phentolamine on standby *in case extravasation occurs; infiltration of the site with 10 to 15 ml saline containing 5 to 10 mg phentolamine is usually effective in saving the area.*
- Provide thorough patient teaching including measures to avoid adverse effects, warning signs of problems, and the need for monitoring and evaluation *to enhance patient knowledge about drug therapy and to promote compliance.*
- Offer support and encouragement *to deal with the drug regimen* (see Patient Teaching Checklist: Adrenergic Agonists).

Evaluation

- Monitor patient response to the drug (improvement in blood pressure, ocular pressure, bronchial airflow).
- Monitor for adverse effects (cardiovascular changes, decreased urine output, headache, GI upset).
- Evaluate the effectiveness of the teaching plan (patient can name drug, dosage, adverse effects to watch for, specific measures to avoid adverse effects).
- Monitor the effectiveness of comfort measures and compliance to regimen (see Nursing Care Guide: Adrenergic Agonists).

Alpha-Specific Adrenergic Agonists

Alpha-specific adrenergic agonists, or ***alpha agonists,*** are drugs that bind primarily to alpha receptors rather than to beta receptors. Currently, two drugs are in this class: phenylephrine (*Neo-Synephrine, Allerest, Ak Dilate,* and others) and clonidine (*Catapres*).

Phenylephrine, a potent vasoconstrictor with little or no effect on the heart or bronchi, is used in many combination cold and allergy products. Parenterally it is used to treat shock or shock-like states, to overcome paroxysmal supraventricular tachycardia, to prolong local anesthesia, and to maintain blood pressure during spinal anesthesia. Topically it is used to treat allergic rhinitis and to relieve the symptoms of otitis media. Ophthalmically it is used

PATIENT TEACHING CHECKLIST

Adrenergic Agonists

Create customized patient teaching materials for a specific adrenergic agonist from your CD-ROM. Your patient teaching should stress the following points for drugs within this class:

An adrenergic agonist, or a sympathomimetic drug, acts by mimicking the effects of the sympathetic nervous system, a particular part of your nervous system that is responsible for your fight or flight response. Because this drug causes many effects in the body, you may experience some undesired adverse effects. It is crucial to discuss the effects of the drug with your health care provider and to try to make them as tolerable as possible.

If your drug is in solution, you should check the solution before each use. If the solution is pink, brown, or black, it should be discarded.

If you are a man with known prostate problems, it might help to void before each dose of the drug.

If your drug is to be taken sublingually (under the tongue), you must be careful to avoid swallowing the tablet; do not swallow until the tablet is completely dissolved. When the tablet is swallowed, it is destroyed in your stomach and you do not receive any of the beneficial effects of the drug.

If your drug is taken with an inhaler, check the manufacturer's instructions that come with the inhaler because each inhaler is slightly different.

Some of the following adverse effects may occur:

- Restlessness, shaking—If these occur, avoid driving, operating heavy machinery, or performing delicate tasks.
- Flushing, sweating—Avoid warm temperatures and heavy clothing; frequent washing with cool water may help.
- Heart palpitations—If you feel your heart is beating too fast, or skipping beats, sit down for a while and rest. If the feeling becomes too uncomfortable, notify your health care provider.
- Sensitivity to light—Avoid glaring lights or wear sun glasses if in bright light. Be careful when moving between extremes of light because your vision may not adjust quickly.

Report any of the following to your health care provider: difficulty voiding, chest pain, difficulty breathing, dizziness, headache, changes in vision.

Do not stop taking this drug suddenly; make sure you have enough of your prescription. This drug should be tapered over 2 to 4 days when you are instructed to discontinue it by your health care provider.

Avoid over-the-counter medications, including cold and allergy remedies and diet pills. If you feel that you need one of these, check with your health care provider first.

Tell any doctor, nurse, or other health care provider that you are taking these drugs.

Keep this drug, and all medications, out of the reach of children. Do not share these drugs with other people.

This Teaching Checklist reflects general patient teaching guidelines. It is not meant to be a substitute for drug-specific teaching information, which is available in nursing drug guides.

to dilate the pupils for eye examination, prior to surgery, or to relieve glaucoma.

Clonidine specifically stimulates CNS alpha$_2$ receptors. This leads to decreased sympathetic outflow from the CNS because the alpha$_2$ receptors moderate the release of norepinephrine from the nerve axon. It is used to treat essential hypertension as a step 2 drug, to treat chronic pain in cancer patients in combination with opiates and other drugs, and to ease withdrawal from opiates. Clonidine is associated with many more CNS effects (bad dreams, sedation, drowsiness, fatigue, headache) than other sympathomimetics. Because it can also cause extreme hypotension, congestive heart failure, and bradycardia owing to its centrally mediated effects, it should be used carefully with any patients susceptible to these conditions.

THERAPEUTIC ACTIONS AND INDICATIONS

The therapeutic effects of the alpha-specific adrenergic agonists come from the stimulation of alpha receptors within the sympathetic nervous system (see Figure 28-1). The uses are varied, depending on the route of the drug and the drug being used. Clonidine is frequently used to treat essential hypertension. Phenylephrine is found in many cold and allergy products because it is so effective in constricting

NURSING CARE GUIDE
Adrenergic Agonists

Assessment	Nursing Diagnoses	Implementation	Evaluation
HISTORY Allergies to any of these drugs, cardiovascular dysfunction, pheochromocytoma, pregnancy and lactation, narrow angle glaucoma, prostatic hypertrophy, thyroid disease, diabetes	Alteration in cardiac output related to CV effects Sensory, perceptual alterations related to CNS effects Alteration in tissue perfusion related to CV effects Knowledge deficit regarding drug therapy	Ensure safe and appropriate administration of drug. Provide comfort and safety measures: assistance/siderails, temperature control, lighting control, mouth care, skin care. Monitor BP, P, respiratory status throughout drug therapy. Provide support and reassurance to deal with drug effects and discomfort. Provide patient teaching regarding drug name, dosage, side effects, precautions, and warning signs to report.	Evaluate drug effects: relief of signs and symptoms being treated. Monitor for adverse effects: CV effects, dizziness, confusion; headache, rash; difficulty voiding; sweating, flushing; pupil dilation. Monitor for drug–drug interactions as indicated for each drug. Evaluate effectiveness of patient teaching program. Evaluate effectiveness of comfort and safety measures.
PHYSICAL EXAMINATION CV: BP, P, peripheral perfusion, ECG CNS: orientation, affect, reflexes, vision Skin: color, lesions, texture GU: urinary output GI: abdominal, liver evaluation Resp: R, adventitious sounds			

topical vessels and decreasing the swelling, signs, and symptoms of rhinitis.

CONTRAINDICATIONS/CAUTIONS

The alpha-specific adrenergic agonists are contraindicated in the presence of allergy to either phenylephrine or clonidine. Phenylephrine is also contraindicated in the presence of severe hypertension and tachycardia because of possible additive effects; with narrow-angle glaucoma, which could be exacerbated by arterial constriction; and during pregnancy because of potential adverse effects on the fetus.

Phenylephrine should be used with caution in the presence of cardiovascular disease or vasomotor spasm because these conditions could be aggravated by the vascular effects of the drug; with thyrotoxicosis and diabetes because of the thyroid-stimulating and glucose-elevating effects of sympathetic stimulation; and with lactation because the drug may be passed to the infant and cause alpha-specific adrenergic stimulation.

Clonidine should be used cautiously with coronary artery disease, vascular disease, and chronic renal failure because of the potential sympathetic effects on these systems; and with pregnancy and lactation because of possible adverse effects on the fetus or neonate.

ADVERSE EFFECTS

Patients receiving these drugs often experience extensions of the therapeutic effects or other sympathetic stimulatory reactions. CNS effects include feelings

CASE STUDY

Adrenergic Agonist Toxicity

PRESENTATION

M. C. is a 26-year-old man who has recently moved to the northeastern United States from New Mexico. He has been suffering from sinusitis, runny nose, and coldlike symptoms for 2 weeks. He appears at an outpatient clinic with complaints of headache, "jitters," inability to sleep, loss of appetite, and a feeling of impending doom. He states that he feels "on edge" and has not been productive in his job as a watch repairman and jewelry maker. According to his history, M. C. has been treated with several different drugs for nocturnal enuresis, a persisting childhood problem. Only ephedrine, which he has been taking for 2 years, has been successful. He has no other significant health problems. He denies any side effects from using ephedrine, but does admit to self-medicating his nagging cold with OTC preparations—a nasal spray used four times a day and a combination decongestant-pain reliever. A physical examination reveals a pulse of 104, BP 154/86, R 16. The patient appears flushed and slightly diaphoretic.

CRITICAL THINKING QUESTIONS

What are the important nursing implications for M. C.? Think about the problems that confront a patient in a new area seeking health care for the first time. What could be causing the problems that M. C. presents with? The diagnosis of ephedrine overdose was eventually made based on the patient history of OTC drug use and the presenting signs and symptoms. Keeping in mind that this means M. C. has an overstimulated sympathetic stress reaction, what other physical problems can be anticipated? Overwhelming feelings of anxiety and stress are influencing M. C.'s response to work and health care. Given this fact, how would the nurse best deal with explaining the problem and how it could have happened—without making the patient feel uninformed or that the practice of his former health care provider is being questioned? What treatment should be planned and what teaching points should be covered for M. C.?

DISCUSSION

The first step in caring for M. C. is establishing a trusting relationship to help alleviate some of the anxiety he is feeling. Being in a new state and seeking health care in a new setting can be very stressful for patients under normal circumstances. In M. C.'s case, the sympathomimetic effects of the drugs that he has been taking will make him feel even more anxious and jittery.

A careful patient history will help determine whether there are any underlying medical problems that could be exacerbated by these drug effects. A review of M. C.'s nocturnal enuresis and the treatments that have been tried will enhance understanding of his former health care and suggest possible implications for further study. This questioning will also give M. C. assurance that he is an important member of the health team and that the information he has to offer is considered to be important and valuable.

A careful review of the OTC drugs that M. C. has been using will be informative for the patient as well as for the health care providers who have not actually checked OTC drugs for those specific ingredients, but combining them to ease signs and symptoms often results in toxic levels and symptoms of overdose. M. C. will need a full teaching program about the effects of his ephedrine and OTC drugs to avoid. The treatment for his current problems involves withdrawal of the OTC drugs; when these drug levels fall, the signs and symptoms will disappear. M. C. may also wish to avoid nicotine and caffeine as these stimulants could increase his "jitters."

To build trust and ensure that the underlying cause of the problem was drug toxicity, M. C. should receive written patient instructions, including warning signs to report including chest pain, palpitations, difficulty voiding. He also should be given the health care provider's telephone number with instructions to call the next day and report on his health status. Finally, the sinusitis should be cultured and antibiotic treatment prescribed, if appropriate.

of anxiety, restlessness, depression, fatigue, strange dreams, blurred vision, and personality changes. Cardiovascular effects can include arrhythmias, ECG changes, blood pressure changes and peripheral vascular problems. Nausea, vomiting and anorexia can occur, related to the GI-depressing effects of the sympathetic system. Genitourinary effects can include decreased urinary output, difficulty urinating, dysuria, and changes in sexual function related to the sympathetic stimulation of these systems.

CLINICALLY IMPORTANT DRUG–DRUG INTERACTIONS

Phenylephrine combined with MAO inhibitors can cause severe hypertension, headache, and hyperpyrexia; this combination should be avoided. Increased sympathomimetic effects occur when phenylephrine is combined with tricyclic antidepressants (TCAs); if this combination must be used, the patient should be monitored very closely.

Clonidine has a decreased antihypertensive effect if taken with TCAs and a paradoxical hypertension occurs if it is combined with propranolol. If these combinations are used, the patient response should be monitored closely and dosage adjustment made as needed.

DATA LINK

Data link to the following alpha-specific adrenergic agonists in your nursing drug guide:

ALPHA-SPECIFIC ADRENERGIC AGONISTS

Name	Brand Name	Usual Indications
clonidine	*Catapres*	Treatment of essential hypertension; chronic pain; to ease opiate withdrawal
P phenylephrine	*Neo-Synephrine*	Cold and allergies; shock and shock-like states; supraventricular tachycardias; glaucoma; allergic rhinitis; otitis media

NURSING CONSIDERATIONS for patients receiving alpha-specific adrenergic agonists

Assessment

HISTORY. Screen for the following: any known allergies to either drug; presence of any cardiovascular diseases, thyrotoxicosis, or diabetes, which would require cautious use; pregnancy or lactation, which could be contraindications or cautions for drug use; and chronic renal failure, which could be exacerbated by drug use.

PHYSICAL ASSESSMENT. Include screening for baseline status before beginning therapy and for any potential adverse effects: orientation, affect, reflexes, and vision to monitor for CNS changes related to drug therapy; blood pressure, pulse, ECG, peripheral perfusion, and cardiac output, to establish a baseline and to monitor drug effects and adverse cardiovascular effects; and urinary output and renal function tests to monitor drug effects on the renal system.

Nursing Diagnoses

The patient receiving an alpha agonist may have the following nursing diagnoses related to drug therapy:

- Sensory–perceptual alteration related to CNS effects
- Potential for injury related to CNS, CV effects of drug
- Alteration in cardiac output related to blood pressure changes, arrhythmias, vasoconstriction
- Knowledge deficit regarding drug therapy

Implementation

- Do not discontinue drug abruptly; *sudden withdrawal can result in rebound hypertension, arrhythmias, flushing, and even hypertensive encephalopathy and death; taper drug over 2 to 4 days.*
- Do not discontinue prior to surgery; mark the patient's chart and monitor blood pressure carefully during surgery. *Sympathetic stimulation may alter the normal response to anesthesia as well as recovery from anesthesia.*
- Monitor blood pressure, pulse, rhythm, and cardiac output regularly, even with ophthalmic preparations *in order to adjust dosage or discontinue the drug if cardiovascular effects are severe.*
- When giving phenylephrine IV, maintain an alpha blocking agent on *standby in case severe reaction occurs;* infiltrate any area of extravasation with phentolamine within 12 hours of extravasation *to preserve tissue.*
- Arrange for supportive care and comfort measures, including rest and environmental control, *to decrease CNS irritation;* headache medication *to relieve discomfort;* safety measures if CNS effects occur *to protect the patient from injury;* and protective measures if CNS effects are severe.
- Provide thorough patient teaching including dosage, potential adverse effects, safety measures, warning signs of problems, and proper administration for each route used *to enhance patient knowledge about drug therapy and to promote compliance* (refer to Patient Teaching Checklist: Adrenergic Agonists).
- Offer support and encouragement to deal with the drug regimen.

Evaluation

- Monitor patient response to the drug (improvement in condition being treated).
- Monitor for adverse effects (GI upset, CNS and cardiovascular changes).
- Evaluate the effectiveness of the teaching plan (patient can name drug, dosage, adverse effects to watch for, and specific measures to avoid adverse effects).
- Monitor the effectiveness of comfort measures and compliance to the regimen (refer to Nursing Care Guide: Adrenergic Agonists).

Beta-Specific Adrenergic Agonists

Most of the drugs that belong to the class of beta-specific adrenergic agonists, or **beta agonists,** are beta$_2$-specific agonists, which are used to manage and treat bronchial spasm, asthma, and other obstructive pulmonary conditions. These drugs, including albuterol, bitolterol, isoetharine, metaproterenol, pirbuterol, salmeterol, and terbutaline, are covered in Chapter 53, which deals with drugs used to treat obstructive pulmonary diseases.

Two other beta agonists are available for use. Ritodrine (*Yutopar*) is used to manage preterm labor. Isoproterenol (*Isuprel, Medihaler-Iso*) is used in an inhaled form to treat obstructive pulmonary disease; as an injection to treat shock and cardiac standstill and to prevent bronchospasm during anesthesia; and in a sublingual form to treat bronchospasm, heart block, and some ventricular arrhythmias.

THERAPEUTIC ACTIONS AND INDICATIONS

The therapeutic effects of these drugs are related to their stimulation of the beta adrenergic receptors. Increased heart rate, conductivity and contractility, bronchodilation, increased blood flow to skeletal muscles and splanchnic beds, and relaxation of the uterus are the desired effects of these drugs. Ritodrine is indicated for the management of preterm labor because of its relaxing effects on the uterus, stopping uterine contractions. Isoproterenol is indicated for the treatment of shock to increase cardiac activity; with cardiac arrest and certain ventricular arrhythmias to stimulate cardiac activity and conduction; and to prevent bronchospasm, if used in the sublingual or inhaled forms. It is especially effective in treating heart blocks in transplanted hearts.

CONTRAINDICATIONS/CAUTIONS

Beta-specific adrenergic agonists are contraindicated in the presence of allergy to the drug or any components of the drug; with pulmonary hypertension; during anesthesia with halogenated hydrocarbons, which sensitize the myocardium to catecholamines and could cause a severe reaction; with eclampsia, uterine hemorrhage, and intrauterine death, which could be complicated by uterine relaxation or increased blood pressure; and during pregnancy and lactation because of potential effects on the fetus or neonate, unless used cautiously to manage preterm labor. Caution should be used with diabetes, thyroid disease, vasomotor problems, degenerative heart disease, or history of stroke, all of which could be exacerbated by the sympathomimetic effects of the drugs.

ADVERSE EFFECTS

Patients receiving these drugs often experience adverse effects related to the stimulation of sympathetic adrenergic receptors. CNS effects include restlessness, anxiety, fear, tremor, fatigue, and headache. Cardiovascular effects can include tachycardia, angina, myocardial infarction, and palpitations. Pulmonary effects can be severe, ranging from difficulty breathing, coughing, and bronchospasm to severe pulmonary edema. GI upset, nausea, vomiting, and anorexia can occur due to the slowdown of the GI system by the SNS. Other anticipated effects can include sweating, pupil dilation, rash, and muscle cramps.

CLINICALLY IMPORTANT DRUG–DRUG INTERACTIONS

Increased sympathomimetic effects can be expected if these drugs are taken with other sympathomimetic drugs. Decreased therapeutic effects can occur if these drugs are combined with beta adrenergic blockers. Ritodrine has been associated with the increased risk of potentially fatal pulmonary hypertension when it is combined with corticosteroids, so this combination should be avoided.

DATA LINK

Data link to the following beta-specific adrenergic agonists in your nursing drug guide:

BETA–SPECIFIC ADRENERGIC AGONISTS

Name	Brand Name	Usual Indications
P isoproterenol	*Isuprel*	Treatment of shock, cardiac standstill; treatment of heart block in transplanted hearts; prevention of bronchospasm during anesthesia; inhaled to treat bronchospasm
ritodrine	*Yutopar*	Management of preterm labor

NURSING CONSIDERATIONS
for patients receiving beta-specific adrenergic agonists

Assessment

HISTORY. Screen for the following: any known allergies to any drug or any components of the drug; pulmonary hypertension; anesthesia with halogenated hydrocarbons, which sensitize the myocardium to catecholamines and could cause severe reaction; eclampsia, uterine hemorrhage, and intrauterine death, which could be complicated by uterine relaxation or increased blood pressure; pregnancy and lactation because of potential effects on the fetus or neonate, unless used cautiously to manage preterm labor; diabetes, thyroid disease, vasomotor problems, degenerative heart disease, or history of stroke, all of which could be exacerbated by the sympathomimetic effects of the drugs.

PHYSICAL ASSESSMENT. Physical assessment should include screening for baseline status before beginning therapy and for any potential adverse effects:

skin color, temperature; pulse, blood pressure, ECG; respiration, adventitious sounds; and urine output and electrolytes.

Nursing Diagnoses

The patient receiving beta agonists may have the following nursing diagnoses related to drug therapy:

- Pain related to CV and systemic effects
- Alteration in cardiac output related to CV effects
- Alteration in tissue perfusion related to CV effects
- Knowledge deficit regarding drug therapy

Implementation

- Monitor patient pulse and blood pressure carefully during administration *in order to arrange to discontinue the drug at any sign of pulmonary edema.*
- Have patients receiving ritodrine lie in the left lateral position during administration *to decrease risk of hypotension.*
- Maintain a beta adrenergic blocker on standby when giving parenteral isoproterenol *in case severe reaction occurs.*
- Use minimal doses of isoproterenol needed to achieve effects *because drug tolerance can occur over time.*
- Arrange for supportive care and comfort measures, including rest and environmental control, *to relieve CNS effects;* provide headache medication and safety measures if CNS effects occur *to provide comfort and prevent injury;* avoid overhydration *to prevent pulmonary edema.*
- Provide thorough patient teaching including the name of the drug, dosage, anticipated adverse effects, measures to avoid drug-related problems, warning signs of problems, and proper administration techniques *to enhance patient knowledge about drug therapy and to promote compliance* (refer to Patient Teaching Checklist: Adrenergic Agonists).
- Offer support and encouragement *to deal with the drug regimen.*

Evaluation

- Monitor patient response to the drug (improvement in condition being treated, stabilization of blood pressure, prevention of preterm labor, cardiac stimulation).
- Monitor for adverse effects (GI upset, CNS changes, respiratory problems).
- Evaluate the effectiveness of the teaching plan (patient can name drug, dosage, adverse effects to watch for, specific measures to avoid adverse effects).
- Monitor the effectiveness of comfort measures and compliance to the regimen (refer to Nursing Care Guide: Adrenergic Agonists).

CHAPTER SUMMARY

- Adrenergic agonists are drugs used to stimulate the adrenergic receptors within the SNS. They are also called sympathomimetic drugs, because they mimic the effects of the SNS.
- Sympathomimetic drugs are used when sympathetic stimulation is needed. The adverse effects associated with these drugs are usually also a result of sympathetic stimulation.
- Alpha and beta adrenergic agonists stimulate all of the adrenergic receptors in the SNS. They are used to induce a fight or flight response and are frequently used to treat shock.
- Alpha-specific adrenergic agonists only stimulate the alpha receptors within the SNS. Clonidine stimulates $alpha_2$ receptors and is used to treat hypertension because its action blocks norepinephrine release from nerve axons. Phenylephrine is used in many cold and allergy remedies because it is a powerful local vasoconstrictor.
- Many of the $beta_2$-specific adrenergic agonists are used to manage and treat asthma, bronchospasm, and other obstructive pulmonary diseases.
- Ritodrine, a $beta_2$-specific agonist, is used to manage preterm labor because of its relaxing effect on the uterus.
- Isoproterenol, a beta-specific adrenergic agonist, is used to treat shock, cardiac standstill, and certain arrhythmias when used systemically; it is especially effective in treating heart block in transplanted hearts and is also used to treat bronchospasm and asthma when used in an inhaled form.

BIBLIOGRAPHY

Bullock, B. L. (2000). *Focus on pathophysiology.* Philadelphia: Lippincott Williams & Wilkins.

Hardman, J. G., Limbird, L. E., Molinoff, P. B., Ruddon, R. W., & Gilman, A. G. (Eds.). (1996). *Goodman and Gilman's the pharmacological basis of therapeutics* (9th ed.). New York: McGraw-Hill.

Karch, A. M. (2000). *2000 Lippincott's nursing drug guide.* Philadelphia: Lippincott Williams & Wilkins.

Malseed, R. (1995). *Textbook of pharmacology and nursing care.* Philadelphia: Lippincott-Raven.

McEvoy, B. R. (Ed.). (1999). *Facts and comparisons 1999.* St. Louis: Facts and Comparisons.

Professional's guide to patient drug facts. (1999). St. Louis: Facts and Comparisons.

CHAPTER 29

Adrenergic Blocking Agents

Alpha and beta adrenergic blocking agents
- carvedilol
- guanadrel
- guanethidine
- **P** labetalol

Alpha adrenergic blocking agents
- phenoxybenzamine
- **P** phentolamine

Alpha$_1$-selective adrenergic blocking agents
- **P** doxazosin
- prazosin
- terazosin

Beta adrenergic blocking agents
- carteolol
- nadolol
- penbutolol
- pindolol
- **P** propranolol
- sotalol
- timolol

Beta$_1$-selective adrenergic blocking agents
- acebutolol
- **P** atenolol
- betaxolol
- bisoprolol
- esmolol
- metoprolol

CHAPTER OUTLINE

KEY TERMS

alpha$_1$-selective adrenergic blocking agents
beta adrenergic blocking agents
beta$_1$-selective adrenergic blocking agents
bronchodilating effect
pheochromocytoma
specific adrenergic receptor sites
sympatholytic

INTRODUCTION

Adrenergic blocking agents are also called ***sympatholytic*** drugs because they lyse, or block, the effects of the sympathetic nervous system (SNS). The therapeutic and adverse effects associated with these drugs are related to their ability to react with ***specific adrenergic receptor sites*** without activating them. By occupying the adrenergic receptor site, they prevent norepinephrine released from the nerve terminal or from the adrenal medulla from activating the receptor, thus blocking the SNS effects.

ADRENERGIC BLOCKERS

The therapeutic and adverse effects associated with these drugs are related to their ability to prevent the signs and symptoms associated with SNS activation. The adrenergic blockers have varying degrees of specificity for the adrenergic receptor sites. For example, some can interact with all of the adrenergic sites, both alpha and beta. Some are specific to alpha receptors or, even more specifically, to alpha$_1$ receptors. Other adrenergic blockers are specific to both beta$_1$ or beta$_2$ receptors, while others interact with just one type of beta receptor, either beta$_1$ or beta$_2$ receptors only. This specificity allows the clinician to select a drug that will have the desired therapeutic effects without undesired effects that occur when the entire sympathetic nervous system is blocked. In general, however, the specificity of these drugs depends on the concentration of drug in the body. Most specificity is lost with higher serum levels (Figure 29-1).

Alpha and Beta Adrenergic Blocking Agents

Drugs that block all adrenergic receptors are primarily used to treat cardiac-related conditions. Amiodarone (*Cordarone*) and bretylium, both alpha and beta adrenergic blockers, are only used as antiarrhythmics (see Chapter 43). Carvedilol (*Coreg*) is used as part of combination therapy in treating hypertension and congestive heart failure (CHF). Guanadrel (*Hylorel*), an older drug, is used to treat hypertension in patients who do not respond to thiazide diuretics. Guanethidine (*Ismelin*), another older drug, is used to treat hypertension and renal hypertension (high blood pressure caused by changes in renal blood flow or response). A newer drug, labetalol (*Normodyne, Trandate*), is used IV and orally to treat hypertension and can be used in conjunction with diuretics. Labetalol has also been used to treat hypertension associated with ***pheochromocytoma*** and clonidine withdrawal hypertension.

THERAPEUTIC ACTIONS AND INDICATIONS

Adrenergic blocking agents competitively block the effects of norepinephrine at both alpha and beta receptors throughout the SNS. This action prevents the signs and symptoms associated with a sympathetic stress reaction and results in lower blood pressure, slower pulse, and increased renal perfusion with decreased renin levels. These drugs are indicated to treat essential hypertension, alone or in combination with diuretics.

CONTRAINDICATIONS/CAUTIONS

The alpha and beta adrenergic blocking agents are contraindicated in the presence of bradycardia or heart blocks, which could be worsened by the slowed heart rate and conduction; asthma, which could be exacerbated by the loss of norepinephrine's ***bronchodilating effect;*** shock or CHF, which could become worse with the loss of the sympathetic reaction; and pregnancy and lactation, because of the potential adverse effects on the fetus or neonate.

These drugs should be used with caution in patients with diabetes because the disorder could be aggravated by the blocked sympathetic response and because the usual signs and symptoms of hypoglycemia and hyperglycemia are lost when the SNS cannot respond. Caution also should be used with bronchospasm, which could progress to respiratory distress with the loss of norepinephrine's bronchodilating actions.

ADVERSE EFFECTS

The adverse effects associated with the use of alpha and beta adrenergic blocking agents are usually associated with the drug's effects on the sympathetic nervous system. These effects can include dizziness, paresthesias, insomnia, depression, fatigue, and vertigo, which are related to the blocked effects of norepinephrine in the central nervous system (CNS). Nausea, vomiting, diarrhea, anorexia, and flatulence are associated with the loss of the balancing sympathetic effect on the gastrointestinal (GI) tract and

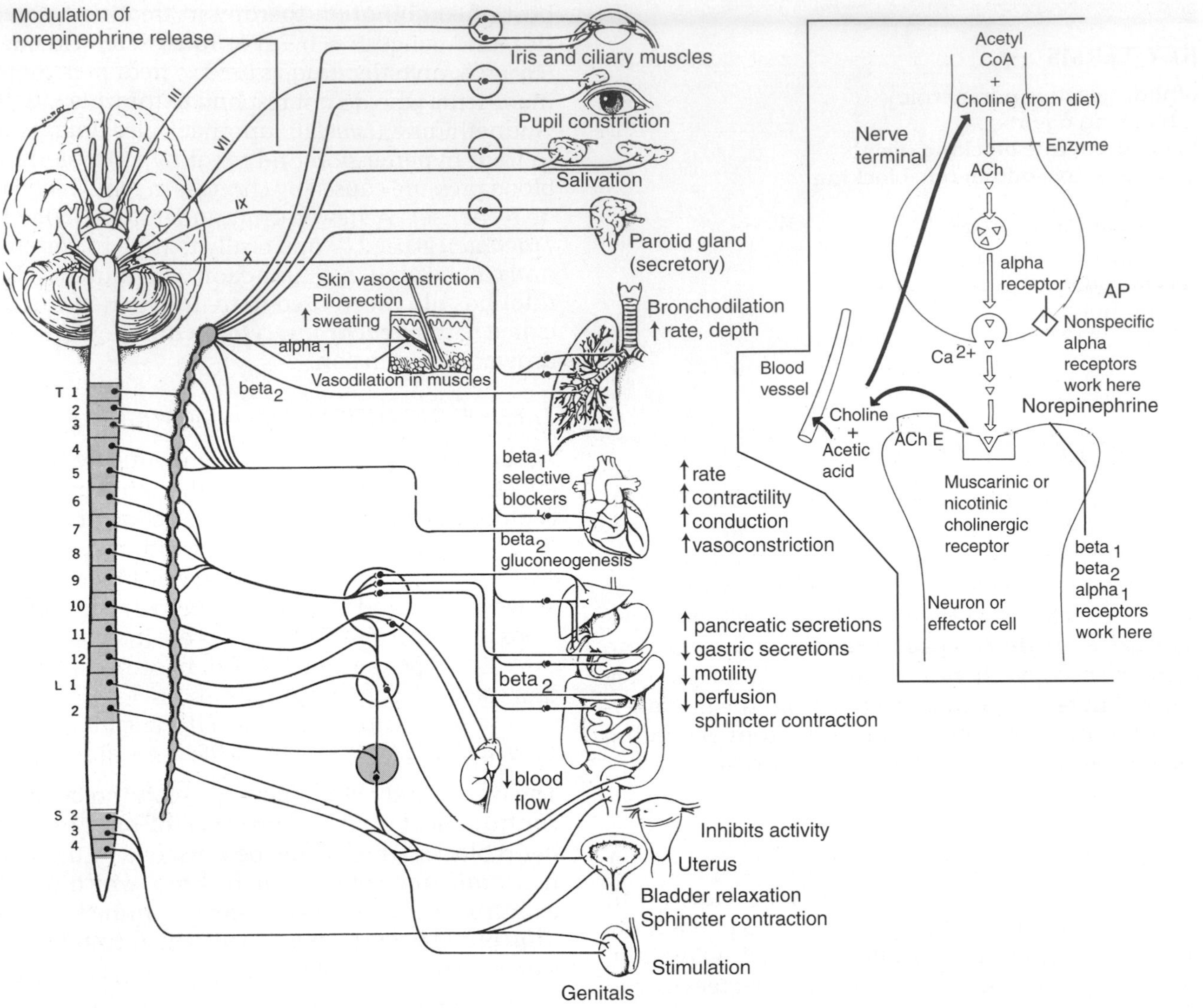

FIGURE 29-1. Site of action of adrenergic blockers and resultant physiologic response. Bar indicates a blocking of the effects indicated by those receptors.

increased parasympathetic dominance. Cardiac arrhythmias, hypotension, CHF, pulmonary edema, and cerebral vascular accident (CVA), or stroke, are related to the lack of stimulatory effects and loss of vascular tone in the cardiovascular (CV) system. Bronchospasm, cough, rhinitis, and bronchial obstruction are related to the loss of the bronchodilating effects on the respiratory tract and vasodilation of the mucous membrane vessels. Other effects reported include decreased exercise tolerance, hypoglycemia, and rash.

CLINICALLY IMPORTANT DRUG–DRUG INTERACTIONS

There is increased risk of excessive hypotension if any of these drugs are combined with enflurane, halothane, or isoflurane anesthetics. There also is an increased effectiveness of diabetic agents when used with these drugs; patients should be monitored closely and dosage adjustments made as needed. In addition, carvedilol has been associated with potentially dangerous conduction system disturbances when combined with verapamil or diltiazem; if this combination is used, the patient should be continuously monitored.

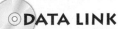

DATA LINK

Data link to the following alpha and beta adrenergic blocking agents in your nursing drug guide:

ALPHA AND BETA ADRENERGIC BLOCKING AGENTS

Name	Brand Name	Usual Indications
carvedilol	*Coreg*	Treatment of hypertension, CHF
guanadrel	*Hylorel*	Treatment of hypertension in patients who do not respond to thiazide diuretics

guanethidine	*Ismelin*	Treatment of hypertension, renal hypertension
P labetalol	*Normodyne, Trandate*	Treatment of hypertension, pheochromocytoma, clonidine withdrawal hypertension

NURSING CONSIDERATIONS
for patients receiving alpha and beta adrenergic blocking agents

Assessment

HISTORY. Screen for the following: any known allergies to these drugs; presence of bradycardia or heart blocks, which could be worsened by the slowing of heart rate and conduction; asthma, which could be exacerbated by the loss of the bronchodilating effect of norepinephrine; shock or CHF, which could become worse with the loss of the sympathetic reaction; pregnancy and lactation, because of the potential adverse effects on the fetus or neonate; diabetes, which could be aggravated by the blocking of the sympathetic response and because the usual signs and symptoms of hypoglycemia and hyperglycemia are lost when the SNS cannot respond; and bronchospasm, which could progress to respiratory distress with the loss of the bronchodilating actions of norepinephrine.

PHYSICAL ASSESSMENT. Include screening for baseline status and any potential adverse effects: skin color, temperature; pulse, blood pressure, cardiac output, ECG; respiration, adventitious sounds; and blood glucose levels and electrolytes.

Nursing Diagnoses

The patient receiving an alpha and beta adrenergic blocker may have the following nursing diagnoses related to drug therapy:

- Pain related to CV and systemic effects
- Alteration in cardiac output related to CV effects
- Ineffective airway clearance related to lack of bronchodilating effects
- Knowledge deficit regarding drug therapy

Implementation

- Do not discontinue abruptly after chronic therapy; *hypersensitivity to catecholamines may develop; taper drug slowly over 2 weeks, monitoring patient.*
- Consult with the physician about withdrawing the drug before surgery *because withdrawal is controversial; effects on the sympathetic system after surgery can cause problems.*
- Encourage the patient to adapt lifestyle changes, including diet, exercise, stopping smoking, and decreasing stress, *to aid in lowering blood pressure.*
- Monitor for orthostatic hypotension and provide safety precautions if this occurs *to prevent injury to the patient.*
- Monitor for any sign of liver failure *in order to arrange to discontinue the drug if this occurs (this effect is more likely to happen with carvedilol).*
- Provide thorough patient teaching including measures to avoid adverse effects, warning signs of problems, and the need for monitoring and evaluation *to enhance patient knowledge about drug therapy and to promote compliance.*
- Offer support and encouragement *to deal with the drug regimen.*

Evaluation

- Monitor patient response to the drug (improvement in blood pressure and CHF).
- Monitor for adverse effects (CV changes, headache, GI upset, bronchospasm, liver failure).
- Evaluate the effectiveness of the teaching plan (patient can name drug, dosage, adverse effects to watch for, specific measures to avoid adverse effects).
- Monitor the effectiveness of comfort measures and compliance to the regimen.

Alpha Adrenergic Blocking Agents

Some adrenergic blocking agents have a specific affinity for alpha receptor sites. Their use is somewhat limited because of the development of even more specific and safer drugs.

Phenoxybenzamine (*Dibenzyline*) is used to manage the signs and symptoms of acute pheochromocytoma episodes. A pheochromocytoma is a tumor of the chromaffin cells of the adrenal medulla that periodically releases large amounts of norepinephrine and epinephrine into the system, with resultant severe hypertension and tachycardia. Phentolamine (*Regitine*) is used to diagnose pheochromocytoma and to prevent severe hypertension reactions due to the manipulation of pheochromocytoma prior to and during surgery. Phenotolamine is most frequently used to prevent cell death and tissue sloughing following extravasation of IV norepinephrine or dopamine.

THERAPEUTIC ACTIONS AND INDICATIONS

These drugs block the postsynaptic $alpha_1$ adrenergic receptors, decreasing sympathetic tone in the vasculature and causing vasodilation, which leads to a lowering of blood pressure. They also block presynaptic $alpha_2$ receptors, preventing the feedback control of norepinephrine release. The result is an increase in the reflex tachycardia that occurs when blood pressure is lowered. These drugs are used to diagnose and manage episodes of pheochromocytoma. Phentolamine is used to rescue cells injured by norepinephrine or dopamine extravasation by causing vasodilation and a return of blood flow.

CONTRAINDICATIONS/CAUTIONS

The alpha adrenergic blocking agents are contraindicated in the presence of allergy to these or similar drugs and in the presence of coronary artery disease or myocardial infarction (MI) because of the potential exacerbation of these conditions; they should be used cautiously in pregnancy and lactation because of the potential adverse effects on the fetus or neonate.

ADVERSE EFFECTS

Patients receiving these drugs often experience extensions of the therapeutic effects, including hypotension, orthostatic hypotension, angina, MI, CVA, flushing, tachycardia, and arrhythmia—all of which are related to vasodilation and decreased blood pressure. Weakness and dizziness often occur as a reaction to the hypotension. Nausea, vomiting, and diarrhea may also occur.

CLINICALLY IMPORTANT DRUG–DRUG INTERACTIONS

There may be decreased hypertensive and vasoconstrictive effects of ephedrine and epinephrine if taken concomitantly with these drugs because these agents work in opposing ways in the body. Increased hypotension may occur if combined with alcohol, which is also a vasodilator.

DATA LINK

Data link to the following alpha adrenergic blocking agents in your nursing drug guide:

ALPHA ADRENERGIC BLOCKING AGENTS

Name	Brand Name	Usual Indications
phenoxybenzamine	*Dibenzylin*	Management of the signs and symptoms of pheochromocytoma
P phentolamine	*Regitine*	Diagnosis of pheochromocytoma, management of severe hypertension during pheochromocytoma surgery; to prevent cell death with IV infiltration of norepinephrine or dopamine

NURSING CONSIDERATIONS
for patients receiving alpha adrenergic blocking agents

Assessment

HISTORY. Screen for the following: any known allergies to either drug; presence of any cardiovascular diseases, which may be contraindications to the use of these drugs; and pregnancy or lactation, which require caution for drug use.

PHYSICAL ASSESSMENT. Include screening for baseline status and for any potential adverse effects: assess orientation, affect, and reflexes to monitor for CNS changes related to drug therapy; blood pressure, pulse, ECG, peripheral perfusion, and cardiac output; and urinary output.

Nursing Diagnoses

The patient receiving an alpha adrenergic blocking agent may also have the following nursing diagnoses related to drug therapy:

- Potential for injury related to CNS, CV effects of drug
- Alteration in cardiac output related to blood pressure changes, arrhythmias, vasodilation
- Knowledge deficit regarding drug therapy

Implementation

- Monitor heart rate and blood pressure very carefully *in order to arrange to discontinue the drug if adverse reactions are severe; provide supportive management if needed.*
- Inject phentolamine directly into the area of extravasation of epinephrine or dopamine *to prevent local cell death.*
- Arrange for supportive care and comfort measures such as rest, environmental control, and other measures *to decrease CNS irritation;* provide headache medication; arrange safety measures if CNS effects or orthostatic hypotension occur *to prevent patient injury.*
- Provide thorough patient teaching including dosage, potential adverse effects, measures to avoid adverse effects, and warning signs of problems *to enhance patient knowledge about drug therapy and to promote compliance.*
- Offer support and encouragement to deal with the drug regimen.

Evaluation

- Monitor patient response to the drug (improvement in signs and symptoms of pheochromocytoma, improvement in tissue condition after extravasation).

• Monitor for adverse effects (orthostatic hypotension, arrhythmias, CNS effects).
• Evaluate the effectiveness of the teaching plan (patient can name drug, dosage, adverse effects to watch for, specific measures to avoid adverse effects).
• Monitor the effectiveness of comfort measures and compliance to the regimen.

Alpha$_1$-Selective Adrenergic Blocking Agents

Alpha$_1$-selective adrenergic blocking agents are drugs that have a specific affinity for alpha 1 receptors. Doxazosin (*Cardura*) is used to treat hypertension and is also effective in treating benign prostatic hypertrophy (BPH) (Chapter 50). Prazosin (*Minipress*) is used to treat hypertension alone or in combination with other drugs. Terazosin (*Hytrin*) is used to treat hypertension as well as BPH (see Chapter 50). Tamsulosin (*Flomax*) is only used in the treatment of BPH and is discussed later (see Chapter 50).

THERAPEUTIC ACTIONS AND INDICATIONS

The therapeutic effects of the alpha$_1$-selective adrenergic blocking agents come from their ability to block the postsynaptic alpha$_1$ receptor sites. This causes a decrease in vascular tone and vasodilation, which leads to a fall in blood pressure. Because these drugs do not block the presynaptic alpha$_2$ receptor sites, the reflex tachycardia that accompanies a fall in blood pressure does not occur. These drugs can be used to treat BPH or to treat hypertension, alone or as part of a combination therapy.

CONTRAINDICATIONS/CAUTIONS

The alpha$_1$-selective adrenergic blocking agents are contraindicated in the presence of allergy to any of these drugs and with lactation because the drugs cross into breast milk and could have adverse effects on the neonate. They should be used cautiously in the presence of CHF or renal failure, because their blood pressure lowering effects could exacerbate these conditions. Caution also should be used during pregnancy because of the potential for adverse effects on the fetus.

ADVERSE EFFECTS

The adverse effects associated with the use of these drugs are usually related to their effects of blocking the sympathetic nervous system. CNS effects include dizziness, weakness, fatigue, drowsiness, and depression. Nausea, vomiting, abdominal pain, and diarrhea may occur as a result of direct effects on the GI tract and sympathetic blocking. Anticipated cardiovascular effects include arrhythmias, hypotension, edema, CHF, and angina. The vasodilation caused by these drugs can also cause flushing, rhinitis, reddened eyes, nasal congestion, and priapism.

CLINICALLY IMPORTANT DRUG–DRUG INTERACTIONS

Increased hypotensive effects may occur if these drugs are combined with any other vasodilating or antihypertensive drugs.

DATA LINK

Data link to the following alpha$_1$-selective adrenergic blocking agents in your nursing drug guide:

ALPHA$_1$-SELECTIVE ADRENERGIC BLOCKING AGENTS

Name	Brand Name	Usual Indications
P doxazosin	*Cardura*	Treatment of hypertension and benign prostatic hypertrophy
prazosin	*Minipress*	Treatment of hypertension
terazosin	*Hytrin*	Treatment of hypertension and benign prostatic hypertrophy

NURSING CONSIDERATIONS
for patients receiving alpha$_1$-selective adrenergic blocking agents

Assessment

HISTORY. Screen for the following: any known allergies to either drug; pregnancy or lactation, which could be contraindications or cautions for drug use; and CHF or renal failure, which could be exacerbated by drug use.

PHYSICAL ASSESSMENT. Include screening for baseline status and for any potential adverse effects: assess orientation, affect, and reflexes to monitor for CNS changes related to drug therapy; blood pressure, pulse, ECG, peripheral perfusion, and cardiac output, monitor cardiovascular effects; and urinary output and renal function to monitor effects on the renal system.

Nursing Diagnoses

The patient receiving an alpha$_1$-selective adrenergic blocking agent may have the following nursing diagnoses related to drug therapy:

• Pain related to headache, GI upset, flushing, nasal congestion
• Potential for injury related to CNS, CV effects of drug
• Alteration in cardiac output related to BP changes, arrhythmias, vasodilation
• Knowledge deficit regarding drug therapy

Implementation

- Monitor blood pressure, pulse, rhythm, and cardiac output regularly in order *to arrange to adjust dosage or discontinue the drug if cardiovascular effects are severe.*
- Establish safety precautions if CNS effects or orthostatic hypotension occur *to prevent patient injury.*
- Arrange for small, frequent meals if GI upset is severe *to relieve discomfort and maintain nutrition.*
- Arrange for supportive care and comfort measures (rest, environmental control, other measures) *to decrease CNS irritation;* provide headache medication; arrange safety measures if CNS effects occur *to prevent patient injury.*
- Provide thorough patient teaching including dosage, adverse effects to anticipate, measures to avoid adverse effects, and warning signs of problems *to enhance patient knowledge about drug therapy and to promote compliance.*
- Offer support and encouragement *to deal with the drug regimen.*

Evaluation

- Monitor patient response to the drug (lowering of blood pressure).
- Monitor for adverse effects (GI upset, CNS or cardiovascular changes).
- Evaluate the effectiveness of the teaching plan (patient can name drug, dosage, adverse effects to watch for, specific measures to avoid adverse effects).
- Monitor the effectiveness of comfort measures and compliance to the regimen.

Beta Adrenergic Blocking Agents

The ***beta adrenergic blocking agents*** are used to treat cardiovascular problems (hypertension, angina, migraines) and to prevent reinfarction following MI. These drugs are widely used today; in fact, propranolol (*Inderal*) was once the most prescribed drug in the country.

Propranolol has been approved for multiples uses, which include treating hypertension, angina, idiopathic hypertrophic subaortic stenosis (IHSS) induced palpitations, angina and syncope, and certain cardiac arrhythmias induced by catecholamines or digoxin; preventing reinfarction following MI; treating pheochromocytoma; prophylaxis for migraine headache (which may be caused by vasodilation and is relieved by vasoconstriction); preventing stage fright (which is a sympathetic stress reaction to a particular situation); and treating essential tremors. It is very effective in blocking all of the beta receptors in the SNS and was one of the first drugs of the class.

Since the introduction of propranolol, newer and more selective drugs have become available that are not associated with some of the adverse effects seen in total blocking of the SNS beta receptors. Carteolol (*Cartrol*) is used for the treatment of hypertension, alone or in combination with other drugs. Penbutolol (*Levator*) and pindolol (*Visken*) are also used for the treatment of hypertension. The drug of choice would depend mostly on personal experience. Nadolol (*Corgard*) is used to treat hypertension and also for the chronic management of angina. It would be a drug of choice in treating an angina patient who is also hypertensive. Sotalol (*Betapace*) is reserved for use in the treatment of potentially life-threatening arrhythmias and is not recommended for any other use. Timolol (*Blocadren, Timoptic*), a newer beta adrenergic blocker, has several recommended uses including treatment of hypertension; prevention of reinfarction after MI; prophylaxis for migraine; and, in ophthalmic form, reduction of intraocular pressure in open-angle glaucoma.

THERAPEUTIC ACTIONS AND INDICATIONS

The therapeutic effects of these drugs are related to their competitive blocking of the beta adrenergic receptors in the SNS. The blockade of the beta receptors in the heart and the juxtoglomerular (JG) apparatus of the nephron account for most of the therapeutic benefit of these drugs. Decreased heart rate, contractility, and excitability as well as a membrane stabilizing effect lead to a decrease in arrhythmias and a decreased cardiac workload and oxygen consumption. The JG cells are not stimulated to release renin, which further decreases blood pressure. These effects are useful in treating hypertension and chronic angina and can help to prevent reinfarction following an MI by decreasing cardiac workload and oxygen consumption.

Blocking of other SNS effects accounts for the use of propranolol in preventing stage fright. That is because decreased feelings of anxiety, decreased pulse and blood pressure, and decreased sweating and flushing help to alleviate situational anxiety. The mechanism of action in treating migraines is not clearly understood.

Timolol is used topically to reduce intraocular pressure by its relaxing effects on the eye muscles. Because it is applied topically, it is generally not absorbed systemically from this route.

CONTRAINDICATIONS/CAUTIONS

These beta adrenergic blocking agents are contraindicated in the presence of allergy to any of these drugs or any components of the drug being used; with bradycardia or heart blocks, shock, CHF (which could be exacerbated by the cardiac suppressing effects of these drugs); bronchospasm, chronic obstructive pulmonary disease (COPD), or acute asthma, which could be made worse by the blocking of the sympathetic bronchodilation; pregnancy because neonatal apnea, bradycardia, and hypoglycemia can occur; and lactation, because of the potential effects on the neonate, which could include slowed heart rate, hypotension, and hypoglycemia. These drugs should be used cautiously with diabetes and hypoglycemia (because of the blocking of the normal signs and symptoms of hypoglycemia and hyperglycemia), with thyrotoxicosis (because of the adrenergic blocking effects on the thyroid gland), and with hepatic dysfunction, which could interfere with the metabolism of these drugs.

ADVERSE EFFECTS

Patients receiving these drugs often experience adverse effects related to the blocking of the sympathetic nervous system's beta receptors. CNS effects include fatigue, dizziness, depression, paresthesias, sleep disturbances, memory loss, and disorientation. Cardiovascular effects can include bradycardia, heart block, CHF, hypotension, and peripheral vascular insufficiency. Pulmonary effects can range from difficulty breathing, coughing, and bronchospasm to severe pulmonary edema and bronchial obstruction. GI upset, nausea, vomiting, diarrhea, gastric pain and even colitis can occur as a result of unchecked parasympathetic activity and the blocking of the sympathetic receptors. Genitourinary effects can include decreased libido, impotence, dysuria, and Peyronie's disease. Other effects that can occur include decreased exercise tolerance (patients often report that their "get up and go" is gone), hypoglycemia or hyperglycemia, and liver changes.

CLINICALLY IMPORTANT DRUG–DRUG INTERACTIONS

A paradoxical hypertension occurs when beta blockers are given with clonidine, and an increased rebound hypertension with clonidine withdrawal may also occur. It is best to avoid this combination. A decreased antihypertensive effect occurs when beta blockers are given with NSAIDs; if this combination is used, the patient should be monitored closely and dosage adjustment made to achieve the desired control of blood pressure. An initial hypertensive episode followed by bradycardia may occur if these drugs are given with epinephrine. There also is a possibility of peripheral ischemia if the beta blockers are taken in combination with ergot alkaloids. When these drugs are given with insulin or antidiabetic agents, there is a potential for change in blood glucose levels. The patient also will not display the usual signs and symptoms of hypoglycemia or hyperglycemia, which are caused by activation of the sympathetic nervous system. When these effects are blocked, the patient will need new indications to alert him or her to potential problems. If this combination is used, the patient should monitor blood glucose frequently throughout the day and should be alert to new warnings about glucose imbalance.

DATA LINK

Data link to the following beta adrenergic blocking agents in your nursing drug guide:

BETA ADRENERGIC BLOCKING AGENTS

Name	Brand Name	Usual Indications
carteolol	*Cartrol*	Treatment of hypertension
nadolol	*Corgard*	Treatment of hypertension, management of angina
penbutolol	*Levator*	Treatment of hypertension
pindolol	*Visken*	Treatment of hypertension
P propranolol	*Inderal*	Treatment of hypertension, angina, ideopathic hypertrophic subaortic stenosis, certain cardiac arrhythmias, pheochromocytoma; prophylaxis for migraine headache, prevention of stage fright
sotalol	*Betapace*	Treatment of potentially life threatening ventricular arrhythmias
timolol	*Blocadren, Timoptic*	Treatment of hypertension; prevention of reinfarction after MI; prophylaxis for migraine; and, in ophthalmic form, reduction of intraocular pressure in open-angle glaucoma

NURSING CONSIDERATIONS
for patients receiving beta adrenergic blocking agents

Assessment

HISTORY. Screen for the following: any known allergies to any drug or any components of the drug; bradycardia or heart blocks, shock, or CHF, which could be exacerbated by the cardiac suppressing effects of these drugs; bronchospasm, COPD, or acute asthma, which could be made worse by the blocking of the sympathetic bronchodilation; pregnancy and lactation, because of the potential effects on the fetus or neonate; diabetes and hypoglycemia; thyrotoxicosis; and hepatic dysfunction, which could interfere with the metabolism of these drugs.

PHYSICAL ASSESSMENT. Include screening for baseline status and for any potential adverse effects: skin color, temperature; pulse, blood pressure, ECG; respiration, adventitious sounds; and abdominal exam, liver function tests, urine output, and electrolytes.

PATIENT TEACHING CHECKLIST

Beta Adrenergic Blocking Agents

Create customized patient teaching materials for a specific beta adrenergic blocking agent from your CD-ROM. Your patient teaching should stress the following points for drugs within this class:

A beta adrenergic blocking agent works to prevent certain stimulating activities that normally occur in your body in response to such factors as stress, injury, or excitement.

You should learn to take your own pulse and monitor it daily, writing the pulse rate on your calendar. Your current pulse rate is ___________.

Never discontinue this medication suddenly. If you find that your prescription is running out, notify your health care provider at once. This drug needs to be tapered over time to prevent severe reactions when it is discontinued.

Some of the following adverse effects may occur:

- Fatigue, weakness: Try to space your activities throughout the day and allow rest periods.
- Dizziness, drowsiness: If these should occur, take care to avoid driving, operating dangerous machinery, or doing delicate tasks. Change position slowly to avoid dizzy spells.
- Change in sexual function: Be assured that this is a drug effect and discuss it with your health care provider.
- Nausea, diarrhea: These gastrointestinal discomforts will often diminish over time. If they become too uncomfortable or do not improve, talk to your health care provider.
- Dreams, confusion: These are drug effects. If they become too uncomfortable, discuss them with your health care provider.

Report any of the following to your health care provider: very slow pulse, need to sleep on more pillows at night, difficulty breathing, swelling in the ankles or fingers, sudden weight gain, mental confusion or personality change, fever, or rash.

Avoid over-the-counter medications, including cold and allergy remedies and diet pills. Many of these preparations contain drugs that could interfere with this medication. If you feel that you need one of these, check with your health care provider first.

Tell any doctor, nurse, or other health care provider that you are taking these drugs.

Keep this drug, and all medications, out of the reach of children. Do not share these drugs with other people.

This Teaching Checklist reflects general patient teaching guidelines. It is not meant to be a substitute for drug-specific teaching information, which is available in nursing drug guides.

Nursing Diagnoses

The patient receiving beta adrenergic blocking agents may have the following nursing diagnoses related to drug therapy:

- Pain related to CNS, GI, and systemic effects
- Alteration in cardiac output related to CV effects
- Alteration in tissue perfusion related to CV effects
- Knowledge deficit regarding drug therapy

Implementation

- Do not stop these drugs abruptly after chronic therapy; taper gradually over 2 weeks, *because long-term use of these drugs can sensitize the myocardium to catecholamines and severe reactions could occur.*
- Give the oral form of these drugs with food *to improve absorption.*
- Continuously monitor any patient receiving an IV form of these drugs *to avert serious complications caused by rapid sympathetic blockade.*
- Arrange for supportive care and comfort measures (rest, environmental control, other measures) *to relieve CNS effects;* institute safety measures if CNS effects occur *to prevent patient injury;* provide small, frequent meals and mouth care *to help relieve discomfort of GI effects.*
- Provide thorough patient teaching including name of the drug, dosage, anticipated adverse effects, measures to avoid drug-related problems, warning signs of problems, and proper administration techniques as needed *to enhance patient knowledge about drug therapy and to promote compliance* (see Patient Teaching Checklist: Beta Adrenergic Blocking Agents).
- Offer support and encouragement *to deal with the drug regimen.*

NURSING CARE GUIDE
Beta Adrenergic Blocking Agents

Assessment	Nursing Diagnoses	Implementation	Evaluation
HISTORY Allergies to any of these drugs, CHF, shock, bradycardia, heart block, hypotension, COPD, pregnancy and lactation, thyroid disease, diabetes	Alteration in cardiac output related to CV effects Pain related to CNS, GI, systematic effects Alteration in tissue perfusion related to CV effects Knowledge deficit regarding drug therapy	Ensure safe and appropriate administration of drug. Provide comfort and safety measures: assistance/siderails; temperature control; rest periods; mouth care; small, frequent meals. Monitor BP, P, respiratory status throughout drug therapy. Provide support and reassurance to deal with drug effects and discomfort, sexual dysfunction, fatigue. Provide patient teaching regarding drug name, dosage, side effects, precautions, and warning signs to report.	Evaluate drug effects: BP within normal limit, decrease in anginal episodes, stabilized cardiac rhythm. Monitor for adverse effects: CV effects: CHF, block; dizziness, confusion; sexual dysfunction; GI effects; hypoglycemia; respiratory problems. Monitor for drug–drug interactions as indicated for each drug. Evaluate effectiveness of patient teaching program. Evaluate effectiveness of comfort and safety measures.
PHYSICAL EXAMINATION CV: BP, P, peripheral perfusion, ECG CNS: orientation, affect, reflexes, vision Skin: color, lesions, texture GU: urinary output, sexual function GI: abdominal, liver evaluation Resp: R, adventitious sounds			

Evaluation

- Monitor patient response to the drug (lowering of blood pressure, decrease in anginal episodes, improvement in condition being treated).
- Monitor for adverse effects (GI upset, CNS changes, respiratory problems, CV effects, loss of libido and impotence).
- Evaluate effectiveness of teaching plan (patient can name drug, dosage, adverse effects to watch for, specific measures to avoid adverse effects).
- Monitor the effectiveness of comfort measures and compliance to the regimen (see Nursing Care Guide: Beta Adrenergic Blocking Agents).

Beta$_1$-Selective Adrenergic Blocking Agents

The ***beta$_1$-selective adrenergic blocking agents*** have an advantage over the nonselective beta blockers in some cases. Because they do not usually block beta$_2$ receptor sites, they do not block the sympathetic bronchodilation that is so important for patients with lung diseases or allergic rhinitis. Consequently, these drugs are preferred for patients who smoke or who have asthma, any other obstructive pulmonary disease, or seasonal or allergic rhinitis. These selective beta blockers are also used for treating hypertension, angina, and some cardiac arrhythmias.

CASE STUDY

Nonspecific Beta Blockers

PRESENTATION

M. R., a 59-year-old male, suffered a diaphragmatic myocardial infarction (MI) last August. He recovered well and returned to work as a salesman within 8 weeks. Shortly after he resumed working, he began to suffer vague, pressure-type chest pains. He was maintained on propranolol (*Inderal*) 10 mg qid with no further problems. The following June, M. R. developed acute respiratory distress while picnicking in a state park with his family. On the way to the emergency room, he suffered an apparent respiratory arrest. He was admitted to the hospital and placed in the respiratory ICU. It was found that M. R. had a history of hay fever and allergic rhinitis during the pollen season, but had never experienced such a severe reaction.

CRITICAL THINKING QUESTIONS

Why did M. R. have such a severe reaction? What appropriate measures should be taken to assure that M. R. recovers fully and does not reexperience this event? What sort of support will M. R. and his family need after going through such a frightening experience? Think about the children who may have witnessed the respiratory arrest and how they should be reassured, depending on their ages. Think about the support M. R.'s wife may need and the fear that may now be associated with M. R.'s condition. M. R. has been on propranolol for several months and will need to be weaned from it, because the drug is somewhat responsible for the reaction that M. R. experienced. What kind of teaching program will need to be developed to help M. R. deal with his drugs, their effects, and his underlying cardiac problem?

DISCUSSION

Propranolol, a nonspecific beta blocker, was prescribed to decrease the workload and oxygen consumption of M. R.'s heart and to prevent reinfarction after his MI. He did well on the drug until pollen season arrived. That is because propranolol, a nonspecific beta blocker, prevented the compensatory bronchodilation that occurs when the sympathetic nervous system is stimulated. When the pollen reacted with M. R.'s airways, his body was unable to dilate the bronchi to allow airflow through the swollen bronchial tubes. The result was bronchial constriction and respiratory distress that, in M. R.'s case, progressed to a respiratory arrest. Prior to his taking propranolol, M. R. had probably been effectively compensating for the swelling of the bronchi through bronchodilation and had never experienced such a reaction. The propranolol will need to be weaned from M. R.'s system. M. R. should then be started on a specific beta$_1$ adrenergic blocker, which should give him the decreased cardiac workload that he needs without interfering with his reflex bronchodilation.

M. R. may want to discuss this frightening incident with his health care provider. He also may want to include his family in this discussion. It should be stressed that he did so well up to this point because he had not been exposed to pollen, and so had not had the problem that brought him into the hospital this time. M. R. probably never reported the occurrence of hay fever to his health care provider when the drug was prescribed because it had never been a problem and probably did not seem significant to him. M. R. and his family should receive support and be encouraged to talk about what happened and how they reacted to it. It is normal to feel frightened and unsure when a loved one is in distress. A full teaching program, including information on M. R.'s heart disease and details about his new specific beta$_1$ adrenergic blocker, should be undertaken. M. R. should receive written information about the drug, warning signs to watch for, and adverse effects that may occur.

Acebutolol (*Sectral*) is used for treating hypertension and premature ventricular contractions (PVCs). Atenolol (*Tenormin*), which is more widely used, is prescribed to treat MI, chronic angina, and hypertension, and for the prophylaxis of migraines. Betaxolol (*Kerlone*) is used to treat hypertension; it is also available as an ophthalmic agent (*Betoptic*) to treat ocular hypertension and open angle glaucoma. Bisoprolol (*Zebeta*) is reserved for use in treating hypertension. Esmolol (*Brevibloc*) is available as an IV agent for the treatment of supraventricular tachycardias such as atrial flutter or atrial fibrillation and noncompensatory tachycardia when the heart rate must be slowed. Metoprolol (*Lopressor, Toprol XL*) is used to treat hypertension and has an extended release form that only needs to be taken once a day. It is also used to treat angina and to prevent reinfarction following MI. The beta$_1$-selective blocker of choice would depend on the condition or combination of conditions being treated and personal experience with the drugs.

THERAPEUTIC ACTIONS AND INDICATIONS

The therapeutic effects of these drugs are related to their ability to selectively block beta$_1$ receptors in the SNS. That selectivity occurs at therapeutic doses, but the selectivity is lost with doses higher than the recommended range. The blockade of the beta$_1$

receptors in the heart and the juxtaglomerular apparatus account for most of the therapeutic benefit of these drugs. Decreased heart rate, contractility, and excitability, as well as a membrane stabilizing effect, lead to a decrease in arrhythmias and a decreased cardiac workload and oxygen consumption. The JG cells are not stimulated to release renin, which further decreases blood pressure. These effects are useful in treating hypertension and chronic angina and can help to prevent reinfarction following an MI by decreasing cardiac workload and oxygen consumption. At therapeutic doses, these drugs do not block the beta$_2$ receptors and so do not prevent sympathetic bronchodilation. These drugs are used to treat cardiac arrhythmias, hypertension, and angina; to prevent reinfarction following MI; and, in ophthalmic form, to decrease intraocular pressure and to treat open-angle glaucoma.

CONTRAINDICATIONS/CAUTIONS

The beta$_1$-selective adrenergic blockers are contraindicated in the presence of allergy to the drug or any components of the drug; with sinus bradycardia or with heart block, cardiogenic shock, CHF, and hypotension, all of which could be exacerbated by the cardiac depressing and blood pressure lowering effects of these drugs; and with lactation because of the potential adverse effects on the neonate. They should be used with caution with diabetes, thyroid disease, and COPD because of the potential for adverse effects on these diseases with sympathetic blocking; and pregnancy, because of the potential for adverse effects on the fetus.

ADVERSE EFFECTS

Patients receiving these drugs often experience adverse effects related to the blocking of the sympathetic nervous system's beta$_1$ receptors. CNS effects include fatigue, dizziness, depression, paresthesias, sleep disturbances, memory loss, and disorientation. CV effects can include bradycardia, heart block, CHF, hypotension, and peripheral vascular insufficiency. Pulmonary effects ranging from rhinitis to bronchospasm and dyspnea can occur; these effects are not as likely to occur with these drugs as with the nonselective beta blockers. GI upset, nausea, vomiting, diarrhea, gastric pain, and even colitis can occur as a result of unchecked parasympathetic activity and the blocking of the sympathetic receptors. Genitourinary effects can include decreased libido, impotence, dysuria, and Peyronie's disease. Other effects that can occur include decreased exercise tolerance (patients often report that their "get up and go" is gone), hypoglycemia or hyperglycemia, and liver changes which are reflected in elevated liver enzymes.

CLINICALLY IMPORTANT DRUG–DRUG INTERACTIONS

A decreased hypertensive effect occurs if these drugs are given with clonidine, NSAIDs, rifampin, or barbiturates. If this combination is used, the patient should be monitored closely and dosage adjustment made. There is an initial hypertensive episode followed by bradycardia if these drugs are given with epinephrine. Increased serum levels and increased toxicity of IV lidocaine will occur if given with these drugs. An increased risk of postural hypotension occurs if these drugs are taken with prazosin. If this combination is used, the patient must be monitored closely and safety precautions taken. There are increased effects of the selective beta$_1$ blockers if taken with verapamil, cimetidine, methimazole, and propylthiouracil. The patient should be monitored closely and appropriate dosage adjustment made.

DATA LINK

Data link to the following beta$_1$-selective adrenergic blocking agents in your nursing drug guide:

BETA$_1$-SELECTIVE ADRENERGIC BLOCKING AGENTS

Name	Brand Name	Usual Indications
acebutolol	*Sectral*	Treatment of hypertension and PVCs
P atenolol	*Tenormin*	Treatment of MI, chronic angina, hypertension; prophylaxis of migraines
betaxolol	*Kerlone,* *Betoptic*	Treatment of hypertension Treatment of ocular hypertension, open angle glaucoma
bisoprolol	*Zebeta*	Treatment of hypertension
esmolol	*Brevibloc*	Treatment of supraventricular tachycardias
metoprolol	*Lopressor, Toprol XL*	Treatment of hypertension, angina; prevention of reinfarction after MI

NURSING CONSIDERATIONS
for patients receiving beta$_1$-selective adrenergic blocking agents

Assessment

HISTORY. Screen for the following: any known allergies to any drug or any components of the drug; bradycardia or heart blocks, shock, and CHF, which could be exacerbated by the cardiac suppressing effects of these drugs; bronchospasm and COPD; pregnancy and lactation, because of the potential effects on the fetus or neonate; diabetes and hypoglycemia; and thyrotoxicosis.

PHYSICAL ASSESSMENT. Include screening for baseline status and for any potential adverse effects: skin color, temperature; pulse, blood pressure, ECG; respiration, adventitious sounds; and abdominal exam, urine output, and electrolytes.

Nursing Diagnoses

The patient receiving $beta_1$ adrenergic blockers may have the following nursing diagnoses related to drug therapy:

- Pain related to CNS, GI, and systemic effects
- Alteration in cardiac output related to cardiovascular effects
- Alteration in tissue perfusion related to cardiovascular effects
- Knowledge deficit regarding drug therapy

Implementation

- Do not stop these drugs abruptly after chronic therapy; *taper gradually over 2 weeks. Long-term use of these drugs can sensitize the myocardium to catecholamines and severe reactions could occur.*
- Consult with the physician about discontinuing these drugs before surgery *because withdrawal is controversial.*
- Give oral forms of the drug with food *to facilitate absorption.*
- Continuously monitor any patient receiving an IV form of these drugs *to detect severe reaction to sympathetic blockade.*
- Arrange for supportive care and comfort measures, including rest, environmental control, and other measures *to relieve CNS effects;* safety measures if CNS effects occur *to protect the patient from injury;* and small, frequent meals and mouth care *to relieve the discomfort of GI effects.*
- Provide thorough patient teaching including the name of the drug, dosage, anticipated adverse effects, measures to avoid drug-related problems, and warning signs of problems, as well as proper administration as needed *to enhance patient knowledge about drug therapy and to promote compliance.*
- Offer support and encouragement *to deal with the drug regimen.*

Evaluation

- Monitor patient response to the drug (lowering of blood pressure, decrease in anginal episodes, lowered intraocular pressure).
- Monitor for adverse effects (GI upset, CNS changes, cardiovascular effects, loss of libido and impotence, potential respiratory effects).
- Evaluate the effectiveness of the teaching plan (patient can name drug, dosage, adverse effects to watch for, specific measures to avoid adverse effects).

Monitor the effectiveness of comfort measures and compliance to the regimen.

WWW.WEB LINKS

Health care providers and patients may want to consult the following Internet sources:

Information on research, alternative methods of therapy, pharmacology from the National Heart, Lung and Blood Institute:
http://www.heartinfo.org/news98/jnvi42398.htm

Patient information on hypertension, treatments, lifestyle adjustments:
http://www.jhbmc/jhu.edu/cardiology/rehab/hypertension.html

Patient information, support groups, diet, exercise, research information on hypertension and other cardiovascular diseases:
http://amhrt.org

Information on cardiovascular research, treatments, hypertension, arrhythmias:
http://www.acc.org/login/index.taf

CULTURAL CONSIDERATIONS ••••

Alternative Therapies and Adrenergic Blocking Effects

Patients who use alternative therapies as part of their daily regimen should be cautioned about potential increased adrenergic blocking effects if the following alternative therapies are combined with adrenergic blocking agents:

- Ginseng, sage—cause increased antihypertensive effects (risk of hypotension and increased CNS effects)
- Xuan seng, nightshade—slow heart rate (risk of severe bradycardia and reflex arrhythmias)
- Celery, coriander, Di huang, fenugreek, goldenseal, Java plum, xuan seng—lower blood glucose (increased risk of severe hypoglycemia)
- Saw palmetto—used to treat BPH, can interact to cause increased urinary tract complications

Patients who are prescribed an adrenergic blocking drug should be cautioned about the use of herbs, teas, and alternative medicines. If a patient feels that one of these agents is needed, the health care provider should be consulted and appropriate precautions taken to ensure that the patient is able to achieve the most therapeutic effects with the least adverse effects while on the drug.

CHAPTER SUMMARY

- Adrenergic blocking agents or sympatholytic drugs lyse or block the effects of the sympathetic nervous system.
- Both the therapeutic and the adverse effects associated with these drugs are related to their blocking of the normal responses of the sympathetic nervous system.
- Alpha and beta adrenergic blocking agents block all of the receptor sites within the SNS, which results in lower blood pressure, slower pulse, and increased renal perfusion with decreased renin levels. These drugs are indicated for the treatment of essential hypertension. They are associated with many adverse effects, including lack of bronchodilation, cardiac suppression, and diabetic reactions.
- Selective adrenergic blocking agents have been developed that, at therapeutic levels, have specific affinity for alpha or beta or for specific $alpha_1$, $beta_1$, or $beta_2$ receptor sites. This specificity is lost at higher-than-therapeutic levels.
- Alpha adrenergic drugs specifically block the alpha receptors of the SNS. At therapeutic levels, they do not block beta receptors.
- Nonspecific alpha adrenergic blocking agents are used to treat pheochromocytoma, a tumor of the adrenal medulla.
- $Alpha_1$-selective adrenergic blocking agents block the postsynaptic $alpha_1$ receptor sites, causing a decrease in vascular tone and a vasodilation which leads to a fall in blood pressure without the reflex tachycardia that occurs when the presynaptic $alpha_2$ receptor sites are blocked also.
- Beta blockers are drugs used to block the beta receptors within the SNS. These drugs are used for a wide range of problems including hypertension, stage fright, migraines, angina, and essential tremors.
- Blocking all beta receptors results in a loss of the reflex bronchodilation that occurs with sympathetic stimulation. This limits the use of these drugs in patients who smoke or have allergic or seasonal rhinitis, asthma, or COPD.
- $Beta_1$-selective adrenergic blocking agents do not block the $beta_1$ receptors responsible for bronchodilation and are therefore preferred in patients with respiratory problems.

BIBLIOGRAPHY

Andrews, M. & Boyle, J. (1999). *Transcultural concepts in nursing care.* Philadelphia: Lippincott Williams & Wilkins.

Bullock, B. L. (2000). *Focus on pathophysiology.* Philadelphia: Lippincott Williams & Wilkins.

Hardman, J. G., Limbird, L. E., Molinoff, P. B., Ruddon, R. W., & Gilman, A. G. (Eds.). (1996). *Goodman and Gilman's the pharmacological basis of therapeutics* (9th ed). New York: McGraw-Hill.

Karch, A. M. (2000). *2000 Lippincott's nursing drug guide.* Philadelphia: Lippincott Williams & Wilkins.

McEvoy, B. R. (1999). *Facts and comparisons 1999.* St. Louis: Fact and Comparisons.

The medical letter on drugs and therapeutics. (1999). New Rochelle, NY: Medical Letter.

Porth, C. M. (1998). *Pathophysiology: Concepts of altered health states* (5th ed.). Philadelphia: Lippincott-Raven.

CHAPTER 30

Cholinergic Agents

Direct-acting cholinergic agonists
- P bethanechol
- carbachol
- pilocarpine

Indirect-acting cholinergic agonists
- ambenonium
- P donepezil
- edrophonium
- neostigmine
- physostigmine
- P pyridostigmine
- tacrine

Reversing agent
- pralidoxime

CHAPTER OUTLINE

KEY TERMS

acetylcholinesterase
Alzheimer's disease
cholinergic
miosis
myasthenia gravis
nerve gas
parasympathomimetic

INTRODUCTION

Cholinergic drugs are chemicals that act at the same site as the neurotransmitter acetylcholine. Because these sites are found extensively throughout the parasympathetic nervous system, the stimulation of these sites produces a response similar to what is seen when the parasympathetic system is activated. As a result, these drugs are often called ***parasympathomimetic*** drugs because their action mimics the action of the parasympathetic nervous system. Because the action of these drugs cannot be limited to a specific site, their effects can be widespread throughout the body; thus, they are usually associated with many undesirable systemic effects.

CHOLINERGIC AGONISTS

Cholinergic agonists are drugs that increase the activity of the acetylcholine receptor sites throughout the body. These drugs work either directly or indirectly. Direct-acting cholinergic agonists occupy receptor sites for acetylcholine on the membranes of the effector cells of the postganglionic cholinergic nerves, causing increased stimulation of the cholinergic receptor. In contrast, indirect-acting cholinergic agonists cause increased stimulation of the acetylcholine receptor sites by reacting with the enzyme ***acetylcholinesterase*** and preventing it from breaking down the acetylcholine that was released from the nerve. These drugs produce their effects indirectly by producing an increase in the levels of acetylcholine in the synaptic cleft, leading to increased stimulation of the cholinergic receptor site (Figure 30-1).

Direct-Acting Cholinergic Agonists

The direct-acting cholinergic agonists are similar to acetylcholine and react directly with receptor sites to cause the same reaction as acetylcholine. These drugs tend to cause stimulation of the muscarinic receptors within the parasympathetic system. They are used to increase bladder tone and urinary excretion and as ophthalmic agents, which are not absorbed systemically. Their use today is infrequent: because they can cause widespread parasympathetic activity, the more specific and less toxic drugs that are now available are preferred.

The agent bethanechol (*Duvoid, Urecholine*) is available for use orally and subcutaneously to treat nonobstructive postoperative and postpartum urinary retention and to treat neurogenic bladder atony by directly increasing muscle tone and relaxing the sphincters. The drugs carbachol (*Miostat*) and pilocarpine (*Pilocar* and others) are available only as ophthalmic agents, which are used to induce ***miosis,*** or pupil constriction, to relieve the increased intraocular pressure of glaucoma and to perform certain surgical procedures.

THERAPEUTIC ACTIONS AND INDICATIONS

The direct-acting cholinergic agonists act at cholinergic receptors in the peripheral nervous system (PNS) to mimic the effects of acetylcholine and parasympathetic stimulation. These parasympathetic effects include slowed heart rate and contractility, vasodilation, bronchoconstriction and increased secretions from bronchial mucus, increase in gastrointestinal (GI) activity and secretions, increased in bladder tone, relaxation of GI and bladder sphincters, and pupil constriction (see Figure 30-1).

The only drug of this type that is used systemically is bethanechol. Bethanechol has an affinity for the cholinergic receptors in the urinary bladder to increase the tone of the detrusor muscle of the bladder and relax the bladder sphincter to improve bladder emptying. Because this drug is not destroyed by acetylcholinesterase, the effects on the receptor site are longer than when stimulated by acetylcholine. Carbachol and pilocarpine are topical drugs that are not generally absorbed systemically, so they are not associated with severe adverse effects.

CONTRAINDICATIONS/CAUTIONS

These drugs are used sparingly because of the potential undesirable systemic effects of parasympathetic stimulation. They are contraindicated in the presence of any condition that would be exacerbated by parasympathetic effects. For example, bradycardia, hypotension, vasomotor instability, and coronary artery disease (CAD) could be made worse by the cardiac- and cardiovascular-suppressing effects of the parasympathetic system. Peptic ulcer, intestinal obstruction, or recent GI surgery could be negatively affected by the GI-stimulating effects of the PNS. Asthma could be exacerbated by the increased parasympathetic effect, overriding the protective sympathetic bronchodilation. Bladder obstruction or healing sites from recent bladder surgery could be aggravated by the stimulatory effects on the bladder. Epilepsy and parkinsonism could be affected by the stimulation of acetylcholine receptors in the brain. Caution should be used during pregnancy and lactation because of the potential adverse effects on the fetus or neonate.

ADVERSE EFFECTS

Patients should be cautioned about the potential adverse effects of these drugs. Even if the drug is being given as a topical ophthalmic agent, there is always a possibility that it will be absorbed. The adverse effects associated with these drugs are related to parasympathetic nervous system stimulation. GI effects

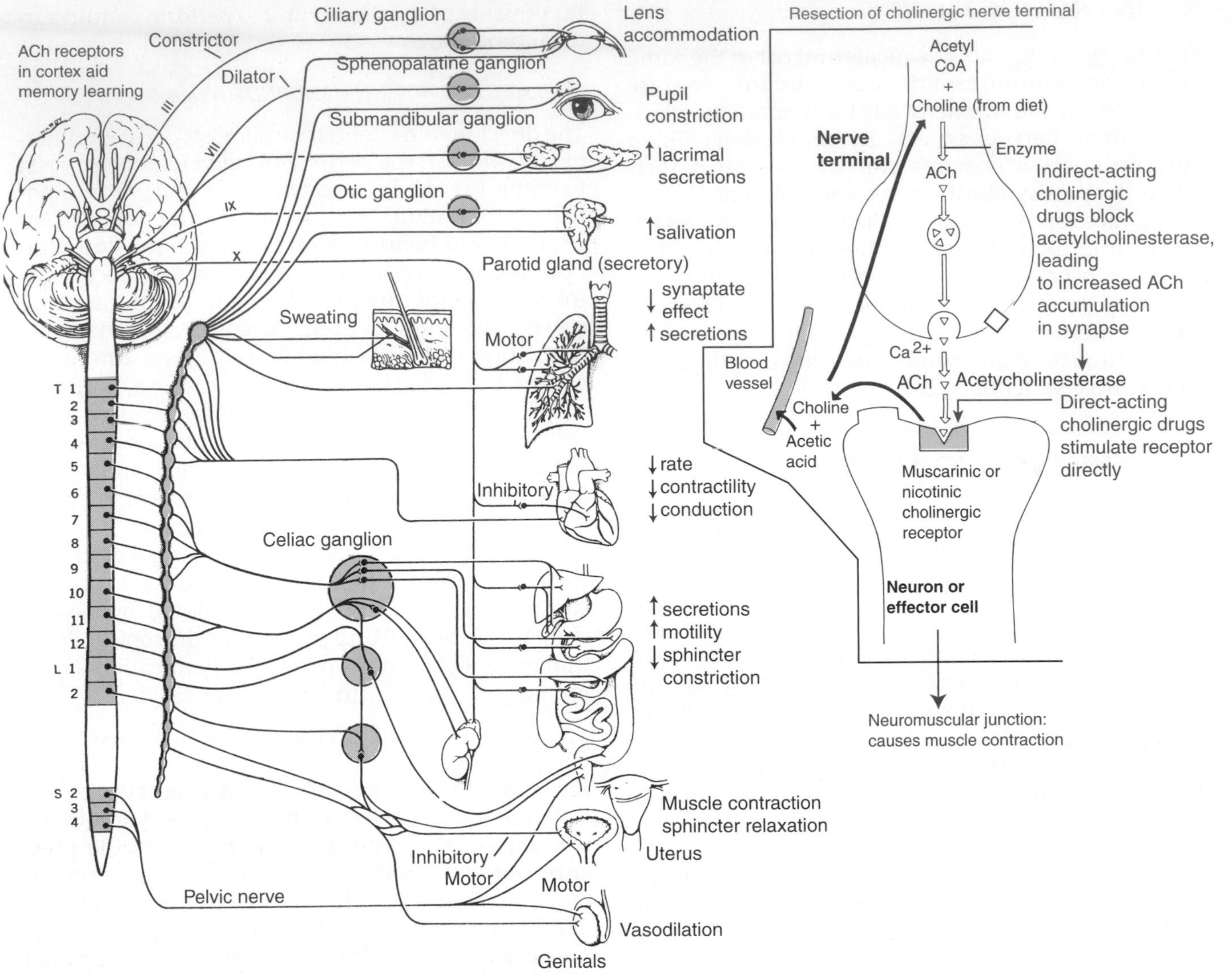

FIGURE 30-1. Site of action of cholinergic drugs and associated physiologic responses.

can include nausea, vomiting, cramps, diarrhea, increased salivation, and involuntary defecation related to the increase in GI secretions and activity. Cardiovascular effects can include bradycardia, heart block, hypotension, and even cardiac arrest related to the cardiac-suppressing effects of the parasympathetic nervous system. Urinary tract effects can include a sense of urgency related to the stimulation of the bladder muscles and sphincter relaxation. Other effects may include flushing and increased sweating secondary to stimulation of the cholinergic receptors in the sympathetic nervous system (SNS).

CLINICALLY IMPORTANT DRUG–DRUG INTERACTIONS

There is an increased risk of cholinergic effects if these drugs are combined or given with acetylcholinesterase inhibitors. The patient should be monitored and appropriate dosage adjustments made.

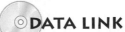

DATA LINK

Data link to the following direct-acting cholinergic agonists in your nursing drug guide:

DIRECT-ACTING CHOLINERGIC AGONISTS

Name	Brand Name	Usual Indications
P bethanechol	*Duvoid, Urecholine*	Nonobstructive urinary retention, neurogenic bladder
carbachol	*Miostat*	Glaucoma, miosis
pilocarpine	*Pilocar*	Glaucoma, miosis

NURSING CONSIDERATIONS
for patients receiving direct-acting cholinergic agonists

Assessment

HISTORY. Screen for the following: any known allergies to these drugs; bradycardia, vasomotor instability, peptic ulcer, obstructive urinary or GI diseases; recent GI or genitourinary surgery; asthma; parkinsonism or epilepsy; pregnancy and lactation, all of which could be exacerbated or complicated by parasympathetic stimulation.

PHYSICAL ASSESSMENT. Include screening for baseline status before beginning therapy and for any potential adverse effects: skin color, lesions, temperature; pulse, blood pressure, ECG; respiration, adventitious sounds; and urine output and bladder tone.

Nursing Diagnoses

The patient receiving a direct-acting cholinergic agonist may have the following nursing diagnoses related to drug therapy:

- Pain related to GI effects
- Alteration in cardiac output related to cardiovascular effects
- Alteration in urinary output related to effects on the bladder
- Knowledge deficit regarding drug therapy

Implementation

- Assure proper administration of ophthalmic preparations *to increase effectiveness of drug therapy.*
- Administer oral drug on an empty stomach *to decrease nausea and vomiting.*
- Monitor patient response closely, including blood pressure, ECG, urine output, and cardiac output, to arrange *to adjust dosage accordingly to assure the most benefit with the least amount of toxicity.* Maintain atropine on standby *to reverse overdose or counteract severe reactions.*
- Provide safety precautions if the patient reports poor visual acuity in dim light *to prevent injury.*
- Provide thorough patient teaching, including measures to avoid adverse effects and warning signs of problems, as well as the need for monitoring and evaluation, *to enhance patient knowledge about drug therapy and to promote compliance* (see Patient Teaching Checklist: Cholinergic Agents).
- Offer support and encouragement *to deal with the drug regimen.*

Evaluation

- Monitor patient response to the drug (improvement in bladder function, miosis).
- Monitor for adverse effects (cardiovascular changes, GI stimulation, urinary urgency, respiratory distress).
- Evaluate the effectiveness of the teaching plan (patient can name drug, dosage, adverse effects to watch for, specific measures to avoid adverse effects, proper administration of ophthalmic drugs).
- Monitor the effectiveness of comfort and safety measures and compliance to the regimen (see Nursing Care Guide: Cholinergic Agents).

Indirect-Acting Cholinergic Agonists

The indirect-acting cholinergic agonists do not react directly with acetylcholine receptor sites, but instead react chemically with acetylcholinesterase, the enzyme responsible for the breakdown of acetylcholine (ACh), in the synaptic cleft to prevent it from breaking down ACh. As a result, the ACh that is released from the presynaptic nerve remains in the area and accumulates, stimulating the ACh receptors. These drugs work at all ACh receptors, in the parasympathetic nervous system, in the central nervous system (CNS), and at the neuromuscular junction. All of these drugs bind reversibly to acetylcholinesterase, so their effects will pass with time. (Certain drugs, however, are irreversible acetylcholinesterase-inhibiting agents, requiring special considerations [Boxes 30-1 and 30-2].)

The indirect-acting cholinergic agents fall into two main categories: (1) agents used to treat ***myasthenia gravis,*** and (2) newer agents used to treat ***Alzheimer's disease.***

MYASTHENIA GRAVIS AGENTS

Myasthenia gravis is a chronic muscular disease that is caused by a defect in neuromuscular transmission. It is thought to be an autoimmune disease in which patients make antibodies to their acetylcholine receptors. These antibodies cause gradual destruction of the ACh receptors, causing the patient to have fewer and fewer receptor sites available for stimulation. The disease is marked by progressive weakness and lack of muscle control with periodic acute episodes. The disease can progress to paralysis of the diaphragm, which prevents the patient from breathing and would prove fatal without intervention.

Drugs used to help patients with this progressive disease are acetylcholinesterase inhibitors. These drugs cause an accumulation of ACh in the synaptic cleft, providing a longer period of time for ACh to stimulate whatever receptors are still available.

Physostigmine (*Escrine*) is a very potent acetylcholinesterase inhibitor. Because it crosses the blood–brain barrier, it is associated with many toxic systemic effects. Its use is now limited to an ophthalmic preparation for the treatment of glaucoma by causing miosis.

PATIENT TEACHING CHECKLIST

Cholinergic Agents

Create customized patient teaching materials for a specific cholinergic agent from your CD-ROM. Your patient teaching should stress the following points for drugs within this class:

Cholinergic drugs get this name because they act at certain nerve–nerve and nerve–muscle junctions in the body that are called cholinergic sites.

If your drug is given as eye drops, it is important to make sure that you are storing them properly. Eye drops should be clear and kept sterile; if you have any doubts about the drug, discard it.

Proper administration of eye drops will help to decrease the adverse effects that you might experience. To administer the drops, follow these instructions: Tilt the head backward slightly. Pull down the lower eyelid, maintaining pressure over the opening of the tear duct in the corner of the eye. Administer the correct number of drops. Do not touch the eyedropper to your eye. Maintain pressure over the tear duct opening for a full minute after putting in the drops.

Some of the following adverse effects may occur:

- Nausea, excessive gas, diarrhea. It is wise to be near bathroom facilities after taking your drug. If these symptoms become too severe, consult with your health care provider.
- Flushing, sweating. Staying in a cool environment and wearing lightweight clothing may help.
- Urgency to void. Maintaining access to a bathroom may relieve some of this discomfort.
- Headache. Aspirin or another headache medication (if not contraindicated in your particular case) will help to alleviate this pain.

Report any of the following to your health care provider: very slow pulse, light-headedness, fainting, excessive salivation, abdominal cramping or pain, weakness or confusion, blurring of vision.

Tell any doctor, nurse, or other health care provider that you are taking these drugs.

Keep this drug, and all medications, out of the reach of children. Do not share these drugs with other people.

This Teaching Checklist reflects general patient teaching guidelines. It is not meant to be a substitute for drug-specific teaching information, which is available in nursing drug guides.

Neostigmine (*Prostigmine*) is a synthetic drug that does not cross the blood–brain barrier, but has a strong influence at the neuromuscular junction. It has a duration of action of 2 to 4 hours and so must be given every few hours, based on patient response, to maintain a therapeutic level.

Pyridostigmine (*Reganol, Mestinol*), which has a longer duration of action than neostigmine (3–6 hours), is preferred in some cases for the management of myasthenia gravis because it does not need to be taken as frequently. It is available in oral and parenteral form, which can be used if the patient is having trouble swallowing.

Ambenonium (*Mytelase*) is a newer drug that is similar to pyridostigmine in that it only needs to be taken four times a day. Its main disadvantage is that it is only available in an oral preparation and cannot be used if the patient is unable to swallow tablets.

Edrophonium (*Tensilon, Enlon*) has a very short duration of action (only 10–20 min). Its primary use is as a diagnostic agent for myasthenia gravis. If a patient has a temporary reversal of symptoms after injection with edrophonium, it indicates a problem with the ACh neuromuscular receptors.

ALZHEIMER'S DISEASE DRUGS

Alzheimer's disease is a progressive disorder with neural degeneration in the cortex leading to a marked loss of memory and ability to carry on activities of daily living. The cause of the disease is not yet known, but there is a progressive loss of ACh-producing neurons and their target neurons. Two drugs are currently available to slow the progression of this disease: Tacrine (*Cognex*), the first drug developed for the treatment of mild to moderate Alzheimer's dementia, and donepezil (*Aricept*), which has once-a-day dosing. The once-a-day dosing offers a great advantage in a disease that affects memory and the patient's ability to remember to take pills throughout the day.

THERAPEUTIC ACTIONS AND INDICATIONS

All of the indirect-acting cholinergic agonists work by blocking acetylcholinesterase at the synaptic cleft. This blocking allows the accumulation of ACh released from the nerve ending and leads to increased and prolonged stimulation of ACh receptor sites at all of the postsynaptic cholinergic sites. These drugs can work to relieve the signs and symptoms of myas-

NURSING CARE GUIDE
Cholinergic Agents

Assessment	Nursing Diagnoses	Implementation	Evaluation
HISTORY			
Allergies to any of these drugs, coronary artery disease, hypotension, bradycardia, heart block, bowel or urinary obstruction, pregnancy and lactation, epilepsy, parkinsonism, recent GI or urinary surgery	Alteration in cardiac output related to CV effects Pain related to GI, systemic effects Alteration in urinary output related to GU effects Knowledge deficit regarding drug therapy	Ensure safe and appropriate administration of drug. Provide comfort and safety measures: assistance/siderails; temperature control; pain relief; small, frequent meals. Monitor cardiac status and urine output throughout drug therapy. Provide support and reassurance to deal with drug effects, discomfort, and GI effects. Provide patient teaching regarding drug name, dosage, side effects, precautions, and warning signs to report.	Evaluate drug effects: miosis; decrease in signs and symptoms of myasthenia gravis, Alzheimer's disease. Monitor for adverse effects: CV effects- bradycardia, heart block, hypotension; urinary problems; GI effects; respiratory problems. Monitor for drug–drug interactions as indicated for each drug. Evaluate effectiveness of patient teaching program. Evaluate effectiveness of comfort and safety measures.
PHYSICAL EXAMINATION			
CV: BP, P, peripheral perfusion, ECG CNS: orientation, affect, reflexes, vision Skin: color, lesions, texture GU: urinary output, bladder tone GI: abdominal exam Resp: R, adventitious sounds			

thenia gravis and increase muscle strength by accumulating ACh in the synaptic cleft at neuromuscular junctions.

The drugs preferred for this use are those that do not cross the blood–brain barrier. Drugs that cross the blood–brain barrier and seem to affect mostly the cells in the cortex to increase ACh concentration are used in the treatment of mild to moderate Alzheimer's disease. Neostigmine and edrophonium, because of their rapid onset of action, are also used to reverse toxicity from nondepolarizing neuromuscular junction blocking drugs, which are used to paralyze muscles during surgery (see Chapter 26).

CONTRAINDICATIONS/CAUTIONS

These drugs are contraindicated in the presence of allergy to any of these drugs; with bradycardia or intestinal or urinary tract obstruction, which could be exacerbated by the stimulation of cholinergic receptors; and in pregnancy (the uterus could be stimulated and labor induced) and lactation because of the potential effects on the baby.

Caution should be used with any condition that could be exacerbated by cholinergic stimulation. Although the effects of these drugs are generally more localized to the cortex and neuromuscular junction, the possibility of parasympathetic effects should be considered carefully in patients with asthma, coronary disease, peptic ulcer, arrhythmias, epilepsy, and parkinsonism.

ADVERSE EFFECTS

The adverse effects associated with these drugs are related to the stimulation of the parasympathetic

BOX 30-1 PRALIDOXIME CHLORIDE: ANTIDOTE FOR IRREVERSIBLE ACETYLCHOLINESTERASE INHIBITING DRUGS

Pralidoxime (*Protopam Chloride*), the antidote for irreversible acetylcholinesterase-inhibiting drugs, is given IM or IV to reactivate the acetylcholinesterase that has been blocked by these drugs. Freeing up the acetylcholinesterase allows it to break down accumulated acetylcholine that has overstimulated acetylcholine receptor sites, causing paralysis.

Pralidoxime does not readily cross the blood–brain barrier and is most useful for treating peripheral drug effects. It reacts within minutes of injection and should be available for any patient receiving indirect-acting cholinergic agonists to treat myasthenia gravis. The patient and a significant other should understand when to use the drug and how to administer it.

Pralidoxime is also used with atropine (which does cross the blood–brain barrier and will block the effects of accumulated ACh at CNS sites) to treat organophosphate pesticide poisonings and nerve gas exposure (see Box 30-2), both of which cause inactivation of acetylcholinesterase.

Adverse effects associated with use of pralidoxime include dizziness, blurred vision, diplopia, headache, drowsiness, hyperventilation, and nausea. These effects are also seen with exposure to nerve gas and organophosphate pesticides, so it can be difficult to differentiate drug effects from the effects of the poisoning.

BOX 30-2 NERVE GAS: AN IRREVERSIBLE ACETYLCHOLINESTERASE INHIBITOR

Recent worldwide events and conflicts have made the development of ***nerve gas*** a major news story. As developed as a weapon, nerve gas is an irreversible acetylcholinesterase inhibitor. The drug is inhaled and quickly spreads throughout the body, where it permanently binds with acetylcholinesterase. This causes an accumulation of ACh at nerve endings and a massive cholinergic response. The heart rate slows and becomes ineffective, pupils and bronchi constrict, the GI tract increases activity and secretions, and muscles contract and remain that way. The muscle contraction soon freezes the diaphragm, causing breathing to stop. The bodies of people who are killed using nerve gas have a characteristic rigor of muscle contraction.

If the presence of nerve gas is expected, individuals who may be exposed are given IM injections of atropine (to temporarily block cholinergic activity and to activate acetylcholine sites in the CNS) and pralidoxime (to free up the acetylcholinesterase to start breaking down acetylcholine). An autoinjector is provided to military personnel who may be at risk. The injector is used to give atropine and then pralidoxime. The injections are repeated in 15 minutes. If symptoms of nerve gas exposure exist after an additional 15 minutes, the injections are repeated. If symptoms still persist after a third set of injections, medical help should be sought.

nervous system. GI effects can include nausea, vomiting, cramps, diarrhea, increased salivation, and involuntary defecation related to the parasympathetic nervous system's increase in GI secretions and activity. Cardiovascular effects can include bradycardia, heart block, hypotension, and even cardiac arrest related to the cardiac-suppressing effects of the parasympathetic nervous system. Urinary tract effects can include a sense of urgency related to the stimulation of the bladder muscles and sphincter relaxation. Miosis and blurred vision, headaches, dizziness, and drowsiness can occur related to effects on CNS cholinergic drugs. Other effects may include flushing and increased sweating secondary to stimulation of the cholinergic receptors in the SNS.

CLINICALLY IMPORTANT DRUG–DRUG INTERACTIONS

There may be an increased risk of GI bleeding if these drugs are used with NSAIDs because of the combination of increased GI secretions and the GI mucosal erosion associated with NSAIDs. If this combination is used, the patient should be monitored closely for any sign of GI bleeding. There will be a decreased effect of anticholinesterase drugs if taken in combination because these work in opposition to each other.

DATA LINK

Data link to the following indirect-acting cholinergic agonists in your nursing drug guide:

INDIRECT-ACTING CHOLINERGIC AGONISTS

Name	Brand Name(s)	Usual Indications
ambenonium	*Mytelase*	Myasthenia gravis
P donepezil	*Aricept*	Alzheimer's disease
edrophonium	*Tensilon, Enlon*	Myasthenia gravis diagnosis, antidote NMJ blockers
neostigmine	*Prostigmine*	Myasthenia gravis diagnosis, antidote NMJ blockers
physostigmine	*Eserine*	Miosis, glaucoma
P pyridostigmine	*Reganol, Mestinol*	Myasthenia gravis
tacrine	*Cognex*	Alzheimer's disease

NURSING CHALLENGE

Myasthenic Crisis Versus Cholinergic Crisis

Myasthenia gravis is an autoimmune disease that runs an unpredictable course throughout the patient's life. Some patients will have a very mild presentation—drooping eyelid, for instance—and will go into remission with no further signs and symptoms for several years. Others will have a more severe course with progressive muscle weakness, confinement to a wheelchair, and so on. Many times, the disease goes through an intense phase called a myasthenic crisis, marked by extreme muscle weakness and respiratory difficulty.

Because of the variability of the disease and the tendency to have crises and periods of remission, managing the drug dosage for a patient with myasthenia gravis is a genuine nursing challenge. If a patient goes into remission, a smaller dosage will be needed. If a patient has a crisis, more drug will be needed. To further complicate the clinical picture, the presentation of a cholinergic overdose or cholinergic crisis is similar to the presentation of a myasthenic crisis. The patient with a cholinergic crisis will present with progressive muscle weakness and respiratory difficulty as the accumulation of acetylcholine (ACh) at the cholinergic receptor site leads to reduced impulse transmission and muscle weakness. This is a crisis when the respiratory muscles are involved.

For a myasthenic crisis, the correct treatment is increased cholinergic drug. However, treatment of a cholinergic crisis requires withdrawal of the drug. The patient's respiratory difficulty usually necessitates acute medical attention. At this point, the drug edrophonium can be used as a diagnostic agent to distinguish the two conditions. If the patient improves immediately after the edrophonium injection, the problem is a myasthenic crisis, which is improved by the cholinergic drug. If the patient gets worse, the problem is probably a cholinergic crisis. Withdrawal of the patient's cholinergic drug along with intense medical support is indicated. Atropine will help to alleviate some of the parasympathetic reactions to the cholinergic drug. But because atropine is not effective at the neuromuscular junction, only time will reverse the drug toxicity.

The patient and significant other will need support, teaching, and encouragement to deal with the tricky regulation of the cholinergic medication throughout the course of the disease. Nurses in the acute care setting need to be mindful of the difficulty in distinguishing drug toxicity from the need for more drug—and be prepared to respond appropriately.

NURSING CONSIDERATIONS
for patients receiving indirect-acting cholinergic agonists

Assessment

HISTORY. Screen for the following: any known allergies to any of these drugs; arrhythmias, coronary artery disease, hypotension, urogenital or GI obstruction, peptic ulcer, pregnancy, lactation, recent GI or genitourinary surgery, which could limit the use of the drugs; and regular use of NSAIDs, which could cause a drug–drug interaction.

PHYSICAL ASSESSMENT. Include screening for baseline status before beginning therapy and for any potential adverse effects: assess orientation, affect, reflexes, ability to carry on ADLs (Alzheimer's drugs), and vision to monitor for CNS changes related to drug therapy; blood pressure, pulse, ECG, peripheral perfusion, and cardiac output; and urinary output, renal and liver function tests to monitor drug effects on the renal system and liver, which could change the metabolism and excretion of the drugs.

Nursing Diagnoses

The patient receiving an indirect-acting cholinergic agonist may also have the following nursing diagnoses related to drug therapy:

- Alteration in thought processes related to CNS effects
- Pain related to GI effects
- Alteration in cardiac output related to blood pressure changes, arrhythmias, vasodilation
- Knowledge deficit regarding drug therapy

Implementation

- If given IV, administer slowly *to avoid severe cholinergic effects.*
- Maintain atropine sulfate on standby *as an antidote in case of overdose or severe cholinergic reaction.*
- Discontinue the drug if excessive salivation, diarrhea, emesis or frequent urination become a problem *to decrease the risk of severe adverse reactions.*
- Administer the oral drug with meals *to decrease GI upset if it is a problem.*
- Mark the patient's chart and notify the surgeon if the patient is to undergo surgery; *prolonged muscle relaxation may occur if succinylcholine-type anesthetics are used. The patient will require prolonged support and monitoring.*
- Monitor the patient being treated for Alzheimer's disease for any progress; *the drug is not a cure and only slows progression; refer families to supportive services.*
- The patient and a significant other should receive instruction in drug administration, warning signs of

CULTURAL/LIFESPAN CONSIDERATIONS

Alzheimer's Disease

Alzheimer's disease has been seen increasingly in the 90s. In the past, many people with Alzheimer's disease would have been diagnosed with senile dementia or dementia. This disease can affect individuals at any age, but it is seen mainly in elderly people and in more men than in women. Currently, the only accurate way to diagnose Alzheimer's disease is at autopsy. However, many companies are working to develop a diagnostic test to permit preautopsy diagnosis.

Alzheimer's is a chronic, progressive disease of the brain's cortex. Eventually, it results in memory loss so severe that patients may not remember how to perform the basic activities of daily living or recognize close family members. Although Alzheimer's disease primarily strikes the elderly, it has a tremendous impact on family members of all ages. For example, adult children of Alzheimer's patients, many of whom are busy raising children of their own, may find themselves in the role of caregivers—in essence, becoming parents of the parent. This new role can put tremendous stress on individuals who are trying to struggle with work, family, and issues related to their parent's care.

When caring for an Alzheimer's patient and family, the nurse must remember that the patient's cultural background can affect how the family copes with the progressive, debilitating nature of the disease. For instance, those who tend to have solid extended families or who are part of communities that offer strong social support and interdependence may be better equipped to deal with the tremendous burden of caring for the patient as the disease progresses. In contrast, families that are more goal and achievement oriented and who value autonomy and independence may find themselves overwhelmed by the patient's needs and may require more support and referrals to community resources.

The nurse is in the best position to evaluate the family situation. By approaching each situation as unique and striving to incorporate cultural and social norms into the considerations for care, the nurse can help ease the family's burden while also maintaining the dignity of the patient and the family through this difficult experience.

drug overdose, and signs and symptoms to report immediately if being treated for myasthenia gravis *to enhance patient knowledge about drug therapy and to promote compliance.*

• Arrange for supportive care and comfort measures, including rest, environmental control, and other measures *to decrease CNS irritation;* headache medication *to relieve pain;* safety measures if CNS effects occur *to prevent injury;* protective measures if CNS effects are severe *to prevent patient injury;* and small, frequent meals if GI upset is severe *to decrease discomfort and maintain nutrition.*

• Provide thorough patient teaching, including dosage and adverse effects to anticipate; measures to avoid adverse effects; and warning signs of problems as well as proper administration for each route used *to enhance patient knowledge about drug therapy and to promote compliance* (refer to Patient Teaching Checklist: Cholinergic Agents).

• Offer support and encouragement *to deal with the drug regimen.*

Evaluation

• Monitor patient response to the drug (improvement in condition being treated).

• Monitor for adverse effects (GI upset, CNS changes, cardiovascular changes, genitourinary changes).

• Evaluate the effectiveness of the teaching plan (patient can name drug, dosage, adverse effects to watch for, specific measures to avoid adverse effects, proper administration).

• Monitor the effectiveness of comfort measures and compliance to the regimen (refer to Nursing Care Guide: Cholinergic Agents).

WWW.WEB LINKS

Health care providers and patients may want to consult the following Internet sources:

Information on Alzheimer's disease research, conferences:
http://dsmallpc.2.path.unimelb.edu.au/ad.html

Information on resources, medical treatments, outreach programs, local support groups involved with Alzheimer's disease:
http://www.alz.org

Information on current research on myasthenia gravis, treatments:
http://www.myasthenia.org

Information on myasthenia gravis educational programs, local support groups, and resources:
http://www.lowvision.org/myasthenia gravis.htm

Information on nerve gas treatment protocols:
http://www.tatrc.org/gobook/nervekit.html

CASE STUDY

Cholinergic Drugs as Causes of Postoperative Abdominal Distention

PRESENTATION

A. J. has been returned to your unit following a lengthy abdominal surgery. She has not eaten since the previous evening, but has no desire for the ice chips that have been offered. Her abdomen appears distended, and no bowel sounds are heard on auscultation. The harried house officer who is called decides that A. J. is probably suffering either from paralytic ileus or atonic bladder and orders an IM injection of neostigmine (to reverse the effects of an NMJ blocker used during surgery) and several oral doses of bethanechol.

CRITICAL THINKING QUESTIONS

What could be responsible for A. J.'s symptoms? Following abdominal surgery, it is not unusual to have some reflex intestinal atony because of the intestinal manipulation during surgery. Do the ordered medications seem to be reasonable? What are the potential adverse effects to consider when giving two cholinergic drugs? What are the potential complications from these drugs following GI surgery? Outline a care plan for A. J. considering her postoperative status, the potential problem she is encountering, the potential effects of the prescribed drug therapy, and the stress and anxiety she may be experiencing as a result of these complications. Do you think you would give the ordered medications? If not, what else should be done?

DISCUSSION

The cholinergic drugs that have been ordered would produce some anticipated adverse effects related to their stimulation of the parasympathetic nervous system. These effects include increased bronchial secretions and bronchoconstriction, which could cause a problem in recovery from general anesthesia, requiring vigorous pulmonary toilet; increased gastric secretions and activity, which could cause major problems following abdominal surgery, including rupture or obstruction; hypotension and bradycardia, which could further complicate recovery from anesthesia and result in poor perfusion to the operative site; increased tone and contractions of the bladder, which could cause some problems in the postoperative patient, depending on the site of the surgery and use of a catheter, and so on.

The most appropriate action in this case would be to question the drugs ordered and to refuse to give the medications until further tests are done to evaluate the actual cause of the abdominal distention. An abdominal x-ray or ultrasound would be helpful in determining the cause of the problem, which could just as easily be internal bleeding.

In the meantime, A. J. should receive support and comfort measures (e.g., positioning, medication). Baseline assessment should be done on all of those parameters most affected by anticholinergic drugs. If the cholinergic drugs are the most appropriate treatment in this case, baseline information will be in place to evaluate for any adverse effects of the drugs. If these drugs are used, very careful patient assessment will be necessary to assure the safety of the patient in the postoperative phase and full recovery later on.

Teaching plans should include the reason for the concerns, the reasons for additional tests, and the actions and anticipated side effects of the drugs, as well as supportive measures that will be taken to help A. J. cope with the therapy and recover fully.

CHAPTER SUMMARY

- Cholinergic drugs are chemicals that act at the same site as the neurotransmitter acetylcholine, stimulating the parasympathetic nerves, some nerves in the brain, and the neuromuscular junction.
- Direct-acting cholinergic drugs react with the ACh receptor sites to cause cholinergic stimulation.
- Use of direct-acting cholinergic drugs is limited by the systemic effects of the drug. They are used to cause miosis to treat glaucoma and one agent is available to treat neurogenic bladder and bladder atony postoperatively or postpartum.
- Indirect-acting cholinergic drugs are acetylcholinesterase inhibitors. They block acetylcholinesterase to prevent it from breaking down ACh in the synaptic cleft.
- Cholinergic stimulation by acetylcholinesterase inhibitors is caused by an accumulation of the ACh released from the nerve ending.
- Myasthenia gravis is an autoimmune disease characterized by antibodies to the ACh receptors. This results in a loss of ACh receptors and eventual loss of response at the neuromuscular junction.
- Acetylcholinesterase inhibitors are used to treat myasthenia gravis because they are able to cause the accumulation of ACh in the synaptic cleft, prolonging stimulation of any ACh sites remaining.
- Alzheimer's disease is a progressive dementia characterized by a loss of ACh-producing neurons and ACh receptor sites in the neurocortex.
- Acetylcholinesterase inhibitors that cross the blood–brain barrier are used to manage this disease

by increasing ACh levels in the brain and slowing the progression of the disease.

- Side effects associated with the use of these drugs are related to stimulation of the parasympathetic nervous system (bradycardia, hypotension, increased GI secretions and activity, increased bladder tone, relaxation of GI and genitourinary sphincters, bronchoconstriction, pupil constriction) and may limit the usefulness of some of these drugs.
- Nerve gas is an irreversible acetylcholinesterase inhibitor that leads to toxic accumulations of ACh at cholinergic receptor sites and can cause parasympathetic crisis and muscle paralysis.
- Pralidoxime is an antidote for the irreversible acetylcholinesterase inhibitors, freeing the acetylcholinesterase that has been inhibited.

Bibliography

Andrews, M. & Boyle, J. (1999). *Transcultural concepts in nursing care.* Philadelphia: Lippincott Williams & Wilkins.

Bullock, B. L. (2000). *Focus on pathophysiology.* Philadelphia: Lippincott Williams & Wilkins.

Hardman, J. G., Limbird, L. E., Molinoff, P. B., Ruddon, R. W. and Gilman, A. G. (Eds.). (1996). *Goodman and Gilman's the pharmacological basis of therapeutics* (9th ed.). New York: McGraw-Hill.

Karch, A. M. (2000). *2000 Lippincott's nursing drug guide.* Philadelphia: Lippincott Williams & Wilkins.

McEvoy, B. R. (1999). *Facts and comparisons 1999.* St. Louis: Facts and Comparisons.

The medical letter on drugs and therapeutics (1999). New Rochelle, NY: Medical Letter.

Porth, C. M. (1998). *Pathophysiology: Concepts of altered health states* (5th ed). Philadelphia: Lippincott-Raven.

CHAPTER 31

Anticholinergic Agents

Anticholinergic agents/ parasympatholytics

- **P** atropine
- dicyclomine
- glycopyrrolate
- propantheline
- scopolamine

CHAPTER OUTLINE

KEY TERMS

anticholinergic
belladonna
cyclopegia
mydriasis
parasympatholytic

INTRODUCTION

Drugs that are used to block the effects of acetylcholine are called ***anticholinergic*** drugs. Because this action lyses, or blocks, the effects of the parasympathetic nervous system, they are also called ***parasympatholytic*** agents. This class of drugs was once very widely used to decrease gastrointestinal (GI) activity and secretions in the treatment of ulcers and to decrease other parasympathetic activities to allow the sympathetic system to become more dominant. Today, more specific and less systemically toxic drugs are available for many of the conditions that would benefit from these effects, so this class of drugs is less commonly used. Atropine remains the only widely used anticholinergic drug.

ANTICHOLINERGICS/ PARASYMPATHOLYTICS

Atropine (generic) has been used for many years and is derived from the plant ***belladonna.*** (Belladonna was once used by fashionable ladies of the European court to dilate the pupils in an effort to make them more innocent-looking and alluring.)

Both atropine and scopolamine (*Transderm-Scop* and generic) work by blocking only the muscarinic effectors in the parasympathetic nervous system and those few cholinergic receptors in the sympathetic nervous system (SNS), for example, those that control sweating. They act by competing with acetylcholine for the muscarinic acetylcholine receptor sites. They do not block the nicotinic receptors and so have little or no effect at the neuromuscular junction.

Atropine is available for parenteral, oral, and topical use to block parasympathetic effects in a variety of situations. Scopolamine is available in a transdermal form as well as oral and parenteral forms (Table 31-1). Dicyclomine (*Antispas, Dibent,* and others) is an oral drug used to relax the GI tract in the treatment of hyperactive or irritable bowel. Glycopyrrolate (*Robinul*), available in oral and parenteral forms, can be used orally as an adjunct in the treatment of ulcers, though it is not a drug of choice. It is widely used systemically to decrease secretions prior to anesthesia or intubation and to protect the patient from the peripheral effects of cholinergic drugs used to reverse neuromuscular blockade. Propantheline (*Probanthine*), an oral drug, was once widely used as an adjunct in the treatment of ulcers but now has been replaced, for the most part by the histamine 2 blockers.

Flavoxate (see Chapter 50), ipratropium (see Chapter 53), and methscopolamine (see Chapter 56) are anticholinergic drugs with very specific indications that are discussed in relation to the systems they affect.

THERAPEUTIC ACTIONS AND INDICATIONS

The anticholinergic drugs competitively block the acetylcholine receptors at the muscarinic cholinergic receptor sites that are responsible for mediating the effects of the parasympathetic postganglionic impulses (Figure 31-1). This means that atropine is used to depress salivation and bronchial secretions and dilate the bronchi, but can thicken respiratory secretions (causing obstruction of airways). Atropine also is used to inhibit vagal responses in the heart, relax the GI and genitourinary tracts, inhibit GI secretions, cause ***mydriasis*** or relaxation of the pupil of the eye (also called a mydriatic effect), and cause cycloplegia or inhibition of the ability of the lens in the eye to accommodate to near vision (also called a cycloplegic effect). They also are thought to block the effects of acetylcholine in the central nervous system (CNS).

Anticholinergic drugs can be used to decrease secretions prior to anesthesia; to treat parkinsonism; to restore cardiac rate and blood pressure following vagal stimulation during surgery; to relieve bradycardia caused by a hyperactive carotid sinus reflex; to relieve pylorospasm and hyperactive bowel, to relax biliary and ureteral colic; to relax bladder detrusor muscles and tighten sphincters, to help to con-

TABLE 31-1

AVAILABLE FORMS OF ANTICHOLINERGIC DRUGS

	Available Forms					
Drug	*Oral*	*IM*	*IV*	*SC*	*Transdermal Patch*	*Ophthalmic*
atropine	x	x	x	x	—	x
dicyclomine	x	x	—	—	—	—
glycopyrrolate	x	x	x	x	—	—
propantheline	x	—	—	—	—	—
scopolamine	—	x	x	x	x	x

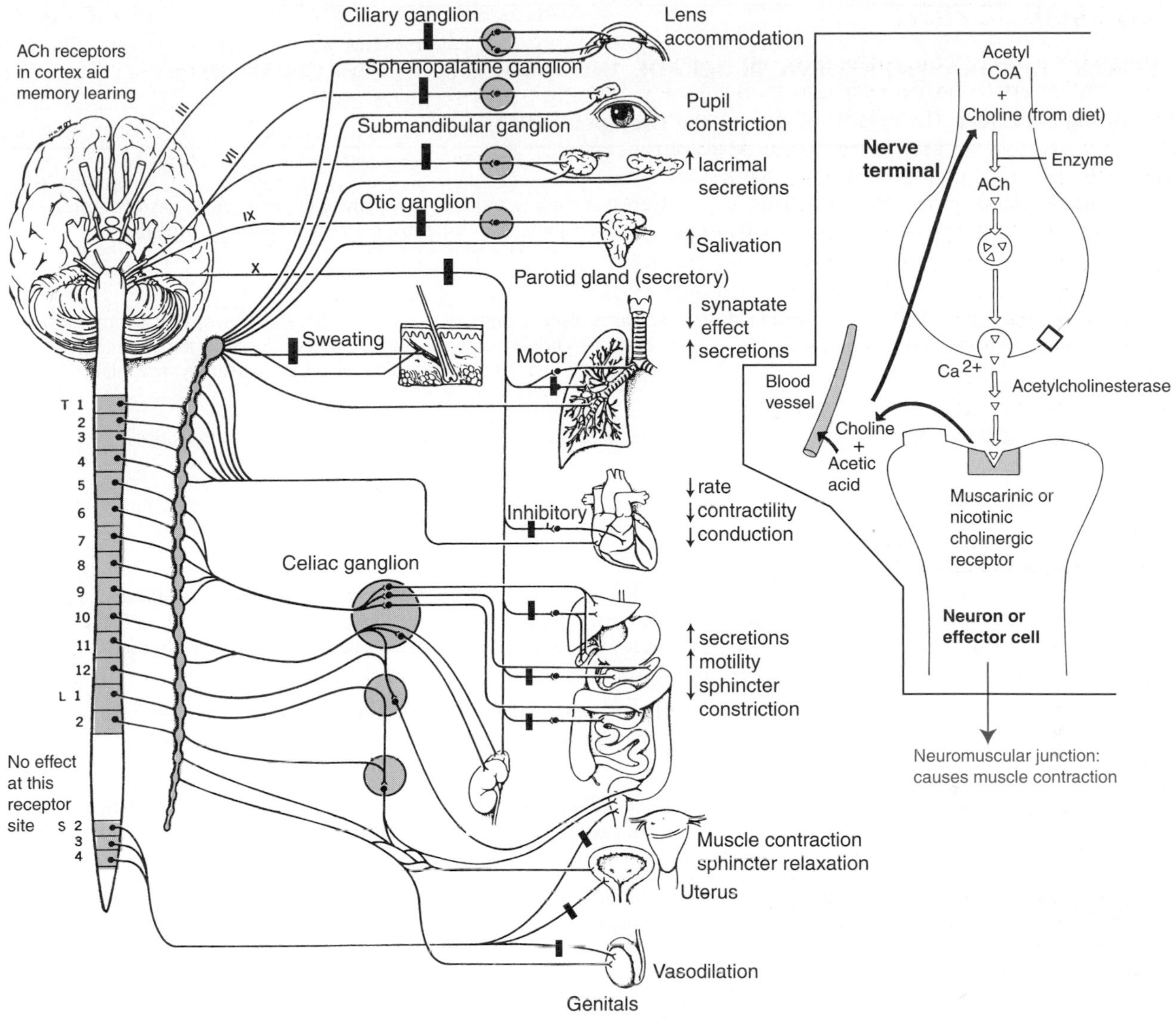

FIGURE 31-1. Site of action of anticholinergic drugs and associated physiologic response bar indicates a block of that activity.

trol crying or laughing episodes in patients with brain injuries; to relax uterine hypertonicity; to help in the management of peptic ulcer; to control rhinorrhea associated with hay fever; as an antidote for cholinergic drugs and for poisoning by certain mushrooms; and as an ophthalmic agent to cause mydriasis or cycloplegia in acute inflammatory conditions.

Scopolamine is also used to decrease the nausea and vomiting associated with motion sickness and has been used to induce obstetric amnesia and relax the mother. Other agents are used for specific indications as noted above and summarized in Table 31-2.

CONTRAINDICATIONS/CAUTIONS

Anticholinergics are contraindicated in the presence of known allergy to any of these drugs. They are also contraindicated with any condition that could be exacerbated by a blocking of the parasympathetic nervous system. These conditions include glaucoma (because of the possibility of increased pressure with pupil dilation); stenosing peptic ulcer, intestinal atony, paralytic ileus, GI obstruction, severe ulcerative colitis, and toxic megacolon (all of which could be intensified with a further slowing of GI activity); prostatic hypertrophy and bladder obstruction (which could be further compounded by a blocking of bladder muscle activity and a blocking of sphincter relaxation in the bladder); cardiac arrhythmias, tachycardia, and myocardial ischemia (which could be exacerbated by the increased sympathetic influence including tachycardia and increased contractility that occurs when the parasympathetic nervous system is blocked); impaired liver or kidney function

TABLE 31-2

EFFECTS OF PARASYMPATHETIC BLOCKADE AND ASSOCIATED THERAPEUTIC USES

Physiological Effect	Therapeutic Use
GI TRACT	
Smooth muscle: blocks spasm, blocks peristalsis Secretory glands: decreases acid and digestive enzyme production	Decreases motility and secretory activity in peptic ulcer, gastritis, cardiospasm, pylorospasm, enteritis, diarrhea, hypertonic constipation
URINARY TRACT	
Decreases tone and motility in the ureters and fundus of the bladder; increases tone in the bladder sphincter	Increases bladder capacity in children with enuresis, spastic paraplegics; decreases urinary urgency and frequency in cystitis; antispasmodic in renal colic and to counteract bladder spasm caused by morphine
BILIARY TRACT	
Relaxes smooth muscle, antispasmodic	Relief of biliary colic; counteracts spasms caused by narcotics
BRONCHIAL MUSCLE	
Weakly relaxes smooth muscle	Aerosol form may be used in asthma; may counteract bronchoconstriction caused by drugs
CARDIOVASCULAR SYSTEM	
Increases heart rate (may decrease heart rate at very low doses); causes local vasodilation and flushing	Counteracts bradycardia caused by vagal stimulation, carotid sinus syndrome, surgical procedures; used to overcome heart blocks following MI; used to counteract hypotension caused by cholinergic drugs.
OCULAR EFFECTS	
Pupil dilation, cyclopegia	Allows ophthalmological examination of the retina, optic disk; relaxes ocular muscles and decreases irritation in iridocyclitis, choroiditis
SECRETIONS	
Reduces sweating, salivation, respiratory tract secretions	Preoperatively before inhalation anesthesia; reduces nasal secretions in rhinitis, hay fever; may be used to reduce excessive sweating in hyperhidrosis
CNS	
Decreases extrapyramidal motor activity Atropine may cause excessive stimulation, psychosis, delirium, disorientation Scopolamine causes depression, drowsiness	Decreases tremor in parkinsonism; helps to prevent motion sickness; scopolamine may be in OTC sleep aids

(which could alter the metabolism and excretion of the drug); and myasthenia gravis (which could worsen with further blocking of the cholinergic receptors; low doses of atropine are sometimes used in myasthenia gravis to block unwanted GI and cardiovascular effects of the cholinergic drugs used to treat that condition).

Caution should be used in the presence of lactation, because of possible suppression of lactation; hypertension, because of the possibility of additive hypertensive effects from the sympathetic system's dominance with parasympathetic nervous system blocking; and spasticity and brain damage, which could be exacerbated by cholinergic blockade within the CNS.

ADVERSE EFFECTS

The adverse effects associated with the use of anticholinergic drugs are caused by the systemic blockade of cholinergic receptors. Adverse effects in some cases may be the desired therapeutic effects in others. The intensity of adverse effects is related to drug dosage: The more of the drug in the system, the greater the systemic effects. These adverse effects could include the CNS effects of blurred vision, pupil dilation and resultant photophobia, cycloplegia, and increased

CULTURAL CONSIDERATIONS ••••

Mydriatric Effects

Nurses working in eye clinics or doing preoperative medications for eye surgery should be aware that mydriatics (including atropine) are much less effective in African Americans than in the general population. Increased dosage may be needed, and there may be a prolonged time to peak effect. This effect, though somewhat less pronounced, is seen in any individual with dark-pigmented eyes.

intraocular pressure. These effects are all related to the blocking of the parasympathetic effects in the eye. Weakness, dizziness, insomnia, mental confusion, and excitement are effects related to the blocking of the cholinergic receptors within the CNS. Dry mouth results from the blocking of GI secretions. Altered taste perception, nausea, heartburn, constipation, bloated feelings, and paralytic ileus are related to a slowing of GI activity. Tachycardia and palpitations are possible effects related to blocking of the parasympathetic effects on the heart. Urinary hesitancy and retention are related to the blocking of bladder muscle activity and relaxation of the sphincter. Decreased sweating and an increased predisposition to heat prostration are related to the inability to cool the body by sweating, a result of the blocking of the sympathetic cholinergic receptors responsible for sweating. Suppression of lactation is related to anticholinergic effects in the breasts and in the CNS (see Table 31-2).

CLINICALLY IMPORTANT DRUG–DRUG INTERACTIONS

There is an increased incidence of anticholinergic effects if these drugs are combined with any other drugs with anticholinergic activity, including antihistamines, antiparkinson drugs, MAO inhibitors, and tricyclic antidepressants (TCAs). If such combinations must be used, the patient should be monitored closely and dosage adjustments made. Patients should be advised to avoid over-the-counter drugs that might contain these products. There is a decreased effectiveness of phenothiazines if combined with anticholinergic drugs, and there is an increased risk of paralytic ileus. This combination should be avoided.

NURSING CHALLENGE

Atropine Toxicity

Atropine is used in a large variety of clinical settings to:

- Decrease secretions, as a preoperative agent
- Treat parkinsonism (relieves tremor and rigidity)
- Restore cardiac rate and arterial pressure during general anesthesia when increased vagal stimulation causes a rapid parasympathetic response
- Relieve bradycardia and syncope with hyperreactive carotid sinus
- Relieve pylorospasm and hypertonic intestine
- Relax the spasm of biliary and ureteral colic and bronchospasm
- Relax the urinary bladder
- Control crying and laughing episodes in patients with brain lesions
- Treat closed head injuries that cause acetylcholine release
- Relax uterine hypertonicity
- Manage peptic ulcer
- Control rhinorrhea or acute rhinitis from hay fever
- Induce mydriasis for ophthalmic procedures

It also is used as an antidote to overdose with cholinergic drugs or cholinesterase inhibitors and as an antidote to poisoning with certain mushrooms.

Atropine can be a poison, causing severe toxicity. Because it is found in many natural products, including the belladonna plant, and may be in herbal or alternative therapy products, atropine toxicity can occur inadvertently. Atropine toxicity should be considered whenever a patient receiving an anticholinergic drug presents with a sudden onset of bizarre mental and neurological symptoms. Toxicity is dose related and usually progresses as follows:

0.5 mg atropine—slight cardiac slowing, dryness of mouth, inhibition of sweating
1.0 mg atropine—definite mouth and throat dryness, thirst, rapid heart rate, pupil dilation
2.0 mg atropine—rapid heart rate, palpitations; marked mouth dryness; dilated pupils; some blurring of vision
5.0 mg atropine—all of the above and marked speech disturbances; difficulty swallowing; restlessness, fatigue, headache; dry and hot skin; difficulty voiding; reduced intestinal peristalsis
10.0 mg atropine—all of the above symptoms, more marked; pulse rapid and weak; iris nearly gone; vision blurred; skin flushed, hot, dry, and scarlet; ataxia; restlessness and excitement; hallucinations; delirium and coma

Treatment: If the poison was taken orally, immediate gastric lavage should be done to limit absorption. Physostigmine can be used as an antidote. A slow IV injection of 0.5 to 4 mg (depending on the size of the patient and the severity of the symptoms) usually reverses the delirium and coma of atropine toxicity. Physostigmine is metabolized rapidly, so the injection may need to be repeated every 1 to 2 hours until the atropine has been cleared from the system. Diazepam is the drug of choice if an anticonvulsant is needed. Cool baths and alcohol sponging may relieve the fever and hot skin. In extreme cases, respiratory support may be needed. It is important to remember that the half-life of atropine is 2.5 hours; at extremely high doses, several hours may be needed to clear the atropine from the body.

CASE STUDY

Anticholinergic Drugs and Heart Disease

PRESENTATION

E. K., a 64-year-old woman with a long history of heart disease, has suffered from repeated bouts of cystitis. With this infection, her course was marked by severe pain, frequency, urgency, and even nocturnal enuresis. She was treated with an antibiotic deemed appropriate after a culture and sensitivity tests were done on her urine and was given atropine to relax the bladder spasm and alleviate some of the unpleasant side effects that she was experiencing. Within the next few days, she plans to travel south for the winter and wants any information that she should have before she goes.

CRITICAL THINKING QUESTIONS

E. K. presents many nursing care problems. What are the implications of giving an anticholinergic drug to a person with a long history of heart disease? Repeated bouts of cystitis are not normal; what potential problems should be addressed in this area? E. K. is about to leave for her winter home in the south; what teaching plans will be essential for her if she is taking atropine when she leaves? What are the medical problems that can arise with people who live in different areas at different times of the year? Considering her age, what written information should E. K. take with her as she travels?

DISCUSSION

E. K. is doing well with her cardiac problems at the moment, but could develop problems as a result of the anticholinergic drug that has been prescribed. The anticipated adverse effect of tachycardia could tip the balance in a compensated heart, leading to CHF or oxygen delivery problems. She will need to be carefully evaluated for the status of her heart disease and potential for problems.

E. K. should be further evaluated for the cause of her repeated bouts with cystitis. Does she have a structural problem, a dietary problem, or a simple hygiene problem? She should receive instruction on ways to avoid bladder infections, such as wiping only from front to back, voiding after sexual intercourse, avoiding baths, avoiding citrus juices and other alkaline ash foods that decrease the acidity of the urine and promote bacterial growth, and pushing fluids as much as possible.

E. K. also should be evaluated to establish a baseline for vision, reflexes, the possibility of glaucoma, GI problems, and so on. She should receive thorough teaching about her atropine, especially adverse effects to anticipate, safety measures to take if vision changes occur, and a bowel program that she can follow to avoid constipation.

Since E. K. is leaving a cold climate and traveling to a warm climate, she will need to be warned that atropine decreases sweating. This means she may be susceptible to heat stroke in the warmer climate. She should be encouraged to take precautions to avoid these problems.

It will be difficult to follow E. K. while she is away. It should be anticipated that patients such as E. K. might have two sets of health care providers who may not communicate with each other. It is important to give E. K. written information about her current diagnosis, including test results; details about her drugs, including dosages; information about the adverse effects she may experience and ways to deal with them; and ways to avoid cystitis in the future. It may be useful to include a phone number that E. K. can use or give to her southern health care provider to use if further tests or follow-up is indicated.

DATA LINK

Data link to the following anticholinergic agents in your nursing drug guide:

ANTICHOLINERGIC AGENTS

Name	Brand Name(s)	Usual Indications
P atropine	generic	Decrease secretions, bradycardia, pylorospasm, ureteral colic, relaxing of bladder, emotional lability with head injuries, antidote for cholinergic drugs, pupil dilation
dicyclomine	*Antispas, Dibent*	Irritable or hyperactive bowel
glycopyrrolate	*Robinul*	Decrease secretions, antidote for neuromuscular blockers
propantheline	*ProBanthine*	Adjunctive therapy for ulcers
scopolamine	*Transderm Scop*	Motion sickness, decrease secretions, obstetric amnesia, relief of urinary problems, adjunctive for ulcers, pupil dilation

NURSING CONSIDERATIONS for patients receiving anticholinergic agents

Assessment

HISTORY. Screen for the following: any known allergies to these drugs; glaucoma; stenosing peptic ulcer, intestinal atony, paralytic ileus, GI obstruction, severe ulcerative colitis, and toxic megacolon; prostatic hypertrophy and bladder obstruction; cardiac ar-

PATIENT TEACHING CHECKLIST

Anticholinergic Agents

Create customized patient teaching materials for a specific anticholinergic agent from your CD-ROM. Your patient teaching should stress the following points for drugs within this class: Parasympathetic blockers, parasympatholytics, or anticholinergics block or stop the actions of a group of nerves that are part of the parasympathetic nervous system. These drugs may decrease the activity of your GI tract, dilate your pupils, or speed up your heart.

Some of the following adverse effects may occur:

- Dry mouth, difficulty swallowing. Frequent mouth care will help to remove dried secretions and keep the mouth fresh. Sucking on sugarless candies will help to keep the mouth moist. Taking lots of fluids with meals (unless you are on a fluid restriction) will help swallowing.
- Blurring vision, sensitivity to light. If your vision is blurred, avoid driving, operating hazardous machinery, or doing close work that requires attention to details until your vision returns to normal. Dark glasses will help protect your eyes from the light.
- Retention of urine. Take the drug just after you have emptied your bladder. Moderate your fluid intake while the drug's effects are the highest; if possible, take the drug before bed when this effect will not be a problem.
- Constipation. Include fluid and roughage in your diet, and follow any bowel regimen that you may have. Monitor your bowel movements so that appropriate laxatives can be taken if necessary.
- Flushing, intolerance to heat, decreased sweating. This drug blocks sweating, which is your body's way of cooling off. This places you at increased risk of developing heat stroke. Avoid extremes of temperature, dress coolly on very warm days, and avoid exercise as much as possible.

Report any of the following to your health care provider: eye pain, skin rash, fever, rapid heart beat, chest pain, difficulty breathing, agitation or mood changes, impotence (a dosage adjustment may help alleviate this problem).

Avoid the use of over-the-counter medications, especially for sleep and nasal congestion; avoid antihistamines, diet pills, cold capsules. These drugs may contain similar drugs which could cause a severe reaction. Consult with your health care provider if you feel that you need medication for symptomatic relief.

Tell any doctor, nurse, or other health care provider that you are taking these drugs.

Keep this drug, and all medications, out of the reach of children. Do not share these drugs with other people.

This Teaching Checklist reflects general patient teaching guidelines. It is not meant to be a substitute for drug-specific teaching information, which is available in nursing drug guides.

rhythmias, tachycardia, and myocardial ischemia, all of which could be exacerbated by parasympathetic blockade; impaired liver or kidney function which could alter the metabolism and excretion of the drug; myasthenia gravis, which could become much worse with further blocking of the cholinergic receptors; lactation, because of possible suppression of lactation; hypertension; and spasticity and brain damage, which require cautious use of these drugs.

PHYSICAL ASSESSMENT. Include screening for baseline status before beginning therapy and for any potential adverse effects: skin color, lesions, temperature; affect, orientation, reflexes, pupil response; pulse, blood pressure, ECG; respiration, adventitious sounds; urine output, bladder tone; and bowel sounds and abdominal exam.

Nursing Diagnoses

The patient receiving anticholinergic drugs may have the following nursing diagnoses related to drug therapy:

- Pain related to GI, CNS, genitourinary, cardiovascular effects
- Alteration in cardiac output related to cardiovascular effects
- Alteration in bowel elimination, constipation, related to GI effects
- Noncompliance related to adverse drug effects
- Knowledge deficit regarding drug therapy

Implementation

- Ensure proper administration of the drug *to assure effective use and decrease the risk of adverse effects.*

NURSING CARE GUIDE
Anticholinergic Agents

Assessment	Nursing Diagnoses	Implementation	Evaluation
HISTORY Allergies to any of these drugs, COPD, narrow-angle glaucoma, myasthenia gravis, bowel or urinary obstruction, pregnancy and lactation, tachycardia, prostatic hypertrophy, recent GI or urinary surgery	Alteration in cardiac output related to CV effects Pain related to GI, GU, CNS, CV effects Alteration in bowel elimination, constipation related to GI effects Knowledge deficit regarding drug therapy Potential for noncompliance related to adverse effects	Ensure safe and appropriate administration of drug. Provide comfort, safety measures: assistance/siderails; temperature control; dark glasses; small, frequent meals; artificial saliva, fluids; sugarless lozenges, mouth care; bowel program. Provide support and reassurance to deal with drug effects, discomfort, and GI effects. Provide patient teaching regarding drug name, dosage, adverse effects, precautions, and warnings to report.	Evaluate drug effects: pupil dilation, decrease in signs and symptoms being treated. Monitor for adverse effects: CV effects—tachycardia, CHF; CNS—confusion, dreams; urinary retention; GI effects—constipation; visual blurring, photophobia. Monitor for drug–drug interactions as indicated for each drug. Evaluate effectiveness of patient teaching program. Evaluate effectiveness of comfort and safety measures.
PHYSICAL EXAMINATION CV: BP, P, peripheral perfusion, ECG CNS: orientation, affect, reflexes, vision Skin: color, lesions, texture, sweating GU: urinary output, bladder tone GI: abdominal exam Resp: R, adventitious sounds			

- Ensure adequate hydration and temperature control *to prevent hyperpyrexia.*
- Provide comfort measures *to help the patient tolerate drug effects:* sugarless lozenges to suck and frequent mouth care for dry mouth, lighting control to alleviate photophobia, small and frequent meals to alleviate GI discomfort, bowel program to alleviate constipation, safety precautions if CNS effects are severe, analgesics if headaches occur, voiding before taking medication if urinary retention is a problem (commonly occurs with benign prostatic hypertrophy [BPH]).
- Monitor patient response closely (blood pressure, ECG, urine output, cardiac output) *in order to arrange to adjust dosage accordingly to ensure benefit with least amount of toxicity.*
- Provide thorough patient teaching including measures to avoid adverse effects, warning signs of problems, and the need for monitoring and evaluation *to enhance patient knowledge about drug therapy and to promote compliance* (see Patient Teaching Checklist: Anticholinergic Agents).
- Offer support and encouragement *to deal with the drug regimen.*

Evaluation

- Monitor patient response to the drug (improvement in disorder being treated).
- Monitor for adverse effects (cardiovascular changes, GI problems, CNS effects, urinary hesitancy and re-

tention, pupil dilation and photophobia, decrease in sweating and heat intolerance).

• Evaluate the effectiveness of the teaching plan (patient can name drug, dosage, adverse effects to watch for, specific measures to avoid adverse effects, proper administration of ophthalmic drugs).

• Monitor the effectiveness of comfort measures and compliance to the regimen (see Nursing Care Guide: Anticholinergic Agents).

WWW.WEB LINKS

Health care providers and patients may want to consult the following Internet sources:

Information on atropine and related anticholinergics:
http://www.infoplease.com/ce5/CE003568.html

Information on atropine research, pharmacokinetics, pharmacodynamics:
http://www.vgernet.net/bkand/state/atrop.html

CHAPTER SUMMARY

- Anticholinergic drugs are drugs that block the effects of acetylcholine at cholinergic receptor sites.
- Anticholinergic drugs are also called parasympatholytic drugs because they block the effects of the parasympathetic nervous system.
- Blocking the parasympathetic system causes increase in heart rate, decrease in GI activity, decrease in urinary bladder tone and function, and pupil dilation and cycloplegia.
- These drugs also block cholinergic receptors in the CNS and sympathetic postganglionic cholinergic receptors, including those that cause sweating.
- There are many systemic adverse effects associated with the use of anticholinergic drugs, caused by the systemic cholinergic blocking effects that can also produce the desired therapeutic effect.
- Atropine is the most commonly used anticholinergic drug. It is indicated for a wide variety of conditions and is available in oral, parenteral, and topical forms.
- Patients receiving anticholinergic drugs must be monitored for dry mouth, difficulty swallowing, constipation, urinary retention, tachycardia, pupil dilation and photophobia, cycloplegia and blurring of vision, and heat intolerance caused by a decrease in sweating.

BIBLIOGRAPHY

Andrews, M. & Boyle, J. (1999). *Transcultural concepts in nursing care.* Philadelphia: Lippincott Williams & Wilkins.

Bullock, B. L. (2000). *Focus on pathophysiology.* Philadelphia: Lippincott Williams & Wilkins.

Hardman, J. G., Limbird, L. E., Molinoff, P. B., Ruddon, R. W., & Gilman, A. G. (Eds). (1996). *Goodman and Gilman's the pharmacological basis of therapeutics* (9th ed). New York: McGraw-Hill.

Karch, A. M. (2000). *2000 Lippincott's nursing drug guide.* Philadelphia: Lippincott Williams & Wilkins.

McEvoy, B. R. (1999). *Facts and comparisons 1999.* St. Louis: Facts and Comparisons.

The medical letter on drugs and therapeutics. (1999). New Rochelle, NY: Medical Letter.

Porth, C. M. (1998). *Pathophysiology: Concepts of altered health states* (5th ed.). Philadelphia: Lippincott-Raven.

PART

6

Drugs Acting on the Endocrine System

CHAPTER 32

Introduction to the Endocrine System

CHAPTER OUTLINE

KEY TERMS

anterior pituitary
diurnal rhythm
hormones
hypothalamic–pituitary axis
hypothalamus
negative feedback system
neuroendocrine system
pituitary gland
posterior pituitary
releasing hormones or factors

INTRODUCTION

The nervous system and the endocrine system work together to maintain internal homeostasis and to integrate the body's response to the external environment. Their activities and functions are so closely related that it is probably more correct to refer to them as the ***neuroendocrine system.*** However, this section deals with drugs affecting the traditional endocrine system, which includes glands that secrete ***hormones,*** or chemical messengers, directly into the blood stream to communicate within the body.

It is important to note that certain hormones that influence body functioning are not secreted by endocrine glands. For example, tissue hormones such as the prostaglandins are produced in various tissues and have effects at their local site. Neurotransmitters such as norepinephrine and dopamine also can be classified as hormones because they are secreted directly into the blood stream for dispersion throughout the body. There also are many gastrointestinal (GI) hormones that are produced in GI cells and that act locally to produce effects. All of these hormones are addressed in the sections most related to their effects.*

HORMONES

Hormones are chemicals that are produced in the body and that meet specific criteria. The following are characteristic of all hormones:

- They are produced in very small amounts.
- They are secreted directly into the bloodstream.
- They travel through the blood to specific receptor sites throughout the body.
- They act to increase or decrease the normal metabolic processes of cells when they react with their specific receptor sites.
- They are immediately broken down.

Hormones may react with specific receptor sites on a cell membrane to stimulate the nucleotide cyclic adenosine monophosphate (cAMP) within the cell to cause an effect. For example, when insulin reacts with an insulin receptor site, it activates intracellular enzymes that cause many effects, including changing the cell membrane's permeability to glucose. Hormones such as insulin that do not enter the cell act very quickly, often within seconds, to produce an effect.

Other hormones, such as estrogen, actually enter the cell and react with a receptor site inside the cell to change messenger RNA and affect the cell's function. These hormones take quite a while to produce an effect. The full effects of estrogen may not be seen for months to years as evidenced by the changes that occur at puberty. Because the neuroendocrine system tightly regulates the body's processes within a narrow range of normal limits, overproduction or underproduction of any hormone can affect the body's activities and other hormones within the system.

THE HYPOTHALAMUS

The ***hypothalamus*** is the coordinating center for the nervous and endocrine responses to internal and external stimuli. The hypothalamus constantly monitors the body's homeostasis by analyzing input from the periphery and the central nervous system (CNS) and coordinating responses through the autonomic, endocrine, and nervous systems. In effect, it is the "master gland" of the neuroendocrine system. This title was once given to the pituitary gland because of its many functions (see below).

Situated at the base of the forebrain, the hypothalamus receives input from virtually all other areas of the brain, including the limbic system and the cerebral cortex. Because of its positioning, the hypothalamus is able to influence, and be influenced by, emotions and thoughts. The hypothalamus is located in an area of the brain that is poorly protected by the blood–brain barrier, so it is able to act as a sensor to various electrolytes, chemicals, and hormones that are in circulation and do not affect other areas of the brain. The hypothalamus has various neurocenters, areas specifically sensitive to certain stimuli, that regulate a number of body functions, including body temperature, thirst, hunger, water retention, sleep and waking, blood pressure, respiration, reproduction, and emotional reactions.

The hypothalamus maintains internal homeostasis by sensing blood chemistries and by stimulating or suppressing endocrine, autonomic, and CNS activity. In essence, it can turn the autonomic nervous system and its effects on or off. The hypothalamus also produces and secretes a number of ***releasing hormones or factors*** that stimulate the pituitary gland to stimulate or inhibit various endocrine glands throughout

* Gastrointestinal hormones are discussed in Part 11: Drugs Acting on the Gastrointestinal System. Neurotransmitters acting like hormones are discussed in Chapter 27: Introduction to the Autonomic Nervous System. The reproductive hormones are discussed in Chapter 37: Introduction to the Reproductive System. Hormones active in the inflammatory and immune responses are discussed in Part 3: Drugs Acting on the Immune System. Specific traditional endocrine glands and hormones are discussed in Chapter 33 (hypothalamic and pituitary hormones), Chapter 34 (adrenocortical hormones), Chapter 35 (thyroid and parathyroid hormones), and Chapter 36 (pancreatic hormones).

the body (Figure 32-1). These releasing hormones include growth hormone–releasing hormone (GHRH), thyrotropin-releasing hormone (TRH), gonadotropin-releasing hormone (GnRH), corticotropin-releasing hormone (CRH), and prolactin releasing hormone (PRH). The hypothalamus also produces two inhibiting factors that act as regulators to shut off the production of hormones when levels become too high; these releasing factors are growth hormone release inhibiting factor (somatostatin) and prolactin inhibiting factor (PIF) (Table 32-1).

Recent research has indicated that PIF may actually be dopamine, a neurotransmitter. Patients who are on dopamine-blocking drugs often develop galactorrhea (inappropriate milk production) and breast engorgement, theoretically because PIF also is blocked. Research is ongoing about the actual chemical structure of several of the releasing factors.

The hypothalamus produces two other hormones, antidiuretic hormone (ADH) and oxytocin, that are stored in the posterior pituitary to be released when stimulated by the hypothalamus. The hypothalamus is connected to the pituitary gland by two networks: a vascular network carries the hypothalamic-releasing factors directly into the anterior pituitary, and a neurological network delivers ADH and oxytocin to the posterior pituitary to be stored.

THE PITUITARY

The ***pituitary gland*** is located in the bony sella turcica under a layer of dura mater. It is divided into three lobes: an anterior lobe, a posterior lobe, and an intermediate lobe. Traditionally, the anterior pituitary was known as the body's master gland

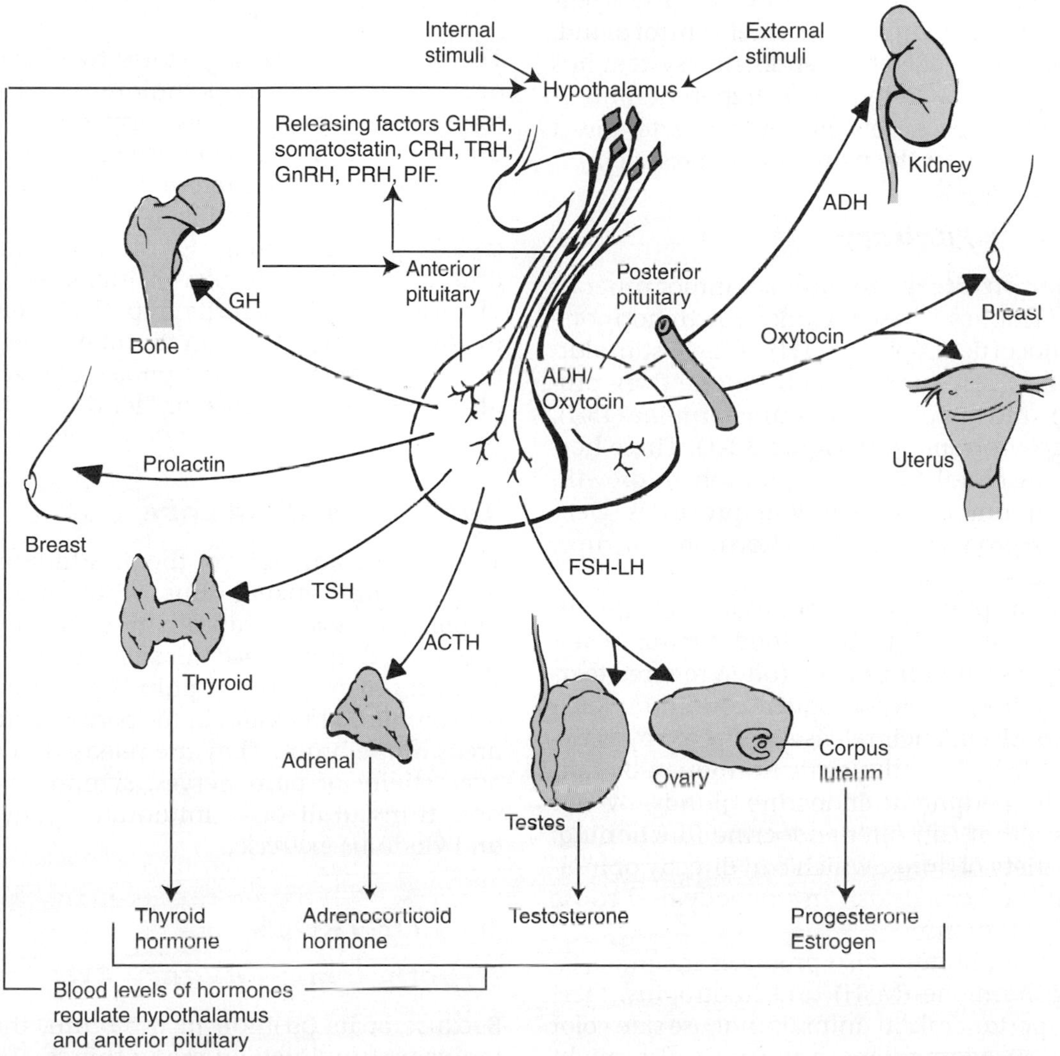

FIGURE 32-1. The traditional endocrine system.

TABLE 32-1

HYPOTHALAMIC RELEASING AND INHIBITING HORMONES AND ASSOCIATED ANTERIOR PITUITARY AND ENDOCRINE GLAND RESPONSE

Hypothalamus Hormones	Anterior Pituitary Hormones	Target Organ Response
STIMULATING HORMONES		
CRH (corticotropin-releasing hormone)	ACTH (adrenocorticotropic hormone)	Adrenal corticosteroid hormones
TRH (thyroid-releasing hormone)	TSH (thyroid-stimulating hormone)	Thyroid hormone
GHRH (growth hormone–releasing hormone)	GH (growth hormone)	Cell growth
GnRH (gonadotropin-releasing hormone)	LH and FSH (leutinizing hormone, follicle-stimulating hormone)	Estrogen and progesterone (females) Testosterone (males)
PRH (prolactin-releasing hormone)	Prolactin	Milk production
INHIBITING HORMONES		
Somatostatin (growth hormone–inhibiting factor)		Stops release of GH
PIF (prolactin inhibiting factors)		Stops release of prolactin

because it has so many important functions and, through feedback mechanisms, regulates the function of many other endocrine glands. Also, its unique and protected position in the brain led early scientists to believe that it must be the chief control gland. However, as knowledge of the endocrine system has grown, scientists now designate the hypothalamus as the master gland because it has even greater direct regulatory effects over the neuroendocrine system.

The Anterior Pituitary

The ***anterior pituitary*** produces six major anterior pituitary hormones. These include growth hormone (GH), adrenocorticotropin (ACTH), follicle-stimulating hormone (FSH), luteinizing hormone (LH), prolactin (PRL), and thyroid-stimulating hormone (TSH), also called thyrotropin (see Figure 32-1). These hormones are essential for the regulation of growth, reproduction, and some metabolic processes. Deficiency or overproduction of these hormones disrupts this regulation.

The anterior pituitary hormones are released in a rhythmic manner into the blood stream. Their secretion varies with time of day (often referred to as ***diurnal rhythm***) or physiological conditions such as exercise or sleep. Their release is affected by activity in the CNS; by hypothalamic hormones; by hormones of the peripheral endocrine glands; by certain diseases that can alter endocrine functioning; and by a variety of drugs, which can directly or indirectly upset the homeostasis in the body and cause an endocrine response.

The anterior pituitary also produces melanocyte-stimulating hormone (MSH) and lipotropins. MSH plays an important role in animals that use skin color changes as an adaptive mechanism. It also might be important for nerve growth and development in humans. Lipotropins stimulate fat mobilization but have not been clearly isolated in humans.

The Posterior Pituitary

The ***posterior pituitary*** stores two hormones that are produced by the hypothalamus and deposited in the posterior lobe via the nerve axons where they are produced. These two hormones are antidiuretic hormone (ADH), also referred to as vasopressin, and oxytocin. ADH is directly released in response to increased plasma osmolarity or decreased blood volume, which often results in increased osmolarity. The osmoreceptors in the hypothalamus stimulate the ADH release. Oxytocin stimulates uterine smooth muscle contraction in late phases of pregnancy and also causes milk release or "let down" in lactating women.

The Intermediate Lobe

The intermediate lobe of the pituitary produces endorphins and enkephalins, which are released in response to severe pain or stress and which occupy specific endorphin-receptor sites in the brain stem to block the perception of pain. These hormones are also produced in tissues in the periphery and in other areas of the brain. They are released in response to overactivity of pain nerves, sympathetic stimulation, transcutaneous stimulation, guided imagery, and vigorous exercise.

CONTROLS

Hypothalamic–Pituitary Axis

Because of its position in the brain, the hypothalamus is stimulated by many things, such as light, emotion, cerebral cortex activity, and a variety of chemical and hormonal stimuli. Together, the hypothalamus and the pituitary function closely to maintain endocrine activity along what is called the ***hypothalamic–pituitary axis*** (HPA). This axis functions using a series of ***negative feedback systems.***

Here is how a negative feedback system works. When the hypothalamus senses a need for a particular hormone, say thyroid hormone, it secretes a releasing factor (thyrotropin-releasing hormone, or TRH) directly into the anterior pituitary. In response to the TRH, the anterior pituitary secretes thyroid-stimulating hormone (TSH), which in turn stimulates the thyroid gland to produce thyroid hormone. When the hypothalamus senses the rising levels of thyroid hormone, it stops secreting TRH, resulting in decreased TSH production and subsequent reduced thyroid hormone levels. The hypothalamus, sensing the falling thyroid hormone levels, secretes TRH again. The negative feedback system continues in this fashion, maintaining the levels of thyroid hormone within a relatively narrow range of normal (Figure 32-2).

It is thought that this feedback system is more complex than once believed. The hypothalamus probably also senses TRH and TSH levels and regulates TRH secretion within a narrow range, even if thyroid hormone is not produced. The anterior pituitary may also be sensitive to TSH levels and thyroid hormone, regulating its own production of TSH. This complex system provides back-up controls and regulation if any part of the hypothalamic–pituitary axis fails. This system also can create complications, especially when there is a need to override or interact with the total system, as is the case with replacement therapy or treatment of endocrine disorders.

Two of the traditional anterior pituitary hormones, growth hormone and prolactin, do not have a target organ and so cannot be regulated by the same feedback mechanism. Growth hormone release and prolactin release are directly inhibited by the hypothalamic inhibiting factors somatostatin and PIF, respectively. The hypothalamus may be stimulated to release inhibiting factors by increased circulating levels of the hormone or by some mediating factor that is stimulated by these hormones. The hypothalamic–pituitary axis functions constantly to keep these particular hormones regulated.

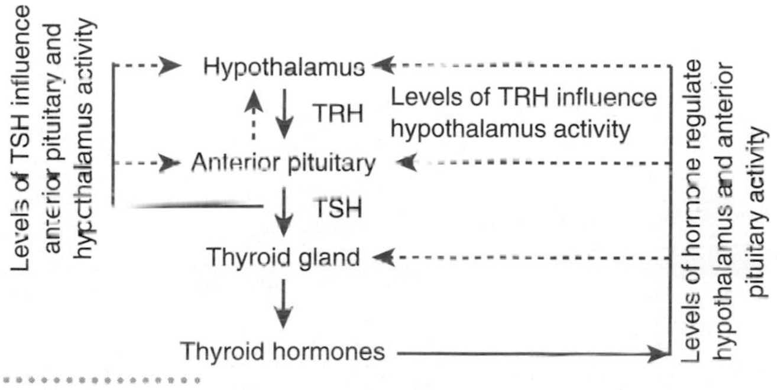

FIGURE 32-2. Negative feedback system. Regulation of thyroid hormone levels is done by a series of negative feedback systems influencing TRH, TSH, and thyroid hormone levels.

Other Controls

Other hormones are released in response to stimuli other than stimulating hormones. For example, the endocrine pancreas produces and releases insulin, glucagon, and somatostatin from various cells in response to varying blood glucose levels. The parathyroid glands release parathormone in response to local calcium levels. The juxtaglomerular cells in the kidney release erythropoietin and renin in response to decreased pressure or decreased oxygenation of the blood flowing into the glomerulus. GI hormones are released in response to local stimuli in the area, such as acid, proteins, or calcium. The thyroid gland produces and secretes another hormone called calcitonin in direct response to serum calcium levels. Many different prostaglandins are released throughout the body in response to local stimuli in the tissues that produce them. Activation of the sympathetic nervous system directly causes release of ACTH and the adrenocorticoid hormones to prepare the body for fight or flight. Aldosterone, an adrenocorticoid hormone, is released in response to ACTH, but also is released directly in response to high potassium levels.

As more is learned about the interactions of the nervous and endocrine systems, new ideas will be formed about how the body controls its intricate homeostasis. When administering any drug that affects the endocrine or nervous systems, it is important for the nurse to remember how closely related all of these activities are. Expected or unexpected adverse effects involving areas of the endocrine and nervous systems often occur.

WWW.WEB LINKS

Students may want to explore up-to-date information from the following sources:

Travel through the virtual endocrine system:

http://www.letsfindout.com/subjects/body

http://www.innerbody.com/image/endoov.html

CHAPTER SUMMARY

- The endocrine system is a regulatory system that communicates through the use of hormones.

- Because the endocrine and nervous systems are tightly intertwined in the regulation of body homeostasis, they are often referred to as the neuroendocrine system.
- A hormone is a chemical that is produced within the body, is needed in only small amounts, travels to specific receptor sites to cause an increase or decrease in cellular activity, and is broken down immediately.
- The hypothalamus is the "master gland" of the neuroendocrine system. It helps regulate the central and autonomic nervous systems and the endocrine system to maintain homeostasis.
- The pituitary is made up of three lobes: anterior, posterior, and intermediate. The anterior lobe produces stimulating hormones in response to hypothalamic stimulation. The posterior lobe stores two hormones produced by the hypothalamus, ADH and oxytocin. The intermediate lobe produces endorphins and enkephalins to modulate pain perception.
- The hypothalamus and pituitary operate by a series of negative feedback mechanisms called the hypothalamic–pituitary axis (HPA). The hypothalamus secretes releasing factors to cause the anterior pituitary to release stimulating hormones, which act with specific endocrine glands to cause the release of hormones or, in the case of growth hormone and prolactin, to stimulate cells directly. This stimulation shuts down the production of releasing factors, which leads to decreased stimulating factors and subsequently decreased hormone release.
- Growth hormone and prolactin are released by the anterior pituitary and directly influence cell activity. These hormones are regulated by the release of hypothalamic inhibiting factors in response to hormone levels or a cellular mediator.
- Some hormones are not influenced by the HPA and are released in response to direct, local stimulation.
- When any drug that affects either the endocrine or the nervous system is given, adverse effects may occur throughout both systems because they are closely interrelated.

BIBLIOGRAPHY

Bullock, B. L. (2000). *Focus on pathophysiology.* Philadelphia: Lippincott Williams & Wilkins.

Girard, J. (1991). *Endocrinology of puberty.* Farmington, CT: Karger Publishers.

Guyton, A. & Hall, J. (1996). *Textbook of medical physiology.* Philadelphia: W. B. Saunders.

Joseph, R. (1996). *Neuropsychiatry, neuropsychology and clinical neurosciences* (2nd ed.). Philadelphia: Williams & Wilkins.

Karch, A. M. (2000). *2000 Lippincott's nursing drug guide.* Philadelphia: Lippincott Williams & Wilkins.

North, W. G. et al. (1993). The neurohypophysis: A window on brain function. *Annals of the New York Academy of Sciences,* 689.

Porth, C. (1998). *Pathophysiology: Concepts of altered health states* (5th ed.). Philadelphia: Lippincott-Raven.

CHAPTER 33

Hypothalamic and Pituitary Agents

Hypothalamic releasing hormones
- corticotropin releasing hormone
- gonadorelin
- goserelin
- histrelin
- **P** leuprolide
- nafarelin
- protirelin
- sermorelin

Anterior pituitary stimulating hormones
- chorionic gonadotropin
- **P** corticotropin
- cosyntropin
- menotropins
- somatropin
- somatrem
- thyrotropin

Growth hormone antagonists
- **P** bromocriptine mesylate
- octreotide acetate

Posterior pituitary hormones
- desmopressin
- lypressin
- **P** vasopressin

CHAPTER OUTLINE

KEY TERMS

acromegaly
diabetes insipidus
dwarfism
gigantism
hypopituitarism

INTRODUCTION

As described in Chapter 32, the endocrine system's main function is to maintain homeostasis. This is achieved through a complex balance of glandular activities that either stimulate or suppress hormone release. Too much or too little glandular activity disrupts the body's homeostasis, leading to various disorders and interfering with the normal functioning of other endocrine glands. The drugs presented in this chapter are those used to either replace or interact with the hormones or factors produced by the hypothalamus and pituitary.

HYPOTHALAMIC RELEASING FACTORS

The hypothalamus uses a number of releasing hormones or factors to stimulate or inhibit the release of hormones from the anterior pituitary. These releasing hormones are growth hormone–releasing hormone (GHRH), thyrotropin-releasing hormone (TRH), gonadotropin-releasing hormone (GnRH), corticotropin-releasing hormone (CRH), and prolactin releasing hormone (PRH). The hypothalamus also releases two inhibiting factors, somatostatin (growth hormone–inhibiting factor) and prolactin inhibiting factor (PIF). These hormones are found in such minute quantities that their actual chemical structures have not been clearly identified. Not all of the hypothalamic hormones are used as pharmacological agents. A number of hypothalamic releasing factors described below are used for diagnostic purposes only, whereas others are used primarily as antineoplastic agents (Table 33-1).

TABLE 33-1

HYPOTHALAMIC RELEASING FACTORS

Name	Brand/ Chemical Name	Usual Indications
CRH	generic	Diagnosis of Cushing's disease
goserelin	*Zoladex*	Treatment of prostatic cancers
histrelin	*Supprelin*	Treatment of precocious puberty in children
P leuprolide	*Lupron*	Treatment of specific cancers, endometriosis, precocious puberty
nafarelin	*Synarel*	Treatment of endometriosis and precocious puberty
TRH	protirelin	Diagnosis of thyroid dysfunction; prevention of respiratory distress of prematurity (orphan drug use)
GHRH	sermorelin	Diagnosis of hypothalamic or pituitary dysfunction in short children; evaluation of response to surgery or irradiation; ovulation induction, AIDS-associated cachexia (orphan drug uses)

CRH stimulates the release of adrenocorticotropin (ACTH) from the anterior pituitary and is used to diagnose Cushing's disease (a condition characterized by hypersecretion of adrenocortical hormones in response to excessive ACTH release).

Gonadorelin (*Lutrepulse, Factrel*) is used to diagnose gonadotropic production of the pituitary. *Lutrepulse* also is used to treat primary amenorrhea, which results from failure of the hypothalamus to produce GnRH. Research into the use of gonadorelin to induce or inhibit ovulation and to treat precocious puberty is ongoing.

Goserelin (*Zoladex*) is an analog of GnRH. After an initial burst of follicle-stimulating hormone (FSH) and luteinizing hormone (LH) release, goserelin inhibits pituitary gonadotropin secretion with a resultant drop in the production of the sex hormones. This drug currently is used as an antineoplastic agent to treat prostatic cancers.

Histrelin (*Supprelin*) is a GnRH agonist. With chronic use, it inhibits gonadotropin secretion and decreases the levels of steroid sex hormones. It is used to treat precocious puberty in children.

Leuprolide (*Lupron*) occupies pituitary GnRH receptor sites so that they no longer respond to GnRH. As a result, there is no stimulation for release of LH and FSH. This drug is used primarily as an antineoplastic agent to treat specific cancers. It is also used to treat endometriosis and precocious puberty that results from hypothalamic activity.

Nafarelin (*Synarel*), a potent agonist of GnRH, is used to decrease the production of gonadal hormones through repeated stimulation of their receptor sites. After about 4 weeks of therapy, gonadal hormone levels fall and the cells they normally stimulate are quiet. This drug is used to treat endometriosis and precocious puberty.

TRH (protirelin) is used only for diagnostic purposes. It stimulates the pituitary to produce thyrotropin (thyroid-stimulating hormone, TSH), which in turn stimulates the thyroid to produce thyroid hormones (see Chapter 35, Thyroid/Parathyroid Agents, for more details). A TRH infusion test is the most sensitive method for diagnosing mild hypothyroidism and hyperthyroidism. TRH has orphan-drug status when used to prevent infant respiratory distress syndrome associated with prematurity. TRH is also under investigation for improving the outcome of spinal cord injuries when it is given within a very specific time frame.

GHRH (sermorelin) stimulates the production of growth hormone by the anterior pituitary. It is used for diagnostic purposes in short children to determine the presence of hypothalamic or pituitary dysfunction. It is also used to evaluate therapeutic response in surgically treated or irradiated patients. It has orphan-drug status with gonadotropin to induce ovulation and to treat AIDS-associated cachexia.

Figure 33-1 displays the sites of action of hypothalamic releasing factors and other hypothalamic and pituitary agents.

NURSING CONSIDERATIONS
for patients receiving hypothalamic releasing factors

The specific nursing care of the patient receiving a hypothalamic releasing factor is related to the hormone (or hormones) that the drug is affecting (see Chapter 34 for adrenocorticoid hormones, Chapter 35 for thyroid hormones, and Chapters 38 and 39 for sex hormones). Drugs used for diagnostic purposes are short-lived; information about these agents should be included in any patient teaching about the diagnostic procedure. Nursing process guidelines for other agents can be found with the therapeutic drug class to which they belong, antineoplastic agents (see Chapter 12).

ANTERIOR PITUITARY HORMONES

Agents that affect pituitary function are used mainly to mimic or antagonize the effect of specific pituitary hormones. They may be used either as replacement therapy for conditions resulting from a hypoactive pituitary or for diagnostic purposes. The anterior pituitary hormones that are in use today include seven different drugs, which are described below (see Figure 33-1).

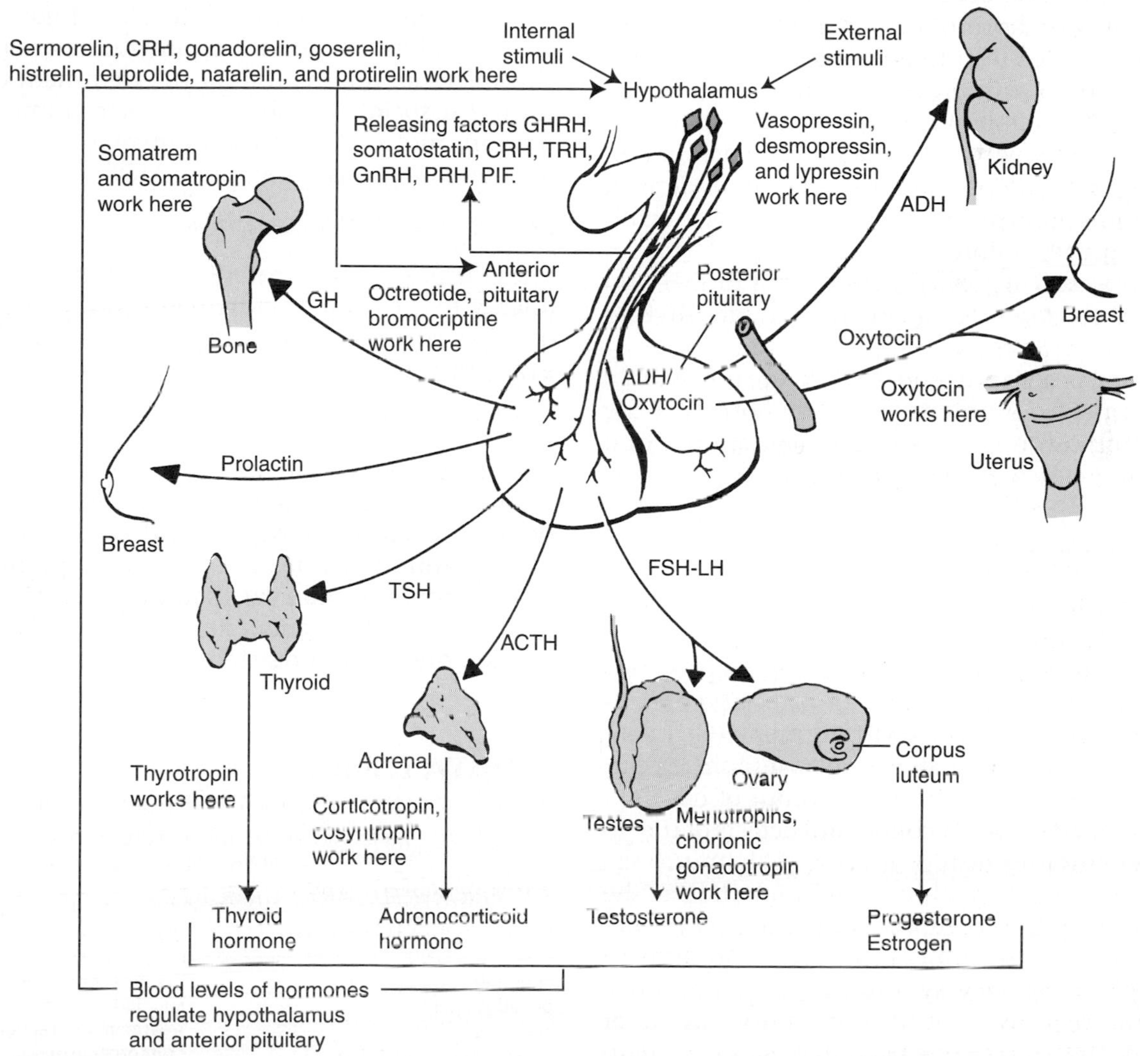

FIGURE 33-1. Sites of action of hypothalamic/pituitary agents.

Chorionic gonadotropin (*Chorex*) acts like LH and stimulates the production of testosterone and progesterone. It is used to treat hypogonadism in males, to induce ovulation in females with functioning ovaries, and to treat prepubertal cryptorchidism when there is no anatomical obstruction to testicular movement. (See Chapters 38 and 39 for nursing implications.)

Corticotropin (*Acthar*), or ACTH, is used for diagnostic purposes to test adrenal function and responsiveness. Because it stimulates steroid release and anti-inflammatory effects, it also is used to treat various inflammatory disorders.

Cosyntropin (*Cortrosyn*) is used to diagnose adrenal dysfunction. Because it has a rapid onset and short duration of activity, it is not used for therapeutic purposes.

Menotropins (*Pergonal*) is a purified preparation of gonadotropins. It is used as a fertility drug to stimulate ovulation in women and spermatogenesis in men. (See Chapters 38 and 39 for nursing implications.)

Somatropin (*Nutropin, Saizen, Biotropin,* and others) is a growth hormone that is produced using recombinant-DNA technology. It is used in the treatment of children with growth failure.

Somatrem (*Protropin*) is a genetically engineered growth hormone with an added amino acid, making it longer acting and purer than animal-derived growth hormone. This drug is also used to treat children with growth failure.

Thyrotropin (*Thytropar*) is equivalent to TSH and is used as a diagnostic agent to evaluate thyroid function.

In clinical practice, the agents that are used purely as replacements for anterior pituitary hormones are those acting as growth hormone—somatropin and somatrem. These will be discussed further.

Growth Hormone

Growth hormone is responsible for linear skeletal growth, the growth of internal organs, protein synthesis, and the stimulation of many other processes that are required for normal growth. ***Hypopituitarism*** is often seen as growth hormone (GH) deficiency before any other signs and symptoms occur. Hypopituitarism may occur as a result of developmental abnormalities or congenital defects of the pituitary, circulatory disturbances (e.g., hemorrhage or infarction), acute or chronic inflammation of the pituitary, and pituitary tumors. GH deficiency in children results in short stature (***dwarfism***). Adults with somatropin deficiency syndrome (SDS) may have hypopituitarism as a result of pituitary tumors or trauma or they may have been treated for GH deficiency as children, resulting in a shutdown of the pituitary production of somatotropin.

GH deficiency was once treated with GH injections extracted from the pituitary glands of cadavers. The supply of GH was therefore rather limited and costly. Synthetic human GH is now available from recombinant DNA sources using genetic engineering. Synthetic GH is expensive, but it is thought to be safer than cadaver GH and is being used increasingly to treat GH deficiencies. Somatropin and somatrem are the two growth hormone replacement drugs in use today (see Figure 33-1).

THERAPEUTIC ACTIONS AND INDICATIONS

As noted previously, somatropin and somatrem are hormones of recombinant DNA origin that are equivalent to human growth hormone.

Somatrem is indicated only for the treatment of children with growth failure due to lack of endogenous growth hormone. It has orphan drug status for the treatment of short stature associated with Turner's syndrome in girls.

Somatropin is indicated for the treatment of growth failure due to lack of growth hormone or to chronic renal failure and for the treatment of short stature associated with Turner's syndrome. It has orphan drug status for use to increase protein production and growth in various AIDS-related states.

CONTRAINDICATIONS/CAUTIONS

These drugs are contraindicated with any known allergy to the drug or ingredients in the drug. They also are contraindicated in the presence of closed epiphyses or with underlying cranial lesions.

ADVERSE EFFECTS

The adverse effects that most often occur when using growth hormone include the development of antibodies to growth hormone and subsequent signs of inflammation and autoimmune-type reactions (much more common with somatrem); swelling and joint pain; and the endocrine reactions of hypothyroidism and insulin resistance.

DATA LINK

Data link to the following anterior pituitary hormones in your nursing drug guide:

ANTERIOR PITUITARY HORMONES

Name	Brand Name	Usual Indication
chorionic gonadotropin	*Chorex*	Treatment of male hypogonadism, induction of ovulation, treatment of prepubertal cryptorchidism

LIFE-SPAN CONSIDERATIONS

Growth Hormone Therapy

In the past, growth hormone therapy was very expensive and rather unsafe. The use of cadaver pituitaries resulted in unreliable hormone levels and, in many cases, hypersensitivity reactions to the proteins found in the drug. With the advent of genetic engineering and the development of safer, more reliable forms of growth hormone, there has been a surge in the use of the drug to treat children with short stature. Even so, the drug is still costly and not without adverse effects.

Growth hormone can be used to treat growth failure due either to lack of growth hormone or renal failure. It also can help children with normal growth hormone levels who are just genetically small. Before the drug is prescribed, the child must undergo screening procedures and specific testing (including x-rays and blood tests)—and display a willingness to have regular injections. The child taking this drug will need to have pretherapy and periodic tests of thyroid function, blood sugar levels, glucose tolerance, and tests for growth hormone antibodies (a risk that increases with the length of time the drug is given). In addition, x-rays of the long bones will need to be taken to monitor for closure of the epiphyses, a sign that the drug must be stopped. Because the child taking growth hormone may experience sudden growth, he or she will need to be monitored for nutritional needs as well as psychological trauma that may occur with the sudden change in body image. Insulin therapy and replacement thyroid therapy may be needed, depending on the child's response to the drug.

The child's family or caregivers will need instructions on the following points:

- Storage of the drug (refrigeration is required)
- Preparation of the drug (the reconstitution procedure varies depending on the brand name used)
- Administration of the drug (sterile technique, need to rotate injection sites, and the need to monitor injection sites for atrophy or extravasation)

They also must be advised to report any lack of growth as well as signs of glucose intolerance (thirst, hunger, voiding pattern changes) and thyroid dysfunction (fatigue, thinning hair, slow pulse, puffy skin, intolerance to the cold).

The use of growth hormone involves an interrelationship of many subspecialists and expensive and regular medical evaluation and care. The key to the success of this therapy may be the attitude and cooperation of the young patient, who will go through so much for this therapy to be effective.

P corticotropin	*Acthar*	Diagnosis of adrenal function, treatment of various inflammatory disorders
cosyntropin	*Cortrosyn*	Diagnosis of adrenal function
menotropins	*Pergonal*	Stimulation of ovulation and spermatogenesis
somatropin	*Nutropin, Saizen,* and others	Treatment of children with growth failure
somatrem	*Protropin*	Treatment of children with growth failure
thyrotropin	*Thytopar*	Diagnosis of thyroid function

NURSING CONSIDERATIONS
for patients receiving growth hormone

Assessment

HISTORY. Screen for history of allergy to any growth hormone or binder, and for closed epiphyses or underlying cranial lesions.

PHYSICAL ASSESSMENT. Include screening for baseline status before beginning therapy and for any potential adverse effects: height, weight, thyroid function tests, glucose tolerance tests, and growth hormone levels.

Nursing Diagnoses

The patient receiving any growth hormone may have the following nursing diagnoses related to drug therapy:

- Alteration in nutrition, less than body requirements, related to metabolic changes
- Pain related to need for injections
- Knowledge deficit regarding drug therapy

Implementation

- Reconstitute following manufacturer's directions *because individual products vary;* administer IM or SC *for appropriate delivery of drug.*
- Monitor response carefully when beginning therapy *to allow appropriate dosage adjustments as needed.*
- Monitor thyroid function, glucose tolerance, and growth hormone levels periodically *to monitor endocrine changes and to institute treatment as needed.*
- Provide thorough patient teaching, including measures to avoid adverse effects, warning signs of problems, and the need for regular evaluation (including blood tests) *to enhance patient knowledge about drug therapy and promote compliance.* Instruct family member in proper preparation and administration technique.

Evaluation

- Monitor patient response to the drug (return of growth hormone levels to normal; growth and development).
- Monitor for adverse effects (hypothyroidism, glucose intolerance, nutritional imbalance).
- Evaluate the effectiveness of the teaching plan (patient can name drug, dosage, adverse effects to watch for, specific measures to avoid adverse effects; family member can demonstrate proper technique for preparation and administration of drug).
- Monitor the effectiveness of comfort measures and compliance to the regimen.

WWW.WEB LINKS

Patients and health care providers may want to consult the following Internet sources:

Information on growth hormone therapy, pediatric challenges, and research—the Pediatric Endocrinology Nursing Society:
http://www.pens.org

Information on disease research and development, latest drug therapy, and links to other resources—National Institutes of Health:
http://www.nih.gov

Information on where to go to find support groups, information on specific diseases and treatments:
http://www.interaccess.com/hpnet/health.html

GROWTH HORMONE ANTAGONISTS

Growth hormone hypersecretion can occur at any time of life. This is often referred to as hyperpituitarism. If it occurs before the epiphyseal plates of the long bones fuse, it causes an acceleration in linear skeletal growth producing ***gigantism*** of 7 to 8 feet in height with fairly normal body proportions. In adults after epiphyseal closure, linear growth is impossible. Instead, hypersecretion of GH causes enlargement in the peripheral parts of the body such as the hands and feet and in internal organs, especially the heart. ***Acromegaly*** is the term used to describe the onset of excessive GH secretion occurring after puberty and epiphyseal plate closure.

Most conditions of GH hypersecretion are caused by pituitary tumors and are treated by radiation therapy or surgery. Drug therapy for GH excess can be used for those patients who are not candidates for surgery or radiation therapy. The drugs used to treat GH excess include a somatostatin analogue (octreotide acetate [*Sandostatin*]) and a dopamine agonist (bromocriptine [*Parlodel*]) (see Figure 33-1).

THERAPEUTIC ACTIONS AND INDICATIONS

Somatostatin is an inhibitory factor released from the hypothalamus. It is not used to decrease GH levels, though it does do that very effectively. Because it also has multiple effects on many secretory systems (e.g., inhibits release of gastrin, glucagon, insulin) and a short duration of action, it is not desirable as a therapeutic agent. An analog of somatostatin, octreotide acetate, is considerably more potent in inhibiting GH release with less of an inhibitory effect on insulin release. Consequently, it is used instead of somatostatin.

Bromocriptine, a semisynthetic ergot alkaloid, is a dopamine agonist frequently used to treat acromegaly. It may be used alone or as an adjunct to irradiation. Dopamine agonists inhibit GH secretion in some patients with acromegaly; the opposite effect occurs in normal individuals. Bromocriptine's GH-inhibiting effect may be explained by the fact that dopamine increases somatostatin release from the hypothalamus. Both of these drugs are indicated for the treatment of acromegaly in patients who are not candidates for or who cannot tolerate other therapy.

CONTRAINDICATIONS/CAUTIONS

These drugs are contraindicated in the presence of any known allergy to the drug. They should be used cautiously in the presence of any other endocrine disorder (e.g., diabetes, thyroid dysfunction) and pregnancy or lactation.

ADVERSE EFFECTS

Octreotide is associated with many gastrointestinal (GI) complaints because of its effects on the GI tract. Constipation or diarrhea, flatulence, and nausea are not uncommon. Octreotide has also been associated with the development of acute cholecystitis, cholestatic jaundice, biliary tract obstruction, and pancreatitis. Patients must be assessed for the possible development of any of these problems. Other, less common adverse effects include headache, sinus bradycardia or other cardiac arrhythmias, and decreased glucose tolerance. Octreotide must be administered SC, and can be associated with discomfort and/or inflammation at injection sites.

Bromocriptine is given orally and is also associated with GI disturbances. Because of its dopamine-blocking effects, it may cause drowsiness and postural hypotension.

CLINICALLY IMPORTANT DRUG–DRUG INTERACTIONS

Increased serum bromocriptine levels and increased toxicity occur if this drug is combined with erythromycin. This combination should be avoided. There also may be a decreased effectiveness of bromocriptine if combined with phenothiazines. If this combination is used, the patient should be monitored carefully.

DATA LINK

Data link to the following growth hormone antagonists in your nursing drug guide:

GROWTH HORMONE ANTAGONISTS

Name	Brand Name	Usual Indications
P bromocriptine	*Parlodel*	Treatment of acromegaly in patients who are not candidates for or who cannot tolerate other therapy.
octreotide	*Sandostatin*	Treatment of acromegaly in patients who are not candidates for or who cannot tolerate other therapy.

NURSING CONSIDERATIONS
for patients receiving growth hormone antagonists

Assessment

HISTORY. Screen for history of allergy to any growth hormone antagonist or binder; other endocrine disturbances; and pregnancy or lactation.

PHYSICAL ASSESSMENT. Include screening for baseline status before beginning therapy and for any potential adverse effects: orientation, affect, reflexes; blood pressure, pulse, orthostatic blood pressure; abdominal exam; glucose tolerance tests, growth hormone levels.

Nursing Diagnoses

The patient receiving any growth hormone antagonist may have the following nursing diagnoses related to drug therapy:

- Alteration in nutrition, more than body requirements related to metabolic changes
- Pain related to need for injections (octreotide)
- Knowledge deficit regarding drug therapy

Implementation

- Reconstitute octreotide following manufacturer's directions; administer SC and rotate injection sites regularly *to prevent skin breakdown and to assure proper delivery of the drug.*
- Monitor thyroid function, glucose tolerance, and growth hormone levels periodically *to detect problems and to institute treatment as needed.*
- Arrange for baseline and periodic ultrasound evaluation of the gallbladder if using octreotide *to detect any gallstone development and to arrange for appropriate treatment.*
- Provide thorough patient teaching, including measures to avoid adverse effects, warning signs of problems, and need for regular evaluation (including blood tests) *to enhance patient knowledge about drug therapy and promote compliance.* Instruct family member in proper preparation and administration technique.

Evaluation

- Monitor patient response to the drug (return of growth hormone levels to normal, growth and development).
- Monitor for adverse effects (hypothyroidism, glucose intolerance, nutritional imbalance, GI disturbances, cholecystitis).
- Evaluate the effectiveness of the teaching plan (patient can name drug, dosage, adverse effects to watch for, specific measures to avoid adverse effects; family member can demonstrate proper technique for preparation and administration of drug).
- Monitor the effectiveness of comfort measures and compliance to the regimen.

POSTERIOR PITUITARY HORMONES

The posterior pituitary stores two hormones, produced in the hypothalamus: antidiuretic hormone (ADH), also known as vasopressin, and oxytocin. Oxytocin stimulates milk ejection or "let down" in lactating women. In pharmacological doses, it can be used to initiate or to improve uterine contractions in labor. This drug is discussed in Chapter 38.

ADH possesses antidiuretic, hemostatic, and vasopressor properties. Posterior pituitary disorders can be secondary to metastatic cancer, lymphomas, disseminated intravascular coagulation (DIC, discussed in Chapter 46), and septicemia. Posterior pituitary disorders that are seen clinically involve ADH release and include ***diabetes insipidus*** (DI), which results from insufficient secretion, and syndrome of inappropriate antidiuretic hormone (SIADH), which occurs with excessive secretion of ADH. Diabetes insipidus can be treated pharmacologically.

Diabetes insipidus is characterized by the production of a large amount of dilute urine containing no glucose. Blood glucose levels will then be higher than normal and the body will respond with polyuria (lots

CASE STUDY

Teaching Plan for Diabetes Insipidus

PRESENTATION

B. T. is a 56-year-old teacher who developed diabetes insipidus. She was eventually regulated on lypressin nasal spray, one or two sprays per nostril qid. B. T. seemed highly interested in her disease and therapy and learned to control her own dosage by symptom control. For several years, B. T. maintained good control of her symptoms. At her last clinical visit, it was noted that she had developed postnasal ulcerations and nasal rhinitis. She also complained of several GI symptoms including upset stomach, abdominal cramps, and diarrhea.

CRITICAL THINKING QUESTIONS

Think about the pathophysiology of diabetes insipidus. What are the effects of lypressin on the body, and what adverse effects might occur if the drug was being absorbed inappropriately? Since B. T. has used the drug for so many years, she may have forgotten some of the teaching points about her disease and drug administration. Outline a care plan for B.T that will include necessary teaching points and will take into consideration her long experience with her disease and her drug therapy. Think about specific warning signs that should be highlighted for B. T. and ways to involve her in the teaching program that might make it more pertinent to her and her needs.

DISCUSSION

An essential aspect of the ongoing nursing process is continual evaluation of the effectiveness of the drug therapy. An evaluation of this situation shows that B. T.'s postnasal mucosa was ulcerated, possibly as a result of overexposure to the vasoconstrictive properties of the drug. B. T.'s GI tract also seemed to show evidence of increased ADH effects. These factors seem to indicate that perhaps the drug was being administered incorrectly, resulting in excessive exposure of the nasal mucosa to the drug, increased absorption, and increased levels of the drug reaching the systemic circulation.

The nurse should ask B. T. to administer a dose of the drug to herself, then discuss the signs and symptoms of problems that B. T. should watch for. In this case, B. T. remembered most of the details of her drug teaching. But when administering the drug, she tilted her head back, tipped the bottle upside down, then squirted the drug into each nostril. When the nurse questioned B. T. about her technique, she explained that she had seen an advertisement on TV about nasal sprays and realized that she had been doing it wrong all these years. The nurse explained the difference in the types of nasal sprays and reviewed the entire teaching plan with B. T. The drug was discontinued and B. T. was placed on SC ADH until the nasal ulcerations healed.

As a patient becomes more familiar with a drug therapy, the details about the drug may be forgotten. It is important to remember that patient teaching needs regular updating and evaluation. This point is often forgotten when dealing with patients who have been on a drug for years. However, remembering to assess the patient's knowledge about the drug can prevent problems such as B. T.'s from developing. Since B. T. is a teacher, she might be interested in developing a teaching protocol that will meet her needs and serve as appropriate reminders about the disease and drug therapy. If B. T. is actively involved in preparing such a plan, it will be more effective and might be remembered much longer.

of urine), polydipsia (lots of thirst), and dehydration. With this rare metabolic disorder, patients produce large quantities of dilute urine and are constantly thirsty. DI is caused by a deficiency in the amount of posterior pituitary ADH and may be caused by pituitary disease or injury (e.g., head trauma, surgery, tumors). The condition can be acute and short in duration, or it can be a chronic, lifelong problem.

ADH itself is never used as therapy for DI. Instead, synthetic preparations of ADH, which are purer and associated with fewer adverse effects, are used. The ADH preparations that are available include vasopressin (*Pitressin Synthetic*), which is available in parenteral and nasal spray forms; lypressin (*Diapid*), which is only available in nasal spray forms; and desmopressin (*DDAVP*) (see Figure 33-1). The drug of choice will depend on the individual response to the drug and the patient's ability or willingness to use a particular dosage form.

THERAPEUTIC ACTIONS AND INDICATIONS

ADH is released in response to increases in plasma osmolarity or decreases in blood volume. It produces its antidiuretic activity in the kidney, causing the cortical and medullary parts of the collecting duct to become permeable to water, thereby increasing water reabsorption and decreasing urine formation. These activities reduce plasma osmolarity and increase blood volume.

The ADH preparations that are available are indicated for the treatment of neurogenic DI. Desmopressin is also indicated for the treatment of hemophilia A and von Willibrand's disease and is used as

PATIENT TEACHING CHECKLIST

Antidiuretic Hormone (ADH)

Create customized patient teaching materials for a specific antidiuretic hormone from your CD-ROM. Your patient teaching should stress the following points for drugs within this class:

Antidiuretic hormone, or ADH, works in the kidneys to limit the loss of water in the urine.

If the drug is to be injected, you and a significant other will need to learn how to prepare and inject the drug, and how to rotate injection sites.

If the drug is to be used intranasally, it should be administered with the head held upright and the bottle also held upright.

When taking the drug, you might experience the following adverse effects:

- Nasal irritation and congestion—Your nasal passages may adjust to the drug over time. If the irritation becomes severe, check with your health care provider.
- Heartburn and GI upset—These symptoms often occur when the nasal preparation drips down the pharynx and may be eliminated with careful administration.
- Abdominal cramps—These occur because the drug acts to increase GI activity and will have to be tolerated. If the cramping becomes severe, talk to your health care provider.

Report any of the following to your health care provider: drowsiness, listlessness, headache; chest pain, shortness of breath; severe abdominal cramps; prolonged nasal congestion; return of the signs of diabetes insipidus, such as large volumes of urine and excessive thirst.

Tell any doctor, nurse or other health care provider that you are taking this drug.

Keep this drug, and all medications, out of the reach of children.

This Teaching Checklist reflects general patient teaching guidelines. It is not meant to be a substitute for drug-specific teaching information, which is available in nursing drug guides.

a nasal spray for the treatment of nocturnal enuresis (bed wetting). Because of vasopressin's actions to increase GI motility, it is also indicated for the prevention and treatment of postoperative abdominal distention and to dispel gas formation before abdominal tests.

CONTRAINDICATIONS/CAUTIONS

ADH preparations are contraindicated with any known allergy to the drug or its components or with severe renal dysfunction. Caution should be used with any known vascular disease (because of its effects on vascular smooth muscle); epilepsy; asthma; and pregnancy or lactation.

ADVERSE EFFECTS

The adverse effects associated with the use of ADH preparations include water intoxication (drowsiness, lightheadedness, headache, coma, convulsions) related to the shift to water retention; tremor, sweating, vertigo, and headache (related to water retention—a "hangover" effect); abdominal cramps, flatulence, nausea, and vomiting (related to stimulation of GI motility); and local nasal irritation related to nasal administration. Hypersensitivity reactions have also been reported, ranging from rash to bronchial constriction.

DATA LINK

Data link to the following posterior pituitary hormones in your nursing drug guide:

POSTERIOR PITUITARY HORMONES

Name	Brand Name	Routes	Usual Indications
desmopressin	*DDAVP*	PO, IV, SC, nasal	Diabetes insipidus, von Willebrand's disease, hemophilia A, treatment of nocturnal enuresis
lypressin	*Diapid*	Nasal	Diabetes insipidus
P vasopressin	Pitressin	IM, SC	Diabetes insipidus, prevention of post-operative abdominal distention, to dispel gas for abdominal exams

NURSING CARE GUIDE
Antidiuretic Hormone (ADH)

Assessment	Nursing Diagnoses	Implementation	Evaluation
HISTORY Allergies to any ADH preparation, pregnancy, lactation, vascular disease, chronic renal disease	Alteration in urinary patterns related to antidiuretic effect Fluid volume excess related to antidiuretic effect Knowledge deficit regarding drug therapy	Prepare and safely administer drug as ordered. Monitor and limit fluid intake as needed. Provide patient teaching regarding drug name, dosage, adverse effects, precautions, proper administration, warning signs to report.	Evaluate drug effects: regulation of fluid volume. Monitor for adverse effects: water intoxication, nasal congestion, GI problems. Monitor for drug–drug interactions as indicated for each drug. Evaluate effectiveness of patient teaching program. Evaluate effectiveness of comfort and safety measures.
PHYSICAL EXAMINATION Neurological: orientation Skin: color, lesions CV: P, cardiac auscultation, BP Respiratory: R, adventitious sounds GI: bowel sounds Renal: output, urinalysis Lab tests: serum electrolytes			

NURSING CONSIDERATIONS
for patients receiving posterior pituitary hormones

Assessment

HISTORY. Screen for history of allergy to any ADH preparation or components; vascular diseases; epilepsy; renal dysfunction; pregnancy; and lactation.

PHYSICAL ASSESSMENT. Include screening for baseline status before beginning therapy and for any potential adverse effects: skin, lesions; orientation, affect, reflexes; blood pressure, pulse; respiration, adventitious sounds; abdominal exam; renal function tests; and serum electrolytes.

Nursing Diagnoses

The patient receiving any posterior pituitary hormone may have the following nursing diagnoses related to drug therapy:

- Alteration in urinary elimination patterns
- Fluid volume excess related to water retention
- Knowledge deficit regarding drug therapy

Implementation

- Monitor patient fluid volume *to watch for signs of water intoxication and fluid excess;* arrange to decrease dosage as needed.
- Monitor patients with vascular disease for any sign of exacerbation *to provide for immediate treatment.*
- Monitor condition of nasal passages if given intranasally *to observe for nasal ulceration which can occur and could affect absorption of the drug.*
- Provide thorough patient teaching, including measures to avoid adverse effects; warning signs of problems; and the need for regular evaluation, including blood tests, *to enhance patient knowledge about drug therapy and promote compliance.* (See Patient Teaching Checklist: Antidiuretic Hormone [ADH].)

Evaluation

- Monitor patient response to the drug (maintenance of fluid balance).
- Monitor for adverse effects (GI problems, water intoxication, headache, skin rash).

- Evaluate the effectiveness of the teaching plan (patient can name drug, dosage, adverse effects to watch for, specific measures to avoid adverse effects; patient can demonstrate proper administration of nasal preparations).
- Monitor the effectiveness of comfort measures and compliance to the regimen (see Nursing Care Guide: ADH).

CHAPTER SUMMARY

- Hypothalamic releasing factors stimulate the anterior pituitary to release hormones.
- The hypothalamic releasing factors are used mostly for diagnostic tests and for treating some forms of cancer.
- Anterior pituitary hormones stimulate endocrine glands or cell metabolisms.
- Growth hormone deficiency can cause dwarfism in children and somatropin deficiency syndrome in adults.
- Growth hormone replacement is done with drugs produced by recombinant DNA processes; these agents are more reliable and cause fewer problems than drugs used in the past.
- Growth hormone excess causes gigantism in patients whose epiphyseal plates have not closed and acromegaly in patients with closed epiphyseal plates.
- Growth hormone antagonists include octreotide and bromocriptine. Blockage of other endocrine activity may occur when these drugs are used.
- Posterior pituitary hormones are produced in the hypothalamus and stored in the posterior pituitary. They include oxytocin and antidiuretic hormone.
- Lack of antidiuretic hormone produces diabetes insipidus, which is characterized by large amounts of dilute urine and excessive thirst.
- Antidiuretic hormone (ADH) replacement uses analogs of ADH and can be administered parenterally or intranasally.
- Fluid balance needs to be monitored when patients are on ADH replacement because water intoxication and dilution of essential electrolytes can occur.

BIBLIOGRAPHY

Andrews, M. & Boyle, J. (1999). *Transcultural concepts in nursing care.* Philadelphia: Lippincott Williams & Wilkins.

Bullock, B. L. (2000). *Focus on pathophysiology.* Philadelphia: Lippincott Williams & Wilkins.

Girard, J. (1991). *Endocrinology of puberty.* Farmington, CT: Karger Publishers.

Guyton, A. & Hall, J. (1996). *Textbook of medical physiology.* Philadelphia: W. B. Saunders.

Hardman, J. G., Limbird, L. E., Molinoff, P. B., Ruddon, R. W., & Gilman, A. G. (Eds.). (1996). *Goodman and Gilman's the pharmacological basis of therapeutics* (9th ed). New York: McGraw-Hill.

Karch, A. M. (2000). *2000 Lippincott's nursing drug guide.* Philadelphia: Lippincott Williams & Wilkins.

McEvoy, B. R. (1999). *Facts and comparisons 1999.* St. Louis: Facts and Comparisons.

The medical letter on drugs and therapeutics. (1999). New Rochelle, NY: Medical Letter.

North, W. G. et al. (1993). The neurohypophysis: A window on brain function. *Annals of the New York Academy of Sciences,* 689.

Porth, C. (1998). *Pathophysiology: Concepts of altered health states* (5th ed.). Philadelphia: Lippincott-Raven.

CHAPTER 34

Adrenocortical Agents

Glucocorticoids
- beclomethasone
- betamethasone
- budenoside
- cortisone
- dexamethasone
- flunisolide
- hydrocortisone
- methylprednisolone
- P prednisolone
- prednisone
- triamcinolone

Mineralocorticoids
- cortisone
- P fludrocortisone
- hydrocortisone

CHAPTER OUTLINE

INTRODUCTION
THE ADRENAL GLANDS
Controls
Adrenal Insufficiency
Adrenal Crisis
GLUCOCORTICOIDS
THERAPEUTIC ACTIONS AND INDICATIONS
CONTRAINDICATIONS/CAUTIONS
ADVERSE EFFECTS
CLINICALLY IMPORTANT DRUG–DRUG INTERACTIONS
NURSING CONSIDERATIONS for patients receiving glucocorticoids
Assessment
HISTORY
PHYSICAL ASSESSMENT
Nursing Diagnoses
Implementation
Evaluation
MINERALOCORTICOIDS
THERAPEUTIC ACTIONS AND INDICATIONS
CONTRAINDICATIONS/CAUTIONS
ADVERSE EFFECTS
CLINICALLY IMPORTANT DRUG–DRUG INTERACTIONS
NURSING CONSIDERATIONS for patients receiving mineralocorticoids
Assessment
HISTORY
PHYSICAL ASSESSMENT
Nursing Diagnoses
Implementation
Evaluation
CHAPTER SUMMARY
BIBLIOGRAPHY

KEY TERMS

adrenal cortex
adrenal medulla
corticosteroids
glucocorticoids
mineralocorticoids

INTRODUCTION

Adrenocortical agents are widely used to suppress the immune system and actually help people to feel better. These drugs do not, however, cure any inflammatory disorders. Once widely used to treat a number of chronic problems, adrenocortical agents are now reserved for short-term use to relieve inflammation during acute stages of illness.

THE ADRENAL GLANDS

The two adrenal glands are flattened bodies that sit on top of each kidney. Each gland is made up of an inner core or ***adrenal medulla*** and an outer shell called the ***adrenal cortex***.

The adrenal medulla is actually part of the sympathetic nervous system (SNS). It is a neuron ganglia that releases the neurotransmitters norepinephrine and epinephrine into circulation when the SNS is stimulated. The secretion of these neurotransmitters directly into the bloodstream allows them to act as hormones, traveling from the adrenal medulla to react with specific receptor sites throughout the body. This is thought to be a back-up system for the sympathetic system, adding an extra stimulus to the "fight or flight" response.

The adrenal cortex surrounds the medulla and consists of three layers of cells, each of which synthesizes chemically different types of steroid hormones that exert physiologic effects throughout the body. The adrenal cortex produces hormones called ***corticosteroids***. There are three types of corticosteroids: androgens, ***glucocorticoids,*** and ***mineralocorticoids***.

Androgens (male and female sex hormones) actually have little effect compared with the sex hormones produced by the testes and ovaries. They are able to maintain a certain level of cellular stimulation and can contribute to cell-sensitive growth in some forms of cancers, particularly prostate, breast, and ovarian cancers. These drugs are addressed in Part 7: Drugs Acting on the Reproductive System.

Glucocorticoids are so named because they stimulate and increase glucose levels for energy. They also increase the rate of protein breakdown and decrease the rate of protein formation from amino acids, another way of preserving energy. Glucocorticoids also cause lipogenesis, or the formation and storage of fat in the body. This stored fat will then be available to be broken down for energy when needed.

Mineralocorticoids affect electrolyte levels and homeostasis. These steroid hormones, like aldosterone, directly affect the levels of electrolytes in the system. Potassium is lost and sodium and water are retained in response to aldosterone. Hydrocortisone and cortisone also have the same effects when present in high levels.

Figure 34–1 displays the sites of action of the glucocorticoids and the mineralocorticoids.

Controls

The adrenal cortex responds to adrenocorticotropic hormone (ACTH) released from the anterior pituitary. ACTH, in turn, responds to corticotropin releasing hormone (CRH) released from the hypothalamus. This happens during a normal day in what is called diurnal rhythm. A person who has a regular cycle of sleep and wakefulness will produce high levels of CRH during sleep, usually around midnight. A resulting peak response of increased ACTH and adrenocortical hormones occurs sometime early in the morning, around 6 to 9 A.M. This high level of hormones will then suppress any further CRH or ACTH release. The corticosteroids will be used up slowly throughout the day and fall to low levels by evening. At this point, the hypothalamus and pituitary will sense low levels of the hormones and begin the production and release of CRH and ACTH again. This will peak around midnight and the cycle will start again.

Activation of the stress reaction, the SNS, will bypass the usual diurnal rhythm and cause release of ACTH and secretion of the adrenocortical hormones—an important aspect of the stress, or fight or flight, response. The stress response is activated with cellular injury or when a person perceives fear or feels anxious. These hormones have many actions, including the following:

- Increasing the blood volume (aldosterone effect)
- Causing the release of glucose for energy
- Slowing the rate of protein production (which reserves energy)
- Blocking the activities of the inflammatory and immune systems (which reserves a great deal of energy)

These actions are important during an acute stress situation, but can cause adverse reactions in periods of extreme or prolonged stress. For instance, a postoperative patient who is very fearful and stressed may not heal well because protein building is blocked, infections may be hard to treat in such a patient because the inflammatory and immune systems are not functioning adequately.

Aldosterone will also be released without ACTH stimulation when the blood surrounding the adrenal gland is high in potassium, since high potassium is a direct stimulus for aldosterone release. Aldosterone causes the kidneys to excrete potassium to restore homeostasis.

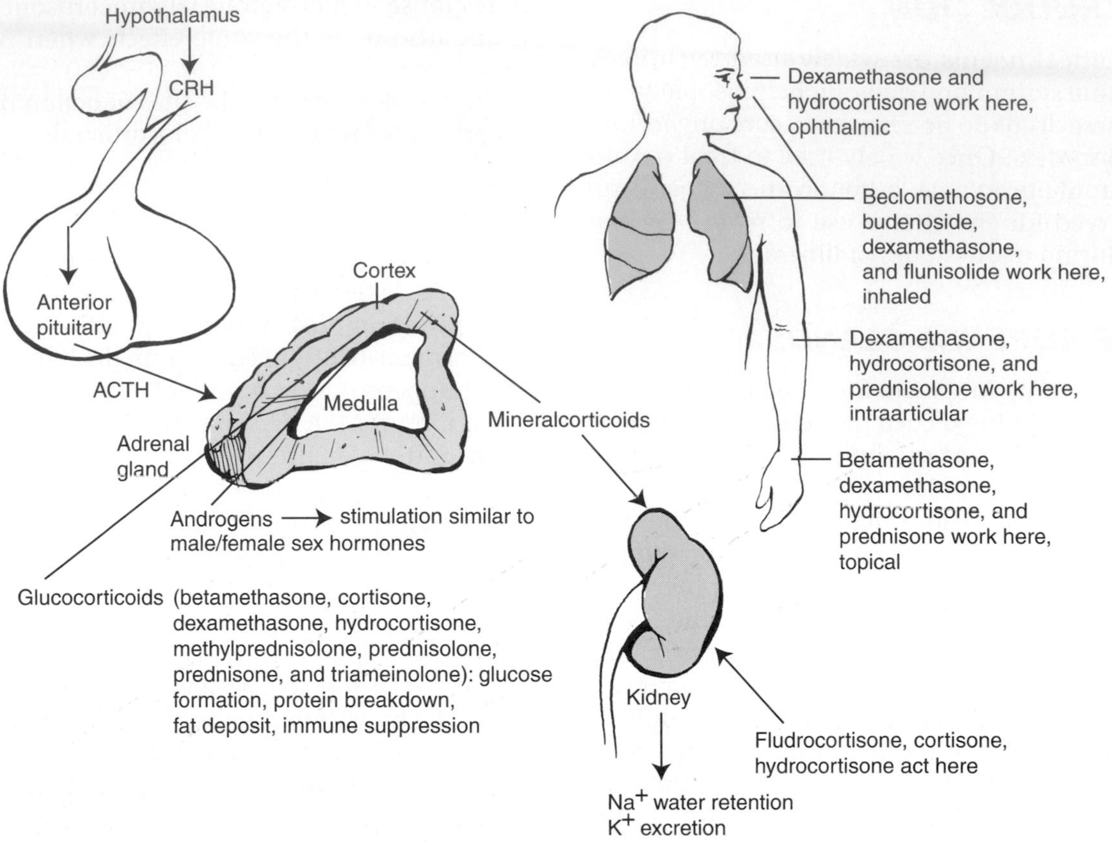

FIGURE 34-1. Sites of action of the adrenocortical agents.

NURSING CHALLENGE

Diurnal Rhythm

The adrenocortical hormones are released in a pattern called the diurnal rhythm. The secretion of CRH, ACTH, and cortisol are high in the morning in day-oriented people—those who have a regular cycle of wakefulness during the day and sleep during the night. In such individuals, the peak levels of cortisol usually come between 6 and 8 A.M. The levels then fall off slowly (with periodic spurts) and reach a low in the late evening, with lowest levels around midnight. It is thought that this cycle is related to the effects of sleeping on the hypothalamus, with the hypothalamus regulating its stimulation of the anterior pituitary in relation to sleep and activity. The cycle may also be connected to the hypothalamic response to light. This is important to keep in mind when treating patients with corticosteroids. In order to mimic the normal diurnal pattern, patients should take these drugs first thing upon awakening in the morning.

Complications to this pattern arise, however, when patients work shifts or change their sleeping patterns (much like college students do). In response, the hypothalamus will shift its release of CRH to correspond to the new cycle. For instance, if a person works all night and goes to bed at 8 A.M. arising at 3 P.M. to carry on the day's activities before going to work at 11 P.M., the hypothalamus will release CRH around 3 P.M. in accordance with the new sleep–wake cycle. It usually takes 2 or 3 days for the hypothalamus to readjust. A patient on this schedule who is taking replacement corticosteroids would then need to take them at 3 P.M. or on arising. Patients who work several different shifts in one week may not have the time to reregulate their hypothalamus, and the corticosteroid cycle may be thrown off. Patients who have to change their sleep patterns repeatedly will often complain about feeling weak, getting sick more easily, or having trouble concentrating. College students frequently develop a pattern of sleeping all day, then staying up all night—a cycle that becomes hard to break as their body and endocrine system try to readjust.

It is a nursing challenge to help patients understand how the body works and to offer ways to decrease the stress of changing sleep patterns—especially if the nurse is also working several different shifts. Many employers are willing to have employees work several days of the same shift before switching back, mainly because they have noticed an increase in productivity and a decrease in absences when employees have enough time to allow their bodies to adjust to the new shift.

Adrenal Insufficiency

Some patients may experience a shortage of adrenocortical hormones and develop signs of adrenal insufficiency. This can occur when a patient does not produce enough ACTH, when the adrenal glands are not able to respond to ACTH, when the adrenal gland is damaged and cannot produce enough hormones (as in Addison's disease), or secondary to surgical removal of the glands.

A more common cause of adrenal insufficiency is prolonged use of corticosteroid hormones. When exogenous corticosteroids are used, they act to negate the regular feedback systems (Figure 34–2). The adrenal glands begin to atrophy because ACTH release is suppressed by the exogenous hormones, so the glands are no longer stimulated to produce or secrete hormones. It takes several weeks to recover from the atrophy caused by this lack of stimulation. To prevent this from happening, patients should receive only short-term steroid therapy and should be weaned slowly from the hormones so that the adrenals have time to recover and start producing hormones again.

Adrenal Crisis

Patients who have an adrenal insufficiency may do quite well until they experience a period of extreme stress, such as a motor vehicle accident, a surgical procedure, or a massive infection. Because they are not able to supplement the energy-consuming effects of the sympathetic reaction, these patients will enter an adrenal crisis, which can include physiologic exhaustion, hypotension, fluid shift, shock, and even death. Patients in adrenal crisis are treated with massive infusion of replacement steroids, constant monitoring, and life support procedures.

GLUCOCORTICOIDS

There are several glucocorticoids available for pharmacological use. They differ by route of administration and duration of action.

Beclomethasone (*Beclovent*) is available as a respiratory inhalant and nasal spray to block inflammation locally in the respiratory tract.

Betamethasone (*Celestone* and others) is a long-acting steroid. It is available for systemic, parenteral use in acute situations. It also is available orally for short-term relief of inflammation and as a topical application for local inflammatory conditions.

Budenoside (*Rhinocort*) is a relatively new steroid for intranasal use. It relieves the signs and symptoms of allergic or seasonal rhinitis with few side effects.

Cortisone (*Cortone Acetate*) was one of the first corticosteroids made available. It is used for replacement therapy in adrenal insufficiency as well as acute inflammatory situations.

Dexamethasone (*Decadron* and others) is widely used and available in multiple forms for dermatologic, ophthalmologic, intra-articular, parenteral, and inhalational uses. It peaks quickly and effects can last for 2 to 3 days.

Flunisolide (*Aerobid, Nasalide*) is another relatively new drug that has proven to be very successful as a respiratory inhalant or intranasal drug.

Hydrocortisone (*Cortef* and others) is a powerful corticosteroid that has both glucocorticoid and mineralocorticoid activity. Because of this, it is used for replacement therapy in adrenal insufficiency. It has largely been replaced for other uses (e.g., intra-articular, IV) by other steroid hormones with less mineralocorticoid effect. It may be preferred for use as a topical or ophthalmic agent.

Methylprednisolone (*Medrol*) has little mineralocorticoid activity at therapeutic doses. Because it has sig-

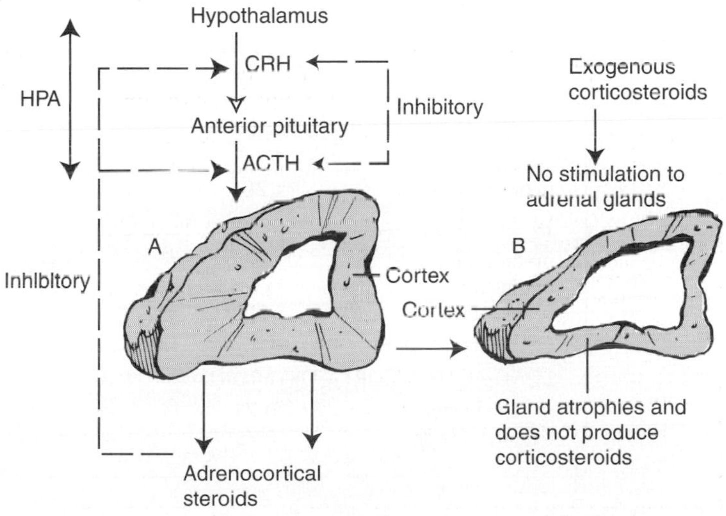

FIGURE 34-2. (*A*) Normal controls of adrenal gland. The hypothalamus releases CRH, which causes release of ACTH from the anterior pituitary. ACTH stimulates the adrenal cortex to produce and release corticosteroids. Increasing levels of corticosteroids inhibit the release of CRH and ACTH. (*B*) Exogenous corticosteroids act to inhibit CRH and ACTH release; the adrenal cortex is no longer stimulated and atrophies. Sudden stopping of steroids results in a crisis of adrenal hypofunction until HPA controls stimulate the adrenal gland again.

nificant anti-inflammatory and immunosuppressive effects, it is a drug of choice for inflammatory and immune disorders in multiple forms, including oral, parenteral, intra-articular, and retention enema.

Prednisolone (*Delta-Cortef* and others) is an intermediate-acting corticosteroid with effects lasting only a day or so. It is used for injection and intralesional and intra-articular injection, and in oral and topical forms.

Prednisone (*Deltasone* and others) is available only as an oral agent and can be used as replacement therapy in adrenal insufficiency. It is also used for short-term and acute therapy to decrease inflammation.

Triamcinolone (*Aristocort, Kenaject* and others) is available in many forms for use in acute inflammatory conditions. It has been used to treat adrenal insufficiency when combined with a mineralocorticoid.

CULTURAL CONSIDERATIONS

Steroid Toxicity in African Americans

African Americans develop increased toxicity to the corticosteroid methylprednisolone—particularly when it is used for immunosuppression following renal transplant. This toxicity can include severe steroid-induced diabetes mellitus. African Americans are nearly four times as likely as whites to develop end-stage renal disease, so this complication is not an unusual problem. If an African American patient is being treated with methylprednisolone, extreme care should be taken to adjust dosages appropriately and to treat adverse effects as they arise.

THERAPEUTIC ACTIONS AND INDICATIONS

Glucocorticoids enter target cells and bind to cytoplasmic receptors, initiating many complex reactions that are responsible for anti-inflammatory and immunosuppressive effects. Hydrocortisone, cortisone, and prednisone also have some mineralocorticoid activity and affect potassium, sodium, and water levels in the body (Table 34-1).

Glucocorticoids are indicated for the short-term treatment of many inflammatory disorders, to relieve discomfort and to give the body a chance to heal from the effects of inflammation. They can be used to treat local inflammation as topical agents, intranasal or inhaled agents, intra-articular injections, and ophthalmic agents. Systemic use is indicated for the treatment of some cancers, hypercalcemia associated with cancer, hematologic disorders, and some neurologic infections. When combined with mineralocorticoids, some of these drugs can be used in replacement therapy for adrenal insufficiency.

CONTRAINDICATIONS/CAUTIONS

These drugs are contraindicated in the presence of any known allergy to any steroid preparation; in the presence of an acute infection (which could become serious or even fatal when the immune and inflammatory responses are blocked); and with lactation (when the anti-inflammatory and immunosuppressive actions could be passed to the baby).

Caution should be used with diabetes (the glucose-elevating effects disrupt glucose control), acute peptic ulcers (steroid use is associated with the development of ulcers); other endocrine disorders (which could be sent into imbalance); and pregnancy.

TABLE 34-1

SELECTED CORTICOSTEROIDS: EQUIVALENT STRENGTH, GLUCOCORTICOID AND MINERALOCORTICOID EFFECTS, AND DURATION OF EFFECTS BY DRUG

Drug	Equivalent Dose (mg)	Glucocorticoid Effects	Mineralocorticoid Effects	Duration of Effects
SHORT-ACTING CORTICOSTEROIDS				
cortisone	25	+	++++	8–12 h
hydrocortisone	20	+	++++	8–12 h
INTERMEDIATE-ACTING CORTICOSTEROIDS				
prednisone	5	++++	++	18–36 h
prednisolone	5	++++	++	18–36 h
triamcinolone	4	+++++	–	18–36 h
methylprednisolone	4	+++++	–	18–36 h
LONG-ACTING CORTICOSTEROIDS				
dexamethasone	0.75	+++++++++	–	36–54 h
betamethasone	0.75	+++++++++	–	35–54 h

ADVERSE EFFECTS

The adverse effects associated with the glucocorticoids are related to the route of administration that is used. Systemic use is associated with endocrine disorders; fluid retention and potential congestive heart failure (CHF); increased appetite and weight gain; fragile skin and loss of hair; weakness and muscle atrophy as protein breakdown occurs and protein is not built; and increased susceptibility to infections and the development of cancers (long-term use). Children are at risk for growth retardation associated with suppression of the hypothalamic-pituitary system. Local use is associated with local inflammations and infections, burning, and stinging (Table 34-2).

CLINICALLY IMPORTANT DRUG–DRUG INTERACTIONS

There are increased therapeutic effects and toxic effects if corticosteroids are given with erythromycin, ketoconazole, or troleandomycin. There is a risk of decreased serum levels and decreased effectiveness if combined with salicylates, barbiturates, phenytoin, or rifampin.

TABLE 34-2

ADVERSE EFFECTS OF CORTICOSTEROID USE ASSOCIATED WITH VARYING ROUTES OF ADMINISTRATION

Systemic: Systemic effects are most likely to occur when the corticosteroid is given orally, IV, IM, or SC. Systemic absorption is possible, however, when other routes of administration are not used correctly or when tissue breakdown or injury allows direct absorption.

CNS: vertigo, headache, parethesias, insomnia, convulsions, psychosis

GI: peptic or esophageal ulcers, pancreatitis, abdominal distention, nausea, vomiting, increased appetite, weight gain

CV: hypotension, shock, CHF secondary to fluid retention, thromboembolism, thrombophlebitis, fat embolism, arrhythmias secondary to electrolyte disturbances

Hematological: sodium and fluid retention, hypokalemia, hypocalcemia, increased blood sugar, increased serum cholesterol, decreased thyroid hormone levels

Musculoskeletal: muscle weakness, steroid myopathy, loss of muscle mass, osteoporosis, spontaneous fractures

EENT: cataracts, glaucoma

Dermatological: frail skin, petechiae, ecchymoses, purpura, striae, subcutaneous fat atrophy

Endocrine: amenorrhea, irregular menses, growth retardation, decreased carbohydrate tolerance, diabetes

Other: immunosuppression, aggravation or masking of infections, impaired wound healing, HPA suppression

IM repository injections: Atrophy at the injection site

Retention enema: Local pain, burning; rectal bleeding

Intra-articular injection: Osteonecrosis, tendon rupture, infection

Intraspinal: Meningitis, adhesive arachnoiditis, conus medullaris syndrome

Intrathecal administration: Arachnoiditis

Topical: Local burning, irritation, acneform lesions, stria, skin atrophy

Respiratory inhalant: Oral, laryngeal, and pharyngeal irritation; fungal infections

Intranasal: Headache, nausea, nasal irritation, fungal infections, epistaxis, rebound congestion, perforation of the nasal septum, anosmia, urticaria

Ophthalmic: Infections, glaucoma, cataracts

Intralesional: Blindness when used on the face and head (rare)

DATA LINK

Data link to the following glucocorticoids in your nursing drug guide:

GLUCOCORTICOIDS

Name	Brand Name	Routes	Usual Indications
beclomethasone	*Beclovent*	Nasal spray, respiratory inhalant	Blocking inflammation in the respiratory tract
betamethasone	*Celestone*	Oral, IM, IV	Management of allergic intra-articular, topical, and inflammatory disorders
budenoside	*Rhinocort*	Intranasal	Relief of symptoms of seasonal and allergic rhinitis
cortisone	*Cortisone Acetate*	Oral, IM	Replacement therapy in adrenal insufficiency; treatment of allergic and inflammatory disorders
dexamethasone	*Decadron*	Oral, IV, IM, inhalation, intranasal, topical, ophthalmic	Management of allergic and inflammatory disorders, adrenal hypofunction
flunisolide	*Nasalide, Aerobid*	Inhalant, intranasal	Control of bronchial asthma; relief of symptoms of seasonal and allergic rhinitis
hydrocortisone	*Cortef*	Oral, IV, IM, topical, ophthalmic, rectal, intra-articular	Replacement therapy, treatment of allergic and inflammatory disorders
methylprednisolone	*Medrol*	Oral, IV, IM	Treatment of allergic and inflammatory disorders
P prednisolone	*Delta-Cortef*	Oral, IV, IM, ophthalmic, intra-articular	Treatment of allergic and inflammatory disorders
prednisone	*Deltasone*	Oral	Replacement therapy for adrenal insufficiency; treatment of allergic and inflammatory disorders

triamcinolone	*Aristocort*	Oral, IM, inhalant, intra-articular, topical	Treatment of allergic and inflammatory disorders, management of asthma

NURSING CONSIDERATIONS
for patients receiving glucocorticoids

Assessment

HISTORY. Screen for history of allergies to any steroid preparations; acute infections; peptic ulcer disease; pregnancy; lactation; endocrine disturbances, and renal dysfunction.

PHYSICAL ASSESSMENT. Include screening for baseline status before beginning therapy and for any potential adverse effects: weight; temperature; orientation, affect, grip strength, eye exam; blood pressure, pulse, peripheral perfusion, vessel evaluation; respiration, adventitious breath sounds; and glucose tolerance, renal function, serum electrolytes, and endocrine function tests as appropriate.

Nursing Diagnoses

The patient receiving any glucocorticoid may have the following nursing diagnoses related to drug therapy:

- Alteration in cardiac output related to fluid retention
- Fluid volume excess related to water retention
- Sensory–perceptual alteration
- Infection related to immunosuppression
- Ineffective individual coping related to body changes caused by drug
- Knowledge deficit regarding drug therapy

Implementation

- Administer daily around 8 to 9 A.M. *to mimic normal peak diurnal concentration levels to minimize hypothalamic–pituitary axis suppression.*
- Space multiple doses evenly throughout the day *to try to achieve homeostasis.*
- Use minimal dose for minimal amount of time *to minimize adverse effects.*
- Taper doses when discontinuing from high doses or from long-term therapy *to give the adrenal glands a chance to recover and produce adrenocorticoids.*
- Arrange for increased dosage when the patient is under stress *to supply increased demand for corticosteroids associated with the stress reaction.*
- Use alternate-day maintenance therapy with short-acting drugs whenever possible *to decrease the risk of adrenal suppression.*
- Do not give live virus vaccines when the patient is immunosuppressed *because there is an increased risk of infection.*
- Protect from unnecessary exposure to infection and invasive procedures *because the steroids suppress the immune system and the patient will be at increased risk of infection.*
- Assess the patient carefully for any potential drug–drug interactions if giving in combination with other drugs *to avoid adverse effects.*
- Provide thorough patient teaching, including measures to avoid adverse effects; warning signs of problems; and the need for regular evaluation, including blood tests *to enhance patient knowledge of drug therapy and promote compliance.* Explain the need to protect the patient from exposure to infections (see Patient Teaching Checklist: Corticosteroids).

Evaluation

- Monitor patient response to the drug (relief of signs and symptoms of inflammation, return of adrenal function to within normal limits).
- Monitor for adverse effects (increased susceptibility to infections, skin changes, endocrine dysfunctions, fatigue, fluid retention, peptic ulcer, psychological changes).
- Evaluate the effectiveness of the teaching plan (patient can name drug, dosage, adverse effects to watch for, specific measures to avoid adverse effects).
- Monitor the effectiveness of comfort measures and compliance to the regimen (see Nursing Care Guide: Corticosteroids).

MINERALOCORTICOIDS

The classic mineralocorticoid is aldosterone, which holds sodium and, with it, water in the body and causes the excretion of potassium. Aldosterone is not available for pharmacological use. When used in high doses, the glucocorticoids cortisone and hydrocortisone have a mineralocorticoid effect. However, this effect is usually not enough to maintain electrolyte balance in adrenal insufficiency. Fludrocortisone (*Florinef*) is a more powerful mineralocorticoid and is preferred for replacement therapy, in combination with a glucocorticoid.

THERAPEUTIC ACTIONS AND INDICATIONS

The mineralocorticoids increase sodium reabsorption in renal tubules and increase potassium and hydrogen excretion, leading to water and sodium

PATIENT TEACHING CHECKLIST

Corticosteroids

Create customized patient teaching materials for a specific corticosteroid from your CD-ROM. Your patient teaching should stress the following points for drugs within this class: Corticosteroids are similar to steroids produced naturally in your body and affect a number of bodily functions.

You should never stop taking your drug suddenly. If your prescription is low, or you are unable to take the medication for *any* reason, notify your health care provider.

Some of the following adverse effects may occur:

- Increased appetite—This may be a welcome change, but if you notice a continual weight gain, you may want to watch your calories.
- Restlessness, trouble sleeping—Some people experience an elation and feeling of new energy; frequent rest periods should be taken.
- Increased susceptibility to infection—Because your body's normal defenses will be decreased, you should avoid crowded places or people with known infections. If you notice any signs of illness or infection, notify your health care provider at once.

If you are taking this drug for a prolonged period of time, limit your intake of salt and salted products and add proteins to your diet.

Avoid the use of any over-the-counter medication without first checking with your health care provider. Several of these medications can interfere with the effectiveness of this drug.

Tell any doctor, nurse, or other health care provider that you are taking this drug.

Because this drug affects your body's natural defenses, you will need special care during any stressful situations. You may want to wear or carry a medical alert tag showing that you are on this medication. This tag alerts any medical personnel taking care of you in an emergency to the fact that you are taking this drug.

Report any of the following to your health care provider: sudden weight gain; fever or sore throat; black, tarry stools; swelling of the hands or feet; any signs of infection; easy bruising.

It is important to have regular medical follow-up. If you are being tapered from this drug, notify your health care provider if any of the following occur: fatigue; nausea, vomiting; diarrhea; weight loss; weakness; dizziness.

Keep this drug out of the reach of children. Do not give this medication to anyone else or take any similar medication that has not been prescribed for you.

This Teaching Checklist reflects general patient teaching guidelines. It is not meant to be a substitute for drug-specific teaching information, which is available in nursing drug guides.

retention (see Figure 34-1). These drugs are indicated, in combination with a glucocorticoid, for replacement therapy in primary and secondary adrenal insufficiency. They are also indicated for the treatment of salt-wasting adrenogenital syndrome when taken with appropriate glucocorticoids. Fludrocortisone is being tried for the treatment of severe orthostatic hypotension because its sodium and water retention effects can lead to increased blood pressure.

CONTRAINDICATIONS/CAUTIONS

These drugs are contraindicated in the presence of any known allergy to the drug; with severe hypertension, CHF, or cardiac disease (because of the resultant increased blood pressure); and lactation. Caution should be used in pregnancy, in the presence of any infection, and with high sodium intake (severe hypernatremia could occur).

ADVERSE EFFECTS

Adverse effects commonly associated with the use of mineralocorticoids are related to the increased fluid volume seen with sodium and water retention (e.g., headache, edema, hypertension, CHF, arrhythmias, weakness, hypokalemia). Allergic reactions, ranging from skin rash to anaphylaxis, have been reported.

CLINICALLY IMPORTANT DRUG–DRUG INTERACTIONS

Decreased effectiveness of salicylates, barbiturates, hydantoins, rifampin, and anticholinesterases has

NURSING CARE GUIDE
Corticosteroids

Assessment	***Nursing Diagnoses***	***Implementation***	***Evaluation***
HISTORY Allergies to any steroids, CHF, pregnancy, lactation, hypertension, acute infection, peptic ulcer, vaccination with a live virus, endocrine disorders	Alteration in cardiac output related to fluid retention Sensory–perceptual alteration related to CNS effects Infection related to immunosuppression Ineffectual individual coping related to body changes caused by drug Fluid volume excess related to water retention Knowledge deficit regarding drug therapy	Administer around 9 A.M. to mimic normal diurnal rhythm. Use minimal dose for minimal period of time dosage is needed. Arrange for increased doses during times of stress. Taper gradually to allow adrenal glands to recover and produce own steroids. Protect patient from unnecessary exposure to infection. Provide support and reassurance to deal with drug therapy. Provide patient teaching regarding drug name, dosage, adverse effects, precautions, and warning signs to report.	Evaluate drug effects: relief of signs and symptoms of inflammation; adrenal replacement as appropriate. Monitor for adverse effects: infection, peptic ulcer, fluid retention, hypertension, electrolyte imbalance endocrine changes. Monitor for drug–drug interactions as indicated for each drug. Evaluate effectiveness of patient teaching program. Evaluate effectiveness of comfort and safety measures.
PHYSICAL EXAMINATION Neurological: orientation, reflexes, affect General: T, weight CV: P, cardiac auscultation, BP, edema Respiratory: R, adventitious sounds Lab tests: urinalysis, blood glucose, stool guaiac test, renal function tests			

been reported when these drugs are combined with mineralocorticoids. The combinations should be avoided if possible, but if necessary, the patient should be monitored closely and dosage increased as needed.

DATA LINK

Data link to the following mineralocorticoids in your nursing drug guide:

MINERALOCORTICOIDS

Name	Brand Name	Routes	Usual Indications
cortisone	*Cortisone Acetate*	Oral, IM	Replacement therapy in adrenal insufficiency; treatment of allergic and inflammatory disorders
P fludrocortisone	*Florinef*	Oral	Replacement therapy and treatment of salt-losing adrenogenital syndrome with a glucocorticoid

hydrocortisone	*Cortef*	Oral, IV, IM, topical, ophthalmic, rectal, intra-articular	Replacement therapy, treatment of allergic and inflammatory disorders

WWW.WEB LINKS

Patients and health care providers may want to consult the following Internet sources:

Information on where to go to learn about diseases, drugs, other therapies:
http://www.healthfinder.gov

Information on disease research and development, latest drug therapy, and links to other resources—National Institutes of Health:
http://www.nih.gov

Information on where to go to find support groups, information on specific diseases, and treatments:
http://www.spinihl/nvap0302.htm

Information on rheumatoid and inflammatory diseases:
http://www.arthritis.org.connections/international/

NURSING CONSIDERATIONS
for patients receiving mineralocorticoids

Assessment

HISTORY. Screen for history of CHF, hypertension, infections, high sodium intake, lactation, and pregnancy.

PHYSICAL ASSESSMENT. Include screening for baseline status before beginning therapy and for any potential adverse effects: blood pressure, pulse, adventitious breath sounds; weight, temperature; tissue turgor; reflexes and bilateral grip strength; and serum electrolyte levels.

Nursing Diagnoses

The patient receiving any mineralocorticoid may have the following nursing diagnoses related to drug therapy:

- Alteration in nutrition, more than required, related to metabolic changes
- Fluid volume excess related to sodium retention
- Alteration in patterns of urinary elimination related to sodium retention
- Knowledge deficit regarding drug therapy

Implementation

- Use only in conjunction with appropriate glucocorticoids *to maintain control of electrolyte balance.*
- Increase dosage in times of stress to prevent adrenal insufficiency *to meet increased demands for corticosteroids under stress.*
- Monitor for hypokalemia (weakness, serum electrolytes) *to detect the loss early and treat appropriately.*
- Discontinue if signs of overdosage occur (excessive weight gain, edema, hypertension, cardiomegaly).
- Provide thorough patient teaching including measures to avoid adverse effects; warning signs of problems; and the need for regular evaluation, including blood tests *to enhance patient knowledge about drug therapy and promote compliance.*

Evaluation

- Monitor patient response to the drug (maintenance of electrolyte balance).
- Monitor for adverse effects (fluid retention, edema, hypokalemia, headache).
- Evaluate the effectiveness of the teaching plan (patient can name drug, dosage, adverse effects to watch for, specific measures to avoid adverse effects).
- Monitor the effectiveness of comfort measures and compliance to the regimen.

CHAPTER SUMMARY

- There are two adrenal glands, one on top of each kidney.
- Each adrenal gland is composed of the adrenal medulla and adrenal cortex. The adrenal medulla is basically a sympathetic nerve ganglia that releases norepinephrine and epinephrine into the blood stream in response to sympathetic stimulation. The adrenal cortex produces three different hormones.
- The adrenal cortex produces three corticosteroids: androgens (male and female sex hormones), glucocorticoids, and mineralocorticoids.
- The corticosteroids are released normally in a diurnal rhythm, with the hypothalamus producing peak levels of CRH around midnight; peak adrenal response occurs around 9 A.M. The steroid levels drop slowly during the day to reach low levels in the evening, when the hypothalamus begins CRH secretion, with peak levels again occurring around midnight. Corticosteroids are also released as part of the sympathetic stress reaction to help the body conserve energy for "fight or flight."
- Prolonged use of corticosteroids will suppress the normal hypothalamic–pituitary axis and lead to adrenal atrophy from lack of stimulation. Cortico-

steroids need to be tapered slowly after prolonged use to allow the adrenals to resume steroid production.

- The glucocorticoids increase glucose production; stimulate fat deposition and protein breakdown; and inhibit protein formation. They are used clinically to block inflammation and the immune response and in conjunction with mineralocorticoids to treat adrenal insufficiency.
- The mineralocorticoids stimulate sodium and water retention and the excretion of potassium. They are used therapeutically in conjunction with glucocorticoids to treat adrenal insufficiency.
- Adverse effects of corticosteroids are related to exaggeration of the physiologic effects, including immunosuppression, peptic ulcer formation, fluid retention, and edema.
- Corticosteroids are used topically and locally to achieve the desired anti-inflammatory effects at a particular site without the systemic adverse effects that limit the usefulness of the drugs.

Bibliography

Andrews, M. & Boyle, J. (1999). *Transcultural concepts in nursing care.* Philadelphia: Lippincott Williams & Wilkins.

Bullock, B. L. (2000). *Focus on pathophysiology.* Philadelphia: Lippincott Williams & Wilkins.

Guyton, A. & Hall, J. (1996). *Textbook of medical physiology.* Philadelphia: W. B. Saunders.

Hardman, J. G., Limbird, L. E., Molinoff, P. B., Ruddon, R. W., & Gilman, A.G. (Eds.). (1996). *Goodman and Gilman's the pharmacological basis of therapeutics* (9th ed.). New York: McGraw-Hill.

Karch, A. M. (2000). *2000 Lippincott's nursing drug guide: 2000.* Philadelphia: Lippincott Williams & Wilkins.

McEvoy, B. R. (1999). *Facts and comparisons 1999.* St. Louis: Facts and Comparisons.

The medical letter on drugs and therapeutics. (1999). New Rochelle, NY: Medical Letter.

North, W. G. et al. (1993). The neurohypophysis: A window on brain function. *Annals of the New York Academy of Sciences,* 689.

Porth, C. (1998). *Pathophysiology: Concepts of altered health states* (5th ed.). Philadelphia: Lippincott-Raven.

CHAPTER 35

Thyroid and Parathyroid Agents

Thyroid hormones
- P levothyroxine
- liothyronine
- liotrix
- thyroid desiccated

Antithyroid agents
- Thioamides
  - methimazole
  - P propylthiouracil
- Iodines
  - sodium iodide I^{131}
  - P strong iodine solution, potassium iodide

Antihypocalcemic agents
- P calcitriol
- dihydrotachysterol

Antihypercalcemic agents
- Bisphosphonates
  - alendronate
  - P etidronate
  - pamidronate
  - risendronate
  - tiludronate
- Calcitonins
  - calcitonin, human
  - P calcitonin, salmon
- Other antihypercalcemic agents
  - gallium

CHAPTER OUTLINE

KEY TERMS

bisphosphonates
calcitonin
cretinism
follicles
hyperparathyroidism
hyperthyroidism
hypoparathyroidism
hypothyroidism
iodine
liothyronine
metabolism
myxedema
Paget's disease
parathormone
postmenopausal osteoporosis
hypocalcemia
thioamides
thyroxine

INTRODUCTION

This chapter will review drugs that are used to affect the function of the thyroid and parathyroid glands. These two glands are closely situated in the middle of the neck and share the common goal of calcium homeostasis. In most respects, however, these glands are very different in structure and function.

THE THYROID GLAND

Structure

The thyroid gland is located in the middle of the neck where it surrounds the trachea like a shield (Figure 35-1). Its name comes from the Greek words *thyros* (shield) and *eidos* (gland). The thyroid is a vascular gland with two lobes, one on each side of the trachea, and a small isthmus connecting the two lobes. The gland is made up of cells arranged in circular ***follicles***. The center of each follicle is composed of colloid tissue where thyroid hormones produced by the gland are stored.

The thyroid gland produces two slightly different thyroid hormones, using iodine that is found in the diet: ***levothyroxine,*** or T_4, so named because it contains four iodine atoms, and triiodothyronine or ***liothyronine,*** or T_3, so named because it contains three iodine atoms. The thyroid cells remove iodine from the blood, concentrate it, and prepare it for attachment to tyrosine, an amino acid. A person must obtain sufficient amounts of dietary iodine to produce thyroid hormones.

When thyroid hormone is needed in the body, the stored thyroid hormone molecule is absorbed into the thyroid cells where the T_3 and T_4 are broken off and released into circulation. These hormones are carried on plasma proteins, which can be measured as the protein-bound iodine (PBI) levels. The thyroid gland produces more T_4 than T_3. More T_4 is released into circulation, but T_3 is approximately four times more active than T_4. Most T_4 (with a half-life of about 12 hours) is converted to T_3 (with a half-life of about 1 week) at the tissue level.

Control

Thyroid hormone production and release are regulated by the anterior pituitary hormone thyroid-stimulating hormone (TSH). The secretion of TSH is regulated by thyrotropin releasing hormone (TRH), a hypothalamic regulating factor. A delicate balance exists between the thyroid, the pituitary, and the hypothalamus in regulating the levels of thyroid hormone. The thyroid gland produces increased thyroid hormone in response to increased levels of TSH. The increased levels of thyroid hormones send a negative feedback message to the pituitary to decrease TSH release and at the same time to the hypothalamus to decrease TRH release. A drop in TRH levels will subsequently result in a drop of TSH levels, which in turn will lead to a drop in thyroid hormone levels. In response to low blood serum levels of thyroid hormone, the hypothalamus sends TRH to the anterior pituitary, which responds by releasing TSH, which in turn stimulates the thyroid gland to again produce and release thyroid hormone. The rising levels of thyroid hormone are sensed by the hypothalamus, and the cycle will begin again. This intricate series of negative feedback mechanisms keep the level of thyroid hormone within a narrow range of normal (Figure 35-2).

Function

The thyroid hormone regulates the rate of ***metabolism,*** that is, the rate at which energy is burned, in almost all the cells of the body. The thyroid hormones affect heat production and body temperature; oxygen

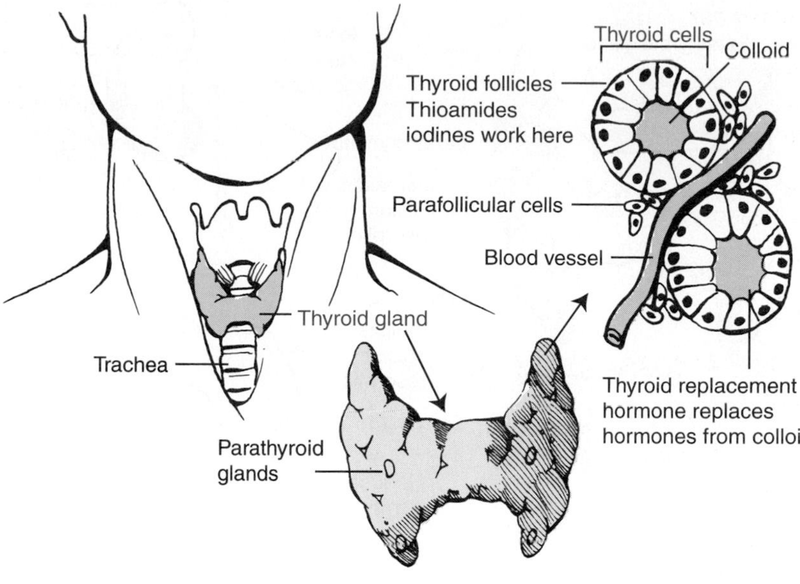

FIGURE 35-1. The thyroid and parathyroid glands. The basic unit of the thyroid gland is the follicle.

consumption and cardiac output; blood volume; enzyme system activity; and metabolism of carbohydrates, fats, and proteins. Thyroid hormone is also an important regulator of growth and development, especially within the reproductive and nervous system. Since the thyroid has such widespread effects throughout the body, any dysfunction of the thyroid gland will have numerous systemic effects.

Cells found around the follicle of the thyroid gland, called parafollicular cells, produce another hormone called ***calcitonin***. This hormone affects calcium levels and acts to balance the effects of parathyroid hormone, parathormone. The release of calcitonin is not controlled by the hypothalamic–pituitary axis but is regulated locally at the cellular level. The cells release calcitonin when the concentration of calcium around them rises. The calcitonin is released into the blood stream and works to reduce calcium levels by blocking bone resorption and enhancing bone formation, pulling calcium out of the serum for deposit into bone (Figure 35-3). When the calcium levels surrounding the cells fall, they will no longer produce calcitonin.

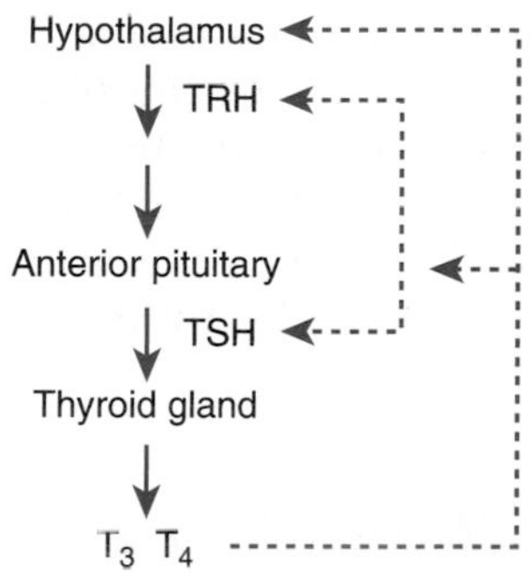

FIGURE 35-2. In response to low blood serum levels of thyroid hormone, the hypothalamus sends the thyrotropin releasing hormone (TRH) to the anterior pituitary, which responds by releasing the thyroid stimulating hormone (TSH) to the thyroid gland, which, in turn, responds by releasing the thyroid hormone (T_3 and T_4) into the blood stream. The anterior pituitary is also sensitive to the increase in blood serum levels of the thyroid hormone and decreases production and release of TSH. As thyroid hormone production and release subside, the hypothalamus senses the lower serum levels and the process is repeated by the release of TRH again. This intricate series of negative feedback mechanisms keeps the level of thyroid hormone within normal limits.

THYROID DYSFUNCTION

Thyroid dysfunction involves either underactivity, called ***hypothyroidism,*** or overactivity, called ***hyperthyroidism***.

Hypothyroidism

Hypothyroidism is a lack of sufficient levels of thyroid hormones to maintain a normal metabolism. This condition occurs in a number of pathophysiologic states:

- Absence of the thyroid gland
- Lack of sufficient iodine in the diet to produce the needed level of thyroid hormone
- Lack of sufficient functioning thyroid tissue due to tumor or autoimmune disorders
- Lack of TSH due to pituitary disease
- Lack of TRH related to a tumor or disorder of the hypothalamus

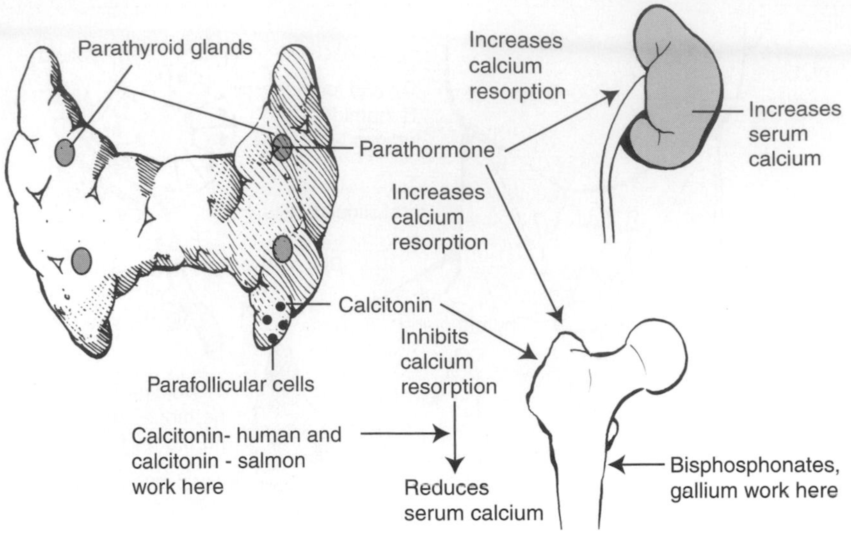

FIGURE 35-3. Calcium control. Parathormone and calcitonin work to maintain calcium homostasis in the body.

Hypothyroidism is the most common type of thyroid dysfunction. It is estimated that approximately 5 to 10% of women over age 50 are hypothyroid. Hypothyroidism is also a common finding in the elderly. The symptoms of hypothyroidism can be varied and vague and are frequently overlooked. The signs and symptoms of hypothyroidism are often mistaken for signs of normal aging. Goiter, or enlargement of the thyroid gland, occurs when the thyroid is overactive. This effect frequently occurs when the thyroid is overstimulated by TSH. This can happen when the thyroid gland cannot make sufficient thyroid hormones to turn off the hypothalamus and anterior pituitary; in an attempt to produce the needed amount of thyroid hormone, it is continually stimulated by increasing levels of TSH.

Children who are born without a thyroid gland or who have a nonfunctioning gland develop a condition called ***cretinism***. If untreated, these children will have poor growth and development and mental retardation because of the lack of thyroid hormone stimulation. Severe adult hypothyroidism is called ***myxedema***. Myxedema usually develops gradually as the thyroid slowly stops functioning. It can develop as a result of autoimmune thyroid disease (Hashimoto's disease), viral infection, or overtreatment with antithyroid drugs, or because of surgical removal or irradiation of the thyroid gland. Patients with myxedema exhibit many signs and symptoms of decreased metabolism, including lethargy, hypoactive reflexes, hypotension, bradycardia, pale and coarse skin, loss of hair, intolerance to the cold, decreased appetite, decreased body temperature, thickening of the tongue and vocal chords, decreased sexual function, and even sterility. Patients with hypothyroidism are treated with replacement thyroid hormone therapy.

Hyperthyroidism

Hyperthyroidism will occur when excessive amounts of thyroid hormones are produced and released into the circulation. Graves' disease, a poorly understood condition that is thought to be an autoimmune problem, is the most common cause of hyperthyroidism. Patients with hyperthyroidism may exhibit many signs and symptoms of overactive cellular metabolism, including increased body temperature, tachycardia, palpitations, hypertension, flushing, thin skin, an intolerance to heat, amenorrhea, weight loss, and goiter. Treatment of hyperthyroidism may involve surgical removal of the gland or portions of the gland; treatment with radiation to destroy parts or all of the gland; or drug treatment to block the production of thyroxine in the thyroid gland or to destroy parts or all of the gland. These patients will then need to be regulated with replacement thyroid hormone therapy.

Table 35-1 outlines the signs and symptoms of thyroid dysfunction.

THYROID HORMONE

Several replacement hormone products are available for treating hypothyroidism. These products contain natural and synthetic thyroid. Replacement hormones act to replace low or absent levels of the thyroid hormones and to suppress overproduction of TSH by the pituitary. (See Figure 35-1, which shows where these drugs act.)

Levothyroxine (*Synthroid*), a synthetic salt of T_4, is the most frequently used replacement hormone because of its predictable bioavailability and reliability. Other brand name and generic products are also available.

TABLE 35-1

SIGNS AND SYMPTOMS OF THYROID DYSFUNCTION

	Hypothyroidism	Hyperthyroidism
CNS	Depressed—hypoactive reflexes, lethargy, sleepiness, slow speech, emotional dullness	Stimulated—hyperactive reflexes, anxiety, nervousness, insomnia, tremors, restlessness
CV	Depressed—bradycardia, hypotension, anemia, oliguria, decreased sensitivity to catecholamine	Stimulated—tachycardia, palpitations, increased pulse pressure, systolic hypertension, increased sensitivity to catecholamines
Skin, hair, nails	Pale, coarse, dry, thickened; puffy eyes and eyelids; hair coarse and thin; nails thick and hard	Flushed, warm, thin, moist, sweating; hair fine and soft; nails soft and thin
Metabolic rate	Decreased—lower body temperature; intolerance to cold; decreased appetite, higher levels of fat and cholesterol, weight gain, and hypercholesterolemia	Increased—low-grade fever; intolerance to heat; increased appetite with weight loss; muscle wasting and weakness, thyroid myopathy
Generalized myxedema	Accumulation of mucopolysaccharides in the heart, tongue, vocal chords; periorbital edema, cardiomyopathy, hoarseness, and thickened speech	Localized with accumulation of mucopolysaccharides in eyeballs, ocular muscles; periorbital edema, lid lag, exophthalmos; pretibial edema
Ovaries	Decreased function—menorrhagia, habitual abortion, sterility	Altered; tendency toward oligomenorrhea, amenorrhea
Goiter	Rare; simple nontoxic type may occur	Diffuse, highly vascular; very frequent

Thyroid desiccated (*Thyroid Strong* and others) is prepared from dried animal thyroid glands and contains both T_3 and T_4. Although the ratio of the hormones is unpredictable and the required dosage and effects vary widely, this drug is inexpensive, making it attractive to some.

Liothyronine (*Cytomel*) is a synthetic salt of T_3. Because it contains only T_3, liothyronine has a rapid onset and long duration of action. It also has a greater incidence of cardiac side effects and is not recommended for use in patients with potential cardiac problems.

Liotrix (*Thyrolar*) is a synthetic preparation of both T_4 and T_3 in a standard 4:1 ratio. Because it is associated with several cardiac and central nervous system (CNS) effects, it may not be the drug of choice for patients who have cardiac problems or are prone to anxiety reactions.

THERAPEUTIC ACTIONS AND INDICATIONS

The thyroid replacement hormones increase the metabolic rate of body tissues, increasing oxygen consumption, respiration, heart rate, growth and maturation, and the metabolism of fats, carbohydrates, and proteins. They are indicated for replacement therapy in hypothyroid states, the treatment of myxedema coma, suppression of TSH in the treatment and prevention of goiters, and the management of thyroid cancer. In conjunction with antithyroid drugs, they also are indicated to treat thyroid toxicity, prevent goiter formation during thyroid overstimulation, and treat thyroid overstimulation during pregnancy.

CONTRAINDICATIONS/CAUTIONS

These drugs should not be used with any known allergy to the drugs or their binders, during acute thyrotoxicosis (unless used in conjunction with antithyroid drugs), or during acute myocardial infarction (MI) (unless complicated by hypothyroidism) because these hormones could exacerbate these conditions. Caution should be used during lactation (because the drug enters breast milk and could suppress the infant's own thyroid production) and with hypoadrenal conditions such as Addison's disease.

ADVERSE EFFECTS

When the correct dosage of the replacement therapy is being used, there are few if any adverse effects associated with these drugs. Skin reactions and loss of hair are sometimes seen, especially in the first few months of treatment in children. Symptoms of hyperthyroidism may occur as the drug dose is regulated. Some of the less predictable effects are associated with cardiac stimulation (arrhythmias, hypertension) and CNS effects (anxiety, sleeplessness, headache).

CLINICALLY IMPORTANT DRUG–DRUG INTERACTIONS

Decreased absorption of the thyroid hormones occurs when taken concurrently with cholestyramine. If this combination is needed, the drugs should be separated by 2 hours. The effectiveness of oral anticoagulants is increased when combined with thyroid hormone. Because this may lead to increased bleeding, the dosage of the oral anticoagulant should be reduced and the bleeding time checked periodically.

NURSING CHALLENGE

Thyroid Hormones for Obesity

Treatment trends for obesity have changed over the years. Not long ago, one of the suggested treatments was the use of thyroid hormone. The thinking was that obese people had slower metabolisms and thus would benefit from a boost in metabolism from extra thyroid hormone.

If an obese patient is truly hypothyroid, this might be a good idea. Unfortunately, many of the patients who received thyroid hormone for weight loss were not tested for thyroid activity—and ended up with excessive thyroid hormone in their systems. This situation triggered a cascade of events. The exogenous thyroid hormone disrupted the hypothalamic-pituitary-thyroid control system, resulting in decreased TRH and TSH production as the hypothalamus and pituitary sensed the rising levels of thyroid hormone. Because the thyroid was no longer stimulated to produce and secrete thyroid hormone, thyroid levels would actually fall. Lacking stimulation by TSH, the thyroid gland would start to atrophy. If exogenous thyroid hormone were stopped, the atrophied thyroid would not be able to immediately respond to the TSH stimulation and produce thyroid hormone. Ultimately, these patients experienced an endocrine imbalance. What's more, they also did not lose weight—and in the long run may actually have gained weight as the body's compensatory mechanisms tried to deal with the imbalances.

Today, thyroid hormone is no longer considered a good choice for treating obesity. Other drugs have come and gone, and new drugs are released each year to attack other aspects of the problem. Many patients, especially middle-aged people who may recall that thyroid was once used for weight loss, ask for thyroid hormone as an answer to their weight problem. Patients have even been know to "borrow" thyroid replacement hormones from others for a quick weight loss solution.

Obese patients need reassurance, understanding, and education about the risks of borrowed thyroid hormone. Insistent patients should undergo thyroid function tests. If the results are normal, patients should receive teaching about the controls and actions of thyroid hormone in the body and an explanation of why taking these hormones can cause problems. Obesity is a chronic and frustrating problem that poses continual challenges for health care providers.

Decreased effectiveness of digitalis glycosides can occur when these drugs are combined. Consequently, digitalis levels should be monitored and increased dosage may be required. Theophylline clearance is decreased in hypothyroid states. As the patient approaches normal thyroid function, theophylline dosage may need to be adjusted frequently.

DATA LINK

Data link to the following thyroid hormones in your nursing drug guide:

THYROID HORMONES

Name	Brand Name	Usual Indications
P levothyroxine	*Synthroid* and others	Replacement therapy in hypothyroidism; suppression of TSH release; treatment of myxedema coma and thyrotoxicosis
liothyronine	*Cytomel*	Replacement therapy in hypothyroidism; suppression of TSH release; treatment of thyrotoxicosis synthetic hormone used in patients allergic to dessicated thyroid—not for use with cardiac or anxiety problems
liotrix	*Thyrolar*	Replacement therapy in hypothyroidism; suppression of TSH release; treatment of thyrotoxicosis—not for use with cardiac dysfunction
thyroid desiccated	*Thyroid Strong*	Replacement therapy in hypothyroidism; suppression of TSH release; treatment of thyrotoxicosis

NURSING CONSIDERATIONS
for patients receiving thyroid hormones

Assessment

HISTORY. Screen for history of allergy to any thyroid hormone or binder; lactation; Addison's disease; acute MI not complicated by hypothyroidism; and thyrotoxicosis.

PHYSICAL ASSESSMENT. Include screening for baseline status before beginning therapy and for any potential adverse effects: the presence of any skin lesions; orientation and affect: baseline pulse and blood pressure, baseline ECG; respiration, adventitious sounds; and thyroid function tests.

Nursing Diagnoses

The patient receiving any thyroid hormone may have the following nursing diagnoses related to drug therapy:

- Alteration in cardiac output related to cardiac effects

CASE STUDY

Hypothyroidism

PRESENTATION

H. R., a 38-year-old white woman, is seen in the clinic with complaints of "exhaustion, lethargy, and sleepiness." Her past history was sketchy, her speech seemed slurred, and her attention span was limited. Mr. R., her husband, reported feeling frustrated with H. R., stating that she had become increasingly lethargic, disorganized, and uninvolved at home. He also noted that she had gained weight and lost interest in her appearance. Physical examination revealed the following remarkable findings: P—52; BP—90/62; T—96.8°F (oral); skin—pale, dry, thick; periorbital edema; tongue thick and asymmetric; height—5′5″; weight—165 lbs. The immediate impression was of hypothyroidism. Laboratory tests confirmed this, with TSH levels elevated, and T3 and T4 levels very low. The patient was begun on *Synthroid* 0.2 mg qd PO.

CRITICAL THINKING QUESTIONS

What teaching plans should be developed for this patient? What interventions would be appropriate in helping Mr. and Mrs. R. accept her diagnosis and the pathophysiological basis for her complaints and the problems they are having. What body image changes will H. R. experience as her body adjusts to the thyroid therapy? How can H. R. be helped to adjust to these changes and reestablish her body image and self concept?

DISCUSSION

Hypothyroidism develops slowly over a period of time. With it comes fatigue, lethargy, and lack of emotional affect—conditions that result in the patient losing interest in appearance, activities, and responsibilities. The patient's husband, not knowing that there was a physical reason for this problem, became increasingly frustrated and even angry. Mr. R. should be involved in the teaching program so that his feelings can be taken into consideration. Any teaching should be written down for later reference. (When H. R. starts to return to normal, her attention span and interest should return; anything that was missed or forgotten can be referred to in the written teaching program.)

H. R. should be encouraged to bring a picture of herself from a year or so ago to help her to understand and appreciate the changes that have occurred. Many patients are totally unaware of changes in appearance and activity because the disease progresses so slowly and brings on lethargy and lack of emotional affect.

The teaching plan should include information about the function of the thyroid gland and the anticipated changes that will be occurring to H. R. over the next week and beyond. The importance of taking the medication daily should be emphasized. The need to return for follow-up to evaluate the effectiveness of the medication and the effects on her body should also be stressed. Both H. R. and her husband will need support and encouragement to deal with past frustrations and the return to normal. Lifelong therapy will most likely be needed, so further teaching will be important once things have stabilized.

- Alteration in nutrition, less than required, related to changes in metabolism
- Alteration in tissue perfusion related to thyroid activity
- Knowledge deficit regarding drug therapy

Implementation

- Administer a single daily dose before breakfast each day *to assure consistent therapeutic levels.*
- Monitor response carefully when beginning therapy *to adjust dosage according to patient response.*
- Monitor cardiac response *to detect cardiac adverse effects.*
- Assess the patient carefully *to detect any potential drug–drug interactions if giving in combination with other drugs.*
- Arrange for periodic blood tests of thyroid function *to monitor the effectiveness of the therapy.*
- Provide thorough patient teaching including measures to avoid adverse effects, warning signs of problems, and the need for regular evaluation if used for longer than recommended *to enhance patient knowledge of drug therapy and promote compliance* (see Patient Teaching Checklist: Thyroid Hormone).

Evaluation

- Monitor patient response to the drug (return of metabolism to normal, prevention of goiter).
- Monitor for adverse effects (tachycardia, hypertension, anxiety, skin rash).
- Evaluate the effectiveness of the teaching plan (patient can name drug, dosage, adverse effects to watch for, specific measures to avoid adverse effects).

PATIENT TEACHING CHECKLIST

Thyroid Hormone

Create customized patient teaching materials for a specific thyroid hormone from your CD-ROM. Your patient teaching should stress the following points for drugs within this class:

This hormone is designed to replace the thyroid hormone that your body is not able to produce. The thyroid hormone is responsible for regulating your body's metabolism, or the speed with which your body's cells burn energy. Because of this action of the thyroid hormone, it affects many body systems. It is very important that you take this medication only as prescribed.

Never stop taking this drug without consulting with your health care provider. The drug is used to replace a very important hormone and will probably have to be taken for life. Stopping the medication can lead to serious problems.

This drug usually causes no adverse effects. You may notice a slight skin rash or hair loss in the first few months of therapy. You should notice that the signs and symptoms of your thyroid deficiency will disappear and you will feel "back to normal."

Report any of the following to your health care provider: chest pain, difficulty breathing, sore throat, fever, chills, weight gain, sleeplessness, nervousness, unusual sweating or intolerance to heat.

Avoid the use of any over-the-counter medication without first checking with your health care provider. Several of these medications can interfere with the effectiveness of this drug.

Tell any doctor, nurse, or other health care provider that you are taking this drug. You may want to wear or carry a medical alert tag showing that you are on this medication. This would alert any medical personnel taking care of you in an emergency to the fact that you are taking this drug.

While you are taking this drug, it is important to have regular medical follow-up, including blood tests to check the activity of your thyroid gland, and to evaluate your response to the drug and any possible underlying problems.

Keep this drug, and all medications, out of the reach of children. Do not give this medication to anyone else or take any similar medication that has not been prescribed for you.

This Teaching Checklist reflects general patient teaching guidelines. It is not meant to be a substitute for drug-specific teaching information, which is available in nursing drug guides.

- Monitor the effectiveness of comfort measures and compliance to the regimen (see Nursing Care Guide: Thyroid Hormone).

ANTITHYROID AGENTS

Drugs used to block production of thyroid hormone and to treat hyperthyroidism include the ***thioamides*** and iodide solutions. Although not chemically related, both groups of drugs block the formation of thyroid hormones within the thyroid gland (see Figure 35-1).

The Thioamides

Propylthiouracil (*PTU*) is the most frequently used thioamide. The other available thioamide is methimazole (*Tapazole*). Hematologic adverse effects are more common with methimazole, so the patient needs to have CBC and differentials monitored regularly. Gastrointestinal (GI) effects are somewhat less pronounced with methimazole, so it may be a drug of choice in patients unable to tolerate PTU.

THERAPEUTIC ACTIONS AND INDICATIONS

The thioamides prevent the formation of thyroid hormone within the thyroid cells, lowering the serum levels of thyroid hormone. They also partially inhibit the conversion of T_4 to T_3 at the cellular level. Thioamides are indicated for the treatment of hyperthyroidism.

CONTRAINDICATIONS/CAUTIONS

Thioamides are contraindicated in the presence of any known allergy to antithyroid drugs and during pregnancy. (If an antithyroid drug is absolutely essential and the mother has been informed about the risk of cretinism in the infant, propylthiouracil is the drug of choice.) They should be used cautiously during lactation because of the risk of antithyroid activity in the infant. (Again, if an antithyroid drug is needed, propylthiouracil is the drug of choice.)

ADVERSE EFFECTS

The adverse effects most commonly seen with these drugs are the effects of thyroid suppression: drowsi-

NURSING CARE GUIDE
Thyroid Hormone

Assessment	Nursing Diagnoses	Implementation	Evaluation
HISTORY Allergies to any of these drugs, Addison's disease; acute MI not complicated by hypothyroidism; lactation; thyrotoxicosis	Alteration in cardiac output related to cardiac effects Alteration in nutrition, less than body requirements, related to effects on metabolism Alteration in tissue perfusion related to thyroid effects Knowledge deficit regarding drug therapy	Administer once a day at breakfast. Provide comfort, safety measures (e.g., temperature control, rest as needed, safety precautions). Provide support and reassurance to deal with drug effects and life-time need. Provide patient teaching regarding drug name, dosage, adverse effects, and precautions, and warning signs to report.	Evaluate drug effects: return of metabolism to normal; prevention of goiter. Monitor for adverse effects: anxiety, tachycardia, hypertension, skin reaction. Monitor for drug–drug interactions as indicated for each drug. Evaluate effectiveness of patient teaching program. Evaluate effectiveness of comfort and safety measures.
PHYSICAL EXAMINATION Neurological: orientation, affect Skin: color, lesions CV: P, cardiac auscultation, BP, ECG Respiratory: R, adventitious sounds Hematological: thyroid function tests			

ness, lethargy, bradycardia, nausea, skin rash, and so on. Propylthiouracil is associated with nausea, vomiting, and GI complaints. Methimazole is also associated with bone marrow suppression, so the patient using this drug must have frequent blood tests to monitor for this effect.

Iodine Solutions

Low doses of iodine are needed in the body for the formation of thyroid hormone. High doses, however, act to block thyroid function; thus, iodine preparations are sometimes used to treat hyperthyroidism. Radioactive iodine (I^{131}) is sometimes used as a diagnostic agent or to destroy thyroid tissue in cases of severe Graves' disease. Strong Iodine Solution, potassium iodide, and sodium iodide (*Thyro-Block*) are taken orally and have a rapid onset of action, with effects seen within 24 hours and peak effects seen in 10 to 15 days. The effects are short-lived and may even precipitate further thyroid enlargement and dysfunction. Because of this, and the availability of the more predictable thioamides, iodides are not used as often as they once were in the clinical setting.

THERAPEUTIC ACTIONS AND INDICATIONS

The thyroid cells become oversaturated with iodine and stop producing thyroid hormone. In some cases, the thyroid cells are actually destroyed. The iodine solutions are reserved for presurgical suppression of the thyroid gland, for treatment of acute thyrotoxicosis until thioamide levels can take effect, or for thyroid blocking during radiation therapy.

The iodine solutions are also used to block thyroid function in radiation emergencies. Radioactive iodine is taken up into the thyroid cells, which are then destroyed by the beta radiation given off by the radioactive iodine. The use of radioactive iodine is reserved for those patients who are not candidates for surgery, for women who cannot become pregnant, or for elderly patients with such severe, complicating conditions that immediate thyroid destruction is needed.

CONTRAINDICATIONS/CAUTIONS

The use of iodine solutions is contraindicated in the presence of pregnancy (because of the effect on the mother's and fetus's thyroid glands) and with pulmonary edema or pulmonary tuberculosis.

ADVERSE EFFECTS

The most common adverse effect to these drugs is hypothyroidism, so the patient will need to be started on replacement thyroid hormone to maintain homeostasis. Other adverse effects include iodism (metallic taste and burning in the mouth, sore teeth and gums, diarrhea, cold symptoms, and stomach upset), staining of teeth, skin rash, and the development of goiter.

CLINICALLY IMPORTANT DRUG–DRUG INTERACTIONS

Since the use of drugs to destroy thyroid function will revert the patient from hyperthyroidism to hypothyroidism, patients on drugs that are metabolized differently in hypothyroid or hyperthyroid states, or that have a small margin of safety which could be altered by the change in thyroid function, should be monitored closely. These drugs include anticoagulants, theophylline, digoxin, metoprolol, and propranolol.

DATA LINK

Data link to the following antithyroid agents in your nursing drug guide:

ANTITHYROID AGENTS

Name	Brand Name	Usual Indications
THIOAMIDES		
methimazole	*Tapazole*	Treatment of hyperthyroidism
P propylthiouracil	*PTU*	Treatment of hyperthyroidism
IODINES		
sodium iodide I^{131}	generic	Treatment of hyperthyroidism, destruction of thyroid tissue in patients who are not candidates for surgery and thyroid destruction is needed
strong iodine solution, potassium iodide	*Thyro-Block*	Treatment of hyperthyroidism, thyroid blocking in radiation emergencies

NURSING CONSIDERATIONS
for patients receiving antithyroid agents

Assessment

HISTORY. Screen for history of allergy to any antithyroid drug, and pregnancy or lactation.

PHYSICAL ASSESSMENT. Include screening for baseline status before beginning therapy and for any potential adverse effects: the presence of any skin lesions; orientation and affect: baseline pulse and blood pressure, baseline ECG; respiration, adventitious sounds; and thyroid function tests.

Nursing Diagnoses

The patient receiving any antithyroid drug may have the following nursing diagnoses related to drug therapy:

- Alteration in cardiac output related to cardiac effects
- Alteration in nutrition, more than body requirements, related to changes in metabolism
- Potential for injury related to bone marrow suppression
- Knowledge deficit regarding drug therapy

Implementation

- Administer propylthiouracil three times a day, around the clock, *to assure consistent therapeutic levels.*
- Give iodine solution through a straw *to decrease staining of teeth;* tablets can be crushed.
- Monitor response carefully; arrange for periodic blood tests *to assess patient response and to monitor for adverse effects.*
- Monitor patients receiving iodine solution for any sign of iodism *so drug can be stopped immediately if such signs appear.*
- Provide thorough patient teaching, including measures to avoid adverse effects, warning signs of problems, and the need for regular evaluation if used for longer than recommended *to enhance patient knowledge of drug therapy and promote compliance.*

Evaluation

- Monitor patient response to the drug (lowering of thyroid hormone levels).
- Monitor for adverse effects (bradycardia, anxiety, blood dyscrasias, skin rash).
- Evaluate the effectiveness of the teaching plan (patient can name drug, dosage, adverse effects to watch for, specific measures to avoid adverse effects).
- Monitor the effectiveness of comfort measures and compliance to the regimen.

THE PARATHYROID GLANDS

Structure and Function

The parathyroid glands are actually four very small groups of glandular tissue located on the back of the thyroid gland. These cells produce parathyroid hormone (PTH) or ***parathormone***. PTH is the most important regulator of serum calcium levels in the body. PTH has many actions, including the following:

- Stimulation of osteoclasts or bone cells to release calcium from the bone
- Increased intestinal absorption of calcium
- Increased calcium resorption from the kidneys
- Stimulation of cells in the kidney to produce calcitriol, the active form of vitamin D, which stimulates intestinal transport of calcium into the blood

Control

Calcium is an electrolyte that is used in many of the body's metabolic processes. These processes include membrane transport systems, conduction of nerve impulses, muscle contraction, and blood clotting. To achieve all of these effects, the serum levels of calcium must be maintained between 9 and 11 mg/dl. This is achieved through regulation of serum calcium by two hormones, PTH and calcitonin (Figure 35-4).

Calcitonin is released when serum calcium levels rise. Calcitonin, produced in the thyroid gland, works to reduce calcium levels by blocking bone resorption and enhancing bone formation. This action pulls calcium out of the serum for deposit into the bone. PTH secretion is also directly regulated by serum calcium levels. When serum calcium levels are low, PTH release is stimulated. When serum calcium levels are high, PTH release is blocked.

Another electrolyte, magnesium, also affects PTH secretion by mobilizing calcium and inhibiting the release of PTH when concentrations rise above or fall below normal. An increased serum phosphate level will indirectly stimulate parathyroid activity. Renal tubular phosphate reabsorption is balanced by calcium secretion into the urine, which will cause a drop in serum calcium, stimulating PTH secretion. The hormones PTH and calcitonin work together to maintain the delicate balance of serum calcium levels in the body and to keep serum calcium levels within the normal range.

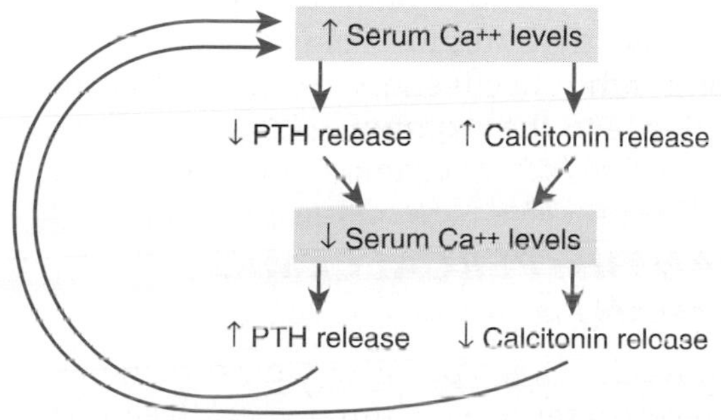

FIGURE 35-4. Control of serum Ca^{++} levels by PTH (parathormone) and calcitonin, showing the negative-feedback cycle in effect.

PARATHYROID DYSFUNCTION AND RELATED DISORDERS

The absence of parathormone, a condition called ***hypoparathyroidism,*** is relatively rare. It is most like to occur with the accidental removal of the parathyroid glands during thyroid surgery. The treatment of hypoparathyroidism consists of calcium and vitamin D therapy to increase serum calcium levels. There is no replacement PTH available.

The excessive production of parathormone, called ***hyperparathyroidism,*** can occur as a result of parathyroid tumor or certain genetic disorders. Patients with hyperparathyroidism may present with decalcification of bone and deposits of calcium in body tissues including the kidney, resulting in kidney stones. Primary hyperparathyroidism occurs more often in women in their 60s and 70s. Secondary hyperparathyroidism occurs most frequently in patients with chronic renal failure. When plasma concentrations of calcium are elevated secondary to high PTH levels, inorganic phosphate levels are usually decreased. Pseudorickets (renal fibrocystic osteosis or renal rickets) may occur as a result of this phosphorus retention (hyperphosphatemia), which results from increased stimulation of the parathyroid glands and increased PTH secretion.

The genetically linked disorder ***Paget's disease*** is a condition of overactive osteoclasts that are eventually replaced by enlarged and softened bony structures. Patients with this disease complain of deep bone pain, headaches, and hearing loss and usually have cardiac failure and bone malformation.

Postmenopausal osteoporosis can occur when dropping levels of estrogen allow calcium to be pulled out of the bone, resulting in weakened and honeycombed bone structure. Estrogen normally causes calcium deposits in the bone; osteoporosis is one of the many complications that accompany the loss of estrogen at menopause.

ANTIHYPOCALCEMIC AGENTS

Deficient levels of parathyroid hormone result in hypocalcemia, or calcium deficiency. Vitamin D stimulates calcium absorption from the intestine and restores the serum calcium to a normal level. Hypoparathyroidism is treated primarily with vitamin D and, if necessary, dietary supplements of calcium. Calcitriol (*Calcijex*) is the most commonly used form of vitamin D. Dihydrotachysterol (*Hytakerol*) is also used.

THERAPEUTIC ACTIONS AND INDICATIONS

Vitamin D compounds regulate the absorption of calcium and phosphate from the small intestine, mineral resorption in bone, and reabsorption of phosphate from the renal tubules. Working along with PTH and calcitonin to regulate calcium homeostasis, vitamin D actually functions as a hormone. Use of these agents is indicated for the management of hypocalcemia in patients on chronic renal dialysis and for the treatment of hypoparathyroidism.

CONTRAINDICATIONS/CAUTIONS

These drugs should not be used in the presence of any known allergy to vitamin D; hypercalcemia; vitamin D toxicity; or pregnancy. Caution should be used with a history of renal stones or during lactation when high calcium levels could cause problems.

ADVERSE EFFECTS

The adverse effects most commonly seen with these drugs are related to GI effects: metallic taste, nausea, vomiting, dry mouth, constipation, and anorexia. CNS effects such as weakness, headache, somnolence, and irritability may also occur. These are possibly related to the changes in electrolytes that occur with these drugs.

CLINICALLY IMPORTANT DRUG–DRUG INTERACTIONS

There is increased risk of hypermagnesemia if these drugs are taken with magnesium-containing antacids. This combination should be avoided. Reduced absorption of these compounds may occur if taken with cholestyramine or mineral oil because they are fat-soluble vitamins. If this combination is used, the drugs should be separated by at least 2 hours.

DATA LINK

Data link to the following antihypocalcemic agents in your nursing drug guide:

ANTIHYPOCALCEMIC AGENTS

Name	Brand Name	Usual Indications
P calcitriol	*Calcijex*	Management of hypocalcemia and reduction of PTH levels
dihydrotachyesterol	*Hytakerol*	Management of hypocalcemia

NURSING CONSIDERATIONS
for patients receiving antihypocalcemic agents

Assessment

HISTORY. Screen for history of allergy to vitamin D; hypercalcemia; vitamin toxicity; renal stone; and pregnancy or lactation.

PHYSICAL ASSESSMENT. Include screening for baseline status before beginning therapy and for any potential adverse effects: the presence of any skin lesions; orientation and affect; liver evaluation; serum calcium, magnesium, and alkaline phosphate levels; and x-ray of bones as appropriate.

Nursing Diagnoses

The patient receiving any antihypocalcemic drug may have the following nursing diagnoses related to drug therapy:

- Pain related to GI and CNS effects
- Alteration in nutrition, less than body requirements related to GI effects
- Knowledge deficit regarding drug therapy

Implementation

- Monitor serum calcium prior to and periodically during treatment *to allow for adjustment of dosage to maintain calcium levels within normal limits.*
- Provide supportive measures *to help the patient deal with GI and CNS effects of the drug* (analgesics, small and frequent meals, help with activities of daily living).
- Arrange for a nutritional consultation if GI effects are severe *to assure nutritional balance.*
- Provide thorough patient teaching, including measures to avoid adverse effects, warning signs of problems, and the need for regular evaluation *to enhance the patient's knowledge about drug therapy and promote compliance.*

Evaluation

- Monitor patient response to the drug (return of serum calcium levels to normal).
- Monitor for adverse effects (weakness, headache, GI effects).
- Evaluate the effectiveness of the teaching plan (patient can name drug, dosage, adverse effects to watch for, specific measures to avoid adverse effects).
- Monitor the effectiveness of comfort measures and compliance to the regimen.

ANTIHYPERCALCEMIC AGENTS

Drugs used to treat parathyroid hormone excess or high levels of serum calcium (hypercalcemia) include the *bisphosphonates,* calcitonin (human and salmon), and gallium. These drugs act on the serum levels of calcium and not directly on the parathyroid gland or parathyroid hormone.

Bisphosphonates

The bisphosphonates include etidronate (*Didronel*), pamidronate (*Aredia*), risedronate (*Actonel*), tiludronate (*Skelid*), and alendronate (*Fosamax*). These drugs act to slow or block bone resorption; by doing this, they help to lower serum calcium levels.

THERAPEUTIC ACTIONS AND INDICATIONS

The bisphosphonates slow normal and abnormal bone resorption but do not inhibit normal bone formation and mineralization. These drugs are used in the treatment of Paget's disease and of postmenopausal osteoporosis in women. Pamidronate and etidronate are also used for the treatment of hypercalcemia of malignancy and osteolytic bone lesions in certain cancer patients. Tiludronate is reserved for use in the treatment of Paget's disease in patients who do not respond to other therapy. Risedronate is used daily for 2 months to treat Paget's disease in symptomatic people at risk for complication.

CONTRAINDICATIONS/CAUTIONS

These drugs should not be used in the presence of hypocalcemia, which could be made worse by lowering calcium levels; during pregnancy and lactation, because of the potential for adverse effects on the fetus or neonate; or with a history of any allergy to bisphosphonates. Caution should be used with renal dysfunction, which could interfere with excretion of the drug, or with upper GI disease, which could be aggravated by the drug.

ADVERSE EFFECTS

The most common adverse effects seen with bisphosphonates are headache, nausea, and diarrhea. There is also an increase in bone pain in patients suffering from Paget's disease, but this effect usually passes after a few days to a few weeks.

CLINICALLY IMPORTANT DRUG–DRUG INTERACTIONS

Oral absorption of bisphosphonates is decreased if taken concurrently with antacids, calcium products, iron, and multiple vitamins. If these drugs need to be taken, they should be separated by at least 30 minutes. There may also be increased GI distress if combined with aspirin; this combination should be avoided if possible.

DATA LINK

Data link to the following bisphosphonates in your nursing drug guide:

GENDER/LIFE-SPAN CONSIDERATIONS

Osteoporosis

Osteoporosis is the most common bone disease found in adults. It results from a lack of bone-building cell (osteoclast) activity and a decrease in bone matrix and mass, with less calcium and phosphorous being deposited in the bone. This can occur with advancing age, when the endocrine system is slowing down and the stimulation to build bone is absent; with menopause, when the calcium-depositing effects of estrogen are lost; with malnutrition states, when vitamin C and proteins essential for bone production are absent from the diet; and with a lack of physical stress on the bones from lack of activity, which promotes calcium removal and does not stimulate osteoclast activity. The inactive, elderly, postmenopausal woman with a poor diet is a prime candidate for osteoporosis. Fractured hips and wrists, shrinking size, and curvature of the spine are all evidence of osteoporosis in this age group. Besides the use of bisphosphonates to encourage calcium deposition in the bone, several other interventions can help prevent severe osteoporosis in this group or in any other people with similar risk factors.

- Aerobic exercise—Walking, even 10 minutes a day, has been shown to help increase osteoclast activity. Encourage people to walk around the block or to park the car far from the door and walk. Exercise does not have to involve vigorous gym activity to be beneficial.
- Proper diet—Calcium and proteins are essential for bone growth. The person who eats only pasta and avoids milk products could benefit from calcium supplements and encouragement to eat protein at least 2 to 3 times/week. Weight loss can also help to improve activity and decrease pressure on bones at rest.
- Hormone replacement therapy (HRT)—For women, HRT has been very successful in decreasing the progression of osteoporosis. Women who are at high risk for breast cancer and do not elect to take HRT are good candidates for bisphosphonates.

The risk of osteoporosis should be taken into consideration as part of the health care regimen for all people as they age. Prevention can save a great deal of pain and debilitation in the long run.

BISPHOSPHATES

Name	Brand Name	Usual Indications
alendronate	*Fosamax*	Treatment of Paget's disease, postmenopausal osteoporosis
P etidronate	*Didronel*	Treatment of Paget's disease, postmenopausal osteoporosis, hypercalcemia of malignancy, osteolytic bone lesions in cancer patients

pamidronate	*Aredia*	Treatment of postmenopausal osteoporosis, hypercalcemia of malignancy, osteolytic bone lesions in cancer patients
risendronate	*Actonel*	Treatment of symptomatic Paget's disease
tiludronate	*Skelid*	Treatment of Paget's disease in patients who do not respond to other treatment

Calcitonins

The calcitonins are hormones secreted by the thyroid gland to balance the effects of parathyroid hormone. They are available as synthetic human calcitonin (*Cibacalcin*) or salmon calcitonin (*Calcimar* and others).

THERAPEUTIC ACTIONS AND INDICATIONS

These hormones inhibit bone resorption; lower serum calcium levels in children and patients with Paget's disease; and increase the excretion of phosphate, calcium, and sodium from the kidney. Human calcitonin is only approved for use in treating Paget's disease. Salmon calcitonin, which has a longer duration of action, has more uses. For example, it is also recommended for the treatment of Paget's disease, for the treatment of postmenopausal osteoporosis in conjunction with vitamin D and calcium supplements, and for the emergency treatment of hypercalcemia. Both of these drugs must be given by injection.

CONTRAINDICATIONS/CAUTIONS

These drugs should not be used during lactation because the calcium-lowering effects could cause problems for the baby. Salmon calcitonin should not be used with a known allergy to salmon or fish products. Caution should be used with renal dysfunction and pernicious anemia, which could be exacerbated by these drugs.

ADVERSE EFFECTS

The most common adverse effects seen with these drugs include flushing of the face and hands; skin rash; nausea and vomiting; urinary frequency; and local inflammation at the site of injection. Many of these side effects will lessen with time, the time varying with each individual patient.

DATA LINK

Data link to the following calcitonins in your nursing drug guide:

CALCITONINS

Name	Brand Name	Usual Indications
calcitonin, human	*Cibacalcin*	Treatment of Paget's disease
P calcitonin, salmon	*Calcimar* and others	Treatment of Paget's disease, postmenopausal osteoarthritis, emergency treatment of hypercalcemia

WWW.WEB LINKS

Patients and health care providers may want to consult the following Internet sources:

Information on thyroid diseases, support groups, treatments, research:
http://the-thyroid-society.org

Information on endocrine diseases, screening, treatment:
http://www.endo-society.org

Information on osteoporosis—support groups, screening, treatment, research:
http://www.nof.org

Information on national and international research on osteoporosis and related bone diseases:
http://www.osteorec.com

Other Antihypercalcemic Agents

Gallium (*Ganite*) is another drug that is used as an antihypercalcemic agent, but that does not fit into either of the above categories.

THERAPEUTIC ACTIONS AND INDICATIONS

Gallium inhibits calcium resorption from bone and reduces bone turnover, producing a lowered serum calcium. Gallium is used IV over 5 days to treat cancer-related hypercalcemia that is symptomatic and does not respond to conventional treatment.

CONTRAINDICATIONS/CAUTIONS

Gallium is contraindicated in the presence of severe renal dysfunction and lactation. Caution should be used with mild hypocalcemia, pregnancy, or any visual or auditory disturbances.

ADVERSE EFFECTS

Because there is a risk of acute renal failure with this drug, renal function tests must be monitored closely for any sign of renal failure. It is crucial to maintain adequate hydration in patients receiving gallium and to closely monitor serum electrolytes. Other adverse effects that occur often are hypocalcemia and decreased serum bicarbonate, which could lead to acidosis.

CLINICALLY IMPORTANT DRUG–DRUG INTERACTIONS

Because of the risk of renal failure, extreme caution should be used if other nephrotoxic drugs are used concurrently, including the aminoglycosides and amphotericin B.

DATA LINK

Data link to the following antihypercalcemic agent in your nursing drug guide:

OTHER ANTIHYPERCALCEMIC AGENTS

Name	Brand Name	Usual Indications
gallium	*Ganite*	Treatment of cancer-related hypercalcemia unresponsive to other treatments

NURSING CONSIDERATIONS
for patients receiving antihypercalcemic agents

Assessment

HISTORY. Screen for history of allergy to any of these products and fish products with salmon calcitonin; pregnancy; lactation; hypocalcemia; and renal dysfunction.

PHYSICAL ASSESSMENT. Include screening for baseline status before beginning therapy and for any potential adverse effects: the presence of any skin lesions; orientation and affect; abdominal exam; serum electrolytes; and renal function tests.

Nursing Diagnoses

The patient receiving any antihypercalcemic agent may have the following nursing diagnoses related to drug therapy:

- Pain related to GI, skin effects
- Alteration in nutrition, less than body requirements, related to GI effects
- Anxiety related to need for parenteral injections (specific drugs)
- Knowledge deficit regarding drug therapy

Implementation

- Assure adequate hydration with any of these agents *to reduce risk of renal complications.*
- Arrange for concomitant vitamin D, calcium supplements, and hormone replacement therapy if used *to treat postmenopausal osteoporosis.*
- Rotate injection sites and monitor for inflammation if using calcitonins *to prevent tissue breakdown and irritation.*
- Monitor serum calcium regularly *to allow for dosage adjustment as needed.*
- Assess the patient carefully for any potential drug–drug interactions if giving in combination with other drugs *to prevent serious effects.*
- Arrange for periodic blood tests of renal function if using gallium *to monitor for renal dysfunction.*
- Provide comfort measures and analgesics *to relieve bone pain if it returns as treatment begins.*
- Provide thorough patient teaching including measures to avoid adverse effects, warning signs of problems, and the need for regular evaluation if used for longer than recommended *to enhance patient knowledge about drug therapy and promote compliance.*

Evaluation

- Monitor patient response to the drug (return of calcium levels to normal; prevention of complications of osteoporosis; control of Paget's disease).
- Monitor for adverse effects (skin rash; nausea and vomiting; hypocalcemia; renal dysfunction).
- Evaluate the effectiveness of the teaching plan (patient can name drug, dosage, adverse effects to watch for, specific measures to avoid adverse effects).
- Monitor the effectiveness of comfort measures and compliance to the regimen.

CHAPTER SUMMARY

- The thyroid gland uses iodine to produce thyroid hormones. Thyroid hormones control the rate at which most body cells use energy (metabolism).
- Control of the thyroid gland is an intricate balance between TRH, released by the hypothalamus; TSH, released by the anterior pituitary; and circulating levels of thyroid hormone.
- Hypothyroidism, or lower-than-normal levels of thyroid hormone, is treated with replacement thyroid hormone.
- Hyperthyroidism, or higher-than-normal levels of thyroid hormone, is treated with thioamides, which block the thyroid from producing thyroid hormone, or with iodines, which prevent thyroid hormone production or destroy parts of the gland.
- The parathyroid glands are located behind the thyroid gland and produce parathormone, which works with calcitonin, produced by thyroid cells, to maintain the calcium balance in the body.

- Hypocalcemia, or low levels of calcium, is treated with vitamin D products and calcium replacement therapy.
- Hypercalcemia and hypercalcemic states include postmenopausal osteoporosis and Paget's disease, as well as hypercalcemia related to malignancy.
- Hypercalcemia is treated with bisphosphonates, calcitonin, or gallium. Bisphosphonates slow or block bone resorption, which will lower serum calcium levels. Calcitonin inhibits bone resorption; lowers serum calcium levels in children and patients with Paget's disease; and increases the excretion of phosphate, calcium, and sodium from the kidney. Gallium inhibits calcium resorption from bone and reduces bone turnover, producing a lowered serum calcium.

Bibliography

AMA drug evaluations. (1999). Chicago: American Medical Association.

Bullock, B. L. (2000). *Focus on pathophysiology.* Philadelphia: Lippincott Williams & Wilkins.

Hardman, J. G., Limbird, L. E., Molinoff, P. B., Ruddon, R. W. & Gilman, A. G. (Eds.). (1996). *Goodman and Gilman's the pharmacological basis of therapeutics* (9th ed.). New York: McGraw-Hill.

Karch, A. M. (2000). *2000 Lippincott's nursing drug guide.* Philadelphia: Lippincott Williams & Wilkins.

McEvoy, B. R. (1999). *Facts and comparisons 1999.* St. Louis: Fact and Comparisons.

The medical letter on drugs and therapeutics. (1999). New Rochelle, NY: Medical Letter.

CHAPTER 36

Antidiabetic Agents

Parenteral antidiabetic agent
- insulin

Oral antidiabetic agents
- Sulfonylureas: First generation
  - acetohexamide
  - P chlorpropamide
  - tolazamide
  - tolbutamide
- Sulfonylureas: Second generation
  - glimepiride
  - glipizide
  - P glyburide
- Nonsulfonylureas
  - P acarbose
  - metformin
  - miglitol
  - repaglinide
  - troglitazone

Glucose-elevating agents
- diazoxide
- glucagon

CHAPTER OUTLINE

KEY TERMS

diabetes mellitus
glycogen
glycosuria
hyperglycemia
hypoglycemia
insulin
ketosis
polydipsia
polyphagia
sulfonylureas

INTRODUCTION

Diabetes mellitus is the most common of all metabolic disorders. It is estimated that eight million people in the United States have been diagnosed with diabetes mellitus, with many others not yet diagnosed. Diabetes is a complicated disorder that affects many end organs and causes numerous clinical complications. Currently, treatment of diabetes is aimed at tightly regulating the blood sugar level through the use of insulin or insulin-stimulating drugs.

GLUCOSE REGULATION

Glucose is the leading energy source for the human body. Glucose is stored in the body for rapid release in times of stress and so that the serum levels of glucose can be maintained at a level that will supply a constant supply of glucose to the neurons. The minute-to-minute control of glucose levels is the function of the endocrine pancreas gland.

The Pancreas Gland

The pancreas is both an endocrine gland, producing hormones, and an exocrine gland, releasing sodium bicarbonate and pancreatic enzymes directly into the common bile duct to be released into the small intestine, where they neutralize the acid chyme from the stomach and aid digestion. The endocrine part of the pancreas produces hormones in collections of tissue called the islets of Langerhans. These islets contain endocrine cells that produce specific hormones. The alpha cells release glucagon in response to low glucose levels. The beta cells release ***insulin*** in response to high glucose levels. Delta cells produce somatostatin, which blocks the secretion of insulin and glucagon. These hormones work together to maintain the serum glucose level within normal limits.

Insulin

Insulin is the hormone produced by the beta cells on the islets of Langerhans. The hormone is released into circulation when the levels of glucose around these cells rise. Insulin circulates through the body and reacts with specific insulin receptor sites to stimulate the transport of glucose into the cells to be used for energy, a process called facilitated diffusion. Insulin also stimulates the synthesis of ***glycogen*** (stored glucose for immediate release during times of stress or low glucose), the conversion of lipids into fat stored in the form of adipose tissue, and the synthesis of needed proteins from amino acids.

Insulin is released after a meal, when the blood glucose levels rise. It will circulate and change metabolism, allowing the body to either store or use the nutrients from the meal effectively. As a result of the insulin release, blood glucose levels will fall and insulin release will drop off. Sometimes, an insufficient amount of insulin is released. This may occur because the pancreas cannot produce enough insulin, the insulin receptor sites have lost their sensitivity to insulin, or the person does not have enough receptor sites to support his or her body size, as in obesity.

When an insufficient amount of insulin is released, several metabolic changes occur, beginning with hyperglycemia or increased blood sugar. Hyperglycemia results in ***glycosuria*** as sugar is spilled into the urine because the concentration of glucose in the blood is too high for complete reabsorption. Because this sugar-rich urine is an ideal environment for bacteria, cystitis is a common finding. The patient experiences fatigue because the body's cells cannot use the glucose that is there, and they need insulin to facilitate the transport of the glucose into the cells. ***Polyphagia*** (increased eating) occurs because the hypothalamic centers cannot take in glucose and sense that they are starving. ***Polydipsia*** (increased thirst) occurs because the tonicity of the blood is increased due to the increased glucose and waste products in the blood and to the loss of fluid with glucose in the urine. (The hypothalamic cells sensitive to fluid levels sense a need to increase fluid in the system and the patient feels thirsty.) Lipolysis or fat breakdown occurs as the body breaks down stored fat for energy because glucose is not usable. The patient will experience ***ketosis*** as metabolism shifts to the use of fat and the ketone wastes cannot be removed effectively. Acidosis also occurs as the liver cannot remove all of the waste products (acid being a primary waste product) resulting from the breakdown of glucose, fat, and proteins. Muscles will break down as proteins are no longer being built and the body will break down proteins for their essential amino acids. The breakdown of proteins results in an increase in nitrogen wastes seen in elevated BUN, and sometimes in protein in the urine. Patients with hyperglycemia do not heal quickly because of this breakdown of proteins and the lack of a stimulus to build proteins. All of these actions will eventually contribute to the development of the complications associated with chronic hyperglycemia or diabetes.

DIABETES MELLITUS

Diabetes mellitus (literally honey urine) is characterized by complex disturbances in metabolism. Diabetes affects carbohydrate, protein, and fat metabolism. The most frequently recognized clinical signs of diabetes are ***hyperglycemia*** (fasting blood sugar level over 126 mg/dl) and ***glycosuria*** (the presence of sugar in the urine). The alteration in the body's ability to effectively deal with carbohydrate, fat, and protein metabolism over a long term results in a thickening of the basement membrane (a thin layer of collagen filament that lies just below the endothelial lining of blood vessels) in large and small blood vessels. This thickening leads to changes in the oxygenation of the lining of the vessel; damage to the vessel lining, which will lead to a narrowing and decreased blood flow through the vessel; and an inability of oxygen to rapidly diffuse across the membrane to the tissue. These changes result in increased incidence of a number of disorders, including the following:

Atherosclerosis—heart attacks and strokes related to the development of atherosclerotic plaques in the vessel lining

Retinopathy—with resultant loss of vision as tiny vessels in the eye are narrowed and closed

Neuropathies—with motor and sensory changes in the feet and legs and progressive changes in other nerves as the oxygen supply to these nerves is slowly cut off

Nephropathy—with renal dysfunction related to changes in the basement membrane of the glomerulus

CULTURAL CONSIDERATIONS

Diabetes and Blood Glucose Variations

Certain cultures tend to have a genetically predetermined variation in routine blood glucose levels, possibly due to a variation in metabolism. For example, American Indians, Hispanic Americans, and Japanese Americans have higher blood glucose levels than white Americans. The clinical importance of this involves proper screening of patients for hypoglycemia and diabetes mellitus. Patients in these cultural groups will need fasting glucose tolerance tests and will need to have the standard readjusted before a diagnosis is made. Such patients will also require an understanding of potential differences in normal levels on home glucose monitoring tests when they are regulating insulin at home.

Cultural groups that are more likely to develop diabetes mellitus include African Americans and Hispanic Americans. People in these groups should be screened regularly for diabetes. They also would benefit from teaching about warning signs of diabetes to watch for.

The overall metabolic disturbances associated with diabetes are thought to be due to a lack of the hormone insulin. There is debate over whether the lack of insulin leads to the basement membrane changes and complications of diabetes, or whether the basement membrane thickening is the initial problem that leads to lack of insulin. Whichever comes first, replacing or stimulating insulin release is the mainstay for treating diabetes mellitus.

Diabetes mellitus is classified as either Type I, IDDM (insulin-dependent diabetes mellitus), or Type II, NIDDM (non–insulin-dependent diabetes mellitus). Type I is usually associated with rapid onset, mostly in younger people, and is connected in many cases to viral destruction of the beta cells of the pancreas. Type I requires insulin replacement.

Type II usually occurs in mature adults and has a slow and progressive onset. The treatment of Type II diabetes usually begins with changes in diet and exercise. Dieting will control the amount and timing of glucose introduced into the body, and weight loss decreases the number of insulin receptor sites that need to be stimulated. Exercise will increase the movement of glucose into the cell by activation of the sympathetic nervous system and by the increase in potassium in the blood directly after exercising. Potassium acts as part of a polarizing system during exercise that will push glucose into the cell.

When diet and exercise no longer work, oral agents (see below) are tried to stimulate the production of insulin in the pancreas, increase the sensitivity of the insulin receptor sites, or control the entry of glucose into the system. Injection of insulin may eventually be needed to replace the missing insulin. This concept is often confusing when learning about diabetes. NIDDM often evolves until insulin is needed. Timing of the injections is correlated to food intake and anticipated increases in blood glucose levels.

Hyperglycemia

Hyperglycemia, or high blood sugar, results when there is insufficient insulin to deal with the glucose in the system. Clinical signs and symptoms of hyperglycemia include fatigue, lethargy, irritation, glycosuria, polyphagia, polydipsia, and itchy skin (from accumulation of wastes that the liver cannot clear). If the hyperglycemia goes unchecked, the patient will experience ketoacidosis and central nervous system (CNS) changes that can progress to coma. Signs of impending dangerous complications to hyperglycemia include the following:

- Fruity breath as the ketones build up in the system and are excreted through the lungs
- Dehydration as fluid and important electrolytes are lost through the kidneys
- Slow, deep respirations (Kussmaul's respirations) as the body tries to rid itself of high acid levels
- Loss of orientation and coma

This level of hyperglycemia needs to be treated immediately with insulin.

Hypoglycemia

Hypoglycemia, or blood sugar level below 40 mg/dl, occurs in a number of clinical situations, including starvation and when treatment of hyperglycemia with insulin or oral agents lowers the blood sugar too far. The body immediately reacts to lowered blood sugar because the cells require glucose to survive, the neurons being some of the most sensitive cells. The initial reaction to falling blood sugar is parasympathetic stimulation—increased GI activity to increase digestion and absorption. Rather rapidly, the sympathetic nervous system (SNS) responds with a fight or flight reaction that increases blood glucose levels by initiating the breakdown of fat and glycogen to release glucose for rapid energy. The pancreas releases glucagon, a hormone that counters the effects of insulin and works to increase glucose levels. In many cases, the response to the hypoglycemic state causes a hyperglycemic state. Balancing the body's responses to glucose is sometimes a difficult job when trying to treat and control diabetes. Table 36-1 offers a comparison of the signs and symptoms of hyperglycemia and hypoglycemia.

REPLACEMENT INSULIN

Replacement insulin is used to treat diabetes mellitus in adults who do not respond to diet, exercise, and oral agents, and for Type I diabetics who require replacement insulin. Originally, insulin was prepared from pork and beef pancreas. Today, virtually all insulin is prepared by recombinant DNA technology and is human insulin produced by genetically altered bacteria. This more pure form of insulin is not associated with the sensitivity problems that many patients developed with the animal products. Animal insulins may still be obtained for patients who are most responsive to these agents, but they are not generally used.

Box 36-1 describes the various forms of insulin delivery that are currently available or under study for future use.

THERAPEUTIC ACTIONS AND INDICATIONS

Insulin is a hormone that promotes the storage of the body's fuels; facilitates the transport of various metabolites and ions across cell membranes; and stimulates the synthesis of glycogen from glucose, of fats from lipids, and of proteins from amino acids. Insulin does these things by reacting with specific receptor sites on the body's cell. Figure 36-1 shows the site of action of replacement insulin and other drugs used to treat diabetic conditions.

Replacement insulin is used to treat Type I diabetes mellitus; Type II diabetes mellitus in patients whose diabetes cannot be controlled by diet or other agents; severe ketoacidosis or diabetic coma; and hyperkalemia with infusion of glucose to produce a shift of potassium into the cells (polarizing solution). It also is used for short courses of therapy during periods of stress (surgery, disease) for Type II diabetics, for newly diagnosed patients getting stabilized, for patients with poor control of glucose levels, and for patients with gestational diabetes. Different preparations of insulin are available to provide short- and long-term coverage (Table 36-2). Frequently, patients use more than one preparation to provide insulin coverage at different times during the day.

CONTRAINDICATIONS/CAUTIONS

Because insulin is used as a replacement hormone, there are no contraindications. Care should be used

TABLE 36-1

SIGNS AND SYMPTOMS OF HYPOGLYCEMIA AND HYPERGLYCEMIA

	Hypoglycemia	Hyperglycemia
CNS	Headache, blurred vision, diplopia; drowsiness progressing to coma; ataxia; hyperactive reflexes	Decreased level of consciousness, sluggishness progressing to coma; hypoactive reflexes
Neuromuscular	Paresthesias; weakness; muscle spasms; twitching progressing to seizures	Weakness, lethargy
CV	Tachycardia; palpitations; normal to high BP	Tachycardia; hypotension
Respiratory	Rapid, shallow respirations	Rapid, deep respirations (Kussmaul's); acetone-like or fruity breath
GI	Hunger, nausea	Nausea; vomiting; thirst
Other	Diaphoresis; cool and clammy skin; normal eyeballs	Dry, warm, flushed skin; soft eyeballs
Laboratory tests	Urine glucose—negative; blood glucose low	Urine glucose—strongly positive; urine ketone levels—positive; blood glucose levels—high
Onset	Sudden; patient appears anxious, drunk; associated with overdose of insulin, missing a meal, increased stress	Gradual; patient is slow and sluggish; associated with lack of insulin, increased stress

BOX 36-1

INSULIN DELIVERY PAST, PRESENT, AND FUTURE

Past

Subcutaneous injection—The delivery of insulin by subcutaneous injection was first introduced in the 1920s and changed the way that diabetic patients were managed clinically, giving them a chance for a normal lifestyle. Research is ongoing to find more efficient and acceptable ways to deliver insulin to diabetic patients.

Present

SC insulin injection—This remains the primary delivery system.

Insulin jet injector—This cylindrical device shoots a fine spray of insulin through the skin under very high pressure. Although it is appealing for people who don't like needles or have problems disposing of needles properly, it can be very expensive.

Insulin pen—This syringe-like device actually looks like a pen. It has a small needle at the tip, and a barrel that holds insulin. The patient "dials" the amount of insulin to be given and injects the insulin SC by pressing on the top of the pen. This is advantageous to people who need insulin two or three times during the day but cannot easily transport syringes and needles. It is a subtle way to given insulin and is popular with students and business people on the go.

External insulin pump—This pump device can be worn on a belt or hidden in a pocket and is attached to a small tube inserted into the subcutaneous tissue of the abdomen. The device slowly leaks a base rate of insulin into the abdomen all day; the patient can pump or inject booster doses throughout the day to correspond with meals and activity. The device does have several disadvantages. For example, it is awkward, the tubing poses an increased risk of infection and requires frequent changing, and the patient has to frequently check blood glucose levels throughout the day to monitor response.

Future

Implantable insulin pump—This pump is surgically implanted into the abdomen and delivers base insulin as well as insulin boluses as needed directly into the abdomen to be absorbed by the liver—like pancreatic insulin. The disadvantages are risk of infection, mechanical problems with the pump, and lack of long-term data on its effectiveness. This method is not yet available for general use.

Insulin patch—The patch is placed on the skin and delivers a constant low dose of insulin. When the patient eats a meal, tabs are pulled on the patch to release more insulin. The problem with this delivery method is that insulin does not readily pass through the skin, so there is tremendous variability in its effects. This route is not yet commercially available.

Inhaled insulin—the lung tissue is one of the best sites for insulin absorption. An aerosol delivery system has been developed that delivers a powder insulin formulation directly into the lung tissue. Research has been very promising, suggesting that this may be a more reliable method of delivering insulin in the future.

Long-acting insulin—Research is ongoing in the development of a subcutaneous insulin that lasts 2 to 3 times longer than NPH insulin. This would decrease the need for multiple injections and may increase glucose control. Adverse effects associated with prolonged changes in metabolism have complicated the studies on these drugs.

For the most up-to-date information on insulin delivery research, web link with: http://www.niddk.nih.gov/health/diabetes/summary/altins/altins.htm

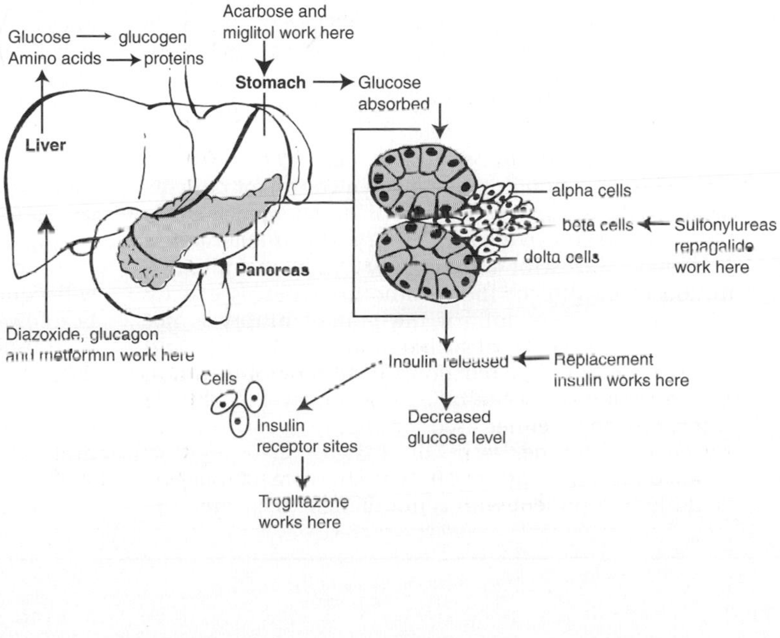

FIGURE 36-1. Sites of action of drugs used to treat diabetic conditions.

TABLE 36-2

COMPARISON OF INSULIN TYPES

Type	Onset	Peak	Duration
Insulin analogue *Humalog*	<15 min	1 hr	3.5–4.5 hr
Regular *Humulin R* *Iletin Regular* *Novolin R* *Velosulin BR*	30–60 min	2–4 hr	6–8 hr
NPH *Humulin N* *Iletin NPH* *Novolin N*	1–2 hr	6–12 hr	18–24 hr
Lente *Humulin L* *Iletin L* *Novolin L*	1–2.5 hr	6–12 hr	18–24 hr
PZI *Humulin U*	4–8hr	8–20 hr	24–48 hr

Insulin is available in various preparations with a wide range of peaks and durations of action. A patient may receive a combination of regular and NPH insulin in the morning to cover the glucose peak from breakfast (regular onset is 30–60 min) and lunch and dinner glucose peaks. The patient may then require another injection before bed. The types of insulin used are determined by the anticipated eating and exercise activities of any particular patient.

during pregnancy and lactation to monitor the glucose levels closely and adjust the insulin dosage accordingly. Patients with allergies to beef or pork products should use only human insulins.

ADVERSE EFFECTS

The most common adverse effects to insulin use are hypoglycemia and ketoacidosis, which can be controlled with proper dosage adjustments, and local reactions at injection sites.

CLINICALLY IMPORTANT DRUG–DRUG INTERACTIONS

Caution should be used when giving a patient stabilized on insulin any drug that will decrease glucose levels (e.g, MAO inhibitors, beta blockers, salicylates, alcohol). Dosage adjustments will be needed when adding or removing any of these drugs. Care should also be taken when combining insulin with any beta blocker. The blocking of the SNS will also block many of the signs and symptoms of hypoglycemia, hindering the patient's ability to recognize problems. Patients taking beta blockers will need to learn other ways to recognize hypoglycemia.

NURSING CHALLENGE

Managing Glucose Levels During Stress

The body has many compensatory mechanisms for assuring that blood glucose levels stay within a safe range. The sympathetic stress reaction elevates the blood glucose levels to provide ready energy for fight or flight (see Chapter 27). The stress reaction causes the breakdown of glycogen to release glucose, and the breakdown of fat and proteins to release other energy. The stress reaction will elevate the blood glucose level above the normal range. In severe stress situations—an acute MI or an automobile accident, for instance—the blood glucose level can be very high (300–400 mg/dl). In these situations, the body will use that energy either to fight the insult or to flee from the stressor.

Nurses in acute care situations need to be aware of this reflex elevation in glucose when caring for patients in acute stress, especially patients in emergency situations with no known medical history. The usual response to a blood glucose of 400 mg/dl would be the administration of insulin. In many situations, that is exactly what is done, especially if the patient history is not known and the effects of such a high glucose level could cause severe systemic reactions. Insulin administration will cause a drop in the blood glucose level as glucose enters cells to be either used for energy or converted to glycogen for storage.

But a problem may arise in the acute care setting, particularly in a patient who is not diabetic. Relieving the stress reaction can also drop glucose levels as the stimulus to increase these levels is lost and the glucose that was there is used for energy. A patient in this situation is at risk for developing potentially severe hypoglycemia. The body's response to low glucose levels is a sympathetic stress reaction, which will again elevate blood glucose levels. If treated, the patient potentially can enter a cycle of high and low glucose levels. Nurses are often the ones in closest contact with the highly stressed patient—in the emergency room, the intensive care unit, the postanesthesia room—and should be constantly aware of the normal and reflex changes in blood glucose that accompany stress. Careful monitoring, with awareness of stress and the relief of stress, can prevent a prolonged treatment program to maintain blood glucose levels within the range of normal, a situation that is not "normal" during a stress reaction.

Diabetic patients who are in severe stress situations will require changes in their insulin dosages. They should be allowed some elevation of blood glucose, even though their inability to produce sufficient insulin will make it difficult for their cells to make effective use of the elevated glucose levels. It is a clinical challenge to balance glucose levels with the needs of the patient because so many factors can affect the glucose level.

CASE STUDY

Type I Diabetes Mellitus

PRESENTATION

M. J. is a 22-year-old woman who has newly diagnosed Type I diabetes mellitus. She was stabilized on insulin while hospitalized for diagnosis and management. One week after discharge, M. J. experienced nausea and anorexia. She was unable to eat, but she took her insulin as usual in the morning. That afternoon, she experienced profuse sweating and was tremulous and apprehensive, so she went to the hospital emergency room. The initial diagnosis was insulin reaction from taking insulin and not eating, combined with the stress of her GI distress. M. J. was treated at the emergency room with intravenous glucose. After she had rested and her glucose levels returned to normal, she was discharged to home.

CRITICAL THINKING QUESTIONS

What instructions should M. J. receive before she leaves? Think about the ways that stress can alter the blood glucose levels. Then consider the stress that a newly diagnosed Type I diabetic patient undergoes when coping with the diagnosis, learning self-injection, and thinking about complications of the disease that may arise in the future. What teaching approaches could help M. J. to decrease her stress and to effectively plan her medical regimen? What sort of support would be useful for M. J. as she adjusts to her new life?

DISCUSSION

The diagnosis of Type I diabetes is a life-changing event. M. J. had to learn about the disease and how to test her own blood and give herself injections; manage a new diet and exercise program; and, perhaps, cope with the knowledge that the long-term complications of diabetes can be devastating. Many patients who are regulated on insulin in the hospital experience a real change in insulin demand after discharge. The sympathetic nervous system (SNS) is active in the hospital, and one of the effects of SNS activity is increased glucose levels—preparing the body for fight or flight. For some patients, returning home often eases the stress that activated the SNS, and glucose levels fall. If the patient continues to use the same insulin dose, hypoglycemia can occur. Other patients, however, may feel protected in the hospital and experience stress when they are sent home. They may feel anxious about taking care of themselves while coping with everyday problems and tensions. These patients will need an increased insulin dose because their stress reaction intensifies when they get home, driving their blood glucose up.

Patients are taught to test their own blood glucose before leaving the hospital. When they get used to doing this and regulating their own insulin based on glucose levels, they usually manage well. But the first few days to weeks are often the hardest. The nurse should review with M. J. how to test her glucose, draw up her insulin, and regulate the dose. The nurse also should give M. J. written information that she can refer to later.

In addition, the nurse should give M. J. a chance to talk and to vent her feelings about her diagnosis and her future. To help decrease M. J.'s stress and to avoid problems during this adjustment period, the nurse can give M. J. a telephone number to call if she has problems or questions. M. J. should return in a few days to review her progress and have any questions answered. In the meantime, the nurse should encourage M. J. to write down any questions or problems that arise so they can be addressed during this follow-up visit. Support and encouragement will be crucial to helping M. J. adjust to her disease and her drug therapy. She can also be referred to the American Diabetic Association, which in many communities offers support services to help diabetics.

DATA LINK

Data link to the following parenteral antihyperglycemic agent in your nursing drug guide:

PARENTERAL ANTIHYPERGLYCEMIC AGENT

Name	Brand Name	Usual Indication
Insulin	(see Table 36-2)	Treatment of diabetes Type I; treatment of diabetes Type II that cannot be controlled by other means; treatment of severe ketoacidosis, treatment of newly diagnosed diabetics, treatment of hyperkalemia as part of a polarizing solution, treatment of gestational diabetes

NURSING CONSIDERATIONS
for patients taking insulin

Assessment

HISTORY. Screen for history of allergy to any insulin, and pregnancy or lactation.

PHYSICAL ASSESSMENT. Include screening for baseline status before beginning therapy and for any potential adverse effects: the presence of any skin lesions; orientation and reflexes; baseline pulse and blood pressure; respiration, adventitious breath sounds; and urinalysis and blood glucose level.

Nursing Diagnoses

The patient receiving insulin may have the following nursing diagnoses related to drug therapy:

- Alteration in nutrition, less than body requirements related to metabolic effects
- Sensory–perceptual alteration related to glucose levels
- Potential for infection related to injections and disease process
- Ineffectual individual coping related to diagnosis and injection therapy
- Knowledge deficit regarding drug therapy

Implementation

- *Ensure uniform suspension of insulin* by gently rotating vial; avoid vigorous shaking.
- Give maintenance doses SC only; rotate injection sites regularly; give regular insulin IM or IV in emergency situations *to avoid damage to muscles and to prevent subcutaneous atrophy.*
- Monitor response carefully *to avoid adverse effects;* blood glucose monitoring is the most effective way to evaluate insulin dosage.
- Use caution when mixing types of insulin; use mixtures of regular and NPH or regular and lente insulins within 15 minutes of combining them *to prevent precipitation and ineffective dosing.*
- Store insulin in a cool place away from direct sunlight. Predrawn syringes are stable for 1 week if refrigerated; these offer a good way *to ensure the proper dosage for patients* with limited vision.
- Monitor patients during times of trauma or severe stress *for potential dosage adjustment needs.*
- Instruct patients also receiving beta blockers in ways to monitor glucose levels and signs and symptoms of glucose abnormalities *to prevent hypoglycemic and hyperglycemic episodes when SNS and warning signs are blocked.*
- Provide thorough patient teaching, including measures to avoid adverse effects, warning signs of problems, proper administration techniques, and the need to monitor disease status *to enhance patient knowledge about drug therapy and promote compliance* (see Patient Teaching Checklist: Insulin).

Evaluation

- Monitor patient response to the drug (stabilization of blood glucose levels).
- Monitor for adverse effects (hypoglycemia, ketoacidosis, injection site irritation).
- Evaluate the effectiveness of the teaching plan (patient can name drug, dosage, adverse effects to watch for, specific measures to avoid adverse effects, proper administration technique).
- Monitor the effectiveness of comfort measures and compliance to the regimen (see Nursing Care Guide: Insulin).

ORAL ANTIDIABETIC AGENTS

Oral drugs are successful in controlling Type II diabetes in patients who still have a functioning pancreas. The ***sulfonylureas*** were the first oral agents introduced. They stimulate the pancreas to release insulin. Other oral agents, called nonsulfonylureas, have been introduced more recently. The nonsulfonylureas act to decrease insulin resistance or alter glucose absorption and uptake. They usually are combined with a sulfonylurea for effectiveness.

Sulfonylureas

The sulfonylureas bind to potassium channels on pancreatic beta cells to increase insulin secretion. They may improve insulin binding to insulin receptors and increase the number of insulin receptors. They are also known to increase the effect of ADH on renal cells. They are effective only in patients who have functioning beta cells. They are not effective for all diabetics and may lose their effectiveness over time with others. All of the sulfonylureas can cause hypoglycemia.

First-Generation Sulfonylureas

The first-generation sulfonylureas include chlorpropamide (*Diabenese*), tolbutamide (*Orinase*), acetohexamide (*Dymelor*), and tolazamide (*Tolinase*). Chlorpropamide is the most frequently used of the group because it has the most predictable effects and has proven to be very reliable. Tolbutamide is preferred for patients with renal dysfunction who may not be able to excrete chlorpropamide, because it is more easily cleared from the body. Acetohexamide and tolazamide, which are used less frequently, are usually tried after the first two drugs are shown to be ineffective. They are not as predictably effective in many patients, but may be very effective in some patients who do not respond to chlorpropamide. Tolbutamide, acetohexamide, and tolazamide are sometimes used in combination with insulin to reduce the insulin dosage and decrease the risk of hypoglycemia in certain Type II diabetics who have begun to use insulin to control blood glucose level.

The first-generation sulfonylureas were associated with an increased risk of cardiovascular disease and death in a somewhat controversial study. They are now thought to possibly cause an increase in cardiovascular deaths.

Second-Generation Sulfonylureas

These drugs have several advantages over the first-generation drugs, including the following:

- Second-generation sulfonylureas are excreted in the urine and the bile, making them safer for patients with renal dysfunction.

PATIENT TEACHING CHECKLIST

Insulin

Create customized patient teaching materials for a specific insulin from your CD-ROM. Your patient teaching should stress the following points for drugs within this class:

Insulin is a hormone that is normally produced by your pancreas. It helps to regulate your energy balance by affecting the way the body uses sugar and fats. The lack of insulin produces a disease called diabetes mellitus. By injecting insulin each day, you can help your body use the sugars and fats in your food effectively.

Check the expiration date on your insulin. Store the insulin at room temperature and avoid extremes of heat and light. Gently rotate the vial between your palms before use to dispense any crystals that may have formed. *Do not shake the vial, because vigorous shaking can inactivate the drug.*

A prescription is required to get the syringes that you will need to administer your insulin. Keep the syringes sealed until ready to use, and dispose of them appropriately. Rotate your injection sites regularly to prevent tissue damage and to ensure that the proper amount of insulin is absorbed.

You should be aware of the signs and symptoms of hypoglycemia (too much insulin). If any of these occur, eat or drink something high in sugar, such as candy, orange juice, honey, or sugar. The signs and symptoms to watch for include the following: nervousness, anxiety, sweating, pale and cool skin, headache, nausea, hunger, shakiness. These may happen if you skip a meal, exercise too much, or experience extreme stress. If these symptoms happen very often, notify your health care provider.

Avoid the use of any over-the-counter medication without first checking with your health care provider. Several of these medications can interfere with the effectiveness of insulin. Avoid the use of alcohol because this will increase the chances of having hypoglycemic attacks.

Tell any doctor, nurse, or other health care provider that you are taking this drug. You may want to wear or carry a medical alert tag showing that you are on this medication. This would alert any medical personnel taking care of you in an emergency to the fact that you are taking this drug.

Report any of the following to your health care provider: loss of appetite, blurred vision, fruity odor to your breath, increased urination, increased thirst, nausea, vomiting.

While you are on this drug, it is important to have regular medical follow-up, including blood tests to monitor your blood glucose levels, to evaluate you for any adverse effects of your diabetes.

Keep this drug and your syringes out of the reach of children. Do not give this medication to anyone else or take any similar medication that has not been prescribed for you.

This Teaching Checklist reflects general patient teaching guidelines. It is not meant to be a substitute for drug-specific teaching information, which is available in nursing drug guides.

- They do not interact with as many protein-bound drugs as the first-generation drugs.
- They have a longer duration of action, making it possible to take them only once or twice a day, thus increasing compliance.

The second-generation drugs include glimepiride (*Amaryl*), glipizide (*Glucotrol*), and glyburide (*DiaBeta* and others). Glimepiride is a much less expensive drug than most of the other sulfonylureas, which has advantages for some people. Prescribers may try different agents with patients, first- or second-generation drugs, before finding the one that is most effective for them.

THERAPEUTIC ACTIONS AND INDICATIONS

The sulfonylureas stimulate insulin release from the beta cells in the pancreas (see Figure 36-1). They improve insulin binding to insulin receptors and may actually increase the number of insulin receptors. They are indicated as an adjunct to diet and exercise to lower blood glucose in Type II diabetes mellitus. They have the unlabeled use of being an adjunct to insulin to improve glucose control in Type II diabetics.

CONTRAINDICATIONS/CAUTIONS

Sulfonylureas are contraindicated in the presence of known allergy to any sulfonylureas and in diabetes complicated by fever, severe infections, severe trauma, major surgery, ketoacidosis, severe renal or hepatic disease, and pregnancy and lactation because insulin should be used in these severe conditions. These drugs are also contraindicated for use in Type I diabetics.

ADVERSE EFFECTS

The most common adverse effects related to the sulfonylureas are hypoglycemia (from imbalance in

NURSING CARE GUIDE
Insulin

Assessment	Nursing Diagnoses	Implementation	Evaluation
HISTORY Allergies to any insulins, pregnancy, lactation	Alteration in nutrition, less than body requirements, related to metabolic effects Sensory–perceptual alteration related to effects on glucose levels Potential for infection related to injcctions and disease process Ineffective individual coping related to diagnosis and injections Knowledge deficit regarding drug therapy	Administer SC and rotate sites. Store in cool place away from light. Use caution when mixing types. Monitor blood glucose to adjust dosage as needed. Monitor during times of stress and trauma and adjust dosage. Provide support and reassurance to deal with drug injections and lifetime need. Provide patient teaching regarding drug name, dosage, adverse effects, precautions, warning signs to report, and proper administration technique.	Evaluate drug effects: return of glucose levels to normal. Monitor for adverse effects: hypoglycemia, injection site reaction. Monitor for drug–drug interactions as indicated for insulin. Evaluate effectiveness of patient teaching program. Evaluate effectiveness of comfort and safety measures.
PHYSICAL EXAMINATION Neurological: orientation, reflexes Skin: color, lesions CV: P, cardiac auscultation, BP Respiratory: R, adventitious sounds Lab tests: urinalysis, blood glucose			

glucose-to-insulin levels) and GI distress, including nausea, vomiting, epigastric discomfort, heartburn, and anorexia. (Anorexia should be monitored, as patients may not eat after taking the sulfonylurea, which could lead to hypoglycemia.) Allergic skin reactions have been reported with some of these drugs and, as mentioned before, there may be an increased risk of cardiovascular mortality, particularly with the first-generation agents.

CLINICALLY IMPORTANT DRUG–DRUG INTERACTIONS

Care should be taken with any drug that acidifies the urine because excretion of the sulfonylurea may be decreased. Caution should also be used with beta blockers, which may mask the signs of hypoglycemia, and with alcohol, which can lead to altered glucose levels when combined with sulfonylureas.

DATA LINK

Data link to the following sulfonylureas in your nursing drug guide:

SULFONYLUREAS

Name	Brand Name	Usual Indication
FIRST GENERATION		
acetohexamide	*Dymelor*	Adjunct to diet for the management of Type II diabetes; adjunct to insulin for the management of certain Type II diabetics, reducing the insulin dose and decreasing the risks of hypoglycemia

P chlorpropamide	*Diabinese*	Adjunct to diet for the management of Type II diabetes
tolazamide	*Tolinase*	Adjunct to diet for the management of Type II diabetes; adjunct to insulin for the management of certain Type II diabetics, reducing the insulin dose and decreasing the risks of hypoglycemia
tolbutamide	*Orinase*	Adjunct to diet for the management of Type II diabetes; adjunct to insulin for the management of certain Type II diabetics, reducing the insulin dose and decreasing the risks of hypoglycemia
SECOND GENERATION		
glimepiride	*Amaryl*	Adjunct to diet for the management of Type II diabetes; adjunct to insulin for the management of certain Type II diabetics, reducing the insulin dose and decreasing the risks of hypoglycemia
glipizide	*Glucotrol*	Adjunct to diet for the management of Type II diabetes; adjunct to insulin for the management of certain Type II diabetics, reducing the insulin dose and decreasing the risks of hypoglycemia
P glyburide	*DiaBeta, Micronase, Glynase PresTab*	Adjunct to diet for the management of Type II diabetes; adjunct to insulin for the management of certain Type II diabetics, reducing the insulin dose and decreasing the risks of hypoglycemia

Nonsulfonylureas

The nonsulfonylureas are oral agents that are structurally unrelated to the sulfonylureas. They frequently are effective when used in combination with sulfonylureas or insulin. These drugs include acarbose (*Precose*), metformin (*Glucophage*), miglitol (*Glyset*), repaglinide (*Prandin*), and troglitazone (*Rezulin*).

Acarbose is an alpha-glucosidase (an enzyme that breaks down glucose for absorption) inhibitor, which delays the absorption of glucose. It has only a mild effect on glucose levels and has been associated with severe hepatic toxicity. It is reserved as an adjunct with other agents for use in patients with uncontrollable glucose levels.

Metformin decreases the production of and increases the uptake of glucose. It is effective in lowering blood glucose levels and does not cause hypoglycemia like the sulfonylureas. It has been associated with the development of lactic acidosis. Both acarbose and metformin can cause GI distress.

Miglitol delays the digestion of carbohydrates, leading to a smaller rise in blood glucose following meals and a decrease in glycosylated hemoglobin (glucose carried on red blood cells). It does not enhance insulin secretion and so its effects are additive to those of the sulfonylureas in controlling blood glucose. It is used in combination with other oral agents for patients who cannot be controlled with a single agent.

Troglitazone decreases insulin resistance and is used in combination with sulfonylureas or metformin to treat patients with insulin resistance. It can cause serious hepatotoxicity and has been removed from the market in some European countries. Box 36-2 describes two drugs that are similar to troglitazone but do not have the associated hepatotoxic effects.

The newest of the nonsulfonylureas is repaglinide, which acts like the sulfonylureas to increase insulin release. It is a rapid-acting drug with a very short half-life. It is used just before meals to lower postprandial glucose levels. It can be used in combination with metformin. Because repaglinide is so new, its long-term effects are not known.

Therapeutic actions and indications, contraindications and cautions, adverse effects, and clinically important drug–drug interactions for nonsulfonylureas are the same as for the sulfonylureas.

DATA LINK

Data link to the following nonsulfonylureas in your nursing drug guide:

NONSULFONYLUREAS

Name	Brand Name	Usual Indication
P acarbose	*Precose*	Adjunct to diet to lower blood glucose in Type II diabetics; in combination with sulfonylureas to control blood sugar in patients who cannot be controlled with either drug alone
metformin	*Glucophage*	Adjunct to diet to lower blood glucose in Type II diabetics
miglitol	*Glyset*	Adjunct to diet to lower blood glucose in Type II diabetics; in combination with sulfonylureas to control blood sugar in patients who cannot be controlled with either drug alone
repaglinide	*Prandin*	Adjunct to diet to lower blood glucose in Type II diabetics; in combination with metformin to control blood sugar in patients who cannot be controlled with either drug alone
troglitazone	*Rezulin*	Adjunct to diet to lower blood glucose in Type II diabetics; in combination with insulin or sulfonylureas to control blood sugar in patients who cannot be controlled with either drug alone

BOX 36-2

AVOIDING TOXIC LIVER REACTIONS

Pioglitazone (*Actos*) and rosiglitazone (*Avandia*), similar to troglitazone but without the associated toxic liver reactions, became available in 1999. These drugs increase insulin receptor site numbers and sensitivity. They are approved as monotherapy or in combination with sulfonylureas or insulin in the treatment of Type II diabetes.

NURSING CONSIDERATIONS for patients taking oral antidiabetic agents

Assessment

HISTORY. Screen for history of allergy to any of the oral agents; severe renal or hepatic dysfunction; and pregnancy or lactation.

PHYSICAL ASSESSMENT. Include screening for baseline status before beginning therapy and for any potential adverse effects: the presence of any skin lesions; orientation and reflexes; baseline pulse and blood pressure; adventitious breath sounds; abdominal sounds and function; urinalysis and blood glucose level; and renal and liver function tests.

Nursing Diagnoses

The patient receiving oral antidiabetic agents may have the following nursing diagnoses related to drug therapy:

- Potential alteration in nutrition, less than body requirements, related to metabolic effects
- Sensory–perceptual alteration related to glucose levels
- Ineffective individual coping related to diagnosis and therapy
- Knowledge deficit regarding drug therapy

Implementation

- Administer the drug as prescribed in the appropriate relationship to meals *to ensure therapeutic effectiveness.*
- Monitor nutritional status *to provide nutritional consultation as needed.*
- Monitor response carefully; blood glucose monitoring is the most effective way *to evaluate dosage.*
- Monitor liver enzymes of patients receiving troglitazone very carefully *to avoid liver toxicity;* arrange to discontinue the drug and avert serious liver damage if liver toxicity develops.
- Monitor patients during times of trauma, pregnancy, or severe stress *to arrange to switch to insulin coverage as needed.*
- Provide thorough patient teaching, including measures to avoid adverse effects, warning signs of problems, proper administration technique, and the need to monitor disease status *to enhance patient knowledge of drug therapy and promote compliance.*

Evaluation

- Monitor patient response to the drug (stabilization of blood glucose levels).
- Monitor for adverse effects (hypoglycemia, GI distress).
- Evaluate the effectiveness of the teaching plan (patient can name drug, dosage, adverse effects to watch for, specific measures to avoid adverse effects).
- Monitor the effectiveness of comfort measures and compliance to the regimen.

GLUCOSE-ELEVATING AGENTS

There are some conditions that are associated with hypoglycemia, or abnormally low blood sugar (<40 mg/dl). These conditions include pancreatic disorders, kidney disease, certain cancers, disorders of the anterior pituitary, and unbalanced treatment of diabetes mellitus (this can occur when the patient takes the wrong dose of insulin or oral agents or when something interferes with food intake or changes stress levels and exercise).

Two agents are used to elevate glucose in these conditions: diazoxide (*Proglycem*), which can be taken orally, and glucagon, the hormone produced by the alpha cells of the pancreas to elevate glucose levels. Glucagon (*GlucaGen*) can only be given parenterally and is preferred for emergency situations. Pure glucose can also be given orally or IV to elevate glucose levels.

THERAPEUTIC ACTIONS AND INDICATIONS

These agents increase blood glucose level by decreasing insulin release and accelerating the breakdown of glycogen in the liver to release glucose. They are indicated for the treatment of hypoglycemic reactions related to insulin or oral antidiabetic agents; treatment of hypoglycemia related to pancreatic or other cancers; and short-term treatment of acute hypoglycemia related to anterior pituitary dysfunction.

CONTRAINDICATIONS/CAUTIONS

Diazoxide is contraindicated with known allergies to sulfonamides or thiazides. Both drugs are contraindicated for use during pregnancy and lactation. Caution should be used with renal and hepatic dysfunction and cardiovascular disease.

ADVERSE EFFECTS

Glucagon is associated with GI upset, nausea, and vomiting. Diazoxide has been associated with vascular effects including hypotension, headache, cerebral ischemia, weakness, congestive heart failure, and arrhythmias; these reactions are associated with diazoxide's ability to relax arteriolar smooth muscle.

CLINICALLY IMPORTANT DRUG–DRUG INTERACTIONS

There is an increased risk of toxicity if diazoxide is taken in combination with thiazide diuretics because it is structurally similar to these diuretics. Increased anticoagulation effects have been noted when glucagon is combined with oral anticoagulants. If this combination is needed, the dosage will need to be adjusted.

DATA LINK

Data link to the following glucose-elevating agents in your nursing drug guide:

GLUCOSE-ELEVATING AGENTS

Name	Brand Name	Usual Indication
diazoxide	*Proglycem, Hyperstat*	Oral management of hypoglycemia; IV use for management of severe hypertension
glucagon	*GlucaGen*	To counteract severe hypoglycemic reactions

NURSING CONSIDERATIONS for patients taking glucose-elevating agents

Assessment

HISTORY. Screen for history of allergy to thiazides if using diazoxide; severe renal or hepatic dysfunction; and pregnancy or lactation.

PHYSICAL ASSESSMENT. Physical assessment should include screening for baseline status before beginning therapy and for any potential adverse effects: orientation and reflexes; baseline pulse, blood pressure, and adventitious sounds; abdominal sounds and function; urinalysis and blood glucose level; and renal and liver function tests.

Nursing Diagnoses

The patient receiving glucose-elevating agents may have the following nursing diagnoses related to drug therapy:

- Alteration in nutrition, more than body requirements, related to metabolic effects and less than body requirements related to GI upset
- Sensory–perceptual alteration related to glucose levels
- Knowledge deficit regarding drug therapy

Implementation

- Monitor blood glucose levels daily *to evaluate the effectiveness of the drug.*
- Have insulin on standby during emergency use *to treat severe hyperglycemia if it occurs.*
- Monitor nutritional status *to provide nutritional consultation as needed.*
- Monitor patients receiving diazoxide for potential cardiovascular effects, including blood pressure, heart rhythm and output, and weight changes *to avert serious adverse reactions.*
- Provide thorough patient teaching, including measures to avoid adverse effects, warning signs of problems, proper administration technique, and the need to monitor glucose levels daily *to enhance patient knowledge of drug therapy and promote compliance.*

Evaluation

- Monitor patient response to the drug (stabilization of blood glucose levels).
- Monitor for adverse effects (hyperglycemia, GI distress).
- Evaluate the effectiveness of the teaching plan (patient can name drug, dosage, adverse effects to watch for, specific measures to avoid adverse effects).
- Monitor the effectiveness of comfort measures and compliance to the regimen.

WWW.WEB LINKS

Patients and health care providers may want to consult the following Internet sources:

Information on diabetes, drugs, research, diet, recipes, support groups, activities.
http://www.diabetes.org

Information on the latest diabetes research and news:
http://www.diabetes.com

Information on diabetes research and information:
http://niddk.nih.gov/health/diabetes/summary/altins/altins.htm

Information on research, treatment, and care of children with diabetes:
http://www.castleweb.com/diabetes/

CHAPTER SUMMARY

- Diabetes mellitus is the most common metabolic disorder. It is characterized by high blood glucose levels and alterations in the metabolism of fats, proteins, and glucose.
- Diabetes mellitus is complicated by many end-organ problems. These are related to thickening of basement membranes and the resultant decrease in blood flow to these areas.

- Treatment of diabetes involves tight control of blood glucose levels using diet and exercise; a combination of oral agents to stimulate insulin release or alter glucose absorption; or the injection of replacement insulin.
- Replacement insulin was once obtained from beef and pork pancreas. Today, most replacement insulin is human, derived from genetically altered bacteria.
- The amount and type of insulin given must be regulated daily. Patients taking insulin must learn to inject the drug, to test their own blood, and to recognize the signs of hypoglycemia and hyperglycemia.
- Insulin is used for Type I diabetes and for Type II diabetes in times of stress or when other therapies have failed.
- Oral antidiabetic agents include first- and second-generation sulfonylureas which stimulate the pancreas to release insulin; and other agents that alter glucose absorption, decrease insulin resistance, or decrease the formation of glucose. These agents are often used in combination to achieve effectiveness.
- Glucose-elevating agents are used to increase glucose when levels become dangerously low. Imbalance in glucose levels while taking insulin or oral agents is a common cause of hypoglycemia.

Bibliography

American Diabetes Association. (1997). Standards of medical care for patients with diabetes mellitus. *Diabetes Care, 20* (Suppl), S11–S12.

Andrews, M. & Boyle, J. (1999). *Transcultural concepts in nursing care.* Philadelphia: Lippincott Williams & Wilkins.

Bullock, B. L. (2000). *Focus on pathophysiology.* Philadelphia: Lippincott Williams & Wilkins.

Hardman, J. G., Limbird, L. E., Molinoff, P. B., Ruddon, R. W. & Gilman, A. G. (Eds.). (1996). *Goodman and Gilman's the pharmacological basis of therapeutics* (9th ed.). New York: McGraw-Hill.

Henderson, D. (1998). Microvascular complications of diabetes. *American Journal of Nursing, 98* (6).

Karch, A. M. (2000). *2000 Lippincott's nursing drug guide.* Philadelphia: Lippincott Williams & Wilkins.

Marks, J. (1998). Diabetes management in the future: A whiff and a long shot? *Clinical Diabetes, 16* (3).

McEvoy, B. R. (1999). *Facts and comparisons 1999.* St. Louis: Facts and Comparisons.

Repaglinide for Type 2 diabetes mellitus. (1998). *The Medical Letter, 40* (1027).

PART

7

Drugs Acting on the Reproductive System

CHAPTER 37

Introduction to the Reproductive Systems

CHAPTER OUTLINE

KEY TERMS

corpus luteum
estrogen
follicle
inhibin
interstitial or Leydig cells
menopause
menstrual cycle
ova
ovaries
progesterone
puberty
seminiferous tubules
sperm
testes
testosterone
uterus

INTRODUCTION

The glands that produce sexual hormones originate from the same fetal cells in both males and females. In the female, those cells stay in the abdomen and develop into the ***ovaries***. In the male, the cells will migrate out of the abdomen, forming the ***testes***, which will be suspended from the body in the scrotum. Both male and female glands respond to follicle stimulating hormone (FSH) and luteinizing hormone (LH) released from the anterior pituitary in response to stimulation from gonadotropic releasing hormone (GnRH) released from the hypothalamus.

FEMALE REPRODUCTIVE SYSTEM

The female reproductive system is composed of two ovaries, which store the ***ova***, or eggs, and which act as endocrine glands and produce ***estrogen*** and ***progesterone***; the ***uterus***, which is the womb for the developing embryo and fetus; and the fallopian tubes, which provide a pathway for released ova from the ovaries to the uterus. Accessory parts include the vagina, clitoris, labia, and breast tissue (Figure 37-1).

Ovaries

The ovaries contain all of the ova that a woman will have at birth. The ova slowly degenerate over time or are released for possible fertilization throughout a woman's life. Each ovum is contained in a storage site called a ***follicle***, which produces the female sex hormones estrogen and progesterone. The primary goal of these hormones is to prepare the body for pregnancy and to maintain the pregnancy until delivery.

In a nonpregnant female, the levels of these hormones fluctuate in a cyclical fashion until all of the ova are gone and ***menopause***, the cessation of menses, occurs. In a pregnant female, the placenta takes over production of estrogen and progesterones and high levels of both hormones help to maintain the pregnancy. The adrenal gland also produces small amounts of androgens, which include testosterone and some estrogens.

Controls

The developing hypothalamus is sensitive to the androgens released by the adrenal glands and does not release GnRH during childhood. As the hypothalamus matures, it loses its sensitivity to the androgens

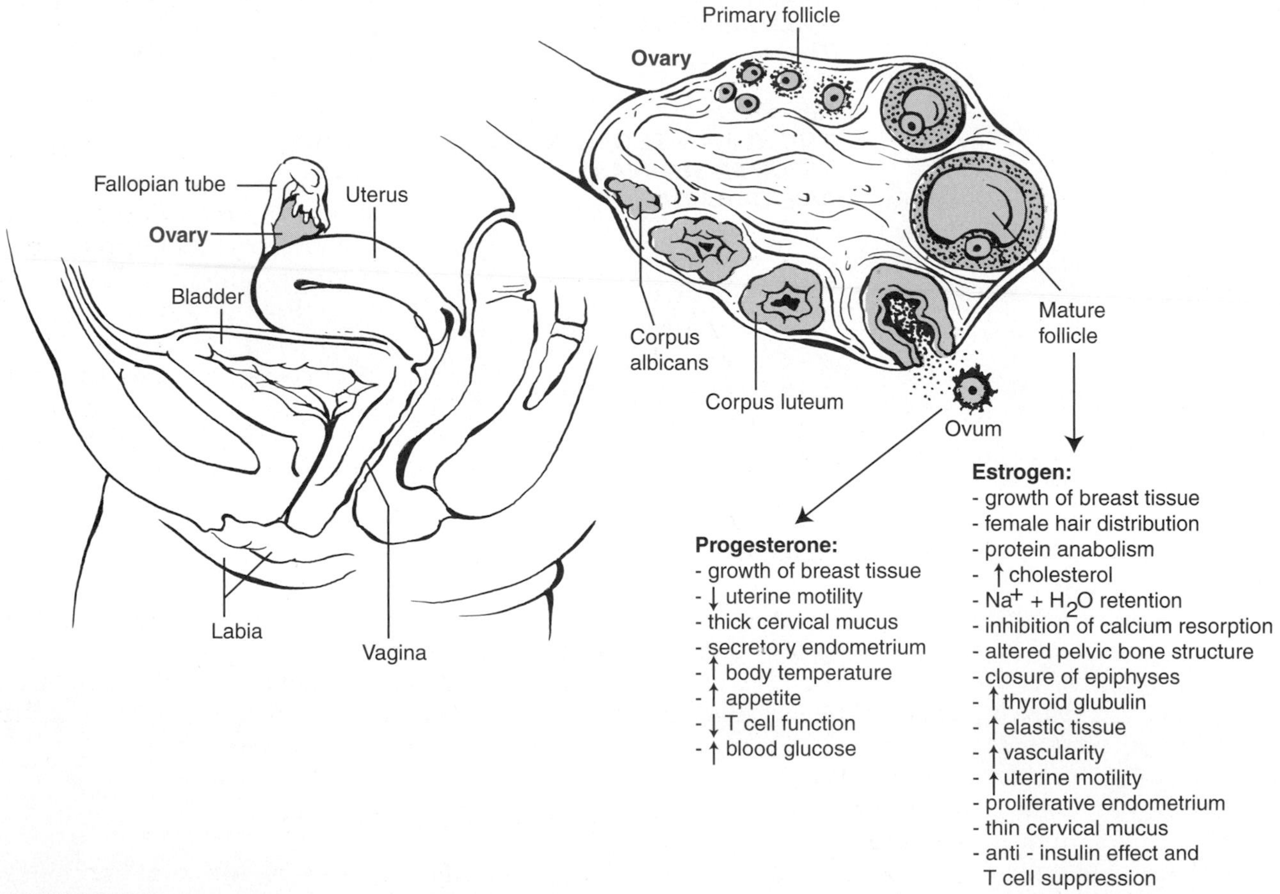

FIGURE 37-1. The female reproductive system.

and starts to release GnRH. This occurs at ***puberty***, or sexual development. The onset of puberty leads to a number of hormonal changes.

To begin with, GnRH stimulates the anterior pituitary to release FSH and LH. FSH and LH stimulate the follicles on the outer surface of the uterus to grow and develop. These follicles are called graafian follicles; they produce progesterone, which is retained in the follicle, and estrogen, which is released into circulation. When the circulating estrogen level rises high enough, it will stimulate a massive release of LH from the anterior pituitary. This is called the "LH surge." This burst of LH causes one of the developing follicles to burst and release the ovum and all the hormones that are inside the follicle into the system. LH also causes the rest of the developing follicles to shrink in on themselves, or involute, and eventually disappear. The release of an ovum from the follicle is called ovulation.

The ovum is released into the abdomen near the end of the fallopian tubes, and the constant movement of cilia within the tube helps to propel the ovum into the fallopian tube and then into the uterus. The ruptured follicle becomes a functioning endocrine gland called the ***corpus luteum***. It will continue to produce estrogen and progesterone for 10 to 14 days unless pregnancy occurs. If the ovum is fertilized and implants in the uterine wall, one of the first hormones that is produced by the junction of the fertilized embryo with the uterine wall is human chorionic gonadotropin. This hormone will stimulate the corpus luteum to continue to produce estrogen and progesterone until placental levels of these hormones are high enough to sustain the pregnancy.

If pregnancy does not occur, the corpus luteum will involute and become a white scar on the ovary. This scar is called the corpus albicans. Initially, the rising levels of estrogen and progesterone produced by the corpus luteum act as a negative feedback system to the hypothalamus and the pituitary, stopping the production and secretion of GnRH, FSH, and LH. Later in the cycle, the corpus luteum atrophies, the falling levels of estrogen and progesterone stimulate the hypothalamus to release GnRH, and the cycle begins again.

When all of the follicles are used up, the ovaries no longer produce estrogen and progesterone and menopause occurs. The hypothalamus and pituitary will produce increased levels of GnRH, FSH, and LH for a while in attempts to stimulate the ovaries to produce estrogen and progesterone. When that does not happen, the levels of these hormones fall back within a normal range in response to their own negative feedback systems. Menopause is associated with the loss of many of the effects of the two hormones on the body, including retention of calcium in the bones, lowered serum lipid levels, and maintenance of secondary sex characteristics.

It should be noted that because of its position in the brain, the hypothalamus is influenced by many internal and external factors. For example, high levels of stress may stop the reproductive cycle; tremendous amounts of energy are expended in reproduction, and if the body needs energy for fight or flight, the hypothalamus shuts down the reproductive activities. In addition to stress, starvation, extreme exercise, and emotional problems are all associated with a decrease in reproductivity, related to the controls of the hypothalamus.

Interestingly, light has been found to have an influence on the functioning of the hypothalamus. Increased light levels boost the release of FSH and LH and increase the release of estrogen and progesterone. This is thought to contribute to the early sexual maturation of girls near the equator. Longer and earlier exposure to light leads to earlier GnRH release by the hypothalamus and earlier sexual development.

Hormones

The hormones produced in the ovaries are estrogen and progesterone. These two hormones influence many other body systems while preparing the body for pregnancy or maintenance of pregnancy.

ESTROGEN

The estrogens produced by the ovaries include estradiol, estrone, and estriol. The estrogens enter cells and bind to receptors within the cytoplasm to promote messenger RNA activity, resulting in specific proteins for cell activity or structure. The effects of estrogen on the body are summarized in Box 37-1. Many of these effects are first noticed at menarche (the onset of the menstrual cycle), when the hormones begin cycling for the first time. Female characteristics are associated with the effects of estrogen on many of the body's systems—wider hips, soft skin, breast growth, and so on.

PROGESTERONE

Progesterone is released into circulation after ovulation. Its effects are summarized in Box 37-2. Progesterone's effects on body temperature are monitored in the "rhythm method" of birth control to indicate that ovulation has just occurred.

The Menstrual Cycle

The cyclic effects of the female sexual hormones on the body produces the ***menstrual cycle***. The onset of the menstrual cycle is called the menarche. The

BOX 37-1 ESTROGEN EFFECTS ON THE BODY

- Growth of genitalia (in preparation for childbirth)
- Growth of breast tissue (in preparation for pregnancy and lactation)
- Characteristic female pubic hair distribution (a triangle)
- Stimulation of protein building (important for the developing fetus)
- Increased total blood cholesterol (for energy for the mother as well as the developing fetus) with an increase in HDL levels (good cholesterol, which serves to protect the female heart against atherosclerosis)
- Retention of sodium and water (provide cooling for the heat generated by the developing fetus and to increase diffusion of these to the fetus through the placenta)
- Inhibition of calcium resorption from the bones (helps to deposit calcium in the fetal bone structure; when this property is lost at menopause, osteoporosis or loss of calcium from the bone is common)
- Alteration of pelvic bone structure to a wider and flaring pelvis (to promote easier delivery)
- Closure of the epiphyses (to conserve energy for the fetus by halting growth of the mother)
- Increased thyroid hormone globulin (metabolism needs to be increased greatly during pregnancy, and the increase in thyroid hormone facilitates this)
- Increased elastic tissue of the skin (to allow for the tremendous stretch of the abdominal skin during pregnancy)
- Increased vascularity of the skin (to allow for radiation loss of heat generated by the developing fetus)
- Increased uterine motility (estrogen is high when the ovum first leaves the ovary, and increased uterine motility helps to move the ovum toward the uterus and to propel the sperm toward the ovum)
- Thin, clear cervical mucous (allows easy penetration of the sperm into the uterus as ovulation occurs; used in fertility programs as an indication that ovulation will soon occur)
- Proliferative endometrium (to prepare the lining of the uterus for implantation with the fertilized egg)
- Anti-insulin effect with increased glucose levels (to allow increased diffusion of glucose to the developing fetus)
- T cell inhibition (to protect the non-self cells of the embryo from the immune surveillance of the mother)

BOX 37-2 PROGESTERONE EFFECTS ON THE BODY

- Decreased uterine motility (to provide increased chance that implantation can occur)
- Development of a secretory endometrium (to provide glucose and a rich blood supply for the developing placenta and embryo)
- Thickened cervical mucous (to protect the developing embryo and keep out bacteria and other pathogens; this is lost at the beginning of labor as the mucus plug)
- Breast growth (to prepare for lactation)
- Increased body temperature (a direct hypothalamic response to progesterone, which stimulates metabolism and promotes activities for the developing embryo; this increase in temperature is monitored in the "rhythm method" of birth control to indicate that ovulation has occurred)
- Increased appetite (this is a direct effect on the satiety centers of the hypothalamus and results in increased nutrients for the developing embryo)
- Depressed T cell function (again, this protects the non-self cells of the developing embryo from the immune system)
- Anti-insulin effect (to generate a higher blood glucose to allow rapid diffusion of glucose to the developing embryo)

cycle starts with release of FSH and LH and stimulation of the follicles on the ovary. For about the next 14 days, these developing follicles will release estrogen into the body. The many effects of estrogen will be noticed by the female (e.g., breast tenderness, water retention, thin cervical mucosa, increased susceptibility to infections, and development of a secretory endometrium).

Around day 14, the estrogen levels have caused the LH surge and ovulation occurs. The female will experience increased body temperature, increased appetite, breast tenderness, bloating and abdominal fullness, constipation, and so on—the effects associated with progesterone. The uterus becomes thicker and more vascular as the cycle progresses and develops a proliferative endometrium. After ovulation, the lining of the uterus begins producing glucose and other nutrients that would nurture a growing embryo; this is called a secretory endometrium. If pregnancy does not occur, after about 14 days the corpus luteum involutes and the levels of estrogen and progesterone drop off (Figure 37-2).

The dropping levels of estrogen and progesterone trigger the release of FSH and LH again, along with the start of the menstrual cycle. Lowered hormone levels also cause the inner lining of the uterus to slough off as it is no longer stimulated by the hormones. High levels of plasminogen in the uterus prevent clotting of the lining as the vessels shear off. Prostaglandins in the uterus will stimulate uterine contraction to clamp off vessels as the lining sheds away. This causes menstrual cramps that can be very uncomfortable for some women. This loss of the uterine lining is called menstruation and repeats approximately every 28 days. Figure 37-3 displays the various phases of the menstrual cycle.

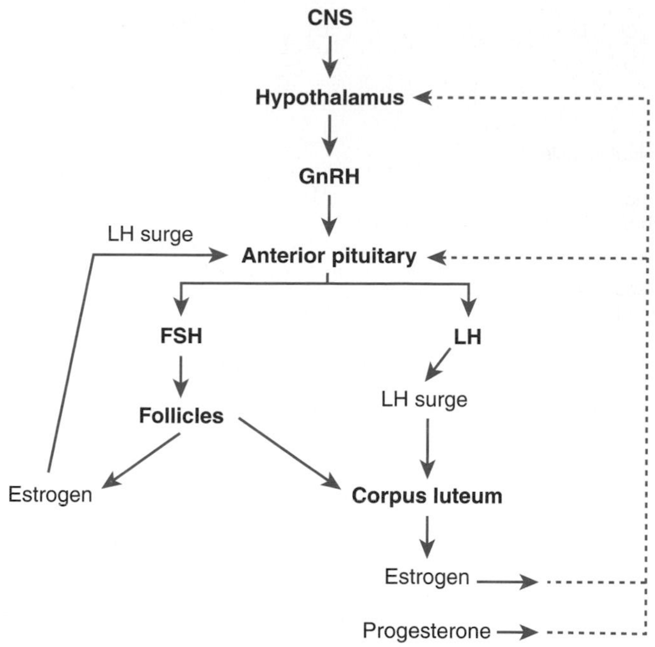

FIGURE 37-2. Interaction of the hypothalamic, pituitary, and ovarian hormones that underlies the menstrual cycle of the female. Dotted lines indicate negative feedback surge.

Pregnancy

When the ovum is fertilized by a sperm, a new cell is produced that rapidly divides to produce the embryo. The embryo implants in the wall of the uterus, and the interface between the fetal cells and the uterus produces the placenta, a large, vascular organ that serves as a massive endocrine gland and a transfer point for nutrients from the mother to the fetus. The placenta maintains high levels of estrogens and progesterone to support the uterus and the developing fetus. When the placenta ages, the levels of progesterone and estrogens fall off.

Eventually, the tendency to block uterine activity (a progesterone effect) is overcome by the stimulation to increase uterine activity by oxytocin (a hypothalamic hormone stored in the posterior pituitary). At this point, local prostaglandins stimulate uterine contraction and the onset of labor. Once the fetus and the placenta have been expelled from the uterus, the hormone levels plummet toward the nonpregnant state. This is a time of tremendous adjustment for the body as it tries to reachieve homeostasis.

MALE REPRODUCTIVE SYSTEM

The male reproductive system originates from the same fetal cells as the female. The two endocrine glands that develop in the male are called the testes. The testes continually produce ***sperm*** as well as the

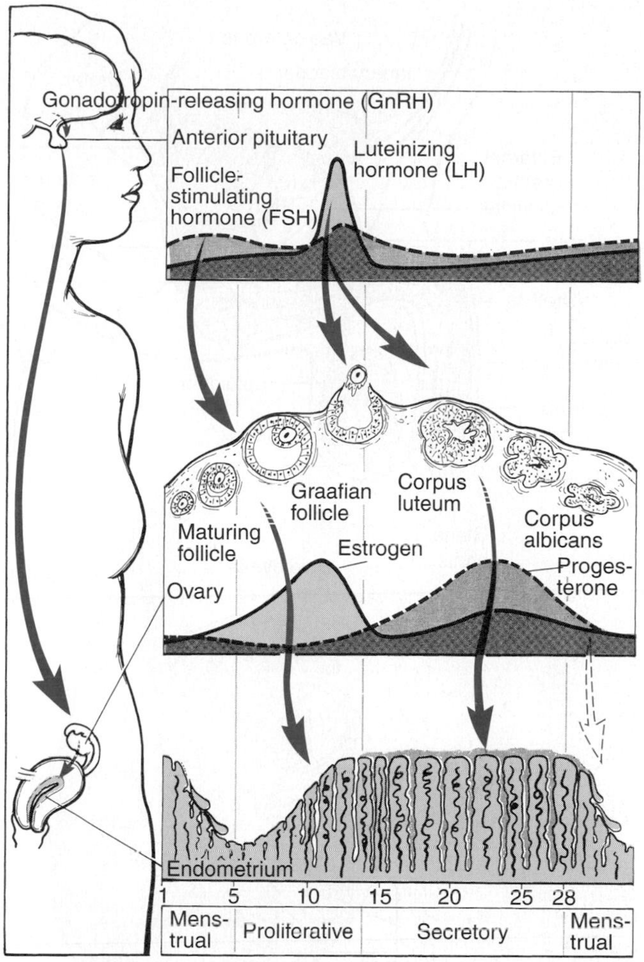

FIGURE 37-3. Relation of pituitary and ovarian hormone levels to the menstrual cycle and to ovarian and endometrial function. (Bullock, B. L. [2000]. *Focus on pathophysiology.* Philadelphia: Lippincott Williams & Wilkins.)

hormone ***testosterone***. The other parts of the male reproductive system include the vas deferens, which stores produced sperm and carries sperm from the testes to be ejaculated from the body; the prostate gland, which produces enzymes to stimulate sperm maturation as well as lubricating fluid; the penis, which includes two corpora cavernosa and a corpus spongiosum, which allow massively increased blood flow and erection; the urethra, through which urine as well as the sperm and seminal fluid are delivered; and other glands and ducts that promote sperm and seminal fluid development (Figure 37-4).

Testes

The two testes migrate down the abdomen and descend into the scrotum outside the body. There they are protected from the heat of the body to prevent injury to the sperm-producing cells. The testes are made up of two distinct parts: the ***seminiferous tubules,*** which produce the sperm, and the ***interstitial or Leydig cells***, which produce the hormone testosterone.

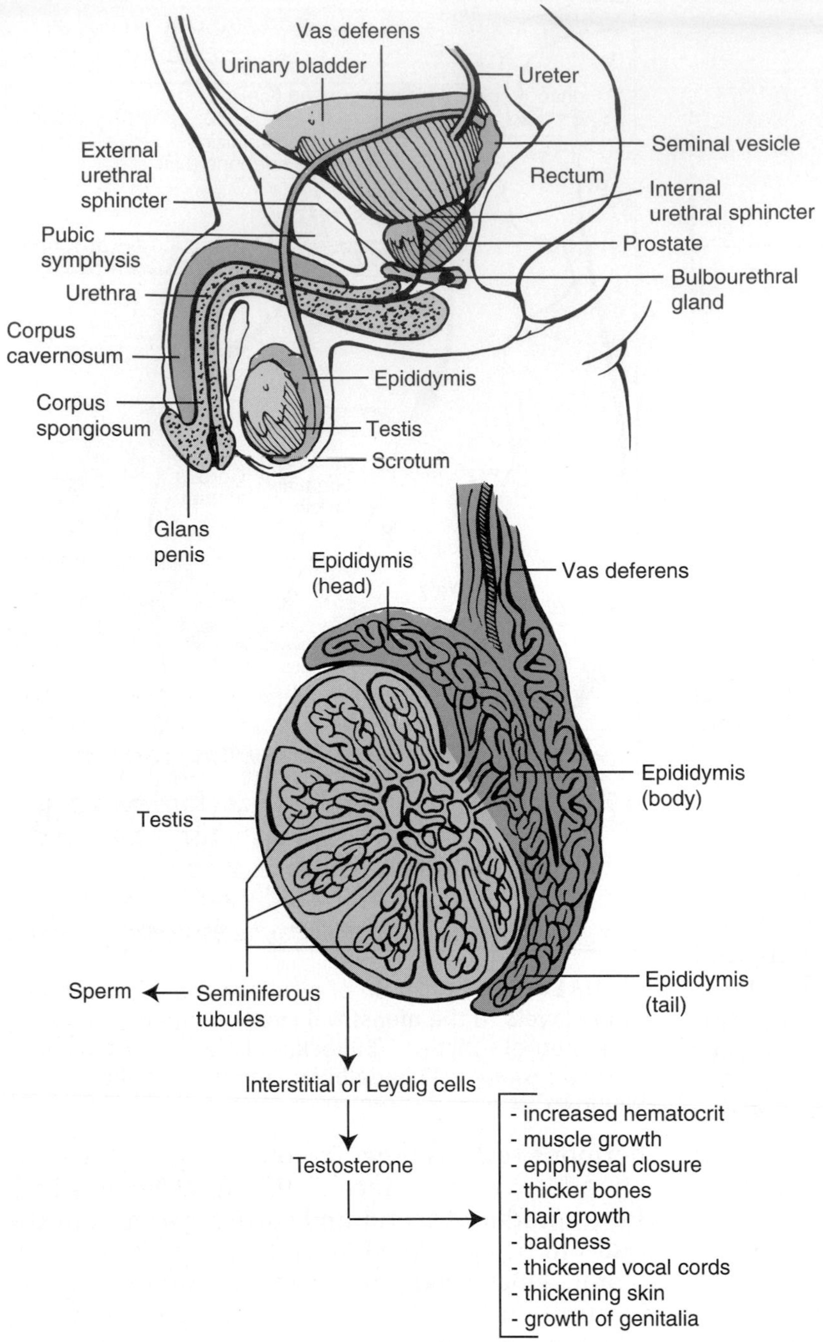

FIGURE 37-4. The male reproductive system.

Controls

The activity of the male sex glands is not thought to be cyclical like that of the female. The hypothalamus in the male child is also sensitive to circulating levels of adrenal androgens and suppresses GnRH release. When the hypothalamus matures, the sensitivity is lost and the hypothalamus releases GnRH. This in turn stimulates the anterior pituitary to release FSH and LH, or what is sometimes called interstitial cell stimulating hormone (ICSH) in males. FSH directly stimulates the seminiferous tubules to stimulate sperm production, a process called spermatogenesis. FSH also stimulates the Sertoli cells in the seminiferous tubules to produce estrogens, which provide negative feedback to the pituitary and hypothalamus to cause a decrease in the release of GnRH, FSH, and LH.

The Sertoli cells also produce a substance called ***inhibin*** (an estrogen-like molecule). The inhibin is sensed by the hypothalamus and anterior pituitary, and a negative feedback response occurs, decreasing the circulating levels of FSH. When the FSH levels fall low enough, the hypothalamus is stimulated to again release GnRH to stimulate FSH release. This feedback system prevents an overproduction of sperm in the testes (Figure 37-5).

Inhibin has been investigated for many years as a possible male birth control drug, since it only affects sperm production. The LH or ICSH stimulates the interstitial cells or Leydig cells to produce testosterone. The levels of testosterone act in a similar negative feedback system with the hypothalamus. When levels are high enough, the hypothalamus will decrease GnRH release, leading to a subsequent decrease in FSH and LH release. The levels of testosterone are thought to remain within a fairly well defined range of normal. It has been documented, however, that light affects the male sexual hormones in a similar fashion to its effect on female hormones. "Spring fever," with the increased exposure time to sunlight, does increase testosterone levels in males. Other factors that may also have an influence on male hormone levels are likely to be identified in the future.

With age, the seminiferous tubules and interstitial cells atrophy and the male climacteric, a period of lessened sexual activity, occurs. This is similar to female menopause, when the hypothalamus and anterior pituitary put out larger amounts of GnRH, FSH, and LH in attempts to stimulate the gland. When no increase in testosterone or inhibin occurs, the levels of GnRH, FSH, and LH will eventually return to normal levels.

Hormones

Testosterone is responsible for many sexual and metabolic effects in the male. Like estrogen, testosterone enters the cell and reacts with a cytoplasmic receptor site to influence messenger RNA (mRNA) activity, resulting in proteins for cell structure or function. The effects of testosterone on the body are summarized in Box 37-3.

Castration, or removal of the testes before puberty, will result in a lack of development of the normal male characteristics as well as in sterility. It has been found, however, that once puberty occurs and the physical changes brought about by testosterone occur, the androgens released by the adrenal glands are sufficient to sustain the male characteristics. This is important information for adult patients undergoing testicular surgery or chemical castration.

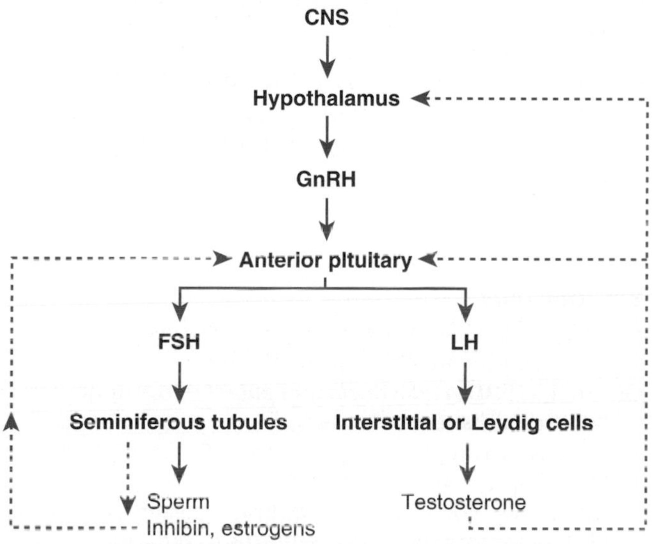

FIGURE 37-5. Interaction of the hypothalamic, pituitary, and testicular hormones that underlies the male sexual hormone system.

THE HUMAN SEXUAL RESPONSE

Humans are the only known animals that can be sexually stimulated and responsive at will. Many animals require particular endocrine stimuli, called an estrous cycle, for sexual response to occur. Humans can be sexually stimulated by thoughts, sights, touch, or a variety of combined stimuli. The human sexual response consists of four different phases:

- A period of stimulation with mild increases in sensitivity and beginning stimulation of the sympathetic nervous system
- A plateau stage when stimulation levels off
- A climax, which results from massive sympathetic stimulation of the body
- A period of recovery or resolution, when the effects of the sympathetic stimulation are resolved (Figure 37-6)

BOX 37-3

TESTOSTERONE EFFECTS ON THE BODY

- Growth of male sexual accessory organs (penis, prostate gland, seminal vesicles, vas deferens)
- Growth of testes and scrotal sac
- Thickening of vocal chords, producing the deep, male voice
- Hair growth on the face, body, arms, legs, and trunk
- Male pattern baldness
- Increased protein anabolism and decreased protein catabolism (this causes larger and more powerful muscle development)
- Increased bone growth in length and width, which ends when the testosterone stimulates closure of the epiphyses
- Thickening of the cartilage and skin, leading to the male gait
- Vascular thickening
- Increased hematocrit

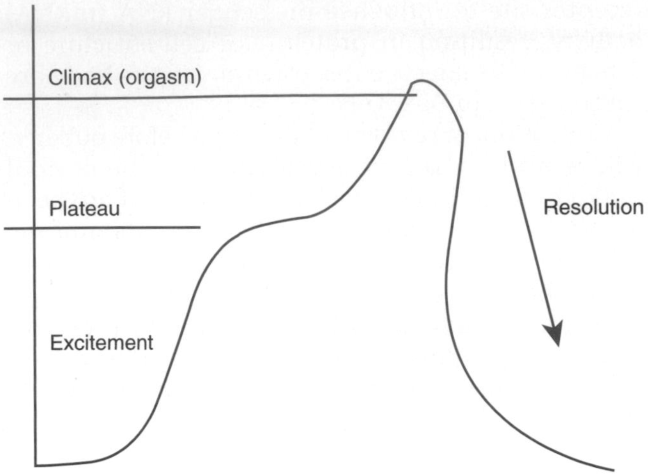

FIGURE 37-6. Human sexual response.

It was once thought that male and female responses were very different, but it is now thought that the physiology of the responses is very similar. Sexual stimulation and activity are a normal response and, in healthy individuals, are probably necessary for complete health of the systems. The sympathetic stimulation will cause increased heart rate, increased blood pressure, sweating, pupil dilation, glycogenolysis (breakdown of stored glycogen to glucose for energy) and other sympathetic responses. This stimulation could be dangerous in some cardiovascular conditions that could be exacerbated by the sympathetic effects. In the male, the increased blood flow to the penis causes erection, which is necessary for penetration of the female and depositing of the sperm. Any drug therapy or disease process that interferes with the sympathetic response or the innervation of the sexual organs will change the person's ability to experience the human sexual response. This is important to keep in mind when doing patient teaching and when evaluating the effects of a drug.

WWW.WEB LINKS

Students may want to explore the following Internet sources:

Explore the virtual reproductive system:

http://www.InnerBody.com

http://www.letsfindout.com/subjects/body

CHAPTER SUMMARY

- Male and female reproductive systems arise from the same fetal cells.
- The female ovary stores ova and produces the sex hormones estrogen and progesterone.
- Male testes produce sperm and the sex hormone testosterone.
- The hypothalamus releases GnRH at puberty to stimulate the anterior pituitary release of FSH and LH, thus stimulating the production and release of the sex hormones. Levels are controlled by a series of negative feedback systems.
- Female sex hormones are released in a cyclical fashion. Male sex hormones are released in a steadier fashion.
- Female sex hormones prepare the body for pregnancy and the maintenance of the pregnancy. Ovulation is the release of an egg for possible fertilization.
- If pregnancy does not occur, the prepared inner lining of the uterus is sloughed off as menstruation in the menstrual cycle so the lining can be prepared again when ovulation reoccurs.
- Menopause in females and the male climacteric occur when the body can no longer produce sex hormones, and the hypothalamus and anterior pituitary respond by releasing increasing levels of GnRH, FSH, and LH in an attempt to achieve higher levels of sex hormones.
- The testes produce sperm in the seminiferous tubules, in response to FSH stimulation, and testosterone in the interstitial cells, in response to LH stimulation.
- Testosterone is responsible for the development of male sex characteristics. These characteristics can be maintained by the androgens from the adrenal gland once the body has undergone the changes of puberty.
- The human sexual response involves activation of the sympathetic nervous system to allow a four-phase response: stimulation, plateau, climax, and resolution.

BIBLIOGRAPHY

Bullock, B. L. (2000). *Focus on pathophysiology.* Philadelphia: Lippincott Williams & Wilkins.

Girard, J. (1991). *Endocrinology of puberty.* Farmington, CT: Karger Publishers.

Guyton, A. & Hall, J. (1996). *Textbook of medical physiology.* Philadelphia: W.B. Saunders.

Karch, A. M. (2000). *2000 Lippincott's nursing drug guide.* Philadelphia: Lippincott Williams & Wilkins.

Muske, L. E. (1993). *The neurobiology of reproductive behavior.* Farmington, CT: Karger Publishers.

CHAPTER 38

Drugs Affecting the Female Reproductive System

Estrogens
- chlorotrianisene
- dienestrol
- diethylstilbestrol
- P estradiol
- estrogens, conjugated
- estrogens, esterified
- estrone
- estropipate

Estrogen receptor modulators
- P raloxifene
- toremifene

Progestins
- hydroxyprogesterone
- P levonorgestrel
- medroxyprogesterone
- norethindrone
- norgestrel
- progesterone

Fertility drugs
- P clomiphene
- follitropin alfa
- follitropin beta
- menotropins
- urofollitropin

Oxytocics
- ergonovine
- methylergonovine
- P oxytocin

Abortifacients
- carboprost
- P dinoprostone
- mifepristone

Tocolytics
- P ritodrine
- terbutaline

CHAPTER OUTLINE

Assessment
HISTORY
PHYSICAL ASSESSMENT
Nursing Diagnoses
Implementation
Evaluation
CHAPTER SUMMARY
BIBLIOGRAPHY

KEY TERMS

abortifacients
fertility drugs
oxytocics
progestins
tocolytics

INTRODUCTION

The female reproductive system uses a cycling balance to maintain homeostasis. Changing any factor in the system can have a wide variety of effects on the entire body. Drugs that are used to affect the female reproductive system include the female steroid hormones estrogen and the ***progestins*** (which include the endogenous female hormone progesterone and its various derivatives); estrogen receptor modulators that are not hormones, but that affect specific estrogen receptor sites; fertility drugs that stimulate the female reproductive system; ***oxytocics***, which stimulate uterine contractions and assist labor; ***abortifacients***, which are used to induce abortion; and ***tocolytics***, which are used to relax the gravid uterus to prolong pregnancy (Figure 38-1).

ESTROGENS

Estrogens are used in many clinical situations. For example, in small doses, they are used for replacement therapy when ovarian activity is blocked or absent. They also are useful in palliative and preventive therapy during menopause, when many of the beneficial effects of estrogen are lost. Estrogens produce a wide variety of systemic effects, including protecting the heart from atherosclerosis, retaining calcium in the bones, and maintaining the secondary female sex characteristics. (See Box 37-1 for a complete listing of estrogen effects.)

Estrogens that are available for use include chlorotrianisene (*Tace*); dienestrol (*Ortho Dienestrol*), which is only available as a topical agent; diethylstilbestrol (*DES*), which has been associated with birth defects and is now only used to treat certain cancers; estradiol (*Estrace, Climara,* and others), which is widely used and found in combination form as an oral contraceptive; estrogens, conjugated (*Premarin*), one of the most popular drugs for postmenopausal treatment; estrogen, esterified (*Estratab*); estrone (*Aquest* and others), which is slow acting and only available for IM administration; and estropipate (*Ortho-Est, Ogen*), a slow-acting oral agent that has been associated with severe hepatic effects. Figure 38-2 summarizes the various forms in which estrogens are available.

THERAPEUTIC ACTIONS AND INDICATIONS

As explained previously, estrogens are important for the development of the female reproductive system and secondary sex characteristics. They affect the release of pituitary follicle-stimulating hormone (FSH) and luteinizing hormone (LH); cause capillary dilatation, fluid retention, and protein anabolism and thin cervical mucous; conserve calcium and phosphorus and encourage bone formation; inhibit ovulation; and prevent postpartum breast discomfort. Estrogens also are responsible for the proliferation of the endometrial lining. An absence of or decrease in estrogen produces the signs and symptoms of menopause in the uterus, vagina, breasts, and cervix. Estrogens are known to compete with androgens for receptor sites; this trait makes them beneficial in certain androgen-dependent prostate cancers.

Estrogens are indicated for the palliation of moderate to severe vasomotor symptoms, atrophic vaginitis, and kraurosis vulvae (atrophy of the female genitalia) associated with menopause; the treatment of female hypogonadism, female castration, and primary ovarian failure; the prevention of postpartum breast engorgement; in combination with progestins as oral contraceptives; as a postcoital contraceptive when taken in particular sequence; to retard osteoporosis in postmenopausal women; to decrease the risk of coronary artery disease (CAD) in postmenopausal women; and as palliation in certain types of prostatic and mammary cancers (Figure 38-3).

CONTRAINDICATIONS/CAUTIONS

Estrogens are contraindicated in the presence of any known allergies to estrogens; with pregnancy (serious fetal defects have occurred); idiopathic vaginal bleeding; breast cancer; any estrogen-dependent cancer; history of thromboembolic disorders (because of the increased risk of thrombus and embolus development); and hepatic dysfunction (because of the effects of estrogen on liver function).

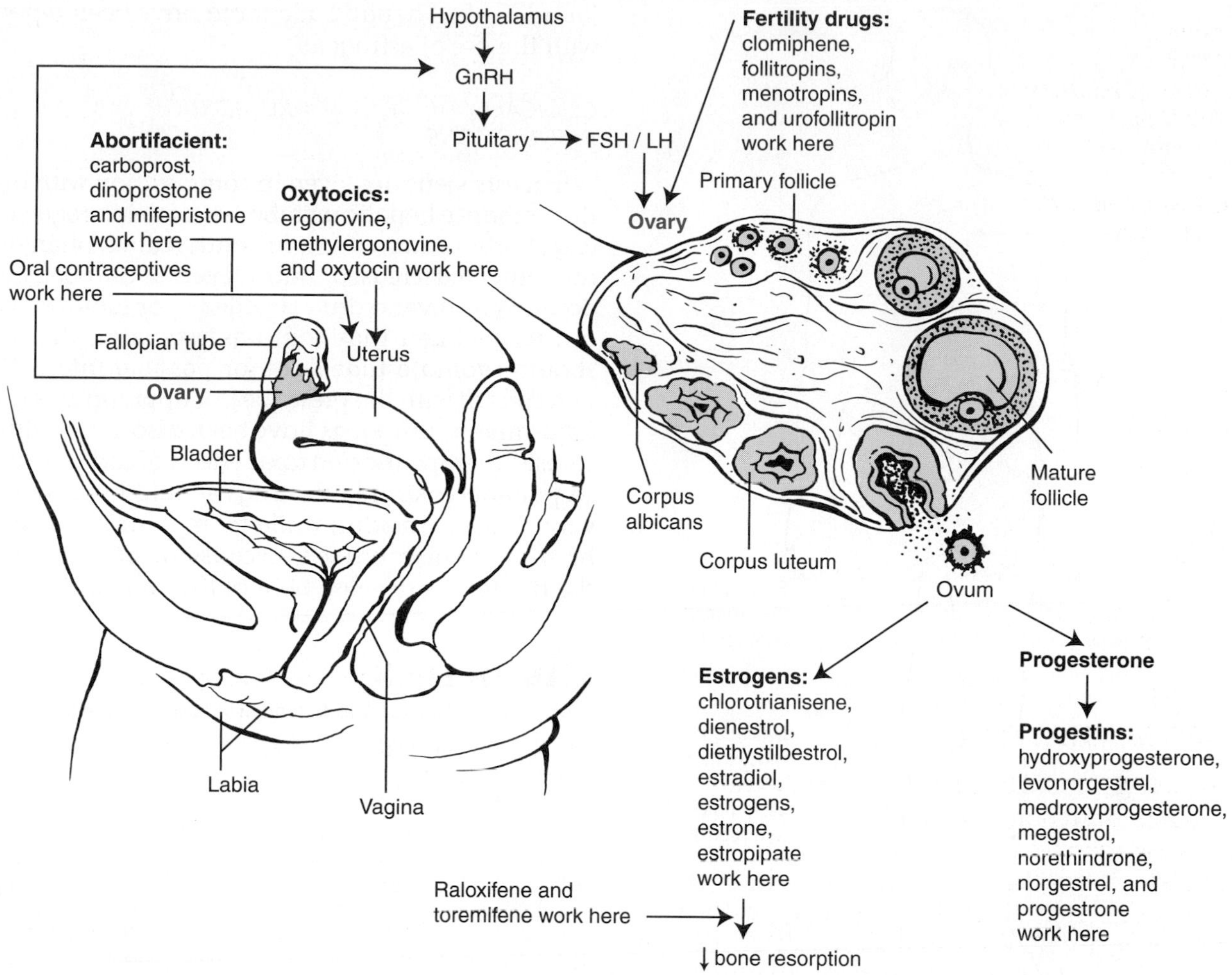

FIGURE 38-1. Sites of action of drugs affecting the female reproductive system.

	Oral	Injection	Vaginal cream or gel	Transdermal patch	Vaginal ring	Implant
Estrogens						
chlorotrianisene	x	–	–	–	–	–
dienestrol	–	–	x	–	–	–
diethystilbestrol	x	x	–	–	–	–
estradiol	x	x	x	x	x	–
estrogens, conjugated	x	x	x	–	–	–
estrogens, esterified	x	–	–	–	–	–
estrone	–	x	–	–	–	–
estropipate	x	–	x	–	–	–
Progestins						
hydroxyprogesterone	–	x	–	–		–
levonorgestrel	–	–	–	–	–	x
medroxyprogestrone	x	x	–	–	–	–
norethindrone	x	–	–	–	–	–
norgestrel	x	–	–	–		–
progesterone	–	x	x	–	–	–

FIGURE 38-2. Available forms of estrogen and progestin products.

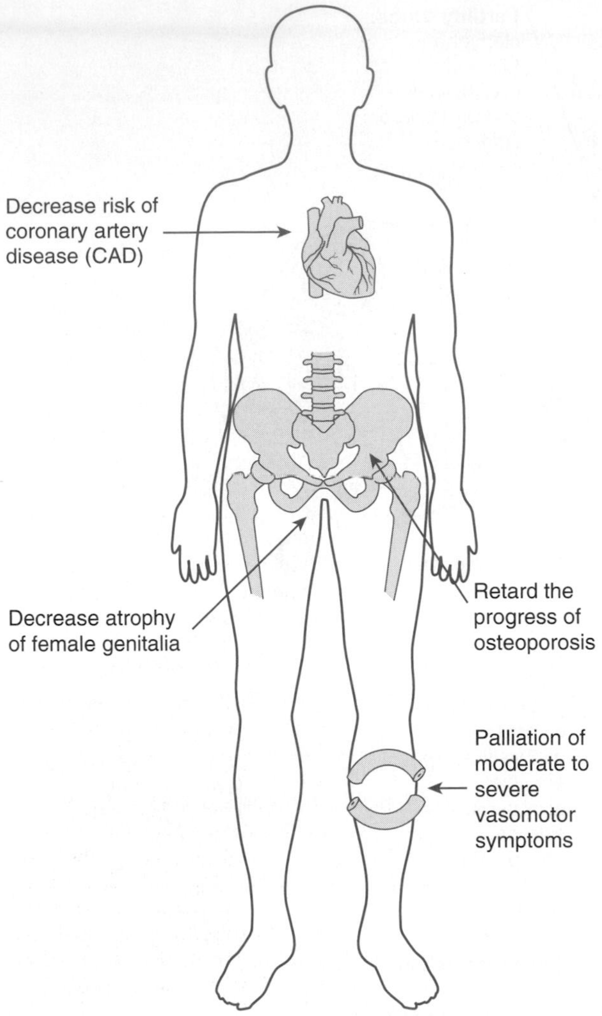

FIGURE 38-3. Sites of action of the estrogens.

Estrogens should be used with caution during lactation (because of possible effects on the neonate), with metabolic bone disease (because of the bone-conserving effect of estrogen), and with renal insufficiency (because of the estrogen's affect on fluid and electrolytes).

ADVERSE EFFECTS

Many of the most common adverse effects associated with estrogens include effects on the genitourinary (GU) tract (e.g., breakthrough bleeding, menstrual irregularities, dysmenorrhea, amenorrhea, changes in libido). Other effects can be due to the systemic effects of estrogens (e.g., fluid retention, electrolyte disturbances, headache, dizziness, mental changes, weight changes, edema). Gastrointestinal (GI) effects also are fairly common (e.g., nausea, vomiting, abdominal cramps and bloating, colitis). Potentially serious GI effects of acute pancreatitis, cholestatic jaundice, and hepatic adenoma have been reported with the use of estrogens.

CLINICALLY IMPORTANT DRUG–DRUG INTERACTIONS

When estrogens are given in combination with drugs that enhance hepatic metabolism of the estrogen drug (e.g., barbiturates, rifampin, tetracyclines, phenytoin, and others) decreased serum levels of estrogens may occur. Whenever a drug is added to or removed from a drug regimen that contains estrogens, the nurse should evaluate that drug for possible interactions and consult with the prescriber for appropriate dosage adjustments. Estrogens have been associated with increased therapeutic and toxic effects of corticosteroids, so patients taking both drugs should be monitored very closely. Smoking while taking estrogens should be strongly discouraged, because nicotine increases the risk for the development of thrombi and emboli.

DATA LINK

Data link to the following estrogens in your nursing drug guide:

ESTROGENS

Name	Brand Name	Usual Indications
chlorotrianisene	*Tace*	Palliation of signs and symptoms of menopause, prostate cancer, treatment of female hypogonadism
dienestrol	*Ortho Dienestrol*	Palliation of signs and symptoms of menopause
diethylstilbestrol	*DES*	Palliation in prostatic and breast cancer
P estradiol	*Estrace*	Palliation of signs and symptoms of menopause, prostate cancer, inoperable breast cancer; treatment of female hypogonadism, postpartum breast engorgement
estrogens, conjugated	*C.E.S.*	Palliation of signs and symptoms of menopause, prostate cancer, inoperable breast cancer; treatment of female hypogonadism, postpartum breast engorgement; to retard the progress of osteoporosis
estrogens, esterified	*Estratab*	Palliation of signs and symptoms of menopause, prostate cancer, inoperable breast cancer; treatment of female hypogonadism
estrone	*Aquest*	Palliation of signs and symptoms of menopause, prostate cancer treatment of female hypogonadism, treatment of abnormal uterine bleeding
estropipate	*Ortho-Est*	Palliation of signs and symptoms of menopause; treatment of female hypogonadism

CASE STUDY

Menopause

PRESENTATION

J. M. is a 52-year-old female who is being seen in her gynecologist's office for a routine annual physical and Pap smear. J. M. reports that her periods are closer together and much heavier than they used to be. Her mother went through menopause in her early 50s, so J. M. is anxious to know if she is about to enter menopause and what to expect.

CRITICAL THINKING QUESTIONS

What teaching and counseling issues will be important for J. M. at this time? Think about myths and stories surrounding menopause and ways that these ideas can affect the experience people have. What important issues should be discussed when suggesting the advisability of HRT (hormone replacement therapy) to this patient? What other measures can be taken to help a patient cope with the signs and symptoms of menopause that do not involve drug therapy?

DISCUSSION

The exact age that a woman experiences menopause or "the change" will vary. The age at which a patient's mother underwent menopause is a good measure for estimating when the patient can expect menopause. The nurse should review with J. M. the cause of menopause (running out of ova, so further production of estrogen and progesterone is drastically reduced). The nurse also should discuss the physical signs and symptoms that J. M. might experience. These include hot flashes (a sign of vasomotor instability with feelings of heat and sweating unrelated to activity or environment); decreased muscle strength; personality changes; irregular and erratic periods; thin, dry skin; dryness of the vaginal area; sleep disturbances; and changes in libido. The nurse also should advise J. M. about changes that she might not be aware of, such as the increased risk of coronary artery disease and heart attack, uterine atrophy, osteoporosis, and possible decrease in cognitive ability.

Nonpharmacological measures to help J. M. through menopause can be explored. Regular exercise can help to protect the heart and to relieve insomnia; environmental control can help to alleviate some of the discomfort of hot flashes; avoiding stimulants like caffeine can be beneficial in alleviating insomnia and in easing some of the mood swings that may occur. J. M. may want to discuss other "remedies" that she has heard about and these can be explored with the health care provider.

The leading cause of death in postmenopausal women is heart disease, but research has shown that treating women with replacement therapy can greatly decrease that risk. The health care provider should give J. M. information about replacement hormones for women in menopause. J. M. may be aware of possible increased risk of breast or cervical cancer while taking these drugs, and the data available on that risk should be discussed (see Age/Gender Considerations).

ESTROGEN RECEPTOR MODULATORS

Estrogen receptor modulators were developed to produce some of the positive effects of estrogen replacement, yet limit the adverse effects. The two estrogen receptor modulators that are currently available are raloxifene (*Evista*), which is used to prevent and treat osteoporosis, and toremifene (*Fareston*), which is used as an antineoplastic agent because of its effects on estrogen receptor sites (see Chapter 12 for information on this drug). The long-term effects of these two drugs are not yet known.

THERAPEUTIC ACTIONS AND INDICATIONS

Raloxifene affects specific estrogen receptor sites to increase bone mineral density without stimulating the endometrium in women. It is indicated for the treatment of postmenopausal osteoporosis.

CONTRAINDICATIONS/CAUTIONS

Raloxifene is contraindicated in the presence of any known allergy to raloxifene, and in pregnancy and lactation (because of potential effects on the fetus or neonate). Caution should be used in the presence of a history of venous thrombosis or smoking because of an increased risk of blood clot formation when smoking and estrogen are combined.

ADVERSE EFFECTS

Raloxifene has been associated with GI upset, nausea, and vomiting. Changes in fluid balance may also cause headache, dizziness, visual changes, and mental changes. Hot flashes, skin rash, edema, and vaginal bleeding may occur. Venous thromboembolism is a potentially dangerous side effect that has been reported.

GENDER/LIFE-SPAN CONSIDERATIONS

Menopause and Hormone Replacement Therapy (HRT)

Females experience the menarche, or onset of the menstrual cycle, in their adolescent years and menopause, or the cessation of the menstrual cycle, in their middle years. The exact age that a woman experiences menopause or "the change" will vary. The family history of onset of menopause is a good guide for when the effects can be expected. Just as the physical changes associated with puberty can take a few years to be accomplished, the changes associated with menopause may also take a few years. The signs and symptoms of menopause are related to the loss of estrogen and progesterone effects on the body (see Case Study).

For centuries, women have proceeded through this time in their lives without pharmacological intervention. Today, with more research and safer drugs available to counteract some of these effects, many women are being advised to use hormone replacement therapy (HRT). The use of HRT can decrease the discomforts associated with menopause and can dramatically decrease the risk of coronary artery disease, the leading cause of death among women over 50 in the western world.

Various forms of HRT have been associated over the years with increased risk of breast cancer and cervical cancer, and many women are reluctant to consider HRT because of these effects. The newer drugs used in HRT have been shown to be associated with only a possible increase in risk of breast and cervical cancer. Patients with many risk factors for developing these cancers are at greater risk than patients with no risk factors. Other drugs, estrogen receptor modulators, have antiestrogen effects on the breast and may remove the cancer risk. But these drugs may be less reliable in their management of the signs and symptoms of menopause.

The woman who is entering menopause should have all the information available before deciding about the use of HRT. A complete family and personal history of cancer and coronary artery disease risk factors should be completed to help the patient balance the benefits versus the risks of this therapy. This is a very difficult decision for many women to make. The nurse is often in the best position to provide information, listen to concerns, and help the patient to decide what is best for her. If the decision is made to use HRT, the patient may need support in dealing with the effects of the drugs and may have to try several different preparations before the one best suited to her is found. This can be a very frustrating time, so the patient will need a consistent, reliable person to turn to with questions and for support. As more research is done in women's health issues, better therapies may be developed to help women through this unavoidable transition in life.

DATA LINK

Data link to the following estrogen receptor modulator in your nursing drug guide:

ESTROGEN RECEPTOR MODULATORS

Name	Brand Name	Usual Indications
P raloxifene	*Evista*	Treatment of postmenopausal osteoporosis

NURSING CONSIDERATIONS
for patients receiving estrogens or estrogen receptor modulators

Assessment

HISTORY. Screen for history of allergy to any estrogen or estrogen product, pregnancy, lactation, hepatic dysfunction, cardiovascular disease, breast or genital cancer, renal disease, metabolic bone disease, history of thromboembolism, smoking, and idiopathic vaginal bleeding.

PHYSICAL ASSESSMENT. Include screening for baseline status before beginning therapy and for any potential adverse effects: skin color, lesions, texture; affect, orientation, mental status, reflexes; blood pressure, pulse, cardiac auscultation, edema, perfusion; abdominal exam, liver exam, pelvic exam, Pap smear, urinalysis, breast exam and ophthalmic exam, particularly if the patient wears contact lenses.

Nursing Diagnoses

The patient receiving estrogens or estrogen receptor modulators may have the following nursing diagnoses related to drug therapy:

- Fluid volume excess related to fluid retention
- Pain related to systemic side effects
- Alteration in tissue perfusion
- Knowledge deficit regarding drug therapy

Implementation

- Administer as prescribed *to prevent adverse effects;* administer with food if GI upset is severe *to relieve GI distress.*
- Provide analgesics *for relief of headache as appropriate.*
- Arrange for at least an annual physical examination, including pelvic examination, Pap smear, and breast examination *to avert adverse effects and monitor drug effects.*

PATIENT TEACHING CHECKLIST

Oral Contraceptives

Create customized patient teaching materials for a specific oral contraceptive from your CD-ROM. Your patient teaching should stress the following points for drugs within this class:

An oral contraceptive (OC) or birth control pill contains specific amounts of female sex hormones that work to make the body unreceptive to pregnancy and to prevent ovulation, the release of the egg from the ovary. Because these hormones affect many systems in your body, it is important to have regular physical check-ups while you are taking this drug.

Many drugs affect the way that OCs work. To be safe, avoid the use of over-the-counter drugs and other drugs, unless you first check with your health care provider.

Some of the following adverse effects may occur:

- Headache, nervousness—Check with your health care provider about the use of an analgesic; this effect usually passes after a few months on the drug.
- Nausea, loss of appetite—This usually passes with time; consult your health care provider if this is a problem.
- Swelling, weight gain—Water retention is a normal effect of these hormones. Limiting salt intake may help. You may have trouble with contact lenses if you wear them, because the body often retains fluid which may change the shape of your eye. This usually adjusts over time.

Cigarette smoking can aggravate serious side effects of OCs, such as the formation of blood clots. When taking OCs, it is advisable to cut down, or preferably to stop, cigarette smoking.

Tell any doctor, nurse, or other health care provider that you are taking this drug.

Report any of the following to your health care provider: pain in the calves or groin; chest pain or difficulty breathing; lump in the breast; severe headache, dizziness, visual changes; severe abdominal pain; yellowing of the skin; pregnancy.

Bleeding (a false menstrual period) should occur during the time that the drug is withdrawn. Report bleeding at *any* other time to your health care provider.

It is important to have regular medical follow-ups, including a Pap smear, while you are taking this drug. If you decide to stop the drug to become pregnant, consult with your health care provider.

Keep this drug and all medications out of the reach of children.

A patient package insert is included with this drug. Read this information and feel free to ask any questions that you might have.

This Teaching Checklist reflects general patient teaching guidelines. It is not meant to be a substitute for drug-specific teaching information, which is available in nursing drug guides.

- Monitor liver function periodically for patient on long-term therapy *to ensure that the drug is discontinued at any sign of hepatic dysfunction.*
- Provide support and reassurance *to deal with the drug and drug effects.*
- Provide thorough patient education, including measures to avoid adverse effects, warning signs of problems, and the need for regular evaluation (including pelvic examination and Pap smear) *to enhance patient knowledge about drug therapy and to promote compliance.*

Evaluation

- Monitor patient response to the drug (palliation of signs and symptoms of menopause, prevention of pregnancy, decreased risk of CAD, palliation of certain cancers).
- Monitor for adverse effects (liver changes, GI upset, edema, changes in secondary sex characteristics, headaches, thromboembolic episodes, breakthrough bleeding).
- Monitor for potential drug–drug interactions as indicated for each particular drug.
- Evaluate the effectiveness of the teaching plan (patient can name drug, dosage, adverse effects to watch for, specific measures to avoid adverse effects). (See Patient Teaching Checklist: Oral Contraceptives.)
- Monitor the effectiveness of comfort measures and compliance to the regimen (see Nursing Care Guide: Estrogens, Progestins).

PROGESTINS

Progestins are used as contraceptives, most effectively in combination with estrogens; to treat amen-

NURSING CARE GUIDE

Estrogens, Progestins

Assessment	Nursing Diagnoses	Implementation	Evaluation
HISTORY Allergies to any estrogens; pregnancy, lactation; breast or genital cancer; hepatic dysfunction; CAD; thromboembolic disease; renal disease; idiopathic vaginal bleeding; metabolic bone disease; diabetes	Fluid volume excess related to fluid retention Pain related to systemic side effects Alteration in tissue perfusion Knowledge deficit regarding drug therapy	Administer as prescribed. Administer with meals. Provide analgesics for headache if appropriate. Provide at least annual physical exam, including Pap smear and breast exam. Provide support and reassurance to deal with drug therapy. Provide patient teaching regarding drug name, dosage, adverse effects, precautions, warnings to report, safe administration.	Evaluate drug effects: prevention of pregnancy; relief of signs and symptoms of menopause; decreased risk of CAD. Monitor for adverse effects: liver changes; GI upset; edema; changes in secondary sex characteristics; headaches; thromboembolic episodes; breakthrough bleeding. Monitor for drug–drug interactions as indicated for each drug. Evaluate effectiveness of patient teaching program. Evaluate effectiveness of comfort and safety measures.
PHYSICAL EXAMINATION Neurological: orientation, reflexes, affect, mental status Skin: color, lesions CV: P, cardiac auscultation, BP, edema, perfusion GI: abdominal exam, liver exam GU: pelvic exam, Pap smear, urinalysis Eye: ophthalmic exam			

orrhea and functional uterine bleeding; and as part of fertility programs. Like the estrogens, some progestins are useful in specific cancers (see Chapter 12) with specific receptor site sensitivity. A number of progestins are available for use. Hydroxyprogesterone (*Hylutin*) is available for IM use to treat amenorrhea and to produce a secretory endometrium. Levonorgestrel (*Norplant System*) is used as an implant system to prevent pregnancy. It also is found in many combination oral contraceptives. Medroxyprogesterone (*Amen, Curretab,* and others) is available orally for treating amenorrhea and by injection for cancer palliation therapy. Norethindrone (*Aygestin*) is used in combination oral contraceptives and alone for the treatment of amenorrhea. Norgestrel (*Ovrette*) is an oral contraceptive that is most effective when used in combination form. Progesterone (*Progestasert* and others) is available in several forms for the treatment of amenorrhea, contraception, and fertility programs. (See Figure 38-2 for a summary of the various forms in which progestins are available.)

THERAPEUTIC ACTIONS AND INDICATIONS

The progestins transform the proliferative endometrium into a secretory endometrium, inhibit the secretion of FSH and LH, prevent follicle maturation and ovulation, inhibit uterine contractions, and may have some anabolic and estrogenic effects. When used as a contraceptive, the exact mechanism of action is not known, but it is thought that circulating progestins and estrogens will "trick" the hypothalamus and pituitary and prevent the release of gonadotropic releasing hormone (GnRH), FSH, and LH, thus preventing follicle development and ovulation. The low levels of these hormones do not produce a lush endometrium that is receptive to implantation, and if ovulation and fertilization were to occur, the chances of implantation are remote.

Progestins are indicated for contraception; as treatment of primary and secondary amenorrhea; as treatment for functional uterine bleeding; and in some fertility protocols. Some progestins are also effective as palliative treatment in specific cancers (see Chapter 12, Antineoplastic Agents).

CONTRAINDICATIONS/CAUTIONS

Progestins are contraindicated in the presence of any known allergies to progestins; pregnancy (serious fetal defects have occurred); idiopathic vaginal bleeding; breast cancer or genital cancer; history of thromboembolic disorders, including cerebrovascular accident (because of the increased risk of thrombus and embolus development); hepatic dysfunction (because of the effects of progestins on the liver function); pelvic inflammatory disease (PID), sexually transmitted diseases (STDs), endometriosis, or pelvic surgery (because of the effects of progestins on the uterus); and lactation (because of potential effects on the neonate).

Progestins should be used with caution with epilepsy, migraine headaches, asthma, and cardiac or renal dysfunction (because of the potential exacerbation of these conditions).

ADVERSE EFFECTS

Adverse effects associated with progestins vary with the administration route used. Oral contraceptives are associated with thromboembolic disorders, particularly when combined with nicotine; increased blood pressure; weight gain; and headache. Vaginal gel use is associated with headache, nervousness, constipation, breast enlargement, and perineal pain. Intrauterine systems are associated with abdominal pain, endometriosis, abortion, PID, and expulsion of the intrauterine device. Parenteral routes are associated with breakthrough bleeding, spotting, changes in the menstrual cycle, breast tenderness, thrombophlebitis, vision changes, weight gain, and fluid retention.

DATA LINK

Data link to the following progestins in your nursing drug guide:

PROGESTINS

Name	Brand Name	Usual Indications
hydroxyprogesterone	*Hylutin*	Treatment of amenorrhea; production of a secretory endometrium for fertility treatment
P levonorgestrel	*Norplant System*	Contraception
medroxyprogesterone	*Amen, Curretab*	Treatment of amenorrhea; palliation of certain cancers
norethindrone	*Aygestin*	Contraception, treatment of amenorrhea
norgestrel	*Ovrette*	Contraception
progesterone	*Progestasert* and others	Contraception, treatment of amenorrhea, fertility programs

NURSING CONSIDERATIONS
for patients receiving progestins

Assessment

HISTORY. Screen for history of allergy to any progestin product, pregnancy, lactation, hepatic dysfunction, cardiovascular disease, breast or genital cancer, renal disease, history of thromboembolism, smoking, idiopathic vaginal bleeding, pelvic diseases, asthma, and epilepsy.

PHYSICAL ASSESSMENT. Include screening for baseline status before beginning therapy and for any potential adverse effects: skin color, lesions, texture; affect, orientation, mental status, reflexes; blood pressure, pulse, cardiac auscultation, edema, perfusion; abdominal exam, liver exam, pelvic exam, Pap smear, urinalysis, breast exam, and ophthalmic exam, particularly if the patient wears contact lenses.

Nursing Diagnoses

Follow the same guidelines as for estrogens.

Implementation

Follow the same guidelines as for estrogens.

Evaluation

Follow the same guidelines as for estrogens (see Nursing Care Guide: Estrogens and Progestins).

FERTILITY DRUGS

Women without primary ovarian failure who cannot get pregnant after a year of trying may be candidates for the use of fertility drugs. These drugs act to stimulate follicle development and ovulation in functioning ovaries and are combined with human chorionic gonadotropin (HCG) to maintain the follicles once ovulation has occurred. The following fertility drugs are in use today.

Clomiphene (*Clomid* and others) is a commonly used oral agent that is also used for the treatment of male infertility. Follitropin alfa (*Gonal-F*) and follitropin beta (*Follistim*) are FSH molecules produced by recombinant DNA technology; they are injected to stimulate follicular development in infertility and for harvesting ova for in vitro fertilization. Menotropins (*Pergonal, Humegon*) is a purified gonadotropin (similar to FSH and LH) that is also used to stimulate spermatogenesis. Urofollitropin (*Fertinex*) is an injected preparation derived from the urine of postmenopausal women; it has been associated with immune-type reactions. With the development of newer, purer drugs, urofollitropin is used less often.

THERAPEUTIC ACTIONS AND INDICATIONS

Fertility drugs work either directly or by stimulating the hypothalamus to increase FSH and LH levels and stimulate ovarian follicular development and ova maturation. Given in sequence with HCG to maintain the follicle and hormone production, these drugs are used to treat infertility in women with functioning ovaries whose partners are fertile. Fertility drugs also may be used to stimulate multiple follicle development for the harvesting of ova for in vitro fertilization. Menotropins also stimulates spermatogenesis in men with low sperm counts and otherwise normally functioning testes.

CONTRAINDICATIONS/CAUTIONS

These drugs are contraindicated in the presence of primary ovarian failure (they only work to stimulate functioning ovaries); thyroid or adrenal dysfunction (because of the effects on the hypothalamic–pituitary axis); ovarian cysts; pregnancy (serious fetal defects have occurred); idiopathic uterine bleeding; and known allergy to any fertility drug. Caution should be used with lactation, thromboembolic diseases, and respiratory diseases.

ADVERSE EFFECTS

Adverse effects associated with fertility drugs include a greatly increased risk of multiple births and birth defects; ovarian overstimulation (abdominal pain, distention, ascites, pleural effusion); and headache, fluid retention, nausea, bloating, uterine bleeding, ovarian enlargement, gynecomastia, and febrile reactions (possibly due to stimulation of progesterone release).

DATA LINK

Data link to the following fertility drugs in your nursing drug guide:

FERTILITY DRUGS

Name	Brand Name	Usual Indications
P clomiphene	*Clomid* and others	Treatment of infertility
follitropin alfa	*Gonal-F*	Stimulation of follicular development for harvesting of ova
follitropin beta	*Follistin*	Stimulation of follicular development for harvesting of ova
menotropins	*Pergonal*	Stimulation of ovulation in women and spermatogenesis in men
urofollitropin	*Fertinex*	Stimulation of ovulation for the treatment of infertility and to stimulate follicular development for harvesting ova

NURSING CONSIDERATIONS for patients receiving fertility drugs

Assessment

HISTORY. Screen for history of allergy to any fertility drug, pregnancy, lactation, ovarian failure, thyroid or adrenal dysfunction, ovarian cysts, idiopathic uterine bleeding, thromboembolic diseases, and respiratory diseases.

PHYSICAL ASSESSMENT. Include screening for baseline status before beginning therapy and for any potential adverse effects: skin, lesions; orientation, affect, reflexes; blood pressure, pulse; respiration, adventitious sounds; hormone levels, Pap smear, breast exam.

Nursing Diagnoses

The patient receiving fertility drugs may have the following nursing diagnoses related to drug therapy:

- Body image disturbance related to drug treatment and diagnosis
- Pain related to headache, fluid retention, GI upset
- Sexual dysfunction
- Knowledge deficit regarding drug therapy

Implementation

- Assess the cause of dysfunction before beginning therapy *to assure appropriate use of the drug.*
- Complete a pelvic exam before each cycle of drug therapy *to rule out ovarian enlargement, pregnancy, or uterine problems.*

- Check urine estrogen and estradiol levels before beginning therapy *to verify ovarian function.*
- Administer with an appropriate dosage of HCG as indicated *to assure beneficial effects.*
- Discontinue the drug at any sign of ovarian overstimulation; *arrange for hospitalization if this occurs.*
- Provide women with a calendar of treatment days, explanations of adverse effects to anticipate, and instructions on when intercourse should occur *to increase the therapeutic effectiveness of the drug.*
- Provide warnings about the risk and hazards of multiple births *so the patient can make informed decisions about drug therapy.*
- Provide thorough patient education, including measures to avoid adverse effects, warning signs of problems, and the need for regular evaluation *to enhance patient knowledge about drug therapy and to promote compliance.*

Evaluation

- Monitor patient response to the drug (ovulation).
- Monitor for adverse effects (abdominal bloating, weight gain, ovarian overstimulation, multiple births).
- Evaluate the effectiveness of the teaching plan (patient can name drug, dosage, adverse effects to watch for, specific measures to avoid adverse effects).
- Monitor the effectiveness of comfort measures and compliance to the regimen.

OXYTOCICS

Oxytocic drugs are used to stimulate contraction of the uterus, much like the action of the hypothalamic hormone oxytocin, which is stored in the posterior pituitary. These drugs include ergonovine (*Ergotrate*), which is given IM or IV and is used to prevent and treat postpartum and postabortion uterine atony; methylergonovine (*Methergine*), which can be given IM or IV directly after delivery, then continued in the oral form to promote uterine involution; and oxytocin (*Pitocin, Syntocinon*), which is used to induce labor and to promote uterine contractions after labor. Oxytocin is available in a nasal form to stimulate milk let-down in lactating women.

THERAPEUTIC ACTIONS AND INDICATIONS

The oxytocics directly affect neuroreceptor sites to stimulate contraction of the uterus. They are especially effective in the gravid uterus. Oxytocin, a synthetic form of the hypothalamic hormone, also stimulates the lacteal glands in the breast to contract, promoting milk ejection in lactating women.

Oxytocics are indicated for the prevention and treatment of uterine atony following delivery. This is important to prevent postpartum hemorrhage. Ergonovine is being tested for use in diagnostic tests for angina during arteriography studies because it has been shown to induce coronary artery contraction. Methylergonovine has been successfully used in stimulating the last stage of labor. Oxytocin is used in a nasal form to stimulate milk let-down in lactating women. It is also being evaluated as a diagnostic agent to test abnormal fetal heart rates (oxytocin challenge) and to treat breast engorgement.

CONTRAINDICATIONS/CAUTIONS

Oxytocics are contraindicated in the presence of any known allergy to oxytocics and with cephalopelvic disproportion, unfavorable fetal position, complete uterine atony, or early pregnancy. Caution should be used with coronary disease, hypertension, lactation, and previous cesarean section.

ADVERSE EFFECTS

The adverse effects most often associated with the oxytocics are related to excessive effects (e.g., uterine hypertonicity and spasm, uterine rupture, postpartum hemorrhage, decreased fetal heart rate). GI upset, nausea, headache, and dizziness are not uncommon. Ergonovine and methylergonovine can produce ergotism (e.g., nausea, blood pressure changes, weak pulse, dyspnea, chest pain, numbness and coldness in extremities, confusion, excitement, delirium, convulsions, and even coma). Oxytocin has caused severe water intoxication (because of related antidiuretic hormone [ADH] effects; ADH is also stored in the posterior pituitary and may be released in response to oxytocin activity, causing water retention in the kidney), with coma and even maternal death when used for a prolonged period of time.

DATA LINK

Data link to the following oxytocics in your nursing drug guide:

OXYTOCICS

Name	Brand Name	Usual Indications
ergonovine	*Ergotrate*	Prevention and treatment of postpartum and postabortion uterine atony
methylergonovine	*Methergine*	Promotion of postpartum uterine involution
P oxytocin	*Pitocin, Syntocinon*	Induction of labor; promotion of uterine contractions postpartum; nasally to stimulate milk let-down in lactating women

NURSING CONSIDERATIONS for patients receiving oxytocics

Assessment

HISTORY. Screen for history of allergy to oxytocics, early pregnancy, lactation, uterine atony, hypertension, history of cesarean section, undesirable fetal position, and cephalopelvic disproportion.

PHYSICAL ASSESSMENT. Include screening for baseline status before beginning therapy and for any potential adverse effects: skin, lesions; orientation, affect, reflexes; blood pressure, pulse; respiration, adventitious sounds; fetal position, fetal heartbeat, uterine tone, and timing of contractions; and bleeding studies and CBC.

Nursing Diagnoses

The patient receiving oxytocics may have the following nursing diagnoses related to drug therapy:

- Pain related to uterine contractions, headache, fluid retention, GI upset
- Potential for altered cardiac output related to ergotism or water intoxication
- Knowledge deficit regarding drug therapy

Implementation

- Ensure fetal position (if appropriate) and cephalopelvic proportions *to prevent serious complications of delivery.*
- Regulate oxytocin delivery between contractions if being given *to stimulate labor.*
- Monitor blood pressure periodically during and after administration *to monitor for adverse effects. Discontinue the drug if blood pressure rises dramatically.*
- Monitor uterine tone and involution and amount of bleeding *to assure safe and therapeutic use of the drug.*
- Discontinue the drug at any sign of uterine hypertonicity *to avoid potentially life-threatening effects; provide life support as needed.*
- Monitor fetal heartbeat if given during labor *to ensure safety of the fetus.*
- Provide nasal oxytocin at bedside with the bottle sitting upright. The patient should be instructed to invert the squeeze bottle and exert gentle pressure *to deliver the drug just before nursing.*
- Provide thorough patient education, including measures to avoid adverse effects and warning signs of problems to report *to enhance patient knowledge about drug therapy and to promote compliance.*

Evaluation

- Monitor patient response to the drug (uterine contraction, prevention of hemorrhage, milk let-down).
- Monitor for adverse effects (blood pressure changes, uterine hypertonicity, water intoxication, ergotism).
- Evaluate the effectiveness of the teaching plan (patient can name drug, dosage, adverse effects to watch for, specific measures to avoid adverse effects).
- Monitor the effectiveness of comfort measures and compliance to the regimen.

ABORTIFACIENTS

Abortifacients are drugs used to evacuate the uterus by stimulating intense uterine contractions. These drugs include carboprost (*Hemabate*), dinoprostone (*Cervidil, Prepidil Gel, Prostin E2*), and mifepristone (*RU-486, Mifegyne*). Carboprost is an IM drug used to terminate early pregnancy, evacuate a missed abortion, or control postpartum hemorrhage. Dinoprostone is a prostaglandin that stimulates uterine contractions; it is given by intravaginal suppository. Besides evacuating the uterus, it is also used to stimulate cervical ripening before labor. Mifepristone is a new, controversial drug that acts as an antagonist of progesterone sites in the endometrium, allowing local prostaglandins to stimulate uterine contractions and dislodge or prevent the implantation of any fertilized egg. This drug is given orally and takes 5 to 7 days to produce the desired effect.

THERAPEUTIC ACTIONS AND INDICATIONS

The abortifacients stimulate uterine activity, dislodging any implanted trophoblast and preventing implantation of any fertilized egg. These drugs are approved for use to terminate pregnancy 12 to 20 weeks from the date of the last menstrual period. Mifepristone is approved for use during the first 49 days of the pregnancy. Carboprost and dinoprostone are also approved for use to evacuate the uterus after a missed abortion or fetal death. Carboprost also is used to treat postpartum hemorrhage that is not responsive to the usual therapy. Because of its local prostaglandin effects, dinoprostone can be used to stimulate cervical ripening before induction of labor.

CONTRAINDICATIONS/CAUTIONS

Abortifacients should not be used with any known allergy to abortifacients or prostaglandins; after 20 weeks from the last menstrual period; and with active PID or acute cardiovascular, hepatic, renal, or pulmonary disease. Caution should be used with any history of asthma, hypertension, or adrenal disease; or with acute vaginitis (inflammation of the vagina) or scarred uterus.

ADVERSE EFFECTS

Adverse effects associated with abortifacients include abdominal cramping, heavy uterine bleeding, perforated uterus, and uterine rupture, related to exaggeration of the desired effects of the drug. Other side effects include headache, nausea and vomiting, diarrhea, diaphoresis (sweating), backache, and rash.

DATA LINK

Data link to the following abortifacients in your nursing drug guide:

ABORTIFACIENTS

Name	Brand Name	Usual Indications
carboprost	*Hemabate*	Termination of early pregnancy, evacuation of missed abortion, control of postpartum hemorrhage
P dinoprostone	*Cervidil* and others	Evacuation of the uterus, cervical ripening before labor
mifepristone	*Mifegyne*	Termination of early pregnancy

NURSING CONSIDERATIONS
for patients receiving abortifacients

Assessment

HISTORY. Screen for history of allergy to any abortifacient or prostaglandin preparation; active PID; cardiac, hepatic, pulmonary, or renal disease; history of asthma; and hypotension, hypertension, epilepsy, scarred uterus, and acute vaginitis.

PHYSICAL ASSESSMENT. Include screening for baseline status before beginning therapy and for any potential adverse effects: skin, lesions; orientation, affect; blood pressure, pulse; respiration, adventitious sounds; vaginal discharge, pelvic exam, uterine tone; and liver and renal function tests, WBC, and urinalysis.

Nursing Diagnoses

The patient receiving abortifacients may have the following nursing diagnoses related to drug therapy:

- Pain related to uterine contractions, headache, fluid retention, GI upset
- Potential for ineffective individual coping related to abortion or fetal death
- Knowledge deficit regarding drug therapy

Implementation

- Administer via route indicated, following the manufacturer's directions for storage and preparation *to assure safe and therapeutic use of the drug.*
- Assure the age of the pregnancy before administering the drug *to assure appropriate use of the drug.*
- Assure that abortion or uterine evacuation is complete *to avoid potential bleeding problems; prepare for dilation and curettage if necessary.*
- Monitor blood pressure periodically during and after administration *to assess for adverse effects; discontinue the drug if blood pressure rises dramatically.*
- Monitor uterine tone and involution and the amount of bleeding during and for several days after using the drug *to assure appropriate response and recovery from the drug.*
- Provide support and appropriate referrals *to deal with abortion or fetal death.*
- Provide thorough patient teaching, including measures to avoid adverse effects and warning signs of problems to report *to enhance patient knowledge about drug therapy and to promote compliance.*

Evaluation

- Monitor patient response to the drug (evacuation of uterus).
- Monitor for adverse effects (GI upset, nausea, blood pressure changes, hemorrhage, uterine rupture).
- Evaluate the effectiveness of the teaching plan (patient can name drug, dosage, adverse effects to watch for, specific measures to avoid adverse effects).
- Monitor the effectiveness of comfort measures and compliance to the regimen.

TOCOLYTICS

Uterine contractions that become strong before term can lead to premature labor and delivery, which can have detrimental effects on the neonate, including death. Drugs used to relax the uterine smooth muscle and prevent contractions leading to premature labor and delivery are called tocolytics. They are usually reserved for use after 20 weeks of gestation, when the neonate has a chance of survival outside the uterus. The tocolytic agents that are in use include ritodrine (*Yutopar*) and terbulatine (*Bricanyl*), a drug that is used as an antiasthmatic in oral and inhaled forms but that is effective in relaxing uterine smooth muscle when given IV.

THERAPEUTIC ACTIONS AND INDICATIONS

The tocolytics are $beta_2$-specific adrenergic agonists that mimic the effects of the sympathetic nervous system at $beta_2$ sites. These effects include relaxation of the uterine smooth muscle. They are indicated for the management of preterm labor in selected patients at more than 20 weeks gestation.

CONTRAINDICATIONS/CAUTIONS

Tocolytics are contraindicated in the presence of known allergy to these drugs or components used in their preparation; with pregnancies of less than 20 weeks because of the low chance of neonatal survival; with antepartum hemorrhage, which could be exacerbated by uterine relaxation; with eclampsia or preeclampsia, which could be exacerbated by sympathetic stimulation; with intrauterine death when uterine evacuation is desirable; and with maternal cardiac disease, uncontrolled diabetes, pulmonary hypertension, or other disorders that could be exacerbated by sympathetic stimulation.

ADVERSE EFFECTS

Maternal adverse effects associated with these drugs are related to the sympathetic stimulation that they can cause and include headache, tremor, nervousness, nausea, vomiting, tachycardia, hypertension, rash, and potentially fatal postpartum pulmonary edema, a condition that is more likely in patients taking corticosteroids. Fetal effects can include tachycardia, hypotension, hypoglycemia, and paralytic ileus.

CLINICALLY IMPORTANT DRUG–DRUG INTERACTIONS

There is an increase in sympathetic effects if tocolytics are combined with other sympathomimetic drugs. Decreased effects will occur if they are combined with beta-adrenergic blockers. The risk of potentially fatal postpartum pulmonary edema is increased if combined with corticosteroids.

DATA LINK

Data link to the following tocolytics in your nursing drug guide:

TOCOLYTICS

Name	Brand Name	Usual Indication
P ritodrine	*Yutopar*	Management of preterm labor in selected patients ≤ 20 wk gestation
terbutaline	*Bricanyl*	Management of preterm labor in selected patients ≤ 20 wk gestation

NURSING CONSIDERATIONS
for patients receiving tocolytics

Assessment

HISTORY. Screen for history of allergy to any tocolytic or components used in the preparation; cardiac or pulmonary disease; history of asthma; gestational age; intrauterine death; uterine hemorrhage; and eclampsia or preeclampsia.

PHYSICAL ASSESSMENT. Include screening for baseline status before beginning therapy and for any potential adverse effects: skin, lesions; orientation, affect; blood pressure, pulse; respiration, adventitious sounds; pelvic exam, uterine tone, and maternal and fetal heart rates; and blood glucose.

Nursing Diagnoses

The patient receiving tocolytics may have the following nursing diagnoses related to drug therapy:

- Increased cardiac output related to sympathetic stimulation
- Anxiety related to potential premature labor and delivery
- Ineffective gas exchange related to pulmonary edema
- Knowledge deficit regarding drug therapy

Implementation

- Monitor maternal pulse and respirations closely; *persistent maternal pulse greater than 140 or respirations higher than 20 may be signs of impending pulmonary edema and require immediate action.*
- Avoid fluid overload; *serial hemograms may indicate the state of hydration.*
- Maintain the patient in the left lateral position during infusion *to minimize hypotension.*
- Provide support and appropriate referrals *to deal with possible premature labor.*
- Provide thorough patient teaching, including measures to avoid adverse effects and warning signs of problems to report *to enhance patient knowledge about drug therapy and to promote compliance.*

Evaluation

- Monitor patient response to the drug (stopping of premature labor).
- Monitor for adverse effects (tachycardia, hypertension, headache, pulmonary edema, GI upset, rash).
- Evaluate the effectiveness of the teaching plan (patient can name drug, dosage, adverse effects to watch for, specific measures to avoid adverse effects).
- Monitor the effectiveness of comfort measures and compliance to the regimen.

WWW.WEB LINKS

Health care providers and patients may want to explore the following Internet sources:

Information on fertility drugs—research, explanations, related information:
http://www.babycenter.com/refcap/4091.html

Information on menopause, specifically for patients and teaching aids with explanations, drugs, choices, support groups:

http://fbhc.org/Patients/BetterHealth/Menopause/home.html

Information on hormone replacement therapy, updated regularly with studies, controversies, and treatment choices, cross-referenced to research studies:

http://pharminfo.com/disease/Cardio/hrt_HD.html

Information on contraceptives—good teaching guidelines, explanations, choices:

http://www.reproline.jhu.edu/english/lcontech/lmethods/lmethods.htm

Information on estrogens—research, uses, and controversies, for professionals:

http://www.ionet.net/~jscott/homepage/drugdb/038.html

CHAPTER SUMMARY

- Estrogens are female sex hormones important in the development of the female reproductive system and secondary sex characteristics.
- Estrogens are used pharmacologically mainly to replace hormones lost at menopause to prevent many of the signs and symptoms associated with menopause, including the development of CAD; to stimulate ovulation in woman with hypogonadism; and in combination with progestins for oral contraceptives.
- Progestins are female sex hormones that are responsible for the maintenance of a pregnancy and the development of some secondary sex characteristics.
- Progestins are used in combination with estrogens for contraceptives, to treat uterine bleeding, and for palliation in certain cancers with sensitive receptor sites.
- Fertility drugs stimulate FSH and LH in women with functioning ovaries to increase follicle development and improve the chances for pregnancy.
- A major adverse effect of fertility drugs is multiple births and birth defects.
- Oxytocic drugs act like the hypothalamic hormone oxytocin to stimulate uterine contractions and induce or speed up labor. They are most frequently used to control bleeding and promote postpartum uterus involution.
- Abortifacients are drugs that stimulate uterine activity to cause uterine evacuation. These drugs can be used to induce abortion in early pregnancy or to promote uterine evacuation following intrauterine fetal death.
- Tocolytics are drugs that relax the uterine smooth muscle; they are used to stop premature labor in patients after 20 weeks gestation.

BIBLIOGRAPHY

Abernathy, K. (1997). Hormone replacement therapy. *Professional Nurse, 21* (10), 717–719.

Bullock, B. L. (2000). *Focus on pathophysiology.* Philadelphia: Lippincott Williams & Wilkins.

Crandall, S. G. (1997). Menopause made easier. *RN, 60* (7), 46–50.

Greendale, G. A. & Sowers, M. (1997). The menopause transition. *Endocrinology and Metabolism Clinics of North America, 26* (2), 262–277.

Hardman, J. G., Limbird, L. E., Molinoff, P. B., Ruddon, R. W., & Gilman, A. G. (Eds.). (1996). *Goodman and Gilman's the pharmacological basis of therapeutics* (9th ed.). New York: McGraw-Hill.

Karch, A. M. (2000). *2000 Lippincott's nursing drug guide.* Philadelphia: Lippincott Williams & Wilkins.

McEvoy, B. R. (1999). *Facts and comparisons 1999.* St. Louis: Fact and Comparisons.

CHAPTER 39

Drugs Affecting the Male Reproductive System

Androgens
- danazol
- fluoxymesterone
- testolactone
- P testosterone

Anabolic steroids
- P nandrolone
- oxandrolone
- oxymetholone
- stanozolol

Drugs for treating penile dysfunction
- alprostadil
- P sildenafil

CHAPTER OUTLINE

KEY TERMS

anabolic steroids
androgenic effects
androgens
hirsutism
hypogonadism
penile erectile dysfunction

INTRODUCTION

Drugs that are used to affect the male reproductive system include male steroid hormones or ***androgens,*** which act like testosterone, the male sex hormone; ***anabolic steroids,*** which are synthetic testosterone preparations that have more anabolic (tissue building) effects than ***androgenic effects*** (effects associated with development of male sexual characteristics); and drugs that act to improve penile dysfunction. These drugs include a prostaglandin, alprostadil, and a new, selective cGMP (a reactive tissue enzyme) inhibitor, sildenafil, which increases nitric oxide in the corpus cavernosum to improve erection (Figure 39-1).

ANDROGENS

The primary natural androgen, testosterone (*Duratest, Testoderm,* and others) is the classic androgen in use today. It is used for replacement therapy in hypogonadism (underdeveloped testes) and to treat certain breast cancers. Other androgens include

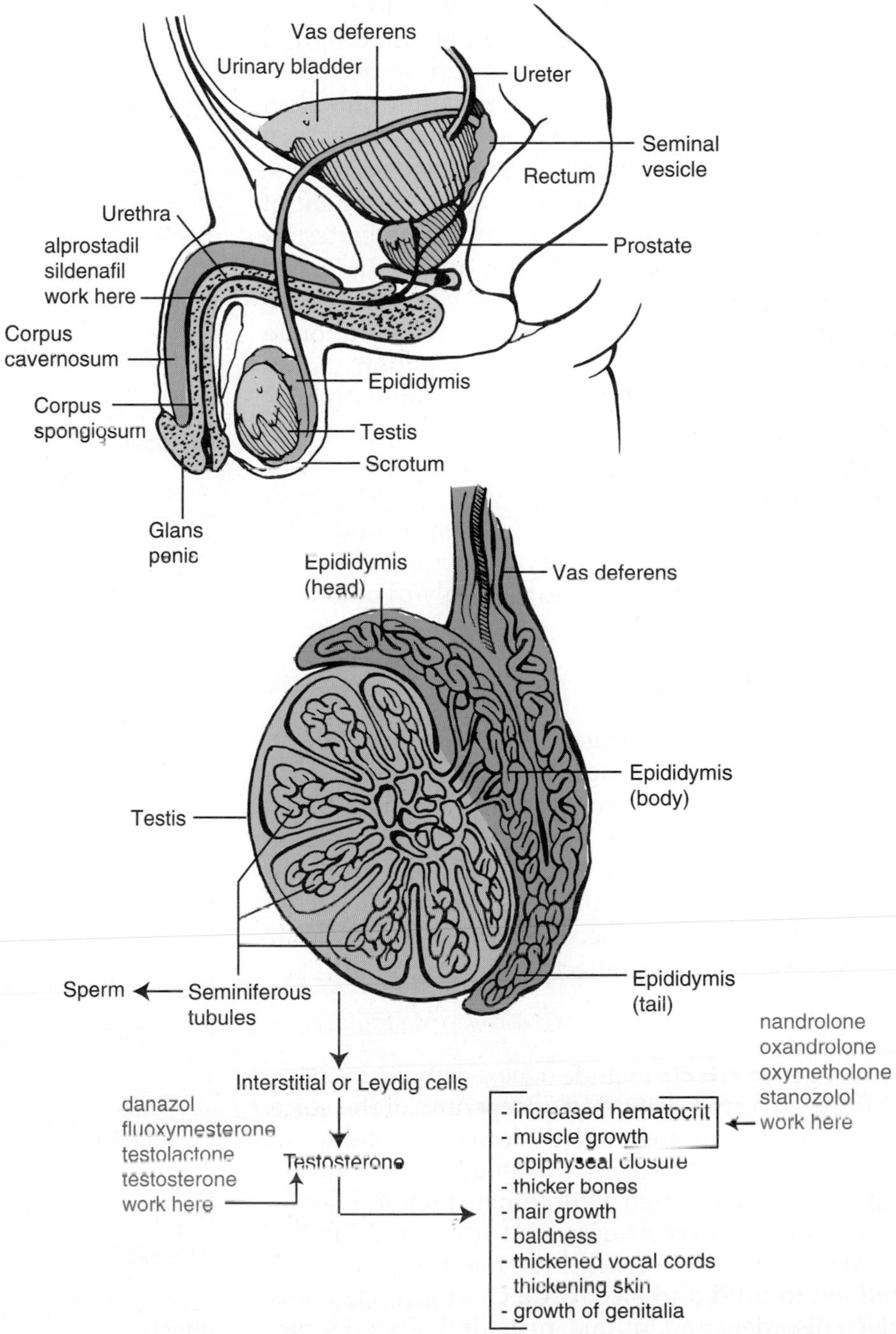

FIGURE 39-1. Sites of action of drugs affecting the male reproductive system.

danazol (*Danocrine*), a synthetic androgen that is used primarily to block follicle-stimulating hormone and luteinizing hormone release in women; fluoxymesterone (*Halotestin*), an analog of testosterone and a controlled substance used for replacement therapy in hypogonadism and to treat certain breast cancers; and testolactone (*Teslac*), a synthetic androgen used for the treatment of specific breast cancers.

THERAPEUTIC ACTIONS AND INDICATIONS

The androgens are forms of testosterone and are responsible for the growth and development of male sex organs and the maintenance of secondary sex characteristics (see Figure 39-1). They act to increase the retention of nitrogen, sodium, potassium, and phosphorus and decrease the urinary excretion of calcium. Testosterones increase protein anabolism and decrease protein catabolism (breakdown). They also increase the production of red blood cells.

Androgens can be indicated for the treatment of hypogonadism and delayed puberty in males (testosterone and fluoxymesterone). They are also indicated for the treatment of certain breast cancers in postmenopausal women; the prevention of ovulation to treat endometriosis (danazol); the prevention of postpartum breast engorgement (testosterone); and the treatment of hereditary angioedema (danazol). Testosterone is long acting and is available in several forms, including depot (deep, slow release) injections and dermal patch. Fluoxymesterone and testolactone are short acting and only available in oral form. Danazol is long acting and only available in oral form.

CONTRAINDICATIONS/CAUTIONS

These drugs are contraindicated with any known allergy to the drug or ingredients in the drug; pregnancy; lactation (because of their potential effects on the neonate); and in the presence of prostate or breast cancer in males. They should be used cautiously in the presence of any liver dysfunction or cardiovascular disease because these disorders could be exacerbated by the effects of the hormones.

ADVERSE EFFECTS

Androgenic effects include acne, edema, ***hirsutism*** (increased hair distribution), deepening of the voice, oily skin and hair, weight gain, decrease in breast size, and testicular atrophy. Antiestrogen effects can be anticipated when used with women: flushing, sweating, vaginitis, nervousness, and emotional lability. Other common effects include headache (possibly related to fluid and electrolyte changes), dizziness, sleep disorders and fatigue, rash, and altered serum electrolytes. A potentially life-threatening effect that has been documented is hepatocellular cancer. This may occur because of the effect of testosterone on hepatic cells. Patients on long-term therapy should have hepatic function tests monitored regularly, prior to beginning therapy and every 6 months during therapy.

CLINICALLY SIGNIFICANT DRUG–LABORATORY TEST INTERFERENCES

While taking androgens, there may be a decrease in thyroid function tests as well as increased creatinine and creatinine clearance that are not associated with disease states. These effects can last up to 2 weeks following the discontinuation of therapy.

DATA LINK

Data link to the following androgens in your nursing drug guide:

ANDROGENS

Name	Brand Name	Usual Indication
danazol	*Danocrine*	Block FSH and LH release in women
fluoxymesterone	*Halotestin*	Replacement therapy in hypogonadism, certain breast cancers
testolactone	*Teslac*	Treatment of specific breast cancers
P testosterone	*Duratest, Testoderm*	Replacement therapy in hypogonadism, certain breast cancers

NURSING CONSIDERATIONS for patients receiving androgens

Assessment

HISTORY. Screen for history of allergy to any testosterone or androgen, pregnancy, lactation, hepatic dysfunction, cardiovascular disease, and breast or prostate cancer in men.

PHYSICAL ASSESSMENT. Include screening for baseline status before beginning therapy and for any potential adverse effects: skin color, lesions, texture, hair distribution; affect, orientation, peripheral sensation; abdominal exam; serum electrolytes, serum cholesterol, and liver function tests; and long bone x-rays in children.

Nursing Diagnoses

The patient receiving any androgen may also have the following nursing diagnoses related to drug therapy:

- Body image disturbance related to androgenic effects
- Pain related to need for injections

- Sexual dysfunction related to androgenic effects
- Knowledge deficit regarding drug therapy

Implementation

- Reconstitute following manufacturer's directions *to assure proper reconstitution and to administer as prescribed.*
- Monitor response carefully when beginning therapy *so that the dosage can be adjusted accordingly.*
- Monitor liver function periodically with long-term therapy; *arrange to discontinue the drug at any sign of hepatic dysfunction.*
- Provide thorough patient teaching, including measures to avoid adverse effects, warning signs of problems, and the need for regular evaluation, including blood tests. Instruct a family member or caregiver in proper preparation and administration techniques as appropriate *to enhance patient knowledge about drug therapy and to promote compliance with drug regimen.*

Evaluation

- Monitor patient response to the drug (onset of puberty; maintenance of male sexual characteristics; palliation of breast cancer; blockage of ovulation; prevention of postpartum breast engorgement; relief of angioedema).
- Monitor for adverse effects (androgenic effects, hypoestrogen effects, serum electrolyte imbalance, headache, sleep disturbances, rash, hepatocellular carcinoma).
- Evaluate the effectiveness of the teaching plan (patient can name drug, dosage, adverse effects to watch for, specific measures to avoid adverse effects; family member or caregiver can demonstrate proper technique for preparation and administration of drug as appropriate).
- Monitor the effectiveness of comfort measures and compliance to the regimen.

ANABOLIC STEROIDS

The anabolic steroids are analogs of testosterone that have been developed to produce the tissue-building effects of testosterone with less androgenic effect. These are controlled substances that are known to be used illegally for the enhancement of athletic performance through increased muscle mass, increased hematocrit, and, theoretically, an increase in strength and endurance. The adverse effects of these drugs can be deadly when used in the amounts needed for enhanced athletic performance. Cardiomyopathy, hepatic carcinomas, personality changes, and sexual dysfunction are all associated with the excessive and nonindicated use of anabolic steroids.

Nandrolone (*Durabolin* and others) is an anabolic steroid that is used to treat anemia. It is used to treat anemia and renal insufficiency because of its effects on the bone marrow to increase red blood cell production. Oxandrolone (*Oxandrin*) has several uses: to promote weight gain in debilitated patients, to increase protein anabolism in patients on prolonged corticosteroid therapy, and to treat certain cancers. Oxymetholone (*Anadrol-50*) is used to treat various anemias. Stanozolol (*Winstrol*) is indicated only for the treatment of angioedema because of its effects on the liver.

THERAPEUTIC ACTIONS AND INDICATIONS

Anabolic steroids promote body tissue-building processes; reverse catabolic or tissue-destroying processes; and increase hemoglobin and red blood cell mass.

Indications for particular anabolic steroids vary with the drug. They can be used to treat anemias, certain cancers, and angioedema, and to promote weight gain and tissue repair in debilitated patients and protein anabolism in patients who are on long-term corticosteroid therapy.

CONTRAINDICATIONS/CAUTIONS

These drugs are contraindicated in the presence of any known allergy to androgens; during pregnancy and lactation (because of potential masculinization in the neonate); and with liver dysfunction, coronary disease (because of cholesterol-raising effects through effects on the liver), and prostate or breast cancer in males.

ADVERSE EFFECTS

In prepubertal males, adverse effects include virilization (e.g., phallic enlargement, hirsutism, increased skin pigmentation). Postpubertal males may experience inhibition of testicular function, gynecomastia, testicular atrophy, priapism (a painful and continual erection of the penis), baldness, and change in libido (increased or decreased). Women may experience hirsutism, hoarseness, deepening of the voice, clitoral enlargement, baldness, and menstrual irregularities. As with the androgens, serum electrolyte changes, liver dysfunction (including life-threatening hepatitis), insomnia, and weight gain may occur. There is an increased risk of prostate problems, especially in geriatric patients.

CLINICALLY IMPORTANT DRUG–DRUG INTERACTIONS

Because the anabolic steroids affect the liver, there is the potential for interaction with oral anticoagulants and a potential decreased need for antidiabetic agents because these may not be metabolized normally. Patients should be monitored closely and appropriate dosage adjustments made.

CASE STUDY

Adverse Effects of Anabolic Steroids

PRESENTATION

K. S. is a senior nursing student who recently became engaged to a college senior. He is training as a javelin thrower and hopes to make it to the Olympics. K. S. noticed that her fiancé has been suffering from GI upset for the last 3 weeks and more recently has developed tremors and muscle cramps. K. S. first suspected that he was suffering from a viral infection, but when the symptoms did not resolve, she became concerned. K. S. tried to get her fiancé to see a doctor, but he refused. Eventually, he admitted that he had begun using anabolic steroids to develop his muscles and improve his athletic prowess. He said that his friend who gave him the drugs told him that stomach upset was normal. He refuses to see a physician because he knows that the use of these drugs is illegal. He feels that using the anabolic steroids for a while will put him closer to his goal. K. S. accepts his explanation but is upset about the use of anabolic steroids. She consults with her clinical instructor about the effects of these drugs.

CRITICAL THINKING QUESTIONS

What does K. S. need to know? Think about the systemic effects of anabolic steroids and the possible long-term effects from their abuse. What implications do these effects have for the athlete? Consider the guilt and concern that K. S. must be experiencing. Suggest ways for K. S. to share the information about the actual effects of anabolic steroids with her fiancé and still cope with her own feelings and concerns. What are the ethical and legal issues involved with a health care provider knowing about illegal drug use and abuse? Outline a plan for helping K. S. and her fiancé cope with this issue and its implications for their futures.

DISCUSSION

Use of anabolic steroids is illegal in almost all organized athletic contests. Random drug testing is done to rule out use of these and other drugs. Not surprisingly, K. S. feels insecure about her fiancé's decision. She needs to know that her discussion will be confidential and that she will receive support for her concerns and her fears. K. S. needs to review the effects of anabolic steroids. Although they do promote muscle development, there has never been any evidence that they actually improve athletic performance. The potential adverse effects of these drugs can be deadly, especially if K. S.'s fiancé is receiving the drugs from a friend and has no medical evaluation or dosage guidance to reduce the risk. Personality changes, cardiomyopathy, liver cancer, and impotence are just a few of the possible adverse effects.

K. S. is in a precarious position, not wanting to interfere with her fiancé's dreams or to cause problems in their relationship. She should be encouraged to explain the adverse effects of the drugs to her fiancé, pointing out that he is already experiencing some of them. Adverse effects associated with the drugs can ultimately interfere with, not enhance, his athletic performance. She might be encouraged to practice what she will tell her fiancé and to seek other support as needed.

The sale or distribution of anabolic steroids without a prescription is illegal, and this fact further complicates the situation for K. S. Because she is planning to become a health care provider, she may be obligated by state law to report this information to the authorities. K. S. should research these issues and discuss them further with her clinical instructor and other resource people.

DATA LINK

Data link to the following anabolic steroids in your nursing drug guide:

ANABOLIC STEROIDS

Name	Brand Name	Usual Indication
P nandrolone	*Durabolin*	Anemia associated with renal dysfunction
oxandrolone	*Oxandrin*	Promotion of weight gain in debilitated patients; treatment of certain cancers
oxymetholone	*Anadrol-50*	Treatment of anemias
stanozolol	*Winstrol*	Treatment of angioedema

NURSING CONSIDERATIONS
for patients receiving anabolic steroids

Assessment

HISTORY. Screen for history of allergy to any androgens or anabolic steroids; pregnancy or lactation (because of masculinization of the neonate); prostrate or breast cancer; coronary disease; and hepatic dysfunction.

PHYSICAL ASSESSMENT. Include screening for baseline status before beginning therapy and for any potential adverse effects: skin color, texture, hair distribution; affect, orientation; abdominal exam; liver

PATIENT TEACHING CHECKLIST

Androgens, Anabolic Steroids

Create customized patient teaching materials for a specific androgen or anabolic steroid from your CD-ROM. Your patient teaching should stress the following points for drugs within this class:

Androgens or anabolic steroids have properties similar to those of the male sex hormones. Because the drug has widespread effects, there are often many adverse effects associated with its use.

Some of the following adverse effects may occur:

GI upset, nausea, vomiting—Taking the drug with food usually helps this.

Acne—This is a hormone effect; washing your face regularly and avoiding oily foods may help.

Increased facial hair, decreased head hair—These are hormonal effects; if they become bothersome, consult with your health care provider.

Menstrual irregularities (women)—This is a normal effect of the androgens; if you suspect that you might be pregnant, consult with your health care provider immediately.

Weight gain, increased muscle development—These are common hormone effects.

Change in sex drive—This can be distressing and difficult to deal with; consult with your health care provider if this is a serious concern.

Tell any doctor, nurse, or other health care provider that you are taking this drug.

Report any of the following to your health care provider: swelling in fingers or legs; continual erection; uncontrollable sex drive; yellowing skin; fever, chills, or rash; chest pain or difficulty breathing; hoarseness, loss of hair or facial hair (women).

It is important to have regular medical follow-up, including blood tests, to monitor your response to this drug.

Keep this drug and all medications out of the reach of children.

Take this medicine only as directed. Do not give this medication to anyone else or take any similar medication that has not been prescribed for you.

This Teaching Checklist reflects general patient teaching guidelines. It is not meant to be a substitute for drug specific teaching information, which is available in nursing drug guides.

evaluation; serum electrolytes, cholesterol levels; and long bone x-rays in children.

Nursing Diagnoses

The patient receiving an anabolic steroid may have the following nursing diagnoses related to drug therapy:

- Body image disturbance related to systemic effects
- Pain related to gastrointestinal (GI), central nervous system effects
- Knowledge deficit regarding drug therapy

Implementation

- Administer with food if GI effects are severe *to relieve GI distress.*
- Monitor endocrine function, hepatic function, and serum electrolytes before and periodically during therapy *so that dosage can be adjusted appropriately and severe adverse effects can be avoided.*
- Arrange for long bone x-rays in children every 3 to 6 months *so that the drug can be discontinued if bone growth reaches the norm for the child's age.*
- Provide thorough patient teaching, including measures to avoid adverse effects and warning signs of problems, as well as the need for regular evaluation including blood tests (see Patient Teaching Checklist: Androgens, Anabolic Steroids) *to enhance patient knowledge about drug therapy and to promote compliance with drug regimen.*

Evaluation

- Monitor patient response to the drug (increase in hematocrit, protein anabolism).
- Monitor for adverse effects (androgenic effects, serum electrolyte disturbances, epiphyseal closure, hepatic dysfunction, personality changes, cardiac effects).

NURSING CARE GUIDE
Androgens, Anabolic Steroids

Assessment	Nursing Diagnoses	Implementation	Evaluation
HISTORY Allergies to any steroids, pregnancy, lactation, breast or prostate cancer in men; hepatic dysfunction; CAD	Body image disturbance related to drug effects Sexual dysfunction Pain related to injections Knowledge deficit regarding drug therapy	Administer as prescribed. Monitor liver function prior to and periodically during therapy. Monitor patient response and adjust dose as appropriate. Discontinue in children if bone age reaches norm. Provide support and reassurance to deal with drug therapy. Provide patient teaching regarding drug name, dosage, adverse effects, precautions, warnings to report, and safe administration.	Evaluate drug effects: onset of puberty, maintenance of male sex characteristics, suppression of lactation. Monitor for adverse effects: androgenic effects, hypoestrogenic effects, hepatic dysfunction, electrolyte imbalance, endocrine changes. Monitor for drug–drug interactions: as indicated for each drug. Evaluate effectiveness of patient teaching program. Evaluate effectiveness of comfort and safety measures.
PHYSICAL EXAMINATION Neurological: orientation, reflexes, affect Skin: color, lesions, hair CV: P, cardiac auscultation, BP, edema GI: abdominal exam, liver exam Lab tests: serum electrolytes, hepatic function tests, long bone x-rays			

- Evaluate the effectiveness of the teaching plan (patient can name drug, dosage, adverse effects to watch for, specific measures to avoid adverse effects).
- Monitor the effectiveness of comfort measures and compliance to the regimen (see Nursing Care Guide: Androgens, Anabolic Steroids).

DRUGS FOR TREATING PENILE ERECTILE DYSFUNCTION

Two very different drugs are approved for the treatment of ***penile erectile dysfunction,*** a condition in which the corpus cavernosum does not fill with blood to allow for penile erection. Penile erection can be compromised by the aging process and by vascular and neurological conditions. Alprostadil (*Caverject, MUSE*) is a prostaglandin that relaxes vascular smooth muscle and allows filling of the corpus cavernosum when injected directly into the cavernosum. Sildenafil (*Viagra*) selectively inhibits receptors and increases nitrous oxide levels, allowing blood flow into the corpus cavernosum. This drug has the advantage of being an oral drug that is taken 1 hour before erection is desired.

THERAPEUTIC ACTIONS AND INDICATIONS

The prostaglandin alprostadil is injected and acts locally to relax vascular smooth muscle and promote blood flow into the corpus cavernosum, causing penile erection. Sildenafil is taken orally and acts to increase nitrous oxide levels in the corpus cavernosum. Nitrous oxide activates the enzyme cGMP, which causes smooth muscle relaxation, allowing the flow of blood into the corpus cavernosum. Sildenafil prevents the breakdown of cGMP by phosphodiesterase, leading to increased cGMP levels and prolonged smooth muscle relaxation and promoting the flow of blood into the corpus cavernosum, resulting in penile erection. These drugs are both indicated for the treatment of penile erectile dysfunction.

CONTRAINDICATIONS/CAUTIONS

These drugs are contraindicated in the presence of any anatomical obstruction or condition that might predispose to priapism; they cannot be used with penile implants; neither is indicated for use in women (though sildenafil is being studied for the treatment of sexual dysfunction in women). Caution should be used with bleeding disorders. Sildenafil should also be used cautiously with coronary artery disease, active peptic ulcer, or retinitis pigmentosa because of risks of exacerbation of these diseases.

ADVERSE EFFECTS

Adverse effects associated with alprostadil are local effects such as pain at the injection site, infection, priapism, fibrosis, and rash. Sildenafil is associated with more systemic effects, including headache, flushing (related to relaxation of vascular smooth muscle), dyspepsia, urinary tract infection, diarrhea, dizziness, and rash.

CLINICALLY IMPORTANT DRUG–DRUG INTERACTIONS

Sildenafil cannot be taken in combination with any organic nitrates; serious cardiovascular effects, including death, have occurred.

DATA LINK

Data link to the following drugs used to treat penile erectile dysfunction in your nursing drug guide:

DRUGS USED TO TREAT PENILE ERECTILE DYSFUNCTION

Name	Brand Name	Usual Indications
alprostadil	*Caverject, MUSE*	Penile erectile dysfunction
P sildenafil	*Viagra*	Penile erectile dysfunction

NURSING CONSIDERATIONS
for patients receiving drugs to treat penile erectile dysfunction

Assessment

HISTORY. Screen for history of allergy to either preparation, penile structural abnormalities, penile

CULTURAL/GENDER CONSIDERATIONS

Viagra—Wonder Drug?

The release of the drug *Viagra* to treat penile erectile dysfunction caused a tremendous stir in American society. This was the first oral drug developed to treat a disorder found to be common in aging men but which was seldom mentioned or discussed. *Viagra,* which facilitates penile erection approximately 1 hour after it is taken, brought the return of sexual function to many of these men.

For many months after its release, the drug was the center of controversy, news coverage, and debate. Stand-up comedians, television sitcoms, and Internet joke networks were buzzing with the latest *Viagra* joke months after the drug's release. Insurance companies debated covering the cost of this drug. Was it like cosmetic surgery, and not a necessary treatment, or was it a necessary part of human physiology? Most insurance companies ended up covering the cost of this drug. Women's rights groups became concerned because there was no drug approved and covered to help facilitate a woman's sexual response.

Viagra has proven to be very effective in increasing sexual functioning for many men. It is in trial stages for treating sexual dysfunction in women; early reports seem to indicate it is effective.

The use of the drug is not without risks. Deaths have occurred when the drug was combined with nitrates (nitroglycerin, for example). Headache, flushing, stomach upset, and urinary tract infections often occur. The drug can only be used once per day and does not work in the absence of sexual stimulation. Its absorption is delayed if taken with high-fat meals, and patients need to know to plan accordingly. Patients also should be reminded that they need to use protection against sexually transmitted diseases.

When *Viagra* was the hot, new drug, there was tremendous demand for it from the public. This demand put health care providers in the position of assuring the drug was right for the patient's actual needs. The cause of penile erectile dysfunction should be determined, if at all possible. If this is a problem that the patient never discussed with the health care provider before, it could reveal underlying medical conditions that should be addressed. The adverse effects, timing of administration, and drug combinations to avoid should be discussed with the patient before giving the drug.

With pharmaceutical companies now advertising in magazines, on television, and over the Internet, health care providers are often asked for specific prescription drugs based on media advertising. This relatively new phenomenon in health care presents new challenges to the health care provider to ensure quality patient teaching to help the patient understand the actual uses, effects, and rationales for specific drug therapy.

implants, bleeding disorders, active peptic ulcer, and coronary artery disease.

PHYSICAL ASSESSMENT. Include screening for baseline status before beginning therapy and for any potential adverse effects: skin, lesions; orientation, affect, reflexes; blood pressure, pulse; respiration, adventitious sounds; local inspection of penis; and bleeding time and liver function tests.

Nursing Diagnoses

The patient receiving drugs for treating penile dysfunction may have the following nursing diagnoses related to drug therapy:

- Body image disturbance related to drug effects and indication
- Pain related to injection of alprostadil
- Sexual dysfunction
- Knowledge deficit regarding drug therapy

Implementation

- Assess cause of dysfunction before beginning therapy *to assure appropriate use of these drugs.*
- Monitor patients with vascular disease for any sign of exacerbation *so that the drug can be discontinued before severe adverse effects occur.*
- Instruct the patient in the injection of alprostadil, storage of the drug, filling of the syringe, sterile technique, site rotation, and proper disposal of needles *to assure safe and proper administration of the drug.*
- Monitor patients on sildenafil for use of nitrates *to avert potentially serious drug–drug interactions.*
- Provide thorough patient teaching, including measures to avoid adverse effects and warning signs of problems as well as the need for regular evaluation *to enhance patient knowledge about drug therapy and to promote compliance with drug regimen.*

Evaluation

- Monitor patient response to the drug (improvement in penile erection).
- Monitor for adverse effects (dizziness, flushing, local inflammation or infection, fibrosis, diarrhea, dyspepsia).
- Evaluate the effectiveness of the teaching plan (patient can name drug, dosage, adverse effects to watch for, specific measures to avoid adverse effects; patient can demonstrate proper administration of injected drug).
- Monitor the effectiveness of comfort measures and compliance to the regimen.

WWW. WEB LINKS

Health care providers and patients may want to consult the following Internet sources:

Information on male fertility—research, explanations, related information, endocrinology research:
http://www.noah.cuny.edu/pregnancy/fertility.htm/MALEINFERTILITY

Information on testosterone and testosterone replacement:
http://www.aace.com/clin/guides/hypogonadism.html

Information on erectile dysfunction—overview, teaching aids, patient information, support groups:
http://www.ivf.com/emotion.html

Information for professionals, research, new drugs:
http://www.ama-assn.org/insight/h_focus/men_hlth/sexdysf/index.htm

Information on BPH—overview, teaching aids, questions, and answers:
http://www.mediconsult.com/mc/mcsite.usf/conditionnav/bph~sectionintroduction

Information on current research, professional issues:
http://www.mediconsult.com/me/mesite.nsf/conditionnav/bph

CHAPTER SUMMARY

- Androgens are male sex hormones, specifically testosterone or testosterone-like compounds.
- Androgens are responsible for the development and maintenance of male sex characteristics and secondary sex characteristics or androgenic effects.
- Side effects related to androgen use involve excess of the desired effects as well as potentially deadly hepatocellular carcinoma.
- Androgens can be used for replacement therapy or to block other hormone effects, as seen with their use in specific breast cancers.
- Anabolic steroids are analogs of testosterone that have been developed to have more anabolic or protein-building effects than androgenic effects.
- Anabolic steroids have been abused to enhance muscle development and athletic performance, often with deadly effects.
- Anabolic steroids are used to increase hematocrit and improve protein anabolism in certain depleted states.
- Penile erectile dysfunction can inhibit erection and male sexual function.

- Alprostadil, a prostaglandin, can be injected into the penis to stimulate erection.
- Sildenafil is an oral agent that acts quickly to promote vascular filling of the corpus cavernosum and promote penile erection.

Bibliography

Bullock, B. L. (2000). *Focus on pathophysiology*. Philadelphia: Lippincott Williams & Wilkins.

Davis, S. R. & Burger, H. G. (1996). Androgens and postmenopausal women. *Journal of Endocrinology & Metabolism, 81* (8), 2759–2763.

Hardman, J. G., Limbird, L. E., Molinoff, P. B., Ruddon, R. W., & Gilman, A. G. (Eds). (1996). *Goodman and Gilman's the pharmacological basis of therapeutics* (9th ed.). New York: McGraw-Hill.

Karch, A. M. (2000). *2000 Lippincott's nursing drug guide*. Philadelphia: Lippincott Williams & Wilkins.

Miller, K. L. (1996). Hormone replacement therapy in the elderly. *Annals of Pharmacotherapy, 31* (7–8), 915–917.

McEvoy, B. R. (1999). *Facts and comparisons 1999*. St. Louis: Facts and Comparisons.

The medical letter on drugs and therapeutics. (1999). New Rochelle, NY: Medical Letter.

Walsh, P. C. et al. (1998). *Campbell's urology* (7th ed.). Philadelphia: W. B. Saunders.

PART

8

Drugs Acting on the Cardiovascular System

CHAPTER 40

Introduction to the Cardiovascular System

CHAPTER OUTLINE

KEY TERMS

actin
arrhythmia
arteries
atrium
auricle
automaticity
capillary
capacitance system
cardiac cycle
conductivity
diastole
electrocardiogram (ECG)
fibrillation
myocardium
myosin
oncotic pressure
pulse pressure
resistance system
sarcomere
sinoatrial (SA) node
Starling's law of the heart
syncytia
systole
troponin
veins
ventricle

INTRODUCTION

The cardiovascular system is responsible for delivering oxygen and nutrients to all of the cells of the body and for removing waste products for excretion. The cardiovascular system consists of a pump—the heart—and an interconnected series of tubes that continually move blood throughout the body.

THE HEART

The heart is a hollow, muscular organ that is divided into four chambers. The heart may actually be viewed as two joined hearts: a right heart and a left heart, each of which is divided into two parts, including an upper part called the ***atrium*** (literally "porch" or entryway) and a lower part called the ***ventricle.***

Attached to each atrium is an appendage called the ***auricle.*** The auricle serves to collect blood, which is then pumped into the ventricles by atrial contraction. The ventricles pump blood out of the heart to the lungs or the body. The right auricle is quite large; the left is very small.

Between the atria and ventricles are two cardiac valves, thin tissues that are anchored to an annulus, or fibrous ring, which also gives the hollow organ some structure and helps to keep the organ open and divided into distinct chambers.

A partition called a septum separates the right half of the heart from the left. The right half receives deoxygenated blood from everywhere in the body through the ***veins*** (vessels that carry blood toward the heart) and directs that blood into the lungs. The left half receives the now oxygenated blood from the lungs and directs it into the aorta. The aorta delivers blood into the systemic circulation by way of arteries (vessels that carry blood away from the heart) (Figure 40-1). The heart is the pump that keeps blood flowing through 60,000 miles of tubes, constituting the cardiovascular system, to deliver oxygen and nutrients to all the cells of the body and to remove metabolic waste products from the tissues.

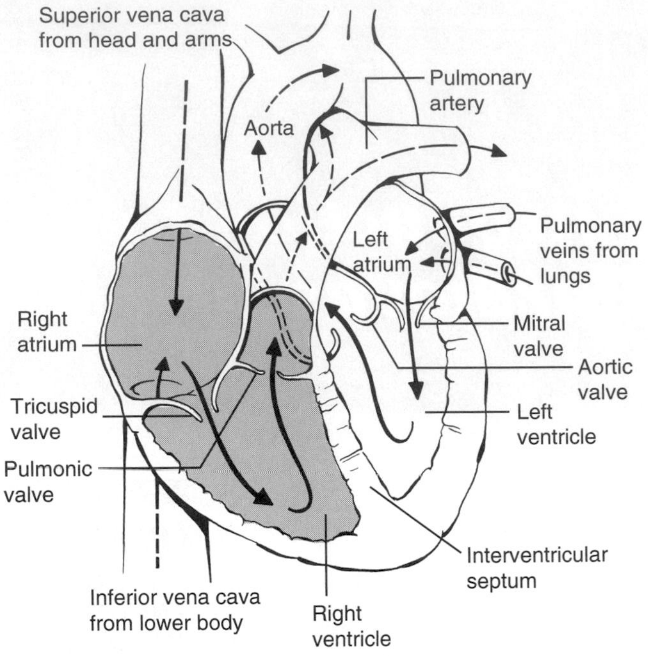

FIGURE 40-1. Blood flow into and out of the heart. Deoxygenated blood enters the right atrium from the superior and inferior venae cavae and falls through the tricuspid valve into the right ventricle, which contracts and sends the blood through the pulmonic valve into the pulmonary artery and to the lungs. Oxygenated blood from the lungs enters the left atrium through the pulmonary veins and passes through the mitral valve into the left ventricle, which contracts and ejects the blood through the aortic valve into the aorta and out to the systemic circulation.

WWW.WEB LINKS

To explore the virtual cardiovascular system, consult the following Internet sources:

http://www.InnerBody.com

The Cardiac Cycle

The heart, which contracts thousands of millions of times in a lifetime, possesses structural and functional properties that are different from other muscles. The fibers of the cardiac muscle, or ***myocardium,*** form two intertwining networks called ***syncytia.*** There are atrial and ventricular syncytia. These interlacing structures enable first the atria and then the ventricles to contract synchronously when excited by the same stimulus. Simultaneous contraction is a necessary property for a muscle that acts as a pump. A hollow pumping mechanism must also pause long enough in the pumping cycle to allow the chambers to fill with fluid. Heart muscle relaxes long enough to ensure adequate filling; the more completely it fills, the stronger the contraction that occurs. This occurs because the muscle fibers of the heart, stretched by the increased volume of blood that has returned to them, will spring back to normal size. This is similar to stretching a rubber band, which returns to its normal size after it is stretched—the further you stretch it, the stronger the spring back to normal. This property is defined in Starling's law of the heart (see p. 487).

During ***diastole,*** the period of cardiac muscle relaxation, blood returns to the heart from the systemic and pulmonic veins, which flow into the right and left atria, respectively. When the pressure generated by the blood volume in the atria is greater than the pressure in the ventricle, blood flows through the atrioventricular valves into the ventricles. The valve on the right side of the heart is called the tricuspid valve because it is composed of three leaflets or cusps (see Figure 40-1). The valve on the left side of the heart, called the mitral or bicuspid valve, is composed of two leaflets or cusps (see Figure 40-1). Just before the ventricles are stimulated to contract, the atria contract, pushing about 1 more tablespoon of blood into each ventricle. The much more powerful ventricles then contract, pumping blood out to the lungs through the pulmonary valve or out to the aorta through the aortic valve and into the systemic circulation. The contraction of the ventricles is referred to as ***systole.*** Each period of systole followed by a period of diastole is called a ***cardiac cycle.***

The heart's series of one-way valves keeps the blood flowing in the correct direction, as follows:

Deoxygenated blood—right atrium through tricuspid valve to right ventricle through pulmonary valve to the lungs

Oxygenated blood—through the pulmonary veins to the left atrium through the mitral valve to the left ventricle, through the aortic valve to the aorta (see Figure 40-1)

The atrioventricular valves close very tightly when the ventricles contract, preventing the blood from flowing backwards into the atria and keeping it moving forward through the system. The pulmonary and aortic valves open with the pressure of ventricular contraction and close tightly during diastole, keeping blood from flowing backward into the ventricles. These valves operate much like one-way automatic doors. You can go through them in the direction that is intended, but if you try to go the wrong way, they close and stop your movement. The proper functioning of the cardiac valves is important in maintaining the functioning of the cardiovascular system.

Conduction System of the Heart

Each cycle of cardiac contraction and relaxation is controlled by impulses that arise spontaneously in certain pacemaker cells of the ***sinoatrial (SA) node*** of the heart. These impulses are conducted from the pacemaker cells by a specialized conducting system that activates all of the parts of the heart muscle almost simultaneously. These continuous, rhythmic contractions are controlled by the heart itself; the brain does not stimulate the heart to beat. This safety feature allows the heart to beat as long as it has enough nutrients and oxygen to survive, regardless of the status of the rest of the body. This property protects the vital cardiovascular function in many disease states; it is the same property that allows the heart to continue functioning in a patient who is "brain dead."

The conduction system of the heart is composed of the SA node, atrial bundles, atrioventricular (AV) node, bundle of His, bundle branches, and the Purkinje fibers (Figure 40-2). The SA node, located in the top of the right atria, acts as the pacemaker of the heart. Atrial bundles conduct the impulse through the atrial muscle. The AV node slows the impulse and sends it from the atria into the ventricles by way of the bundle of His, which enters the septum then divides into three bundle branches. These bundle branches, which conduct the impulses through the ventricles, break into a fine network of conducting fibers called the Purkinje fibers, which deliver the impulse to the ventricular cells.

AUTOMATICITY

The cells of the impulse-forming and conducting system are rather primitive, uncomplicated cells called pale or P cells. Because of their simple cell membrane, these cells possess a special property that differenti-

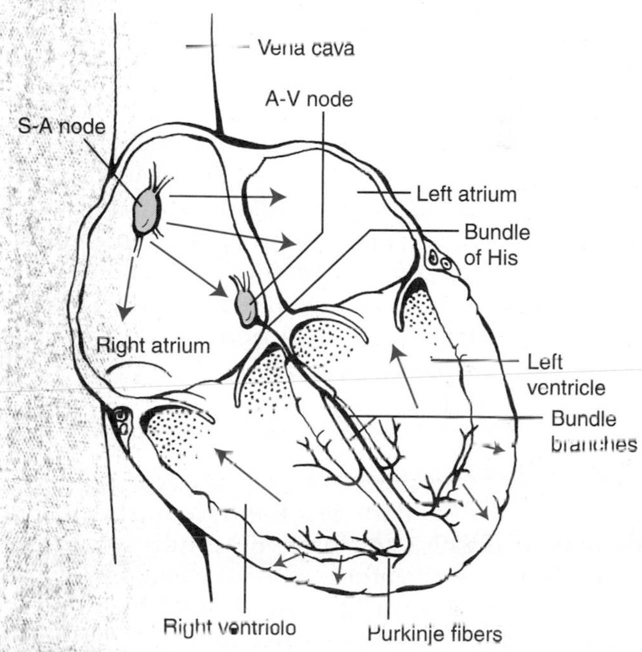

FIGURE 40-2. The conducting system of the heart. Impulses originating in the S-A node are transmitted through the atrial bundles to the A-V node and down the bundle of His and the bundle branches by way of the Purkinje fibers through the ventricles.

ates them from other cells: they can generate action potentials or electrical impulses, without being excited to do so by external stimuli. This property is called ***automaticity.***

All cardiac cells possess some degree of automaticity. During diastole or rest, these cells undergo a spontaneous depolarization because they decrease the flow of potassium ions out of the cell and probably leak sodium into the cell causing an action potential. This action potential is basically the same as the action potential of the neuron (described in Chapter 17). The action potential of the cardiac muscle cell consists of five phases:

- Phase 0 occurs when the cell reaches a point of stimulation. The sodium gates open along the cell membrane, and sodium rushes into the cell and causes a positive flow of electrons into the cell—an electrical potential. This is called depolarization.
- Phase 1 is a very short period when the sodium ions equalize inside and outside of the cell.
- Phase 2, or the plateau stage, occurs as the cell membrane becomes less permeable to sodium. Calcium slowly enters the cell and potassium begins to leave the cell. The cell membrane is trying to return to its resting state, a process called repolarization.
- Phase 3 is a period of rapid repolarization as the gates are closed and potassium rapidly moves out of the cell.
- Phase 4 occurs when the cell comes to rest as the sodium-potassium pump returns the membrane to its previous state with sodium outside and potassium inside the cell, and spontaneous depolarization begins again.

Each area of the heart has an action potential that appears slightly different from the other action potentials, reflecting the complexity of the cells in that particular area. Because of these differences in the action potential, each area of the heart has a slightly different rate of rhythmicity. The SA node generates an impulse about 70 to 80 times a minute; the AV node about 40 to 50 times a minute; and the complex ventricular muscle cells, only about 10 to 20 times a minute (Figure 40-3).

CONDUCTIVITY

Normally, the SA node sets the pace for heart rate because it depolarizes faster than any cell in the heart. However, the other cells in the heart are capable of generating an impulse if anything were to happen to the SA node, another protective feature of the heart. As noted above, the SA node is said to be the pacemaker of the heart because it acts to stimulate the rest of the cells to depolarize at its rate. When the SA node sets the pace for the heart rate, the person is said to be in sinus rhythm.

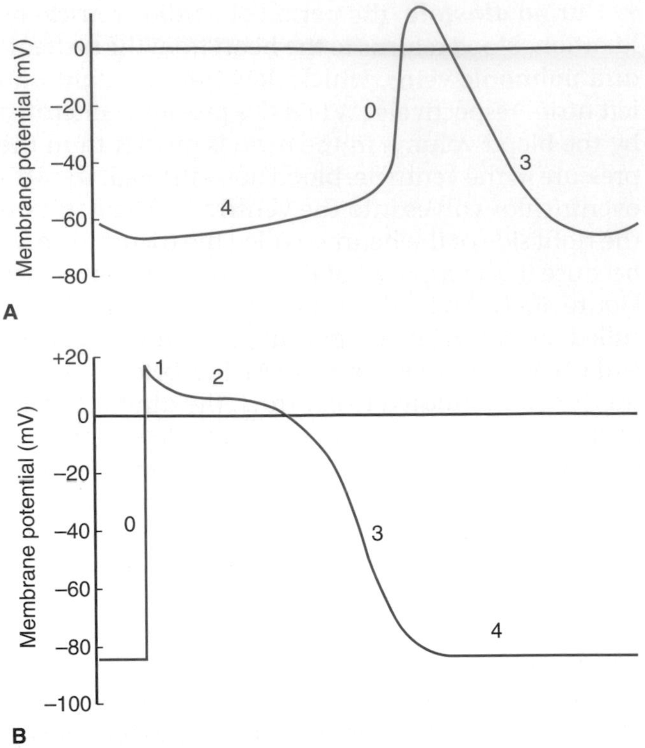

FIGURE 40-3. Action potentials. (*A*) Recorded from a cell in the SA node, showing diastolic depolarization in phase 4; (*B*) recorded from a ventricular muscle cell. (*phase 0*) The cell is stimulated, sodium rushes into the cell, and the cell is depolarized; (*phase 1*) sodium levels equalize; (*phase 2*) the plateau phase, in which calcium enters the cell (the slow current), and potassium and sodium leave; (*phase 3*) the slow current stops, and sodium and potassium leave the cell; (*phase 4*) the resting membrane potential returns and the pacemaker potential begins in the SA node cell.

The specialized cells of the heart can conduct an impulse rapidly through the system so that the muscle cells of the heart are stimulated at approximately the same time. This property of cardiac cells is called ***conductivity.***

The conduction velocity, or speed at which the cells can pass on the impulse, is slowest in the AV node and fastest in the Purkinje fibers.

This delay in conduction at the AV node, right between the atria and the ventricles, accounts for the fact that the atria contract a fraction of a second before the ventricles contract. This allows extra time for the ventricles to fill completely before they contract. The almost simultaneous spread of the impulse through the Purkinje fibers permits a simultaneous and powerful contraction of the ventricle muscles, making them an effective pump.

After a cell membrane has conducted an action potential, there is a period of time, called the absolute refractory period, in which it is impossible to stimulate that area of membrane. The absolute refractory period is the minimal amount of time that must elapse between two stimuli applied at one site in the heart for each of these stimuli to cause an action potential. This time reflects the responsiveness of the heart cells to stimuli. Cardiac drugs may affect the refractory period of the cells to make the heart more or less responsive.

AUTONOMIC INFLUENCES

The heart can generate action potentials on its own and could function without connection to the rest of the body. The autonomic nervous system (Chapter 27) can influence the heart rate and rhythm and the strength of contraction. The parasympathetic nerves, primarily the vagus or 10th cranial nerve, can slow the heart rate and decrease the speed of conduction through the AV node. This allows the heart to rest and conserve its strength. The parasympathetic influence on the SA node is the dominant influence most of the time.

The sympathetic nervous system stimulates the heart to beat faster, speeds conduction through the AV node, and causes the heart muscle to contract harder. This action is important during exercise or stress, when the body's cells need to have more oxygen delivered. These two branches of the autonomic nervous system work together to help the heart meet the body's demands. Drugs that influence either of these branches of the autonomic nervous system have autonomic effects on the heart.

Mechanical Activity

The end result of the electrical stimulation of the heart cells is the unified contraction of the atria and ventricles, which moves the blood throughout the vascular system. The basic unit of the cardiac muscle is called a ***sarcomere.*** A sarcomere is made up of two contractile proteins: ***actin,*** a thin filament, and ***myosin,*** a thick filament with small projections on it. These proteins like to react with each other, but at rest they are kept apart by the protein ***troponin.***

When a cardiac muscle cell is stimulated, calcium enters the cell though channels in the cell membrane as well as from storage sites within the cell. This occurs during phase 2 of the action potential, when the cell is starting to repolarize. The calcium reacts with the troponin and inactivates it. This action allows the actin and myosin proteins to react with each other, forming actomyosin bridges. These bridges then break quickly, and the myosin slides along to form new ones.

As long as calcium is present, the actomyosin bridges continue to form. This action slides the proteins together, shortening or contracting the sarcomere. Cardiac muscle cells are linked together, so when one cell is stimulated to contract, they are all stimulated to contract.

The shortening of numerous sarcomeres causes the contraction and pumping action of the heart muscle. As the cell reaches its repolarized state, calcium is removed from the cell by a sodium–calcium pump and calcium released from storage sites within the cell returns to the storage sites. The contraction process requires energy and oxygen for the chemical reaction, which allows the formation the actomyosin bridges and calcium to allow the bridge formation to occur.

The degree of shortening, or the strength of contraction, is determined by the amount of calcium present (the more calcium is present, the more bridges will be formed) and by the stretch of the sarcomere before contraction begins. The further apart the actin and myosin proteins are before the cell is stimulated, the more bridges will be formed and the stronger the contraction will be. This correlates with ***Starling's law of the heart.*** The more the cardiac muscle is stretched, the greater the contraction will be. The more blood you put into the heart, the greater the contraction will be to empty the heart, up to a point. If the bridges are stretched too far apart, they will not be able to reach each other to form the actomyosin bridges, and no contraction will occur (Figure 40-4).

Cardiac Arrhythmias

Various factors—drugs, acidosis, decreased oxygen levels, changes in the electrolytes in the area, build-up of waste products—can change the cardiac rate and rhythm. A disruption in cardiac rate or rhythm is called an ***arrhythmia*** or a dysrhythmia. Arrhythmias interfere with the work of the heart and can disrupt cardiac output, which affects every cell in the body. Arrhythmias can arise because of changes to the automaticity or conductivity of the heart cells. Some arrhythmias occur when there is a shift in the

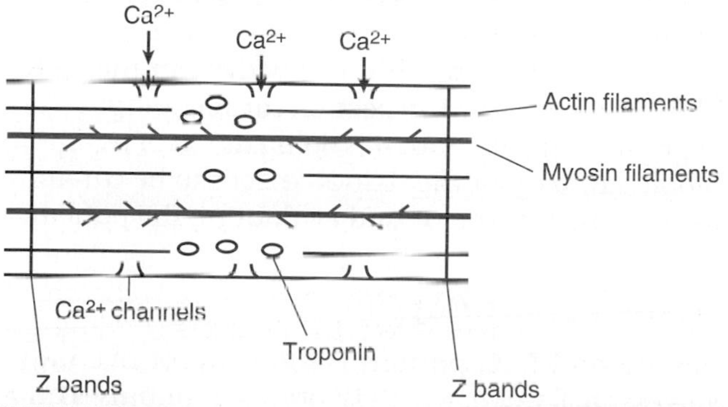

FIGURE 40-4. A sarcomere, the functional unit of cardiac muscle.

pacemaker of the heart from the SA node to some other site, called an ectopic focus. This occurs most frequently with damage to the heart muscle and can be seen in the form of premature contractions or extrasystoles. These premature beats may be unimportant and sporadic, but in some cases they can be the prelude to more serious or even fatal arrhythmias when the coordinated pumping action of the muscle is lost.

A lack of or decrease in conductivity through the AV node produces a condition called heart block. In first degree heart block, all of the impulses from the SA node arrive in the ventricles, but it takes a longer time than normal. In second degree heart block, some of the impulses are lost and do not get through, resulting in a slow rate of ventricular contraction. In third degree or complete heart block, no impulses from the SA node get through to the ventricles, and the much slower ventricular automaticity takes over. Very serious arrhythmias arise when the combination of ectopic foci and altered conduction set off an irregular, uncoordinated twitching of the atrial or ventricular muscle, called ***fibrillation.*** In this situation, the pumping action of the heart is lost, and the cardiac output falls. Individuals can live quite normally with atrial fibrillation, but if the ventricles fibrillate, there is total loss of cardiac output; death can occur if treatment is not initiated.

THE ELECTROCARDIOGRAM

Electrocardiography is a process of recording the patterns of electrical impulses as they move through the heart. It has become a very important diagnostic tool in the care of the cardiac patient. The electrocardiography machine detects the patterns of electrical impulse generation and conduction through the heart and translates that information to a recorded pattern, seen on a cardiac monitor or printed out on calibrated paper as a wave form. It is very important to remember that an ***electrocardiogram (ECG)*** is a measure of electrical activity; it provides no information about the mechanical activity of the heart. The very important aspect of cardiac output—the degree to which the heart is doing its job of pumping blood out to all of the tissues—needs to be carefully assessed by looking at and evaluating the patient.

Normal Sinus Rhythm

The normal ECG pattern is made up of five main waves: the P wave, which is formed as impulses originating in the sinoatrial node or pacemaker pass through the atrial tissues; the QRS complex, which represents depolarization of the bundle of His (Q) and the ventricles (RS); and the T wave, which represents repolarization of the ventricles.

The P wave immediately precedes the contraction of the atria. The QRS complex immediately precedes the contraction of the ventricles and relaxation of the ventricles during the T wave. The repolarization of the atria, the Ta wave, occurs during the QRS complex and is usually not seen on an ECG. In certain conditions of atrial hypertrophy, the Ta wave may appear around the QRS complex (Figure 40-5).

The critical points of the ECG are as follows:

P–R interval—reflects the normal delay of conduction at the AV node

Q–T interval—reflects the critical timing of repolarization of the ventricles

S–T segment—reflects important information about the repolarization of the ventricles

Abnormalities in the shape or timing of each part of an ECG tracing reveal the presence of particular cardiac disorders. A person with a normal ECG pattern and a heart rate within the normal range for that person's age group is said to be in normal sinus rhythm.

Types of Arrhythmias

A disruption in cardiac rate or rhythm is called an arrhythmia (or dysrhythmia). Arrhythmias are significant because they interfere with the work of the heart and can disrupt the cardiac output, which eventually will affect every cell in the body.

SINUS ARRHYTHMIAS

The SA node is influenced by the autonomic nervous system to change the rate of firing in order to meet the body's demands for oxygen. A faster-than-normal heart rate, usually anything over 100 beats per minute in adults, with a normal-appearing ECG pattern is called sinus tachycardia. Sinus bradycardia is a slower-than-normal heart rate (usually less than 60 beats per minute) with a normal-appearing ECG pattern.

SUPRAVENTRICULAR ARRHYTHMIAS

Arrhythmias that originate above the ventricles but not in the SA node are called supraventricular arrhythmias. These arrhythmias feature an abnormally shaped P wave, because the site of origin is not the sinus node; however, they will feature normal QRS complexes because the ventricles are still conducting impulses normally. Supraventricular arrhythmias include the following:

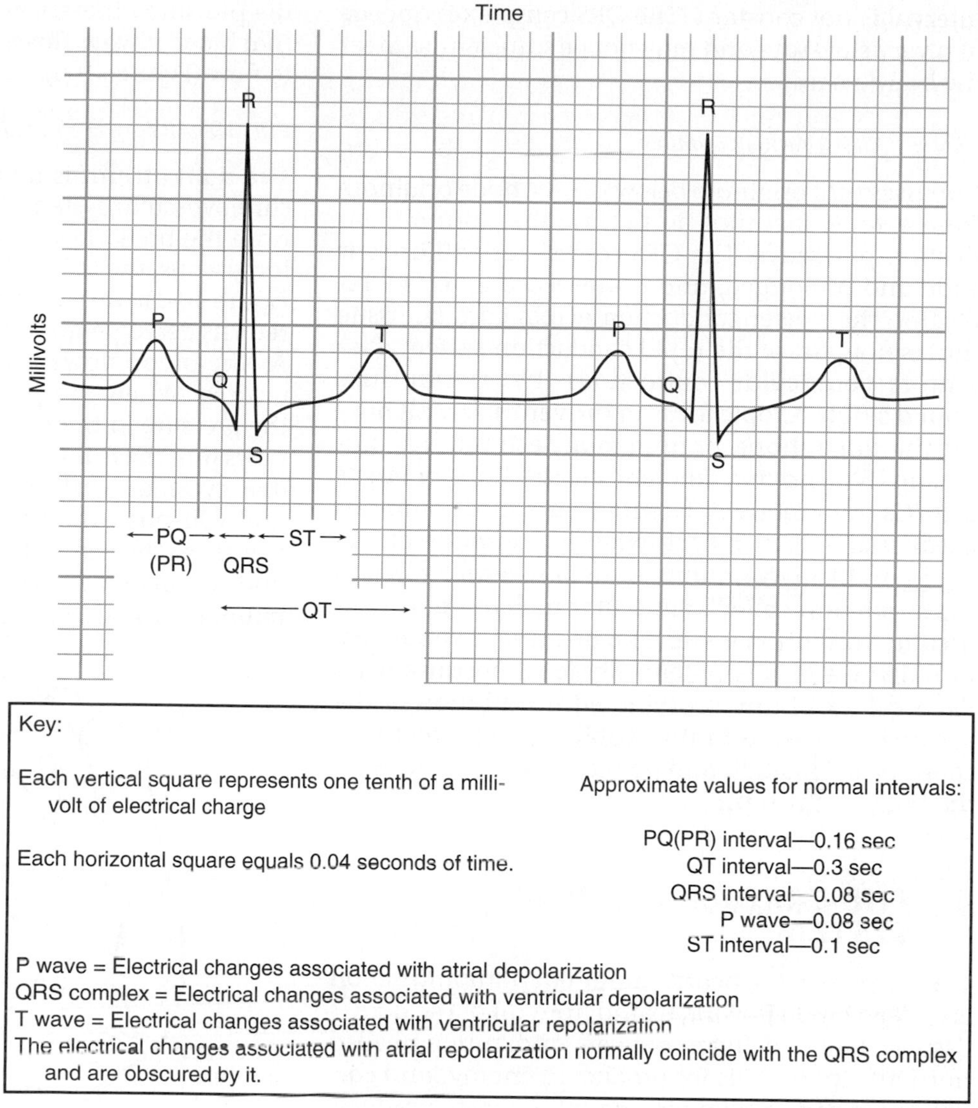

Time
Millivolts
P
Q
R
S
T
P
Q
R
S
T
←PQ→ (PR)
←→ QRS
←ST→
←QT→
Key:
Each vertical square represents one tenth of a millivolt of electrical charge
Each horizontal square equals 0.04 seconds of time.
Approximate values for normal intervals:
PQ(PR) interval—0.16 sec
QT interval—0.3 sec
QRS interval—0.08 sec
P wave—0.08 sec
ST interval—0.1 sec
P wave = Electrical changes associated with atrial depolarization
QRS complex = Electrical changes associated with ventricular depolarization
T wave = Electrical changes associated with ventricular repolarization
The electrical changes associated with atrial repolarization normally coincide with the QRS complex and are obscured by it.

FIGURE 40-5. The normal ECG pattern.

- Premature atrial contractions (PACs), which reflect an ectopic focus in the atria generating an impulse out of the normal rhythm
- Paroxysmal atrial tachycardia (PAT), sporadically occurring runs of rapid heart rate originating in the atria
- Atrial flutter, characterized by sawtooth-shaped P waves reflecting a single ectopic focus generating a regular, fast atrial depolarization
- Atrial fibrillation with irregular P waves representing many ectopic foci firing in an uncoordinated manner through the atria

With atrial flutter, often one of every two or one of every three impulses is transmitted to the ventricles. The person may have a 2:1 or 3:1 ratio of P waves to QRS complexes. The ventricles will beat faster than normal, losing some efficiency. With atrial fibrillation, so many impulses are bombarding the AV node that an unpredictable number of impulses will be transmitted to the ventricles. The ventricles will be stimulated to beat in a fast, irregular, and inefficient manner.

AV BLOCK

Atrioventricular (AV) block, also called heart block, reflects a slowing or lack of conduction at the AV node. This can occur because of structural damage, hypoxia, or injury to the heart muscle. First degree heart block is characterized by a lengthening of the P–R interval beyond the normal 0.16 to 0. 20 seconds. Each P wave is followed by a QRS complex. In second degree heart block, a QRS complex may follow one, two, three, or four P waves. Third degree heart block, or complete heart block, shows a total dissociation of P waves from QRS complexes and T waves. Because the P waves can come at any time, the P–R interval is not constant. The QRS complexes appear at a very slow rate and may not be sufficient to meet the body's needs.

VENTRICULAR ARRHYTHMIAS

Impulses that originate below the AV node originate from ectopic foci that do not use the normal conduction pathways. The QRS complexes will appear wide and prolonged, and T waves are inverted, reflecting the slower conduction across cardiac tissue that is not part of the rapid conduction system. Premature ventricular contractions (PVCs) can arise from a single ectopic focus in the ventricles, all having the same shape, or from many ectopic foci, producing PVCs having different shapes. Runs or bursts of PVCs from many different foci are more ominous because they can reflect extensive damage or hypoxia in the myocardium. Runs of several PVCs at a rapid rate are called ventricular tachycardia. Ventricular fibrillation is seen as a bizarre, irregular, distorted wave and is potentially fatal because it reflects a lack of any coordinated stimulation of the ventricles, leading to the inability to contract in a coordinated fashion and no blood being pumped to the body or the brain.

THE CARDIOVASCULAR SYSTEM

The purpose of the heart's continual pumping action is to keep blood flowing to and from all of the body's tissues. Blood delivers oxygen and much-needed nutrients to the cells for producing energy, and carries away carbon dioxide and other waste products of metabolism. The steady circulation of blood is essential for the proper functioning of all of the body's organs, including the heart itself.

Circulation

The circulation of the blood follows two courses:

1. Heart–lung or pulmonary circulation: the right side of the heart sends blood to the lungs, where carbon dioxide and some waste products are removed from the blood and oxygen is picked up by the red blood cells.
2. Systemic circulation: the left side of the heart sends oxygenated blood out to all of the cells in the body.

The blood moves through the circulatory system from areas of high pressure to areas of lower pressure. The system is a "closed" system; that is, it has no openings or holes that would allow blood to leak out. The closed nature of the system is what keeps the pressure differences in the proper perspective so that blood always flows in the direction it is intended to flow (Figure 40-6).

PULMONARY AND SYSTEMIC CIRCULATION

The right atrium is a very-low-pressure area in the cardiovascular system. All of the deoxygenated blood from the body flows into the right atrium from the large veins, the inferior and superior vena cavae (see Figure 40-1), and from the great cardiac vein, which returns deoxygenated blood from the heart muscle. As the blood flows into the atria, the pressure increases. When the pressure becomes greater than the pressure in the right ventricle, most of the blood flows into the right ventricle. At this point in the cardiac cycle, the atrium will be stimulated to contract and will push the remaining blood into the right ventricle. The ventricle is then stimulated to contract and will generate pressure that will push open the pulmonic valve (see Figure 40-1) and send blood into

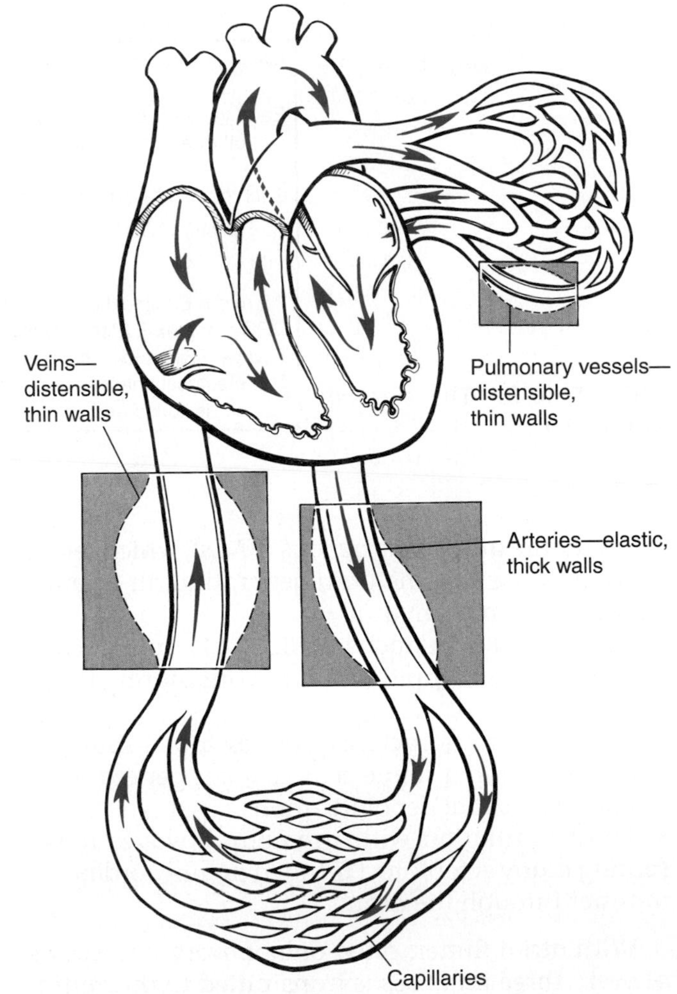

FIGURE 40-6. Blood flow through the systemic and pulmonary vasculature circuit. (Bullock, B. L. [2000]. *Focus on pathophysiology.* Philadelphia: Lippincott Williams & Wilkins.)

the pulmonary artery, which will take the blood into the lungs, a very-low-pressure area. The blood will circulate around the alveoli of the lungs, pick up oxygen and get rid of carbon dioxide, and flow through pulmonary capillaries (the tiny blood vessels that connect arteries and veins) to the pulmonary veins, which flow into the left atrium. When the pressure of blood volume in the left atrium is greater than the pressure in the large left ventricle, this oxygenated blood will flow into the left ventricle. The left atrium will contract and push any remaining blood into the left ventricle, which is stimulated to contract and generates tremendous pressure to push the blood out the aorta, carrying the blood throughout the body.

ARTERIES, CAPILLARIES, AND VEINS

The aorta and other large arteries have thick, muscular walls. The entire arterial system contains muscles in the walls of the vessels all the way to the terminal branches or arterioles, which consist of fragments of muscle and endothelial cells. These muscles offer resistance to the blood that is sent pumping into the arterial system by the left ventricle, generating pressure. The arterial system is referred to as a ***resistance system.*** The vessels can constrict or dilate, increasing or decreasing resistance, based on the needs of the body. The arterioles are able to completely shut off blood flow to some areas of the body, that is, they can shunt blood to another area where it is needed more. The arterioles, because of their ability to increase or decrease resistance in the system, are one of the main regulators of blood pressure.

Blood from the tiny arterioles flows into the ***capillary*** system that connects the arterial and venous systems. These microscopic vessels are composed of loosely connected endothelial cells. Oxygen, fluid, and nutrients are able to pass through the arterial end of the capillaries and enter the interstitial area between tissue cells. Fluid at the venous end of the capillary is drawn back into the vessel and contains carbon dioxide and other waste products. This shifting of fluid in the capillaries, called the capillary fluid shift, is carefully regulated by a balance between hydrostatic (fluid pressure) forces on the arterial end of the capillary and ***oncotic pressure*** (the pulling pressure of the large, vascular proteins) on the venous end of the capillary. In a normal situation, the higher pressure at the arterial end of a capillary will force fluid out of the vessel and into the tissue, and the now-concentrated proteins (which are too large to leave the capillary) will exert a pull on the fluid at the venous end of the capillary to pull the fluid back in. A disruption in the hydrostatic pressure or the concentration of proteins in the capillary can lead to fluid being left in the tissue or edema. The capillaries merge into venules, which merge into veins, which are responsible for returning the blood to the heart (Figure 40-7).

The veins are thin-walled, very elastic, low-pressure vessels that can hold large quantities of blood if necessary. The venous system is referred to as a ***capacitance system*** because the veins have the capacity to hold large quantities of fluid as they distend with fluid volume. These capacitance vessels have a great deal of influence on the venous return to the heart, the amount of blood that is delivered to the right atrium.

CORONARY CIRCULATION

The heart muscle itself requires a constant supply of oxygenated blood to keep contracting. The myocardium receives its blood through two main coronary arteries that branch off the base of the aorta from an area called the sinuses of Valsalva. These arteries encircle the heart in a pattern resembling a crown, which is why they are called coronary arteries.

The artery arising from the left side of the aorta bifurcates, or divides, into two large vessels called the left circumflex (which travels down the left side of the heart and feeds most of the left ventricle) and the left anterior descending (which travels down the front of the heart and feeds the septum and anterior areas, including much of the conduction system). The artery arising from the right side of the aorta feeds most of the right side of the heart, including the sinus node.

The coronary arteries receive blood during diastole, when the muscle is at rest and relaxed so that blood can flow freely down into the muscle. When the ventricle contracts, it forces the aortic valve open and the leaflets of the valve cover the openings of the coronary arteries. When the ventricles relax, the blood is no longer pumped forward and starts to flow back toward the ventricle. The blood flowing down the sides of the aorta closes the aortic valve and fills up the coronary arteries. The pressure that fills the coronary arteries is the difference between the systolic ejection pressure and the diastolic resting pressure. This is called the ***pulse pressure*** (systolic–diastolic blood pressure readings). The pulse pressure is monitored clinically to evaluate the filling pressure of the coronary arteries. The oxygenated blood that is fed into the heart by the coronary circulation will reach every cardiac muscle fiber as the vessels divide and subdivide throughout the myocardium.

The heart has a pattern of circulation called end-artery circulation. The arteries go into the muscle and end without a great deal of back-up or collateral circulation. Normally this is an efficient system and is able to meet the needs of the heart muscle. The heart's supply of and demand for oxygen is met by

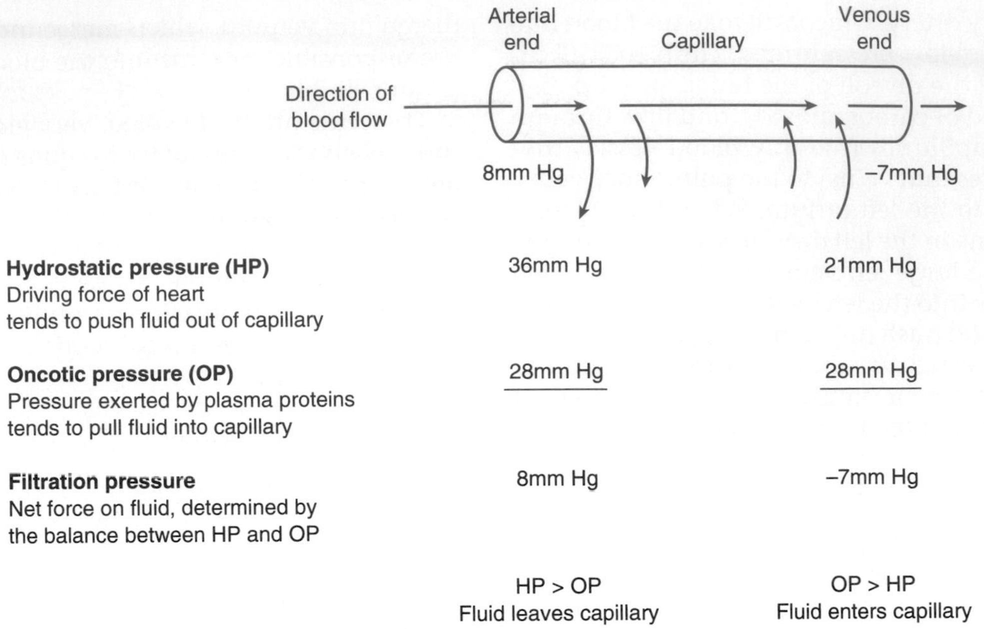

FIGURE 40-7. The net shift of fluid out of and into the capillary is determined by the balance between the hydrostatic pressure (*HP*) and the oncotic pressure (*OP*). HP tends to push fluid out of the capillary, and OP tends to pull it back into the capillary. At the arterial end of the capillary bed, blood pressure (HP) is higher than at the venous end. At the arterial end, HP exceeds OP, and fluid filters out. At the venous end, HP has fallen and HP is less than OP; fluid is pulled back into the capillary from the surrounding tissue. The lymphatic system also returns fluids and substances from the tissues to the circulation.

changes in the delivery of oxygen through the coronary system. Problems can arise, however, when an imbalance develops between the supply of oxygen delivered to the heart muscle and the myocardial demand for oxygen. The main forces that determine the heart's use of oxygen or oxygen consumption are as follows:

1. Heart rate: The more the heart has to pump, the more oxygen it will require to do that.
2. Preload (amount of blood that is brought back to the heart to be pumped around): The more blood that is returned to the heart, the harder it will have to work to pump it around. The volume of blood in the system is a determinant of preload.
3. Afterload (resistance against which the heart has to beat): The higher the resistance in the system, the harder the heart will have to contract to force open the valves and pump the blood along. Blood pressure is a measure of afterload.
4. Stretch on the ventricles: If the ventricular muscle is stretched before it is stimulated to contract, more actomyosin bridges will be formed (which will take more energy): or if the muscle is stimulated to contract harder than usual (which happens with sympathetic stimulation), more bridges will be formed, which will require more energy.

The muscle can be stretched with ventricular hypertrophy related to chronic hypertension or cardiac muscle damage, or with heart failure when the ventricle does not empty completely and blood backs up in the system.

The supply of blood to the myocardium can be altered when the heart fails to pump effectively and cannot deliver blood to the coronary arteries. This happens in congestive heart failure and cases of hypotension. The supply is most frequently altered, however, when the coronary vessels become narrowed and unresponsive to stimuli to dilate and deliver more blood. This happens in atherosclerosis or coronary artery disease. The end result of this narrowing can be total blockage of a coronary artery and hypoxia and eventual death of the cells that depend on that vessel for oxygen. This is called a myocardial infarction, which is the leading cause of death in the United States (Figure 40-8).

Systemic Arterial Pressure

The contraction of the left ventricle, which sends blood surging out into the aorta, creates a pressure that continues to force blood into all of the branches of the aorta. This pressure against arterial walls is greatest during systole (cardiac contraction), and falls to its lowest level during diastole. The measurement of both the systolic and diastolic pressure indi-

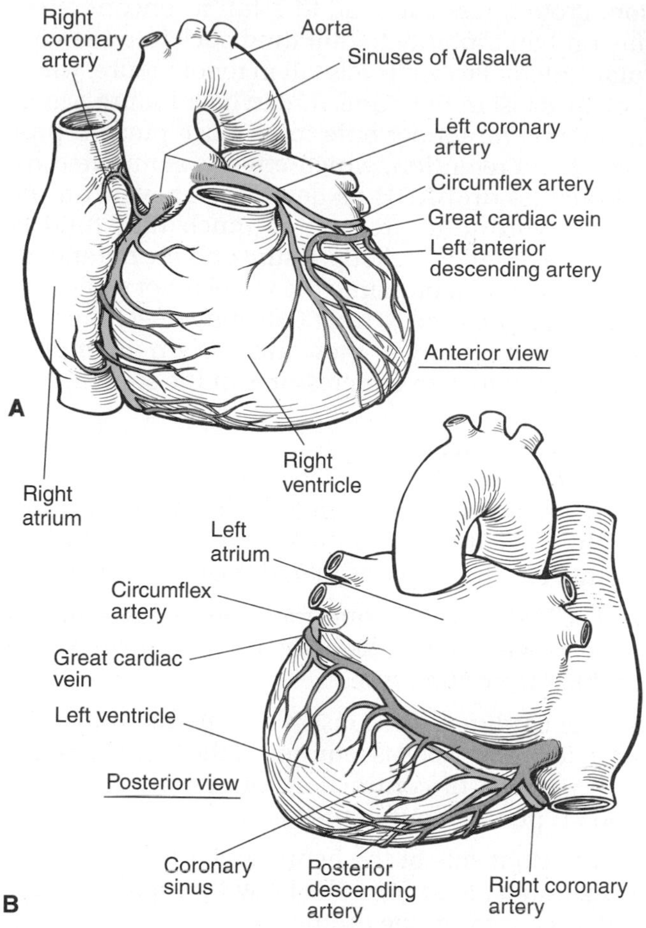

FIGURE 40-8. Coronary arteries and veins. (*A*) Anterior view; (*B*) posterior view. (Bullock, B. L. [2000]. *Focus on pathophysiology.* Philadelphia: Lippincott Williams & Wilkins.)

cates the pumping pressure of the ventricle and the generalized pressure in the system, or the pressure the ventricle has to overcome to pump blood out of the heart.

HYPOTENSION

The pressure in the arteries needs to remain relatively high to ensure that blood is delivered to every cell in the body and to keep the blood flowing from high-pressure areas to low-pressure areas. Hypotension can occur if the blood pressure falls dramatically, either from loss of blood volume or failure of the heart muscle to pump effectively. Severe hypotension can progress to shock and even death as cells are cut off from their oxygen supply.

HYPERTENSION

Constant, excessive high blood pressure, called hypertension, can damage the fragile inner lining of blood vessels and cause a disruption of blood flow to the tissues. It also puts a tremendous strain on the heart muscle, increasing myocardial oxygen consumption and putting the heart muscle itself at risk. Hypertension can be caused by neurostimulation to the blood vessels to constrict and to raise pressure, or by increased volume in the system. In most cases, the cause of hypertension is not known and drug therapy to correct it is aimed at changing one or more of the normal reflexes that control vascular resistance or the force of cardiac muscle contraction.

VASOMOTOR TONE

The smooth muscles in the walls of the arteries receive constant input from nerve fibers of the sympathetic nervous system. These impulses work to dilate the vessels if more blood flow is needed in an area; constrict vessels if increased pressure is needed in the system; and maintain muscle tone so that the vessel remains patent and responsive.

The coordination of these impulses is regulated through the medulla in an area called the cardiovascular center. If increased pressure is needed, this center will increase sympathetic flow to the vessels. If pressure rises too high, this is sensed by baroreceptors or pressure receptors and the sympathetic flow is decreased. Chapter 41 discusses drugs that are used to influence that stimulation of vessels to alter blood pressure.

RENIN–ANGIOTENSIN SYSTEM

Another determinant of blood pressure is the renin–angiotensin system. This system is activated when blood flow to the kidneys is decreased.

Cells in the kidney release an enzyme called renin. Renin will be transported to the liver, where it will convert angiotensinogen (produced in the liver) to angiotensin I. Angiotensin I travels to the lungs, where it is converted by angiotensin converting enzyme (ACE) to angiotensin II. Angiotensin II travels through the body and reacts with angiotensin II receptor sites on blood vessels to cause a severe vasoconstriction. This will increase blood pressure and should increase blood flow to the kidneys to decrease the release of renin. Angiotensin II also causes the release of aldosterone from the adrenal cortex, which causes retention of sodium and water, leading to the release of ADH to retain water and increased blood volume. Increasing blood volume increases blood flow to the kidney. This system works constantly, whenever a position change alters either flow to the kidney or blood volume or pressure changes, to help to maintain the blood pressure within a range that will ensure perfusion (delivery of blood to all of the tissues) (Figure 40-9).

Venous Pressure

Pressure in the veins may also sometimes rise above normal. This can happen when the heart is not

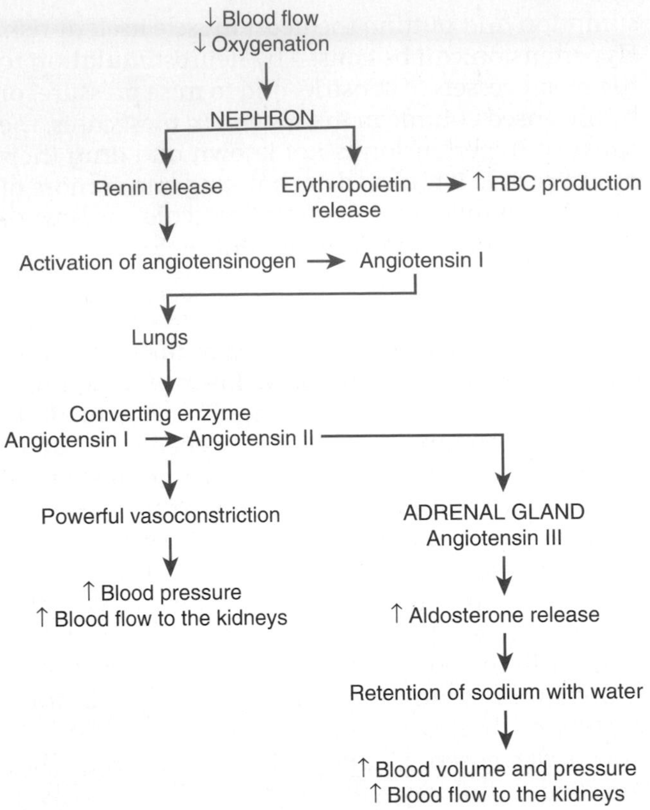

FIGURE 40-9. The renin-angiotensin system for reflex maintenance of blood pressure control.

pumping effectively and cannot pump out all of the blood that is trying to return to it. This results in a back-up or congestion of blood waiting to enter the heart. Pressure rises in the right atrium and then in the veins that are trying to return blood to the heart as they encounter resistance. The venous system then begins to back up, or become congested with blood.

CONGESTIVE HEART FAILURE AND EDEMA

When the heart muscle fails to do its job of effectively pumping blood through the system, blood backs up and the system becomes congested. This is called congestive heart failure (CHF). The rise in venous pressure that results from this back-up of blood increases the hydrostatic pressure on the venous end of the capillaries. Hydrostatic pressure pushing fluid out of the capillary will soon be higher than the oncotic pressure trying to pull the fluid back into the vessel, causing fluid to be lost into the tissues. This shift of fluid accounts for the edema seen with CHF. Pulmonary edema results when the left side of the heart is failing; peripheral, abdominal, and liver edema occur when the right side of the heart is failing.

Other factors that can contribute to this loss of fluid in the tissues include protein loss and fluid retention. Protein loss can lead to a fall in oncotic pressure and an inability to pull fluid back into the vascular system. Protein levels fall in renal failure, when protein is lost in the urine, and in liver failure, when the liver is no longer able to produce plasma proteins. Fluid retention, which often is stimulated by aldosterone and ADH as described above, can increase hydrostatic pressure so much that fluid is pushed out under higher pressure and the balancing pressure to pull it back into the vessel is not sufficient. Drugs that are used to treat CHF may affect the vascular system at any of these areas in an attempt to return a balance to the pressures in the system.

CHAPTER SUMMARY

- The heart is a hollow muscle that is divided into a right and left side by a thick septum, and into four chambers—the upper atria and the lower ventricles.
- The heart is responsible for pumping oxygenated blood to every cell in the body and picking up waste products from the tissues.
- The cardiac cycle consists of a period of rest, or diastole, when blood is returned to the heart by veins, and a period of contraction, or systole, when the blood is pumped out of the heart.
- The right side of the heart receives all of the deoxygenated blood from the body through the veins and directs it into the lungs.
- The left side of the heart receives oxygenated blood from the lungs and pumps it out to every cell in the body through the arteries.
- The heart muscle possesses the properties of automaticity (the ability to generate an action potential in the absence of stimulation) and conductivity (the ability to rapidly transmit an action potential).
- The heart muscle is stimulated to contract by impulses generated in the heart, not by stimuli from the brain. The autonomic nervous system can affect the heart to increase (sympathetic) or decrease (parasympathetic) activity.
- The normal conduction or stimulatory system of the heart consists of the SA node, the atrial bundles, the AV node, the bundle of His, the bundle branches, and the Purkinje fibers.
- In normal sinus rhythm, cells in the SA node generate an impulse which is transmitted through the atrial bundles and delayed slightly at the AV node before being sent down the bundle of His into the ventricles. When cardiac muscle cells are stimulated, they contract.
- Alterations in the generation of conduction of impulses in the heart cause arrhythmias (dysrhythmias), which can upset the normal balance in the

cardiovascular system and lead to a decrease in cardiac output, affecting all of the cells of the body.

- Heart muscle contracts by the sliding of actin and myosin filaments in a functioning unit called a sarcomere. Contraction requires energy and calcium to allow the filaments to react with each other and slide together.

- The heart muscle needs a constant supply of blood, furnished by the coronary arteries. Increase in demand for oxygen can occur with changes in heart rate, preload, afterload, or stretch on the muscle.

- The cardiovascular system is a closed pressure system that uses arteries (muscular, pressure or resistance tubes) to carry blood from the heart, veins (flexible, distensible capacitance vessels) to return blood to the heart, and capillaries (which connect arteries to veins) to keep blood flowing from areas of high pressure to areas of low pressure.

- Blood pressure is maintained by stimulus from the sympathetic system and reflex control of blood volume and pressure by the renin–angiotensin system and the aldosterone–ADH system. Alterations in blood pressure (hypotension or hypertension) can upset the balance of the cardiovascular system and lead to problems in blood delivery.

- Fluid shifts out of the blood at the arterial ends of capillaries to deliver oxygen and nutrients to the tissues. It is pushed out of the vessel by the hydrostatic or fluid pressure in the arterial side of the system. Fluid returns to the system at the venous end of the capillaries because of the oncotic pull of proteins in the vessels. Disruptions in these pressures can lead to edema or loss of fluid in the tissues.

Bibliography

Bullock, B. L. (2000). *Focus on pathophysiology.* Philadelphia: Lippincott Williams & Wilkins.

Ganong, W. (1999). *Review of medical physiology* (19th ed.). Norwalk, CT: Appleton & Lange.

Guyton, A. & Hall, J. (1996). *Textbook of medical physiology.* Philadelphia: W. B. Saunders.

Hardman, J. G., Limbird, L. E., Molinoff, P. B., Ruddon, R. W., & Gilman, A. G. (Eds.). (1996). *Goodman and Gilman's the pharmacological basis of therapeutics* (9th ed.). New York: McGraw-Hill.

Karch, A. M. (2000). *2000 Lippincott's nursing drug guide.* Philadelphia: Lippincott Williams & Wilkins.

Porth, C. M. (1998). *Pathophysiology: Concepts of altered health states* (5th ed.). Philadelphia: Lippincott-Raven.

CHAPTER

41

Drugs Affecting Blood Pressure

Antihypertensive agents
- Angiotensin-converting enzyme (ACE) inhibitors
  - benazepril
  - P captopril
  - enalapril
  - fosinopril
  - lisinopril
  - moexipril
  - quinapril
  - ramipril
  - trandolapril
- Angiotensin II receptor blockers
  - candesartan
  - irbesartan
  - P losartan
  - telmisartan
  - valsartan
- Calcium channel blockers
  - amlodipine
  - P diltiazem
  - felodipine
  - isradipine
  - nicardipine
  - nifedipine
  - nisoldipine
- Vasodilators
  - diazoxide
  - hydralazine
  - minoxidil
  - P nitroprusside
  - tolazoline
- Ganglionic blocker
  - mecamylamine

Antihypotensive agent
- midodrine

CHAPTER OUTLINE

Assessment
HISTORY
PHYSICAL ASSESSMENT
Nursing Diagnoses
Implementation
Evaluation
CHAPTER SUMMARY
BIBLIOGRAPHY

KEY TERMS

ACE inhibitor
angiotensin II receptors
baroreceptor
cardiovascular center
essential hypertension
hypotension
peripheral resistance
renin-angiotensin system
shock
stroke volume

INTRODUCTION

The cardiovascular system is a closed system of blood vessels responsible for delivering oxygenated blood to the tissues and removing waste products from the tissues. The blood in this system flows from areas of high pressure to areas of low pressure. The area of highest pressure is always the left ventricle during systole. The pressure in this area propels the blood out of the aorta and into the system. The lowest pressure is in the right atrium, which collects all of the deoxygenated blood from the body. The maintenance of this pressure system is controlled by specific areas of the brain and various hormones. If the pressure becomes too high, the person is said to be hypertensive. If the pressure becomes too low and blood cannot be delivered effectively, the person is said to be hypotensive. Helping the patient to maintain the blood pressure within normal limits is the goal of drug therapy affecting blood pressure.

BLOOD PRESSURE CONTROL

The pressure in the cardiovascular system is determined by three elements:

1. Heart rate
2. **Stroke volume,** or the amount of blood that is pumped out of the ventricle with each heart beat (primarily determined by the volume of blood in the system)
3. Total **peripheral resistance,** or the resistance of the muscular arteries to the blood being pumped through

The small arterioles are thought to be the most important factors in determining peripheral resistance. That is because the arterioles have the smallest diameter and so are able to nearly stop blood flow into capillary beds when they constrict, building up tremendous pressure in the arteries behind them as they prevent the blood from flowing through. The arterioles are very responsive to stimulation from the sympathetic nervous system, constricting when the sympathetic system is stimulated, and increasing total peripheral resistance and blood pressure. The body uses this responsiveness to regulate blood pressure on a minute-to-minute basis, to assure that there is enough pressure in the system to deliver sufficient blood to the brain.

Baroreceptors

As the blood leaves the left ventricle through the aorta, it influences specialized cells in the arch of the aorta called **baroreceptors** (pressure receptors). Similar cells are located in the carotid arteries and deliver blood to the brain. If there is sufficient pressure in these vessels, the baroreceptors are stimulated, sending that information to the brain. If the pressure falls, the stimulation of the baroreceptors falls off. That information is also sent up to the brain.

The sensory input from the baroreceptors is received in the medulla, in an area called the **cardiovascular center** or vasomotor center. If the pressure is high, the medulla will stimulate vasodilation and a decrease in cardiac rate and output, and the pressure in the system will drop. If the pressure is low, the medulla will directly stimulate an increase in cardiac rate and output and vasoconstriction; this will increase total peripheral resistance and raise blood pressure. The medulla mediates these effects through the autonomic nervous system (see Chapter 27).

The baroreceptor reflex functions continually to maintain blood pressure within a predetermined range of normal. For example, if you have been lying down flat and suddenly stand up, the blood will rush to your feet (an effect of gravity). You may even feel light-headed or dizzy for a short period of time. When you stand and the blood flow drops, the baroreceptors are not stretched. The medulla senses this drop in stimulation of the baroreceptors and stimulates a rise in heart rate and cardiac output and a generalized vasoconstriction, which increases total peripheral resistance and blood pressure. These increases should raise pressure in the system, which will restore blood flow to the brain and stimulate the baroreceptors. The stimulation of the baroreceptors will lead to a decrease in stimulatory impulses from the medulla, and the blood pressure will fall back within normal limits (Figure 41-1).

Renin–Angiotensin System

Another compensatory system will kick in when the blood pressure in the kidneys falls. Because the kidneys require a constant perfusion to function properly, they have a compensatory mechanism to help ensure that blood flow is maintained. This mechanism is called the ***renin–angiotensin system***. (It is also sometimes referred to as the renin-angiotensin-aldosterone system.)

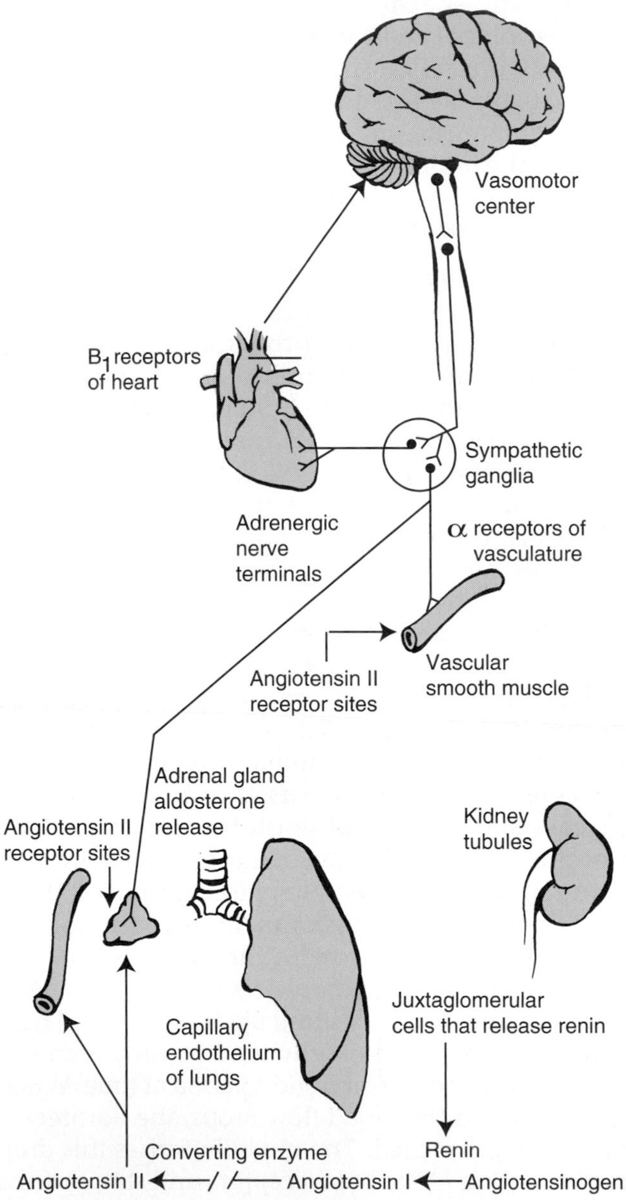

FIGURE 41-1. Control of blood pressure. The vasomotor center in the medulla responds to stimuli from aortic and carotid baroreceptors to cause sympathetic stimulation. The kidneys release renin to activate the renin-angiotensin system, causing vasoconstriction and increased blood volume.

Low blood pressure or poor oxygenation of a nephron causes the release of renin from the juxtaglomerular cells, a group of cells monitoring blood pressure and flow into the glomerulus. Renin is released into the blood stream and arrives in the liver to convert the compound angiotensinogen (produced in the liver) to angiotensin I. Angiotensin I travels in the bloodstream to the lungs, where the metabolic cells of the alveoli convert it, using angiotensin-converting enzyme, to angiotensin II. Angiotensin II reacts with specific angiotensin II receptor sites on blood vessels to cause intense vasoconstriction. This effect will raise the total peripheral resistance and raise the blood pressure, restoring blood flow to the kidneys and decreasing the release of renin.

Angiotensin II, most likely after conversion to angiotensin III, also stimulates the adrenal cortex to release aldosterone. Aldosterone acts on the nephrons to cause the retention of sodium and water. This effect will increase blood volume, which should also contribute to increasing blood pressure. The sodium-rich blood will stimulate the osmoreceptors in the hypothalamus to cause the release of antidiuretic hormone (ADH), which will cause the retention of water in the nephrons, further increasing the blood volume. This increase in blood volume will increase blood pressure, which should increase blood flow to the kidneys. This should lead to a decrease in the release of renin, thus causing the compensatory mechanisms to stop (Figure 41-2).

Hypertension

When a person's blood pressure is above normal limits for a sustained period of time, a diagnosis of hypertension is made (Box 41-1). It is estimated that at least 20% of the people in the United States have hypertension, many of whom are not even aware of it. Ninety percent of the people with hypertension have what is called *essential hypertension,* or hypertension with no known underlying cause. People with essential hypertension usually have an elevated total peripheral resistance. Their organs are being perfused effectively, and they usually display no symptoms. A few people develop secondary hypertension, or high blood pressure resulting from a known cause. For instance, a tumor in the adrenal medulla, called a pheochromocytoma, can cause hypertension that is resolved when the tumor is removed.

The underlying danger of hypertension of any type is the prolonged force on the vessels of the vascular system. The muscles in the arterial system eventually become thickened, leading to a loss of responsiveness in the system. The left ventricle will thicken

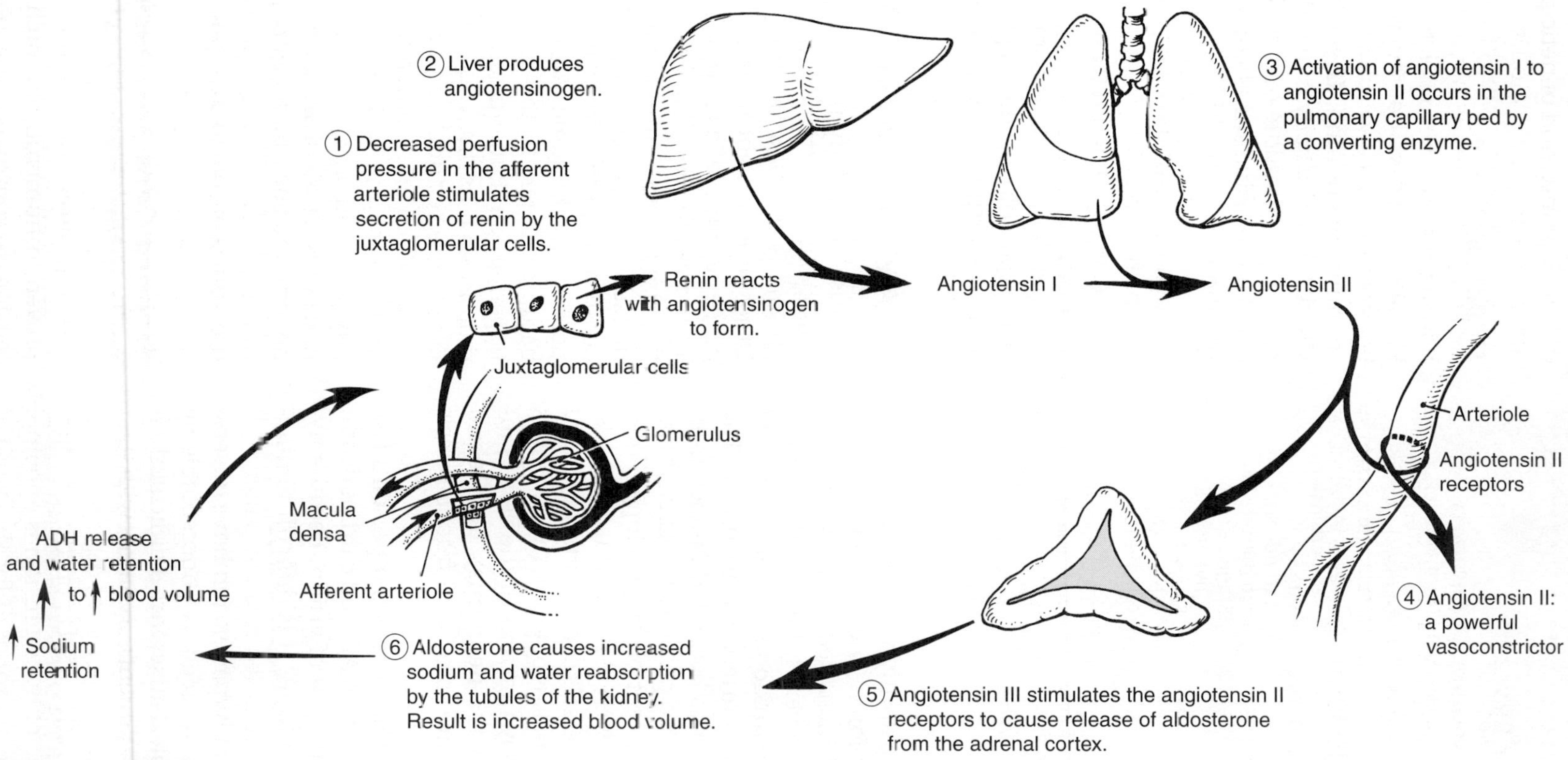

2 Liver produces angiotensinogen.
1 Decreased perfusion pressure in the afferent arteriole stimulates secretion of renin by the juxtaglomerular cells.
3 Activation of angiotensin I to angiotensin II occurs in the pulmonary capillary bed by a converting enzyme.
Renin reacts with angiotensinogen to form.
Angiotensin I
Angiotensin II
Juxtaglomerular cells
Glomerulus
Arteriole
Angiotensin II receptors
Macula densa
ADH release and water retention
to ↑ blood volume
↑ Sodium retention
Afferent arteriole
4 Angiotensin II: a powerful vasoconstrictor
6 Aldosterone causes increased sodium and water reabsorption by the tubules of the kidney. Result is increased blood volume.
5 Angiotensin III stimulates the angiotensin II receptors to cause release of aldosterone from the adrenal cortex.

FIGURE 41-2. The renin-angiotensin system.

BOX 41-1

CATEGORIES RATING THE SEVERITY OF HYPERTENSION

BP Range		
Systolic Pressure	*Diastolic Pressure*	**Category**
<130 mm Hg	<85 mm Hg	Normal blood pressure
130–139	85–89	High normal blood pressure
140–159	90–99	Stage 1 (mild) hypertension
160–179	100–109	Stage 2 (moderate) hypertension
180–209	110–119	Stage 3 (severe) hypertension
≥210	≥120	Stage 4 (very severe) hypertension

Risk of developing complications increases as category severity increases. When systolic and diastolic pressure are noted to be in different categories, the person's blood pressure category is identified at the higher level.

as the muscle must constantly work hard to pump blood out at a greater force. The thickening of the heart muscle and the increased pressure that the muscle has to generate every time that it contracts leads to an increased workload on the heart and increased risk of coronary artery disease (CAD). The inner linings of the arteries become damaged from the force of the blood being propelled against them, making these vessels susceptible to developing atherosclerosis and a narrowing of the lumen of the vessels (Chapter 44). Tiny vessels can become damaged and destroyed, leading to loss of vision (if the vessels are in the retina), kidney function (if the vessels include the glomeruli in the nephrons), or cerebral function (if the vessels are small and fragile vessels in the brain).

Untreated hypertension increases a person's risk for the following conditions: CAD and cardiac death, stroke, renal failure, and loss of vision. Because hypertension has no symptoms, it is difficult to diagnose and treat; it is often called a "silent killer." All of the drugs used to treat hypertension have adverse effects, many of which are seen as unacceptable by otherwise healthy people. Nurses face a difficult challenge trying to convince patients to comply with their drug regimens when they experience adverse effects and do not see any positive effects on their bodies. Research into the cause of hypertension is ongoing. Many theories have been proposed for the cause of the disorder, and it may well be a mosaic of many contributing factors leading to the problem. Factors that have been shown to increase blood pressure in some people include high levels of psychological stress, exposure to high-frequency noises, high-salt diet, lack of rest, and genetic predisposition.

Hypotension

If blood pressure becomes too low, the vital centers in the brain as well as the rest of the tissues of the body may not receive sufficient oxygenated blood to continue functioning. ***Hypotension*** can progress to ***shock,*** when the body is in serious jeopardy as waste products accumulate and cells die from lack of oxygen. Hypotensive states can occur in the following situations:

- When the heart muscle is damaged and unable to pump effectively
- With severe blood loss, where volume drops dramatically
- When there is extreme stress and the body's levels of norepinephrine are depleted, leaving the body unable to respond to stimuli to raise blood pressure

ANTIHYPERTENSIVE AGENTS

Because an underlying cause of hypertension is not usually known, altering the body's regulatory mechanisms is the best treatment currently available. Drugs used to treat hypertension work to alter one of the normal reflexes that control blood pressure. Treatment for essential hypertension does not cure the disease but is aimed at maintaining the blood pressure within normal limits to prevent the damage that hypertension can cause. All patients will not respond the same way to antihypertensive drugs because different factors may be contributing to their hypertension. Patients may have complicating conditions, such as diabetes or acute MI, making it unwise to use certain drugs. Several different types of drugs, which affect different areas of blood pressure control, may need to be used in combination to actually maintain a patient's blood pressure within normal limits. Trials of drugs and combinations of drugs are often needed to develop an individual regimen that is effective yet does not have adverse effects that are unacceptable to the patient.

Stepped Care Approach to Treating Hypertension

The importance of treating hypertension has been proven in numerous research studies. When hypertension is controlled, the patient's risk of cardiovascular death and disease is reduced. The risk of developing cardiovascular complications is directly

NURSING CHALLENGE

"White Coat" Hypertension

The diagnosis of hypertension is accompanied by the impact of serious ramifications, such as increased risk for numerous diseases and cardiovascular death, the potential need for significant lifestyle changes, and the potential need for drug therapy, which may include many unpleasant adverse effects. Consequently, it is important that a patient is properly diagnosed before being labeled hypertensive.

Researchers in the 1990s discovered that some patients were hypertensive only when they were in their doctor's office having their blood pressure taken. This was correlated to a sympathetic stress reaction (which elevates systolic blood pressure) and a tendency to tighten the muscles (isometric exercise, which elevates diastolic blood pressure) while waiting to be seen and during the blood pressure measurement. The researchers labeled this "white coat hypertension."

The American Heart Association has put forth new guidelines for the diagnosis of hypertension. A patient should have three consecutive blood pressure readings above normal, when taken by a nurse, over a period of 2 to 3 weeks. (It was assumed that nurses were not as threatening or stress provoking as doctors.) These guidelines point out the importance of using the correct technique when taking a patient's blood pressure, especially when the results can have such a tremendous impact on a patient. It is good practice to periodically review the process for performing this routine task. For example, the nurse should:

- Select a cuff that is the correct size for the patient's arm (a cuff that is too small may give a high reading; a cuff that is too large may give a lower reading).
- Try to put the patient at ease; remember that waiting alone in a cold room can be stressful to the body and mind and increase blood pressure.
- Ensure that the arm that will be used for the cuff is supported.
- Make sure the rest of the patient's muscles are not tensed up while the blood pressure is being taken.
- Place both the cuff and the stethoscope directly on the patient instead of on clothing.
- Listen carefully and record the first sound heard, the muffling of sounds, and the absence of sound (the actual diastolic pressure is thought to be between these two sounds).

Blood pressure machines found in grocery stores and pharmacies often give higher readings than the actual blood pressure, so the patient should not be encouraged to use these for follow-up readings. The American Heart Association offers many good guidelines for accurate blood pressure measurement. Nurses are often the health care providers most likely to be taking and recording patient blood pressure, so it is important to always use proper technique and record accurately.

related to the patient's degree of hypertension (see Box 41-1). Lowering the degree of hypertension lowers the risk.

The Joint National Committee on Detection, Evaluation and Treatment of Hypertension, from the National Institutes of Health, has established a stepped care approach to treating hypertension that has proved effective in national studies (Box 41-2). There are four steps involved:

Step 1: Lifestyle modifications are instituted. These include weight reduction, smoking cessation, reduction in the use of alcohol and salt in the diet (all of which have been shown to increase blood pressure), and an increase in physical exercise (which has been shown to decrease blood pressure and improve cardiovascular tone and reserve).

Step 2: If the measures in Step 1 are not sufficient to lower the blood pressure to an acceptable level, drug therapy is added. The drug of choice may be a diuretic, which decreases serum sodium levels and blood volume; a beta blocker, which leads to a decrease in heart rate and strength of contraction as well as vasodilation; an ***ACE inhibitor,*** which blocks the conversion of angiotensin I to II; a calcium channel blocker, which relaxes muscle contraction; or other autonomic blockers.

Step 3: If the patient's response to Step 2 is inadequate, the drug dose or class may be changed or another drug may be added for a combined effect.

Step 4: This step includes all of the above measures with the addition of more antihypertensive agents until the desired level of blood pressure control is achieved.

Hypertensive treatment is further complicated by the presence of other chronic conditions. The Joint National Committee on Prevention, Detection, Evaluation and Treatment of High Blood Pressure published an algorithm for the treatment of hypertension to help prescribers select an antihypertensive agent in light of complicating conditions (Figure 41-3). The actual patient's response to an antihypertensive is

BOX 41-2 STEPPED CARE MANAGEMENT OF HYPERTENSION FROM THE JOINT NATIONAL COMMITTEE ON DETECTION, EVALUATION AND TREATMENT OF HYPERTENSION

Step 1: Lifestyle Modifications
- Weight reduction
- Reduction of sodium intake
- Moderation of alcohol intake
- Smoking cessation
- Physical activity increase

Step 2: Inadequate response
- Continue lifestyle modifications
- Initial drug selection:
  1. Diuretic or beta blocker
  2. ACE inhibitor, calcium channel blocker, alpha blocker, alpha/beta blocker

Step 3: Inadequate response
1. Increase drug dose, or
2. Substitute another drug, or
3. Add a second drug from another class

Step 4: Inadequate response
Add a second or third agent or diuretic if not already prescribed

very individual, so the drug of choice for one patient may have little to no effect on another patient.

Diuretics

Diuretics are drugs that increase the excretion of sodium and water from the kidney (see Chapter 49) (Figure 41-4). These drugs are often the first agents tried in mild hypertension and affect blood sodium levels and blood volume. Although these drugs cause increased urination and can cause electrolyte and acid–base disturbances, they are usually tolerated well by most patients (Table 41-1).

Sympathetic Nervous System Blockers

Drugs that block the effects of the sympathetic nervous system (see Chapter 29) are useful in blocking many of the compensatory effects of the sympathetic nervous system (see Figure 41-4).

- Beta blockers block vasoconstriction, increased heart rate, and increased cardiac muscle contraction and tend to increase blood flow to the kidney, leading to a decrease in the release of renin. These drugs have many adverse effects and are not recommended for all people. They are often used as monotherapy in step 2 treatment and in some patients will control blood pressure adequately.
- Alpha and beta blockers are useful in conjunction with other agents and tend to be somewhat more powerful, blocking all of the receptors in the sympathetic system. Patients often complain of fatigue, loss of libido, inability to sleep, and gastrointestinal (GI) and genitourinary disturbances, and may not be willing to continue taking these drugs.
- Alpha adrenergic blockers inhibit the postsynaptic $alpha_1$ adrenergic receptors, decreasing sympathetic tone in the vasculature and causing vasodilation, leading to a lowering of blood pressure. However, these drugs also block presynaptic $alpha_2$ receptors, preventing the feedback control of norepinephrine release. The result is an increase in the reflex tachycardia that occurs when blood pressure is lowered. These drugs are used to diagnose and manage episodes of pheochromocytoma but have limited usefulness in essential hypertension because of the associated adverse effects.
- $Alpha_1$ blockers are used to treat hypertension because of their ability to block the postsynaptic $alpha_1$ receptor sites. This causes a decrease in vascular tone and a vasodilation that leads to a fall in blood pressure. These drugs do not block the presynaptic $alpha_2$ receptor sites and therefore the reflex tachycardia that accompanies a fall in blood pressure does not occur.
- $Alpha_2$ agonists stimulate the $alpha_2$ receptors in the central nervous system (CNS) and inhibit the cardiovascular centers, leading to a decrease in sympathetic outflow from the CNS and a resultant drop in blood pressure. These drugs are associated with many adverse CNS and GI effects as well as cardiac arrhythmias (see Table 41-1).

ANGIOTENSIN-CONVERTING ENZYME INHIBITORS

The angiotensin-converting enzyme (ACE) inhibitors block the conversion of angiotensin I to angiotensin II in the lungs (see Figure 41-4). This stops that phase of the renin–angiotensin system before vasoconstriction or aldosterone release can occur. The ACE inhibitors are used as monotherapy in step 2 of hypertension management or may be combined with diuretics. ACE inhibitors that are used include the following:

- Benazepril (*Lotensin*), a frequently used oral drug, is only approved for use in treating hypertension; it is usually well tolerated but has been associated with an unrelenting cough.
- Captopril (*Capoten*) is indicated for use in hypertension, in treating congestive heart failure (CHF), diabetic nephropathy, and left ventricular dysfunction following myocardial infarction (MI); it has been associated with a sometimes fatal pancytopenia, cough, and unpleasant GI distress.

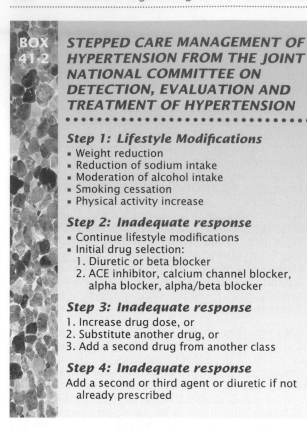

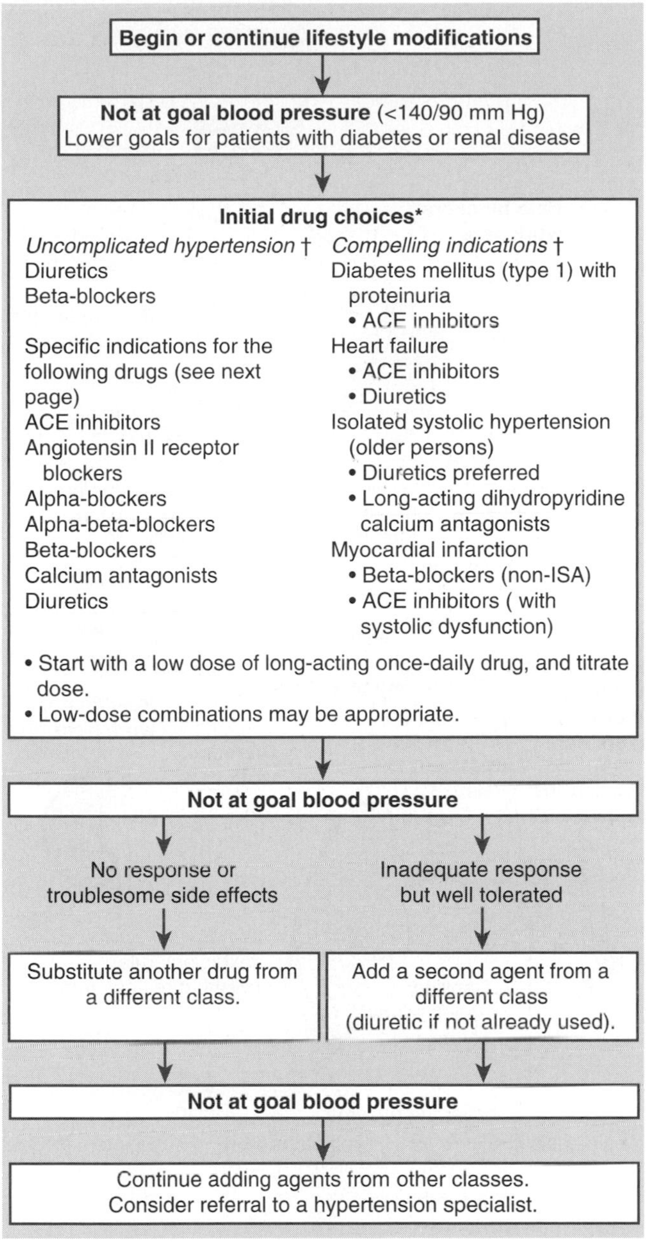

Begin or continue lifestyle modifications
Not at goal blood pressure (<140/90 mm Hg)
Lower goals for patients with diabetes or renal disease
Initial drug choices*
Uncomplicated hypertension †
Diuretics
Beta-blockers
Specific indications for the following drugs (see next page)
ACE inhibitors
Angiotensin II receptor blockers
Alpha-blockers
Alpha-beta-blockers
Beta-blockers
Calcium antagonists
Diuretics
Compelling indications †
Diabetes mellitus (type 1) with proteinuria
• ACE inhibitors
Heart failure
• ACE inhibitors
• Diuretics
Isolated systolic hypertension (older persons)
• Diuretics preferred
• Long-acting dihydropyridine calcium antagonists
Myocardial infarction
• Beta-blockers (non-ISA)
• ACE inhibitors (with systolic dysfunction)
• Start with a low dose of long-acting once-daily drug, and titrate dose.
• Low-dose combinations may be appropriate.
Not at goal blood pressure
No response or troublesome side effects
Inadequate response but well tolerated
Substitute another drug from a different class.
Add a second agent from a different class (diuretic if not already used).
Not at goal blood pressure
Continue adding agents from other classes.
Consider referral to a hypertension specialist.

Considerations for individualizing antihypertensive drug therapy*

Indication	Drug Therapy
Compelling indications unless contraindicated	
Diabetes mellitus (type 1) with proteinuria	ACE I
Heart failure	ACE I, diuretics
Isolated systolic hypertension (older patients)	Diuretics (preferred), CA (long-acting DHP)
Myocardial infarction	Beta-blockers (non-ISA), ACE I (with systolic dysfunction)
May have favorable effects on comorbid conditions†	
Angina	Beta-blockers, CA
Atrial tachycardia and fibrillation	Beta-blockers, CA (non-DHP)
Cyclosporine-induced hypertension (caution with the dose of cyclosporine)	CA
Diabetes mellitus (types 1 and 2) with proteinuria	ACE I (preferred), CA
Diabetes mellitus (type 2)	Low-dose diuretics
Dyslipidemia	Alpha-blockers
Essential tremor	Beta-blockers (non-CS)
Heart failure	Carvedilol, losartan potassium
Hyperthyroidism	Beta-blockers
Migraine	Beta-blockers (non-CS), CA (non-DHP)
Myocardial infarction	Diltiazem hydrochloride, verapamil hydrochloride
Osteoporosis	Thiazides
Preoperative hypertension	Beta-blockers
Prostatism (BPH)	Alpha-blockers
Renal insuffiency (caution in renovascular hypertension and creatinine ≥265.2 mmol/L [3 mg/dL])	ACE I
May have unfavorable effects on comorbid conditions†‡	
Bronchospastic disease	Beta-blockers§
Depression	Beta-blockers, central alpha-agonists, reserpine§
Diabetes mellitus (types 1 and 2)	Beta-blockers, high-dose diuretics
Dyslipidemia	Beta-blockers (non-ISA), diuretics (high dose)
Gout	Diuretics
2° to 3° heart block	Beta-blockers,§ CA (non-DHP)§
Heart failure	Beta-blockers (except carvedilol), CA (except amlodipine besylate, felodipine)
Liver disease	Labetalol hydrochloride, methyldopa§
Peripheral vascular disease	Beta-blockers
Pregnancy	ACE I,§ angiotensin II receptor blockers§
Renal insuffiency	Potassium-sparing agents
Renovascular disease	ACE I, angiotensin II receptor blockers

*For initial drug therapy recommendations, see preceding page. ACE I indicates angiotensin-converting enzyme inhibitors; BPH, benign prostatic hyperplasia; CA, calcium antagonists; DHP, dihydropyridine; ISA, intrinsic sympathomimetic activity; MI, myocardial infarction; and non-CS, noncardioselective.
†Conditions and drugs are listed in alphabetical order.
‡These drugs may be used with special monitoring unless contraindicated.
§Contraindicated.

FIGURE 41-3. Algorithm for the treatment of hypertension. (From the Sixth Report of the Joint National Committee on Prevention, Detection, Evaluation, and Treatment of High Blood Pressure. National Institutes of Health Publication No. 98-4080, November 1997.)

TABLE 41-1

OTHER DRUG CLASSES USED TO TREAT HYPERTENSION

DIURETICS (CHAPTER 49)

Thiazide and thiazide-like diuretics
bendroflumethiazide, benzthiazide, chlorothiazide, hydrochlorothiazide, hydroflumethiazide, methyclothiazide, polythiazide, trichlormethiazide, chlorthalidone, indapamide, metolazone, quinethazone

Loop diuretics
bumetanide, ethacrynic acid, furosemide torsemide

Carbonic anhydrase inhibitors
acetazolamide, methazolamide

Potassium sparing diuretics
amiloride, spironolactone, triamterene

SYMPATHETIC NERVOUS SYSTEM DRUGS (CHAPTER 29)

Beta blockers
acebutolol, atenolol, betaxolol, bisoprolol, carteolol, metoprolol, nadolol, penbutolol, pindolol, propranolol, timolol

Alpha and beta blockers
carvedilol, labetalol, guanabenz, guanadrel, guanethidine

Alpha adrenergic blockers
phenoxybenzamine, phentolamine

$Alpha_1$ blockers
doxazosin, prazosin, terazosin

$Alpha_2$ agonists
clonidine, guanfacine, methyldopa

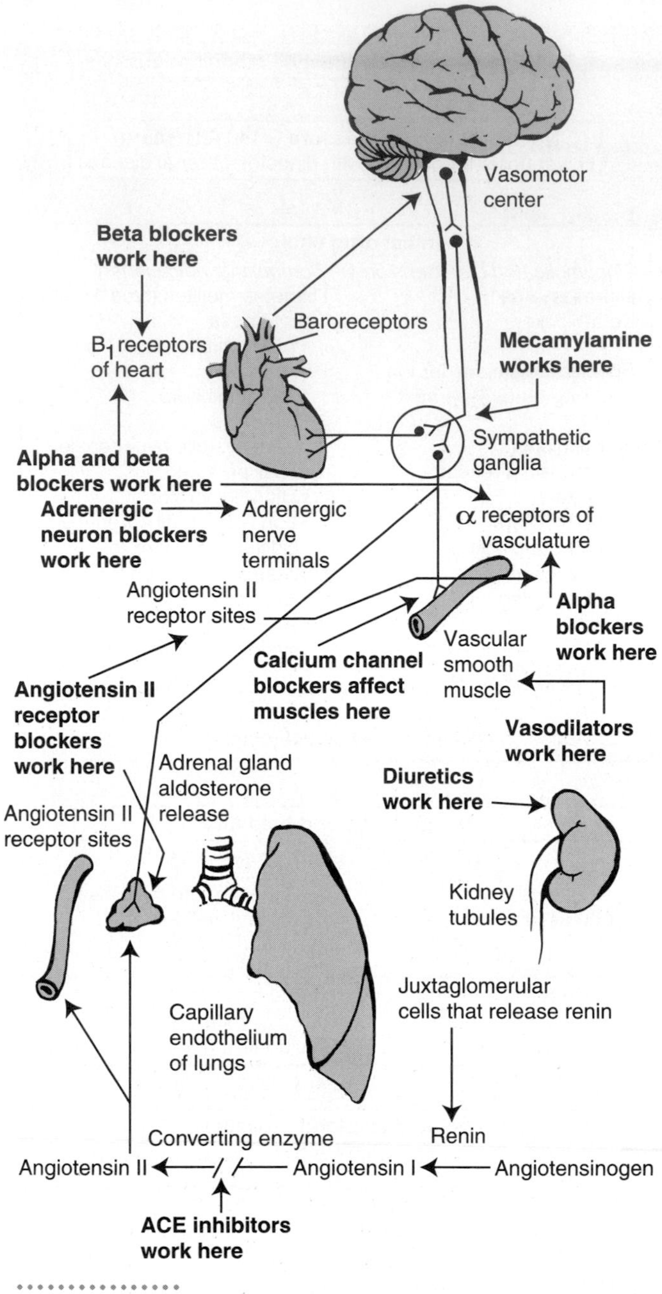

FIGURE 41-4. Sites of action of antihypertensive drugs.

• Enalapril (*Vasotec*), an oral drug, is used for the treatment of hypertension, CHF, and left ventricular dysfunction; it has the advantage of parenteral use (enalaprilat [*Vasotec IV*]) if oral use is not feasible or rapid onset is desirable.
• Fosinopril (*Monopril*) is a well-tolerated oral drug used for the treatment of hypertension and for adjunctive therapy in CHF; it is also associated with a cough.
• Lisinopril (*Prinvil, Zestril*) is an oral drug used in treating hypertension and CHF, and in the treatment of stable patients within 24 hours of acute MI to improve the likelihood of survival.
• Moexipril (*Univasc*) is a less well tolerated oral drug used in the treatment of hypertension; it is associated with many unpleasant GI and skin effects, cough, and cardiac arrhythmias. Sometimes fatal MI and pancytopenia have been associated with this drug.
• Quinapril (*Accupril*) is used orally for the treatment of hypertension and adjunct treatment of CHF; it is not associated with as many adverse effects as some of the other agents.
• Ramipril (*Altace*) is used orally for the treatment of hypertension and adjunct treatment of CHF; it is not associated with as many adverse effects as some of the other agents.
• Trandolapril (*Mavik*), used orally for the treatment of hypertension, is a fairly well tolerated drug.

THERAPEUTIC ACTIONS AND INDICATIONS

ACE inhibitors prevent angiotensin-converting enzyme from converting angiotensin I to angiotensin II, a powerful vasoconstrictor and stimulator of aldosterone release. This action leads to a decrease in blood pressure and in aldosterone secretion with a resultant slight increase in serum potassium and a loss of serum sodium and fluid. These drugs are indicated for the treatment of hypertension, alone or in combination with other drugs. They are also used

CULTURAL CONSIDERATIONS

Hypertension and Antihypertensive Therapy

In the United States, African Americans are at highest risk for developing hypertension, with males more likely than females to develop the disease. African Americans have documented differences in response to antihypertensive therapy. For example, they are:

- Most responsive to single drug therapy (as opposed to combination drug regimens)
- More responsive to diuretics, calcium channel blockers, and alpha adrenergic blockers
- Less responsive to ACE inhibitors and beta blockers

Increased adverse effects (depression, fatigue, drowsiness) often occur when using thiazide and thiazide-like diuretics, potentially requiring the use of different diuretics or lower doses of the thiazide diuretics.

Screening for hypertension among African Americans is very important to detect hypertension early and prevent the organ damage that occurs with prolonged hypertension. Because African Americans are more responsive to diuretics, the stepped care approach should include the first-line use of a diuretic in combination with diet and other lifestyle changes. The use of calcium channel blockers or alpha adrenergic blockers should follow.

in conjunction with digoxin and diuretics for the treatment of CHF and left ventricular dysfunction. Their therapeutic effect in these cases is thought to be related to a decrease in cardiac workload associated with the decrease in peripheral resistance and blood volume.

CONTRAINDICATIONS/CAUTIONS

ACE inhibitors are contraindicated in the presence of allergy to any of the ACE inhibitors; with impaired renal function, which could be exacerbated by the effects of this drug in decreasing renal blood flow; and with pregnancy because of the potential for adverse effects on the fetus. Caution should be used with CHF, because the change in hemodynamics could be detrimental in some cases; during lactation, because of potential decrease in milk production and effects on the neonate; and with salt/volume depletion, which could be exacerbated by the drug effects.

ADVERSE EFFECTS

The adverse effects most commonly associated with the ACE inhibitors are related to the effects of vasodilation and alterations in blood flow. Such effects include reflex tachycardia, chest pain, angina, CHF, and cardiac arrhythmias; GI irritation, ulcers, constipation, and liver injury; renal insufficiency, renal failure, proteinuria; and rash, alopecia, dermatitis, and photosensitivity. Many of these drugs cause an unrelenting cough, possibly related to effects in the lungs where the ACE is inhibited, which may lead to the patient discontinuing the drug. Some of these drugs have been associated with fatal pancytopenia and MI.

CLINICALLY IMPORTANT DRUG–DRUG INTERACTIONS

There is an increased risk of hypersensitivity reactions if these drugs are taken with allopurinol.

CLINICALLY IMPORTANT DRUG–FOOD INTERACTIONS

There is decreased absorption of oral ACE inhibitors if they are taken with food. They should be taken on an empty stomach, 1 hour before or 2 hours after meals.

DATA LINK

Data link to the following ACE inhibitors in your nursing drug guide:

ANGIOTENSIN CONVERTING ENZYME (ACE) INHIBITORS

Name	Brand Name(s)	Usual Indications
benazepril	*Lotensin*	Treatment of hypertension
P captopril	*Capoten*	Treatment of hypertension; adjunct therapy for CHF; treatment of left ventricular dysfunction following MI, diabetic nephropathy
enalapril enalaprilat	*Vasotec* *Vasotec IV*	Treatment of hypertension, CHF, left ventricular dysfunction
fosinopril	*Monopril*	Treatment of hypertension, CHF
lisinopril	*Prinvil, Zestril*	Treatment of hypertension, CHF; treatment of stable patients within 24 hours of acute MI to increase survival
moexipril	*Univasc*	Treatment of hypertension
quinapril	*Accupril*	Treatment of hypertension; adjunctive treatment of CHF
ramipril	*Altace*	Treatment of hypertension; adjunctive treatment of CHF
trandolapril	*Mavik*	Treatment of hypertension

NURSING CONSIDERATIONS
for patients receiving ACE inhibitors

Assessment

HISTORY. Screen for the following: any known allergies to these drugs; impaired kidney function, which could be exacerbated by these drugs; pregnancy and lactation because of the potential adverse effects on the fetus or neonate; salt/volume depletion, which could be exacerbated by these drugs; and CHF.

PHYSICAL ASSESSMENT. Include screening for baseline status before beginning therapy and for any potential adverse effects. Assess the following: body temperature, weight; skin color, lesions, temperature; pulse, blood pressure, baseline ECG, perfusion; respirations, adventitious breath sounds; bowel sounds, abdominal exam; and renal function tests, CBC with differential, and serum electrolytes.

Nursing Diagnoses

The patient receiving an ACE inhibitor may have the following nursing diagnoses related to drug therapy:

- Alteration in tissue perfusion related to changes in cardiac output
- Alteration in skin integrity related to dermatologic effects
- Pain related to GI distress, cough
- Knowledge deficit regarding drug therapy

Implementation

- Encourage the patient to implement lifestyle changes, including weight loss, smoking cessation, decrease in alcohol and salt in the diet, and increased exercise, *to increase the effectiveness of antihypertensive therapy.*
- Administer on an empty stomach, 1 hour before or 2 hours after meals *to ensure proper absorption of drug.*
- Alert the surgeon and mark the patient's chart prominently if the patient is to undergo surgery *to alert medical personnel that the blockage of compensatory angiotensin II could result in hypotension following surgery that will need to be reversed with volume expansion.*
- Give parenteral forms only if an oral form is not feasible; transfer to an oral form as soon as possible *to avert increased risk of adverse effects.*
- Consult with the prescriber to reduce dosage in patients with renal failure *to account for their decreased production of renin and lower-than-normal levels of angiotensin II.*
- Monitor the patient carefully in any situation that might lead to a drop in fluid volume (e. g, excessive sweating, vomiting, diarrhea, dehydration) *to detect and treat excessive hypotension that may occur.*
- Provide comfort measures *to help the patient tolerate drug effects.* These include small, frequent meals, access to bathroom facilities, bowel program as needed, environmental control, safety precautions, and appropriate skin care as needed.
- Provide thorough patient teaching, including the name of the drug, dosage prescribed, measures to avoid adverse effects, warning signs of problems, and the need for periodic monitoring and evaluation *to enhance patient knowledge about drug therapy and to promote compliance* (see Patient Teaching Checklist: ACE Inhibitors).
- Offer support and encouragement *to deal with diagnosis and drug regimen.*

Evaluation

- Monitor patient response to the drug (maintenance of blood pressure within normal limits).
- Monitor for adverse effects (hypotension, cardiac arrhythmias, renal dysfunction, skin reactions, cough, pancytopenia, CHF).
- Evaluate the effectiveness of the teaching plan (patient can name drug, dosage, adverse effects to watch for, specific measures to avoid adverse effects, importance of continued follow-up).
- Monitor the effectiveness of comfort measures and compliance to the regimen (see Nursing Care Guide: ACE Inhibitors).

ANGIOTENSIN II RECEPTOR BLOCKERS

The angiotensin II receptor blockers selectively bind the **angiotensin II receptors** in blood vessels and in the adrenal cortex to prevent the vasoconstriction and release of aldosterone that is caused by reaction of these receptors with angiotensin II. These actions will lead to a decrease in blood pressure caused by a decrease in total peripheral resistance and blood volume. The angiotensin II receptor blockers include the following:

- Candesartan (*Atacand*), which is used alone or as part of combination therapy to treat hypertension; it is contraindicated during the second and third trimesters of pregnancy because of associated fetal abnormalities.
- Irbesartan (*Avapro*), which is used as monotherapy in the treatment of hypertension; it also is contraindicated during the second and third trimesters of pregnancy because of associated fetal abnormalities and death.
- Losartan (*Cozaar*), which can be used alone or as part of combination therapy for hypertension; it should not be used at any time during pregnancy.
- Telmisartan (*Micardis*), which is used alone or as part of combination therapy to treat hypertension;

PATIENT TEACHING CHECKLIST

ACE Inhibitors

Create customized patient teaching materials for a specific ACE inhibitor from your CD-ROM. Your patient teaching should stress the following points for drugs within this class:

An ACE inhibitor is an antihypertensive drug that is used to treat high blood pressure. High blood pressure is a disorder that may have no symptoms but that can cause serious problems, such as heart attack, stroke, or kidney problems, if left untreated. It is very important to take your medication every day, as prescribed, even if you feel perfectly well without the medication. It is possible that you may feel worse because of the adverse effects associated with the medication when you take it. Even if this happens, it is crucial that you take your medication. If you find that the adverse effects of this drug are too uncomfortable, discuss the possibility of taking a different antihypertensive medication with your health care provider.

Common effects of these drugs include:

- Dizziness, drowsiness, lightheadedness—These effects often pass after the first few days. Until they do, avoid driving or performing hazardous or delicate tasks that require concentration. If these effects occur, change positions slowly to decrease the lightheadedness.
- Nausea, vomiting, change in taste perception—Small, frequent meals may help ease these effects, which may pass with time. If they persist and become too uncomfortable, consult with your health care provider.
- Skin rash, mouth sores—Frequent mouth care may help. Keep skin dry and use prescribed skin care (lotions, coverings, medication) if needed.
- Cough—Although this can be very irritating, do not try to treat the cough with over-the-counter medications. Consult with your health care provider if this occurs and persists.

Report any of the following to your health care provider; difficulty breathing; mouth sores; swelling of the feet, hands, or face; chest pain; palpitations; sore throat; fever or chills.

Do not stop taking this drug for any reason. Consult with your health care provider if you have problems taking this medication.

Tell any doctor, nurse, or other health care provider that you are taking this drug.

Keep this drug, and all medications, out of the reach of children.

Avoid the use of over-the-counter medications while you are on this drug. If you feel that you need one of these, consult with your health care provider for the best choice. Many of these drugs may interfere with the antihypertensive effect that usually occurs with this drug.

Be extremely careful in any situation that might lead to a drop in blood pressure (e.g., excessive sweating, vomiting, diarrhea, dehydration). If you experience lightheadedness or dizziness in any of these situations, consult your health care provider immediately.

This Teaching Checklist reflects general patient teaching guidelines. It is not meant to be a substitute for drug specific teaching information, which is available in nursing drug guides.

it is contraindicated during the second and third trimesters of pregnancy because of associated fetal abnormalities.

- Valsartan (*Diovan*), which can be used alone or as part of combination therapy for hypertension; it should not be used at any time during pregnancy.

THERAPEUTIC ACTIONS AND INDICATIONS

The angiotensin II receptor blockers selectively bind with angiotensin II receptor sites in vascular smooth muscle and in the adrenal gland to block vasoconstriction and the release of aldosterone. These actions will block the blood pressure–raising effects of the renin–angiotensin system and lower blood pressure. They are indicated to be used alone or in combination therapy for the treatment of hypertension.

CONTRAINDICATIONS/CAUTIONS

The angiotensin II receptor blockers are contraindicated in the presence of allergy to any of these drugs; during pregnancy because of associated fetal death and severe abnormalities; and during lactation because of potential adverse effects on the neonate. Caution should be used in the presence of hepatic or

NURSING CARE GUIDE

ACE Inhibitors

Assessment	Nursing Diagnoses	Implementation	Evaluation
HISTORY Allergies to any of these drugs, renal dysfunction, pregnancy, salt/volume depletion, sedation, sleep shock, CHF, hypotension	Alteration in tissue perfusion related to changes in cardiac output Alteration in skin integrity related to skin effects Pain related to GI effects, cough Knowledge deficit regarding drug therapy	Encourage lifestyle changes to increase drug effectiveness. Administer on an empty stomach. Provide comfort and safety measures: Reduce dosage in renal failure; Clearly mark chart before surgery; Use parenteral form only if PO not possible; Monitor for any situation that might lead to a drop in blood pressure. Provide support and reassurance to deal with drug effects. Provide patient teaching regarding drug, dosage, adverse effects, what to report, and safety precautions.	Evaluate drug effects: maintenance of blood pressure within normal limits. Monitor for adverse effects: sedation, dizziness; hypotension, CHF, arrhythmias; skin reactions; renal dysfunction; cough; pancytopenia. Monitor for drug–drug interactions as indicated for each drug. Evaluate effectiveness of patient teaching program. Evaluate effectiveness of comfort and safety measures.
PHYSICAL EXAMINATION CV: BP, P, perfusion, baseline ECG CNS: orientation, affect Skin: color, lesions, texture, temperature Resp: R, adventitious sounds GI: abdominal exam, bowel sounds Lab tests: renal function tests, CBC, electrolytes			

renal dysfunction, which could alter the metabolism and excretion of these drugs, and with hypovolemia because of the blocking of potentially life-saving compensatory mechanisms.

ADVERSE EFFECTS

The adverse effects most commonly associated with angiotensin II receptor blockers include the following: headache, dizziness, syncope, and weakness, which could be associated with drops in blood pressure; hypotension; GI complaints including diarrhea, abdominal pain, nausea, dry mouth, and tooth pain; symptoms of upper respiratory tract infections and cough; and rash, dry skin, and alopecia. In preclinical trials, these drugs have been associated with the development of cancers.

CLINICALLY IMPORTANT DRUG–DRUG INTERACTIONS

There is an increased risk of decreased serum levels and loss of effectiveness of the angiotensin II receptor blocker if taken in combination with phenobarbital. If this combination is used, the patient should be monitored closely and dosage adjustments made.

DATA LINK

Data link to the following angiotensin II receptor blockers in your nursing drug guide:

ANGIOTENSIN II RECEPTOR BLOCKERS

Name	Brand Name	Usual Indication
candesartan	*Atacand*	Alone or as part of combination therapy to treat hypertension
irbesartan	*Avapro*	Monotherapy in the treatment of hypertension
P losartan	*Cozaar*	Alone or as part of combination therapy to treat hypertension
telmisartan	*Micardis*	Alone or as part of combination therapy to treat hypertension
valsartan	*Diovan*	Alone or as part of combination therapy to treat hypertension

NURSING CONSIDERATIONS
for patients receiving angiotensin II receptor blockers

Assessment

HISTORY. Screen for the following: any known allergies to these drugs; impaired kidney or liver function, which could be exacerbated by these drugs; pregnancy and lactation because of the potential adverse effects on the fetus and neonate; and hypovolemia.

PHYSICAL ASSESSMENT. Include screening for baseline status before beginning therapy and for any potential adverse effects. Assess the following: body temperature, weight; skin color, lesions, temperature; pulse, blood pressure, baseline ECG, perfusion; respirations, adventitious breath sounds; bowel sounds, abdominal exam; and renal and liver function tests.

Nursing Diagnoses

The patient receiving an angiotensin II receptor blocker may have the following nursing diagnoses related to drug therapy:

- Alteration in tissue perfusion related to changes in cardiac output
- Alteration in skin integrity related to dermatologic effects
- Pain related to GI distress, cough, skin effects, headache
- Knowledge deficit regarding drug therapy

Implementation

- Encourage the patient to implement lifestyle changes, including weight loss, smoking cessation, decrease in alcohol and salt in the diet, and increased exercise, *to increase the effectiveness of antihypertensive therapy.*
- Administer without regard to meals; give with food *to decrease GI distress if needed.*
- Alert the surgeon and mark the patient's chart prominently if the patient is to undergo surgery *to notify medical personnel that the blockage of compensatory angiotensin II could result in hypotension following surgery that will need to be reversed with volume expansion.*
- Ensure that the patient is not pregnant before beginning therapy and suggest the use of barrier contraceptives while on this drug *to avert potential fetal death or abnormalities that have been associated with these drugs.*
- Find an alternative method of feeding the baby if the patient is nursing *to prevent the potentially dangerous block of the renin–angiotensin system in the neonate.*
- Monitor the patient carefully in any situation that might lead to a drop in fluid volume (e. g., excessive sweating, vomiting, diarrhea, dehydration) *to detect and treat excessive hypotension that may occur.*
- Provide comfort measures *to help the patient tolerate drug effects* (e. g., small, frequent meals; access to bathroom facilities; safety precautions if CNS effects occur; environmental control; appropriate skin care as needed; analgesics as needed).
- Provide thorough patient teaching, including the name of the drug, dosage prescribed, measures to avoid adverse effects, warning signs of problems, and the need for periodic monitoring and evaluation *to enhance patient knowledge about drug therapy and to promote compliance.*
- Offer support and encouragement *to deal with the diagnosis and drug regimen.*

Evaluation

- Monitor patient response to the drug (maintenance of blood pressure within normal limits).
- Monitor for adverse effects (hypotension, GI distress, skin reactions, cough, headache, dizziness).
- Evaluate the effectiveness of the teaching plan (patient can name drug, dosage, adverse effects to watch for, specific measures to avoid adverse effects, importance of continued follow-up).
- Monitor the effectiveness of comfort measures and compliance to the regimen.

CALCIUM CHANNEL BLOCKERS

The calcium channel blockers prevent the movement of calcium into the cardiac and smooth muscle cells when the cells are stimulated. This blocking of calcium will interfere with the muscle cell's ability to contract, leading to a loss of smooth muscle tone, vasodilation, and a decrease in peripheral resistance. These effects will decrease blood pressure, cardiac workload, and myocardial oxygen consumption. Calcium channel blockers are very effective in the treatment of angina (see Chapter 44) because they decrease the cardiac workload.

Not all calcium channel blockers are used to treat hypertension. Some of the calcium channel blockers are only considered safe and effective in treating hypertension if they are sustained-release or extended-release preparations. The calcium channel blockers that are used in the treatment of hypertension include the following:

- Amlodipine (*Norvasc*), an oral drug that may be used alone or in combination with other agents to treat hypertension and is used for angina.
- Diltiazem (*Cardizem, Tiamate*). A sustained release preparation only is recommended for the treatment of hypertension.
- Felodipine (*Plendil*), which is not used for angina but is indicated alone or in combination with other agents for the treatment of hypertension.
- Isradipine (*DynaCirc*), which is not used for angina but is indicated alone or in combination with thiazide diuretics for the treatment of hypertension.
- Nicardipine (*Cardene*), which is used alone or in combination with other agents to treat hypertension and angina; it is available in IV form for short-term use when oral administration is not feasible.
- Nifedipine (*Procardia XL*). A sustained release preparation only is indicated for the treatment of hypertension.
- Nisoldipine (*Sular*). Extended release tablets are indicated for the treatment of hypertension as monotherapy or as part of combination therapy.

THERAPEUTIC ACTIONS AND INDICATIONS

Calcium channel blockers inhibit the movement of calcium ions across the membranes of myocardial and arterial muscle cells, altering the action potential and blocking muscle cell contraction. This effect will depress myocardial contractility, slow cardiac impulse formation in the conductive tissues, and relax and dilate arteries, causing a fall in blood pressure and a decrease in venous return.

CONTRAINDICATIONS/CAUTIONS

These drugs are contraindicated in the presence of allergy to any of these drugs; with heart block or sick sinus syndrome because these could be exacerbated by the conduction-slowing effects of these drugs; with renal and hepatic dysfunction, which could alter the metabolism and excretion of these drugs; and with pregnancy and lactation because of the potential for adverse effects on the fetus and neonate.

ADVERSE EFFECTS

The adverse effects associated with these drugs are related to their effects on cardiac output and on smooth muscle. CNS effects include dizziness, lightheadedness, headache, and fatigue. GI problems can include nausea and hepatic injury related to direct toxic effects on hepatic cells. Cardiovascular effects include hypotension, bradycardia, peripheral edema, and heart block. Skin flushing and rash may also occur.

CLINICALLY IMPORTANT DRUG–DRUG INTERACTIONS

Drug–drug interactions vary with each of the calcium channel blockers used to treat hypertension. A potentially serious effect to keep in mind is an increase in serum levels and toxicity of cyclosporine if taken with diltiazem.

DATA LINK

Data link to the following calcium channel blockers in your nursing drug guide:

CALCIUM CHANNEL BLOCKERS USED IN HYPERTENSION

Name	Brand Name(s)	Usual Indications
amlodipine	*Norvasc*	Alone or in combination with other agents for the treatment of hypertension
P diltiazem	*Cardizem, Tiamate*	Extended release preparation used to treat hypertension
felodipine	*Plendil*	Alone or in combination with other agents for the treatment of hypertension
isradipine	*DynaCirc*	Alone or in combination with other agents for the treatment of hypertension
nicardipine	*Cardene*	Alone or in combination with other agents to treat hypertension and angina; IV form for short-term use when oral route is not feasible
nifedipine	*Procardia XL*	Sustained release preparation only is indicated for the treatment of hypertension
nisoldipine	*Sular*	Extended release tablets for the treatment of hypertension as monotherapy or part of combination therapy

NURSING CONSIDERATIONS
for patients receiving calcium channel blockers

The main use of calcium channel blockers is the treatment of angina. See Chapter 44 for the nursing considerations of calcium channel blockers.

VASODILATORS

When other drug therapies do not achieve the desired reduction in blood pressure, it is sometimes necessary to use a direct vasodilator. Vasodilators produce relaxation of the vascular smooth muscle, decreasing peripheral resistance and reducing blood pressure. They do not block the reflex tachycardia that will occur when blood pressure drops. Most of the vasodilators are reserved for use in severe hypertension or hypertensive emergencies. The vasodilators that might be used to treat severe hypertension include the following:

- Diazoxide (*Hyperstat*), which is used as an IV drug in hospitalized patients with severe hypertension; this drug also increases blood glucose levels by blocking insulin release, so it must be used with extreme caution with functional hypoglycemia.
- Hydralazine (*Apresoline*), which is available for oral and IV or IM use for the treatment of severe hypertension; it is thought to maintain or increase renal blood flow while relaxing smooth muscle.
- Minoxidil (*Loniten*), which is an oral agent used only for the treatment of severe and unresponsive hypertension; it is associated with reflex tachycardia and increased renin release leading to volume increase. (The oral drug is associated with changes in body hair growth and distribution, which led to a topical preparation [*Rogaine*] for the treatment of baldness.)
- Nitroprusside (*Nitropress*), which is used IV for the treatment of hypertensive crisis and to maintain controlled hypotension during surgery; toxic levels cause cyanide toxicity.
- Tolazoline (*Priscoline*), which is only used IV to treat persistent pulmonary hypertension of the newborn; it increases cardiac output and GI activity.

THERAPEUTIC ACTIONS AND INDICATIONS

The vasodilators act directly on vascular smooth muscle to cause muscle relaxation, leading to vasodilation and drop in blood pressure. They are indicated for the treatment of severe hypertension that has not responded to other therapy.

CONTRAINDICATIONS/CAUTIONS

The vasodilators are contraindicated in the presence of known allergy to the drug; with pregnancy and lactation because of the potential for adverse effects on the fetus and neonate; and with any condition that could be exacerbated by a sudden fall in blood pressure, such as cerebral insufficiency. Caution should be used with peripheral vascular disease, CAD, CHF, or tachycardia, all of which could be exacerbated by the fall in blood pressure.

ADVERSE EFFECTS

The adverse effects most frequently seen with these drugs are related to the changes in blood pressure. These include dizziness, anxiety, headache; reflex tachycardia, CHF, chest pain, edema; skin rash, lesions (abnormal hair growth with minoxidil); and GI upset, nausea, and vomiting. Cyanide toxicity (dyspnea, headache, vomiting, dizziness, ataxia, loss of consciousness, imperceptible pulse, absent reflexes, dilated pupils, pink color, distant heart sounds, shallow breathing) may occur with nitroprusside, which is metabolized to cyanide and which also suppresses iodine uptake and can cause hypothyroidism.

CLINICALLY IMPORTANT DRUG–DRUG INTERACTIONS

Each of these drugs works differently in the body, so each drug should be checked for potential drug–drug interactions before use.

DATA LINK

Data link to the following vasodilators in your nursing drug guide:

VASODILATORS

Name	Brand Name	Usual Indication
diazoxide	*Hyperstat*	IV use for the treatment of severe hypertension in hospitalized patients
hydralazine	*Apresoline*	Treatment of severe hypertension
minoxidil	*Loniten*	Treatment of severe hypertension unresponsive to other therapy
P nitroprusside	*Nitropress*	IV use for the treatment of hypertensive crisis; to maintain controlled hypotension during surgery
tolazoline	*Priscoline*	Treatment of persistent pulmonary hypertension of the newborn

NURSING CONSIDERATIONS
for patients receiving vasodilators

Assessment

HISTORY. Screen for the following: any known allergies to these drugs; impaired kidney or liver function; pregnancy and lactation because of the potential adverse effects on the fetus and neonate; and cardiovascular dysfunction, which could be exacerbated by a fall in blood pressure.

PHYSICAL ASSESSMENT. Include screening for baseline status before beginning therapy and for any potential adverse effects. Assess the following: body temperature, weight; skin color, lesions, temperature; pulse, blood pressure, baseline ECG, perfusion; respirations, adventitious breath sounds; bowel sounds, abdominal exam; renal and liver function tests; and blood glucose.

Nursing Diagnoses

The patient receiving a vasodilator may have the following nursing diagnoses related to drug therapy:

- Alteration in tissue perfusion related to changes in cardiac output
- Alteration in skin integrity related to dermatologic effects
- Pain related to GI distress, skin effects, headache

Knowledge deficit regarding drug therapy

Implementation

- Encourage the patient to implement lifestyle changes, including weight loss, smoking cessation, decrease in alcohol and salt in the diet, and increased exercise, *to increase the effectiveness of antihypertensive therapy.*
- Monitor blood pressure closely during administration *to evaluate for effectiveness and to ensure quick response if blood pressure falls rapidly or too much.*
- Monitor blood glucose and serum electrolytes *to avoid potentially serious adverse effects.*
- Monitor the patient carefully in any situation that might lead to a drop in fluid volume (e.g., excessive sweating, vomiting, diarrhea, dehydration) *to detect and treat excessive hypotension that may occur.*
- Provide comfort measures *to help the patient tolerate drug effects* (e.g., small, frequent meals, access to bathroom facilities, safety precautions if CNS effects occur, environmental control, appropriate skin care as needed, analgesics as needed).
- Provide thorough patient teaching, including the name of the drug, dosage prescribed, measures to avoid adverse effects, warning signs of problems, and the need for periodic monitoring and evaluation *to enhance patient knowledge about drug therapy and to promote compliance.*
- Offer support and encouragement *to deal with the diagnosis and drug regimen.*

Evaluation

- Monitor patient response to the drug (maintenance of blood pressure within normal limits).
- Monitor for adverse effects (hypotension, GI distress, skin reactions, tachycardia, headache, dizziness).
- Evaluate the effectiveness of the teaching plan (patient can name drug, dosage, adverse effects to watch for, specific measures to avoid adverse effects, importance of continued follow-up).
- Monitor the effectiveness of comfort measures and compliance to the regimen.

OTHER ANTIHYPERTENSIVE AGENT

One other drug that has proven useful in the treatment of severe hypertension is mecamylamine (*Inversine*). Mecamylamine is a ganglionic blocker that occupies cholinergic receptor sites of autonomic neurons, blocking the effects of acetylcholine at both the sympathetic and parasympathetic ganglia. It decreases the effectiveness of both of these branches of the autonomic system. Blocking the sympathetic system leads to vasodilation, decreased blood pressure, and a blocking of reflex tachycardia as well as the release of catecholamines from the adrenal gland. It can cause severe hypotension, CHF, and CNS symptoms of dizziness, syncope, weakness, and vision changes; parasympathetic blocking symptoms of dry mouth, glossitis, nausea, vomiting, constipation, and urinary retention; and impotence. It is reserved for use in severe or malignant hypertension when other drugs are not successful. The patient receiving this drug must be monitored very closely because of the loss of autonomic reflexes.

WWW.WEB LINKS

Health care providers and patients may want to consult the following Internet sources:

Information on research, alternative methods of therapy, pharmacology from the National Heart, Lung and Blood Institute:

http://www.heartinfo.org/news98/jnvi42398.htm

Patient information on hypertension, treatments, lifestyle adjustments:

http://www.jhbmc/jhu.edu/cardiology/rehab/hypertension.html

Patient information, support groups, diet, exercise, research information on hypertension and other cardiovascular diseases:

http://www.amhrt.org

Specific information on the care of the pediatric hypertensive patient:

http://www.medscape.com/jobson/MedTrib/familyphys/1996/v37.n20/ChildhoodHypertensionGuide.html

ANTIHYPOTENSIVE AGENTS

As mentioned earlier, if blood pressure becomes too low (hypotension) the vital centers in the brain and the rest of the tissues of the body may not receive sufficient oxygenated blood to continue functioning.

CASE STUDY

Initiating Antihypertensive Therapy

PRESENTATION

B. R., a 46-year-old African-American male business executive, was seen for a routine insurance physical. His examination was negative except for a blood pressure of 164/102. He also was approximately 20 pounds overweight. Urinalysis and blood work all came back within normal limits. He was given a 1200-calorie-per-day diet to follow and was encouraged to cut down on salt and alcohol intake, start exercising, and stop smoking. He was asked to return in 3 weeks for a follow-up appointment (step 1). Three weeks later, B. R. returned with a 7-pound weight loss and an average blood pressure reading (of three) of 145/92. Discussion was held about starting B. R. on a diuretic (step 2) in addition to the lifestyle changes that B. R. was undertaking. B. R. was reluctant to take a diuretic and asked to be given more time to bring his pressure to a normal range without drug therapy.

CRITICAL THINKING QUESTIONS

What nursing interventions should be done at this point? Consider the risk factors that B. R. has for hypertension and the damage that hypertension can cause. What are the chances that B. R. can bring his blood pressure within a normal range? What additional teaching points should be covered with B. R. before a treatment decision is made? What implications does the diagnosis of hypertension have for B. R.'s insurance and job security? What effects could diuretic therapy have on B. R.'s busy business day?

DISCUSSION

B. R. was asked to change many things in his life over the last 3 weeks. These changes themselves can be stressful and can increase a person's blood pressure. B. R.'s reluctance to take a diuretic is understandable for a business executive who might not want his day interrupted by many bathroom stops. African Americans often show a good response to diuretic therapy and a return to normal blood pressure, but they also tend to have more adverse CNS effects to the most commonly used diuretics, the thiazides. This may have an impact on B. R.'s business and home life. B. R. should receive a complete teaching program outlining what is known about hypertension and all of the risk factors involved with the disease. The good effects of weight loss, exercise, and the other lifestyle changes should be stressed, and B. R. should be praised for his success over the last 3 weeks.

B. R. may benefit from trying for a couple more weeks to make lifestyle changes that will help bring his blood pressure into normal range. He will then feel that he has some control and input into the situation, so if drug therapy is needed, he may be more willing to comply with the prescribed treatment. The diagnosis of hypertension may be delayed for these 2 weeks while B. R. changes his lifestyle. Such a diagnosis should be made only after three consecutive blood pressure readings in the high range are recorded. B. R. may be able to have his blood pressure checked at work in a comfortable environment, which will improve the accuracy of the reading.

Many insurance companies, and some employers, will see hypertension as an increased risk. This could have a tremendous impact on B. R.'s ability to get health and life insurance, and even on any future promotions or job changes. Being a business executive, B. R. may be well aware of these possibilities—another reason to give him a little more time. He may wish to look into biofeedback for relaxation, a fitness program, smoking cessation programs (if appropriate), and stress reduction. As long as B. R. receives regular follow-up and frequent blood pressure checks, it may be a good idea to allow him to take some control and continue lifestyle changes. If at the end of the 2 weeks no further progress has been made or B. R.'s blood pressure has gone up, drug therapy will need to be considered. Teaching should be aimed at helping B. R. to incorporate the drug effects into his lifestyle, to improve his compliance and tolerance of the therapy.

Severe hypotension or shock puts the body in serious jeopardy; it is often an acute emergency situation to treat the shock to save the patient's life. The first choice drug for treating shock is usually a sympathomimetic drug.

Sympathetic Adrenergic Agonists

Sympathomimetic drugs react with sympathetic adrenergic receptors to cause the effects of a sympathetic stress response: increased blood pressure, increased blood volume, and increased strength of cardiac muscle contraction. These actions will increase blood pressure and may restore balance to the cardiovascular system while the underlying cause of the shock (volume depletion, blood loss, and so forth) is treated. The sympathomimetic drugs are discussed in Chapter 28. Table 41-2 lists the sympathomimetics used in the treatment of severe hypotension and shock.

Midodrine

Midodrine (*ProAmatine*) is a drug that is used for the treatment of orthostatic hypotension—hypotension that occurs with position change—that interferes

TABLE 41-2

DRUGS USED TO TREAT SEVERE HYPOTENSION AND SHOCK STATES

SYMPATHOMIMETIC DRUGS (CHAPTER 28)

dobutamine, dopamine, ephedrine, epinephrine, isoproterenol, metaraminol

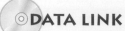

with a person's ability to function and has not responded to any other therapy.

THERAPEUTIC ACTIONS AND INDICATIONS

Midodrine activates alpha receptors in arteries and veins to produce an increase in vascular tone and an increase in blood pressure. It is indicated for the symptomatic treatment of orthostatic hypotension in patients whose lives are impaired by the disorder and who have not responded to any other therapy.

CONTRAINDICATIONS/CAUTIONS

Midodrine is contraindicated in the presence of supine hypertension, CAD, or pheochromocytoma because of the risk of precipitating a hypertensive emergency; with acute renal disease, which might interfere with the excretion of the drug; with urinary retention because the stimulation of alpha receptors can exacerbate this problem; and with thyrotoxicosis, which could further increase blood pressure. Caution should be used with pregnancy and lactation because of the potential for adverse effects on the fetus or neonate; with visual problems, which could be exacerbated by vasoconstriction; and with renal or hepatic impairment, which could alter the metabolism and excretion of the drug.

ADVERSE EFFECTS

The most common adverse effects associated with this drug are related to the stimulation of alpha receptors and include piloerection, chills, and rash; hypertension and bradycardia; dizziness, vision changes, vertigo, and headache; and problems with urination.

CLINICALLY IMPORTANT DRUG–DRUG INTERACTIONS

There is a risk of increased effects and toxicity of cardiac glycosides, beta blockers, alpha adrenergic agents, and corticosteroids if taken with midodrine. Patients receiving any of these combinations should be monitored carefully for the need for a dosage adjustment.

DATA LINK

Data link to midodrine in your nursing drug guide:

ANTIHYPOTENSIVE: MIDODRINE

Name	Brand Name	Usual Indication
midodrine	*ProAmatine*	Treatment of orthostatic hypotension

NURSING CONSIDERATIONS for patients receiving midodrine

Assessment

HISTORY. Screen for the following: any known allergy to midodrine; impaired kidney or liver function; pregnancy and lactation because of the potential adverse effects on the fetus and neonate; cardiovascular dysfunction; visual problems; urinary retention; and pheochromocytoma.

PHYSICAL ASSESSMENT. Include screening for baseline status before beginning therapy and for any potential adverse effects. Assess the following: body temperature, weight; skin color, lesions, temperature; pulse, blood pressure, orthostatic blood pressure, perfusion; respiration, adventitious sounds; bowel sounds, abdominal exam; and renal and liver function tests.

Nursing Diagnoses

The patient receiving midodrine may have the following nursing diagnoses related to drug therapy:

- Alteration in tissue perfusion related to changes in cardiac output
- Sensory–perceptual alteration related to CNS effects
- Pain related to GI distress, piloerection, chills, headache
- Knowledge deficit regarding drug therapy

Implementation

- Monitor blood pressure carefully *to monitor effectiveness.*
- Do not administer to patients who are bedridden; only administer to patients who are up and mobile *to ensure therapeutic effects and decrease the risk of severe hypertension.*
- Monitor heart rate regularly when beginning therapy *to monitor for bradycardia, which commonly occurs at the beginning of therapy; if bradycardia persists, it may indicate a need to discontinue the drug.*
- Monitor patients with known visual problems carefully *to ensure that the drug is discontinued if visual fields change.*

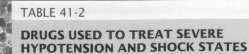

• Encourage patients to void before taking a dose of the drug *to decrease the risk of urinary retention problems.*
• Provide comfort measures *to help the patient tolerate drug effects* (e.g., small, frequent meals, access to bathroom facilities, safety precautions if CNS effects occur, environmental control, appropriate skin care as needed, analgesics as needed).
• Provide thorough patient teaching, including the name of the drug, dosage prescribed, measures to avoid adverse effects, warning signs of problems, and the need for periodic monitoring and evaluation *to enhance patient knowledge about drug therapy and to promote compliance.*
• Offer support and encouragement *to deal with the diagnosis and drug regimen.*

Evaluation

• Monitor patient response to the drug (maintenance of blood pressure within normal limits).
• Monitor for adverse effects (hypertension, dizziness, visual changes, piloerection, chills, urinary problems).
• Evaluate the effectiveness of the teaching plan (patient can name drug, dosage, adverse effects to watch for, specific measures to avoid adverse effects, importance of continued follow-up).
• Monitor the effectiveness of comfort measures and compliance to the regimen.

CHAPTER SUMMARY

- The cardiovascular system is a closed system that depends on pressure differences to ensure the delivery of blood to the tissues and the return of that blood to the heart.
- Blood pressure is related to heart rate, stroke volume, and the total peripheral resistance against which the heart has to push the blood.
- Peripheral resistance is primarily controlled by constriction or relaxation of the arterioles. Constricted arterioles raise pressure; dilated arterioles lower pressure.
- Control of blood pressure involves baroreceptor (pressure receptor) stimulation of the medulla to activate the sympathetic nervous system, which causes vasoconstriction and increased fluid retention when pressure is low in the aorta and carotid arteries, and vasodilation and loss of fluid when pressure is too high.
- The kidneys activate the renin–angiotensin system when blood flow to the kidneys is decreased.
- Renin activates angiotensinogen to angiotensin I in the liver; angiotensin I is converted by angiotensin-converting enzyme to angiotensin II in the lungs; angiotensin II reacts with specific receptor sites on blood vessels to cause vasoconstriction to raise blood pressure and in the adrenal gland to cause release of aldosterone, which leads to retention of fluid and increased blood volume.
- Hypertension is a sustained state of higher-than-normal blood pressure that can lead to damage of blood vessels, increased risk of atherosclerosis development, and damage to small vessels in end organs. Because hypertension often has no signs or symptoms, it is called the silent killer.
- Essential hypertension has no underlying cause, and treatment can vary widely from individual to individual. A stepped care approach is recommended; lifestyle changes are tried first, followed by careful addition and adjustment of various antihypertensive drugs.
- Drug treatment of hypertension is aimed at altering one or more of the normal reflexes that control blood pressure: diuretics decrease sodium levels and volume; sympathetic nervous system drugs alter the sympathetic response and lead to vascular dilation and decreased pumping power of the heart; ACE inhibitors prevent the conversion of angiotensin I to II; angiotensin II receptor blockers prevent the body from responding to angiotensin II; calcium channel blockers interfere with the ability of muscles to contract and lead to vasodilation; and vasodilators directly cause the relaxation of vascular smooth muscle.
- Hypotension is a state of lower-than-normal blood pressure that can result in decreased oxygenation of the tissues, cell death, tissue damage, and even death. Hypotension is most often treated with sympathomimetic drugs, which stimulate the sympathetic receptor sites to cause vasoconstriction, fluid retention, and return of normal pressure.

BIBLIOGRAPHY

Andrews, M. & Boyle, J. (1999). *Transcultural concepts in nursing care.* Philadelphia: Lippincott Williams & Wilkins.

Bullock, B. L. (2000). *Focus on pathophysiology.* Philadelphia: Lippincott Williams & Wilkins.

Hardman, J. G., Limbird, L. E., Molinoff, P. B., Ruddon, R. W., and Gilman, A. G. (Eds.). (1996.) *Goodman and Gilman's the pharmacological basis of therapeutics* (9th ed.). New York: McGraw-Hill.

Karch, A. M. (2000). *2000 Lippincott's nursing drug guide.* Philadelphia: Lippincott Williams & Wilkins.

McEvoy, B. R. (1999). *Facts and comparisons 1999.* St. Louis: Facts and Comparisons.

Medical letter on drugs and therapeutics. (1999). New Rochelle, NY: Medical Letter.

Porth, C. M. (1998). *Pathophysiology: Concepts of altered health states* (5th ed.). Philadelphia: Lippincott-Raven.

CHAPTER

42

Cardiotonic Agents

Cardiac glycosides
- digitoxin
- P digoxin

Phosphodiesterase inhibitors
- P amrinone
- milrinone

Digoxin antidote
- digoxin immune Fab

CHAPTER OUTLINE

KEY TERMS

cardiomegaly
congestive heart failure
dyspnea
hemoptysis
nocturia
orthopnea
positively inotropic
pulmonary edema
tachypnea

INTRODUCTION

Congestive heart failure (CHF) is a condition in which the heart *fails* to effectively pump blood around the body. Because the cardiac cycle normally involves a tight balance between the pumping of the right and left sides of the heart, any failure of the muscle to pump blood out of either side of the heart can result in a back-up of blood cells. If this happens, the blood vessels become congested; eventually, the body's cells are deprived of oxygen and nutrients, and waste products build up in the tissues. The primary treatment for CHF involves helping the muscle to contract more efficiently to bring the system back into balance.

REVIEW OF CARDIAC MUSCLE FUNCTION

The underlying problem in CHF usually involves muscle function: (1) the muscle could be damaged by atherosclerosis or cardiomyopathy (a disease of the heart muscle leading to an enlarged heart and eventually complete muscle failure and death); (2) the muscle could be forced to work too hard to maintain an efficient output, as with hypertension or valvular disease; or (3) the structure of the heart could be abnormal, as with congenital cardiac defects.

The basic unit of the heart muscle, the sarcomere, contains two contractile proteins, actin and myosin, which like to react with each other but at rest are kept apart by troponin. When a cardiac muscle cell is stimulated, calcium enters the cell and inactivates the troponin, allowing the actin and myosin to form actomyosin bridges. The formation of these bridges allows the muscle to fibers to slide together or to contract (Figure 42-1). (See Chapter 40 for a review of heart muscle contraction processes.)

The contraction process requires energy, oxygen, and calcium to allow the formation of the actomyosin bridges. The degree of shortening, or the strength of contraction, is determined by the amount of calcium present (the more calcium present, the more bridges formed) and by the stretch of the sarcomere before contraction begins. The farther apart the actin and myosin proteins are before the cell is stimulated, the more bridges will be formed and the stronger the contraction will be. This correlates with Starling's law of the heart. The more the cardiac muscle is stretched, the greater the contraction will be. The more blood you put into the heart, the greater the contraction will be to empty the heart, up to a point. If the bridges are stretched too far apart, they won't be able to reach each other to form the actomyosin bridges and no contraction will occur. This severe response can be seen with severe cardiomyopathy when the muscle cells are stretched and distorted and eventually stop contracting because the muscle cells can no longer respond.

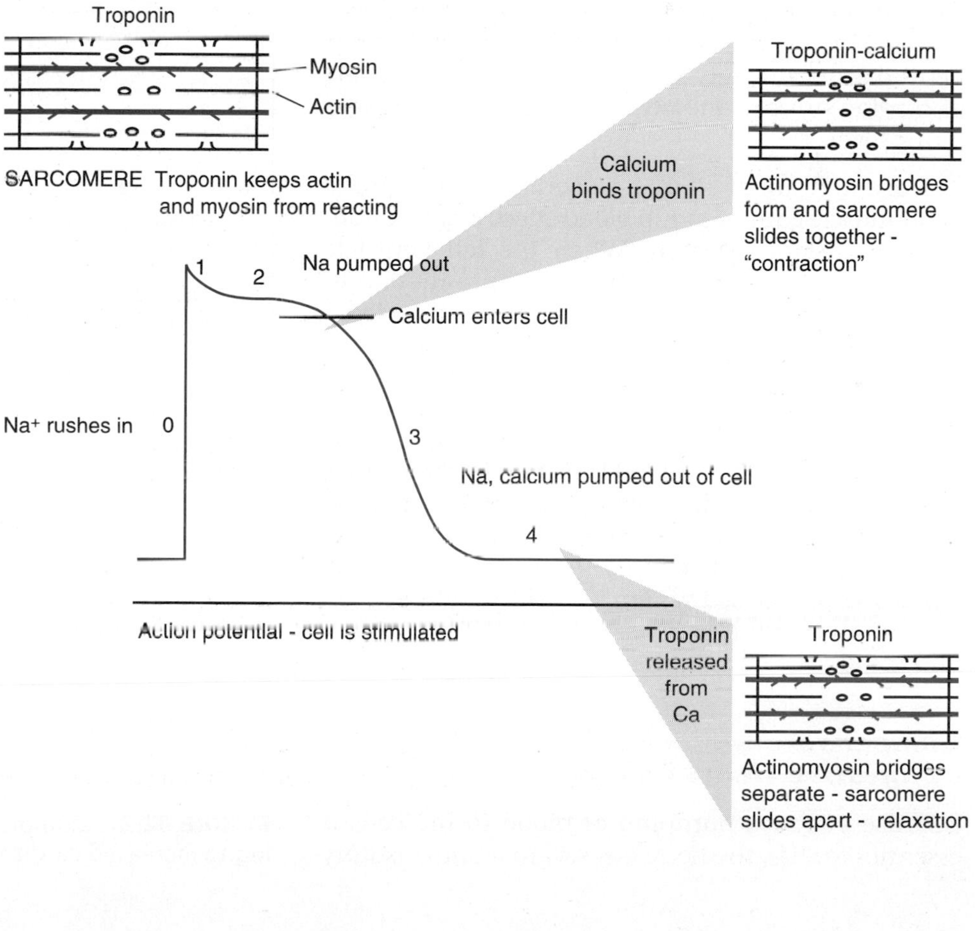

FIGURE 42-1. The sliding filaments of myocardial muscles. Calcium entering the cell deactivates troponin and allows actin and myosin to react, causing contraction. Calcium pumped out of the cell frees troponin to separate actin and myosin; the sarcomere filament slides apart and the cell relaxes.

CONGESTIVE HEART FAILURE

Congestive heart failure, a condition which was once called "dropsy" or decompensation, is a syndrome that can occur with any of the disorders that damage or overwork heart muscle.

- Coronary artery disease (CAD) is the leading cause of CHF, accounting for approximately 95% of the cases diagnosed (see Chapter 45 for a discussion of CAD). CAD results in an insufficient supply of blood to meet the myocardium's oxygen demands. Consequently, the muscles become hypoxic and can no longer function efficiently. When CAD evolves into a myocardial infarction (MI), muscle cells die or are damaged, leading to an inefficient pumping effort.
- Cardiomyopathy can occur as a result of a viral infection, alcoholism, anabolic steroid abuse, and collagen disorders. It causes muscle alterations and ineffective contraction and pumping.
- Hypertension eventually leads to an enlarged cardiac muscle because the heart has to work harder than normal to pump against the high pressure in the arteries. Hypertension puts constant, increased demands for oxygen on the system because the heart is pumping so hard all of the time.
- Valvular heart disease leads to an overload of the ventricles because the valves do not close tightly, allowing blood to leak backwards into the ventricles. This overloading causes muscle stretching and increased demand for oxygen and energy as the heart muscle has to constantly contract harder. (Valvular heart disease is rarely seen today due to the success of cardiac surgery and effective treatment for rheumatic fever.)

The end result of all of these conditions is that the heart muscle cannot pump blood effectively throughout the vascular system. When the left ventricle pumps inefficiently, blood backs up into the lungs, causing pulmonary vessel congestion and fluid leakage into the alveoli and lung tissue. In severe cases, ***pulmonary edema*** (rales, wheezes, blood-tinged sputum, low oxygenation, S_3 [third heart sound] development) can occur. When the right side of the heart is the primary problem, blood backs up in the venous system leading to the right side of the heart. Liver congestion and edema of the legs and feet reflect right-sided failure. Because the cardiovascular system works as a closed system, one-sided failure, if left untreated, eventually leads to failure of both sides, and the signs and symptoms of total CHF occur.

Compensatory Mechanisms in Congestive Heart Failure

Because effective pumping of blood to the cells is essential for life, the body has several compensatory mechanisms that function if the heart muscle starts to fail (Figure 42-2). Decreased cardiac output will stimulate the baroreceptors in the aortic arch and the carotid arteries, causing a sympathetic stimulation (see Chapter 27). This sympathetic stimulation will cause an increase in heart rate, blood pressure, and rate and depth of respirations as well as a ***positively inotropic*** effect (increased force of contraction) on the heart and increase in blood volume (through the release of aldosterone). The decrease in cardiac output will also stimulate the release of renin from the kidneys and activate the renin–angiotensin system, which will further increase blood pressure and blood volume.

When these compensatory mechanisms work effectively, the patient may have no signs and symptoms of CHF and is said to be compensated. Unfortunately, over time, all of these effects will increase the workload of the heart, contributing to further development of CHF. Eventually, the heart muscle will stretch out from overwork, and the chambers of the heart will dilate secondary to the increased blood volume that they have had to handle. This hypertrophy (enlargement) of the heart muscle, called ***cardiomegaly,*** will lead to inefficient pumping and eventually increased CHF.

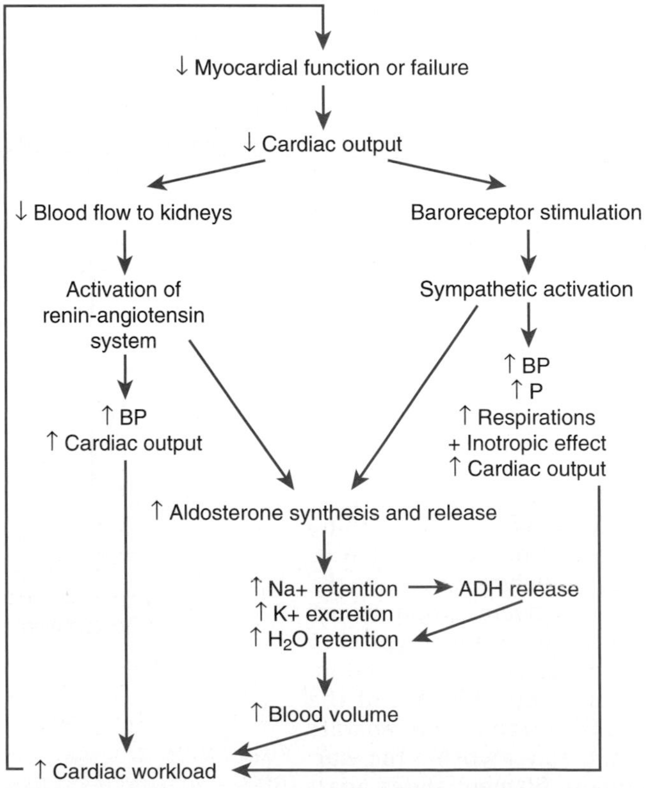

FIGURE 42-2. Compensatory mechanisms in CHF leading to increased cardiac workload and further CHF.

Cellular Changes in Congestive Heart Failure

The myocardial cells are changed with prolonged CHF. Unlike healthy heart cells, the failing heart cells seem to lack the ability to produce energy and use it for effective contractions. They are no longer able to effectively move calcium ions into and out of the cell. This defect in the calcium movement process may lead to further deterioration, as the muscle contracts ineffectively and is unable to deliver blood to the cardiac muscle.

Signs and Symptoms of Congestive Heart Failure

The patient with CHF presents a predictable clinical picture that reflects not only the problems with heart pumping, but also the compensatory mechanisms that are working to balance the problem. Cardiomegaly can be detected using x-rays, ECGs, or direct percussion and palpation. Heart rate will be rapid secondary to sympathetic stimulation, and the patient may develop atrial flutter or fibrillation as atrial cells are stretched and damaged. Anxiety often occurs as the body stimulates the sympathetic stress reaction. Heart murmurs may develop when the muscle is no longer able to support the papillary muscles or the annuli supporting the cardiac valves. Peripheral congestion and edema occur as the blood starts to engorge vessels as it waits to be pumped through the heart. Enlarged liver (hepatomegaly); enlarged spleen (splenomegaly); decreased blood flow to the gastrointestinal (GI) tract causing feelings of nausea and abdominal pain; swollen legs and feet; dependent edema in the coccyx or other dependent areas, with decreased peripheral pulses and hypoxia of those tissues; and, with left sided failure, edema of the lungs reflect the engorged vessels and increased hydrostatic pressure throughout the cardiovascular system (Figure 42-3).

LEFT-SIDED CONGESTIVE HEART FAILURE

Left-sided CHF reflects engorgement of the pulmonary veins, which eventually leads to difficulty breathing. Patients complain of ***tachypnea*** (rapid, shallow respirations); ***dyspnea*** (discomfort with breathing often accompanied by a panicked feeling of being unable to breathe); and ***orthopnea*** (increased difficulty breathing when lying down). Orthopnea occurs in the supine position when the pattern of blood flow changes because of the effects of gravity, which causes increased pressure and perfusion in the lungs. Orthopnea is usually relieved when the patient sits up, thereby reducing the blood flow through the lungs. The degree of CHF is often calculated by the number of pillows required to get relief (e.g., one-pillow, two-pillow, or three-pillow orthopnea).

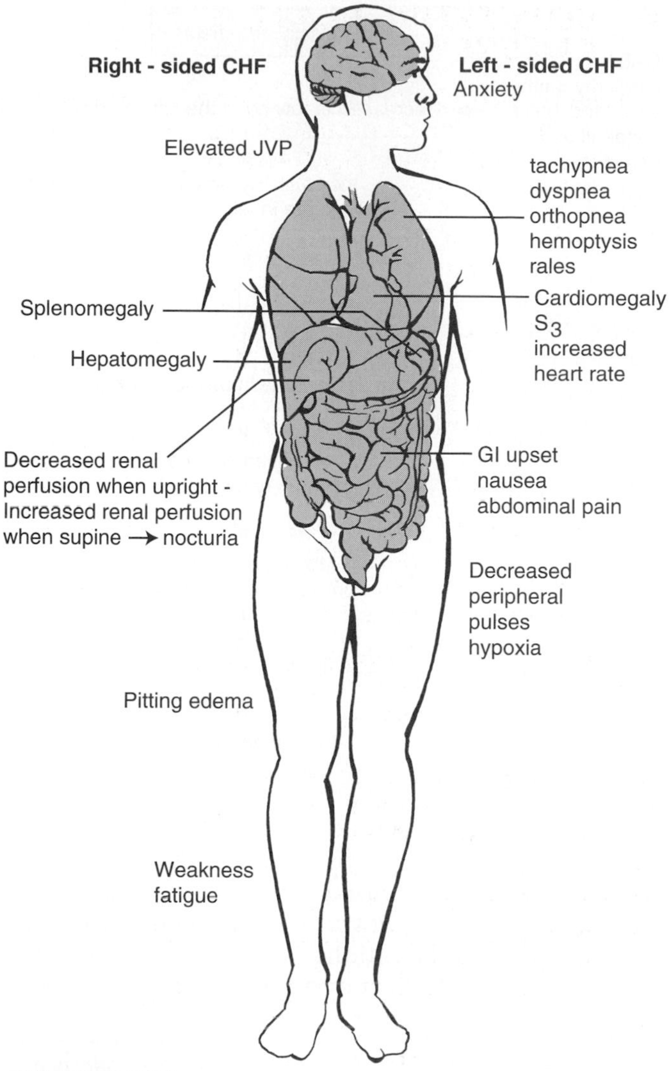

FIGURE 42-3. Signs and symptoms of congestive heart failure.

The patient with left-sided CHF may also experience coughing and ***hemoptysis*** (coughing up of blood). Rales may be present, signaling the presence of fluid in the lung tissue. In severe cases, the patient may develop pulmonary edema; this can be life threatening because as the spaces in the lungs fill up with fluid, there will be no place for gas exchange to occur (Figure 42-4).

RIGHT-SIDED CONGESTIVE HEART FAILURE

Right-sided CHF usually occurs as a result of chronic obstructive pulmonary disease (COPD) or other lung diseases that elevate the pulmonary pressure. It often results when the right side of the heart, normally a very low pressure system, must generate more and more force to move the blood into the lungs (Figure 42-5).

In right-sided CHF, venous return to the heart is decreased because of the increased pressure in the right side of the heart. This causes a congestion and back

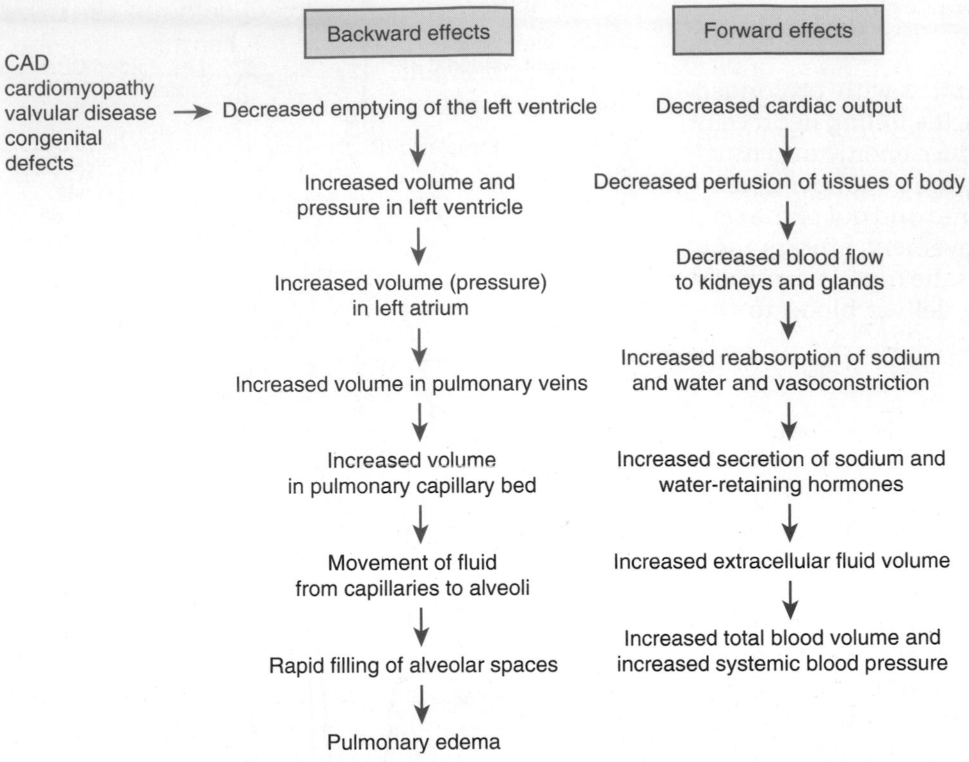

FIGURE 42-4. Highly schematic representation of the pathophysiology of left heart failure.

up of blood in the systemic system. An elevated jugular venous pressure (JVP) is seen with distended neck veins, reflecting increased central venous pressure (CVP). The liver enlarges and become congested with blood, which leads initially to pain and tenderness and, eventually, to liver dysfunction and jaundice.

Dependent areas develop edema or swelling of the tissues as fluid leaves the congested blood vessels and pools in the tissues. Pitting edema in the legs is a common finding of CHF, reflecting a pool of fluid in the tissues. When the patient with right-sided CHF changes position and the legs are no longer depen-

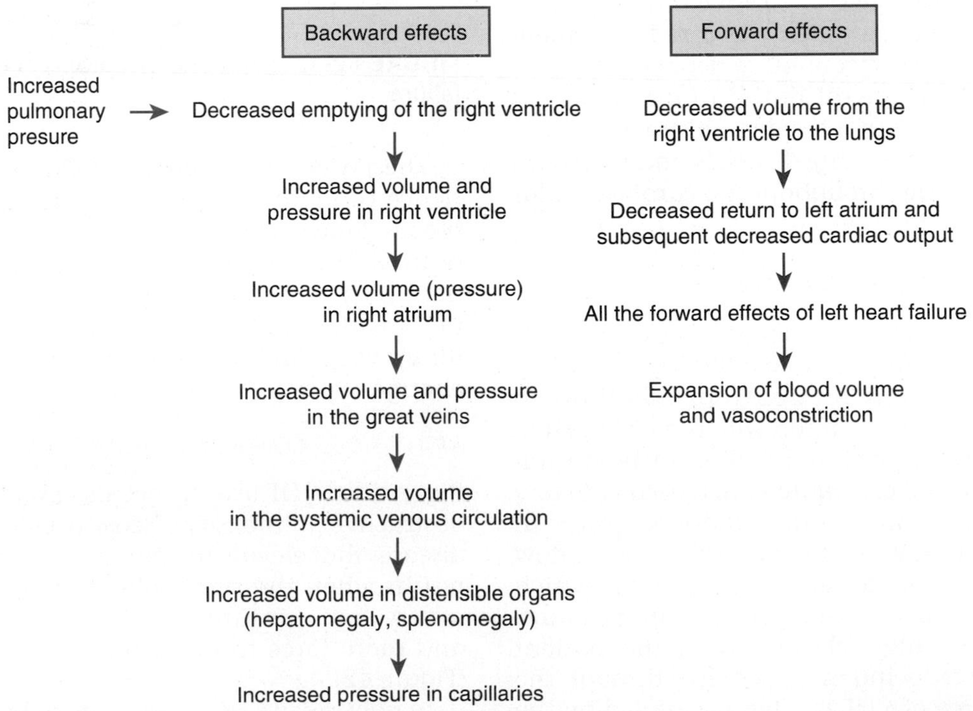

FIGURE 42-5. Highly schematic representation of the pathophysiology of right heart failure.

dent, for example, the fluid will be pulled back into circulation and returned to the heart. This increase in cardiovascular volume will increase blood flow to the kidneys, causing increased urine output. This is often seen as ***nocturia*** (excessive voiding during the night), when a person who is up and around during the day is supine at night. The person may need to get up during the night to eliminate all of the urine that has been produced due to the fluid shift.

TREATMENTS FOR CONGESTIVE HEART FAILURE

Several different approaches are used to treat CHF. This chapter will discuss the cardiotonic drugs (also called inotropic drugs) that work to directly increase the force of cardiac muscle contraction. Other drug therapies used to treat CHF are discussed in other chapters and so will be discussed only briefly here.

Vasodilators (ACE Inhibitors and Nitrates)

Vasodilators are used to treat CHF because they can decrease the workload of the overworked cardiac muscle. By relaxing vascular smooth muscle, these drugs decrease the pressure the heart has to pump against (afterload). They also cause a pooling of blood in stretchable veins when the vessels relax, thus decreasing the venous return to the heart and decreasing the preload the muscle has to deal with.

ACE inhibitors block the enzyme that converts angiotensin I to angiotensin II in the lungs, thus blocking the vasoconstriction and the release of aldosterone from the adrenal gland caused by angiotensin II (Figure 42-6). This in turn will decrease the afterload by relieving vasoconstriction and by decreasing blood volume through the effects on aldosterone, which will also decrease the afterload. ACE inhibitors are the vasodilators of choice in treating CHF. They are most effective in mild CHF and in patients who are at high risk for developing CHF or who have only beginning signs and symptoms.

Nitrates directly relax vascular muscle and cause a decrease in blood pressure and a pooling of blood in the veins (see Figure 42-6). These two actions will also decrease preload and afterload. Nitrates are often used in treating more severe CHF. (See Chapters 41 and 44 for additional information.)

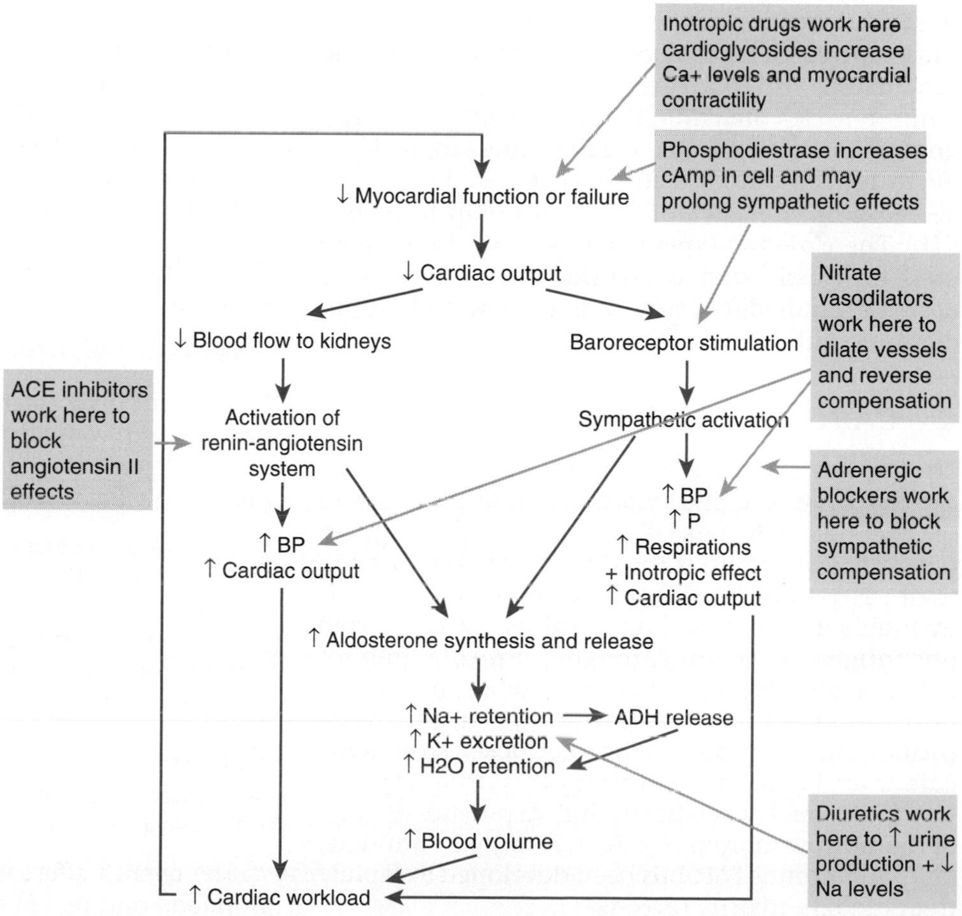

FIGURE 42-6. Sites of action of drugs used to treat CHF.

Diuretics

Diuretics are used to decrease blood volume, which will decrease venous return and blood pressure (see Figure 42-6). The end result is a decrease in afterload and preload and a decrease in the heart's workload. Diuretics are available in mild to potent compounds and are frequently used as adjunctive therapy in the treatment of all degrees of CHF. (See Chapter 49 for additional information.)

Beta Adrenergic Agonists

Beta adrenergic agonists stimulate the beta receptors in the sympathetic nervous system, increasing calcium flow into the myocardial cells and causing increased contraction, a positively inotropic effect (see Figure 42-6). Other sympathetic stimulation effects can cause increased CHF as the heart's workload is increased by most sympathetic activity. Dobutamine is the beta agonist most frequently used to treat CHF. Because it must be given by IV infusion in an acute care setting, it is usually reserved for use in acute CHF. (See Chapter 28 for additional information.)

CARDIOTONIC DRUGS

Cardiotonic (inotropic) drugs affect the intracellular calcium levels in the heart muscle, leading to increased contractility. This increase in contraction strength leads to increased cardiac output, which causes increased renal blood flow and increased urine production. Increased renal blood flow decreases renin release, breaking the effects of the renin–angiotensin system, and increases urine output, leading to decreased blood volume. Together, these effects decrease the heart's workload and help to relieve CHF. There are two types of cardiotonic drugs being used: the classic cardiac glycosides, which have been used for hundreds of years, and the newer phosphodiesterase inhibitors.

CARDIAC GLYCOSIDES

The cardiac glycosides were originally derived from the foxglove or digitalis plant. These plants were once ground up to make digitalis leaf. Today, digoxin (*Lanoxin, Lanoxicaps*) is the drug most often used to treat CHF; it has a very rapid onset of action and is available for parenteral and oral use. It is excreted unchanged in the urine, making it a safe drug for patients with liver dysfunction. Digoxin has a very narrow margin of safety (meaning that the therapeutic dose is very close to the toxic dose), so extreme care must be taken when using this drug. Digoxin toxicity is a real possibility in clinical practice because of the narrow margin of safety. A digoxin antidote, digoxin immune Fab, has been developed to rapidly treat digoxin toxicity (Box 42-1).

BOX 42-1

DIGOXIN ANTIDOTE: DIGOXIN IMMUNE FAB

Digoxin immune Fab (*Digibind*) is an antigen binding fragment (Fab) derived from specific antidigoxin antibodies. These antibodies bind molecules of digoxin, making them unavailable at their site of action. The digoxin antibody-antigen complexes accumulate in the blood and are excreted through the kidney. Digoxin immune Fab is used for the treatment of life-threatening digoxin intoxication (serum levels >10 ng/ml with serum K >5 mEq/L in a setting of digoxin intoxication) and the treatment of potential life-threatening digoxin overdose.

The amount of digoxin immune Fab that is infused IV is determined by the amount of digoxin ingested or on the serum digoxin level if the ingested amount is unknown. The patient's cardiac status should be monitored continually while the drug is given and for several hours after the infusion is finished. Because there is a risk of hypersensitivity reaction to the infused protein, life-support equipment should be on standby.

Serum digoxin levels will be very high and unreliable for about 3 days after the digoxin immune Fab infusion because of the high levels of digoxin in the blood. The patient should not be redigitalized for several days to a week after digoxin immune fab has been used because of the potential of remaining fragments in the blood.

Another digitalis compound, digitoxin (*Crystodigin*), is also still available for use to treat CHF. Digitoxin is only available in oral form and has a slow onset of action and a very long duration, making it less useful than digoxin in managing acute CHF. It, too, has a narrow margin of safety. It is metabolized in the liver and can reach toxic levels in patients who do not have good liver function. This is not a drug of choice.

THERAPEUTIC ACTIONS AND INDICATIONS

The cardiac glycosides increase intracellular calcium and allow more calcium to enter myocardial cells during depolarization (see Figure 42-6), causing the following effects:

- Increased force of myocardial contraction (a positive inotropic effect)
- Increased cardiac output and renal perfusion (which has a diuretic effect, increasing urine output and decreasing blood volume while decreasing renin release and activation of the renin–angiotensin system)
- Slowed heart rate by slowing the rate of cellular repolarization (a negative chronotropic effect)
- Decreased conduction velocity through the AV node

The overall effect is a decrease in the myocardial workload and relief of CHF (Table 42-1). The cardiac

NURSING CHALLENGE

Lanoxin versus Lanoxicaps

Digoxin comes in two similar-sounding, brand-name preparations: *Lanoxin* and *Lanoxicaps*. These drugs both provide digoxin, but the bioavailability of these two drugs is dramatically different. *Lanoxicaps* are absorbed much more effectively—a 0.2-mg dose of *Lanoxicaps* is the equivalent of a 0.25-mg dose of *Lanoxin*, and the 0.1-mg capsule of *Lanoxicaps* is equivalent to the 0.125-mg tablet of *Lanoxin*. Digoxin has a very small margin of safety to begin with, and the room for error is much smaller with *Lanoxicaps*.

Extreme care must be taken when administering either of these drugs to ensure the right dose goes with the right brand name. Patient education should clearly identify the drug and dose being ordered. Patients should be warned not to trade or share medication because of the potential for serious problems. Here is an example of what can happen: A patient on vacation ran out of his *Lanoxin* tablets, which were ordered at 0.25 mg/day, and borrowed 0.1 mg *Lanoxicaps* from a friend. He took two and a half *Lanoxicaps* each day because he knew he should have 0.25 mg. But during his vacation, the patient became digoxin toxic and required hospitalization to regulate his arrhythmias.

The names of these two drugs are so close that it is easy to make a similar mistake in a patient care setting. By being alert to the possibility of a problem, the nurse may avert adverse consequences for the patient.

glycosides are indicated for the treatment of CHF, atrial flutter, atrial fibrillation, and paroxysmal atrial tachycardia.

CONTRAINDICATIONS/CAUTIONS

Cardiac glycosides are contraindicated in the presence of allergy to any digitalis preparation. These drugs also are contraindicated in the following conditions: ventricular tachycardia or fibrillation (which are potentially fatal arrhythmias and should be treated with other drugs); heart block or sick sinus syndrome (which could be made worse by slowing of conduction through the AV node); idiopathic hypertrophic subaortic stenosis (IHSS) (because the increase in force of contraction could obstruct the outflow tract to the aorta and cause severe problems); acute MI (because the increase in force of contraction could cause more muscle damage and infarct); renal insufficiency (because the drug is excreted through the kidneys and toxic levels could develop); and electrolyte abnormalities (e.g., increased calcium, decreased potassium, or decreased magnesium) that could alter the action potential and change the effects of the drug.

Cardiac glycosides should be used cautiously with pregnancy or lactation because of the potential for adverse effects on the fetus or neonate.

ADVERSE EFFECTS

The adverse effects most frequently seen with the cardiac glycosides include headache, weakness, drowsiness, and vision changes (a yellow halo around

TABLE 42-1

CONGESTIVE HEART FAILURE AND RESPONSE TO CARDIAC GLYCOSIDES

	Response	
Signs and Symptoms*	*During Congestive Heart Failure*	*After Full Digitalization*†
Heart rate, rhythm, and size	Heart hypertrophied, dilated; rate rapid, irregular; "palpitations"; auscultation—S_3	Dilatation decreased, hypertrophy remains; rate, 70–80, may be regular; auscultation—no S_3
Lungs	Dyspnea on exertion; orthopnea; tachypnea; paroxysmal nocturnal dyspnea; wheezing, rales, cough, hemoptysis (pulmonary edema)	↓ rate of respiration; wheezes, rales gone
Peripheral congestion	Pitting edema of dependent parts; hepatomegaly; ↑ JVP; cyanosis; oliguria; nocturia	↑cardiac output and renal blood flow leads to ↑ urine flow, ↓ edema, ↓ signs and symptoms of poor perfusion
Other	Weakness, fatigue, anorexia, insomnia, nausea, vomiting, abdominal pain	↑ appetite: ↑ strength, energy

*Because the clinical picture in heart failure various with the stage and degree of severity, the signs and symptoms may vary considerably in different patients.

†Digitalization will not overcome similar symptoms when they are caused by conditions other than heart failure. Overdosage may actually cause symptoms similar to those of heart failure (e.g., anorexia, nausea, and vomiting, cardiac arrhythmias peripheral congestion).

LIFE-SPAN CONSIDERATIONS

Digoxin Toxicity in Children and the Elderly

Pediatric and geriatric patients are at increased risk for the development of digoxin toxicity. Individuals in both of these groups have body masses that are smaller than average adult body masses, and may have immature or aging kidneys. Digoxin is excreted unchanged in the kidney, so any change in kidney function can result in increased serum digoxin levels and subsequent digoxin toxicity. Extreme care should be taken when administering digoxin to patients in either of these age groups.

Many institutions require that pediatric digoxin doses be checked by a second nurse before administration. This practice provides an extra check to help prevent the toxicity of this potentially dangerous drug. The patient should then be assessed before the drug is given, including careful cardiac auscultation and apical pulse measurement to monitor heart rate and rhythm to detect any possible toxic effects.

Geriatric patients may not receive the same kind of attention in policy, but should be monitored for any factor that might affect digoxin levels when the drug is administered. Such factors may include:

- Renal function (is the BUN elevated?)
- Low body mass (is the patient underweight, undernourished, taking laxatives?)
- Current pulse, including quality and rhythm
- Hydration (is skin loose? Are mucous membranes dry? The presence of these conditions could signal potential electrolyte disturbances.)

Many geriatric patients eventually need a decrease in dose from 0.25 mg once a day to 0.125 mg once a day or 0.25 mg every other day. The nurse administering the drug is often in the best position to detect any changes in the patient's condition that might indicate a need for further evaluation.

objects is often reported with digoxin toxicity). GI upset and anorexia also commonly occur. A risk of arrhythmia development exists because the glycosides affect the action potential and conduction system of the heart.

CLINICALLY IMPORTANT DRUG–DRUG INTERACTIONS

There is a risk of increased therapeutic effects and toxic effects of digoxin if taken with verapamil, amiodarone, quinidine, quinine, erythromycin, tetracycline, or cyclosporine. If digoxin is combined with any of these drugs, it may be necessary to decrease the digoxin dose to prevent toxicity. If one of these drugs has been part of a medical regimen with digoxin and it is discontinued, the digoxin dose may need to be increased. An increased risk of cardiac arrhythmias exists if these drugs are taken with potassium-losing diuretics. If this combination is used, the patient's potassium levels should be checked regularly and appropriate replacement done. Digoxin may be less effective if it is combined with thyroid hormones, metoclopramide, or penicillamine, and increased digoxin dosage may be needed. Absorption of oral digoxin may be decreased if it is taken with cholestyramine, charcoal, colestipol, bleomycin, cyclophosphamide, or methotrexate. If it is used in combination with any of these agents, the drugs should not be taken at the same time, but should be administered 2 to 4 hours apart.

DATA LINK

Data link to the following cardiac glycosides in your nursing drug guide:

CARDIAC GLYCOSIDES

Name	Brand Name(s)	Usual Indications
digitoxin	*Crystodigin*	Treatment of CHF, atrial arrhythmias
P digoxin	*Lanoxin, Lanoxicaps*	Treatment of acute CHF, atrial arrhythmias

NURSING CONSIDERATIONS for patients receiving cardiac glycosides

Assessment

HISTORY. Screen for the following: any known allergies to any digitalis product; impaired kidney function, which could alter the excretion of the drug; ventricular tachycardia or fibrillation; heart block or sick sinus syndrome; IHSS; acute MI; electrolyte abnormalities (increased calcium, decreased potassium, or decreased magnesium); and pregnancy and lactation because of the potential adverse effects on the fetus or neonate.

PHYSICAL ASSESSMENT. Include screening for baseline status before beginning therapy and for any potential adverse effects. Assess the following: weight, skin color, lesions; affect, orientation, reflexes; pulse, blood pressure, perfusion, baseline ECG, cardiac auscultation; respirations, adventitious sounds; abdominal exam, bowel sounds; renal function tests; and serum electrolyte levels.

Nursing Diagnoses

The patient receiving a cardiac glycoside may have the following nursing diagnoses related to drug therapy:

- Alteration in cardiac output related to cardiac effects
- Fluid volume depletion related to diuresis
- Alteration in tissue perfusion related to change in cardiac output

- Alteration in gas exchange related to changes in cardiac output
- Knowledge deficit regarding drug therapy

Implementation

- Consult with the prescriber about the need for a loading dose when beginning therapy *to achieve desired results as soon as possible.*
- Monitor apical pulse for 1 full minute before administering the drug *to monitor for adverse effects.* Hold the dose if pulse is less than 60 in adults or less than 90 in infants; retake pulse in 1 hour. If pulse remains less than 60 in adults or less than 90 in infants, document pulse, hold the drug, and notify the prescriber *as the pulse rate could indicate toxic levels of digoxin and digoxin toxicity.*
- Monitor pulse for any change in quality or rhythm *to detect arrhythmias, early signs of toxicity.*
- Check the dosage and preparation carefully *because digoxin has a very small margin of safety and inadvertent drug errors can cause serious problems.*
- Check pediatric dosage with extreme care *because children are more apt to develop digoxin toxicity.* Have the dosage double checked before administration.
- Follow dilution instructions carefully for IV use; use promptly *to avoid drug degradation.*
- Administer IV doses very slowly over at least 5 minutes *to avoid cardiac arrhythmias and adverse effects.*
- Avoid IM administration, *which could be quite painful.*
- Arrange for the patient to be weighed at the same time each day, in the same clothes, *to monitor for fluid retention and CHF.*
- Avoid administering the oral drug with food or antacids *to avoid delays in absorption.*
- Maintain emergency equipment on standby: potassium salts, lidocaine (*for treatment of arrhythmias*), phenytoin (*for treatment of seizures*), atropine (*to increase heart rate*), and a cardiac monitor *in case severe toxicity should occur.*
- Monitor the patient for therapeutic digoxin level (0.5–2 ng/ml) *to evaluate therapeutic dosing and to monitor for the development of toxicity.*
- Provide comfort measures *to help the patient tolerate drug effects.* These include small, frequent meals, access to bathroom facilities if GI upset is severe, environmental control, safety precautions, adequate lighting if vision changes occur, positioning for comfort, and frequent rest periods to balance supply and demand of oxygen.
- Provide thorough patient teaching, including the name of the drug, dosage prescribed, proper administration, measures to avoid adverse effects, warning signs of problems, and the need for periodic monitoring and evaluation *to enhance patient knowledge about drug therapy and to promote compliance.* (See Patient Teaching Checklist: Digoxin.)
- Offer support and encouragement *to deal with the diagnosis and drug regimen.*

Evaluation

- Monitor patient response to the drug (improvement in signs and symptoms of CHF, resolution of atrial arrhythmias, serum digoxin level of 0.5–2 ng/ml).
- Monitor for adverse effects (vision changes, arrhythmias, CHF, headache, dizziness, drowsiness, GI upset, nausea).
- Evaluate the effectiveness of the teaching plan (patient can name drug, dosage, proper administration, adverse effects to watch for, specific measures to avoid adverse effects, importance of continued follow-up).
- Monitor the effectiveness of comfort measures and compliance to the regimen (see Nursing Care Guide: Digoxin).

PHOSPHODIESTERASE INHIBITORS

The phosphodiesterase inhibitors belong to a second class of drugs that act as cardiotonic (inotropic) agents. Amrinone (*Inocor*) is only available for IV use and is approved only for use in CHF patients who have not responded to digoxin, diuretics, or vasodilators. Milrinone (*Primacor*) is available only for IV use for the short-term management of CHF patients who are receiving digoxin and diuretics. Because these drugs have been associated with the development of potentially fatal ventricular arrhythmias, their use is limited to severe situations.

THERAPEUTIC ACTIONS AND INDICATIONS

The phosphodiesterase inhibitors block the enzyme phosphodiesterase. This blocking effect leads to an increase in myocardial cell cAMP, which increases calcium levels in the cell (see Figure 42-6). Increased cellular calcium causes a stronger contraction and prolongs the effects of sympathetic stimulation, which can lead to vasodilation, increased oxygen consumption, and arrhythmias. These drugs are indicated for the short-term treatment of CHF in patients who are not responding to digoxin or diuretics alone or who have poor response to digoxin, diuretics, and vasodilators.

CONTRAINDICATIONS/CAUTIONS

Phosphodiesterase inhibitors are contraindicated in the presence of allergy to either of these drugs or to bisulfites. They also are contraindicated in the following conditions: severe aortic or pulmonic valvular disease, which could be exacerbated by increased contraction; acute MI, which could be exacerbated by increased oxygen consumption and increased force of contraction; fluid volume deficit, which could be made worse by increased renal perfusion; and ven-

PATIENT TEACHING CHECKLIST

Digoxin

Create customized patient teaching materials for digoxin from your CD-ROM. Your patient teaching should stress the following points for drugs within this class:

Digoxin is a digitalis preparation. Digitalis has many helpful effects on the heart; for example, it helps the heart to beat more slowly and efficiently. These effects lead to better circulation and should help to reduce the swelling in your ankles or legs. It also should increase the amount of urine that you produce every day. Digoxin is a very powerful drug and must be taken *exactly* as prescribed. It is important to have regular medical checkups to ensure that the dosage of the drug is correct for you and that it is having the desired effect on your heart.

Do not stop taking this drug without consulting your health care provider. Never skip doses and never try to "catch up" any missed doses because serious adverse effects could occur.

You should learn to take your own pulse. Take it each morning before engaging in any activity. Write your pulse rate on a calendar so you will be aware of any changes and can notify your health care provider if the rate of rhythm of your pulse shows a consistent change. Your normal pulse rate is: ___________

You should monitor your weight fairly closely. Weigh yourself every other day, at the same time of the day and in the same amount of clothing. Record your weight on your calendar for easy reference. If you gain or lose three or more pounds in one day, it may indicate a problem with your drug. Consult your health care provider.

Some of the following adverse effects may occur:

- Dizziness, drowsiness, headache—Avoid driving or performing hazardous tasks or delicate tasks that require concentration if these occur. Consult your health care provider for an appropriate analgesic if the headache is a problem.
- Nausea, GI upset, loss of appetite—Small, frequent meals may help; monitor your weight loss and if it becomes severe, consult your health care provider.
- Vision changes, "yellow" halos around objects—These effects may pass with time. Take extra care in your activities for the first few days. If these reactions do not go away after 3 to 4 days, consult with your health care provider.

Report any of the following to your health care provider: unusually slow or irregular pulse; rapid weight gain; "yellow vision"; unusual tiredness or weakness; skin rash or hives; swelling of the ankles, legs, or fingers; difficulty breathing.

Tell any doctor, nurse, dentist, or other health care provider that you are taking this drug.

Keep this drug, and all medications, out of the reach of children.

Avoid the use of over-the-counter medications while you are on this drug. If you feel that you need one of these, consult with your health care provider for the best choice. Many of these drugs may contain ingredients that could interfere with your digoxin.

It might be helpful to wear or carry a Medic-Alert tag to alert any medical personnel who might take care of you in an emergency that you are taking this drug.

Regular medical follow-up is important to evaluate the actions of the drug and to adjust the dosage if necessary.

This Teaching Checklist reflects general patient teaching guidelines. It is not meant to be a substitute for drug-specific teaching information, which is available in nursing drug guides.

tricular arrhythmias, which could be exacerbated by these drugs.

Caution should be used with the elderly, who are more likely to develop adverse effects, and with pregnancy and lactation because of potential adverse effects on the fetus or neonate.

ADVERSE EFFECTS

The adverse effects most frequently seen with these drugs are ventricular arrhythmias (which can progress to fatal ventricular fibrillation), hypotension, and chest pain. GI effects include nausea, vomiting, anorexia, and abdominal pain. Thrombocytopenia occurs frequently with amrinone; it also can occur with milrinone. Hypersensitivity reactions associated with these drugs include vasculitis, pericarditis, pleuritis, and ascites. Burning at the injection site is also a frequent adverse effect.

CLINICALLY IMPORTANT DRUG–DRUG INTERACTIONS

Precipitates form when these drugs are given in solution with furosemide. Avoid this combination in solution. Use alternate lines if both of these drugs are being given IV.

NURSING CARE GUIDE
Digoxin

Assessment	Nursing Diagnoses	Implementation	Evaluation
HISTORY Allergies to any digitalis product, renal dysfunction, IHSS, pregnancy, lactation, arrhythmias, heart block, electrolyte abnormalities	Alteration in cardiac output related to cardiac effects Fluid volume depletion related to diuretic effects Alteration in tissue perfusion related to changes in cardiac output Alterations in gas exchange related to changes in cardiac output Knowledge deficit regarding drug therapy	Administer a loading dose to provide rapid therapeutic effects. Monitor apical pulse for 1 full minute before administering to assess for adverse and therapeutic effects. Check dosage very carefully. Provide comfort and safety measures: give small, frequent meals; ensure access to bathroom facilities; avoid IM injection; administer IV over 5 min; keep emergency equipment on standby. Provide support and reassurance to deal with drug effects. Provide patient teaching regarding drug, dosage, adverse effects, what to report, safety precautions.	Evaluate drug effects: relief of signs and symptoms of CHF, resolution of atrial arrhythmias, serum digoxin levels 0.5–2 ng/ml. Monitor for adverse effects: - arrhythmias - vision changes (yellow halo) - GI upset - headache, drowsiness Monitor for drug–drug interactions as indicated for each drug. Evaluate effectiveness of patient teaching program. Evaluate effectiveness of comfort and safety measures.
PHYSICAL EXAMINATION CV: BP, P, perfusion, ECG CNS: orientation, affect, reflexes, vision Skin: color, lesions, texture, perfusion Resp: R, adventitious sounds GI: abdominal exam, bowel sounds Lab tests: serum electrolytes, body weight			

DATA LINK

Data link to the following phosphodiesterase inhibitors in your nursing drug guide:

PHOSPHODIESTERASE INHIBITORS

Name	Brand Name	Usual Indication
P amrinone	*Inocor*	Treatment of CHF in patients who are not responsive to digoxin, diuretics, or vasodilators
milrinone	*Primacor*	Short-term management of CHF in patients receiving digoxin and diuretics

NURSING CONSIDERATIONS
for patients receiving phosphodiesterase inhibitors

Assessment

HISTORY. Screen for the following: any known allergies to these drugs or bisulfites; acute aortic or

CASE STUDY

Inadequate Digoxin Absorption

PRESENTATION

G. J. is an 82-year-old white woman with a 50-year history of rheumatic mitral valve disease. G. J. has been stabilized on digoxin for 10 years in a compensated state of congestive heart failure (CHF). G. J. recently moved into an extended care facility, having had difficulty caring for herself independently. She was examined by the admitting facility physician and was found to be stable. A note was made of an irregular pulse of 76, with ECG documentation of her chronic atrial fibrillation.

Three weeks after her arrival at the nursing home, G. J. began to develop progressive weakness, dyspnea on exertion, two-pillow orthopnea, and peripheral 2 + pitting edema. These signs and symptoms became progressively worse, and 5 days after the first indication that her CHF was returning, G. J. was admitted to the hospital with a diagnosis of CHF. Physical examination revealed a heart rate of 96 with atrial fibrillation, S3, rales, wheezes, 2 + pitting edema bilaterally up to the knees, elevated jugular venous pressure, cardiomegaly, weak pulses, and poor peripheral perfusion. G. J.'s serum digoxin level was 0.12 ng/ml (therapeutic range 0.5–2 ng/ml). G. J. was treated with diuretics and was redigitalized in the hospital with close cardiac monitoring. After she was stabilized, G. J. reported that she knew she had been taking her digoxin every day because she recognized the pill. The only difference she could identify was that she was given the pill in the afternoon with a dish of ice cream, while at home she always took it on an empty stomach first thing in the morning. The nursing home staff confirmed that G. J. had received the drug daily in the afternoon and that it was the same brand name she had used at home.

CRITICAL THINKING QUESTIONS

What nursing interventions should be done at this point? Think about the signs and symptoms of CHF and how they show the progression of the heart failure. How could the change in the drug administration timing be related to the decreased serum digoxin levels noted on G. J.'s admission? Consider the factors that affect the absorption of a drug. What alterations in dosing could be suggested that would prevent this from happening to G. J. again? What potential problems with trust could develop for G. J. on her return to the nursing home? Suggest an explanation for what happened to G. J. and possible ways that this could have been averted.

DISCUSSION

G. J.'s immediate needs involve trying to alleviate the alteration to her cardiac output that occurred when she lost the therapeutic effects of digoxin. Positioning, cool environment, small and frequent meals, and rest periods can help to decrease the workload on her heart. Digoxin has a small margin of safety and requires an adequate serum level to be therapeutic. G. J. was not absorbing enough digoxin to achieve a therapeutic serum level and consequently, her body began to go through the progression of congestive heart failure, right- and then left-sided.

Consultation with a clinical pharmacologist determined that ice cream, which is cold and causes a vasoconstriction in the stomach and slowing of muscle contraction, contains protein and calcium, two things that increase acid production in the stomach. Taking the digoxin with the ice cream exposed the drug to increased acid levels in the stomach for a longer period of time than normal. This effect destroyed much of the digoxin, leaving only a small amount to be absorbed. This change was enough to lower G. J.'s serum digoxin level below a therapeutic range, leading to the development of CHF over the 3-week period.

G. J. should receive extensive patient teaching about her disease, her drugs, and the adverse effects that may signal the development of drug toxicity or lack of therapeutic effectiveness. G. J. should receive this information in writing to take back to the facility with her. To avoid friction when teaching the facility staff about G. J.'s situation, the hospital staff might explain the kind of research that was needed to determine what happened, then discuss how much the nurses learned about the drug and drug mechanics from this process. Working together, both staffs can establish a better timing of G. J.'s digoxin dose that can successfully be incorporated into the routine at the extended care facility. G. J. should have serum digoxin levels drawn in 1 week to determine the effectiveness of the dosing and the drug.

Many factors can change the way that a drug is absorbed or biotransformed in the body—diet, brand of the drug, environmental stresses, disease states, interactions with other drugs. Because digoxin must be maintained within a limited range to be effective, any of these factors could greatly influence its bioavailability and effectiveness. Careful patient monitoring is very important with the use of digoxin to ensure a therapeutic effect and to prevent adverse effects.

pulmonic valvular disease, acute MI or fluid volume deficit, or ventricular arrhythmias, which could be exacerbated by these drugs; and pregnancy and lactation because of the potential adverse effects on the fetus and neonate.

PHYSICAL ASSESSMENT. Include screening for baseline status before beginning therapy and for any potential adverse effects. Assess the following: skin color, lesions, temperature; affect, orientation, reflexes; pulse, blood pressure, perfusion, baseline ECG;

respirations, adventitious sounds; abdominal exam; and serum electrolytes and CBC.

Nursing Diagnoses

The patient receiving a phosphodiesterase inhibitor may have the following nursing diagnoses related to drug therapy:

- Alteration in cardiac output related to arrhythmias, hypotension
- High risk for injury related to CNS, CV effects
- Alteration in tissue perfusion related to hypotension, thrombocytopenia, arrhythmias
- Knowledge deficit regarding drug therapy

Implementation

- Protect the drug from light *to prevent drug degradation.*
- Monitor pulse and blood pressure periodically during administration *to monitor for adverse effects so that dosage can be altered if needed to avoid toxicity.*
- Monitor input and output and record daily weights *to evaluate resolution of CHF.*
- Monitor platelet counts prior to and regularly during therapy *to ensure the dose is appropriate;* consult with the prescriber about the need to decrease the dose at the first sign of thrombocytopenia.
- Monitor injection sites and provide comfort measures *if infusion is painful.*
- Provide life support equipment on standby *in case of severe reaction to the drug or development of ventricular arrhythmias.*
- Provide comfort measures *to help the patient tolerate drug effects.* These include small, frequent meals, access to bathroom facilities if GI upset is severe and if diuresis occurs, environmental control, safety precautions, and orientation to surroundings.
- Provide thorough patient teaching including the name of the drug, dosage prescribed, proper administration, measures to avoid adverse effects, warning signs of problems, and the need for periodic monitoring and evaluation *to enhance patient knowledge about drug therapy and to promote compliance.*
- Offer support and encouragement *to help the patient deal with the diagnosis and drug regimen.*

Evaluation

- Monitor patient response to the drug (alleviation of signs and symptoms of CHF).
- Monitor for adverse effects (hypotension, cardiac arrhythmias, GI upset, thrombocytopenia).
- Evaluate the effectiveness of the teaching plan (patient can name drug, dosage, adverse effects to watch for, specific measures to avoid adverse effects, importance of continued follow-up).
- Monitor the effectiveness of comfort measures and compliance to the regimen.

WWW.WEB LINKS

Health care providers and patients may want to consult the following Internet sources:

Information on diet, exercise, drug therapy, cardiac rehabilitation:
http://www.jhbmc/jhu.edu/cardiology/rehab/rehab.html

Patient information on latest resources, diets, programs:
http://www.jhbmc/jhu.edu/cardiology/rehab/patientinfo.html

Patient information, support groups, diet, exercise, research information on heart disease and CHF:
http://www.amhrt.org

Specific information on the acute care of CHF (American Association of Critical Care Nurses):
http://www.aacn.org

CHAPTER SUMMARY

- Congestive heart failure (CHF) is a condition in which the heart muscle fails to effectively pump blood through the cardiovascular system, leading to a build up of blood or congestion in the system.
- CHF can be the result of a damaged heart muscle and increased demand to work harder secondary to coronary artery disease, hypertension, cardiomyopathy, valvular disease, or congenital heart abnormalities.
- The sarcomere is the functioning unit of the heart muscle that is made up of protein fibers: thin actin fibers and thick myosin fibers.
- Actin and myosin fibers will react with each other and slide together, contracting the sarcomere when calcium is present to inactivate troponin, an inhibitory compound that prevents this reaction. This sliding action requires the use of energy.
- Calcium enters the cell during the action potential after the cell has been stimulated. It gains entrance to the cell through calcium channels in the cell membrane and from storage sites within the cell.
- Failing cardiac muscle cells lose the ability to effectively use energy to move calcium into the cell, and contractions become weak and ineffective.

- Treatment for CHF can include the use of vasodilators (to reduce the heart's workload); diuretics (to reduce blood volume and the heart's workload); beta blockers (which decrease the heart's workload precipitated by the activation of the sympathetic reaction); and cardiotonic (inotropic) agents (which directly stimulate the muscle to contract more effectively).
- Signs and symptoms of CHF reflect the back-up of blood in the vascular system and the loss of fluid in the tissues. Edema, liver congestion, elevated jugular venous pressure, and nocturia reflect right-sided CHF. Tachypnea, dyspnea, orthopnea, hemoptysis, anxiety, and low blood oxygenation reflect left-sided CHF.
- Cardiac glycosides increase the movement of calcium into the heart muscle. This results in increased force of contraction, which increases blood flow to the kidneys (causing a diuretic effect), slows the heart rate, and slows conduction through the AV node. All of these effects decrease the heart's workload, helping to bring the system back into balance or compensation.
- Phosphodiesterase inhibitors block the breakdown of cAMP in the cardiac muscle. This allows more calcium to enter the cell (leading to more intense contraction) and increases the effects of sympathetic stimulation (which can lead to vasodilation but also can increase pulse, blood pressure, and workload on the heart). Because these drugs are associated with severe effects, they are reserved for use in extreme situations.

Bibliography

Abramowicz, M. (1996). *Drugs for chronic heart failure. The Medical Letter on Drugs and Therapeutics, 38* (985). New Rochelle, NY: Medical Letter.

Bullock, B. L. (2000). *Focus on pathophysiolgy*. Philadelphia: Lippincott Williams & Wilkins.

Hardman, J. G., Limbird, L. E., Molinoff, P. B., Ruddon, R.W., & Gilman, A. G. (Eds.). (1996). *Goodman and Gilman's the pharmacological basis of therapeutics* (9th ed.). New York: McGraw-Hill.

Karch, A. M. (2000). *2000 Lippincott's nursing drug guide*. Philadelphia: Lippincott Williams & Wilkins.

McEvoy, B. R. (1999). *Facts and comparisons 1999*. St. Louis: Facts and Comparisons.

Medical letter on drugs and therapeutics. (1999). New Rochelle, NY: Medical Letter.

Porth, C. M. (1998). *Pathophysiology: Concepts of altered health states* (5th ed.). Philadelphia: Lippincott-Raven.

CHAPTER 43

Antiarrhythmic Agents

Class Ia antiarrhythmics
- disopyramide
- moricizine
- procainamide
- **P** quinidine

Class Ib antiarrhythmics
- **P** lidocaine
- mexiletine
- tocainide

Class Ic antiarrhythmics
- **P** flecainide
- propafenone

Class II antiarrhythmics
- acebutolol
- esmolol
- **P** propranolol

Class III antiarrhythmics
- amiodarone
- **P** bretylium
- ibutilide
- sotalol

Class IV antiarrhythmics
- **P** diltiazem
- verapamil

Other
- adenosine
- digoxin

CHAPTER OUTLINE

KEY TERMS

antiarrhythmics
bradycardia
cardiac output
cardiac arrhythmia suppression trial (CAST)
heart blocks
hemodynamics
premature ventricular contraction (PVC)
premature atrial contraction (PAC)
proarrhythmic
tachycardia

INTRODUCTION

As discussed in earlier chapters, disruptions in the impulse formation and conduction of impulses through the myocardium are called arrhythmias. (These also are called dysrhythmias by some health care providers.) Arrhythmias occur in the heart because all of the cells of the heart possess the property of automaticity (see below) and so can generate an excitatory impulse. Disruptions in the normal rhythm of the heart can interfere with myocardial contractions and affect the ***cardiac output.*** Arrhythmias that seriously disrupt the cardiac output can be fatal. Drugs used to treat arrhythmias suppress automaticity or alter the conductivity of the heart.

REVIEW OF CARDIAC CONDUCTION

As discussed in Chapter 40, each cycle of cardiac contraction and relaxation is controlled by impulses that arise spontaneously in the sinoatrial or SA node of the heart. These impulses are conducted from the pacemaker cells by a specialized conducting system that activates all of the parts of the heart muscle almost simultaneously. These continuous, rhythmic contractions are controlled by the heart itself. This property allows the heart to beat as long as it has enough nutrients and oxygen to survive, regardless of the status of the rest of the body.

The conduction system of the heart is composed of the following:

The sinoatrial (SA) node is located in the top of the right atria and acts as the pacemaker of the heart.

Atrial bundles conduct the impulse through the atrial muscle.

The atrioventricular (AV) node slows the impulse and sends it from the atria into the ventricles by way of the bundle of His.

The bundle of His enters the septum and then divides into three bundle branches.

The bundle branches conduct the impulses through the ventricles; these branches break into a fine network of conducting fibers called the Purkinje fibers.

The Purkinje fibers deliver the impulse to the ventricular cells (Figure 43-1).

AUTOMATICITY OF THE HEART

All cardiac cells possess some degree of automaticity as described in Chapter 40. These cells undergo a spontaneous depolarization during diastole or rest because they decrease the flow of potassium ions out of the cell and probably leak sodium into the cell, causing an action potential. This action potential is basically the same as the action potential of the neuron (described in Chapter 17).

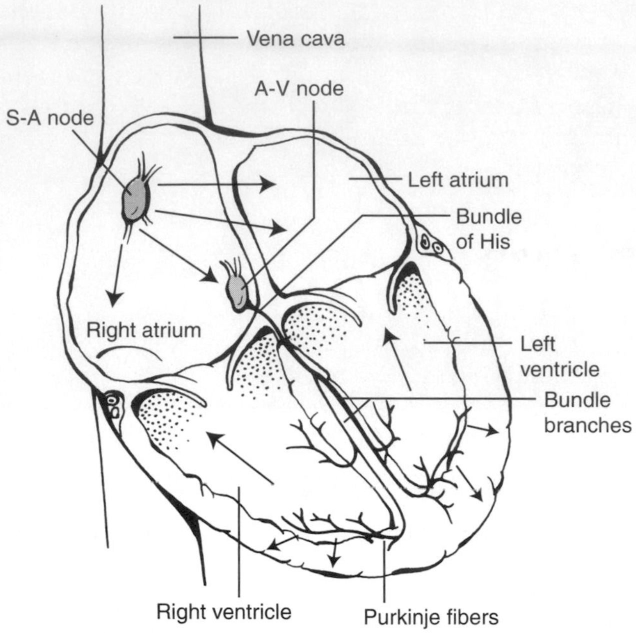

FIGURE 43-1. The conducting system of the heart. Impulses originating in the S-A node are transmitted through the atrial bundles to the A-V node and down the bundle of His and the bundle branches by way of the Purkinje fibers through the ventricles.

The action potential of the cardiac muscle cell consists of five phases:

Phase 0 occurs when the cell reaches a point of stimulation. The sodium gates open along the cell membrane, and sodium rushes into the cell and causes a positive flow of electrons into the cell—an electrical potential. This is called depolarization.

Phase 1 is a very short period when the sodium ions will equalize inside and outside of the cell.

Phase 2, or the plateau stage, occurs as the cell membrane becomes less permeable to sodium, calcium slowly enters the cell, and potassium begins to leave the cell. The cell membrane is trying to return to its resting state, a process called repolarization.

Phase 3 is a time of rapid repolarization as the sodium gates are closed and potassium flows out of the cell.

Phase 4 occurs when the cell comes to rest; the sodium-potassium pump returns the membrane to its resting membrane potential, and spontaneous depolarization begins again.

Each area of the heart has a slightly different appearing action potential that reflects the complexity of the cells in that area. Because of these differences in the action potential, each area of the heart has a slightly different rate of rhythmicity. The SA node will generate an impulse about 70 to 80 times a minute; the AV node about 40 to 50 times a minute; and the complex ventricular muscle cells, only about 10 to 20 times a minute.

CARDIAC ARRHYTHMIAS

As noted before, various factors can change the cardiac rate and rhythm. Arrhythmias can be caused by changes in rate (***tachycardia,*** which is a faster-than-normal heart rate; or ***bradycardia,*** which is a slower-than-normal heart rate), by stimulation from an ectopic focus (such as ***premature atrial contractions [PACs]*** or ***premature ventricular contractions [PVCs],*** atrial flutter, and atrial or ventricular fibrillation), or by alterations in conduction through the muscle (such as ***heart blocks,*** bundle branch blocks). Figure 43-2 displays an ECG strip showing normal sinus rhythm; Figures 43-3 through 43-6 display ECG strips showing various arrhythmias.

Causes

The underlying causes of arrhythmias can arise from changes to the automaticity or the conductivity of the heart cells. These changes can be due to several factors, including:

- Electrolyte disturbances that can alter the action potential
- Decreases in the oxygen delivered to the cells, which lead to hypoxia or anoxia and which change the cell's action potential and ability to maintain a membrane potential
- Structural damage that changes the conduction pathway through the heart
- Acidosis or the accumulation of waste products that alter the action potential in that area

In some cases, changes to the heart's automaticity or conductivity may result from drugs altering the action potential or cardiac conduction.

Hemodynamics

The study of the forces moving blood throughout the cardiovascular system is called ***hemodynamics.*** The ability of the heart to effectively pump blood depends on the coordinated contraction of the atrial and ventricular muscles. The muscular walls of these chambers are activated to contract by impulses that arise at the SA node, travel through the atria, are delayed slightly at the AV node, and then stimulate the His-Purkinje system through the ventricles. The conduction system is designed so that atrial stimulation is followed by total atrial contraction and ventricular stimulation follows with total ventricular contraction.

To be an effective pump, these muscles need to contract together. When this orderly initiation and conduction of impulses is altered, the result can be a poorly coordinated contraction of the ventricles that is unable to deliver an adequate supply of oxygenated blood to the brain and other organs, including the heart muscle itself. If these hemodynamic alterations are severe, serious complications can occur. For example, lack of sufficient blood flow to the brain can cause syncope or precipitate strokes; lack of sufficient blood flow to the myocardium can exacerbate atherosclerosis and cause angina or myocardial infarction (MI).

ANTIARRHYTHMIC DRUGS

Antiarrhythmics affect the action potential of the cardiac cells, altering their automaticity, conductivity, or both. Because of this effect, antiarrhythmic drugs can also produce new arrhythmias; that is, they are ***proarrhythmic.*** Antiarrhythmics are used in emergency situations when the hemodynamics arising from the arrhythmia are severe and could potentially be fatal.

Antiarrhythmics were widely used on a long-term basis to suppress any abnormal arrhythmia until the publication of the ***Cardiac Arrhythmia Suppression***

(text continues on page 536)

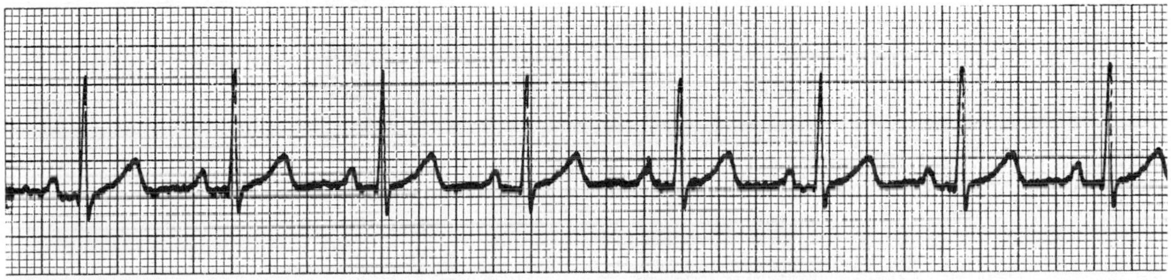

FIGURE 43-2. Normal sinus rhythm. Rhythm: regular. Rate: 60–100. P-R interval: =.12 to 0.20 seconds. QRS: 0.06–0.10 seconds. (Hudak, C. M. & Gallo, B. M. [1998]. *Critical care nursing* [7th ed.]. Philadelphia: Lippincott-Raven.)

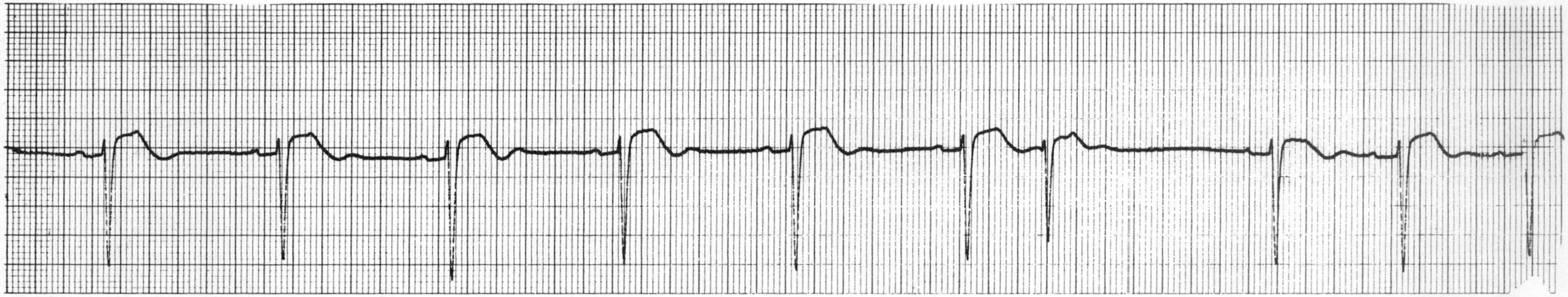

FIGURE 43-3. Premature atrial contractions (PACs). Rhythm: irregular due to the origination of a beat outside the normal conduction system (ectopic). Rate: does not interfere with the normal sinus rate, except for PACs. P-R: P wave is abnormal and interval may be slightly shortened in ectopic beat. QRS: normal. (Hudak, C. M. & Gallo, B. M. [1998]. *Critical care nursing* [7th ed.]. Philadelphia: Lippincott-Raven.)

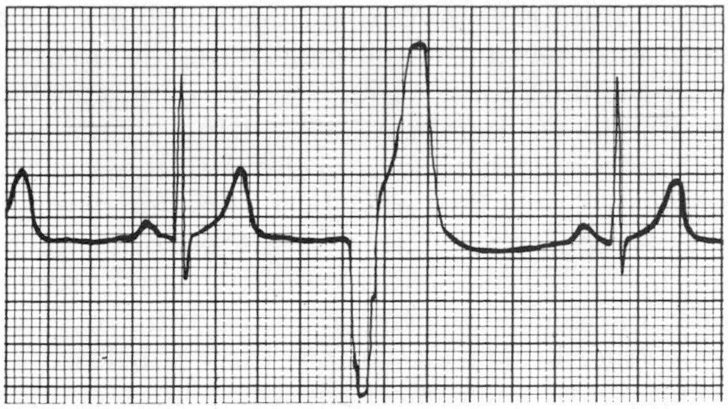

A

Ventricular premature contraction.

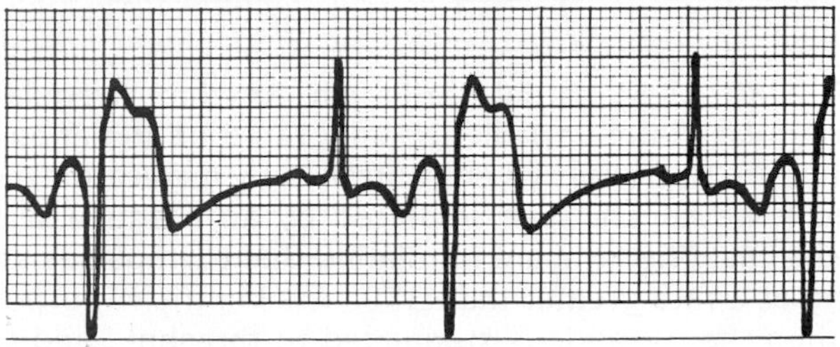

B

Ventricular bigeminy. (Every other beat is a VPB.)

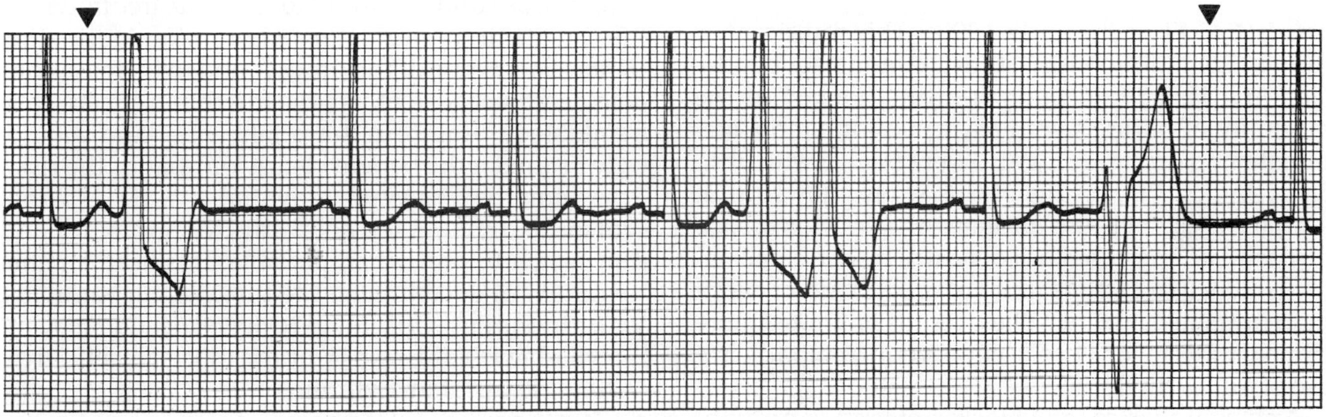

C

Multiformed PVCs.

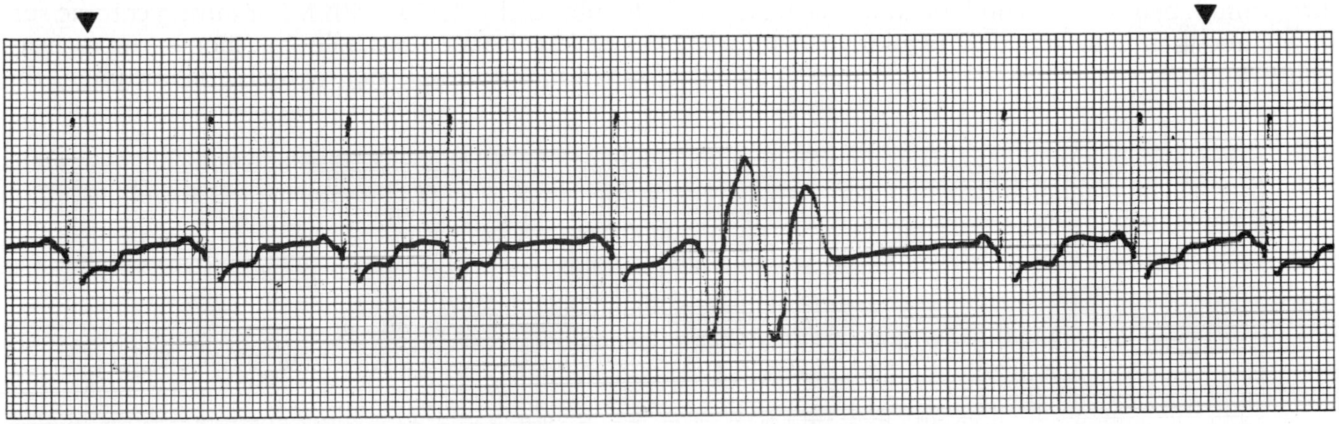

D

Couplet (two PVCs in a row).

FIGURE 43-4. Premature ventricular contractions (PVCs) or ventricular premature beats (VPBs). Rhythm: irregular. Rate: variable. Only interrupts the cycle of the ectopic, ventricular contraction. P-R: normal in sinus beats, not measurable in PVC. QRS: wide, bizarre, greater than 0.12 seconds. (Hudak, C. M. & Gallo, B. M. [1998]. *Critical care nursing* [7th ed.]. Philadelphia: Lippincott-Raven.)

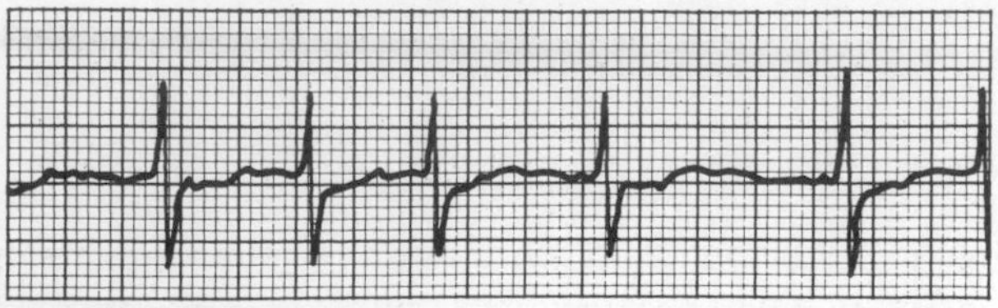

FIGURE 43-5. Atrial fibrillation. Rhythm: irregularly irregular. Rate: variable. Usually rapid on initiation of rhythm. Decreases when controlled by medication. P-R: no P waves are seen, replaced by an irregular wavy baseline. The atria are fibrillating due to impulses arising at a rate greater than 350. The ventricles respond when the AV node is stimulated to threshold and can receive the impulse. QRS: normal. (Hudak, C. M. & Gallo, B. M. [1998]. *Critical care nursing* [7th ed.]. Philadelphia: Lippincott-Raven.)

Trial (CAST) in the early 1990s. This multicenter, randomized, long-term study, conducted by the National Heart and Lung Institute, looked at the mortality of patients with asymptomatic, non–life-threatening arrhythmias who were treated with antiarrhythmics. The results of this study showed that long-term use of some antiarrhythmics was associated with an increased risk of death. In fact, some patients were two to three times at greater risk of death than untreated patients. These results prompted more clinical trials to look at the effectiveness of long-term use of antiarrhythmics.

Antiarrhythmics may block some reflex arrhythmias that help keep the cardiovascular system in balance, or may precipitate new, deadly arrhythmias. Therefore, it is important to document the arrhythmia being treated and the rationale for treatment, and to monitor a patient regularly when using these drugs.

CLASS I ANTIARRHYTHMICS

Class I antiarrhythmics are drugs that block the sodium channels in the cell membrane during an action potential (Figure 43-7). The class I drugs are local anesthetics or membrane stabilizing agents. They bind more quickly to sodium channels that are open or inactive, ones that have been stimulated and are not yet repolarized. This makes these drugs preferable in conditions like tachycardia, when the sodium gates are open frequently. The class I antiarrhythmics are further broken down into three subclasses, reflecting how their blockage of sodium channels affects the action potential.

- *Class Ia drugs* depress phase 0 of the action potential and prolong the action potential duration. Disopyramide (*Norpace*) is an oral drug also available for pediatric use and recommended for the treatment of life-threatening ventricular arrhythmias. Moricizine (*Ethmozine*) is one of the drugs found to increase cardiac death because of its proarrhythmic effects. It is available in oral form, for adults only, and should only be used if the benefit clearly outweighs the risk. Procainamide (*Pronestyl*) is available in IM, IV, and oral forms, making it a good drug to start treatment and switch to oral when possible. It is used for the treatment of documented life-threatening ventricular arrhythmias. Quinidine (*Quinaglute, Cardioquin*) is available PO, IM, and IV and is especially effective in treating atrial arrhythmias.
- *Class Ib drugs* depress phase 0 somewhat and actually shorten the duration of the action potential. Lidocaine (*Xylocaine*), the most frequently used antiarrhythmic, is used IM or IV to manage acute ventricular arrhythmias with MI or during cardiac surgery. It is also used as a bolus injection in emergencies when monitoring is not available to document the

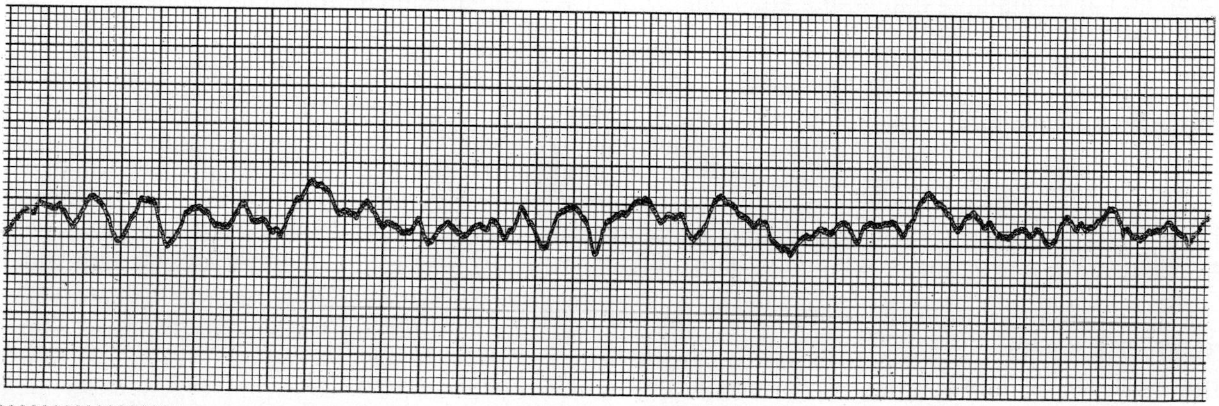

FIGURE 43-6. Ventricular fibrillation. Rhythm: irregular. Rate: not measurable. P-R: not measurable. QRS: not measurable, replaced by an irregular wavy baseline. No coordinated electrical or mechanical activity in the ventricle, no cardiac output. (Hudak, C. M. & Gallo, B. M. [1998]. *Critical care nursing* [7th ed.]. Philadelphia: Lippincott-Raven.)

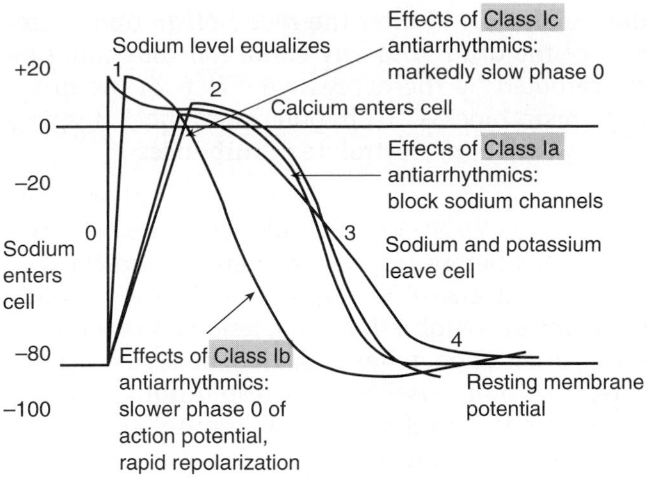

FIGURE 43-7. The cardiac action potentials, showing the effects of class Ia, Ib, and Ic antiarrhythmics.

exact arrhythmia. Mexiletine (*Mexitil*) is an oral drug only approved for use in life-threatening arrhythmias. The CAST showed that its use may not affect mortality. Tocainide (*Tonocard*) is an oral drug also approved for use only in the treatment of potentially life-threatening ventricular arrhythmias. This drug is being studied for the treatment of myotonic dystrophy and trigeminal neuralgia because of its effects on action potentials.

- *Class Ic drugs* markedly depress phase 0 with a resultant extreme slowing of conduction. They have little effect on the duration of the action potential. Flecainide (*Tambocor*) is a class Ic drug that was found to increase the risk of death in the CAST study. It is available as an oral drug for use in the treatment of life-threatening ventricular arrhythmias and for the prevention of paroxysmal atrial tachycardia (PAT) in symptomatic patients without structural heart disease. Propafenone (*Rhythmol*) is also an oral class Ic drug that can be used to treat potentially life-threatening ventricular arrhythmias as well as for prevention of PAT in symptomatic patients without structural heart defects.

THERAPEUTIC ACTIONS AND INDICATIONS

The class I antiarrhythmics stabilize the cell membrane by binding to sodium channels, depressing phase 0 of the action potential, and changing the duration of the action potential. They have a local anesthetic effect. These drugs are indicated for the treatment of potentially life-threatening ventricular arrhythmias and should not be used to treat other arrhythmias because of the risk of a proarrhythmic effect. Quinidine is especially effective in the treatment of atrial arrhythmias. Flecainide and propafenone are also used to prevent PAT in symptomatic patients who do not have structural heart defects.

CONTRAINDICATIONS/CAUTIONS

These drugs are contraindicated in the presence of allergy to any of these drugs; with bradycardia or heart block unless an artificial pacemaker is in place, as changes in conduction could lead to complete heart block; with congestive heart failure (CHF), hypotension, or shock, which could be exacerbated by effects on the action potential; with pregnancy and lactation because of the potential for adverse effects on the fetus or neonate; and with electrolyte disturbances, which could alter the effectiveness of these drugs. Caution should be used with renal or hepatic dysfunction, which could interfere with the biotransformation and excretion of these drugs.

ADVERSE EFFECTS

The adverse effects of the class I antiarrhythmics are associated with their membrane-stabilizing effects and effects on action potentials. Central nervous system (CNS) effects can include dizziness, drowsiness, fatigue, twitching, mouth numbness, slurred speech, vision changes, and tremors that can progress to convulsions. Gastrointestinal (GI) symptoms include changes in taste, nausea, and vomiting. Cardiovascular effects include the development of arrhythmias (including heart blocks), hypotension, vasodilation, and the potential for cardiac arrest. Respiratory depression progressing to respiratory arrest can also occur. Other adverse effects include rash, hypersensitivity reactions, loss of hair, and potential bone marrow depression.

CLINICALLY IMPORTANT DRUG–DRUG INTERACTIONS

Several drug–drug interactions have been reported with these drugs, so the possibility of an interaction should always be considered before adding any drug to a drug regimen containing an antiarrhythmic. There is increased risk for arrhythmia development if these drugs are combined with other drugs that are known to cause arrhythmias, such as digoxin and the beta blockers. Because quinidine competes for renal transport sites with digoxin, the combination of these two drugs can lead to increased digoxin levels and digoxin toxicity. If these drugs are used in combination, the patient's digoxin level should be monitored and appropriate dosage adjustment made. Cimetidine increases serum levels and toxicity of the class I antiarrhythmics if these are combined; extreme caution should be used if patients are receiving this combination. There is increased risk of bleeding effects if these drugs are combined with oral anticoagulants; patients receiving this combination should be monitored closely and have their anticoagulant dose reduced as needed. Check individual drug monographs for specific interactions associated with each drug.

CLINICALLY IMPORTANT DRUG–FOOD INTERACTIONS

Quinidine requires a slightly acidic urine (normal state) for excretion. Patients receiving quinidine should avoid foods that alkalinize the urine (citrus juices, vegetables, antacids, milk products), which could lead to increased quinidine levels and toxicity.

DATA LINK

Data link to the following class I antiarrhythmics in your nursing drug guide:

CLASS I ANTIARRHYTHMICS

Name	Brand Name(s)	Usual Indication(s)
Class Ia		
disopyramide	*Norpace*	Treatment of life-threatening ventricular arrhythmias
moricizine	*Ethmozine*	Treatment of life-threatening ventricular arrhythmias
procainamide	*Pronestyl*	Treatment of life-threatening ventricular arrhythmias
P quinidine	*Quinaglute, Cardioquin*	Treatment of atrial arrhythmias
Class Ib		
P lidocaine	*Xylocaine*	Treatment of life-threatening ventricular arrhythmias during MI or cardiac surgery; emergency treatment of ventricular arrhythmias when diagnostic tests are not available
mexiletine	*Mexitil*	Treatment of life-threatening ventricular arrhythmias
tocainide	*Tonocard*	Treatment of life-threatening ventricular arrhythmias; studied for the treatment of myotonic dystrophy, trigeminal neuralgia
Class Ic		
P flecainide	*Tambocor*	Treatment of life-threatening ventricular arrhythmias; prevention of PAT in symptomatic patients with no structural heart defect
propafenone	*Rhythmol*	Treatment of life-threatening ventricular arrhythmias; prevention of PAT in symptomatic patients with no structural heart defect

NURSING CONSIDERATIONS
for patients receiving class I antiarrhythmics

Assessment

HISTORY. Screen for the following: any known allergies to these drugs; impaired liver or kidney function, which could alter the metabolism and excretion of the drug; and any condition that could be exacerbated by the depressive effects of the drugs (e.g., heart block, CHF, hypotension, shock, respiratory dysfunction, electrolyte disturbances).

PHYSICAL ASSESSMENT. Include screening for baseline status before beginning therapy and for any potential adverse effects. Assess the following: body temperature, weight; skin color, lesions, temperature; affect, orientation, reflexes, speech; pulse, blood pressure, perfusion, baseline ECG; respirations, adventitious sounds; bowel sounds, abdominal exam; and renal and liver function tests.

Nursing Diagnoses

The patient receiving an antiarrhythmic may have the following nursing diagnoses related to drug therapy:

- Alteration in thought processes and sensory–perceptual alteration related to CNS effects
- Risk for injury related to CNS effects
- Alteration in cardiac output related to cardiac effects
- Knowledge deficit regarding drug therapy

Implementation

- Continually monitor cardiac rhythm when initiating or changing dose *to detect potentially serious adverse effects and to evaluate drug effectiveness.*
- Maintain life support equipment on standby *to treat severe adverse reactions that might occur.*
- Give parenteral forms only if the oral form is not feasible; transfer to the oral form as soon as possible *to decrease the potential for severe adverse effects.*
- Titrate the dose to the smallest amount needed to achieve control of the arrhythmia *to decrease the risk of severe adverse effects.*
- Consult with the prescriber to reduce the dosage in patients with renal or hepatic dysfunction; reduced dosage may be needed *to ensure therapeutic effects without increased risk of toxic effects.*
- Establish safety precautions, including side rails, lighting, and noise control, if CNS effects occur *to ensure patient safety.*
- Arrange for periodic monitoring of cardiac rhythm when the patient is on long-term therapy *to evaluate effects on cardiac status.*
- Provide comfort measures *to help the patient tolerate drug effects.* These include small, frequent meals, access to bathroom facilities, bowel program as

PATIENT TEACHING CHECKLIST

Antiarrhythmics

Create customized patient teaching materials for a specific antiarrhythmic from your CD-ROM. Your patient teaching should stress the following points for drugs within this class:

An antiarrhythmic acts to stop irregular rhythm in the heart, helping it to beat more regularly and therefore more efficiently. The drug may work by making the heart less irritable and by slowing it down to a more effective rate.

- Procainamide must be taken around the clock. You will need to have an alarm clock at night to awaken you to take your medication. It should be taken on an empty stomach. The best times for you to take procainamide are: ___________, ___________, ___________, ___________.
- Quinidine and disopyramide may be taken with food if gastrointestinal upset occurs.
- Verapamil should be taken on an empty stomach, 1 hour before or 2 hours after a meal.

If quinidine has been prescribed for you, plan to limit your intake of certain foods (e.g., citrus juices, milk, vegetables) and avoid over-the-counter drugs (e.g., antacids) that make your urine alkaline. If your urine become alkaline, you may develop signs of an overdose of quinidine.

It is helpful to take your pulse on a regular basis. You should count the number of beats in 1 minute and determine if your pulse is regular or irregular. Your usual resting heart rate is ___________. Record your pulse on your calendar for easy reference.

Some of the following adverse effects may occur:

- Tiredness, weakness—Space your activities throughout the day and take periodic rest periods to help conserve your energy and rest your heart.
- Nausea, vomiting, loss of appetite—These problems may pass over time; taking the drug with meals, if appropriate, or eating small, frequent meals may help.
- Sensitivity to light (more pronounced with disopyramide)—Avoid prolonged exposure to ultraviolet light or sunlight.
- Constipation or diarrhea—These reactions are very common; if either occurs and becomes too uncomfortable, consult your health care provider.

Report any of the following to your health care provider: chest pain, difficulty breathing, ringing in the ears, swelling in the ankles or legs, unusually slow pulse (<35 beats/min), unusually fast pulse (>15 beats/min above your normal rate), suddenly irregular pulse, fever, rash.

Tell any doctor, nurse, or other health care provider that you are taking this drug.

Keep this drug, and all medications, out of the reach of children.

Avoid the use of over-the-counter medications while you are on this drug. If you feel that you need one of these, consult with your health care provider for the best choice. Many of these drugs may interfere with your benzodiazepine.

It is important to get regular medical follow-up while you are on this drug to have your heart rhythm evaluated as well as your response to the drug.

Do not stop taking this medication. If you have to stop the medication for any reason, contact your health care provider immediately.

This Teaching Checklist reflects general patient teaching guidelines. It is not meant to be a substitute for drug-specific teaching information, which is available in nursing drug guides.

needed, food with drug if GI upset is severe, environmental control, orientation, and appropriate skin care as needed.

- Provide thorough patient teaching, including the name of the drug, dosage prescribed, measures to avoid adverse effects, and warning signs of problems as well as the need for periodic monitoring and evaluation *to enhance patient knowledge about drug therapy and promote compliance with the drug regimen* (see Patient Teaching Checklist: Antiarrhythmics).
- Offer support and encouragement to deal with the diagnosis and drug regimen.

Evaluation

- Monitor patient response to the drug (stabilization of cardiac rhythm and output).
- Monitor for adverse effects (sedation, hypotension, cardiac arrhythmias, respiratory depression, CNS effects).

NURSING CARE GUIDE
Antiarrhythmics

Assessment	Nursing Diagnoses	Implementation	Evaluation
HISTORY Allergies to any of these drugs, renal or hepatic dysfunction, pregnancy, lactation, heart block, CHF, shock, hypotension, electrolyte disturbances	Alteration in thought processes and sensory–perceptual alteration related to CNS effects Potential for injury related to CNS effects Alteration in cardiac output related to CV effects Knowledge deficit regarding drug therapy	Continually monitor cardiac rhythm when initiating or changing doses. Provide comfort and safety measures: have life support equipment on standby; use parenteral form only if oral form cannot be used; titrate dose to smallest needed for therapeutic effects; reduce dosage with renal or hepatic dysfunction; lower dose with renal, hepatic impairment; use side rails, environmental control as needed for safety; provide small frequents meals, access to bathroom facilities, skin care. Provide support and reassurance to deal with drug effects. Provide patient teaching regarding drug, dosage, adverse effects, what to report, and safety precautions.	Evaluate drug effects: stabilization of cardiac rhythm and output. Monitor for adverse effects: sedation, dizziness, insomnia; cardiac arrhythmias; GI upset; respiratory depression. Monitor for drug–drug interactions as indicated for each drug. Evaluate effectiveness of patient teaching program. Evaluate effectiveness of comfort and safety measures.
PHYSICAL EXAMINATION CV: BP, P, perfusion CNS: orientation, affect, reflexes, vision Skin: color, lesions, texture Resp: R, adventitious sounds GI: abdominal exam, bowel sounds Lab tests: liver and renal function tests, CBC			

• Evaluate the effectiveness of the teaching plan (patient can name drug, dosage, adverse effects to watch for, specific measures to avoid adverse effects, importance of continued follow-up).
• Monitor the effectiveness of comfort measures and compliance to the regimen (see Nursing Care Guide: Antiarrhythmics).

CLASS II ANTIARRHYTHMICS

The class II antiarrhythmics are beta adrenergic blockers that block beta receptors, causing a depression of phase 4 of the action potential (Figure 43-8). By doing this, these drugs slow the recovery of the cells, leading to a slowing of conduction and dec-

CASE STUDY

Recognizing Quinidine Toxicity

PRESENTATION

R. A., a 56-year-old post-MI patient with a documented duodenal ulcer, has felt highly "stressed" lately. He called the nurse with complaints of dizziness, confusion, headaches, nausea, vomiting, and a very slow pulse. The nurse requested that R. A. come in immediately to be evaluated. On examination, pulse was 52, with an ECG showing second degree heart block with occasional escape beats; BP 82/60. R. A. reported that he was still taking quinidine, which had been started post-MI to regulate arrhythmias. He states that he has been taking *Mylanta* (an antacid) for ulcer pain, about 12 tablets a day, and that he has been drinking a lot of orange juice to treat a cold.

CRITICAL THINKING QUESTIONS

Based on your knowledge of the drug quinidine and the symptoms reported by R. A., what do you think happened? If R. A. is found to be quinidine toxic, what should be done to alleviate his signs and symptoms and to return him to his normal cardiac rhythm? What teaching points will be essential to convey to R. A. before he goes home? Should any other problems be addressed while R. A. is being evaluated at this time?

DISCUSSION

R. A. has many of the signs and symptoms of quinidine toxicity—slow pulse, AV heart block, hypotension, nausea, vomiting, dizziness, headache, confusion. The initial treatment for this condition includes withholding all medications, ordering blood drawn for a serum quinidine level determination, and careful monitoring of R. A., with emergency life support equipment on standby in case his condition deteriorates. (This equipment should include sodium lactate, which blocks the drug's effects on the myocardium, and adrenergic stimulants, which can increase blood pressure, pulse, and cardiac output.)

R. A. stabilized rapidly, and patient teaching on the current drug therapy was initiated. The effects of foods and drugs on urine pH and on quinidine excretion were stressed, and R. A. received a written list of foods and antacids that cause an alkaline urine (citrus juices, milk, vegetables). The alkaline urine prevents quinidine excretion, leading to build-up of toxic levels. The combination of the orange juice and the numerous doses of antacid probably made R. A.'s urine quite alkaline, leading to increased serum levels of quinidine and a toxic response to the drug. The signs and symptoms of quinidine toxicity should be reviewed with R. A., as well as precautionary measures that he should take. He should be told that he did the correct thing in calling and should be encouraged to do so again if problems occur again. The teaching program should be directed at preventing future problems.

While R. A. is within the health care system, it is important to offer him support and encouragement. His ulcer can be evaluated at this time, as well as his feelings of stress. R. A. may need to ventilate his feelings and explore new ways of coping with or avoiding stressful situations. The effects of stress on the heart can be reviewed with R. A. to help him realize the importance of stress management. It would also be helpful to review the problems of self-medication for various complaints while taking a prescription drug. R. A. should receive all information in writing for future reference. Eventually, he may be reevaluated to determine the actual need for continuing this medication. In the meantime, good patient education can help prevent serious complications while he is using the drug.

reased automaticity. There are several beta adrenergic blockers that are used as antiarrhythmics.

Acebutolol (*Sectral*), an oral drug also used as an antihypertensive, is especially effective in the treatment of premature ventricular contractions (PVCs). Esmolol (*Brevibloc*), an IV drug, is used for the short-term management of supraventricular tachycardia and tachycardia that is not responding to other measures. Propranolol (*Inderal*) is used as an antihypertensive, antianginal, antimigraine headache drug and as an antiarrhythmic to treat supraventricular tachycardias caused by digoxin or catecholamines.

THERAPEUTIC ACTIONS AND INDICATIONS

The class II antiarrhythmics competitively block beta receptor sites in the heart and kidneys, thereby decreasing heart rate, cardiac excitability, and cardiac output, and slowing conduction through the AV node and decreasing the release of renin. These effects stabilize excitable cardiac tissue and decrease blood pressure, which decreases the heart's workload and may further stabilize hypoxic cardiac tissue. These drugs are indicated for the treatment of supraventricular tachycardias and PVCs.

CONTRAINDICATIONS/CAUTIONS

The use of these drugs is contraindicated in the presence of sinus bradycardia (rate < 45) and AV block, which could be exacerbated by the effects of these drugs; with cardiogenic shock, CHF, asthma, or respiratory depression which could be made worse by the blocking of beta receptors; and with pregnancy

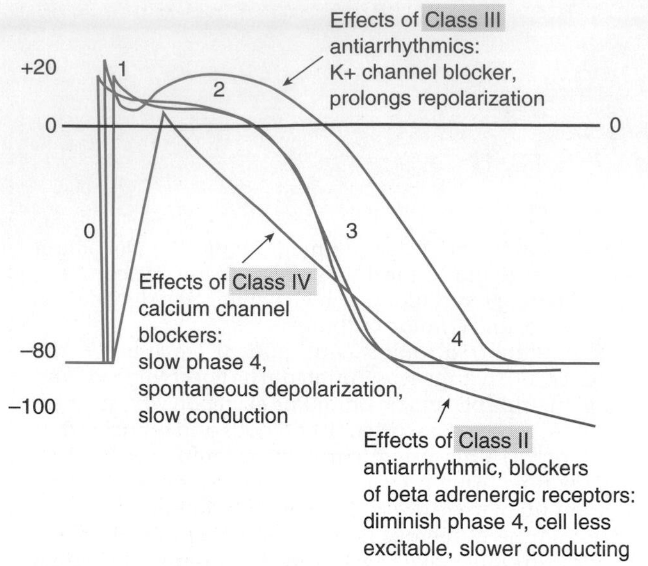

FIGURE 43-8. The cardiac action potential, showing the effects of class II, III, and IV antiarrhythmics.

and lactation because of the potential for adverse effects on the neonate. Caution should be used with diabetes and thyroid dysfunction, which could be altered by the blocking of the beta receptors, and with renal and hepatic dysfunction, which could alter the metabolism and excretion of these drugs.

ADVERSE EFFECTS

The adverse effects associated with class II antiarrhythmics are related to the effects of blocking beta receptors in the sympathetic nervous system. CNS effects include dizziness, insomnia, dreams, and fatigue. Cardiovascular symptoms can include hypotension, bradycardia, AV block, arrhythmias, and alterations in peripheral perfusion. Respiratory effects can include bronchospasm and dyspnea. GI problems frequently include nausea, vomiting, anorexia, constipation, and diarrhea. Other effects to anticipate include a loss of libido, decreased exercise tolerance, and alterations in blood glucose levels.

CLINICALLY IMPORTANT DRUG–DRUG INTERACTIONS

There is a risk of increased effects if these drugs are taken with verapamil; if this combination is used, dosage adjustment will be needed. There is a possibility of increased hypoglycemia if combined with insulin; patients should be monitored closely. Other specific drug interactions may occur with each drug; check your drug reference before combining these drugs with any others.

DATA LINK

Data link to the following class II antiarrhythmics in your nursing drug guide:

CLASS II ANTIARRHYTHMICS

Name	Brand Name	Usual Indication(s)
acebutolol	*Sectral*	Management of PVCs
esmolol	*Brevibloc*	Short-term management of supraventricular tachycardia
P propranolol	*Inderal*	Treatment of supraventricular tachycardias caused by digoxin or catecholamines; treatment of hypertension, angina, migraine, situational anxiety

NURSING CONSIDERATIONS
for patients receiving class II antiarrhythmics

The nursing considerations for patients taking any antiarrhythmic are outlined above under class I antiarrhythmics.

CLASS III ANTIARRHYTHMICS

The class III antiarrhythmics block potassium channels, prolonging phase 3 of the action potential, which prolongs repolarization and slows the rate and conduction of the heart (see Figure 43-3). Class III antiarrhythmics include a number of agents.

Amiodarone (*Cordarone*) is available as an oral and IV drug. It should only be used to treat documented life-threatening arrhythmias because it has been associated with serious and even fatal toxic reactions; other drugs should always be tried first. Bretylium (generic), which is used IV or IM, is indicated for the short-term treatment of ventricular fibrillation or ventricular arrhythmias that do not respond to other drugs. Ibutilide (*Corvert*) is used IV to rapidly convert atrial fibrillation or atrial flutter of recent onset; it is most effective if onset is less than 90 days. Sotalol (*Betapace*) is an oral drug that is only indicated for the treatment of documented life-threatening arrhythmias. Because it is known to be proarrhythmic, it is undesirable for any other use.

THERAPEUTIC ACTIONS AND INDICATIONS

The class III antiarrhythmics block potassium channels and slow the outward movement of potassium during phase 3 of the action potential. This action prolongs the action potential. All of these drugs are proarrhythmic and have the potential of inducing arrhythmias. These drugs are indicated for the treatment of life-threatening ventricular arrhythmias

NURSING CHALLENGE

Atrial Fibrillation

Atrial fibrillation (AF) is a relatively common arrhythmia of the atria. It has been associated with CAD, myocardial inflammation, valvular disease, cardiomegaly, and rheumatic heart disease. The cells of the atria are connected side to side and top to bottom and are relatively simple cells. In contrast, the cells of the ventricles are connected only from top to bottom, with one cell connected only to one or two other cells. It is much easier, therefore, for an ectopic focus in the atria to spread that impulse throughout the entire atria, setting up a cycle of chaotic depolarization and repolarization. It is more difficult to stimulate fibrillation in the ventricles, as one ectopic site cannot rapidly spread impulses to many other cells, only the cells connected in its two- or three-cell set.

Fibrillation results in lack of any coordinated pumping action because the muscles are not stimulated to contract and pump out blood. In the ventricles, this is a life-threatening situation. If the ventricles do not pump blood, no blood is delivered to the brain, the tissues of the body, or to the heart muscle itself. However, loss of pumping action in the atria does not usually cause much of a problem in itself. The atrial contraction is like an extra kick of blood into the ventricles; it provides a nice backup to the system, but the blood will still flow normally without that kick.

One of the problems with AF occurs when the AF is present over a period of more than 1 week. The auricles (those appendages hanging on the atria to collect blood; see Chapter 40) fill with blood that is not effectively pumped into the ventricles. Over time, this somewhat stagnant blood tends to clot. Because the auricles are sacks of striated muscle fibers, blood clots form around these fibers. In this situation, if the atria were to contract in a coordinated manner, there is a substantial risk that those clots or emboli will be pumped into the ventricles and then into the lungs (from the right auricle), which could lead to pulmonary emboli, or to the brain or periphery (from the left auricle), which could cause a stroke or occlusion of peripheral vessels.

Treatment of AF can be complicated if the length of time that a patient has been in AF is not known. If a patient goes into AF acutely, drug therapy is now available for rapid conversion of the AF. For example, ibutilide is often very effective when given IV for rapid conversion. Quinidine IM also may convert a patient effectively. In some situations, digoxin has been effective in converting AF. Electrocardioversion, a DC current shock to the chest, may break the cycle of fibrillation and convert a patient to sinus rhythm, after which the rhythm will need to be stabilized with drug therapy. Quinidine is often the drug of choice for long-term stabilization.

If the onset of AF is not known and it is suspected that the atria may well have been fibrillating for over a week, the patient is better off staying in AF without drug therapy or electrocardioversion. Prophylactic oral anticoagulants are given to decrease the risk of clot formation and emboli being pumped into the system. Converting this person could result in potentially life-threatening embolization of the lungs, brain, or other tissues.

The other danger of AF is rapid ventricular response to the atrial stimuli, a condition called supraventricular tachycardia (SVT). With the atria firing impulses, possibly 200 to 300 a minute, the number of stimuli conducted into the ventricles will be erratic and irregular. If the ventricle is responding too rapidly—over 120 times a minute—filling time of the ventricles will be greatly reduced, causing cardiac output to fall dramatically. In these situations, and when AF is anticipated (such as with atrial flutter or PAT), drugs may be given to slow conduction and protect the ventricles from rapid rates. Flecainide, propafenone, and propranolol are often used to convert rapid SVTs. Esmolol, diltiazem, and verapamil are used IV to convert SVT with rapid ventricular response, which could progress to atrial fibrillation.

Careful patient assessment is essential before beginning treatment for AF: if a history cannot be established from patient information and medical records are not available, it is usually recommended that AF be left untreated and anticoagulant therapy begun. This can pose a real challenge for the nurse in trying to teach a patient about why the rapid and irregular heart rate will not be treated and explaining all of the factors involved in the long-term use of oral anticoagulants.

(bretylium and sotalol) or the conversion of recent onset atrial fibrillation or atrial flutter to normal sinus rhythm (ibutilide).

CONTRAINDICATIONS/CAUTIONS

When these drugs are used to treat life-threatening arrhythmias for which no other drug has been effective, there are no contraindications. Ibutilide should not be used in the presence of AV blocks, which could be exacerbated by the drug. Caution should be used with all of these drugs in the presence of shock, hypotension, or respiratory depression (which could be made worse by the depressive effects on action potentials), and with renal or hepatic disease (which could alter the biotransformation and excretion of these drugs).

ADVERSE EFFECTS

The adverse effects associated with these drugs are related to the changes they cause in action potentials. Nausea, vomiting, and GI distress; weakness and dizziness; and hypotension, CHF, and arrhythmia are common. Amiodarone has been associated with a potentially fatal liver toxicity, ocular abnormalities, and the development of very serious cardiac arrhythmias.

CLINICALLY IMPORTANT DRUG–DRUG INTERACTIONS

These drugs can cause serious toxic effects if combined with digoxin or quinidine. Other specific drug–drug interactions have been reported with individual drugs; a drug reference should always be consulted when adding a new drug to a regimen containing any of these drugs.

DATA LINK

Data link to the following class III antiarrhythmics in your nursing drug guide:

CLASS III ANTIARRHYTHMICS

Name	Brand Name	Usual Indication
amiodarone	*Cordarone*	Treatment of life-threatening ventricular arrhythmias not responding to any other drug
P bretylium	generic	Treatment of ventricular fibrillation and ventricular tachycardias not responsive to other drugs
ibutilide	*Corvert*	Conversion of recent onset atrial fibrillation or atrial flutter
sotalol	*Betapace*	Treatment of life-threatening ventricular arrhythmias not responding to any other drug

NURSING CONSIDERATIONS
for patients receiving class III antiarrhythmics

The nursing considerations for patients taking any antiarrhythmic are outlined above under class I antiarrhythmics.

CLASS IV ANTIARRHYTHMICS

The class IV antiarrhythmics act to block calcium channels in the cell membrane, leading to a depression of depolarization and a prolongation of phases 1 and 2 of repolarization, which will slow automaticity and conduction (see Figure 43-3). The calcium channel blockers are used as antihypertensives (see Chapter 41) and to treat angina (see Chapter 45). The two calcium channel blockers that seem to have special effects on the heart muscle are diltiazem (*Cardizem*), which is used IV to treat paroxysmal supraventricular tachycardia, and verapamil (*Calan, Covera*), which is used parenterally to treat supraventricular tachycardia and to temporarily control rapid ventricular response to atrial flutter or fibrillation.

THERAPEUTIC ACTIONS AND INDICATIONS

The class IV antiarrhythmics block the movement of calcium ions across the cell membrane, depressing the generation of action potentials, delaying phase I and 2 of repolarization, and slowing conduction through the AV node. They are indicated for the treatment of supraventricular tachycardia and to control ventricle response to rapid atrial rates. They are given IV for these purposes.

CONTRAINDICATIONS/CAUTIONS

These drugs are contraindicated with known allergy to any calcium channel blocker; with sick sinus syndrome or heart block (unless an artificial pacemaker is in place) because the block could be exacerbated by these drugs; with pregnancy or lactation because of the potential for adverse effects on the fetus or neonate; and with CHF or hypotension because of the hypotensive effects of these drugs. Caution should be used with idiopathic hypertrophic subaortic stenosis (IHSS), which could be exacerbated, or with impaired renal or liver function, which could affect the metabolism or excretion of these drugs.

ADVERSE EFFECTS

The adverse effects associated with these drugs are related to their vasodilation of blood vessels throughout the body. CNS effects include dizziness, weakness, fatigue, depression, and headache. GI upset, nausea, and vomiting can occur. Hypotension, CHF, shock, arrhythmias, and edema have also been reported.

CLINICALLY IMPORTANT DRUG–DRUG INTERACTIONS

Verapamil has been associated with many drug–drug interactions including increased risk of cardiac depression with beta blockers; additive AV slowing with digoxin; increased serum levels and toxicity of digoxin, carbemazepine, prazosin, and quinidine; increased respiratory depression with atracurium, gallamine, metocurine, pancuronium, rocuronium, tubocurarine, and vecuronium; and decreased effects if combined with calcium products or rifampin. There is a risk of severe cardiac effects if given IV within 48 hours of IV beta adrenergic drugs; avoid this combination. Diltiazem can increase the serum levels and toxicity of cyclosporine if taken concurrently.

DATA LINK

Data link to the following class IV antiarrhythmics in your nursing drug guide:

CLASS IV ANTIARRHYTHMICS

Name	Brand Name(s)	Usual Indication(s)
P diltiazem	*Cardizem*	IV to treat paroxysmal supraventricular tachycardia
verapamil	*Calan, Covera*	IV to treat paroxysmal supraventricular tachycardia; slow ventricular response to rapid atrial rates

NURSING CONSIDERATIONS
for patients receiving class IV antiarrhythmics

The nursing considerations for patients taking any antiarrhythmic are outlined above under class I antiarrhythmics.

WWW.WEB LINKS

Patients and health care providers may want to consult the following Internet sources:

Information on arrhythmias, drug therapy, current research, the National Heart, Lung, and Blood Institute:
http://www.nscardiology.com/factsarrhythmia.htm

Patient information on patient teaching, supports, other educational programs:
http://www.cardioassoc.com/patient_pgs/conditions/arrhythmias.asp

Information on interpreting arrhythmias, therapy, research:
http://sageunix.uvm.edu/dana/vtchip/arrhythm.htm

Patient information, support groups, research information on heart disease, scientific programs:
http://www.amhrt.org

OTHER DRUGS USED TO TREAT ARRHYTHMIAS

Adenosine (*Adenocard*) is another antiarrhythmic that is used to convert supraventricular tachycardia to sinus rhythm when vagal maneuvers have been ineffective. It is often the drug of choice for terminating supraventricular tachycardias, including those associated with the use of alternate conduction pathways around the AV node (e. g., Wolff-Parkinson-White syndrome), for two reasons: (1) it has a very short duration of action (about 15 seconds); and (2) it is associated with very few adverse effects (headache, flushing, and dyspnea of short duration). This drug slows conduction through the AV node, prolongs the refractory period, and decreases automaticity in the AV node. It is given IV with the patient continually monitored.

Digoxin (see Chapter 42) is also used at times to treat arrhythmias. This drug slows calcium from leaving the cell, prolonging the action potential and slowing conduction and heart rate. Digoxin is effective in the treatment of atrial arrhythmias. The drug is also positively inotropic, leading to increased cardiac output, which will increase perfusion of the coronary arteries and may eliminate the cause of some arrhythmias as hypoxia is resolved and waste products are removed more effectively.

Table 43-1 provides a summary of the types of arrhythmias and specific drugs used to treat each.

TABLE 43-1

TYPES OF ARRHYTHMIAS AND DRUGS OF CHOICE FOR TREATMENT

Arrhythmia	Antiarrhythmic Drugs
ATRIAL	
Flutter or fibrillation	Class Ia: quinidine* (long-term) Class III: ibutilide* (conversion of recent onset) Other: digoxin
Paroxysmal atrial tachycardia (PAT)	Class Ic: flecainide, propafenone*
Supraventricular tachycardia (SVT)	Class II: esmolol* (short-term), propranolol Class IV: diltiazem (IV), verapamil (IV) Other: adenosine* (SVT, including those caused by using alternate conduction pathways)
VENTRICULAR	
Premature ventricular contractions (PVCs)	Class Ib: lidocaine* Class II: acebutolol
Tachycardia or fibrillation	Class Ib: lidocaine* Class III: bretylium
Life-threatening ventricular arrhythmias	Class Ia: disopyramide, moricizine (X), procainamide Class Ib: mexiletine, tocainide Class Ic: flecainide (X), propafenone Class III: amiodarone (X), sotalol (X)

* drug of choice
(X) not drug of choice; proarrhythmic

DATA LINK

Data link to these other antiarrhythmics in your nursing drug guide:

OTHER ANTIARRHYTHMICS

Name	Brand Name(s)	Usual Indication(s)
adenosine	*Adenocard*	Treatment of supraventricular tachycardias, including those caused by the use of alternate conduction pathways
digoxin	*Lanoxin, Lanoxicaps*	Treatment of atrial flutter, atrial fibrillation, paroxysmal atrial tachycardia

NURSING CONSIDERATIONS
for patients receiving other antiarrhythmics

The nursing considerations for patients taking any of these antiarrhythmics are outlined above under class I antiarrhythmics.

CHAPTER SUMMARY

- Disruptions in the normal rate of rhythm of the heart are called arrhythmias (also known as dysrhythmias).
- Cardiac rate and rhythm are normally determined by the heart's specialized conduction system starting with the SA node, progressing through the atria to the AV node, through the bundle of His into the ventricles, and down bundle branches to the fibers of the Purkinje system.
- The cardiac cells possess the property of automaticity which allows them to generate an action potential and stimulate the cardiac muscle without stimulation from external sources.
- Disruptions in the automaticity of the cells or the conduction of the impulse resulting in arrhythmias can be caused by changes in heart rate (tachycardias or bradycardias); stimulation from ectopic foci in the atria or ventricles which cause an uncoordinated muscle contraction; or blocks in the conduction system (AV heart block or bundle branch blocks) which alter the normal movement of the impulse through the system.
- Arrhythmias can arise because of changes to the automaticity or the conductivity of the heart cells due to electrolyte disturbances, decreases in the oxygen delivered to the cells leading to hypoxia or anoxia, structural damage that changes the conduction pathway, acidosis or the accumulation of waste products, or drug effects.
- Arrhythmias cause problems because they alter the hemodynamics of the cardiovascular system. They can cause a decrease in cardiac output related to the uncoordinated pumping action of the irregular rhythm, leading to lack of filling time for the ventricles. Any of these can interfere with the delivery to blood to the brain, the other tissues, or the heart muscle itself.
- Antiarrhythmics are drugs that alter the action potential of the heart cells and interrupt arrhythmias. The CAST study found that the long-term treatment of arrhythmias may actually cause cardiac death, so these drugs are now indicated for the short-term treatment of potentially life-threatening ventricular arrhythmias.
- Class I antiarrhythmics block sodium channels, depress phase 0 of the action potential, and generally prolong the action potential, leading to a slowing of conduction and automaticity.
- Class II antiarrhythmics are beta adrenergic receptor blockers that prevent sympathetic stimulation.
- Class III antiarrhythmics block potassium channels and prolong phase 3 of the action potential.
- Class IV antiarrhythmics are calcium channel blockers that shorten the action potential, disrupting ineffective rhythms and rates.
- A patient receiving an antiarrhythmic drug needs to be constantly monitored while being stabilized and during the use of the drug to detect the development of arrhythmias or other adverse effects associated with altering the action potentials of other muscles or nerves.

BIBLIOGRAPHY

Bullock, B. L. (2000). *Focus on pathophysiology.* Philadelphia: Lippincott Williams & Wilkins.

Epstein, A. E. et al. (1993). Mortality following ventricular arrhythmic suppression. The original design concept of the CAST study. *Journal of the American Medical Association, 270*(20).

Hardman, J. G., Limbird, L. E., Molinoff, P. B., Ruddon, R. W., & Gilman, A. G. (Eds.). (1996). *Goodman and Gilman's the pharmacological basis of therapeutics* (9th ed.). New York: McGraw-Hill.

Karch, A. M. (2000). *2000 Lippincott's nursing drug guide.* Philadelphia: Lippincott Williams & Wilkins.

McEvoy, B. R. (1999). *Facts and comparisons 1999.* St. Louis: Facts and Comparisons.

Medical letter on drugs and therapeutics. (1999). New Rochelle, NY: Medical Letter.

Porth, C. M. (1998). *Pathophysiology: Concepts of altered health states* (5th ed.). Philadelphia: Lippincott-Raven.

CHAPTER 44

Antianginal Agents

Nitrates
- amyl nitrate
- isosorbide dinitrate
- **P** nitroglycerin

Beta blockers
- nadolol
- **P** propranolol

Calcium channel blockers
- amlodipine
- bepridil
- **P** diltiazem
- nicardipine
- nifedipine
- verapamil

CHAPTER OUTLINE

KEY TERMS

angina pectoris
atheromas
atherosclerosis
coronary artery disease (CAD)
myocardial infarction
nitrates
Prinzmetal's angina
pulse pressure

INTRODUCTION

Coronary artery disease (CAD) has for many years been the leading cause of death in the United States and most western nations. Despite great strides in the understanding of the contributing causes of this disease and ways to prevent it, CAD claims more lives than any other disease. The drugs discussed in this chapter are used to prevent myocardial death when the coronary vessels are already seriously damaged and having trouble maintaining the blood flow to the heart muscle. Chapters 45 and 46 will discuss drugs that are used to reverse or prevent the blocking of the coronary arteries before they become narrowed and damaged.

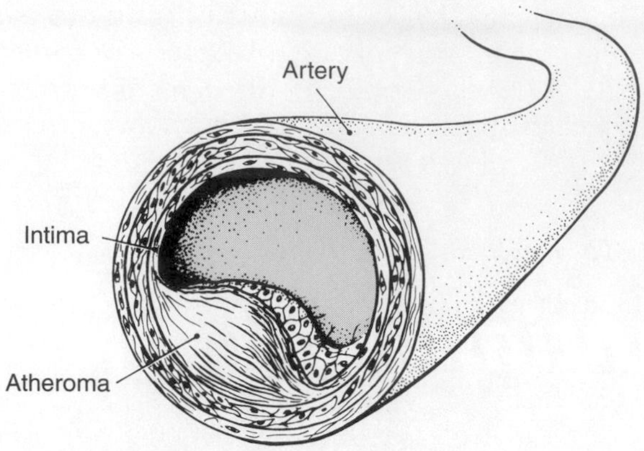

FIGURE 44-1. Schematic illustration of an atheromatous plaque. (Bullock, B. L. [2000]. *Focus on pathophysiology.* Philadelphia: Lippincott Williams & Wilkins.)

CORONARY ARTERY DISEASE

The myocardium, or heart muscle, must receive a constant supply of blood in order to have the oxygen and nutrients needed to maintain a constant pumping action. The myocardium receives all of its blood from two coronary arteries that exit the sinuses of Valsalva at the base of the aorta. These vessels divide and subdivide to form the capillaries that will deliver oxygen to heart muscle fibers.

Unlike other tissues in the body, the heart muscle receives its blood supply during diastole, while it is at rest. This is important because when the heart muscle contracts, it becomes tight and clamps the blood vessels closed, rendering them unable to receive blood during systole, which is when all other tissues receive fresh blood. The openings in the sinuses of Valsalva, which are the beginnings of the coronary arteries, are positioned so that they can be filled when the blood flows back against the aortic valve when the heart is at rest. The pressure that fills these vessels is the pulse pressure (systolic-diastolic pressure)—the pressure of the column of blood falling back onto the closed aortic valve. The heart has just finished contracting and using energy and oxygen. The acid and carbon dioxide built up in the muscle will cause a local vasodilation and the blood will flow freely through the coronary arteries and into the muscle cells.

In CAD, the openings in the blood vessels become narrowed so blood is no longer able to flow freely to the muscle cells. The narrowing of the vessels is caused by the development of ***atheromas,*** or fatty tumors in the intima of the vessels (Figure 44-1). This is a process called ***atherosclerosis.*** These fatty deposits cause damage to the intimal lining of the vessels, attracting platelets and immune factors and causing swelling and the development of a larger deposit. Over time, these deposits severely decrease the size of the vessel. While the vessel is being narrowed by the deposits in the intima, the vessels are also losing their natural elasticity and becoming unable to respond to the normal stimuli to dilate or constrict to meet the needs of the tissues.

The person with atherosclerosis has a classic supply and demand problem. The heart may do just fine until there is increased activity or other stresses that put a demand on it to beat faster or harder. The normal heart would stimulate the vessels to deliver more blood when this occurs, but the narrowed vessels are not able to respond and cannot supply the blood needed by the working heart (Figure 44-2). The heart muscle then becomes hypoxic. As a result, the heart demands increased blood supply in order to function properly, but the supply cannot be delivered. This happens with ***angina pectoris,*** literally "suffoca-

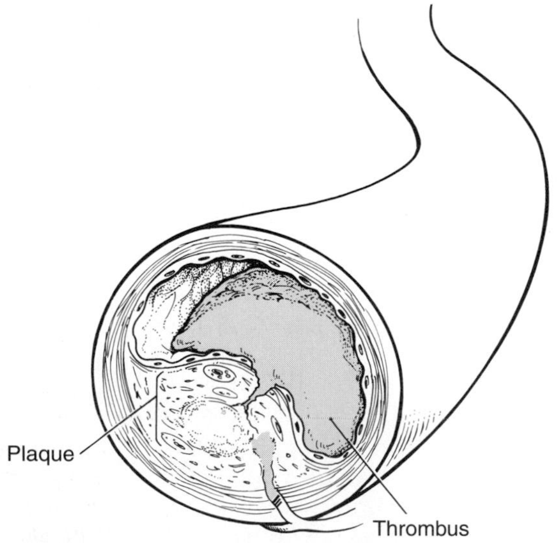

FIGURE 44-2. Thrombosis of an atherosclerotic plaque. It may partially or completely occlude the lumen of the vessel. (Bullock, B. L. [2000]. *Focus on pathophysiology.* Philadelphia: Lippincott Williams & Wilkins.)

tion of the chest." If the supply and demand issue becomes worse, or if a vessel becomes so narrow it actually occludes, the cells in the myocardium may actually become necrotic and die from a lack of oxygen. This is called a ***myocardial infarction.***

Stable Angina

The body's response to a lack of oxygen to the heart muscle is pain. Though the heart muscle does not have any pain fibers, a substance called factor P is released from ischemic myocardial cells, and pain is felt wherever substance P reacts with a pain receptor. For many people this is the chest, for others it is the left arm, still others have pain in the jaw and teeth. The basic response to this type of pain is to stop whatever one is doing and to wait for the pain to go away. In cases of minor limitations to the blood flow through vessels, stopping activity may bring the supply and demand for blood back into balance. This condition is called stable angina. There is no damage to heart muscle, and the basic reflexes surrounding the pain will restore blood flow to the heart muscle.

Unstable Angina

When the narrowing of the coronary arteries becomes more pronounced, the heart may experience episodes of ischemia even when the patient is at rest. This condition is called unstable angina. Though there is still no damage to heart muscle, the person is at great risk of completely cutting off the blood supply to the heart muscle if the heart should have to work hard or increase demand.

Prinzmetal's Angina

Prinzmetal's angina is an unusual form of angina because it seems to be caused by spasm of the blood vessels and not just by vessel narrowing. The person with this type of angina will have angina at rest, often at the same time each day, and usually with an associated ECG pattern change.

Acute Myocardial Infarction

When a coronary vessel becomes completely occluded and is unable to deliver blood to the cardiac muscle, the area of muscle that is dependent on that vessel for oxygen becomes ischemic, then necrotic. This is called a myocardial infarction (MI). The pain associated with this event can be excruciating; the person may also have nausea and a severe sympathetic stress reaction. A serious danger of an MI is that arrhythmias can develop in nearby tissue that is ischemic and very irritable. Most of the deaths caused by MI occur as a result of fatal arrhythmias. If the heart muscle has a chance to heal, within 6 to 10 weeks the dead area will be replaced with a scar and the muscle will compensate for the injury. When the area of the muscle that is damaged is very large, the muscle may not be able to compensate for the loss, and congestive heart failure and even cardiogenic shock may occur. These conditions can be fatal or can leave a person severely limited by the weakened heart muscle.

ANTIANGINAL DRUGS

In early cases of angina, avoidance of exertion or stressful situations may be sufficient to prevent anginal pain. Antianginal drugs are used to help restore the supply and demand ratio in oxygen delivery to the myocardium when rest is not enough. These drugs can work to improve the blood delivery to the heart muscle in one of two ways: (1) by dilating blood vessels (that is, by increasing the supply of oxygen), or (2) by decreasing the work of the heart (that is, by decreasing the demand for oxygen). Nitrates, beta adrenergic blockers, and calcium channel blockers are used to treat angina (Figure 44-3). They are all effective and are sometimes used in combination to achieve good control of the anginal pain. The type of drug that is best for a patient is determined by tolerance of adverse effects and response to the drug.

NITRATES

Nitrates are drugs that act directly on smooth muscle to cause relaxation and to depress muscle tone. Because the action is direct, it does not have to influence any nerve or other activity. The response to this

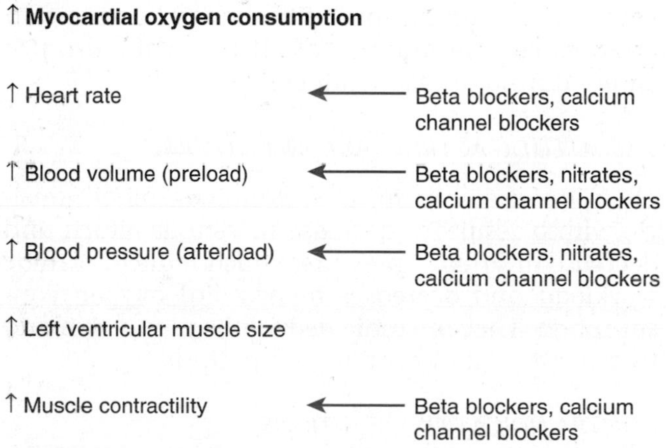

FIGURE 44-3. Factors affecting myocardial oxygen demand and points where antianginal drugs have their effects.

type of drug is usually quite fast. The nitrates relax and dilate veins, arteries, and capillaries, allowing increased blood flow through these vessels and lowering systemic blood pressure because of a drop in resistance. Because CAD causes a stiffening and lack of responsiveness in the coronary arteries, the nitrates probably have very little effect on increasing blood flow through these arteries. They do increase blood flow through healthy coronary arteries, so there will be an increased supply of blood through any healthy vessels in the heart, which could help the heart to compensate somewhat.

The main effect of nitrates, however, seems to be related to the drop in blood pressure that occurs. The vasodilation pools blood in veins and capillaries, decreasing the volume of blood that the heart has to pump around (the preload), while the relaxation of the vessels decreases the resistance the heart had to pump against (the afterload). The combination of these effects greatly reduces the cardiac workload and the demand for oxygen, thus bringing the supply and demand ratio back into balance.

Nitroglycerin (*Nitrobid, Nitrostat,* and others) is the nitrate of choice in an acute anginal attack. It can be given sublingually, as a translingual spray, IV, transdermally, topically, or as a transmucosal agent. It is rapidly absorbed and has an onset of action within minutes. It can be carried with the patient, who can use it when the need arises. It can also be used for prevention of anginal attacks in the slowed release forms. Other nitrates also are available for treating angina. Amyl nitrate (generic) is inhaled and has an onset of action of about 30 seconds. It comes as a capsule that has to be broken and waved under the patient's nose. The administration is somewhat awkward and usually requires a person other than the patient to give it properly. Isosorbide dinitrate (*Isordil* and others), an oral drug, has a slower onset of action but may last up to 4 hours. It is taken before chest pain begins in situations when exertion or stress can be anticipated. It is not the drug of choice during an acute attack.

THERAPEUTIC ACTIONS AND INDICATIONS

The nitrates cause direct relaxation of smooth muscle with a resultant decrease in venous return and decrease in arterial pressure, which reduces cardiac workload and decreases myocardial oxygen consumption. They are indicated for the prevention and treatment of attacks of angina pectoris.

CONTRAINDICATIONS/CAUTIONS

Nitrates are contraindicated in the presence of any allergy to nitrates. These drugs also are contraindicated in the following conditions: severe anemia because the decrease in cardiac output could be detrimental; head trauma or cerebral hemorrhage because the relaxation of cerebral vessels could cause intracranial bleeding; and pregnancy or lactation because of potential adverse effects on the neonate and ineffective blood flow to the fetus.

Caution should be used with hepatic or renal disease, which could alter the metabolism and excretion of these drugs. Caution also is required with hypotension, hypovolemia, or conditions limiting cardiac output (e.g., tamponade, low ventricular filling pressure, low pulmonary capillary wedge pressure) because these conditions could be exacerbated, resulting in serious adverse effects.

ADVERSE EFFECTS

The adverse effects associated with these drugs are related to the vasodilation and decrease in blood flow that occurs. Central nervous system (CNS) effects include headache, dizziness, and weakness. Gastrointestinal (GI) symptoms can include nausea, vomiting, and incontinence. Cardiovascular problems include hypotension, which can be severe and must be monitored; reflex tachycardia that occurs when blood pressure falls; syncope; and angina. Skin-related effects include flushing, pallor, sweating, and increased perspiration. When using the transdermal preparation, there is a risk of contact dermatitis and local hypersensitivity reactions.

CLINICALLY IMPORTANT DRUG—DRUG INTERACTIONS

There is a risk of hypertension and decreased antianginal effects if these drugs are given with ergot derivatives. There is also a risk of decreased therapeutic effects of heparin if these drugs are given together; if this combination is used, the patient should be monitored and appropriate dosage adjustments made.

DATA LINK

Data link to the following nitrates in your nursing drug guide:

NITRATES

Name	Brand Name(s)	Usual Indication(s)
amyl nitrate	generic	Relief of acute anginal pain
isosorbide dinitrate	*Isordil* and others	Prevention and treatment of angina
P nitroglycerin	*Nitrobid, Nitrostat* and others	Treatment of acute angina attack; prevention of anginal attacks

NURSING CONSIDERATIONS
for patients receiving nitrates

Assessment

HISTORY. Screen for the following: any known allergies to nitrates; impaired liver or kidney function, which could alter the metabolism and excretion of the drug; any condition that could be exacerbated by the hypotension and change in blood flow caused by these drugs (e.g., early MI, head trauma, cerebral hemorrhage, hypotension, hypovolemia, anemia, low cardiac output states); and pregnancy and lactation because of the potential adverse effects on the fetus or neonate.

PHYSICAL ASSESSMENT. Include screening for baseline status before beginning therapy and for any potential adverse effects. Assess the following: skin color, lesions, temperature; affect, orientation, reflexes; pulse, blood pressure, perfusion, baseline ECG; respirations, adventitious sounds; liver and renal function tests; CBC; and hemoglobin levels.

Nursing Diagnoses

The patient receiving a nitrate may have the following nursing diagnoses related to drug therapy:

- Alteration in cardiac output related to hypotensive effects
- Risk for injury related to CNS, cardiovascular effects
- Alteration in tissue perfusion related to hypotension, change in cardiac output
- Knowledge deficit regarding drug therapy

Implementation

- Give sublingual preparations under the tongue or in the buccal pouch; encourage the patient not to swallow *to ensure therapeutic effectiveness is achieved.* Ask the patient if the tablet "fizzles" or burns, *which indicates potency.* Always check the expiration date on the bottle and protect the medication from heat and light *because these drugs are volatile and lose their potency.*
- Give sustained release forms with water; caution patient not to chew or crush these preparations *because these preparations need to reach the GI tract intact.*
- Rotate the sites of topical forms *to decrease the risk of skin abrasion and breakdown;* monitor for signs of skin breakdown *and arrange for appropriate skin care as needed.*
- Ensure that translingual spray is used under the tongue and not inhaled *to ensure that the therapeutic effects can be achieved.*
- Break an amyl nitrate capsule and wave it under the nose of the angina patient *to provide rapid relief using the inhalation form of the drug;* this may be repeated with another capsule in 3 to 5 minutes if needed.
- Provide life support equipment on standby *in case of severe reaction to the drug or myocardial infarction.*
- Taper the dosage gradually (over 4–6 weeks) after long-term therapy *because abrupt withdrawal could cause a severe reaction including MI.*
- Provide comfort measures *to help the patient tolerate drug effects.* These include small, frequent meals, access to bathroom facilities if GI upset is severe, environmental control, safety precautions, orientation, and appropriate skin care as needed.
- Provide thorough patient teaching, including the name of the drug, dosage prescribed, proper administration, measures to avoid adverse effects, warning signs of problems, and the importance of periodic monitoring and evaluation *to enhance patient knowledge about drug therapy and promote compliance to the drug regimen* (see Patient Teaching Checklist: Antianginal Nitrates).
- Offer support and encouragement *to help the patient deal with the diagnosis and drug regimen.*

Evaluation

- Monitor patient response to the drug (alleviation of signs and symptoms of angina, prevention of angina).
- Monitor for adverse effects (hypotension, cardiac arrhythmias, GI upset, skin reactions, headache).
- Evaluate the effectiveness of the teaching plan (patient can name drug, dosage, proper administration, adverse effects to watch for, specific measures to avoid adverse effects, importance of continued follow-up).
- Monitor the effectiveness of comfort measures and compliance to the regimen (see Nursing Care Guide: Antianginal Nitrates).

BETA BLOCKERS

As discussed in Chapter 29, beta adrenergic blockers are used to block the stimulatory effects of the sympathetic nervous system. These drugs block beta adrenergic receptors and vasoconstriction (thereby stopping an increase in blood pressure) and prevent the increase in heart rate and increased intensity of myocardial contraction that occurs with sympathetic stimulation such as exertion or stress. These effects decrease the cardiac workload and the demand for oxygen.

PATIENT TEACHING CHECKLIST

Antianginal Nitrates

Create customized patient teaching materials for a specific antianginal nitrate from your CD-ROM. Your patient teaching should stress the following points for drugs within this class:

A nitrate is given to patients with chest pain that occurs because the heart muscle is not receiving enough oxygen. The nitrates act by decreasing the heart's workload and thus its need for oxygen, which it uses for energy. This relieves the pain of angina.

Besides taking the drug as prescribed, you can also help your heart by decreasing the work that it must do. For example, you can:

- Reduce weight, if necessary.
- Decrease or avoid the use of coffee, cigarettes, or alcoholic beverages.
- Avoid going outside in very cold weather; if this can't be avoided, dress warmly and avoid exertion while outside.
- Avoid stressful activities, especially in combination. For example, if you eat a big meal, don't drink coffee or alcoholic beverages with that meal. If you have just eaten a big meal, don't climb stairs; rest for a while.
- Determine which social interactions cause you to feel stressed or anxious, then find ways to limit or avoid these situations.
- Determine ways to ventilate your feelings (throwing things, screaming, diversions).
- Learn to slow down, rest periodically, and schedule your activities to allow your heart to pace its use of energy throughout the day and to help you to maintain your activities without pain.

Nitroglycerin tablets are taken sublingually. Place one tablet under your tongue. Do not swallow until the tablet has dissolved. The tablet should burn slightly or "fizzle" under your tongue; if this does not occur, the table is not effective and you should get a fresh supply of tablets. Ideally, take the nitroglycerin before your chest pain begins. If you know that a certain activity usually causes pain (for example, eating a big meal, attending a business meeting, engaging in sexual intercourse) take the tablet before undertaking the particular activity.

Dermal patches should be applied daily. They can be placed on the chest, upper arm, upper thigh, or back. They should be placed on an area that is free of body hair. The site of the application should be changed slightly each day to avoid excess irritation to the skin.

Sublingual nitroglycerin is a very unstable compound. Do not buy large quantities at a time, because it does not store well. Keep the drug in a dark, dry place and in a dark-colored glass container, not a plastic bottle, with a tight lid. Leave it in its own bottle. Do not combine it with other drugs.

Some of the following adverse effects may occur:

- Dizziness, lightheadedness—This will often pass as you adjust to the drug. Use great care if you are taking sublingual or transmucosal forms of the drug. Sit or lie down to avoid dizziness or falls. Change position slowly to help decrease the dizziness.
- Headache—This is a common problem. Over-the-counter headache remedies often provide no relief for the pain. Lying down in a cool environment and resting may help alleviate some of the discomfort.
- Flushing of the face and neck—This is usually a very minor problem that passes as the drug's effects pass.

Report any of the following to your health care provider: blurred vision, persistent or severe headache, skin rash, more frequent or more severe angina attacks, fainting.

Sublingual nitroglycerin usually relieves chest pain within 3 to 5 minutes. If pain is not relieved within 5 minutes, take another tablet. If pain continues, take another tablet in 5 minutes. A total of ____________ tablets can be used, spaced every 5 minutes. If the pain is not relieved after that time, call your health care provider or go to a hospital emergency room as soon as possible.

Tell any doctor, nurse, or other health care provider that you are taking this drug.

Keep this drug, and all medications, out of the reach of children.

Avoid the use of over-the-counter medications while you are on this drug. If you feel that you need one of these, consult with your health care provider for the best choice. Many of these drugs may change the effects of this drug and cause problems.

Avoid alcohol while you are on this drug because the combination can cause serious problems.

If you are on this drug for a prolonged period of time, do not stop taking it suddenly. Your body will need time to adjust to the loss of the drug. The dosage will need to be gradually reduced to prevent serious problems from developing.

This Teaching Checklist reflects general patient teaching guidelines. It is not meant to be a substitute for drug-specific teaching information which is available in nursing drug guides.

NURSING CARE GUIDE
Antianginal Nitrates

Assessment	Nursing Diagnoses	Implementation	Evaluation
HISTORY Allergies to any nitrates, renal or hepatic dysfunction, pregnancy, lactation, early MI, head trauma, hypotension, hypovolemia	Alteration in cardiac output related to hypotension Risk for injury related to CNS, CV effects Alteration in tissue perfusion related to CV effects Knowledge deficit regarding drug therapy	Ensure proper administration of drug. Provide comfort and safety measures: -Protect drug from heat and light. -Rotate transdermal sites. -Offer environmental control for headaches. -Give drug with food if GI upset occurs. -Provide skin care as needed. -Taper dosage after long-term use. Provide support and reassurance to deal with drug effects. Provide patient teaching regarding drug, dosage, adverse effects, what to report, safety precautions.	Evaluate drug effects: relief of signs and symptoms of angina, prevention of angina. Monitor for adverse effects: -headache, dizziness; arrhythmias; -GI upset; -skin reactions; -hypotension, CV effects. Monitor for drug–drug interactions as indicated for each drug. Evaluate effectiveness of patient teaching program. Evaluate effectiveness of comfort and safety measures.
PHYSICAL EXAMINATION CV: BP, P, perfusion, ECG CNS: orientation, affect, reflexes, vision Skin: color, lesions, texture Resp: R, adventitious sounds GI: abdominal exam, bowel sounds Lab tests: liver and renal function tests, CBC Hgb			

These drugs are sometimes used in combination with nitrates to increase exercise tolerance. Beta blockers have many adverse effects associated with the blocking of the sympathetic nervous system. The dose that is used to prevent angina is lower than doses used to treat hypertension, so there is a decreased incidence of adverse effects associated with this specific use of beta blockers. They are not recommended for use with patients with diabetes, peripheral vascular disease, or chronic obstructive pulmonary disease (COPD) because the effects on the sympathetic nervous system could exacerbate these problems. The beta blockers that are recommended for use in angina are propranolol (*Inderal*) and nadolol (*Corgard*).

THERAPEUTIC ACTIONS AND INDICATIONS

The beta blockers competitively block beta-adrenergic receptors in the heart and juxtaglomerular apparatus, decreasing the influence of the sympathetic nervous system on these tissues and thereby decreasing the excitability of the heart, cardiac output, and cardiac oxygen compensation, and lowering blood pressure. They are indicated for the long-term management of angina pectoris caused by atherosclerosis.

CASE STUDY

Handling an Angina Attack

PRESENTATION

S. W. is a 50-year-old white woman with a 2-year history of angina pectoris. She was given sublingual nitroglycerin to use in case of chest pain. For the past 6 months, she has been stable, experiencing little chest pain. This morning after her exercise class, S. W. had an argument with her daughter and experienced severe chest pain that was unrelieved by four nitroglycerin tablets taken over a 20-minute period. S. W.'s daughter rushed her to the hospital, where she was given oxygen through nasal prongs and placed on a cardiac monitor, which showed a sinus tachycardia of 110. A 12-lead ECG showed no changes from her previous ECG of 7 months ago. The chest pain subsided within 3 minutes of receiving another sublingual nitroglycerin. It was decided that S.W. should stay in the emergency room (ER) for a few hours for observation. The diagnosis of angina attack was made.

CRITICAL THINKING QUESTIONS

What nursing interventions should be done with S. W. while she is still in the ER? Consider the progression of CAD and the ways in which that progression can be delayed and chest pain avoided. What teaching points should be stressed with this patient? What type of guilt may the daughter experience after the fight with S. W.? What interventions would be useful in dealing with mother and daughter during this crisis? Should any further tests or treatments be addressed with S. W. when discussing her heart disease?

DISCUSSION

S. W.'s vital signs should be monitored closely while she is in the ER. If her attack subsides, she will be discharged with review of her teaching for CAD. It would be a good time to discuss angina with S.W. and her daughter, reviewing the pathophysiology of the disease and ways to avoid upsetting the supply and demand ratio in the heart muscle.

Because S. W. took four nitroglycerin tablets with no effects before coming to the ER, it would be important to find out the age and potency of her drug. Review the storage requirements for the drug, ways to tell if it is potent, and the importance of replacing the pills at least every 6 months.

S. W. and her daughter should be encouraged to ventilate their feelings about this episode; for example, guilt or anger may be precipitated by this scare. They should have the opportunity to explore other ways of handling their problems, how to space activities to avoid excessive demand for oxygen, and what to do if this happens again. They should both receive support and encouragement to cope with the angina and its implications.

Written information should be given to S. W., including drug information. Once S. W. is stabilized, further studies may be indicated to monitor the progress of S. W.'s disease. The use of hormone therapy in this patient may be explored, as well as dietary implications, avoidance of smoking as appropriate, and the need to control blood pressure and monitor activities.

They are not indicated for the treatment of Prinzmetal's angina because they could actually cause vasospasm when they block beta receptor sites. Propranolol is also used to prevent reinfarction in stable patients 1 to 4 week post-MI. This effect is thought to be due to the suppression of myocardial oxygen demand for a prolonged period.

CONTRAINDICATIONS/CAUTIONS

The beta blockers are contraindicated in the presence of bradycardia, heart block, cardiogenic shock, asthma, and COPD because their blocking of the sympathetic response could exacerbate these diseases. They also are contraindicated with pregnancy and lactation because of the potential for adverse effects on the fetus or neonate. Caution should be used in the presence of diabetes, peripheral vascular disease, and thyrotoxicosis because the blocking of the sympathetic response will block normal reflexes necessary for maintaining homeostasis with these diseases.

ADVERSE EFFECTS

The adverse effects associated with these drugs are related to their blockade of the sympathetic nervous system. CNS effects include dizziness, fatigue, emotional depression, and sleep disturbances. GI problems include gastric pain, nausea, vomiting, colitis, and diarrhea. Cardiovascular effects can include congestive heart failure, reduced cardiac output, and arrhythmias. Respiratory symptoms can include bronchospasm, dyspnea, and cough. Decreased exercise tolerance and malaise are also common complaints.

CLINICALLY IMPORTANT DRUG–DRUG INTERACTIONS

A paradoxical hypertension occurs when clonidine is given with beta blockers, and an increased rebound hypertension with clonidine withdrawal may also occur; it is best to avoid this combination. A decreased antihypertensive effect occurs when beta blockers are given with NSAIDs; if this combination is used, the patient should be monitored closely and a dosage adjustment made. An initial hypertensive episode followed by bradycardia occurs if these drugs are given with epinephrine. A possibility of peripheral ischemia exists if the beta blockers are taken in combination with ergot alkaloids. There also is a potential for change in blood glucose levels if these drugs are given with insulin or antidiabetic agents, and the patient will not have the usual signs and symptoms of hypoglycemia or hyperglycemia to alert him or her to potential problems. If this combination is used, the patient should monitor blood glucose frequently throughout the day and should be alert to new warnings about glucose imbalance.

DATA LINK

Data link to the following beta blockers used to treat angina in your nursing drug guide:

BETA BLOCKERS

Name	Brand Name	Usual Indication(s)
nadolol	*Corgard*	Long-term management of angina
P propranolol	*Inderal*	Long-term management of angina and prevention of reinfarction in patients 1 to 4 weeks post-MI

NURSING CONSIDERATIONS
for patients receiving beta blockers

See Chapter 29 for the nursing considerations associated with beta blockers.

WWW.WEB LINKS

Patients and health care providers may want to explore information from the following Internet sources:

Information on angina, drug therapy, current research, the National Heart, Lung and Blood Institute:
http://www.nscardiology.com/factsarrhythmia.htm

Patient information on patient teaching, supports, other educational programs:
http://www.cardioassoc.com/patient_pgs/conditions/arrhythmias.asp

Patient information, support groups, research information on heart disease, scientific programs:
http://www.amhrt.org

Information on diet, exercise, drug therapy, cardiac rehabilitation, and prevention of CAD:
http://heartdisease.miningco.com/mbody.htm?PID-2370&COB-home

CALCIUM CHANNEL BLOCKERS

The calcium channel blockers prevent the movement of calcium into the cardiac and smooth muscle cells when the cells are stimulated, interfering with the muscle cell's ability to contract. This leads to a loss of smooth muscle tone, vasodilation, and decreased peripheral resistance. These effects decrease venous return (preload) and the resistance the heart muscle has to pump against (afterload), which in turn decreases cardiac workload and oxygen consumption. Table 44-1 lists the calcium channel blockers that are used in treating angina. The drug of choice depends on the patient's diagnosis and ability to tolerate adverse drug effects.

THERAPEUTIC ACTIONS AND INDICATIONS

Calcium channel blockers inhibit the movement of calcium ions across the membranes of myocardial and arterial muscle cells, altering the action potential and blocking muscle cell contraction. This effect will depress myocardial contractility; slow cardiac impulse formation in the conductive tissues; and relax and dilate arteries, causing a fall in blood pressure and a decrease in venous return. These effects will decrease the workload of the heart and myocardial oxygen consumption and, in Prinzmetal's angina, will relieve the vasospasm of the coronary artery which will increase blood flow to the muscle cells. Research also indicates that these drugs will block the proliferation of cells in the endothelial layer of the blood vessel, slowing the progress of the atherosclerosis. These drugs are indicated for the treatment of Prinzmetal's angina, chronic angina, effort-associated angina, and hypertension. Verapamil is also used to treat rapid cardiac arrhythmias because it slows conduction more than the other calcium channel blockers.

CONTRAINDICATIONS/CAUTIONS

These drugs are contraindicated in the presence of allergy to any of these drugs; with heart block or sick sinus syndrome because these could be exacerbated by the conduction-slowing effects of these drugs; with renal and hepatic dysfunction which could alter the metabolism and excretion of these drugs; and with pregnancy and lactation because of the potential for adverse effects on the fetus or neonate.

ADVERSE EFFECTS

The adverse effects associated with these drugs are related to their effects on cardiac output and on smooth

TABLE 44-1

CALCIUM CHANNEL BLOCKERS USED TO TREAT ANGINA

Drug	Brand Name	Route(s)	Usual Indications	Special Notes
amlodipine	*Norvasc*	Oral	Prinzmetal's angina; chronic angina, hypertension	Use with caution with CHF; can cause headache, arrhythmias, edema
bepridil	*Vascor*	Oral	Chronic, stable angina in patients who cannot tolerate other antianginals	Can cause serious arrhythmias and agranulocytosis; limit use to patients unable to take other agents; monitor very closely
P diltiazem	*Cardizem*	Oral, IV	Prinzmetal's angina; chronic angina in patients not controlled by nitrates or beta blockers; effort-associated angina; hypertension	Can cause serious cardiac arrhythmias, monitor patient closely at initiation of therapy and with any change in dose
nicardipine	*Cardene*	Oral, IV	Chronic stable angina, hypertension, IV for short-term treatment of hypertension when oral use is not possible	Can cause angina and arrhythmias, monitor patient closely; also causes severe GI upset
nifedipine	*Procardia*	Oral	Prinzmetal's angina; chronic angina; hypertension (SR only)	GI upset; dizziness, lightheadedness; edema, arrhythmias are common; may also cause nasal congestion and cough
verapamil	*Calan*	Oral, IV	Prinzmetal's angina; chronic angina; unstable, preinfarction angina; hypertension; treatment of supra-ventricular tachycardia	Depresses cardiac conduction, do not use with any heart block; has strong negatively inotropic effects, use caution in low output states; increases digoxin levels, monitor patients receiving both drugs very carefully

muscle. CNS effects include dizziness, lightheadedness, headache, and fatigue. GI effects can include nausea and hepatic injury related to direct toxic effects on hepatic cells. Cardiovascular effects include hypotension, bradycardia, peripheral edema, and heart block. Skin effects include flushing and rash.

CLINICALLY IMPORTANT DRUG–DRUG INTERACTIONS

Drug–drug interactions vary with each of the calcium channel blockers. Potentially serious effects to keep in mind include increased serum levels and toxicity of cyclosporine if taken with diltiazem and increased risk of heart block and digoxin toxicity if combined with verapamil because verapamil increases digoxin serum levels. Both drugs depress myocardial conduction. If any combinations of these drugs must be used, the patient should be monitored very closely and appropriate dosage adjustments made. Verapamil has also been associated with serious respiratory depression when given with general anesthetics and adjuncts to anesthesia.

DATA LINK

Data link to the calcium channel blockers used to treat angina, which are listed in Table 44-1, in your nursing drug guide.

NURSING CONSIDERATIONS
for patients receiving calcium channel blockers

Assessment

HISTORY. Screen for the following: any known allergies to any of these drugs; impaired liver or kidney function, which could alter the metabolism and excretion of the drug; heart block, which could be exacerbated by the conduction depression of these drugs; and pregnancy and lactation because of the potential adverse effects on the fetus or neonate.

PHYSICAL ASSESSMENT. Include screening for baseline status before beginning therapy and for any potential adverse effects. Assess the following: skin color, lesions, temperature; affect, orientation, reflexes; pulse, auscultation, blood pressure, perfusion, baseline ECG; respirations, adventitious sounds; and liver and renal function tests.

Nursing Diagnoses

The patient receiving a calcium channel blocker may have the following nursing diagnoses related to drug therapy:

- Alteration in cardiac output related to hypotension
- Potential for injury related to CNS, cardiovascular effects

- Alteration in tissue perfusion related to hypotension, change in cardiac output
- Knowledge deficit regarding drug therapy

Implementation

- Monitor the patient carefully (blood pressure, cardiac rhythm, cardiac output) while the drug is being titrated or dosage is being changed *to assure early detection of potentially serious adverse effects.*
- Monitor blood pressure very carefully if the patient is also on nitrates *because there is an increased risk of hypotensive episodes.*
- Periodically monitor blood pressure and cardiac rhythm while using these drugs *because of the potential for adverse cardiovascular effects.*
- Provide comfort measures *to help the patient tolerate drug effects.* These include small, frequent meals, access to bathroom facilities if GI upset is severe, environmental control, and safety precautions.
- Provide thorough patient teaching, including the name of the drug, dosage prescribed, proper administration, measures to avoid adverse effects, warning signs of problems, and the need for periodic monitoring and evaluation *to enhance patient knowledge about drug therapy and to promote compliance with the drug regimen.*
- Offer support and encouragement *to help the patient deal with the diagnosis and drug regimen.*

Evaluation

- Monitor patient response to the drug (alleviation of signs and symptoms of angina, prevention of angina).
- Monitor for adverse effects (hypotension, cardiac arrhythmias, GI upset, skin reactions, headache).
- Evaluate the effectiveness of the teaching plan (patient can name drug, dosage, proper administration, adverse effects to watch for, specific measures to avoid adverse effects, importance of continued follow-up).
- Monitor the effectiveness of comfort measures and compliance to the regimen.

CHAPTER SUMMARY

- Coronary artery disease is the leading cause of death in the United States and most western nations.
- Coronary artery disease develops when changes in the intima of coronary vessels leads to the development of atheromas or fatty tumors, accumulation of platelets and debris, and a thickening of arterial muscles resulting in a loss of elasticity and responsiveness to normal stimuli.
- Narrowing of the coronary arteries secondary to the atheroma build-up is called atherosclerosis.
- Narrowed coronary arteries eventually become unable to deliver all the blood that is needed by the myocardial cells, causing a problem of supply and demand.
- Angina pectoris, or "suffocation of the chest," occurs when the myocardial demand for oxygen cannot be met by the narrowed vessels. Pain, anxiety, and fatigue develop when the supply and demand ratio is upset.
- Stable angina occurs when the heart muscle is perfused adequately except during exertion or increased demand. People usually respond to the pain of angina by stopping all activity and resting, which decreases the demand for oxygen and restores the supply–demand balance.
- Unstable or preinfarction angina occurs when the vessels are so narrowed that the myocardial cells are low on oxygen even at rest.
- Prinzmetal's angina occurs as a result of a spasm of a coronary vessel, leading to decreased blood flow through the narrowed lumen.
- Myocardial infarction occurs when a coronary vessel is completely occluded and the cells depending on that vessel for oxygen become ischemic, then necrotic, and die.
- Angina can be treated by drugs that either increase the supply of oxygen or decrease the heart's workload, which decreases the demand for oxygen.
- Nitrates and beta blockers are used to cause vaso dilation and decrease the venous return and arterial resistance, effects that decrease cardiac workload and oxygen consumption.
- Calcium channel blockers block muscle contraction in smooth muscle and decrease the heart's workload, relax spasm in Prinzmetal's angina, and possibly block the proliferation of the damaged endothelium in coronary vessels.

BIBLIOGRAPHY

Bullock, B. L. (2000). *Focus on pathophysiology.* Philadelphia: Lippincott Williams & Wilkins.

Hardman, J. G., Limbird, L. E., Molinoff, P. B., Ruddon, R. W., & Gilman, A. G. (Eds.). (1996). *Goodman and Gilman's the pharmacological basis of therapeutics* (9th ed.). New York: McGraw-Hill.

Karch, A. M. (2000). *2000 Lippincott's nursing drug guide.* Philadelphia: Lippincott Williams & Wilkins.

McEvoy, B. R. (1999). *Facts and comparisons 1999.* St. Louis: Facts and Comparisons.

Medical letter on drugs and therapeutics. (1999). New Rochelle, NY: Medical Letter.

Porth, C. M. (1998). *Pathophysiology: Concepts of altered health states* (5th ed.). Philadelphia: Lippincott-Raven.

CHAPTER 45

Lipid-Lowering Agents

Bile acid sequestrants
- P cholestyramine
- colestipol

HMG CoA reductase inhibitors
- atorvastatin
- cerivastatin
- fluvastatin
- P lovastatin
- pravastatin
- simvastatin

Other antihyperlipidemic agents
- clofibrate
- dextrothyroxine
- fenofibrate
- gemfibrozil
- niacin

CHAPTER OUTLINE

KEY TERMS

bile acids
cholesterol
chylomicron
high density lipoprotein (HDL)
HMG CoA reductase
hyperlipidemia
low density lipoprotein (LDL)
risk factors

INTRODUCTION

The drugs discussed in this chapter lower serum levels of cholesterol and lipids. There is mounting evidence that the incidence of coronary artery disease (CAD), the leading killer of adults in the western world, is higher among people with high serum lipid levels. The cause of CAD is poorly understood, but some evidence indicates that cholesterol and fat play a major role in disease development.

CORONARY ARTERY DISEASE

As explained in Chapter 44, coronary artery disease is characterized by the progressive growth of atheromatous plaques, or atheromas, in the coronary arteries. These plaques, which begin as fatty streaks in the endothelium, eventually injure the endothelial lining of the artery, causing an inflammatory reaction. This inflammatory process triggers the development of characteristic foam cells, containing fats and white blood cells, that further injure the endothelial lining. Over time, platelets, fibrin, other fats, and remnants collect on the injured vessel lining and cause the atheroma to grow, further narrowing the interior of the blood vessel and limiting blood flow.

The injury to the vessel also causes scarring and a thickening of the vessel wall. As the vessel thickens, it becomes less distensible and less reactive to many neurological and chemical stimuli that would ordinarily dilate or constrict it. As a result, the coronary vessels no longer are able to balance the myocardial demand for oxygen with increased blood supply.

Strong evidence exists that atheroma development occurs more quickly in patients with elevated cholesterol and lipid levels. Patients who consume high-fat diets are more likely to develop high lipid levels. However, patients without elevated lipid levels can also develop atheromas leading to coronary artery disease, so other factors evidently contribute to this process. Although the exact mechanism of atherogenesis (atheroma development) is not understood, certain ***risk factors*** increase the likelihood that a person will develop CAD. Following is a list of untreatable and treatable risk factors:

Untreatable risk factors

Genetic predispositions: CAD is more likely to occur in people who have a family history of the disease.

Age: The incidence of CAD increases with age.

Gender: Men are more likely to have CAD than premenopausal women; however, the incidence is nearly equal in men and postmenopausal women, a possible link to a protective effect of estrogens.

Treatable risk factors

Gout: Increased uric acid levels seem to injure vessel walls.

Cigarette smoking: Nicotine causes vasoconstriction; over time, smoking can lower oxygen levels in the blood.

Sedentary lifestyle: Exercise increases the levels of chemicals that seem to protect the coronary arteries.

High stress levels: Constant sympathetic reactions increase the myocardial oxygen demand while causing vasoconstriction.

Hypertension: High pressure in the arteries causes endothelial injury and increases afterload and myocardial oxygen demand.

Obesity: This may reflect altered fat metabolism, which increases the heart's workload.

Diabetes: Diabetics have a capillary membrane thickening, which accelerates the effects of atherosclerosis, and an abnormal fat metabolism.

Other factors that, if untreated, may contribute to CAD include bacterial infections (chlamydia infections have been correlated with onset of CAD, and treatment with tetracycline and fluororoentgenography has been associated with decreased incidence of CAD, indicating a possible bacterial link) and an autoimmune process (some plaques contain antibodies and other products of immune reactions, making autoimmune reactions a possibility).

Because an exact cause of CAD is not known, successful treatment involves manipulating a number of these risk factors (Table 45-1). Overall treatment and prevention of CAD should include the following measures: decreasing dietary fats (a decrease in

TABLE 45-1

RISK FACTORS FOR THE DEVELOPMENT OF CORONARY ARTERY DISEASE

Untreatable Risks	Treatable Risks	Suggested Treatments
Family history	Sedentary lifestyle	Exercise
Age	High-fat diet	Low-fat diet
Gender	Smoking	Stop smoking
	Obesity	Weight loss
	High stress levels	Stress management
	Bacterial infections	Antibiotic treatment
	Diabetes	Control blood glucose levels
	Hypertension	Control blood pressure
	Gout	Control uric acid levels
	Menopause	Hormone replacement therapy

saturated fats seems to have the most impact on serum lipid levels); losing weight; eliminating smoking; increasing exercise levels; decreasing stress; and treating hypertension, diabetes, gout, and estrogen deficiency.

METABOLISM OF FATS

Fats are taken into the body as dietary animal fats, then broken down in the stomach to fatty acids, lipids, and cholesterol (Figure 45-1). The presence of these products in the duodenum stimulates contraction of the gall bladder and the release of bile. ***Bile acids,*** which contain high levels of ***cholesterol*** (fat), act like a detergent in the small intestine, breaking up fats. (Imagine ads for dishwashing detergents that break up the grease and fats in the dishwashing water; bile acids do much the same thing.)

GENDER CONSIDERATIONS

Women and Heart Disease

Until the late 1990s, heart disease was considered to be a condition that primarily affected men. Because of that belief, women were seldom screened for heart disease, and when they did experience acute cardiac events, they were not treated promptly or adequately. However, recent research has shown that heart disease is the leading cause of death among women, surpassing such diseases as breast and colon cancers. This finding led to further research, still ongoing, about women and heart disease.

Women enjoy a protective hormone effect against the development of CAD until menopause, when estrogen loss seems to rapidly increase the production of atheromas and the development of CAD. In several studies, women who received hormone replacement therapy (HRT) at menopause had a significantly reduced risk of CAD and myocardial infarction (MI). Convincing women of a certain age group to use HRT has been a challenge for health care professionals, possibly because many of those women recall that early HRT was associated with an increased risk of breast cancer—a disease that scares women more than heart disease.

Women should be encouraged to consider HRT if they do not have risk factors that predispose them to breast cancer. They also should be advised to reduce other cardiac risk factors by eating a diet low in saturated fats, exercising regularly, not smoking, controlling weight, managing stress, and seeking treatment for gout, hypertension, and diabetes.

Clearly, heart disease is not just a disease of men. Research will continue to offer health care professionals new information on preventing and treating heart disease in women.

CULTURAL CONSIDERATIONS

Variations in Coronary Artery Disease Risk Among Cultures

Despite the fact that white Americans have the highest incidence of coronary artery disease, certain known risk factors may place other ethnic groups at greater risk. For example, hypertension and diabetes occur more frequently among African Americans and Native Americans than whites. Irrespective of race, all adults should be screened both for risk factors and for signs and symptoms of coronary artery disease.

Cultural variations in key parameters:

- Serum cholesterol levels—Whites > African Americans, Native Americans
- HDL levels—African Americans, Asian Americans > Whites; Mexican Americans < Whites
- LDL levels—African Americans < Whites
- HDL: cholesterol ratio—African Americans < Whites

Bile acids break down the fats into small units called micelles that can be absorbed into the wall of the small intestine. The bile acids are then reabsorbed and recycled to the gall bladder, where they remain until the gall bladder is again stimulated to release them to facilitate fat absorption.

Because fats and water do not mix, the fats cannot be absorbed directly into the plasma but need to be transported on a plasma protein. To allow absorption, micelles are carried on ***chylomicron,*** a package of fats and proteins. The chylomicrons pass through the wall of the small intestine, where they are picked up by the lymphatic system surrounding the intestines. The chylomicrons travel through the lymphatic system to the heart, then are sent out into circulation. The proteins that are exposed on the chylomicron, called apoproteins, determine the fate of the lipids or fats being carried. For example, some of these packages are broken down in the tissues to be used for energy, some are stored in fat deposits for future use as energy, and some continue to the liver, where they are further processed into lipoproteins.

The lipoproteins produced in the liver that have known clinical implications are the ***low density lipoproteins (LDL)*** and the ***high density lipoproteins (HDL).*** LDLs enter circulation as tightly packed cholesterol, triglycerides, and lipids—all of which are carried by proteins that enter circulation to be broken down for energy or stored for future use as energy. When an LDL package is broken down, many remnants or leftovers need to be returned to the liver for recycling. If a person has many of these remnants in the blood vessels, it is thought that the inflamma-

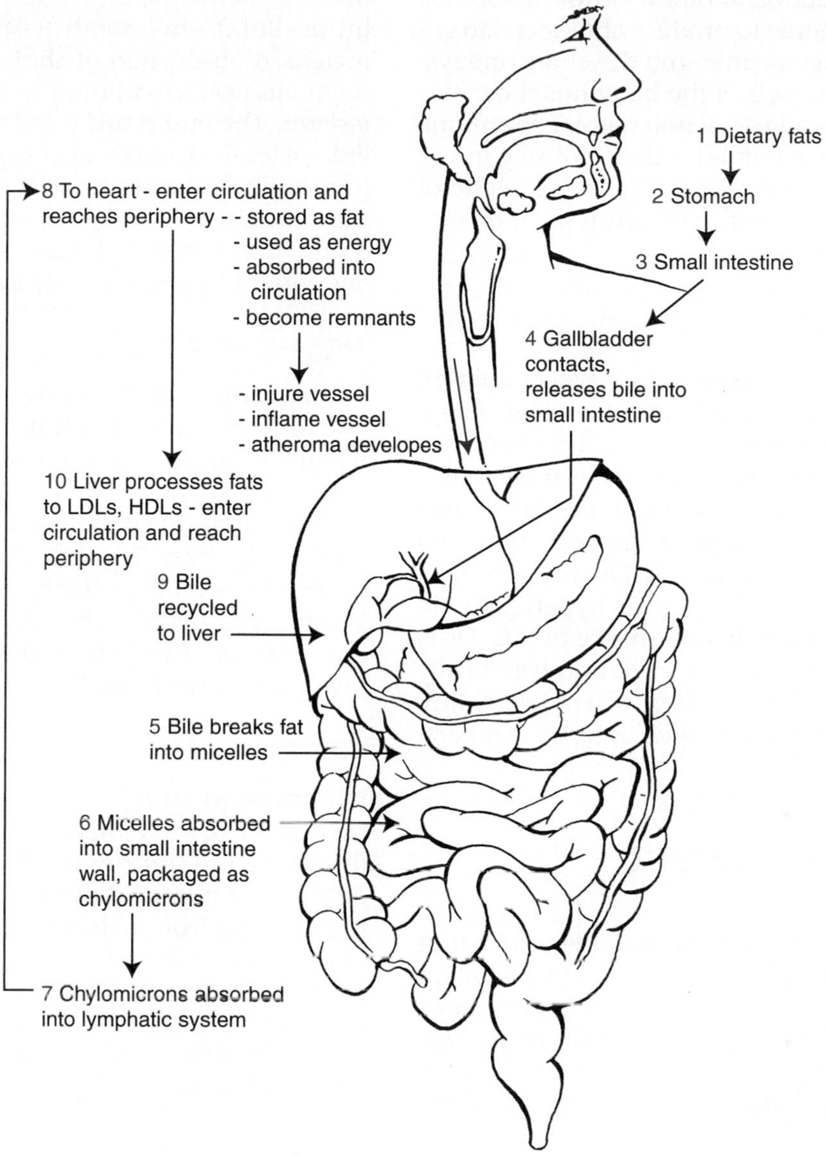
1 Dietary fats
2 Stomach
3 Small intestine
4 Gallbladder contacts, releases bile into small intestine
5 Bile breaks fat into micelles
6 Micelles absorbed into small intestine wall, packaged as chylomicrons
7 Chylomicrons absorbed into lymphatic system
8 To heart - enter circulation and reaches periphery - - stored as fat
- used as energy
- absorbed into circulation
- become remnants
- injure vessel
- inflame vessel
- atheroma developes
9 Bile recycled to liver
10 Liver processes fats to LDLs, HDLs - enter circulation and reach periphery

FIGURE 45-1. Metabolism of fats in the body.

tory process is initiated to help remove this debris. Some experts feels that this may be the underlying process involved in atherogenesis.

HDLs enter circulation as loosely packed lipids that are used for energy and to pick up remnants of fats and cholesterol that are left in the periphery by LDL breakdown. HDLs serve a protective role in cleaning up remnants in blood vessels. It is known that HDL levels increase during exercise, which could explain why people who exercise regularly lower their risk of CAD. HDL levels also increase in response to estrogen, which could explain some of the protective effect of estrogen before menopause and of hormone replacement therapy after menopause.

Cholesterol

The body needs fats, particularly cholesterol, to maintain normal function. Cholesterol is the base unit for the formation of the steroid hormones (the sex hormones as well as the adrenal cortical hormones). It is also a basic unit in the formation and maintenance of cell membranes. Cholesterol is usually provided through the diet and the fat metabolism process described above. If dietary cholesterol falls off, the body is prepared to produce cholesterol to ensure that the cell membranes and the endocrine system are intact. Every cell in the body has the metabolic capability of producing cholesterol. The enzyme ***HMG CoA reductase*** regulates the final step in the cellular synthesis of cholesterol. If dietary cholesterol is severely limited, the cellular synthesis of cholesterol will increase (Figure 45-2).

Hyperlipidemias

Hyperlipidemia, an increase in the level of lipids in the blood, increases a person's risk for the development of CAD. It can result from excessive dietary intake of fats or genetic alterations in fat metabolism leading to a variety of elevated fats in the blood, such as hypercholesterolemia, hypertriglyceridemia, and alterations in LDL and HDL levels. Dietary modifications are often successful in treating hyperlipidemia resulting from excessive dietary intake of fats. Drug therapy is needed, however, in treating genetically linked alterations in lipid levels or when dietary limits do not decrease the serum lipid levels to an acceptable range.

ANTIHYPERLIPIDEMIC AGENTS

Drugs that are used to treat hyperlipidemia include bile acid sequestrants, HMG CoA inhibitors, fibrates, a thyroid hormone, and niacin. These drugs are often used in combination and should be part of an overall health care regimen that includes exercise, dietary restrictions, and lifestyle changes to decrease the risk of CAD.

BILE ACID SEQUESTRANTS

Bile acid sequestrants bind with bile acids, leading to their excretion in the feces. The resulting low levels of bile acids reentering hepatic circulation stimulate the production of more bile acids in the liver. Bile acids contain cholesterol. Because the liver must use cholesterol to manufacture bile acids, the hepatic intracellular cholesterol level falls, leading to an increased absorption of cholesterol-containing LDL segments from circulation to replenish the cell's cholesterol. The end result is a decrease in plasma cholesterol levels. Two bile acid sequestrants are currently in use. Cholestyramine (*Questran*) is a powder that must be mixed with liquids and taken up to six times a day. Colestipol (*Colestid*), available in both powder and tablet form, is only taken four times a day.

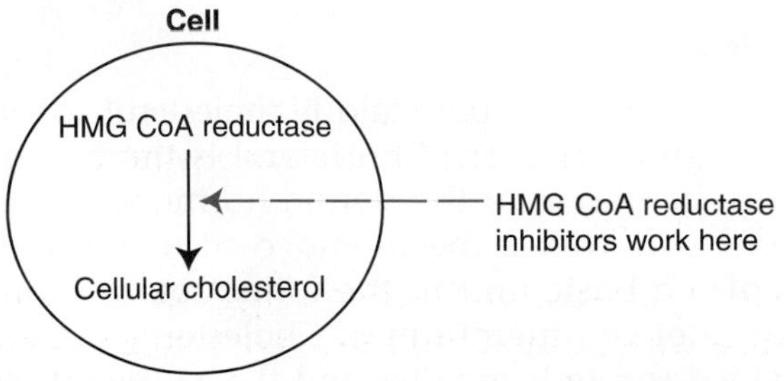

FIGURE 45-2. Cellular production of cholesterol.

THERAPEUTIC ACTIONS AND INDICATIONS

Bile acid sequestrants bind with bile acids in the intestine to form a complex that is excreted in the feces (Figure 45-3). As a result, the liver must use cholesterol to make more bile acids, so the serum levels of cholesterol and LDL decrease to provide the cholesterol for the liver. These drugs are used to reduce serum cholesterol in patients with primary hypercholesterolemia (with high LDLs) as an adjunct to diet and exercise. Cholestyramine is also used to treat pruritus associated with partial biliary obstruction.

CONTRAINDICATIONS/CAUTIONS

Bile acid sequestrants are contraindicated in the presence of allergy to either bile acid sequestrant. These drugs also are contraindicated in the following conditions: complete biliary obstruction, which would prevent bile from being secreted into the intestine; abnormal intestinal function, which could be aggravated by the presence of these drugs; and pregnancy and lactation, because the potential decrease in the absorption of fat-soluble vitamins could have a detrimental effect on the fetus or neonate.

ADVERSE EFFECTS

Adverse effects associated with the use of these drugs include headache, anxiety, fatigue, and drowsiness, which could be related to changes in serum cholesterol levels. Direct GI irritation, including nausea, and constipation that may progress to fecal impaction and aggravation of hemorrhoids may occur. Other effects include increased bleeding times related to a decreased absorption of vitamin K and consequent decreased production of clotting factors; vitamin A and D deficiencies related to decreased absorption of fat-soluble vitamins; rash; and muscle aches and pains.

CLINICALLY IMPORTANT DRUG–DRUG INTERACTIONS

Malabsorption of fat-soluble vitamins occurs when combined with these drugs. There is decreased or delayed absorption of thiazide diuretics, digoxin, warfarin, thyroid hormones, and corticosteroids if

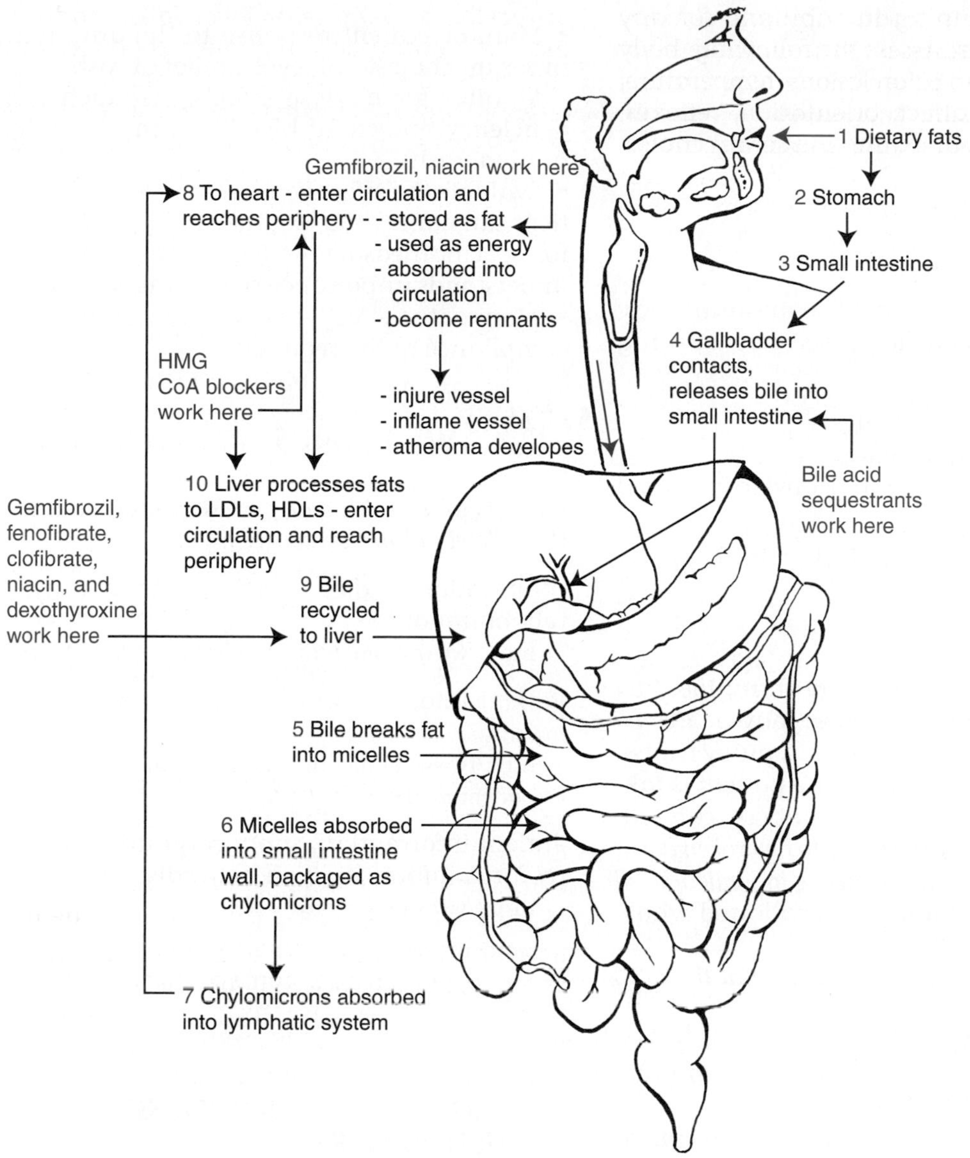
1 Dietary fats
2 Stomach
3 Small intestine
4 Gallbladder contacts, releases bile into small intestine
Bile acid sequestrants work here
5 Bile breaks fat into micelles
6 Micelles absorbed into small intestine wall, packaged as chylomicrons
7 Chylomicrons absorbed into lymphatic system
8 To heart - enter circulation and reaches periphery - - stored as fat
- used as energy
- absorbed into circulation
- become remnants
- injure vessel
- inflame vessel
- atheroma developes
Gemfibrozil, niacin work here
HMG CoA blockers work here
10 Liver processes fats to LDLs, HDLs - enter circulation and reach periphery
9 Bile recycled to liver
Gemfibrozil, fenofibrate, clofibrate, niacin, and dexothyroxine work here

FIGURE 45-3. Sites of action of lipid-lowering agents.

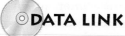

DATA LINK

Data link to the following bile acid sequestrants in your nursing drug guide:

BILE ACID SEQUESTRANTS

Name	Brand Name	Usual Indications
P cholestyramine	*Questran*	Adjunctive treatment of primary hypercholesterolemia; pruritus associated with partial biliary obstruction
colestipol	*Colestid*	Adjunctive treatment of primary hypercholesterolemia

taken with bile acid sequestrants. Consequently, any of these drug should be taken 1 hour before or 4 to 6 hours after the bile acid sequestrant.

NURSING CONSIDERATIONS
for patients receiving bile acid sequestrants

Assessment

HISTORY: Screen for the following: known allergies to these drugs; impaired intestinal function, which could be exacerbated by these drugs; biliary obstruction; and pregnancy and lactation.

PHYSICAL ASSESSMENT. Include screening for baseline status before beginning therapy and for any potential adverse effects. Assess the following: body temperature, weight; skin color, lesions, temperature; pulse, blood pressure; affect, orientation, reflexes; bowel sounds, abdominal exam; and serum cholesterol and lipid levels.

Nursing Diagnoses

The patient receiving a bile acid sequestrant may have the following nursing diagnoses related to drug therapy:

- Pain related to CNS and GI effects
- Constipation related to GI effects
- Altered general tissue perfusion related to increased bleeding
- Knowledge deficit regarding drug therapy

Implementation

- Do not administer powder in dry form; *the drug must be mixed in fluids to be effective* (may be mixed with fruit juices, soups, liquids, cereals, pulpy fruits). Stir and swallow all of the dose. If the patient is taking tablets, ensure that tablets are not cut, chewed, or crushed *because they are designed to be broken down in the GI tract and if crushed, the active ingredients will not be effective.* Tablets should be swallowed whole with plenty of fluid.
- Give the drug before meals *to ensure that the drug is in the GI tract with food.*
- Administer other oral medications 1 hour before or 4 to 6 hours after the bile sequestrant *to avoid drug–drug interactions.*
- *Arrange for a bowel program as appropriate* if constipation occurs.
- Provide comfort measures *to help the patient tolerate the drug effects.* These include small, frequent meals, access to bathroom facilities, safety precautions to prevent injury if bleeding is a problem, replacement of fat-soluble vitamins, skin care as needed, and analgesics for headache.
- Provide thorough patient teaching, including the name of the drug, dosage prescribed, proper administration, measures to avoid adverse effects, warning signs of problems, the importance of periodic monitoring and evaluation, and the need to avoid overdose and poisoning *to enhance patient knowledge about drug therapy and promote compliance with the drug regimen.*
- Offer support and encouragement *to help the patient deal with the diagnosis and drug regimen;* refer the patient to services that might help with the high cost of these drugs.

Evaluation

- Monitor patient response to the drug (reduction in serum cholesterol levels, relief of rash).
- Monitor for adverse effects (headache, vitamin deficiency, increased bleeding times, constipation, nausea, rash).
- Evaluate the effectiveness of the teaching plan (patient can name drug, dosage, adverse effects to watch for, specific measures to avoid adverse effects; patient understands importance of continued follow-up).
- Monitor the effectiveness of comfort measures and compliance to the regimen.

WWW.WEB LINKS

Patients and health care providers may want to consult the following Internet sources:

Information on diet, exercise, drug therapy, cardiac rehabilitation:
http://www.jhbmc/jhu.edu/cardiology/rehab/rehab.html

Patient information on latest resources, diets, programs:
http://www.jhbmc/jhu.edu/cardiology/rehab/patientinfo.html

Patient information, support groups, diet, exercise, research information on heart disease:
http://www.amhrt.org

Specific information on exercise programs and safety:
http://nhlbi.nih.gov/health/prof/heart

HMG CoA REDUCTASE INHIBITORS

The final step in the synthesis of cellular cholesterol involves the enzyme HMG CoA reductase (hydroxymethylglutaryl-coenzyme A). If this enzyme is blocked, serum cholesterol and LDL levels will decrease because more LDLs will be absorbed by the cells for processing into cholesterol. In contrast, HDL levels increase slightly with this alteration in fat metabolism. HMG CoA reductase inhibitors block HMG CoA reductase from completing the synthesis of cholesterol. Most of these drugs are chemical modifications of compounds produced by fungi. As a group, they are frequently referred to as statins.

The HMG CoA reductase inhibitors include the following:

- Atorvastatin (*Lipitor*), which is associated with severe renal and liver complications.
- Cerivastatin (*Baycol*), which is recommended for combination use with other drugs.

- Fluvastatin (*Lescol*), which is actually a fungal product and should not be used with any known allergies to fungal byproducts.
- Lovastatin (*Mevacor*), one of the oldest HMG CoA drugs available, is very long acting and not associated with some of the severe liver and renal toxicity seen with the other agents.
- Pravastatin (*Pravachol*), which has been proven to be effective in preventing a first MI even in patients who do not have a documented increased cholesterol, an effect that may be related to a blocking of the formation of foam cells in injured arteries; this drug is not associated with the severe renal and liver toxicities of some of the other statins.
- Simvastatin (*Zocor*), which is indicated for lowering cholesterol and preventing MI in patients with known hypercholesterolemia and CAD; this drug is not associated with the severe renal and liver toxicities of some of the other statins.

THERAPEUTIC ACTIONS AND INDICATIONS

HMG CoA reductase inhibitors block the formation of cellular cholesterol, leading to a decrease in serum cholesterol and a decrease in serum LDLs, with a slight increase or no change in the levels of HDLs (see Figure 45-2). Since these drugs undergo a marked first-pass effect in the liver, most of their effects are seen in the liver. These drugs may also have some effects on the process that generates atheromas in vessel walls. That exact mechanism of action is not understood. These drugs are indicated as adjuncts with diet and exercise for the treatment of elevated cholesterol and LDL levels in patients unresponsive to dietary restrictions alone; to slow the progression of CAD in patients with documented CAD (pravastatin and simvastatin); and to prevent first MI in patients who are at risk for MI development (pravastatin).

CONTRAINDICATIONS/CAUTIONS

These drugs are contraindicated in the presence of allergy to any of the statins or to fungal byproducts or compounds. They also are contraindicated with active liver disease, which could be exacerbated, leading to severe liver failure, and with pregnancy and lactation because of the potential for adverse effects on the fetus and neonate. Caution should be used with impaired endocrine function because of the potential alteration in formation of steroid hormones.

ADVERSE EFFECTS

The most common adverse effects associated with these drugs reflect their effects on the GI system: flatulence, abdominal pain, cramps, nausea, vomiting, and constipation. CNS effects can include headache, dizziness, blurred vision, insomnia, fatigue, and cataract development and may reflect changes in the cell membrane and synthesis of cholesterol. Elevated liver enzymes commonly occur, and acute liver failure has been reported with the use atorvastatin, cerivastatin, and fluvastatin. Rhabdomyolysis (an acute, sometimes fatal disease characterized by destruction of the muscles, often associated with renal failure as myoglobin builds up in the kidney) with acute renal failure has also occurred with the use of atorvastatin, cerivastatin, and fluvastatin.

CLINICALLY IMPORTANT DRUG–DRUG INTERACTIONS

There is an increased risk of rhabdomyolysis if any of these drugs are combined with erythromycin, cyclosporine, gemfibrozil, niacin, or antifungal drugs; these combinations should be avoided. Increased serum levels and resultant toxicity can occur if these drugs are combined with digoxin or warfarin; if this combination is used, serum digoxin levels and/or clotting times should be monitored carefully and the prescriber consulted for appropriated dosage changes. Increased estrogen levels can occur if these drugs are taken with oral contraceptives; the patient should be monitored carefully if this combination is used.

DATA LINK

Data link to the following HMG CoA reductase inhibitors in your nursing drug guide:

HMG COA REDUCTASE INHIBITORS

Name	Brand Name	Usual Indications
atorvastatin	*Lipitor*	Adjunctive therapy for reduction of elevated cholesterol and LDL levels
cerivastatin	*Baycol*	Adjunctive therapy for reduction of elevated cholesterol and LDL levels, recommended for combination use with other drugs
fluvastatin	*Lescol*	Adjunctive therapy for reduction of elevated cholesterol and LDL levels
P lovastatin	*Mevacor*	Adjunctive therapy for reduction of elevated cholesterol and LDL levels
pravastatin	*Pravachol*	Prevention of first MI even in patients who do not have a documented increased cholesterol, slowing of the progression of CAD; adjunctive therapy for reduction of elevated cholesterol and LDL levels
simvastatin	*Zocor*	Prevention of first MI in patients with known hypercholesterolemia and CAD; adjunctive therapy for reduction of elevated cholesterol and LDL levels

NURSING CONSIDERATIONS for patients receiving HMG CoA reductase inhibitors

Assessment

HISTORY. Screen for the following: any known allergies to these drugs or to fungal byproducts; active liver disease, which could be exacerbated by the effects of these drugs; pregnancy and lactation because of potential adverse effects on the fetus or neonate; and impaired endocrine function, which could be exacerbated by effects on steroid hormones.

PHYSICAL ASSESSMENT. Include screening for baseline status before beginning therapy and for any potential adverse effects. Assess the following: body temperature, weight; skin color, lesions, temperature; affect, orientation, reflexes; pulse, blood pressure, perfusion; respirations, adventitious sounds; bowel sounds, abdominal exam; renal and liver function tests; and serum lipid levels.

Nursing Diagnoses

The patient receiving an HMG CoA reductase inhibitor may have the following nursing diagnoses related to drug therapy:

- Sensory–perceptual alteration related to CNS effects
- Potential for injury related to CNS, liver, and renal effects
- Pain related to headache, myalgia, and GI effects
- Knowledge deficit regarding drug therapy

Implementation

- Administer the drug at bedtime because the highest rates of cholesterol synthesis occur between midnight and 5 a.m. and the *drug should be taken when it will be most effective.*
- Monitor serum cholesterol and LDL levels prior to and periodically during therapy *to evaluate the effectiveness of this drug.*
- Arrange for periodic ophthalmic examinations *to monitor for cataract development.*
- Monitor liver function tests prior to and periodically during therapy *to monitor for liver damage;* consult with the prescriber to discontinue drug if AST or ALT levels increase to three times normal.
- Ensure that the patient has attempted a cholesterol-lowering diet and exercise program for at least 3 to 6 months before beginning therapy *to ensure the need for drug therapy.*
- Encourage the patient to make the lifestyle changes necessary *to decrease the risk of CAD and to increase the effectiveness of drug therapy.*
- Withhold atorvastatin, cerivastatin, or fluvastatin in any acute, serious medical condition (e.g., infection, hypotension, major surgery or trauma, metabolic endocrine disorders, or seizures) *that might suggest myopathy or serve as a risk factor for the development of renal failure.*
- Suggest the use of barrier contraceptives for women of childbearing age *because there is a risk of severe fetal abnormalities if these drugs are taken during pregnancy.*
- Provide comfort measures *to help the patient tolerate drug effects.* These include small, frequent meals, access to bathroom facilities, bowel program as needed, food with drug if GI upset is severe, environmental control, safety precautions, and orientation as needed.
- Provide thorough patient teaching, including the name of the drug, dosage prescribed, measures to avoid adverse effects, warning signs of problems, and the need for periodic monitoring and evaluation *to enhance the patient's knowledge of drug therapy and to promote compliance with the drug regimen* (see Patient Teaching Checklist: HMG CoA reductase inhibitors).
- Offer support and encouragement *to deal with the diagnosis, needed lifestyle changes, and drug regimen.*

Evaluation

- Monitor patient response to the drug (lowering of serum cholesterol and LDL levels, prevention of first MI, slowing of progression of CAD).
- Monitor for adverse effects (headache, dizziness, blurred vision, cataracts, GI upset, liver failure, rhabdomyolysis, renal failure).
- Evaluate the effectiveness of the teaching plan (patient can name drug, dosage, adverse effects to watch for, specific measures to avoid adverse effects; patient understands importance of continued follow-up).
- Monitor the effectiveness of comfort measures and compliance to the regimen (see Nursing Care Guide: HMG CoA reductase inhibitors).

OTHER DRUGS USED TO AFFECT LIPID LEVELS

Other drugs that are used to affect lipid levels do not fall into one of the classes discussed above. These include the fibrates (derivatives of fibric acid), a thyroid hormone, and the vitamin niacin (see Figure 45-3).

The fibrates stimulate the breakdown of lipoproteins and their removal from the plasma. Fibrates in use today include the following agents:

- Clofibrate (*Atromid S*), which also inhibits liver synthesis of LDL and cholesterol, lowers serum lipids, and has an antiplatelet effect. It is used to treat genetic hyperlipidemia that does not respond to diet

PATIENT TEACHING CHECKLIST

HMG CoA Reductase Inhibitors

Create customized patient teaching materials for a specific HMG CoA reductase inhibitor from your CD-ROM. Your patient teaching should stress the following points for drugs within this class:

An HMG CoA reductase inhibitor, or statin, is an antihyperlipidemia agent, which means it works to decrease the levels of certain lipids, or fats, in your blood. An increase in serum lipid levels has been associated with the development of many blood vessel disorders including coronary artery disease, which can lead to a heart attack. This drug must be used in conjunction with a low-calorie, low-saturated-fat diet and an exercise program.

Some of the following adverse effects may occur:

- Headache, blurred vision, nervousness, insomnia—Avoid driving or performing hazardous or delicate tasks that require concentration; these effects may pass with time.
- Nausea, vomiting, flatulence, constipation—Small, frequent meals may help. If constipation becomes a problem, consult with your health care provider for appropriate interventions.

Report any of the following to your health care provider: severe GI upset, vision changes, unusual bleeding, dark urine, or light-colored stools.

You will need to have regular medical examinations to monitor the effectiveness of this drug on your lipid levels and to detect for any adverse effects. These examinations will include blood tests and eye examinations.

Tell any doctor, nurse, or other health care provider that you are taking this drug.

Keep this drug, and all medications, out of the reach of children.

To help decrease your risk of heart disease, follow these guidelines: adhere to a diet that is low in calories and saturated fat, exercise regularly, stop smoking, and reduce stress.

This Teaching Checklist reflects general patient teaching guidelines. It is not meant to be a substitute for drug-specific teaching information, which is available in nursing drug guides.

and adults with very high triglycerides with abdominal pain and pancreatitis.

- Fenofibrate (*Tricor*), which inhibits triglyceride synthesis in the liver, resulting in reduction of LDLs; increases uric acid secretion; and may stimulate triglyceride breakdown. It is used to treat adults with very high triglyceride levels who are at risk for pancreatitis and do not respond to strict dietary measures.
- Gemfibrozil (*Lopid*) inhibits peripheral breakdown of lipids, reduces triglyceride production and LDL production, and increases HDL concentrations. It is associated with GI and muscle discomfort. This drug cannot be combined with statins for 3 weeks to several months after therapy because of the risk of rhabdomyolysis.

Dextrothyroxine (*Choloxin*), a thyroid hormone, stimulates liver breakdown and excretion of cholesterol in bile and feces. It is also used to lower serum cholesterol and LDLs in patients who have normal thyroid function. It cannot be used with patients who have thyroid dysfunction and should be used cautiously with other endocrine problems.

The vitamin niacin (*Niaspan*) inhibits release of free fatty acids from adipose tissue, increases the rate of triglyceride removal from plasma, and generally reduces LDL and triglyceride levels and increases HDL levels. It may also decrease levels of apoproteins needed to form chylomicrons. Niacin is associated with an intense cutaneous flushing, nausea, and abdominal pain, making its use somewhat limited. It also increases serum levels of uric acid and may predispose patients to the development of gout. Niacin is often combined with bile acid sequestrants for increased effect. It is given at bedtime to make the maximum use of nighttime cholesterol synthesis and it must be given 4 to 6 hours after the bile sequestrant to assure absorption.

DATA LINK

Data link to the following antihyperlipidemic drugs in your nursing drug guide:

OTHER ANTIHYPERLIPIDEMIC DRUGS

Name	Brand Name	Usual Indications
clofibrate	*Atromid S*	Genetic hyperlipidemia; severely elevated triglyceride levels
dextrothyroxine	*Choloxin*	Lowering of elevated serum cholesterol and LDLs in patients with normal thyroid function

NURSING CARE GUIDE
HMG CoA Reductase Inhibitors

Assessment	Nursing Diagnoses	Implementation	Evaluation
HISTORY Allergies to any of these drugs or fungal byproducts; hepatic dysfunction, pregnancy, lactation, endocrine disorders	Sensory–perceptual alteration related to CNS effects Potential for injury related to CNS, liver, renal effects Pain related to headache, myalgia, and GI effects Knowledge deficit regarding drug therapy	Administer drug at bedtime. Monitor serum lipids prior to therapy. Provide comfort and safety measures: Give small meals. Arrange for periodic ophthalmic exams to screen for cataracts. Give drug with food if GI upset occurs Institute bowel program as needed Provide safety measures if needed Monitor liver function and arrange to stop drug if liver impairment occurs. Provide support and reassurance to deal with drug effects and need to make lifestyle, diet, and exercise changes. Provide patient teaching regarding drug, dosage, adverse effects, what to report, safety precautions.	Evaluate drug effects: lowering of serum cholesterol and lipid levels, prevention of first MI, slowed progression of CAD. Monitor for adverse effects: sedation, dizziness, headache, cataracts, GI upset; hepatic or renal dysfunction; rhabdomyolysis. Monitor for drug–drug interactions as indicated for each drug. Evaluate effectiveness of patient teaching program. Evaluate effectiveness of comfort and safety measures.
PHYSICAL EXAMINATION CV: BP, P, perfusion CNS: orientation, affect, reflexes, vision Skin: color, lesions, texture Resp: R, adventitious sounds GI: abdominal exam, bowel sounds Lab tests: liver and renal function tests, serum lipids			

fenofibrate	*Tricor*	Treatment of adults with very high triglyceride levels at risk for pancreatitis and not responsive to dietary measures
gemfibrozil	*Lopid*	Treatment of adults with very high triglyceride levels with abdominal pain and potential pancreatitis
niacin	*Niaspan*	Treatment of hyperlipidemia; to slow progression of CAD when combined with a bile acid sequestrant

COMBINATION THERAPY

Frequently, patients who do not respond to strict dietary modification, exercise and lifestyle changes, and the use of one lipid-lowering agent may require combination therapy to achieve a desirable serum LDL and cholesterol level. For example, a bile acid sequestrant might be combined with niacin; the combination would decrease the synthesis of LDLs

CASE STUDY

Treating Hyperlipidemia

PRESENTATION

M. M., a 55-year-old white businessman, was seen for a routine insurance physical examination. He was found to be obese and borderline hypertensive, with a nonfasting LDL level of 325 (very high). M.M. reported smoking 2 packs of cigarettes a day and noted in his family history that both of his parents died of heart attacks before age 50. He described himself as a "workaholic" with no time to exercise and a tendency to eat most of his meals in restaurants. The primary medical regimen suggested for M. M. included decreased smoking, weight loss, dietary changes to eliminate saturated fats, and decreased stress. On a return visit after 4 weeks, M. M. had lost 7 pounds and reported a decrease in smoking, but his LDL levels were unchanged. The use of an antihyperlipidemia drug was discussed.

CRITICAL THINKING QUESTIONS

What nursing interventions are appropriate at this point? Consider all of the known risk factors for coronary artery disease (CAD), then rank M. M.'s risk based on those factors. What lifestyle changes can help M. M. reduce his risk of heart disease? What support services should be consulted to help M. M.? Should other tests be done before considering any drug therapy for M. M.? Think about the kind of patient teaching that would help M. M. cope with the overwhelming lifestyle changes that have been suggested, yet remain compliant to his medical regimen.

DISCUSSION

M. M.'s description of himself as a workaholic should alert the nurse to the possibility that he will have trouble adapting to any prescribed lifestyle changes. (Workaholics tend to be very organized, goal-driven, and somewhat controlling individuals.) M. M. should first receive extensive teaching about CAD, his risk factors, and his options. The benefits of decreasing or eliminating risk factors should be discussed. M. M. may be more compliant if he exercises some control over his situation, so he should be invited to suggest possible lifestyle changes or adaptations. M. M. also should be encouraged to set short-range goals that are achievable, to help him feel successful.

Referral to a dietician and to an exercise program may help M. M. select foods and exercises that fit into his lifestyle. A stress test, angiogram, or both may be ordered to evaluate the actual state of M. M.'s coronary arteries. The results of these tests could serve as powerful teaching tools and motivators.

M. M. needs to understand that antihyperlipidemia drugs can cause dizziness, headaches, GI upset, and constipation. Because of his busy lifestyle, M. M. may have trouble coping with these adverse effects. M. M.'s health care provider may need to try a variety of different drugs or combinations of drugs to find ones that are effective but do not cause unacceptable adverse effects.

The American Heart Association (AHA) has numerous booklets, diets, support groups, and counselors who can help M. M. as he tries to adapt to his medical regimen. He can even contact the AHA online at http://www.ahmrt.org for a quick reference and referrals to other sources. M. M. will benefit from having a consistent health care provider who can offer him encouragement, answer any questions, and allow him to vent his feelings. This health care provider can help to coordinate all of his various referrals and activities and act as a consistent base for reassurance and questions. Many times, lifestyle changes are the most difficult part of this medical regimen, so M. M. will need constant support.

while lowering the serum levels of LDLs. This combination is thought to help slow the progression of CAD. However, care must be taken not to combine agents that increase the risk of rhabdomyolysis. For example, HMG CoA reductase inhibitors should not be combined with niacin or gemfibrozil.

CHAPTER SUMMARY

- Coronary artery disease (CAD) is the leading cause of death in the Western world. It is associated with the development of atheromas or plaques in arterial lining that leads to narrowing of the lumen of the artery and hardening of the artery wall, with loss of distensibility and responsiveness to stimuli to contract or dilate.

- The cause of CAD is not known, but many contributing risk factors have been identified including increasing age, male gender, genetic predisposition, high-fat diet, sedentary lifestyle, smoking, obesity, high stress levels, bacterial infections, diabetes, hypertension, gout, and menopause.

- Treatment and prevention of CAD is aimed at manipulating the known risk factors to decrease CAD development and progression.

- Fats are metabolized using bile acids, which act as a detergent to break fats into small molecules called micelles. Micelles are absorbed into the intestinal wall and combined with proteins to become chylomicrons, which can be transported throughout the circulatory system.

- Some fats are used immediately for energy or stored in adipose tissue, while other fats are processed in the liver to LDLs, which are associated with the development of CAD. LDLs are broken down in the periphery and leave many remnants of fats and so forth that must be removed from blood vessels. This process involves the inflammatory reaction and may initiate or contribute to atheroma production.
- Some fats are processed into HDLs, which are able to absorb fats and remnants from the periphery and offer a protective effect against the development of CAD.
- Cholesterol is an important fat that is used to make bile acids. It is the base for steroid hormones and provides necessary structure for cell membranes. All cells can produce cholesterol.
- HMG CoA reductase is an enzyme that controls the final step in production of cellular cholesterol. Blocking this enzyme results in lower serum cholesterol levels, a resultant breakdown of LDLs, and a slight increase in HDLs.
- Bile acid sequestrants bind with bile acids in the intestine and lead to their excretion in the feces. This results in low bile acid levels as the liver uses cholesterol to produce more bile acids. The end result is a decrease in serum cholesterol and LDL levels as the liver changes its metabolism of these fats to meet the need for more bile acids.
- Overall treatment of patients on lipid-lowering drugs should include diet, exercise, and lifestyle changes to reduce the risk of CAD. Such lifestyle changes include stopping smoking; managing stress; and treating hypertension, gout, diabetes, estrogen deficiencies, and bacterial infections (particularly chlamydial infections).

Bibliography

Abramowicz, M. (1996). Choice of lipid-lowering drugs. *Medical Letter, 38* (980), 67–70.

Bullock, B. L. (2000). *Focus on pathophysiology.* Philadelphia: Lippincott Williams & Wilkins.

Hardman, J. G., Limbird, L. E., Molinoff, P. B., Ruddon, R. W., & Gilman, A. G. (Eds.). (1996). *Goodman and Gilman's the pharmacological basis of therapeutics* (9th ed.). New York: McGraw-Hill.

Karch, A. M. (2000). *2000 Lippincott's nursing drug guide.* Philadelphia: Lippincott Williams & Wilkins.

McEvoy, B. R. (1999). *Facts and comparisons 1999.* St. Louis: Facts and Comparisons.

Medical letter on drugs and therapeutics. (1999). New Rochelle, NY: Medical Letter.

Porth, C. M. (1998). *Pathophysiology: Concepts of altered health states* (5th ed.). Philadelphia: Lippincott-Raven.

CHAPTER 46

Drugs Affecting Blood Coagulation

Anticoagulants
- Antiplatelet drugs
  - abciximab
  - P aspirin
  - clopidogrel
  - dipyridamole
  - eptifibatide
  - sulfinpyrazone
  - ticlopidine
  - tirofiban
- Anticoagulants
  - antithrombin
  - P heparin
  - warfarin
- Low-molecular-weight heparins
  - ardeparin
  - dalteparin
  - danaparoid
  - P enoxaparin
- Anticoagulant adjunctive therapy
  - lepirudin
  - P protamine sulfate
  - vitamin K
- Hemorrheologic agent
  - pentoxifylline
- Thrombolytic agents
  - alteplase
  - anistreplase
  - reteplase
  - P streptokinase
  - urokinase

Drugs used to control bleeding
- Antihemophilic agents
  - P antihemophilic factor
  - anti-inhibitor coagulation complex
  - factor IX complex
- Systemic hemostatic agents
  - P aminocaproic acid
  - aprotinin
- Topical hemostatic agents
  - P absorbable gelatin
  - micro collagen
  - thrombin

CHAPTER OUTLINE

Nursing Diagnoses
Implementation
Evaluation
TOPICAL HEMOSTATIC AGENTS
CHAPTER SUMMARY
BIBLIOGRAPHY

KEY TERMS

anticoagulants
clotting factors
coagulation
extrinsic pathway
Hageman factor
hemorrhagic disorders
hemostatic drugs
intrinsic pathway
plasminogen
platelet aggregation
thromboembolic disorders
thrombolytic drugs

INTRODUCTION

The cardiovascular system is a closed system, and blood remains in a fluid state while in it. Because the blood is trapped in a closed space, it maintains the difference in pressures required to keep the system moving along. If the vascular system is injured—from a cut, a puncture, or capillary destruction—the fluid blood could leak out, causing the system to lose pressure and potentially shut down entirely.

To deal with the problem of blood leaking and potentially shutting down the system, blood that is exposed to an injury in a vessel almost immediately forms into a solid state, or clot, which plugs the hole in the system and keeps the rest of the blood moving along. These little injuries to the blood vessels occur all the time (e. g., coughing too hard with a cold, knocking into the corner of the desk when sitting down). Consequently, the system must maintain an intricate balance between the tendency to clot, or form a solid state called ***coagulation,*** and the need to "unclot" or reverse coagulation to keep the vessels open and the blood flowing. When a great deal of vascular damage occurs, such as with a major cut or incision, the balance in the area shifts to a procoagulation mode and a large clot is formed. At the same time, the enzymes in the plasma work to dissolve this clot before blood flow to tissues is lost, with resultant hypoxia and potential cell death.

Drugs that affect blood coagulation work at various steps in the blood clotting and clot dissolving processes to restore the balance that is needed to maintain the cardiovascular system.

BLOOD COAGULATION

Blood coagulation is a complex process that involves vasoconstriction, platelet clumping or aggregation, and a cascade of ***clotting factors*** produced in the liver that eventually react to break down fibrinogen (a protein also produced in the liver) into fibrin threads. When a clot is formed, plasmin (another blood protein) acts to break it down. Blood coagulation can be affected at any step in this complicated process to alter the way that blood clotting occurs.

Vasoconstriction

The first reaction to a blood vessel injury is local vasoconstriction (Figure 46-1). If the injury to the blood vessel is very small, this vasoconstriction could seal off any break and allow the area to heal.

Platelet Aggregation

Injury to a blood vessel exposes blood to the collagen and other substances under the endothelial lining of the vessel. This exposure causes platelets in the circulating blood to stick or adhere to the site of the injury. Once they stick, the platelets release ADP and other chemicals that attract other platelets, causing them to gather or aggregate and to stick. ADP is also a precursor of the prostaglandins from which thromboxane A2 is formed. Thromboxane A2 causes local vasoconstriction and further ***platelet aggregation*** and adhesion. This series of events forms a platelet plug at the site of the vessel injury. In many injuries, the combination of vasoconstriction and platelet aggregation is enough to seal off the injury and keep the cardiovascular system intact (Figure 46-2).

Intrinsic Pathway

As blood comes in contact with the exposed collagen of the injured blood vessel, one of the clotting factors, *Hageman factor* (also called factor XII), a chemical substance that is found circulating in the blood, is activated. (Clotting factors are often known by a name and by a Roman numeral. When one of these factors becomes activated, the lower-case letter *a* is added. Activated Hageman factor would also be called factor XIIa.) The activation of Hageman factor starts a number of reactions in the area: the clot formation process is activated, the clot dissolving process is activated, and the inflammatory response is started (see Chapter 13). The activation of Hageman factor first activates clotting factor XI, then activates a cascading series of coagulant substances, called the ***intrinsic pathway*** (Figure 46-3), that end

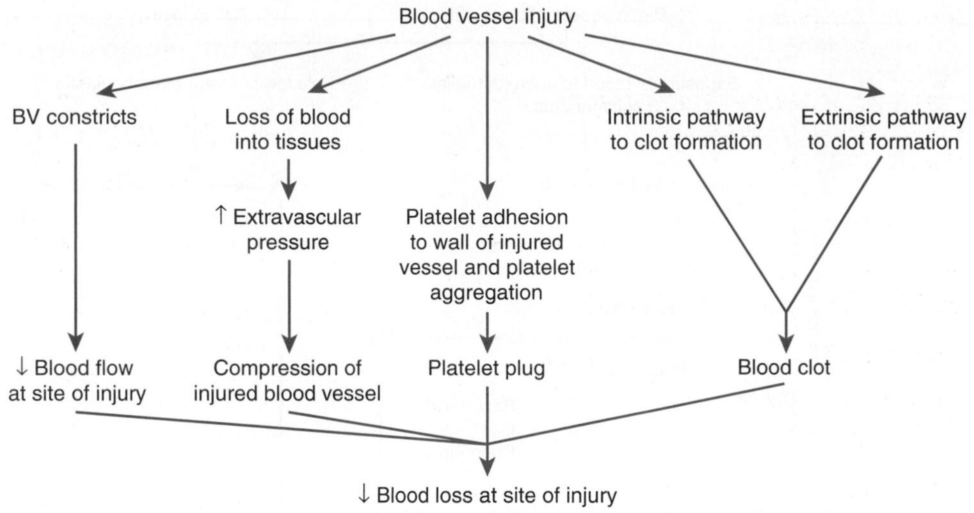

FIGURE 46-1. Process of blood coagulation.

with the conversion of prothrombin to thrombin. Activated thrombin breaks down fibrinogen to form fibrin threads, which form a clot inside the blood vessel. The clot, called a thrombus, acts to plug the injury and seal the system.

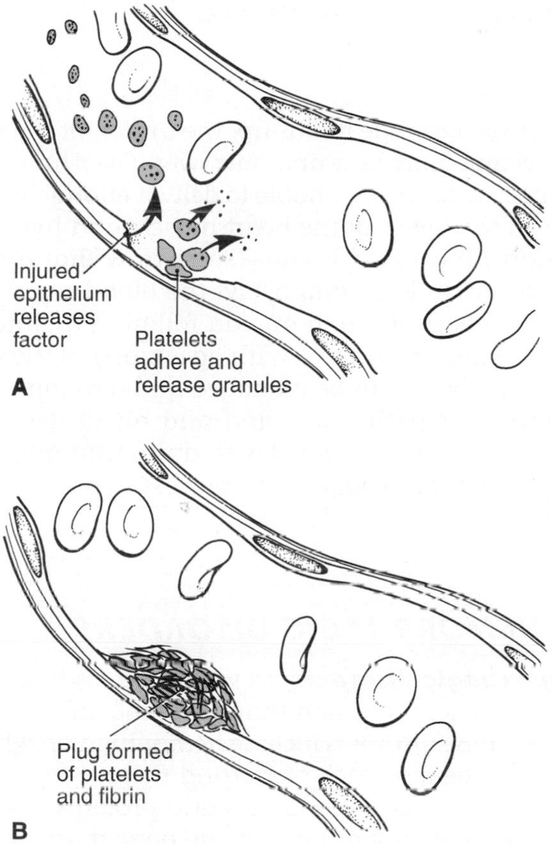

FIGURE 46-2. *A.* Damaged vessel endothelium is a stimulus to circulating platelets, causing platelet adhesion. Platelets release mediators *B.* Platelet aggregation results. (Bullock, B. L. [2000]. *Focus on pathophysiology.* Philadelphia: Lippincott Williams & Wilkins.)

Extrinsic Pathway

While that coagulation process is going on inside the blood vessel, the blood that has leaked out of the vascular system and into the surrounding tissues is caused to clot by the ***extrinsic pathway.*** Injured cells release a substance called tissue thromboplastin, which activates clotting factors in the blood and starts the clotting cascade to form a clot on the outside of the blood vessel. The injured vessel is now vasoconstricted and has a platelet plug as well as a clot both on the inside and the outside of the blood vessel in the area of the injury. These actions maintain the closed nature of the cardiovascular system (see Figure 46-3).

CLOT RESOLUTION AND ANTICLOTTING

Blood plasma also contains anticlotting substances that inhibit clotting reactions that might otherwise lead to an obstruction of blood vessels by blood clots. For example, antithrombin III prevents the formation of thrombin, thus stopping the breakdown of the fibrin threads.

Another substance in the plasma, called plasmin or fibrinolysin, dissolves clots to ensure free movement of blood through the system. Plasmin is a protein-dissolving substance that breaks down the fibrin framework of blood clots and opens up vessels. Its precursor, called ***plasminogen,*** is found in the plasma. The conversion of plasminogen to plasmin begins with the activation of Hageman factor and is facilitated by a number of other factors, including antidiuretic hormone (ADH), epinephrine, pyrogens, emotional stress, physical activity, and the chemicals urokinase and streptokinase. Plasmin helps keep blood vessels open and functional. Very high levels of plasmin are found in the lungs (which contain

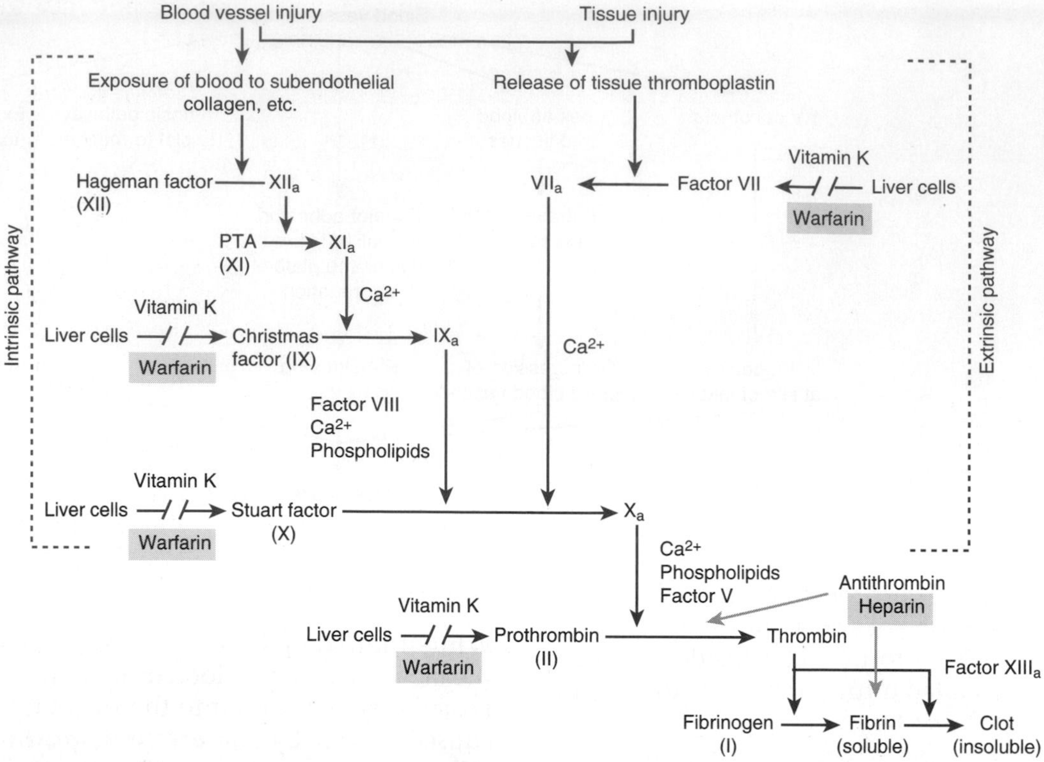

FIGURE 46-3. Details of the intrinsic and extrinsic clotting pathways. The sites of action of some of the drugs that can influence these processes are shown in blue.

millions of tiny, easily injured capillaries) and in the uterus (which in pregnancy must maintain a constant blood flow for the developing fetus). The action of plasmin is evident in the female menstrual flow in that clots do not form rapidly when the lining of the uterus is shed; the blood oozes slowly over a period of days (Figure 46-4).

THROMBOEMBOLIC DISORDERS

Medical conditions that involve the formation of thrombi result in decreased blood flow through or total occlusion of a blood vessel. These conditions are marked by the signs and symptoms of hypoxia, anoxia, or even necrosis in areas affected by the decreased blood flow. In some of these disorders, pieces of the thrombus, called emboli, can break off and travel through the cardiovascular system until they become lodged in a tiny vessel, thus plugging it up.

Conditions that predispose a person to the formation of clots and emboli are called ***thromboembolic disorders.*** Coronary artery disease (CAD) involves a narrowing of the coronary arteries caused by damage to the endothelial lining of these vessels. Thrombi tend to form along the damaged endothelial lining, and as the damage builds up, the lumen of the vessels become narrower and narrower. Over time, the coronary arteries are unable to deliver enough blood to meet the needs of the heart muscle and hypoxia develops. If a vessel become so narrow that a tiny clot can occlude it completely, the blood supply to that area is cut off and anoxia followed by infarction and necrosis occurs. With age, many of the vessels in the body can be damaged and develop similar problems with narrowing and blood delivery. These disorders are treated with drugs that interfere with the normal coagulation process to prevent the formation of clots in the system.

HEMORRHAGIC DISORDERS

Hemorrhagic disorders, in which excess bleeding occurs, are less common than thromboembolic disorders. These disorders include hemophilia, in which there is a genetic lack of clotting factors; liver disease, in which clotting factors and proteins needed for clotting are not produced; and bone marrow disorders, in which platelets are not formed in sufficient quantity to be effective. These disorders are treated with clotting factors and drugs that promote the coagulation process.

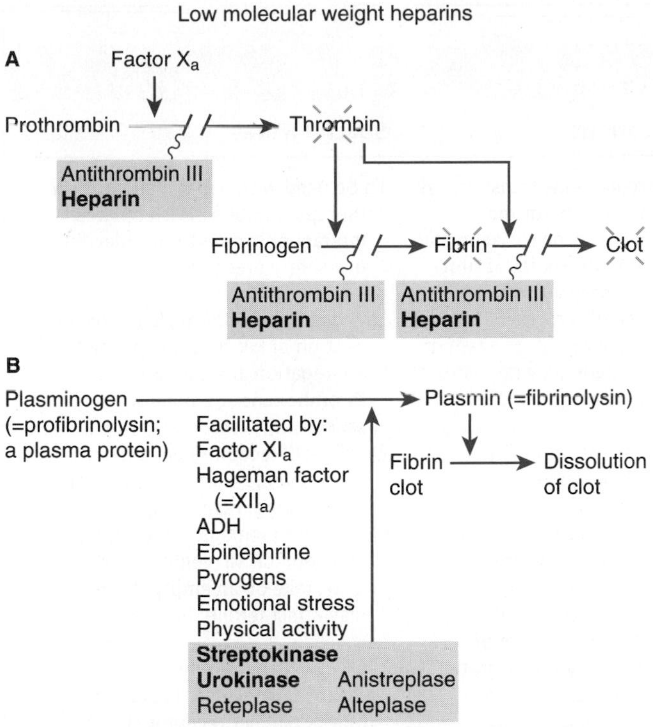

FIGURE 46-4. (*A*) Anticlotting process: prevents clotting. Antithrombin III (in plasma) inhibits the activity of Stuart factor (factor X_a) and thrombin; the drug, Heparin, enhances the activity of antithrombin III. Steps in clot formation that are inhibited by heparin are shown in red. (*B*) Fibrinolytic process: clots are dissolved. The step that is facilitated by the clot-dissolving drugs and by other agents is shown in blue.

ANTICOAGULANTS

Anticoagulants are drugs that interfere with the normal coagulation process. They can affect the process at any step to slow or prevent clot formation. Antiplatelet drugs alter the formation of the platelet plug. Anticoagulants interfere with the clotting cascade and thrombin formation. ***Thrombolytic*** drugs break down the thrombus that has been formed by stimulating the plasmin system.

ANTIPLATELET DRUGS

Antiplatelet drugs decrease the formation of the platelet plug by decreasing the responsiveness of the platelets to stimuli that would cause them to stick and aggregate on a vessel wall. These drugs are used effectively in treating cardiovascular diseases that are prone to occluded vessels; for the maintenance of venous and arterial grafts; to prevent cerebrovascular occlusion; and as adjuncts to thrombolytic therapy in the treatment of myocardial infarction and the prevention of reinfarction. Table 46-1 shows the antiplatelet drugs used today and their usual indications. The prescriber's choice of drug will depend on the intended use and the patient's tolerance of the associated adverse effects.

THERAPEUTIC ACTIONS AND INDICATIONS

The antiplatelet drugs inhibit platelet adhesion and aggregation by blocking receptor sites on the platelet membrane, preventing platelet–platelet interaction or the interaction of platelets with other clotting chemicals. These drugs are used to decrease the risk of fatal MI, to prevent reinfarction after MI, to prevent thromboembolic stroke, and to maintain the patency of grafts; an unlabeled use is the treatment of other thromboembolic disorders.

CONTRAINDICATIONS/CAUTIONS

Antiplatelet drugs are contraindicated in the presence of allergy to the specific drug and with pregnancy and lactation because of the potential adverse effects on the fetus or neonate. Caution should be used in the following conditions: the presence of any known bleeding disorder because of the risk of excessive blood loss; recent surgery because of the risk of increased bleeding in unhealed vessels; and closed head injuries because of the risk of bleeding from the injured vessels in the brain.

ADVERSE EFFECTS

The most common adverse effect seen with these drugs is bleeding, which often occurs as increased bruising and bleeding while brushing the teeth. Other common problems include headache, dizziness, and weakness; the cause of these reactions is not understood. Nausea and gastrointestinal (GI) distress may occur because of direct irritating effects of the oral drug on the GI tract. Skin rash, another common effect, may be related to direct drug effects on the dermis.

CLINICALLY IMPORTANT DRUG–DRUG INTERACTIONS

There is an increased risk of excessive bleeding if any of these drugs are combined with other drugs that affect blood clotting.

DATA LINK

Data link to the antiplatelet drugs, which are listed in Table 46-1, in your nursing drug guide.

NURSING CONSIDERATIONS for patients receiving antiplatelet drugs

Assessment

HISTORY. Screen for the following: any known allergies to these drugs; pregnancy and lactation because of the potential adverse effects on the fetus or

TABLE 46-1
ANTIPLATELET DRUGS

Drug	Brand Name	Route(s)	Usual Indications	Special Notes
abciximab	*ReoPro*	IV (bolus, infusion of up to 12 hours)	Adjunct to percutaneous transluminal coronary angioplasty for the prevention of acute coronary ischemia in patients at high risk for abrupt closure of coronary vessels.	To be used with heparin and aspirin therapy; inhibits platelet-platelet interactions; monitor for bleeding, use safety precautions.
P aspirin	*Bayer*, etc.	Oral, rectal	Reduction of risk of recurrent TIAs in males; reduction of risk of death or nonfatal MI in patients with history of MI or unstable angina.	Low dose (300–325 mg/day) for prevention of MI: prevents platelet aggregation and the formation of thromboxane A_2; monitor for salicylism.
clopidogrel	*Plavix*	Oral	Treatment of patients at high risk for ischemic events—history of MI, peripheral artery disease, stroke.	Blocks ADP receptors on platelets and prevents clumping; monitor for bleeding, rash, GI upset.
dipyridamole	*Persantine*	Oral, IV	With warfarin to prevent thromboembolism in patients with prosthetic heart valves; diagnostic aid IV for patients who cannot exercise; prevention of MI; maintenance of patency of coronary artery grafts.	Monitor for pulmonary edema, fatal and nonfatal MI; ventricular arrhythmias; take on an empty stomach; may affect fertility of women.
eptifibatide	*Integrelin*	IV	Treatment of acute coronary syndrome; prevention of cardiac ischemic complications in patients undergoing percutaneous coronary intervention.	Can cause headache, dizziness; blocks platelet receptor sites to prevent adhesion and clot formation; monitor for bleeding.
sulfinpyrazone	*Anturane*	Oral	Prevention of sudden death post-MI; reduction of emboli in rheumatic valve disease.	Inhibits prostaglandin formation and prevents platelet aggregation associated with GI disturbances; must be given with meals or antacids.
ticlopidine	*Ticlid*	Oral	Prevention of thrombotic stroke in patients who have had a thrombotic stroke, especially if intolerant to aspirin; unlabeled use for other thromboembolic disorders.	Inhibits platelet–platelet interactions; irreversible effects on platelet membranes; associated with severe GI upset, must be given with food; monitor for neutropenia.
tirofiban	*Aggrastat*	IV	Treatment of acute coronary syndrome in combination with heparin; prevention of cardiac ischemic complications in patients undergoing percutaneous coronary intervention.	Can cause headache, dizziness; blocks platelet receptors to prevent adhesion and clot formation; monitor for bleeding.

neonate; and bleeding disorders, recent surgery, or closed head injury because of the potential for excessive bleeding.

PHYSICAL ASSESSMENT. Include screening for baseline status before beginning therapy and for any potential adverse effects: body temperature; skin color, lesions, temperature; affect, orientation, reflexes; pulse, blood pressure, perfusion; respirations, adventitious sounds; and clotting studies.

Nursing Diagnoses

The patient receiving antiplatelet drugs may have the following nursing diagnoses related to drug therapy:

- Potential for injury related to bleeding effects, CNS effects
- Pain related to GI, CNS effects
- Knowledge deficit regarding drug therapy

Implementation

- Provide small, frequent meals *to relieve GI discomfort* if GI upset is a problem.
- Provide comfort measures and analgesia for headache *to relieve pain and improve patient compliance to the drug regimen.*
- Suggest safety measures, including the use of an electric razor and avoidance of contact sports *to decrease the risk of bleeding.*

• Provide increased precautions against bleeding during invasive procedures; use pressure dressings and ice *to decrease excessive blood loss due to anticoagulation.*
• Mark the chart of any patient receiving this drug *to alert medical staff that there is a potential for increased bleeding.*
• Provide thorough patient teaching, including the name of the drug, dosage prescribed, measures to avoid adverse effects, warning signs of problems, the need for periodic monitoring and evaluation, and the need to wear or carry a Medic-Alert notification *to enhance patient knowledge about drug therapy and to promote compliance with the drug regimen.*
• Offer support and encouragement *to help the patient deal with the diagnosis and drug regimen.*

Evaluation

• Monitor patient response to the drug (increased bleeding time).
• Monitor for adverse effects (bleeding, GI upset, dizziness, headache).
• Evaluate the effectiveness of the teaching plan (patient can name drug, dosage, adverse effects to watch for, specific measures to avoid adverse effects; patient understands importance of continued follow-up).
• Monitor the effectiveness of comfort measures and compliance to the regimen.

BOX 46-1

VITAMIN K: REVERSING WARFARIN'S EFFECTS

Phytonadione (*AquaMEPHYTON*), a form of vitamin K, is used to reverse the effects of warfarin. Vitamin K is responsible for promoting the liver synthesis of several clotting factors. When these pathways have been inhibited by warfarin, clotting time is increased. By providing an increased level of vitamin K, more of these factors are produced and the clotting time can be brought back within a normal range.

Because of the way that vitamin K exerts its effects on clotting, there is at least a 24-hour delay from the time that the drug is given until some change can be seen. This is because there is no direct effect on the warfarin itself, but an increased stimulation of the liver, which must then produce the clotting factors. The usual dosage for the treatment of anticoagulant-induced prothrombin (PT) deficiency is 2.5 to 10 mg IM or SC, or (rarely) 25 mg IM or SC. Oral doses can be used if injection is not feasible. A PT response within 6 to 8 hours after parenteral doses or 12 to 48 hours after oral doses will determine the need for a repeat dose. If a response is not seen, and the patient is bleeding excessively, fresh frozen plasma or an infusion of whole blood may be needed.

ANTICOAGULANTS

Anticoagulants interfere with the coagulation process by interfering with the clotting cascade and thrombin formation. Drugs in this class include warfarin, heparin, and antithrombin. These drugs can be used orally (warfarin) or parenterally (heparin and antithrombin).

• Warfarin (*Coumadin*), an oral drug, is used to maintain a state of anticoagulation in situations in which the patient is susceptible to potentially dangerous clot formation. Warfarin works by interfering with the formation of vitamin-K–dependent clotting factors in the liver. The eventual effect is a depletion of these clotting factors and a prolongation of clotting times. Warfarin's onset of action is about 3 days; its effects last for about 4 to 5 days. Because of the time delay, warfarin is not the drug of choice in an acute situation, but is convenient and useful for prolonged effects (Box 46-1). It is used to treat patients with atrial fibrillation, artificial heart valves, or valvular damage that makes them susceptible to thrombus and embolus formation. It also is used to treat and prevent venous thrombosis and embolization after acute MI and pulmonary embolism.
• Heparin (generic) is a naturally occurring substance that inhibits the conversion of prothrombin to thrombin, thus blocking the conversion of fibrinogen to fibrin—the final step in clot formation. It is injected IV or SC and has an almost immediate onset of action. Its usual indications include acute treatment and prevention of venous thrombosis and pulmonary embolism; treatment of atrial fibrillation with embolization; prevention of clotting in blood samples and dialysis and venous tubing; and diagnosis and treatment of disseminated intravascular coagulation (DIC), as well as an adjunct in the treatment of MI and stroke. Because heparin must be injected, it is often not the drug of choice for outpatients who would be responsible for injecting the drug several times during the day. Patients may be started on heparin in the acute situation, then switched to the oral drug warfarin (Boxes 46-2 and 46-3).
• Antithrombin (*Thrombate III*) is a naturally occurring anticoagulant. It is used IV for patients with hereditary antithrombin III deficiencies who are undergoing surgery or obstetric procedures that might put them at risk for thromboembolism. It also is used for replacement therapy in congenital antithrombin III deficiency.

THERAPEUTIC ACTIONS AND INDICATIONS

As noted above, the anticoagulants interfere with the normal cascade of events involved in the clotting

BOX 46-2

PROTAMINE SULFATE: ANTIDOTE FOR HEPARIN OVERDOSE

The antidote for heparin overdose is protamine sulfate (generic). This strongly basic protein drug forms stable salts with heparin as soon as the two drugs come in contact, immediately reversing heparin's anticoagulant effects. Paradoxically, if protamine is given to a patient who has not received heparin, it has anticoagulant effects.

The dosage of protamine that is used is determined by the amount of heparin that has been given and the time that has elapsed since the drug was administered. A dose of 1 mg IV protamine neutralizes 90 USP of heparin derived from lung tissue or 110 USP of heparin derived from intestinal mucosa. The drug must be administered very slowly IV, not to exceed 50 mg in any 10-minute period. Care must be taken to calculate the amount of heparin that has been given to the patient. Potentially fatal anaphylactic reactions have been reported with the use of this drug, so life support equipment should be readily available when it is used.

process. Warfarin causes a decrease in the production of vitamin-K–dependent clotting factors in the liver. Heparin blocks the formation of thrombin from prothrombin. Antithrombin interferes with the formation of thrombin from prothrombin. These drugs are used to treat thromboembolic disorders such as atrial fibrillation, MI, pulmonary embolus, and evolving stroke, and to prevent the formation of thrombi in such disorders.

CONTRAINDICATIONS/CAUTIONS

The anticoagulants are contraindicated in the presence of known allergy to the drugs. They also should not be used with any conditions that could be compromised by increased bleeding tendencies; these include hemorrhagic disorders, recent trauma, spinal puncture, GI ulcers, recent surgery, intrauterine device placement, tuberculosis, the presence of indwelling catheters, and threatened abortion. In addition, anticoagulants are contraindicated with pregnancy (fetal injury and death has occurred); lactation (use of heparin is suggested if an anticoagulant is needed during lactation); and renal or hepatic disease, which could interfere with the metabolism and effectiveness of these drugs.

Caution should be used with congestive heart failure (CHF), thyrotoxicosis, senile or psychotic individuals (because of the potential for unexpected effects), and diarrhea and fever, which could alter the normal clotting process by loss of vitamin K from the intestine (caused by diarrhea) and by activation of plasminogen (caused by fever).

ADVERSE EFFECTS

The most commonly encountered adverse effect of the anticoagulants is bleeding, ranging from bleeding gums with tooth brushing to severe internal hemorrhage. Clotting times should be monitored closely to avoid these problems. Nausea, GI upset, diarrhea, and hepatic dysfunction also may occur secondary to direct drug toxicity. Warfarin has been associated with alopecia and dermatitis as well as bone marrow depression and, less frequently, prolonged and painful erections.

CLINICALLY IMPORTANT DRUG–DRUG INTERACTIONS

Increased bleeding can occur if heparin is combined with oral anticoagulants, salicylates, penicillins, and cephalosporins. Decreased anticoagulation can occur if heparin is combined with nitroglycerin. Warfarin has documented drug–drug interactions with a vast number of other drugs (Table 46-2). It is a wise practice never to add or take away a drug from the drug regimen of a patient receiving warfarin without careful patient monitoring and adjustment of the warfarin dosage to prevent serious adverse effects.

BOX 46-3

LEPIRUDIN: TREATING HEPARIN ALLERGY

Lepirudin (*Refludan*) is an IV drug that was developed to treat a rare allergic reaction to heparin. In some patients, an allergy to heparin precipitates a heparin-induced thrombocytopenia with associated thromboembolic disease. Lepirudin directly inhibits thrombin, blocking the thromboembolic effects of this reaction. A 0.4 mg/kg initial IV bolus followed by a continuous infusion of 0.15 mg/kg for 2 to 10 days is the recommended treatment. The patient needs to be monitored closely for bleeding from any sites and for the development of direct hepatic injury.

DATA LINK

Data link to the following anticoagulants in your nursing drug guide:

ANTICOAGULANTS

Name	Brand Name(s)	Usual Indications
antithrombin	*Thrombate III*	Replacement in antithrombin III deficiency; treatment of patients with this deficiency who are to undergo surgery or obstetrical procedures
P heparin	generic	Prevention and treatment of venous thrombosis, pulmonary embolus, clotting in blood samples and venous lines; diagnosis and treatment of DIC

TABLE 46-2

CLINICALLY IMPORTANT DRUG–DRUG INTERACTIONS WITH WARFARIN

↑ Bleeding effects	↓ Anticoagulation	↑ Activity and effects of phenytoin
Salicylates	Barbiturates	
Chloral hydrate	Griseofulvin	
Phenylbutazone	Rifampin	
Clofibrate	Phenytoin	
Disulfiram	Glutethimide	
Chloramphenicol	Carbamazepine	
Metronidazole	Vitamin K	
Cimetidine	Vitamin E	
Ranitidine	Cholestyramine	
Cotrimoxazole	Aminoglutethimide	
Sulfinpyrazone	Ethchlorvynol	
Quinidine		
Quinine		
Oxyphenbutazone		
Thyroid drugs		
Glucagon		
Danazol		
Erythromycin		
Androgens		
Amiodarone		
Cefamandole		
Cefoperazone		
Cefotetan		
Moxalactam		
Cefazolin		
Cefoxitin		
Ceftriaxone		
Meclofenamate		
Mefenamic acid		
Famotidine		
Nizatidine		
Nalidixic acid		

warfarin	*Coumadin*	Prevention and treatment of venous thrombosis, pulmonary embolus, embolus with atrial fibrillation, systemic emboli post-MI

NURSING CONSIDERATIONS
for patients receiving anticoagulants

Assessment

HISTORY. Screen for any known allergies to these drugs. Also screen for conditions that could be exacerbated by increased bleeding tendencies; these include hemorrhagic disorders, recent trauma, spinal puncture, GI ulcers, recent surgery, intrauterine device placement, tuberculosis, the presence of indwelling catheters, threatened abortion, pregnancy (fetal injury and death has occurred), lactation (use of heparin is suggested if an anticoagulant is needed during lactation), renal or hepatic disease (which could interfere with the metabolism and effectiveness of these drugs), CHF, thyrotoxicosis, senility or psychoses (because of the potential for unexpected effects), and diarrhea and fever (which could alter the normal clotting process).

PHYSICAL ASSESSMENT. Include screening for baseline status before beginning therapy and for any potential adverse effects. Assess the following: body temperature; skin color, lesions, temperature; affect, orientation, reflexes; pulse, blood pressure, perfusion; respirations, adventitious sounds; clotting studies, renal and hepatic function tests, CBC, and stool guaiac; ECG is appropriate.

Nursing Diagnoses

The patient receiving an anticoagulant may have the following nursing diagnoses related to drug therapy:

- Potential for injury related to bleeding effects, bone marrow depression
- Body image disturbance related to alopecia, skin rash
- Potential alteration in perfusion related to blood loss
- Knowledge deficit regarding drug therapy

Implementation

- Evaluate for therapeutic effects of warfarin: prothrombin time (PT) 1.5 to 2.5 times the control value or PT/INR (international normalized ratio) ratio of 2 to 3 *to evaluate the effectiveness of the drug dose.*
- Evaluate for therapeutic effects of heparin: whole blood clotting time (WBCT) of 2.5 to 3 times control or activated partial thromboplastin time (APTT) of 1.5 to 3 times control value *to evaluate the effectiveness of the drug dose.*
- Evaluate the patient regularly for any sign of blood loss (petechiae, bleeding gums, bruises, dark-colored stools, dark-colored urine) *to evaluate the effectiveness of the drug dose and to consult with the prescriber if bleeding becomes apparent.*
- Establish safety precautions *to protect the patient from injury.*
- Provide safety measures, e.g., electric razor, avoidance of contact sports, *to decrease the risk of bleeding.*
- Provide increased precautions against bleeding during invasive procedures; use pressure dressings. Avoid IM injections; do not rub SC injection sites *because the state of anticoagulation will increase the risk of blood loss.*
- Mark the chart of any patient receiving this drug *to alert the medical staff that there is a potential for increased bleeding.*
- Maintain antidotes on standby (protamine sulfate for heparin, vitamin K for warfarin) *in case of overdose.*

PATIENT TEACHING CHECKLIST

ORAL ANTICOAGULANTS

Create customized patient teaching materials for a specific oral anticoagulant from your CD-ROM. Your patient teaching should stress the following points for drugs within this class:

An anticoagulant slows the body's normal blood clotting processes to prevent harmful blood clots from forming. This type of drug is often called a "blood thinner"; however, it cannot dissolve any clots that have already formed.

Never change any medication that you are taking—such as adding or stopping another drug, taking a new over-the-counter medication, or stopping one that you have been taking regularly—without consulting with your health care provider. Many other drugs affect the way that your anticoagulant works; starting or stopping another drug can cause excessive bleeding or interfere with the desired effects of the drug.

Some of the following adverse effects may occur:

- Stomach bloating, cramps—These problems often pass with time; consult your health care provider if they persist or become too uncomfortable.
- Loss of hair, skin rash—These problems can be very frustrating; you may wish to discuss these with your health care provider.
- Orange-yellow discoloration of the urine—This can be frightening, but may just be an effect of the drug. If you are concerned that this might be blood, simply add vinegar to your urine; the color should disappear. If the color does not disappear, it may be caused by blood and you should contact your health care provider.

Report any of the following to your health care provider: unusual bleeding (when brushing your teeth, excessive bleeding from an injury, excessive bruising); black or tarry stools; cloudy or dark urine; sore throat, fever, chills; severe headache or dizziness.

Tell any doctor, nurse, or other health care provider that you are taking this drug. You should carry or wear a Medic-Alert bracelet stating that you are on this drug to alert emergency medical personnel that you are at increased risk for bleeding.

It is important to avoid situations in which you could be easily injured—for example, engaging in contact sports or using a straight razor.

Keep this drug, and all medications, out of the reach of children.

Avoid the use of over-the-counter medications while you are on this drug. If you feel that you need one of these, consult with your health care provider for the best choice. Many of these drugs may interfere with your anticoagulant.

You will need to have regular, periodic blood tests while you are on this drug in order to monitor the effects of the drug on your body and adjust your dosage as needed.

This Teaching Checklist reflects general patient teaching guidelines. It is not meant to be a substitute for drug-specific teaching information, which is available in nursing drug guides.

- Monitor the patient carefully when any drug is added to or withdrawn from the drug regimen of the patient on warfarin *because of the risk of drug–drug interactions changing the effectiveness of the anticoagulant.*
- Ensure that the patient receives regular follow-up and monitoring, including clotting times, *to ensure maximum therapeutic effects.*
- Provide thorough patient teaching, including the name of the drug, dosage prescribed, measures to avoid adverse effects, warning signs of problems, the need for periodic monitoring and evaluation, and the need to wear or carry a Medic-Alert notification *to enhance patient knowledge about drug therapy and to promote compliance with the drug regimen* (see Patient Teaching Checklist: Oral Anticoagulants).
- Offer support and encouragement *to help the patient deal with the diagnosis and drug regimen.*

Evaluation

- Monitor patient response to the drug: increased bleeding time; warfarin, PT 1.5 to 2.5 times the control value or PT/INR ratio of 2 to 3; heparin, WBCT of 2.5 to 3 times control value or APTT of 1.5 to 3 times control.
- Monitor for adverse effects (bleeding, bone marrow depression, alopecia, GI upset, rash).
- Evaluate the effectiveness of the teaching plan (patient can name drug, dosage, adverse effects to watch for, specific measures to avoid adverse effects; patient understands importance of continued follow-up).

NURSING CARE GUIDE
Oral Anticoagulants

Assessment	Nursing Diagnoses	Implementation	Evaluation
HISTORY Allergies to any of these drugs, renal or hepatic dysfunction, pregnancy, lactation, gastric ulcers, tuberculosis, indwelling catheters	Alteration in tissue perfusion related to alteration in clotting effects Potential for injury related to anticoagulant effects Alteration in self-concept related to alopecia, skin rash Knowledge deficit regarding drug therapy	Ensure proper administration of drug. Provide comfort and safety measures: - Give small meals - Provide protection from injury - Provide safety measures with invasive procedures - Institute bowel program as needed - Have antidote on standby (vitamin K) - Provide skin care Provide support and reassurance to deal with drug effects. Provide patient teaching regarding drug, dosage, adverse effects, what to report, safety precautions.	Evaluate drug effects: increased bleeding times, PT 1.5–2.5x control or PT/INF ratio of 2–3. Monitor for adverse effects: bleeding, alopecia, rash, gi upset, excessive bleeding. Monitor for drug–drug interactions (numerous). Evaluate effectiveness of patient teaching program. Evaluate effectiveness of comfort and safety measures.
PHYSICAL EXAMINATION CV: BP, P, perfusion, baseline ECG CNS: orientation, affect, reflexes, vision Skin: color, lesions, texture Resp: R, adventitious sounds GI: abdominal exam, stool guaiac Lab tests: liver and renal function tests, prothrombin time (PT)			

• Monitor the effectiveness of comfort measures and compliance to the regimen (see Nursing Care Guide: Oral Anticoagulants).

LOW-MOLECULAR-WEIGHT HEPARINS

In the late 1990s, a series of low-molecular-weight heparins were developed. These drugs inhibit thrombus and clot formation by blocking factors Xa and IIa. Because of the size and nature of their molecules, these drugs do not greatly affect thrombin, clotting, or prothrombin times. Therefore, they cause fewer systemic adverse effects. These drugs are indicated for very specific uses in the prevention of clots and emboli formation following certain surgeries; however, each of these drugs is being studied for use following additional types of surgery. The nursing care of a patient receiving one of these drugs is similar to the care of a patient receiving heparin. They are given just before or after the surgery (depending on the drug), then are continued for 7 to 10 days during the postoperative recovery process.

CASE STUDY

Using Oral Anticoagulants to Protect Against Emboli

PRESENTATION

G. R. is a 68-year-old woman with a history of severe mitral valvular disease. For the last several years, she has been able to manage her condition with digoxin, a diuretic, and a potassium supplement. However, a recent visit to her physician revealed that she had been experiencing periods of breathlessness, palpitations, and dizziness. Tests showed that G. R. was having frequent periods of atrial fibrillation (AF), with a heart rate of up to 140. Because of the danger of emboli as a result of her valvular disease and the bouts of atrial fibrillation, G. R. was started on warfarin.

CRITICAL THINKING QUESTIONS

What nursing interventions should be done at this point? Why do people with mitral valve disease frequently develop AF? Think about why emboli form when the atria fibrillate. Stabilizing G. R. on warfarin may take several weeks of blood tests and dosage adjustments. How can this process be made easier? What patient teaching points should be covered with G. R. to ensure that she is protected from emboli and does not experience excessive bleeding?

DISCUSSION

G. R.'s situation is complex. She has a progressive degenerative valve disease that usually leads to congestive heart failure (CHF), and frequently to other complications such as AF and emboli formation. Her digoxin and potassium levels should be checked to determine whether her CHF is stabilized or the digoxin is causing the AF because of excessive doses or potassium imbalance. If these tests are within normal limits, G. R. may be experiencing AF because of irritation to the atrial cells caused by the damaged mitral valve and associated swelling and scarring. If this is the case, an anticoagulant will help protect G. R. against emboli, which form in the auricles when blood pools there while the atria are fibrillating. There is less chance of emboli formation if clotting is slowed.

G. R. will need extensive teaching about warfarin, including the need for frequent blood tests, the list of potential drug–drug interactions, the importance of being alert to the many factors that can affect dosage needs (including illness and diet), and how to monitor for subtle blood loss. This would be a good opportunity to review teaching about her valve disease and CHF and answer any questions that she might have about how all of these things interrelate. If possible, it would be useful to teach G. R. or a significant other how to take her pulse so she can be alerted to potential arrhythmias and avert problems before they begin. It also would be a good idea to check on support services for G. R., to ensure that her blood tests can be done and that her response to the drug is monitored carefully.

DATA LINK

Data link to the following low-molecular-weight heparins in your nursing drug guide:

LOW-MOLECULAR-WEIGHT HEPARINS

Name	Brand Name	Usual Indication
ardeparin	*Normiflo*	Prevention of deep vein thrombosis that may lead to pulmonary emboli following knee replacement surgery
dalteparin	*Fragmin*	Prevention of deep vein thrombosis that may lead to pulmonary emboli following abdominal surgery
danaparoid	*Orgaran*	Prevention of deep vein thrombosis that may lead to pulmonary emboli following elective hip replacement surgery
P enoxaparin	*Lovenox*	Prevention of deep vein thrombosis that may lead to pulmonary emboli following hip replacement surgery

BOX 46-4 PENTOXIFYLLINE: HEMORRHEOLOGIC AGENT

Pentoxifylline (*Trental*) is known as a hemorrheologic agent, or a drug that can induce hemorrhage. It is a xanthine that, like coffee and theophylline, decreases platelet aggregation and decreases fibrinogen concentration in the blood. These effects can decrease blood clot formation and increase blood flow through narrowed or damaged vessels. The mechanism of action by which pentoxifylline does these things is not known. It is one of the very few drugs found to be effective in treating intermittent claudication, a painful vascular problem of the legs.

Because pentoxifylline is a xanthine, it is associated with many cardiovascular stimulatory effects; patients with underlying cardiovascular problems need to be monitored carefully when taking this drug. Pentoxifylline can also cause headache, dizziness, nausea and upset stomach. It is taken orally three times a day for at least 8 weeks to evaluate its effectiveness.

THROMBOLYTIC AGENTS

If a thrombus has already formed in a vessel (e.g., during an acute MI), it may be necessary to dissolve that clot to open up the vessel and restore blood flow to the dependent tissue. All of the drugs that are available for this purpose work to activate the natural anticlotting system, conversion of plasminogen to plasmin. The activation of this system breaks down fibrin threads and dissolves any formed clot. The thrombolytic drugs are effective only if the patient has plasminogen in the plasma. Table 46-3 indicates the thrombolytic agents that are available for use.

THERAPEUTIC ACTIONS AND INDICATIONS

The thrombolytic agents work by activating plasminogen to plasmin, which in turn breaks down fibrin threads in a clot to dissolve a formed clot. They are indicated for the treatment of acute MI (to dissolve the clot and prevent further tissue damage, if used within 6 hours of the onset of symptoms); to treat pulmonary emboli and ischemic stroke; and to open clotted IV catheters.

CONTRAINDICATIONS/CAUTIONS

The use of thrombolytic agents is contraindicated in the presence of allergy to any of these drugs. These drugs also should not be used with any condition that could be worsened by the dissolution of clots; these include recent surgery, active internal bleeding, cerebrovascular accident (CVA) within the last 2 months, aneurysm, obstetric delivery, organ biopsy, recent serious GI bleeding, rupture of a noncompressible blood vessel, recent major trauma (including cardiopulmonary resuscitation), known blood clotting defects, cerebrovascular disease, uncontrolled hypertension, liver disease (which could affect normal clotting factors and the production of plasminogen), and lactation, because of the possible adverse effects on the neonate.

ADVERSE EFFECTS

The most common adverse effect associated with the use of thrombolytic agents is bleeding. Patients should be monitored closely for the occurrence of cardiac arrhythmias (with coronary reperfusion) and hypotension. Hypersensitivity reactions are not uncommon and range from rash and flushing to bronchospasm and anaphylactic reaction.

CLINICALLY IMPORTANT DRUG–DRUG INTERACTIONS

There is an increased risk of hemorrhage if thrombolytic agents are used with any anticoagulant or antiplatelet drugs.

DATA LINK

Data link to the thrombolytic agents, listed in Table 46-3, in your nursing drug guide.

TABLE 46-3

THROMBOLYTIC DRUGS

Drug	Brand Name(s)	Route	Usual Indications	Special Notes
alteplase	*Activase*	IV	Treatment of acute MI; acute, massive pulmonary embolism; acute ischemic stroke	APTT should be less than 2× control
anistreplase	*Eminase*	IV	Management of acute MI to open obstructed coronary arteries, improve LV function and decrease mortality	Streptokinase, plasminogen activator; monitor for bleeding
reteplase	*Retevase*	IV	Treatment of coronary thrombosis associated with acute MI	Converts plasminogen to plasmin; monitor for bleeding
P streptokinase	*Streptase, Kabikinase*	IV	Treatment of coronary artery thrombosis if within 6 hours of onset of symptoms; pulmonary embolism; occluded A-V cannulae; deep vein thrombosis; LV thrombosis and embolism	Converts plasminogen to plasmin; institute treatment within 2–6 hours of onset of MI and within 7 days of other thrombotic events; monitor for severe bleeding
urokinase	*Abbokinase*	IV	IV catheter clearance: coronary artery thrombosis within 6 hours of onset of symptoms; lysis of pulmonary emboli	Institute treatment within 2–6 hours of onset of MI; monitor cardiac rhythm; monitor for excessive bleeding.

NURSING CONSIDERATIONS for patients receiving thrombolytic agents

Assessment

HISTORY. Screen for any known allergies to these drugs. Also screen for any conditions that could be worsened by the dissolution of clots; these include recent surgery, active internal bleeding, CVA within the last 2 months, aneurysm, obstetric delivery, organ biopsy, recent serious GI bleeding, rupture of a noncompressible blood vessel, recent major trauma (including cardiopulmonary resuscitation), known blood clotting defects, cerebrovascular disease, uncontrolled hypertension, liver disease (which could affect normal clotting factors and the production of plasminogen), and lactation because of the possible adverse effects on the neonate.

PHYSICAL ASSESSMENT. Include screening for baseline status before beginning therapy and for any potential adverse effects. Assess the following: body temperature; skin color, lesions, temperature; affect, orientation, reflexes; pulse, blood pressure, perfusion; respirations, adventitious sounds; and clotting studies, renal and hepatic function tests, CBC, stool guaiac, and ECG.

Nursing Diagnoses

The patient receiving a thrombolytic drug may have the following nursing diagnoses related to drug therapy:

- Potential for injury related to clot dissolving effects
- Alteration in perfusion related to possible blood loss
- Alteration in cardiac output related to bleeding, arrhythmias
- Knowledge deficit regarding drug therapy

Implementation

- Discontinue heparin if it is being given before administration of a thrombolytic agent, unless specifically ordered for coronary artery infusion *to prevent excessive loss of blood.*
- Evaluate the patient regularly for any sign of blood loss (petechiae, bleeding gums, bruises, dark-colored stools, dark-colored urine) *to evaluate drug effectiveness and to consult with the prescriber if blood loss becomes apparent.*
- Monitor coagulation studies regularly; *consult with the prescriber to adjust the drug dose appropriately.*
- Institute treatment within 6 hours of the onset of symptoms of acute MI *to achieve optimum therapeutic effectiveness.*
- Arrange to type and cross match blood *in case of serious blood loss that will require whole blood transfusion.*
- Monitor cardiac rhythm continuously if being given for acute MI *because of the risk of alteration in cardiac function;* have life support equipment on standby as needed.
- Provide increased precautions against bleeding during invasive procedures; use pressure dressings and ice. Avoid IM injections; do not rub SC injection sites *because of the risk of increased blood loss in the anticoagulated state.*
- Mark the chart of any patient receiving this drug *to alert medical staff that there is a potential for increased bleeding.*
- Provide thorough patient teaching, including the name of the drug, dosage prescribed, measures to avoid adverse effects, warning signs of problems, and the need for periodic monitoring and evaluation *to enhance patient knowledge about drug therapy and to promote compliance with the drug regimen.*
- Offer support and encouragement *to help the patient deal with the diagnosis and drug regimen.*

Evaluation

- Monitor patient response to the drug (dissolution of the clot and return of blood flow to the area).
- Monitor for adverse effects (bleeding, arrhythmias, hypotension, hypersensitivity reaction).
- Evaluate the effectiveness of the teaching plan (patient can name drug, adverse effects to watch for, specific measures to avoid adverse effects).
- Monitor the effectiveness of comfort measures and compliance to the regimen.

WWW.WEB LINKS

Health care providers and patients may want to explore the following Internet sources:

Information on thrombosis, process, interventions, pathology:
http://lef.org/protocols/prtcl-104a.shtml

Information designed for patients and families regarding the home use of warfarin:
http://www.stjames.ie/nmic/warfarin/warfcoun.html

Information on heparin—use, research, complications:
http://www-heparin.pharmacy.uiowa.edu

Information on heparin and the low-molecular-weight heparins—comparisons, use, toxicity:
http://www.heparin.com/index/html

DRUGS USED TO CONTROL BLEEDING

On the other end of the spectrum of coagulation problems are various bleeding disorders. These include the following:

Hemophilia: a disorder in which there is a genetic lack of clotting factors, leaving the patient vulnerable to excessive bleeding with any injury.
Liver disease: in which clotting factors and proteins needed for clotting are not produced.
Bone marrow disorders: in which platelets are not formed in sufficient quantity to be effective.

These disorders are treated with clotting factors and drugs that promote the coagulation process.

ANTIHEMOPHILIC AGENTS

The drugs used to treat hemophilia are replacement factors for the specific clotting factors that are genetically missing in that particular type of hemophilia.

- Antihemophilic factor (*Bioclate, Koate-HP,* and others) is factor VIII, the clotting factor that is missing in classical hemophilia (hemophilia A). It is used to correct or prevent bleeding episodes or to allow necessary surgery.
- Anti-inhibitor coagulation complex (*Autoplex T*) is a preparation made from pooled human blood and contains variable amounts of preformed clotting factors. Because of the risk involved in receiving blood and blood products, this is not a preferred drug. However, it is useful when patients with hemophilia A require surgery and need immediate relief from bleeding.
- Factor IX complex (*Benefix, Profilnine SD,* and others) contains plasma fractions of many of the clotting factors and increases blood levels of factors II, VII, IX, and X. It is given IV to prevent or treat hemophilia B (Christmas disease, a deficiency of factor IX), control bleeding episodes in hemophilia A, and control bleeding episodes in cases of factor VII deficiency.

THERAPEUTIC ACTIONS AND INDICATIONS

The antihemophilic drugs replace clotting factors that are either genetically missing or low in each particular hemophilia. They are used to prevent blood loss due to injury or surgery and to treat bleeding episodes. The drug of choice depends on the particular hemophilia that is being treated.

CONTRAINDICATIONS/CAUTIONS

Antihemophilic factor is contraindicated in the presence of known allergy to mouse proteins. Factor IX is contraindicated in the presence of liver disease with signs of intravascular coagulation or fibrinolysis. Because these drugs are used to prevent serious bleeding problems or to treat bleeding episodes, there are few contraindications to their use.

ADVERSE EFFECTS

The most common adverse effects associated with antihemophilic agents involve risks associated with the use of blood products (e.g., hepatitis, AIDS). Headache, flushing, chills, fever, and lethargy may occur as a reaction to the injection of a foreign protein. Nausea and vomiting and stinging, itching, and burning at the site of the injection may also occur.

DATA LINK

Data link to the following antihemophilic agents in your nursing drug guide:

ANTIHEMOPHILIC AGENTS

Name	Brand Name	Usual Indication
P antihemophilic factor	*Bioclate* and others	Treatment of hemophilia A; to correct bleeding episodes or to allow surgery
factor IX complex	*Benefix* and others	Treatment of hemophilia B; treatment of bleeding episodes with factor VII and factor VIII deficiencies

NURSING CONSIDERATIONS for patients receiving antihemophilic agents

Assessment

HISTORY. Screen for the following: any known allergies to these drugs or to mouse proteins with antihemophilic factor; and liver disease.

PHYSICAL ASSESSMENT. Include screening for baseline status before beginning therapy and for any potential adverse effects. Assess the following: body temperature; skin color, lesions, temperature; affect, orientation, reflexes; pulse, blood pressure, perfusion; respirations, adventitious sounds; clotting studies; and hepatic function tests.

Nursing Diagnoses

The patient receiving an antihemophilic drug may have the following nursing diagnoses related to drug therapy:

- Alteration in perfusion related to thrombosis
- Pain related to GI, CNS, and skin effects
- Fear and anxiety related to the diagnosis and the use of blood-related products
- Knowledge deficit regarding drug therapy

Implementation

- Administer by IV route only *to ensure therapeutic effectiveness.*
- Monitor clinical response and clotting factor levels regularly *in order to arrange to adjust dosage as needed.*
- Monitor the patient for any sign of thrombosis *to arrange to use comfort and support measures as needed (e.g., support hose, positioning, ambulation, exercise).*
- Decrease the rate of infusion if headache, chills, fever, or tingling occur *to prevent severe drug reaction;* in some individuals the drug will need to be discontinued.
- Arrange to type and cross match blood *in case of serious blood loss that will require whole blood transfusion.*
- Mark the chart of any patient receiving this drug *to alert medical staff that there is a potential for increased bleeding.*
- Provide thorough patient teaching, including the name of the drug, dosage prescribed, measures to avoid adverse effects, warning signs of problems, and the need for periodic monitoring and evaluation, *to enhance patient knowledge about drug therapy and to promote compliance with the drug regimen.*
- Offer support and encouragement *to help the patient deal with the diagnosis and drug regimen.*

Evaluation

- Monitor patient response to the drug (control of bleeding episodes, prevention of bleeding episodes).
- Monitor for adverse effects (thrombosis, CNS effects, nausea, hypersensitivity reaction, hepatitis, AIDS).
- Evaluate the effectiveness of the teaching plan (patient can name drug, dosage of drug, adverse effects to watch for, specific measures to avoid adverse effects, warning signs to report).
- Monitor the effectiveness of comfort measures and compliance to the regimen.

SYSTEMIC HEMOSTATIC AGENTS

Some situations result in a fibrinolytic state with excessive plasminogen activity and risk of bleeding from clot dissolution. For example, patients undergoing repeat coronary artery bypass surgery are especially prone to excessive bleeding and may require blood transfusion. ***Hemostatic*** drugs are used to stop bleeding. The hemostatic drugs that are used systemically include the following:

- Aprotinin (*Trasylol*), an IV drug derived from bovine lung tissue, forms complexes with kinins, plasmin, and other clot-dissolving factors to block the activation of the plasminogen system. It is used during repeat coronary bypass surgery and in certain unusual cases of first-time coronary bypass surgery when the patient is at increased risk of bleeding.
- Aminocaproic acid (*Amicar*) inhibits plasminogen-activating substances and has some antiplasmin activity. It is available in oral and IV forms and is used to limit excessive bleeding in hyperfibrinolysis states, to prevent recurrence of subarachnoid hemorrhage (SAH), and (sometimes) to treat attacks of hereditary angioedema. When taking the oral form, the patient

NURSING CHALLENGE

Disseminated Intravascular Coagulation

Disseminated intravascular coagulation (DIC) is a syndrome in which bleeding and thrombosis may be found together. It can occur as a complication of many problems, including severe infection with septic shock, traumatic childbirth or missed abortion, and massive injuries. In these disorders, local tissue damage causes the release of coagulation stimulating substances into circulation. These substances then stimulate the coagulation process, causing fibrin clot formation in small vessels in the lungs, kidneys, brain, and other organs. This continuing reaction consumes excessive amount of fibrinogen, other clotting factors, and platelets. The end result of this is increased bleeding. In essence, the patient clots too much, resulting in the possibility of bleeding to death.

The first step in treating this disorder is controlling the problem that initially precipitated it. For example, treating the infection, performing dilation and curettage to clear the uterus, or stabilizing injuries can help stop this continuing process. Whole blood infusions or the infusion of fibrinogen may be used to buy some time until the patient is stable and can form clotting factors again. There are associated problems with giving whole blood (e.g., development of hepatitis or AIDS), and there is a risk that fibrinogen may set off further intravascular clotting. Paradoxically, the treatment of choice for DIC is the anticoagulant heparin. Heparin prevents the clotting phase from being completed, thus inhibiting the breakdown of fibrinogen. It may also help avoid hemorrhage by preventing the body from depleting its entire store of coagulation factors.

It can be a real challenge for the nursing staff to feel comfortable administering heparin to a patient who is bleeding to death, but understanding the disease process can help alleviate any doubts about the treatment.

may need to take 10 tablets in the first hour and then continue taking the drug around the clock.

THERAPEUTIC ACTIONS AND INDICATIONS

The systemic hemostatic agents stop the natural plasminogen clot-dissolving mechanism by blocking its activation, or by directly inhibiting plasmin. These drugs are used to prevent or treat excess bleeding in hyperfibrinolytic states, including repeat coronary artery bypass graft surgery.

CONTRAINDICATIONS/CAUTIONS

Systemic hemostatic agents are contraindicated in the presence of allergy to these drugs and with acute DIC because of the risk of tissue necrosis. Caution should be used with the following conditions: cardiac disease, because of the risk of arrhythmias; renal and hepatic dysfunction, which could alter the excretion of these drugs and the normal clotting processes; and lactation, because of the potential for adverse effects on the neonate.

ADVERSE EFFECTS

The most common adverse effect associated with systemic hemostatic agents is excessive clotting. CNS effects can include hallucinations, drowsiness, dizziness, headache, and psychotic states, all of which could be related to changes in cerebral blood flow associated with changes in clot dissolution. GI effects, including nausea, cramps, and diarrhea, may be related to excessive clotting in the GI tract, causing reflex GI stimulation. Weakness, fatigue, malaise, and muscle pain can occur as small clots build up in muscles. Intrarenal obstruction and renal dysfunction have also been reported.

Aprotinin has been associated with cardiac arrhythmias, MI, CHF, and hypotension. These effects may be related to the fact that this drug is used during coronary bypass surgery. Anaphylactic and respiratory reactions have also been reported with aprotinin, possibly related to immune reactions to the bovine protein.

CLINICALLY IMPORTANT DRUG–DRUG INTERACTIONS

There is an increased risk of bleeding if given with heparin. Aminocaproic acid is associated with the development of hypercoagulation states if combined with oral contraceptives or estrogens.

DATA LINK

Data link to the following systemic hemostatic agents in your nursing drug guide:

SYSTEMIC HEMOSTATIC AGENTS

Name	Brand Name	Usual Indication
P aminocaproic acid	*Amicar*	Treatment of excessive bleeding in hyperfibrinolytic states; prevention of recurrence of bleeding with SAH
aprotinin	*Trasylol*	Prevention of blood loss and need for transfusion following repeat coronary artery bypass graft surgery; in rare instances, first coronary artery bypass surgery in patients prone to bleeding.

NURSING CONSIDERATIONS
for patients receiving systemic hemostatic agents

Assessment

HISTORY. Screen for the following: any known allergies to these drugs; acute DIC because of the risk of tissue necrosis; cardiac disease because of the risk of arrhythmias; renal and hepatic dysfunction, which could alter the excretion of these drugs and the normal clotting processes; and lactation because of the potential for adverse effects on the neonate.

PHYSICAL ASSESSMENT. Include screening for baseline status before beginning therapy and for any potential adverse effects. Assess the following: body temperature; skin color, lesions, temperature; affect, orientation, reflexes; pulse, blood pressure, perfusion; respirations, adventitious sounds; bowel sounds, normal output; urinalysis, clotting studies; and renal and hepatic function tests.

Nursing Diagnoses

The patient receiving a systemic hemostatic drug may have the following nursing diagnoses related to drug therapy:

- Sensory–perceptual alterations related to CNS effects
- Pain related to GI, CNS, muscle effects
- High risk for injury related to CNS, blood clotting effects
- Knowledge deficit regarding drug therapy

Implementation

- Monitor clinical response and clotting factor levels regularly *in order to arrange to adjust dosage as needed.*
- Monitor the patient for any sign of thrombosis *in order to arrange to use comfort and support measures as needed (e.g., support hose, positioning, ambulation, exercise).*

- Orient patient and offer support and safety measures if hallucinations or psychoses occur *to prevent patient injury.*
- Offer comfort measures *to help the patient deal with the effects of the drug.* These include small, frequent meals; mouth care; environmental control; and safety measures.
- Provide thorough patient teaching, including the name of the drug, dosage prescribed, measures to avoid adverse effects, warning signs of problems, and the need for periodic monitoring and evaluation *to enhance patient knowledge about drug therapy and to promote compliance with the drug regimen.*
- Offer support and encouragement *to help the patient deal with the diagnosis and drug regimen.*

Evaluation

- Monitor the patient response to the drug (control of bleeding episodes).
- Monitor for adverse effects (thrombosis, CNS effects, nausea, hypersensitivity reaction).
- Evaluate the effectiveness of the teaching plan (patient can name drug, dosage of drug, adverse effects to watch for, specific measures to avoid adverse effects, warning signs to report).
- Monitor the effectiveness of comfort measures and compliance to the regimen.

TOPICAL HEMOSTATIC AGENTS

Some surface injuries involve so much damage to the small vessels in the area that clotting does not occur and blood is slowly and continually lost. For these situations, topical or local hemostatic agents are often used.

Absorbable gelatin (*Gelfoam*) and microfibrillar collagen (*Avitene*) are available in sponge form and are applied directly to the injured area until the bleeding stops. Use of these products can pose a risk of infection because bacteria can become trapped in the vascular area when the sponge is applied. Immediate removal of the sponge and cleaning of the area can help to decrease this risk. Thrombin (*Thrombinar, Thrombostat*), which is derived from bovine sources, is applied topically and mixed in with the blood. Because this drug comes from animal sources, it may precipitate an allergic response; the patient needs to be carefully monitored for such a reaction.

The use of these drugs is incorporated into the care of the wound or decubitus ulcer as adjunctive therapy. The drug of choice depends on the nature of the injury and the prescriber's personal preference.

DATA LINK

Data link to the following local hemostatic agents in your nursing drug guide:

TOPICAL HEMOSTATIC AGENTS

Name	Brand Name(s)	Usual Indications
P absorbable gelatin	*Gelfoam*	All of these agents are indicated to control bleeding from surface cuts or injury
microfibrillar collagen	*Avitene*	
thrombin	*Thrombostat, Thrombinar*	

CHAPTER SUMMARY

- Coagulation is the transformation of fluid blood to a solid state to plug up breaks in the vascular system.
- Coagulation involves several processes, including vasoconstriction, platelet aggregation to form a plug, and intrinsic and extrinsic clot formation initiated by Hageman factor to plug up any breaks in the system.
- The final step of clot formation is the conversion of prothrombin to thrombin, which breaks down fibrinogen to form insoluble fibrin threads.
- Once a clot is formed, it must be dissolved to prevent the occlusion of blood vessels and loss of blood supply to tissues.
- Plasminogen is the basis of the clot dissolving system. It is converted to plasmin (fibrinolysin) by several factors, including Hageman factor. Plasmin dissolves fibrin threads and resolves the clot.
- Anticoagulants block blood coagulation by interfering with one or more of the steps involved, such as blocking platelet aggregation or inhibiting the intrinsic or extrinsic pathways to clot formation.
- Thrombolytic drugs dissolve clots or thrombi that have formed. They activate the plasminogen system to stimulate natural clot dissolution.
- Hemostatic drugs are used to stop bleeding. They may replace missing clotting factors or prevent the plasminogen system from dissolving formed clots.
- Hemophilia, a genetic lack of essential clotting factors, results in excessive bleeding. It is treated by replacing missing clotting factors.

BIBLIOGRAPHY

Bullock, B. L. (2000). *Focus on pathophysiology.* Philadelphia: Lippincott Williams & Wilkins.

Hardman, J. G., Limbird, L. E., Molinoff, P. B., Ruddon, R. W., & Gilman, A. G. (Eds.). (1996). *Goodman and Gilman's the pharmacological basis of therapeutics* (9th ed.). New York: McGraw-Hill.

Karch, A. M. (2000). *2000 Lippincott's nursing drug guide.* Philadelphia: Lippincott Williams & Wilkins.

McEvoy, B. R. (1999). *Facts and comparisons 1999.* St. Louis: Facts and Comparisons.

Medical letter on drugs and therapeutics. (1999). New Rochelle, NY: Medical Letter.

Porth, C. M. (1998). *Pathophysiology: Concepts of altered health states* (5th ed.). Philadelphia: Lippincott-Raven.

CHAPTER 47

Drugs Used to Treat Anemias

Erythropoietin
- epoetin alfa

Iron preparations
- ferrous fumarate
- ferrous gluconate
- P ferrous sulfate
- ferrous sulfate exsiccated
- iron dextran

Folic acid derivatives
- P folic acid
- leucovorin

Vitamin B_{12}
- cyanocobalamin
- P hydroxocobalamin

CHAPTER OUTLINE

KEY TERMS

anemia
erythrocytes
erythropoiesis
erythropoietin
iron deficiency anemia
megaloblastic anemia
pernicious anemia
plasma
reticulocyte

INTRODUCTION

The cardiovascular system exists to pump blood to all of the body's cells. Blood is essential for cell survival because it contains oxygen and nutrients and removes waste products that could be toxic to the tissues. It also contains clotting factors that help maintain the vascular system and keep it sealed. In addition, blood contains the important components of the immune system that protect the body from infection. This chapter discusses drugs that are used to treat anemias, which are disorders that involve too few or ineffective red blood cells and that can alter the blood's ability to carry oxygen.

BLOOD COMPONENTS

Blood is composed of liquid and formed elements. The liquid part of blood is called ***plasma.*** Plasma is mostly water but also contains proteins that are essential for the immune response and for blood clotting. The formed elements of the blood include leukocytes (white blood cells), which are an important part of the immune system (see Chapter 13); ***erythrocytes*** (red blood cells), which carry oxygen to the tissues and remove carbon dioxide for delivery to the lungs; and platelets, which play an important role in coagulation (see Chapter 46).

ERYTHROPOIESIS

Erythropoiesis is the process of red blood cell (RBC) production. RBCs are produced in the myeloid tissue of the bone marrow. The rate of red blood cell production is controlled by the glycoprotein erythropoietin, which is released from the kidneys in response to decreased blood flow or decreased oxygen tension in the kidneys. Under the influence of erythropoietin, an undifferentiated cell in the bone marrow becomes a hemocytoblast. This cell uses certain amino acids, lipids, carbohydrates, vitamin B_{12}, folic acid, and iron to turn into an immature red blood cell. In the last phase of RBC production, the cell loses its nucleus and enters circulation. This cell, called a reticulocyte, will finish the maturing process in circulation (Figure 47-1).

Although the mature RBC has no nucleus, it does have a vast surface area to improve its ability to transport oxygen and carbon dioxide. Because it lacks a nucleus, the RBC cannot reproduce or maintain itself, so it will eventually wear out. The average life span of an RBC is about 120 days. At that time, the elderly RBC is lysed in the liver, spleen, or bone marrow. The building blocks of the RBC (e.g., iron, vitamin B_{12}) are then recycled and returned to the bone marrow for the production of new RBCs (see Figure 47-1). The only part of the RBC that cannot be recycled is the toxic pigment, bilirubin, which is conjugated in the liver, passed into the bile, and excreted from the body in the feces or the urine. Bilirubin is what gives color to both of these excretions. Erythropoiesis is a constant process, where about 1% of the RBCs are destroyed and replaced each day.

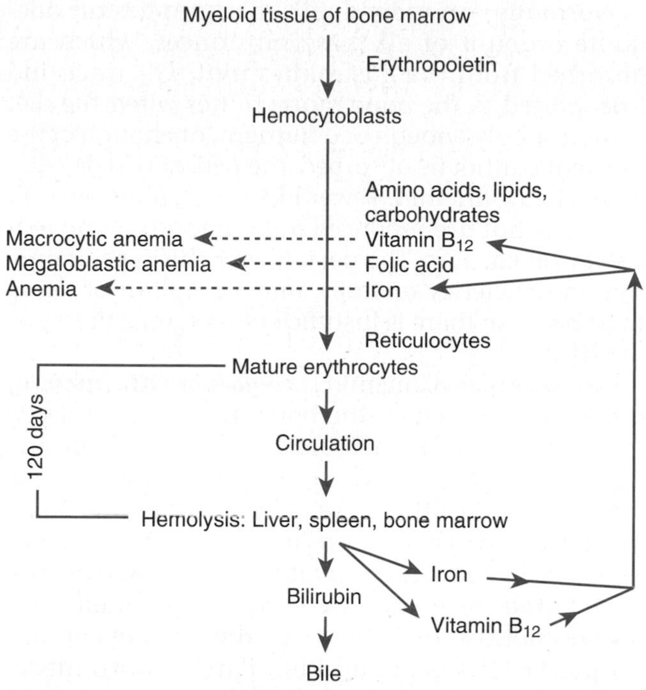

FIGURE 47-1. Erythropoiesis. Red blood cells are produced in the myeloid tissue of the bone marrow in response to the hormone erythropoietin. The hemocytoblasts require various essential factors to produce mature erythrocytes. A lack of any one of these can result in an anemia of the type indicated opposite each factor. Mature erythrocytes survive for about 120 days, and are then lysed in the liver, spleen, or bone marrow.

ANEMIA

Anemia, a decrease in the number of RBCs, can occur when erythropoietin levels are low. This is seen in renal failure, when the kidneys are no longer able to produce erythropoietin. It can also occur if the body does not have enough of the building blocks necessary to form RBCs. To produce healthy RBCs, the bone marrow must have the following:

- Adequate amounts of iron, which is used in forming hemoglobin rings to carry the oxygen.
- Minute amounts of vitamin B_{12} and folic acid to form a strong supporting structure that can survive being battered through blood vessels for 120 days.
- Essential amino acids and carbohydrates to complete the hemoglobin rings, cell membrane, and basic structure.

Normally, an individual's diet supplies an adequate amount of all these substances, which are absorbed from the gastrointestinal (GI) tract and transported to the bone marrow. But when the diet cannot supply enough of a nutrient, or enough of the nutrient cannot be absorbed, the person can develop a deficiency anemia. Fewer RBCs are produced, and the ones that are produced are not mature and efficient iron carriers. The person with this type of anemia, a deficiency anemia, may complain of being tired because there is insufficient oxygen delivery to the tissues.

Another type of anemia is ***megaloblastic anemia,*** a condition in which the bone marrow contains a large number of megaloblasts, or large, immature RBCs. Because these RBCs are so large, they become very crowded in the bone marrow and fewer RBCs are produced. There is an increase in these immature cells in circulation. Overall, fewer RBCs are produced, and those that are produced are ineffective and do not usually survive for the 120 days that is normal for the life of an RBC. Patients with megaloblastic anemia usually have a lack of vitamin B_{12} or folic acid.

CULTURAL CONSIDERATIONS

Sickle Cell Anemia

Sickle cell anemia is a chronic hemolytic anemia that occurs almost exclusively in blacks. (Hemolytic anemias involve a lysing of red blood cells due to genetic factors or from exposure to toxins.) Sickle cell anemia is characterized by a genetically inherited hemoglobin S, which gives the RBCs a sickle-shaped appearance. The patient with sickle cell anemia produces fewer than normal RBCs, which are unable to carry oxygen efficiently. The patient may be of short stature with stubby fingers and toes; these characteristics are related to the body's response to the inability to deliver oxygen to the tissues.

The sickle-shaped RBCs can become lodged in tiny blood vessels, where they stack up onto one another and occlude the vessel. This occlusion leads to anoxia and infarction of the tissue in that area, which is characterized by severe pain and an acute inflammatory reaction—a condition often called sickle cell crisis. (The patient may have ulcers on the extremities as a result of such occlusions.) Severe, acute episodes of sickling with vessel occlusion may be associated with acute infections and the body's reactions to the immune and inflammatory responses.

In the past, the only treatment for sickle cell anemia was pain medication and support of the patient. Now hydroxyurea (*Hydrea*) has been found to effectively treat this disease. Hydroxyurea is a cytotoxic antineoplastic agent that is used to treat leukemia, ovarian cancer, and melanoma. It has been shown that it increases the amount of fetal hemoglobin produced in the bone marrow and dilutes the formation of the abnormal hemoglobin S in sickle cell patients. The process takes several months, but once effective, it prevents the clogging of small vessels and the painful, anoxic effects of RBC sickling. Because this drug is associated with several uncomfortable adverse effects—including GI problems, rash, headache, and possible bone marrow depression—the decision to use it is not made lightly. However, it has been found to be effective in preventing the painful crises of sickle cell anemia.

Iron Deficiency Anemias

All cells in the body require some amount of iron, but iron can be very toxic to cells, especially neurons. To maintain the needed iron levels and avoid toxic levels, the body has developed a system for controlling the amount of iron that can enter the body through intestinal absorption. Only enough iron is absorbed to replace the amount of iron that is lost each day. Once iron is absorbed, it is carried by a plasma protein called transferrin, a beta globulin. This protein carries iron to various tissues to be stored, and transports iron from RBC lysis back to the bone marrow for recycling.

Only about 1 mg of iron is actually lost each day in sweat, in sloughed skin, and from GI and urinary tract linings. Because of the body's efficient iron recycling, very little iron is usually needed in the diet, and most diets quite adequately replace the iron that is lost. However, in situations in which blood is being lost, such as from internal bleeding or heavy menstrual flow, a negative iron balance might occur, and the patient could develop ***iron deficiency anemia.*** This can also occur in certain GI diseases in which the patient is unable to absorb iron from the GI tract. These conditions are usually treated with iron replacement therapy.

Megaloblastic Anemias

Megaloblastic anemias occur when there is not sufficient folic acid or vitamin B_{12} to adequately create the stromal structure needed in a healthy RBC. The lack of these two chemicals causes a slowing of nuclear DNA synthesis in human cells. This effect is seen in other rapidly dividing cells, not just bone marrow cells. For example, cells in the GI tract are often affected, resulting in the appearance of a characteristic red and glossy tongue and diarrhea.

FOLIC ACID DEFICIENCY

Folic acid is essential for cell division in all types of tissue. Deficiencies in folic acid are noticed first in

CULTURAL CONSIDERATIONS ••••

Hematological Laboratory Test Variations

Hemoglobin/hematocrit: African Americans are generally 1 g lower than other groups.

Serum transferrin levels* (children ages 1–3.5 years): The mean value for African American children is 22 mg/100 ml > white children.

Because of these variations, the diagnosis and treatment of anemia in African Americans should be based on a different norm than with other groups of patients.

* This may be because African Americans have lower hematocrit and hemoglobin; transferrin levels increase normally in the presence of anemia.

rapidly growing cells, such as those in cancerous tissues, in the GI tract, and in the bone marrow. Most people can get all of the folic acid needed from their diet. For example, folic acid is found in green leafy vegetables, milk, eggs, and liver. Deficiency in folic acid may occur in certain malabsorption states, such as sprue and celiac diseases. Malnutrition that accompanies alcoholism is also a common cause of folic acid deficiency. Repeated pregnancies and extended treatment with certain antiepileptic medications can also contribute to folic acid deficiency. This disorder is treated by the administration of folic acid or folate.

VITAMIN B_{12} DEFICIENCY

Vitamin B_{12} is used in minute amounts by the body and is stored for use if dietary intake falls. It is necessary not only for the health of the RBCs, but also for the formation and maintenance of the myelin sheath in the central nervous system (CNS). It is found in the diet in meats, seafood, eggs, and cheese. Strict vegetarians who eat nothing but vegetables may develop a vitamin B_{12} deficiency. Such individuals with a dietary insufficiency of vitamin B_{12} typically respond to vitamin B_{12} replacement therapy to reverse their anemia.

The most common cause of this deficiency, however, is the GI tract's inability to absorb the needed amounts of the vitamin. Gastric mucosal cells produce a substance called intrinsic factor, which is necessary for the absorption of vitamin B_{12} by the upper intestine. ***Pernicious anemia*** occurs when the gastric mucosa cannot produce intrinsic factor and vitamin B_{12} cannot be absorbed. The person with pernicious anemia will complain of fatigue and lethargy and will also have CNS effects because of the damage to the myelin sheath. Patients will complain of numbness, tingling, and eventually lack of coordination and motor activity. Pernicious anemia was once a fatal disease, but is now treated with injections of vitamin B_{12} to replace the amount that can no longer be absorbed.

ERYTHROPOIETIN

Patients who are no longer able to produce enough erythropoietin in the kidneys may benefit from treatment with erythropoietin (EPO), which is available as the drug epoetin alfa (*Epogen, Procrit*).

Epogen is used to treat anemia associated with renal failure, including patients on dialysis. It is also used to decrease the need for blood transfusions in surgical patients and to treat anemias related to treatment for AIDS. It is not approved to treat severe anemia associated with other causes, and it is not meant to replace whole blood for an emergency treatment of anemia. There is a risk of decreasing the normal levels of erythropoietin if this drug is given to patients with normal renal functioning and adequate levels of erythropoietin. A negative feedback occurs with the renal cells, and less endogenous erythropoietin is produced when exogenous erythropoietin is given. Administering this drug to an anemic patient with normal renal function may actually cause more anemia when the endogenous levels fall and no longer stimulate RBC production.

Procrit is also used to treat severe anemia related to chemotherapy in cancer patients, when bone marrow is depressed and kidneys may be affected by the toxic drugs (Figure 47-2).

THERAPEUTIC ACTIONS AND INDICATIONS

Epoetin alfa acts like the natural glycoprotein erythropoietin to stimulate the production of RBC in the bone marrow (Figure 47-3). It is indicated for the treatment of anemia associated with renal failure or for patients on dialysis. It is also used to decrease the need for blood transfusions in surgical patients, for the treatment of anemia associated with AIDS treatment, and for the treatment of anemia associated with cancer chemotherapy (*Procrit* only).

CONTRAINDICATIONS/CAUTIONS

Epoetin alfa is contraindicated in the presence of uncontrolled hypertension because of the risk of even further hypertension when RBC numbers increase; with allergy to mammalian cell-derived products or to human albumin; and with lactation because

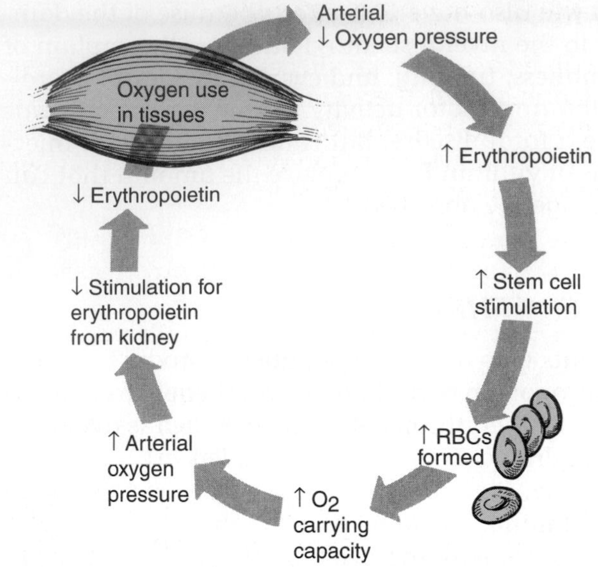

FIGURE 47-2. Erythropoiesis controls the rate of blood cell production. (Bullock, B. L. [2000]. *Focus on pathophysiology*. Philadelphia: Lippincott Williams & Wilkins.)

of the potential for allergic-type reactions with the neonate.

ADVERSE EFFECTS

The adverse effects most commonly associated with this drug include the CNS effects of headache, fatigue, asthenia, and dizziness, and the potential for serious seizures. These effects may be due to a cellular response to the glycoprotein. Nausea, vomiting, and diarrhea also are common effects. Cardiovascular symptoms can include hypertension, edema, and possible chest pain and can be related to the increase in RBC numbers changing the balance within the cardiovascular system. Patients receiving IV administration must also be monitored for possible clotting of the access line related to direct cellular effects of the drug.

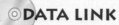

DATA LINK

Data link to erythropoietin in your nursing drug guide:

ERYTHROPOIETIN

Name	Brand Name(s)	Usual Indications
epoetin alfa	*Epogen*	Treatment of anemia associated with renal failure; reduction in need for transfusions in surgical patients; treatment of anemia associated with AIDS treatments
	Procrit	Treatment of anemia associated with cancer chemotherapy

NURSING CONSIDERATIONS for patients receiving erythropoietin

Assessment

HISTORY. Screen for the following: any known allergies to this drug, mammalian cell-derived products, or human albumin; severe hypertension, which could be exacerbated; and lactation because of potential adverse effects on the neonate.

PHYSICAL ASSESSMENT. Include screening for baseline status before beginning therapy and for any potential adverse effects. Assess the following: affect, orientation, reflexes; pulse, blood pressure, perfusion; respirations, adventitious breath sounds; and renal function tests, CBC, hematocrit, iron levels, and electrolytes.

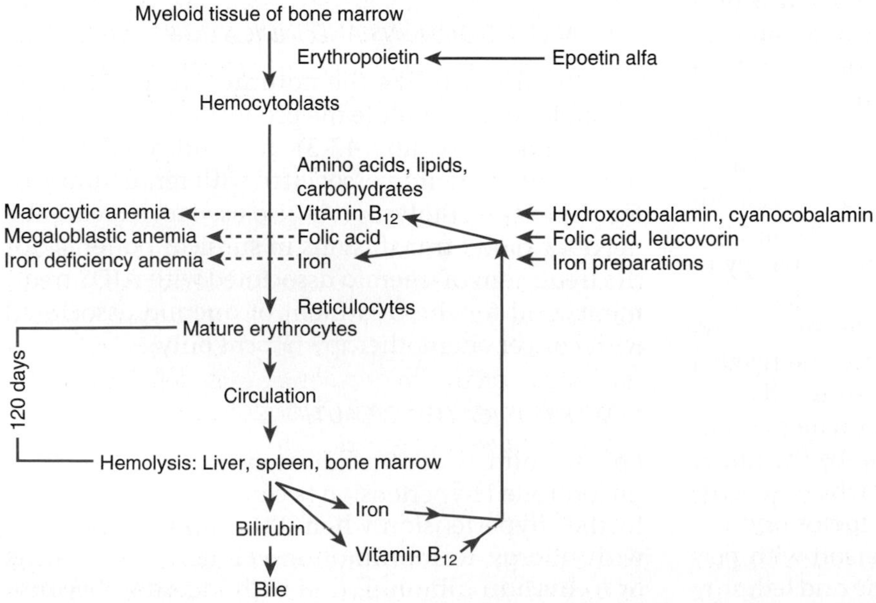

FIGURE 47-3. Sites of action of drugs used to treat anemia.

Nursing Diagnoses

The patient receiving epoetin alfa may have the following nursing diagnoses related to drug therapy:

- Alteration in comfort related to CNS, GI effects
- Potential for alteration in cardiac output related to cardiovascular effects
- Knowledge deficit regarding drug therapy

Implementation

- Confirm chronic, renal nature of anemia before administering *to assure proper use of drug.*
- Must be given 3 times per week, either IV or SC, *to achieve appropriate therapeutic drug levels.* The patient should receive a calendar of marked days *to increase compliance to drug regimen.*
- Do not give with any other drug solution *to avoid drug–drug interactions.*
- Monitor access lines for clotting and *arrange to clear line as needed.*
- Arrange for hematocrit reading before administration *to determine correct dosage.* If the patient does not respond within 8 weeks, reevaluate the cause of anemia.
- Evaluate iron stores prior to and periodically during therapy *because supplemental iron may be needed as the patient makes more RBCs.*
- Maintain seizure precautions on standby *in case seizures occur as a reaction to the drug.*
- Provide comfort measures *to help the patient tolerate the drug effects.* These include small, frequent meals, access to bathroom facilities, and analgesia for headache or arthralgia.
- Provide thorough patient teaching, including the name of the drug, dosage prescribed, measures to avoid adverse effects, warning signs of problems, and the need for periodic monitoring and evaluation *to enhance patient knowledge about drug therapy and to promote compliance with the drug regimen.*
- Offer support and encouragement *to help the patient deal with the diagnosis and drug regimen.*

Evaluation

- Monitor patient response to the drug (alleviation of anemia).
- Monitor for adverse effects (headache, hypertension, nausea, vomiting, seizures, dizziness).
- Evaluate the effectiveness of the teaching plan (patient can name drug, dosage, adverse effects to watch for, specific measures to avoid adverse effects; patient understands importance of continued follow-up).
- Monitor the effectiveness of comfort measures and compliance to the regimen.

IRON PREPARATIONS

Though most people should get all the iron that they need through diet, there are some situations in which diet alone may not be adequate. Iron deficiency anemia is a relatively common problem in certain age groups, including the following:

- Menstruating women who lose RBCs monthly.
- Pregnant and nursing women who have increased demands for iron.
- Rapidly growing adolescents, especially those who do not have a nutritious diet.
- Persons with GI bleeding; even individuals with slow bleeding associated with NSAIDs may develop this disorder.

Oral iron preparations are often used to help these patients regain a positive iron balance; these preparations need to be supplemented with adequate dietary intake of iron. Ferrous fumarate (*Feostat*), ferrous gluconate (*Fergon*), ferrous sulfate (*Feosol*), and ferrous sulfate exsiccated (*Ferralyn Lanacaps, Slow FE*) are the oral iron preparations that are available for use. Most of the drug that is taken will be lost in the feces, but slowly some of the metal will be absorbed into the intestine and transported to the bone marrow. It can take 2 to 3 weeks to see improvement and up to 6 to 10 months to return to a stable iron level once a deficiency exists. The drug of choice will depend on the prescriber's personal preference and experience, and often on what kinds of samples are available to give the patient.

Iron dextran (*InFeD*) is a parenteral form of iron that can be used when the oral form cannot be given or cannot be tolerated. Patients with severe GI absorption problems may require this form of iron. If given IM, it must be given by the Z-track method because it can stain the tissues brown and can be very painful. Patients should be switched to the oral form if at all possible. Severe hypersensitivity reactions have been associated with the parenteral form of iron.

THERAPEUTIC ACTIONS AND INDICATIONS

Iron preparations elevate the serum iron concentration (see Figure 47-3). They are then either converted to hemoglobin or trapped in reticuloendothelial cells for storage and eventual release for conversion into a useable form of iron for RBC production. They are indicated for the treatment of iron deficiency anemias and may also be used for adjunctive therapy in patients receiving epoetin alfa.

CONTRAINDICATIONS/CAUTIONS

These drugs are contraindicated with known allergy to any of these preparations. They also are contraindicated in the following conditions: hemochromatosis (excessive iron); hemolytic anemias, which may increase serum iron levels and cause toxicity; normal iron balance because the drug will not be absorbed and will just pass through the body; and peptic ulcer, colitis, and regional enteritis because the drug can be directly irritating to these tissues and can cause exacerbation of the diseases.

ADVERSE EFFECTS

The most common adverse effects associated with oral iron are related to direct GI irritation; these include GI upset, anorexia, nausea, vomiting, diarrhea, dark stools, and constipation. With increasing serum levels, iron can be directly CNS toxic, causing coma and even death. (Box 47-1 discusses iron toxicity and drugs that are used to counteract this effect.) Parenteral iron is associated with severe anaphylactic reactions, local irritation, staining of the tissues, and phlebitis.

CLINICALLY IMPORTANT DRUG–DRUG INTERACTIONS

There is decreased iron absorption if taken with antacids or cimetidine; if these drugs must be used, they should be spaced at least 2 hours apart. There can be a decreased anti-infective response to ciprofloxacin, enoxacin, norfloxacin, or ofloxacin if taken with iron because of a decrease in absorption; these drugs also should be taken at least 2 hours apart. Increased iron levels occur if taken with chloramphenicol; patients receiving this combination should be monitored closely for any sign of iron toxicity. There may be decreased effects of levodopa if taken with iron preparations; patients receiving both of these drugs should take them at least 2 hours apart.

CLINICALLY IMPORTANT DRUG–FOOD INTERACTIONS

Iron is not absorbed if taken with antacids, eggs, milk, coffee, or tea. These should not be administered concurrently.

DATA LINK

Data link to the following iron preparations in your nursing drug guide:

IRON PREPARATIONS

Name	Brand Name	Usual Indications
ferrous fumarate	*Feostat*	Treatment of iron deficiency anemia
ferrous gluconate	*Fergon*	Treatment of iron deficiency anemia
P ferrous sulfate	*Feosol*	Treatment of iron deficiency anemia
ferrous sulfate exsiccated	*Ferralyn Lanacaps, Slow FE*	Treatment of iron deficiency anemia
iron dextran	*InFeD*	Parenteral treatment of iron deficiency anemia

BOX 47-1

CHELATING AGENTS

Heavy metals, including iron, lead, arsenic, mercury, copper, and gold, can cause toxicity in the body by their ability to tie up chemicals in living tissues that need to be free in order for the cell to function normally. When these vital substances (thiols, sulfurs, carboxyls, and phosphoryls) are bound to the metal, certain cellular enzyme systems become deactivated, resulting in failure of cellular function and eventual cell death. Drugs that have been developed to counteract metal toxicity are called chelating agents.

Chelating (from the Greek word for "claw") agents grasp and hold a toxic metal so that it can be carried out of the body before it has time to harm the tissues. The chelating agent binds the molecules of the metal, preventing it from damaging the cells within the body. The complex that is formed by the chelating agent and the metal is nontoxic and is excreted by the kidneys.

Chelating Agent	***Toxic Metal***	***Special Notes***
calcium disodium edetate	lead	Given IM or IV; monitor renal and hepatic function because serious and even fatal toxicity can occur
deferoxamine mesylate (*Desferal*)	iron	Given IM, SC, or IV; rash and vision changes common
dimercaprol (*BAL in Oil*)	arsenic, gold, mercury	Given IM only for 7–10 days; CV toxicity may occur; push fluids and alkalinize urine to increase excretion

NURSING CONSIDERATIONS
for patients receiving iron preparations

Assessment

HISTORY. Screen for the following: any known allergies to this drug; hyperchromatosis; and colitis, enteritis, peptic ulcer, and hemolytic anemias.

PHYSICAL ASSESSMENT. Include screening for baseline status before beginning therapy and for any potential adverse effects. Assess the following: skin color, gums, teeth; affect, orientation, reflexes; pulse, blood pressure, perfusion; respirations, adventitious sounds; bowel sounds; and CBC, hematocrit, hemoglobin, and serum ferritin assays.

Nursing Diagnoses

The patient receiving iron may have the following nursing diagnoses related to drug therapy:

- Pain related to CNS, GI effects
- Alteration in self concept related to drug staining
- High risk for injury related to CNS effects
- Knowledge deficit regarding drug therapy

Implementation

- Confirm iron deficiency anemia before administering drugs *to ensure proper use of the drug.*
- Consult with the physician to arrange for treatment of the underlying cause of anemia if possible, *as iron replacement will not correct the cause of the iron loss.*
- Administer with meals (avoiding eggs, milk, coffee, tea) *to relieve GI irritation* if GI upset is severe.
- Caution the patient that stool may be dark or green *to prevent undue alarm if this occurs.*
- Administer IM only by Z-track technique *to ensure proper administration and to avoid staining.*
- Arrange for hematocrit and hemoglobin levels before administration and periodically during therapy *to monitor drug effectiveness.*
- Provide comfort measures *to help the patient tolerate drug effects.* These include small, frequent meals and access to bathroom facilities.
- Provide thorough patient teaching, including the name of the drug, dosage prescribed, measures to avoid adverse effect, warning signs of problems, and the need for periodic monitoring and evaluation *to enhance patient knowledge about drug therapy and to promote compliance with drug regimen* (see Patient Teaching Checklist: Iron Preparations).
- Offer support and encouragement *to help the patient deal with the diagnosis and drug regimen.*

Evaluation

- Monitor patient response to the drug (alleviation of anemia).
- Monitor for adverse effects (GI upset and reaction, CNS toxicity, coma).
- Evaluate the effectiveness of the teaching plan (patient can name drug, dosage, adverse effects to watch for, specific measures to avoid adverse effects; patient understands importance of continued follow-up).
- Monitor the effectiveness of comfort measures and compliance to the regimen (see Nursing Care Guide: Iron Preparations).

MEGALOBLASTIC ANEMIA TREATMENTS

Megaloblastic anemia is treated with folic acid and vitamin B_{12}. Folate deficiencies usually occur secondary to increased demand (as in pregnancy, growth spurts) because of absorption problems in the small intestine; because of drugs that cause folate deficiencies; or secondary to the malnutrition of alcoholism. Vitamin B_{12} deficiencies can result from poor diet or increased demand, but the usual cause is lack of intrinsic factor in the stomach, which is necessary for absorption. The drugs are usually given together to ensure that the problem is addressed and the blood cells can be formed properly.

FOLIC ACID DERIVATIVES

Folic acid (*Folvite*) can be given in oral, IM, IV, and SC forms. The parenteral drugs are preferred for patients with potential absorption problems; all other patients should be given the oral form if at all possible. Leucovorin (*Wellcovorin*) is a reduced form of folic acid that is available for oral, IM, and IV use. (It is used for the "leucovorin rescue" of patients receiving high doses of methotrexate for osteocarcinoma, allowing noncancerous cells to survive the chemotherapy. It is also used with 5-FU for palliative treatment of colorectal cancer. See Chapter 12.)

VITAMIN B_{12}

Hydroxocobalamin (*Hydro-Crysti 12*) is the traditional treatment for pernicious anemia and vitamin B_{12} deficiency. It must be given IM every day for 5 to 10 days to build up levels, then once a month for life. It cannot be taken orally because the problem with pernicious anemia is the inability to absorb vitamin B_{12} secondary to low levels of intrinsic factor. It can be used in states of increased demand (pregnancy, growth spurts) and cases of dietary deficiencies, but oral vitamins are preferred in most of those cases. Cyanocobalamin (*Nascobal*), a newer vitamin B_{12} preparation, is an intranasal gel that allows vitamin B_{12} absorption directly through the nasal mucosa. It is used once a week as an intranasal spray in one nostril.

PATIENT TEACHING CHECKLIST

Iron Preparations

Create customized patient teaching materials for a specific iron preparation from your CD-ROM. Your patient teaching should stress the following points for drugs within this class:

Iron is a naturally occurring mineral found in many foods. It is used by the body to make red blood cells, which carry oxygen to all parts of the body. Supplemental iron needs to be taken when the body does not have enough iron available to make healthy red blood cells, a condition called anemia. Iron is a toxic substance if too much is taken. You must avoid self-medicating with over-the-counter preparations containing iron while you are on this drug. You will need to return for regular medical check-ups while taking this drug to determine its effectiveness.

Take your medication as follows, depending on the specific iron preparation that has been prescribed:

- Dissolve *ferrous salts* in orange juice to improve the taste.
- Take *liquid iron preparations* with a straw, as this will prevent the iron from staining teeth.
- Place *iron drops* on the back of the tongue to prevent staining teeth.

Some of the following adverse effects may occur:

- Dark, tarry, or green stools—The iron preparations stain the stools; the color will remain as long as you are taking the drug and should not cause concern.
- Constipation—This is a common problem; if it becomes too uncomfortable, consult with your health care provider for an appropriate remedy.
- Nausea, indigestion, vomiting—This problem can often be solved by taking the drug with food, making sure to avoid the foods listed above.

Report any of the following to your health care provider: severe diarrhea, severe abdominal pain or cramping, unusual tiredness or weakness, bluish tint to the lips or fingernail beds.

Tell any doctor, nurse, or other health care provider that you are taking this drug.

Keep this drug, and all medications, out of the reach of children. Because iron can be very toxic, seek emergency medical help immediately if you suspect that a child has taken this preparation unsupervised.

Because iron can interfere with the absorption of some drugs, do not take iron at the same time as *tetracycline* or *antacids*. These drugs must be taken at intervals when iron is not in the stomach.

This Teaching Checklist reflects general patient teaching guidelines. It is not meant to be a substitute for drug-specific teaching information, which is available in nursing drug guides.

THERAPEUTIC ACTIONS AND INDICATIONS

Folic acid and vitamin B_{12} are essential to cell growth and division and for the production of a strong stroma in RBCs (see Figure 47-3). Vitamin B_{12} is also necessary for the maintenance of the myelin sheath in nerve tissue. They are given as replacement therapy for dietary deficiencies; as replacement in high-demand states such as pregnancy and lactation; and to treat megaloblastic anemia. Folic acid is used as a rescue for cells exposed to some toxic chemotherapeutic agents.

CONTRAINDICATIONS/CAUTIONS

These drugs are contraindicated in the presence of known allergies to these drugs or to drug components. They should be used cautiously with pregnancy and lactation and with other anemias. Cyanocobalamin should be used with caution in the presence of nasal erosion or ulcers.

ADVERSE EFFECTS

These drugs have relatively few adverse effects as they are used as replacement for required chemicals. Pain and discomfort can occur at injection sites. Nasal irritation can occur with the use of intranasal spray.

DATA LINK

Data link to the following drugs used to treat megaloblastic anemia in your nursing drug guide:

NURSING CARE GUIDE
Iron Preparations

Assessment	Nursing Diagnoses	Implementation	Evaluation
HISTORY			
Allergies to any iron preparation, colitis, enteritis, hepatic dysfunction, peptic ulcer	Pain related to GI, CNS effects Potential for injury related to CNS effects Alteration in self-concept related to drug staining Knowledge deficit regarding drug therapy	Confirm iron deficiency anemia before administering the drug: Provide comfort and safety measures: - Give small meals - Ensure access to bathroom facilities - Use Z-track method for IM administrations - Give drug with food if GI upset occurs - Institute bowel program as needed Arrange for treatment of underlying cause of anemia. Provide support and reassurance to deal with drug effects. Provide patient teaching regarding drug, dosage, adverse effects, what to report, safety precautions.	Evaluate drug effects: relief of signs and symptoms of anemia, hematocrit within normal limits Monitor for adverse effects: GI upset, CNS toxicity, coma. Monitor hematocrit and hemoglobin periodically. Monitor for drug–drug interactions as indicated for each drug. Evaluate effectiveness of patient teaching program. Evaluate effectiveness of comfort and safety measures.
PHYSICAL EXAMINATION			
CV: BP, P, perfusion CNS: orientation, affect, reflexes, vision Skin: color, lesions, gums, teeth Resp: R, adventitious sounds GI: abdominal exam, bowel sounds Lab tests: CBC, Hgb, Hct, serum ferritin assays			

FOLIC ACID DERIVATIVES/VITAMIN B_{12}

Name	Brand Name	Usual Indications
Folic acid derivatives		
P folic acid	*Folvite*	Replacement therapy and treatment of megaloblastic anemia
leucovorin	*Wellcovorin*	Replacement therapy and treatment of megaloblastic anemia; rescue following chemotherapy
Vitamin B_{12}		
P hydroxocobalamin	*Hydro-Crysti 12*	Replacement therapy; treatment of megaloblastic anemia, pernicious anemia
cyanocobalamin	*Nascobal*	Replacement therapy; treatment of megaloblastic anemia (as nasal gel)

CASE STUDY

Iron Preparations and Toxicity

PRESENTATION

L. L., a 28-year-old woman, suffered a miscarriage 6 weeks ago. She lost a great deal of blood during the miscarriage and underwent a dilation and curettage to control the bleeding. On her 6-week routine follow-up visit, she was found to have recovered physically from the event but was still depressed over her loss. Her hematocrit was 31, and she admitted feeling tired and weak. She was offered emotional support and given a supply of ferrous sulfate tablets, with instructions to take one tablet three times a day.

At home, L. L. transferred the pills to a decorative bottle that had once held vitamins and left it on her table as a reminder to take the tablets. The next day, she discovered her 2-year-old daughter eating the tablets and punished her for getting into them. About an hour later, the toddler complained of a really bad "tummy ache" and started vomiting. She then became lethargic, and L. L. called the pediatrician, who told them to go immediately to the emergency room and bring the remaining tablets with them. The toddler was found to have a weak, rapid pulse (156); rapid, shallow respirations (32); and a low BP (60/42). When a diagnosis of acute iron toxicity was made, L. L. became distraught. She said she had no idea that iron could be dangerous because it can be bought over the counter in so many preparations. She had not read the written information given to her because it was "just iron."

CRITICAL THINKING QUESTIONS

What nursing interventions should be done at this point? What sort of crisis intervention would be most appropriate for L. L.? Think about the combined depression from the miscarriage, the fear and anxiety related to this crisis, and L. L.'s iron-depleted state. What kind of reserve does she have for dealing with this crisis? Which measures would be appropriate for helping the mother cope with this crisis, and for treating the toddler?

DISCUSSION

The first priority is to support and detoxify the child in iron toxicity. In cases of acute iron poisoning, the patient should be induced to vomit and given eggs and milk to bind the iron and prevent absorption. Gastric lavage, using a 1% sodium bicarbonate solution, can be done in a medical facility. This procedure is safe for about the first hour after ingestion. However, after that time, there is an increased risk of gastric erosion caused by the corrosive iron, making the lavage very dangerous. Because this toddler is well beyond the first hour, other measures will be needed. Supportive measures to deal with shock, dehydration, and GI damage will be necessary. In addition, an iron chelating agent such as deferoxamine mesylate may be tried.

During this crisis, L. L. will need a great deal of support, including a significant other who can stay with her. She also will need reassurance and a place to rest. When the situation is stabilized, L. L. will need teaching and additional support. For example, she should be reassured that most people do not take over-the-counter (OTC) drugs seriously; many do not even read the labels. However, the nurse can use this opportunity to stress the importance of reading all of the labels and following the directions that come with OTC drugs. L. L. also should be commended for calling the pediatrician and getting medical care for the toddler quickly. Finally, she should receive a review of the iron teaching information and be encouraged to ask questions.

This case is a good example for a staff in-service program, stressing not only the dangers of iron toxicity but also the vital importance of providing good patient education before sending a patient home with a new drug. Simply giving a patient written information is often not enough.

NURSING CONSIDERATIONS
for patients receiving folic acid derivatives or vitamin B_{12}

Assessment

HISTORY. Screen for the following: any known allergies to these drugs or drug components, other anemias, pregnancy, lactation, and nasal erosion.

PHYSICAL ASSESSMENT. Include screening for baseline status before beginning therapy and for any potential adverse effects. Assess the following: affect, orientation, reflexes; pulse, blood pressure, perfusion; respirations, adventitious sounds; and renal function tests, CBC, hematocrit, iron levels, and electrolytes.

Nursing Diagnoses

The patient receiving folic acid/vitamin B_{12} may have the following nursing diagnoses related to drug therapy:

- Pain related to injection, nasal irritation
- Alteration in cardiac output related to CV effects
- Knowledge deficit regarding drug therapy

Implementation

- Confirm nature of megaloblastic anemia *to ensure proper drug regimen is being used.*
- Give both types of drug in cases of pernicious anemia *to ensure therapeutic effectiveness.*

• Parenteral vitamin B must be given IM each day for 5 to 10 days and then once a month for life *if used to treat pernicious anemia.*
• Liquid forms of iron should be given through a straw *to avoid staining of teeth.*
• Arrange for nutritional consultation *to ensure a well-balanced diet.*
• Monitor for the possibility of hypersensitivity reactions; *have life support on standby in case reactions occur.*
• Arrange for hematocrit readings before and periodically during therapy *to monitor drug effectiveness.*
• Provide comfort measures *to help the patient tolerate drug effects.* These include small, frequent meals, access to bathroom facilities, and analgesia for muscle or nasal pain.
• Provide thorough patient teaching, including the name of the drug, dosage prescribed, measures to avoid adverse effects, warning signs of problems, and the need for periodic monitoring and evaluation *to enhance patient knowledge about drug therapy and to promote compliance with drug regimen.*
• Offer support and encouragement *to help the patient deal with the diagnosis and drug regimen.*

Evaluation

• Monitor patient response to the drug (alleviation of anemia).
• Monitor for adverse effects (nasal irritation, pain at injection site, nausea).
• Evaluate the effectiveness of the teaching plan (patient can name drug, dosage, adverse effects to watch for, specific measures to avoid adverse effects; patient understands importance of continued follow-up).
• Monitor the effectiveness of comfort measures and compliance to the regimen.

WWW.WEB LINKS

Health care providers and patients may want to explore the following Internet sources:

Information on various forms of anemias, causes, characteristics, diagnosis, treatment:
http://www.aplastic.org/index.html

Information designed for patients and families regarding anemias:
http://thedailyapple.com

Information on iron toxicity—treatment, diagnosis, and complications, for patients and health care providers:
http://www.ansci.cornell.edu/plants/toxicagents/iron.html

Information on erythropoietin—action, uses:
http://www.noblood.com/wf/arficles/00200545.htm

Information about chelating agents—uses, actions, dosage:
http://www.medicalmaze.com/hompchel.html

CHAPTER SUMMARY

- The cardiovascular system exists to pump blood to all of the body's cells.
- Blood contains oxygen and nutrients that are essential for cell survival; it delivers these to the cells and removes waste products from the tissues.
- Blood is composed of a liquid plasma (containing water, proteins, glucose, and electrolytes) and formed components including white blood cells, red blood cells (RBCs), and platelets.
- RBCs are produced in the bone marrow in a process called erythropoiesis, which is controlled by the glycoprotein erythropoietin, produced by the kidneys.
- RBCs do not have a nucleus and have a life span of about 120 days, at which time they are lysed and the building blocks recycled to make new RBCs.
- The bone marrow uses iron, amino acids, carbohydrates, folic acid, and vitamin B_{12} to produce healthy, efficient RBCs.
- An insufficient number or maturity of RBCs will result in low oxygen levels in the tissues and tiredness, fatigue, and loss of reserve.
- Anemia is a state of too few RBCs. Anemia can be caused by a lack of erythropoietin or by a lack of the components needed to produce RBCs.
- Iron deficiency anemia occurs when there is inadequate iron intake in the diet or an inability to absorb iron from the GI tract. Iron is needed to produce hemoglobin, which carries the oxygen. Iron deficiency anemia is treated with iron replacement.
- Iron is a very toxic mineral at high levels. The body controls the absorption of iron and carefully regulates its storage and movement in the body.
- Folic acid and vitamin B_{12} are needed to produce a strong supporting structure in the RBC so that it can survive 120 days of being propelled through the vascular system. These are usually found in adequate amounts in the diet.
- A dietary lack of or inability to absorb folic acid, vitamin B_{12}, or both will produce a megaloblastic anemia with large, immature RBCs with a short life span.
- Pernicious anemia is a lack of vitamin B_{12}, which is also used by the body to maintain the myelin sheath on nerve axons. If vitamin B_{12} is lacking, these neurons will degenerate and cause many CNS effects.

- Pernicious anemia is caused by a deficient production of intrinsic factor by gastric cells.
- Intrinsic factor is needed to allow the body to absorb vitamin B_{12}. To treat this, vitamin B_{12} must be given parenterally or intranasally for life to ensure absorption.

BIBLIOGRAPHY

Bullock, B. L. (2000). *Focus on pathophysiology*. Philadelphia: Lippincott Williams & Wilkins.

Hardman, J. G., Limbird, L. E., Molinoff, P. B., Ruddon, R. W., & Gilman, A. G. (Eds.). (1996). *Goodman and Gilman's the pharmacological basis of therapeutics* (9th ed.). New York: McGraw-Hill.

Karch, A. M. (2000). *2000 Lippincott's nursing drug guide*. Philadelphia: Lippincott Williams & Wilkins.

McEvoy, B. R. (1999). *Facts and comparisons 1999*. St. Louis: Facts and Comparisons.

Medical letter on drugs and therapeutics. (1999). New Rochelle, NY: Medical Letter.

Porth, C. M. (1998). *Pathophysiology: Concepts of altered health states* (5th ed.). Philadelphia: Lippincott-Raven.

PART

9

Drugs Acting on the Renal System

CHAPTER

48

Introduction to the Kidney and the Urinary Tract

CHAPTER OUTLINE

KEY TERMS

aldosterone
antidiuretic hormone (ADH)
carbonic anhydrase
counter-current mechanism
filtration
glomerulus
nephron
prostate gland
reabsorption
renin–angiotensin system
secretion

INTRODUCTION

The renal system is composed of the kidneys and the organs of the urinary tract: the ureters, the urinary bladder, and the urethra. This system has four major functions in the body: (1) maintaining the volume and composition of body fluids within normal ranges, which includes clearing nitrogenous wastes from protein metabolism, maintaining acid–base balance and electrolyte levels, and excreting various drugs and drug metabolites; (2) regulating vitamin D activation, which helps to maintain and regulate calcium levels; (3) regulating blood pressure through the renin–angiotensin system; and (4) regulating red blood cell production through the production and secretion of erythropoietin.

THE KIDNEYS

The kidneys are two small organs making up about 0.5% of total body weight, but receiving about 25% of the cardiac output. Approximately 1600 liters of blood flow through these two small organs each day for cleansing. Most of the fluid that is filtered out by the kidneys is returned to the body, while the waste products that remain are excreted in a relatively small amount of water as urine.

The kidneys are located under the ribs, for protection from injury, and have three protective layers that make up the renal capsule: a fiber layer, a perirenal or brown fat layer, and the renal parietal layer. The capsule contains pain fibers, which are stimulated if the capsule is stretched secondary to an inflammatory process. The kidney has three identifiable regions: the outer cortex, the inner medulla, and the renal pelvises, into which collecting ducts drain into the ureters. The ureters are muscular tubes that lead into the urinary bladder, where urine is stored until it is excreted (Figure 48-1).

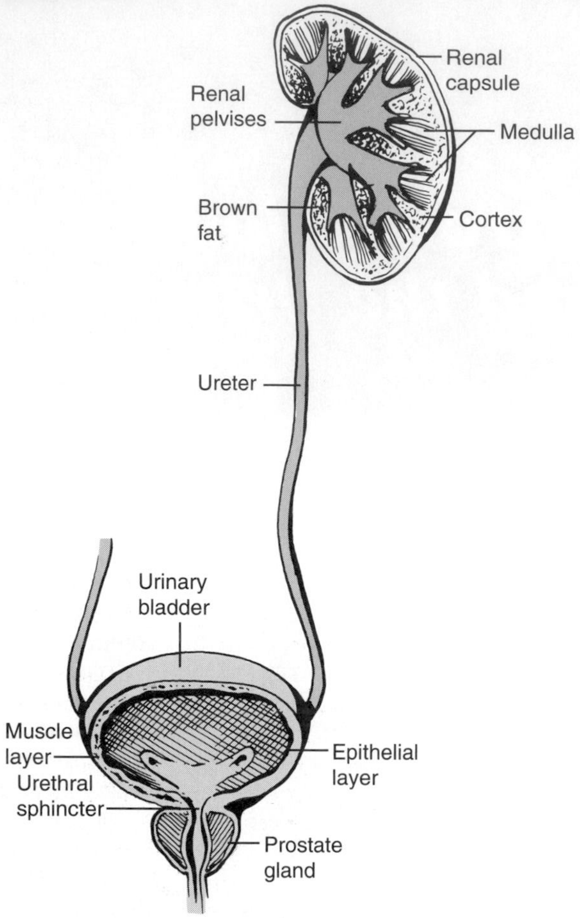

FIGURE 48-1. The kidney and organs of the urinary tract.

The functional unit of the kidney is called the ***nephron.*** There are approximately 2.4 million nephrons in an adult. All of the nephrons filter fluid and make urine, but only the medullary nephrons can concentrate or dilute urine. It is estimated that only about 25% of the total number of nephrons are necessary to maintain healthy renal function. That means that the renal system is well protected from failure with a large back-up system. It also means that by the time a patient has signs and symptoms of renal failure, extensive damage to the kidneys has already occurred.

The nephron is basically a tube (Figure 48-2). It begins with Bowman's capsule, which has a fenestrated or "windowed" epithelium that works like a sieve or a strainer to allow fluid to flow through, but keeps large things (such as proteins) from entering. The nephron then curls around in a section called the proximal convoluted tubule. From there, it narrows to form the descending and ascending loop of Henle, widens as the distal convoluted tubule, then flows into the collecting ducts, which meet at the renal pelvis. Each section of the tubule functions in a slightly different manner to maintain balance in the body.

The blood flow to the nephron is unique. The renal arteries come directly off the aorta and enter each kidney. A renal artery enters each of the kidneys and divides to form interlobar arteries, which become smaller arcuate (bowed) arteries, then afferent arterioles. The afferent arterioles form the ***glomerulus*** inside Bowman's capsule. The glomerulus is like a tuft of blood vessels with a capillary-like endothelium that allows easy passage of fluid and waste products. The efferent arteriole exits from the glomerulus and forms the peritubular capillary system, which returns fluid and electrolytes that have been reabsorbed from the tubules to the blood stream. These capillaries flow

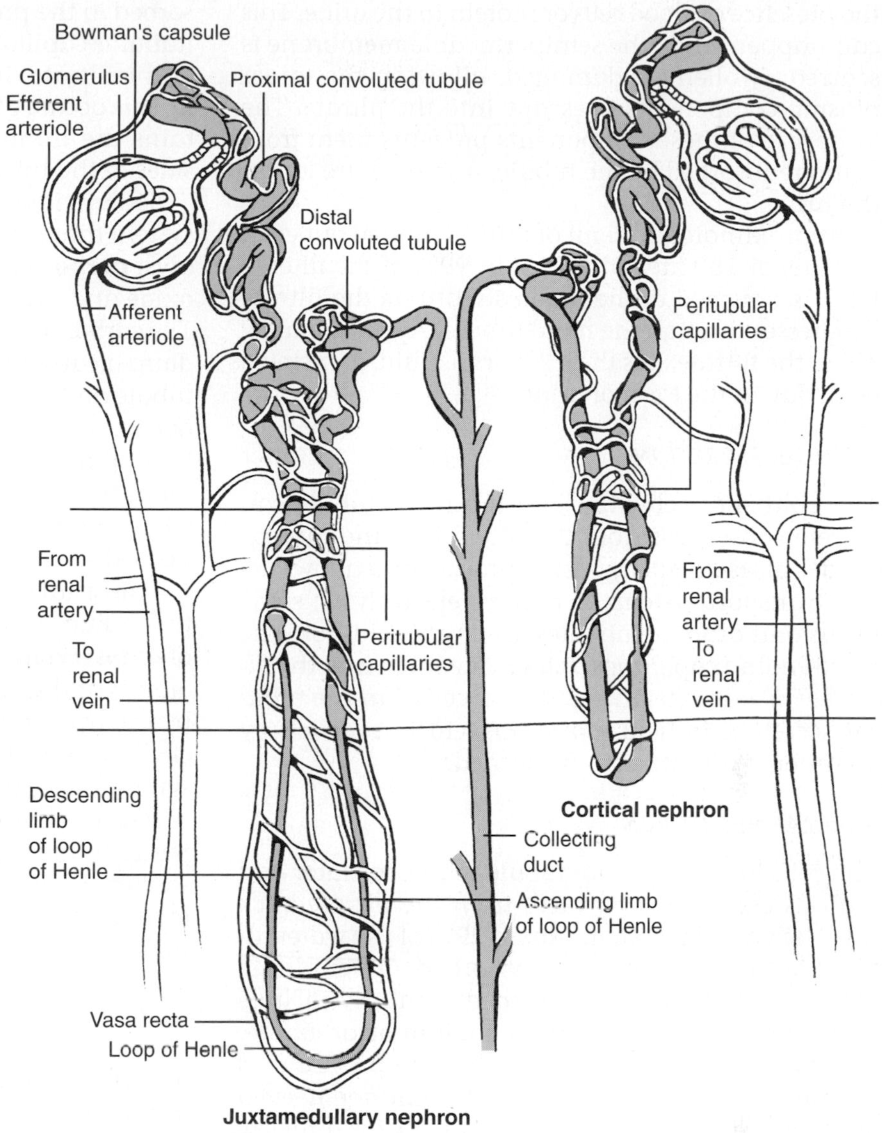

FIGURE 48-2. The nephron, the functional unit of the kidney. Secretion and reabsorption of water, electrolytes, and other solutes in the various segments of the renal tubule, the loop of Henle, and the collecting duct can be influenced by diuretics, other drugs, and endogenous substances, including certain hormones. In the kidney, the distal convoluted tubule wraps around and is actually next to the afferent arteriole.

into the vasa recta, which flows into intralobar veins, which, in turn, drain into the inferior vena cava. The two arterioles around the glomerulus work together to closely regulate the flow of fluid into the glomerulus, increasing or decreasing pressure on either side of the glomerulus as needed.

A small group of cells, called the juxtoglomerular apparatus, connects the afferent arteriole to the distal convoluted tubule (see Figure 48-2) and is the location where erythropoietin and renin are produced. Because of their proximity to the afferent arteriole, these cells are especially sensitive to the volume and quality of blood flow into the glomerulus.

Surrounding the nephrons is an area called the macula densa, which is full of immune system cells and chemicals that can respond quickly to any cellular damage or injury.

Renal Processes

The nephrons function by using three basic processes: glomerular ***filtration*** (straining of fluid into the nephron), tubular ***secretion*** (actively removing components from the capillary system and depositing them into the tubule), and tubular ***reabsorption*** (removing components from the tubule to return to the capillary system and circulation).

GLOMERULAR FILTRATION

The glomerulus acts as an ultrafine filter for all of the blood that flows into it. The semipermeable membrane keeps blood cells, proteins, and lipids inside the vessel, while the hydrostatic pressure from the blood pushes water and smaller components of the plasma into the tubule. A clinical sign of renal damage is the presence of blood cells or protein in the urine. This can happen when the semipermeable membrane is scarred, swollen, or damaged, allowing the larger plasma components to escape into the filtrate. The large size of these components prevents them from being reabsorbed by the tubule, and they are lost in the urine.

Approximately 125 ml of fluid is filtered out each minute, or 180 liters/day. About 99% of the filtered fluid is returned to the blood stream as the filtrate progresses through the renal tubule. Approximately 1% of the filtrate, less than 2 liters of fluid, is excreted each day in the form of urine.

TUBULAR SECRETION

The epithelial cells that line the renal tubule can secrete substances from the blood into the tubular fluid. This is an energy-using process and allows active transport systems to remove electrolytes, some drugs and drug metabolites, and uric acid from the surrounding capillaries and secrete them into the filtrate. For instance, the epithelial cells can use tubular secretion to help maintain acid–base levels by secreting hydrogen ions as needed.

TUBULAR REABSORPTION

The cells lining the renal tubule reabsorb water and various essential substances from the filtrate back into the vascular system. About 99% of the water filtered at the glomerulus is reabsorbed. Other filtrate components that are reabsorbed regularly include vitamins, glucose, electrolytes, sodium bicarbonate, and sodium chloride. The reabsorption process uses a series of transport systems that exchange needed ions for unwanted ones (see Chapter 5 for a review of cellular transport systems). Drugs that affect renal function frequently overwhelm one of these transport systems or interfere with its normal activity, leading to an imbalance in acid–base or electrolyte levels. The precision of the reabsorption process allows the body to maintain the correct extracellular fluid volume as well as composition.

Maintenance of Volume and Composition of Body Fluids

The kidney regulates the composition of body fluids by balancing the levels of the key electrolytes. The volume of body fluids is controlled by diluting or concentrating the urine.

SODIUM REGULATION

Sodium is one of the body's major cations or positively charged ions. It filters through the glomerulus and enters the renal tubule, then is actively reabsorbed in the proximal convoluted tubule to the peritubular capillaries. As sodium is actively moved out of the filtrate, it takes chloride ions and water with it. This occurs by passive diffusion as the body maintains the osmotic and electrical balances on both sides of the tubule.

Sodium ions are also reabsorbed using a transport system that functions under the influence of the catalyst ***carbonic anhydrase,*** which allows carbon dioxide and water to combine, forming carbonic acid. The carbonic acid immediately dissociates to form sodium bicarbonate using a sodium ion-from the renal tubule and a free hydrogen ion—an acid. The hydrogen ion is then left in the filtrate, causing the urine to be slightly acidic. The bicarbonate is stored in the renal tubule as the body's alkaline reserve, for use when the body becomes too acidic and a buffer is needed.

The distal convoluted tubule acts to further adjust the sodium levels in the filtrate under the influence of ***aldosterone*** (a hormone produced by the adrenal gland) and naturetic hormone (probably produced by the hypothalamus). Aldosterone is released into circulation in response to high potassium levels, to sympathetic stimulation, and to angiotensin III. Aldosterone stimulates a sodium–potassium exchange pump in the cells of the distal tubule that reabsorbs sodium in exchange for potassium (see Chapter 5 for a review of the sodium pump). As a result of aldosterone stimulation, sodium is reabsorbed into the system and potassium is lost in the filtrate. Naturetic hormone causes a decrease in sodium reabsorption from the distal tubules with a resultant dilute urine or increased volume. Naturetic hormone is released in response to fluid overload or hemodilution.

Counter-Current Mechanism

Sodium is further regulated in the medullary nephrons in what is known as the ***counter-current mechanism*** in the loop of Henle. In the descending loop of Henle, the cells are freely permeable to water and sodium. Sodium is actively reabsorbed into the surrounding peritubular tissue, and water flows out of the tubule into this sodium-rich tissue to maintain osmotic balance. The filtrate at the end of the descending loop of Henle is concentrated in comparison to the rest of the filtrate.

In contrast, the ascending loop of Henle is impermeable to water, so water that remains in the tubule is trapped there. Chloride is actively transported out of the tubule using energy in a process that is referred to as the chloride pump; sodium leaves with the chloride to maintain electrical neutrality. As a result, the fluid in the ascending loop of Henle becomes hypotonic in comparison to the hypertonic situation in the peritubular tissue.

Antidiuretic hormone (ADH), which is produced by the hypothalamus and stored in the posterior pituitary gland, is important in maintaining fluid balance. ADH is released in response to falling blood volume, sympathetic stimulation, and rising sodium levels (a concentration that is sensed by the osmotic cells of the hypothalamus).

If ADH is present at the distal convoluted tubule and the collecting duct, the permeability of the membrane to water will be increased. Consequently, the water remaining in the tubule rapidly flows into the hypertonic tissue surrounding the loop of Henle, where it is either absorbed by the peritubular capillaries or reenters the descending loop of Henle in a counter-current style. The resulting urine is hypertonic and of small volume. If ADH is not present, the tubule remains impermeable to water. The water that has been trapped in the ascending loop of Henle passes into the collection duct, resulting in a hypotonic urine of greater volume. This counter-current mechanism allows the body to finely regulate fluid volume by regulating the control of sodium and water (Figure 48-3).

POTASSIUM REGULATION

Potassium is another cation vital to proper functioning of the nervous system, muscles, and cell membranes. About 65% of the potassium that is filtered at the glomerulus is reabsorbed at Bowman's capsule and the proximal convoluted tubule. Another 25% to 30% is reabsorbed in the ascending loop of Henle. The fine tuning of potassium levels occurs in the distal convoluted tubule, where aldosterone activates the sodium–potassium exchange, leading to a loss of potassium. If potassium levels are very high, the retention of sodium in exchange for potassium also leads to a retention of water and a dilution of the blood volume, which further decreases potassium concentration (see Figure 48-3).

CHLORIDE REGULATION

Chloride is an important anion, a negatively charged ion, which helps to maintain electrical neutrality with the movement of cations across the cell membrane. Chloride is primarily reabsorbed in the loop of Henle where it promotes the movement of sodium out of the cell.

Regulation of Vitamin D Activation

Calcium is another important cation that is regulated by the kidney. The absorption of calcium from the gastrointestinal (GI) tract is regulated by vitamin D. Vitamin D is taken in as part of the diet and then must be activated in the kidney to a form that will promote the absorption of calcium from the GI tract. Once absorbed from the GI tract, calcium levels are maintained within a very tight range by the activity of parathyroid hormone and calcitonin.

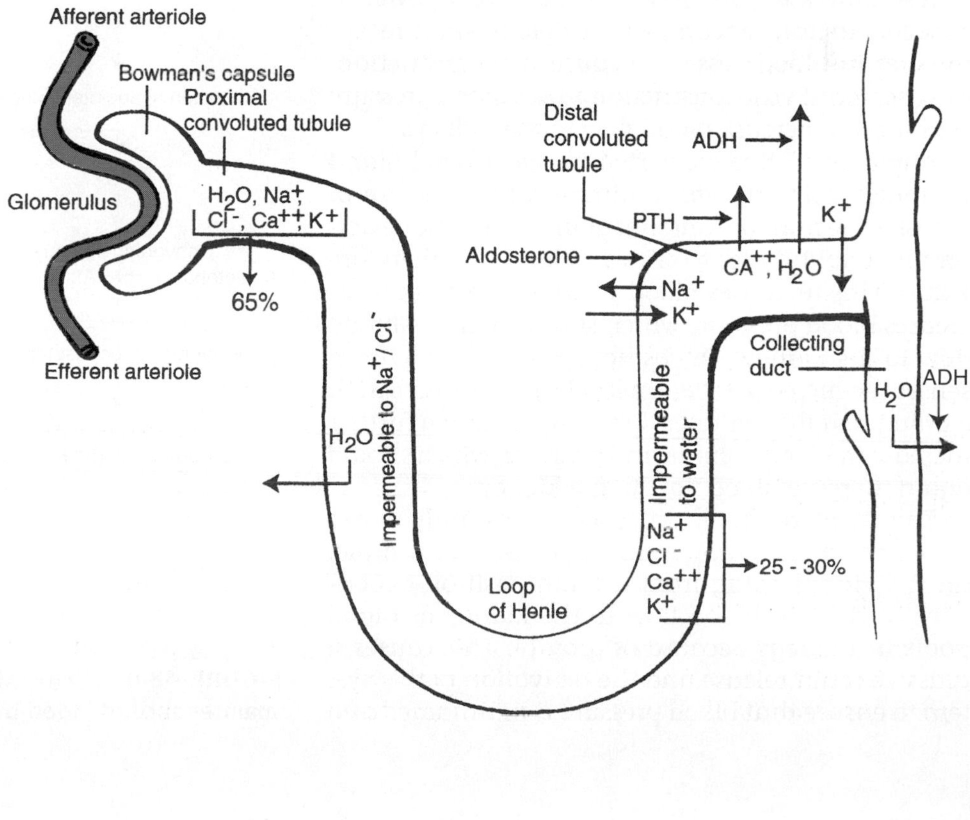

FIGURE 48-3. Nephron and points of regulation of sodium, chloride, potassium, calcium, and water.

CALCIUM REGULATION

Calcium is important in muscle function, blood clotting, bone formation, contraction of cell membranes, and muscle movement. Calcium is filtered at the glomerulus and mostly reabsorbed in the proximal convoluted tubule and ascending loop of Henle. Fine tuning of calcium reabsorption occurs in the distal convoluted tubule, where the presence of parathyroid hormone stimulates reabsorption of calcium to increase serum calcium levels when they are low (see Figure 48-3; see Chapter 35).

Blood Pressure Control: Renin–Angiotensin System

The fragile nephrons require a constant supply of blood and are equipped with a system to ensure that they are perfused. This mechanism, called the ***renin–angiotensin system,*** involves a total body reaction to decreased blood flow to the nephrons.

Whenever blood flow or oxygenation to the nephron is decreased (due to hemorrhage, shock, congestive heart failure, hypotension), renin is released from the juxtoglomerular cells. (These cells, which are positioned next to the glomerulus, are stimulated by decreased stretch and decreased oxygen levels.) The released renin immediately is absorbed into the capillary system and into circulation.

The released renin activates angiotensinogen, a substrate produced in the liver, which becomes angiotensin I. Angiotensin I is then converted to angiotensin II by a converting enzyme found in the lungs and some vessels. Angiotensin II is a very powerful vasoconstrictor, reacting with angiotensin II receptor sites in blood vessels to cause vasoconstriction. This powerful vasoconstriction raises blood pressure and should increase blood flow to the kidneys.

Angiotensin II is converted in the adrenal gland to angiotensin III, which stimulates the release of aldosterone from the adrenal gland. Aldosterone acts on the renal tubules to retain sodium and therefore water. This increases blood volume and further increases blood pressure, which should increase blood flow to the kidney. The osmotic center in the brain senses the increased sodium levels and releases ADH, leading to a further retention of water and a further increase in blood volume and pressure, which should again increase blood flow to the kidney.

The renin–angiotensin system constantly works to maintain blood flow to the kidneys. For example, an individual rising from a lying position experiences a drop in blood flow to the kidney as blood pools in the legs because of gravity. This causes a massive renin release and the activation of this system to ensure that blood pressure is maintained and the kidneys are perfused. Blood loss from injury or during surgery also activates this system to increase blood flow through the kidneys.

It is important to note that drugs that interfere with any aspect of this system will cause a reflex response. For instance, taking a drug such as a diuretic to decrease fluid volume can lead to decreased blood flow to the kidney as blood volume drops. This in turn leads to a rebound retention of fluid as part of the renin–angiotensin system's effects (Figure 48-4).

Regulation of Red Blood Cell Production

Whenever blood flow or oxygenation to the nephron is decreased (due to hemorrhage, shock, congestive heart failure, or hypotension), the hormone erythropoietin is also released from the juxtoglomerular cells. This hormone stimulates the bone marrow to increase production of red blood cells, which act to bring oxygen to the kidneys. Erythropoietin is the only known factor that can regulate the rate of red blood cell production. When a patient develops renal failure and the production of erythropoietin drops, the production of red blood cells falls and the patient becomes anemic.

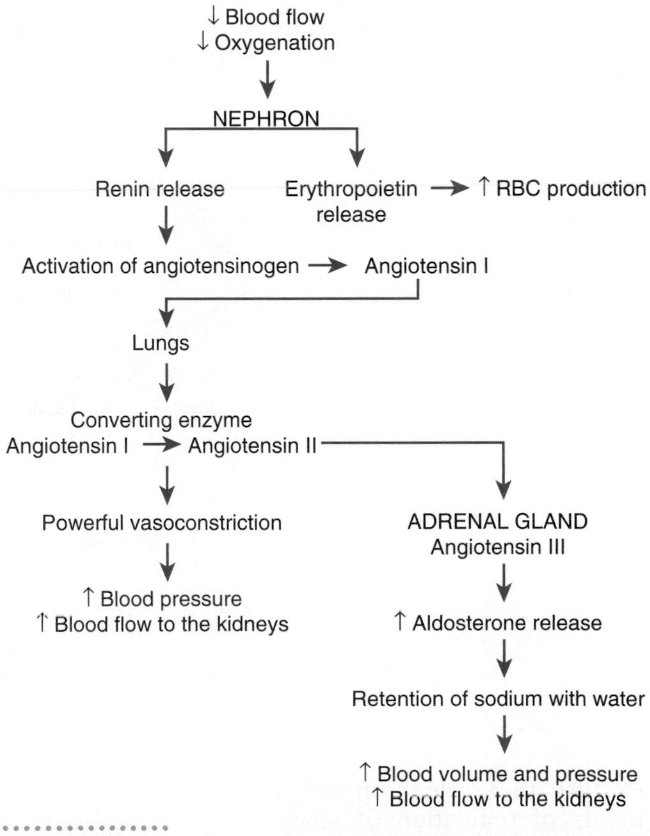

FIGURE 48-4. The renin-angiotensin system for reflex maintenance of blood pressure control.

THE URINARY TRACT

As noted above, the urinary tract is composed of the ureters, urinary bladder, and urethra (see Figure 48-1). One ureter exits each kidney, draining the filtrate from the collecting ducts. The ureters have a smooth endothelial lining and circular muscular layers. Urine entering the ureter stimulates a peristaltic wave that pushes the urine down toward the urinary bladder.

The urinary bladder is a muscular pouch that stretches and holds the urine until it is excreted from the body. Urine is usually a slightly acidic fluid; this acidity helps to maintain the normal transport systems and destroy bacteria that may enter the bladder.

In the female, the urethra is very short and leads to an area populated by normal flora including *E. coli,* which causes frequent bladder infections or cystitis. In the male, the urethra is much longer and passes through the ***prostate gland,*** a small gland that produces an acidic fluid important in maintaining the sperm and lubricating the tract. Enlargement and infection in the prostate gland are often problems in older males. Control of bladder emptying is learned control over the urethral sphincter; once established, a functioning nervous system is necessary to maintain control.

CHAPTER SUMMARY

- The kidneys are two small organs that receive about 25% of the cardiac output.
- The functional unit of the kidney is called the nephron, which is composed of Bowman's capsule, the proximal convoluted tubule, the loop of Henle, the distal convoluted tubule, and the collecting duct.
- The blood flow to the nephron is unique, allowing autoregulation of blood flow through the glomerulus.
- The nephrons function by using three basic processes: glomerular filtration (straining of fluid into the nephron), tubular secretion (actively removing components from the capillary system and depositing them into the tubule), and tubular reabsorption (removing components from the tubule to return to the capillary system and circulation).
- Sodium levels are regulated throughout the tubule by active and passive movement and are fine-tuned by the presence of aldosterone in the distal tubule.
- The counter-current mechanism in the medullary nephrons allows for the concentration or dilution of urine under the influence of ADH secreted by the hypothalamus.
- Potassium concentration is regulated throughout the tubule, with aldosterone being the strongest influence for potassium loss.
- The kidneys play a key role in the regulation of calcium by activating vitamin D to allow GI calcium reabsorption and by reabsorbing or excreting calcium from the tubule under the influence of parathyroid hormone.
- The kidneys influence blood pressure control, releasing renin to activate the renin–angiotensin system and increase blood pressure and thus blood flow to the kidney. The balance of this reflex system can lead to water retention or excretion and has an impact on drug therapy that promotes water or sodium loss.
- The ureters, urinary bladder, and urethra make up the rest of the urinary tract. The longer male urethra passes through the prostate gland, which may enlarge or become infected, a problem often associated with advancing age.

WWW.WEB LINKS

To explore the virtual kidney and urinary tract, visit the following Internet sites:

http://www. InnerBody.com
http://wwwl.biostr.washington.edu/DigitalAnatomist.html

BIBLIOGRAPHY

Bullock, B. L. (2000). *Focus on pathophysiology.* Philadelphia: Lippincott Williams & Wilkins.

Fox, S. (1991). *Perspectives on human biology.* Dubuque, IA: Wm. C. Brown Publishers.

Ganong, W. (1999). *Review of medical physiology* (19th ed.). Norwalk, CT: Appleton & Lange.

Guyton, A. & Hall, J. (1996). *Textbook of medical physiology.* Philadelphia: W.B. Saunders.

Hardman, J. G., Limbird, L. E., Molinoff, P. B., Ruddon, R. W., & Gilman, A. G. (Eds.). (1996). *Goodman and Gilman's the pharmacological basis of therapeutics* (9th ed.). New York: McGraw-Hill.

CHAPTER 49

Diuretic Agents

Thiazide diuretics
- bendroflumethiazide
- benzthiazide
- chlorothiazide
- P hydrochlorothiazide
- hydroflumethiazide
- methyclothiazide
- polythiazide
- trichlormethiazide

Thiazide-like diuretics
- P chlorthalidone
- indapamide
- metolazone
- quinethazone

Loop diuretics
- bumetanide
- ethacrynic acid
- P furosemide
- torsemide

Carbonic anhydrase inhibitors
- P acetazolamide
- methazolamide

Potassium-sparing diuretics
- amiloride
- P spironolactone
- triamterene

Osmotic diuretics
- glycerin
- isosorbide
- P mannitol
- urea

CHAPTER OUTLINE

KEY TERMS

alkalosis
edema
fluid rebound
high-ceiling diuretics
hyperaldosteronism
hypokalemia
osmotic pull

INTRODUCTION

There are five classes of diuretics, each working at a slightly different site in the nephron or using a different mechanism. Diuretic classes include the thiazide and thiazide-like diuretics, the loop diuretics, the carbonic anhydrase inhibitors, the potassium-sparing diuretics, and the osmotic diuretics. The overall nursing care of a patient receiving a diuretic is similar for any drug of this class. The diuretics classes will be discussed starting with the most frequently used drugs.

DIURETIC AGENTS

Diuretic agents are commonly thought of simply as drugs that increase the amount of urine produced by the kidneys. Most diuretics do increase the volume of urine produced to some extent, but the greater clinical significance of diuretics is related to their ability to increase sodium excretion.

THERAPEUTIC ACTIONS AND INDICATIONS

Diuretics prevent the cells lining the renal tubules from reabsorbing an excessive proportion of the sodium ions in the glomerular filtrate. As a result, sodium and other ions (and the water in which they are dissolved) are lost in the urine instead of being returned to the blood, where they would cause increased intravascular volume and therefore hydrostatic pressure, resulting in a leaking of fluids at the capillary level.

Diuretics are indicated for the treatment of ***edema*** associated with congestive heart failure, acute pulmonary edema, liver disease (including cirrhosis), and renal disease, and for the treatment of hypertension. They are also used to decrease fluid pressure in the eye (intraocular pressure), which is useful in treating glaucoma. Diuretics that decrease potassium levels may also be indicated in the treatment of conditions which present with hyperkalemia.

Congestive heart failure (CHF) can cause edema as a result of several factors. The failing heart muscle does not pump sufficient blood to the kidneys, causing activation of the renin–angiotensin system and resulting in increased blood volume and increased sodium retention. Because the failing heart muscle cannot respond to the usual reflex stimulation, the increased volume is slowly pushed out into the capillary level as venous pressure increases because the blood is not being pumped effectively (see Chapter 42).

Pulmonary edema, or left-sided CHF, develops when the increased volume of fluids backs up into the lungs. The fluid pushed out into the capillaries in the lungs interferes with gas exchange; when this condition develops rapidly, it can be life threatening.

Liver failure and cirrhosis will often present with edema and ascites. This is caused by (1) reduced plasma protein production, resulting in less oncotic pull in the vascular system and fluid loss at the capillary level; and (2) obstructed blood flow through the portal system resulting from increased pressure from congested hepatic vessels.

Renal disease produces edema because of the loss of plasma proteins into the urine when there is damage to the glomerular basement membrane. Other types of renal disease produce edema because of activation of the renin–angiotensin system or because of failure of the renal tubules to regulate electrolytes effectively. Decreasing blood volume due to the loss of fluid into the urine decreases vascular pressure, resulting in a drop in blood pressure.

Hypertension is predominantly an idiopathic disorder; in other words, the underlying pathology is not known. Treatment of hypertension is aimed at reducing the higher-than-normal blood pressure, which can damage end organs and lead to serious cardiovascular disorders. Diuretics were once the key element in antihypertensive therapy, the goal of which was to decrease volume and sodium, which would then decrease pressure in the system. Now several other classes of drugs, including angiotensin converting enzyme (ACE) inhibitors, beta blockers, and calcium channel blockers are used more frequently for the initial treatment of hypertension. Currently, diuretics are often used as an adjunct to improve the effectiveness of these other drugs.

Glaucoma is an eye disease that is characterized by increased pressure in the eye (intraocular pressure, IOP), which can cause optic nerve atrophy and blindness. Diuretics are used to provide osmotic pull to remove some of the fluid from the eye, which will decrease IOP, or as adjunctive therapy to reduce fluid volume and pressure in the cardiovascular system, which will also somewhat decrease pressure in the eye.

CONTRAINDICATIONS/CAUTIONS

Diuretic use is contraindicated in the presence of allergy to any of the drugs given. Other conditions in which diuretics are contraindicated include fluid and electrolyte imbalances, which can be potentiated by the fluid and electrolyte changes caused by the diuretics, and severe renal disease, which may prevent the diuretic from working or could be pushed into a crisis stage by the blood flow changes brought about by the diuretic.

Caution should be used with the following conditions: systemic lupus erythematosus, which frequently causes glomerular changes and renal dysfunction that could precipitate renal failure in some cases; glucose tolerance abnormalities or diabetes mellitus, which are worsened by the glucose-elevating effects of many diuretics; gout, which reflects an abnormality in normal tubule reabsorption and secretion; liver disease, which could interfere with the normal metabolism of the drugs, leading to an accumulation of the drug or toxicity; and pregnancy and lactation, which are conditions that could be jeopardized by changes in fluid and electrolyte balance.

ADVERSE EFFECTS

Adverse effects associated with diuretics are specific to the particular class used. For details, see the section on adverse effects for each class of diuretics discussed in this chapter; also refer to Table 49-1. The most common adverse effects seen with diuretics include GI upset, fluid and electrolyte imbalances, hypotension, and electrolyte disturbances.

CLINICALLY IMPORTANT DRUG–DRUG INTERACTIONS

When diuretics are used, there is a potential for interactions with drugs that depend on a particular electrolyte balance to have therapeutic effects (e.g., antiarrhythmics such as digoxin), with drugs that depend on urine alkalinity for proper excretion (e.g., quinidine), or with drugs that depend on normal reflexes to balance their effects (e.g., antihypertensives, antidiabetic agents) because these reflexes are altered by the action of diuretics.

Other specific drug–drug interactions that might relate to the chemical make-up of a particular diuretic are noted below.

THIAZIDE AND THIAZIDE-LIKE DIURETICS

Hydrochlorothiazide (*Hydrodiuril*), the most frequently used of the thiazide diuretics, is often used in combination with other drugs for the treatment of hypertension. It can be used in a smaller doses because it is more potent than chlorothiazide (*Diuril*), which is the oldest drug of this class and is considered the prototype. Other thiazides include bendroflumethiazide (*Naturetin*), benzthiazide (*Exna*), hydroflumethiazide (*Diucardin*), methyclothiazide (*Aquatensen*), polythiazide (*Renese*), and trichlormethiazide (*Diurese*).

The thiazide-like diuretics include chlorthalidone (*Hygroton*), indapamide (*Lozol*), metolazone (*Mykrox*), and quinethazone (*Hydromox*). All of these drugs are used less often than hydrochlorothiazide and are typically chosen according to the prescriber's personal preference.

THERAPEUTIC ACTIONS AND INDICATIONS

The thiazide diuretics belong to a chemical class of drugs called the sulfonamides. Thiazide-like diuret-

TABLE 49-1

COMPARISON OF DIURETICS

Diuretic Class	Major Site of Action	Usual Indications	Major Adverse Effects
Thiazide, thiazide-like	Distal convoluted tubule	Edema of CHF, liver and renal disease Adjunct for hypertension	GI upset, CNS complications, hypovolemia
Loop	Loop of Henle	Acute CHF Acute pulmonary edema Hypertension Edema of CHF, renal and liver disease	Hypokalemia, volume depletion, hypotension, CNS effects, GI upset, hyperglycemia
Carbonic anhydrase inhibitors	Proximal tubule	Glaucoma Diuresis in CHF Mountain sickness Epilepsy	GI upset, urinary frequency
Potassium-sparing	Distal tubule and collecting duct	Adjunct for edema of CHF, liver and renal disease Treatment of hypokalemia Adjunct for hypertension Hyperaldosteronism	Hyperkalemia, CNS effects, diarrhea
Osmotic	Glomerulus, tubule	Reduction of intracranial pressure Prevention of oliguric phase of renal failure Reduction of intraocular pressure Renal clearance of toxic substances	Hypotension, GI upset, fluid and electrolyte imbalances

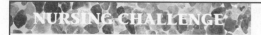

NURSING CHALLENGE

Avoiding Fluid Rebound

Care must be taken when using diuretics to avoid ***fluid rebound,*** which is associated with fluid loss. If a patient stops taking in water and takes the diuretic, the result will be a concentrated plasma of smaller volume. The decreased volume is sensed by the nephrons, which activate the renin–angiotensin cycle. When the concentrated blood is sensed by the osmotic center in the brain, ADH is released to hold water to dilute the blood. The result can be a "rebound" edema as fluid is retained.

Many patients who are taking a diuretic will markedly decrease their fluid intake to decrease the number of trips to the bathroom. The result is a rebound of water retention after the diuretic effect. This effect can also be seen in many "immediate result" diets, which contain a key provision to increase fluid intake to 8 to 10 full glasses of water daily. The reflex result of diluting the system with so much water is a drop in ADH release and fluid loss. Some people can lose 5 pounds in a few days by doing this. However, the body's reflexes will soon kick in, causing rebound retention of fluid to reestablish fluid and electrolyte balance. Most people get frustrated at this point and give up the fad diet. It is important to be able to explain this effect. Balancing the desired diuretic effect with the actions of the normal reflexes is a real clinical challenge.

ics have a slightly different chemical structure but work in the same way that thiazide diuretics do. Their action is to block the chloride pump. Chloride is actively pumped out of the tubule by cells lining the ascending limb of the loop of Henle and the distal tubule. Sodium passively moves with the chloride to maintain an electrical neutrality. (Chloride is a negative ion and sodium is a positive ion.) Blocking the chloride pump keeps the chloride and the sodium in the tubule to be excreted in the urine, thus preventing the reabsorption of both chloride and sodium in the vascular system (Figure 49-1). Because these segments of the tubule are impermeable to water, there is little increase in the volume of urine produced, but it will be sodium rich, a saluretic effect. Thiazides are considered to be mild diuretics compared to the more potent loop diuretics.

Thiazide and thiazide-like diuretics are usually indicated for the treatment of edema associated with CHF and with liver and renal disease. These drugs also are used as adjuncts for the treatment of hypertension.

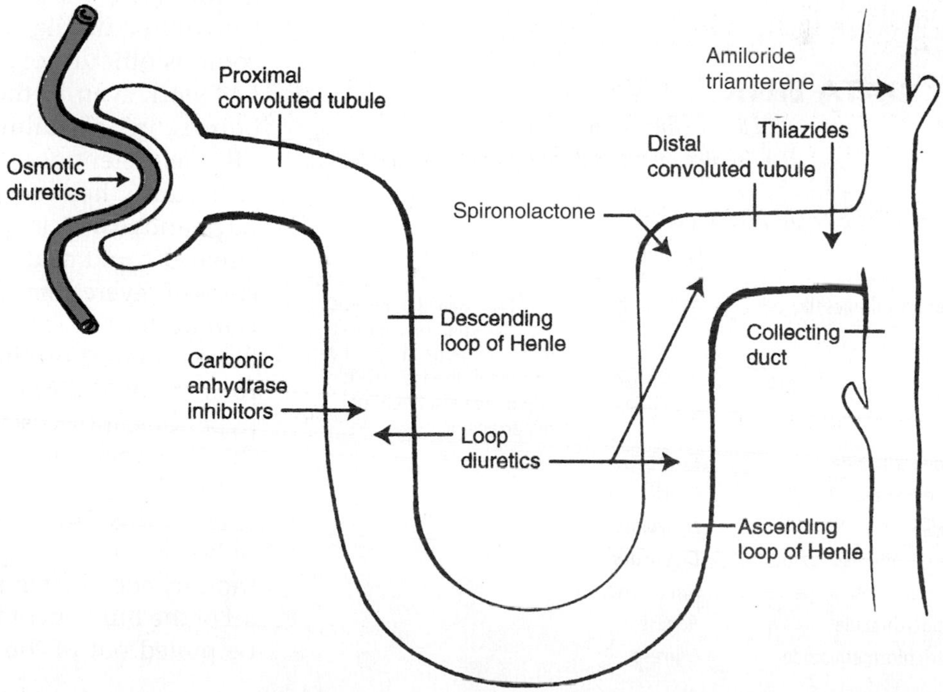

FIGURE 49-1. Sites of action of diuretics in the nephron.

ADVERSE EFFECTS

Adverse effects of thiazide use are related to the interference with the normal regulatory mechanisms of the nephron. Potassium is lost at the distal tubule because of the actions on the pumping mechanism, and ***hypokalemia*** (low blood levels of potassium) may result. Signs and symptoms of hypokalemia include weakness, muscle cramps, and arrhythmias. Another adverse effect is decreased calcium excretion, leading to increased calcium levels. Uric acid excretion also is decreased because the thiazides interfere with its secretory mechanism. High levels of uric acid can result in a condition called gout.

When these drugs are used over a prolonged period of time, blood glucose levels may be increased. This may result from the changes in potassium levels (which keep glucose out of the cells), or it may relate to some other mechanism of glucose control.

Urine will be slightly alkalinized when the thiazides are used because they block the reabsorption of bicarbonate. This effect can cause problems for patients who are susceptible to bladder infections and for those taking quinidine, which requires an acid urine for excretion.

CLINICALLY IMPORTANT DRUG–DRUG INTERACTIONS

Decreased absorption of these drugs may occur if combined with cholestyramine or colestipol. If this combination is used, the drugs should be separated by at least 2 hours.

DATA LINK

Data link to the following thiazides and thiadize-like diuretics in your nursing drug guide:

THIAZIDE DIURETICS

Name	Brand Name	Usual Indications
bendroflumethiazide	*Naturetin*	All of the thiazide diuretics are indicated for the treatment of edema of CHF, liver, and renal disease, and for adjunctive treatment of hypertension
benzthiazide	*Exna*	
chlorothiazide	*Diuril*	
P hydrochlorothiazide	*Hydrodiuril*	
hydroflumethiazide	*Diucardin*	
methyclothiazide	*Aquatensen*	
polythiazide	*Renese*	
trichlormethiazide	*Diurese*	
P chlorthalidone	*Hygroton*	All of the thiazide-like diuretics are indicated for the treatment of edema of CHF, liver and renal disease, and for adjunctive treatment of hypertension
indapamide	*Lozol*	
quinethazone	*Hydromox*	
metolazone	*Mykrox*	

LOOP DIURETICS

Loop diuretics are so named because they work in the loop of Henle. There are currently four loop diuretics available. Furosemide (*Lasix*), the most commonly used loop diuretic, is less powerful than the new loop diuretics, bumetanide (*Bumex*) and torsemide (*Demadex*), so it has a larger margin of safety for home use. Ethacrynic acid (*Edecrin*), the first loop diuretic introduced, is used less frequently in the clinical setting because of the improved potency and reliability of the newer drugs.

THERAPEUTIC ACTIONS AND INDICATIONS

Loop diuretics are also referred to as ***high-ceiling diuretics*** because they cause a greater degree of diuresis than other diuretics. These drugs block the chloride pump in the ascending loop of Henle, where normally 30% of all filtered sodium is reabsorbed. This action decreases the reabsorption of sodium and chloride. The loop diuretics have a similar effect in the descending loop of Henle and in the distal convoluted tubule, resulting in the production of a copious amount of sodium-rich urine. These drugs will work even in the presence of acid–base disturbances, renal failure, electrolyte imbalances, or nitrogen retention.

Because they can produce a loss of fluid of up to 20 pounds a day, loop diuretics are the drugs of choice when a rapid and extensive diuresis is needed. In cases of severe edema or acute pulmonary edema, it is important to remember that these drugs can only have an effect on the blood that reaches the nephrons. A rapid diuresis will occur, producing a more hypertonic intravascular fluid. In pulmonary edema, this fluid then circulates back to the lungs, pulls fluid out of the interstitial spaces by its oncotic pull, and delivers this fluid to the kidneys where the water is pulled out, thus completing the cycle. In treating pulmonary edema, it may sometimes take hours to move all of the fluid out of the lungs because the fluid must be pulled out of the interstitial spaces in the lungs

CASE STUDY

Using Furosemide (Lasix) in Congestive Heart Failure

PRESENTATION

M. R. is a 68-year-old female with rheumatic mitral valve heart disease. She has refused any surgical intervention and has developed progressively worsening congestive heart failure (CHF). M. R. recently received a prescription for furosemide (*Lasix*), 40 mg PO qd, along with digoxin. After 10 days with the new prescription, M. R. calls to tell you that she is allergic to the new medicine and can't take it any more. She reports extensive ankle swelling and difficulty breathing and is referred to a cardiologist for immediate review.

CRITICAL THINKING QUESTIONS

Think about the physiology of mitral valve disease and the progression of CHF in this patient. How does furosemide work in the body? What additional activities will be important to help maintain some balance in this patient's cardiac status? What is the nature of M. R.'s allergy, and what other options could be tried?

DISCUSSION

Over time, an incompetent mitral valve leads to an enlarged and overworked left ventricle as the backup of blood "waiting to be pumped" continues to progress. Drug therapy for a patient with this disorder is usually aimed at decreasing the workload of the heart as much as possible to maintain cardiac output. Digoxin increases the contractility of the heart muscle, which should lead to better perfusion of the kidneys. Furosemide, a loop diuretic, acts on the loop of Henle to block the reabsorption of sodium and water and lead to a diuresis, which decreases the volume of blood the heart needs to pump and makes the blood that is pumped more efficient. This blood then has an oncotic pull to move fluid from the tissues into circulation, where it can be acted on by the kidney, leading to further diuresis.

M. R. should be encouraged to maintain fluid intake and to engage in activity as much as possible, but to take frequent rest periods. Her potassium should be monitored regularly (this is especially important because she is also taking digoxin, which is very sensitive to potassium levels), her edematous limbs should be elevated periodically during the day, and she should monitor her sodium intake.

When M. R. was questioned about her reported allergy, it was discovered that her "allergic reaction" was actually increased urination (a therapeutic effect). M. R. requires teaching about the actions of the drug. She also needs information about the timing of administration so that the resultant diuresis will not interfere with rest or with her daily activities. CHF is a progressive, incurable disease, making patient education a very important part of the overall management regimen.

before it can be circulated to the kidneys for removal. Remembering how the drugs work and the way fluid moves in the vascular system will make it easier to understand the effects to anticipate.

Loop diuretics are commonly indicated for the treatment of acute CHF, acute pulmonary edema, edema associated with CHF and renal and liver disease, and hypertension.

ADVERSE EFFECTS

Adverse effects are related to the imbalance in electrolytes and fluid that these drugs cause. Hypokalemia is a very common adverse effect as potassium is lost when the transport systems in the tubule try to save some of the sodium being lost. *Alkalosis* may occur as bicarbonate is lost in the urine. Calcium is also lost in the tubules along with the bicarbonate, which may result in hypocalcemia and tetany. The fast loss of fluid may cause hypotension and dizziness in cases where it causes a rapid imbalance in fluid levels. Long-term use of these drugs may also result in hyperglycemia because of the diuretic effect on blood glucose levels, so susceptible patients need to be monitored for this effect. Ototoxicity and even deafness have been reported with these drugs, but the loss of hearing is usually reversible when the drug is stopped. This effect may be due to the electrolyte changes that occur on the conduction of fragile nerves in the central nervous system.

CLINICALLY IMPORTANT DRUG–DRUG INTERACTIONS

There is an increased risk of ototoxicity if loop diuretics are combined with aminoglycosides or cisplatin. There may be a decreased loss of sodium and decreased antihypertensive effects if these drugs are combined with indomethacin, ibuprofen, or other NSAIDs. The patient receiving this combination should be monitored closely and appropriate dosage adjustments made.

DATA LINK

Data link to the following loop diuretics in your nursing drug guide:

LOOP DIURETICS

Name	Brand Name	Usual Indications
bumetanide	*Bumex*	All of the loop diuretics are indicated for the treatment of acute CHF; acute pulmonary edema; hypertension; and edema of CHF, renal, or liver disease
ethacrynic acid	*Edecrin*	
P furosemide	*Lasix*	
torsemide	*Demadex*	

CARBONIC ANHYDRASE INHIBITORS

The carbonic anhydrase inhibitors are relatively mild diuretics. More often, they are used to treat glaucoma, as the inhibition of carbonic anhydrase results in decreased secretion of the aqueous humor of the eye. Available agents include acetazolamide (*Diamox*) and methazolamide (*Neptazane*).

THERAPEUTIC ACTIONS AND INDICATIONS

The enzyme carbonic anhydrase is a catalyst for the formation of sodium bicarbonate, stored as the alkaline reserve in the renal tubule, and the excretion of hydrogen, resulting in a slightly acidic urine. Diuretics that block the effects of carbonic anhydrase slow down the movement of hydrogen ions; as a result, more sodium and bicarbonate are lost in the urine.

These drugs are used as adjuncts to other diuretics when a more intense diuresis is needed. Acetazolamide is used to treat glaucoma, in conjunction with other drugs to treat epilepsy, and to treat mountain sickness. Methazolamide (*Neptazane*) is used primarily for the treatment of glaucoma.

ADVERSE EFFECTS

Adverse effects of carbonic anhydrase inhibitors are related to the disturbances in acid–base and electrolyte balance. Metabolic acidosis is a relatively common and potentially dangerous effect that occurs when bicarbonate is lost. Hypokalemia is also common as potassium excretion is increased as the tubule loses potassium in an attempt to retain some of the sodium that is being excreted. Patients also complain of paresthesias (tingling) of the extremities, confusion, and drowsiness, all of which are probably related to the neural effect of the electrolyte changes.

CLINICALLY IMPORTANT DRUG–DRUG INTERACTIONS

There may be an increased excretion of salicylates and lithium if combined with these drugs. Caution should be used to monitor serum levels of patients on lithium.

DATA LINK

Data link to the following carbonic anhydrase inhibitors in your nursing drug guide:

CARBONIC ANHYDRASE INHIBITORS

Name	Brand Name	Usual Indications
P acetazolamide	*Diamox*	Treatment of glaucoma; adjunctive treatment of epilepsy, mountain sickness
methazolamide	*Neptazane*	Treatment of glaucoma

POTASSIUM-SPARING DIURETICS

The potassium-sparing diuretics include amiloride (*Midamor*), spironolactone (*Aldactone*), and triamterene (*Dyrenium*). These diuretics are used in patients in which a high risk of hypokalemia associated with diuretic use exists (patients on digitalis, patients with cardiac arrhythmias). They are not as powerful as the loop diuretics, but retain potassium instead of wasting it.

THERAPEUTIC ACTIONS AND INDICATIONS

Certain diuretics act to cause the loss of sodium while retaining potassium. Spironolactone acts as an aldosterone antagonist, blocking the actions of aldosterone in the distal tubule. Amiloride and triamterene act to block potassium secretion through the tubule. The diuretic effect of these drugs comes from the balance achieved in losing sodium to offset potassium retained.

Potassium-sparing diuretics are often used as adjuncts with thiazide or loop diuretics or with patients who are especially at risk if hypokalemia develops, for example, patients on certain antiarrhythmics or digoxin, or who have particular neurological conditions. Spironolactone, the most frequently prescribed of these drugs, is the drug of choice for treating ***hyperaldosteronism,*** a condition seen in cirrhosis of the liver and nephrotic syndrome.

ADVERSE EFFECTS

The most common adverse effect of potassium-sparing diuretics is hyperkalemia, which can cause lethargy, confusion, ataxia, muscle cramps, and cardiac arrhythmias. Patients on these drugs need to be evaluated regularly for signs of increased potassium and informed about the signs and symptoms to watch for. They also should be advised to avoid foods high in potassium (Box 49-1).

CLINICALLY IMPORTANT DRUG–DRUG INTERACTIONS

There is a decreased diuretic effect if potassium-sparing diuretics are combined with salicylates. Dosage adjustment may be necessary to achieve therapeutic effects.

DATA LINK

Data link to the following potassium-sparing diuretics in your nursing drug guide:

POTASSIUM-SPARING DIURETICS

Name	Brand Name	Usual Indications
amiloride	*Midamor*	All of the potassium-sparing diuretics are indicated for the adjunctive treatment of edema of CHF, liver and renal disease; hypertension; hyperkalemia; and hyperaldosteronism
P spironolactone	*Aldactone*	
triamterene	*Dyrenium*	

OSMOTIC DIURETICS

Osmotic diuretics pull water into the renal tubule without sodium loss. They are the diuretics of choice in cases of increased cranial pressure and acute renal failure due to shock, drug overdose, or trauma. The osmotic diuretics include two mild agents (glycerin [*Osmoglyn*] and isosorbide [*Ismotic*]) and two powerful ones (mannitol [*Osmitrol*] and urea [*Ureaphil*]). Glycerin can be given IV to treat elevated intracranial pressure and is used orally to treat glaucoma. Isosorbide is only available orally and is a preferred drug for treating glaucoma. Mannitol, which is only available for IV use, is the mainstay for treatment of elevated intracranial pressure and acute renal failure. Urea also is only available for IV use and is indicated for reduction of intracranial pressure and the treatment of acute glaucoma.

THERAPEUTIC ACTIONS AND INDICATIONS

Some nonelectrolytes are used intravenously to increase the volume of fluid produced by the kidneys. Mannitol, for example, a sugar that is not well reabsorbed by the tubules, acts to pull large amounts of fluid into the urine by the ***osmotic pull*** of the large sugar molecule. Because the tubule is not able to reabsorb all of the sugar pulled into it, large amounts of fluid are lost in the urine. The effects of these osmotic drugs are not limited to the kidney, as the injected substance pulls fluid into the vascular system from extravascular spaces, including the aqueous humor. For this reason, these drugs are often used in acute situations when it is necessary to decrease intraocular pressure before eye surgery or during acute attacks of glaucoma. Mannitol is also used to decrease intracranial pressure, to prevent the oliguric phase of renal failure, and to promote the movement of toxic substances through the kidneys.

ADVERSE EFFECTS

The most common and potentially dangerous adverse effect related to osmotic diuretics is the sudden drop in fluid levels. Nausea, vomiting, hypotension, lightheadedness, confusion, and headache can be accompanied by cardiac decompensation and even shock. Patients receiving these drugs should be closely monitored for fluid and electrolyte imbalance.

DATA LINK

Data link to the following osmotic diuretics in your nursing drug guide:

OSMOTIC DIURETICS

Name	Brand Name	Usual Indications
glycerin	*Osmoglyn*	Treatment of elevated intracranial pressure (IV); glaucoma (PO)
isosorbide	*Ismotic*	Treatment of glaucoma

BOX 49-1

POTASSIUM-RICH FOODS (IMPORTANT TO EAT WITH POTASSIUM-WASTING DIURETICS)

avocados	bananas	broccoli	cantaloupe	dried fruits
grapefruit	lima beans	nuts	navy beans	oranges
peaches	potatoes	prunes	rhubarb	*Sanka* coffee
sunflower seeds	spinach	tomatoes		

P mannitol	*Osmitrol*	Treatment of elevated intracranial pressure; renal failure; acute glaucoma
urea	*Ureaphil*	Treatment of elevated intracranial pressure; acute glaucoma

NURSING CONSIDERATIONS for patients receiving diuretics

Assessment

HISTORY. Screen for the following: any known allergies to diuretics; fluid or electrolyte disturbances, which could be exacerbated by the diuretic or render the diuretic ineffective; gout, which reflects an abnormal tubule function and could be worsened by the diuretic or reflect a condition that would render the diuretic ineffective; glucose tolerance abnormalities, which may be exacerbated by the glucose-elevating effects of some diuretics; liver disease, which could alter the metabolism of the diuretic leading to toxic levels; systemic lupus erythematosus (SLE), which frequently affects the glomerulus and could be exacerbated by the use of a diuretic; and pregnancy and lactation, which could be affected by the change in fluid and electrolyte balance.

PHYSICAL ASSESSMENT. Physical assessment should include the following: thorough skin examination (including color, texture, and the presence of edema) to provide a baseline as a reference for drug effectiveness; assessment of blood pressure, pulse, cardiac auscultation to provide a baseline for effects on blood pressure and volume; body weight, to provide a baseline to monitor fluid load; liver evaluation to determine potential problems in drug metabolism; check of urinary output to establish a baseline of renal function; and evaluation of blood tests to provide a baseline reference for electrolyte balance, glucose levels, uric acid levels, and liver function tests.

Nursing Diagnoses

The patient receiving a diuretic may have the following nursing diagnoses related to drug therapy:

- Fluid volume deficit related to diuretic effect
- Alteration in urinary elimination related to diuretic effect
- Alteration in nutrition related to GI upset and metabolic changes
- Knowledge deficit regarding drug therapy

Implementation

- Administer oral drug with food or milk *to buffer the drug effect on stomach lining if GI upset is a problem.*
- Administer IV drug slowly *to prevent severe changes in fluid and electrolytes;* protect the drug from light *because disintegration can occur;* discard diluted drug after 24 hours *to prevent contamination or ineffective drug use.*
- Continuously monitor urinary output, cardiac response, and rhythm of patients receiving IV diuretics *to monitor for rapid fluid switch and potential electrolyte disturbances leading to cardiac arrhythmia.* Switch to the oral form, *which is less potent and easier to monitor, as soon as possible.*
- Administer early in the day *so increased urination will not interfere with sleep.*
- Monitor the dose carefully and reduce the dosage of one or both drugs if given with antihypertensive agents; *loss of fluid volume can precipitate hypotension.*
- Monitor the patient response to the drug (e.g., blood pressure, urinary output, weight, serum electrolytes, hydration, periodic blood glucose monitoring) *to evaluate the effectiveness of the drug and monitor for adverse effects.*
- Provide comfort measures, including skin care and nutrition consult, *to increase compliance to drug therapy and decrease severity of adverse effects;* provide safety measures if dizziness and weakness are a problem.
- Provide potassium-rich or poor diet as appropriate for drug being given *to maintain electrolyte balance and replace lost potassium.*
- Provide thorough patient teaching, including measures to avoid adverse effects and warning signs of problems as well as ways to incorporate diuretic effect in planning the day's activities *to enhance patient knowledge about drug therapy and to promote compliance* (see Patient Teaching Checklist: Diuretic Agents).

Evaluation

- Monitor patient response to the drug (weight, urinary output, edema changes, blood pressure).
- Monitor for adverse effects (electrolyte imbalance, orthostatic hypotension, rebound edema, hyperglycemia, increased uric acid levels, acid–base disturbances, dizziness).
- Evaluate the effectiveness of the teaching plan (patient can name drug, dosage, adverse effects to watch for, specific measures to avoid adverse effects).
- Monitor the effectiveness of comfort measures and compliance to the regimen (see Nursing Care Guide: Diuretic Agents).

WWW.WEB LINKS

Health care providers and patients may want to consult the following Internet sources:

Information on diuretics, good teaching guides and aids:

http://www.med.virginia.edu/med-ed/handouts/physiology/renal/diuretic.html

PATIENT TEACHING CHECKLIST

Diuretic Agents

Create customized patient teaching materials for a specific diuretic agent from your CD-ROM. Your patient teaching should stress the following points for drugs within this class:

A diuretic, or "water pill," will help to reduce the amount of fluid that is in your body by causing the kidneys to pass larger amounts of water and salt into your urine. By removing this fluid, the diuretic helps to decrease the work of the heart, lower blood pressure, and get rid of edema or swelling in your tissues.

This drug can be taken with food, which may eliminate any stomach upset. When taking a diuretic, you should maintain your usual fluid intake and try to avoid excessive intake of salt.

Because your diuretic causes potassium loss, you should eat foods that are high in potassium (e.g., orange juice, raisins, bananas). You also may be asked to take a potassium substitute, if appropriate. Your diuretic also can cause potassium retention, so you should avoid foods high in potassium as well as salt substitutes, as appropriate.

Weigh yourself each day, at the same time of day and in the same clothing. Record these weights on a calendar. Report any loss or gain of 3 or more pounds in 1 day.

Common effects of this drug include:

- Increased volume and frequency of urination—Have ready access to bathroom facilities. Once you are used to the drug you will know how long the effects last for you.
- Dizziness, feeling faint on arising, drowsiness—Loss of fluid can lower blood pressure and cause these feelings. Change positions slowly; if you feel drowsy avoid driving or dangerous activities. These feelings are often increased if alcohol is consumed. Avoid this combination or take special precautions if you combine these two.
- Increased thirst—As fluid is lost, you may experience a feeling of thirst. Sucking on sugarless lozenges and frequent mouth care might help alleviate this feeling. Do not drink an excessive amount of fluid while taking a diuretic. Try to maintain your usual fluid intake.

Report any of the following to your health care provider: muscle cramps or pain, loss or gain of more than 3 pounds in one day, swelling in your fingers or ankles, nausea or vomiting, unusual bleeding or bruising, trembling or weakness.

Avoid the use of any over-the-counter medication without first checking with your health care provider. Several of these medications can interfere with the effectiveness of this drug.

Tell any doctor, nurse, or other health care provider that you are taking this drug.

Keep this drug, and all medications, out of the reach of children.

This Teaching Checklist reflects general patient teaching guidelines. It is not meant to be a substitute for drug-specific teaching information, which is available in nursing drug guides.

Information on congestive heart failure, pathophysiology, treatment, research:
http://www.plgrm.com/health/C/Congestive_Heart_Failure.HTM

Information on liver disease and related treatment:
http://cpmcnet.columbia.edu/dept/gi/other.html

Information on glaucoma, prevention and treatment:
http://www.eyenet.org

CHAPTER SUMMARY

- Diuretics are drugs that increase the excretion of sodium and therefore water from the kidneys.
- Diuretics are used in the treatment of edema associated with congestive heart failure and pulmonary edema, liver failure and cirrhosis, and various types of renal disease, and as adjuncts in the treatment of hypertension.
- Diuretics must be used cautiously in any condition that would be exacerbated by changes in fluid and electrolyte balance.
- Adverse effects associated with diuretics include electrolyte imbalance (potassium, sodium, chloride); hypotension and hypovolemia; hypoglycemia; and metabolic alkalosis.
- Classes of diuretics differ in their site of action and intensity of effects. Thiazide diuretics work to

NURSING CARE GUIDE

Diuretic Agents

Assessment	Nursing Diagnoses	Implementation	Evaluation
HISTORY Allergies to diuretics, fluid or electrolyte disturbances, gout, glucose tolerance abnormalities, liver disease, SLE, pregnancy and lactation.	Fluid volume deficit related to diuretic effect Alteration in urinary elimination Alteration in nutrition Knowledge deficit regarding drug therapy	Obtain daily weights, monitor output. Provide comfort and safety measures: sugarless lozenges, mouth care, safety precautions, skin care, nutrition. Administer with food, early in day. Provide support and reassurance to deal with drug effects and lifestyle changes. Provide patient teaching regarding drug name, dosage, side effects, precautions, warnings to report, daily weighing, and recording dietary changes as needed.	Evaluate drug effects: urinary output, weight changes, status of edema, BP changes. Monitor for adverse effects: hypotension, hypokalemia hyperkalemia, hypocalcemia hypercalcemia, hyperglycemia, increased uric acid levels. Monitor for drug–drug interactions as indicated for each drug. Evaluate effectiveness of patient teaching program. Evaluate effectiveness of comfort/safety measures.
PHYSICAL EXAMINATION Neurological: orientation, reflexes, strength Skin: color, texture, edema CV: BP, P, cardiac auscultation GI: liver evaluation GU: urinary output Lab tests: hematologic; serum electrolytes, glucose, uric acid; liver function tests			

block the chloride pump in the distal convoluted tubule. This effect leads to a loss of sodium and potassium and a minor loss of water. Thiazides are frequently used in combination with other drugs to treat hypertension. These are considered to be mild diuretics.

- Loop diuretics work in the loop of Henle and have a powerful diuretic effect, leading to the loss of water, sodium, and potassium. These drugs are the most potent diuretics and are used in acute situations as well as chronic conditions not responsive to milder diuretics.
- Carbonic anhydrase inhibitors work to block the formation of carbonic acid and bicarbonate in the renal tubule. These drugs can cause an alkaline urine and the loss of the bicarbonate buffer. Carbonic anhydrase inhibitors are used in combination with other diuretics when a stronger diuresis is needed, and they are frequently used to treat glaucoma as they decrease the amount of aqueous humor produced in the eye.
- Potassium-sparing diuretics are mild diuretics that act to spare potassium in exchange for the loss of sodium and water in the urine. These diuretics are preferable if potassium loss could be detrimental to a patient's cardiac or neuromuscular condition. Patients must be careful not to become hyperkalemic while on these drugs.

- Osmotic diuretics use hypertonic pull to remove fluid from the intravascular spaces and to deliver large amounts of water into the renal tubule. There is a danger of sudden change of fluid volume and massive fluid loss with some of these drugs. These drugs are used to decrease intracranial pressure, treat glaucoma, and help push toxic substances through the kidney.
- Patients receiving diuretics need to be monitored for fluid loss and retention (daily weights, blood pressure, skin evaluation, urinary output), have periodic electrolyte evaluations and blood glucose determinations, and have evaluations of the effectiveness of their teaching program.

Bibliography

Bullock, B. L. (2000). *Focus on pathophysiology.* Philadelphia: Lippincott Williams & Wilkins.

Hardman, J. G., Limbird, L. E., Molinoff, P. B., Ruddon, R. W., & Gilman, A. G. (Eds.). (1996). *Goodman and Gilman's the pharmacological basis of therapeutics* (9th ed.). New York: McGraw-Hill.

Karch, A. M. (2000). *2000 Lippincott's nursing drug guide.* Philadelphia: Lippincott Williams & Wilkins.

Malseed, R. (1995). *Textbook of pharmacology and nursing care.* Philadelphia: J. B. Lippincott.

McEvoy, B. R. (Ed.). (1999). *Facts and comparisons 1999.* St. Louis: Facts and Comparisons.

Professional's guide to patient drug facts. (1999). St. Louis: Facts and Comparisons.

CHAPTER 50

Drugs Affecting the Urinary Tract and the Bladder

Urinary tract anti-infectives
- cinoxacin
- fosfomycin
- methenamine
- methylene blue
- nalidixic acid
- nitrofurantoin
- P norfloxacin

Urinary tract antispasmodics
- flavoxate
- P oxybutynin

Urinary tract analgesic
- phenazopyridine

Bladder protectant
- pentosan polysulfate sodium

Drugs used to treat benign prostatic hyperplasia
- P doxazosin
- finasteride
- tamsulosin
- terazosin

CHAPTER OUTLINE

KEY TERMS

acidification
antispasmodics
benign prostatic hyperplasia (BPH)
cystitis
dysuria
interstitial cystitis
nocturia
pyelonephritis
urgency
urinary frequency

TABLE 50-1

DRUGS USED TO TREAT URINARY TRACT PROBLEMS

Urinary Tract Problem	Drugs of Choice
Infection	Urinary tract anti-infectives: fosfomycin, cinoxacin, methenamine, nalidixic acid, methylene blue, nitrofurantoin, norfloxacin
Spasm	Antispasmodics: flavoxate, oxybutynin
Pain	Urinary tract analgesic: phenazoypyridine
	Bladder protectant for interstitial cystitis: pentosan
BPH	Alpha adrenergic blockers: doxazosin, terazosin
	Testosterone inhibitor: finasteride

INTRODUCTION

Acute urinary tract infections occur second in frequency only to respiratory tract infections in the American population. Females, with shorter urethras, are particularly vulnerable to repeated bladder and even kidney infections. Patients with indwelling catheters or intermittent catheterizations often are affected by bladder infections or ***cystitis,*** which can result from bacteria introduced into the bladder by these devices. Blockage anywhere in the urinary tract can lead to back-flow problems and the spread of bladder infections into the kidney.

The signs and symptoms of a urinary tract infection are uncomfortable and include ***urinary frequency; urgency;*** burning on urination (associated with cystitis); and chills, fever, flank pain, and tenderness (associated with acute ***pyelonephritis***). To treat these infections, clinicians use antibiotics (see Chapter 7) as well as specific agents that reach antibacterial levels only in the kidney and bladder and are thought to sterilize the urinary tract.

Drugs also are available to block spasms of the urinary tract muscles, decrease urinary tract pain, protect the cells of the bladder from irritation, and treat enlargement of the prostate gland in males. All of these agents will be discussed in this chapter. (Table 50-1 provides a summary of urinary tract problems and the drugs of choice to treat them.)

URINARY TRACT ANTI-INFECTIVES

Urinary tract anti-infectives are of two types. One type is the antibiotics, which include cinoxacin (*Cinobac Pulvules*), the newer and more broad spectrum drug norfloxacin (*Noroxin*), the new one-dose drug fosfomycin (*Monurol*), and the older drugs nalidixic acid (*NegGram*) and nitrofurantoin (*Furadantin*). The other type of urinary tract anti-infectives work to acidify the urine, killing bacteria that might be in the bladder. These include methenamine (*Hiprex*) and methylene blue (*Urolene Blue*).

THERAPEUTIC ACTIONS AND INDICATIONS

Urinary tract anti-infectives act specifically within the urinary tract to destroy bacteria, either through a direct antibiotic effect or through ***acidification*** of the urine. They do not have an antibiotic effect systemically, being activated or effective only in the urinary tract (Figure 50-1). They are used to treat chronic urinary tract infections, as adjunctive therapy in acute cystitis and pyelonephritis, and as prophylaxis with urinary tract anatomic abnormalities and residual urine disorders. Fosfomycin, a relatively new agent, is a one-dose only antibacterial. Ease of treatment makes this a very desirable agent; however, many patients experience unpleasant adverse effects, especially gastrointestinal (GI) effects, with this drug.

CONTRAINDICATIONS/CAUTIONS

These drugs are contraindicated in the presence of any known allergy to any of these drugs. They should be used with caution in the presence of renal dysfunction, which could interfere with the excretion and action of these drugs; and with pregnancy and lactation because of the potential for adverse effects on the neonate.

ADVERSE EFFECTS

Adverse effects associated with these drugs include nausea, vomiting, diarrhea, anorexia, bladder irritation, and dysuria. Infrequent symptoms include pruritus, urticaria, headache, dizziness, nervousness, and confusion. These effects may be due to GI irritation

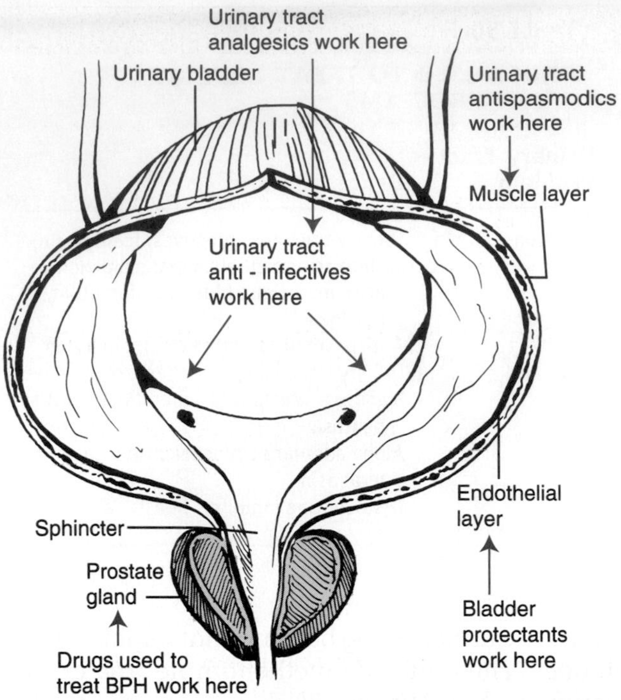

FIGURE 50-1. Sites of action of drugs acting on the urinary tract.

caused by the agent, which may be somewhat alleviated if the drug is taken with food, or to a systemic reaction to the urinary tract irritation.

CLINICALLY IMPORTANT DRUG–DRUG INTERACTIONS

Because these drugs are from several different chemical classes, the drug–drug interactions that can occur with these drugs are very specific to the drug being used. Consult your nursing drug guide for specific interactions.

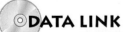

DATA LINK

Data link to the following urinary tract anti-infectives in your nursing drug guide:

URINARY TRACT ANTI-INFECTIVES

Name	Brand Name	Usual Indications
cinoxacin	*Cinobac Pulvules*	Treatment of urinary tract infections caused by susceptible bacteria
fosfomycin	*Monurol*	Treatment of urinary tract infections caused by susceptible bacteria (one-dose drug)
methenamine	*Hiprex*	Suppression or elimination of bacteriuria associated with urinary tract infections and anatomical abnormalities
methylene blue	*Urolene Blue*	Suppression or elimination of bacteriuria associated with urinary tract infections and anatomical abnormalities
nalidixic acid	*NegGram*	Treatment of urinary tract infections caused by susceptible bacteria
nitrofurantoin	*Furadantin*	Treatment of urinary tract infections caused by susceptible bacteria
P norfloxacin	*Noroxin*	Treatment of urinary tract infections caused by susceptible bacteria (broad-spectrum agent)

NURSING CONSIDERATIONS
for patients receiving urinary tract anti-infectives

Assessment

HISTORY: Screen for the following: any history of allergy to antibacterials; liver or renal dysfunction that might interfere with the drug's metabolism and excretion; and pregnancy or lactation, which are contraindications to the use of these drugs.

PHYSICAL ASSESSMENT: Physical assessment should be done to establish baseline data for assessing the effectiveness of the drug and the occurrence of any adverse effects associated with drug therapy. Assess for the following: skin to evaluate for the development of rash or hypersensitivity reactions; orientation and reflex assessment to evaluate any central nervous system (CNS) effects of the drug; and renal and hepatic function tests to determine baseline function of these organs.

Nursing Diagnoses

The patient receiving a urinary tract anti-infective may have the following nursing diagnoses related to drug therapy:

- Pain related to GI, CNS, skin effects of drug
- Sensory–perceptual alteration related to CNS effects
- Knowledge deficit regarding drug therapy

Implementation

- Ensure that culture and sensitivity tests are performed before beginning therapy and repeated if the response is not as expected *to ensure appropriate treatment of the infection.*
- Administer the drugs with food *to decrease GI adverse effects if they occur.*
- Institute safety precautions if the patient experiences CNS effects *to prevent patient injury.*

PATIENT TEACHING CHECKLIST

Urinary Tract Anti-infectives

Create customized patient teaching materials for a specific urinary tract anti-infective from your CD-ROM. Your patient teaching should stress the following points for drugs within this class:

A urinary tract anti-infective works to treat urinary tract infections by destroying bacteria and by helping produce an environment that is not conducive to bacterial growth.

If this drug causes stomach upset, it can be taken with food. It is important to avoid foods that alkalinize the urine, such as citrus fruits and milk, because they decrease the effectiveness of the drug. Cranberry juice is one juice that can be used. As much fluid as possible (8–10 glasses of water a day) should be taken to help treat the infection.

Avoid the use of any over-the-counter (OTC) medication that might contain sodium bicarbonate (e.g., antacids, baking soda) because these drugs will alkalinize the urine and will interfere with the ability of the drugs to treat the infection. If you question the use of any OTC drug, check with your health care provider.

Take the full course of your prescription. Do not use this drug to self-treat any other infection.

Common adverse effects of this drug may include:

- Stomach upset, nausea—Taking the drug with food or eating small, frequent meals may help.
- Painful urination—If this occurs, report it to your health care provider. A dosage adjustment may be needed.

The following activities can help to decrease urinary tract infections:

- Avoid bubble baths.
- Void whenever you feel the urge; try not to wait.
- Always try to void after sexual intercourse to flush the urethra.
- *For women:* Always wipe from front to back, never from back to front.

Report any of the following to your health care provider: skin rash or itching, severe GI upset, GI upset that prevents adequate fluid intake, very painful urination, pregnancy.

Tell any doctor, nurse, or other health care provider that you are taking this drug.

Keep this drug, and all medications, out of the reach of children.

This Teaching Checklist reflects general patient teaching guidelines. It is not meant to be a substitute for drug-specific teaching information; which is available in nursing drug guides.

- Advise patients to continue the full course of the drug ordered and to not stop taking it as soon as the uncomfortable signs and symptoms pass *to ensure eradication of the infection and prevent the emergence of resistant strains of bacteria.*
- Encourage the patient to push fluids (unless contraindicated by other conditions) *to flush the bladder and urinary tract frequently and decrease the opportunity for bacteria growth.*
- Educate patients with chronic urinary tract infections about additional activities *that can facilitate an acidic urine and increase the effectiveness of urinary tract anti-infectives.* For example, all patients should:
  - Avoid foods that cause an alkaline ash, producing an alkaline urine (e.g., citrus juices, fruits, antacids).
  - Drink high-acid cranberry juice.
  - Void immediately after sexual intercourse, to help clear any invading organisms.
  - *For women:*
  - Avoid baths if possible, especially bubble baths (because the bubbles act as transport agents to deliver bacteria through the short urethra).
  - Wipe front to back and never back to front, which introduces *E. coli* and other agents to the urethra.
- Provide thorough patient teaching, including the drug name and prescribed dosage, measures to help avoid adverse effects, warning signs that may indicate problems, and the need for periodic monitoring and evaluation *to enhance patient knowledge about drug therapy and to promote compliance* (see Patient Teaching Checklist: Urinary Tract Anti-infectives).

NURSING CARE GUIDE
Urinary Tract Anti-infectives

Assessment	***Nursing Diagnoses***	***Implementation***	***Evaluation***
HISTORY Allergies to antibacterials, liver or renal dysfunction, pregnancy and lactation.	Pain related to GI, CNS, skin effects of drug Sensory–perceptual alteration related to CNS effects Knowledge deficit regarding drug therapy	Obtain culture and sensitivity test of urine. Provide comfort and safety measures: safety precautions, skin care, nutrition. Encourage acidifying foods. Push fluids. Teach hygiene measures. Administer with food if GI upset is a problem. Provide support and reassurance to deal with drug effects and lifestyle changes. Provide patient teaching regarding drug name, dosage, adverse effects, precautions, warnings to report, hygiene measures, and dietary changes as needed.	Evaluate drug effects: relief of symptoms, resolution of infection. Monitor for adverse effects: GI upset, headache, dizziness, confusion, dysuria, pruritus, urticaria. Monitor for drug–drug interactions as indicated for each drug. Evaluate effectiveness of patient teaching program. Evaluate effectiveness of comfort and safety measures.
PHYSICAL EXAMINATION Neurological: orientation, reflexes, strength Skin: color, texture, edema GI: liver evaluation GU: urinary output Lab tests: liver function tests, urinalysis, urine for culture & sensitivity			

Evaluation

- Monitor patient response to the drug (resolution of urinary tract infection and relief of signs and symptoms); repeat culture and sensitivity tests are recommended for evaluation of the effectiveness of all of these drugs.
- Monitor for adverse effects (skin evaluation, orientation and reflexes, GI effects).
- Evaluate the effectiveness of the teaching plan (patient can name drug, dosage, adverse effects to watch for, specific measures to avoid adverse effects, and measures to take to increase the effectiveness of the drug).
- Monitor the effectiveness of comfort and safety measures and compliance to the regimen (see Nursing Care Guide: Urinary Tract Anti-infectives).

URINARY TRACT ANTISPASMODICS

Urinary tract ***antispasmodics*** block the spasms of urinary tract muscles caused by various conditions. Flavoxate (*Urispas*) prevents smooth muscle spasm specifically in the urinary tract, but is associated with CNS effects (blurred vision, dizziness, confusion) that make it less desirable to use in certain patients.

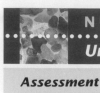

CASE STUDY

Teaching Plan for Treating Cystitis

PRESENTATION

J. K. is a 6-year-old girl with a history of repeated urinary tract infections. She is seen with complaints of dysuria, frequency, urgency, and a low-grade fever. A urine sample is sent for culture and sensitivity testing J. K. is started on methenamine, 500 mg qid, and referred to the nurse for teaching.

CRITICAL THINKING QUESTIONS

What is the best approach for this patient? What key teaching points (at least five) should be emphasized to assist the pharmacological therapy in treating this infection? Think about the following points: what the drug is doing, how it works, and how it works best.

DISCUSSION

Cystitis is very difficult to treat in young girls and can become a chronic problem. Patient and parent education is very important for trying to block the growth of bacteria and cure the infection. Teaching points should emphasize activities that will decrease the number of bacteria introduced into the bladder, acidify the urine to make the bladder an unpleasant environment for bacterial growth, and flush the bladder to prevent stagnant urine from encouraging bacteria growth.

To decrease the number of bacteria introduced into the bladder, patient education should cover the following hygiene measures: always wipe from front to back and never from back to front to avoid the introduction of intestinal bacteria into the urethra; avoid baths, particularly bubble baths, which facilitate the entry of bacteria into the urethra on the bubbles; and wear dry, cotton underwear to discourage bacteria growth.

Patient education also should stress the importance of avoiding alkaline ash foods (e.g., citrus fruits, certain vegetables) and encouraging foods that acidify the urine. Cranberry juice is often recommended as a choice for fruit juice because it helps to acidify the bladder and destroy bacteria. Fluid, especially water, should be pushed as much as possible to keep the bladder flushed out. Finally, the patient should be encouraged to complete the full course of medication prescribed and to not stop taking the drug when symptoms disappear.

Oxybutynin (*Ditropan*) is a potent urinary antispasmodic, but has numerous anticholinergic effects, making it undesirable in certain conditions or situations that might be aggravated by decreased sweating, urinary retention, tachycardia, and changes in GI activity.

THERAPEUTIC ACTIONS AND INDICATIONS

Inflammation in the urinary tract, such as cystitis, prostatitis, urethritis, and urethrocystitis/urethrotrigonitis, causes smooth muscle spasms along the urinary tract. Irritation of the urinary tract leading to muscle spasm also occurs with patients who have uninhibited neurogenic and neurogenic bladders. These spasms lead to the uncomfortable effects of ***dysuria,*** urgency, incontinence, ***nocturia,*** and suprapubic pain. The urinary tract antispasmodics act to relieve these spasms by blocking parasympathetic activity and relaxing the detrusor and other urinary tract muscles (see Figure 50-1).

CONTRAINDICATIONS/CAUTIONS

These drugs are contraindicated in the presence of known allergy to the drugs; with pyloric or duodenal obstruction or recent surgery, because the anticholinergic effects can cause serious complications; with obstructive urinary tract problems, which could be further aggravated by the blocking of muscle activity; with glaucoma, myasthenia gravis, or acute hemorrhage, which could all be exacerbated by the anticholinergic effects of these drugs. Caution should be used in the presence of renal or hepatic dysfunction, which could alter the metabolism and excretion of the drugs; and with pregnancy and lactation because of potential adverse effects on the neonate secondary to the anticholinergic effects of the drugs.

ADVERSE EFFECTS

Adverse effects of urinary tract antispasmodics are related to the blocking of the parasympathetic system and include nausea, vomiting, dry mouth, nervousness, tachycardia, and vision changes.

CLINICALLY IMPORTANT DRUG–DRUG INTERACTIONS

Decreased effectiveness of phenothiazines and haloperidol has been associated with the combination of these drugs with oxybutynin. If any such combinations must be used, the patient should be monitored closely and appropriate dosage adjustments made.

DATA LINK

Data link to the following urinary tract antispasmodics in your nursing drug guide:

URINARY TRACT ANTISPASMODICS

Name	Brand Name	Usual Indications
flavoxate	*Urispas*	Symptomatic relief of urinary bladder spasm
P oxybutynin	*Ditropan*	Symptomatic relief of urinary bladder spasm

NURSING CONSIDERATIONS
for patients receiving urinary tract antispasmodics

Assessment

HISTORY: Screen for the following: any history of allergy to these drugs; pyloric or duodenal obstruction or other GI lesions or obstructions, which could be dangerously exacerbated by these drugs; obstructions of the lower urinary tract, which could also be exacerbated by these drugs; glaucoma, which requires caution because of the blockage of the parasympathetic nervous system and potential for increased intraocular pressure; and pregnancy or lactation, which require caution if using these drugs.

PHYSICAL ASSESSMENT: Physical assessment should be done to establish baseline data for assessing the effectiveness of the drug and the occurrence of any adverse effects associated with drug therapy. Assess the following: skin to evaluate for the development of rash or hypersensitivity reactions; orientation and reflex assessment to evaluate any CNS effects of the drug; ophthalmic examination including intraocular pressure to assess for any developing glaucoma; and pulse to establish a baseline for evaluating extent of parasympathetic block.

Nursing Diagnoses

The patient receiving a urinary tract antispasmodic may have the following nursing diagnoses related to drug therapy:

- Pain related to GI, CNS, ophthalmologic effects of drug
- Sensory–perceptual alteration related to CNS, ophthalmologic effects
- Knowledge deficit regarding drug therapy

Implementation

- Arrange for appropriate treatment of any underlying urinary tract infection, *which may be causing the spasm.*
- Arrange for an ophthalmologic examination at the beginning of therapy and periodically during long-term treatment *to evaluate drug effects on intraocular pressure so that the drug can be stopped if intraocular pressure increases.*
- Institute safety precautions if the patient experiences CNS effects *to prevent patient injury.*
- Encourage the patient to continue treatment for the underlying cause of the spasm *to treat the cause and prevent the return of the signs and symptoms.*
- Provide thorough patient teaching, including the drug name and prescribed dosage, measures to help avoid adverse effects, warning signs that may indicate problems, and the need for periodic monitoring and evaluation *to enhance patient knowledge about drug therapy and to promote compliance.*
- Offer support and encouragement *to deal with the discomfort of the drug therapy.*

Evaluation

- Monitor patient response to the drug (resolution of urinary tract spasms and relief of signs and symptoms); repeat culture and sensitivity tests are recommended for evaluation of the effectiveness of all of these drugs.
- Monitor for adverse effects (skin evaluation, orientation and reflexes, intraocular pressure).
- Evaluate the effectiveness of the teaching plan (patient can name drug, dosage, adverse effects to watch for, specific measures to avoid adverse effects).
- Monitor the effectiveness of comfort and safety measures and compliance to the regimen.

URINARY TRACT ANALGESIC

Urinary tract pain can be very uncomfortable and lead to urinary retention and increased risk of infection. The agent phenazopyridine (*Azo-Standard, Baridium,* and others) is a dye that is used to relieve that pain.

THERAPEUTIC ACTIONS AND INDICATIONS

When phenazopyridine is excreted in the urine, it exerts a direct, topical analgesic effect on the urinary tract mucosa (see Figure 50-1). It is used to relieve symptoms (burning, urgency, frequency, pain, discomfort) related to urinary tract irritation from infection, trauma, or surgery.

CONTRAINDICATIONS/CAUTIONS

Phenazopyridine is contraindicated in the presence of known allergy to the drug and with serious renal dysfunction which would interfere with the excretion and effectiveness of the drug. Caution should be used with pregnancy and lactation because of the potential for adverse effects on the neonate.

ADVERSE EFFECTS

Adverse effects associated with this drug include GI upset, headache, rash, and a reddish-orange coloring of the urine, all of which are related to the drug's chemical actions in the system. There also is potential for renal or hepatic toxicity. This drug should not be used longer than 2 days because the toxic effects may be increased.

CLINICALLY IMPORTANT DRUG–DRUG INTERACTIONS

There is an increased risk of toxic effects of this drug if combined with antibacterial agents used for treating urinary tract infections. If this combination is used, the phenazopyridine should not be used longer than 2 days.

DATA LINK

Data link to the following urinary tract analgesic in your nursing drug guide:

URINARY TRACT ANALGESIC

Name	Brand Name(s)	Usual Indications
phenazopyridine	*Azo-Standard, Baridium*	Symptomatic relief of the discomforts associated with urinary tract trauma or infection

NURSING CONSIDERATIONS
for patients receiving a urinary tract analgesic

Assessment

HISTORY: Screen for the following: history of allergy to these drugs or renal insufficiency, which are contraindications to the use of this drug; pregnancy or lactation, which require caution if using this drug.

PHYSICAL ASSESSMENT: Physical assessment should be done to establish baseline data for assessing the effectiveness of the drug and the occurrence of any adverse effects associated with drug therapy. Assess for the following: skin to evaluate for the development of rash or hypersensitivity reactions; normal GI function and liver evaluation to establish baseline data to assess adverse effects of the drug; renal and hepatic function tests to assess for any underlying condition that might affect the metabolism or excretion of this drug; urinalysis to assess for underlying infection or renal problems.

Nursing Diagnoses

The patient receiving a urinary tract analgesic may have the following nursing diagnoses related to drug therapy:

- Pain related to GI effects of drug and headache
- Knowledge deficit regarding drug therapy

Implementation

- Arrange for appropriate treatment of any underlying urinary tract infection *which may be causing the pain.*
- Caution the patient that urine may be reddish-brown and may stain fabrics *to prevent undue anxiety when this adverse effect occurs.*
- Administer the drug with food *to alleviate GI irritation if GI upset is a problem.*
- Teach the patient to discontinue the drug and contact the health care provider if sclera or skin become yellowish—*a sign of drug accumulation in the body and a possible sign of hepatic toxicity.*
- Provide thorough patient teaching, including the drug name and prescribed dosage, measures to help avoid adverse effects, warning signs that may indicate problems, and the need for periodic monitoring and evaluation *to enhance patient knowledge about drug therapy and to promote compliance.*

Evaluation

- Monitor patient response to the drug (resolution of urinary tract pain).
- Monitor for adverse effects (skin evaluation, GI upset and complaints, headache).
- Evaluate the effectiveness of the teaching plan (patient can name drug, dosage, adverse effects to watch for, specific measures to avoid adverse effects).
- Monitor the effectiveness of comfort measures and compliance to the regimen.

BLADDER PROTECTANT

The bladder protectant pentosan polysulfate sodium (*Nipent*) is used to coat or adhere to the bladder mucosal wall and protect it from irritation related to solutes in the urine.

THERAPEUTIC ACTIONS AND INDICATIONS

Pentosan polysulfate sodium is a heparin-like compound that has anticoagulant and fibrinolytic effects. This drug adheres to the bladder wall mucosal membrane and acts as a buffer to control cell permeability, preventing irritating solutes in the urine from reaching the bladder wall cells (see Figure 50-1). It is used specifically to decrease the pain and discomfort associated with *interstitial cystitis.*

CONTRAINDICATIONS/CAUTIONS

Because of its heparin-like effects it should not be used with any condition that involves an increased risk of bleeding (surgery, pregnancy, anticoagulation, hemophilia). It is also contraindicated in the presence of a history of heparin-induced thrombocytopenia, which could recur with this drug. Caution should be used with hepatic or splenic dysfunction which could be affected by the heparin-like actions of the drug; and with pregnancy and lactation because of the potential for adverse effects on the fetus.

ADVERSE EFFECTS

Adverse effects associated with pentosan use include bleeding that may progress to hemorrhage (related to the drug's heparin effects), headache, alopecia (seen with heparin-type drugs), and GI disturbances related to local irritation on the GI tract with administration.

CLINICALLY IMPORTANT DRUG–DRUG INTERACTIONS

There is a potential for increased bleeding risks if combined with anticoagulants, aspirin, or NSAIDs. If this combination is used, the patient should be monitored very closely for any signs of bleeding and appropriate dosage adjustments should be made.

DATA LINK

Data link to the following bladder protectant in your nursing drug guide:

BLADDER PROTECTANT

Name	Brand Name	Usual Indications
pentosan polysulfate sodium	*Nipent*	Relief of bladder pain or discomfort associated with interstitial cystitis

NURSING CONSIDERATIONS
for patients receiving a bladder protectant

Assessment

HISTORY: Screen for the following: history of allergy to this drug; history of bleeding abnormalities, splenic disorders, or hepatic dysfunction, which could result in bleeding when combined with the heparin-like effect of this drug; and pregnancy and lactation, which require cautious use of this drug.

PHYSICAL ASSESSMENT: Physical assessment should be done to establish baseline data for assessing the effectiveness of the drug and the occurrence of any adverse effects associated with drug therapy. Assess the following: skin to evaluate for the development of rash or hypersensitivity reactions; orientation, affect, and reflexes to establish a baseline to evaluate CNS effects of the drug; and liver function tests and bleeding times to establish a baseline to monitor safe use of the drug and occurrence of adverse effects.

Nursing Diagnoses

The patient receiving a bladder protectant may have the following nursing diagnoses related to drug therapy:

- Alteration in perfusion related to bleeding related to heparin effects of the drug
- Pain related to headache, CNS effects, and GI effects of the drug
- Potential alteration in safety related to bleeding and CNS effects
- Knowledge deficit regarding drug therapy

Implementation

- Establish the presence of interstitial cystitis by biopsy or cytoscopy before beginning therapy *to ensure appropriate therapy is being used.*
- Administer the drug on an empty stomach, 1 hour before or 2 hours after meals, *to relieve GI discomfort and improve absorption.*
- Monitor bleeding times periodically during therapy *to assess for excessive heparin effect.*
- Arrange for wig or appropriate head covering *if alopecia develops as a result of drug therapy.*
- Provide thorough patient teaching, including the drug name and prescribed dosage, measures to help avoid adverse effects, warning signs that may indicate problems, and the need for periodic monitoring and evaluation *to enhance patient knowledge about drug therapy and to promote compliance.*

Evaluation

- Monitor patient response to the drug (relief of bladder pain and discomfort).
- Monitor for adverse effects (skin evaluation, GI upset and complaints, headache, bleeding time).
- Evaluate the effectiveness of the teaching plan (patient can name drug, dosage, adverse effects to watch for, specific measures to avoid adverse effects).
- Monitor the effectiveness of comfort measures and compliance with the regimen.

WWW.WEB LINKS

Health care providers and patients may want to consult the following Internet sources:

Information on BPH, support groups, research, treatment for patients:
http://www.pslgroup.com/ENLARGPROST.HTM

Information on BPH research and medical information:
http://www.uro.com/bph.htm

Information on neurogenic bladder:
http://www.a-urology.com/BladComm.HTM

Information on interstitial cystitis:
http://www.ichelp.org

Information on cystitis—research, prevention, treatment, pathology:
http://thedailyapple.com/Level3/w3/cyhmw3.htm

DRUGS FOR TREATING BENIGN PROSTATIC HYPERPLASIA (BPH)

Two types of drugs are currently used to relieve the symptoms of benign prostatic hyperplasia (BPH) in males. Alpha adrenergic blockers doxazosin (*Cardura*), tamsulosin (*Flomax*), and terazosin (*Hytrin*) are used to block the dilation of arterioles in the bladder and urinary tract. Tamsulosin was developed specifically for the treatment of BPH and is not associated with as many of the adverse adrenergic blocking effects as the other two drugs. Finasteride (*Proscar*) is specifically used to treat BPH by blocking testosterone production and is associated with more androgen blocking effects than the other drugs.

THERAPEUTIC ACTIONS AND INDICATIONS

BPH is a common problem in males, increasing in incidence with age. This enlargement of the gland surrounding the urethra leads to discomfort, difficulty in initiating a stream of urine, feelings of bloating, and an increased incidence of cystitis. Alpha adrenergic blockers are indicated for the treatment of symptomatic BPH. These drugs block postsynaptic $alpha_1$-adrenergic receptors, which results in a dilation of arterioles and veins and a relaxation of sympathetic effects on the bladder and urinary tract. These drugs are also indicated for the treatment of hypertension (see Chapter 41).

Finasteride, another drug used for treating BPH, inhibits the intracellular enzyme that converts testosterone to a potent androgen (DHT), which the prostate gland depends on for its development and maintenance (see Figure 50-1). This drug is used for long-term therapy to shrink the prostate and relieve the symptoms of hyperplasia. It is also used to prevent male-pattern baldness in patients with a strong family history.

When any of these drugs are used, it is important to make sure that the prostate enlargement is benign and not caused by cancer, infection, stricture, or hypotonic bladder. Patients on long-term therapy will need to be reassessed periodically.

CONTRAINDICATIONS/CAUTIONS

These drugs are contraindicated in the presence of allergy to the drugs, and with pregnancy and lactation (though not a consideration if used to treat BPH). Caution should be used in the presence of hepatic or renal dysfunction which could alter the metabolism and excretion of the drugs. The adrenergic blockers should be used with caution in the presence of congestive heart failure or known coronary disease.

ADVERSE EFFECTS

Adverse effects of alpha adrenergic blockers include headache, fatigue, dizziness, postural dizziness, lethargy, tachycardia, hypotension, GI upset, and sexual dysfunction, all of which are effects seen with the blocking of the alpha receptors. Finasteride is associated with decreased libido, impotence, and sexual dysfunction, all of which are related to decreased DHT levels.

CLINICALLY IMPORTANT DRUG–DRUG INTERACTIONS

There is a possibility of decreased theophylline levels if combined with these drugs. The patient should be monitored and appropriate dosage adjustment made if this combination is used.

DATA LINK

Data link to the following drugs to treat BPH in your nursing drug guide:

DRUGS USED TO TREAT BPH

Name	Brand Name	Usual Indications
P doxazosin	*Cardura*	Relief of symptoms of BPH; hypertension
finasteride	*Proscar*	Relief of symptoms of BPH; prevention of male-pattern baldness
tamsulosin	*Flomax*	Treatment of BPH
terazosin	*Hytrin*	Relief of symptoms of BPH; hypertension

NURSING CONSIDERATIONS for patients receiving drugs to treat BPH

Assessment

HISTORY: Screen for the following: history of allergy to this drug; history of congestive heart failure; and renal or hepatic failure, which would require caution when using these drugs.

PHYSICAL ASSESSMENT: Physical assessment should be done to establish baseline data for assessing the effectiveness of the drug and the occurrence of any adverse effects associated with drug therapy. Assess the following: skin to evaluate for the development of rash or hypersensitivity reactions; blood pressure, pulse, auscultation, perfusion to evaluate the cardiovascular effects of alpha adrenergic blockade; urinalysis and normal urinary function; prostate palpation and appropriate tests, including prostate-specific antigen (PSA) levels to evaluate prostate problems.

Nursing Diagnoses

The patient receiving a bladder protectant may have the following nursing diagnoses related to drug therapy:

- Potential alteration in sexual function related to drug effects
- Pain related to headache, CNS effects, and GI effects of the drug
- Knowledge deficit regarding drug therapy

Implementation

- Determine the presence of BPH and periodically evaluate *to reconfirm that no other problem is occurring through prostate exam and PSA levels.*
- Administer the drug without regard to meals, but give with meals *if GI upset is a problem.*
- Provide thorough patient teaching, including the drug name and prescribed dosage, measures to help avoid adverse effects, warning signs that may indicate problems, and the need for periodic monitoring and evaluation *to enhance patient knowledge about drug therapy and to promote compliance.*
- Offer support and encouragement *to cope with potential decreases in sexual functioning.*

Evaluation

- Monitor patient response to the drug (relief of signs and symptoms of BPH, improved urine flow, and decrease in discomfort).
- Monitor for adverse effects (skin evaluation, GI upset and complaints, headache, cardiovascular effects).
- Evaluate the effectiveness of the teaching plan (patient can name drug, dosage, adverse effects to watch for, specific measures to avoid adverse effects).
- Monitor the effectiveness of comfort measures and compliance with the regimen.

CHAPTER SUMMARY

- Acute urinary tract infections are second in frequency to respiratory tract infections in the American population.
- Urinary tract anti-infectives are drugs used to kill bacteria in the urinary tract by producing an acidic urine, which is undesirable to bacteria growth, or by acting to destroy bacteria in the urinary tract.
- Many activities are necessary to help decrease the bacteria in the urinary tract (e.g., hygiene measures, proper diet, and forcing fluids) to facilitate the treatment of urinary tract infections and help the urinary tract anti-infectives to be more effective.
- Inflammation and irritation of the urinary tract can cause smooth muscle spasms along the urinary tract. These spasms lead to the uncomfortable effects of dysuria, urgency, incontinence, nocturia, and suprapubic pain.
- The urinary tract antispasmodics act to relieve spasms of the urinary tract muscles by blocking parasympathetic activity and relaxing the detrusor and other urinary tract muscles.
- The urinary tract analgesic, phenazopyridine, is used to provide relief of symptoms (burning, urgency, frequency, pain, discomfort) related to urinary tract irritation from infection, trauma, and surgery.
- Pentosan polysulfate sodium is a heparin-like compound that has anticoagulant and fibrinolytic effects and adheres to the bladder wall mucosal membrane to act as a buffer to control cell permeability. This action prevents irritating solutes in the urine from reaching the bladder wall cells. It is used specifically to decrease the pain and discomfort associated with interstitial cystitis.
- Benign prostatic hyperplasia (BPH) is a common enlargement of the prostate gland in older males.
- Drugs commonly used to relieve the signs and symptoms of prostate enlargement include alpha adrenergic blockers, which relax the sympathetic effects on the bladder and sphincters, and finasteride, which blocks the body's production of a powerful androgen. The prostate is dependent on testosterone for its maintenance and development; blocking the androgen leads to shrinkage of the gland and relief of symptoms.

BIBLIOGRAPHY

Bullock, B. L. (2000). *Focus on pathophysiology.* Philadelphia: Lippincott Williams & Wilkins.

Hardman, J. G., Limbird, L. E., Molinoff, P. B., Ruddon, R. W., & Gilman, A. G. (Eds.). (1996). *Goodman and Gilman's the pharmacological basis of therapeutics* (9th ed.). New York: McGraw-Hill.

Karch, A. M. (2000). *2000 Lippincott's nursing drug guide.* Philadelphia: Lippincott Williams & Wilkins.

Malseed, R. (1995). *Textbook of pharmacology and nursing care.* Philadelphia: J. B. Lippincott.

McEvoy, B. R. (Ed.). (1999). *Facts and comparisons 1999.* St. Louis: Facts and Comparisons.

Professional's guide to patient drug facts. (1999). St. Louis: Facts and Comparisons.

PART

10

Drugs Acting on the Respiratory System

CHAPTER 51

Introduction to the Respiratory System

CHAPTER OUTLINE

KEY TERMS

alveoli
asthma
bronchial tree
chronic obstructive pulmonary disease (COPD)
cilia
common cold
cough
larynx
lower respiratory tract
pneumonia
respiration
respiratory membrane
seasonal rhinitis
sinuses
sinusitis
sneeze
surfactant
trachea
upper respiratory tract
ventilation

INTRODUCTION

The respiratory system is essential for survival. It brings oxygen into the body, allowing for the exchange of gases and expelling carbon dioxide and other waste products. The normal functioning of the respiratory system depends on an intricate balance of the nervous, cardiovascular, and musculoskeletal systems. The respiratory system consists of two parts: the ***upper respiratory tract*** and the ***lower respiratory tract.*** The upper portion, or conducting airways, is composed of the nose, mouth, pharynx, larynx, trachea, and the upper ***bronchial tree*** (Figure 51-1). The lower portion is made up of the smallest bronchi and the ***alveoli*** (respiratory sacs), which make up the lungs.

THE UPPER RESPIRATORY TRACT

Air usually moves into the body through the nose and into the nasal cavity. The nasal hairs catch and filter foreign substances that may be present in the inhaled air. The air is warmed and humidified as it passes by blood vessels close to the surface of the epithelial lining in the nasal cavity. The epithelial lining contains goblet cells that produce mucus, which traps dust, microorganisms, pollen, and any other foreign substances. The epithelial cells of this lining contain ***cilia,*** microscopic, hair-like projections of the cell membrane, which are constantly moving and directing the mucus and any trapped substances down toward the throat (Figure 51-2).

Pairs of ***sinuses*** (air-filled passages through the skull) open into the nasal cavity. Because the epithelial lining of the nasal passage is continuous with the lining of the sinuses, the mucus produced in the sinuses drains into the nasal cavity. From there, the mucus drains into the throat and is swallowed into the gastrointestinal tract, where stomach acid destroys foreign materials.

Air moves from the nasal cavity into the pharynx and ***larynx.*** The larynx contains the vocal chords and the epiglottis, which close during swallowing to protect the lower respiratory tract from any foreign particles. From the larynx, air proceeds to the ***trachea,*** the main conducting airway into the lungs. The trachea bifurcates, or divides, into two main bronchi, which further divide into smaller and smaller branches. All of these tubes contain mucus-producing goblet cells and cilia to entrap any particles that may have escaped the upper protective mechanisms. The cilia in these tubes move the mucus up the trachea into the throat, where again it is swallowed.

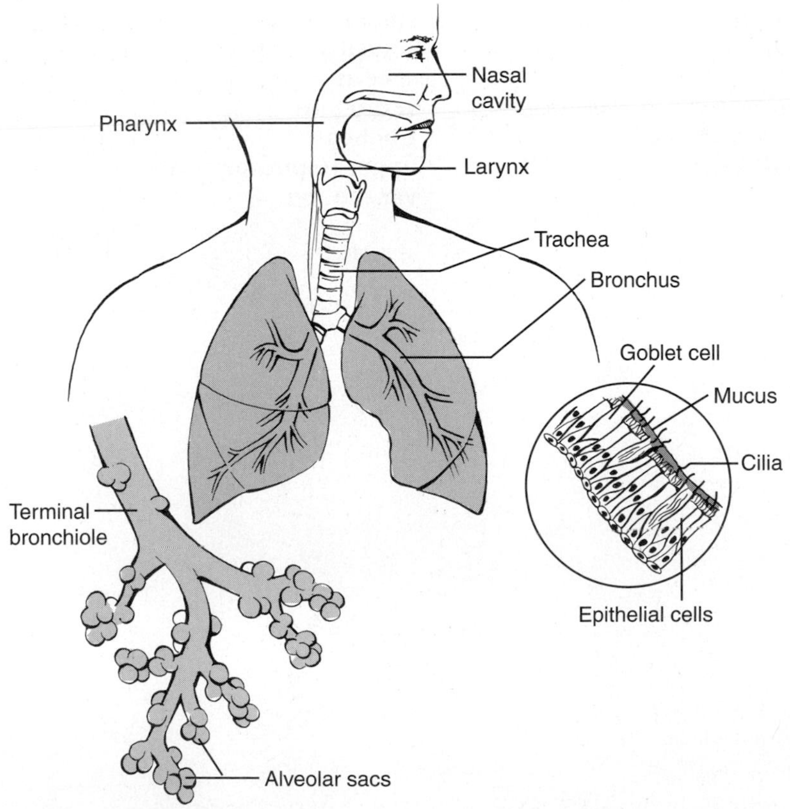

FIGURE 51-1. The respiratory tract.

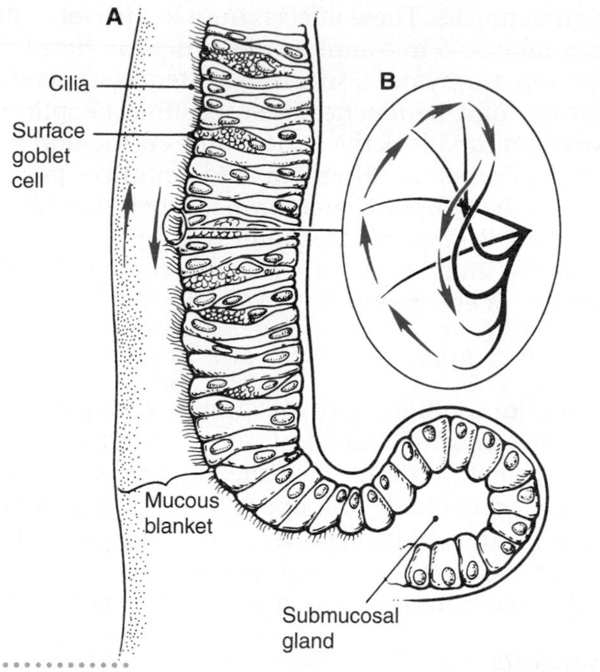

FIGURE 51-2. (*A*) The mucociliary escalator. (*B*) Conceptual scheme of ciliary movement, which allows forward motion to move the viscous gel layer and backward motion to occur entirely within the more fluid sol layer. (Bullock, B. L. [2000]. *Focus on pathophysiology.* Philadelphia: Lippincott Williams & Wilkins.)

The bronchial tubes are composed of three layers: cartilage, muscle, and epithelial cells. The cartilage keeps the tube open and becomes progressively less abundant as the bronchi divide and get smaller. The muscles keep the bronchi open; the muscles in the bronchi become smaller and less abundant, with only a few muscle fibers remaining in the terminal bronchi and alveoli. The epithelial cells are very similar in structure and function to the epithelial cells in the nasal passage.

The walls of the trachea and conducting bronchi are highly sensitive to irritation. When receptors in the walls are stimulated, a central nervous system reflex is initiated and a ***cough*** results. The cough causes air to be pushed through the bronchial tree under tremendous pressure, cleaning out any foreign irritant. This reflex, along with the similar ***sneeze*** reflex (which is initiated by receptors in the nasal cavity), forces foreign materials directly out of the system, opening it for more efficient flow of gas.

Throughout the airways, many macrophage scavengers freely move about the epithelium and destroy invaders. Mast cells are present in abundance and release histamine, serotonin, adenosine triphosphate (ATP), and other chemicals to assure a rapid and intense inflammatory reaction to any cell injury. The end result of these various defense mechanisms is that the lower respiratory tract is virtually sterile—an important protection against respiratory infection that could interfere with essential gas exchange.

THE LOWER RESPIRATORY TRACT

The lower respiratory tract, or the respiratory airways, is composed of the smallest bronchioles and the alveoli (see Figure 51-1). These structures are the functional units of the lungs. Within the lungs are a network of bronchi, alveoli, and blood vessels. The lung tissue receives its blood supply from the bronchial artery, which branches directly off the aorta. The alveoli receive unoxygenated blood from the right ventricle via the pulmonary artery. The delivery of this blood to the alveoli is referred to as perfusion.

Gas exchange occurs in the alveoli. In this process, carbon dioxide is lost from the blood and oxygen is transferred to the blood. The exchange of gases at the alveolar level is called ***ventilation.*** The alveolar sac holds the gas, allowing needed oxygen to diffuse across the ***respiratory membrane*** into the capillary while carbon dioxide, which is more abundant in the capillary blood, diffuses across the membrane and enters the alveolar sac to be expired.

The respiratory membrane is made up of the capillary endothelium, the capillary basement membrane, the interstitial space, the alveolar basement membrane, the alveolar epithelium, and the surfactant layer (Figure 51-3). The sac is able to stay open because the surface tension of the cells is decreased by the lipoprotein ***surfactant.*** Absence of surfactant leads to alveolar collapse. Surfactant is produced by the type-2 cells in the alveoli. These cells have other

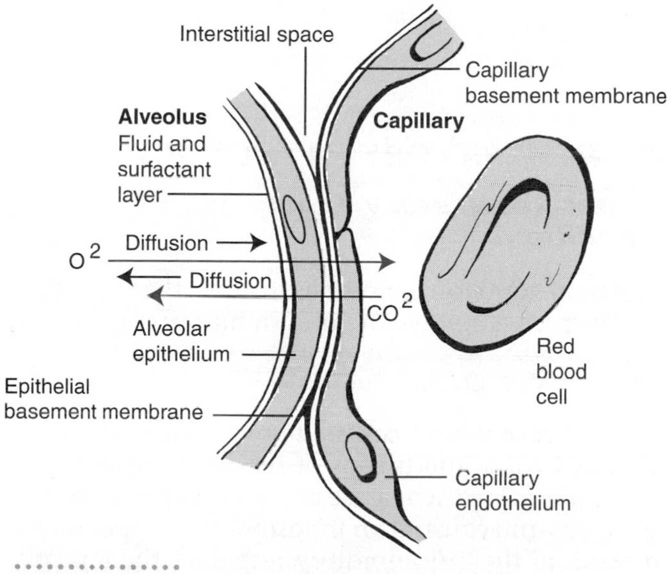

FIGURE 51-3. The respiratory membrane.

metabolic functions including the conversion of angiotensin I to angiotensin II, the degradation of serotonin, and possibly the metabolism of various hormones. The oxygenated blood is returned to the left atrium via the pulmonary veins and from there is pumped throughout the body to deliver oxygen to the cells and to pick up waste products.

RESPIRATION

Respiration, or the act of breathing, is controlled by the central nervous system. The inspiratory muscles—diaphragm, external intercostals, and abdominal muscles—are stimulated to contract by the respiratory center in the medulla. The medulla receives input from chemoreceptors (neuroreceptors sensitive to carbon dioxide and acid levels) and increases the rate and/or depth of respiration to maintain homeostasis in the body.

The vagus nerve, a predominantly parasympathetic nerve, plays a key role in stimulating diaphragm contraction and inspiration. The vagal stimulation also leads to a bronchoconstriction or tightening. The sympathetic system also innervates the respiratory system. Stimulation of the sympathetic system leads to increased rate and depth of respiration and dilation of the bronchi to allow freer air flow through the system.

WWW.WEB LINKS

To explore the virtual respiratory tract, refer to the following Internet sources:

http://www.InnerBody.com

http://www.biostr.washington.edu/DigitalAnatomist.html

RESPIRATORY PATHOLOGY

Upper Respiratory Tract Conditions

The most common conditions to affect the upper respiratory tract involve the inflammatory response.

THE COMMON COLD

A number of viruses cause the ***common cold.*** These viruses invade the tissues of the upper respiratory tract, initiating the release of histamine and prostaglandins and causing an inflammatory response. As a result of the inflammatory response, the mucous membranes become engorged with blood, the tissues swell, and the goblet cells increase the production of mucus. These effects cause the person with a common cold to complain of sinus pain, nasal congestion, runny nose, sneezing, watery eyes, scratchy throat, and headache. In susceptible people, this swelling can block the outlet of the eustachian tube, which drains the inner ear and equalizes pressure across the tympanic membrane. When this outlet is blocked, feelings of ear stuffiness and pain can occur and the individual is more likely to develop otitis media, or ear infection.

SEASONAL RHINITIS

A similar condition that afflicts many people is allergic or ***seasonal rhinitis*** (an inflammation of the nasal cavity), commonly called hay fever. This condition occurs when the upper airways respond to a specific antigen (e.g., pollen, mold, dust) with a vigorous inflammatory response resulting again in nasal congestion, sneezing, stuffiness, and watery eyes.

SINUSITIS

Other areas of the upper respiratory tract can become irritated or infected with a resultant inflammation of that particular area. ***Sinusitis*** occurs when the epithelial lining of the sinus cavities becomes inflamed. The resultant swelling that occurs often causes severe pain as the bony cavity cannot stretch and the swollen tissue pushes against the bone and blocks the sinus passage. The danger of a sinus infection is that if untreated, microorganisms can move up the sinus passages and into brain tissue.

PHARYNGITIS AND LARYNGITIS

Pharyngitis and laryngitis are infections of the pharynx and larynx respectively. These infections are frequently caused by common bacteria or viruses. Pharyngitis and laryngitis are frequently seen with influenza, which is caused by a variety of different viruses and produces the uncomfortable respiratory symptoms of other inflammations along with a fever, muscle aches and pains, and malaise.

Lower Respiratory Tract Conditions

A number of disorders affect the lower respiratory tract, including atelectasis, ***pneumonia*** (bacterial, viral, or aspiration), bronchitis or inflammation of the bronchi (acute and chronic), bronchiectasis, and the obstructive disorders—asthma, chronic obstructive pulmonary disease (COPD), cystic fibrosis, and respiratory distress syndrome. Tuberculosis, discussed in Chapter 7, is a bacterial infection. Once known as consumption, this disease was responsible for many respiratory deaths throughout the centuries. All of these disorders involve, to some degree, an alteration in the ability to move gases in and out of the respiratory system.

ATELECTASIS

Atelectasis, the collapse of once-expanded lung tissue, can occur as a result of outside pressure against the alveoli, for example, from a pulmonary tumor, a pneumothorax (air in the pleural space exerting high pressure against the alveoli), or a pleural effusion. Atelectasis most commonly occurs as a result of blockage of the airway, preventing air from entering the alveoli and keeping it expanded. This occurs when a mucous plug, edema of the bronchioles, or a collection of pus or secretions occludes an airway and prevents the movement of air. Patients may experience atelectasis following surgery, when the effects of anesthesia on the lungs, pain, and decreased coughing reflexes can lead to a decreased tidal volume and accumulation of secretions in the lower airways. Patients may present with rales, dyspnea, fever, cough, hypoxia, and changes in chest wall movement. Treatment may involve clearing the airways, delivery of oxygen, and assisted ventilation.

PNEUMONIA

Pneumonia is an inflammation of the lungs caused either by bacterial or viral invasion of the tissue, or by aspiration of foreign substances into the lower respiratory tract. The rapid inflammatory response to any foreign presence in the lower respiratory tract leads to a localized swelling, engorgement, and exudation of protective sera. The respiratory membrane is affected, resulting in decreased gas exchange. Patients complain of difficulty breathing and fatigue and present with fever, noisy breath sounds, and poor oxygenation.

BRONCHITIS

Acute bronchitis occurs when bacteria, viruses, or foreign materials infect the inner layer of the bronchi. The person with bronchitis may have a narrowed airway during the inflammation; this condition can be very serious in a person with obstructed or narrowed airflow. Chronic bronchitis is an inflammation of the bronchi that does not clear.

BRONCHIECTASIS

Bronchiectasis is a chronic disease that involves the bronchi and bronchioles. It is characterized by dilation of the bronchial tree and chronic infection and inflammation of the bronchial passages. With chronic inflammation, the bronchial epithelial cells are replaced by a fibrous scar tissue. The loss of the protective mucous and ciliary movement of the epithelial cell membranes, combined with the dilation of the bronchial tree, leads to chronic infections in the now unprotected lower areas of the lung tissue. Patients with bronchiectasis often have an underlying medical condition that makes them more susceptible to infections (e.g., immune suppression, AIDS, chronic inflammatory conditions). Patients present with the signs and symptoms of acute infection, including fever, malaise, myalgia, and arthralgia, and with a purulent, productive cough.

OBSTRUCTIVE PULMONARY DISEASES

As noted previously, the obstructive pulmonary diseases include asthma, cystic fibrosis, COPD, and respiratory distress syndrome.

Asthma is characterized by reversible bronchospasm, inflammation, and hyperactive airways (Figure 51-4). The hyperactivity is triggered by allergens or non-allergic inhaled irritants or by factors such as exercise and emotions. The triggers cause an immediate release of histamine, causing bronchospasm in about 10 minutes. The later response (3–5 hours) is cytokine-mediated inflammation, mucus production, and edema contributing to the obstruction. Appropriate treatment depends on understanding the early and late responses. The extreme case of asthma is called status asthmaticus; this is a life-threatening bronchospasm that does not

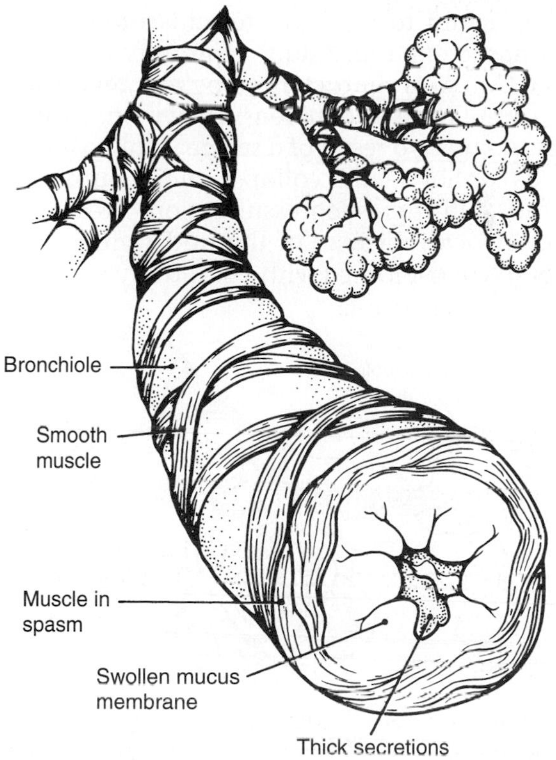

FIGURE 51-4. Asthma. The bronchiole is obstructed on expiration, particularly by muscle spasm, edema of the mucosa, and thick secretions. (Bullock, B. L. [2000]. *Focus on pathophysiology*. Philadelphia: Lippincott Williams & Wilkins.)

respond to usual treatment and occludes air flow into the lungs.

Chronic obstructive pulmonary disease (COPD) is a permanent, chronic obstruction of airways, often related to cigarette smoking. It is caused by two related disorders: emphysema and chronic bronchitis, both resulting in airflow obstruction on expiration; and overinflated lungs and poor gas exchange. Emphysema is characterized by loss of the elastic tissue of the lungs, destruction of alveolar walls, and a resultant hyperinflation and tendency to collapse with expiration. Chronic bronchitis is a permanent inflammation of the airways, with mucus secretion, edema, and poor inflammatory defenses. Characteristics of both disorders often are present in the person with COPD (Figure 51-5).

Cystic fibrosis is a hereditary disease that results in an accumulation of copious amounts of very thick secretions in the lungs. Eventually, the secretions will obstruct the airways, leading to destruction of the lung tissue. Treatment is aimed at keeping the secretions fluid and moving and maintaining airway patency as much as possible.

Respiratory distress syndrome is frequently seen in premature babies delivered before the lungs have fully developed and surfactant levels are still very low. Surfactant is necessary for lowering the surface tension in the alveoli so that they can stay open to allow the flow of gases. Treatment is aimed at instilling surfactant to prevent atelectasis and to allow the lungs to expand. Adult respiratory distress syndrome (ARDS) is characterized by progressive loss of lung compliance and increasing hypoxia. This syndrome occurs as a result of a severe insult to the body, such as cardiovascular collapse, major burns, severe trauma, and rapid depressurization. Treatment of ARDS involves reversal of the underlying cause of the problem combined with ventilatory support.

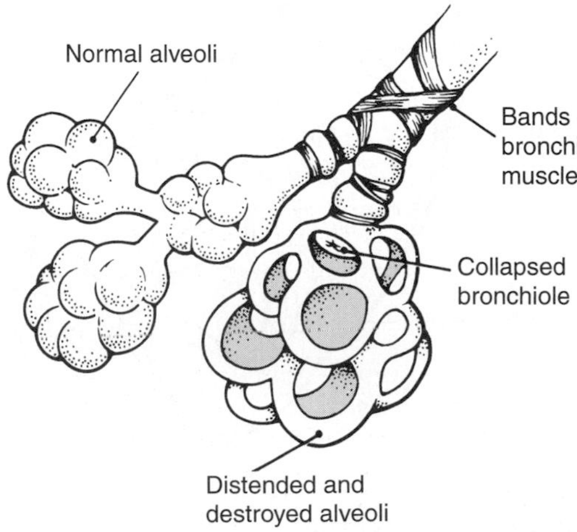

FIGURE 51-5. Distended and destroyed alveoli versus normal alveoli. (Bullock, B. L. [2000]. *Focus on pathophysiology*. Philadelphia: Lippincott Williams & Wilkins.)

CHAPTER SUMMARY

- The respiratory system is composed of the upper respiratory tract, or conducting airways (nose, mouth, pharynx, larynx, trachea, and the bronchial tree), and the lower respiratory tract, made up of alveoli (respiratory sacs), which make up the lungs.
- The respiratory system is essential for survival, bringing oxygen into the body (ventilation), allowing for the exchange of gases, and expelling carbon dioxide and other waste products.
- The upper airways have many features to protect the fragile alveoli: hairs filter the air; goblet cells produce mucus to trap material; cilia move the trapped material toward the throat for swallowing; blood supply close to the surface warms the air and adds humidity to improve gas movement and gas exchange; and the cough and sneeze reflexes clear the airways.
- The alveolar sac is where gas exchange occurs across the respiratory membrane. The alveoli produce surfactant to decrease surface tension within the sac and have other metabolic functions.
- Respiration is controlled through the medulla in the central nervous system and depends on a balance between the sympathetic and parasympathetic systems and a functioning muscular system.
- Inflammation of the upper respiratory tract results in many uncomfortable disorders, including the common cold, seasonal rhinitis, sinusitis, pharyngitis, and laryngitis.
- Inflammation of the lower respiratory tract can result in serious disorders that interfere with gas exchange; these include bronchitis and pneumonia.
- Obstructive disorders interfere with the ability to deliver gases to the alveoli because of obstructions in the conducting airways and eventually in the respiratory airways. These disorders include asthma, COPD, cystic fibrosis, and respiratory distress syndrome.

BIBLIOGRAPHY

Bullock, B. L. (2000). *Focus on pathophysiology*. Philadelphia: Lippincott Williams & Wilkins.

Fox, S. (1991). *Perspectives on human biology*. Dubuque, IA: Wm. C. Brown Publishers.

Ganong, W. (1999). *Review of medical physiology* (19th ed.). Norwalk, CT: Appleton & Lange.

Guyton, A. & Hall, J. (1996). *Textbook of medical physiology*. Philadelphia: W. B. Saunders.

Hardman, J. G., Limbird, L. E., Molinoff, P. B., Ruddon, R. W., & Gilman, A. G. (Eds). (1996). *Goodman and Gilman's the pharmacological basis of therapeutics* (9th ed). New York: McGraw-Hill.

CHAPTER 52

Drugs Acting on the Upper Respiratory Tract

Antitussives
- benzonatate
- codeine
- **P** dextromethorphan
- hydrocodone
- terpin hydrate

Decongestants
- Topical nasal decongestants
  - **P** ephedrine
  - oxymetazoline
  - phenylephrine
  - tetrahydrozoline
  - xylometazoline
- Oral decongestants
  - phenylpropanolamine
  - **P** pseudoephedrine
- Topical nasal steroid decongestants
  - beclomethasone
  - budesonide
  - dexamethasone
  - **P** flunisolide
  - fluticasone
  - triamcinolone

Antihistamines
- azatadine
- azelastine
- brompheniramine
- buclizine
- cetirizine
- chlorpheniramine
- clemastine
- cyclizine
- cyproheptadine
- dexchlorpheniramine
- dimenhydrinate
- **P** diphenhydramine
- fexofenidine
- hydroxyzine
- loratidine
- meclizine
- methdilazine
- promethazine
- tripelennamine

Expectorants
- **P** guaifenesin
- terpin hydrate

Mucolytics
- **P** acetylcysteine
- dornase alfa

CHAPTER OUTLINE

KEY TERMS

antihistamines
antitussives
decongestants
expectorants
mucolytics
rebound congestion
rhinitis medicamentosa

INTRODUCTION

Drugs that affect the respiratory system work to keep the airways open and gases moving efficiently. The classes discussed in this chapter mainly act on the upper respiratory tract and include the following:

- ***Antitussives***—block the cough reflex
- ***Decongestants***—decrease the blood flow to the upper respiratory tract and decrease the overproduction of secretions
- ***Antihistamines***—block the release or action of histamine, a chemical released during inflammation that increases secretions and narrows airways
- ***Expectorants***—increase productive cough to clear the airways
- ***Mucolytics***—increase or liquefy respiratory secretions to aid the clearing of the airways

Figure 52-1 displays the sites of action of these drugs.

ANTITUSSIVES

Antitussives are drugs that suppress the cough reflex. Many disorders of the respiratory tract, including the common cold, sinusitis, pharyngitis, and pneumonia, are accompanied by an uncomfortable, unproductive cough. Persistent coughing can be exhausting and can cause muscle strain and further irritation of the respiratory tract. A cough that occurs without the presence of any active disease process or persists following treatment may be a symptom of another disease process and should be investigated before any medication is given to alleviate it.

THERAPEUTIC ACTIONS AND INDICATIONS

The traditional antitussives, including codeine (generic only), hydrocodone (*Hycodan*), and dextromethorphan (*Benylin* and many others), act directly on the medullary cough center of the brain to depress the cough reflex. Because they are centrally acting, they are not the drugs of choice for anyone with head injury or who could be impaired by central nervous system (CNS) depression.

Other antitussives have a direct effect on the respiratory tract. Terpin hydrate (generic only) stimulates the secretory cells in the respiratory tract lining, leading to more copious secretions, which buffer the irritation in the respiratory tract wall that stimulates the cough. This drug would not be recommended for patients already impaired by copious secretion. Benzonatate (*Tessalon*) acts as a local anesthetic on the respiratory passages, lungs, and pleura, blocking the effectiveness of the stretch receptors that stimulate a cough reflex. These drugs are indicated for the treatment of nonproductive cough.

CONTRAINDICATIONS/CAUTIONS

Antitussives are contraindicated in patients who need to cough to maintain the airways (e.g., postoperative patients and those who have undergone abdominal or thoracic surgery). Careful use is recommended for patients with asthma and emphysema because cough suppression in these patients can lead to an accumulation of secretions and a loss of respiratory reserve. Caution should also be used with patients who are hypersensitive to or have a history of addiction to narcotics (codeine, hydrocodone). Codeine is a narcotic and has addiction potential. Patients who need to drive or to be alert should use codeine, hydrocodone, and dextromethorphan

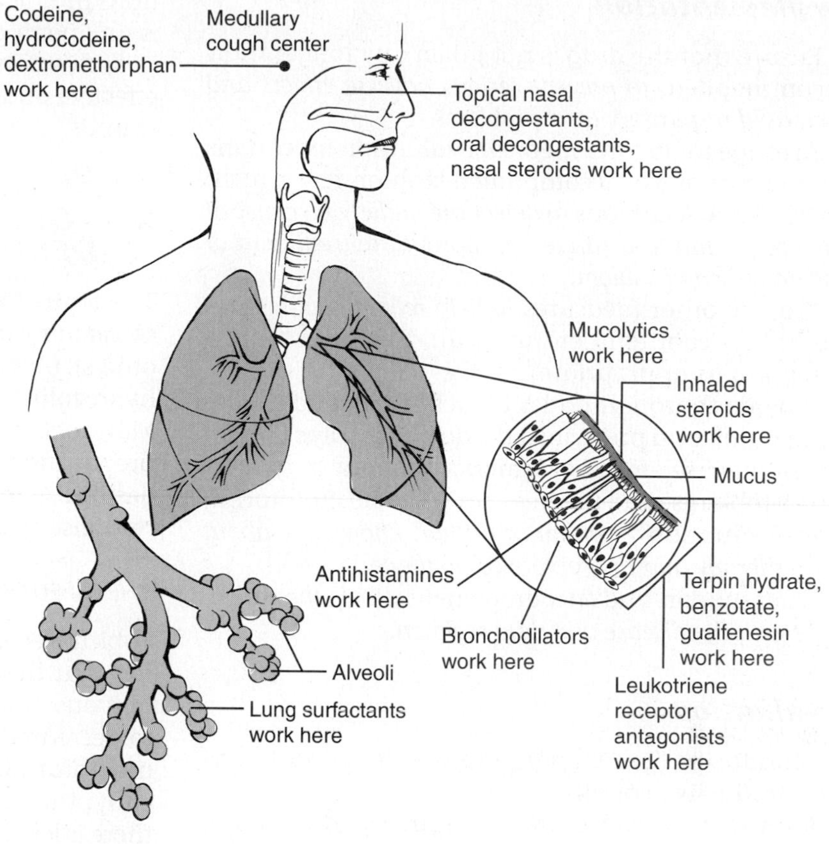

FIGURE 52-1. Sites of action of drugs acting on the upper respiratory tract.

with extreme caution, as these can cause sedation and drowsiness.

ADVERSE EFFECTS

Traditional antitussives have a drying effect on the mucous membranes and can increase the viscosity of respiratory tract secretions. Because they affect centers in the brain, these antitussives are associated with CNS adverse effects including drowsiness and sedation. Their drying effect can lead to nausea, constipation, and complaints of dry mouth. The locally acting antitussives are associated with GI upset, headache, feelings of congestion, and sometimes dizziness.

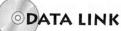

DATA LINK

Data link to the following antitussives in your nursing drug guide:

ANTITUSSIVES

Name	Brand Name	Usual Indication
benzonatate	*Tessalon*	All of the antitussives are indicated for treatment of nonproductive cough
codeine	generic	
P dextromethorphan	*Benylin*	
hydrocodone	*Hycodan*	
terpin hydrate	generic	

NURSING CONSIDERATIONS
for patients receiving antitussives

Assessment

HISTORY. Screen for the following: any history of allergy to any component of the drug or drug vehicle; cough that persists longer than a week or is accompanied by other signs and symptoms; and pregnancy and lactation.

PHYSICAL ASSESSMENT. Physical assessment should be done to establish baseline data for assessing the effectiveness of the drug and the occurrence of any adverse effects associated with drug therapy. Assess the following: temperature (to evaluate for possible underlying infection), respirations and adventitious sounds (to assess drug effectiveness and to monitor for accumulation of secretions), and orientation and affect (to monitor for CNS effects of the drug).

Nursing Diagnoses

The patient receiving an antitussive may have the following nursing diagnoses related to drug therapy:

- Ineffective airway clearance related to excessive drug effects
- Sensory–perceptual alteration related to CNS effects
- Knowledge deficit regarding drug therapy

Implementation

- Ensure that the drug is not taken any longer than recommended, *to prevent serious adverse effects and increased respiratory tract problems.*
- Arrange for further medical evaluation for coughs that persist or are accompanied by high fever, rash, or excessive secretions *to detect the underlying cause of the cough and to arrange for appropriate treatment of the underlying problem.*
- Provide other measures *to help relieve cough* (e.g., humidity, cool temperatures, fluids, use of topical lozenges) as appropriate.
- Provide thorough patient teaching, including the drug name and prescribed dosage, measures to help avoid adverse effects, warning signs that may indicate problems, and the need for periodic monitoring and evaluation *to enhance patient knowledge about drug therapy and to promote compliance.*
- Offer support and encouragement *to help the patient cope with the disease and drug regimen.*

Evaluation

- Monitor patient response to the drug (control of nonproductive cough).
- Monitor for adverse effects (respiratory depression, dizziness, sedation).
- Evaluate the effectiveness of the teaching plan (patient can name drug, dosage, adverse effects to watch for, specific measures to avoid adverse effects, measures to take to increase the effectiveness of the drug).
- Monitor effectiveness of other measures to relieve cough.

DECONGESTANTS

Decongestants are drugs, usually adrenergics or sympathomimetics, that cause local vasoconstriction and therefore decrease the blood flow to the irritated and dilated capillaries of the mucous membranes lining the nasal passages and sinus cavities. This vasoconstriction leads to a shrinking of swollen membranes and tends to open up clogged nasal passages, providing relief from the discomfort of a blocked nose and promoting drainage of secretions and improved airflow. An adverse effect that accompanies frequent or prolonged use of these drugs is a ***rebound congestion,*** officially called ***rhinitis medicamentosa.*** The reflex reaction to vasoconstriction is a rebound vasodilation which often leads to prolonged overuse of decongestants.

Topical steroids are also used as decongestants. Topical steroids act to directly block the effects of inflammation on the nasal mucous membranes. This blocks the swelling, congestion, and increased secretions that accompany inflammation. The end result is an opening of the nasal passages and an increase in airflow. These drugs take several weeks to be really effective and are more often used in cases of chronic rhinitis.

TOPICAL NASAL DECONGESTANTS

The topical nasal decongestants include ephedrine (*Kondon's Nasal*), oxymetazoline (*Afrin, Allerest,* and others), phenylephrine (*Coricidin,* many others), tetrahydrozoline (*Tyzine*), and xylometazoline (*Otrivin*). Many of these are available as over-the-counter (OTC) preparations. The choice of a topical nasal decongestant is individual. Some patients may have no response to one and respond very well to another.

THERAPEUTIC ACTIONS AND INDICATIONS

Topical decongestants are sympathomimetics, meaning that they imitate the effects of the sympathetic nervous system to cause vasoconstriction, leading to decreased edema and inflammation of the nasal membranes. Because these drugs are applied topically, the onset of action is almost immediate and there is less chance of systemic effects. They are available as nasal sprays used to relieve the discomfort of nasal congestion that accompanies the common cold, sinusitis, and allergic rhinitis. These drugs can also be used when dilation of the nares is desired to facilitate medical examination and to relieve the pain and congestion of otitis media. Opening the nasal passage allows better drainage of the eustachian tube, relieving pressure in the middle ear.

CONTRAINDICATIONS/CAUTIONS

Caution should be used when there is any lesion or erosion in the mucous membranes which could lead to systemic absorption. Because these agents have adrenergic properties, caution should also be used with patients with any condition that might be exacerbated by sympathetic activity (e.g., glaucoma, hypertension, diabetes, thyroid disease, coronary disease, prostate problems).

ADVERSE EFFECTS

Adverse effects associated with topical decongestants include local stinging and burning that may occur the first few times the drug is used. If the sensation does not pass, the drug should be discontinued because it may indicate lesions or erosion of the mucous membranes. Use for longer than 3 to 5 days can lead to a rebound congestion. (Rebound congestion occurs when the nasal passages become congested as the drug effect wears off. As a result, patients tend to use more drug to decrease the congestion, thus initiating a vicious cycle of congestion, drug, congestion, which leads to abuse of the decongestant.) Sympathomimetic effects (e.g., increased pulse, blood pressure; urinary retention) should be monitored because some systemic absorption may occur, though these effects are less likely with topical administration than with other routes.

CLINICALLY IMPORTANT DRUG–DRUG INTERACTIONS

The use of the topical nasal decongestants is contraindicated with concurrent use of cyclopropane or halothane anesthesia because serious cardiovascular effects could occur. Combined use with any other sympathomimetic drug or sympathetic blocking drug could result in toxic or noneffective responses. Monitor the use of these combinations carefully.

DATA LINK

Data link to the following topical nasal decongestants in your nursing drug guide:

TOPICAL NASAL DECONGESTANTS

Name	Brand Name(s)	Usual Indications
P ephedrine	*Kondon's Nasal*	Relief of the discomfort of nasal congestion associated with the common cold, sinusitis, allergic rhinitis; relief of pressure of otitis media
oxymetazoline	*Afrin, Allerest*	Relief of the discomfort of nasal congestion associated with the common cold, sinusitis, allergic rhinitis
phenylephrine	*Coricidin*	Relief of the discomfort of nasal congestion associated with the common cold, sinusitis, allergic rhinitis
tetrahydrozoline	*Tyzine*	Relief of the discomfort of nasal congestion associated with the common cold, sinusitis, allergic rhinitis; relief of pressure of otitis media
xylometazoline	*Otrivin*	Relief of the discomfort of nasal congestion associated with the common cold, sinusitis, allergic rhinitis; relief of pressure of otitis media

NURSING CONSIDERATIONS
for patients receiving topical nasal decongestants

Assessment

HISTORY. Screen for the following: any history of allergy to the drug or component of the drug vehicle; glaucoma, hypertension, diabetes, thyroid disease, coronary disease, and prostate problems, all of which could be exacerbated by the sympathomimetic effects; and pregnancy or lactation, which require cautious use of the drug.

PHYSICAL ASSESSMENT. Physical assessment should be done to establish baseline data for assessing the effectiveness of the drug and the occurrence of any adverse effects associated with drug therapy. Assess the following: skin color and temperature (to assess sympathetic response); orientation and reflexes (to evaluate CNS effects of the drug); pulse, blood pressure, cardiac auscultation (to monitor cardiovascular, sympathomimetic effects); respirations, adventitious breath sounds (to assess effectiveness of drug and potential excess effect); bladder percussion (to monitor for urinary retention related to sympathomimetic effects); and nasal mucous membrane evaluation (to monitor for lesions that could lead to systemic absorption and to evaluate decongestant effect).

Nursing Diagnoses

The patient receiving a topical nasal decongestant may have the following nursing diagnoses related to drug therapy:

- Pain related to GI, CNS, local effects of drug
- Sensory–perceptual alteration related to CNS effects (less likely with this route of administration)
- Knowledge deficit regarding drug therapy

Implementation

- Teach the patient the proper administration of the drug *to ensure therapeutic effect.* The patient should be instructed to clear the nasal passages before use, to tilt the head back when applying the drops or spray, and to keep it tilted back for a few seconds after administration. This technique *helps ensure contact with the affected mucous membranes and decreases the chances of letting the drops trickle down the back of throat, which may lead to more systemic effects.*
- Caution patients not to use the drug for more than 5 days, and to seek medical care if signs and symptoms persist after that time *to facilitate detection of underlying medical conditions that may require treatment.*
- Caution patients that these drugs are found in many OTC preparations and *care should be taken not to inadvertently combine drugs with the same ingredients, leading to overdose.*
- Provide safety measures if dizziness or sedation occur as a result of drug therapy *to prevent patient injury.*
- Institute other measures *to help relieve the discomfort of congestion* (e.g., humidity, increased fluid intake,

cool environment, avoidance of smoke-filled areas) as appropriate.

- Provide thorough patient teaching, including the drug name and prescribed dosage, measures to help avoid adverse effects, warning signs that may indicate problems, and the need for periodic monitoring and evaluation *to enhance patient knowledge about drug therapy and to promote compliance.*
- Offer support and encouragement *to help the patient cope with the disease and drug regimen.*

Evaluation

- Monitor patient response to the drug (relief of nasal congestion).
- Monitor for adverse effects (local burning and stinging; adrenergic effects such as increased pulse, blood pressure, urinary retention, cool and clammy skin).
- Evaluate the effectiveness of the teaching plan (patient can name drug, dosage, adverse effects to watch for, specific measures to avoid adverse effects, measures to take to increase the effectiveness of the drug, proper administration technique).
- Monitor the effectiveness of comfort and safety measures and compliance with the regimen.

ORAL DECONGESTANTS

Oral decongestants are drugs taken orally to decrease nasal congestion related to the common cold, sinusitis, and allergic rhinitis. They are also used to relieve the pain and congestion of otitis media. Opening the nasal passage allows better drainage of the eustachian tube, relieving pressure in the middle ear. Oral decongestants include phenylpropanolamine (available in multiple OTC combination products) and pseudoephedrine (*Dorcol, Decofed,* and others).

THERAPEUTIC ACTIONS AND INDICATIONS

Oral decongestants shrink the nasal mucous membrane by stimulating the alpha-adrenergic receptors in the nasal mucous membranes. This shrinkage results in a decrease in membrane size, promoting drainage of the sinuses and improving air flow. Because these drugs are taken systemically, adverse effects related to their sympathomimetic effects (e.g., cardiac stimulation, feelings of anxiety) are more likely to occur.

CONTRAINDICATIONS/CAUTIONS

Because oral decongestants have adrenergic properties, caution should be used with patients with any condition that might be exacerbated by sympathetic activity (e.g., glaucoma, hypertension, diabetes, thyroid disease, coronary disease, prostate problems).

ADVERSE EFFECTS

Adverse effects associated with oral decongestants include rebound congestion. Sympathetic effects include feelings of anxiety, tenseness, restlessness, tremors, hypertension, arrhythmias, sweating, and pallor.

DATA LINK

Data link to the following oral decongestants in your nursing drug guide:

ORAL DECONGESTANTS

Name	Brand Name(s)	Usual Indications
phenylpropanolamine	numerous	Decrease nasal congestion associated with the common cold, allergic rhinitis; relief of pain and congestion of otitis media
P pseudoephedrine	*Dorcal, Decofed*	Decrease nasal congestion associated with the common cold, allergic rhinitis; relief of pain and congestion of otitis media

NURSING CONSIDERATIONS
for patients receiving oral decongestants

Assessment

HISTORY. Screen for the following: any history of allergy to the drug and pregnancy and lactation, which are contraindications to drug use; hypertension and coronary artery disease, which require cautious use; and hyperthyroidism, diabetes mellitus, and prostate enlargement, all of which could be exacerbated by these drugs.

PHYSICAL ASSESSMENT. Physical assessment should be done to establish baseline data for assessing the effectiveness of the drug and the occurrence of any adverse effects associated with drug therapy. Assess the following: skin color and lesions to monitor for adverse reactions; orientation, reflexes, and affect to monitor CNS effects of the drug; blood pressure, pulse, and auscultation to monitor cardiovascular stimulations; respiration and adventitious sounds to monitor drug effectiveness; and urinary output to evaluate for urinary retention.

Nursing Diagnoses

The patient receiving an oral decongestant may have the following nursing diagnoses related to drug therapy:

- Pain related to GI, CNS, skin effects of drug
- Alteration in cardiac output related to sympathomimetic actions of the drug

- Sensory–perceptual alteration related to CNS effects
- Knowledge deficit regarding drug therapy

Implementation

- Note that these drugs are found in many OTC products, especially combination cold and allergy preparations. *Care should be taken to prevent inadvertent overdose or excessive adverse effects.*
- Provide safety measures as needed if CNS effects occur *to prevent patient injury.*
- Monitor pulse, blood pressure, and cardiac response to the drug, especially in patients who are at risk for cardiac stimulation *to detect adverse effects early and arrange to reduce dosage or discontinue the drug.*
- Encourage the patient not to use this drug for longer than 1 week and to seek medical evaluation if symptoms persist after that *to encourage the detection of underlying medical conditions that could be causing these symptoms and to arrange for appropriate treatment.*
- Provide thorough patient teaching, including the drug name and prescribed dosage, measures to help avoid adverse effects, warning signs that may indicate problems, and the need for periodic monitoring and evaluation *to enhance patient knowledge about drug therapy and to promote compliance.*
- Offer support and encouragement *to help the patient cope with the disease and drug regimen.*

Evaluation

- Monitor patient response to the drug (improvement in nasal congestion).
- Monitor for adverse effects (sympathomimetic reactions including increased pulse, blood pressure, pallor, sweating, arrhythmias, feelings of anxiety, tension, dry skin).
- Evaluate the effectiveness of the teaching plan (patient can name drug, dosage, adverse effects to watch for, specific measures to avoid adverse effects, measures to take to increase the effectiveness of the drug).
- Monitor the effectiveness of comfort and safety measures and compliance with the regimen.

TOPICAL NASAL STEROID DECONGESTANTS

Topical nasal steroid decongestants are currently very popular for the treatment of allergic rhinitis. They have been found to be effective in patients who no longer respond to other decongestants. The topical nasal steroid decongestants include beclomethasone (*Beclovent* and others), budesonide (*Rhinocort*), dexamethasone (*Decaderm* and others), flunisolide (*AeroBid* and others), fluticasone (*Flovent*), and triamcinolone (*Kenacort*).

THERAPEUTIC ACTIONS AND INDICATIONS

The exact mechanism of action of topical steroids is not known. Their anti-inflammatory action results from their ability to produce a direct local effect that blocks many of the complex reactions responsible for the inflammatory response. Applied topically, there is less of a chance of systemic absorption and associated adverse effects. Onset of action is not immediate and may actually require up to a week to cause any changes. If no effects are seen after 3 weeks, the drug should be discontinued. Topical nasal steroidal preparations are used to treat seasonal allergic rhinitis for patients who do not respond to other decongestant preparations. They are frequently used to relieve inflammation following the removal of nasal polyps.

CONTRAINDICATIONS/CAUTIONS

Because nasal steroids block the inflammatory response, their use is contraindicated in the presence of acute infections. Increased incidence of *Candida albicans* has been reported with their use, related to the anti-inflammatory and anti-immune activities associated with steroids. Caution should be used with any patients with active infection, including tuberculosis, because systemic absorption would interfere with the inflammatory and immune responses. Patients using nasal steroids should avoid exposure to any airborne infection, such as chickenpox or measles.

ADVERSE EFFECTS

The most common adverse effects associated with the use of topical nasal steroids are local burning, irritation, stinging, dryness of the mucosa, and headache. Because healing is suppressed by steroids, patients who have recently experienced nasal surgery or trauma should be monitored closely until healing has occurred.

DATA LINK

Data link to the following topical steroid nasal decongestants in your nursing drug guide:

TOPICAL STEROID NASAL DECONGESTANTS

Name	Brand Name	Usual Indications
beclomethasone	*Beclovent*	All of the topical steroid nasal decongestants are indicated for treatment of seasonal allergic rhinitis in patients who do not respond to other decongestant preparations and for relief of inflammation following the removal of nasal polyps.
budesonide	*Rhinocort*	
dexamethasone	*Decaderm*	

P flunisolide	*Aerobid*
fluticasone	*Flovent*
triamcinolone	*Kenacort*

NURSING CONSIDERATIONS
for patients receiving topical steroid nasal decongestants

Assessment

HISTORY. Screen for the following: any history of allergy to steroid drugs or any components of the drug vehicle, which would be a contraindication; and for acute infection, which would require cautious use.

PHYSICAL ASSESSMENT. Physical assessment should be done to establish baseline data for assessing the effectiveness of the drug and the occurrence of any adverse effects associated with drug therapy. Intranasal examination should be performed to determine the presence of any lesions that would increase the risk of systemic absorption of drug. Assess the following: respiration and adventitious sounds (to evaluate drug effectiveness) and temperature (to monitor for the possibility of acute infection).

Nursing Diagnoses

The patient receiving topical nasal steroid nasal decongestants may have the following nursing diagnoses related to drug therapy:

- Pain related to local effects of the drug
- Potential for injury related to suppression of inflammatory reaction
- Knowledge deficit regarding drug therapy

Implementation

- Teach the patient the proper administration of these drugs, *which is very important to ensure effectiveness and prevent systemic effects.* A variety of preparations is available (e.g., sprays, aerosols, powder disks). Advise the patient about the proper administration technique for whichever preparation is recommended.
- Have the patient clear nasal passages before using the drug *to improve the effectiveness of the drug.*
- Encourage the patient to continue using the drug regularly, even if results are not seen immediately *because benefits may take 2 to 3 weeks to appear.*
- Monitor the patient for the development of acute infection *that would require medical intervention. Encourage the patient to avoid areas where airborne infections could be a problem, because steroid use decreases the effectiveness of the immune and inflammatory responses.*
- Provide thorough patient teaching, including the drug name and prescribed dosage, measures to help avoid adverse effects, warning signs that may indicate problems, and the need for periodic monitoring and evaluation *to enhance patient knowledge about drug therapy and to promote compliance.*
- Offer support and encouragement *to help the patient cope with the disease and drug regimen.*

Evaluation

- Monitor patient response to the drug (relief of nasal congestion).
- Monitor for adverse effects (local burning and stinging).
- Evaluate the effectiveness of the teaching plan (patient can name drug, dosage, adverse effects to watch for, specific measures to avoid adverse effects, measures to take to increase the effectiveness of the drug).
- Monitor the effectiveness of comfort and safety measures and compliance with the regimen.

ANTIHISTAMINES

Antihistamines are found in multiple OTC preparations designed to relieve respiratory symptoms and to treat allergies. These agents block the effects of histamine, bringing relief to patients suffering from itchy eyes, swelling, congestion, and drippy nose.

Numerous antihistamines are available, including first- and second-generation agents. First-generations antihistamines have greater anticholinergic effects, with resultant drowsiness. These drugs include azatadine (*Optimine*), azelastine (*Astelin*), brompheniramine (*Dimetane* and others), buclizine (*Bucladin-S*), cetirizine (*Reactine*), chlorpheniramine (*Aller-Chlor* and others), clemastine (*Tavist*), cyclizine (*Marazine*), cyproheptadine (*Periactin*), dexchlorpheniramine (*Dexchlor*), dimenhydrinate (*Dimentabs* and others), diphenhydramine (*Benadryl* and others), hydroxyzine (*Vistaril* and others), meclizine (*Bonine*), methdilazine (*Tacaryl*), promethazine (*Phenergan* and others), and tripelennamine (*PBZ*). Second-generation antihistamines, including fexofenidine (*Allegra*) and loratidine (*Claritin*), have fewer anticholinergic effects than first-generation agents.

When choosing an antihistamine, the individual patient's reaction to the drug is usually the governing factor. If a person needs to be alert, one of the second-generation, nonsedating antihistamines would be the drug of choice. Because of their OTC availability, these drugs are often misused to treat colds and influenza.

THERAPEUTIC ACTIONS AND INDICATIONS

The antihistamines selectively block the effects of histamine at the H_1 receptor sites, decreasing the allergic response. They also have anticholinergic (atropine-like) and antipruritic effects. Antihistamines are used for the relief of symptoms associated with seasonal and perennial allergic rhinitis, allergic conjunctivitis, uncomplicated urticaria, and angioedema. They are also used for amelioration of allergic reactions to blood or blood products; for relief of discomfort associated with dermographism; and as adjunctive therapy in anaphylactic reactions. Other uses that are being explored include relief of exercise-and hyperventilation-induced asthma and histamine-induced bronchoconstriction in asthmatics. They are most effective if used before the onset of symptoms.

CONTRAINDICATIONS/CAUTIONS

Antihistamines are contraindicated during pregnancy or lactation. They should be used with caution in renal or hepatic impairment, which could alter the metabolism and excretion of the drug. Special care should be taken when these drugs are used by any patient with a history of arrhythmias or prolonged Q-T intervals because fatal cardiac arrhythmias have been associated with the use of certain antihistamines and drugs that increase Q-T intervals, including erythromycin.

ADVERSE EFFECTS

The adverse effects most often seen with antihistamine use are drowsiness and sedation, though second-generation antihistamines are less sedating in many people. The anticholinergic effects that can be anticipated include drying of the respiratory and GI mucous membranes, GI upset and nausea, arrhythmias, dysuria, urinary hesitancy, and skin eruption and itching associated with dryness.

DATA LINK

Data link to the following antihistamines in your nursing drug guide:

ANTIHISTAMINES

Name	Brand Name(s)	Usual Indications
First generation		
azatadine	*Optimine*	Relief of symptoms of seasonal and perennial allergic rhinitis; allergic conjunctivitis; uncomplicated urticaria and angioedema; amelioration of allergic reactions; relief of discomfort associated with dermographism; and as an adjunctive therapy in anaphylactic reactions
azelastine	*Astelin*	Relief of symptoms of seasonal and perennial allergic rhinitis
brompheniramine	*Dimetane* and others	Relief of symptoms of seasonal and perennial allergic rhinitis; allergic conjunctivitis; uncomplicated urticaria and angioedema; amelioration of allergic reactions; relief of discomfort associated with therapy in anaphylactic reactions
buclizine	*Bucladin-S*	Relief of nausea and vomiting associated with motion sickness
cetirizine	*Reactine*	Relief of symptoms of seasonal and perennial allergic rhinitis; management of chronic urticaria
chlorpheniramine	*Aller-Chlor* and others	Relief of symptoms of seasonal and perennial allergic rhinitis; allergic conjunctivitis; uncomplicated urticaria and angioedema; amelioration of allergic reactions; relief of discomfort associated with dermographism; and as an adjunctive therapy in anaphylactic reactions
clemastine	*Tavist*	Relief of symptoms of seasonal and perennial allergic rhinitis; allergic conjunctivitis; uncomplicated urticaria and angioedema; amelioration of allergic reactions; relief of discomfort associated with dermographism; and as an adjunctive therapy in anaphylactic reactions
cyclizine	*Marazine*	Relief of nausea and vomiting associated with motion sickness
cyproheptadine	*Periactin*	Relief of symptoms of seasonal and perennial allergic rhinitis; allergic conjunctivitis; uncomplicated urticaria and angioedema; amelioration of allergic reactions; relief of discomfort associated with dermographism; and as an adjunctive therapy in anaphylactic reactions
dexchlorpheniramine	*Dexchlor*	Relief of symptoms of seasonal and perennial allergic rhinitis; allergic conjunctivitis; uncomplicated urticaria and angioedema; amelioration of allergic reactions; relief of discomfort associated with dermographism; and as an adjunctive therapy in anaphylactic reactions
dimenhydrinate	*Dimentabs* and others	Relief of nausea and vomiting associated with motion sickness
P diphenhydramine	*Benadryl* and others	Relief of symptoms of seasonal and perennial allergic rhinitis; allergic conjunctivitis; uncomplicated urticaria and angioedema; amelioration of allergic reactions; relief of discomfort associated with dermographism; and as an adjunctive therapy in anaphylactic reactions; sleeping aid; parkinsonism
hydroxyzine	*Vistaril* and others	Relief of symptoms of seasonal and perennial allergic rhinitis; allergic conjunctivitis; uncomplicated urticaria and

		angioedema; amelioration of allergic reactions; relief of discomfort associated with dermographism; and as an adjunctive therapy in anaphylactic reactions; sedation
meclizine	*Bonine*	Relief of nausea and vomiting associated with motion sickness
methdilazine	*Tacaryl*	Relief of symptoms of seasonal and perennial allergic rhinitis; allergic conjunctivitis; uncomplicated urticaria and angioedema; amelioration of allergic reactions; relief of discomfort associated with dermographism
promethazine	*Phenergan* and others	Relief of symptoms of seasonal and perennial allergic rhinitis; allergic conjunctivitis; uncomplicated urticaria and angioedema; amelioration of allergic reactions; relief of discomfort associated with dermographism; and as an adjunctive therapy in anaphylactic reactions; sedation
tripelennamine	*PBZ*	Relief of symptoms of seasonal and perennial allergic rhinitis; allergic conjunctivitis; uncomplicated urticaria and angioedema; amelioration of allergic reactions; relief of discomfort associated with dermographism; and as an adjunctive therapy in anaphylactic reactions
Second generation—nonsedating		
fexofenadine	*Allegra*	Relief of symptoms of seasonal and perennial allergic rhinitis
loratidine	*Claritin*	Relief of symptoms of seasonal and perennial allergic rhinitis; allergic conjunctivitis; uncomplicated urticaria and angioedema; amelioration of allergic reactions; relief of discomfort associated with dermographism; and as an adjunctive therapy in anaphylactic reactions

NURSING CONSIDERATIONS
for patients receiving antihistamines

Assessment

HISTORY. Screen for the following: any history of allergy to antihistamines, pregnancy or lactation, and prolonged Q-T interval, which are contraindications to the use of the drug; and renal or hepatic impairment, which require cautious use of the drug.

PHYSICAL ASSESSMENT. Physical assessment should be done to establish baseline data for assessing the effectiveness of the drug and the occurrence of any adverse effects associated with drug therapy. Assess the following: skin color, texture, and lesions (to monitor for anticholinergic effects or allergy); orientation, affect, and reflexes (to monitor for changes due to central nervous system effects); respirations and adventitious sounds (to monitor drug effects); and serum liver and renal function tests (to monitor for factors that could affect the metabolism or excretion of the drug).

Nursing Diagnoses

The patient receiving antihistamines may have the following nursing diagnoses related to drug therapy:

- Pain related to GI, CNS, skin effects of the drug
- Sensory–perceptual alteration related to CNS effects
- Knowledge deficit regarding drug therapy

Implementation

- Administer the drug on an empty stomach, 1 hour before or 2 hours after meals, *to increase the absorption of the drug;* the drug may be given with meals if GI upset is a problem.
- Note that a patient may have poor response to one of these agents but a very effective response to another. The prescriber may need to try several different agents *to find the one that is most effective.*
- Because of the drying nature of antihistamines, patients often experience dry mouth, which may lead to nausea and anorexia. *Suggest sugarless candies or lozenges to relieve some of this discomfort.*
- Provide safety measures as appropriate if CNS effects occur *to prevent patient injury.*
- Increase humidity and push fluids *to decrease the problem of thickened secretions and dry nasal mucosa.*
- Have the patient void before each dose *to decrease urinary retention if this is a problem.*
- Provide skin care as needed if skin dryness and lesions become a problem, *to prevent skin breakdown.*
- Caution the patient to avoid excessive dosage and *to check OTC drugs for the presence of antihistamines, which could cause toxicity and which are found in many OTC preparations.*
- Caution the patient to avoid alcohol while on these drugs *because serious sedation can occur.*
- Provide thorough patient teaching, including the drug name and prescribed dosage, measures to help avoid adverse effects, warning signs that may indicate problems, and the need for periodic monitoring and evaluation, *to enhance patient knowledge about drug therapy and to promote compliance* (see Patient Teaching Checklist: Antihistamines).

PATIENT TEACHING CHECKLIST

Antihistamines

Create customized patient teaching materials for a specific antihistamine from your CD-ROM. Your patient teaching should stress the following points for drugs within this class:

Antihistamines are used to treat the signs and symptoms of various allergic reactions. Your drug has been prescribed to treat ________. Because these drugs work throughout the body, many systemic effects can occur with their use (e.g., dry mouth, dizziness, drowsiness).

Take this drug only as prescribed. Do not increase the dosage if symptoms are not relieved. Consult your health care provider if this occurs.

Common effects of this drug include:

- Drowsiness, dizziness—Do not drive or operate dangerous machinery if this occurs. Use caution to prevent injury.
- GI upset, nausea, vomiting, heartburn—Taking the drug with food may help this problem.
- Dry mouth—Frequent mouth care and sucking sugarless lozenges may help.
- Thickening of the mucus, difficulty coughing, tightening of the chest—Use a humidifier, or if you do not have one, place pans of water throughout the house to increase the humidity of the room air; avoid smoke-filled areas; drink plenty of fluids.

Avoid the use of alcoholic beverages while you are taking this drug. Serious drowsiness or sedation can occur if these are combined.

Report any of the following to your health care provider: difficulty breathing, rash, hives, difficulty in voiding, abdominal pain, visual changes, disorientation or confusion.

Avoid the use of any over-the-counter medication without first checking with your health care provider. Several of these medications contain drugs that can interfere with the effectiveness of this drug.

Tell any doctor, nurse, or other health care provider that you are taking this drug.

Take this drug only as prescribed. Do not give this drug to anyone else and do not take similar preparations that have been prescribed for someone else.

Keep this drug, and all medications, out of the reach of children.

This Teaching Checklist reflects general patient teaching guidelines. It is not meant to be a substitute for drug-specific teaching information; which is available in nursing drug guides.

- Offer support and encouragement *to help the patient cope with the disease and drug regimen.*

Evaluation

- Monitor patient response to the drug (relief of the symptoms of allergic rhinitis).
- Monitor for adverse effects (skin dryness; GI upset; sedation and drowsiness; urinary retention; thickened secretions; glaucoma).
- Evaluate the effectiveness of the teaching plan (patient can name drug, dosage, adverse effects to watch for, specific measures to avoid adverse effects, measures to take to increase the effectiveness of the drug).
- Monitor the effectiveness of comfort and safety measures and compliance with the regimen (see Nursing Care Guide: Antihistamines).

EXPECTORANTS

Expectorants liquefy the lower respiratory tract secretions, reducing the viscosity of these secretions and making it easier for the patient to cough them up. Expectorants are available in many OTC preparations, making them widely available to the patient without advice from a health care provider. Available expectorants include guaifenesin (*Anti-Tuss* and others) and terpin hydrate (also an antitussive) (generic only).

THERAPEUTIC ACTIONS AND INDICATIONS

Guaifenesin enhances the output of respiratory tract fluids by reducing the adhesiveness and surface tension of these fluids, allowing easier movement of the less viscous secretions. The result of this thinning of

NURSING CARE GUIDE
Antihistamines

Assessment	Nursing Diagnoses	Implementation	Evaluation
HISTORY			
Allergies, GI stenosis or obstruction, bladder obstruction, narrow-angle glaucoma, BPH, pregnancy, and lactation.	Pain related to GI effects, dry mouth Alteration in cardiac output Sensory–perceptual alteration Alteration in urinary elimination related to thickening mucus Knowledge deficit regarding drug therapy	Provide comfort and safety measures: - Give drug with meals. - Provide mouth care. - Have male patients void before dose (BPH). - Increase humidity. - Institute safety measures if dizziness occurs. Provide support and reassurance to deal with drug effects and allergy. Provide patient teaching regarding drug name, dosage, adverse effects, precautions, and warnings to report.	Evaluate drug effects: relief of respiratory symptoms. Monitor for adverse effects: CNS effects, thickening of secretions, urinary retention, glaucoma. Monitor for drug–drug interactions as indicated for each drug. Evaluate effectiveness of patient teaching program. Evaluate effectiveness of comfort and safety measures. Evaluate effectiveness of support and encouragement as needed.
PHYSICAL EXAMINATION			
Neurological: orientation, reflexes, affect, coordination Skin: lesions CV: BP, P, peripheral perfusion GI: bowel sounds, abdominal exam Hematological: CBC Respiratory: R, nares, adventitious sounds GU: urinary output			

secretions is a more productive cough and thus decreased frequency of coughing. Terpin hydrate, an iodine preparation, stimulates the glands of the respiratory tract to increase the amount of fluid secreted. Iodine preparations have been used for many years to stimulate an increase in the fluid produced by the lungs. These drugs tend to have a very bitter taste, limiting their popularity. They also must be used with caution in many conditions because of the effect of iodine on the thyroid gland. Expectorants are used for the symptomatic relief of respiratory conditions characterized by a dry, nonproductive cough, including the common cold, acute bronchitis, and influenza.

ADVERSE EFFECTS

The most common adverse effects associated with expectorants are GI symptoms (e.g., nausea, vomiting, anorexia). Some patients experience headache and/or dizziness; occasionally, mild rash will develop. The most important consideration in the use of these drugs is discovering the cause of the underlying cough. Prolonged use of the OTC preparation could result in the masking of important symptoms of a serious underlying disorder. These drugs should not be used for more than a week; if the cough persists, encourage the patient to seek health care.

CASE STUDY

Dangers of Self-Medicating for Seasonal Rhinitis

PRESENTATION

K. E. is a 46-year-old businessman who has been self-treating for seasonal rhinitis and a cold. His wife calls the physician's office concerned that her husband is dizzy, has lost his balance several times, and is very drowsy. He is unable to drive to work or to stay awake. She wants to take him to the emergency department of the local hospital.

CRITICAL THINKING QUESTIONS

What is the best approach for this patient? What crucial patient history questions should you ask before proceeding any further? If you do not know this patient, given his presenting story, what medical conditions would need to be ruled out before proceeding further? If K. E. is self-medicating for the signs and symptoms of seasonal rhinitis, what could be causing his drowsiness and dizziness? What teaching points should be emphasized with this patient and his wife?

DISCUSSION

The first impression of K. E.'s condition is that it is a neurological disorder. K. E. should be evaluated by a health care provider to rule out significant neurological problems. After a careful patient history and physical examination, K. E.'s condition seemed to be related to high levels of over-the-counter (OTC) medications.

There are a multitude of OTC cold and allergy remedies, most of which contain the same ingredients in varying proportions. A patient may be taking one to stop his nasal drip, another to help his cough, another to relieve his congestion, and so on. By combining OTC medications like this, a patient is at great risk for inadvertently overdosing or at least allowing the medication to reach toxic levels.

In this situation, the first thing to determine is exactly what medication is being taken and how often. K. E. seems to have received toxic levels of antihistamine, decongestant, or other upper respiratory tract agents. The nurse should encourage K. E.—and all patients—to check the labels of any OTC medications being taken and to check with the health care provider if there are any questions. K. E. and his wife should receive written information about the drugs that K. E. is taking. They also should be shown how to read OTC bottles or boxes for information on the contents of various preparations. In addition, they should be encouraged to use alternative methods to relieve the discomfort of seasonal rhinitis—using a humidifier, drinking lots of liquids, avoiding smoky areas—to decrease the belief that many OTC drugs are needed. Finally, K. E. and his wife should be advised to check with their health care provider if they have any questions about an OTC or prescription drug, or if they have continued problems coping with seasonal allergic reactions. Other prescription medication may prove more effective.

DATA LINK

Data link to the following expectorants in your nursing drug guide:

EXPECTORANTS

Name	Brand Name	Usual Indications
P guaifenesin	*Anti-Tuss* and others	Symptomatic relief of dry, nonproductive cough
terpin hydrate	generic	Symptomatic relief of dry, nonproductive cough

NURSING CONSIDERATIONS
for patients receiving expectorants

Assessment

HISTORY. Screen for the following: any history of allergy to the drug; persistent cough due to smoking, asthma, or emphysema, which would be cautions to the use of the drug; and very productive cough, which would indicate an underlying problem that should be evaluated.

PHYSICAL ASSESSMENT. Physical assessment should be done to establish baseline data for assessing the effectiveness of the drug and the occurrence of any adverse effects associated with drug therapy. Assess the following: skin, for presence of lesions and color (to monitor for any adverse reaction); temperature (to monitor for an underlying infection); respirations and adventitious sounds (to evaluate the respiratory response to the drug effects); and orientation and affect (to monitor CNS effects of the drug).

Nursing Diagnoses

The patient receiving an expectorant may have the following nursing diagnoses related to drug therapy:

- Pain related to GI, CNS, skin effects of the drug
- Sensory–perceptual alteration related to CNS effects
- Knowledge deficit regarding drug therapy

Implementation

• Caution the patient not to use these drugs for longer than 1 week and to seek medical attention if the cough still persists after that time, *to evaluate for any underlying medical condition and to arrange for appropriate treatment.*
• Advise the use of small, frequent meals *to alleviate some of the GI discomfort associated with these drugs.*
• Advise the patient to avoid driving or performing dangerous tasks if dizziness and drowsiness occur, *to prevent patient injury.*
• Alert the patient that these drugs may be found in OTC *preparations and care should be taken to avoid excessive dosage.*
• Provide thorough patient teaching, including the drug name and prescribed dosage, measures to help avoid adverse effects, warning signs that may indicate problems, and the need for periodic monitoring and evaluation, *to enhance patient knowledge about drug therapy and to promote compliance.*
• Offer support and encouragement *to help the patient cope with the disease and drug regimen.*

Evaluation

• Monitor patient response to the drug (improved effectiveness of cough).
• Monitor for adverse effects (skin rash, GI upset, CNS effects).
• Evaluate the effectiveness of the teaching plan (patient can name drug, dosage, adverse effects to watch for, specific measures to avoid adverse effects, measures to take to increase the effectiveness of the drug).
• Monitor the effectiveness of comfort and safety measures and compliance with the regimen.

WWW.WEB LINKS

Health care providers and patients may want to consult the following Internet sources:

Information on allergic rhinitis and seasonal rhinitis, including support groups, research, treatment:
http://www.allergy.pair.com

Information on education programs, research, and other information related to allergies and seasonal rhinitis:
http://www.healthy.net/clinic/dandc/hayfever/index.html

Information about allergy research and treatment:
http://www.healthline.com/articles/ac970102.htm

Information for patients, including special pediatric information on seasonal allergies, hayfever, resources, references:
http://allergy.mcg.edu/media/rhinit.html

Information on cystic fibrosis, including research, treatments, resources:
http://www.cff.org

MUCOLYTICS

Mucolytics work to break down mucus in order to aid the high-risk respiratory patient in coughing up thick, tenacious secretions. The medication may be administered by nebulization or by direct instillation into the trachea via an endotracheal tube or tracheostomy. The mucolytics include acetylcysteine (*Mucomyst* and others) and dornase alfa (*Pulmozyme*).

THERAPEUTIC ACTIONS AND INDICATIONS

Mucolytics are usually reserved for patients who have difficulty mobilizing and coughing up secretions, such as individuals with chronic obstructive pulmonary disease (COPD), cystic fibrosis, pneumonia, and tuberculosis. These drugs are also indicated for patients who develop atelectasis because of thick mucus secretions. They can be used during diagnostic bronchoscopy to clear the airway and to facilitate the removal of secretions, and postoperatively and in patients with tracheostomies to facilitate airway clearance and suctioning. Acetylcysteine is used orally to protect liver cells from being damaged during episodes of acetaminophen toxicity because it normalizes hepatic glutathione levels and binds with a reactive hepatotoxic metabolite of acetaminophen. Acetylcysteine affects the mucoproteins in the respiratory secretions by splitting apart disulfide bonds that are responsible for holding the mucus material together. The result is a decrease in the tenacity and viscosity of the secretions. Dornase alfa is a mucolytic prepared by recombinant DNA which selectively breaks down respiratory tract mucous by separating extracellular DNA from proteins. This drug is used to relieve the build-up of secretions in cystic fibrosis to help keep the airways open and functioning longer.

CONTRAINDICATIONS/CAUTIONS

Caution should be used in cases of acute bronchospasm, peptic ulcer, and esophageal varices because the increased secretions could aggravate the problem.

ADVERSE EFFECTS

Adverse effects most commonly associated with mucolytic drugs include GI upset and stomatitis, rhinorrhea, bronchospasm, and occasionally a rash.

DATA LINK

Data link to the following mucolytics in your nursing drug guide:

MUCOLYTICS

Name	Brand Name	Usual Indications
P acetylcysteine	*Mucomyst* and others	Liquification of secretions in patients with difficulty moving secretions; clearing of secretions for diagnostic tests; postoperatively to facilitate clearing of secretions; orally to protect liver from acetaminophen toxicity
dornase alfa	*Pulmozyme*	To relieve the build-up of secretions in cystic fibrosis to keep airways open longer

NURSING CONSIDERATIONS for patients receiving mucolytics

Assessment

HISTORY. Screen for the following: any history of allergy to the drug and the presence of acute bronchospasm, which are contraindications to the use of these drugs; and peptic ulcer and esophageal varices, which would require careful monitoring and cautious use.

PHYSICAL ASSESSMENT. Physical assessment should be done to establish baseline data for assessing the effectiveness of the drug and the occurrence of any adverse effects associated with drug therapy. Assess the following: skin color and lesions to monitor for adverse reactions; blood pressure and pulse to evaluate cardiac response to drug treatment; and respirations and adventitious sounds to monitor drug effectiveness.

Nursing Diagnoses

The patient receiving a mucolytic may have the following nursing diagnoses related to drug therapy:

- Pain related to GI, CNS, skin effects of the drug
- Sensory–perceptual alteration related to CNS effects
- Alteration in airflow related to bronchospasm
- Knowledge deficit regarding drug therapy

Implementation

- Avoid combining with other drugs in the nebulizer *to avoid the formation of precipitates and potential loss of effectiveness of either drug.*
- Dilute the concentrate with sterile water for *injection if build-up becomes a problem that could impede drug delivery.*
- Note that patients receiving acetylcysteine by face mask should have the residue wiped off the face mask and their face with plain water *to prevent skin breakdown.*
- Review the use of the nebulizer with patients receiving dornase alfa at home, *to assure the most effective use of the drug.* They should be cautioned to store the drug in the refrigerator, protected from light.
- Caution cystic fibrosis patients receiving dornase alfa about the need to continue all therapies for their cystic fibrosis *because dornase alfa is only a palliative therapy that improves respiratory symptoms.*
- Provide thorough patient teaching, including the drug name and prescribed dosage, measures to help avoid adverse effects, warning signs that may indicate problems, and the need for periodic monitoring and evaluation *to enhance patient knowledge about drug therapy and to promote compliance.*
- Offer support and encouragement *to help the patient cope with the disease and drug regimen.*

Evaluation

- Monitor patient response to the drug (improvement of respiratory symptoms, loosening of secretions).
- Monitor for adverse effects (CNS effects, skin rash, bronchospasm, GI upset).
- Evaluate the effectiveness of the teaching plan (patient can name drug, dosage, adverse effects to watch for, specific measures to avoid adverse effects, measures to take to increase the effectiveness of the drug).
- Monitor the effectiveness of comfort and safety measures and compliance with the regimen.

CHAPTER SUMMARY

- The classes of drugs that affect the upper respiratory system work to keep the airways open and gases moving efficiently.
- Antitussives are drugs that suppress the cough reflex. They can act centrally, to suppress the medullary cough center, or locally, to increase secretion and buffer irritation or to act as local anesthetics. These drugs should not be used longer than a week; patients with persistent cough after that time should seek medical evaluation.
- Decongestants are drugs that cause local vasoconstriction and therefore decrease the blood flow to the irritated and dilated capillaries of the mucous membranes lining the nasal passages and sinus cavities.
- An adverse effect that accompanies frequent or prolonged use of decongestants is rebound vasodilation, called rhinitis medicamentosa. The reflex

reaction to vasoconstriction is a rebound vasodilation, which often leads to prolonged overuse of decongestants.

- Topical nasal decongestants are preferable in patients who need to avoid systemic adrenergic effects. Oral decongestants are associated with systemic adrenergic effects and require caution in patients with cardiovascular disease, hyperthyroidism, and diabetes mellitus.

- Topical nasal steroid decongestants block the inflammatory response from occurring. These drugs, which take several days to weeks to reach complete effectiveness, are preferred for patients with allergic rhinitis who need to avoid the complications of systemic steroid therapy.

- The antihistamines selectively block the effects of histamine at the H_1 receptor sites, decreasing the allergic response. Antihistamines are used for the relief of symptoms associated with seasonal and perennial allergic rhinitis, allergic conjunctivitis, uncomplicated urticaria, and angioedema.

- Patients taking antihistamines may react to dryness of the skin and mucous membranes. The nurse should encourage them to drink plenty of fluids, to use a humidifier if possible, to avoid smoke-filled rooms, and to use good skin care and moisturizers.

- Antihistamines should be avoided with any patient who has a prolonged Q-T interval because serious cardiac complications and even death have occurred.

- Expectorants are drugs that liquefy the lower respiratory tract secretions. They are used for the symptomatic relief of respiratory conditions characterized by a dry, nonproductive cough.

- Mucolytics work to break down mucus in order to aid high-risk respiratory patients in coughing up thick, tenacious secretions.

- Many of the drugs that act on the upper respiratory tract are found in different OTC cough and allergy preparations. Patients need to be advised to always read the labels carefully to avoid inadvertent overdose and toxicity.

Bibliography

Bullock, B. L. (2000). *Focus on pathophysiology.* Philadelphia: Lippincott Williams & Wilkins.

Hardman, J. G., Limbird, L. E., Molinoff, P. B., Ruddon, R. W., & Gilman, A. G. (Eds.). (1996). *Goodman and Gilman's the pharmacological basis of therapeutics* (9th ed.). New York: McGraw-Hill.

Karch, A. M. (2000). *2000 Lippincott's nursing drug guide.* Philadelphia: Lippincott Williams & Wilkins.

Malseed, R. (1995). *Textbook of pharmacology and nursing care.* Philadelphia: J. B. Lippincott.

McEvoy, B. R. (Ed.). (1999). *Facts and comparisons 1999.* St. Louis: Facts and Comparisons.

Professional's guide to patient drug facts. (1999). St. Louis: Facts and Comparisons.

CHAPTER 53

Drugs for Treating Obstructive Pulmonary Disorders

Bronchodilators/antiasthmatics
Xanthines
- aminophylline
- caffeine
- dyphylline
- oxtriphylline
- pentoxifylline
- **P** theophylline

Sympathomimetics
- albuterol
- bitolterol
- ephedrine
- **P** epinephrine
- isoetharine
- isoproterenol
- metaproterenol
- pirbuterol
- salmeterol
- terbutaline

Anticholinergics
- ipratropium

Inhaled steroids
- beclomethasone
- **P** flunisolide
- triamcinolone

Leukotriene receptor antagonists
- **P** zafirkulast
- zileuton

Lung surfactants
- **P** beractant
- colfosceril

Other antiallergy/antiasthmatic drugs
- **P** cromolyn
- nedocromil

CHAPTER OUTLINE

KEY TERMS

bronchodilator
xanthine
Cheyne-Stokes respiration
sympathomimetics
leukotriene receptor antagonists
mast cell stabilizer
respiratory distress syndrome (RDS)

INTRODUCTION

Pulmonary obstructive diseases include asthma and chronic obstructive pulmonary disease (COPD), which includes emphysema. These diseases present with obstruction to the major airways. The obstruction of asthma, emphysema, and COPD can be related to inflammation resulting in the narrowing of the interior of the airway and to muscular constriction resulting in the narrowing of the conducting tube (Figure 53-1). With chronic inflammation, muscular and cilial action is lost, and complications related to the loss of these protective processes can occur, for example, infections, pneumonia, and movement of inhaled substances deep into the respiratory system. In severe COPD, air is trapped in the lower respiratory tract, the alveoli degenerate and fuse together, and the exchange of gases is greatly impaired. Treatment of these disorders is aimed at either opening the conducting airways through muscular bronchodilation or decreasing the effects of inflammation on the lining of the airway.

Another obstructive disease, ***respiratory distress syndrome,*** presents with an obstruction at the alveolar level. The obstruction of respiratory distress syndrome in the neonate is related to a lack of the lipoprotein surfactant, leading to an inability to maintain an open alveolus. Surfactant is essential in decreasing the surface tension in the tiny alveolus, allowing it to expand and remain open. If surfactant is lacking, the alveoli collapse and gas exchange cannot occur. Pharmacological therapy for this condition involves instilling surfactant into the alveoli. Adult respiratory distress syndrome (ARDS) is characterized

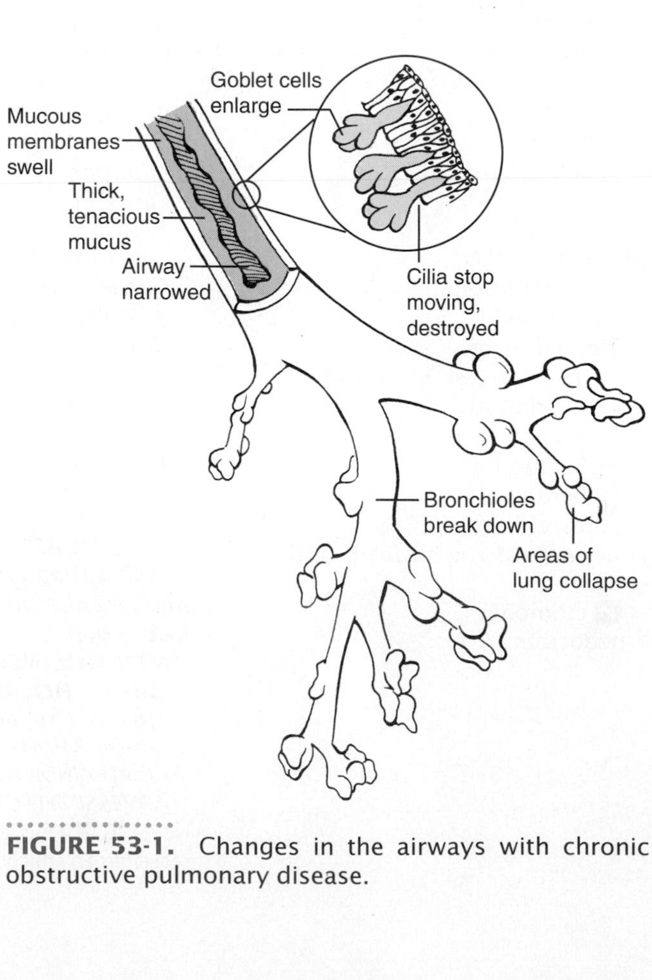

FIGURE 53-1. Changes in the airways with chronic obstructive pulmonary disease.

by progressive loss of lung compliance and increasing hypoxia. This syndrome occurs as a result of a severe insult to the body, such as cardiovascular collapse, major burns, severe trauma, and rapid depressurization. Treatment of ARDS involves reversal of the underlying cause of the problem combined with ventilatory support.

BRONCHODILATORS/ ANTIASTHMATICS

Bronchodilators are medications used to facilitate respirations by dilating the airways. They are helpful in symptomatic relief or prevention of bronchial asthma and bronchospasm associated with COPD. Several of the bronchodilators are administered orally and absorbed systemically, giving them the potential for many systemic adverse effects. Other medications are administered directly into the airways by nebulizers. These medications have the advantage of a decreased number of systemic adverse reactions.

XANTHINES

The ***xanthines,*** including caffeine and theophylline (*Theo-Dur*), come from a variety of naturally occurring sources. These drugs were once the main choice for treatment of asthma and bronchospasm. However, they have a relatively narrow margin of safety and interact with many other drugs. Consequently, they are no longer considered the first-choice bronchodilators. Xanthines include aminophylline (*Truphylline*), caffeine (*Caffedrine* and others), dyphylline (*Dilor* and others), oxtriphylline (*Choledyl-SA*), pentoxifylline (*Trental*), and theophylline (*Slo-Bid, Theo-Dur*).

THERAPEUTIC ACTIONS AND INDICATIONS

The xanthines have a direct effect on the smooth muscles of the respiratory tract, both those in the bronchi and the blood vessels (Figure 53-2). Although the exact mechanism of action is not known, one theory suggests that xanthines work by directly affecting the mobilization of calcium within the cell. It does this by stimulating two prostaglandins, resulting in smooth muscle relaxation. The effect of smooth muscle relaxation increases the vital capacity that has been impaired by bronchospasm or air-trapping. Xanthines also inhibit the release of slow-reacting substance of anaphylaxis (SRSA) and histamine, decreasing the bronchial swelling and narrowing that occurs as a result of these two chemicals.

Xanthines are indicated for the symptomatic relief or prevention of bronchial asthma and reversal of

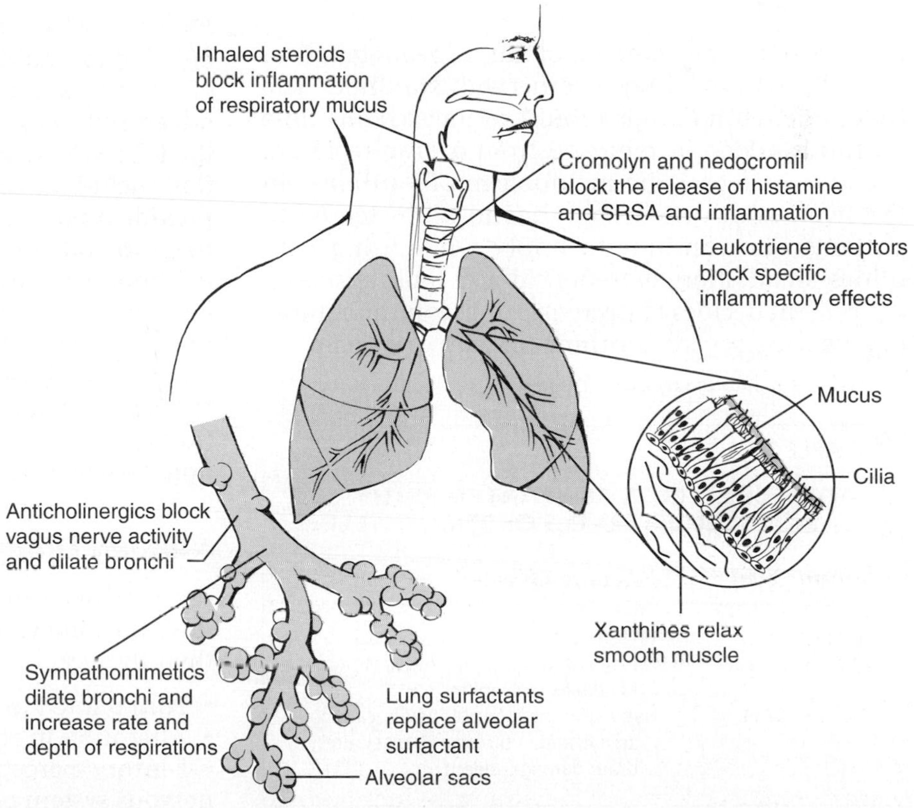

FIGURE 53-2. Sites of action of drugs used to treat obstructive pulmonary disorders.

bronchospasm associated with COPD. Unlabeled uses include stimulation of respirations in ***Cheyne-Stokes respiration*** and the treatment of apnea and bradycardia in premature infants.

CONTRAINDICATIONS/CAUTIONS

Caution should be taken with any patient with gastrointestinal (GI) problems, coronary disease, respiratory dysfunction, renal or hepatic disease, alcoholism, or hyperthyroidism because these conditions can be exacerbated by the systemic effects of xanthines. Xanthines are available for oral and parenteral use; the drug should be switched to the oral form as soon as possible because the systemic effects are less acute and more manageable.

ADVERSE EFFECTS

Adverse effects associated with xanthines are related to theophylline levels in the blood. Therapeutic theophylline levels are from 10 to 20 μg/ml. With increasing levels, predictable adverse effects are seen, ranging from GI upset, nausea, irritability, and tachycardia to seizures, brain damage, and even death (Table 53-1). Consult your drug guide for detailed lists of theophylline levels and associated adverse effects.

CLINICALLY IMPORTANT DRUG–DRUG INTERACTIONS

Because of the mechanism of xanthine metabolism in the liver, many drugs interact with xanthines. The list of interacting drugs should be checked any time a drug is added or removed from a drug regimen. Nicotine increases the metabolism of xanthines in the liver; xanthine dosage has to be increased in patients who continue to smoke while using xanthines. In addition, extreme caution must be used if the patient decides to decrease or discontinue smoking, because severe xanthine toxicity can occur.

TABLE 53-1

ADVERSE EFFECTS ASSOCIATED WITH VARIOUS SERUM LEVELS OF THEOPHYLLINE

Serum Level	Adverse Effects
<20 μg/mL	Uncommon
>20–25 μg/mL	Nausea, vomiting, diarrhea, insomnia, headache, irritability
>30–35 μg/mL	Hyperglycemia, hypotension, cardiac arrhythmias, tachycardia, seizures, brain damage, death

DATA LINK

Data link to the following xanthine bronchodilators in your nursing drug guide:

XANTHINE BRONCHODILATORS

Name	Brand Name	Usual Indications
aminophylline	*Truphylline*	All of the xanthine bronchodilators are indicated for symptomatic relief or prevention of bronchial asthma and reversal of bronchospasm associated with COPD
caffeine	generic	
dyphylline	*Dilor*	
oxtriphylline	*Choledyl-SA*	
pentoxifylline	*Trental*	
P theophylline	*Slo-Bid, Theo-Dur*	

NURSING CONSIDERATIONS
for patients receiving xanthines

Assessment

HISTORY. Screen for the following: any known allergies; cigarette use (which would affect the metabolism of the drug); peptic ulcer, gastritis, renal or hepatic dysfunction, and coronary disease, all of which require cautious use; and pregnancy and lactation (which are contraindications).

PHYSICAL ASSESSMENT. Physical assessment should be done to establish baseline data for assessing the effectiveness of the drug and the occurrence of any adverse effects associated with drug therapy. Perform the following assessments: thorough skin examination including color and the presence of lesions (to provide a baseline as a reference for drug effectiveness); blood pressure, pulse, cardiac auscultation, peripheral perfusion, and baseline EKG (to provide a baseline for effects on the cardiovascular system); and bowel sounds, liver evaluation, and blood tests (to provide a baseline for renal and hepatic function tests). In addition, evaluate serum theophylline levels (to provide a baseline reference and identify conditions that may require caution in the use of diuretics).

Nursing Diagnoses

The patient receiving a xanthine bronchodilator may have the following nursing diagnoses related to drug therapy:

- Pain related to headache and GI upset
- Alteration in cardiac output
- Sensory–perceptual alterations related to central nervous system (CNS) effects

PATIENT TEACHING CHECKLIST

Xanthines

Create customized patient teaching materials for a specific xanthine from your CD-ROM. Your patient teaching should stress the following points for drugs within this class:

Bronchodilators work by relaxing the airways, helping to make breathing easier and to decrease wheezes and shortness of breath. To be effective, this drug must be taken exactly as prescribed.

This drug should be taken on an empty stomach with a full glass of water. If GI upset is severe, you can take the drug with food. Do not chew the enteric-coated or timed-release capsules or tablets—they have to be swallowed whole to be effective.

Common effects of this drug include:

- GI upset, nausea, vomiting, heartburn—Taking the drug with food may help this problem.
- Restlessness, nervousness, difficulty in sleeping—The body often adjusts to these effects over time. Avoiding other stimulants, like caffeine, may help decrease some of these symptoms.
- Headache—This often goes away with time. If headaches persist or become worse, notify your health care provider.

Many foods can change the way that your drug works; if you decide to change your diet, consult with your health care provider.

Adverse effects of the drug can be avoided by avoiding foods that contain caffeine or other xanthine derivatives (coffee, cola, chocolate, tea) or by using them in moderate amounts. This is especially important if you experience nervousness, restlessness or sleeplessness.

Cigarette smoking affects the way your body uses this drug. If you decide to change your smoking habits, such as increasing or decreasing the number of cigarettes you smoke each day, consult with your health care provider regarding the possible need to adjust your dosage.

Report any of the following to your health care provider: vomiting, severe abdominal pain, pounding or fast heartbeat, confusion, unusual tiredness, muscle twitching, skin rash, hives.

Avoid the use of any over-the-counter medication without first checking with your health care provider. Several of these medications can interfere with the effectiveness of this drug.

Tell any doctor, nurse, or other health care provider that you are taking this drug.

Keep this drug, and all medications, out of the reach of children.

This Teaching Checklist reflects general patient teaching guidelines. It is not meant to be a substitute for drug-specific teaching information; which is available in nursing drug guides.

- Ineffective rest–activity pattern
- Knowledge deficit regarding drug therapy

Implementation

- Administer oral drug with food or milk *to relieve GI irritation, if GI upset is a problem.*
- Monitor patient response to the drug, for example, relief of respiratory difficulty and improved air flow, *to determine the effectiveness of the drug dosage and to adjust dosage as needed.*
- Provide comfort measures, including rest periods, quiet environment, dietary control of caffeine, and headache therapy as needed, *to help the patient cope with the effects of drug therapy.*
- Provide periodic follow-up including blood tests *to monitor serum theophylline levels.*
- Provide thorough patient teaching, including the drug name and prescribed dosage, measures to help avoid adverse effects, warning signs that may indicate problems, and the need for periodic monitoring and evaluation, *to enhance patient knowledge about drug therapy and to promote compliance* (see Patient Teaching Checklist: Xanthines).

Evaluation

- Monitor patient response to the drug (improved air flow, ease of respirations).
- Monitor for adverse effects (CNS effects, cardiac arrhythmias, GI upset, local irritation).
- Monitor for potential drug–drug interactions; consult with the prescriber to adjust dosages as appropriate.

NURSING CARE GUIDE
Xanthines

Assessment	Nursing Diagnoses	Implementation	Evaluation
HISTORY Allergies, peptic ulcer, gastritis, renal or hepatic dysfunction, coronary disease, cigarette use, pregnancy, and lactation.	Pain related to GI effects Alteration in cardiac output Sensory–perceptual alteration Ineffective rest–activity pattern Knowledge deficit regarding drug therapy	Provide comfort and safety measures: - Give drug with meals. - Allow for rest periods. - Provide a quiet environment. - Ensure dietary control of caffeine. - Provide headache therapy as needed. Provide support and reassurance to deal with drug effects and lifestyle changes. Provide patient teaching regarding drug name, dosage, adverse effects, precautions, warnings to report, dietary cautions, and need for follow-up.	Evaluate drug effects: relief of respiratory difficulty, improvement of air movement. Monitor for adverse effects: GI upset, CNS effects, cardiac arrhythmias, local irritation (suppositories). Monitor for drug–drug interactions as indicated for each drug. Evaluate effectiveness of patient teaching program. Evaluate effectiveness of comfort and safety measures.
PHYSICAL EXAMINATION Neurological: orientation, reflexes, affect, coordination Skin: color, lesions CV: BP, P, peripheral perfusion, baseline EKG GI: bowel sounds, abdominal exam Lab tests: serum theophylline levels, renal, hepatic function tests			

• Evaluate the effectiveness of the teaching plan (patient can name drug, dosage, adverse effects to watch for, specific measures to avoid adverse effects).
• Monitor effectiveness of comfort measures and compliance with the regimen (see Nursing Care Guide: Xanthines).

SYMPATHOMIMETICS

Sympathomimetics are drugs that mimic the effects of the sympathetic nervous system. One of the actions of the sympathetic nervous system is dilation of the bronchi and increased rate and depth of respiration. This is the desired effect when selecting a sympathomimetic as a bronchodilator.

Sympathomimetics that are used as bronchodilators include the following:

• Albuterol (*Proventil* and others), which is long-acting and available in inhaled and oral forms.
• Bitolterol (*Tornalate*), which is long-acting and inhaled; preferred for prophylaxis of bronchospasm.
• Ephedrine (generic), which is used parenterally for acute bronchospasm, though epinephrine is the drug of choice.
• Epinephrine (*Sus-Phrine, EpiPen,* and others), which is the drug of choice for the treatment of acute bronchospasm, including that which is caused by anaphylaxis; also available for inhalation. Because epinephrine is associated with systemic sympathomimetic effects, it is not the drug of choice for patients with cardiac conditions.

CASE STUDY

Toxic Reaction to Theophylline

PRESENTATION

M. K. has a medical diagnosis of chronic bronchitis and has been stabilized on theophylline for the past 3 years. She has been labeled as noncompliant to medical therapy because she continues to smoke cigarettes (more than 3 packs per day) knowing that she has a progressive pulmonary disease. M. K. was referred to a student nurse for teaching. After several sessions, in which the student presented posters and pictures and gave M. K. a great deal of personal attention and encouragement, it was determined that M. K. had a good understanding of her problem and would stop or at least cut down on her smoking. Three days later, M. K. presented to the emergency department with complaints of dizziness, nausea, vomiting, confusion, grouchiness, and palpitations. Her admission heart rate was 96 with occasional to frequent PVCs.

CRITICAL THINKING QUESTIONS

What probably happened to M. K.? What information should the student have known before conducting the teaching program? How could that information have been included in the patient teaching program? What would the best approach be to this patient now?

DISCUSSION

M. K. probably did cut down on her smoking. However, she was not aware that cigarette smoking increases the metabolism of theophylline and that she had been stabilized on a dose that took that information into account. By cutting down on smoking, theophylline was not metabolized as quickly and began to accumulate, leading to the toxic reaction that brought M. K. into the emergency department. This is a real nursing challenge. By following the teaching program and doing what she was asked to do, M. K. became sicker and felt awful. A careful teaching approach will be necessary to encourage M. K. to continue cutting down on cigarette smoking. Staff should be educated on the numerous variables that affect drug therapy and encouraged to check drug interactions frequently when making any changes in a patient's regimen. Regular follow-up and support will be important to help M. K. regain trust in her medical care providers and to continue her progress in cutting down smoking. Frequent checks of theophylline levels should be done while M. K. is cutting back, and dosage adjustments should be made by her prescriber to maintain therapeutic levels of theophylline and avoid toxic levels.

- Isoetharine (*Bronkosol* and others), which is an inhaled drug used for prophylaxis and treatment of bronchospasm.
- Isoproterenol (*Isuprel* and others), which is used for treatment of bronchospasm during anesthesia and as an inhalant for treatment of bronchospasm; it is associated with more cardiac side effects than some other drugs.
- Metaproterenol (*Alupent*), which is available as an oral or inhaled agent and is used for both treatment and prophylaxis of bronchospasm.
- Pirbuterol (*Maxair*), which is an inhaled drug used for both treatment and prophylaxis of bronchospasm.
- Salmeterol (*Serevent*), which is an inhaled drug successfully used to prevent exercise-induced asthma and for prophylaxis of bronchospasm in select patients.
- Terbutaline (*Brethaire* and others), which can be used orally, parenterally, and by inhalation for both prophylaxis and treatment of bronchospasm.

THERAPEUTIC ACTIONS AND INDICATIONS

Most of the sympathomimetics used as bronchodilators are beta$_2$-selective adrenergic agonists. That means that at therapeutic levels, their actions are specific to the beta$_2$ receptors found in the bronchi (see Chapter 28). This specificity is lost at higher levels. Other systemic effects of sympathomimetics include increased blood pressure, increased heart rate, vasoconstriction, and decreased renal and GI blood flow-all actions of the sympathetic nervous system. These overall effects limit the systemic usefulness of these drugs in certain patients.

The sympathomimetic epinephrine is given by injection during acute asthma attacks, when the need for bronchodilation outweighs the risk of adverse effects. Other sympathomimetics are used in the treatment of bronchospasm in reversible obstructive airway disease, such as acute and chronic asthma and chronic bronchitis. They have also been effective in preventing exercise-induced bronchospasm (see Figure 53-2).

CONTRAINDICATIONS/CAUTIONS

These drugs are contraindicated or should be used with caution, depending on the severity of the underlying condition, in conditions that would be aggravated by the sympathetic stimulation. Such conditions include cardiac disease, vascular disease, arrhythmias, diabetes, hyperthyroidism, pregnancy, and lactation.

ADVERSE EFFECTS

Adverse effects of these drugs, which can be attributed to sympathomimetic stimulation, include CNS stimulation, GI upset, cardiac arrhythmias, hypertension, bronchospasm, sweating, pallor, and flushing.

CLINICALLY IMPORTANT DRUG–DRUG INTERACTIONS

Special precautions need to be used to avoid the combination of sympathomimetic bronchodilators with the general anesthetics cyclopropane and halogenated hydrocarbons. Because these drugs sensitize the myocardium to catecholamines, serious cardiac complications could occur.

DATA LINK

Data link to the following sympathomimetic bronchodilators in your nursing drug guide:

SYMPATHOMIMETIC BRONCHODILATORS

Name	Brand Name	Usual Indications
albuterol	*Proventil*	Treatment and prophylaxis of bronchospasm
bitolterol	*Tornalate*	Prophylaxis for bronchospasm
ephedrine	generic	Treatment of acute bronchospasm
P epinephrine	*Sus-phrine*	Drug of choice for treatment of acute bronchospasm
isoetharine	*Bronkosol*	Treatment and prophylaxis of bronchospasm
isoproterenol	*Isuprel*	Treatment of bronchospasm during anesthesia and prophylaxis of bronchospasm
metaproterenol	*Alupent*	Treatment and prophylaxis of bronchospasm
pirbuterol	*Maxair*	Treatment and prophylaxis of bronchospasm
salmeterol	*Serevent*	Prophylaxis of bronchospasm and prevention of exercise-induced asthma
terbutaline	*Brethaire*	Treatment and prophylaxis of bronchospasm

NURSING CONSIDERATIONS
for patients receiving sympathomimetic bronchodilators

Assessment

HISTORY. Screen for the following: allergy to any sympathomimetic or drug vehicle; pregnancy or lactation, which would require cautious use of the drug; acute asthma attack, which would be a contraindication for use of the drug; cardiac disease, vascular disease, arrhythmias, diabetes, and hyperthyroidism, which may be exacerbated by sympathomimetic effects; and the use of the general anesthetics cyclopropane and halogenated hydrocarbons, which sensitize the myocardium to catecholamines and could cause serious cardiac complications if used with these drugs.

PHYSICAL ASSESSMENT. Physical assessment should be done to establish baseline data for assessing the effectiveness of the drug and the occurrence of any adverse effects associated with drug therapy. Assess the following: reflexes, orientation (to evaluate CNS effects of the drug); respirations, adventitious sounds (to establish a baseline for drug effectiveness and possible adverse effects); pulse, blood pressure, and, in certain cases, a baseline EKG (to monitor the cardiovascular effects of sympathetic stimulation); and liver function tests (to assess for changes that could interfere with metabolism of the drug and require dosage adjustment).

Nursing Diagnoses

The patient receiving a sympathomimetic bronchodilator may have the following nursing diagnoses related to drug therapy:

- Alteration in cardiac output related to sympathomimetic effects
- Pain related to CNS, GI, cardiac effects of the drug
- Alteration in thought processes related to CNS effects
- Knowledge deficit related to drug therapy

Implementation

- Assure the patient that the drug of choice will vary with each individual. *These sympathomimetics are slightly different chemicals and are prepared in a variety of delivery systems. A patient may have to try several different sympathomimetics before the most effective one is found.*
- Advise patients to use the minimal amount needed for the shortest period of time necessary, *to prevent adverse effects and accumulation of drug levels.*
- Teach patients who use one of these drugs for exercise-induced asthma to use it 30 to 60 minutes before exercising *to ensure peak therapeutic effects when they are needed.*
- Provide safety measures as needed if CNS effects become a problem, *to prevent patient injury.*
- Provide small, frequent meals and nutritional consultation if GI effects interfere with eating *to ensure proper nutrition.*
- Carefully teach the patient about the proper use of the prescribed delivery system. Review that proce-

dure periodically *as improper use may result in ineffective therapy.*

- Provide thorough patient teaching, including the drug name and prescribed dosage, measures to help avoid adverse effects, warning signs that may indicate problems, and the need for periodic monitoring and evaluation *to enhance patient knowledge about drug therapy and to promote compliance.*
- Offer support and encouragement *to help the patient cope with the disease and drug regimen.*

Evaluation

- Monitor patient response to the drug (improved breathing).
- Monitor for adverse effects (CNS effects, increased pulse and blood pressure, GI upset).
- Evaluate the effectiveness of the teaching plan (patient can name drug, dosage, adverse effects to watch for, specific measures to avoid adverse effects, measures to take to increase the effectiveness of the drug).
- Monitor the effectiveness of other measures to ease breathing.

ANTICHOLINERGIC BRONCHODILATOR

Patients who are not able to tolerate the sympathetic effects of the sympathomimetics might respond to the anticholinergic drug ipratropium (*Atrovent*). This drug is not as effective as the sympathomimetics, but can provide some relief to those patients who cannot tolerate the other drugs.

THERAPEUTIC ACTIONS AND INDICATIONS

Anticholinergics are used as bronchodilators because of their effect on the vagus nerve, which is to block or antagonize the action of the neurotransmitter acetylcholine at vagal-mediated receptor sites (see Figure 53-2). Normally, vagal stimulation results in a stimulating effect on smooth muscle, causing contraction. By blocking the vagal effect, relaxation of smooth muscle in the bronchi occurs, leading to bronchodilation. Ipratropium is the only anticholinergic recommended for bronchodilation. It is indicated for the maintenance treatment of patients with COPD, including bronchospasm and emphysema.

CONTRAINDICATIONS/CAUTIONS

Caution should be used in any condition that would be aggravated by the anticholinergic or atropine-like effects of the drug, such as narrow-angle glaucoma (drainage of the vitreous humor can be blocked by smooth muscle relaxation), bladder neck obstruction or prostatic hypertrophy (relaxed muscle causes decreased bladder tone), and conditions aggravated by dry mouth and throat. The use of ipratropium is contraindicated in the presence of known allergy to the drug.

ADVERSE EFFECTS

Adverse effects are related to the anticholinergic effects of the drug when it is absorbed systemically. These effects include dizziness, headache, fatigue, nervousness, dry mouth, sore throat, palpitations, and urinary retention.

DATA LINK

Data link to the following anticholinergic bronchodilator in your nursing drug guide:

ANTICHOLINERGIC BRONCHODILATOR

Name	Brand Name	Usual Indication
ipratropium	*Atrovent*	Maintenance treatment of patients with COPD

NURSING CONSIDERATIONS for patients receiving an anticholinergic bronchodilator

Assessment

HISTORY. Screen for the following: allergy to atropine or other anticholinergics; acute bronchospasm, which would be a contraindication; narrow-angle glaucoma (drainage of the vitreous humor can be blocked by smooth muscle relaxation), bladder neck obstruction or prostatic hypertrophy (relaxed muscle causes decreased bladder tone), and conditions aggravated by dry mouth and throat, all of which could be exacerbated by the use of this drug; and pregnancy and lactation, which would require cautious use.

PHYSICAL ASSESSMENT. Physical assessment should be done to establish baseline data for assessing the effectiveness of the drug and the occurrence of any adverse effects associated with drug therapy. Assess the following: skin color and lesions (to assess for dryness or allergic reaction); orientation, affect, and reflexes (to evaluate CNS effects); pulse and blood pressure (to monitor cardiovascular effects of the drug); respirations and adventitious sounds (to monitor drug effectiveness and possible adverse effects); and urinary output and prostate palpation as appropriate (to monitor anticholinergic effects).

Nursing Diagnoses

The patient receiving an anticholinergic bronchodilator may have the following nursing diagnoses related to drug therapy:

- Pain related to CNS, GI, respiratory effects of drug
- Alteration in nutrition related to dry mouth and GI upset
- Knowledge deficit regarding drug therapy

Implementation

- Ensure adequate hydration and provide environmental control, such as the use of a humidifier, *to make the patient more comfortable.*
- Encourage the patient to void before each dose of medication *to prevent urinary retention related to drug effects.*
- Provide safety measures if CNS effects occur *to prevent patient injury.*
- Provide small, frequent meals and sugarless lozenges *to relieve dry mouth and GI upset.*
- Review use of the inhalator with the patient. Caution the patient not to exceed 12 inhalations in 24 hours *to prevent serious adverse effects.*
- Advise the patient not to drive or use hazardous machinery if nervousness, dizziness, and drowsiness occur with this drug, *to prevent injury.*
- Provide thorough patient teaching, including the drug name and prescribed dosage, measures to help avoid adverse effects, warning signs that may indicate problems, and the need for periodic monitoring and evaluation, *to enhance patient knowledge about drug therapy and to promote compliance.*
- Offer support and encouragement *to help the patient cope with the disease and drug regimen.*

Evaluation

- Monitor patient response to the drug (improved breathing).
- Monitor for adverse effects (CNS effects, increased pulse, blood pressure; GI upset; dry skin and mucous membranes).
- Evaluate the effectiveness of the teaching plan (patient can name drug, dosage, adverse effects to watch for, specific measures to avoid adverse effects, measures to take to increase the effectiveness of the drug).
- Monitor the effectiveness of other measures to ease breathing.

INHALED STEROIDS

Inhaled steroids have been found to be a very effective treatment for bronchospasm. Agents approved for this use include beclomethasone (*Beclovent* and others), flunisolide (*AeroBid*), and triamcinolone (*Azmacort* and others). The drug of choice depends on the individual patient's response. For example, a patient may have little response to one agent and do very well on another. It is usually useful to try another preparation if one is not effective within 2 to 3 weeks.

THERAPEUTIC ACTIONS AND INDICATIONS

Inhaled steroids are used to decrease the inflammatory response in the airway. In an airway swollen and narrowed by inflammation and swelling, this action will increase airflow and facilitate respiration. Inhaling the steroid tends to decrease the numerous systemic effects that are associated with steroid use. When administered into the lungs by inhalation, steroids decrease the effectiveness of the inflammatory cells. This has two effects: decreased swelling associated with inflammation and promotion of beta adrenergic receptor activity, which may promote smooth muscle relaxation and inhibit bronchoconstriction (see Figure 53-2).

These drugs are used for the prevention and treatment of asthma, to treat chronic steroid-dependent bronchial asthma, and as adjunct therapy for patients whose asthma is not controlled by traditional bronchodilators. These drugs are rapidly absorbed, but take from 2 to 3 weeks to reach effective levels.

CONTRAINDICATIONS/CAUTIONS

Inhaled corticosteroids are not for emergency use and not for use during an acute asthma attack or status asthmaticus. They should not be used during pregnancy or lactation. These preparations should be used with caution in any patient with an active infection of the respiratory system, as the depression of the inflammatory response could result in serious illness.

ADVERSE EFFECTS

Adverse effects are limited because of the route of administration. Sore throat, hoarseness, coughing, dry mouth, and pharyngeal and laryngeal fungal infections are the most common side effects encountered. If a patient does not administer the drug appropriately or develops lesions that allow absorption of the drug, the systemic side effects associated with steroids may occur.

DATA LINK

Data link to the following inhaled steroids in your nursing drug guide:

INHALED STEROIDS

Name	Brand Name	Usual Indications
beclomethasone	*Beclovent*	All of the inhaled steroids are used for the prevention and treatment of asthma; for treatment of chronic

		steroid-dependent bronchial asthma; and as adjunct therapy for asthma patients who do not respond to traditional bronchodilators
P flunisolide	*Aerobid*	
triamcinolone	*Azmacort*	

NURSING CONSIDERATIONS
for patients receiving inhaled steroids

Assessment

HISTORY. Screen for the following: acute asthmatic attacks; allergy to the drugs; pregnancy and lactation, which are contraindications; and systemic infections, which require cautious use.

PHYSICAL ASSESSMENT. Physical assessment should be done to establish baseline data for assessing the effectiveness of the drug and the occurrence of any adverse effects associated with drug therapy. Assess the following: temperature (to monitor for possible infections); blood pressure, pulse, and auscultation (to evaluate cardiovascular response); and respirations and adventitious sounds (to monitor drug effectiveness). In addition, conduct an examination of the nares to evaluate for any lesions which might lead to systemic absorption of the drug.

Nursing Diagnoses

The patient receiving an inhaled steroid may have the following nursing diagnoses related to drug therapy:

- Potential for injury related to immunosuppression
- Pain related to local effects of the drug
- Knowledge deficit regarding drug therapy

Implementation

- Do not administer the drug to treat an acute asthma attack or status asthmaticus, *as these drugs are not intended for treatment of acute attack.*
- Taper systemic steroids carefully during the transfer to inhaled steroids; *deaths have occurred from adrenal insufficiency with sudden withdrawal.*
- Have the patient use decongestant drops before using the inhaled steroid *to facilitate penetration of the drug if nasal congestion is a problem.*
- Have the patient rinse the mouth after using the inhaler, as this will help *to decrease systemic absorption and decrease GI upset and nausea.*
- Monitor the patient for any sign of respiratory infection; *continued use of steroids during an acute infection can lead to serious complications related to the depression of the inflammatory and immune responses.*
- Provide thorough patient teaching, including the drug name and prescribed dosage, measures to help avoid adverse effects, warning signs that may indicate problems, and the need for periodic monitoring and evaluation *to enhance patient knowledge about drug therapy and to promote compliance.*
- Offer support and encouragement *to help the patient cope with the disease and drug regimen.*

Evaluation

- Monitor patient response to the drug (improved breathing).
- Monitor for adverse effects (nasal irritation, fever, GI upset).
- Evaluate the effectiveness of the teaching plan (patient can name drug, dosage, adverse effects to watch for, specific measures to avoid adverse effects, measures to take to increase the effectiveness of the drug).
- Monitor the effectiveness of other measures to ease breathing.

WWW.WEB LINKS

Health care providers and patients may want to consult the following Internet sources:

Information on living with COPD, aimed at patients and families:
http://olinda.freeservers.com

Information on education programs, research, smoking cessation, adjusting lifestyles, support groups:
http://www.combivent.com/fam_index.htm

Information on support groups, treatment programs, resources, and research involving COPD and asthma:
http://www.newtechpub.com/health.html

Information on respiratory distress syndrome:
http://www.uia.org/uiademo/str/j1189.htm

Information on lung diseases, community support groups, getting involved, treatment, research, definitions:
http://www.lungusa.org/index.html

LEUKOTRIENE RECEPTOR ANTAGONISTS

A new class of drugs, the ***leukotriene receptor antagonists,*** was developed to act more specifically at the site of the problem associated with asthma. Zafirkulast (*Accolate*) was the first drug of this class to be developed. Zileuton (*Zyflo*) is the newest drug of this class. Because this class is new, long-term effects and the benefits of one drug over another have not yet been determined.

THERAPEUTIC ACTIONS AND INDICATIONS

Leukotriene receptor antagonists selectively and competitively block (zafirkulast) or antagonize (zileuton) receptors for the production of leukotriene D4 and E4, components of slow-reacting substance of anaphylaxis (SRSA). As a result of these actions, these drugs block many of the signs and symptoms of asthma, such as neutrophil and eosinophil migration, neutrophil and monocyte aggregation, leukocyte adhesion, increased capillary permeability, and smooth muscle contraction. These actions contribute to inflammation, edema, mucus secretion, and bronchoconstriction seen in patients with asthma. These drugs are indicated for the prophylaxis and chronic treatment of bronchial asthma in patients younger than 12 years of age. They are not indicated for the treatment of acute asthmatic attacks (see Figure 53-2).

CONTRAINDICATIONS/CAUTIONS

These drugs should be used cautiously with hepatic or renal impairment because these conditions can affect the drug's metabolism and excretion.

ADVERSE EFFECTS

Adverse effects associated with leukotriene receptor antagonists include headache, dizziness, myalgia, nausea, diarrhea, abdominal pain, elevated liver enzymes, vomiting, generalized pain, fever, and myalgia.

CLINICALLY IMPORTANT DRUG–DRUG INTERACTIONS

Caution should be used if propranolol, theophylline, terfenadine, or warfarin are taken with these drugs, as increased toxicity can occur. Toxicity may also occur when combined with calcium channel blockers, cyclosporine, and aspirin; decreased dosage of either drug may be necessary.

DATA LINK

Data link to the following leukotriene receptor antagonists in your nursing drug guide:

LEUKOTRIENE RECEPTOR ANTAGONISTS

Name	Brand Name	Usual Indication
P zafirkulast	*Accolate*	Prophylaxis and chronic treatment of bronchial asthma
zileuton	*Zyflo*	Prophylaxis and chronic treatment of bronchial asthma

NURSING CONSIDERATIONS
for patients receiving leukotriene receptor antagonists

Assessment

HISTORY. Screen for the following: allergy to the drug, pregnancy or lactation, and acute bronchospasm or asthmatic attack, all of which would be contraindications to the use of the drug; and impaired renal or hepatic function, which could alter the metabolism and excretion of the drug and might require a dosage adjustment.

PHYSICAL ASSESSMENT. Physical assessment should be done to establish baseline data for assessing the effectiveness of the drug and the occurrence of any adverse effects associated with drug therapy. Assess the following: temperature (to monitor for underlying infection); orientation and affect (to monitor for CNS effects of the drug); respirations and adventitious breath sounds (to monitor the effectiveness of the drug); liver and renal function tests (to assess for impairments); and abdominal evaluation (to monitor GI effects of the drug).

Nursing Diagnoses

The patient receiving a leukotriene receptor antagonist may have the following nursing diagnoses related to drug therapy:

- Pain related to headache, GI upset, myalgia
- Potential for injury related to CNS effects
- Knowledge deficit regarding drug therapy

Implementation

- Administer the drug on an empty stomach, 1 hour before or 2 hours after meals. *The bioavailability of these drugs is decreased markedly by the presence of food.*
- Caution the patient that these drugs are not to be used during an acute asthmatic attack or bronchospasm; *instead, regular emergency measures will be needed.*
- Caution the patient to take the drug continuously and not to stop the medication during symptom-free periods *to assure therapeutic levels are maintained.*
- Provide appropriate safety measures if dizziness occurs *to prevent patient injury.*
- Urge the patient to avoid OTC preparations containing aspirin, *which might interfere with the effectiveness of these drugs.*
- Provide thorough patient teaching, including the drug name and prescribed dosage, measures to help avoid adverse effects, warning signs that may indicate problems, and the need for periodic monitoring

and evaluation, *to enhance patient knowledge about drug therapy and to promote compliance.*
- Offer support and encouragement *to help the patient cope with the disease and drug regimen.*

Evaluation

- Monitor patient response to the drug (improved breathing).
- Monitor for adverse effects (drowsiness, headache, abdominal pain, myalgia).
- Evaluate the effectiveness of the teaching plan (patient can name drug, dosage, adverse effects to watch for, specific measures to avoid adverse effects, measures to take to increase the effectiveness of the drug).
- Monitor the effectiveness of other measures to ease breathing.

LUNG SURFACTANTS

Lung surfactants are naturally occurring compounds or lipoproteins containing lipids and apoproteins that reduce the surface tension within the alveoli, allowing expansion of the alveoli for gas exchange. Two lung surfactants currently available for use are beractant (*Survanta*) and colfosceril (*Exosurf Neonatal*).

THERAPEUTIC ACTIONS AND INDICATIONS

These drugs are used to replace the surfactant missing in the lungs of neonates suffering from respiratory distress syndrome (see Figure 53-2). These agents are indicated for the rescue treatment of infants who have developed RDS. They are also used for prophylactic treatment of infants at high risk for developing RDS (those with a birth weight of less than 1350 grams or a birth weight of greater than 1350 grams who have evidence of respiratory immaturity).

ADVERSE EFFECTS

Adverse effects that are associated with the use of lung surfactants include patent ductus arteriosus, hypotension, intraventricular hemorrhage, pneumothorax, pulmonary air leak, hyperbilirubinemia, and sepsis. These effects may be related to the immaturity of the patient, the invasive procedures used, or reactions to the lipoprotein. Since lung surfactants are used as emergency drugs, there are no contraindications.

DATA LINK

Data link to the following lung surfactants in your nursing drug guide:

LUNG SURFACTANTS

Name	Brand Name	Usual Indications
P beractant	*Survanta*	Rescue treatment of infants who have developed RDS; prophylactic treatment of infants at high risk for developing RDS
colfosceril	*Exosurf Neonatal*	Rescue treatment of infants who have developed RDS; prophylactic treatment of infants at high risk for developing RDS

NURSING CONSIDERATIONS
for patients receiving lung surfactants

Assessment

HISTORY. Screen for time of birth and exact weight to determine appropriate dosages. Since this drug is used as an emergency treatment, there are no contraindications to screen for.

PHYSICAL ASSESSMENT. Physical assessment should be done to establish baseline data for assessing the effectiveness of the drug and the occurrence of any adverse effects associated with drug therapy. Assess the following: skin temperature and color to evaluate perfusion; respirations, adventitious sounds, endotracheal tube placement and patency, and chest movements to evaluate the effectiveness of the drug and drug delivery; blood pressure, pulse, and arterial pressure to monitor infant status; blood gases and oxygen saturation to monitor drug effectiveness; and temperature and CBC to monitor for sepsis.

Nursing Diagnoses

The patient receiving a lung surfactant may have the following nursing diagnoses related to drug therapy:

- Alteration in cardiac output related to cardiovascular and respiratory effects of the drug
- High risk for injury related to prematurity and risk of infection
- Ineffective airway clearance related to the possibility of mucous plugs
- Knowledge deficit regarding drug therapy (for parents)

Implementation

- Monitor the patient continuously during administration and until stable *to provide life support measures as needed.*
- Ensure proper placement of the endotracheal tube with bilateral chest movement and lung sounds *to provide adequate delivery of the drug.*
- Have staff view the manufacturer's teaching video before regular use *to review the specific technical aspects of administration.*

• Suction the infant immediately before administration, but do not suction for 2 hours after administration unless clinically necessary, *to allow the drug time to work.*
• Provide support and encouragement to parents of the patient, explaining the use of the drug in the teaching program, *to help them cope with the diagnosis and treatment of their infant.*
• Continue other supportive measures related to the immaturity of the infant *as this is only one aspect of medical care needed for premature infants.*

Evaluation

• Monitor patient response to the drug (improved breathing, alveolar expansion).
• Monitor for adverse effects (pneumothorax, patent ductus arteriosus [PDA], bradycardia, sepsis).
• Evaluate the effectiveness of the teaching plan and support parents as appropriate.
• Monitor the effectiveness of other measures to support breathing and stabilize the patient.
• Evaluate effectiveness of other supportive measures related to the immaturity of the infant.

OTHER ANTIASTHMATIC/ ANTIALLERGY DRUGS

Two other drugs that are often used in the treatment of asthma and allergy are cromolyn (*Intal*) and nedocromil (*Tilade*). Because these drugs do not fit into the pharmacological class of any other drugs, they are considered alone.

CROMOLYN

Cromolyn is a drug that is frequently used in the treatment of asthma. It does not have bronchodilating or anticholinergic effects and does not fit into any other pharmacological class.

THERAPEUTIC ACTIONS AND INDICATIONS

Cromolyn is a ***mast cell stabilizer.*** It works at the cellular level to inhibit the release of histamine (released from mast cells in response to inflammation or irritation) and inhibits the release of SRSA (see Figure 53-2). By blocking these chemical mediators of the immune reaction, cromolyn prevents the allergic asthmatic response when the respiratory tract is exposed to the offending allergen. It is inhaled from a capsule and may not reach its peak effect for 1 week. It is recommended for the treatment of chronic bronchial asthma, exercise-induced asthma, and allergic rhinitis.

CONTRAINDICATIONS/CAUTIONS

Cromolyn cannot be used during an acute attack, and patients need to be instructed in this precaution. It is not recommended for pregnant or nursing women or children under the age of 6 years.

ADVERSE EFFECTS

Few adverse effects have been reported with the use of cromolyn; those that do occur on occasion include swollen eyes, headache, dry mucosa, and nausea. Careful patient management (avoiding a dry or smokey environment, analgesics, use of proper inhalation technique, using a humidifier, and pushing fluids as appropriate) can help to make drug-related discomfort tolerable.

DATA LINK

Data link to cromolyn in your nursing drug guide:

CROMOLYN

Name	Brand Name	Usual Indication
cromolyn	*Intal*	Treatment of chronic bronchial asthma, exercise-induced asthma, and allergic rhinitis

NURSING CONSIDERATIONS
for patients receiving cromolyn

Assessment

HISTORY. Screen for the following: allergy to cromolyn; impaired renal or hepatic function, which could interfere with the metabolism or excretion of the drug leading to a need for dosage adjustment; and pregnancy or lactation, which require cautious administration.

PHYSICAL ASSESSMENT. Physical assessment should be done to establish baseline data for assessing the effectiveness of the drug and the occurrence of any adverse effects associated with drug therapy. Assess the following: skin color and lesions (to monitor for adverse effects of the drug); respirations and adventitious sounds (to evaluate drug effectiveness); patency of nares (to determine efficacy of inhaled preparations); orientation (to monitor adverse effects and headache); and liver and renal function tests (to assess for potential problems with drug metabolism or excretion).

Nursing Diagnoses

The patient receiving cromolyn may have the following nursing diagnoses related to drug therapy:

- Pain related to local effects, headache, GI effects
- High risk for injury related to CNS effects
- Knowledge deficit regarding drug therapy

Implementation

- Review administration procedures with the patient periodically; *proper use of the delivery device is important in maintaining the effectiveness of this drug.*
- Caution the patient not to discontinue use abruptly; *cromolyn should be tapered slowly if discontinuation is necessary to prevent rebound adverse effects.*
- Caution the patient to continue taking this drug, even in symptom-free periods, *to ensure therapeutic levels of the drug.*
- Administer oral drug one-half hour before meals and at bedtime, *which will promote continual drug levels and relief of asthma.*
- Advise the patient not to wear soft contact lenses; *if cromolyn eye drops are used, lenses can be stained or warped.*
- Provide thorough patient teaching, including the drug name and prescribed dosage, measures to help avoid adverse effects, warning signs that may indicate problems, and the need for periodic monitoring and evaluation *to enhance patient knowledge about drug therapy and to promote compliance.*
- Offer support and encouragement *to help the patient cope with the disease and drug regimen.*

Evaluation

- Monitor patient response to the drug (improved breathing).
- Monitor for adverse effects (drowsiness, headache, GI upset, local irritation).
- Evaluate the effectiveness of the teaching plan (patient can name drug, dosage, adverse effects to watch for, specific measures to avoid adverse effects, measures to take to increase the effectiveness of the drug).
- Monitor the effectiveness of other measures to ease breathing.

NEDOCROMIL

Like cromolyn, nedocromil is used to treat allergy and asthma, but does not fit into the pharmacological class of other drugs. This drug blocks many effects of the inflammatory response.

THERAPEUTIC ACTIONS AND INDICATIONS

Nedocromil inhibits the mediators of a variety of inflammatory cells, including eosinophils, neutrophils, macrophages, and mast cells (see Figure 53-2). By blocking these effects, nedocromil decreases the release of histamine and blocks the overall inflammatory response. This drug is indicated for the management of patients with mild to moderate bronchial asthma who are older than 12 years of age. This drug should be taken continually for best results and is often used concomitantly with corticosteroids.

CONTRAINDICATIONS/CAUTIONS

This drug is contraindicated in the presence of known allergy to the drug and during pregnancy and lactation because of the potential for adverse effects on the neonate.

ADVERSE EFFECTS

Adverse effects include headache, dizziness, fatigue, tearing, GI upset, and cough. The drug should not be discontinued abruptly.

DATA LINK

Data link to nedocromil in your nursing drug guide:

NEDOCROMIL

Name	Brand Name	Usual Indication
nedocromil	*Tilade*	Management of patients with mild to moderate bronchial asthma

NURSING CONSIDERATIONS
for patients receiving nedocromil

Assessment

HISTORY. Screen for the following: allergy to nedocromil; and pregnancy and lactation, which are contraindications to drug use.

PHYSICAL ASSESSMENT. Physical assessment should be done to establish baseline data for assessing the effectiveness of the drug and the occurrence of any adverse effects associated with drug therapy. Assess the following: skin color and lesions to assess for adverse effects; orientation to monitor for CNS effects; respirations and adventitious sounds to evaluate drug effectiveness; patency of nasal passages to assess the efficacy of the route of administration; and liver and kidney function tests to monitor for conditions which may interfere with drug metabolism or excretion and require dosage adjustment.

Nursing Diagnoses

The patient receiving nedocromil may have the following nursing diagnoses related to drug therapy:

- Pain related to local effects, headache, GI effects
- High risk for injury related to CNS effects
- Knowledge deficit regarding drug therapy

Implementation

- Do not administer during acute asthmatic attack or acute bronchospasm. *This drug does not provide immediate bronchodilation; regular emergency procedures should be followed.*
- Review administration procedures with the patient periodically; *proper use of the delivery device is important in maintaining the effectiveness of this drug.*
- Administer corticosteroids concomitantly *for best therapeutic results.*
- Caution the patient not to discontinue use abruptly; *nedocromil should be tapered slowly if discontinuation is necessary, to prevent serious rebound effects.*
- Caution the patient to continue taking this drug, even in symptom-free periods, *to ensure therapeutic levels of the drug, which will help prevent asthmatic attacks.*
- Initiate safety precautions if dizziness and fatigue are a problem *to prevent patient injury.*
- Provide thorough patient teaching, including the drug name and prescribed dosage, measures to help avoid adverse effects, warning signs that may indicate problems, and the need for periodic monitoring and evaluation, *to enhance patient knowledge about drug therapy and to promote compliance.*

Evaluation

- Monitor patient response to the drug (improved breathing).
- Monitor for adverse effects (drowsiness, headache, GI upset, local irritation).
- Evaluate the effectiveness of the teaching plan (patient can name drug, dosage, adverse effects to watch for, specific measures to avoid adverse effects, measures to take to increase the effectiveness of the drug).
- Monitor the effectiveness of other measures to ease breathing.

CHAPTER SUMMARY

- Pulmonary obstructive diseases include asthma, emphysema, and chronic obstructive pulmonary disease (COPD), which present with obstruction to the major airways, and respiratory distress syndrome, which presents with an obstruction at the alveolar level.
- Drugs used to treat asthma and COPD include drugs to block inflammation and drugs to dilate bronchi.
- The xanthine derivatives have a direct effect on the smooth muscle of the respiratory tract, both in the bronchi and the blood vessels.
- The adverse effects of the xanthines are directly related to the theophylline levels in the blood and can progress to coma and death.
- Sympathomimetics are drugs that mimic the effects of the sympathetic nervous system and are used for dilation of the bronchi and increased rate and depth of respiration.
- Anticholinergics can be used as bronchodilators because of their effect on the vagus nerve, resulting in a relaxation of smooth muscle in the bronchi leading to bronchodilation.
- Steroids are used to decrease the inflammatory response in the airway. Inhaling the steroid tends to decrease the numerous systemic effects that are associated with steroid use.
- Leukotriene receptor antagonists block or antagonize receptors for the production of leukotriene D4 and E4, thus blocking many of the signs and symptoms of asthma.
- Lung surfactants are instilled into the respiratory system of premature infants who do not have enough surfactant to ensure alveolar expansion.
- Cromolyn and nedocromil are antiasthmatic drugs that block mediators of inflammation and help to decrease swelling and blockage in the airways.

BIBLIOGRAPHY

Bullock, B. L. (2000). *Focus on pathophysiology.* Philadelphia: Lippincott Williams & Wilkins.

Drazen, J. (1998). New directions in asthma drug therapy. *Hospital Practice,:33*(2).

Hardman, J. G., Limbird, L. E., Molinoff, P. B., Ruddon, R. W., & Gilman, A. G. (Eds.). (1996). *Goodman and Gilman's the pharmacological basis of therapeutics* (9th ed.). New York: McGraw-Hill.

Karch, A. M. (2000). *2000 Lippincott's nursing drug guide.* Philadelphia: Lippincott Williams & Wilkins.

Malseed, R. (1995). *Textbook of pharmacology and nursing care.* Philadelphia: J. B. Lippincott.

McEvoy, B. R. (Ed.). (1999). *Facts and comparisons 1999.* St. Louis: Facts and Comparisons.

Professional's guide to patient drug facts. (1999). St. Louis: Facts and Comparisons.

PART

11

Drugs Acting on the Gastrointestinal System

CHAPTER
54

Introduction to the Gastrointestinal System

CHAPTER OUTLINE

KEY TERMS

bile
chyme
gallstones
gastrin
histamine$_2$ receptors
hydrochloric acid
local gastrointestinal reflexes
nerve plexus
pancreatic enzymes
peristalsis
saliva
segmentation
swallowing
vomiting

INTRODUCTION

The gastrointestinal (GI) system is the only system in the body that is open to the external environment. The gastrointestinal system is composed of one continuous tube that begins at the mouth, progresses through the esophagus, stomach, and small and large intestines, and ends at the anus. The pancreas, liver, and gallbladder are accessory organs that support the functions of the GI system (Figure 54-1). The GI system has four major activities:

1. Secretion—of enzymes, acid, bicarbonate, and mucus
2. Absorption—of water and nearly all of the essential nutrients needed by the body
3. Digestion—of food into usable and absorbable components
4. Motility—movement of food and secretions through the system (what is not used is excreted in the form of feces)

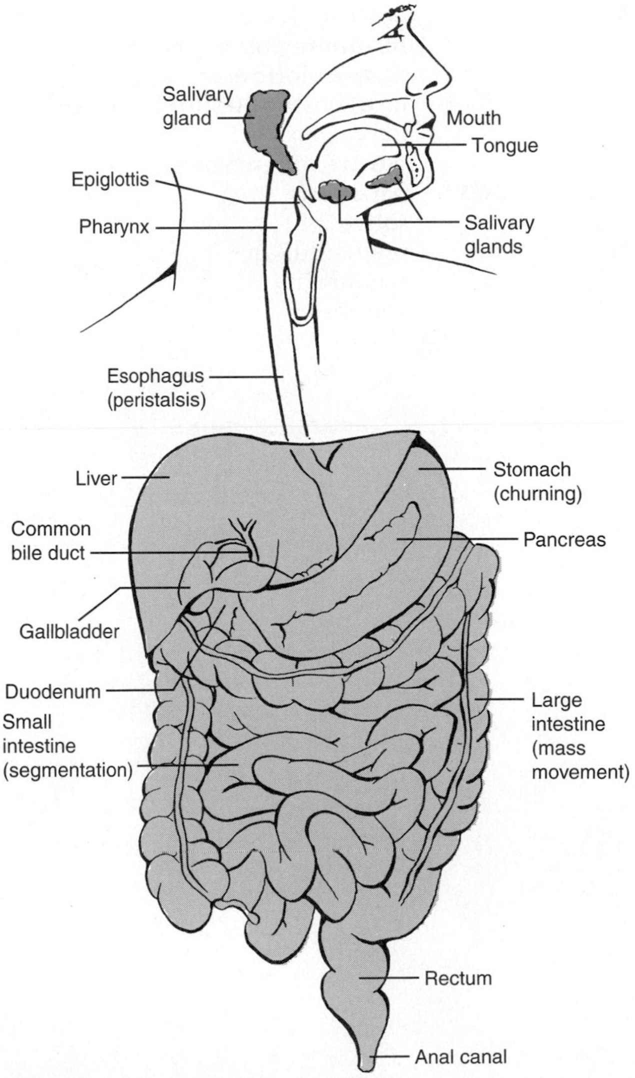

FIGURE 54-1. The gastrointestinal tract.

The GI system is responsible for only a very small part of waste excretion. The kidneys and lungs are responsible for excreting most of the waste products of normal metabolism.

COMPOSITION OF THE GASTROINTESTINAL TRACT

The tube that comprises the GI tract is continuous with the external environment, opening at the mouth and again at the anus. Because of this, the GI tract contains many foreign agents and bacteria that are not found in the rest of the body. The peritoneum lines the abdominal wall and also the viscera with a small "free space" between the two layers. It helps keep the GI tract in place and prevents a build-up of friction with movement. The greater and lesser omentum hang from the stomach over the lower GI tract and are full of lymph nodes, lymphocytes, monocytes, and other components of the mononuclear phagocyte system. This barrier provides rapid protection for the rest of the body if any of the bacteria or other foreign agents in the GI tract should be absorbed into the body (see Figure 54-1).

The GI tube is composed of four layers: the mucosa, the muscularis mucosa, the ***nerve plexus,*** and the adventitia.

- The mucosal layer provides the inner lining of the GI tract. It can be seen in the mouth and is fairly consistent throughout the tube. It is important to remember when assessing a patient that if the mouth is very dry or full of lesions, that is a reflection of the state of the entire GI tract and may indicate that the patient has difficulty digesting or absorbing nutrients. This layer has an epithelium component and a connective tissue component.
- The muscularis mucosa layer is made up of muscles. Most of the GI tract has two muscle layers. One layer runs circularly around the tube, helping keep the tube open and squeezing the tube to aid digestion and motility. The other layer runs horizontally, which helps propel things down the tract. The stomach has a third layer of muscle, which runs obliquely and gives the stomach the ability to move contents in a churning motion.
- The nerve plexus has two layers of nerves, one submucosal layer and one myenteric layer. These nerves give the GI tract local control of movement, secretions, and digestion. The nerves respond to local stimuli and act on the contents of the GI tract accordingly. The GI tract is also innervated by the sympathetic and parasympathetic nervous systems. These

systems can slow down or speed up the activity in the GI tract but cannot initiate local activity. The sympathetic system is stimulated during times of stress (e.g., "fight or flight" response) when digestion is not a priority. To slow the GI tract, the sympathetic system decreases muscle tone, secretions, and contractions, and increases sphincter tone. By shutting down the GI activity, the body saves energy for other activities. In contrast, the parasympathetic system stimulates the GI tract, increasing muscle tone, secretions and contractions and decreasing sphincter tone, allowing easy movement.

- The adventitia, the outer layer of the GI tract, serves as a supportive layer and helps the tube maintain its shape and to stay in position (Figure 54-2).

GASTROINTESTINAL ACTIVITIES

The GI tract has four functions: secretion, digestion, absorption, and motility. These are discussed in detail below.

Secretion

The GI tract secretes various compounds to aid the movement of the food bolus through the GI tube, to protect the inner layer of the GI tract from injury, and to facilitate the digestion and absorption of nutrients (see Figure 54-1). Secretions begin in the mouth. ***Saliva,*** which contains water and digestive enzymes, is secreted from the salivary glands to begin the digestive process and to facilitate ***swallowing*** by making the bolus slippery. Mucus is also produced in the mouth to protect the epithelial lining and to aid swallowing. The esophagus produces mucus to protect the inner lining of the GI tract and to further facilitate the movement of the bolus down the tube.

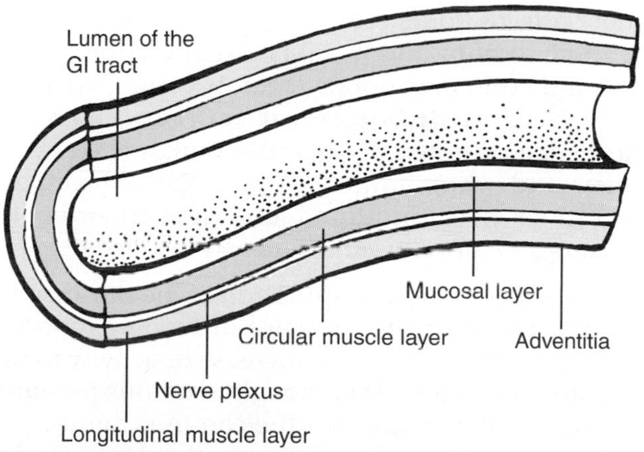

FIGURE 54-2. Layers of the gastrointestinal tract.

The stomach produces acid and digestive enzymes. In addition, it generates a large amount of mucus to protect the stomach lining from the acid and the enzymes. In the stomach, secretion begins with what is called the cephalic phase of digestion. The sight, smell, or taste of food stimulates the stomach to begin secreting before any food reaches the stomach. Once the bolus of food arrives at the stomach, ***gastrin*** is secreted. Gastrin stimulates the stomach muscles to contract, the parietal cells to release ***hydrochloric acid,*** and the chief cells to release pepsin. Parasympathetic stimulation also leads to acid release. Gastrin and the parasympathetic system stimulate ***histamine$_2$ receptors*** near the parietal cells, causing the cells to release hydrochloric acid into the lumen of the stomach. The presence of proteins, calcium, alcohol, and caffeine in the stomach increases gastrin secretion. High levels of acid decrease the secretion of gastrin. Other digestive enzymes are released appropriately in response to proteins and carbohydrates to begin digestion. Peptic ulcers can develop when there is a decrease in the protective mucosal layer or an increase in acid production.

As the now acidic bolus leaves the stomach and enters the small intestine, secretin is released, which stimulates the pancreas to secrete large amounts of sodium bicarbonate (to neutralize the acid bolus), the ***pancreatic enzymes*** chymotrypsin and trypsin (to break down proteins to smaller amino acids), other lipases (to break down fat), and amylases (to break down sugars). These enzymes are delivered to the GI tract through the common duct, shared with the gallbladder.

If fat is present in the bolus, the gallbladder contracts and releases bile into the small intestine. ***Bile*** contains a detergent-like substance that breaks apart fat molecules so that they can be processed and absorbed. The bile in the gallbladder is produced by the liver during normal metabolism. Once delivered to the gallbladder for storage, it is concentrated; water is removed by the walls of the gallbladder. Some people are prone to develop ***gallstones*** in the gallbladder when the concentrated bile crystallizes. These stones can move down the duct and cause severe pain or even blockage of the bile duct.

In response to the presence of food, the small and large intestines may secrete various endocrine hormones, including growth hormone, aldosterone, and glucagon. They also secrete large amounts of mucus to facilitate the movement of the bolus through the rest of the GI tract.

Digestion

Digestion is the process of breaking food into usable, absorbable nutrients. Digestion begins in the mouth with the enzymes in the saliva starting the process of breaking down sugars and proteins. The stomach continues the digestion process with the muscular churning breaking down some foodstuffs while mixing them thoroughly with the hydrochloric acid and enzymes. The acid and enzymes further break down sugars and proteins into building blocks and separate vitamins, electrolytes, minerals, and other nutrients from ingested food for absorption. The beginning of the small intestine introduces bile to the food bolus, which is now called ***chyme.*** Bile breaks down fat molecules for processing and absorption into the bloodstream. Digestion is finished at this point, and absorption of the nutrients begins.

Absorption

Absorption is the active process of removing water, nutrients, and other elements from the GI tract and delivering them to the blood stream for use by the body. The portal system drains all of the lower GI tract where absorption occurs and delivers what is absorbed into the venous system directly into the liver. The liver filters, clears, and further processes most of what is absorbed before it is delivered to the body (see Figure 54-1). Some absorption occurs in the lower end of stomach (e.g., water and alcohol are absorbed here). The small intestine absorbs about 8500 cc, including nutrients, drugs, and anything that is taken into the GI tract, as well as any secretions, each day. The small intestine mucosal layer is specially designed to facilitate this absorption with long villi on the epithelial layer providing a vast surface area for absorption. The large intestine absorbs approximately 350 cc, of mostly sodium and water, each day.

Motility

The GI tract depends on an inherent motility to keep things moving through the system. The nerve plexus maintains a basic electrical rhythm (BER), much like the pacemaker rhythm in the heart. The cells within the plexus are somewhat unstable and leak electrolytes, leading to the regular firing of an action potential. This rhythm maintains the tone of the GI tract muscles and can be affected by local or autonomic stimuli to increase or decrease the rate of firing.

The basic movement seen in the esophagus is ***peristalsis,*** a constant wave of contraction that moves from the top to the bottom of the esophagus. The act of swallowing, a response to a food bolus in the back of the throat, stimulates the peristaltic movement that directs the food bolus into the stomach. The stomach uses its three muscle layers to produce a churning action. This action mixes the digestive enzymes and acid with the food to increase digestion. A contraction of the lower end of the stomach sends the chyme into the small intestine.

The small intestine uses a process of ***segmentation*** with an occasional peristalsis to clear the segment. Segmentation involves contraction of one segment of small intestine while the next segment is relaxed. The contracted segment then relaxes, and the relaxed segment contracts. This action exposes the chyme to a vast surface area to increase the absorption from the chyme. The small intestine maintains a BER of 11 contractions per minute.

The large intestine uses a process of mass movement with an occasional peristaltic wave. When the beginning segment of the large intestine is stimulated, it contracts and sends a massive peristaltic movement throughout the entire large intestine. The end result of the mass movement is usually excretion of waste products. Rectal distention following mass movement stimulates a defecation reflex that causes relaxation of the external and internal sphincters. Control of the external sphincter is a learned behavior. The receptors in the external sphincter adopt relatively quickly to stretch and require more and more distention to stimulate the reflex if the reflex is ignored.

WWW.WEB LINKS

To explore the virtual gastrointestinal system, consult the following Internet sources:

http://www.InnerBody.com

http://wwwl.biostr.washington.edu/DigitalAnatomist.html

LOCAL GASTROINTESTINAL REFLEXES

Stimulation of local nerves within the GI tract causes increased or decreased movement within the system, maintaining a homeostasis. Loss of reflexes or stimulation can result in constipation and the lack of movement of the bolus along the GI tract or diarrhea, with increased motility and excretion. The longer a fecal bolus remains in the large intestine, the more sodium and water is absorbed from it and the harder and less mobile it can become. There are many ***local gastrointestinal reflexes,*** and some knowledge of how they operate makes it easier to understand what happens when the reflexes are blocked or overstimulated and how therapeutic measures are often used to cause reflex activity.

Gastroenteric reflex: stimulation of the stomach by stretching or the presence of food or cephalic stimulation causes an increase in activity in the small intestine. It is thought that this prepares the small intestine for the coming chyme.

Gastrocolic reflex: stimulation of the stomach also causes increased activity in the colon, again preparing to empty any contents to provide space for the new chyme.

Duodenal colic reflex: presence of food or stretch in the duodenum to stimulate colon activity and mass movement, again to empty the colon for the new chyme.

It is important to remember the gastroenteric, gastrocolic, and duodenal reflexes when helping patients to maintain GI movement. Taking advantage of stomach stimulation (e.g., having the patient drink prune juice or hot water or eat bran) and providing the opportunity for time and privacy for a bowel movement allow normal reflexes to keep things in control.

Other local GI reflexes include:

Ileogastric reflex: introduction of chyme or stretch to the large intestine, which slows stomach activity and the introduction of chyme into the small and large intestine and allows time for absorption. In part, this reflex explains why patients who are constipated often have no appetite; the continued stretch on the ileum that comes with constipation continues to slow the activity in the stomach and makes the introduction of new food into the stomach undesirable.

Intestinal–intestinal reflex: excessive irritation to one section of the small intestine, which causes a cessation of activity above that section to prevent further irritation and an increase in activity below that section, leading to a flushing of the irritant. This reflex is active in "Montezuma's revenge" (traveler's diarrhea), when local irritation of the intestine causes increased secretions and movement below that section, resulting in watery diarrhea and a cessation of movement above that section. Loss of appetite or even nausea may occur. An extreme reaction to this reflex can be seen following abdominal surgery, when the handling of the intestines causes intense irritation and the reflex can cause the entire intestinal system to cease activity, leading to a paralytic ileus.

Peritoneointestinal reflex: irritation of the peritoneum due to inflammation or injury, which leads to a cessation of GI activity, preventing continued movement of the GI tract from further irritating the peritoneum.

Renointestinal reflex: irritation or swelling of the renal capsule, which causes a cessation of movement in the GI tract, again to prevent further irritation to the capsule.

Vesicointestinal reflex: irritation or overstretching of the bladder, which can cause a reflex cessation of movement in the GI tract, again to prevent further irritation to the bladder from the GI movement. Many patients with cystitis or overstretched bladders from occupational constraints or neurological problems complain of constipation, which can be attributable to this reflex.

Somatointestinal reflex: taut stretching of the skin and muscles over the abdomen, which irritates the nerve plexus and causes a slowing or cessation of GI activity to prevent further irritation. During the era when tight girdles were commonly worn, this reflex was often seen among women, and constipation was a serious problem for many women who wore such constraining garments. Tight-fitting clothing (e.g., jeans) can have the same effect. Patients who complain of chronic constipation may be suffering from overactivity of the somatointestinal reflex.

CENTRAL REFLEXES

Two centrally mediated reflexes—***swallowing*** and ***vomiting***—are very important to the functioning of the GI tract.

The swallowing reflex is stimulated whenever a food bolus stimulates pressure receptors in the back of the throat and pharynx. These receptors send impulses to the medulla, which stimulates a series of nerves that cause the following actions: the soft palate elevates and seals off the nasal cavity; respirations cease in order to protect the lungs; the larynx raises and the glottis closes to seal off the airway; the pharyngeal constrictor muscles contract and force the food bolus into the top of the esophagus, where pairs of muscles contract in turn to move the bolus down the esophagus into the stomach. This reflex is complex, involving over 25 pairs of muscles.

There are a number of ways that this reflex can be facilitated if swallowing (food or medication) is a problem. Icing the tongue by sucking on a popsicle or an ice cube blocks external nerve impulses and allows this more basic reflex to respond. Icing the sternal notch or the back of the neck, though not as appealing, has also proven effective in stimulating the swallowing reflex. In addition, keeping the head straight, not turned to one side, allows the muscle pairs to work together and helps the process. Providing stimulation of the receptors in the mouth through temperature variations and textured foods helps initiate the reflex. Patients who do not produce their own saliva can be given artificial saliva to increase digestion and to lubricate the food bolus, which also help the swallowing reflex.

The vomiting reflex is another basic reflex that is centrally mediated and important in protecting the system from unwanted irritants. The vomiting reflex is stimulated by two centers in the medulla. The more primitive center is called the emetic zone. When stimulated it initiates a projectile vomiting. This type of intense reaction is seen in young children and when increased pressure in the brain or brain damage allows the more primitive center to override the more mature chemoreceptor trigger zone (CTZ). The CTZ is stimulated in several ways:

- Tactile stimulation of the back of the throat, a reflex to get rid of something that is too big or too irritating to be swallowed
- Excessive stomach distention
- Increasing intracranial pressure by direct stimulation
- Stimulation of the vestibular receptors in the inner ear (a reaction often seen with dizziness after wild rides in amusement parks)
- Stimulation of stretch receptors in the uterus and bladder (a possible explanation for early pregnancy vomiting and predelivery vomiting)
- Intense pain fiber stimulation
- Direct stimulation of various chemicals including fumes, certain drugs, and debris from cellular death (a reason for vomiting following chemotherapy or radiation therapy with resultant cell death).

Once the CTZ is stimulated, a series of reflexes occurs. Salivation increases, and there is a large increase in the production of mucus in the upper GI tract, which is accompanied by a decrease in gastric acid production. This action protects the lining of the GI tract from potential damage by the acidic stomach contents. (Nauseated patients who start swallowing repeatedly or complain about secretions in their throat are in the process of preparing for vomiting.) The sympathetic system is stimulated with a resultant increase in sweating, increased heart rate, deeper respirations, and nausea. This prepares the body for fight or flight and the insult of vomiting. The esophagus then relaxes and becomes distended, and the gastric sphincter relaxes. The patient takes one deep respiration and the glottis closes and the palate rises, trapping the air in the lungs and sealing off the entry to the lungs. The abdominal and thoracic muscles contract, increasing intra-abdominal pressure. The stomach then relaxes and the lower section of the stomach contracts in waves, approximately six times per minute. With nothing in the stomach, this movement is seen as retching and can be quite tiring and uncomfortable. This action causes a backward peristalsis and movement of stomach contents up the esophagus and out the mouth. The body then rids itself of offending irritants.

The vomiting reflex is complex and protective but can be undesirable in certain clinical situations when the stimulant is not something that can be vomited or when the various components of the vomiting reflex can be detrimental to a patient's health status.

CHAPTER SUMMARY

- The gastrointestinal (GI) system is composed of one long tube starting at the mouth, which includes the esophagus, the small intestine, and the large intestine, and ending at the anus. The GI system is responsible for digestion and absorption of nutrients.
- Secretion of digestive enzymes, acid, bicarbonate, and mucus facilitates the digestion and absorption of nutrients.
- The GI system is controlled by a nerve plexus, which maintains a basic electrical rhythm and responds to local stimuli to increase or decrease activity. The autonomic system can influence the activity of the GI tract, the sympathetic system slowing it and the parasympathetic system increasing activity. Initiation of activity depends on local reflexes.
- A series of local reflexes within the GI tract helps maintain homeostasis within the system. Overstimulation of any of these reflexes can result in constipation (underactivity) or diarrhea (overactivity).
- Swallowing is a centrally mediated reflex that is important in delivering food to the GI tract for processing. It is controlled by the medulla and involves a complex series of timed reflexes.
- Vomiting is controlled by the chemoreceptor trigger zone (CTZ) in the medulla or by the emetic zone in immature or injured brains. The CTZ is stimulated by several different processes and initiates a complex series of responses that first prepare the system for vomiting and then cause a strong backward peristalsis to rid the stomach of its contents.

BIBLIOGRAPHY

Bullock, B. L. (2000). *Focus on pathophysiology.* Philadelphia: Lippincott Williams & Wilkins.

Fox, S. (1991). *Perspectives on human biology.* Dubuque, IA: Wm. C. Brown.

Ganong, W. (1999). *Review of medical physiology* (19th ed.). Norwalk, CT: Appleton & Lange.

Guyton, A. & Hall, J. (1996). *Textbook of medical physiology.* Philadelphia: W. B. Saunders.

Hardman, J. G., Limbird, L. E., Molinoff, P. B., Ruddon, R. W., & Gilman, A. G. (Eds.). (1996). *Goodman and Gilman's the pharmacological basis of therapeutics* (9th ed.). New York: McGraw-Hill.

CHAPTER 55

Drugs Affecting Gastrointestinal Secretions

Histamine H_2 antagonists
- **P** cimetidine
- famotidine
- nizatadine
- ranitidine

Antacids
- aluminum
- calcium salts
- magaldrate
- magnesium salts
- **P** sodium bicarbonate

Proton pump inhibitors
- lanisoprazole
- **P** omeprazole

Antipeptic agent
- sucralfate

Prostaglandin
- misoprostol

Digestive enzymes
- pancrelipase
- **P** pancreatin
- saliva substitute

CHAPTER OUTLINE

KEY TERMS

acid rebound
antipeptic
histamine H_2 antagonist
peptic ulcer
prostaglandin
proton pump inhibitor

INTRODUCTION

Gastrointestinal (GI) disorders are among the most common complaints seen in clinical practice. Many products are available for the self-treatment of upset stomach, heartburn, and sour stomach. The underlying causes of these disorders can range from dietary excess, stress, hiatal hernia, esophageal reflux, and adverse drug effects, to the more serious peptic ulcer disease.

Drugs that affect GI secretions can decrease GI secretory activity, block the action of GI secretions, form protective coverings on the GI lining to prevent erosion from GI secretions, or replace missing GI enzymes that the GI tract or ancillary glands and organs can no longer produce (Figure 55-1).

Peptic Ulcers

Erosions in the lining of the stomach and adjacent areas of the GI tract are called ***peptic ulcers.*** Ulcer patients present with a predictable description of gnawing, burning pain, often occurring a few hours after meals. Many of the drugs that are used to affect

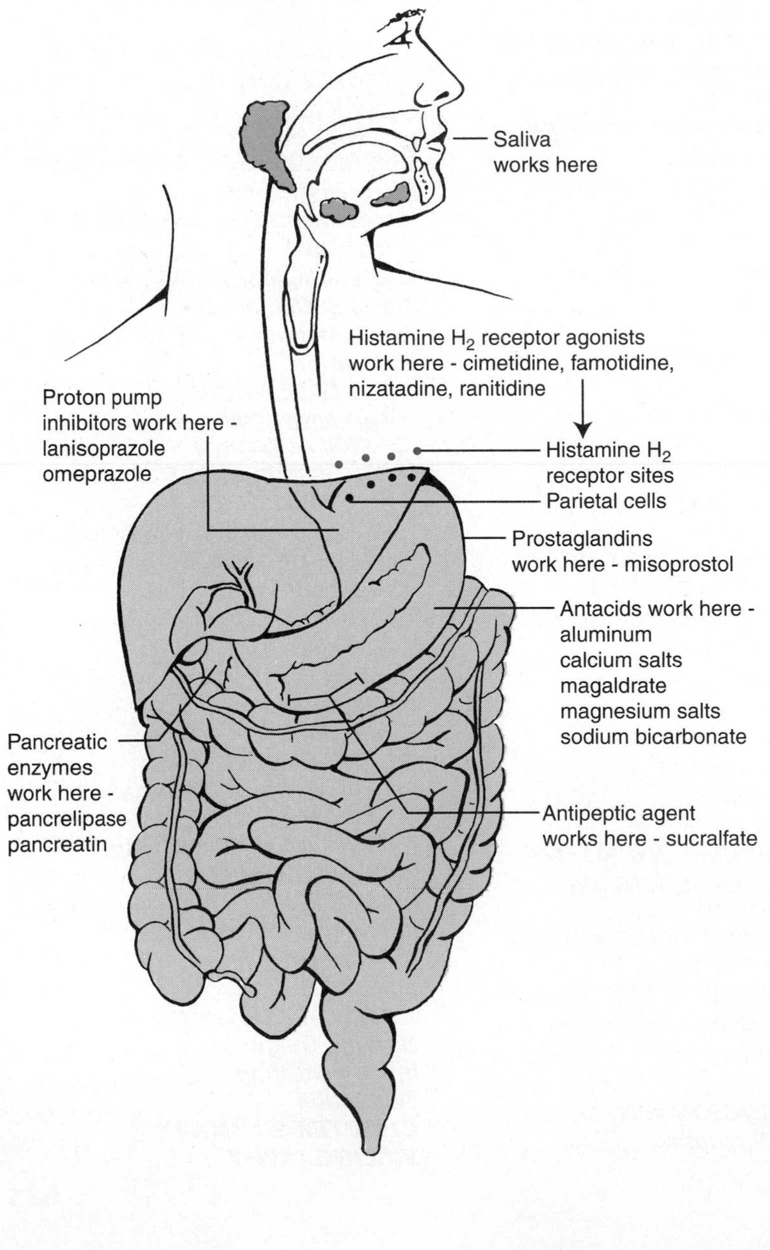

FIGURE 55-1. Sites of action of drugs affecting gastrointestinal secretions.

GI secretions are designed to prevent, treat, or aid in the healing of these ulcers. The actual cause of chronic peptic ulcers is not completely understood. For many years it was believed that ulcers were caused by excessive acid production, and treatment was aimed at neutralizing acid or blocking the parasympathetic system to decrease normal GI activity and secretions. Further research led many to believe that because production was often normal in ulcer patients, ulcers were caused by a defect in the mucous lining that coats the inner lumen of the stomach to protect it from acid and digestive enzymes. Treatment was aimed at improving the balance between the acid produced and the mucous layer that protects the stomach lining. Currently it is believed that chronic ulcers may be the result of bacterial infection by *Helicobacter pylori* bacteria. Combination antibiotics have been found to be quite effective in treating patients with chronic ulcers.

Acute ulcers or "stress ulcers" are often seen in situations that involve acute stress—trauma, burns, or prolonged illness. The activity of the sympathetic nervous system during stress decreases blood flow to the GI tract, leading to weakening of the mucosal layer of the stomach and erosion from acid in the stomach.

Many of the drugs available for treating various peptic ulcers act to alter acid-producing activities of the stomach. Five types of drugs are used in the treatment of ulcers:

1. ***Histamine H_2 antagonists*** block the release of hydrochloric acid in response to gastrin.
2. Antacids interact with acids at the chemical level to neutralize them.
3. ***Proton pump inhibitors*** suppress the secretion of hydrochloric acid into the lumen of the stomach.
4. ***Antipeptic*** agents coat any injured area in the stomach to prevent further injury from acid.
5. ***Prostaglandins*** inhibit the secretion of gastrin and increase the secretion of the mucous lining of the stomach, providing a buffer.

Digestive Enzyme Dysfunction

Some patients may require a supplement to the production of digestive enzymes. Patients with strokes, salivary gland disorders, or extreme surgery of the head and neck may not be able to produce saliva. Saliva is important in beginning the digestion of sugars and proteins and is essential in initiating the swallowing reflex. Artificial saliva may be necessary for these patients. Patients with common duct problems, pancreatic disease, or cystic fibrosis may not be able to produce or secrete pancreatic enzymes. These enzymes may need to be administered to allow normal digestion and absorption of nutrients.

HISTAMINE H_2 ANTAGONISTS

The histamine H_2 antagonists selectively block histamine H_2 receptors. These receptors are located on the parietal cells; blocking them prevents gastrin, which causes local release of histamine and stimulation of these receptors, from stimulating the production of hydrochloric acid. This action will also decrease pepsin production by the chief cells.

Four histamine H_2 antagonists are available:

- Cimetidine (*Tagamet, Tagamet HB*) was the first drug in this class to be developed. It has been associated with antiandronergic effects, including gynecomastia and galactorrhea. It is metabolized mainly in the liver and can slow the metabolism of many other drugs using the same metabolizing enzyme system.
- Ranitidine (*Zantac*), which is longer acting and more potent than cimetidine, is not associated with the antiandronergic adverse effects or the marked slowing of metabolism in the liver.
- Famotidine (*Pepcid, PepcidAC*) is similar to ranitidine in terms of its actions and adverse effects, but is much more potent than either cimetidine or ranitidine.
- Nizatadine (*Axid*), the newest drug in this class, is similar to ranitidine in its effectiveness and adverse effects. It differs from the other three drugs by being eliminated by the kidneys, with no first-pass metabolism in the liver. It is the drug of choice for patients with liver dysfunction and for those who are taking other drugs whose metabolism is slowed by the hepatic activity of the other three histamine H_2 antagonists.

THERAPEUTIC ACTIONS AND INDICATIONS

Histamine H_2 antagonists selectively block H_2 receptor sites. This blocking leads to a reduction in gastric acid secretion and reduction in overall pepsin production (see Figure 55-1). H_2 receptor sites are also found in the heart, and high levels of these drugs can produce cardiac arrhythmias.

These drugs are used in the following conditions:

- Short-term treatment of active duodenal ulcer or benign gastric ulcer (reduction in the overall acid level can promote healing and decrease discomfort)
- Treatment of pathologic hypersecretory conditions such as Zollinger-Ellison syndrome (blocking the overproduction of hydrochloric acid associated with these conditions)

- Prophylaxis of stress-induced ulcers and acute upper GI bleeding in critical patients (blocking the production of acid protects the stomach lining, which is at risk because of decreased mucus production associated with extreme stress)
- Treatment of erosive gastroesophageal reflux (decreasing the acid being regurgitated into the esophagus will promote healing and decrease pain)
- Relief of symptoms of heart burn, acid indigestion, and sour stomach (OTC preparations)

CONTRAINDICATIONS/CAUTIONS

The histamine H_2 antagonists should not be used with any known allergy to any drugs of this class. Caution should be used in pregnancy, lactation, and with hepatic (not as much of a problem with nizatidine) or renal dysfunction that could interfere with drug metabolism and excretion. Care should also be taken if prolonged or continual use of these drugs is necessary, because they may mask serious underlying conditions.

ADVERSE EFFECTS

The adverse effects most commonly associated with histamine H_2 antagonists include the following: GI effects of diarrhea or constipation; CNS effects of dizziness, headache, somnolence, confusion, or even hallucinations (thought to be related to possible histamine H_2 receptor effects in the CNS); cardiac arrhythmias and hypotension (related to histamine H_2 cardiac receptor blocking; more commonly seen with IV or IM administration or with prolonged use); and gynecomastia (more common with long-term use of cimetidine) and impotence.

CLINICALLY IMPORTANT DRUG–DRUG INTERACTIONS

The three histamine H_2 antagonists that are metabolized in the liver (cimetidine, famotidine, and ranitidine) can slow the metabolism of the following drugs, leading to increased serum levels and possible toxic reactions: warfarin anticoagulants, phenytoin, beta-adrenergic blockers, alcohol, quinidine, lidocaine, theophylline, chloroquine, benzodiazepines, nifedipine, pentoxifylline, tricyclic antidepressants, procainamide, and carbamazepine. It is a good idea to review a patient's other medications carefully any time a histamine H_2 antagonist is prescribed or a patient reports taking the OTC form.

DATA LINK

Data link to the following histamine H_2 antagonists in your nursing drug guide:

HISTAMINE H_2 ANTAGONISTS

Name	Brand Name(s)	Usual Indications
P cimetidine	*Tagamet, Tagamet HB*	Treatment of duodenal ulcer, benign gastric ulcer, pathological hypersecretory syndrome, GERD; prophylaxis of stress ulcers; relief of symptoms of heartburn, acid indigestion, sour stomach
famotidine	*Pepcid, Pepcid AC*	Treatment of duodenal ulcer, benign gastric ulcer, pathological hypersecretory syndrome, GERD; relief of symptoms of heartburn, acid indigestion, sour stomach
nizatidine	*Axid*	Treatment of duodenal ulcer, benign gastric ulcer, pathological hypersecretory syndrome, GERD; relief of symptoms of heartburn, acid indigestion, sour stomach
ranitidine	*Zantac*	Treatment of duodenal ulcer, benign gastric ulcer, pathological hypersecretory syndrome, GERD; relief of symptoms of heartburn, acid indigestion, sour stomach

NURSING CONSIDERATIONS for patients receiving histamine H_2 antagonists

Assessment

HISTORY. Screen for history of allergy to any histamine H_2 antagonists; impaired renal or hepatic function; pregnancy or lactation; and a detailed description of the GI problem, including length of time of the disorder and medical evaluation.

PHYSICAL ASSESSMENT. Include screening for presence of any skin lesions; orientation and affect; baseline pulse and blood pressure, ECG (if IV use is needed); liver and abdominal examination; and liver and renal function tests.

Nursing Diagnoses

The patient receiving any histamine H_2 antagonist may have the following nursing diagnoses related to drug therapy:

- Pain related to CNS and GI effects
- Sensory-perceptual alterations related to CNS effects
- Alteration in cardiac output related to cardiac arrhythmias
- Knowledge deficit regarding drug therapy

PATIENT TEACHING CHECKLIST

Histamine H_2 Antagonists

Create customized patient teaching materials for a specific histamine H_2 antagonist from your CD-ROM. Your patient teaching should stress the following points for drugs within this class:

A histamine H_2 antagonist decreases the amount of acid that is produced in the stomach. It is used to treat conditions that are aggravated by excess acid.

Some of the following adverse effects may occur with this drug:

- Diarrhea—Have ready access to bathroom facilities. This usually becomes less severe over time.
- Dizziness, feeling faint on arising, headache—These usually lessen as your body adjusts to the drug. Change positions slowly. If you feel drowsy, avoid driving or dangerous activities.

Report any of the following to your health care provider: sore throat, unusual bleeding or bruising, confusion, muscle or joint pain, heart palpitations.

Avoid the use of any over-the-counter medication without first checking with your health care provider. Several of these medications can interfere with the effectiveness of this drug. If an antacid has been ordered for you, take it exactly as prescribed.

Tell any physician, nurse, or other health care provider that you are taking this drug.

If you are taking any other medications, do not vary the drug schedules. Consult with your primary health care provider if anything should happen to change any of these drugs or your scheduled doses. It is important to have regular medical follow-up while you are taking this drug to evaluate your response to the drug and any possible underlying problems.

Keep this drug, and all other medications, out of the reach of children.

This Teaching Checklist reflects general patient teaching guidelines. It is not meant to be a substitute for drug-specific teaching information, which is available in nursing drug guides.

Implementation

- Administer oral drug with or before meals and at bedtime (exact timing varies with product) *to ensure therapeutic levels when the drug is most needed.*
- Arrange for decreased dosage in cases of hepatic or renal dysfunction *to prevent serious toxicity.*
- Monitor patient continually if giving IV doses *to allow early detection of potentially serious adverse effects, including cardiac arrhythmias.*
- Assess patient carefully for any potential drug–drug interactions if giving in combination with other drugs *because of the drug effects on liver enzyme systems.*
- Provide comfort and safety measures, including analgesics, ready access to bathroom facilities, assistance with ambulation, and periodic orientation if GI or CNS effects occur *to ensure patient safety and improve patient tolerance of the drug and drug effects.*
- Arrange for regular follow-up *to evaluate drug effects and underlying problem.*
- Provide thorough patient teaching, including drug name, prescribed dosage, measures for avoidance of adverse effects, and warning signs that may indicate possible problems. Instruct patients about the need for periodic monitoring and evaluation, *to enhance patient knowledge about drug therapy and to promote compliance* (see Patient Teaching Checklist: Histamine H_2 Antagonists).
- Offer support and encouragement *to help patients cope with the disease and drug regimen.*

Evaluation

- Monitor patient response to the drug (relief of GI symptoms, ulcer healing, prevention of progression of ulcer).
- Monitor for adverse effects (dizziness, confusion, hallucinations, GI alterations, cardiac arrhythmias, hypotension, gynecomastia).
- Evaluate effectiveness of teaching plan (can the patient name drug, dosage, adverse effects to watch for, and specific measures to avoid adverse effects?).
- Monitor effectiveness of comfort measures and compliance with regimen (see Nursing Care Guide: Histamine H_2 Antagonists).

ANTACIDS

The antacids are a group of inorganic chemicals that have long been used to neutralize stomach acid. Antacids are available OTC, and many patients use them to self-treat a variety of GI symptoms. All ant-

NURSING CARE GUIDE
Histamine H_2 Antagonists

Assessment	Nursing Diagnoses	Implementation	Evaluation
HISTORY Allergies to any of these drugs, renal or hepatic failure, pregnancy and lactation, other drugs being taken	Pain related to GI, CNS effects Sensory-perceptual alteration, related to CNS effects Alteration in cardiac output related to cardiac effects Knowledge deficit regarding drug therapy	Administer with meals and at bedtime. Provide comfort and safety measures: analgesics, access to bathroom, safety precautions. Arrange for decreased dose in renal/hepatic disease. Provide support and reassurance to deal with drug effects and life-style changes. Provide patient teaching regarding drug name, dosage, adverse effects, precautions, warnings to report.	Evaluate drug effects: relief of GI symptoms, ulcer healing, prevention of ulcer progression. Monitor for adverse effects: dizziness, confusion; gynecomastia; arrhythmias; GI alterations. Monitor for drug-drug interactions as indicated for each drug. Evaluate effectiveness of patient teaching program. Evaluate effectiveness of comfort and safety measures.
PHYSICAL EXAMINATION Neurological: orientation, affect Skin: color, lesions CV: P, cardiac auscultation GI: liver evaluation Lab tests: CBC, liver, renal function tests			

acids have adverse effects, and there is no perfect antacid.

Administering an antacid frequently causes *acid rebound.* Neutralizing the stomach contents to an alkaline level stimulates gastrin production to cause an increase in acid production and return the stomach to its normal acidic state. In many cases, the acid rebound causes an increase in symptoms, which results in an increased intake of the antacid. This leads to more acid production, and a cycle develops. When more and more antacid is used, the risk for systemic effects rises.

The choice of an antacid depends on adverse effect and absorption factors. Available agents are described below:

- Sodium bicarbonate (*Bell/Ans*), the oldest drug in this group, is readily available in many preparations, including baking soda. It can cause serious electrolyte imbalance in people with renal impairment.
- Calcium carbonate (*Calciday, Tums,* and others), the next antacid to be developed, is actually precipitated chalk. The main drawbacks to this agent are constipation and acid rebound. It can be absorbed systemically and cause calcium imbalance.
- Magnesium salts (*Milk of Magnesia* and others) are very effective in buffering acid in the stomach, but have been known to cause diarrhea. Although these agents are not generally absorbed systemically, absorbed magnesium may lead to nerve damage and even coma.
- Aluminum salts (*Basojel, Amphogel,* and others) do not cause acid rebound but are not very effective in neutralizing acid. They have been related to severe constipation. Aluminum binds dietary phosphates and cause hypophosphotemia, which can then cause calcium imbalance throughout the system.
- Magaldrate (*Lowsium, Riopan*), an aluminum and magnesium salt combination, minimizes the GI effects of constipation and diarrhea by combining these

CASE STUDY

Histamine$_2$ Antagonists

PRESENTATION

W. T., a 48-year old traveling salesman, had experienced increasing epigastric discomfort over a 7-month period. When he finally sought medical care, the diagnosis was a duodenal ulcer. He began taking magaldrate (*Riopan*) for relief of his immediate discomfort as well as cimetidine (*Tagamet*), 300 mg qid. W. T. was referred to the nurse for patient teaching and given an appointment for a follow-up visit in 3 weeks.

CRITICAL THINKING QUESTIONS

Think about the physiology of duodenal ulcers and the various factors that can contribute to aggravating the problem. What patient teaching points should be covered with this patient regarding diet, stress factors, and use of alcohol and tobacco? What adverse effects of the drug should this patient be aware of? What lifestyle changes may be necessary to ensure ulcer healing, and how can W. T. be assisted in making these changes fit into the demands of his job?

DISCUSSION

Further examination indicated that W. T. is a healthy man except for the ulcer. Because he is basically healthy and does not seek medical care unless very uncomfortable (7 months of pain), he may find it difficult to comply with his drug therapy and any suggested lifestyle changes.

W. T. needs patient education, which, for purposes of building trust, should preferably be with the same nurse. The instruction should include information on the duodenal ulcer disease; ways to decrease acid production (e.g., avoiding cigarettes, acid-stimulating foods, alcohol, and caffeine); and ways to improve the protective mucous layer of the stomach by decreasing stress and anxiety-causing situations. Cimetidine may cause dizziness and drowsiness, which could be a major problem if W. T. needs to drive to meet his clients. Because of this adverse effect, another histamine H_2 inhibitor may be preferable. Dizziness and drowsiness are more often associated with use of cimetidine than with some of the newer histamine H_2 inhibitors. This effect should be discussed with W. T. If driving is an important part of W. T.'s job demands, he may want to explore other means of dealing with his ulcer pain and healing.

In addition, spacing of the cimetidine and antacid doses should be stressed. Cimetidine should be taken 1 hour before or 2 hours after any antacids because they can interfere with the absorption of cimetidine and the patient may not receive a therapeutic dose. W. T. should be encouraged to avoid over-the-counter medications and self-medication, because several of these products may contain ingredients that could aggravate his ulcer or interfere with the effectiveness of the drugs that have been prescribed. W. T. should be encouraged to return for regular medical evaluation of his drug therapy and his underlying condition.

Finally, W. T. should feel that he has some control over his situation. Because he does not routinely seek medical care, he may be more comfortable with a medical regimen in which he has participated in planning. Allow him to suggest ways to decrease stress, ways to cut down on smoking or the use of alcohol without interfering with the demands of his job, and the best times to take his drugs in his schedule. He will learn in time what foods and situations irritate his condition. However, research has not shown that bland or restrictive diets are particularly effective in decreasing ulcer pain or spread, and they may actually increase patient anxiety. W. T. should be encouraged to jot down the situations or times of day that seem to cause him the most problems. This information can help to provide a guide for adjusting lifestyle and/or dietary patterns to aid ulcer healing and prevent further development of ulcers.

---

two salts. It may cause a rebound hyperacidity and alkalosis.

Many of these antacids are available in combination forms to take advantage of the acid-neutralizing effect and block adverse effects. For example, a combination of calcium and aluminum salts (*Maalox*) buffers acid and produces neither constipation nor diarrhea.

Antacids can greatly effect the absorption of drugs from the GI tract. Most drugs are prepared for an acidic environment, and an alkaline environment can prevent them from being broken down for absorption or can actually neutralize them so that they cannot be absorbed. Patients taking antacids should be advised to separate them from any other medications by 1 to 2 hours.

THERAPEUTIC ACTIONS AND INDICATIONS

Antacids neutralize stomach acid by direct chemical reaction (see Figure 55-1). They are recommended for the symptomatic relief of upset stomach associated with hyperacidity as well as the hyperacidity associated with peptic ulcer, gastritis, peptic esophagitis, gastric hyperacidity, and hiatal hernia.

CONTRAINDICATIONS/CAUTIONS

The antacids are contraindicated in the presence of any known allergy to antacid products. Caution should be used in the following instances: any condition that can be exacerbated by electrolyte or acid-base imbalance; in the presence of any electrolyte imbalance; GI obstruction, which could cause systemic absorption; allergy to any component of the drug; or renal dysfunction, which can lead to electrolyte disturbance if any absorbed antacid cannot be neutralized properly.

ADVERSE EFFECTS

The adverse effects associated with these drugs relate to their effects on acid-base levels and electrolytes. Rebound acidity, in which the stomach produces more acid in response to the alkaline environment, is common. Alkalosis with resultant metabolic changes (nausea, vomiting, neuromuscular changes, headache, irritability, muscle twitching, and even coma) may occur. The use of calcium salts may lead to hypercalemia and milk-alkali syndrome (seen as alkalosis, renal calcium deposits, severe electrolyte disorders). Constipation and diarrhea may result, depending on the antacid being used. Hypophosphatemia can occur with aluminum salts. Finally, fluid retention and CHF can occur with sodium bicarbonate because of its high sodium content.

DATA LINK

Data link to the following antacids in your nursing drug guide:

ANTACIDS

Name	Brand Name(s)	Usual Indications
aluminum salts	*Basojel, Amphogel*	Symptomatic relief of GI hyperacidity; treatment of hyperphosphatemia; prevention of formation of phosphate urinary stones
calcium salts	*Calciday, Tums*	Symptomatic relief of GI hyperacidity, treatment of calcium deficiency, prevention of hypocalcemia
magaldrate	*Lowsium, Riopan*	Symptomatic relief of GI hyperacidity
magnesium salts	*Milk of Magnesia and others*	Symptomatic relief of GI hyperacidity; prophylaxis of stress ulcers; relief of constipation
P sodium bicarbonate	*Bell/Ans*	Symptomatic relief of GI hyperacidity, minimization of uric acid crystalluria, adjunctive treatment in severe diarrhea

NURSING CONSIDERATIONS
for patients receiving antacids

Assessment

HISTORY. Screen for the following: any history of allergy to antacids; renal dysfunction that might interfere with the drug's metabolism and excretion; and electrolyte disturbances that could be exacerbated by the effects of the drug.

PHYSICAL ASSESSMENT. Include screening for baseline data for assessing the effectiveness of the drug and the occurrence of any adverse effects associated with drug therapy. Assess the following: abdominal sounds (to ensure GI motility); mucous membrane status (to evaluate potential problems with absorption); and serum electrolytes and renal function tests.

Nursing Diagnoses

The patient receiving antacids may have the following nursing diagnoses related to drug therapy:

- Alteration in GI function related to diarrhea or constipation
- Alteration in nutrition related to GI effects
- Alteration in fluid volume related to systemic effects
- Knowledge deficit regarding drug therapy

Implementation

- Administer the drug apart from any other oral medications (1 hour before or 2 hours after) *to ensure adequate absorption of the other medications.*
- Have patients chew tablets thoroughly and follow with *water to ensure therapeutic levels reach stomach to decrease acid.*
- Periodically monitor serum electrolytes *to evaluate drug effects.*
- Assess patients for any signs of acid-base or electrolyte imbalance *to arrange for appropriate interventions.*
- Provide thorough patient teaching, including drug name, prescribed dosage, measures for avoidance of adverse effects, and warning signs that may indicate possible problems. Instruct patients about the need for periodic monitoring and evaluation, *to enhance patient knowledge about drug therapy and to promote compliance.*
- Offer support and encouragement *to help patients cope with the disease and drug regimen.*

Evaluation

- Monitor patient response to the drug (relief of GI symptoms caused by hyperacidity).
- Monitor for adverse effects (GI effects, serum electrolytes, and acid-base levels).
- Evaluate effectiveness of teaching plan (can the patient give the drug and dosage, as well as describe adverse effects to watch for, specific measures to avoid adverse effects, and measures to take to increase the effectiveness of the drug?).

- Monitor effectiveness of comfort measures and compliance with regimen.

PROTON PUMP INHIBITORS

The gastric acid pump or proton pump inhibitors suppress gastric acid secretion by specifically inhibiting the hydrogen/potassium ATPase enzyme system on the secretory surface of the gastric parietal cells. This action blocks the final step of acid production, lowering the acid levels in the stomach.

Two proton pump inhibitors are currently available:

- Omeprazole (*Prilosec*) is the faster acting and more quickly excreted of the two drugs. It is used in combination therapy to treat ulcers caused by *H. pylori* bacteria. Omeprazole is also recommended for the relief of symptoms of heartburn.
- Lanisoprazole (*Prevacid*) is used in the treatment of gastric ulcers, GER, and pathological hypersecretory syndromes; as part of maintenance therapy for healing duodenal ulcers and esophagitis; and in combination therapy for the eradication of *H. pylori* infection.

THERAPEUTIC ACTIONS AND INDICATIONS

Proton pump inhibitors act at specific secretory surface receptors to prevent the final step of acid production and thus decrease the level of acid in the stomach (see Figure 55-1). They are recommended for the short-term treatment of active duodenal ulcers, gastroesophageal reflux disease, erosive esophagitis, and benign active gastric ulcer; for the long-term treatment of pathological hypersecretory conditions; as maintenance therapy for healing of erosive esophagitis; and in combination with amoxicillin and clarithromycin for the treatment of *H. pylori* infection.

CONTRAINDICATIONS/CAUTIONS

These drugs are contraindicated in the presence of known allergy to either drug or the drug components. Caution should be used with pregnancy and lactation.

ADVERSE EFFECTS

The adverse effects associated with these drugs are related to their effects on the hydrogen/potassium ATPase enzyme pump on the parietal and other cells. CNS effects of dizziness and headache are commonly seen; asthenia (loss of strength), vertigo, insomnia, apathy, and dream abnormalities may also be seen. GI effects can include diarrhea, abdominal pain, nausea, vomiting, dry mouth, and tongue atrophy. Upper respiratory symptoms, including cough, stuffy nose, hoarseness, and epistaxis, are frequently seen. Other, less common adverse effects include rash, alopecia, pruritus, dry skin, back pain, and fever. In preclinical studies, long-term effects of proton pump inhibitors included the development of gastric cancer.

DATA LINK

Data link to the following protein pump inhibitors in your nursing drug guide:

PROTEIN PUMP INHIBITORS

Name	Brand Name	Usual Indications
lanisoprazole	*Prevacid*	Treatment of gastric ulcers, GERD, pathological hypersecretory syndromes; maintenance therapy for healing duodenal ulcers and esophagitis; in combination therapy for the eradication of *H. pylori* infection
P omeprazole	*Prilosec*	Treatment of gastric ulcers, GERD, pathological hypersecretory syndromes; maintenance therapy for healing duodenal ulcers and esophagitis; in combination therapy for the eradication of *H. pylori* infection

NURSING CONSIDERATIONS
for patients receiving proton pump inhibitors

Assessment

HISTORY. Screen for any history of allergy to a protein pump inhibitor, pregnancy, or lactation.

PHYSICAL ASSESSMENT. Include screening for assessment to establish baseline data for assessing the effectiveness of the drug and the occurrence of any adverse effects associated with drug therapy. Assess skin color and lesions as well as reflexes, affect, and orientation. In addition, perform an abdominal and respiratory examination.

Nursing Diagnoses

The patient receiving proton pump inhibitors may have the following nursing diagnoses related to drug therapy:

- Alteration in GI function related to diarrhea or constipation
- Alteration in nutrition related to GI effects
- Sensory-perceptual alteration related to CNS effects
- Knowledge deficit regarding drug therapy

Implementation

- Administer drug before meals; ensure that patient does not open, chew, or crush capsules; they should be swallowed whole *to ensure therapeutic effectiveness of the drug.*

- Provide appropriate safety and comfort measures if CNS effects occur *to prevent patient injury.*
- Arrange for medical follow-up if symptoms are not resolved after 4 to 8 weeks of therapy, *because serious underlying conditions could be causing the symptoms.*
- Provide thorough patient teaching, including drug name, prescribed dosage, measures for avoidance of adverse effects, and warning signs that may indicate possible problems. Instruct patients about the need for periodic monitoring and evaluation, *to enhance patient knowledge about drug therapy and to promote compliance.*
- Offer support and encouragement *to help patients cope with the disease and drug regimen.*

Evaluation

- Monitor patient response to the drug (relief of GI symptoms caused by hyperacidity; healing of erosive GI lesions).
- Monitor for adverse effects (GI effects, CNS changes, dermatologic effects, respiratory effects).
- Evaluate effectiveness of teaching plan (can the patient give the drug and dosage and describe adverse effects to watch for, specific measures to avoid adverse effects, and measures to take to increase the effectiveness of the drug?).
- Monitor effectiveness of comfort/safety measures and compliance with regimen.

ANTIPEPTIC AGENT

The antipeptic agent sucralfate (*Carafate*) is given to protect eroded ulcer sites in the GI tract from further damage by acid and digestive enzymes.

THERAPEUTIC ACTIONS AND INDICATIONS

Sucralfate forms an ulcer-adherent complex at duodenal ulcer sites, protecting the sites against acid, pepsin, and bile salts. This action prevents further breakdown of the area and promotes ulcer healing. The drug also inhibits pepsin activity in gastric juices, preventing further breakdown of proteins in the stomach, including the protein wall of the stomach (see Figure 55-1).

Sucralfate is recommended for the short-term treatment of duodenal ulcers. It is used at a reduced dose for maintenance of duodenal ulcers after healing. In addition, this agent is undergoing investigation for the treatment of gastric ulcers; NSAID-induced gastric damage; prevention of stress ulcers in acutely ill individuals; and the treatment of oral and esophageal ulcers due to radiation, chemotherapy, or sclerotherapy.

CONTRAINDICATIONS/CAUTIONS

Sucralfate should not be given to any person with known allergy to the drug or any of its components or with renal failure/dialysis because a buildup of aluminum may occur if used with aluminum-containing products. Caution should be used with pregnancy and lactation.

ADVERSE EFFECTS

The adverse effects associated with sucralfate are primarily related to its GI effects. Constipation is the most frequently seen adverse effect. Diarrhea, nausea, indigestion, gastric discomfort, and dry mouth may also occur. Other adverse effects that have been reported with the use of this drug include dizziness, sleepiness, vertigo, skin rash, and back pain.

CLINICALLY IMPORTANT DRUG–INTERACTIONS

If aluminum salts are combined with sucralfate, there is a risk of high aluminum levels and aluminum toxicity. Extreme care should be taken if this combination is used. In addition, if phenytoin, fluoroquinolone antibiotics (e.g., ciprofloxacin, norfloxacin), or penicillamine is combined with sucralfate, decreased serum levels and drug effectiveness may result. In such combinations, the individual agents should be administered separately, with at least 2 hours between drugs.

DATA LINK

Data link to the following antipeptic agent in your nursing drug guide:

ANTIPEPTIC AGENT

Name	Brand Name	Usual Indications
sucralfate	*Carafate*	Short-term treatment of duodenal ulcers; maintenance of duodenal ulcers after healing

NURSING CONSIDERATIONS
for patients receiving an antipeptic agent

Assessment

HISTORY. Screen for any history of allergy to sucralfate, renal dysfunction or dialysis, and pregnancy or lactation.

PHYSICAL ASSESSMENT. Include screening for establishing baseline data for assessing the effectiveness of the drug and the occurrence of any adverse effects associated with drug therapy. Assess the following:

skin color and lesions; reflexes, affect, and orientation; abdominal examination; and mucous membranes.

Nursing Diagnoses

The patient receiving sucralfate may have the following nursing diagnoses related to drug therapy:

- Alteration in GI function related to diarrhea or constipation
- Alteration in nutrition related to GI effects
- Sensory-perceptual alteration related to CNS effects
- Knowledge deficit regarding drug therapy

Implementation

- Administer drug on an empty stomach, 1 hour before or 2 hours after meals and at bedtime, *to ensure therapeutic effectiveness of the drug.*
- Monitor patient for GI pain, *to arrange to administer antacids to relieve pain if needed.*
- Administer antacids between doses of sucralfate, not within ½ hour of sucralfate dose, *because sucralfate can interfere with the absorption of oral agents.*
- Provide comfort and safety measures if CNS effects occur *to prevent patient injury.*
- Provide frequent mouth care; sugarless lozenges to suck; bowel training as needed; and small, frequent meals *if GI effects are uncomfortable.*
- Provide thorough patient teaching, including drug name, prescribed dosage, measures for avoidance of adverse effects, and warning signs that may indicate possible problems. Instruct patients about the need for periodic monitoring and evaluation, *to enhance patient knowledge about drug therapy and to promote compliance.*
- Offer support and encouragement *to help patients cope with the disease and drug regimen.*

Evaluation

- Monitor patient response to the drug (relief of GI symptoms caused by hyperacidity; healing of erosive GI lesions).
- Monitor for adverse effects (GI effects, CNS changes, dermatologic effects).
- Evaluate effectiveness of teaching plan (can the patient name drug and dosage ad describe adverse effects to watch for, specific measures to avoid adverse effects, and measures to take to increase the effectiveness of the drug?).
- Monitor effectiveness of comfort/safety measures and compliance with regimen.

PROSTAGLANDIN

The synthetic prostaglandin E_1 analog, misoprostol (*Cytotec*), is used to protect the lining of the stomach in situations that might lead to serious GI complications.

THERAPEUTIC ACTIONS AND INDICATIONS

Prostaglandin E_1 inhibits gastric acid secretion and increases bicarbonate and mucous production in the stomach, thus protecting the stomach lining (see Figure 55-1). Misoprostol is used to prevent NSAID-induced gastric ulcers in patients at high risk for complications from a gastric ulcer (e.g., elderly or debilitated patients, patients with a past history of ulcer). It has also been found to be effective in treating duodenal ulcers in patients who are not responsive to histamine H_2 antagonists, and it is being investigated for this purpose.

CONTRAINDICATIONS/CAUTIONS

This drug is contraindicated during pregnancy; it is an abortifacient. Women of childbearing age should be advised to have a negative serum pregnancy test within 2 weeks of beginning treatment and should begin the drug on the second or third day of the next menstrual cycle. In addition, they should be instructed to use barrier contraceptives during therapy. Caution should be used during lactation and with any known allergy to prostaglandins.

ADVERSE EFFECTS

The adverse effects associated with this drug are primarily related to its GI effects—nausea, diarrhea, abdominal pain, flatulence, vomiting, dyspepsia, and constipation. GU effects, which are related to the actions of prostaglandins on the uterus, include miscarriages, excessive bleeding, spotting, cramping, hypermenorrhea, dysmenorrhea, and other menstrual disorders. Women taking this drug should be notified, both in writing and verbally, of these potential effects of this drug.

DATA LINK

Data link to the following prostaglandin in your nursing drug guide:

PROSTAGLANDIN

Name	Brand Name	Usual Indication
misoprostol	*Cytotec*	Prevention of NSAID-induced ulcers in patients at high risk for developing these gastric ulcers

NURSING CONSIDERATIONS
for patients receiving prostaglandin

Assessment

HISTORY. Screen for any history of allergy to misoprostol and pregnancy or lactation.

PHYSICAL ASSESSMENT. Include screening for establishment of baseline data for assessing the effectiveness of the drug and the occurrence of any adverse effects associated with drug therapy. Assess abdominal examination, pregnancy test, and normal menstrual activity.

Nursing Diagnoses

The patient receiving misoprostol may have the following nursing diagnoses related to drug therapy:

- Alteration in GI function related to GI effects
- Alteration in nutrition related to GI effects
- Sexual dysfunction related to GU effects
- Knowledge deficit regarding drug therapy

Implementation

- Administer to patients at high risk for NSAID-induced ulcers during the full course of NSAID therapy *to prevent the development of gastric ulcers.* Administer four times a day—with meals and at bedtime.
- Arrange for serum pregnancy test within 2 weeks of beginning treatment; begin therapy on second or third day of menstrual period *to ensure that women of childbearing age are not pregnant to prevent abortifacient effects associated with this drug.*
- Provide patient with both written and oral information regarding the associated risks of pregnancy *to ensure that patient understands the risks involved;* advise the use of barrier contraceptives during therapy *to ensure prevention of pregnancy.*
- Assess nutritional status if GI effects are severe, *in order to arrange for appropriate measures to relieve discomfort and ensure nutrition.*
- Provide thorough patient teaching, including drug name, prescribed dosage, measures for avoidance of adverse effects, and warning signs that may indicate possible problems. Instruct patients about the need for periodic monitoring and evaluation, *to enhance patient knowledge about drug therapy and to promote compliance.*
- Offer support and encouragement *to help patients cope with the disease and drug regimen.*

Evaluation

- Monitor patient response to the drug (prevention of GI ulcers related to NSAIDs).
- Monitor for adverse effects (GI, GU).
- Evaluate effectiveness of teaching plan (can the patient name drug and dosage and describe adverse effects to watch for, specific measures to avoid adverse effects, and measures to take to increase the effectiveness of the drug?).
- Monitor effectiveness of comfort/safety measures and compliance with regimen.

WWW.WEB LINKS

Health care providers and patients may want to consult the following Internet sources:

Information on the anatomy and physiology of the GI tract, pathophysiology of various gastrointestinal ulcer disorders, treatments, and research:
http://www.wvhealth.wvu.edu/clinical/digestive/ulcers.htm

Information for patients and families on ulcers, including treatments and causes:
http://www.aafp.org/patientinfo/ulcers.html

Information on gastroesophageal reflux disorders:
http://www.merck-medco.com/oh/dh/pu.htm

Information about *Helicobacter pylori* research and treatment:
http://www.cdc.gov/ncidod/dbmd/md/htm

Educational materials on a variety of gastrointestinal disorders:
http://www.healthanswers.com

DIGESTIVE ENZYMES

Some patients—those who have suffered strokes, salivary gland disorders, or extreme surgery of the head and neck, or those with cystic fibrosis or pancreatic dysfunction—may require a supplement to the production of digestive enzymes. Three digestive enzymes are available for replacement in conditions that result in lower than normal levels of these enzymes.

- Saliva substitute (*Mouthkote, Salivart*) helps in conditions resulting in dry mouth—stroke, radiation therapy, chemotherapy, and other illnesses.
- Pancreatin (*Creon Capsules*) is used to aid the digestion and absorption of fats, proteins, and carbohydrates in conditions that result in a lack of this enzyme.
- Pancrelipase (*Cotazym, Ilozyme*) is used like pancreatin in conditions that result in a lack of pancrelipase.

THERAPEUTIC ACTIONS AND INDICATIONS

Saliva substitute contains electrolytes and carboxymethocellulose to act as a thickening agent in dry mouth conditions. This makes the food bolus easier to swallow and begins the early digestion process. The pancreatic enzymes are replacement enzymes that help the digestion and absorption of fats, proteins, and carbohydrates (see Figure 55-1). They are used as replacement therapy in cystic fibrosis, chronic pancreatitis, postpancreatectomy, ductal obstructions, pancreatic insufficiency, steatorrhea or malabsorption syndrome, and postgastrectomy.

CONTRAINDICATIONS/CAUTIONS

Saliva substitute is contraindicated in the presence of known allergy to parabens or any component of the drug. It should be used cautiously with CHF and in hypertension or renal failure because there may be an abnormal absorption of electrolytes, including sodium, leading to increased cardiovascular load. Pancreatic enzymes should not be used with known allergy to the product or to pork products. In addition, they should be used cautiously with pregnancy and lactation.

ADVERSE EFFECTS

The adverse effects most commonly seen with saliva substitute involve complications from abnormal electrolyte absorption, such as elevated levels of magnesium, sodium, or potassium. The adverse effects that most often occur with pancreatic enzymes are related to GI irritation—nausea, abdominal cramps, and diarrhea.

DATA LINK

Data link to the following digestive enzymes in your nursing drug guide:

DIGESTIVE ENZYMES

Name	Brand Name(s)	Usual Indications
P pancreatin	*Creon Capsules*	An aid for digestion and absorption of fats, proteins, and carbohydrates in conditions that result in a lack of this enzyme
pancrelipase	*Cotazym, Ilozym*	An aid for digestion and absorption of fats, proteins, and carbohydrates in conditions that result in a lack of this enzyme
saliva substitute	*Mouthkote, Salivart*	An aid in conditions resulting in dry mouth—stroke, radiation therapy, chemotherapy, and other illnesses

NURSING CONSIDERATIONS
for patients receiving digestive enzymes

Assessment

HISTORY. Screen for the following: any history of allergy to any of the drugs or to pork products (pancreatic enzymes); pregnancy or lactation; CHF or hypertension (saliva substitute).

PHYSICAL ASSESSMENT. Include screening for establishment of baseline data for assessing the effectiveness of the drug and the occurrence of any adverse effects associated with drug therapy. Assess the following: abdominal examination, mucous membranes; blood pressure, cardiac evaluation, and pancreatic enzyme levels (pancreatic enzymes).

Nursing Diagnoses

The patient receiving digestive enzymes may have the following nursing diagnoses related to drug therapy:

- Alteration in GI function related to GI effects
- Alteration in nutrition related to GI effects
- Knowledge deficit regarding drug therapy

Implementation

- Have patient swish a saliva substitute around the mouth as needed for dry mouth and throat *to coat mouth and ensure therapeutic effectiveness of the drug.*
- Monitor swallowing, *because it may be impaired and additional therapy may be needed.*
- Administer pancreatic enzymes with meals and snacks, *so that enzyme is available when it is needed.* Avoid spilling powder on the skin, *because it may be irritating.* Do not crush the capsule or allow the patient to chew it; it must be swallowed whole, *to ensure full therapeutic effects.*
- Assess nutritional status if GI effects *in order to arrange for appropriate measures to relieve discomfort and ensure nutrition.*
- Provide thorough patient teaching, including drug name, prescribed dosage, measures for avoidance of adverse effects, and warning signs that may indicate possible problems. Instruct patients about the need for periodic monitoring and evaluation, *to enhance patient knowledge about drug therapy and to promote compliance.*
- Offer support and encouragement *to help patients cope with the disease and drug regimen.*

Evaluation

- Monitor patient response to the drug (e.g., relief of dry mouth and throat; digestion of fats, proteins, and carbohydrates).
- Monitor for adverse effects (e.g., electrolyte imbalance, GI effects).
- Evaluate effectiveness of teaching plan (can the patient name the drug and dosage and describe adverse

effects to watch for, specific measures to avoid adverse effects, and measures to take to increase the effectiveness of the drug?).

- Monitor effectiveness of comfort/safety measures and compliance with regimen.

CHAPTER SUMMARY

- GI complaints are some of the most common symptoms seen in clinical practice.
- Peptic ulcers may result from increased acid production, decrease in the protective mucous lining of the stomach, infection with *H. pylori* bacteria, or a combination of these.
- Agents used to decrease the acid content of the stomach include histamine H_2 antagonists, which block the release of acid in response to gastrin or parasympathetic release; antacids, which chemically react with the acid to neutralize it; and proton pump inhibitors, which block the last step of acid production to prevent release.
- Acid rebound occurs when the stomach produces more gastrin and more acid in response to lowered acid levels in the stomach. Balancing reducing the stomach acid without increasing acid production is a clinical challenge.
- The antipeptic agent sucralfate forms a protective coating over the eroded stomach lining to protect it from acid and digestive enzymes and to aid healing.
- The prostaglandin misoprostol blocks gastric acid secretion while increasing the production of bicarbonate and mucous lining in the stomach.
- Digestive enzymes such as substitute saliva and pancreatic enzymes may be needed in cases where normal enzyme levels are very low and proper digestion cannot take place.

BIBLIOGRAPHY

Bullock, B. L. (2000). *Focus on pathophysiology.* Philadelphia: Lippincott Williams & Wilkins.

Hardman, J. G., Limbird, L. E., Molinoff, P. B., Ruddon, R. W., & Gilman, A. G. (Eds.). (1996). *Goodman and Gilman's the pharmacological basis of therapeutics* (9th ed.). New York: McGraw-Hill.

Karch, A. M. (2000). *2000 Lippincott's nursing drug guide.* Philadelphia: Lippincott Williams & Wilkins.

Malseed, R. (1995). *Textbook of pharmacology and nursing care.* Philadelphia: J. B. Lippincott.

McEvoy, B. R. (Ed.) (1999). *Facts and comparisons 1999.* St. Louis: Facts and Comparisons.

Professional's guide to patient drug facts (1999). St. Louis: Facts and Comparisons.

CHAPTER

56

Laxative and Antidiarrheal Agents

Laxatives
- bisacodyl
- cascara
- **P** castor oil
- docusate
- glycerin
- lactulose
- **P** magnesium citrate
- magnesium hydroxide
- magnesium sulfate
- **P** mineral oil
- phenolphthalein
- polycarbophil
- psyllium
- senna

GI stimulants
- dexpanthenol
- **P** metoclopramide
- cisapride

Antidiarrheal drugs
- bismuth subsalicylate
- **P** loperamide
- opium

CHAPTER OUTLINE

KEY TERMS

antidiarrheal drug
bulk stimulant
cathartic dependence
chemical stimulant
constipation
diarrhea
lubricant

INTRODUCTION

Drugs used to affect the motor activity of the GI tract can do so in several different ways. They can be used to speed up or improve the movement of intestinal contents along the GI tract when movement becomes too slow or sluggish to allow for proper absorption or nutrients and excretion of wastes, as in ***constipation.*** Drugs are also used to increase the tone of the GI tract and to stimulate motility throughout the system. They can also be used to decrease movement along the GI tract when rapid movement decreases the time for absorption of nutrients, leading to a loss of water and nutrients and the discomfort of ***diarrhea*** (Figure 56–1).

LAXATIVES

Laxative, or cathartic, drugs are used in several ways to speed the passage of the intestinal contents through the GI tract. Laxatives may be either ***chemical stimulants,*** which chemically irritate the lining of the GI tract; ***bulk*** (mechanical) ***stimulants,*** which cause the fecal matter to increase in bulk; or ***lubricants,*** which help the intestinal contents move more smoothly (Table 56–1).

Chemical Stimulants

Drugs that act as chemical stimulants directly stimulate the nerve plexus in the intestinal wall, causing increased movement and the stimulation of local reflexes. Such laxatives include the following agents:

- Cascara (generic), a reliable agent, may have a slow, steady effect or may cause severe cramping and rapid evacuation of the contents of the large intestine.
- Senna (*Senokot*) is another reliable drug with effects similar to cascara.
- Phenolphthalein (*Lax Pills*), found in many over-the-counter (OTC) preparations, acts as a stimulant when it is broken down in the large intestine. Hypersensitivity reactions, including dermatological reactions, are not uncommon with this agent. Neurotoxicity, particularly in small children or pets who accidentally ingest this drug, has led to removal of this particular stimulant from many popular OTC chocolate or chewing gum laxative preparations.
- Castor oil (*Neolid*), an old standby, is used when a thorough evacuation of the intestine is desirable. This agent begins working at the beginning of the small intestine and increases motility throughout the rest of the GI tract. Because castor oil blocks absorption of fats (including fat-soluble vitamins) and may lead to constipation from GI tract exhaustion when there is no stimulus to movement, its frequent use is not desirable.
- Bisacodyl (*Dulcolax*) is chemically related to phenolphthalein. This drug, which causes a slow and steady increase in movement in the large intestine, is often the drug of choice if mild stimulation is needed to prevent constipation and straining after GI surgery or MI.

Bulk Stimulants

Bulk stimulants are rapid-acting, aggressive laxatives that increase the motility of the GI tract by increasing the fluid in the intestinal contents, which enlarges bulk, stimulates local stretch receptors, and activates local activity. Available bulk stimulants include the following agents:

- Magnesium sulfate (*Epsom Salts*), a very potent laxative, is used when total evacuation of the GI tract is needed rapidly, as in cases of GI poisoning. This agent acts by exerting a hypertonic pull against the mucosal wall, drawing fluid into the intestinal contents.
- Magnesium citrate (*Citrate of Magnesia*), found in a citrus-flavored base, is often used to stimulate bowel evacuation before many GI tests and examinations.
- Magnesium hydroxide (*Milk of Magnesia*) is used to stimulate bulk and is a milder and slower-acting laxative. It also works by a saline pull, bringing fluids into the lumen of the GI tract.
- Lactulose (*Chronulac*) is the alternative choice for patients with cardiovascular problems. This saltless osmotic laxative pulls fluid out of the venous system and into the lumen of the small intestine.
- Polycarbophil (*FiberCon*) is a natural substance that forms a gelatin-like bulk out of the intestinal contents. This agent stimulates local activity. It is considered milder and less irritating than many other bulk stimulants. Patients must use caution and take polycarbophil with plenty of water. If only a little water is used, it may absorb enough fluid in the esophagus to swell into a gelatin-like mass that can obstruct the esophagus and cause severe problems.
- Psyllium (*Metamucil*), another gelatin-like bulk stimulant, is similar to polycarbophil in action and effect.

Lubricating Laxatives

Sometimes it is desirable to make defecation easier without stimulating the movement of the GI tract by the use of lubricants. Patients with hemorrhoids or who have recently had rectal surgery may need lubrication of the stool. Some patients who could be harmed by straining might also benefit from this type of laxative.

- Docusate (*Colace*) has a detergent action on the surface of the intestinal bolus, increasing the admixture of fat and water and making a softer stool. This drug is frequently used as prophylaxis for patients

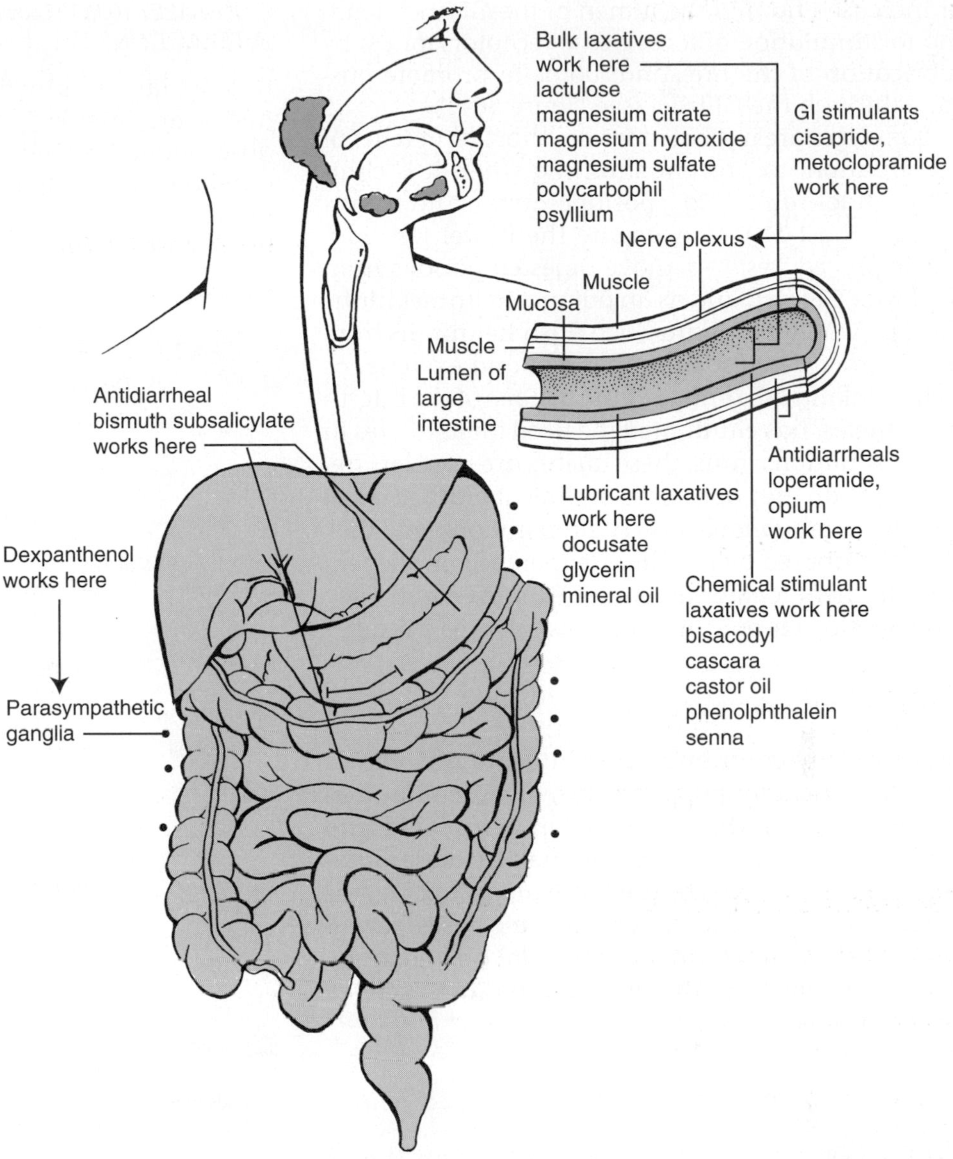

FIGURE 56-1. Sites of action of drugs affecting gastrointestinal motility.

who should not strain (e, g., postoperative, post-MI, postpartum).

- Glycerin (*Sani-Supp*) is a hyperosmolar laxative that is used in suppository form to gently evacuate the rectum without systemic effects higher in the GI tract.

TABLE 56-1

LAXATIVES

Type	Names
Chemical stimulants	bisacodyl, cascara, castor oil, phenolphthalein, senna
Bulk stimulants	lactulose, magnesium citrate, magnesium hydroxide, magnesium sulfate, polycarbophil, psyllium
Lubricants	docusate, glycerin, mineral oil

- Mineral oil (*Agoral Plain*) is the oldest of these laxatives. It is not absorbed and forms a slippery coat on the contents of the intestinal tract. When the intestinal bolus is coated with mineral oil, less water is absorbed out of the bolus and the bolus is less likely to become hard or impacted. Frequent use of mineral oil can interfere with absorption of the fat-soluble vitamins A, D, E, and K. In addition, leakage and staining may be a problem when mineral oil is used when the stool cannot be retained by the external sphincter.

The type of laxative recommended depends on the condition of the patient, the speed of relief needed, and the possible implication of various adverse effects.

THERAPEUTIC ACTIONS AND INDICATIONS

Laxatives work in three ways: (1) by direct chemical stimulation of the GI tract; (2) by production of bulk or increased fluid in the lumen of the GI tract, leading to stimulation of local nerve receptors; or (3) by lubrication of the intestinal bolus to promote passage through the GI tract (see Figure 56–1).

Laxatives are indicated for the short-term relief of constipation; to prevent straining when it is clinically undesirable (e.g., postoperative states, postpartum, post-MI); to evacuate the bowel for diagnostic procedures; to remove ingested poisons from the lower GI tract; and as an adjunct in anthelmintic therapy when it is desirable to flush helminths from the GI tract. The use of proper diet and exercise, as well as taking advantage of the actions of the intestinal reflexes, has eliminated the need for laxatives in many situations; thus, these agents are used less frequently than they once were in clinical practice. Most laxatives are available in OTC preparations, and they are often abused by people who then become dependent on them for stimulation of GI movement. They may develop chronic intestinal disorders as a result.

CONTRAINDICATIONS/CAUTIONS

Laxatives are contraindicated in acute abdominal disorders, including appendicitis, diverticulitis, and ulcerative colitis when increased motility could lead to rupture or further exacerbation of the inflammation. Laxatives should be used with great caution during pregnancy and lactation. In some cases, stimulation of the GI tract can precipitate labor, and many of these agents cross the placenta and are excreted in breast milk.

ADVERSE EFFECTS

The adverse effects most commonly associated with laxatives are GI effects such as diarrhea, abdominal cramping, and nausea; CNS effects, including dizziness, headache, and weakness, are not uncommon and may relate to loss of fluid and electrolyte imbalances that may accompany laxative use. Sweating, palpitations, flushing, and even fainting have been reported following laxative use. These effects may be related to a sympathetic stress reaction to intense neurostimulation of the GI tract or to the loss of fluid and electrolyte imbalance.

A very common adverse effect that is seen with frequent laxative use or laxative abuse is ***cathartic dependence.*** This reaction occurs when patients use laxatives over a long period of time, and the GI tract becomes dependent on the vigorous stimulation of the laxative. Without this stimulation, the GI tract does not move for a period of time (i.e., several days), which could lead to constipation and drying of the stool and ultimately result in impaction.

CLINICALLY IMPORTANT DRUG–DRUG INTERACTIONS

Because laxatives increase the motility of the GI tract and some interfere with the timing or process of absorption, it is advisable not to take laxatives with other prescribed medications. The administration of laxatives and other medications should be separated by at least ½ hour.

DATA LINK

Data link to the following laxatives in your nursing drug guide:

LAXATIVES

Name	Brand Name	Usual Indications
CHEMICAL STIMULANTS		
bisacodyl	*Dulcolax*	Prevention of constipation and straining after GI surgery, MI, delivery; short-term treatment of constipation
cascara	generic	Short-term treatment of constipation; evacuation of the large intestine for diagnostic examination
P castor oil	*Neolid*	Emptying of the GI tract for diagnostic testing; short-term treatment of constipation
phenolphthalein	*Lax Pills*	Short-term treatment of constipation; in many OTC preparations
senna	*Senokot*	Short-term treatment of constipation; treatment of encopresis
BULK LAXATIVES		
lactulose	*Chronulac*	Short-term treatment of constipation; especially useful in patients with CV disorders
P magnesium citrate	*Citrate of Magnesia*	Bowel evacuation before GI diagnostic tests and examinations
magnesium hydroxide	*Milk of Magnesia*	Short-term treatment of constipation; prevention of straining following GI surgery, delivery, MI
magnesium sulfate	*Epsom Salts*	Treatment of GI poisoning; rapid evacuation of the GI tract
polycarbophil	*FiberCon*	Mild laxative; short-term treatment of constipation
psyllium	*Metamucil*	Mild laxative; short-term treatment of constipation
LUBRICANTS		
docusate	*Colace*	Prevention of straining in postoperative, post-MI and postpartum patients
glycerin	*Sani-Supp*	Short-term treatment of constipation
P mineral oil	*Agoral Plain*	Short-term treatment of constipation

NURSING CONSIDERATIONS
for patients receiving laxatives

Assessment

HISTORY. Screen for the following conditions: history of allergy to laxative, fecal impaction, or intestinal obstruction; acute abdominal pain, nausea, and vomiting; and pregnancy and lactation.

PATIENT TEACHING CHECKLIST

Laxatives

Create customized patient teaching materials for a specific laxative from your CD-ROM. Your patient teaching should stress the following points for drugs within this class:

A laxative prevents constipation and helps keep the GI tract functioning on a regular basis. It is used when straining could be dangerous or when a situation arises that may result in constipation. This drug should be taken only as a temporary measure to relieve constipation.

Common effects of this drug include:

- Diarrhea—Have ready access to bathroom facilities. Consult with your health care provider if this becomes a problem.
- Dizziness, weakness—Change positions slowly. If you feel drowsy, avoid driving or dangerous activities.

Report any of the following conditions to your health care provider: sweating, flushing, dizziness, muscle cramps, excessive thirst.

Increase your intake of dietary fiber and fluid, and try to maintain daily exercise to encourage bowel regularity.

Tell any doctor, nurse, or other health care provider that you are taking this drug.

Keep this drug and all medications out of the reach of children.

This Teaching Checklist reflects general patient teaching guidelines. It is not meant to be a substitute for drug-specific teaching information, which is available in nursing drug guides.

PHYSICAL ASSESSMENT. Include screening for the presence of any skin lesions; orientation and affect; baseline pulse; abdominal examination, including bowel sounds; and serum electrolytes.

Nursing Diagnoses

The patient receiving any laxative may have the following nursing diagnoses related to drug therapy:

- Pain related to CNS and GI effects
- Alteration in bowel function related to diarrhea
- Knowledge deficit regarding drug therapy

Implementation

- Administer only as a temporary measure *to prevent development of cathartic dependence.*
- Arrange for appropriate dietary measures, exercise, and environmental control *to encourage return of normal bowel function.*
- Administer with a full glass of water, and caution the patient not to chew tablets *to ensure that laxative reaches the GI tract to allow for therapeutic effects.* Encourage fluid intake throughout the day as appropriate *to maintain fluid balance and improve GI movement.*
- Do not administer in the presence of acute abdominal pain, nausea, or vomiting, *which could indicate serious underlying medical problems that could be exacerbated by laxative use.*
- Monitor bowel function *to evaluate drug effectiveness.* If diarrhea or cramping occurs, discontinue the drug *to relieve discomfort and to prevent serious fluid and electrolyte imbalance.*
- Provide comfort and safety measures *to improve patient compliance and to ensure patient safety,* including ready access to bathroom facilities, assistance with ambulation, and periodic orientation if GI or CNS effects occur.
- Offer support and encouragement *to help patient deal with discomfort of condition and drug therapy.*
- Provide thorough patient teaching, including name of drug, dosage prescribed, proper administration, measures to avoid adverse effects, warning signs of problems, and the importance of periodic monitoring and evaluation *to enhance patient knowledge about drug therapy and promote compliance with the drug regimen* (see Patient Teaching Checklist: Laxatives).
- Offer support and encouragement *to help patient deal with the diagnosis and drug regimen.*

Evaluation

- Monitor patient response to the drug (relief of GI symptoms, absence of straining, evacuation of GI tract).
- Monitor for adverse effects (dizziness, confusion, GI alterations, sweating, electrolyte imbalance, cathartic dependence).

NURSING CARE GUIDE
Laxatives

Assessment	Nursing Diagnoses	Implementation	Evaluation
HISTORY Allergies to any of these drugs, acute abdominal pain, nausea, vomiting, Pregnancy and lactation	Pain related to GI, CNS effects Alteration in bowel function, related to GI effects Knowledge deficit regarding drug therapy	Administer only as a temporary measure. Provide comfort and safety measures: - assistance - access to bathroom - safety precautions. Do not administer in presence of acute abdominal pain, nausea, or vomiting. Monitor bowel function. Provide support and reassurance for coping with drug effects and discomfort. Provide patient teaching regarding - drug name and dosage - adverse effects and precautions - warnings to report	Evaluate drug effects: - relief of GI symptoms - ulcer healing - prevention of ulcer progression Monitor for adverse effects: - GI alterations - dizziness, confusion - cathartic dependence - electrolyte imbalance Monitor for drug–drug interactions as indicated for each drug. Evaluate effectiveness of patient teaching program. Evaluate effectiveness of comfort and safety measures.
PHYSICAL EXAMINATION Neurological: orientation, affect Skin: color, lesions CV: P GI: abdominal evaluation Lab tests: serum electrolytes			

• Evaluate effectiveness of teaching plan (patient can name the drug and dosage as well as describe adverse effects to watch for and specific measures to use to avoid adverse effects).
• Monitor effectiveness of comfort measures and compliance with regimen (see Nursing Care Guide: Laxatives).

GI STIMULANTS

Some drugs are available for more generalized GI stimulation that results in generally increased GI activity and secretions. These drugs stimulate parasympathetic activity or make the GI tissues more sensitive to parasympathetic activity. Such stimulants include:

• Cisapride (*Propulsid*), which increases the release of acetylcholine in the myenteric plexus.
• Dexpanthenol (*Ilopan*), which increases acetylcholine levels and stimulates the parasympathetic system.
• Metoclopramide (*Reglan*), which blocks dopamine receptors and makes the GI cells more sensitive to acetylcholine, leading to increased GI activity and rapid movement of food through the upper GI tract.

THERAPEUTIC ACTIONS AND INDICATIONS

By stimulating parasympathetic activity within the GI tract, these drugs act to increase GI secretions and motility on a general level throughout the tract (see Figure 56–1). They do not have the local effects of laxatives to increase activity only in the intestines. These drugs are indicated when more rapid movement of GI contents is desirable. Cisapride is preferred for moving stomach contents into the intestine, thus relieving the heartburn associated with gastroesophageal reflux disease. Dexpanthenol is indicated in many postoperative situations when intestinal atony or loss of tone could become a problem. Metoclopramide is indicated for relief of symptoms of gastroesophageal reflux disease; prevention of nausea and vomiting after emetogenic chemotherapy or postoperatively; relief of symptoms of diabetic gastroparesis; and for the promotion of GI movement during small bowel intubation or to promote rapid movement of barium.

CONTRAINDICATIONS/CAUTIONS

GI stimulants should not be used with any history or allergy to any of these drugs or with any GI obstruction or perforation. They should be used with caution during pregnancy or lactation.

ADVERSE EFFECTS

The most common adverse effects seen with GI stimulants involve GI stimulation and include nausea, vomiting, diarrhea, intestinal spasm, and cramping. Other adverse effects, such as declining blood pressure and heart rate, weakness, and fatigue, may be related to parasympathetic stimulation.

CLINICALLY IMPORTANT DRUG–DRUG INTERACTIONS

Cisapride has been associated with serious cardiac arrhythmias when combined with ketoconazole, itraconazole, miconazole, and troleandomycin. Extreme caution and constant monitoring should be used if any of these drugs is taken with cisapride.

DATA LINK

Data link to the following GI stimulants in your nursing drug guide:

GI STIMULANTS

Name	Brand Name	Usual Indications
cisapride	*Propulsid*	Relief of heartburn associated with GERD
dexpanthenol	*Ilopan*	Prevention of intestinal atony in postoperative situations
P metoclopramide	*Reglan*	Relief of symptoms of GERD; prevention of nausea and vomiting after emetogenic chemotherapy or postoperatively; relief of symptoms of diabetic gastroparesis; promotion of GI movement during small bowel intubation or promotion of rapid movement of barium

NURSING CONSIDERATIONS
for patients receiving GI stimulants

Assessment

HISTORY. Screen for any history of allergy to these drugs; intestinal obstruction, bleeding, or perforation; or pregnancy or lactation.

PHYSICAL ASSESSMENT. Include screening for establishment of baseline data for assessing the effectiveness of the drug and the occurrence of any adverse effects associated with drug therapy. Perform an abdominal evaluation, checking bowel sounds to ensure GI motility; assess pulse and blood pressure to monitor for adverse effects; and check skin color and lesions to assess for hypersensitivity reactions.

Nursing Diagnoses

The patient receiving GI stimulants may have the following nursing diagnoses related to drug therapy:

- Alteration in GI function related to diarrhea
- Pain related to GI effects
- Knowledge deficit regarding drug therapy

Implementation

- Administer at least 15 minutes before each meal and at *bedtime to ensure therapeutic effectiveness.*
- Monitor BP carefully if giving IV *to detect and consult with the prescriber about treatment for sudden drops in BP.*
- Monitor diabetic patients *in order to arrange for alteration in insulin dose or timing as appropriate.*
- Provide thorough patient teaching, including name of drug, dosage prescribed, proper administration, measures to avoid adverse effects, warning signs of problems, and the importance of periodic monitoring and evaluation *to enhance patient knowledge about drug therapy and promote compliance with the drug regimen.*
- Offer support and encouragement *to help the patient deal with the diagnosis and drug regimen.*

Evaluation

- Monitor patient response to the drug (increased tone and movement of GI tract).
- Monitor for adverse effects (GI effects, parasympathetic activity).
- Evaluate effectiveness of teaching plan (patient can name the drug and dosage, as well as describe adverse effects to watch for and specific measures to take to avoid adverse effects and increase the effectiveness of the drug).
- Monitor effectiveness of comfort measures and compliance with regimen.

WWW.WEB LINKS

Health care providers and patients may want to consult the following Internet sources:

Information on traveler's diarrhea:
http://moon.com/travel_matters/11/health.html

Information for the traveler about causes, treatments, and prevention of traveler's diarrhea:
http://www.bu.edu/cohis/nutrition/disease/diarrhea/travel.htm

Information on constipation—causes, diagnosis, research, treatment, and prevention across the life span:
http://medlineplus.nlm.nih.gov/medlineplus/constipation.html

Information on diarrhea—guidelines for prevention and treatment:
http://webmd.lycos.com/topic_summary/162/

ANTIDIARRHEAL DRUGS

Antidiarrheal drugs, which block stimulation of the GI tract, are used for symptomatic relief from diarrhea. Available agents include the following:

- Bismuth subsalicylate (*Pepto Bismol*) acts locally to coat the lining of the GI tract and soothe any irritation that might be stimulating local reflexes to cause excessive GI activity and diarrhea. This agent has been found to be very helpful in treating traveler's diarrhea and preventing cramping and distention associated with dietary excess and some viral infections.
- Loperamide (*Imodium*) has a direct effect on the muscle layers of the GI tract to slow peristalsis and allow increased time for absorption of fluid and electrolytes.
- Opium derivatives (paregoric) act to stimulate spasm within the GI tract, stopping peristalsis and diarrhea and the discomfort associated with it.

THERAPEUTIC ACTIONS AND INDICATIONS

Antidiarrheal agents slow the motility of the GI tract through direct action on the lining of the GI tract, inhibiting local reflexes (bismuth subsalicylate); through direct action on the muscles of the GI tract to slow activity (loperamide); or by action on CNS centers that cause GI spasm and slowing (opium derivatives). These drugs are indicated for the relief of symptoms of acute and chronic diarrhea; reduction of volume of discharge from ileostomies; and prevention and treatment of traveler's diarrhea (see Figure 56–1).

CONTRAINDICATIONS/CAUTIONS

Antidiarrheal drugs should not be given to anyone with known allergy to the drug or any of its components. Caution should be used with pregnancy and lactation. Care should also be taken in individuals with any history of GI obstruction, acute abdominal conditions, or diarrhea due to poisonings.

ADVERSE EFFECTS

The adverse effects associated with antidiarrheal drugs, such as constipation, distention, abdominal discomfort, nausea, vomiting, dry mouth, and even toxic megacolon, concern their effects on the GI tract. Other adverse effects that have been reported include fatigue, weakness, dizziness, and skin rash.

DATA LINK

Data link to the following antidiarrheals in your nursing drug guide:

ANTIDIARRHEALS

Name	Brand Name	Usual Indications
bismuth subsalicylate	*Pepto Bismol*	Treatment of traveler's diarrhea; prevention of cramping and distention associated with dietary excess and some viral infections
P loperamide	*Imodium*	Short-term treatment of diarrhea associated with dietary problems, viral infections
opium derivatives (paregoric)	generic	Short-term treatment of cramping and diarrhea

NURSING CONSIDERATIONS
for patients receiving antidiarrheals

Assessment

HISTORY. Screen for any history of allergy to these drugs; acute abdominal conditions; poisoning; and pregnancy or lactation.

PHYSICAL ASSESSMENT. Include screening for establishment of baseline data for assessing the effectiveness of the drug and the occurrence of any adverse effects associated with drug therapy. Assess skin color and lesions; abdominal examination; and orientation and affect.

Nursing Diagnoses

The patient receiving antidiarrheal drugs may have the following nursing diagnoses related to drug therapy:

- Alteration in GI function related to GI slowing
- Pain related to GI effects

CASE STUDY

Traveler's Diarrhea

PRESENTATION

P. F. had received an all-expenses-paid trip to Mexico in honor of his graduation from college. He was very excited about getting away for a week of sun and fun and had arranged to stay in the same hotel as two college friends who were also celebrating. The three men had a wonderful time visiting the beaches, bars, and nightclubs in the area. On the third day of the trip, P. F. began experiencing nausea, some vomiting, and a low-grade fever. Several hours later he began experiencing intense cramping and diarrhea. For the next 2 days, P. F. felt so ill he was unable to leave his hotel room. The next morning, he called to arrange for an emergency trip home.

CRITICAL THINKING QUESTIONS

What is probably happening to P. F.? Think about the gastrointestinal reflexes and explain the underlying cause for his signs and symptoms. What treatment should be started now? What could have been done to prevent this problem from occurring? What possible drug therapy might have been helpful for P. F.?

DISCUSSION

P. F. is probably experiencing the common disorder called traveler's diarrhea. This disorder occurs when pathogens found in the food and water of a foreign environment are ingested. (Because these pathogens are commonly found in the environment, they do not normally cause problems for the people who live in the area.) When the pathogen, usually a strain of *Escherichia coli,* enters a host that is not accustomed to the bacteria, it releases enterotoxins and sets off an intestinal-intestinal reaction in the host.

The intestinal-intestinal reaction results in a slowing of activity above the point of irritation (which will cause nausea and in some cases vomiting) and an increase in activity below the point of irritation. The body is trying to flush the invader from the body. A low-grade fever may occur as a reaction to the toxins released by the bacteria. Muscle aches and pains, malaise, and fatigue are often common symptoms. It is important at this stage of the disease to maintain fluid intake to prevent dehydration from occurring.

P. F. may want to fly home, but with intense cramping and diarrhea, it might not be a good idea to try. Bismuth subsalicylate (*Pepto-Bismol*), taken four times a day, has been shown to be effective in preventing traveler's diarrhea and associated problems. Taken during a course of traveler's diarrhea, it may relieve the stomach upset and nausea and some of the discomfort of the diarrhea. Some patients respond to the prophylactic antibiotics *Bactrim* and *Septra,* combinations of trimethoprim and sulfamethoxazole that are often prescribed as prophylactic measures for patients who are traveling to areas known to be associated with traveler's diarrhea or for those who are known to be very susceptible to the disorder.

The best course of action, however, is prevention. Several measures can be taken to avoid ingestion of the local bacteria: drinking only bottled or mineral water; avoiding fresh fruits and vegetables that may have been washed in the local water, unless they are peeled; avoiding ice cubes in drinks, because the ice cubes are made from the local water; avoiding any food that might be undercooked or rare, including shellfish; and even being cautious about using water to brush the teeth or gargle. People who have suffered a bout of traveler's diarrhea are very cautious about exposure to local bacteria when they travel again, often combining prophylactic drug therapy with careful avoidance of local pathogens. P. F. can be assured that in a few days the diarrhea and associated signs and symptoms should pass and he will regain his strength and energy.

- Sensory-perceptual alteration related to CNS effects
- Knowledge deficit regarding drug therapy

Implementation

- Monitor response carefully. If no response is seen within 48 hours, *the diarrhea could be related to an underlying medical condition.* Arrange to discontinue the drug and arrange for medical evaluation *to allow for diagnosis of underlying medical conditions.*
- Provide appropriate safety and comfort measures if CNS effects occur, *to prevent patient injury.*
- Administer drug after each unformed stool *to assure therapeutic effectiveness.* Keep track of exact amount given *to assure that dosage does not exceed recommended daily maximum dose.*
- Provide thorough patient teaching, including name of drug, dosage prescribed, proper administration, measures to avoid adverse effects, warning signs of problems, and the importance of periodic monitoring and evaluation *to enhance patient knowledge about drug therapy and promote compliance with the drug regimen.*
- Offer support and encouragement *to help the patient deal with the diagnosis and drug regimen.*

Evaluation

- Monitor patient response to the drug (relief of diarrhea).
- Monitor for adverse effects (GI effects, CNS changes, dermatologic effects).

- Evaluate effectiveness of teaching plan (patient can name the drug and dosage, as well as describe adverse effects to watch for, specific measures to use to avoid adverse effects, and measures to take to increase the effectiveness of the drug).
- Monitor effectiveness of comfort/safety measures and compliance with regimen.

CHAPTER SUMMARY

- Laxatives are drugs used to stimulate movement along the GI tract and to aid excretion. They may be used to prevent or treat constipation.
- Laxatives can be chemical stimulants, directly irritating the local nerve plexus; bulk stimulants, increasing the size of the food bolus and stimulating stretch receptors in the wall of the intestine; or lubricants, facilitating the movement of the bolus through the intestines.
- Use of proper diet and exercise, as well as taking advantage of the actions of the intestinal reflexes, has eliminated the need for laxatives in many situations.
- Cathartic dependence can occur with the chronic use of laxatives, leading to a need for external stimuli for normal functioning of the GI tract.
- GI stimulants act to increase parasympathetic stimulation in the GI tract and increase tone and general movement throughout the GI system.
- Antidiarrheal drugs are used to soothe irritation to the intestinal wall; block GI muscle activity to decrease movement; or affect CNS activity to cause GI spasm and stop movement.

BIBLIOGRAPHY

Bullock, B. L. (2000). *Focus on pathophysiology.* Philadelphia: Lippincott Williams & Wilkins.

Hardman, J. G., Limbird, L. E., Molinoff, P. B., Ruddon, R. W., & Gilman, A. G. (Eds.) (1996). *Goodman and Gilman's the pharmacological basis of therapeutics* (9th ed.). New York: McGraw-Hill.

Karch, A. M. (2000). *2000 Lippincott's nursing drug guide.* Philadelphia: Lippincott Williams & Wilkins.

McEvoy, B. R. (1999). *Facts and comparisons 1999.* St. Louis: Facts and Comparisons.

Medical letter on drugs and therapeutics. (1999). New Rochelle, NY: Medical Letter.

Porth, C. M. (1998). *Pathophysiology: Concepts of altered health states* (5th ed.). Philadelphia: Lippincott-Raven.

CHAPTER

57

Emetic and Antiemetic Agents

Emetic agent
- **P** ipecac syrup

Antiemetic agents
- benzquinamide
- buclizine
- chlorpromazine
- cyclizine
- dolasetron
- dronabinol
- granisetron
- hydroxyzine
- **P** meclizine
- **P** metoclopramide
- **P** ondansetron
- perphenazine
- **P** prochlorperazine
- promethazine
- thiethylperazine
- triflupromazine
- trimethobenzamide

CHAPTER OUTLINE

KEY TERMS

antiemetic
emetic
intractable hiccough
phenothiazine
photosensitivity
vestibular

INTRODUCTION

One of the most common and most uncomfortable complaints encountered in clinical practice is that of nausea and vomiting. Vomiting is a complex reflex reaction to various stimuli (see Chapter 54). In some cases of overdose or poisoning, it may be desirable to induce vomiting to rapidly rid the body of a toxin. This can be accomplished by physical stimuli, often to the back of the throat or by treatment with an ***emetic*** agent such as syrup of ipecac. In some cases, gastric lavage is used to wash out the contents of the stomach.

In many clinical conditions, the reflex reaction of vomiting is not beneficial in ridding the body of any toxins but is uncomfortable and even clinically hazardous to the patient's condition. In such cases, an ***antiemetic*** is used to decrease or prevent nausea and vomiting. Antiemetic agents can be centrally acting or locally acting and have varying degrees of effectiveness.

EMETIC AGENTS

Ipecac syrup is the standard emetic agent in use today. It can be purchased in prepackaged 1-ounce containers without a prescription to have on hand in case of emergency.

THERAPEUTIC ACTIONS AND INDICATIONS

Ipecac syrup irritates the GI mucosa locally (Figure 57-1), which stimulates the CTZ to induce vomiting within 20 minutes. Ipecac syrup is used to induce vomiting as a treatment for drug overdose and certain poisonings.

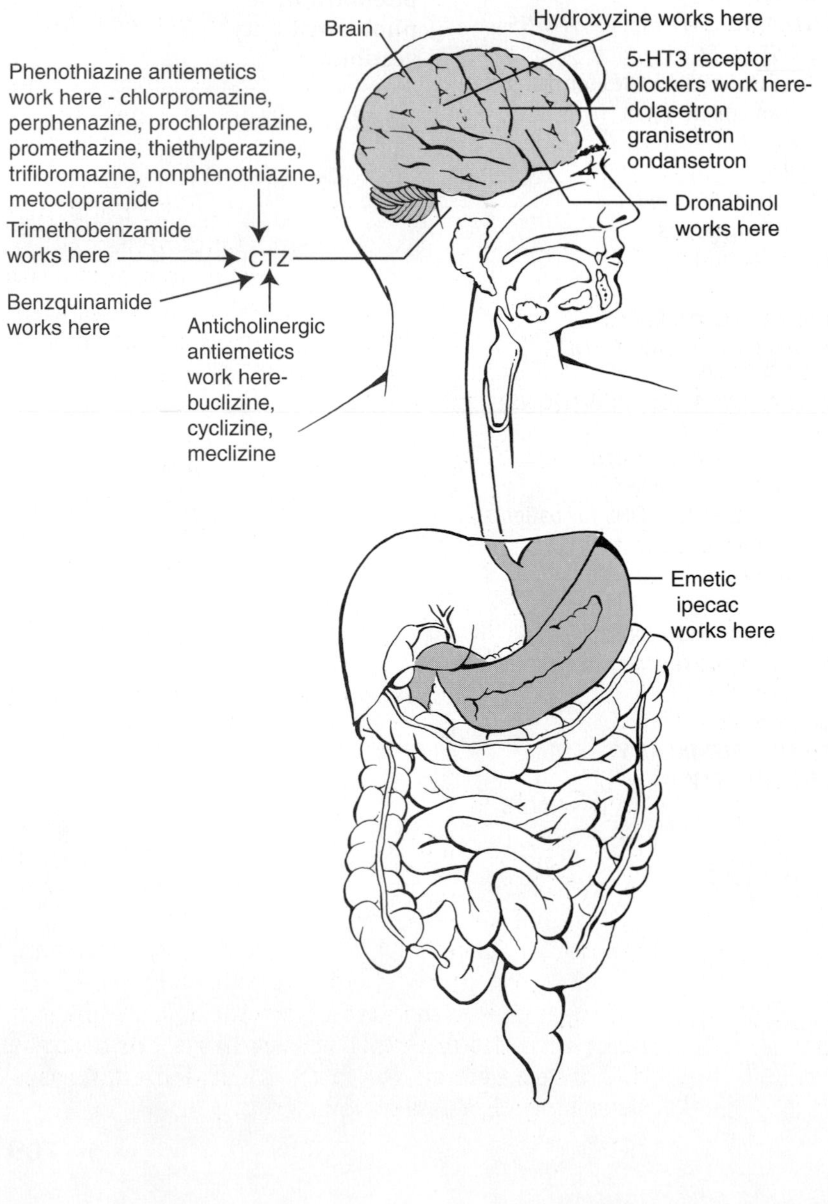

FIGURE 57-1. Sites of action of emetics/antiemetics.

CONTRAINDICATIONS/CAUTIONS

The use of ipecac syrup is contraindicated in the following conditions: when caustic alkali or corrosive mineral acids have been ingested, because the potential for serious damage to the upper GI tract and airways overrides any benefit; when a volatile petroleum distillate such as kerosene has been swallowed, because the risk of aspiration into the lungs, with a resultant fulminant and untreatable pneumonia, is serious; when a patient is comatose or semicomatose or shows signs of convulsing, again because the risk of aspiration is too great; or when a rapid-acting and specific antidote to the poison is available and that treatment would be the most appropriate. These contraindications are summarized in Box 57-1.

ADVERSE EFFECTS

The adverse effects associated with the use of ipecac syrup, such as nausea, diarrhea, and GI upset, are related to its irritating effect on the GI mucosa. Its central nervous system (CNS) effects include mild CNS depression. Cardiotoxicity may occur if large amounts of the drug are absorbed, not vomited.

DATA LINK

Data link to the following emetic in your nursing drug guide:

EMETIC AGENT

Name	Brand Name	Usual Indication
P ipecac	generic	Induction of vomiting as a treatment for drug overdose or certain poisoning

NURSING CONSIDERATIONS for patients receiving an emetic agent

Assessment

HISTORY. Screen for the exact poison or toxin that might have been swallowed; history or convulsions; and semiconscious state.

PHYSICAL ASSESSMENT. Include screening for orientation, affect, baseline pulse, auscultation, and bowel sounds.

BOX 57-1 CONTRAINDICATIONS TO INDUCED VOMITING

- Ingestion of caustic or corrosive mineral acid
- Ingestion of a volatile petroleum distillate
- Comatose or semicomatose patient
- Signs of convulsions

Nursing Diagnoses

The patient receiving an emetic agent may have the following nursing diagnoses related to drug therapy:

- Pain related to CNS and GI effects
- Alteration in cardiac output related to cardiotoxicity
- Knowledge deficit regarding drug therapy

Implementation

- Administer the drug to conscious patients only, *in order to prevent aspiration of the liquid.*
- Administer the drug as soon after poisoning or overdose as possible *to increase effectiveness of induced vomiting and to decrease risk of absorption of the drug or poison.*
- Use caution to differentiate ipecac syrup from ipecac fluid concentrate, *which is 14 times stronger and has caused deaths.*
- Consult with a poison control center *if in doubt about using ipecac syrup or if vomiting has not occurred within 20 minutes of a second dose.*
- Administer with a large amount of water *to assure that the drug reaches the GI tract and to assure that the stomach contains fluid to vomit to decrease the incidence of acid burns during vomiting.*
- Maintain emergency equipment on standby *in case poisoning is not reversed or ipecac is not vomited.*
- Provide comfort and safety measures, including analgesics, ready access to bathroom facilities, assistance with ambulation, and periodic orientation if GI or CNS effects occur, *to prevent patient injury and increase patient comfort.*
- Provide thorough patient teaching, including name of drug, dosage prescribed, proper administration, measures to avoid adverse effects, warning signs of problems, and the importance of periodic monitoring and evaluation and the need to avoid overdose and poisoning *to enhance patient knowledge about drug therapy and promote compliance with the drug regimen.*
- Offer support and encouragement *to help the patient deal with the drug effects and the effects of the poison.*

Evaluation

- Monitor patient response to the drug (vomiting within 20 minutes after the first dose of the drug or within 20 minutes of second dose of drug).
- Monitor for adverse effects (dizziness, confusion, GI upset, diarrhea, cardiac arrhythmias).
- Evaluate effectiveness of teaching plan (patient can name the drug and dosage as well as describe the adverse effects to watch for and specific measures to avoid these adverse effects).

- Monitor effectiveness of comfort measures and compliance with regimen.

WWW.WEB LINKS

Health care providers and patients may want to consult the following Internet sources:

Information on nausea and vomiting associated with cancer chemotherapy:
http://www.anzemet.com/cinv/intro1.htm

Information on nausea and vomiting, including causes, research, and alternative therapies:
http://www.aomc.org/HOD2/general/general-NAUSEA.html

Information on drugs used to treat nausea and vomiting:
http://www.stomachpain.com/pharm/pVomit.html

Information for patients and healthcare workers on ipecac and home treatment of various poisons:
http://noah.cuny.edu/healthliving/ushc/ipecac.html

ANTIEMETIC AGENTS

Drugs used in the management of nausea and vomiting are called antiemetics. All of them work by reducing the hyperactivity of the vomiting reflex in one of two ways: (1) locally, to decrease the local response to stimuli that is being sent to the medulla to induce vomiting; or (2) centrally, to directly block the CTZ or suppress the vomiting center. The locally acting antiemetics may be antacids, local anesthetics, adsorbents, protective drugs that coat the GI mucosa, or drugs that prevent distention and stretch stimulation of the GI tract. These agents are often reserved for use in mild nausea. Many of these drugs are discussed in Chapter 56.

Centrally acting antiemetics can be divided into several groups: ***phenothiazines,*** nonphenothiazines, 5-HT_3 receptor blockers, anticholinergics/antihistamines, and a miscellaneous group (Table 57-1).

TABLE 57-1
ANTIEMETIC AGENTS

Type	Names
Phenothiazines	chlorpromazine, perphenazine, prochlorperazine, promethazine, thiethylperazine, triflupromazine
Nonphenothiazine	metoclopropamide
Anticholinergic/antihistamines	buclizine, cyclizine, meclizine
5-HT_3 receptor blockers	dolasetron, granisetron, ondanesetron
Miscellaneous	benzquinamide, dronabinol, hydroxyzine, trimethobenzamide

The two most commonly used phenothiazines are prochlorperazine (*Compazine*) and promethazine (*Phenergan*), both of which have rapid onset and limited adverse effects. Other drugs in this group include chlorpromazine (*Thorazine*), perphenazine (*Triaflon*), thiethylperazine (*Torecan*), and triflupromazine (*Vesprin*).

The nonphenothiazine available for use is metoclopramide (*Reglan*), which acts to reduce the responsiveness of the nerve cells in the CTZ to circulating chemicals that induce vomiting.

Anticholinergics/antihistamines include buclizine (*Bucladin*), cyclizine (*Marezine*), and meclizine (*Antivert*). These drugs are anticholinergics that act as antihistamines and block the transmission of impulses to the CTZ.

The 5-HT_3receptor blockers of those receptors are associated with nausea and vomiting in the CTZ and locally, and include dolasetron (*Anzemet*), granisetron (*Kytril*), and ondansetron (*Zofran*).

Miscellaneous agents include benzquinamide (*Emete-Con*), which acts similarly to phenothiazine; dronabinol (*Marinol*), which contains the active ingredient of cannabis (marijuana) and has antiemetic effects and whose exact mechanism of action is not understood; hydroxyzine (Vistaril), which may suppress cortical areas of the CNS; and trimethobenzamide (*Tigan*), which is similar to the antihistamines but is not an antihistamine and is not as sedating. Trimethobenzamide is often a drug of choice in this group because it is not associated with as much sedation and CNS suppression. Benzquinamide is preferred for treatment of nausea and vomiting associated with anesthesia and surgery. Hydroxyzine is used for pre- and postpartum and pre- and postoperative nausea and vomiting. Dronabinol is approved for use in managing the nausea and vomiting associated with cancer chemotherapy in those patients who have not responded to other treatment. This drug must be used under close supervision because of the possibility of altered mental status.

THERAPEUTIC ACTIONS AND INDICATIONS

As stated earlier, the locally active antiemetics are used to relieve mild nausea. The centrally acting antiemetics change the responsiveness or stimulation of the CTZ in the medulla (see Figure 57-1). The phenothiazines are recommended for the treatment of nausea and vomiting, including that specifically associated with anesthesia; severe vomiting; ***intractable hiccoughs,*** which occur with repetitive stimulation of the diaphragm and lead to persistent diaphragm spasm; and nausea and vomiting. The anticholinergics that act as antihistamines are recommended for the nausea and vomiting associated with motion sickness or ***vestibular*** (inner ear) problems. Some of these agents are available over-the-counter in a reduced dose to prevent or self-treat motion sickness. The 5-HT_3 receptor blockers are specific for the treatment of nausea and vomiting associated with emetogenic chemotherapy. These are relatively new drugs, and the drug of choice depends on personal preference and experience.

CONTRAINDICATIONS/CAUTIONS

In general, antiemetics should not be used in patients who suffer from coma or severe CNS depression or who have experienced brain damage or injury because of the risk of further CNS depression. Other contraindications include severe hypo- or hypertension and severe liver dysfunction, which might interfere with the metabolism of the drug. Caution should be used with renal dysfunction, active peptic ulcer, and pregnancy and lactation.

ADVERSE EFFECTS

Adverse effects associated with antiemetics are linked to their interference with normal CNS stimulation or response. Drowsiness, dizziness, weakness, tremor, and headache are common adverse effects. As previously stated, some of the antiemetics are thought to have fewer CNS effects. Other not uncommon adverse effects include hypotension, hypertension, and cardiac arrhythmias. When the phenothiazines and antihistamines are used as antiemetics, autonomic effects such as dry mouth, nasal congestion, anorexia, pallor, sweating, and urinary retention often occur. ***Photosensitivity*** (increased sensitivity to the sun and ultraviolet light) is a common adverse reaction with many of the antiemetics. Patients should be advised to use sunscreens and protective garments if exposure cannot be avoided.

CLINICALLY IMPORTANT DRUG–DRUG INTERACTIONS

Additive CNS depression can be seen with any antiemetics if the agents are combined with other CNS depressants, including alcohol. Patients should be advised to avoid this combination and any OTC preparation unless they check with their health care provider. Other drug–drug interactions are specific to each drug (see your nursing drug guide).

DATA LINK

Data link to the following antiemetic agents in your nursing drug guide:

ANTIEMETIC AGENTS

Name	Brand Name	Usual Indications
PHENOTHIAZINES		
chlorpromazine	*Thorazine*	Treatment of nausea and vomiting, including that specifically associated with anesthesia; severe vomiting; intractable hiccoughs
perphenazine	*Triaflon*	
P prochlorperazine	*Compazine*	
promethazine	*Phenergan*	
thiethylperazine	*Torecan*	
triflupromazine	*Vesprin*	
NONPHENOTHIAZINE		
P metoclopropamide	*Reglan*	Treatment of nausea and vomiting, especially related to chemical stimulation of the CTZ
ANTICHOLINERGICS/ANTIHISTAMINES		
buclizine	*Bucladin*	Treatment of nausea and vomiting associated with motion sickness
cyclizine	*Marezine*	
P meclizine	*Antivert*	
5-HT_3 RECEPTOR BLOCKERS		
dolasetron	*Anzemet*	Treatment of nausea and vomiting associated with emetogenic chemotherapy
granisetron	*Kytril*	
P ondansetron	*Zofran*	
MISCELLANEOUS DRUGS		
benzquinamide	*Emete-Con*	Treatment of nausea and vomiting associated with anesthesia and surgery
dronabinol	*Marinol*	Management of nausea and vomiting associated with cancer chemotherapy
hydroxyzine	*Vistaril*	Treatment of pre- and postpartum and pre- and postoperative nausea and vomiting
trimethobenzamide	*Tigan*	Treatment of nausea and vomiting (not sedating)

NURSING CONSIDERATIONS
for patients receiving an antiemetic

Assessment

HISTORY. Screen for history of allergy to antiemetic: impaired renal or hepatic function; pregnancy or lactation; coma or semiconscious state, CNS depression;

PATIENT TEACHING CHECKLIST

Antiemetics

Create customized patient teaching materials for a specific antiemetic from your CD-ROM. Your patient teaching should stress the following points for drugs within this class:

An antiemetic helps prevent nausea and vomiting and the discomfort they cause.

Common effects of this drug include:

- Dizziness, weakness—Change positions slowly. If you feel drowsy, avoid driving or dangerous activities (such as the use of heavy machinery or tasks requiring coordination).
- Sensitivity to the sun—Avoid exposure to the sun and ultraviolet light, because serious reactions may occur. If exposure cannot be prevented, use sunscreen and protective clothing to cover the skin.
- Dehydration—Avoid excessive heat exposure and try to drink fluids as much as possible, as you will have an increased risk for heat stroke.

Report any of the following conditions to your health care provider: fever, rash, yellowing of the eyes or skin, dark urine, pale stools, easy bruising, rash, and vision changes.

Avoid over-the-counter medications. If you feel that you need one, check with your health care provider first.

Tell any doctor, nurse, or other health care provider that you are taking this drug.

Keep this drug and all medications out of the reach of children.

This Teaching Checklist reflects general patient teaching guidelines. It is not meant to be a substitute for drug-specific teaching information, which is available in nursing drug guides.

hypo- or hypertension; active peptic ulcer; and CNS injury.

PHYSICAL ASSESSMENT. Include screening for orientation, affect, and reflexes: baseline pulse and blood pressure; skin lesions and color; liver and abdominal examination; and liver and renal function tests.

Nursing Diagnoses

The patient receiving an antiemetic may have the following nursing diagnoses related to drug therapy:

- Pain related to CNS, skin, and GI effects
- High risk for injury related to CNS effects
- Alteration in cardiac output related to cardiac effects
- Knowledge deficit regarding drug therapy

Implementation

- Assess the patient carefully for any potential drug–drug interactions if giving antiemetics in combination with other drugs *to avert potentially serious drug–drug interactions.*
- Provide comfort and safety measures, including mouth care, ready access to bathroom facilities, assistance with ambulation and periodic orientation, ice chips to suck, protection from sun exposure, and remedial measures to treat dehydration if it occurs, *to protect the patient from injury and to increase patient comfort.*
- Provide support and encouragement, as well as other measures (quiet environment, carbonated drinks, deep breathing), *to help the patient cope with the discomfort of nausea and vomiting and drug effects.*
- Provide thorough patient teaching, including name of drug, dosage prescribed, proper administration, measures to avoid adverse effects, warning signs of problems, and the importance of periodic monitoring and evaluation and the need to avoid overdose and poisoning *to enhance patient knowledge about drug therapy and promote compliance with the drug regimen* (see Patient Teaching Checklist: Antiemetics).

Evaluation

- Monitor patient response to the drug (relief of nausea and vomiting).
- Monitor for adverse effects (dizziness, confusion, GI alterations, cardiac arrhythmias, hypotension, gynecomastia).
- Evaluate effectiveness of teaching plan (patient can name the drug and dosage as well as describe adverse effects to watch for and specific measures to avoid these adverse effects).

NURSING CARE GUIDE
Antiemetics

Assessment	Nursing Diagnoses	Implementation	Evaluation
HISTORY Allergies to any of these drugs, Coma, CNS depression, Severe hypotension, Liver dysfunction, Bone marrow depression, Epilepsy, Pregnancy and lactation	Pain related to GI, skin, CNS effects High risk for injury related related to CNS, CV effects Knowledge deficit regarding drug therapy	Administer only as a temporary measure. Provide comfort and safety measures: - assistance - access to bathroom - safety precautions - mouth care - ice chips. Protect from sun exposure: -coverings - sunscreen Monitor for dehydration; provide remedial measures as needed. Provide support and reassurance for coping with drug effects and discomfort. Provide patient teaching regarding drug name, dosage, adverse effects, precautions, warning to report.	Evaluate drug effects: - relief of nausea - vomiting. Monitor for adverse effects: GI alterations - orthostatic hypotension - dizziness, confusion - sun sensitivity - dehydration. Monitor for drug-drug interactions as indicated for each drug. Evaluate effectiveness of patient teaching program. Evaluate effectiveness of comfort and safety measures.
PHYSICAL EXAMINATION Neurological: orientation, affect Skin: color, lesions CV: P, BP, orthostatic BP GI: abdominal, liver evaluation Lab tests: hematological, CBC, liver function tests			

• Monitor effectiveness of comfort measures and compliance with regimen (see Nursing Care Guide: Antiemetics).

CHAPTER SUMMARY

- Emetic drugs are used to induce vomiting in cases of poisoning or drug overdose.
- Ipecac syrup, the standard emetic agent, can be toxic if absorbed and not vomited.
- Antiemetics are used to manage nausea and vomiting in situations in which they are not beneficial and could actually cause harm to the patient.
- Antiemetics act by depressing the hyperactive vomiting reflex, either locally or through alteration of CNS actions.
- The choice of an antiemetic depends on the cause of the nausea and vomiting and the expected actions of the drug.
- Most antiemetics cause some CNS depression with resultant dizziness, drowsiness, and weakness.

CASE STUDY

Handling Postoperative Nausea and Vomiting

PRESENTATION

A. J. is a 16-year-old boy who has undergone reconstructive knee surgery following a football injury. After the surgery, A. J. complained of nausea and vomited three times in 2 hours. A. J. became increasingly agitated, and rectal prochlorperazine (*Compazine*) was ordered to relieve the nausea, to be followed by an oral order when tolerated. The prochlorperazine was somewhat helpful in relieving the nausea. But A. J. expressed a desire to try cannabis, which he had read was good for the relief of nausea.

CRITICAL THINKING QUESTIONS

What are the important nursing implications in this case? What other measures could be taken to relieve A. J.'s nausea? What explanation could be given to the request for cannabis?

DISCUSSION

It is often impossible to pinpoint an exact cause of a patient's nausea and vomiting in a hospital setting. For example, the underlying cause may be related to the pain, a reaction to the pain medication being given, or a response to what A. J. described as the "awful hospital smell." A combination of factors should be considered when dealing with nausea and vomiting. A. J., as a teenager, may become increasingly agitated by the discomfort and possible embarrassment of vomiting. The administration of rectal prochlorperazine may "take the edge off" the nausea. A. J. will have to be reminded that the drug he is being given may make him dizzy, weak, or drowsy and that he should ask for assistance if he needs to move.

When the nausea and vomiting have diminished somewhat, it will be possible to try other interventions to help stop the vomiting reflex. One such intervention is removing the offending odor that A. J. described, if possible, as doing so may relieve a chemical stimulus to the CTZ. Administration of pain medication, as prescribed, may relieve the CTZ stimulus that comes with intense pain. Other interventions include providing a relaxed, quiet environment and encouraging A. J. to take slow, deep breaths, which stimulate the parasympathetic system (vagus nerve) and partially override the sympathetic activity stimulated by the CTZ to activate vomiting. For many patients, mouth care, ice chips, or small sips of water may also help to relieve the discomfort and ease the sensation of nausea.

After A. J. has relaxed a bit and his nausea has abated, the use of cannabis for treating nausea can be discussed. This may be a good opportunity to explain the many effects of cannabis to A. J. The drug has been shown to relieve nausea and vomiting, especially in chemotherapy patients. It also has been shown to decrease activity in the respiratory tract, to affect the development of sperm in males, and to alter thinking patterns and brain chemistry. The FDA has approved the use of the active ingredient in cannabis—delta-9-tetrahydracannabinol—in an oral form (dronabinol [*Marinol*]) for the relief of nausea and vomiting in cancer chemotherapy patients who have not responded to other therapies and for the treatment of anorexia associated with AIDS. It is not approved for use in the postoperative setting.

Care must be taken to protect the patient and advise him or her to avoid dangerous situations.

- Photosensitivity is another common adverse effect with antiemetics. Patients should be protected from exposure to the sun and ultraviolet light. Sunscreens and protective clothing are essential if exposure cannot be prevented.

Bibliography

Bullock, B. L. (2000). *Focus on pathophysiology.* Philadelphia: Lippincott Williams & Wilkins.

Hardman, J. G., Limbird, L. E., Molinoff, P. B., Ruddon, R. W., & Gilman, A. G. (Eds.) (1996). *Goodman and Gilman's the pharmacological basis of therapeutics* (9th ed.). New York: McGraw-Hill.

Karch, A. M. (2000). *2000 Lippincott's nursing drug guide.* Philadelphia: Lippincott Williams & Wilkins.

McEvoy, B. R. (1999). *Facts and comparisons 1999.* St Louis: Facts and Comparisons.

Medical letter on drugs and therapeutics. (1999). New Rochelle, NY: Medical Letter.

Porth, C. M. (1998). *Pathophysiology: Concepts of altered health states* (5th ed.). Philadelphia: Lippincott-Raven.

CHAPTER 58

Gallstone Solubilizers

P chenodiol
mono-octanoin
ursodiol

CHAPTER OUTLINE

KEY TERMS

cholesterol
gallstone
radiolucent

INTRODUCTION

Gallstones were once thought to be a common diagnosis among fat, fair, and 50ish females. Today it is a rather common diagnosis that occurs among all age groups and sizes and in both genders.

Bile is secreted by the liver cells during their normal metabolism and is stored and concentrated in the gall bladder. It is then released into the duodenum by way of the common bile duct in response to stimuli in the duodenum, such as the presence of fat or the hormone cholecystokinin. Bile contains ***cholesterol*** (a necessary component of human cells that is produced and processed in the liver), bilirubin, and several organic acids that combine to form bile salts. Bile salts act like detergents in the duodenum, breaking up fat into very small globules. Lipases further break up these globules into fatty acids, which can then be absorbed by the small intestine. Bile salts that are absorbed from the intestine stimulate the liver cells to produce more bile.

In some conditions, when the stored bile is concentrated in the gall bladder, the cholesterol becomes supersaturated and crystals are formed. As concentration continues, the crystals can become larger and form ***gallstones.*** Gallstones can become large enough to block the duct leading out of the gall bladder or even the common duct. This condition can precipitate inflammation of the gall bladder and common duct. Such inflammation can cause serious nutritional problems when fats cannot be absorbed for energy or steroid formation and when waste products found in the bile cannot be excreted but are trapped in the body. Although surgical removal of the gall bladder is the standard treatment in these situations, not all affected patients are candidates for surgical procedures. They need a pharmacological solution to their problem.

CULTURAL/GENDER CONSIDERATIONS

Who Is at Risk for Gallstone Development?

- Women are twice as likely as men to develop gallstones. This is thought to be due to the effects of estrogen on the gallbladder. Data from the ongoing Nurses Healthy Study, a 16-year study of more than 47,000 women, suggests that women who experienced episodes of "weight cycling" have an increased risk of developing gallstones. (The study described weight cycling as the loss of 10 pounds or more; which is regained in a short period of time.) Women who reported steep declines in weight while dieting had a 68% risk of developing gallstones.
- African Americans and Far East Asians have a higher risk of developing gallstones. The gallstones in these groups tend to be pigmented stones—white or brown in color—and are related to the metabolism of fats.
- Native Americans are at a higher risk of developing cholesterol gallstones. This is thought to be related to a genetic alteration in the formation and storage of cholesterol in the gall bladder.

GALLSTONE SOLUBILIZERS

Gallstone solubilizers are used to dissolve certain gallstones. Available drugs are:

- Chenodiol *(Chenix),* which was the first such drug developed. Because this agent causes serious diarrhea and sometimes hepatitis and even colon cancer, its use must be weighed carefully against the dangers of the obstructed gall bladder.
- Ursodiol *(Actigall),* another oral gallstone solubilizer, which is not associated with such severe adverse effects but may require months of therapy to achieve an outcome. It is best used when the gallstones are small and not obstructing.
- Mono-octanoin (*Moctanin*), which is a semisynthetic glycerol that must be delivered by a continuous perfusion pump through a catheter inserted into the common bile duct. Treatment with mono-octanoin must continue for 7 to 21 days. Mono-octanoin is reserved for postcholecystectomy patients who still have gallstones in the biliary tract.

WWW.WEB LINKS

Health care providers and patients may want to consult the following Internet sources:

Information on gallstones—development, complications, and treatments:
http://www.wdxcyberstore.com/wdxcyberstore/galandtheirt.html

Information on dietary practices and their influence on the development of gallstones:
http://www.mesomorphosis.com/columns/niddk/nih943677.htm

Information on the relationship of weight-loss diets and the formation of gallstones:
http://thedailyapple.com/level3/ds3/dietgall.htm

Information specifically designed for the African-American patient relating to gallstones:
http://blackhealthnet.com

THERAPEUTIC ACTIONS AND INDICATIONS

Chenodiol and ursodiol suppress synthesis of cholesterol and cholic acid by the liver. This leads to a decreased concentration of cholesterol in the bile and the formation of a bile that dissolves the cholesterol stones. This bile does not precipitate cholesterol. Mono-octanoin dissolves cholesterol in the biliary tract (Figure 58-1). Gallstone solubilizing drugs are used for the dissolution of ***radiolucent*** gallstones (ones that are not calcified) when surgery is contraindicated.

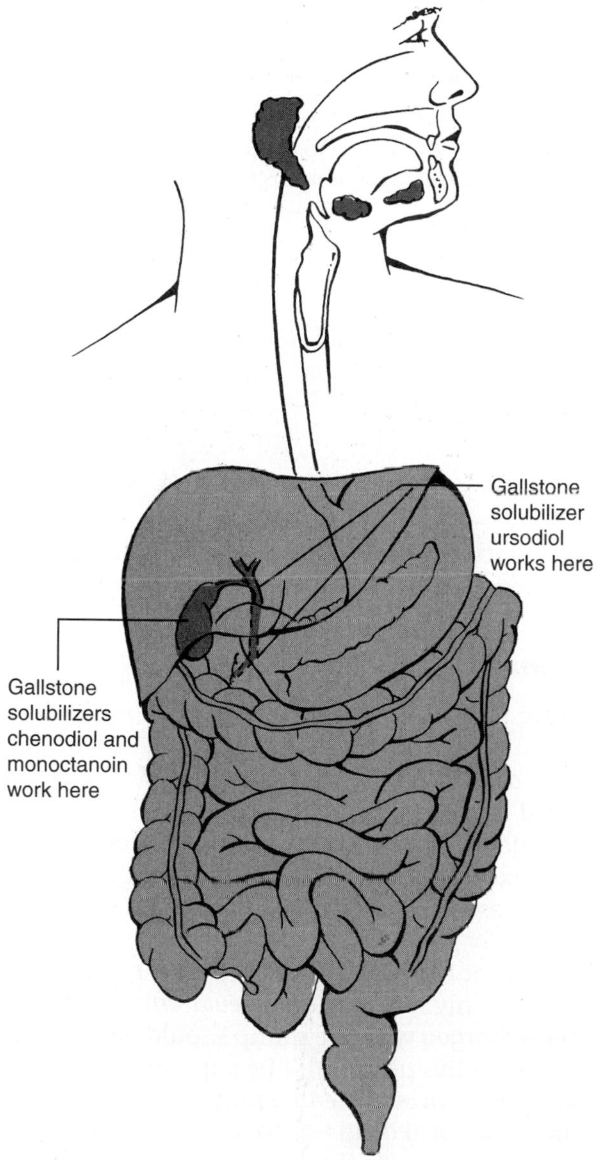

FIGURE 58-1. Sites of action of gallstone solubilizers.

CONTRAINDICATIONS/CAUTIONS

Gallstone solubilizers are contraindicated in the following conditions: with known allergy to any of these drugs; with calcified stones, which are not dissolved; with hepatic dysfunction (chenodiol and ursodiol interfere with hepatic activity and could precipitate hepatitis or hepatic failure); and biliary tract obstruction or bile duct abnormalities. Chenodiol, which is in Pregnancy Category X, should never be used during pregnancy and lactation because it can cause serious adverse effects in the fetus. Ursodiol and mono-octanoin should also be avoided during pregnancy and lactation, because their effects are not clearly known and they may cross the placenta and enter breast milk.

ADVERSE EFFECTS

Adverse effects commonly associated with gallstone solubilizers are related to effects on the liver—hepatitis, liver enzyme changes, and elevated cholesterol and triglyceride levels—and the GI tract—diarrhea, abdominal pain, nausea, vomiting, anorexia, flatulence, and dyspepsia. Dermatologic effects may include rash, pruritus, urticaria, and dry skin. Ursodiol and mono-octanoin are associated with headache, fatigue, anxiety, sleep disorders, and depression. As stated earlier, chenodiol has been associated with colon cancer.

CLINICALLY IMPORTANT DRUG–DRUG INTERACTIONS

Absorption of chenodiol and ursodiol may be decreased if taken in combination with cholestyramine and colestipol. Ursodiol may also not be absorbed if combined with aluminum-based antacids. If such drug–drug combinations are used, the different agents should be spaced at least 2 hours apart to avoid interacting.

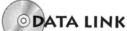

DATA LINK

Data link to the following gallstone solubilizing agents in your nursing drug guide:

GALLSTONE SOLUBILIZERS

Name	Brand Name	Usual Indication
P chenodiol	*Chenix*	Dissolution of radiolucent gallstones when surgery is contraindicated
mono-octanoin	*Moctanin*	Dissolution of gallstones left in the biliary tract post-cholecystectomy
ursodiol	*Actigall*	Dissolution of radiolucent gallstones when surgery is contraindicated

PATIENT TEACHING CHECKLIST

Gallstone Solubilizers

Create customized patient teaching materials for a specific gallstone solubilizer from your CD-ROM. Your patient teaching should stress the following points for drugs within this class:

A gallstone solubilizer prevents the formation of gallstones and dissolves some gallstones that may have already formed.

Common effects of this drug include:

- Diarrhea—Have ready access to bathroom facilities. Consult with your health care provider if this becomes a problem, as the drug dose may be changed.
- Nausea, GI upset, flatulence—Small, frequent meals may help.

Report any of the following conditions to your health care provider: gallstone attack (abdominal pain, nausea, vomiting) and yellowing of the skin or eyes.

Do not take this drug if you are pregnant. Serious problems could occur. The use of a barrier contraceptive is advised while using this drug. If you should become pregnant, consult with your health care provider immediately.

You should have periodic x-rays and ultrasound tests of your gallbladder; you will also need periodic blood tests to monitor the effects of this drug on your body. It is very important to try to keep appointments for these tests.

Tell any doctor, nurse, or other health care provider that you are taking this drug.

Keep this drug and all medications out of the reach of children.

This Teaching Checklist reflects general patient teaching guidelines. It is not meant to be a substitute for drug-specific teaching information, which is available in nursing drug guides.

NURSING CONSIDERATIONS
for patients receiving gallstone solubilizers

Assessment

HISTORY. Screen for the following conditions: history of allergy to any gallstone solubilizer; impaired hepatic function; history of biliary obstruction or malformation; and pregnancy or lactation.

PHYSICAL ASSESSMENT. Include screening for the following conditions: presence of any skin lesions; orientation and affect; abdominal examination; liver function tests and serum cholesterol; radiographic study of the gallbladder and biliary ultrasound.

Nursing Diagnoses

The patient receiving any gallstone solubilizer may have the following nursing diagnoses related to drug therapy:

- Pain related to CNS and GI effects
- Alteration in GI function related to GI effects
- Alteration in nutrition related to GI effects
- Knowledge deficit regarding drug therapy

Implementation

- Ensure that the patient is a proper candidate for treatment with one of these drugs *to avoid unnecessary use of these potential toxic drugs if they are not indicated.*
- Arrange for pretreatment and periodic radiographic examinations, biliary ultrasounds, and liver function tests *to monitor the effectiveness of the drug and assess for possible complications.*
- Administer mono-octanoin via continuous perfusion pump only *to assure therapeutic effectiveness.* Patients discharged with the pump should be instructed in the use of the pump and be supplied with standby batteries *to avoid potential problems at home.*
- Administer oral drug two to three times per day as prescribed *to promote therapeutic effects.*
- Ensure ready access to bathroom facilities *in case diarrhea occurs.*

NURSING CARE GUIDE
Gallstone Solubilizers

Assessment	Nursing Diagnoses	Implementation	Evaluation
HISTORY Allergies to any of these drugs, Hepatic dysfunction, Bile duct abnormalities, Pregnancy (Category X) and lactation	Alteration in comfort related to GI, hepatic effects Alteration in bowel function, related to diarrhea Knowledge deficit regarding drug therapy	Administer twice a day, morning and night. Provide comfort and safety measures: - small, frequent meals - access to bathroom. Arrange for regular monitoring of blood tests, radiological examinations Monitor bowel function; arrange to decrease dose if diarrhea occurs. Provide support and reassurance to cope with drug effects, cost, and long-term therapy. Provide patient teaching regarding the drug name and dosage as well as adverse effects and precautions, plus warnings to report.	Evaluate drug effects: dissolution of gallstones. Monitor for adverse effects: - GI alterations - Hepatic dysfunction - Elevated cholesterol. Evaluate effectiveness of patient teaching program. Evaluate effectiveness of comfort and safety measures.
PHYSICAL EXAMINATION GI: abdominal evaluation Lab tests: hematological, liver function tests, serum lipids, WBC, serum cholesterol Other tests: hepatic and biliary radiological studies			

- Provide small, frequent meals *to relieve GI discomfort if GI upset is severe,* and arrange for nutritional consult *if intake is limited by GI effects.*
- Offer support and encouragement *to help patient cope with long-term therapy and adverse effects.*
- Provide thorough patient teaching, including name of drug, dosage prescribed, proper administration, measures to avoid adverse effects, warning signs of problems, and the importance of periodic monitoring and evaluation and the need to avoid overdose and poisoning *to enhance patient knowledge about drug therapy and promote compliance with the drug regimen* (see Patient Teaching Checklist: Gallstone Solubilizers).

Evaluation

- Monitor patient response to the drug (dissolution of cholesterol gallstones).
- Monitor for adverse effects (GI effects, liver dysfunction, skin lesions, CNS effects).
- Evaluate effectiveness of teaching plan (can the patient name the drug and dosage as well as describe adverse effects to watch for and specific measures to avoid adverse effects?).
- Monitor effectiveness of comfort measures and compliance with regimen (see Nursing Care Guide: Gallstone Solubilizers).

CASE STUDY

Managing Chronic Gallstone Attacks

PRESENTATION

H. P., a 63-year-old retired steel worker, has been suffering from chronic gallstone attacks for several months. Because of the cardiovascular disease he has had for many years, he is not considered a good candidate for surgery. Radiographic examinations reveal several small, radiolucent cholesterol gallstones. To dissolve the stones, H. P. begins taking chenodiol (*Chenix*).

CRITICAL THINKING QUESTIONS

What are the important nursing implications for H. P.? Does his cardiovascular disease change the way that he should be cared for while he is on the chenodiol? What specific issues should be discussed with H. P.? What other clinical implications should be considered?

DISCUSSION

Chenodiol is not a cure for gallstones; it will dissolve gallstones that are already formed but will not prevent the formation of new ones. Dietary factors are important, and H. P. should receive nutritional counseling to avert the development of additional gallstones. He should know that this drug must be taken for a prolonged period time—several weeks or even several months—to achieve any success. Periodic blood tests are needed to monitor the drug effects on the liver, and periodic radiographic examinations are necessary to evaluate the status of the stones.

Diarrhea is a common problem with chenodiol, and H. P. should be cautioned to consult with his health care provider if this is a problem, because a lower dose might be needed. H. P. may need to be extra careful about fluid and electrolyte balance with his cardiovascular disease. A nutritional consultation may also be helpful in this area. Small, frequent meals might help relieve other GI problems that accompany the use of this drug.

Because chenodiol is quite expensive, it might be necessary to consult with social services if H. P. does not have insurance coverage for this type of treatment. He may already be taking several other drugs for his cardiovascular problems and have a fixed income with which to handle the financial strain. Support and encouragement will be needed for a long period of time for this patient. A consistent care giver would be helpful in establishing a trusting relationship so that H. P. will feel free to call with questions or to discuss problems as they rise.

CHAPTER SUMMARY

- Gallstones form when bile becomes concentrated and high levels of cholesterol in the bile crystallize. Gallstones can block the flow of bile from the gall bladder into the common duct or can block the common duct.
- Patients who are at high risk for surgery to remove gallstones may require treatment with gallstone solubilizers to prevent nutritional and other problems associated with a blocked common duct.
- Oral gallstone solubilizers, which are not effective if the gallstones have calcified, decrease the production of cholesterol in the liver. This leads to the formation of bile that is low in cholesterol, allowing the cholesterol stones to dissolve.
- Serious adverse effects are associated with the use of gallstone solubilizers, including liver dysfunction, high cholesterol levels, severe diarrhea, and colon cancer. Their use should be limited to those patients who could benefit from this treatment.
- Support and encouragement of compliance with the prescribed regimen is important with these drugs, which will need to be taken for several months.
- Mono-octanoin dissolves stones directly and is administered only through a continuous perfusion pump via a catheter inserted directly into the common duct.

BIBLIOGRAPHY

Bullock, B. L. (2000). *Focus on pathophysiology.* Philadelphia: Lippincott Williams & Wilkins.

Hardman, J. G., Limbird, L. E., Molinoff, P. B., Ruddon, R. W., & Gilman, A. G. (Eds.) (1996). *Goodman and Gilman's The pharmacological basis of therapeutics* (9th ed.). New York: McGraw-Hill.

Karch, A. M. (2000). *2000 Lippincott's nursing drug guide.* Philadelphia: Lippincott Williams & Wilkins.

McEvoy, B. R. (1999). *Facts and comparisons 1999.* St. Louis: Facts and Comparisons.

Medical letter on drugs and therapeutics. (1999). New Rochelle, NY: Medical Letter.

Porth, C. M. (1998). *Pathophysiology: Concepts of altered health states* (5th ed). Philadelphia: Lippincott-Raven.

Glossary

A fibers: large-diameter nerve fibers that carry peripheral impulses associated with touch and temperature to the spinal cord

abortifacients: drugs used to stimulate uterine contractions and promote evacuation of the uterus to cause abortion or empty the uterus following fetal death

absence seizure: type of generalized seizure that is characterized by sudden, temporary loss of consciousness, sometimes with staring or blinking for 3 to 5 seconds; formerly known as a petit mal seizure

absorption: what happens to a drug from the time it enters the body until it enters the circulating fluid; IV administration causes the drug to directly enter the circulating blood, bypassing the many complications of absorption from other routes

ACE inhibitor: drug that blocks the enzyme responsible for converting angiotensin I to angiotensin II in the lungs; this blocking prevents the vasoconstriction and aldosterone release related to angiotensin II

acetylcholine receptor site: area on the muscle cell membrane where acetylcholine reacts with a specific receptor site to cause stimulation of the muscle in response to nerve activity

acetylcholinesterase: enzyme responsible for the immediate breakdown of acetylcholine when released from the nerve ending; prevents overstimulation of cholinergic receptor sites

acid rebound: reflex response of the stomach to lower-than-normal acid levels; when acid levels are lowered through the use of antacids, gastrin production and secretion are increased to return the stomach to its normal acidity

acidification: the process of increasing the acid level; used to treat bladder infections, making the bladder an undesirable place for bacteria

acquired immunodeficiency syndrome (AIDS): collection of opportunistic infections and cancers that occurs when the immune system is severely depressed by a decrease in the number of functioning helper T cells; caused by infection with HIV (human immunodeficiency virus)

acromegaly: thickening of bony surfaces in response to excess growth hormone after the epiphyseal plates have closed

actin: thin filament that makes up a sarcomere or muscle unit

action potential: sudden change in electrical charge of a nerve cell membrane; the electrical signal by which neurons send information

active immunity: the formation of antibodies secondary to exposure to a specific antigen; leads to the formation of plasma cells, antibodies, and memory cells to immediately produce antibodies if exposed to that antigen in the future; imparts life-long immunity

A-delta and C fibers: small-diameter nerve fibers that carry peripheral impulses associated with pain to the spinal cord

adrenal cortex: outer layer of the adrenal gland; produces glucocorticoids and mineralocorticoids in response to ACTH stimulation; also responds to sympathetic stimulation

adrenal medulla: inner layer of the adrenal gland; sympathetic ganglia, releases norepinephrine and epinephrine into circulation in response to sympathetic stimulation

adrenergic agonist: a drug that stimulates the adrenergic receptors of the sympathetic nervous system, either directly (by reacting with receptor sites) or indirectly (by increasing norepinephrine levels)

adrenergic receptor: receptor sites on effectors that respond to norephinephrine

adrenergic receptor site specificity: a drug's affinity for only adrenergic receptor sites; certain drugs may have specific affinity for only alpha or beta sites

adverse effects: drug effects that are not the desired therapeutic effects; may be unpleasant or even dangerous

aerobic: bacteria that depend on oxygen for survival

affect: feeling that a person experiences when he or she responds emotionally to the environment

afferent: neurons or groups of neurons that bring information to the central nervous system; sensory nerve

agonist: a drug that acts like or increases the effects of a specific neurotransmitter or hormone

AIDS-related complex (ARC): collection of less serious opportunistic infections with HIV infection; the decrease in the number of helper T cells is less severe than in fully developed AIDS

aldosterone: hormone produced by the adrenal gland that causes the distal tubule to retain sodium and therefore water, while losing potassium into the urine

alkalosis: state of not having enough acid to maintain normal homeostatic processes; seen with loop diuretics, which cause loss of bicarbonate in the urine

alopecia: hair loss; a common adverse effect of many antineoplastic drugs, which are more effective against rapidly multiplying cells such as those of hair follicles

alpha agonist: specifically stimulating to the alpha receptors within the SNS, causing body responses seen when the alpha receptors are stimulated

alpha$_1$ selective adrenergic blocking agents: drugs that block the postsynaptic alpha$_1$ receptor sites, causing a decrease in vascular tone and a vasodilation that leads to a fall in blood pressure; these drugs do not block the presynaptic alpha$_2$ receptor sites, and therefore the reflex tachycardia that accompanies a fall in blood pressure does not occur

alpha receptors: adrenergic receptors that are found in smooth muscles

alveoli: the respiratory sac, the smallest unit of the lungs where gas exchange occurs

Alzheimer's disease: degenerative disease of the cortex with loss of acetylcholine-producing cells and cholinergic receptors; characterized by progressive dementia

amebiasis: amebic dysentery, which is caused by intestinal invasion of the trophozoite stage of the protozoan *Entamoeba histolytica*

amnesia: loss of memory of an event or procedure
anabolic steroids: androgens developed with more anabolic or protein-building effects than androgenic effects
anaerobic: bacteria that survive without oxygen, which are often seen when blood flow is cut off to an area of the body
analgesia: loss of pain sensation
analgesic: compounds with pain-blocking properties, capable of producing analgesia
anaplasia: loss of organization and structure; property of cancer cells
androgenic effects: effects associated with development of male sexual characteristics and secondary characteristics, e.g., deepening of voice, hair distribution, genital development, acne
androgens: male sex hormones, primarily testosterone; produced in the testes and adrenal glands
anemia: a decrease in the number of RBCs, leading to an inability to effectively deliver oxygen to the tissues
angina pectoris: "suffocation of the chest"; pain caused by the imbalance between oxygen being supplied to the heart muscle and demand for oxygen by the heart muscle
angiotensin II receptors: specific receptors found in blood vessels and in the adrenal gland that react with angiotensin II to cause vasoconstriction and release of aldosterone
***Anopheles* mosquito:** type of mosquito that is essential to the life cycle of *Plasmodium;* injects the protozoa into humans for further maturation
anterior pituitary: lobe of the pituitary gland that produces stimulating hormones as well as growth hormone, prolactin, and melanocyte stimulating hormone
antiarrhythmics: drugs that affect the action potential of cardiac cells and are used to treat arrhythmias and return normal rate and rhythm
antibiotic: chemical that is able to inhibit the growth of specific bacteria or cause the death of susceptible bacteria
antibodies: immunoglobulins; produced by B cell plasma cells in response to specific protein; react with the protein to cause its destruction directly or through activation of the inflammatory response
anticholinergic: drug that opposes the effects of acetylcholine at acetylcholine receptor sites
anticoagulants: drugs that block or inhibit any step of the coagulation process, preventing or slowing clot formation
antidiarrheal drug: drug that blocks the stimulation of the GI tract, leading to decreased activity and increased time for absorption of needed nutrients and water
antidiuretic hormone (ADH): hormone produced by the hypothalamus and stored in the posterior pituitary gland; important in maintaining fluid balance; causes the distal tubule and collecting duct to become permeable to water, leading to an antidiuretic effect and fluid retention
antiemetic: agent that blocks the hyperactive response of the CTZ to various stimuli, the response that produces non-beneficial nausea and vomiting
antiepileptic: drug used to treat the abnormal and excessive energy bursts in the brain that are characteristic of epilepsy
antigen: foreign protein
antihistamines: drugs that block the release or action of histamine, a chemical released during inflammation that increases secretions and narrows airways
antiinflammatory: blocking the effects of the inflammatory response
antineoplastic agent: drug used to combat cancer or the growth of neoplasms
antipeptic: drug that coats any injured area in the stomach to prevent further injury from acid or pepsin
antipsychotic: drug used to treat disorders involving thought processes; dopamine receptor blocker that helps affected people organize their thoughts and respond appropriately to stimuli
antipyretic: blocking fever, often by direct effects on the thermoregulatory center in the hypothalamus or by blocking prostaglandin mediators
antispasmodics: agents that block muscle spasm associated with irritation or neurological stimulation
antitoxins: immune sera that contains antibodies to specific toxins produced by invaders; may prevent the toxin from adhering to body tissues and causing disease
antitussives: drugs that block the cough reflex
anxiety: unpleasant feeling of tension, fear, or nervousness in response to an environmental stimulus, whether real or imaginary
anxiolytic: drug used to depress the CNS; prevents the signs and symptoms of anxiety
arachidonic acid: released from injured cells to stimulate the inflammatory response through activation of various chemical substances
arrhythmia: a disruption in cardiac rate or rhythm
arteries: vessels that take blood away from the heart; muscular, resistance vessels
assessment: information gathering regarding the current status of a particular patient, including evaluation of past history and physical examination; provides a baseline of information and clues to effectiveness of therapy
asthma: disorder characterized by recurrent episodes of bronchospasm, i.e., bronchial muscle spasm leading to narrowed or obstructed airways
atheroma: plaque in the endothelial lining of arteries; contains fats, blood cells, lipids, inflammatory agents, platelets; leads to a narrowing of the lumen of the artery and a stiffening of the artery and loss of distensibility and responsiveness
atherosclerosis: narrowing of the arteries caused by build up of atheromas, swelling and accumulation of platelets; leads to a loss of elasticity and responsiveness to normal stimuli
atrium: top chamber of the heart, receives blood from veins
attention-deficit disorder: behavioral syndrome characterized by an inability to concentrate for longer than a few minutes and excessive activity
auricle: appendage on the atria of the heart, holds blood to be pumped out with atrial contraction
autoimmune: having antibodies to self-cells or self-proteins; leads to chronic inflammatory disease and cell destruction
automaticity: property of heart cells to generate an action potential without an external stimulus
autonomic nervous system: portion of the CNS and peripheral nervous systems that, with the endocrine system, functions to maintain internal homeostasis
autonomy: loss of the normal controls and reactions that inhibit growth and spreading; property of cancer cells
axon: long projection from a neuron that carries information from one nerve to another nerve or effector

B cells: lymphocytes programmed to recognize specific proteins; when activated, these cells cause the production of antibodies to react with that protein
bactericidal: substance that causes the death of bacteria, usually by interfering with cell membrane stability or proteins or enzymes necessary to maintain the cellular integrity of the bacteria
bacteriostatic: substance that prevents the replication of bacteria, usually by interfering with proteins or enzyme systems necessary for reproduction of the bacteria
balanced anesthesia: use of several different types of drugs to achieve the quickest, most effective anesthesia with the fewest adverse effects
barbiturate: former mainstay drug used for the treatment of anxiety and for sedation and sleep induction; associated with potentially severe adverse effects and many drug–drug interactions, which makes it less desirable than some of the newer agents
baroreceptor: pressure receptor; located in the arch of the aorta and in the carotid artery; responds to changes in pressure and influences the medulla to stimulate the sympathetic system to increase or decrease blood pressure
basal ganglia: lower area of the brain associated with coordination of unconscious muscle movements that involve movement and position

bella donna: a plant containing atropine as an alkaloid; used to dilate the pupils as a fashion statement in the past; used in herbal medicine much as atropine is used today

benign prostatic hyperplasia (BPH): enlargement of the prostate gland, associated with age and inflammation

benzodiazepine: drug that acts in the limbic system and the reticular activating system to make gamma-aminobutyric acid, an inhibitory neurotransmitter, more effective, causing interference with neuron firing; depresses CNS to block the signs and symptoms of anxiety and may cause sedation and hypnosis (extreme sedation with further CNS depression and sleep) in higher doses

beta receptors: adrenergic receptors that are found in the heart, lungs, and vascular smooth muscle

beta agonist: specifically stimulating to the beta receptors within the SNS, causing body responses seen when the beta receptors are stimulated

beta adrenergic blocking agents: drugs that, at therapeutic levels, selectively block the beta receptors of the sympathetic nervous system

$beta_1$ selective adrenergic blocking agents: drugs that, at therapeutic levels, specifically block the $beta_1$ receptors in the SNS, while not blocking the $beta_2$ receptors and resultant effects on the respiratory system

bile acids: cholesterol-containing acids found in the bile, which act like detergents to break up fats in the small intestine

bile: fluid stored in the gallbladder that contains cholesterol and bile salts; essential for the proper breakdown and absorption of fats

biogenic amine: one of the neurotransmitters norepinephrine, serotonin, or dopamine; it is thought that a deficiency of these substances in key areas of the brain results in depression

biotransformation: the alteration of a drug by the body into new chemicals that are less active, less toxic, and more easily excreted by the body; this action usually occurs in the liver

bisphosphonates: drugs used to block bone resorption and lower serum calcium levels in several conditions

blood dyscrasia: bone marrow depression caused by drug effects on the rapidly multiplying cells of the bone marrow; lower than normal levels of blood components can be seen

bone marrow suppression: inhibition of the blood-forming components of the bone marrow; a common adverse effect of many antineoplastic drugs, which are more effective against rapidly multiplying cells such as those in bone marrow, and seen in anemia, thrombocytopenia, and leukopenia

bradycardia: slower than normal heart rate (usually <60 beats/min)

bradykinesia: difficulty in performing intentional movements and extreme slowness and sluggishness; characteristic of Parkinson's disease

brand name: name given to a drug by the pharmaceutical company that developed it; also called trade name

bronchial tree: the conducting airways leading into the alveoli, branching smaller and smaller and appearing much like a tree

bronchodilation: relaxation of the muscles in the bronchi, resulting in a widening of the bronchi; an effect of sympathetic stimulation

bronchodilator: medication used to facilitate respirations by dilating the airways; helpful in symptomatic relief or prevention of bronchial asthma and bronchospasm associated with COPD

bulk stimulant: agent that increases in bulk, frequently by osmotic pull of fluid into the feces; the increased bulk stretches the GI wall, causing stimulation and increased GI movement

calcitonin: hormone produced by the parafollicular cells of the thyroid; counteracts the effects of parathyroid hormone to maintain calcium levels

calor: heat, one of the four cardinal signs of inflammation; caused by the activation of the inflammatory response

***Candida*:** fungus that is normally found on mucous membranes; can cause yeast infections or thrush of the GI tract and vagina in immunosuppressed patients

capacitance system: the venous system; distensible, flexible veins that are capable of holding large amounts of blood

capillary: small vessel made up of loosely connected endothelial cells that connect arteries to veins

carbonic anhydrase: a catalyst that speeds up the chemical reaction combining water and carbon dioxide, which react to form carbonic acid and which immediately dissociate to form sodium bicarbonate

carcinoma: tumor that originates in epithelial cells

cardiac cycle: a period of cardiac muscle relaxation (diastole) followed by a period of contraction (systole) in the heart

cardiac output: the amount of drug the heart can pump per beat; influenced by the coordination of cardiac muscle contraction, heart rate, and blood return to the heart

Cardiac Arrhythmia Suppression Test (CAST): a large research study run by the National Heart and Lung Institute that found that long-term treatment of arrhythmias may have questionable effect on mortality, and in some cases actually led to increased cardiac death; the basis for the current indication for antiarrhythmics that they are used short term to treat life-threatening ventricular arrhythmias

cardiomegaly: enlargement of the heart seen with chronic hypertension, valvular disease, and congestive heart failure

cardiovascular center: area of the medulla whose stimulation will activate the sympathetic nervous system to increase blood pressure, heart rate, and so forth

cathartic dependence: overuse of laxatives that can lead to the need for strong stimuli to initiate movement in the intestines; local reflexes become resistant to normal stimuli after prolonged use of harsher stimulants, leading to further laxative use

cell membrane: lipoprotein structure that separates the interior of a cell from the external environment; regulates what can enter and leave a cell

cell cycle: life cycle of a cell, which includes the phases G_0, G_1, S, G_2, and M; during the M phase, the cell divides into two identical daughter cells

cerebellum: lower portion of the brain associated with coordination of muscle movements, including voluntary motion, as well as extrapyramidal control of unconscious muscle movements

cestode: tapeworm with a head and segmented body parts that is capable of growing to several yards in the human intestine

chemical name: name that reflects the chemical structure of a drug

chemical stimulant: agent that stimulates the normal GI reflexes by chemically irritating the lining of the GI wall, leading to increased activity in the GI tract

chemotaxis: property of drawing neutrophils to an area

chemotherapeutic agents: synthetic chemicals used to interfere with the functioning of foreign cell populations; this term is frequently used to refer to the drug therapy of neoplasms, but it also refers to drug therapy affecting any foreign cell

Cheyne-Stokes respiration: abnormal pattern of breathing characterized by apneic periods followed by periods of tachypnea; may reflect delayed blood flow through the brain

cholesterol: necessary component of human cells that is produced and processed in the liver; stored in the bile until stimulus causes the gallbladder to contract and send the bile into the duodenum via the common bile duct; a fat that is essential for the formation of steroid hormones and cell membranes; produced in cells and taken in by dietary sources

cholinergic: responding to acetylcholine; refers to receptor sites stimulated by acetylcholine as well as neurons that release acetylcholine

cholinergic receptor: receptor sites on effectors that respond to acetylcholine

chronic obstructive pulmonary disease (COPD): chronic condition that occurs over time; often the result of chronic bronchitis or repeated and severe asthma attacks; leads to the destruction of the respiratory defense mechanisms and physical structure

chrysotherapy: treatment with gold salts; gold is taken up by macrophages, which then inhibit phagocytosis; is reserved for use in patients who are unresponsive to conventional therapy; can be very toxic

chylomicron: carrier for lipids in the blood stream, consist of proteins and lipids, cholesterol, and so forth

chyme: contents of the stomach that contains ingested food and secreted enzymes, water, and mucus

cilia: microscopic, hairlike projections of the epithelial cell membrane lining the upper respiratory tract, which are constantly moving and directing the mucous and any trapped substance toward the throat

cinchonism: syndrome of quinine toxicity characterized by nausea, vomiting, tinnitus, and vertigo

clotting factors: substances formed in the liver, many requiring vitamin K, that react in a cascading sequence to cause the formation of thrombin from prothrombin, which will break down fibrin threads from fibrinogen to form a clot

coagulation: the process of blood changing from a fluid state to a solid state to plug injuries to the vascular system

common cold: viral infection of the upper respiratory tract initiating the release of histamine and prostaglandins and causing an inflammatory response

complement: series of cascading proteins that react with the antigen-antibody complex to destroy the protein or stimulate an inflammatory reaction

conductivity: property of heart cells to rapidly conduct an action potential of electrical impulse

congestive heart failure: a condition in which the heart muscle fails to adequately pump blood around the cardiovascular system leading to a backup or congestion of blood in the system

constipation: slower than normal evacuation of the large intestine, which can result in increased water absorption from the feces and lead to impaction

convulsion: tonic-clonic muscular reaction to excessive electrical energy arising from nerve cells in the brain

coronary artery disease (CAD): characterized by progressive narrowing of coronary arteries, leading to a decreased delivery of oxygen to cardiac muscle cells; leading killer of adults in the Western world

corpus luteum: remains of follicle that releases mature ovum at ovulation; becomes an endocrine gland producing estrogen and progesterone

corpus striatum: part of the brain that reacts with the substantia nigra to maintain a balance of suppression and stimulation

corticosteroids: steroid hormones produced by the adrenal cortex; include androgens, glucocorticoids, and mineralcorticoids

cough: reflex response to irritation in the respiratory membrane, results in forced air expelled through the mouth

counter-current mechanism: the process used by medullary nephrons to concentrate or dilute the urine in response to body stimuli to maintain fluid and electrolyte balance

cretinism: lack of thyroid hormone in the infant; if untreated, leads to mental retardation

critical concentration: the concentration a drug must reach in the tissues that respond to the particular drug to cause the desired effect

culture: sample of the bacteria (e.g., from sputum, cell scrapings, urine) to grow in a laboratory to determine the species of bacteria that is causing an infection

cyclopegia: inability of the lens in the eye to accommodate to near vision, causing blurring and inability to see near objects

cystitis: inflammation of the bladder, caused by infection or irritation

cytomegalovirus (CMV): DNA virus that accounts for many respiratory, ophthalmic, and liver infections

cytoplasm: interior of a cell; contains organelles for producing proteins, energy, and so on

decongestants: drugs that decrease the blood flow to the upper respiratory tract and decrease the overproduction of secretions

dendrite: short projection on a neuron that transmits information

depolarization: opening of the sodium channels in a nerve membrane to allow the influx of positive sodium ions, reversing the membrane charge from negative to positive

depolarizing NMJ: stimulation of the muscle cell, causing it to contract, with no allowance for repolarization and restimulation of the muscle; characterized by contraction and then paralysis

depression: affective disorder in which a person experiences sadness that is much more severe and long-lasting than is warranted by the event that seems to have precipitated it, with a more intense mood; the condition may not even be traceable to a specific event or stressor

dermatological reactions: skin reactions commonly seen as adverse effects to drugs; can range from simple rash to potentially fatal exfoliative dermatitis

diabetes insipidus: lack of ADH resulting in the production of copious amounts of glucose-free urine

diabetes mellitus: a metabolic disorder characterized by high blood glucose levels and altered metabolism of proteins and fats; associated with thickening of the basement membrane, leading to numerous complications

diarrhea: more frequent than normal bowel movements, often characterized as fluid-like and watery because time for absorption is not allowed in the passage of the food through the intestines

diastole: resting phase of the heart; blood is returned to the heart during this phase

diffusion: movement of solutes from an area of high concentration to an area of low concentration across a concentration gradient

distribution: movement of a drug to body tissues; the places where a drug may be distributed depend on the drug's solubility, perfusion of the area, cardiac output, and binding of the drug to plasma proteins

diurnal rhythm: response of the hypothalamus and then pituitary and adrenals to wakefulness and sleeping; normally, the hypothalamus begins corticotropic releasing factor (CRF) secretion in the evening, peaking around midnight; adrenocortical peak response is between 6 and 9 AM; levels fall during the day until evening when the low level is picked up by the hypothalamus and CRF secretion begins again

dolor: pain, one of the four cardinal signs of inflammation; caused by the activation of the inflammatory response

dopaminergic: drug that increases the effects of dopamine at receptor sites

drug allergy: formation of antibodies to a drug or drug protein; causes an immune response when the person is next exposed to that drug

drugs: chemicals that are introduced into the body to bring about some sort of change

dwarfism: small stature, resulting from lack of growth hormone in children

dyspnea: discomfort with respirations, often with a feeling of anxiety and inability to breathe, seen with left-sided CHF

dysuria: painful urination

edema: movement of fluid into the interstitial spaces; occurs when the balance between osmotic pull (from plasma proteins) and hydrostatic push (from blood pressure) is upset

effector: cell stimulated by a nerve; may be a muscle, a gland, or another nerve

efferent: neurons or groups of neurons that carry information from the central nervous system to an effector; motor neurons

electrocardiogram (ECG): an electrical tracing reflecting the conduction of an electrical impulse through the heart muscle; does not reflect mechanical activity

emetic: agent used to induce vomiting to rid the stomach of toxins or drugs

endocytosis: engulfing substances and moving them into a cell by extending the cell membrane around the substance; pinocytosis and phagocytosis are two kinds of endocytosis

engram: short-term memory made up of a reverberating electrical circuit of action potentials

epilepsy: collection of different syndromes, all of which are characterized by seizures

ergosterol: steroid-type protein found in the cell membrane of fungi; similar in configuration to adrenal hormones and testosterone

ergot derivative: drug that causes a vascular constriction in the brain and the periphery; relieves or prevents migraine headaches but is associated with many adverse effects

erythrocytes: red blood cells, responsible for carrying oxygen to the tissues and removing carbon dioxide; have no nucleus and live approximately 120 days

erythropoiesis: process of RBC production and life cycle; formed by mega cells in the bone marrow, using iron, folic acid, carbohydrates, vitamin B_{12}, and amino acids; circulate in the vascular system for about 120 days, then are lysed and recycled

erythropoietin: glycoprotein produced by the kidneys, released in response to decreased blood flow or oxygen tension in the kidney; controls the rate of RBC production in the bone marrow

essential hypertension: sustained blood pressure above normal limits with no discernible underlying cause

estrogen: hormone produced by the ovary, placenta, and adrenal gland; stimulates development of female characteristics and prepares the body for pregnancy

excretion: removal of a drug from the body; primarily occurs in the kidneys but can occur through the skin, lungs, bile, and feces

exocytosis: removal of substances from a cell by pushing them through the cell membrane

expectorants: drugs that increase productive cough to clear the airways

extrapyramidal tract: cells from the cortex and subcortical areas, including the basal ganglia and the cerebellum, which coordinate unconsciously controlled muscle activity; allows the body to make automatic adjustments in posture or position and balance

extrinsic pathway: cascading of clotting factors in blood that has escaped the vascular system to form a clot on the outside of the injured vessel

fertility drugs: drugs used to stimulate ovulation and pregnancy in women with functioning ovaries who are having trouble conceiving

fibrillation: rapid, irregular stimulation of the cardiac muscle resulting in lack of pumping activity

filtration: the passing of fluid and small components of the blood through the glomerulus into the nephron tubule

first-pass effect: a phenomenon in which drugs given orally are carried directly to the liver after absorption where they may be largely inactivated by liver enzymes before they can enter the general circulation; oral drugs frequently are given in higher doses than drugs given by other routes because of this early breakdown

fluid rebound: reflex reaction of the body to the loss of fluid or sodium; the hypothalamus causes the release of ADH, which retains water, and stress related to fluid loss combines with decreased blood flow to the kidneys to activate the renin-angiotensin system, leading to further water and sodium retention

focal seizure: seizure that involves one area of the brain and does not spread throughout the entire brain; also known as a partial seizure

follicle: storage site of each ovum in the ovary; allows the ovum to grow and develop, produces estrogen and progesterone

follicles: structural unit of the thyroid gland; cells arranged in a circle

Food and Drug Administration (FDA): federal agency responsible for the regulation and enforcement of drug evaluation and distribution policies

forebrain: upper level of the brain; consists of the two cerebral hemispheres, where thinking and coordination of sensory and motor activity occur

fungus: a cellular organism with a hard cell wall that contains chitin and many polysaccharides as well as a cell membrane that contains ergosterols

gallstone: crystallization of cholesterol in the gall bladder as the bile is concentrated for storage, leading to the formation of crystal clusters or stones; gallstones can become large enough to block the bile duct and common duct

ganglia: a closely packed group of nerve cell bodies

gastrin: secreted by the stomach in response to many stimuli to stimulate the release of hydrochloric acid from the parietal cells and pepsin from the chief cells; causes histamine release at $histamine_2$ receptors to effect the release of acid

gate control theory: theory that states that the transmission of a nerve impulse can be modulated at various points along its path by descending fibers from the brain that close the "gate" and block transmission of pain information and by A fibers that are able to block transmission in the dorsal horn by closing the gate for transmission for the A-delta and C fibers

general anesthetic: drug that induces a loss of consciousness, amnesia, analgesia, and loss of reflexes to allow performance of painful surgical procedures

generalized seizure: seizure that begins in one area of the brain and rapidly spreads throughout both hemispheres

generic drugs: drugs sold by their chemical name; not brand (or trade) name products

generic name: the original designation that a drug is given when the drug company that developed it applies for the approval process

genetic engineering: process of altering DNA, usually of bacteria, to produce a chemical to be used as a drug

giardiasis: protozoal intestinal infection that causes severe diarrhea and epigastric distress; may lead to serious malnutrition

giganticism: response to excess levels of growth hormone before the epiphyseal plates close; heights of 7 to 8 feet are not uncommon

glomerulus: the tuft of blood vessel between the afferent and efferent arterioles in the nephron; fenestrated membrane of the glomerulus allows filtration of fluid from the blood into the nephron tubule

glucocorticoids: steroid hormones released from the adrenal cortex; increase blood glucose levels, fat deposits, and protein breakdown for energy

glycogen: storage form of glucose; can be broken down for rapid glucose level increases during times of stress

glycogenolysis: breakdown of stored glucose to increase the blood glucose levels

glycosuria: presence of glucose in the urine

gram-negative: bacteria that accept a negative stain and are frequently associated with infections of the GU or GI tract

gram-positive: bacteria that take a positive stain and are frequently associated with infections of the respiratory tract and soft tissues

grand mal seizure: see *tonic-clonic seizure*

Hageman factor: first factor activated when a blood vessel is injured; starts the cascading reaction of the clotting factors, activates the conversion of plasminogen to plasmin to dissolve clots, and activates the kinin system responsible for activation of the inflammatory response

half-life: the time it takes for the amount of drug in the body to decrease to one-half of the peak level it previously achieved

heart blocks: blocks to conduction of an impulse through the cardiac conduction system; can be a block at the AV node, interrupting conduction from the atria into the ventricles, or blocks in the bundle branches within the ventricles preventing the normal conduction of the impulse

helminth: worm that can cause disease by invading the human body

helper T cell: human lymphocyte that helps initiate immune reactions in response to tissue invasion

hemodynamics: the study of the forces moving blood throughout the cardiovascular system

hemoptysis: blood-tinged sputum, seen in left-sided CHF when blood backs up into the lungs and fluid leaks out into the lung tissue

hemorrhagic disorders: disorders characterized by a lack of clot forming substances, leading to states of excess bleeding

hemostatic drugs: drugs that stop blood loss, usually by blocking the plasminogen mechanism and preventing clot dissolution

herpes: DNA virus that accounts for many diseases, including shingles, cold sores, genital herpes, and encephalitis

high ceiling diuretics: powerful diuretics that work in the loop of Henle to inhibit the reabsorption of sodium and chloride, leading to a sodium-rich diuresis

high density lipoprotein: loosely packed chylomicron containing fats, able to absorb fats and fat remnants in the periphery; thought to have a protective effect, decreasing the development of CAD

hindbrain: most primitive area of the brain, the brainstem; consists of the pons and medulla, which control basic, vital functions and arousal, and the cerebellum, which controls motor functions that regulate balance

hirsutism: hair distribution associated with male secondary sex characteristics, e.g., increased hair on trunk, arms, legs, face

histamine H_2 antagonist: drug that blocks the histamine H_2 receptor sites; used to decrease acid production in the stomach (histamine H_2 sites are stimulated to cause the release of acid in response to gastrin or parasympathetic stimulation)

histamine$_2$ receptors: sites near the parietal cells of the stomach which, when stimulated, cause the release of hydrochloric acid into the lumen of the stomach; also found near cardiac cells

histocompatibility antigens: proteins found on the surface of the cell membrane, which are determined by genetic code; provide cellular identity as self-cell

HMG CoA reductase: enzyme that regulates the last step in cellular cholesterol synthesis

hormones: a chemical messenger working within the endocrine system to communicate within the body

human immunodeficiency virus (HIV): retrovirus that attacks helper T cells, leading to a decrease in immune function and AIDS or ARC

hydrochloric acid: acid released by the parietal cells of the stomach in response to gastrin release or parasympathetic stimulation; makes the stomach contents more acidic to aid digestion and breakdown of food products

hyperaldosteronism: excessive output of aldosterone from the adrenal gland, leading to increased sodium and water retention and loss of potassium

hyperglycemia: elevated blood glucose levels (>110 mg/dl) leading to multiple signs and symptoms and abnormal metabolic pathways

hyperlipidemia: increased levels of lipids in the serum, associated with increased risk of CAD development

hyperparathyroidism: excessive parathormone

hypersensitivity: excessive responsiveness to either the primary or secondary effects of a drug; may be due to a pathological or individual condition

hyperthyroidism: excess levels of thyroid hormone

hypertonia: state of excessive muscle response and activity

hypnotic: drug used to depress the CNS; causes sleep

hypocalcemia: calcium deficiency

hypoglycemia: lower than normal blood sugar (<40 mg/dl); often results from imbalance between insulin or oral agents and patient's eating, activity, and stress

hypogonadism: underdevelopment of the gonads (testes in the male)

hypokalemia: low potassium in the blood, which often occurs following diuretic use; characterized by weakness, muscle cramps, trembling, nausea, vomiting, diarrhea, and cardiac arrhythmias

hypnosis: extreme sedation resulting in CNS depression and sleep

hypoparathyroidism: rare condition of absence of parathormone; may be seen following thyroidectomy

hypopituitarism: lack of adequate function of the pituitary; reflected in many endocrine disorders

hypotension: sustained blood pressure that is lower than that required to adequately perfuse all of the body's tissues

hypothalamic-pituitary axis: interconnection of the hypothalamus and pituitary to regulate the levels of certain endocrine hormones through a complex series of negative feedback systems

hypothalamus: "master gland" of the neuroendocrine system; regulates both nervous and endocrine responses to internal and external stimuli

hypothyroidism: lack of sufficient thyroid hormone to maintain metabolism

immune stimulant: drug used to energize the immune system when it is exhausted from fighting prolonged invasion or needs help fighting a specific pathogen or cancer cell

immune suppressant: drug used to block or suppress the actions of the T cells and antibody production; used to prevent transplant rejection and treat autoimmune diseases

immune sera: preformed antibodies found in immune globulin from animals or humans who have had a specific disease and developed antibodies to it

immunization: the process of stimulating active immunity by exposing the body to weakened or less toxic proteins associated with specific disease-causing organisms; the goal is to stimulate immunity without suffering the full course of a disease

induction: time from the beginning of anesthesia until achievement of surgical anesthesia

influenza A: RNA virus that invades tissues of the respiratory tract, causing the signs and symptoms of the common cold or "flu"

inhibin: estrogen-like substance produced by seminiferous tubules during sperm production; acts as a negative feedback stimulus to decrease FSH release

insulin: hormone produced by the beta cells in the pancreas; stimulates insulin receptor sites to move glucose into the cells; promotes storage of fat and glucose in the body

interferon: tissue hormone that is released in response to viral invasion; blocks viral replication

interleukines: chemicals released by white cells to communicate with other white cells and to support the inflammatory and immune reactions

interneuron: neuron in the CNS that communicates with other neurons, not muscles or glands

interstitial or Leydig cells: part of the testes that produce testosterone in response to LH stimulation

interstitial cystitis: chronic inflammation of the interstitial connective tissue of the bladder; may extend into deeper tissue

intractable hiccough: repetitive stimulation of the diaphragm that leads to hiccough, a diaphragmatic spasm that persists over time

intrinsic pathway: cascade of clotting factors leading to the formation of a clot within the injured vessel

iodine: important dietary element used by the thyroid gland to produce thyroid hormone

iron deficiency anemia: low RBC count with low iron available because of high demand, poor diet, or poor absorption; treated with iron replacement

ketosis: breakdown of fats for energy, resulting in an increase in ketones to be excreted from the body

kinin system: system activated by Hageman factor as part of the inflammatory response; includes bradykinin

larynx: the vocal chords and the epiglottis, which close during swallowing to protect the lower respiratory tract from any foreign particles

leishmaniasis: skin, mucous membrane, or visceral infection caused by a protozoan passed to humans by the bites of sand flies
leukocytes: white blood cells; can be neutrophils, basophils, or eosinophils
leukotriene receptor antagonists: drugs that selectively and competitively block or antagonize receptors for the production of leukotriene D4 and E4, components of slow-reacting substance of anaphylaxis (SRS-A)
limbic system: area in the midbrain that is rich in epinephrine, norepinephrine, and serotonin, which seems to control emotions
liothyronine: T_3; the most potent thyroid hormone, with a short half-life of 12 hours
lipoprotein: structure composed of proteins and lipids; bipolar arrangement of the lipids monitors substances passing in and out of the cell
local GI reflex: reflex response to various stimuli, allowing the GI tract local control of its secretions and movements based on the contents or activity of the whole GI system
local anesthetic: powerful nerve blocker that prevents depolarization of nerve membranes, blocking the transmission of pain stimuli and, in some cases, motor activity
low density lipoprotein (LDL): tightly packed fats that are thought to contribute to the development of CAD when remnants left over from the LDL are processed in the arterial lining
lower respiratory tract: the smallest bronchi and the alveoli that make up the lungs; the area where gas exchange takes place
lubricant: agent that increases the viscosity of the feces, making it difficult to absorb water from the bolus and easing movement of the bolus through the intestines
lymphocytes: white blood cells with large, varied nuclei; can be T cells or B cells
lysosomes: encapsulated, digestive enzymes found within a cell; digest old or damaged areas of the cell and are responsible for destroying the cell when the membrane ruptures and the cell dies

macrophages: mature leukocytes that are capable of phagocytizing an antigen (foreign protein); also called monocytes or mononuclear phagocytes
major tranquilizer: former name of antipsychotic drugs; no longer used because it implies that its primary effect is sedation, which is no longer thought to be the desired therapeutic action
malaria: protozoal infection with *Plasmodium,* which is characterized by cyclic fever and chills as the parasite is released from ruptured red blood cells; causes serious liver, CNS, heart, and lung damage
malignant hyperthermia: reaction to some NMJ drugs in susceptible individuals; characterized by extreme muscle rigidity, severe hyperpyrexia, acidosis, and in some cases death
mania: state of hyperexcitability; one phase of bipolar disorders, which alternate between periods of severe depression and mania
mast cell stabilizer: drug that works at the cellular level to inhibit the release of histamine (released from mast cells in response to inflammation or irritation) and the release of slow-reacting substance of anaphylaxis (SRS-A)
megaloblastic anemia: anemia caused by lack of vitamin B_{12} and/or folic acid; RBCs are fewer in number and have a weak stroma and a short life span; treated by replacement of folic acid and vitamin B_{12}
menopause: depletion of the female ova; results in lack of estrogen and progesterone
menstrual cycle: cycling of female sex hormones in interaction with the hypothalamus and anterior pituitary feedback systems
metabolism: rate at which the cells burn energy
metastasis: ability to enter the circulatory or lymphatic system and travel to other areas of the body that are conducive to growth and survival; property of cancer cells
midbrain: the middle area of the brain; consists of the hypothalamus and thalamus and includes the limbic system
migraine headache: headache characterized by severe, unilateral, pulsating head pain and associated with systemic effects, including GI upset and light and sound sensitization; related to a hyperperfusion of the brain from arterial dilation
mineralcorticoids: steroid hormones released by the adrenal cortex; cause sodium and water retention and potassium excretion
miosis: constriction of the pupil; relieves intraocular pressure in some types of glaucoma
mitochondria: rod-shaped organelles; produce ATP for energy within the cell
monoamine oxidase (MAO): enzyme that breaks down norephinphrine to make it inactive
monoamine oxidase (MAO) inhibitor: drug that prevents the enzyme monoamine oxidase from breaking down norepinephrine (NE), leading to increased NE levels in the synaptic cleft; relieves depression and also causes sympathomimetic effects
monoclonal antibodies: specific antibodies produced by a single clone of B cells to react with a very specific antigen
mononuclear phagocyte system (MPS): system composed of the thymus gland, the lymphatic tissue, leukocytes, lymphocytes, and numerous chemical mediators; previously called the reticuloendothelial system
mucolytics: drugs that increase or liquefy respiratory secretions to aid the clearing of the airways
muscarinic receptors: cholinergic receptors that also respond to stimulation by muscarine
myasthenia gravis: autoimmune disease characterized by antibodies to cholinergic receptor sites, leading to destruction of the receptor sites and decreased response at the neuromuscular junction; progressive and debilitating, leading to paralysis
mycosis: disease caused by a fungus
mydriasis: relaxation of the muscles around the pupil, leading to pupil dilation
myocardial infarction: end result of vessel blockage in the heart, leads to ischemia and then necrosis of the area cut off from the blood supply; can heal, replacing the dead cells with scar tissue
myocardium: the muscle of the heart
myosin: thick filament with projections that makes up a sarcomere or muscle unit
myxedema: severe lack of thyroid hormone in adults

narcolepsy: mental disorder characterized by daytime sleepiness and periods of sudden loss of wakefulness
narcotic agonists-antagonists: drugs that react with some opioid receptors to stimulate their activity and react at other opioid receptors to block activity
narcotic agonists: drugs that react at opioid receptor sites to stimulate the effects of the receptors
narcotic antagonists: drugs that block the opioid receptor sites; used to counteract the effects of narcotics or to treat an overdose of narcotics
narcotics: drugs that were originally derived from opium, which react with specific opioid receptors throughout the body
negative feedback system: control system in which increasing levels of a hormone lead to decreased levels of releasing and stimulating hormones, which lead to decreased hormone levels, which stimulates the release of releasing and stimulating hormones; allows tight control of the endocrine system
nematode: roundworm such as the commonly encountered pinworm, whipworm, threadworm, Ascaris, or hookworm
neoplasm: new or cancerous growth; occurs when abnormal cells have the opportunity to multiply and grow
nephron: functional unit of the kidney, composed of Bowman's capsule, the proximal and distal convoluted tubules, and the collecting duct
nerve gas: irreversible acetylcholinesterase inhibitor used in warfare to cause paralysis and death by prolonged muscle contraction and parasympathetic crisis

nerve plexus: network of nerve fibers running through the wall of the GI tract, allowing local reflexes and control

neuroendocrine system: the combination of the nervous and endocrine systems; both work closely together to maintain regulatory control and homeostasis in the body

neuron: structural unit of the nervous system

neurotransmitter: chemical produced by a nerve and released when the nerve is stimulated; reacts with a specific receptor site to cause a reaction

nicotinic receptors: cholinergic receptors that also respond to stimulation by nicotine

nitrates: drugs used to cause direct relaxation of smooth muscle, leading to vasodilation and decreased venous return to the heart and decreased resistance to blood flow; this rapidly decreases oxygen demand in the heart and can restore the balance of blood delivered to blood needed in the heart muscle of angina patients

nocturia: getting up to void at night, reflecting increased renal perfusion with fluid shifts in the supine position when a person has gravity-dependent edema related to CHF; other medical conditions, including urinary tract infection, increase the need to get up and void

nondepolarizing NMJ: no stimulation or depolarization of the muscle cell; prevents depolarization and stimulation by blocking the effects of Ach

nonsteroidal anti-inflammatory drugs (NSAIDs): block prostaglandin synthesis and act as antiinflammatory, antipyretic, and analgesic agents

nucleosides: drugs that inhibit cell protein synthesis by HIV, leading to viral death

nucleus: part of a cell that contains the DNA and genetic material; regulates cellular protein production and cellular properties

nursing: the art of nurturing and administering to the sick combined with the scientific application of chemistry, anatomy, physiology, biology, nutrition, psychology, and pharmacology to the particular clinical situation

nursing diagnosis: statement of an actual or potential problem based on the assessment of a particular clinical situation, which directs needed nursing interventions

nursing process: the problem-solving process used to provide efficient nursing care; it involves gathering information, formulating a nursing diagnosis statement, carrying out interventions, and evaluating the process

oncotic pressure: the pulling pressure of the plasma proteins, responsible for returning fluid to the vascular system at the capillary level

opioid receptors: receptor sites on nerves that react with endorphins and enkephalins, which are receptive to narcotic drugs

organelles: distinct structures found within the cell cytoplasm

orphan drugs: drugs that have been discovered but are not available for use by those who could benefit from them, usually because they are not financially profitable

orthopnea: difficulty breathing when lying down, often referred to by the number of pillows required to allow a person to breath comfortably

osmosis: movement of water from an area of low solute concentration to an area of high solute concentration in an attempt to equalize the concentrations

osmotic pull: drawing force of large molecules on water, pulling it into the tubule or capillary; essential for maintaining normal fluid balance within the body; used to draw out excess fluid into the vascular system or the renal tubule

ova: eggs; the female gamete; contain half of the information needed in a human nucleus

ovaries: female sexual glands that store ova and produce estrogen and progesterone

over-the-counter (OTC) drugs: drugs that are available without a prescription for self-treatment of a variety of complaints

oxytocics: drugs acting like the hypothalamic hormone oxytocin; stimulate uterine contraction and contraction of the lacteal glands in the breast, promoting milk ejection

Paget's disease: a genetically linked disorder of overactive osteoclasts that are eventually replaced by enlarged and softened bony structures

pancreatic enzymes: digestive enzymes secreted by the exocrine pancreas, including pancreatin and pancrelipase, which are needed for the proper digestion of fats, proteins, and carbohydrates

paralysis: lack of muscle function

parasympathetic nervous system: "rest and digest" response mediator that contains CNS cells from the cranium or sacral area of the spinal cord, long preganglionic axons, ganglia near or within the effector tissue, and short postganglionic axons that react with cholinergic receptors

parasympatholytic: lysing or preventing parasympathetic effects

parasympathomimetic: mimicking the effects of the parasympathetic nervous system: bradycardia, hypotension, pupil constriction, increased GI secretions and activity, increased bladder tone, relaxation of sphincters, bronchoconstriction

parathormone: hormone produced by the parathyroid glands; responsible for maintaining calcium levels in conjunction with calcitonin

Parkinson's disease: debilitating disease characterized by progressive loss of coordination and function, which results from the degeneration of dopamine-producing cells in the substantia nigra

passive immunity: the injection of preformed antibodies into a host at high risk for exposure to a specific disease; immunity is limited by the amount of circulating antibody

penile erectile dysfunction: condition in which the corpus cavernosum does not fill with blood allowing for penile erection; can be related to aging, neurological, or vascular conditions

peptic ulcer: erosion of the lining of stomach or duodenum, caused by imbalance between acid produced and mucous protection of the GI lining or possibly due to infection by *Helicobacter pylori* bacteria

peripheral resistance: force that resists the flow of blood through the vessels, mostly determined by the arterioles, which contract to increase resistance; important in determining overall blood pressure

peristalsis: type of GI movement to move food bolus forward; characterized by a progressive wave of muscle contraction

pernicious anemia: megaloblastic anemia characterized by lack of vitamin B_{12} secondary to low production of intrinsic factor by gastric cells; vitamin B_{12} must be replaced by IM injection of nasal spray as it cannot be absorbed through the GI tract

petit mal seizure: see *absence seizure*

phagocytes: neutrophils that are able to engulf and digest foreign material

phagocytosis: the process of engulfing and digesting foreign material

pharmacodynamics: the science that deals with the interactions between the chemical components of living systems and the foreign chemicals, including drugs, that enter living organisms; the way a drug affects a body

pharmacokinetics: the way the body deals with a drug, including absorption, distribution, biotransformation, and excretion

pharmacotherapeutics: clinical pharmacology, the branch of pharmacology that deals with drugs; chemicals that are used in medicine for the treatment, prevention, and diagnosis of disease in humans

phase I study: a pilot study of a potential drug done with a small number of selected, healthy human volunteers

phase II study: a clinical study of a drug by selected physicians using actual patients who have the disorder the drug is designed to treat; patients must provide informed consent

phase III study: use of a drug on a wide scale in the clinical setting with patients who have the disease the drug is thought to treat

phase IV study: continual evaluation of a drug after it has been released for marketing

phenothiazine: antianxiety drug that blocks the responsiveness of the CTZ to stimuli, leading to a decrease in nausea and vomiting

pheochromocytoma: a tumor of the chromaffin cells of the adrenal medulla that periodically releases large amounts of norepinephrine and epinephrine into the system with resultant severe hypertension and tachycardia

photosensitivity: hypersensitive reaction to the sun or ultraviolet light, seen as an adverse reaction to various drugs; can lead to severe skin rash and lesions and damage to the eye

pinworm: nematode that causes a common helminthic infection in humans; lives in the intestine and causes anal and possible vaginal irritation and itching

pituitary gland: gland found in the sella turcica of the brain; produces hormones, endorphins, and enkephalins and stores two hypothalamic hormones

placebo effect: documented effect of the mind on drug therapy; if a person perceives that a drug will be effective, the drug is much more likely to actually be effective

plasma: the liquid part of the blood, mostly water and plasma proteins, glucose, and electrolytes

plasma esterase: enzyme found in plasma that immediately breaks down ester-type local anesthetics

plasminogen: natural clot-dissolving system; converted to plasmin, also called fibrinolysin, by many substances to dissolve clots that have formed and maintain the patency of the injured vessels

Plasmodium: a protozoa that causes malaria in humans; its life cycle includes the *Anopheles* mosquito, which injects protozoa into humans

platelet aggregation: property of platelets to adhere to an injured surface and then attract other platelets, which clump together or aggregate at the area, plugging up an injury to the vascular system

platyhelminth: flatworm or fluke such as the tapeworm

***Pneumocystis carinii* pneumonia (PCP):** opportunistic infection that occurs when the immune system is depressed; a frequent cause of pneumonia in patients with acquired immunodeficiency syndrome (AIDS) or in those who are receiving immunosuppressive therapy

pneumonia: inflammation of the lungs that can be caused by bacterial or viral invasion of the tissue or by aspiration of foreign substances

poisoning: overdose of a drug, causing damage to multiple body systems and the potential for fatal reactions

polydipsia: increased thirst; seen in diabetes when loss of fluid and increased tonicity of the blood lead the hypothalamic thirst center to make the patient feel thirsty

polyphagia: increased hunger; sign of diabetes when cells cannot use glucose for energy and feel that they are starving, causing hunger

positively inotropic: causing an increased force of contraction

posterior pituitary: lobe of the pituitary that receives ADH and oxytocin via neuroaxons from the hypothalamus and stores them to be released when stimulated by the hypothalamus

postmenopausal osteoporosis: dropping levels of estrogen allow calcium to be pulled out of the bone, resulting in a weakened and honeycombed bone structure

preclinical trials: initial trial of a chemical thought to have therapeutic potential; uses laboratory animals, not human subjects

premature atrial contraction (PAC): caused by an ectopic focus in the atria stimulating an atrial response

premature ventricular contraction (PVC): an ectopic focus in the ventricles stimulating the cells and causing an early contraction

Prinzmetal's angina: drop in blood flow through the coronary arteries caused by a vasospasm in the artery, not by atherosclerosis

proarrhythmic: tending to cause arrhythmias; many of the drugs used to treat arrhythmias have been found to generate arrhythmias

progesterone: hormone produced by the ovary, placenta, and adrenal gland; promotes maintenance of pregnancy

progestin: female sex hormone; important in maintaining a pregnancy and supporting many secondary sex characteristics

prophylaxis: treatment to prevent an infection before it occurs, as in the use of antibiotics to prevent disease such as bacterial endocarditis or antiprotozoals to prevent malaria

prostaglandin: any one of numerous tissue hormones that have local effects on various systems and organs of the body, including vasoconstriction, vasodilation, increased or decreased GI activity, increased or decreased pancreatic enzyme release

prostate gland: gland located around the male urethra; responsible for producing an acidic fluid that maintains sperm and lubricates the urinary tract

protease inhibitors: drugs that block the activity of the enzyme protease in HIV; protease is essential for the maturation of infectious virus, and its absence leads to the formation of an immature and noninfective HIV particle

proton pump inhibitor: drug that blocks the hydrogen/potassium ATPase enzyme system on the secretory surface of the gastric parietal cells, thus interfering with the final step of acid production and lowering the acid levels in the stomach

protozoa: a single-celled organism that passes through several stages in its life cycle, including at least one phase as a human parasite; found in areas of poor sanitation and hygiene and crowded living conditions

puberty: point at which the hypothalamus starts releasing GnRF to stimulate the release of FSH and LH and begin sexual development

pulmonary edema: severe left-sided congestive heart failure with backup of blood into the lungs, leading to loss of fluid into the lung tissue

pulse pressure: the systolic blood pressure minus the diastolic blood pressure; reflects the filling pressure of the coronary arteries

pyelonephritis: inflammation of the pelvises of the kidney, frequently caused by backward flow problems or bacteria ascending the ureter

pyramidal tract: fibers within the CNS that control precise, intentional movement

pyrogen: substance that resets the thermoregulatory center in the hypothalamus to elevate the body temperature, which subsequently speeds metabolism; some pyrogens are released by active neutrophils as part of the inflammatory response

radiolucent: radiographic indication (appearing clear on x-ray) that gallstones have not yet become calcified and can be treated with gallstone solubilizers

reabsorption: the movement of substances from the renal tubule back into the vascular system

rebound congestion: occurs when the nasal passages become congested as the drug effect wears off; patients tend to use more drug to decrease the congestion and a vicious circle of congestion, drug, and congestion develops, leading to abuse of the decongestant; also called rhinitis medicamentosa

receptor sites: sites on cell membranes that react with specific other chemicals to cause an effect; a drug may be effective because it reacts with a specific receptor site on particular cells in the body

recombinant DNA technology: use of bacteria to produce chemicals normally produced by human cells

releasing hormones or factors: chemicals released by the hypothalamus into the anterior pituitary to stimulate the release of anterior pituitary hormones

renin-angiostensin system: important compensatory process that leads to increased blood pressure and blood volume to ensure perfusion of the kidneys; important in the day-to-day regulation of blood pressure

repolarization: return of a membrane to a resting state, with more sodium ions outside the membrane and a relatively negative charge inside the membrane

resistance: ability of bacteria over time to adapt to an antibiotic and produce cells that are no longer affected by the drug

resistance system: the arteries; the muscles of the arteries provide resistance to the flow of blood, leading to control of blood pressure
respiration: the act of breathing
respiratory distress syndrome (RDS): disorder found in premature neonates whose lungs have not had time to mature and who are lacking sufficient surfactant to maintain open airways to allow for respiration
respiratory membrane: area through which gas exchange must be made; made up of the capillary endothelium, the capillary basement membrane, the interstitial space, the alveolar basement membrane, the alveolar endothelium, and the surfactant layer
reticulocyte: RBC that has lost its nucleus and entered circulation just recently, not yet fully matured
reverse transcriptase inhibitors: drugs that block the transfer of both RNA- and DNA-dependent DNA polymerase activities; prevents the transfer of information that allows the virus to replicate and survive
rhinitis medicamentosa: reflex reaction to vasoconstriction caused by decongestants; a rebound vasodilation that often leads to prolonged overuse of decongestants; also called rebound congestion
ribosomes: fibrous structures that are the sites of protein production within a cell
risk factors: factors that have been identified to increase the risk of the development of CAD, including genetic predisposition, gender, age, high-fat diet, sedentary lifestyle, gout, hypertension, diabetes, and estrogen deficiency
roundworm: worm such as *Ascaris* that causes a common helminthic infection in humans; can cause intestinal obstruction as the adult worms clog the intestinal lumen or severe pneumonia when the larvae migrate to the lungs and form a pulmonary infiltrate
rubor: redness, one of the four cardinal signs of inflammation; caused by the activation of the inflammatory response

salicylates: salicylic acid compounds, used as antiinflammatory, antipyretic, and analgesics agents; block the prostaglandin system
saliva: fluid produced by the salivary glands in the mouth in response to tactile stimuli and cerebral stimulation; contains enzymes to begin digestion as well as water and mucus to make the food bolus slippery and easier to swallow
sarcoma: tumor that originates in the mesenchyma and is made up of embryonic connective tissue cells
sarcomere: functional unit of a muscle cell, composed of actin and myosin molecules arranged in layers to give the unit a striped or striated appearance
schistosomiasis: infection with blood fluke that is carried by a snail that poses a common problem in tropical countries, where the snail is the intermediary in the life cycle of the worm; larvae burrow into the skin in fresh water and migrate throughout the human body, causing a rash and then symptoms of diarrhea and liver and brain inflammation
Schwann cell: insulating cell found on nerve axons; allows "leaping" electrical conduction to speed the transmission of information and prevent the neuron from tiring
seasonal rhinitis: inflammation of the nasal cavity, commonly called hay fever; caused by reaction to a specific antigen
secretion: the active movement of substances from the blood into the renal tubule
sedation: loss of awareness and reaction to environmental stimuli
sedative: drug that depresses the CNS; produces a loss of awareness of and reaction to the environment
segmentation: GI movement characterized by contraction of one segment of small intestine while the next segment is relaxed; the contracted segment then relaxes, and the relaxed segment contracts; exposes the chyme to a vast surface area to increase absorption from the chyme
seizure: sudden discharge of excessive electrical energy from nerve cells in the brain
selective serotonin reuptake inhibitor (SSRI): drug that specifically blocks the reuptake of serotonin and increases its concentration in the synaptic cleft; relieves depression and is not associated with anticholinergic or sympathomimetic adverse effects
selective toxicity: property of a chemotherapeutic agent to affect only systems found in foreign cells, and not affect healthy human cells (e.g., specific antibiotics can affect certain proteins or enzyme systems used by bacteria but not by human cells)
seminiferous tubules: part of the testes that produce sperm in response to FSH stimulation
sensitivity testing: evaluation of bacteria obtained in a culture to determine to which antibiotics the organisms are sensitive and which agent would be appropriate for treatment of a particular infection
serum sickness: reaction of a host to injected antibodies or foreign sera; host cells make antibodies to the foreign proteins and a massive immune reaction can occur
shock: severe hypotension that can lead to accumulation of waste products and cell death
sinoatrial (SA) node: the normal pacemaker of the heart; composed of primitive cells that constantly generate an action potential
sinuses: air-filled passages through the skull that open into the nasal passage
sinusitis: inflammation of the epithelial lining of the sinus cavities
sliding filament theory: theory explaining muscle contraction as a reaction of actin and myosin molecules when freed to react by the inactivation of troponin by calcium allowed to enter the cell during depolarization
sneeze: reflex response to irritation in the nasal passages; results in forced air expelled through the nose
soma: cell body of a neuron; contains the nucleus, cytoplasm, and various granules
spasticity: sustained muscle contractions
spectrum: range of bacteria against which an antibiotic is effective (e.g., broad-spectrum antibiotics are effective against a wide range of bacteria)
sperm: male gamete; contains half of the information needed for a human cell nucleus
spinothalamic tract: nerve pathway from the spine to the thalamus along which pain impulses are carried to the brain
Starling's law of the heart: addresses the contractile properties of the heart; the more the muscle is stretched, the stronger it will react until stretched to a point at which it will not react at all
status epilepticus: state in which seizures rapidly recur; most severe form of generalized seizure
stomatitis: inflammation of the mucous membranes related to drug effects; can lead to alterations in nutrition and dental problems
stroke volume: the amount of blood pumped out of the ventricle with each beat; important in determining blood pressure
substantia nigra: part of the brain rich in dopamine and dopamine receptors; site of degenerating neurons in Parkinson's disease
sulfonylureas: oral antidiabetic agents used to stimulate the pancreas to release more insulin
superinfections: infections caused by the destruction of normal flora bacteria by certain drugs, allowing other bacteria to enter the body and cause infection; may occur during the course of antibiotic therapy
surfactant: lipoprotein that reduces surface tension in the alveoli, allowing them to stay open to allow gas exchange
swallowing: complex reflex response to a bolus in the back of the throat; allows passage of the bolus into the esophagus and movement of ingested contents into the GI tract
sympathetic nervous system: "fight or flight" response mediator; composed of CNS cells from the thoracic or lumbar areas, short preganglionic axons, ganglia near the spinal cord, and long postganglionic axons that react with adrenergic receptors
sympatholytic: a drug that lyses, or blocks, the effects of the sympathetic nervous system

sympathomimetic: mimicking the sympathetic nervous system with the signs and symptoms seen when the SNS is stimulated

sympathomimetics: drugs that mimic the effects of the sympathetic nervous system

synapse: junction between a nerve and an effector; consists of the presynaptic nerve ending, a space called the synaptic cleft, and the postsynaptic cell

syncytia: intertwining network of muscle fibers making up the atria and the ventricles of the heart; allows for a coordinated pumping contraction

synergistic: drugs that work together to increase drug effectiveness

systole: contracting phase of the heart; blood is pumped out of the heart in this phase

T cells: lymphocytes programmed in the thymus gland to recognize self cells; may be effector T cells, helper T cells, or suppressor T cells

tachycardia: faster than normal heart rate (usually >100 beats/minute)

tachypnea: rapid and shallow respirations, seen with left-sided CHF

teratogenic: having adverse effects on the fetus

testes: male sexual gland that produces sperm and testosterone

testosterone: male sex hormone; produced by the interstitial or Leydig cells of the testes

thiazide: type of diuretic acting in the renal tubule to block the chloride pump, which prevents the reabsorption of sodium and chloride, leading to a loss of sodium and water in the urine

thioamides: drugs used to prevent the formation of thyroid hormone in the thyroid cells, lowering thyroid hormone levels

threadworm: pervasive nematode that can send larvae into the lungs, liver, and CNS; can cause severe pneumonia or liver abscess

thromboembolic disorders: a disorder characterized by the formation of clots or thrombi on injured blood vessels with potential breaking of the clot to form emboli, which will travel to smaller vessels where they become lodged and occlude the vessel

thrombolytic drugs: drugs that lyse, or break down, a clot that has formed; these drugs activate the plasminogen mechanism to dissolve fibrin threads

thyroxine: T_4, a thyroid hormone, converted to T_3 in the tissues; has a half-life of 1 week

tinea: fungus called ringworm that causes such infections as athlete's foot, jock itch, and others

tocolytics: drugs used to relax the gravid uterus to prolong pregnancy

tonic-clonic seizure: type of a generalized seizure that is characterized by serious clonic-tonic muscular reactions, loss of consciousness, and exhaustion and little memory of the event on awakening; formerly known as a grand mal seizure

trachea: the main conducting airway leading into the lungs

trichinosis: disease that results from ingestion of encysted roundworm larvae in undercooked pork; larvae migrate throughout the body to invade muscle, nervous tissue, etc; can cause pneumonia, heart failure, and encephalitis

trichomoniasis: infestation with a protozoan that causes vaginitis in women but no signs or symptoms in men

tricyclic antidepressant (TCA): drug that blocks the reuptake of norepinephrine and serotonin; relieves depression and has anticholinergic and sedative effects

triptan: selective serotonin receptor blocker that causes a vascular constriction of cranial vessels; used to treat acute migraine attacks

trophozoite: a developing stage of a parasite, using the host for essential nutrients needed for growth

troponin: chemical in heart muscle that prevents actin and myosin from reacting, leading to muscle relaxation; inactivated by calcium during muscle stimulation to allow actin and myosin to react, causing muscle contraction

trypanosomiasis: African sleeping sickness caused by a protozoan that inflames the central nervous system (CNS), spread to humans by the bite of the tsetse fly; or Chagas' disease, which causes a serious cardiomyopathy following the bite of the house fly

tumor: swelling, one of the four cardinal signs of inflammation; caused by the activation of the inflammatory response

tyramine: an amine found in food that causes vasoconstriction and raises blood pressure; ingesting food high in tyramine while on an MAO inhibitor poses the risk of a severe hypertensive crisis

unconsciousness: loss of awareness of one's surroundings

upper respiratory tract: the conducting airways, composed of the nose, mouth, pharynx, larynx, trachea, and the upper bronchial tree

urgency: the feeling that one needs to void immediately, associated with infection and inflammation in the urinary tract

urinary frequency: the need to void often; usually seen in response to irritation of the bladder, age, and inflammation

uterus: the womb; site of the growth and development of the embryo and fetus

vaccine: immunization containing weakened or altered protein antigens to stimulate a specific antibody formation against a specific disease; refers to a product used to stimulate active immunity

veins: vessels that return blood to the heart; distensible tubes

ventilation: the exchange of gases at the alveolar level across the respiratory membrane

ventricle: bottom chamber of the heart, which contracts to pump blood out of the heart

vestibular: referring to the apparatus of the inner ear that controls balance and sense of motion; stimulus to this area can cause motion sickness

virus: particle of DNA or RNA surrounded by a protein coat that survives by invading a cell to alter its functioning

volatile liquid: liquid that is unstable at room temperature and releases vapors; used as an inhaled general anesthetic, generally in the form of a halogenated hydrocarbon

vomiting: complex reflex mediated through the medulla after stimulation of the CTZ; protective reflex to remove possibly toxic substances from the stomach

whipworm: worm that attaches itself to the intestinal mucosa and sucks blood; may cause severe anemia and disintegration of the intestinal mucosa

xanthines: naturally occurring substances, including caffeine and theophylline, that have a direct effect on the smooth muscle of the respiratory tract, both in the bronchi and the blood vessels

APPENDIX A

Parenteral Agents

Parenteral preparations are fluids that are given either intravenously (IV) or through a central line.

THERAPEUTIC ACTIONS AND INDICATIONS

Parenteral agents are used for the following purposes: to provide replacement fluids, sugars, electrolytes, and nutrients to patients who are unable to take these in orally; to provide ready access for administering drugs in an emergency situation; to provide rehydration; and to restore electrolyte balance. The composition of the IV fluids needed for a patient depends on the patient's fluid and electrolyte status. Parenteral nutrition (PN) is the administration of essential proteins, amino acids, carbohydrates, vitamins, minerals, trace elements, lipids, and fluid. PN is used to improve or stabilize the nutritional status of cachectic or debilitated patients who cannot take in or absorb oral nutrition to the extent required to maintain their nutritional status. The exact composition of the PN solution is determined after a nutritional assessment and must take into account the patient's current health status, age, and metabolic needs.

CONTRAINDICATIONS/CAUTIONS

Parenteral nutrition is contraindicated in anyone with known allergies to any component of the solution. (Multiple combination products are available, so a suitable solution may be found.) PN should be used with caution in patients with unstable cardiovascular status because of the change in fluid volume that may occur and the resultant increased workload on the heart. These preparations also should be used with caution in patients with unstable fluid and electrolyte status who could react adversely to sudden changes in the fluids and electrolytes.

ADVERSE EFFECTS

Adverse effects associated with the use of PN include IV irritation, extravasation of the fluid into the tissues, infection of the insertion site, fluid volume overload, vascular problems related to fluid shifts, and potential electrolyte imbalance related to dilution of the blood. PN also is associated with mechanical problems with insertion of the line, such as pneumothorax, infections, or air emboli; emboli related to protein or lipid aggregation; infections related to nutrient-rich solution and invasive administration; metabolic imbalances related to the composition of the solution; gallstone development (especially in children); and nausea (especially related to the administration of lipids).

CLINICALLY IMPORTANT DRUG–DRUG INTERACTIONS

Some IV drugs can only be diluted with particular IV solutions to avoid precipitation or inactivation of the drug. A drug guide should be checked before diluting any IV drug in solution.

NURSING CONSIDERATIONS

Assessment

HISTORY. Obtain a nutritional assessment. Screen for any medical conditions and drugs being taken.

PHYSICAL ASSESSMENT. Evaluate insertion site; skin hydration; orientation and affect; height and weight; pulse, blood pressure, and respirations; blood chemistries, CBC with differential and glucose levels.

Nursing Diagnoses

The patient receiving a parenteral agent may have the following nursing diagnoses related to drug therapy:

- Pain related to administration of the fluid
- Potential for infection related to invasive delivery system
- Alteration in nutrition related to fluid composition
- Knowledge deficit regarding drug therapy

Implementation

- Assess patient's general physical condition before beginning test *to decrease the potential for adverse effects.*
- Monitor IV insertion site or central line regularly; consult with prescriber *to discontinue site of infusion and treat any infection or extravasation as soon as it occurs.*
- Follow these administration guidelines *to provide the most therapeutic use of PN with the fewest adverse effects:*
  - Refrigerate PN solutions until ready to use.
  - Check contents before hanging to ensure that no precipitates are present.
  - Do not hang for longer than 24 hours.
  - Suggest the use of on-line filters to decrease bacterial invasion and infusion of aggregate.
- Discontinue PN only when an alternative source of nutrition has been established *to ensure continued nutrition* for the patient; taper slowly *to avoid severe reactions.*
- Provide comfort measures *to help patient tolerate drug effects* (e.g., provide proper skin care as needed, analgesics, hot soaks to extravasation sites).
- Include information about the solution being used in a test (e.g., what to expect, adverse effects that may occur, follow-up tests that may be needed)

to enhance patient knowledge about drug therapy and promote compliance with drug regimen.

Evaluation

- Monitor patient response to the drug (stabilization of nutritional state; fluid and electrolyte balance and lab values).
- Monitor for adverse effects (local irritation, infection, fluid and electrolyte imbalance).
- Evaluate effectiveness of teaching plan (patient can name adverse effects to watch for, specific measures to avoid adverse effects; patient understands importance of follow-up that will be needed).
- Monitor effectiveness of comfort measures and compliance with regimen.

TABLE A

PARENTERALS

	Caloric Content (calories/L)	Osmolarity (mOsm/L)	Usual Indications
IN SOLUTIONS			
Dextrose Solutions			
2.5% (25 g/L)	85	126	Provide calories and fluid
5% (50 g/L)	170	253	Provide calories and fluid, keep vein open for administration of IV drugs; frequent choice for dilution of IV drugs
10% (100 g/L)	340	505	Hypertonic solution used after admixture with other fluids; provide calories and fluid
20% (200 g/L)	680	1010	Hypertonic solution used after admixture with other fluids; provide calories and fluid
25% (250 g/L)	850	1330	Hypertonic solution used after admixture with other fluids; provide calories and fluid; treatment of acute hypoglycemic episodes in infants to restore glucose levels and suppress symptoms; sclerosing agent for varicose veins
30% (300 g/L)	1020	1515	Hypertonic solution used after admixture with other fluids; provide calories and fluid
40% (400 g/L)	1360	2020	Hypertonic solution used after admixture with other fluids; provide calories and fluid
50% (500 g/L)	1700	2525	Hypertonic solution used after admixture with other fluids; provide calories and fluid; treatment of hyperinsulinemia; sclerosing agent for varicose veins
60% (600 g/L)	2040	3030	Hypertonic solution used after admixture with other fluids; provide calories and fluid
70% (700 g/L)	2380	3535	Hypertonic solution used after admixture with other fluids; provide calories and fluid

	Sodium Content (mEq/L)	Chloride Content (mEq/L)	Osmolarity (mOsm/L)	Usual Indications
Saline Solutions				
0.45% (1/2 normal saline)	77	77	155	Hydrating solution; may be used to evaluate kidney function; treatment of hyperosmolar diabetes
0.9% (normal saline)	154	154	310	Replacement of fluid, sodium, and chloride; flushing lines and catheters; dilution of IV medications; priming of dialysis machines; neonate blood transfusions
3%	513	513	1030	Hypertonic solution to treat sodium and chloride depletion; emergency treatment of water intoxication or severe salt depletion
5%	855	855	1710	Hypertonic solution to treat sodium and chloride depletion; emergency treatment of water intoxication or severe salt depletion

COMMONLY USED COMBINATION FLUIDS

	Na Content (mEq/L)	K Content (mEq/L)	Cl Content (mEq/L)	Ca Content (mEq/L)	Mg Content (mEq/L)	Lactate (mEq/L)	Acetate (mEq/L)	Osmolarity (mOsm/L)
Plasma-Lyte-56	40	13	40	-	3	-	18	111
Ringer's Injection	147	4	156	4	-	-	-	310

TABLE A

PARENTERALS (Continued)

	Na Content (mEq/L)	K Content (mEq/L)	Cl Content (mEq/L)	Ca Content (mEq/L)	Mg Content (mEq/L)	Lactate (mEq/L)	Acetate (mEq/L)	Osmolarity (mOsm/L)
Lactated Ringer's	130	4	109	3	-	28	-	273
Normosol-R	140	5	96	-	3	-	27	295

TYPICAL CENTRAL PARENTERAL NUTRITION SOLUTION—1 LITER

(Actual concentration of solution and components of any particular solution will be determined by the assessment of the patient's current status and nutritional needs.)

Component	Purpose	Dosage	Special considerations
10% amino acids	Provides 50 g protein for growth and healing	500 mL	Monitor BP, cardiac output, blood chemistries, urine to determine effect of intravascular protein pull.
50% dextrose	Provides 850 calories for energy	500 mL	Monitor blood sugar; evaluate injection site for any sign of infection, irritation.
20% fat emulsion	Provides 500 fat calories, ready energy	250 mL	Monitor for any sign of emboli (e.g., shortness of breath, chest pain, deep leg pain, neurological changes). Carefully monitor patients for any sign of increased vascular workload, especially very young and geriatric patients.
sodium chloride	Provides sodium and chloride needed for various chemical reactions within the body	40 mEq	Monitor cardiac rhythm, serum electrolytes.
calcium gluconate	Provides essential calcium for muscle contraction, blood clotting, numerous chemical reactions	4.8 mEq	Monitor cardiac rhythm, muscle strength, serum electrolytes.
magnesium sulfate	Provides magnesium for various chemical reactions within the body	8 mEq	Monitor BP, deep tendon reflexes, and serum electrolytes.
potassium phosphate	Provides needed potassium for nerve functioning, muscle contractions, etc.	9 mMoles	Monitor P, including rhythm, muscle function, and serum electrolytes.
multi-vitamins	Provide a combination of essential vitamins to maintain cell integrity, promote healing	10 mL	Monitor for signs of vitamin deficiency or toxicity.
Trace Elements	Provide small amounts of elements essential for numerous chemical reactions in the body and maintenance of cell integrity and healing		Periodically monitor blood chemistries to determine adequacy of replacement.
zinc		3 mg	
copper		1.2 mg	
manganese		0.3 mg	
chromium		12 mcg	
selenium		20 mcg	

Total non-protein calories: 1350
Total volume of solution: 1250 ml
Dextrose concentration: 25%
Amino acid concentration: 5%
Osmolarity: 1900 mOsm/L

(continued)

TABLE A

PARENTERALS (Continued)

TYPICAL PERIPHERAL PARENTERAL NUTRITION SOLUTION—1 LITER

(Actual concentration of solution and components of any particular solution will be determined by the assessment of the patient's current status and nutritional needs. Solutions used for peripheral therapy are usually less concentrated and less irritating to the vessel.)

Component	Purpose	Dosage	Special Considerations
8.5% amino acids	Provides 41 g protein for growth and healing	500 mL	Monitor BP, cardiac output, blood chemistries, urine to determine effect of intravascular protein pull.
20% dextrose	Provides 340 calories for energy	500 mL	Monitor blood sugar; evaluate injection site for any sign of infection, irritation.
20% fat emulsion	Provides 500 fat calories, ready energy	250 mL	Monitor for any sign of emboli (e.g., shortness of breath, chest pain, deep leg pain, neurological changes). Carefully monitor patients for any sign of increased vascular workload, especially very young and geriatric patients.
sodium chloride	Provides sodium and chloride needed for various chemical reactions within the body	40 mEq	Monitor cardiac rhythm, serum electrolytes.
calcium gluconate	Provides essential calcium for muscle contraction, blood clotting, numerous chemical reactions	4.8 mEq	Monitor cardiac rhythm, muscle strength, serum electrolytes.
magnesium sulfate	Provides magnesium for various chemical reactions within the body	8 mEq	Monitor BP, deep tendon reflexes, and serum electrolytes.
potassium phosphate	Provides needed potassium for nerve functioning, muscle contractions, etc.	9 mMoles	Monitor P, including rhythm, muscle function and serum electrolytes.
multi-vitamins	Provide a combination of essential vitamins to maintain cell integrity, promote healing, etc.	10 mL	Monitor for signs of vitamin deficiency or toxicity.
Trace Elements	Provide small amounts of elements essential for numerous chemical reactions in the body and maintenance of cell integrity and healing.		Periodically monitor blood chemistries to determine adequacy of replacement.
zinc		3 mg	
copper		1.2 mg	
manganese		0.3 mg	
chromium		12 mcg	
selenium		20 mcg	

Total non-protein calories: 840
Total volume of solution: 1250 mL
Dextrose concentration: 10%
Amino acid concentration: 4.25%
Osmolarity: 900 mOsm/L

Note: Multiple combination preparations are available commercially. Each preparation varies in the concentration of one or more components and should be checked carefully before hanging.

APPENDIX B

Diagnostic Agents

Some pharmacological agents are used solely to diagnose particular conditions. Diagnostic tests that use these agents include:

- In vitro tests, which are done outside the body to measure the presence of particular elements (e.g., proteins, blood glucose, bacteria)
- In vivo tests, which introduce drugs into the body to evaluate specific physiologic functions (e.g., cardiac output, intestinal absorption, gastric acid secretion)

THERAPEUTIC ACTIONS AND INDICATIONS

In vitro tests are often performed as part of the nursing evaluation of a patient, or they may be done at home by the patient as part of a medical regimen. These drugs can include reagents that react with specific enzymes or chemicals, such as glucose, blood, or HCG (human chorionic gonadotropin). Drugs used for in vivo tests may stimulate or suppress normal body reactions, such as a glucose challenge to evaluate insulin release or thyroid suppression tests to evaluate thyroid response. Specific tests of blood, urine, or other bodily fluids are often needed to evaluate the body's response to these drugs and to make a diagnosis. Drugs given as part of in vivo tests are administered under the supervision of medical personnel who are either conducting the test or making the diagnosis. They are usually given only once or used over a short period of time. Their use is part of an overall diagnostic plan to determine the underlying source of a particular problem.

CONTRAINDICATIONS/CAUTIONS

The use of any of the in vivo drugs is contraindicated in cases of allergy to the drugs themselves or to the colorants or preservatives used in them. Specific agents may be contraindicated in conditions that could be exacerbated by the stimulation of particular body responses. These drugs should be used cautiously during pregnancy or lactation.

ADVERSE EFFECTS

The adverse effects seen with the use of diagnostic agents are usually associated with the suppression or stimulation of the response they are being used to test. Because these drugs are given only as part of a test, the adverse effects usually last for a short period of time and can usually be tolerated by the patient.

CLINICALLY IMPORTANT DRUG–DRUG INTERACTIONS

Drug interactions vary with the particular agent that is being used. Consult a drug guide for specific information before giving any diagnostic agent.

CLINICALLY IMPORTANT DRUG–FOOD INTERACTIONS

Since these tests are designed to elicit very specific responses, there is often the possibility that food will interfere with the actions or sensitivity of the test. Consult a drug guide for specific information about drug–food interactions before giving any diagnostic agent.

NURSING CONSIDERATIONS

Assessment

HISTORY. Screen for the following: presence of any known allergy to any of these drugs or to the colorants or preservatives used in these drugs.

PHYSICAL ASSESSMENT. Include screening for baseline status before beginning therapy and for any potential adverse effects. Assess the following: skin and mucous membrane condition; orientation, affect, and reflexes; pulse, blood pressure, respirations; abdominal examination; bowel sounds; blood and urine tests are required for the particular test being performed.

Nursing Diagnoses

The patient receiving a diagnostic agent may have the following nursing diagnoses related to drug therapy:

- Pain related to effects of the drugs
- Fear related to the test being done and possible test results
- Alteration in self-concept related to testing procedure and related tests that must be done
- Knowledge deficit regarding drug therapy

Implementation

- Assess patient's general physical condition before beginning test *to decrease the potential for adverse effects.*
- Provide comfort measures *to help patient tolerate drug effects* (e.g., give drug with food to decrease GI upset, provide proper skin care as needed, administer analgesics for headache as appropriate, provide privacy for the collection and storage of urine samples).
- Include information about the drug being used in a test (e.g., what to expect, adverse effects that may

occur, follow-up tests that may be needed) *to enhance patient knowledge about drug therapy and promote compliance with the drug regimen.*

Evaluation

- Monitor patient response to the drug (adverse reactions, collection of diagnostic information).
- Monitor for adverse effects (neurological effects, GI upset, skin reaction, hypoglycemia, constipation).
- Evaluate effectiveness of teaching plan (patient can name adverse effects to watch for, specific measures to avoid adverse effects; patient understands importance of follow-up that will be needed).
- Monitor effectiveness of comfort measures and compliance with regimen.

TABLE B

DIAGNOSTIC AGENTS

IN VITRO TESTS

Test Object	Brand Names	Usual Indication	Special Considerations
acetone	*Acetest* *Chemstrip K* *Ketostix*	Test for ketones in urine, blood, serum, or plasma	Most frequently used to test urine; *Acetest* is the only product that is also used for blood products
albumin	*Albustix* *Chemstrip Micral*	At-home urine test for the presence of proteins	Advise patient to follow product storage instructions
urine bacteria	*Microstix-3* *Uricult* *Isocult for Bacteruria*	Test for urine nitrates, uropathogens, gram-negative bacteria	Most accurate if used with a clean-catch urine sample
bilirubin	*Icotest*	Test for urine bilirubin levels	Most accurate if used with a clean-catch urine sample
blood urea nitrogen	*Azostix*	Estimate of BUN	Used as a reagent strip with whole blood
Candida tests	*Isocult for Candida* *CandidaSure*	Culture paddles or reagent slides for testing vaginal smears	Rapid test for presence of *Candida* with vaginal examination
Chlamydia trachomatis	*Chlamydiazyme* *MicroTrak for Chlamydia* *Sure Cell Chlamydia*	Kits and slides for testing urogenital, rectal, conjunctival, nasopharyngeal specimens for the presence of *Chlamydia*	Kits are specific for testing specimens
cholesterol	*Advanced Care Cholesterol Test*	At-home cholesterol test	Kit includes audio cassette with instructions; patients should be cautioned to seek medical care and advice
glucose, blood	*Chemstrip bG* *Dextrostip* *Glucostix* *Glucometer Elite* *Accu-Check Advantage* and others	At-home testing of blood glucose levels	Patients should be taught how to calibrate the machine, proper blood drawing technique, and importance of seeking follow-up medical care
glucose, urine	*Clinitest* *Clinistix* *Diastix*	At-home testing of urine glucose levels	Patient should be taught how to read strips, proper storage of products and importance of seeking follow-up medical care
gonorrhea	*Biocult-GC* *Gonozyme Diagnostic* *Isocult for Neisseria gonorrhoeae*	Kits, culture paddles for the detection of *Neisseria gonorrhea* on endocervical, rectal, urethral, and oropharyngeal specimens	Test kits containing reagents, preservatives as needed for detection of *Neisseria gonorrhea* during physical examination
mononucleosis	*Mono-Spot* *Mono-Diff* *Mono-Sure* and others	Kits, reagents, slides for the testing of serum, blood for mononucleosis	Rapid tests for suspected cases of mononucleosis; all necessary reagents and preservatives included in kit
occult blood	*ColoCare* *EZ Detect* *Hemoocult II* and others	Kits and slides for the testing of fecal swabs for the presence of occult blood	Card forms can be used by patients at home in routine screening programs
ovulation	*Answer* *OvuQuick Self-Test* *First Response Ovulation Detector* and others	Kits to determine the levels of LH in the urine as a predictor of ovulation	Used at home by patients as part of fertility programs; patients may need instruction
pregnancy	*Advance First Response Pregnosis* and others	Kits or urine strips to detect the presence of HCG (human chorionic gonadotropin) as a predictor of pregnancy	May be used at home; patients may need instruction and should be advised to seek follow-up medical care

TABLE B
DIAGNOSTIC AGENTS (Continued)

Test Object	Brand Names	Usual Indication	Special Considerations
rheumatoid factor	*Rheumatrex* *Rheumaton*	Slide tests for the presence of rheumatoid factor in blood, serum, or synovial fluid	An aid in the diagnosis of auto-immune diseases
sickle cell	*Sickledex*	Kit for the testing of blood for the presence of hemoglobin S	Diagnostic for sickle cell anemia
streptococci	*Sure Cell Streptococci* *Culturette 10 Minute Group A Strep ID* *Bactigen Strep B* and others	Kits, slides, culture paddles for the identification of streptococcal infection in blood, serum, urine, throat, cerebrospinal fluid	Early detection of streptococcal infection to facilitate beginning of treatment before culture and sensitivity results are known

IN VIVO TESTS

Drug	Brand Names	Usual Indication	Special Considerations
aminohippurate	*PAH* *Aminohippurate Sodium*	Estimation of renal plasma flow and to measure the functional capacity of the renal secretory mechanism	Injected as a 20% aqueous solution; requires careful urine collection
arbutamine	*GenESA*	Diagnosis of CAD in patients who cannot exercise adequately	Causes stress to evaluate body response; must be given with its own delivery device
arginine	*R-Gene 10*	Diagnostic aid to assess pituitary reserve of growth hormone	IV infusion, followed by blood tests to monitor response
bentiromide	*Chymex*	Diagnosis of pancreatic exocrine insufficiency	Given orally following overnight fast and bladder emptying; carefully collect urine for evaluation
benzylpenicilloyl-polylysine	*Pre-Pen*	Skin test to evaluate sensitivity to penicillin and safety of administering penicillin in potentially sensitive individuals	Intradermal or scratch test is used; positive reaction is usually seen within 10–15 minutes
d-xylose	*Xylo-Pan*	Evaluation of intestinal absorption; diagnosis of malabsorptive states	Available over-the-counter for pre-examination use; oral
gonadorelin	*Factrel*	Evaluation of gonadotropic capacity of the pituitary gland	Given IV or SC; monitor closely for potential hypersensitivity reactions
histamine phosphate	*Histamine-Phosphate*	SC—to evaluate ability of gastric mucosa to produce HCl IV—diagnosis of pheochromocytoma	May cause severe symptoms, including shock, cardiovascular collapse, even death; monitor patient closely
indocyanine green	*Cardio-Green*	Determining cardiac output, hepatic function, liver blood flow; also used for ophthalmic angiography	Use caution with known allergy to dyes
inulin	*Inulin Injection*	Measurement of glomerular filtration rate	Requires blood tests and urine collection
methacholine chloride	*Provocholine*	Diagnosis of bronchial airway hypersensitivity in patients without documented asthma	Inhaled with pulmonary function test immediately; may cause hypotension, chest pain, GI upset
pentagastrin	*Peptavlon*	Evaluation of gastric acid secretory function	Given SC; may cause abdominal pain, flushing, nausea, vomiting, diarrhea, tachycardia
protirelin	*Thypinone* *Relefact TRH*	Diagnosis and assessment of thyroid function	Given IV over 15–30 seconds; patient should remain supine for at least 15 minutes because of risk of hypotension
secretin	*Secretin-Kabi*	Diagnosis of pancreatic exocrine disease Diagnosis of gastrinoma	Requires a 12–15-hour fast; passing of a radiopaque tube for pancreatic function or repeated blood samples for gastrinoma diagnosis
sermorelin	*Geref*	Evaluation of pituitary ability to secrete growth hormone	Single IV injection; follow-up blood tests will be needed to determine response

(continued)

TABLE B

DIAGNOSTIC AGENTS (Continued)

Drug	Brand Names	Usual Indication	Special Considerations
sodium iodide	*Sodium Iodide I[123]*	Diagnosis of thyroid function or morphology	Handle with care; oral capsules are radioactive, dispose of properly; thyroid can be evaluated for radiation content within 6 hours of dose
thyrotropin	*Thytropar*	Differentiation of thyroid function to estimate thyroid reserve	Given IM or SC qd for 10 days; follow with radioactive iodine test—no response shows thyroid failure
tolutamide	*Orinase Diagnostic*	Diagnosis of pancreatic islet cell adenoma	Given IV after 3 days of high-carbohydrate diet; prepare to support patient if severe hypoglycemia occurs

APPENDIX C

Topical Agents

Topical agents are intended for surface use only and are not meant for ingestion or injection. They may be toxic if absorbed into the system, but have several useful purposes when applied to the surface of the skin or mucous membranes. Some forms of drugs are prepared to be absorbed through the skin for systemic effects. These drugs may be prepared as transdermal patches (e.g., nitroglycerin, estrogens, nicotine), which are designed to provide a slow release of the drug from the vehicle. Drugs prepared for this type of administration are discussed with the specific drug in the text and are not addressed in this appendix.

THERAPEUTIC ACTIONS AND INDICATIONS

Topical agents are used to treat a variety of disorders in a localized area. Table C describes the usual use for the many different types of topical agents.

CONTRAINDICATIONS/CAUTIONS

The use of topical agents is contraindicated in cases of allergy to the drugs and in the presence of open wounds or abrasions, which could lead to the systemic absorption of the drugs. Caution should be used during pregnancy if there is any possibility that the agent might be absorbed. Caution should also be used in the presence of any known allergy to the vehicles of preparation (creams, lotions).

ADVERSE EFFECTS

Because these drugs are not intended to be absorbed systemically, the adverse effects usually associated with topical agents are local effects, including local irritation, stinging, burning, or dermatitis. Toxic effects are associated with inadvertent systemic absorption.

NURSING CONSIDERATIONS

Assessment

HISTORY. Screen for the presence of any known allergy to drugs.

PHYSICAL ASSESSMENT. Include screening for baseline status before beginning therapy and for any potential adverse effects. Assess the following: condition of area to be treated.

Nursing Diagnoses

The patient receiving a topical agent may have the following nursing diagnoses related to drug therapy:

- Potential for injury related to toxic effects associated with absorption
- Pain related to local effects of the drug
- Knowledge deficit regarding drug therapy

Implementation

- Ensure proper administration of drug *to provide best therapeutic effect and least adverse effects* as follows:
  - Apply sparingly. Some preparations come with applicators, some should be applied while wearing protective gloves, and others are dropped onto the site with no direct contact. Consult information regarding the individual drug being used for specifics.
  - Do not use with open wounds or broken skin.
  - Avoid contact with the eyes.
  - Do not use with occlusive dressings, which could increase the risk of systemic absorption.
- Monitor area being treated *to evaluate drug effects on condition being treated.*
- Provide comfort measures *to help patient tolerate drug effects* (e.g., analgesia as needed for local pain, itching).
- Provide patient teaching *to enhance patient knowledge about drug therapy and promote compliance with drug regimen:*
  - Teach the patient the proper administration technique for the topical agent ordered.
  - Caution patient that transient stinging or burning may occur.
  - Instruct patient to report severe irritation, allergic reaction, or worsening of the condition being treated.

Evaluation

- Monitor patient response to the drug (improvement in condition being treated).
- Monitor for adverse effects (local stinging or inflammation).
- Evaluate effectiveness of teaching plan (patient can name drug, dosage, adverse effects to watch for, specific measures to avoid adverse effects; patient understands importance of continued follow-up).
- Monitor effectiveness of comfort measures and compliance with regimen.

TABLE C

TOPICAL AGENTS

Drug	Brand Name(s)	Dosage	Usual Indication/ Special Considerations
EMOLLIENTS			
boric acid ointment	*Borofax*	Apply as needed	Relieves burns, itching, irritation.
dexpanthenol	*Panthoderm*	Apply qd–bid	Relieves itching and aids in healing for mild skin irritations.
glycerin	generic	Combined with other ingredients—rose water	Moisturizing effect for dry skin.
lanolin		Ointment base, applied generously	Allergy to sheep or sheep products—use caution; base for many ointments.
urea	*Aquacare* *Nutraplus* *Carmol* *Gormel* *Lanaphilic* *Ureacin* *Gordon's Urea*	2–4 times/day to area affected	Rub in completely. Used to restore nails—cover with plastic wrap; keep dry and remove in 3, 7, or 14 days.
vitamin A & D		Apply locally with gentle massage bid–qid.	Relieves minor burns, chafing, skin irritations. Consult health care provider if not improved within 7 days.
zinc oxide		Apply as needed	Relieves burns, abrasion, diaper rash.
GROWTH FACTOR			
becaplermin	*Regranax Gel*	Apply to diabetic foot ulcers bid–qid	Increases the incidence of healing of diabetic foot ulcers as adjunctive therapy; must have an adequate blood supply.
LOTIONS AND SOLUTIONS			
Burow's solution aluminum acetate	*Bluboro Powder* *Buropak Powder* *Domeboro Powder* *Pedi-Boro Soak Paks*	Dissolve one packet in a pint of water; apply q15–30 min for 4–8h	Astringent wet dressing for relief of inflammatory conditions, insect bites, athlete's foot, bruise, sores; do not use occlusive dressing.
calamine lotion	*Calamax* *Resinol* *Calamatum*	Apply to affected area tid–qid	Relieves itching, pain of poison ivy, poison sumac and oak, insect bites, and minor skin irritations.
hamamelis water	*Witch Hazel* *Tucks* *A-E-R*	Apply locally up to 6 times/day	Relieves itching and irritation of vaginal infection, hemorrhoids, postepisiotomy discomfort, post hemorrhoidectomy care.
quaternium-18 bentonite	*Ivy Block*	Apply at least 15 minutes before exposure to poison ivy; q4h for continued protection	Barrier lotion to prevent poison ivy/sumac/oak reactions.
ANTISEPTICS			
benzalkonium chloride	*BAC* *Benza* *Zephiran*	Mix in solution as needed; spray for preoperative	Thoroughly rinse detergents and soaps from skin before use; add anti-rust tablets for instruments stored in solution; dilute solution as indicated for use.
chlorhexidine gluconate	*Hibiclens* *Dyna-Hex* *Exidine ibistat*	Scrub or rinse; leave on for 15 seconds; for surgical scrub—3 minutes	Use for surgical scrub, preoperative skin preparation, wound cleansing; preoperative bathing and showering.
hexachlorphene	*pHisoHex* *Septisol*	Apply as wash	Surgical wash, scrub; do not use with burns or on mucous membranes; rinse thoroughly.
iodine	generic	Wash affected area	Highly toxic; avoid occlusive dressings; stains skin and clothing. Iodine allergy is common.
povidone iodine	*Betadine* *Aerodine* *ACU-dyne* *Betagen* *Iodex*	Apply as needed	Treated areas may be bandaged. HIV is inactivated in this solution; causes less irritation than iodine; less toxic.
sodium hypochlorite	*Dakin's*	Apply as antiseptic	Caution—chemical burns can occur.

TABLE C

TOPICAL AGENTS (Continued)

Drug	Brand Name(s)	Dosage	Usual Indication/ Special Considerations
thimersol	*Mersol* *Aerouid*	Apply qd–bid	Contains mercury compound; used preoperatively and as first aid for abrasions, wounds.
mupirocin	*Bactroban*	Apply small amount to affected area tid	Used to treat impetigo caused by *S. aureus, Streptococcus, S. pathogens;* may be covered with a gauze pad; monitor for signs of superinfection, reevaluate if not clinical response in 3–5 days.
imiquimod	*Aldara*	Apply thin layer to warts and rub in 3×/wk at bedtime for 16 wk	For treatment of genital warts and perianal warts; remove with soap and water after 6–10 hours.
penciclovir	*Denavir*	Apply thin layer to affected area q2h while awake for 4 d	Treatment of cold sores in healthy patients; begin use at first sign of cold sore. Reserve use for herpes labialis on lips and face; avoid mucous membranes.
ammoniated mercury	*Emersal*	Apply qd–bid	Protect from light; potential sensitizer provoking severe allergic reactions.
anthralin	*Anthra-Derm* *Lasan*	Apply qd only to psoriatic lesions	May stain fabrics, skin, hair, fingernails; use protective dressing.
calcipotriene	*Dritocreme* *Dovonex*	Apply thin layer twice a day	Monitor serum calcium levels with extended use; use only for disorder prescribed; may cause local irritation; is a synthetic vitamin D_3.
selenium sulfide	*Selsun Blue* *Exsel*	Massage 5–10 ml into scalp; rest 2–3 minutes, rinse	May damage jewelry, remove before use; discontinue if local irritation occurs.
chloroxine	*Capitrol*	Massage into wet scalp; leave lather on for 3 minutes	May discolor blond, gray, bleached hair. Do not use on active lesions.
butenafine HCl	*Mentax*	Apply to affected area only once a day for 4 weeks	Treatment of athlete's foot (intradigital pedia), tinea corporis, ringworm, tinea cruris.
butoconazole	*Femstat* *Femstat One*	Apply intravaginally hs for 3–6 days	Treatment of vaginal yeast infections; culture fungus, if no response, reculture. Ensure full course of therapy.
clotrimazole	*Lotrimin* *Mycelex*	Gently massage into affected area bid	Cleanse area before applying; use for up to 4 weeks. Discontinue if irritation, worsening of condition occurs.
econozole nitrate	*Spectazole*	Apply locally qd–bid	Treatment of athlete's foot (intradigital pedia), tinea corporis, ringworm, tinea cruris; cleanse area before applying; treat for 2–4 weeks; for athlete's foot, change socks and shoes at least once a day.
gentian violet	generic	Apply locally bid	May stain skin and clothing; do not apply to active lesions.
naftitine HCl	*Naftin*	Gently massage into affected area bid	Avoid occlusive dressings; wash hands thoroughly after application. Do not use longer than 4 weeks.
oxiconazole	*Oxistat*	Apply qd–bid	May be needed for up to 1 month.
terbinafine	*Lamisil*	Apply to area bid until clinical signs are improved; 1–4 weeks	Do not use occlusive dressings; report local irritation; discontinue if local irritation occurs.
tolnaftate	*Tinactin* *Genaspor* *Ting* *Aftate*	Apply small amount bid for 2–3 weeks, 4–6 weeks may be needed if skin is very thick	Cleanse skin with soap and water before applying drug, dry thoroughly; wear loose, well-fitting shoes; change socks at least qid.
PEDICULOCIDES/SCABICIDES			
lindane	*G-Well* *Scabene*	Apply thin layer to entire body; leave on 8–12 hours wash thoroughly; shampoo 1–2 oz into dry hair and leave in place for 4 minutes	Single application is usually sufficient; reapply after 7 days at signs of live lice. Teach hygiene and prevention; treat all contacts. Assure parents this is a readily communicable disease.

(continued)

TABLE C

TOPICAL AGENTS (Continued)

Drug	Brand Name(s)	Dosage	Usual Indication/ Special Considerations
crotamiton	*Eurax*	Thoroughly massage into skin over entire body, repeat in 24 hours. Take a cleansing bath or shower 48 hours after last application	Change all bed linens and clothing the next day. Contaminated clothing can be dry cleaned or washed in hot water. Shake well before using.
permethrin	*Elimite* Nix	Thoroughly massage into all skin areas; wash off after 8–14 hours. Shampoo into freshly washed, rinsed, and towel-dried hair, leave on for 10 minutes, rinse	Single application is usually curative. Notify health care provider if rash, itch becomes worse. Approved for prophylactic use during head lice epidemics.
KERATOLYTICS			
cantharidin		Apply to lesion; cover with tape; remove in 24 hours	Replace tape with loose bandage; may cause itching and burning; may be tender for 2–6 days; if spilled on skin, wipe off with acetone or tape remover; if contacts eyes, flush immediately and contact physician.
podophyllium resin	*Pod-Ben-25* *Podocon-25* *Podofin*	Applied only by physician	Do not use if wart is inflamed or irritated. Very toxic; minimum amount possible is used to avoid absorption.
podofilox	*Condylox*	Apply q12h for 3 consecutive days	Allow to dry before using area; dispose of used applicator; may cause burning and discomfort.
TOPICAL HEMOSTATICS			
absorbable gelatin	*Gelfoam*	Smear or press to cut surface; when bleeding stops, remove excess. Apply sponge and allow to remain in place; will be absorbed	Prepare paste by adding 3–4 mL sterile saline to contents of jar. Apply sponge dry or saturated with saline. Assess for signs of infection. Do not use in presence of infection.
microfibrillar collagen	*Avitene*	Use dry. Apply directly to source of bleeding, apply pressure for 3–5 minutes. Discard leftover product.	Monitor for infection. Remove any excess material once bleeding has stopped.
thrombin	*Thrombinar* *Thrombostat*	Prepare in Sterile Distilled Water. Mix freely with blood on the surface of the injury	Contraindicated in the presence of any bovine allergies. Watch for severe allergic reactions in sensitive individuals.
TOPICAL WOUND DRESSING			
skin collagen	*Apligraf*	Used as a dressing in conjunction with standard dressing	Bilayered skin construct from bovine collagen and human infant foreskins. Enhances wound healing in skin ulcers caused by venous insufficiency.
PAIN RELIEF			
capsaicin	*Zostrix*	Do not apply more than 3–4 ×/day	Provides temporary relief from the pain of osteoarthritis, rheumatoid arthritis, neuralgias. Do not bandage tightly. Stop use and seek medical help if condition worsens or persists after 14–28 days.
BURN PREPARATIONS			
mafenide	*Sulfamylon*	Apply to a clean, debrided wound, 1–2 ×/day burns at all times with drug; reapply as needed	Bathe patient in a whirlpool daily to debride wound. Continue debridement with a gloved hand. Cover. Continue until healing occurs. Monitor for infection and toxicity, especially acidosis. May cause severe discomfort requiring premedication before application.

TABLE C

TOPICAL AGENTS (Continued)

Drug	Brand Name(s)	Dosage	Usual Indication/ Special Considerations
nitrofurazone	*Furacin*	Apply directly to burn or place on gauze; reapply qd	Flushing the dressing with sterile water will facilitate removal. Monitor for superinfections and treat appropriately. Rash is common.
silver sulfadiazine	*Silvadene* *Thermazene*	Apply qd–bid to a clean, debrided wound; use 1/16-inch thickness	Bathe patient in a whirlpool to aid debridement. Dressings are not necessary but may be used; reapply when necessary. Monitor for fungal infections.
ESTROGENS			
dienestrol	*DV* *Ortho Dienestrol*	1–2 applicators intravaginally for 1–2 weeks; reduce to 1/2 initial dose for 1–2 weeks maintenance dose 1 applicator 1–3x/week	Treatment of postmenopausal atrophic vaginitis and kraurosis vulvae. Lie down for 15 minutes after dose; wear a pad to protect clothing.
ACNE PRODUCTS			
adapalene	*Differin*	Apply a thin film to affected area after washing	Do not use near cuts or open wounds; avoid sunburned areas; do not combine with other products; limit exposure to the sun. Less drying than most acne products.
azelaic acid	*Azelex*	Wash and dry skin; massage thin layer into skin bid	Wash hands thoroughly after application. Improvement usually seen within 4 weeks. Initial irritation usually passes with time.
metronidazole	*Noritate*	Apply cream to affected area	Treatment of rosacea.
sodium sulfacetamide	*Klaron*	Apply a thin film bid	Wash affected area with mild soap and water, pat dry. Avoid use in denuded or abraded areas.
tarazotene	*Tazorac*	Apply thin film qd in the evening	Avoid use in pregnancy. Drying, causes photosensitivity. Do not use with products containing alcohol.
tretinoin, 0.025% cream	*Avita*	Apply thin layer qd	Discomfort, peeling, redness and worsening of acne may occur for first 2–4 weeks.
tretinoin, gel	*Retin-A micro*	Apply to cover qd, after cleansing	Exacerbation of inflammation may occur at first. Therapeutic effects usually seen in first 2 weeks.
MOUTH PRODUCTS			
amlexanox	*Aphthasol*	Apply to aphthous ulcers qid after meals and hs, following oral hygiene; for 10 days	Consult with dentist if ulcers are not healed within 10 days. May cause local pain.
ANTIADHESION AGENT			
sodium hyaluronidase and carboxymethycellulose	*Seprafilm*	Placed during open abdominal or pelvic surgery to reduce the occurrence and extent of postoperative adhesion	Turns to gel within 24–48 hours, resorbed within 1 week, excreted within 28 days. Monitor for abscess formation and pulmonary emboli.
ANTIHISTAMINE			
azelastine HCl	*Astelin*	2 sprays per nostril bid	Avoid use of alcohol and OTC antihistamines; dizziness and sedation may occur.
NASAL CORTICOSTEROID			
fluticonosone	*Flonase* *Flovent* *Flovent Rotodisk*	Adult: 88–440 mcg intranasal bid; lower dose if also on corticosteroids Pediatric: 500–600 mcg bid via rotodisk	Preventive treatment for asthma, not a primary treatment. May take several weeks to see effects. Pediatric use for children 4–11 years.

(continued)

TABLE C

TOPICAL AGENTS (Continued)

Drug	Brand Name	Preparation	Special Considerations
TOPICAL CORTICOSTEROIDS			
These drugs enter cells and bind to cytoplasmic receptors, initiating complex reactions that are responsible for the anti-inflammatory, anti-pruritic, and anti-proliferative effects of these drugs. They are used to relieve the inflammation and pruritic manifestations of corticosteroid-sensitive dermatoses and for temporary relief of minor skin irritations and rashes. These agents should always be applied sparingly because of the risk of systemic corticosteroid effects if absorbed systemically. Occlusive dressings and tight coverings should be avoided. Prolonged use should also be avoided because of the risk of systemic effects and local irritation and breakdown. These agents are applied topically bid–tid.			
alclometasone dipropionate	*Aclovate*	Ointment, cream: 0.05% concentration	Occlusive dressings may be used for the management of refractory lesions of psoriasis and deep-seated dermatoses.
amcinonide	*Cyclocort*	Ointment, cream, lotion: 0.1% concentration	
betamethasone benzoate	*Uticort*	Cream, lotion, gel: 0.025% concentration	
betamethasone dipropionate	*Alphatres, Diprosone, Maxivate, Teledar*	Ointment, cream, lotion, aerosol: 0.05% concentration	
betamethasone dipropionate, augmented	*Diprolene*	Ointment, cream, lotion: 0.05% concentration	
betamethasone valerate	*Betatrex, Beta-Val, Dermabet, Valisone*	Ointment, cream, lotion: 0.1% concentration	
clobetasol propionate	*Temovate*	Ointment, cream: 0.05% concentration	
clocortolone pivalate	*Cloderm*	Cream: 0.1% concentration	
desonide	*DesOwen, Tridesiolon*	Ointment, cream: 0.05% concentration	
desoximetasone	*Topicort*	Ointment, cream: 0.25% concentration Gel: 0.05% concentration	
dexamethasone	*Decaderm*	Gel: 0.1% concentration	
	Aeroseb-Dex	Aerosol: 0.01% concentration	
	Decaspray	Aerosol: 0.04% concentration	
dexamethasone sodium phosphate	*Decadron phosphate*	Cream: 0.1% concentration	
diflorasone diacetate	*Florone, Maxiflor, Psorcon Florone E*	Ointment, cream: 0.05% concentration Cream: 0.5% concentration	
fluocinolone acetonide	*Flurosyn, Synalar*	Ointment: 0.025% concentration Cream: 0.01% concentration	
	Flurosyn, Synalar, Synemol	Cream: 0.025% concentration	
	Fluonid, Flurosyn, Synalar	Solution: 0.01% concentration	
fluocinonide	*Lidex*	Ointment: 0.05% concentration	
	Fluonex, Lidex, Vasoderm	Cream: 0.05% concentration	
	Lidex	Solution, gel: 0.05% concentration	
flurandrenolide	*Cordran*	Ointment, cream: 0.025% concentration Ointment, cream, lotion: 0.05% concentration Tape: 4 mcg/cm^2	
fluticasone propionate	*Cutivate*	Cream: 0.05% concentration Ointment: 0.005% concentration	
halcinonide	*Halog*	Ointment, cream, solution: 0.1% concentration Cream: 0.025% concentration	
halobetasol propionate	*Ultravate*	Ointment, cream: 0.05% concentration	
hydrocortisone	*Cortizone 5, Bactine Hydrocortisone, Cort-Dome, Dermolate, Dermtex HC, Hydrotex*	Lotion: 0.25%	
	Cortizone 10, Hycort, Tegrin-HC	Cream, lotion, ointment, aerosol: 0.5%, 1% concentration	
	Hytone	Cream, lotion, ointment, solution: 1% concentration	

TABLE C

TOPICAL AGENTS (Continued)

Drug	Brand Name	Preparation	Special Considerations
hydrocortisone acetate	*Cortaid, Lanacort-5*	Ointment: 0.5% concentration (OTC preparations)	
	Corticaine (R_x), FoilleCort, Gynecort, Lanacort 5	Cream: 0.5% concentration (OTC preparations)	
	Anusol-HC, U-Cort	Cream: 1% concentration	
	Caldecort, Cortaid with Aloe	Cream: 0.5%, 1% concentration (OTC preparation)	
	CortaGel	Gel: 0.5% concentration (OTC preparation)	
hydrocortisone butyrate	*Locoid*	Ointment, cream: 0.1% concentration	
hydrocortisone valerate	*Westcort*	Ointment, cream: 0.2% concentration	
mometasone furoate	*Elocon*	Ointment, cream, lotion: 0.1% concentration	
prednicarbate	*Dermatop*	Cream: 0.1% concentration: preservative free	
triamcinolone acetonide	*Flutex, Kenalog*	Ointment: 0.025% concentration	
	Aristocort, Flutex, Kenalog	Ointment: 0.1% concentration and 0.5% concentration	
	Aristocort, Flutex, Kenalog, Triacet, Triderm	Cream: 0.025% concentration and 0.5% concentration	
		Cream: 0.1% concentration	
	Kenalog	Lotion: 0.025% and 0.1% concentration	

APPENDIX C-1

Canadian Drug Information

Following is a list of Canadian brand or trade names for frequently used drugs. The brand name appears in *italics* with the corresponding generic name listed in parentheses.

A

Abenol (acetaminophen)
Acet-Amp (theophylline)
Acilac (lactulose)
Acti-B (hydroxocobalamin)
Actiprofen (ibuprofen)
Aerosporin (polymyxin B)
Albert Glyburide (glyburide)
Albert Oxybutynin (oxybutynin)
Alcomicin (gentamicin)
Allerdryl (diphenhydramine)
Acyclovir (acyclovir)
Alti-Diltiazem (diltiazem)
Alti-Doxepin (doxepin)
Alti-Ibuprofen (ibuprofen)
Alti-Ipratropium (ipratropium)
Alti-Minocycline (minocycline)
Alti-MPA (medroxyprogesterone)
Alti-Nadolol (nadolol)
Alti-Piroxicam (piroxicam)
Alti-Ranitidine (ranitidine)
Alti-Sulfasalazine (sulfasalazine)
Alti-Trazadone (trazodone)
Alti-Triazolam (triazolam)
Alti-Valproic (valproic acid)
Amatine (midodrine)
Ampicin (ampicilline)
Anandron (nilutamide)
Anapolon (oxymetholone)
Anexate (flumazenil)
Anturan (sulfinpyrazone)
Apo-Acetazolamide (acetazolamide)
Apo-Allopurinol (allopurinol)
Apo-Alpraz (alprazolam)
Apo-Amoxi (amoxicillin)
Apo-Ampi (ampicillin)
Apo-Asa (aspirin)
Apo-Atenol (atenolol)
Apo-Baclofen (baclofen)
Apo-Benztropine (benztropine)
Apo-Bromocriptine (bromocriptine)
Apo-Cal (calcium carbonate)
Apo-Capto (captopril)
Apo-Carbamazepine (carbamazepine)
Apo-Ceclor (cefaclor)
Apo-Cephalex (cephalexin)
Apo-Chlorodiazepoxide (chlordiazepoxide)
Apo-Chlorpropamide (chlorpropamide)
Apo-Chlorthalidone (chlorthalidone)
Apo-Cimetidine (cimetidine)
Apo-Clomipramine (clomipramine)
Apo-Clonazepam (clonazepam)
Apo-Clonidine (clonidine)
Apo-Clorazepate (clorazepate)
APO-Cloxi (cloxacillin)
Apo-Cyclobenzaprine (cyclobenzaprine)
Apo-Desipramine (desipramine)
Apo-Diazepam (diazepam)
Apo-Diflunisal (diflunisal)
Apo-Diltiaz (diltiazem)
Apo-Diltiazem (diltiazem)
Apo-Dimenhydrinate (dimenhydrinate)
Apo-Dipyridamole (dipyridamole)
Apo-Doxepin (doxepin)
Apo-Doxy (doxycycline)
Apo-Erythro (erythromycin)
Apo-Erythro EES (erythromycin)
Apo-Erythro-S (erythromcyin)
Apo-Famotidine (famotidine)
Apo-Ferrous Gluconate (ferrous gluconate)
Apo-Ferrous Sulfate (ferrous sulfate)
Apo-Fluoxetine (fluoxetine)
Apo-Fluphenazine (fluphenazine)
Apo-Flurbiprofen (flurbiprofen)
Apo-Fluvoxamine (fluvoxamine)
Apo-Furosemide (furosemide)
Apo-Gemfibrozil (gemfibrozil)
Apo-Haloperidol (haloperidol)
Apo-Hydralazine (hydralazine)
Apo-Hydro (hydrochlorothiazide)
Apo-Hydroxyzine (hydroxyzine)
Apo-Ibuprofen (ibuprofen)
Apo-Imipramine (imipramine)
Apo-Indomethacin (indomethacin)
Apo-Ipravent (ipratropium)
Apo-ISDN (isosorbide dinitrate)
Apo-K (potassium chloride)
Apo-Lisinopril (lisinopril)
Apo-Loperamide (loperamide)
Apo-Lorazepam (lorazepam)
Apo-Lovastatin (lovastatin)
Apo-Mefenamic (mefenamic acid)
Apo-Megestrol (megestrol)
Apo-Meprobamate (meprobamate)
Apo-Metoclop (metoclopramide)
Apo-Metoprolol (metoprolol)
Apo-Metronidazole (metronidazole)
Apo-Nadolol (nadolol)
Apo-Napro-Na (naproxen)
Apo-Naproxen (naproxen)
Apo-Nifed (nifedipine)
Apo-Nitrofurantoin (nitrofurantoin)

Apo-Nizataidine (nizatidine)
Apo-Nortriptyline (nortriptyline)
Apo-Oxazepam (oxazepam)
Apo-Oxtriphylline (oxtriphylline)
Apo-Oxybutynin (oxybutynin)
Apo-Perphenazine (perphenazine)
Apo-Pindol (pindolol)
Apo-Piroxicam (piroxicam)
Apo-Prazo (prazosin)
Apo-Prednisone (prednisone)
Apo-Primidone (primidone)
Apo-Procainamide (procainamide)
Apo-Propranolol (propranolol)
Apo-Quinidine (quinidine)
Apo-Sotalol (sotalol)
Apo-Sucralfate (sucralfate)
Apo-Sulfinpyrazone (sulfinpyrazone)
Apo-Sulin (sulindac)
Apo-Tamox (tamoxifen)
Apo-Temazepam (temazepam)
Apo-Tetra (tetracycline)
Apo-Thioridazine (thioridazine)
Apo-Timol (timolol)
Apo-Tolbutamide (tolbutamide)
Apo-Trazadone (trazodone)
Apo-Triazo (triazolam)
Apo-Trifluoperazine (trifluoperazine)
Apo-Trihex (trihexyphenidyl)
Apo-Trimip (trimipramine)
Apo-Zidovudine (zidovudine)
Aquacort (hydrocortisone)
Asmavent (albuterol)
Atasol (acetaminophen)
Avirax (acyclovir)
Avlosulfan (dapsone)
Ayercillin (penicillin G procaine)

B

Bacitin (bacitracin)
Balminin DM (dextromethorphan)
Barbilixir (phenobarbital)
Barbita (phenobarbital)
Beclodisk (beclomethasone)
Beclovent Rotocaps (beclomethasone)
Benemid (probenecid)
Bentylol (dicyclomine)
Benuryl (probenecid)
Bepadin (bepridil)
Bepen (betamethasone)
Betabloc (metoprolol)
Betacort (betamethasone)
Betaderm (betamethasone)
Beta-Tim (timolol)
Betnesol (betamethasone)
Betnovate (betamethasone)
Bonamine (meclizine)
Bretylate (bretylium)
Bronalide (flunisolide)
Burinex (bumetanide)
Busodium (butabarbital)
Butalan (butabarbital)

C

Calcite (calcium carbonate)
Calsan (calcium carbonate)
Caltine (calcitonin, salmon)
Candistatin (nystatin)
Canesten (clotrimazole)
Canesten Vaginal (clotrimazole)
Carbolith (lithium)
Cedocard SR (isosorbide dinitrate)
Celestoderm (betamethasone)
C.E.S. (estrogens, conj.)
Charcolate (charcoal)
Chlorprom (chlorpromazine)
Chlorpromanyl (chlorpromazine)
Chlor-Tripolon (chlorpheniramine)
Cibalith-S (lithium)
Ciloxin (ciprofloxacin)
Citro-Mag (magnesium citrate)
Claripex (clofibrate)
Clinda-Derm (clindamycin)
Clonapam (clonazepam)
Clotrimaderm (clotrimazole)
Combantrin (pyrantel)
Congest (estrogens, conj.)
Corax (chlordiazepoxide)
Creon (pancrelipase)
Crysticillin-AS (penicillin G procaine)
Cyclomen (danazol)

D

Dalacin C (clindamycin)
Dehydral (methenamine)
Deproic (valproic acid)
Dermovate (clobetasol)
Diarr-Eze (loperamide)
Diazemuls (diazepam)
Digess (pancrelipase)
Dihydroergotamine Sandoz (dihydroergotamine)
Dimelor (acetohexamide)
Diodoquin (iodoquinol)
Diomycin (erythromycin)
Dioptic's Atropine (atropine)
Diphenylan (phenytoin)
Dipridacot (dipyridamole)
Dixarit (clonidine)
Dopamet (methyldopa)
Doxytec (doxycycline)

Drixoral Cough Liquid Caps (dextromethorphan)
Duralith (lithium)
Duretic (methyclothiazide)
D-Vert (meclizine)

E

Eltor (pseudoephedrine)
Endantadine (amantadine)
Entocort (budenoside)
Entrophen (aspirin)
Epimorph (morphine)
Epival (valproic acid)
Eprex (epoetin)
Ergomar (ergotamine)
Erybid (erythromycin)
Erythrocin (erythromycin)
Erythrocin I.V. (erythromycin)
Erythromid (erythromycin)
Estromed (estrogens, esterified)
Etibi (ethambutol)
Euflex (flutamide)
Euglucon (glyburide)

F

Falapen (penicillin G potassium)
Ferodan (ferrous salts)
Fero-Grad (ferrous salts)
Fertinorm HP (urofollitropin)
Fluor-A-Day (sodium fluoride)
Fluotic (sodium fluoride)
Formulex (dicyclomine)
Froben (flurbiprofen)
Froben-SR (flurabiprofen)
Furoside (furosemide)

G

Gen-Amantadine (amantadine)
Gen-Atenolol (atenolol)
Gen-Baclofen (baclofen)
Gen-Captopril (captopril)
Gen-Cimetidine (cimetidine)
Gen-Clomipramine (clomipramine)
Gen-Clonazepam (clonazepam)
Gen-Diltiazem (diltiazem)
Gen-Fibro (gemfibrozil)
Gen-Glybe (glyburide)
Gen-Medroxy (medroxyprogesterone)
Gen-Minocycline (minocycline)
Gen-Nifedipine (nifedipine)
Gravol (dimenhydrinate)

H

Haldol LA (haloperidol)
Hepalean (heparin)
Hepalean-Lok (heparin)
Heparin Leo (heparin)
Hip-Rex (methenamine)
Honvol (diethylstilbestrol)
Humulin U (insulin)
Hycort (hydrocortisone)
Hydromorph Contin (hydromorphone)
Hy/Gestrone (hydroxyprogesterone)

I

Iletin PZI (insulin)
Immunine VH (factor IX)
Impril (imipramine)
Indocid (indomethacin)
Indocid P.D.A (indomethacin)
Indotec (indomethacin)
Infufer (iron dextran)
Inocid (indomethacin)
Isotamine (isoniazid)
Isotrex (isotretinoin)

K

Kabolin (nandrolone)
Kalium Durules (potassium chloride)
K-Exit (sodium polystyrene)
Kidrolase (asparaginase)
Koffex (dextromethorphan)

L

Lactulax (lactulose)
Lanvis (thioguanine)
Largactil (chlorpromazine)
Laxilose (lactulose)
Levate (amitriptyline)
Lithizine (lithium)
Lopresor (metoprolol)
LoSec (omeprazole)
Loxapac (loxapine)
Lyderm Cream (fluocinonide)

M

Malogen in Oil (testosterone)
Marzine (cyclizine)
Maxeran (metoclopramide)
Meclomen (meclofenamate)
Medrol Veriderm (methylprednisolone)
Megace OS (megestrol)
Megacillin (penicillin G benzathine)
Meprolone (methylprednisolone)
M-Eslon (morphine)
Methadose (methadone)
MetroCream (mitronidazole)
Micozole (miconazole)

Minims (atropine)
Minims Sodium Chloride (sodium chloride)
Minox (minoxidil)
Minoxigaine (minoxidil)
Mireze (nedocromil)
Mobenol (tolbutamide)
Modecate Deconate (fluphenazine)
Moditen Enanthate (fluphenazine)
Monazole (miconazole)
Monitan (acebutolol)
Multipax (hydroxyzine)
Mycifradin (neomycin)
Mycil (chlorphenesin)
Myclo (clotrimazole)
Myrosemide (furosemide)

N
Nadopen-V (penicillin V)
Nadostine (nystatin)
Nalcrom (cromolyn)
Natulan (procarbazine)
Naxen (naproxen)
Neo-Tric (metronidazole)
Nephronex (nitrofurantoin)
NidaGel (metronidazole)
Nobesin (diethylpropion)
Norlutate (norethindrone)
Norventyl (nortriptyline)
Norzine (thiethylperazine)
Novahistex DM (dextromethorphan)
Novahistine DM (dexttomethorphan)
Novamoxin (amoxicillin)
Novasen (aspirin)
Novo-Alprozol (alprazolam)
Novo-Ampicillin (ampicillin)
Novo-Atenol (atenolol)
Novo-AZT (zidovudine)
Novo-Baclofen (baclofen)
Novo-Butamide (tolbutamide)
Novo-Captopril (captopril)
Novo-Carbamaz (carbamazepine)
Novo-Cholamine (cholestyramine)
Novo-Cholamine Light (cholestryamine)
Novo-Cimetine (cimetidine)
Novo-Clopamine (clomipramine)
Novo-Clopate (clorazepate)
Novo-Cloxin (cloxacillin)
Novo-Cycloprine (cyclobenzaprine)
Novo-Desipramine (desipramine)
Novo-Difenac (diclofenac)
Novo-Diflunisal (diflunisal)
Novo-Digoxin (digoxin)
Novo-Diltazem (diltiazem)
Novo-Doxepin (doxepin)
Novo-Doxylin (doxycycline)
Novo-Famotidine (famotidine)
Novo-Fibrate (clofibrate)
Novo-Fluoxetine (fluoxetine)
Novo-Flurbiprofen (flurbiprofen)
Novo-Flutamide (flutamide)
Novo-Furan (nitrofurantoin)
Novo-Gemfibrozil (gemfibrozil)
Novo-Hylazin (hydralazine)
Novo-Hydrazide (hydrochlorothiazide)
Novo-Hydroxyzin (hydroxyzine)
Novo-Ipramide (ipratropium)
Novo-Levamisole (levamisole)
Novo-Lexin (cephalexin)
Novolin ge (insulin)
Novolin ge lente (insulin)
Novolin ge Toronto (insulin)
Novolin ge ultralente (insulin)
Novo-Loperamide (loperamide)
Novo-Lorazem (lorazepam)
Novo-Maprotiline (maprotiline)
Novo-Medopa (methyldopa)
Novo-Medrone (medroxyprogesterone)
Novo-Meprazine (methotrimeprazine)
Novomepro (meprobamate)
Novomethacin (indomethacin)
Novo-Metoprol (metoprolol)
Novo-Mexiletine (mexiletine)
Novo-Minocycline (minocycline)
Novo-Naddol (nadolol)
Novo-Naprox (naproxen)
Novo-Nidazol (metronidazole)
Novo-Nifedin (nifedipine)
Novo-Oxybutynin (oxybutynin)
Novo- Pen G (penicillin G)
Novo-Pen VK (penicillin V)
Novo-Pentobarb (pentobarbital)
Novoperidol (haloperidol)
Novo-Pindol (pindolol)
Novo-Pirocam (piroxicam)
Novo-Pramine (imipramine)
Novo-Pranol (propranolol)
Novo-Prazin (prazosin)
Novo-Prednisolone (prednisolone)
Novo-Prednisone (prednisone)
Novo-Profen (ibuprofen)
Novo-Propoxyn (propoxyphene)
Novo-Pyrazone (sulfinpyrazone)
Novo-Ranidine (ranitidine)
Novo-Rectal (pentobarbital)
Novo-Rythro (erythromycin)
Novo-Salmol (albuterol)
Novo-Secobarb (secobarbital)
Novo-Sotalol (sotalol)
Novosoxazole (sulfisoxazole)
Novo-Spiroton (spironolactone)
Novo-Sucralfate (sucralfate)
Novo-Sundac (sulindac)
Nova-Tamoxifen (tamoxifen)
Novo-Temazepam (temazepam)
Novotetra (tetracycline)

Novo-Timol (timolol)
Novo-Tolmetin (tolmetin)
Novo-Triolam (triazolam)
Novo-Triphyl (oxtriphylline)
Novo-Tripramine (trimipramine)
Novo-Triptyn (amitriptyline)
Novoxapam (oxazepam)
Nozinan (methotrimeprazine)
Nu-Alpraz (alprazolam)
Nu-Amoxi (amoxicillin)
Nu-Ampi (ampicillin)
Nu-Capto (captopril)
Nu-Cephalex (cephalexin)
Nu-Cimet (cimetidine)
Nu-Clonidine (clonidine)
Nu-Cloxi (cloxacillin)
Nu-Diclo (diclofenac)
Nu-Diflunisal (diflunisal)
Nu-Diltiaz (diltiazem)
Nu-Doxycycline (doxycycline)
Nu-Erythromycin-S (erythromycin)
Nu-Hydral (hydralazine)
Nu-Ketoprofen (ketoprofen)
Nu-Loraz (lorazepam)
Nu-Medopa (methyldopa)
Nu-Metoclopramide (metoclopramide)
Nu-Metop (metoprolol)
Nu-Pindol (pindolol)
Nu-Pirox (piroxicam)
Nu-Prazo (prazosin)
Nu-Ranit (ranitidine)
Nu-Tetra (tetracycline)
Nu-Trazodone (trazodone)

O

Occulcort (betamethasone)
Octostim (desmopressin)
Ocupress (carteolol)
Opium TCT (opium)
Orafen (ketoprofen)
Orbenin (cloxacillin)
Orcipren (metaproterenol)
Orfenace (orphenadrine)

P

Palafer (ferrous fumarate)
Parvolex (acetylcysteine)
PCE (erythromycin)
PDF (sodium fluoride)
Pedi-Dent (sodium fluoride)
Penbec V (penicillin V)
Penbritin (ampicillin)
Penglobe (bacampicillin)
Pentacarinat (pentamidine)
Pentids (penicillin G)
Pentids (pencillin G potassium)
Peptol (cimetidine)
Peridol (haloperidol)
Phazyme (simethicone)
Phenazine (perphenazine)
Phenazo (phenazopyridine)
Phenytex (phenytoin)
PMS-ASA (aspirin)
PMS Benztropine (benztropine)
PMS Bethanecol Chloride (bethanechol)
PMS-Ceclor (cefaclor)
PMS-Cephalexin (cephalexin)
PMS-Chloral Hydrate (chloral hydrate)
PMS-Cyproheptadine (cyproheptadine)
PMS-Desipramine (despiramine)
PMS-Egozinc (zinc)
PMS-Fluoxetine (fluoxetine)
PMS-Haloperidol (haloperidol)
PMS-Hydromorphone (hydromorphone)
PMS-Ipecac (ipecac)
PMS-Isoniazid (isoniazid)
PMS-Lithium Carbonate (lithium)
PMS-Loxapine (loxapine)
PMS-Mefenamic Acid (mefenamic acid)
PMS-Methylphenidate (methylphenidate)
PMS Metronidazole (metronidazole)
PMS-Neostigmine Methylsulfate (neostigmine)
PMS-Nortriptyline (nortriptyline)
PMS-Nystatin (nystatin)
PMS-Prochlorperazine (prochlorperazine)
PMS-Procyclidine (procyclidine)
PMS-Promethazine (promethazine)
PMS-Propranolol (propranolol)
PMS-Pyrazinamide (pyrazinamide)
Ponstan (mefenamic acid)
Prepulsid (cisapride)
Pressyn (vasopressin)
Prevex B (betamethasone)
Primazine (promazine)
Primene (amino acids)
Procan SR (procainamide)
Procyclid (procyclidine)
Procytox (cyclophosphamide)
Prodox (hydroxyprogesterone)
Progestilin (progesterone)
Propaderm (beclomethasone)
Propanthel (propantheline)
Propoint (diethylpropion)
Propyl-Thyracil (propylthiouracil)
Puregon (follitropin beta)
Purinol (allopurinol)
Pyribenzamine (tripelennamine)

Q

Quinate (quinidine)
Quintasa (mesalamine)

R
Reactine (cetirizine)
Regibon (diethylpropion)
Renedil (felodipine)
Retin-A (tretinoin)
Revimine (dopamine)
Rhinalar (flunisolide)
Rhinocort Tubuhaler (budenoside)
Rhodacine (indomethacin)
Rhodis (ketoprofen)
Rho-Fluphenazine Deconate (fluphenazine)
Rholosone (betamethasone)
Rhoprosone (betamethasone)
Rhotral (acebutolol)
Rhotrimine (trimipramine)
Rhovail (ketoprofen)
Riphenidate (methylprednisolone)
Rivotril (clonazepam)
R.O. Atropine (atropine)
Robidex (dextromethorphan)
Rofact (rifampin)
Rogitine (phentolamine)
Roychlor (potassium chloride)
Rylosol (sotalol)
Rynacron m (cromolyn)
Rythmodan (disopyramide)

S
Salazopyrin (sulfasalazine)
Salbutamol (albuterol)
Saline from Otrivin (sodium chloride)
Salinex (sodium chloride)
Salofalk (mesalamine)
Sarisol #2 (butabarbital)
S.A.S. (sulfasalazine)
Scheinpharm Testone-cyp (testostersone)
Sotacar (sotalol)
Stemitil (prochlorperazine)
Stemitil Suppositories (prochlorperazine)
Sterine (methenamine)
StieVA-A (tretinoin)
Sulcrate (sucralfate)
Supeudol (oxycodone)
Synacthen Depot (cosyntropin)
Synflex (naproxen)

T
Tamone (tamoxifen)
Tanta Orciprenaline (metaproterenol)
Taro-Sone (betamethasone)
Tebrazid (pyrazinamide)
Teejel (choline salicylate)
Tegopen (cloxacillin)
Tenolin (atenolol)
Texacort (hydrocortisone)
Tija (oxytetracycline)
Topsyn Gel (fluocinonide)
Travel Tabs (dimenhydrinate)
Trexan (naltrexone)
Triadapin (doxepin)
Trichlorex (trichlormethiazide)
Trikacide (metronidazole)
Triptil (protriptyline)

U
Ultracef (cefadroxil)
Ultradol (etodolac)
UltraMOP (methoxsalen)
Urasal (methenamine)
Urozide (hydrochlorothiazide)
Ursofalk (ursodiol)

V
Vamin (amino acids)
Velbe (vinblastine)
Ventodisk (albuterol)
Vivelle (estradiol)
Vivol (diazepam)
Voltaren Ophtha (diclofenac)
Voltaren Rapide (diclofenac)

W
Warfilone (warfarin)
Winpred (prednisone)

X
Xanax-TS (alprazolam)

Y
Yodoquinal (iodoquinol)

Z
Zapex (oxazepam)
Zoladex L.A. (goserelin)
Zonalon (doxepin)

APPENDIX C-2

CANADIAN IMMUNIZATION SCHEDULES FOR INFANTS AND CHILDREN*

The following is an overview on routine immunization schedules for infants and children. This information is not intended to present a comprehensive review; the reader is therefore encouraged to seek additional and confirmatory information.

Reviewed 1999 by V. Marchessault.

Few measures in preventive medicine are of such proven value and as easy to implement as routine immunization against infectious diseases. Immunizations carried out as recommended in the following schedules (Table I, II and III) will provide protection for most children against the diseases shown.

Both live and inactivated polio vaccines have been used in Canada with equal success in preventing the occurrence of paralytic poliomyelitis, but inactivated vaccine is now preferred.

Following a standard schedule ensures complete and adequate protection. However, modifications of the recommended schedule may be necessary because of missed appointments or illness. Interruption of a recommended series does not require starting the series over again, regardless of the interval elapsed.

Similar vaccines are now available from different manufacturers but they may not be identical. It is therefore essential for the user to read the appropriate chapter in the current *Canadian Immunization Guide,* as well as the manufacturer's package insert.

* Reprinted by permission from *Compendium of pharmaceuticals and specialties,* 34th ed., pp. L6–L7. Published by the Canadian Pharmacists Association, Ottawa, © 1999.

REFERENCE

1. National Advisory Committee on Immunization, Canadian immunization guide, 5th ed. Ottawa, ON: Health Canada, 1998.

TABLE I

ROUTINE IMMUNIZATION SCHEDULE FOR INFANTS AND CHILDREN

Age/Time	DTaP[a]	IPV	Hib[b]	MMR	Td[c]	Hep B[d] (3 doses)
2 months old	X	X	X			Infancy
4 months old	X	X	X			
6 months old	X	X[e]	X			or
12 months old				X		
18 months old	X	X	X	X[f] or		
4–6 years old	X	X		X[f]		preadolescence
Grade 3–7						(9–13 yrs)
14–16 years old					X	

Legend: DTaP = diphtheria, tetanus and pertussis (acellular) vaccine, Hep B = recombinant hepatitis B vaccine series, Hb = Haemophilus influenza b conjugate vaccine, IPV = inactivated polio vaccine, MMR = measles, mumps and rubella vaccine, Td = tetanus and diphtheria toxoid, "adult type".

TABLE II

ROUTINE IMMUNIZATION SCHEDULE FOR CHILDREN <7 YEARS OF AGE NOT IMMUNIZED IN EARLY INFANCY

Timing	DTaP[a]	IPV	Hib	MMR	Td[c]	Hep B[d] (3 doses)
1st visit	X	X	X	X[g]		
2 months after 1st visit	X	X	X[h]	X[f]		
2 months after 2nd visit	X	X[e]				
6–12 months after 3rd visit	X	X	X[h]			
4–6 years of age[i]	X	X				Preadolescence
14–16 years of age					X	(9–13 yrs)

TABLE III

ROUTINE IMMUNIZATION SCHEDULE FOR CHILDREN =7 YEARS OF AGE NOT IMMUNIZED IN EARLY INFANCY

Timing	Td[c]	IPV	MMR	Hep B[d] (3 doses)
1st visit	X	X	X	
2 months after 1st visit	X	X	X[f]	
6–12 months after 2nd visit	X	X		Preadolescence
10 years after 3rd visit	X			(9–13 yrs)

FOR ALL TABLES:

[a] DTaP (diphtheria, tetanus, acellular or component pertussis) vaccine is the preferred vaccine for all doses in the vaccination series, including completion of the series in children who have received =1 dose of DPT (whole cell) vaccine.
[b] Hib schedule shown is for PRP-T (e.g., Act-HIB) or HbOC (e.g., Hib TITER) vaccine. If PRP-OMP (e.g., PedVax HIB), give at 2, 4 and 12 months of age.
[c] Td (tetanus and diphtheria toxoid), a combined adsorbed "adult type" preparation for use in persons =7 years of age contains less diphtheria toxoid than preparations given to younger children and is less likely to cause reactions in older persons.
[d] Hepatitis B vaccine can be routinely given to infants or pre-adolescents, depending on the provincial/territorial policy; three doses at 0, 1 and 6 month intervals are preferred. The second dose should be administered at least 1 month after the first dose, and the third dose should be administered at least 4 months after the first dose, and at least 2 months after the second dose.
[e] This dose is not needed routinely, but can be included for convenience.
[f] A second dose of MMR is recommended, at least 1 month after the first dose given. For convenience, options include giving it with the next scheduled vaccination at 18 months of age or with school entry vaccinations at 4–6 years of age (depending on the provincial/territorial policy), or at any intervening age that is practicable.
[g] Delay until subsequent visit if child is <12 months of age.
[h] Recommended schedule and number of doses depend on the product used and the age of the child when vaccination is begun (see the current Canadian Immunization Guide or the product monograph for specific recommendations). Not required past age 5.
[i] Omit these doses if the previous doses of DTaP and polio were given after the 4th birthday.

Adapted from Canadian Immunization Guide, 5th edition, Health Canada, 1998, with permission of the Minister of Public Works and Government Services Canada, 1998.

APPENDIX C-3

CANADIAN NARCOTIC AND CONTROLLED DRUGS*

Table I summarizes the requirements for prescribing, dispensing and record keeping for narcotic and controlled drugs. This information is not intended to present a comprehensive review; the reader is therefore encouraged to seek additional and confirmatory information (e.g., Controlled Drugs and Substances Act, Narcotic Control Regulations, Food and Drugs Regulations).

* Reprinted by permission from *Compendium of pharmaceuticals and specialties,* 34th ed., pp. L6–L7. Published by the Canadian Pharmacists Association, Ottawa, © 1999.

Reviewed 1999 by the Bureau of Drug Surveillance, Health Canada.

TABLE I

NARCOTIC AND CONTROLLED DRUGS SUMMARY

Classification and Description	Legal Requirements
NARCOTIC DRUGS[a] ▪ 1 narcotic (e.g., cocaine, codeine, hydromorphone, morphine) ▪ 1 narcotic + 1 active non-narcotic ingredient (e.g., *Cophylac, Empracet-30, Penntuss, Tylenol No. 4*) ▪ All narcotics for parenteral use (e.g., fentanyl, pethidine) ▪ All products containing diamorphine (hospitals only), hydrocodone, oxycodone, methadone or pentazocine ▪ Dextropropoxyphene, propoxyphene (straight) (e.g., *Darvon-N, 642*)	▪ Written prescription required. ▪ Verbal prescriptions not permitted. ▪ Refills not permitted. ▪ Written prescription may be prescribed to be dispensed in divided portions (part-fills). ▪ For part-fills, copies of prescriptions should be made in reference to the original prescription. Indicate on the original prescription: the new prescription number, the date of the part-fill, the quantity dispensed and the pharmacist's initials. ▪ Record and retain all drug sales and purchases in a manner that permits an audit. ▪ Report the loss or theft of narcotic/controlled drugs as well as forged prescriptions within 10 days to your Regional Office, Drug Programme at the address indicated at the back of the Drug Forgery Report or the Drug Loss/Theft Report forms.
NARCOTIC PREPARATIONS[a] ▪ Verbal prescription narcotics: 1 narcotic + 2 or more active non-narcotic ingredients (e.g., *Cophylac Expectorant, Darvon-N Compound, Fiorinal with Codeine, 692, 282, 292, Tylenol No. 2* and *No. 3*) ▪ Exempted codeine compounds: contain codeine up to 8 mg/solid dosage form or 20 mg/30 mL liquid + 2 or more active non-narcotic ingredients (e.g., *Atasol-8, Robitussin with Codeine*).	▪ Written or verbal prescriptions permitted. ▪ Refills not permitted. ▪ Written or verbal prescriptions may be prescribed to be dispensed in divided portions (part-fills). ▪ For part-fills, copies of prescriptions should be made in reference to the original prescription. Indicate on the original prescription: the new prescription number, the date of the part-fill, the quantity dispensed and the pharmacist's initials. ▪ Exempted codeine compounds when dispensed pursuant to a prescription follow the same regulations as for verbal prescription narcotics. ▪ Record and retain all drug sales and purchases in a manner that permits an audit. ▪ Report the loss or theft of narcotic/controlled drugs as well as forged prescriptions within 10 days to your Regional Office, Drug Programme at the address indicated at the back of the Drug Forgery Report or the Drug Loss/Theft Report forms.
CONTROLLED DRUGS[a] ▪ Part I e.g., amphetamines (*Dexedrine*) methylphenidate (*Ritalin*) pentobarbital (*Nembutal*) secobarbital (*Seconal, Tuinal*) lipreparations: 1 controlled drug + 1 or more active noncontrolled drug(s) (*Cafergot-PB*)	▪ Written or verbal prescriptions permitted. ▪ Refills not permitted for verbal prescriptions. ▪ Refills permitted for written prescriptions if the prescriber has indicated in writing the number of refills and dates for, or intervals between, refills. ▪ Written or verbal prescriptions may be prescribed to be dispensed divided portions (part-fills). ▪ For refills and part-fills, copies of prescriptions should be made in reference to the original prescription. Indicate on the original

TABLE I

NARCOTIC AND CONTROLLED DRUGS SUMMARY (Continued)

Classification and Description	Legal Requirements
	prescription: the new prescription number, the date of the repeat of part-fill, the quantity dispensed and the pharmacist's initials. ▪ Record and retain all drug sales and purchases in a manner that permits an audit. ▪ Report the loss or theft of narcotic/controlled drugs as well as forged prescriptions within 10 days to your Regional Office, Drug Programme at the address indicated at the back of the Drug Forgery Report or the Drug Loss/Theft Report forms.
▪ Part II e.g., barbiturates (amobarbital, phenobarbital) butorphanol (*Stadol NS*) diethylpropion (*Tenuate*) nalbuphine (*Nubain*) phentermine (*Fastin, Lonamin*) preparations: 1 controlled drug + 1 or more active non-controlled ingredients (*Fiorinal, Neo-Pause, Tecnal*) ▪ Part III e.g., anabolic steroids (methyltestosterone, nandrolone decanoate)	▪ Written or verbal prescriptions permitted. ▪ Refills permitted for written or verbal prescriptions if the prescriber has authorized in writing or verbally (at the time of issuance) the number of refills and dates for, or intervals between, refills. ▪ Written or verbal prescriptions may be prescribed to be dispensed in divided portions (part-fills). ▪ For refills and part-fills, copies of prescriptions should be made in reference to the original prescription. Indicate on the original prescription: the new prescription number, the date of the repeat or part-fill, the quantity dispensed and the pharmacist's initials. ▪ Record and retain all drug sales and purchases in a manner that permits an audit. ▪ Report the loss or theft of narcotic/controlled drugs as well as forged prescriptions within 10 days to your Regional Office, Drug Programme at the address indicated at the back of the Drug Forgery Report or the Drug Loss/Theft Report forms.

[a] The products noted are examples only.

INDEX

Page numbers with "t" denote tables; those with "f" denote figures; those with "b" denote boxes

B

C

E

F

M

N

O

Q

R

Study Guide

CHAPTER 1: INTRODUCTION TO DRUGS

MATCHING EXERCISE

Match the word with its definition:

1. ________ Genetic engineering
2. ________ FDA
3. ________ Pharmacology
4. ________ Phase I study
5. ________ OTC drugs
6. ________ Preclinical study
7. ________ Teratogenic
8. ________ Pharmacotherapeutics
9. ________ Generic drugs
10. ________ Drugs

A. The study of the actions of chemicals on living organisms
B. Drugs sold by their chemical names, not brand name products
C. Having adverse effects on the fetus
D. Chemicals that are introduced into the body to bring about some sort of change
E. A drug that is available without a prescription
F. Federal agency responsible for the regulation and enforcement of drug evaluation and distribution policies
G. Process of altering DNA to produce a chemical to be used as a drug
H. Pilot study of a potential drug done with a small number of selected, healthy human volunteers
I. Initial trial of a chemical thought to have therapeutic potential; uses laboratory animals, not human subjects
J. Clinical pharmacology, the branch of pharmacology that deals with drugs

WWW. WEB EXERCISE

Go to the Food and Drug Administration home page on the Internet. Find one drug that was released within the last 3 months. (The FDA site will list drugs approved by year and month. Click on a year, then a month, then scroll down the page to find a drug). Identify the brand name, generic name, and therapeutic class of the drug. Connect to the manufacturer's web page to get specific information regarding the therapeutic use, adverse effects, and dosage of the drug. (This can be done by entering the generic name of the drug into a search.) Return to the FDA site and try this search for another drug released with the last 3 months.

IDENTIFY THE CORRECT TERMS USED FOR THE FOLLOWING DRUG

chlordiazepoxide hydrochloride	Therapeutic class
metaminodiazepoxide hydrochloride	Safety for use during pregnancy
Librium	Chemical name
Pregnancy Category B	Generic name
Benzodiazepine	Pharmacological class
Antianxiety agent	Brand name

FILL IN THE BLANKS

Describe what occurs in each phase of the drug development process.

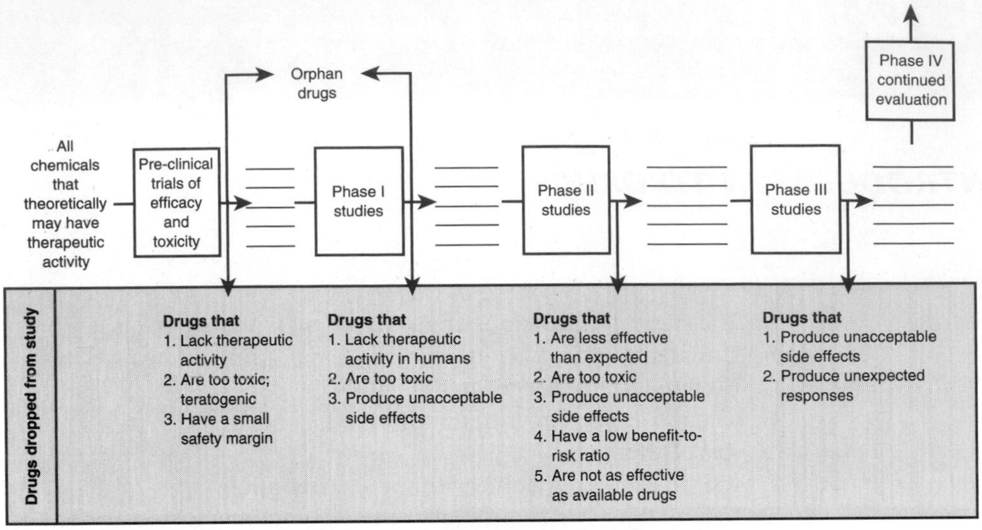

CHAPTER 2: DRUGS AND THE BODY

WORD SEARCH

Circle the following words, related to drugs and the body, hidden in the grid below. Words may be horizontal, vertical or diagonal.

pharmacodynamics
pharmacokinetics
absorption
chemotherapeutic
receptor
selective
toxicity
critical
distribution
biotransformation
concentration
excretion
half-life
first-pass
site

A	P	C	S	M	N	O	M	D	H	L	S	T	W	M	N	V
B	R	T	O	I	L	E	O	C	I	E	E	H	O	I	O	T
T	R	I	P	L	H	L	M	F	F	G	L	N	O	P	Q	R
S	E	L	E	C	T	I	V	I	S	W	E	R	N	E	L	S
C	C	C	O	M	H	E	O	R	T	U	C	S	O	U	C	S
I	E	O	L	I	E	V	B	S	R	S	T	B	I	I	R	P
M	P	N	N	J	N	O	I	T	U	B	I	R	T	S	I	D
A	T	C	H	O	L	H	D	P	H	I	V	U	A	O	T	S
N	O	E	M	S	I	T	R	A	O	L	E	D	M	I	I	R
Y	R	N	E	L	E	T	I	S	A	P	V	E	R	T	C	S
D	I	T	T	O	V	R	P	S	A	C	L	H	O	A	A	C
O	U	R	T	S	L	A	R	R	L	I	N	N	F	R	L	I
C	H	A	D	F	G	S	E	E	O	K	I	E	S	T	T	S
A	C	T	I	L	M	H	F	N	E	S	R	M	N	N	B	E
M	L	I	V	K	T	I	S	M	N	R	B	I	A	E	L	N
R	S	O	T	O	L	W	D	P	H	L	O	A	R	C	E	A
A	B	N	M	F	O	Y	T	I	C	I	X	O	T	N	J	L
H	L	E	L	E	X	C	R	E	T	I	O	N	O	O	P	V
P	H	A	R	M	A	C	O	K	I	N	E	T	I	C	S	O
C	H	L	O	R	N	E	H	O	B	S	L	X	B	W	I	C

FILL IN THE BLANKS

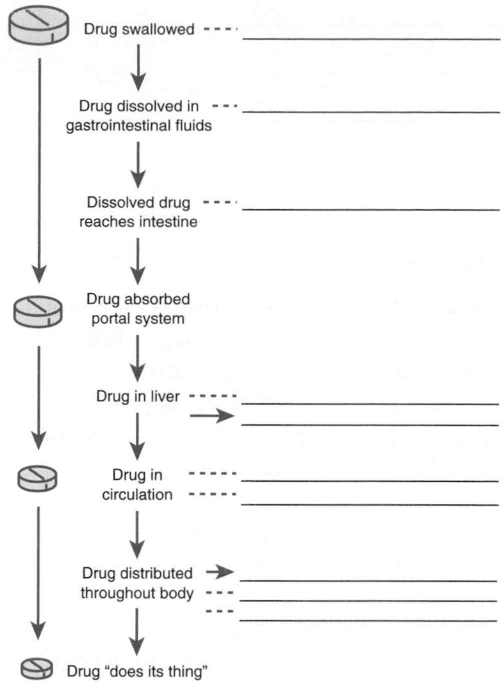

MULTIPLE CHOICE

1. The absorption of a drug given IM can be affected by:
   a. food in the stomach
   b. patient's age
   c. blood supply to the area injected
   d. presence of interacting foods in the stomach
2. The absorption of a drug given SC can be affected by:
   a. age of the patient
   b. temperature of the drug being given
   c. fat content of the tissue being injected
   d. muscle tension
3. The half-life of a drug is 1 hour. A patient receives 50 mg of the drug. What would the expected concentration be in 2 hours.
   a. 25 mg
   b. 12.5 mg
   c. 10 mg
   d. 0 mg
4. Drugs do not act at specific receptor sites to:
   a. increase the activity of the cell
   b. decrease the activity of the cell
   c. block the receptor site to prevent stimulation
   d. change the makeup and function of the cell
5. Excretion of drugs from the body does not occur:
   a. from the kidneys
   b. from the pancreas
   c. from the lungs
   d. through the GI tract

CHAPTER 3: TOXIC EFFECTS OF DRUGS

DESCRIBING ADVERSE EFFECTS

Describe the following adverse reactions:

Anaphylactic reaction: ______________________________

____

Cytotoxic reaction: ______________________________

____

Serum sickness reaction: ______________________________

____

Superinfection: ______________________________

____

Blood dyscrasia: ______________________________

____

MATCH THE ADVERSE DRUG EFFECT WITH THE APPROPRIATE INTERVENTION

1. ________ hypoglycemia
2. ________ hyperglycemia
3. ________ hypokalemia
4. ________ superinfection
5. ________ cholinergic effects
6. ________ Parkinson-like effects

A. Replace serum potassium and carefully monitor serum levels; provide supportive therapy (safety precautions to prevent injury or falls, orient patient, comfort measures for pain and discomfort).
B. Provide sugarless lozenges, mouth care to help mouth dryness. Arrange for bowel program; have the patient void before taking the drug; provide safety measures if vision changes occur.
C. Administer insulin therapy to decrease blood glucose as appropriate; provide support to help the patient deal with signs and symptoms (access to bathroom facilities, controlled environment, reassurance, mouth care).
D. Discontinue the drug, if necessary; treat with antichlolinergics or antiparkinson drugs if recommended and if the benefit outweighs the discomfort of adverse effects; provide small, frequent meals if swallowing becomes difficult; provide safety measures.
E. Restore glucose, IV or PO if possible; provide supportive measures (skin care, environmental control of light and temperature, rest). Institute safety measures to prevent injury or falls.
F. Provide supportive measures (frequent mouth care, skin care, access to bathroom facilities, small and frequent meals); administer anti-fungal therapy as appropriate.

CHAPTER 4: NURSING MANAGEMENT

LIST THE SEVEN POINTS TO CONSIDER IN THE SAFE AND EFFECTIVE ADMINISTRATION OF A DRUG

1. ______________
2. ______________
3. ______________
4. ______________
5. ______________
6. ______________
7. ______________

FILL IN THE BLANKS

Fill in the blanks in the nursing process chart below:

BOX 4-1

THE STEPS OF THE NURSING PROCESS

Nursing Process

↓

Assessment

Past history

____

____

____

____

____

____

____

Physical assessment

____

____

____

____

↓

Nursing Diagnosis

↓

Interventions

Proper drug administration

____

____

____

____

____

____

____

Comfort measures

____

____

____

Patient/family education

↓

Evaluation

LIST EIGHT FACTORS THAT SHOULD ALWAYS BE CONSIDERED WHEN PREPARING A PATIENT TEACHING PLAN FOR DRUG THERAPY

1. ________________
2. ________________
3. ________________
4. ________________
5. ________________
6. ________________
7. ________________
8. ________________

CHAPTER 5: INTRODUCTION TO CELL PHYSIOLOGY

WWW. WEB EXERCISE

Look up information on cell physiology, theories of cell formation, and ongoing cellular research at http://www.historyoftheuniverse.com/cell/html. Correlate the structure of the cell membrane with the cell processes discussed in this chapter.

FILL IN THE BLANKS

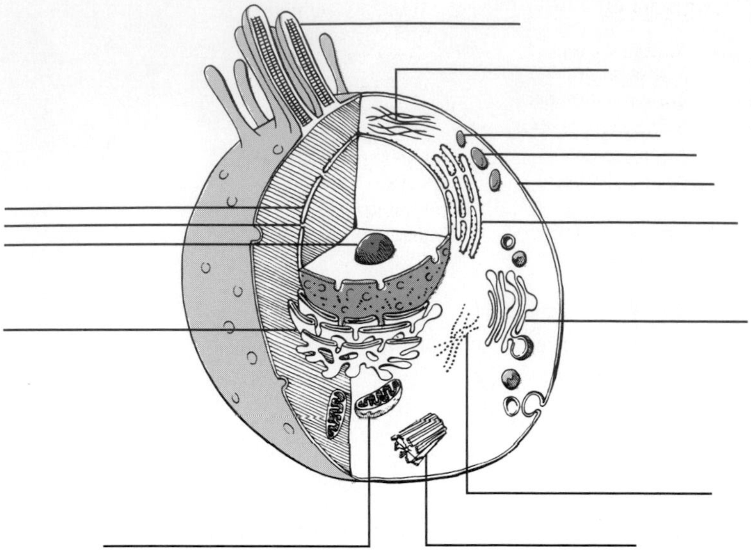

UNSCRAMBLE THE FOLLOWING LETTERS TO FIND BASIC CELLULAR PROCESSES

1. ifsnofidu
2. ctoyseondsi
3. ipysonictos
4. shipgoytacos
5. smooiss
6. tosimsi
7. vissape tatrrsopn
8. evicate protstran

MATCHING

Match the phase of the cell cycle with the cell activity during that phase:

1. ________ G_0 phase
2. ________ G_1 phase
3. ________ S phase
4. ________ G_2 phase
5. ________ M phase

A. Cell splits to form two identical daughter cells
B. Synthesis of DNA
C. Manufacture of substances needed to form mitotic spindles
D. Synthesis of substances needed for DNA production
E. Resting phase

CHAPTER 6: ANTI-INFECTIVE AGENTS

DEFINE THE FOLLOWING TERMS

culture:

prophylaxis:

resistance:

selective toxicity:

sensitivity testing:

spectrum:

CROSSWORD PUZZLE

ACROSS

2 Antibiotics that interfere with protein synthesis
5 Basic units of life
6 Antibiotic class developed from molds
7 Ranges of anti-infective activity

DOWN

1 Production of certain substances by a cell
2 Type of immunity that develops after exposure to an organism
3 Ability of a chemical to affect only certain types of cells
4 First scientist to develop a synthetic anti-infective

MATCHING

Match the antibiotic with the appropriate description:

1. ________ polymyxin B
2. ________ meropenem
3. ________ chloramphenicol
4. ________ vancomycin
5. ________ spectinomycin
6. ________ bacitracin

A. Can cause potentially fatal pseudomembranous colitis
B. Associated with "gray baby syndrome"
C. Very toxic to human cells; nephrotoxicity, neurotoxicity common
D. Use led to development of many resistant strains
E. Used for staphylococci infections in patients who cannot take penicillin or cephalosporins
F. Treatment of specific strains of *Neisseria gonorrhoeae*

CHAPTER 7: ANTIBIOTICS

TRUE OR FALSE

Indicate whether the following statements are true (T) or false (F).

_____ 1. Aerobic bacteria depend on oxygen for survival.
_____ 2. Bactericidal refers to a substance that prevents the replication of bacteria.
_____ 3. Bacteriostatic refers to a drug that causes the death of bacteria.
_____ 4. Anaerobic bacteria survive without oxygen.
_____ 5. Gram-negative refers to bacteria that take a positive stain and are frequently associated with infections of the respiratory tract and soft tissues.
_____ 6. An antibiotic is a chemical that inhibits the growth of specific bacteria or causes the death of susceptible bacteria.
_____ 7. Antibiotics usually eradicate all of the bacteria that have entered the body.
_____ 8. Synergistic drugs are drugs that work together to increase a drug's effectiveness.

WWW. WEB EXERCISE

Log on to: http://www.cdc.gov. Select Health Information. Select the letter T, then find tuberculosis. Develop an information sheet for a patient with tuberculosis, including teaching points, ways to remember to take the medication, family pointers, and drug effects.

UNSCRAMBLE THE FOLLOWING TO FIND THE NAMES OF COMMONLY USED CEPHALOSPORINS

1. pnrciepiha
2. lrcfeoa
3. xcifeldaor
4. afblroecra
5. xciemfetzoi
6. nettacoef
7. toxinefic
8. nozfileca

CHAPTER 8: ANTIVIRAL AGENTS

IDENTIFY THE SITE OF ACTION OF THE FOLLOWING DRUGS USED TO TREAT HIV/AIDS

1. reverse transcriptase inhibitors ____________________

____

2. protease inhibitors ____________________

____

3. nucleosides ____________________

____

4. antiretrovirus drugs ____________________

____

MATCH THE LOCALLY ACTING ANTIVIRAL DRUG WITH THE CONDITION IT IS USUALLY USED TO TREAT

1. _______ idoxuridine
2. _______ imiquimod
3. _______ fomivirsen
4. _______ penciclovir
5. _______ trifluridine
6. _______ vidarabine

A. herpes simplex eye infections
B. herpes simplex eye infections not responsive to idoxuridine
C. cold sores on the face and lips
D. genital and perianal warts
E. CMV retinitis
F. herpes simplex keratitis

PATIENT TEACHING CHECKLIST

Mr. Jones, a 48-year-old piano tuner with a positive HIV titer, has recently begun developing signs of AIDS. He is still asymptomatic but was recently started on ziduovudine, 100 mg q4h while awake. He has been referred to the nurse for drug teaching. Use the patient teaching checklist format to prepare a drug sheet specifically for Mr. Jones.

CHAPTER 9: ANTIFUNGAL AGENTS

WWW. WEB EXERCISE

The basketball coach at the local high school is concerned about an epidemic of athlete's foot that is affecting his entire team. Go on to the Internet to find information that will allow you to prepare a teaching protocol to help the coach with the treatment and prevention of this problem. Log on to http://www.athletesfoot.com/ to get all sorts of information to help you prepare the teaching protocol; http://www.cdc.gov will give you information about available treatments and preventive measures that should be taken.

WORD SEARCH

Circle the following names of antifungal drugs hidden in the grid below. Words may be horizontal, vertical, or diagonal.

amphotericin B
butenafine
butoconazole
clotrimazole
econazole
fluconazole
flucytosine
gentian violet
itraconazole
ketoconazole
miconazole
naftifine
nystatin
oxiconazole
terbinafine
tolnaftate

T	E	R	B	I	N	A	F	I	N	E	Z	O	L	E	C	O	N	C	T
F	N	O	Z	L	E	T	O	L	N	A	F	T	A	T	E	X	F	O	O
L	I	M	G	R	A	O	L	I	C	B	L	B	C	O	N	K	E	N	H
U	S	F	E	A	N	V	F	J	T	H	E	U	A	N	P	E	L	A	P
C	O	L	T	C	I	I	R	L	U	R	Z	T	R	I	E	T	O	Z	M
O	T	U	U	O	T	O	E	E	N	E	A	O	G	L	R	O	Z	O	A
Z	Y	C	B	F	A	L	L	L	L	N	A	C	B	A	I	C	A	L	C
O	C	O	A	N	T	E	O	O	O	I	C	O	O	R	Z	O	M	E	E
L	U	N	E	A	S	T	Z	Z	Z	F	I	N	N	N	O	N	I	M	B
E	L	A	L	Z	Y	A	A	A	O	A	T	A	F	G	A	A	R	H	U
Y	F	Z	O	L	N	G	N	N	L	N	A	Z	I	E	L	Z	T	L	F
I	R	O	Z	O	E	E	O	O	E	E	N	O	C	N	E	O	O	F	L
N	I	L	C	R	L	N	C	C	V	T	O	L	O	T	S	L	L	L	O
E	N	E	I	O	Z	T	I	I	I	U	L	E	L	I	A	E	C	S	E
B	U	T	O	C	O	I	X	M	O	B	C	R	E	A	B	L	H	T	H
R	L	G	A	M	P	H	O	T	E	R	I	C	I	N	B	E	L	R	A

FILL IN THE BLANKS IN THE FOLLOWING SENTENCES

1. A fungus is a cellular organism with a _______________ cell wall that contains chitin and polysaccharides and a cell membrane that contains _______________.
2. Any infection with a fungus is called a _______________.
3. Systemic antifungals can be very toxic; adverse effects may include _______________ and _______________ failure.
4. Vaginal and oral yeast infections are often caused by _______________.
5. Athlete's foot and jock itch are examples of _______________ infections.
6. Topical antifungals can be very toxic and should not be absorbed _______________.
7. Topical antifungals should not be used near _______________ or lesions, which could increase absorption.
8. Topical antifungals can cause serious local _______________, _______________, _______________.

CHAPTER 10: ANTIPROTOZOAL AGENTS

MATCHING

Match the route or causative organism with the associated disease.

1. ________ leishmaniasis
2. ________ amebiasis
3. ________ malaria
4. ________ giardiasis
5. ________ PCP
6. ________ trichomoniasis
7. ________ trypanosomiasis

A. *Pneumocystis carinii*
B. plasmodium
C. tsetse fly bite
D. sand fly bite
E. *Entamoeba histolytica*
F. intestinal protozoan
G. vaginal protozoan

FILL IN THE BLANKS

Fill in the stages of the life cycle of the Anopheles *mosquito.*

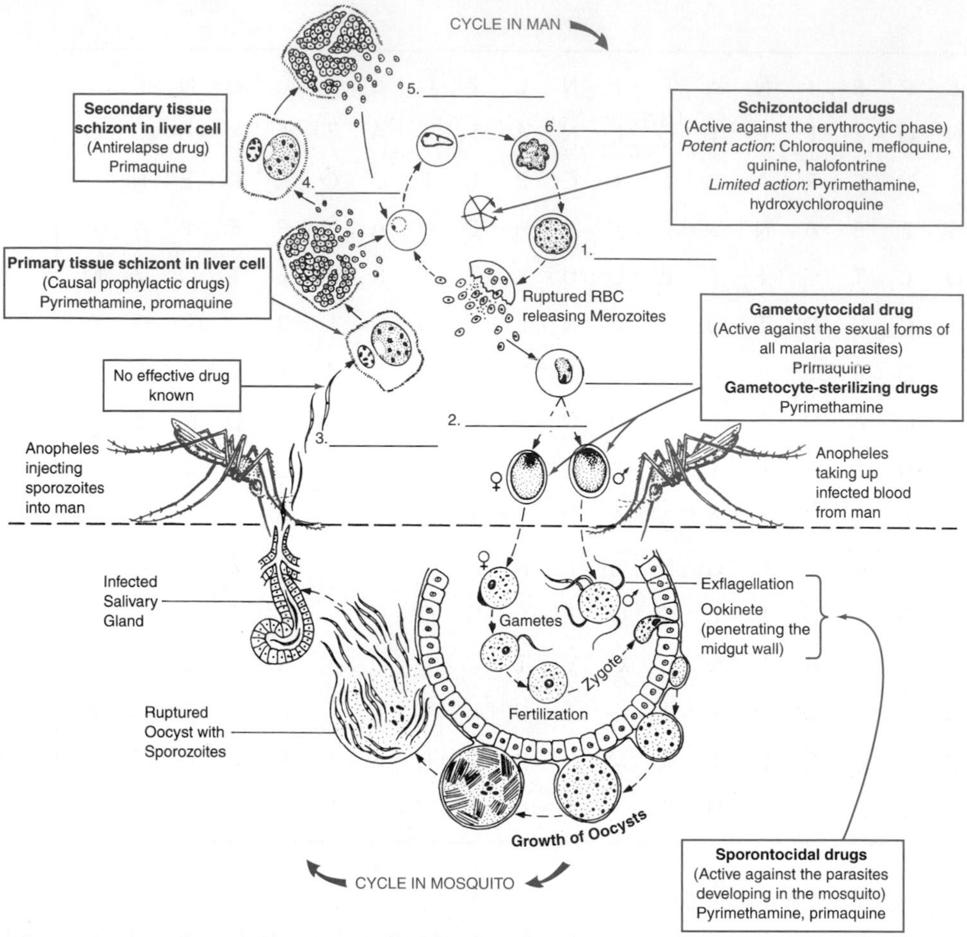

WWW. WEB EXERCISE

A friend of yours has won a trip around the world to many exotic places. You are asked if any shots are needed before the trip. Go to http://www.cdc.gov/travel and prepare a summary of suggested vaccinations or prophylactic measures that should be taken.

CHAPTER 11: ANTHELMINTIC AGENTS

DEFINE THE TERMS

1. cestode
2. nematode
3. pinworm
4. roundworm
5. schistosomiasis
6. trichinosis

7. thread worm

8. whip worm

PATIENT TEACHING CHECKLIST

Prepare a patient teaching checklist for an individual who has been diagnosed with pinworms and has been prescribed mebendazole. The patient will be at home during treatment of this disease.

FILL IN THE BLANKS

Fill in the phases of the life cycle of the worms associated with schistosomiasis.

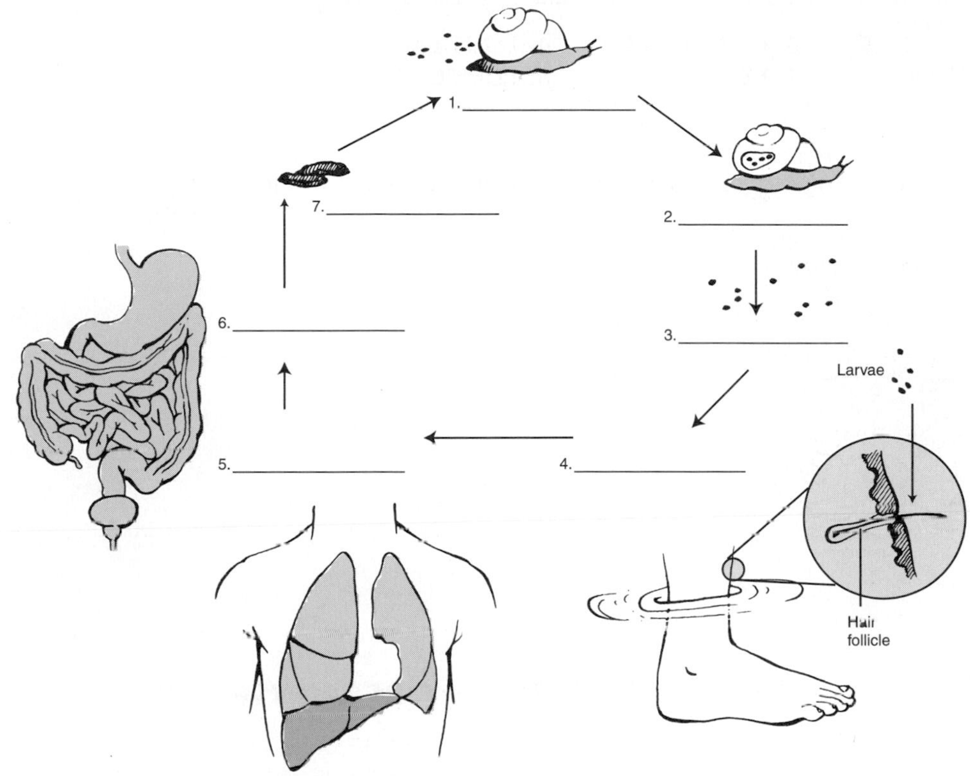

CHAPTER 12: ANTINEOPLASTIC AGENTS

NURSING CARE GUIDE

Jim Jackson has chronic myelogenous leukemia, Philadelphia chromosome positive. He is coming to the chemotherapy center to receive busulfan. Prepare a nursing care guide for Mr. Jackson to ensure continuity of care during his treatment program.

MATCHING

Match the word with the appropriate definition.

1. ________ anaplasia
2. ________ alopecia
3. ________ carcinoma
4. ________ metastasize
5. ________ neoplasm
6. ________ sarcoma
7. ________ autonomy
8. ________ antineoplastic

A. tumors in the mesenchyma, made up of embryonic connective tissue cells
B. drugs used to combat cancer
C. tumors starting in epithelial cells
D. loss of organization and structure
E. to travel throughout the body via lymph and circulation
F. new growth or cancer
G. loss of hair
H. loss of normal controls and reactions that limit cell growth and spreading

WORD SCRAMBLE

Unscramble the following words to find the names of commonly used antineoplastic agents:

1. TLVNIINSAEB 2. MCENUALTIRS 3. CNBPORATALI 4. PSNITILAC
5. FNXIOMETA 6. CMBYLOEN I 7. EZABACADN I 8. PDETEOSOI

FILL IN THE BLANKS

Identify the phases of the cell cycle that are affected by the types of antineoplastic drugs noted in the following diagram.

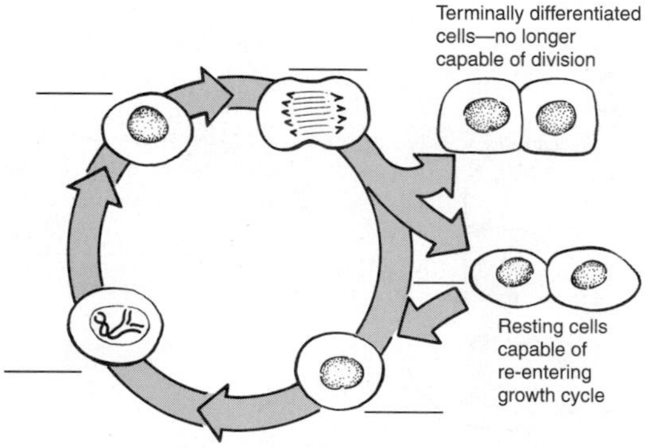

CHAPTER 13: INTRODUCTION TO THE IMMUNE RESPONSE AND INFLAMMATION

MULTIPLE CHOICE

Select the best answer to the following:

1. The inflammatory response is characterized by all of the following ***except:***
   a. Local tissue swelling
   b. Tissue tenderness
   c. Tissue redness
   d. RBC phagocytosis
2. B and T cells are similar in that they both:
   a. Secrete antibodies
   b. Play roles in the humoral immune response
   c. Stem from precursors in the bone marrow
   d. Are phagocytic lymphocytes
3. Antibodies are:
   a. proteins
   b. secreted by T cells
   c. enzymes
   d. effective against any antigens
4. Specific immune responses involve a B lymphocyte system and a T lymphocyte system. Which of the following statements is true about these systems?
   a. T and B lymphocytes have entered the thymus.
   b. T lymphocytes are involved in cell-mediated immunity; B lymphocytes are involved in antibody related immunity.
   c. T lymphocytes cannot influence B lymphocyte activity.
   d. T lymphocytes are important in regulating antibody production.

5. Interleukin 2:
   a. Is released from leukocytes as a means of communicating with other leukocytes
   b. Causes a decrease in temperature by directly affecting the hypothalamus
   c. Can induce REM sleep
   d. Stimulates the production of more B cells in the bone marrow

6. Clonal theory states that:
   a. Each clone of B cells can recognize and bind with many different foreign proteins
   b. Humans develop their B clones sometime after birth
   c. Plasma cells derive from one clone of B cells and will secrete only one kind of antibody
   d. Most humans will be able to develop new B clones when exposed to previously unencountered antigens

FILL IN THE BLANKS

Fill in the blanks below, indicating the clinical signs and symptoms of the inflammatory response and the major catalysts of these signs and symptoms.

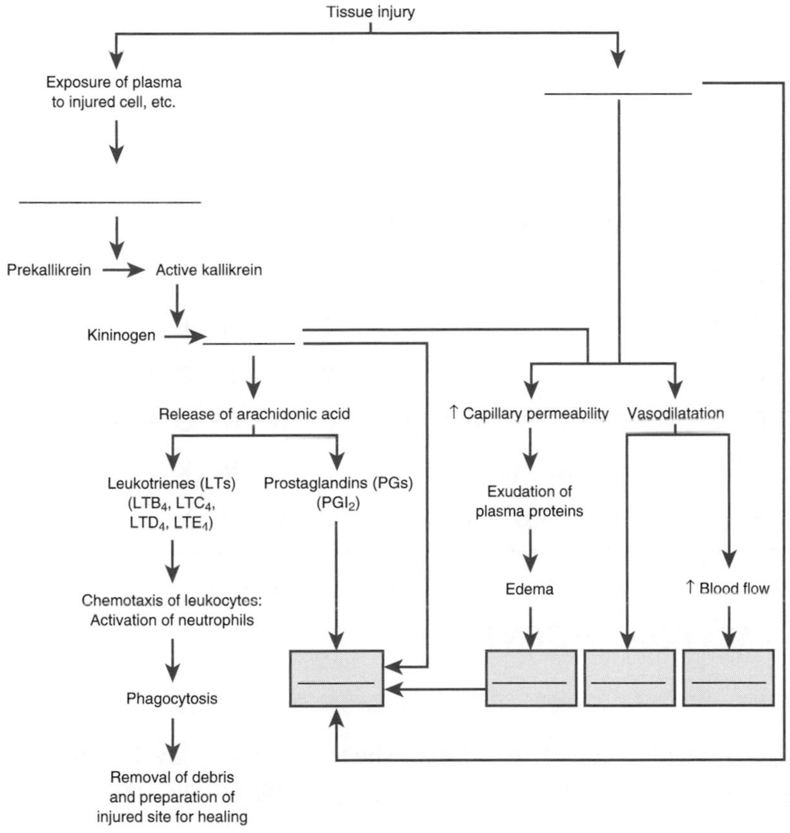

WORD SEARCH

Circle the following words relating to the immune system and the inflammatory response hidden in the grid below. Words may be horizontal, vertical, or diagonal.

neutrophil
eosinophil
basophil
interferon
interleukin
lymphocyte
complement
plasma cell
antibody
cytotoxin
phagocyte
Hageman factor
leukocyte
autoimmune
thymus
kinin
arachidonic acid
chemotaxis

B	Q	E	S	T	U	N	L	O	I	P	M	W	R	Y	O	I
D	L	S	H	I	M	N	T	P	S	H	O	H	E	S	C	N
A	C	O	M	P	L	E	M	E	N	T	R	E	S	E	H	T
L	H	S	P	O	I	U	N	R	O	H	E	R	T	R	E	E
H	A	M	F	A	C	T	O	R	R	Y	L	E	I	S	M	R
L	M	R	S	L	B	R	T	A	S	M	B	P	K	X	O	L
K	E	U	A	I	R	O	H	L	E	U	K	O	C	Y	T	E
U	R	M	L	C	A	P	E	S	L	S	E	L	H	N	A	U
E	S	B	E	O	H	H	L	I	O	H	K	Q	N	Y	X	K
L	E	L	A	N	T	I	B	O	D	Y	P	U	I	M	I	I
E	N	Y	M	T	I	L	D	P	E	K	H	I	X	N	S	N
U	U	S	P	I	A	B	O	O	R	I	A	S	O	B	I	K
O	M	P	H	A	G	E	M	A	N	N	G	H	T	A	T	E
L	M	O	I	R	U	R	I	L	O	I	O	E	O	S	R	U
W	I	N	T	E	R	F	E	R	O	N	C	A	T	O	N	E
E	O	S	I	N	O	P	H	I	L	A	Y	A	Y	P	S	O
S	T	A	G	N	A	N	Y	S	V	E	T	E	C	H	N	O
P	U	L	L	P	L	A	S	M	A	C	E	L	L	I	N	K
A	A	P	E	P	E	T	Y	C	O	H	P	M	Y	L	D	Y

CHAPTER 14: ANTI-INFLAMMATORY AGENTS

WWW. WEB EXERCISE

You are caring for a patient who is newly diagnosed with rheumatoid arthritis. The family is very involved and supportive and would like information on the disease, treatment options, and any new information. Log on to: http://www.arthritis.org/ and prepare an information sheet for this family using data from that site.

WORD SCRAMBLE

Unscramble the following words to find the names of commonly used antiinflammatory agents:

1. EXONRHAP
2. CLAUSIND
3. RALOOCTEK
4. FIDONECCAL
5. BROUPFINE
6. ZOLASNALIE
7. THANNAPOCEINE
8. SLATASLAE
9. PRISAIN
10. FROTNOKEEP

MATCHING

Match the word with the appropriate definition.

1. _______ antiinflammatory
2. _______ antipyretic
3. _______ analgesic
4. _______ salicylates
5. _______ NSAIDs
6. _______ pyrogens
7. _______ chryrostherapy

A. treatment with gold salts
B. non-steroidal antiinflammatory drugs
C. block the prostaglandin system to prevent inflammation
D. blocking the effects of the inflammatory response
E. blocking pain sensation
F. substances that elevate the body's temperature
G. blocking fever

CHAPTER 15: IMMUNE MODULATORS

DEFINE THE TERMS

1. autoimmune
2. interferon
3. interleukin
4. monoclonal antibodies
5. immune suppressant

MATCHING

Match the interferon with its usual indication for use.

1. _______ interferon alfa 2a
2. _______ interferon alfa 2b
3. _______ interferon alfacon 1
4. _______ interferon alfa n3
5. _______ interferon beta 1a
6. _______ interferon beta 1b
7. _______ interferon gamma 1b

A. Treatment of multiple sclerosis
B. Treatment of leukemias, Kaposi's sarcoma, warts, hepatitis B, malignant melanoma
C. Treatment of multiple sclerosis
D. Treatment of serious, chronic granulomatous disease
E. Treatment of leukemias, Kaposi's sarcoma
F. Treatment of chronic hepatitis C
G. Intralesional treatment of warts

FILL IN THE BLANKS

1. _______________ _______________ are specific antibodies produced by a single clone of B cells to react with a very specific antigen.
2. The following monoclonal antibodies are used in the prevention of renal transplant rejection: _______________, _______________, _______________.
3. Infliximab is used to treat _______________ disease in patients who do not respond to other therapy.
4. Palivizumab was developed for the prevention of _______________ _______________ _______________ in high-risk children.
5. Treatment of metastatic breast cancer with tumors that overexpress human epidermal growth factor receptor 2 (HER2) is specifically the indication for _______________.
6. _______________ is used for the treatment of relapsed follicular B-cell non-Hodgkin's lymphoma B lymphocytes.

CHAPTER 16: VACCINES AND SERA

WWW. WEB EXERCISE

Your patient, a new mother, has arrived at the clinic with her 2-week-old baby for routine postpartum health care. She has been watching a TV talk show about the hazards of vaccinations and asks some good questions about vaccinating her baby. Go to the Internet and find some useful information that can be printed out to help your patient understand vaccinations and to make good decisions about her child's health care.

TRUE OR FALSE

Indicate whether the following statements are true (T) or false (F).

_____ 1. Tetanus vaccines will provide active immunity against tetanus toxins.

_____ 2. Active immunity occurs when the host is stimulated to make antibodies to a specific antigen.

_____ 3. Gamma globulin provides a good form of passive immunity to patients exposed to a specific antigen.

_____ 4. Vaccines are used to promote active immunity.

_____ 5. Vaccines are only used to prevent infection with future exposures.

_____ 6. Serious reactions have occurred to routine immunizations in the past.

_____ 7. Patients will not experience any discomfort following an immunization injection.

_____ 8. Serum sickness—a massive immune reaction—occurs more frequently with vaccines than with immune sera

FILL IN THE BLANKS

Fill in the blanks in the figure below to indicate the timing of routine immunizations.

Immunization	*Birth*	*2 mo*	*4 mo*	*6 mo*	*12–15 mo*	*18 mo*	*4–6 y*	*11–12 y*	*14–16 y*
Hepatitis B									
DPT									
Rotavirus									
Tetanus/diphtheria booster									
H. influenzae b									
Measles, mumps, rubella									
Poliovirus									

Suggested by the American Academy of Pediatrics, 1998.

CHAPTER 17: INTRODUCTION TO NERVES AND THE NERVOUS SYSTEM

LABELING

Insert the following labels as they apply to the nerve: soma, cell nucleus, dendrites, axon hillock, axon, Schwann cell, node of Ranvier

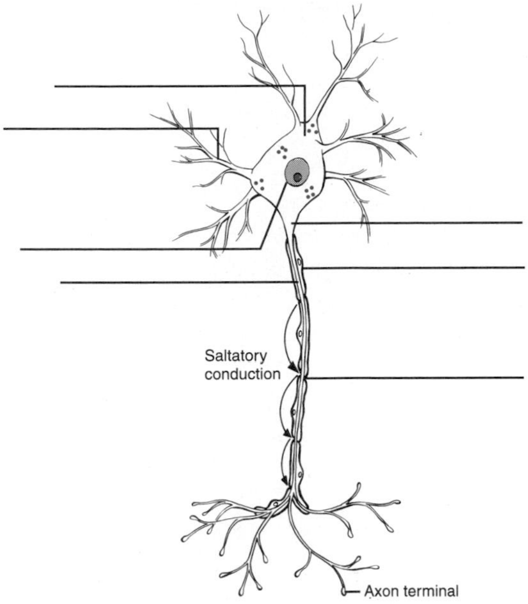

MATCHING

Match the word with the appropriate definition:

1. ________ action potential
2. ________ afferent
3. ________ axon
4. ________ dendrite
5. ________ depolarization
6. ________ effector
7. ________ efferent
8. ________ engram
9. ________ forebrain
10. ________ hindbrain

A. motor neurons
B. long projection from a neuron that carries information from one nerve to another nerve or effector
C. neurons or groups of neurons that bring information to the CNS
D. the brainstem
E. upper level of the brain
F. short-term memory
G. the electrical signal by which neurons send information
H. muscle, a gland, or another nerve stimulated by a nerve
I. reversing the membrane charge from negative to positive
J. short projection on a neuron that transmits information

DIAGRAM

Diagram an action potential and label the cellular events that are occurring during each phase of the action potential.

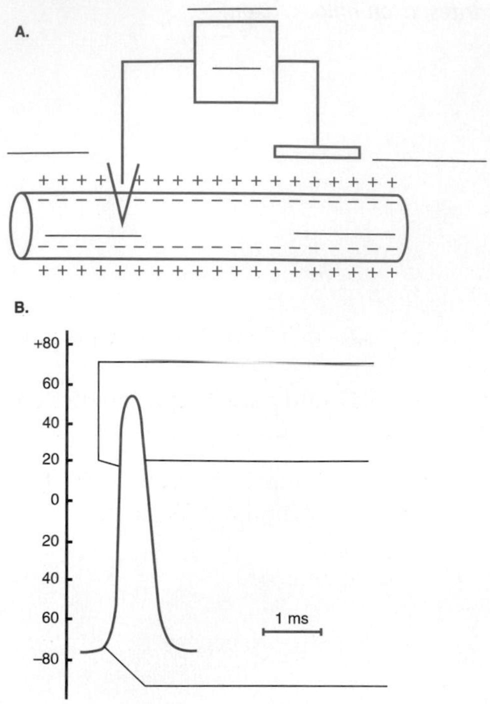

CHAPTER 18: ANXIOLYTIC AND HYPNOTIC AGENTS

FILL IN THE BLANKS

1. ______________ is a feeling of tension, nervousness, apprehension or fear that usually involves unpleasant reactions to a stimulus, which is actual or unknown.
2. Mild anxiety may serve as a stimulus or ______________ in some situations.
3. ______________ are drugs that can calm patients and make them unaware of their environment.
4. Drugs that can cause sleep are called ______________.
5. Anxiolytics can prevent feelings of ______________ or ______________.
6. Patients who are restless, nervous, irritable or overreacting to stimuli could benefit from ______________.
7. Hynosis or sleep can be caused by drugs that ______________ the CNS.
8. ______________ are the most frequently used anxiolytic drugs.

MATCHING

Match the generic name of these commonly used anxiolytic drugs with the associated brand name.

1. ________	clonazepam	A. *Restoril*
2. ________	lorazepam	B. *Xanax*
3. ________	temazepam	C. *Klonopin*
4. ________	alprazolam	D. *Valium*
5. ________	oxazepam	E. *Ativan*
6. ________	triazolam	F. *Librium*
7. ________	diazepam	G. *Serax*
8. ________	chlordiazepoxide	H. *Halcion*
9. ________	flurazepam	I. *Tranxene*
10. ________	clorazepate	J. *Dalmane*

WWW. WEB EXERCISE

One of your patients has acute anxiety disorder. His family members are upset and feeling alone and hopeless. Log onto the Internet and find support groups and educational information that might help this family.

CHAPTER 19: ANTIDEPRESSANT AGENTS

MULTIPLE CHOICE

1. Affect refers to:
   a. people's feelings in response to their environment
   b. people's thought processes
   c. is not a normal part of everyday life
   d. alterations in perceiving the environment
2. Depression:
   a. is always traceable to a precipitating event
   b. is a very common affective disorder
   c. involves anger and excited states
   d. is easily diagnosed with the proper tests
3. Antidepressants may be classified as:
   a. GABA inhibitors, tricylics, and SSRIs
   b. Tricyclic antidepressants (TCAs), the MAO inhibitors, and the selective serotonin reuptake inhibitors (SSRIs)
   c. Benzodiazepines, MAO inhibitors, phenothiazines
   d. Barbiturates, phenothiazines, miscellaneous drugs
4. Tricyclic antidepressants:
   a. Reduce the release of 5HT and norepinephrine from nerves
   b. Block the metabolism of released 5HT and norephinephrine
   c. Reduce the reuptake of 5HT and norepinephrine by nerves
   d. Occupy specific 5HT and norepinephrine sites on stimulated nerves
5. Tyramine containing foods must be limited with the use of MAO inhibitors. Tyramine is found in:
   a. green, leafy vegetables
   b. yellow fruits and vegetables
   c. aged cheeses and wines
   d. chicken—especially white meat

WORD SEARCH

Circle the names of the following antidepressants hidden in the grid below. Words may be horizontal, vertical, or diagonal.

amoxapine
nortriptyline
bupropion
clomipramine
isocarboxazid
nefazodone
desipramine
phenelzine
trazodone
doxepin
citalopram
venlafaxine
imipramine
paroxetine
maprotiline
sertraline

H	L	N	E	O	B	H	T	H	I	N	E	O	N
B	C	L	M	T	U	C	K	U	M	O	L	P	O
A	M	O	X	A	P	I	N	E	I	R	S	H	R
L	A	D	I	N	R	M	B	O	P	R	I	E	T
O	P	R	E	L	O	N	C	L	R	U	N	N	R
P	R	I	N	S	P	O	H	I	A	I	E	E	I
D	O	X	E	P	I	N	E	G	M	E	F	L	P
I	T	S	G	Y	O	P	V	A	I	L	A	Z	T
Z	I	P	I	L	N	O	R	E	N	X	Z	I	Y
A	L	R	O	M	O	P	I	A	E	L	O	N	L
X	I	E	M	O	I	O	S	T	M	O	D	E	I
O	N	N	R	M	N	P	T	R	E	I	O	N	N
B	E	S	O	T	R	A	Z	O	D	O	N	E	E
R	E	L	I	U	E	P	E	N	E	L	E	E	D
A	C	I	T	A	L	O	P	R	A	M	R	D	S
C	V	E	N	L	A	F	A	X	I	N	E	M	O
O	E	N	E	N	I	T	E	X	O	R	A	P	Y
S	E	R	T	R	A	L	I	N	E	L	M	N	I
I	L	S	H	E	N	E	F	O	M	Y	O	I	L

WORD SCRAMBLE

1. PORBPNUIO
2. OTLINUEXFE
3. MAMICOPRLINE
4. FLAXIVENAEN
5. ZIPNEEHLNE
6. TNEXOPRAEI
7. PIMIMINRAE
8. DOZENFAENO

CROSSWORD PUZZLE

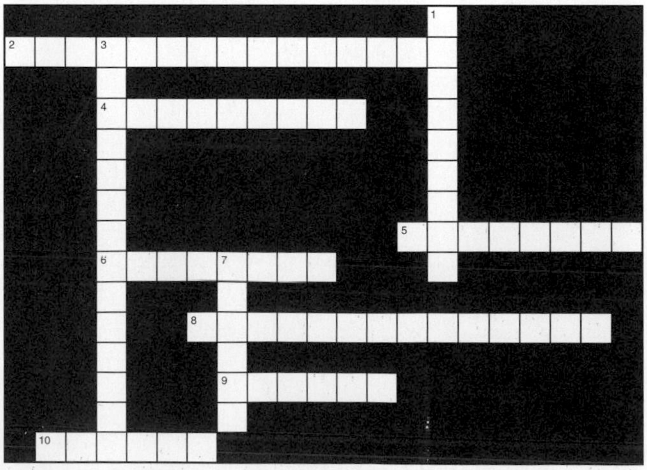

ACROSS

2 Enzyme that breaks down norepinephrine
4 Drug that blocks the reuptake of norepinephrine and serotonin
5 An amine associated with brain chemistry
6 Specific site on a cell that reacts with neurotransmitters
8 Neurotransmitter whose lack is associated with depression
9 State of feeling about one's environment
10 Reabsorption of a chemical into a cell

DOWN

1 Neurotransmitter whose low levels are associated with depression
3 Drug used to relieve affective disorder associated with sadness and lethargy
7 Popular SSRI

CHAPTER 20: PSYCHOTHERAPEUTIC AGENTS

MATCHING

Match the following words with the corresponding definitions.

1. ________ schizophrenia
2. ________ narcolepsy
3. ________ attention-deficit disorder
4. ________ neuroleptic
5. ________ major tranquilizer
6. ________ mania
7. ________ antipsychotic

A. a state of hyperexcitability
B. behavioral syndrome characterized by an inability to concentrate
C. a mental disorder characterized by daytime sleepiness and period and sudden loss of wakefulness
D. name once used to describe antipsychotic drugs
E. a drug used to treat a disorder of the thought processes; a dopamine receptor blocker
F. a psychotic disorder characterized by delusions, hallucinations, and thinking and speech disturbances
G. antipsychotic drug, so named because of the numerous neurologic adverse effects caused by these drugs

PATIENT TEACHING CHECKLIST

Mr. Brown is a landscaper who is very busy in the spring and summer of the year. He has been treated for manifestations of a psychotic disorder, but has had drug sensitivity reactions to most of the drugs he has tried. The psychiatrist has ordered chlorpromazine, 10 mg PO q6h, to try to control his behavior. Mr. Brown is referred to the nurse for drug teaching. Using the patient teaching checklist as a template, prepare a written drug card for Mr. Brown.

WWW. WEB EXERCISE

Your patient has been diagnosed with seasonal affective disorder (SAD). She does not want to take any medication, though her signs and symptoms are nearly incapacitating. Help your patient investigate alternative treatment plans for SAD. Log on to http://www.mhsource.com/

CHAPTER 21: ANTIEPILEPTIC AGENTS

FILL IN THE BLANKS

1. ______________, the most prevalent of the neurologic disorders, is a collection of different syndromes, all characterized by a sudden discharge of excessive electrical energy from nerve cells located within the brain.
2. Sudden discharge of excessive electrical energy in the brain leads to a ______________.
3. If motor nerves are stimulated by this sudden discharge of electrical energy, a ______________ may occur with tonic-clonic muscle contractions.
4. Epilepsy is managed using a class of drugs called ______________.
5. Tonic-clonic seizures, formerly known as ______________, involve dramatic tonic-clonic muscle contractions, loss of consciousness, and a recovery period that is characterized by confusion and exhaustion.
6. A petit mal seizure, now called an ______________, involves abrupt, brief (3–5 seconds) periods of loss of consciousness.
7. Seizures that involve short, sporadic periods of muscle contractions that last for several minutes are called ______________.
8. Seizures that are related to very high fevers and usually involve convulsions are called ______________.
9. The most dangerous of seizure conditions is a state in which seizures rapidly recur again and again; it is referred to as ______________.
10. Partial or ______________ seizures involve one area of the brain and do not spread throughout the entire brain.

NURSING CARE GUIDE

Meghan Smith, a college student, is found beside her car having a tonic-clonic seizure. Safety precautions were taken to avoid injury, and Meghan was transported to the infirmary for evaluation. She has no history of seizure disoders and denies drug or alcohol use. Her parents are called and the attending physician starts her on phenytoin (Dilantin) as a precautionary measure until further tests can be done. Meghan's parents have her transported to a hospital near their home. Prepare a nursing care plan to be transported with Meghan. As a healthy young adult with no other known problems, the care plan will reflect drug therapy.

CROSSWORD PUZZLE

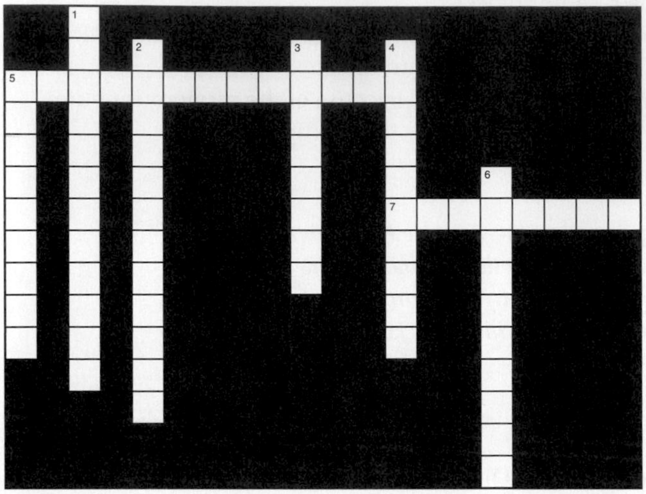

ACROSS

5 Sedative/hypnotic used to treat many forms of seizures

7 Drug of choice for petit mal seizures

DOWN

1 Saved for use in the treatment of petit mal seizures in patients refractory to other agents

2 Used to prevent seizures following neurosurgery

3 Also used to relieve tension and muscle spasm

4 Used to treat petit mal seizures, myoclonic seizures

5 Dilantin

6 Used as an adjunct in treating petit mal seizures

CHAPTER 22: ANTIPARKINSONISM AGENTS

FILL IN THE BLANKS

Label the following diagram, indicating the interrelationship of neurons that leads to Parkinson's disease.

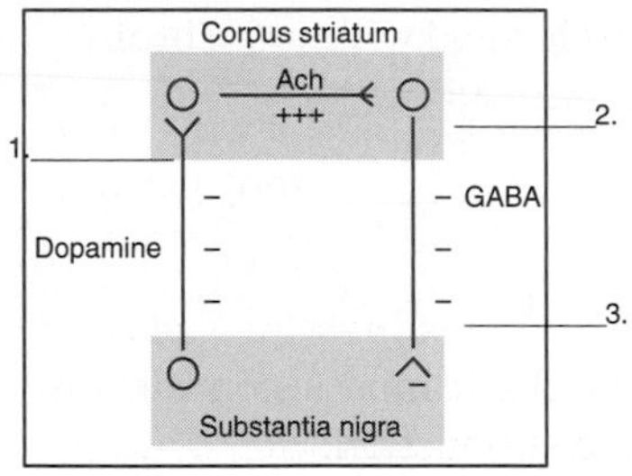

WORD SCRAMBLE

Unscramble the following letters to form the names of commonly used antiparkinsonism drugs.

1. POOLAVED	2. YOPCLICDINRE	3. GLOIERPED	4. PEDRINIBE
5. TANMADAENI	6. POORINIREL	7. ZOPTREBNINE	8. INETRIPCOROMB

WWW. WEB EXERCISE

M. J. was diagnosed with Parkinson's disease at the age of 42, when tremors began to interfere with his job as a watch repairman. He was well controlled on carbidopa, levodopa (*Sinemet*) for 7 years, but now the disease seems to be progressing rapidly. You are trying to work with the family to prepare them for what is to come and to help them to make the most of M. J.'s abilities while they struggle with his prognosis. Go to http://www.ninds.nih.gov/ and find information that will be helpful for this family.

CHAPTER 23: MUSCLE RELAXANTS

MATCHING

Match the following words with the corresponding definitions.

1. ________ spasticity
2. ________ hypertonia
3. ________ hypotonia
4. ________ basal ganglia
5. ________ intraneurons
6. ________ pyramidal tract
7. ________ extrapyramidal tract
8. ________ cerebellum

A. neurons that communicate between other neurons
B. fibers with the CNS that control precise, intentional movement
C. sustained contractions of muscles
D. lower portion of the brain associated with coordination of muscle movements and voluntary muscle movement
E. state of excessive muscle response and activity
F. lower area of the brain associated with coordination of unconscious muscle movements
G. cells that coordinate unconsciously controlled muscle activity
H. state of limited or absent muscle response and activity

FILL IN THE BLANKS

Label the parts of the nerve and muscle reflex.

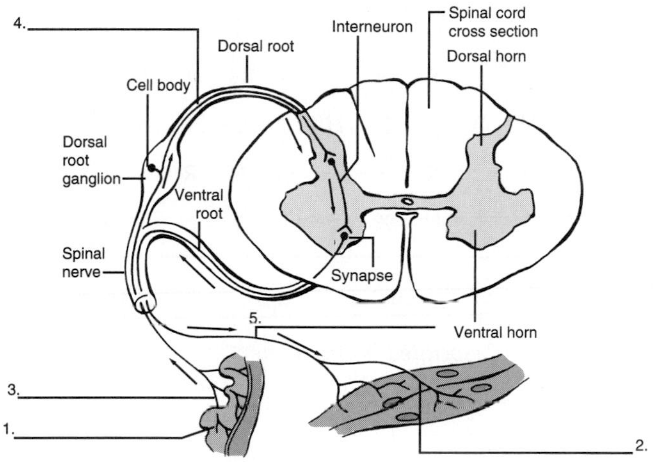

TRUE OR FALSE

Indicate whether the following statements are true (T) or false (F).

_____ 1. The nerves that affect movement, position, and posture are the spinal sensory neurons.

_____ 2. The basal ganglia and the cerebellum modulate spinal motor nerve activity and help coordinate activity between various muscle groups.

_____ 3. Fibers that control precise, intentional movement make up the extrapyramidal tract.

_____ 4. The pyramidal tract modulates or coordinates unconsciously controlled muscle activity and allows the body to make automatic adjustments in posture, position, and balance.

_____ 5. Muscle spasticity is the result of damage to neurons within the CNS rather than injury to peripheral structures.

_____ 6. Excessive stimulation of muscles is referred to as hypotonia.

_____ 7. Centrally acting skeletal muscle relaxants work in the CNS to interfere with the reflexes that are causing the muscle spasm.

_____ 8. antrolene acts within skeletal muscle fibers, interfering with the release of potassium from the muscle tubules, to prevent the fibers from contracting.

_____ 9. The primary indication for the use of centrally acting skeletal muscle agents is the relief of discomfort associated with acute, painful musculoskeletal conditions.

_____ 10. Centrally acting muscle relaxants should be used as an adjunct to rest, physical therapy, and other measures.

CHAPTER 24: NARCOTICS AND ANTIMIGRAINE AGENTS

WORD SEARCH

Circle the names of the following frequently used narcotics hidden in the grid below. Words may be horizontal, vertical, or diagonal.

alfentanil
codeine
fentanyl
hydrocodone
hydromorphone
levorphanol
meperidine
methadone
morphine
oxycodone
oxymorphone
propoxyphene
sufentanil

A	S	T	E	O	X	Y	M	O	R	P	H	I	N	E	P	R	O
E	N	I	D	I	R	E	P	E	M	H	E	N	O	N	R	T	L
E	E	O	E	L	N	P	E	M	E	L	N	O	R	O	O	O	L
N	A	N	P	I	O	S	N	N	H	I	Y	M	S	D	P	L	I
O	D	S	E	O	P	H	E	N	T	I	O	N	G	A	O	X	N
D	I	D	O	P	J	H	N	I	H	O	T	R	A	H	X	I	A
O	O	R	A	H	I	L	O	T	A	N	R	I	M	T	Y	L	T
C	N	E	M	O	X	Y	C	O	D	O	N	E	S	E	P	O	N
O	X	Y	M	O	P	H	N	I	O	R	I	N	S	M	H	E	E
R	Y	N	M	O	R	P	H	I	N	E	C	O	Q	A	E	L	F
D	O	R	U	L	I	P	Y	S	U	F	E	N	T	A	N	I	L
Y	L	E	V	O	R	P	H	A	N	O	L	C	H	L	E	M	A
H	Y	D	R	O	M	O	R	P	H	O	N	E	I	O	N	R	I
D	E	P	R	U	N	L	Y	N	A	T	N	X	E	T	Y	S	T

MATCHING

Match the generic name of these commonly used narcotic agonists with the associated brand name.

1. ________ fentanyl
2. ________ hydrocodone
3. ________ hydromorphone
4. ________ levomethadyl
5. ________ levorphanol
6. ________ meperidine
7. ________ methadone
8. ________ morphine
9. ________ oxycodone
10. ________ propoxyphene

A. *Darvon*
B. *Dolophine*
C. *Demerol*
D. *Dilaudid*
E. *OxyContin*
F. *Hycodan*
G. *Duragesic*
H. *ORLAAM*
I. *Roxanal*
J. *Levo-Dromoran*

MULTIPLE CHOICE

1. The term migraine headache is used to describe several different types of syndromes, all of which include:
   a. severe, throbbing headaches on one side of the head
   b. blinding headaches in the frontal lobe
   c. loss of consciousness
   d. the presence of an anticipatory aura

2. Cluster headaches:
   a. are frequently occurring migraine headaches
   b. start during sleep and involve sharp, steady eye pain lasting for 15–90 minutes with sweating, flushing, tearing, and nasal congestion
   c. occur in conjunction with airborn allergies
   d. are tension headaches

3. Tension headaches:
   a. are migraine headaches
   b. usually occur during stress and feel like a dull band around the entire head
   c. last for up to 2 hours
   d. are cluster headaches

4. Ergot derivatives are used to treat migraines because they:
   a. are not associated with any adverse effects
   b. are inexpensive because they come from molds
   c. cause constriction of cranial blood vessels, decreasing the pulsation of cranial arteries and decreasing the hyperperfusion of the basilar artery vascular bed
   d. are very slow acting and have prolonged effects

5. The triptans are a group of drugs that:
   a. bind to selective serotonin receptor sites to cause vasoconstriction of cranial vessels, relieving the signs and symptoms of migraine headache
   b. must be delivered by injection
   c. have many more adverse effects than the ergot derivatives
   d. can be safely used in the elderly and patients with known vascular disease

CHAPTER 25: GENERAL AND LOCAL ANESTHETIC AGENTS

FILL IN THE BLANKS

Describe what occurs at each of the four stages of anesthesia.

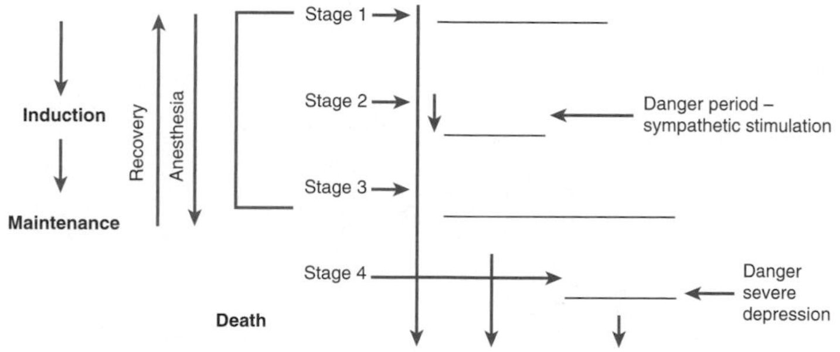

NURSING CARE GUIDE

Lorne Perkins, a 26-year-old football player, is admitted to your short-term surgery unit for repair of an inguinal hernia. He has elected to have a spinal anesthetic for the surgery. Prepare a nursing care guide that can follow him to the recovery area following surgery.

FILL IN THE BLANKS

1. General anesthetics are drugs used to produce ______________, ______________, ______________, ______________ and to block muscle reflexes that could interfere with a surgical procedure or put the patient at risk for harm.
2. Anesthesia proceeds through predictable stages from ______________ to total CNS depression and ______________.
3. ______________ is the time from the beginning of anesthesia administration until the patient reaches surgical anesthesia.
4. ______________ involves giving a variety of drugs, including anticholinergics, rapid IV anesthetics, inhaled anesthetics, NMJ blockers, and narcotics.
5. Local anesthetics block the ______________, preventing the transmission of pain sensations and motor stimuli.
6. The use of general anesthetics involves a widespread ______________ that could be harmful, especially in patients with underlying CNS, CV or respiratory diseases.
7. Patients receiving general anesthetics should be monitored for any adverse effects, offered reassurance, and provided with safety precautions until the recovery of ______________, ______________, and ______________.
8. The adverse effects of local anesthetics may be related to their local blocking of sensation; such effects may include: ______________, ______________, and ______________.

CHAPTER 26: NEUROMUSCULAR JUNCTION BLOCKING AGENTS

FILL IN THE BLANKS

Indicate the actions and functions of the neuromuscular junction and the sliding filament theory of muscle contraction.

BOX 23-1 SUMMARY OF MUSCLE CONTRACTION AND RELAXATION

Stimulus from nerve axon to myoneural junction

↓

____

↓

Increased permeability of muscles cell membrane to sodium

↓

____

____

↓

Transmission of action potential through T tubules

↓

____

↓

Binding of calcium with troponin–tropomyosin

↓

____

____

↓

Contraction of the muscle fiber

↓

____

____

↓

Unbinding of troponin–tropomyosin

↓

____

↓

Lengthening of sarcomere unit

↓

____

CROSSWORD PUZZLE

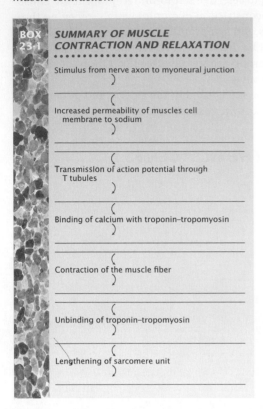

ACROSS

1 Depolarizing neuromuscular junction blocker
4 Neurotransmitter at the neuromuscular junction
6 Loss of muscle function
7 Prevents the formation of actinomyosin bridges

DOWN

1 Functional unit of a muscle
2 Ion needed for muscle contraction
3 Preventing, not causing cell depolarization
5 Poison used on the tips of arrows and spears

WWW. WEB EXERCISE

While you are doing a pre-op assessment, the patient tells you that her family has a history of not waking up from anesthesia. You get as much information as you can from the patient, then research cholinesterase deficiencies to see if this could be a problem for the patient. Log on to patienthttp://www.anesthesia.wisc.edu/Topics/Physiology/pseudocholin.html.

CHAPTER 27: INTRODUCTION TO THE AUTONOMIC NERVOUS SYSTEM

SYMPATHETIC/PARASYMPATHETIC COMPARISON

Fill in the following table describing the characteristics of the sympathetic and parasympathetic branches of the autonomic nervous system.

TABLE 27-1

COMPARISON OF THE SYMPATHETIC AND PARASYMPATHETIC NERVOUS SYSTEMS

Characteristic	Sympathetic	Parasympathetic
CNS nerve origin		
Preganglionic neuron		
Preganglionic neurotransmitter		
Ganglia location		
Postganglionic neuron		
Postganglionic neurotransmitter		
Neurotransmitter terminator		
General response		

MATCHING

Match each of the following words with the appropriate definition.

1. ________ autonomic nervous system
2. ________ sympathetic nervous system
3. ________ parasympathetic nervous system
4. ________ ganglia
5. ________ adrenergic receptors
6. ________ cholinergic receptors
7. ________ beta receptors
8. ________ alpha receptors
9. ________ muscarinic receptors
10. ________ nicotinic receptors
11. ________ acetylcholinesterase
12. ________ MAO

A. adrenergic receptors that are found in smooth muscles
B. closely packed group of nerve cell bodies
C. "fight or flight" response mediator
D. enzyme that breaks down norepinephrine
E. cholinergic receptors that also respond to stimulation by nicotine
F. "rest and digest" response mediator
G. receptor sites on effectors that respond to acetylcholine
H. adrenergic receptors that are found in the heart, lungs, and vascular smooth muscle
I. receptor sites on effectors that respond to norepinephrine
J. cholinergic receptors that also respond to stimulation by muscarine
K. portion of the central and peripheral nervous systems that, with the endocrine system, functions to maintain internal homeostasis
L. enzyme that deactivates acetylcholine released from the nerve axon

FILL IN THE CHART

Fill in the following chart, which shows the effects of the sympathetic and parasympathetic systems on the body's organ system. Insert the specific sympathetic receptor type in column 3 as appropriate.

TABLE 27-2

EFFECTS OF AUTONOMIC STIMULATION

Effector Site	Sympathetic Reaction	Receptor	Parasympathetic Reaction
Heart			
Blood vessels			
Skin, mucous membranes			
Skeletal muscle			
Bronchial muscle			
GI system			
Muscle motility and tone			
Sphincters			
Secretions			
Salivary glands			
Gallbladder			
Liver			
Urinary bladder			
Detrusor muscle			
Trigone muscle and sphincter			
Eye structures			
Iris radial muscle			
Iris sphincter muscle			
Ciliary muscle			
Lacrimal glands			
Skin structures			
Sweat glands			
Piloerector muscles			
Sex organs			
Male			
Female			

(—— means no reaction or response)

CHAPTER 28: ADRENERGIC AGENTS

MULTIPLE CHOICE

1. Adrenergic agonists are:
   a. drugs used to stimulate the cholinergic receptors within the SNS
   b. also called sympathomimetic drugs
   c. drugs used to block the effects of the sympathetic system
   d. used to treat hypertension

2. Alpha and beta adrenergic agonists:
   a. stimulate all of the adrenergic receptors in the SNS
   b. are used to prevent a fight or flight response
   c. are most useful in treating hypertension
   d. are associated with few adverse effects

3. Clonidine:
   a. is a beta-specific adrenergic agonist
   b. is used to treat shock
   c. stimulates alpha $_2$ receptors and blocks norepinephrine release from nerve axons
   d. may be useful in treating asthma

4. Beta-$_2$ specific adrenergic agonists are:
   a. used to manage and treat asthma, bronchospasm, and other obstructive pulmonary diseases
   b. used to stimulate bronchoconstriction
   c. not associated with any cardiovascular effects
   d. useful for stimulating labor

5. Isoproterenol, a beta agonist:
   a. is used to treat hypertension
   b. can be used to treat arrhythmias and also to treat bronchospasm and asthma
   c. can only be given parenterally
   d. blocks the effects of the SNS on the heart

WORD SCRAMBLE

Unscramble the following words to find the names of frequently used adrenergic agonists:

1. redhepnie
2. indocline
3. modanpie
4. torridine
5. Aboutdimen
6. reproninineheр
7. ratammnolie
8. yepphhnneeirl
9. nineppehire
10. pontlioreesor

FILL IN THE BLANKS

Insert the alpha adrenergic drugs discussed in this chapter at their appropriate sites of action.

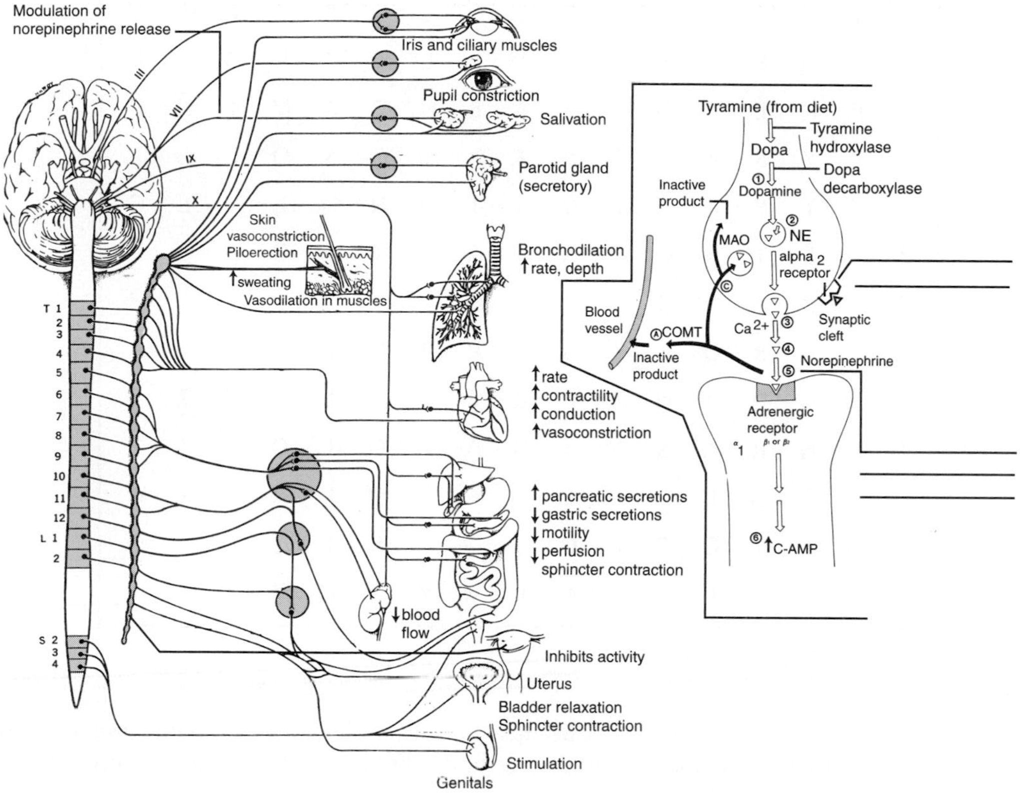

CHAPTER 29: ADRENERGIC BLOCKING AGENTS

WORD SEARCH

Circle the following names of adrenergic blocking agents that are hidden in the grid below:

guanadrel
labetalol
phenoxybenzamine
prazosin
terazosin
carteolol
nadolol
pindolol
sotalol
timolol
atenolol
bisoprolol
esmolol
metoprolol

L	K	U	I	N	O	Z	A	S	O	N	A	C	E	T	A	C
I	O	B	M	O	R	T	X	I	T	E	C	A	M	H	A	D
B	I	B	P	I	N	D	O	L	O	L	H	R	E	E	T	H
L	P	M	E	N	I	O	Z	I	L	L	E	T	S	O	E	P
C	P	H	E	N	O	X	Y	B	E	N	Z	A	M	I	N	E
H	X	Y	S	A	Z	O	S	I	N	I	O	S	O	L	O	X
O	X	Y	P	R	A	Z	O	S	I	N	N	H	L	Y	L	G
Z	A	S	I	N	O	O	X	C	A	R	T	E	O	L	O	L
T	E	R	A	Z	O	S	I	N	M	L	Y	L	L	I	L	Z
M	I	R	R	O	B	I	S	O	P	R	O	L	O	L	I	E
O	S	G	U	A	N	A	D	R	E	L	L	L	Y	X	Z	B
T	H	H	R	A	S	N	I	N	A	D	O	L	O	L	A	F
H	I	R	O	L	A	B	E	T	A	L	O	L	X	M	Y	W
O	M	E	T	O	P	R	O	L	O	L	K	L	Y	S	I	O
P	P	T	O	P	H	S	L	L	M	Y	Y	O	Z	A	S	T

WWW. WEB EXERCISE

Your patient has been diagnosed with essential hypertension. Because his father died at a young age from a heart attack, he is very concerned about his risk of developing heart disease and asks you for more Information. Go to the Internet and develop a teaching packet to address his concerns.

TRUE OR FALSE

Indicate if the following statements are true (T) or false (F).

_____ 1. Adrenergic blocking agents are also called sympathomimetic drugs.

_____ 2. Drugs that block all adrenergic receptors are primarily used to treat cardiac related conditions.

_____ 3. Adrenergic blocking agents competitively block the effects of norepinephrine at both alpha and beta receptors throughout the SNS, causing the signs and symptoms associated with a sympathetic stress reaction.

_____ 4. The adverse effects associated with adrenergic blocking agents of cardiac arrhythmias, hypotension, congestive heart failure, pulmonary edema, cerebral vascular accident or stroke are related to the lack of stimulatory effects and loss of vascular tone in the cardiovascular system.

_____ 5. The therapeutic effects of the alpha-1 selective adrenergic blocking agents come from their ability to block the postsynaptic alpha-1 receptor sites. This causes a decrease in vascular tone and vasodilation, which leads to a fall in blood pressure.

_____ 6. The beta adrenergic blocking agents are used to treat asthma and obstructive pulmonary diseases.

_____ 7. Propranolol is a widely prescribed drug that has been used to treat migraine headaches and stage fright (situational anxiety).

_____ 8. Beta adrenergic blocking agents should not be stopped abruptly after chronic therapy but should be tapered gradually over 2 weeks.

CHAPTER 30: CHOLINERGIC AGENTS

FILL IN THE BLANKS

Fill in the pertinent information regarding the cholinergic receptor site and indicate where direct acting and indirect acting cholinergic agonists work.

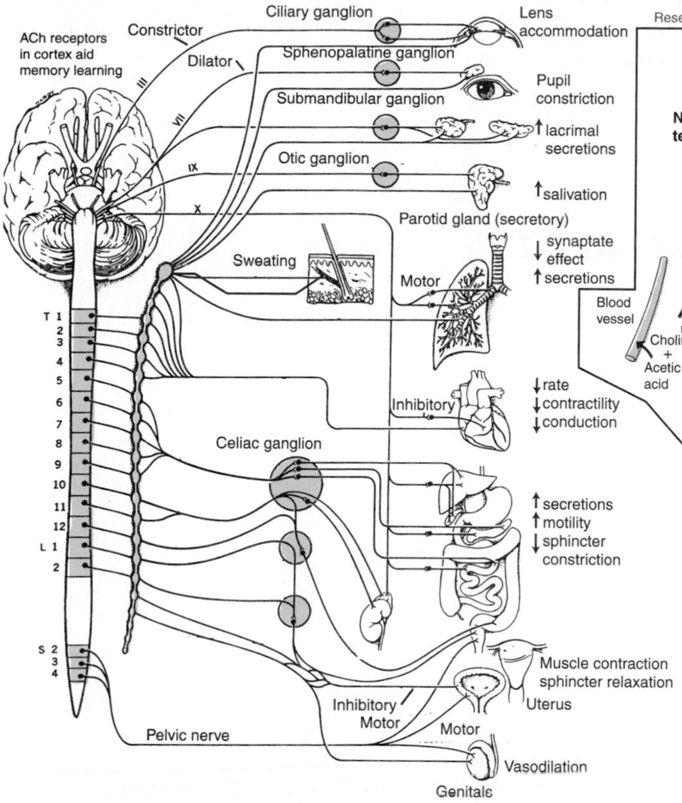

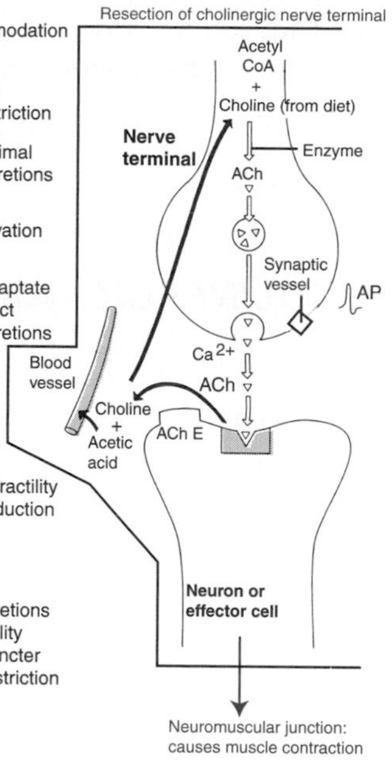

CROSSWORD PUZZLE

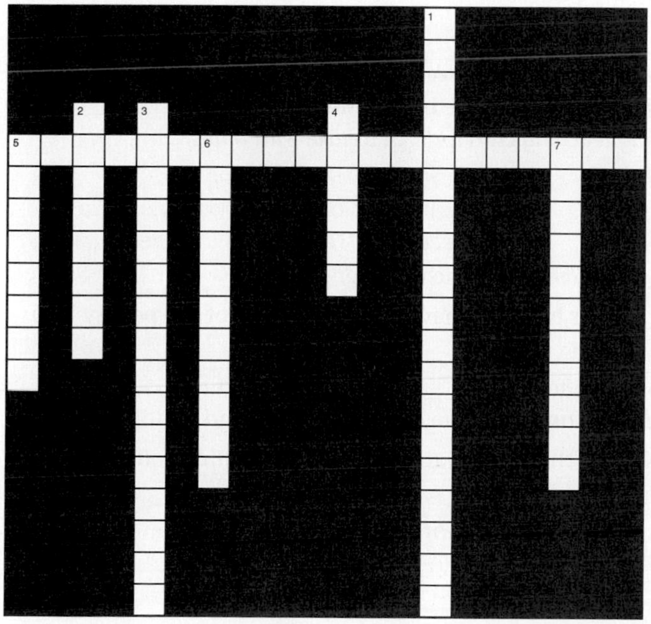

ACROSS

5 Enzyme responsible for the break down of acetylcholine

DOWN

1 Mimicking the effects of the parasympathetic nervous system
2 Irreversible acetylcholinesterase inhibitor used in warfare
3 Autoimmune disorder characterized by destruction of receptor sites
4 Constriction of the pupils
5 Drugs that increase effects or activity
6 Responding to acetylcholine
7 Degenerative disease of the cortex with loss of acetylcholine-producing cells

MATCHING

Match the drug with its usual indication. (Some drugs may have more than one indication.)

1. ________ pilocarpine
2. ________ tacrine
3. ________ neostigmine
4. ________ ambenonium
5. ________ pyridostigmine
6. ________ edrophonium
7. ________ physostigmine
8. ________ donepezil

A. Diagnosis of myasthenia gravis
B. Treatment of myasthenia gravis
C. Antidote for NMJ blockers
D. Glaucoma, miosis
E. Alzheimer's disease

CHAPTER 31: ANTICHOLINERGIC AGENTS

FILL IN THE CHART

Fill in the chart below with the effects of anticholinergic agents:

Physiological Effect	Therapeutic Use
GI tract	
Smooth muscle:	
Secretory glands:	
Urinary tract	
Biliary tract	
Bronchial muscle	
Cardiovascular system	
Ocular effects	
Secretions	
CNS	

PATIENT TEACHING CHECKLIST

E. S. is a 60-year-old bread delivery man with mild prostatic hypertrophy. He is seen in the clinic for recurring bouts of irritable bowel syndrome, which make his job very difficult. He is to be started on dicyclomine and will need teaching information. Prepare a drug teaching card for E. S. to take with him as he leaves the clinic.

FILL IN THE BLANKS

1. Anticholinergic drugs block the effects of ______________ at cholinergic receptor sites.
2. Anticholinergic drugs are also called ______________ drugs because they block the effects of the parasympathetic nervous system.
3. Blocking the parasympathetic system causes the following effects: ______________ in heart rate, ______________ in GI activity and in urinary bladder tone and function, pupil dilation, and cyclopegia.
4. These drugs also block cholinergic receptors in the CNS and those sympathetic postganglionic cholinergic receptors, including those that cause ______________.
5. ______________ is the prevention of accommodation of the lens for near vision.
6. Relaxation of the pupil of the eye is called a ______________ effect.
7. ______________ is the most commonly used anticholinergic drug.
8. Patients receiving anticholinergic drugs must be monitored for problems related to eating because of the adverse effects of ______________ and ______________.

CHAPTER 32: INTRODUCTION TO THE ENDOCRINE SYSTEM

FILL IN THE BLANKS

Fill in the names of the endocrine glands and their hormones in the diagram of the traditional endocrine system.

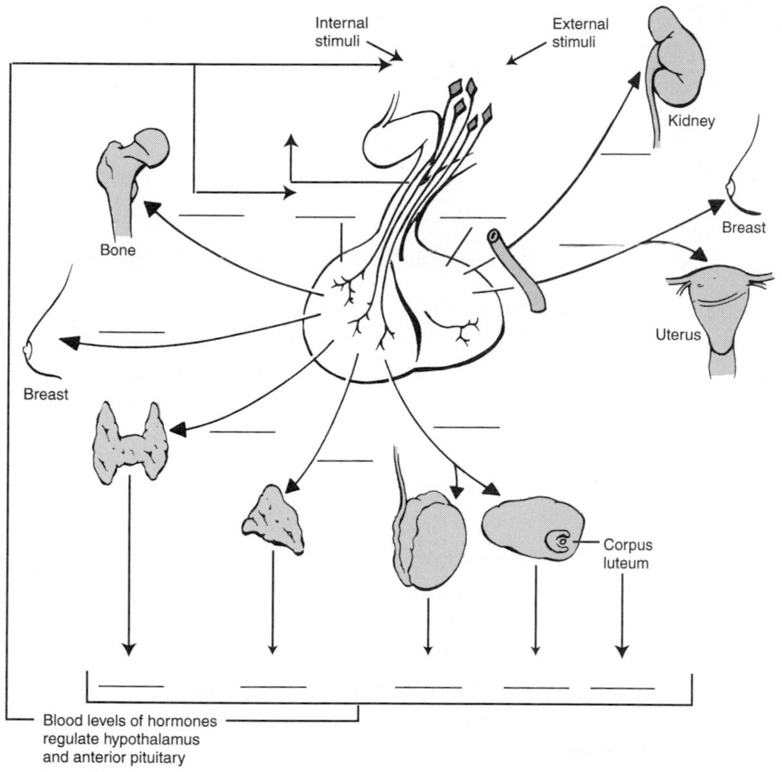

LIST

List the five characteristics of a hormone. All hormones:

____

____

____

____

____

MATCHING

Match the anterior pituitary hormone with the endocrine response it elicits.

1. ________ ACTH
2. ________ GH
3. ________ PRL
4. ________ TSH
5. ________ FSH
6. ________ LH
7. ________ MSH
8. ________ Lipoproteins

A. Production of thyroid hormone
B. Stimulation of fat mobilization
C. Stimulation of ovulation
D. Release of cortisol, aldosterone
E. Nerve growth and development
F. Milk production in the mammary glands
G. Stimulation of follicle development in the ovaries
H. Protein catabolism and cell growth

CHAPTER 33: HYPOTHALAMIC AND PITUITARY AGENTS

MATCHING

Match the hypothalamic releasing or inhibiting factor with the corresponding pituitary hormones that are released or inhibited by their stimulation:

1. ________	GHRH	A. release of ACTH
2. ________	TRH	B. release of FSH and LH
3. ________	GnRH	C. inhibition of growth hormone release
4. ________	CRF	D. release of prolactin
5. ________	PRF	E. inhibition of prolactin release
6. ________	PIF	F. release of growth hormone
7. ________	Somatostatin	G. release of TSH

WWW. WEB EXERCISE

You have been asked to present an inservice to staff of the pediatric endocrine unit, where you are doing your current rotation, about the use of growth hormone for treatment of Turner's syndrome and small stature. You want to ensure that your information is up to date because this presentation represents 25% of your grade. Go to the Internet to research current information.

MATCHING

Match the drug with its usual indication:

1. ________	CRF	A. treatment of children with growth failure
2. ________	nafarelin	B. treatment of specific cancers, endometriosis
3. ________	consyntropin	C. diagnosis of Cushing's disease
4. ________	somatrem	D. treatment of prostatic cancers
5. ________	goserelin	E. treatment of precocious puberty, endometriosis
6. ________	histrelin	F. stimulation of ovulation and spermatogenesis
7. ________	euprolide	G. diagnosis of adrenal failure
8. ________	enotropins	H. treatment of precocious puberty

CHAPTER 34: ADRENOCORTICAL AGENTS

WORD SCRAMBLE

Unscramble the letters below to find the names of adrenocortical agents:

1. SONNDERPIE	2. TOOLNINEMACIR	3. SOTHATOBEEMEN	4. COORSDYRTHINOE
5. SODDUBENIE	6. SOLIDEFUNLIE	7. SORTICONE	8. MEXDATESHOEN

CROSSWORD PUZZLE

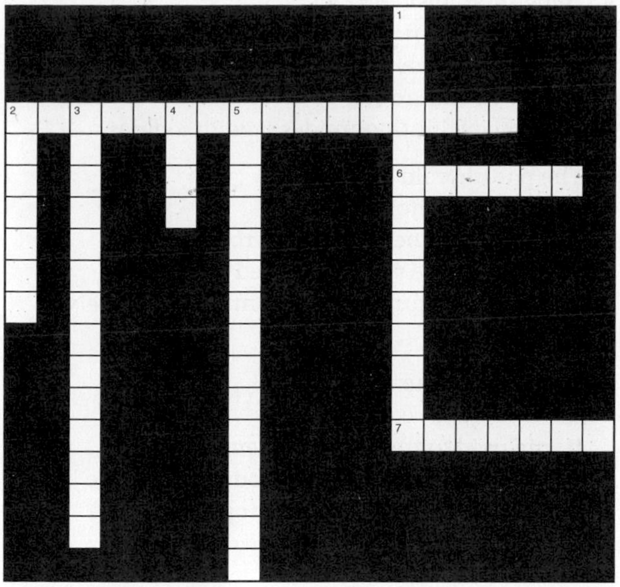

ACROSS

2 Steroid hormone that affects sodium and water retention and potassium excretion

6 Outer layer of the adrenal gland

7 Pattern of steroid hormone release

DOWN

1 Steroid hormone that increases blood glucose levels and fat deposits and breaks down protein for energy

2 Inner layer of the adrenal gland

3 Neurotransmitter released from the adrenal medulla

4 Anterior pituitary hormone that causes release of corticosteroids

5 Steroid hormones produced by the adrenal cortex

TRUE OR FALSE

Indicate if the following statements are true (T) or false (F).

_____ 1. There are two adrenal glands, one on either side of the kidney.

_____ 2. The adrenal cortex is basically a sympathetic nerve ganglia that releases norepinephrine and epinephrine into the bloodstream in response to sympathetic stimulation.

_____ 3. The adrenal medulla produces three corticosteroids: androgens (male and female sex hormones), glucocorticoids, and mineralocorticoids.

_____ 4. The corticosteroids are released normally in a diurnal rhythm.

_____ 5. Prolonged use of corticosteroids will suppress the normal hypothalamic-pituitary axis and lead to adrenal atrophy from lack of stimulation.

_____ 6. The glucocorticoids decrease glucose production; stimulate fat deposition and protein breakdown, and increase protein formation.

_____ 7. The mineralocorticoids stimulate sodium and water excretion and potassium retention.

_____ 8. Adverse effects of corticosteroids are related to exaggeration of their physiological effects, including immunosuppression, peptic ulcer formation, fluid retention, and edema.

_____ 9. Corticosteroids are used topically and locally to achieve the desired anti-inflammatory effects.

_____ 10. Glucocorticoids are used in conjunction with mineralocorticoids to treat adrenal insufficiency.

CHAPTER 35: THYROID AND PARATHYROID AGENTS

PATIENT TEACHING CHECKLIST

P. K. is a 34-year-old mother of three who has been experiencing increasing fatigue, hair loss, apathy, sweating spells, and heart palpitations. After several diagnostic tests, it was discovered that she was hypothyroid. She was started on levothyroxine, 150 mcg/day. Her dose will be adjusted based on her response to the medication. Prepare a drug teaching card for P. K. to take with her as she leaves the office today.

MULTIPLE CHOICE

1. Thyroid hormones control:
   a. the rate at which most body cells use energy (metabolism)
   b. release of ACTH
   c. the growth of long bones
   d. ovulation
2. Control of the thyroid gland involves:
   a. parathyroid hormones
   b. balanced levels of ACTH
   c. an intricate balance between the hypothalamus, the anterior pituitary, and circulating levels of thyroid hormone
   d. a positive feedback system
3. Hypothyroidism is:
   a. treatable with diet changes
   b. easily diagnosed in the elderly
   c. lower-than-normal levels of thyroid hormone
   d. treated with thioamides
4. Hyperthyroidism is:
   a. lower-than-normal levels of thyroid hormone
   b. treatable only with surgical intervention
   c. treated with radioactive iodine
   d. treated with thioamides or with iodines
5. The parathyroid glands:
   a. secrete calcitonin
   b. are located behind the thyroid gland
   c. are palpable when enlarged
   d. secrete calcium when serum calcium levels are low
6. Bisphosphonates:
   a. raise serum calcium levels
   b. are used to treat hypocalcemia
   c. increase the excretion of sodium from the kidney
   d. slow or block bone resorption

MATCHING

Match each of the following words with the appropriate definition:

1. ________ iodine	A.	T_4
2. ________ thyroxine	B.	hormone produced by the thyroid
3. ________ liothyronine	C.	lack of thyroid hormone in the infant
4. ________ calcitonin	D.	excess levels of thyroid hormone
5. ________ hypothyroidism	E.	dietary element used to produce thryoid hormone
6. ________ cretinism	F.	T_3
7. ________ myxedema	G.	drugs used to prevent the formation of thyroid hormone
8. ________ hyperthyroidism	H.	severe lack of thyroid hormone in adults
9. ________ thioamides	I.	disorder of overactive osteoclasts
10. ________ Paget's disease	J.	lack of sufficient thyroid hormone to maintain metabolism

CHAPTER 36: ANTIDIABETIC AGENTS

WORD SEARCH

Circle the following names of antidiabetic agents that are hidden in the grid below:

acarbose
acetohexamide
chlorpropamide
glimepiride
glipizide
glyburide
insulin
metformin
miglitol
repaglinide
sulfonylurea
tolazamide
tolbutamide
troglitazone

I	N	S	L	U	G	L	I	P	I	M	I	R	D	E	I
S	T	R	O	G	L	I	T	A	Z	O	N	E	N	D	P
G	L	O	T	R	Y	N	U	L	I	O	S	P	A	I	N
E	M	I	I	P	B	U	L	I	Z	I	A	A	L	M	P
S	P	I	L	R	U	L	I	N	O	E	R	G	N	A	T
O	H	L	G	L	R	U	L	S	R	I	N	L	I	Z	O
B	O	P	I	M	I	L	R	U	S	T	O	I	M	A	L
R	Z	O	M	E	D	I	L	L	I	O	N	N	R	L	B
A	Y	N	U	R	E	Y	N	I	E	L	O	I	O	O	U
C	G	L	I	P	N	I	Z	N	I	D	E	D	F	T	T
A	C	E	T	O	H	E	X	A	M	I	D	E	T	R	A
C	A	R	F	G	L	I	P	I	Z	I	D	E	E	S	M
A	G	L	I	M	E	P	I	R	I	D	E	N	M	O	I
B	U	T	A	M	I	D	E	T	O	L	B	U	T	L	D
S	I	Z	C	H	L	O	P	R	O	P	A	M	I	D	E

WWW. WEB EXERCISE

J. L. is a 53-year-old traveling salesman, recently diagnosed with Type II diabetes. He is referred to the nurse with his family for education about his disease, diet, drugs, and medical regimen. Go to the Internet to find the latest information for J. L. and to prepare the best teaching resources for him and his family.

NURSING CARE PLAN

*P. G. is a 78-year-old S/P MI, diabetic who is admitted to your assisted living facility. He is on propranolol (*Inderal*) to prevent reinfarction and insulin. Prepare a nursing care plan to go into his chart to promote continuity of care with in his insulin therapy.*

CHAPTER 37: INTRODUCTION TO THE REPRODUCTIVE SYSTEMS

FILL IN THE BLANKS

Identify the parts of the female reproductive system. Indicate where the ova are stored and the site of estrogen and progesterone production.

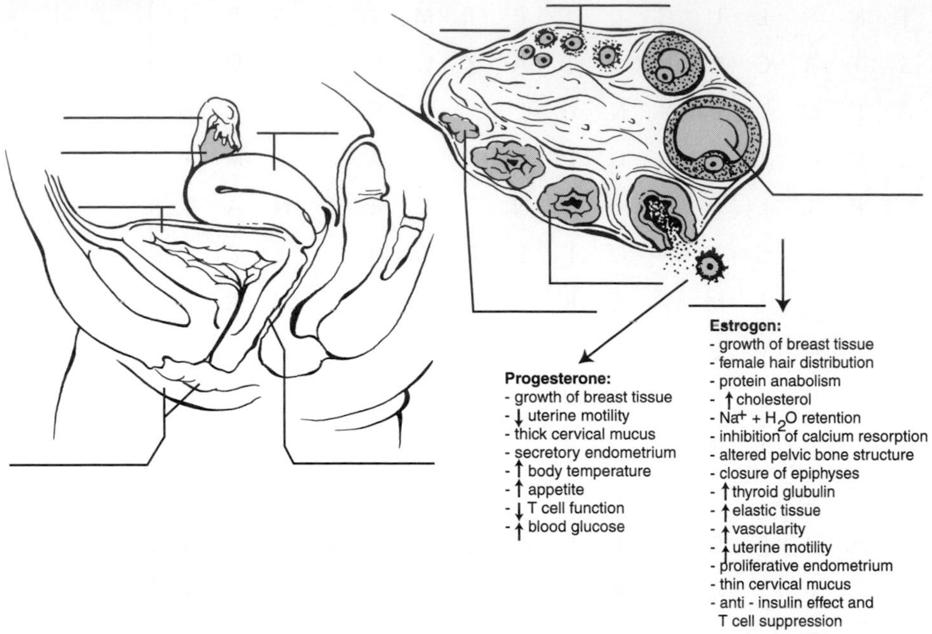

FILL IN THE BLANKS

Identify the parts of the male reproductive system. Indicate the site of sperm and testosterone production.

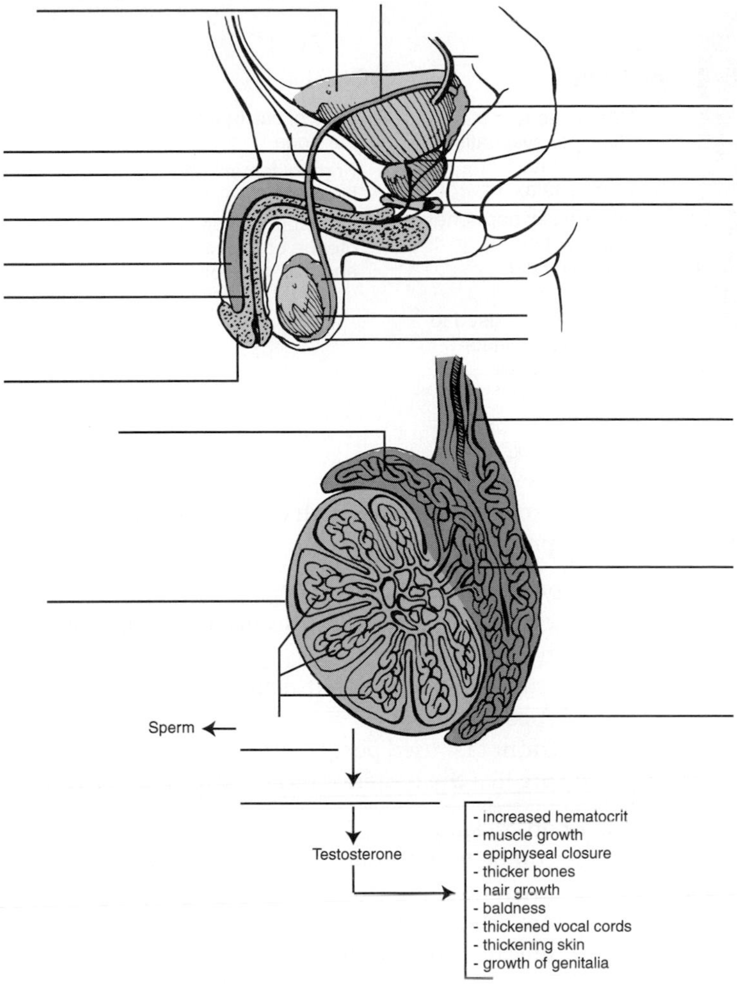

COMPLETE THE CYCLE

Fill in the names of the hormones involved in the negative feedback system that controls the male reproductive system.

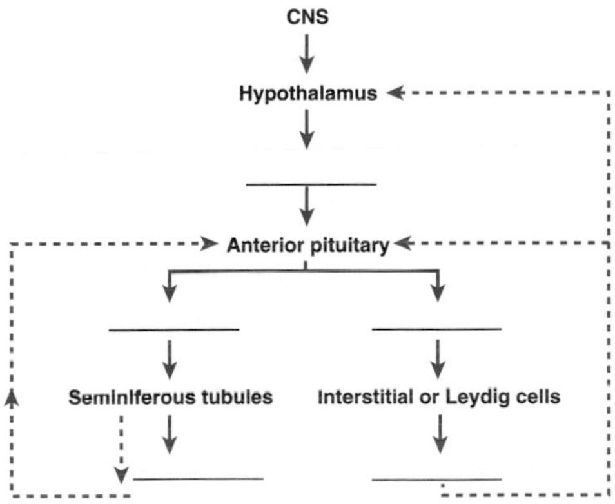

CHAPTER 38: DRUGS AFFECTING THE FEMALE REPRODUCTIVE SYSTEM

CROSSWORD PUZZLE

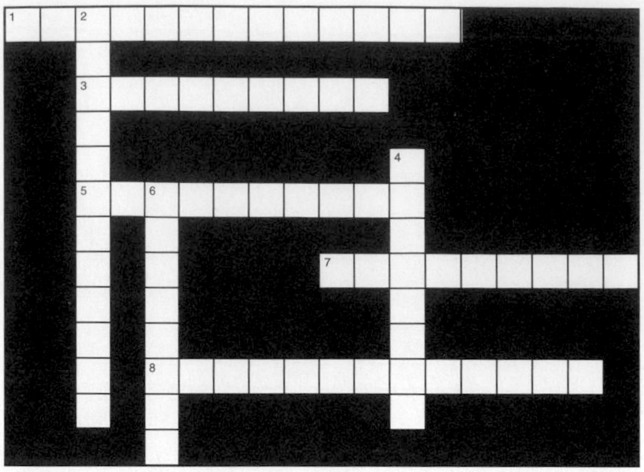

ACROSS

1 Drug used to stimulate evacuation of the uterus
3 Uterine relaxant
5 Female sex hormones, important in maintaining a pregnancy
7 Type of drugs used to stimulate ovulation and pregnancy
8 Birth control measure

DOWN

2 Loss of calcium from the bone
4 Primary female sex hormone
6 Drug that stimulates uterine contraction and milk ejection

MULTIPLE CHOICE

1. Estrogens are **not:**
   a. female sex hormones important in the development of the female reproductive system and secondary sex characteristics
   b. used pharmacologically mainly to replace hormones lost at menopause
   c. used to stimulate ovulation in woman with hypogonadism
   d. used to treat uterine bleeding problems

2. Progestins:
   a. are used in combination with estrogens for oral contraceptives
   b. are not necessary during pregnancy and lactation
   c. are responsible for a thin, clear cervical mucous
   d. cause growth of long bones at puberty

3. Fertility drugs:
   a. can stimulate ovulation in postmenopausal women
   b. have a major adverse effect of multiple births and birth defects
   c. directly stimulate GnRH release from the hypothalamus
   d. are not associated with adverse effects unless pregnancy occurs

4. Oxytocic drugs:
   a. can act as fertility drugs since they stimulate the hypothalamus
   b. stimulate uterine contractions and induce or speed up labor
   c. cannot be used postpartum
   d. are like the posterior pituitary hormone ADH

5. Abortifacients:
   a. can be used through the third trimester of pregnancy
   b. are drugs that stimulate uterine activity to cause uterine evacuation
   c. can be used to induce labor at term
   d. are not associated with any adverse effects

6. Tocolytics:
   a. stimulate uterine contractions
   b. are good fertility drugs
   c. relax the uterine smooth muscle to stop premature labor
   d. can be used as contraceptives

WORD SCRAMBLE

Unscramble the following letters to find the names of commonly used estrogens and estrogen receptor modulators.

1. morefinete	2. dotrailse	3. noreest	4. foxnarliee
5. notsiederl	6. potrestapei	7. stillbesthiedyrotl	8. cehnleosriontari

CHAPTER 39: DRUGS AFFECTING THE MALE REPRODUCTIVE SYSTEM

TRUE OR FALSE

Mark the following statements as true (T) or false (F).

_____ 1. Androgens are male sex hormones, specifically testosterone or testosterone-like compounds.

_____ 2. Androgens are responsible for the development and maintenance of male sex characteristics and secondary sex characteristics or estrogenic effects.

_____ 3. Adverse effects related to androgen use involve potentially deadly hepatocellular carcinoma.

_____ 4. Androgens can be used for replacement therapy or to block other hormone effects.

_____ 5. Anabolic steroids are analogs of estrogen that have been developed to have protein building effects.

_____ 6. Anabolic steroids are used pharmacologically to enhance muscle development and athletic performance, with often deadly effects.

_____ 7. Anabolic steroids are used to increase hematocrit and improve protein anabolism in certain depleted states.

_____ 8. Erectile penile dysfunction can inhibit erection and male sexual function.

_____ 9. Alprostadil, a prostaglandin, is an oral agent used to stimulate penile erection.

_____ 10. Silfenadil is an injected agent that acts quickly to promote vascular filling of the corpus cavernosum and promote penile erection.

MATCHING

Match the drug with its usual indication.

1. ________ nandrolone
2. ________ oxandrolone
3. ________ oxymetholone
4. ________ stanozolol
5. ________ danazol
6. ________ fluoxymesterone
7. ________ testolactone
8. ________ testosterone

A. treatment of anemias
B. treatment of specific breast cancers
C. blocks FSH and LH release in women
D. anemia associated with renal dysfunction
E promotion of weight gain
F. primary male sex hormone—treatment of hypogonadism and certain breast cancers
G. treatment of angioedema
H. replacement therapy in hypogonadism

FILL IN THE BLANKS

1. ______________ effects are associated with development of male sexual characteristics.
2. ______________ effects are tissue building effects associated with androgen use.
3. ______________ is the primary natural androgen.
4. Because they cause an increase in red blood cell production, androgens may be indicated to treat various ______________.
5. ______________ is a condition in which the corpus cavernosum does not fill with blood to allow for penile erection.
6. Alprostadil is a ______________ that relaxes vascular smooth muscle and allows filling of the corpus cavernosum when ______________ directly into the cavernosum.
7. ______________ is taken orally and acts to increase nitrous oxide levels in the corpus cavernosum.
8. The penile erection that accompanies oral use of *Viagra* occurs only with ______________.

CHAPTER 40: INTRODUCTION TO THE CARDIOVASCULAR SYSTEM

FILL IN THE BLANKS

Fill in the blanks indicating the structures in the heart.

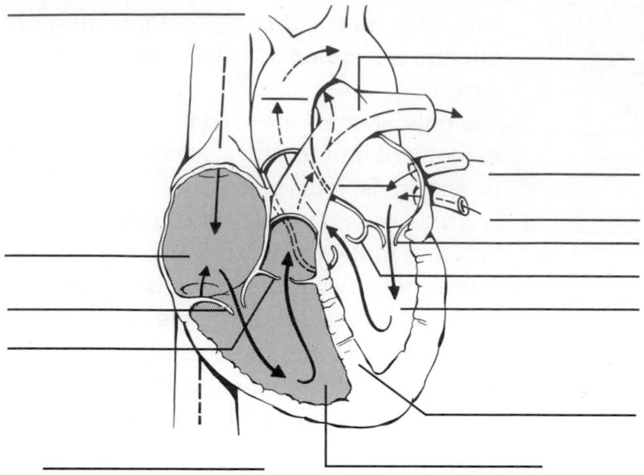

DEFINITIONS

Define the following terms:

1. troponin
2. actin
3. myosin
4. arrhythmia
5. Starling's law of the heart
6. fibrillation
7. capillary
8. resistance system

MATCHING

Match the word with the appropriate definition.

1. ________ atrium
2. ________ ventricle
3. ________ auricle
4. ________ vein
5. ________ artery
6. ________ myocardium
7. ________ syncytia
8. ________ diastole
9. ________ systole
10. ________ automaticity
11. ________ conductivity
12. ________ pulse pressure

A. resting phase of the heart
B. reflects the filling pressure of the coronary arteries
C. bottom chamber of the heart
D. vessel that takes blood away from the heart
E. vessel that returns blood to the heart
F. appendage on the atria of the heart
G. property of heart cells to generate an action potential
H. top chamber of the heart
I. property of heart cells to rapidly conduct an action potential of electrical impulse
J. intertwining network of muscle fibers
K. contracting phase of the heart
L. muscle of the heart

CHAPTER 41: DRUGS AFFECTING BLOOD PRESSURE

MATCHING

Match the following drugs with their appropriate class of antihypertensive agents. (Some classes may be used more than once.)

1. _______ candesartan
2. _______ quinapril
3. _______ mecamylamine
4. _______ losartan
5. _______ nitroprusside
6. _______ tolazoline
7. _______ lisinopril
8. _______ valsartan
9. _______ nicardipine
10. _______ minoxidil
11. _______ fosinopril
12. _______ amlodipine

A. angiotensin-converting enzyme inhibitor
B. angiotensin II receptor blocker
C. calcium channel blocker
D. vasodilator
E. ganglionic blocker

WORD SEARCH

Circle the following names of antihypertensive agents that are hidden in the grid below:

benazepril
candesartan
diazoxide
captopril
losartan
minoxidil
enalapril
valsartan
nitroprusside
ramipril
amlodipine
mecamylamine
trandolapril
diltiazem
nicardipine

M	I	N	O	X	I	D	I	P	I	N	E	N	A	L
P	E	R	L	I	R	P	A	L	A	N	E	I	L	E
B	R	A	M	L	O	D	I	P	I	N	E	I	V	E
S	N	I	C	A	R	D	I	P	I	N	E	T	A	L
D	I	A	Z	E	P	U	L	M	D	E	D	R	L	L
I	N	A	L	A	P	R	A	B	I	D	I	A	S	I
L	O	R	S	A	R	L	I	S	I	B	S	N	A	R
T	O	R	A	V	Y	A	Z	I	D	E	S	D	R	P
I	N	A	L	M	E	T	R	O	P	L	U	O	T	O
A	E	W	A	O	I	R	I	U	I	E	R	L	A	T
Z	E	C	H	I	P	P	N	O	L	S	P	A	N	P
E	E	S	L	O	S	A	R	T	A	N	O	P	O	A
M	E	D	I	A	Z	O	X	I	D	E	R	R	N	C
B	E	N	A	Z	E	P	R	I	L		T	I	E	A
R	L	I	O	M	I	N	O	X	I	D	I	L	L	N
O	C	A	N	D	E	S	A	R	T	A	N	E	L	D

TRUE OR FALSE

Mark the following statements true (T) or false (F)

_____ 1. The cardiovascular system is an open system that depends on pressure differences to ensure the delivery of blood.

_____ 2. Blood pressure is related to heart rate, stroke volume, and the total peripheral resistance.

_____ 3. Constricted arterioles lower pressure; dilated arterioles raise pressure.

_____ 4. Control of blood pressure involves baroreceptor (pressure receptor) stimulation of the medulla to activate the parasympathetic nervous system.

_____ 5. The kidneys activate the renin-angiotensin system when blood flow to the kidneys is decreased.

_____ 6. Renin activates angiotensinogen to angiotensin I in the lung using angiotensin-converting enzyme.

_____ 7. Hypertension is a sustained state of higher than normal blood pressure.

_____ 8. Essential hypertension has no underlying cause, and treatment can vary widely.

_____ 9. Angiotensin II receptor blockers prevent the body from responding to angiotensin II and blocking calcium channels.

_____ 10. Hypotension can result in decreased oxygenation of the tissues, cell death, tissue damage, and even death.

CHAPTER 42: CARDIOTONIC AGENTS

PATIENT TEACHING CHECKLIST

F. A. is a 72-year-old woman with mitral valve disease. She has been doing fairly well until this summer, when she went into congestive heart failure. She has been stabilized on digoxin (Lanoxin). She moves to Florida every November for 6 months. Prepare a teaching card for her to take with her to ensure continuity of care as she switches to her Florida health care provider.

CROSSWORD PUZZLE

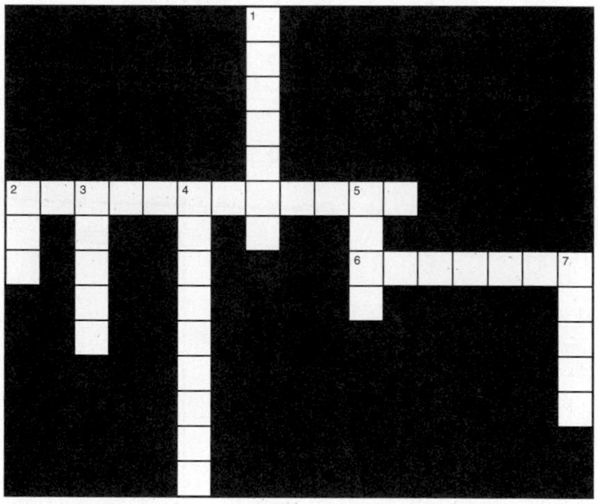

ACROSS

2 Enlargement of the heart

6 Lack of energy

5 Side of the heart associated with pulmonary edema

7 Swelling

DOWN

1 Difficulty breathing

2 Congestive heart failure

3 Side of the heart associated with total body congestion

4 Difficulty breathing while lying down

WWW. WEB EXERCISE

J. D. calls your clinic asking for information about congestive heart failure (CHF). Her mother has been diagnosed with CHF, and J. D. is moving her to town so that she can care for her. However, J. D. does not know anything about CHF and wants to find out what she can expect. Use the Internet to obtain information that might be useful to J. D.

CHAPTER 43: ANTIARRHYTHMIC AGENTS

IDENTIFY THE STRUCTURES

Identify the parts of the cardiac conduction system.

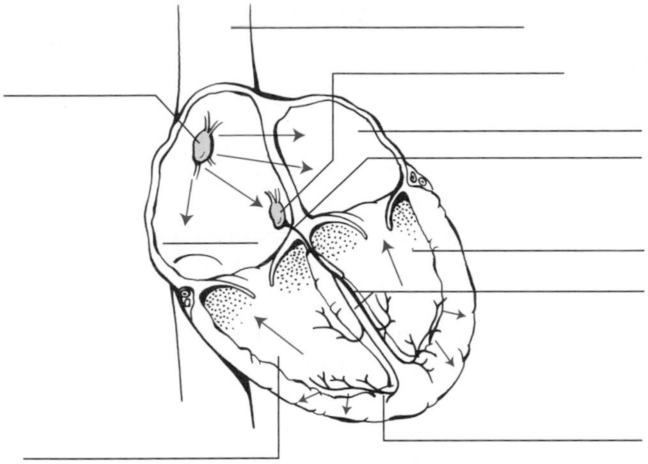

MATCHING

Match the arrhythmia below with the name of the arrhythmia and a drug commonly used to treat it.

1. 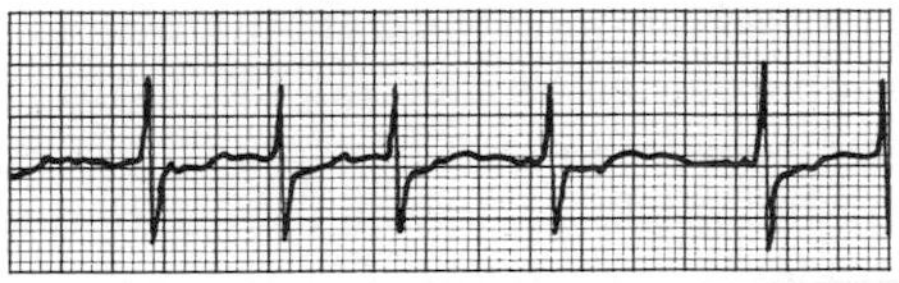

2. 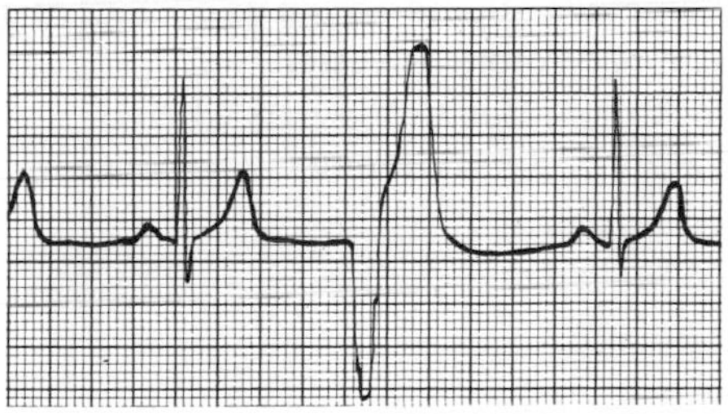

3. 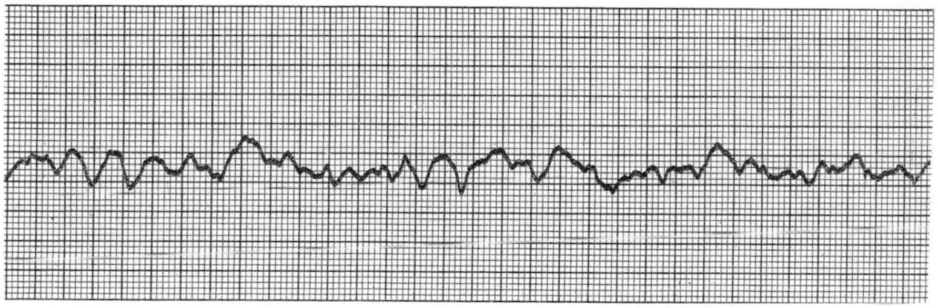

a. PVC
b. atrial fibrillation
c. ventricular flutter
d. quinidine
e. amiodarone
f. lidocaine

WORD SCRAMBLE

Unscramble the letters below to find the names of commonly used antiarrhythmic agents.

1. NAMEDOORIA
2. MOOLESL
3. BYTERMIUL
4. APEVIRMAL
5. MOPERACNIDIA
6. PDOLPRORAN
7. INIFLEDECA
8. ONIDIGX

CHAPTER 44: ANTIANGINAL AGENTS

MATCHING

Match the word with the appropriate definition.

1. ________ CAD
2. ________ pulse pressure
3. ________ atheroma
4. ________ atherosclerosis
5. ________ angina pectoris
6. ________ Prinzmetal's angina
7. ________ myocardial infarction
8. ________ nitrates

A. "suffocation of the chest"
B. drop in blood flow through the coronary arteries caused by a vasospasm in the artery
C. coronary artery disease
D. end result of vessel blockage in the heart
E. fatty tumor in the intima of a coronary artery
F. filling pressure of the coronary arteries
G. narrowing of the arteries caused by build up of atheromas
H. drugs used to cause direct relaxation of smooth muscle

TRUE OR FALSE

Indicate whether the following statements are true (T) or false (F).

_____ 1. Coronary artery disease (CAD) is second to cancer as the leading cause of death in the United States and most Western nations.

_____ 2. Coronary artery disease develops when changes in the intima of coronary vessels lead to the development of atheromas, or fatty tumors.

_____ 3. Narrowing of the coronary arteries secondary to the atheroma buildup is called angina.

_____ 4. Angina pectoris, or "suffocation of the chest," occurs when the myocardial demand for oxygen cannot be met by the narrowed vessels.

_____ 5. Stable angina occurs when the heart muscle is perfused adequately except at rest.

_____ 6. Unstable or preinfarction angina occurs when the vessels are so narrowed that the myocardial cells are low on oxygen during exertion.

_____ 7. Prinzmetal's angina occurs as a result of a spasm of a coronary vessel.

_____ 8. Myocardial infarction occurs when a coronary vessel is completely occluded.

CROSSWORD PUZZLE

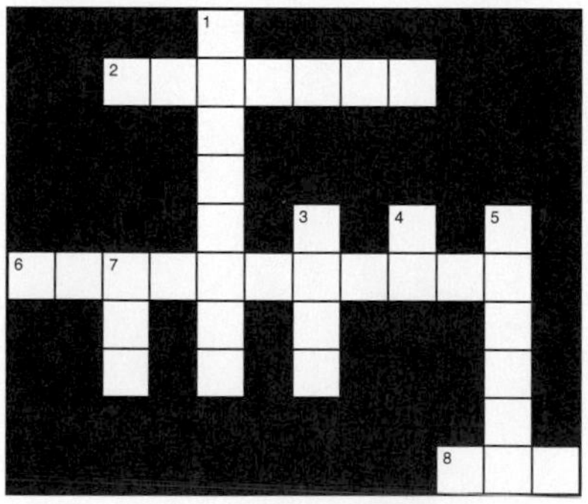

ACROSS

2 Vasodilator
6 Lack of oxygen
8 Leading cause of death in U.S.

DOWN

1 Fatty tumor in the lumen of a vessel
3 Symptom of angina
4 Myocardial infarction
5 Suffocation of the chest
7 Component of an atheroma

CHAPTER 45: LIPID LOWERING AGENTS

WWW. WEB EXERCISE

R. K. is a 46-year-old man who is diagnosed with hypertension and elevated LDLs during a routine insurance physical. He has a strong family history of heart disease and is very concerned about the findings. He is referred to the nurse for appropriate teaching. Use the Internet to obtain the most recent information that might be useful for R. K., then prepare a teaching program for him.

LIST

List the leading risk factors for the development of coronary artery disease. Indicate the ones that are treatable with a T.

1. ______________
2. ______________
3. ______________
4. ______________
5. ______________
6. ______________
7. ______________
8. ______________
9. ______________
10. ______________

IDENTIFY

Identify the process of fat metabolism in humans by filling in the blanks in the figure below. Indicate the site of action of the major classes of lipid lowering agents.

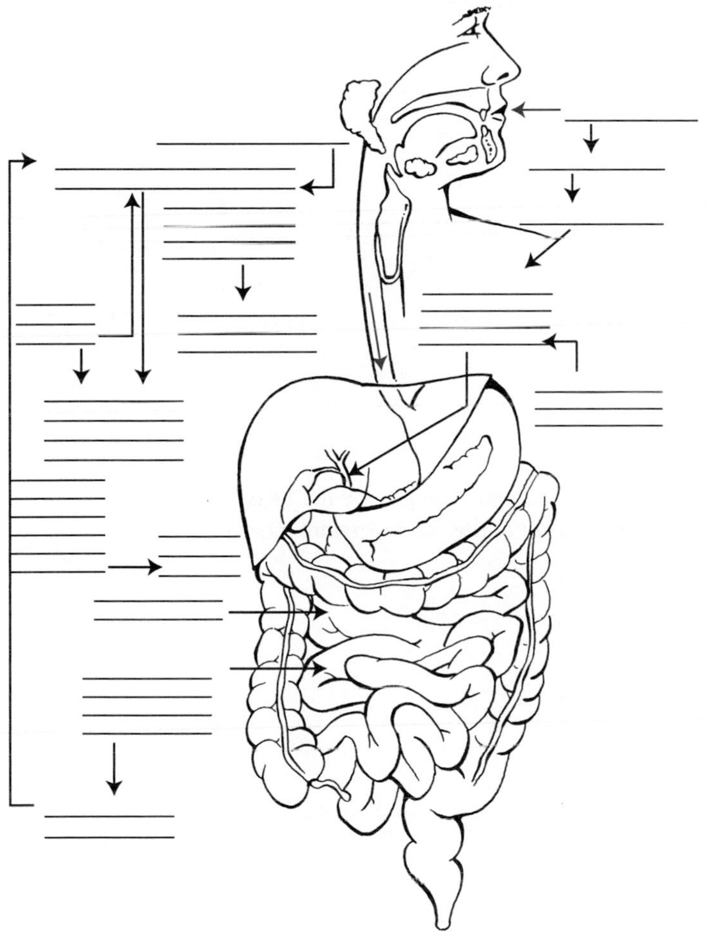

CHAPTER 46: DRUGS AFFECTING BLOOD COAGULATION

TRUE OR FALSE

Indicate whether the following statements are true (T) or false (F).

_____ 1. Coagulation is the transformation of fluid blood to a solid state.

_____ 2. Coagulation involves vasodilation, platelet aggregation, and intrinsic and extrinsic clot formation.

_____ 3. Coagulation is initiated by Hageman factor to plug up any holes in the cardiovascular system.

_____ 4. The final step of clot formation is the conversion of prothrombin to thrombin, which breaks down fibrinogen to form soluble fibrin threads.

_____ 5. Once a clot is formed, it must be dissolved to prevent the occlusion of blood vessels and loss of blood supply to tissues.

_____ 6. Plasminogen is the basis of the coagulation system.

_____ 7. Plasmin dissolves fibrin threads and resolves the clot.

_____ 8. Anticoagulants dissolve clots that have formed.

_____ 9. Thrombolytic drugs block coagulation and prevent the formation of clots.

_____ 10. Hemophilia is a genetic lack of essential clotting factors that results in excessive bleeding situations.

FILL IN THE BLANKS

Fill in the blanks in the figure below to identify the steps in the coagulation process.

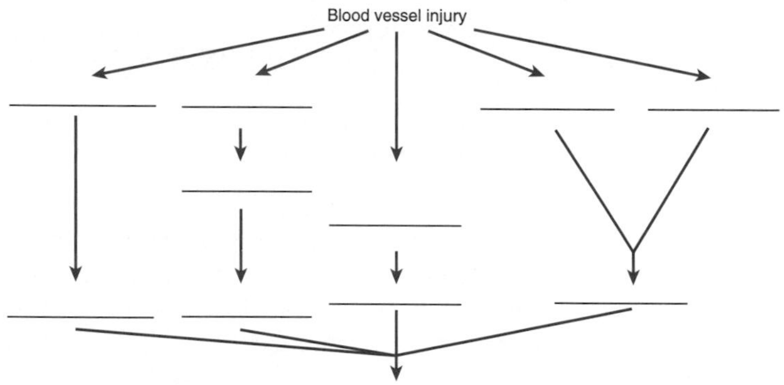

PATIENT TEACHING CHECKLIST

C. F. is a 36-year-old mother of three who has recently undergone a mitral valve replacement. She is being stabilized on Coumadin to prevent the formation of clots as a result of the valve. Prepare a drug teaching card for C. F. that she can refer to at home.

CHAPTER 47: DRUGS USED TO TREAT ANEMIAS

FILL IN THE BLANKS

Fill in the blanks below to identify the steps of erythropoiesis.

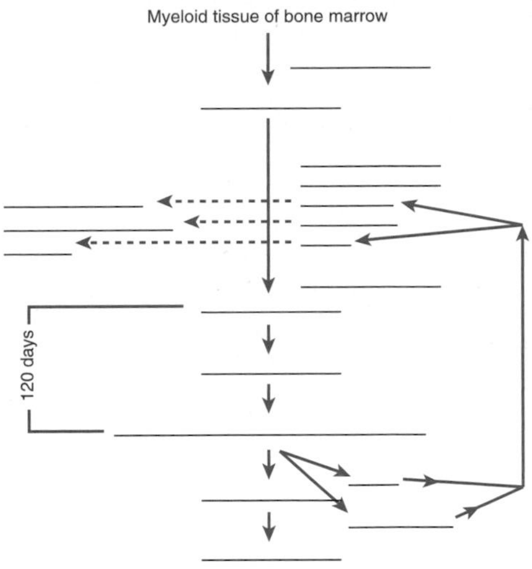

MULTIPLE CHOICE

1. Blood is composed of:
   a. a liquid plasma (containing water, proteins, glucose, and electrolytes)
   b. formed components including nitrogen and urea
   c. endothelial cells
   d. alveolar cells

2. Erythropoiesis is controlled by:
   a. iron formation
   b. carbohydrate availability
   c. erythropoietin which is, produced by the kidneys
   d. bilirubin

3. RBCs:
   a. have a nucleus
   b. have a life span of about 120 days
   c. are mostly bilirubin
   d. have many different shapes

4. Anemia cannot be caused by:
   a. a lack of erythropoietin
   b. a lack of the components needed to produce RBCs
   c. a depressed bone marrow
   d. increased RBC production

5. Iron deficiency anemia occurs:
   a. when there is inadequate iron intake in the diet
   b. when too much iron is absorbed from the GI tract
   c. when oxygen levels are very low
   d. when bilirubin is unconjugated

6. Pernicious anemia:
   a. is a lack of folic acid
   b. is a lack of iron
   c. is a lack of vitamin B_{12}
   d. is not a life-threatening condition

CROSSWORD PUZZLE

ACROSS

2 Hormone that controls RBC production

8 Lack of RBCs

DOWN

1 Main constituent of plasma

3 Immature RBC

4 Red blood cell

5 Liquid part of the blood

6 Factor that activates folic acid

7 Component of the RBC that allows the cell to carry oxygen

CHAPTER 48: INTRODUCTION TO THE KIDNEY AND THE URINARY TRACT

FILL IN THE BLANKS

Fill in the blanks in the figure below to identify the parts of the nephron.

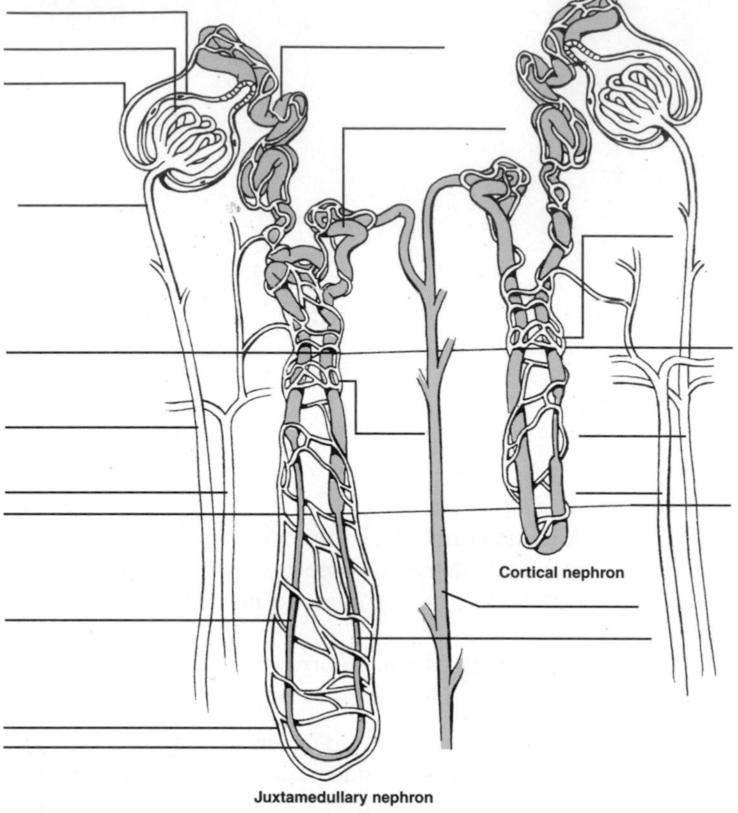

WORD SCRAMBLE

Unscramble the letters below to identify terms associated with the renal system.

1. RUMSOULGEL
2. NATTROFILI
3. TONISCEER
4. ENROOTLADSE
5. PROBEROSTANI
6. UBLUETU
7. NINER
8. STREATPO

FILL IN THE BLANKS

1. The kidneys are two small organs that receive about ______________ of the cardiac output.
2. The functional unit of the kidney is called the ______________, which is composed of ______________, the proximal convoluted tubule, ______________, the distal convoluted tubule, and the ______________.
3. The nephrons function by using three basic processes: ______________, ______________, and ______________.
4. Sodium levels are regulated throughout the tubule by active and passive movement and is fine-tuned by the presence of ______________ in the distal tubule.
5. The counter-current mechanism in the medullary nephrons allows for the ______________ or ______________ of urine under the influence of ADH secreted by the hypothalamus.
6. Potassium concentration is regulated throughout the tubule, with ______________ being the strongest influence for potassium loss.
7. The kidneys play a key role in the regulation of calcium by activating ______________.
8. The kidneys have an important role in blood pressure control, releasing ______________ to activate the renin-angiotensin system.

CHAPTER 49: DIURETIC AGENTS

WORD SEARCH

Circle the commonly used diuretics that are hidden in the grid below:

bendroflumethiazide
hydrochlorothiazide
indapamide
trichlormethiazide
metolazone
bumetanide
furosemide
torsemide
acetazolamide
amiloride
spironolactone
glycerin
urea

B	I	D	E	Z	O	N	E	T	H	I	A	Z	I	Z	O	N	E	Y	L
E	H	A	M	I	N	U	R	T	I	Z	I	D	E	K	L	I	N	D	A
N	I	Y	G	L	Y	A	T	H	U	A	I	Z	I	D	E	O	T	O	M
D	Z	E	D	O	E	H	H	I	L	S	O	E	N	O	E	P	R	M	I
R	A	C	A	R	B	O	S	T	H	I	A	D	I	D	E	Z	O	S	T
O	I	F	U	R	O	S	E	M	I	D	E	I	I	O	D	R	I	P	S
F	H	U	R	O	S	C	M	I	Z	I	D	M	E	L	I	S	M	I	N
L	T	H	E	I	A	Z	H	I	A	Z	A	E	L	O	Z	N	E	R	T
U	E	I	D	E	R	O	I	L	Z	L	Z	S	I	N	A	D	R	O	S
M	M	N	I	R	G	H	I	O	O	I	I	R	N	O	I	R	I	N	T
E	U	E	R	O	L	O	O	Z	L	R	N	O	I	N	H	O	Z	O	E
T	L	F	O	R	Y	U	A	S	E	M	O	T	A	I	T	D	O	L	E
H	F	U	L	R	C	T	F	U	I	A	Z	T	I	D	E	G	H	A	C
I	O	N	I	L	E	H	I	T	L	M	E	H	H	I	F	R	H	C	H
A	R	O	M	C	R	U	N	I	M	M	I	O	Z	I	O	B	E	T	H
Z	D	R	A	I	I	N	U	R	U	N	E	O	S	M	A	T	I	O	I
I	N	E	N	L	N	O	R	B	E	M	E	T	O	L	A	Z	O	N	E
D	E	D	I	M	A	P	A	D	N	I	N	E	Z	I	D	E	I	E	L
E	B	T	R	I	C	H	L	O	R	M	E	T	H	I	A	Z	I	D	E
B	Y	R	O	L	H	I	O	M	O	E	L	H	I	A	Z	D	E	I	E

DEFINITIONS

Define the following terms:

1. edema
2. fluid rebound
3. thiazide diuretic
4. hypokalemia
5. high ceiling diuretics
6. alkalosis
7. hyperaldosteronism
8. osmotic pull

MATCHING

Match the diuretic with the appropriate class. (Some classes will be used more than once.)

1. _______ glycerin
2. _______ acetazolamide
3. _______ furosemide
4. _______ benzthiazide
5. _______ indapamide
6. _______ mannitol
7. _______ spironolactone
8. _______ hydrochlorothiazide
9. _______ amiloride
10. _______ bumetanide

A. osmotic
B. thiazide
C. loop
D. potassium sparing
E. carbonic anhydrase inhibitor

CHAPTER 50: DRUGS AFFECTING THE URINARY TRACT AND BLADDER

WWW. WEB EXERCISE

H. H. and his wife are referred to you for teaching after a diagnosis of BPH is made on a routine physical. They do not understand the problem and are somewhat shy talking about it. Go to the Internet to get information for them about the disease, treatment, and research.

PATIENT TEACHING CHECKLIST

J. W., a 14-year-old with chronic cystitis, has recently moved from a small town and is seen for the first time at your clinic. She has an active cystitis and is started on cinoxacin. Prepare a teaching checklist for J. W. that includes information regarding prevention of urinary tract infections.

TRUE OR FALSE

Indicate whether the following statements are true (T) or false (F).

_____ 1. Acute urinary tract infections are second in frequency to respiratory tract infections in the American population.

_____ 2. Urinary tract anti-infectives are used to kill bacteria in the urinary tract by producing an alkaline urine or by acting to destroy bacteria in the urinary tract.

_____ 3. There is nothing that can be done to help decrease the bacteria in the urinary tract.

_____ 4. Inflammation and irritation of the urinary tract can cause smooth muscle spasms leading to the uncomfortable effects of dysuria, urgency, incontinence, nocturia, and suprapubic pain.

_____ 5. The urinary tract antispasmodics act to relieve spasms of the urinary tract muscles by blocking sympathetic activity.

_____ 6. Pentosan polysulfate sodium is a heparin-like compound that has anticoagulant and fibrinolytic effects and is used specifically to decrease the pain and discomfort associated with interstitial cystitis.

_____ 7. Benign prostatic hyperplasia (BPH) is a rare condition involving enlargement of the prostate gland in older males.

_____ 8. Drugs commonly used to relieve the signs and symptoms of prostate enlargement include alpha adrengergic blockers, which relax the sympathetic effects on the bladder and sphincters, and finasteride, which blocks the body's production of a powerful androgen.

CHAPTER 51: INTRODUCTION TO THE RESPIRATORY SYSTEM

FILL IN THE BLANKS

Label the parts of the respiratory system in the figure below.

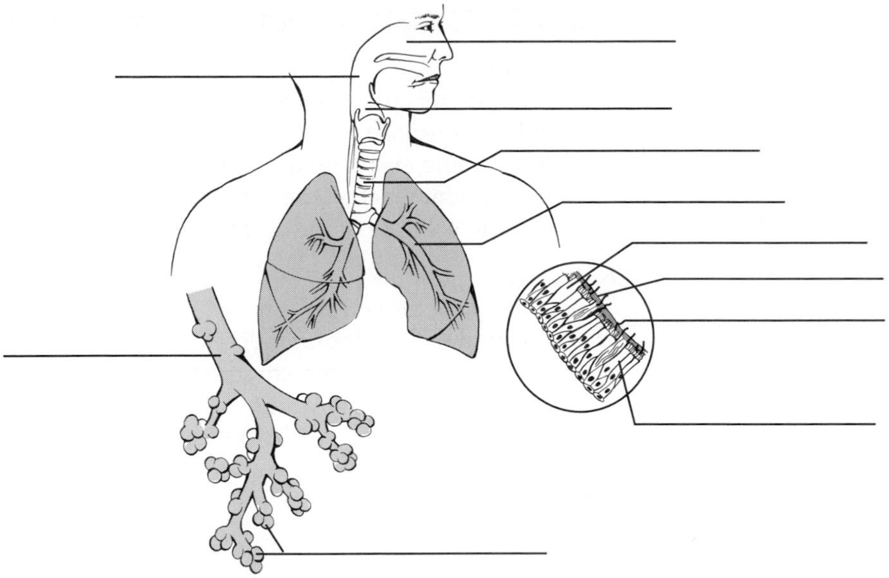

MATCHING

Match the word with the appropriate definition:

1. ________ upper respiratory tract
2. ________ bronchial tree
3. ________ lower respiratory tract
4. ________ alveoli
5. ________ cilia
6. ________ sinuses
7. ________ larynx
8. ________ trachea
9. ________ cough
10. ________ ventilation
11. ________ respiratory membrane
12. ________ surfactant

A. air-filled passages through the skull
B. the area where gas exchange takes place
C. the vocal chords and the epiglottis
D. the conducting airways leading into the alveoli
E. microscopic hairlike projections of the epithelial cell membrane
F. the exchange of gases at the alveolar level
G. the main conducting airway leading into the lungs
H. lipoprotein that reduces surface tension in the alveoli
I. the surface through which gas exchange must occur
J. the respiratory sacs
K. the nose, mouth, pharynx, larynx, trachea, and upper bronchial tree area through which gas exchange must be made
L. reflex response in the respiratory membrane; results in forced air expelled through the mouth

MULTIPLE CHOICE

1. A sneeze:
   a. is a reflex response to irritation in the nasal passages
   b. results in forced air expelled through the mouth
   c. involves tight closure of the larynx
   d. involves sequential contraction of muscles in the esophagus

2. Ventilation is:
   a. the delivery of blood to the tissues
   b. the movement of air into the nares
   c. the exchange of gases at the alveolar level respiratory membrane
   d. not affected by changes in the respiratory membrane

3. The respiratory membrane is made up of:
   a. the capillary cell, the alveolar cell, and the surfactant layer
   b. the capillary cell, the capillary basement membrane, a fluid layer, a thickened basement membrane, and the alveolar cell

c. the capillary basement membrane, the adventitia, the pleura, the alveolar cell, and the surfactant layer
d. the capillary cell, the capillary basement membrane, the interstitial space, the alveolar basement membrane, the alveolar cell, and the surfactant layer

4. The common cold:
a. blocks the inflammatory response
b. prevents the release of histamine and prostaglandins giving a stuffy feeling
c. is a viral infection of the upper respiratory tract
d. is caused by not wearing a hat in the winter

5. Seasonal rhinitis is:
a. another name for the common cold
b. caused by a common virus
c. caused by an autoimmune reaction
d. caused by a reaction to a specific antigen

6. Pneumonia is:
a. an inflammation of the epithelial lining of the nasal sinuses
b. an inflammation of the lungs
c. an inherited deficiency
d. usually caused by a reaction to a specific antigen

7. Asthma:
a. is a disorder characterized by recurrent episodes of bronchospasm
b. is a chronic, never an acute, reaction
c. results from repeated attacks of COPD
d. leads to collapse of the alveoli

8. COPD:
a. is an acute bronchospasm
b. is a chronic condition that occurs over time
c. does not alter the physical structure of the lungs
d. affects only the very young

CHAPTER 52: DRUGS ACTING ON THE UPPER RESPIRATORY TRACT

CROSSWORD PUZZLE

ACROSS

1 Common upper respiratory complaint caused by a virus
3 Drug that blocks the release of histamine and resultant vasodilation
5 Inflammation of the nares
6 Drug that stops membrane swelling and congestion

DOWN

1 Reflex to irritation in the upper respiratory tract
2 Drug that increases the cough reflex and removal of respiratory secretions
3 Drug that blocks the cough reflex
4 Drug that liquifies secretions in the respiratory tract

WWW. WEB EXERCISE

R. W. has recently moved to the area and has developed seasonal rhinitis. He had asthma as a child and is concerned that it might be returning. He asks for up-to-date information on the two disorders and how to survive the discomfort. Go to the Internet and find information that would be useful in preparing a teaching program for R. W.

WORD SCRAMBLE

Unscramble the letters below to find the names of drugs commonly used in treating upper respiratory tract problems.

1. MACTELSENI
2. EXTRAMODERNPHHOT
3. INPEERHED
4. HATZOOTERYLRIDEN
5. HEEDNORIPESUEPD
6. DOBNUDESIE
7. CATFLUNUSOE
8. MAZETILESO

CHAPTER 53: DRUGS FOR TREATING OBSTRUCTIVE PULMONARY DISORDERS

TRUE OR FALSE

Indicate whether the following statements are true (T) or false (F).

_____ 1. Pulmonary obstructive diseases include asthma, emphysema, and chronic obstructive pulmonary disease (COPD), respiratory distress syndrome, and seasonal rhinitis.

_____ 2. Drugs used to treat asthma and COPD include agents that block inflammation and dilate bronchi.

_____ 3. The xanthine derivatives have a direct effect on the smooth muscle of the respiratory tract.

_____ 4. The adverse effects of the xanthines are directly related to the theophylline levels and are fairly insignificant.

_____ 5. Sympathomimetics block the effects of the sympathetic nervous system and are used to cause dilation of the bronchi.

_____ 6. Anticholinergics can be used as bronchodilators because of their effect on the sympathetic nervous system receptor sites.

_____ 7. Steroids are used to decrease the inflammatory response in the airway.

_____ 8. Leukotriene receptor antagonists block or antagonize receptors for the production of leukotriene D_4 and E_4, thus blocking many of the signs and symptoms of asthma.

WWW. WEB EXERCISE

You have a summer job as a nursing assistant and are required to have a physical and tuberculosis (TB) test. Having had many of these in the past, you are not concerned. However, the test site becomes red and hard and is read as positive. You are very concerned and make an appointment at the health service for the next morning. Until then, you decide to find out all you can about this disease on the Internet to share with your family and roommates.

WORD SEARCH

Circle the names of the following drugs used to treat obstructive pulmonary disease that are hidden in the grid below:

aminophylline
caffeine
oxtriphylline
pentoxifylline
albuterol
isoproterenol
pirbuterol
ipratropium
flunisolide
zafirkulast
zileuton
cromolyn
nedocromil
beractant
colfosceril

B	O	X	T	R	I	P	H	Y	L	L	I	N	E	X	E
R	I	N	E	O	P	H	Y	L	L	I	N	E	E	P	R
E	A	M	I	N	R	B	E	R	A	C	T	A	N	T	S
N	O	M	I	N	A	O	Z	I	L	E	U	T	O	N	T
I	N	E	I	S	T	H	Y	P	B	E	R	A	C	Y	S
L	I	N	E	N	R	O	P	H	U	T	A	L	I	L	A
L	P	H	I	S	O	P	R	O	T	E	R	E	N	O	L
Y	M	I	N	O	P	P	I	N	E	X	C	A	R	M	U
F	I	N	E	P	I	P	H	Y	R	I	S	T	O	O	K
I	N	E	Y	Z	U	L	I	Y	O	P	H	Y	L	R	R
X	O	O	H	Y	M	I	N	E	L	U	K	A	S	C	I
O	O	L	I	R	E	C	S	O	F	L	O	C	H	E	F
T	P	H	Y	L	L	C	A	F	F	E	I	N	E	X	A
N	E	D	O	C	R	O	M	I	L	X	O	N	E	A	Z
E	Z	A	F	L	U	N	I	S	O	L	I	D	E	N	E
P	I	R	B	U	T	E	R	O	L	I	O	N	P	H	Y

CHAPTER 54: INTRODUCTION TO THE GASTROINTESTINAL SYSTEM

IDENTIFY

Identify the parts of the GI system in the figure below.

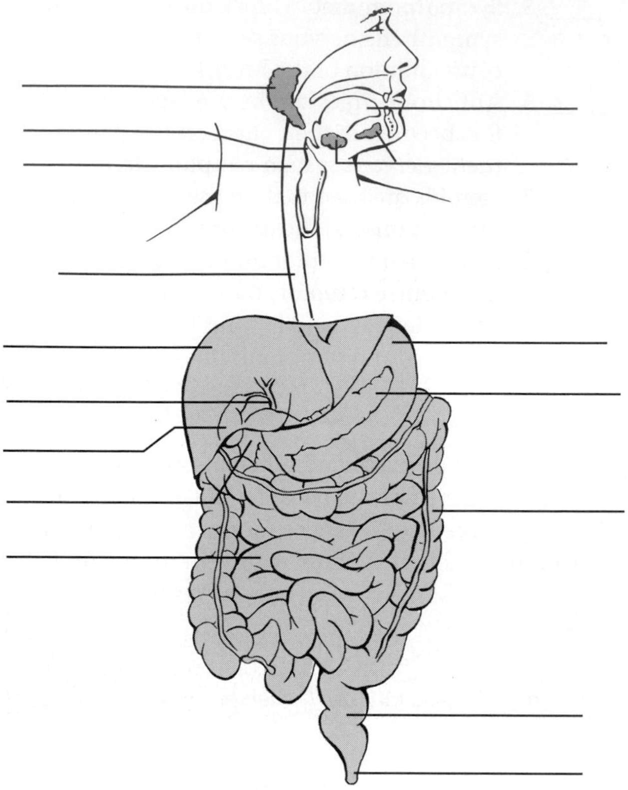

MATCHING

Match the following words with the appropriate definition.

1. ________ bile
2. ________ chyme
3. ________ gallstones
4. ________ gastrin
5. ________ histamine$_2$ receptors
6. ________ hydrochloric acid
7. ________ nerve plexus
8. ________ pancreatic enzymes
9. ________ peristalsis
10. ________ segmentation

A. acid released in response to gastrin
B. sites near the parietal cells of the stomach that cause the release of hydrochloric acid into the stomach
C. contents of the stomach
D. pancreatin and pancrelipase
E. network of nerve fibers running through the wall of the GI tract
F. fluid stored in the gallbladder
G. crystallization of cholesterol in the gallbladder
H. secreted by the stomach to stimulate the release of hydrochloric acid
I. GI movement characterized by contraction of one segment of small intestine while the next segment is relaxed
J. GI movement characterized by a progressive wave of muscle contraction

FILL IN THE BLANKS

1. The gastrointestinal (GI) system is composed of one long tube and is responsible for ______________ and ______________ of nutrients.
2. Secretion of digestive enzymes, ______________, bicarbonate, and ______________ facilitates the digestion and absorption of nutrients.

3. The GI system is controlled by a _______________, which maintains a basic electrical rhythm and responds to local stimuli to increase or decrease activity.
4. The autonomic system can influence the activity of the GI tract; the _______________ system slows it and the _______________ system increases activity.
5. Initiation of activity in the GI tract depends on _______________.
6. Overstimulation of any of the GI reflexes can result in _______________ (underactivity) or _______________ (overactivity).
7. Swallowing is a centrally mediated reflex that is important in delivering food to the GI tract for processing. It is controlled by the _______________.
8. Vomiting is controlled by the _______________ in the medulla or by the emetic zone in immature or injured brains.

CHAPTER 55: DRUGS AFFECTING GASTROINTESTINAL SECRETIONS

WWW. WEB EXERCISE

You are doing a rotation on medicine and working on a GI unit. You are asked to prepare an inservice for the staff covering various GI diseases, treatments, research, and nursing implications involved in the care of patients with these disorders. Because this program will determine 20% of your course grade, you want to be current and thorough. Go to the Internet to prepare the teaching session.

CROSSWORD PUZZLE

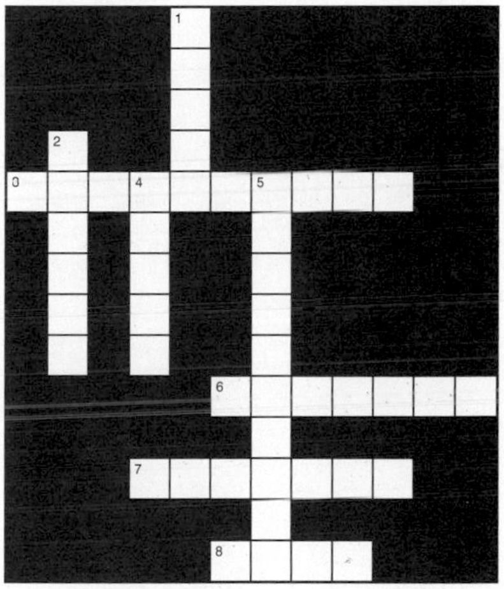

ACROSS

3 Digestive enzyme from the exocrine pancreas

6 Reflex increase in acid following a lowering of acid levels in the stomach

7 Digestive enzyme that results in the release of hydrochloric acid from cells in the stomach

8 Contributes to erosion of the stomach lining in peptic ulcer disease

DOWN

1 Erosion of the stomach or duodenal lining

2 Digestive and lubricating fluid in the mouth

4 Stomach contents

5 A drug that coats any injured area in the stomach

MATCHING

Match the drugs below with the appropriate class of drugs used to affect GI secretions. (Some classes may be used more than once.)

1. ________ misoprostol
2. ________ lanisoprazole
3. ________ sucralfate
4. ________ cimetidine
5. ________ saliva
6. ________ aluminum
7. ________ sodium bicarbonate
8. ________ pancrelipase
9. ________ omeprazole
10. ________ famotidine

A. histamine H_2 antagonists
B. antacids
C. proton pump inhibitors
D. antipeptic agent
E. prostaglandin
F. digestive enzymes

CHAPTER 56: LAXATIVES AND ANTIDIARRHEAL AGENTS

PATIENT TEACHING CHECKLIST

M. A. is a 55-year-old who has recently undergone a vaginal reconstruction. She is pain free and healing well, but has become constipated and is afraid to move her bowels because of her fear of pain or ripping. An order is written for docusate. Prepare a drug teaching card for M. A. to take with her as she leaves.

WORD SCRAMBLE

Unscramble the letters below to find the names of frequently used laxatives or antidiarrheal agents.

1. SACCARA 2. EPROMLEDIA 3. DISCPAIRE 4. SLYUMIPL
5. ANNSE 6. ROMIMCATPELODE 7. UMOIP 8. OCATSUDE

TRUE OR FALSE

Indicate whether the following statements are true (T) or false (F).

_____ 1. Laxatives are used to stop movement along the GI tract.

_____ 2. Laxatives are used to prevent or treat constipation.

_____ 3. Chemical stimulants directly irritate the local nerve plexus of the GI tract.

_____ 4. Bulk stimulants decrease the size of the food bolus and stimulate stretch receptors in the intestinal wall.

_____ 5. For many patients, eating a proper diet, exercising, and taking advantage of the actions of the intestinal reflexes has eliminated the need for laxatives.

_____ 6. Cathartic dependence can occur with the occasional use of laxatives, leading to a need for external stimuli for normal functioning of the GI tract.

_____ 7. GI stimulants act to increase sympathetic stimulation in the GI tract.

_____ 8. Antidiarrheal drugs are used to soothe irritation to the intestinal wall, block GI muscle activity to decrease movement, or affect central nervous system activity to cause GI spasm and stop movement.

CHAPTER 57: EMETIC AND ANTIEMETIC AGENTS

LIST

List four major contraindications for the induction of vomiting.

1. _______________
2. _______________
3. _______________
4. _______________

CROSSWORD PUZZLE

ACROSS

1 Protective response to vomiting reflex

2 Cancer treatment associated with nausea and vomiting

5 Vomiting is a centrally mediated ________

6 A common cause of nausea

DOWN

1 Site of the CTZ

2 Chemoreceptor trigger zone

3 Inducing vomiting

4 Repetitive stimulation of the diaphragm

FILL IN THE BLANKS

1. Emetic drugs are used to induce ______________ in cases of poisoning or drug overdose.
2. ______________ is the standard antiemetic in use.
3. ______________ are used to manage nausea and vomiting in situations in which they are not beneficial and could actually cause harm to the patient.
4. Antiemetics act by depressing the ______________, either locally or through alteration of central nervous system actions.
5. Vomiting is a complex reflex mediated through the ______________ located in the ______________.
6. The CTZ can be stimulated by ______________, ______________, ______________ or several other mechanisms.
7. Most antiemetics cause some ______________ with resultant dizziness, drowsiness, weakness.
8. ______________ is another common adverse effect with antiemetics. Patients should be protected from exposure to the sun and ultraviolet light.

CHAPTER 58: GALLSTONE SOLUBILIZERS

NURSING CARE GUIDE

E. W. is a 34-year-old teacher who has a history of severe gallstones. She is not a candidate for surgery because of a cardiac condition. She is being started on chenodiol. Preapare a nursing care guide to keep with E. W. chart to promote continuity of care.

WWW. WEB EXERCISE

There is some indication that people on weight loss diets are more apt to develop gallstones. A neighborhood friend who is dieting calls to ask you about this because you are a nurse, but this information is new to you. Go to the Internet to find out what is known about this, then prepare a short fact sheet to share.

TRUE OR FALSE

Indicate whether the following statements are true (T) or false (F).

_____ 1. Gallstones form when bile is concentrated and high levels of cholesterol in the bile crystallize.

_____ 2. Gallstones can prevent the formation of bile in the gallbladder.

_____ 3. Gallstones can block the flow of bile from the gallbladder into the common duct or can block the common duct.

_____ 4. The treatment of choice for gallstones is treatment with gallstone solubilizers.

_____ 5. Oral gallstone solubilizers decrease the production of cholesterol in the liver, leading to the formation of bile that is low in cholesterol.

_____ 6. Oral gallstone solubilizers are most effective if stones have calcified.

_____ 7. Serious adverse effects are associated with the use of oral gallstone solubilizers, including liver dysfunction, high cholesterol levels, severe diarrhea, and colon cancer.

_____ 8. Monoctanoin dissolves stones directly and is administered only through a continuous perfusion pump via a catheter inserted directly into the esophagus.

Study Guide Key

CHAPTER 1: INTRODUCTION TO DRUGS

MATCHING

1. G 2. F 3. A 4. H 5. E 6. I 7. C 8. J 9. B 10. D

WEB EXERCISE: Start at http://www.fda.gov

USE OF TERMS

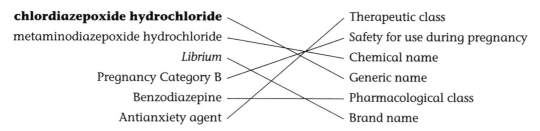

chlordiazepoxide hydrochloride	Therapeutic class
metaminodiazepoxide hydrochloride	Safety for use during pregnancy
Librium	Chemical name
Pregnancy Category B	Generic name
Benzodiazepine	Pharmacological class
Antianxiety agent	Brand name

FILL IN THE BLANKS

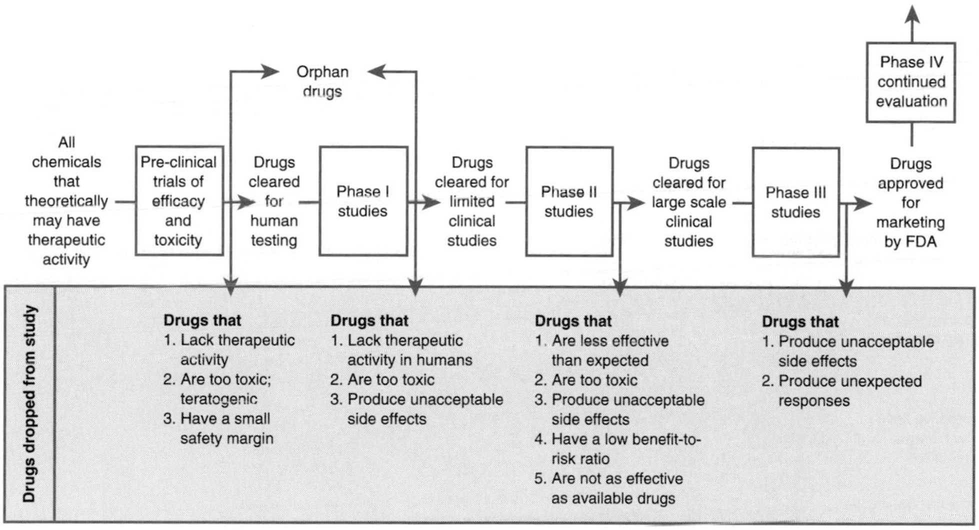

CHAPTER 2: DRUGS AND THE BODY

WORD SEARCH

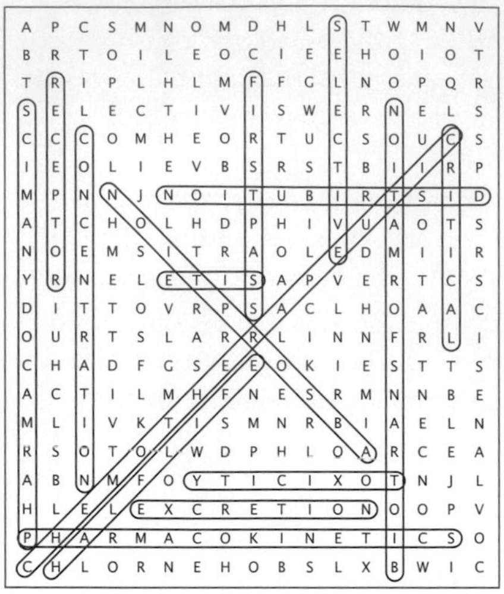

FILL IN THE BLANKS

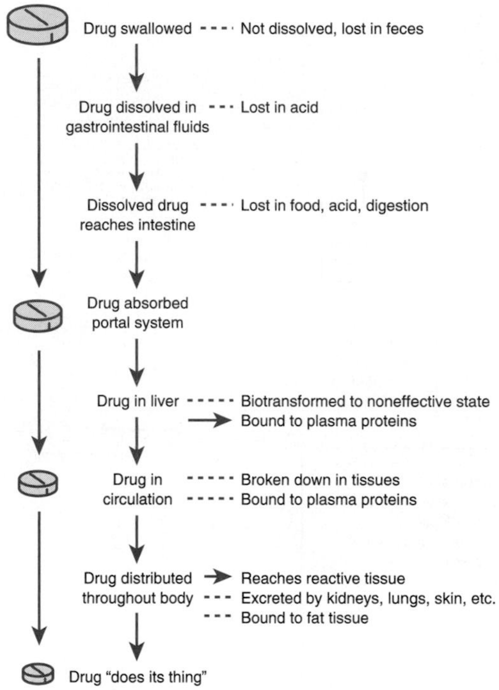

MULTIPLE CHOICE

1. c 2. c 3. b 4. d 5. b

CHAPTER 3: TOXIC EFFECTS OF DRUGS

DESCRIPTION

1. Anaphylactic reaction: An allergy involving an antibody that reacts with specific sites in the body to cause the release of chemicals, including histamine, that produce immediate reactions—mucous membrane swelling and constricting bronchi—that can lead to respiratory distress and even respiratory arrest.
2. Cytotoxic reaction: An allergy involving antibodies that circulate in the blood and attack antigens (the drug) on cell sites, causing death of that cell. This reaction is not immediate but may be seen over a few days.
3. Serum sickness reaction: An allergy involving antibodies that circulate in the blood and cause damage to various tissues by depositing in blood vessels. This reaction may occur up to a week or more after exposure to the drug.
4. Superinfection: Infections caused by the destruction of normal flora bacteria by certain drugs, allowing other bacteria to enter the body and cause infection.
5. Blood dyscrasia: Bone marrow depression caused by drug effects that occur when drugs that can cause cell death (antineoplastics, antibiotics) are used.

MATCHING

1. E 2. C 3. A 4. F 5. B 6. D

CHAPTER 4: NURSING MANAGEMENT

LIST

1. Drug
2. Storage
3. Route
4. Dosage
5. Preparation
6. Timing
7. Recording

FILL IN THE BLANKS

BOX 4-1 THE STEPS OF THE NURSING PROCESS

Nursing Process

↓

Assessment

Past history
- Chronic conditions
- Drug use
- Allergies
- Level of education
- Level of understanding of disease and therapy
- Social supports
- Financial supports
- Pattern of health care

Physical assessment
- Weight
- Age
- Physical parameters related to the disease state or known drug effects

↓

Nursing Diagnosis

↓

Interventions

Proper drug administration
- Drug
- Storage
- Route
- Dosage
- Preparation
- Timing
- Recording

Comfort measures
- Placebo effect
- Managing side effects
- Lifestyle adjustments

Patient/family education

↓

Evaluation

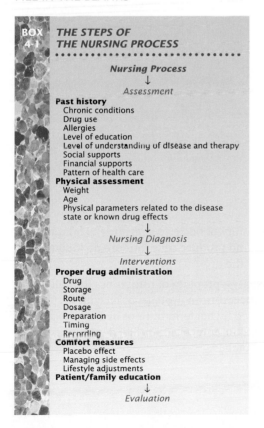

LIST EIGHT TEACHING FACTORS

1. Name, dose, and action of drug
2. Timing of administration
3. Special storage and preparation
4. Specific OTC drugs to avoid
5. Special comfort or safety measures
6. Safety measures
7. Specific points about drug toxicity
8. Specific warnings about drug discontinuation

CHAPTER 5: INTRODUCTION TO CELL PHYSIOLOGY

WEB EXERCISE: Follow web on-line instructions

FILL IN THE BLANKS

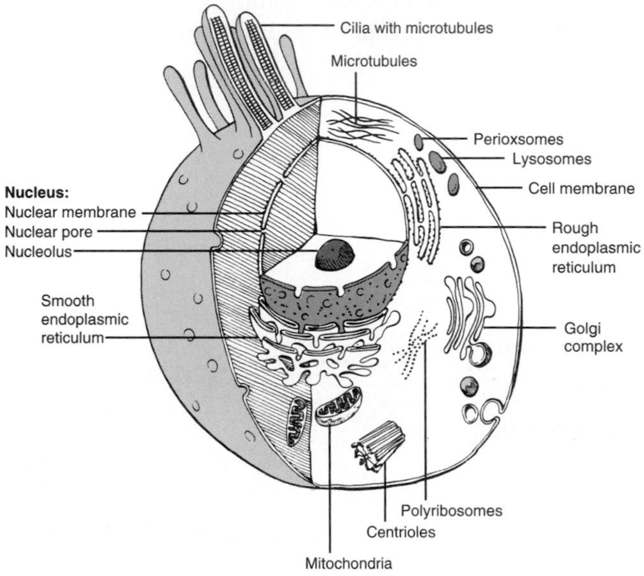

WORD SCRAMBLE

1. diffusion 2. endocytosis 3. pinocytosis 4. phagocytosis
5. osmosis 6. mitosis 7. passive transport 8. active transport

MATCHING

1. E 2. D 3. B 4. C 5. A

CHAPTER 6: ANTI-INFECTIVE AGENTS

DEFINITIONS

culture—sample of the bacteria (e.g., from sputum, cell scrapings, urine) to grow in a laboratory to determine the species of bacteria that is causing an infection

prophylaxis—treatment to prevent an infection before it occurs, as in the use of antibiotics to prevent disease such as bacterial endocarditis or antiprotozoals to prevent malaria

resistance—ability of bacteria over time to adapt to an antibiotic and produce cells that are no longer affected by the drug

selective toxicity—property of antibiotics that allows them to affect certain proteins or enzyme systems that are used by bacteria but not by human cells, sparing the human cells from the destructive effects of the antibiotic

sensitivity testing—evaluation of bacteria obtained in a culture to determine to what antibiotics the organisms are sensitive and which agent would be appropriate for treatment of a particular infection

spectrum—range of bacteria against which an antibiotic is effective (e.g., broad-spectrum antibiotics are effective against a wide range of bacteria)

CROSSWORD PUZZLE

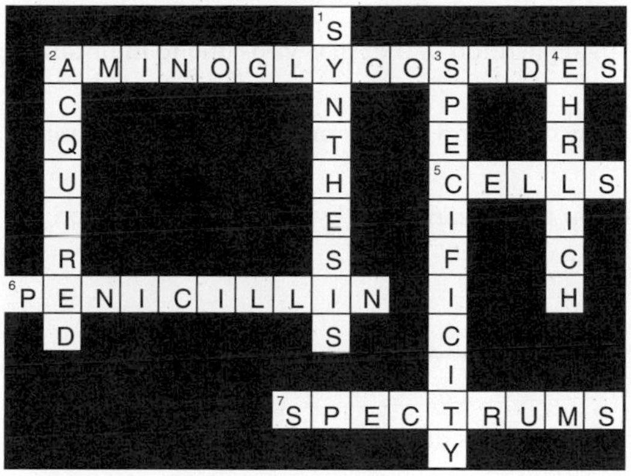

MATCHING

1. C 2. A 3. B 4. E 5. F 6. D

CHAPTER 7: ANTIBIOTICS

TRUE OR FALSE

1. T 2. F 3. F 4. T 5. F 6. T 7. F 8. T

WEB EXERCISE: Use www.cdc.gov to obtain the information. Development of the information will be individual

WORD SCRAMBLE

1. cephipirin 2. cefaclor 3. cefadroxil 4. loracarbef
5. ceftizoxime 6. cefotetan 7. cefoxitin 8. cefazolin

CHAPTER 8: ANTIVIRAL AGENTS

IDENTIFY SITE OF ACTION

1. Reverse transcriptase inhibitors bind directly to HIV to reverse transcriptase, which blocks both RNA and DNA-dependent DNA polymerase activities. This prevents the transfer of information that would allow the virus to replicate and survive.
2. Protease inhibitors block protease, which is essential for the maturation of infectious virus, within the HIV virus; an immature and noninfective virus is produced.
3. Nucleosides inhibit HIV replication by inhibiting cell protein synthesis, leading to viral death.
4. Antiretrovirus drugs act to prevent replication in various retroviruses, including HIV; action is related to their conversion to triphosphates in the body.

MATCHING

1. F 2. D 3. E 4. C 5. A 6. B

PATIENT TEACHING GUIDE

PATIENT TEACHING CHECKLIST

Zidovudine

An antiviral works in combination with other antivirals to stop the replication of the AIDS virus and to maintain the functioning of your immune system.

This drug is not a cure for AIDS or ARC; opportunistic infections may occur and regular medical follow-up should be sought to deal with the disease.

This drug does not reduce the risk of transmission of HIV to others by sexual contact or by blood contamination; use appropriate precautions.

Common effects of this drug include:

- Dizziness, weakness, loss of feeling—Change positions slowly; if you feel drowsy, avoid driving or performing dangerous activities.
- Headache, fever, muscle aches—Analgesics may be ordered to alleviate this discomfort. Consult with your health care provider.
- Nausea, loss of appetite, change in taste—Small, frequent meals may help. It is important to try to maintain your nutrition. Consult your health care provider if this becomes a severe problem.

Report any of the following to your health care provider: excessive fatigue, lethargy, severe headache, difficulty breathing, skin rash.

Avoid over-the-counter medications. If you feel that you need one of these, check with your health care provider first.

Regular medical evaluations, including blood tests, will be needed to monitor the effects of these drugs on your body and to adjust dosages as needed.

Tell any doctor, nurse or other health care provider that you are taking these drugs.

Keep this drug, and all medications, out of the reach of children. Do not share these drugs with other people.

CHAPTER 9: ANTIFUNGAL AGENTS

WEB EXERCISE: Looking up both Internet sources will provide patient teaching materials that can be organized into a usable format.

WORD SEARCH

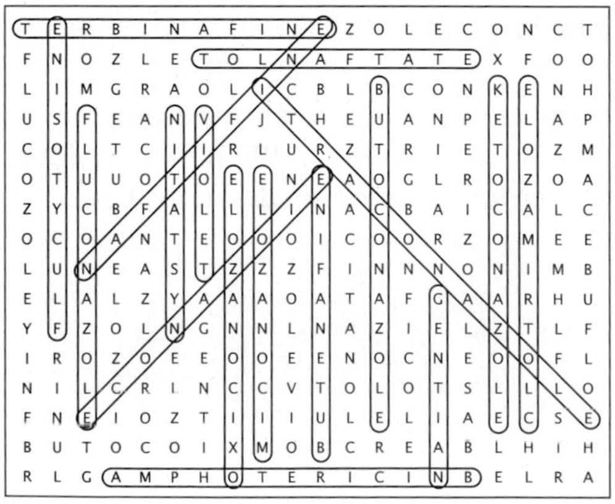

FILL IN THE BLANKS

1. *hard, ergosterol*
2. *mycosis*
3. *hepatic, renal*
4. *Candida*
5. *tinea*
6. *systemically*
7. *wounds*
8. *burning, irritation, pain*

CHAPTER 10: ANTIPROTOZOAL AGENTS

MATCHING

1. D 2. E 3. B 4. F 5. A 6. G 7. C

FILL IN THE BLANKS

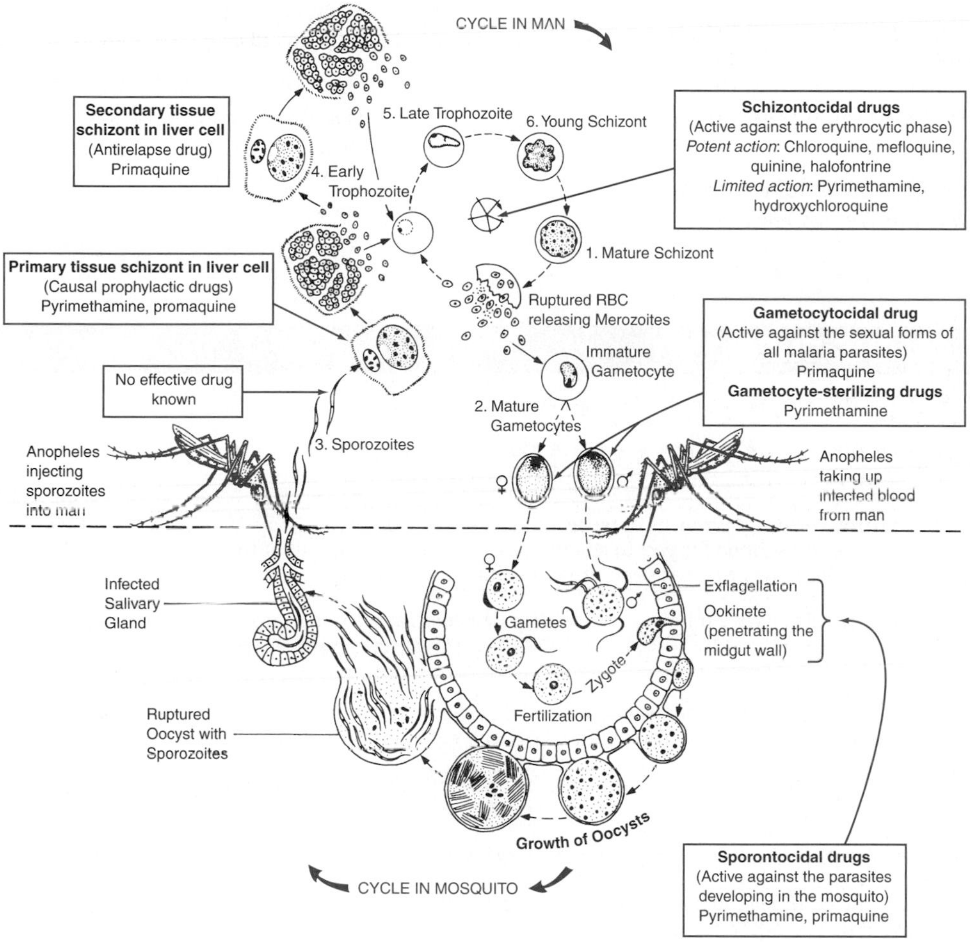

WEB EXERCISE: Log on to www.cdc.gov/travel. Select the graphic travel map. This will show you a map of the world with certain areas highlighted. Using your friend's itinerary, select each area that will be visited. Health risks, suggested vaccinations, and health precautions will be presented (and can be printed). Back on the home page, you can select summary sheets for travel hazards, precautions, and even areas of unrest and political precautions.

CHAPTER 11: ANTHELMINTIC AGENTS

DEFINE THE TERMS

1. cestode—tapeworm with a head and segmented body parts that is capable of growing to several yards in the human intestine
2. nematode—roundworm such as the commonly encountered pinworm, whipworm, threadworm, *Ascaris,* or hookworm
3. pinworm—nematode that causes a common helmintic infection in humans; lives in the intestine and causes anal and possible vaginal irritation and itching
4. round worm—worm such as *Ascaris* that causes a common helmintic infection in humans; can cause intestinal obstruction as the adult worms clog the intestinal lumen or severe pneumonia when the larvae migrate to the lungs and form a pulmonary infiltrate
5. schistosomiasis—infection with blood fluke that is carried by a snail, poses a common problem in tropical countries, where the snail is the intermediary in the life cycle of the worm; larvae burrow into the skin in fresh water and migrate throughout the human body, causing a rash and then symptoms of diarrhea and liver and brain inflammation
6. trichinosis—disease that results from ingestion of encysted roundworm larvae in undercooked pork; larvae migrate throughout the body to invade muscle, nervous tissue; can cause pneumonia, heart failure, and encephalitis
7. thread worm—pervasive nematode that can send larvae into the lungs, liver, and CNS; can cause severe pneumonia or liver abscess
8. whip worm—worm that attaches itself to the intestinal mucosa and sucks blood; may cause severe anemia and disintegration of the intestinal mucosa

PATIENT TEACHING CHECKLIST

PATIENT TEACHING CHECKLIST

Mebendazole

An anthelmintic acts to destroy certain helminths or worms that have invaded your body. You must take the full course of the drug that has been prescribed for you to ensure that you have cleared all of the worms, in all phases of their life cycle, from your body. Your drug has been prescribed to treat pinworms.

Your drug can be taken with meals or with a light snack to help decrease any stomach upset that you may experience.

Common effects of this drug include:

- Nausea, vomiting, loss of appetite—Take the drug with meals and eat small, frequent meals.
- Dizziness, drowsiness—If this happens, avoid driving a car or operating dangerous machinery; change positions slowly to avoid falling or injury.

Report any of the following to your health care provider: fever, chills, rash, headache, weakness or tremors.

It is very important to take the complete prescription that has been ordered for you. Never use this drug to self-treat any other infection or give it to any other person.

Tell any doctor, nurse, or other health care provider that you are taking this drug.

Keep this drug, and all medications, out of the reach of children.

Follow the guidelines below to help to prevent reinfection with the worms or spread to other family members:

- Wash hands vigorously with soap after using toilet facilities.
- Shower in the morning to wash away any ova deposited in the anal area during the night.
- Change and launder undergarments, bed linens, and pajamas every day.
- Disinfect toilets and toilet seats daily and bathroom and bedroom floors periodically.

FILL IN THE BLANKS

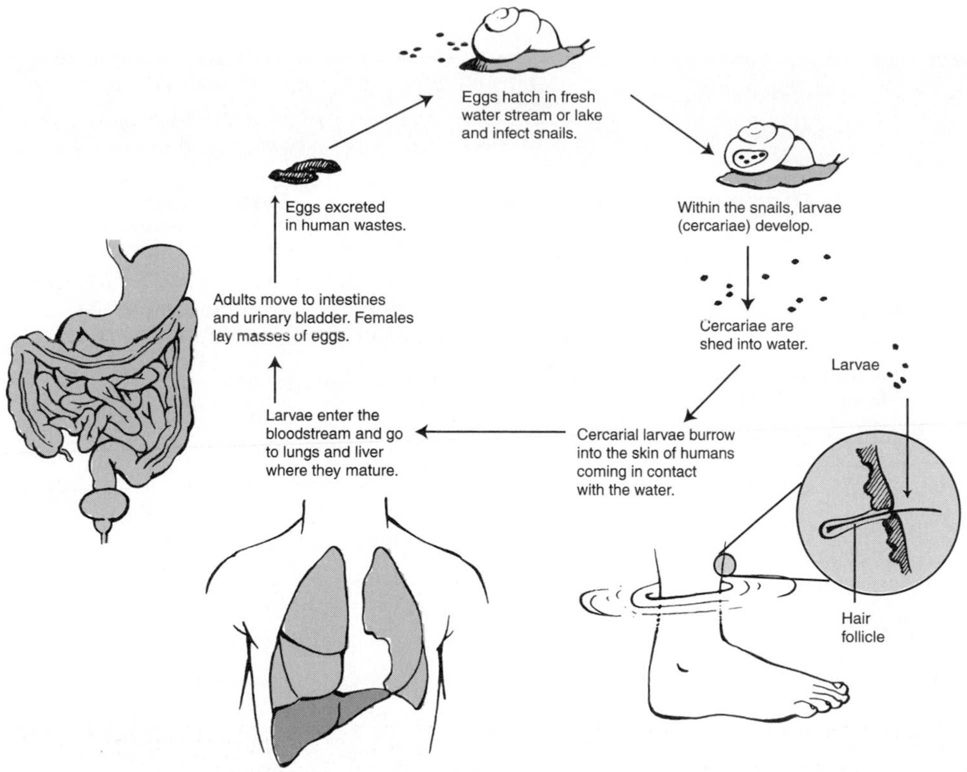
Eggs hatch in fresh water stream or lake and infect snails.
Within the snails, larvae (cercariae) develop.
Cercariae are shed into water.
Larvae
Cercarial larvae burrow into the skin of humans coming in contact with the water.
Hair follicle
Larvae enter the bloodstream and go to lungs and liver where they mature.
Adults move to intestines and urinary bladder. Females lay masses of eggs.
Eggs excreted in human wastes.

CHAPTER 12: ANTINEOPLASTIC AGENTS

NURSING CARE GUIDE

NURSING CARE GUIDE
Busulfan

Assessment	Nursing Diagnoses	Implementation	Evaluation
HISTORY Allergies to busulfan, renal or liver dysfunction, pregnancy and lactation, bone marrow depression, GI ulceration	Pain related to GI, CNS, skin effects Alteration in nutrition related to GI effects Alteration in self-concept related to diagnosis, therapy, side effects Knowledge deficit regarding drug therapy	Ensure safe preparation and administration of the drug. Provide comfort and safety measures: - mouth and skin care - rest periods - safety precautions - antiemetics as needed - maintenance of nutrition - head covering. Provide small, frequent meals and monitor nutritional status. Provide support and reassurance to deal with drug effects, discomfort, and diagnosis. Provide patient teaching regarding drug name, dosage, adverse effects, precautions, warnings to report, and comfort measures to observe.	Evaluate drug effects: resolution of cancer being treated. Monitor for adverse effects: - GI toxicity - bone marrow depression - CNS changes - renal, hepatic damage - alopecia - extravasation of drug. Evaluate effectiveness of patient teaching program. Evaluate effectiveness of comfort and safety measures.
PHYSICAL EXAMINATION Local: injection site evaluation CNS: orientation, affect, reflexes Skin: color, lesions, texture GI: abdominal, liver evalution Hematological: renal and hepatic function tests, CBC with differential			

MATCHING

1. D 2. G 3. C 4. E 5. F 6. A 7. H 8. B

WORD SCRAMBLE

1. VINBLASTINE 2. CARMUSTINE 3. CARBOPLASTIN 4. CISPLATIN
5. TAMOXIFEN 6. BLEOMYCIN 7. DACARBAZINE 8. ETOPOSIDE

FILL IN THE BLANKS

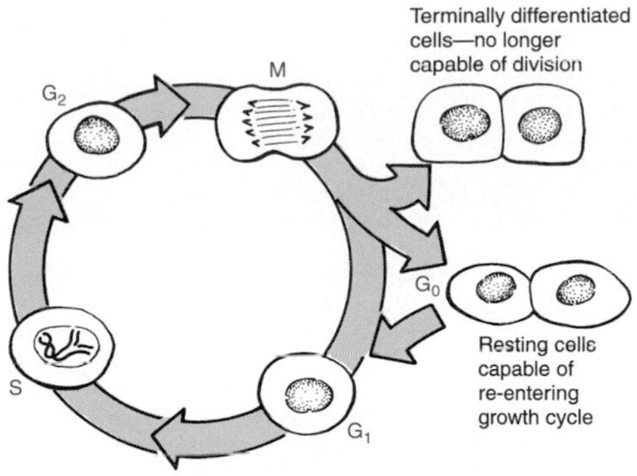

CHAPTER 13: INTRODUCTION TO THE IMMUNE RESPONSE AND INFLAMMATION

MULTIPLE CHOICE

1. d 2. c 3. a 4. b 5. a 6. c

FILL IN THE BLANKS

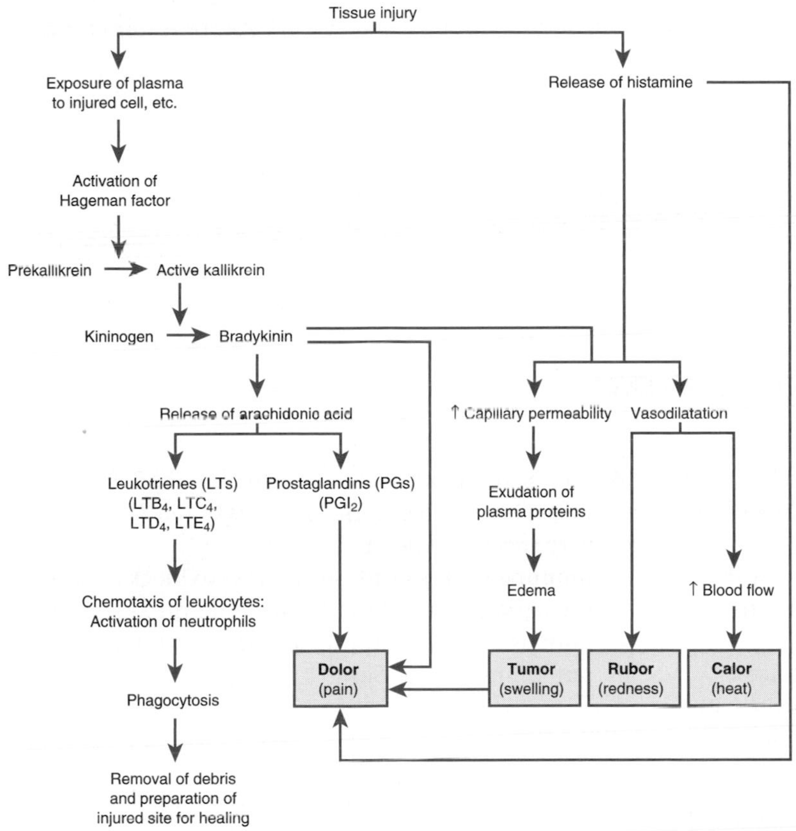

WORD SEARCH

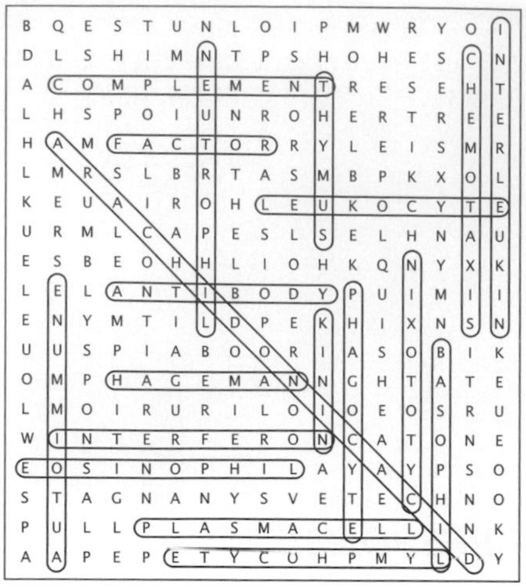

CHAPTER 14: ANTI-INFLAMMATORY AGENTS

WEB EXERCISE: Log on to http://www.arthritis.org/. At the top of the home page is a "search" slot where you can enter any key word—research, drugs, etc. Or select the menu under "Offerings" and select "What's new," "Order brochures," or "Getting a Grip on Rheumatoid Arthritis." You can also go to the lower part of the home page and find local groups that might be appropriate for your patient as support groups, exercise groups, or information sources.

WORD SCRAMBLE

1. naproxen
2. sulindac
3. ketorolac
4. diclofenac
5. ibuprofen
6. olsalazine
7. acetaminophen
8. salsalate
9. aspirin
10. ketoprofen

MATCHING

1. D 2. G 3. E 4. C 5. B 6. F 7. A

CHAPTER 15: IMMUNE MODULATORS

DEFINE THE TERMS

1. autoimmune—having antibodies to self-cells or self-proteins; leads to chronic inflammatory disease and cell destruction
2. interferon—protein released by cells in response to viral invasion; prevents viral replication in other cells
3. interleukin—"between white cells"; substance released by active white cells to communicate with other white cells and to support the inflammatory and immune reactions
4. monoclonal antibodies—specific antibodies produced by a single clone of B cells to react with a very specific antigen
5. immune suppressant—drug used to block or suppress the actions of the T cells and antibody production; used to prevent transplant rejection and treat autoimmune diseases

MATCHING

1. E 2. B 3. F 4. G 5. A 6. C 7. D

FILL IN THE BLANKS

1. Monoclonal antibodies
2. basiliximab, daclizumab, muromonab-CD3
3. Crohn's
4. respiratory syncytial virus
5. trastuzumab
6. Rituximab

CHAPTER 16: VACCINES AND SERA

WEB EXERCISE: Log on to http://www.aap.org/family/parents/vaccine.htm. This page, maintained by the American Academy of Pediatrics, can be printed out and offers answers to the most frequently asked parent questions about vaccinations. A permanent record of vaccinations can be printed out from the bottom of the page if other forms are not available.

TRUE OR FALSE

1. F 2. T 3. T 4. T 5. T 6. T 7. F 8. F

FILL IN THE BLANKS

Immunization	Birth	2 mo	4 mo	6 mo	12–15 mo	18 mo	4–6 y	11–12 y	14–16 y
Hepatitis B	X	X			X				
DPT		X	X	X		X			
Rotavirus		X	X	X					
Tetanus/diphtheria booster							X	X	
H. influenzae b		X	X	X	X				
Measles, mumps, rubella					X		X		
Poliovirus		X	X		X		X		

Suggested by the American Academy of Pediatrics, 1998.

CHAPTER 17: INTRODUCTION TO NERVES AND THE NERVOUS SYSTEM

LABELING

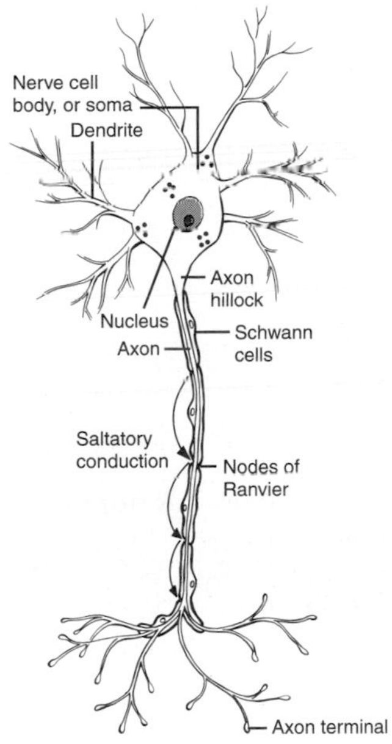

MATCHING

1. G 2. C 3. B 4. I 5. J 6. H 7. A 8. F 9. E 10. D

DIAGRAM

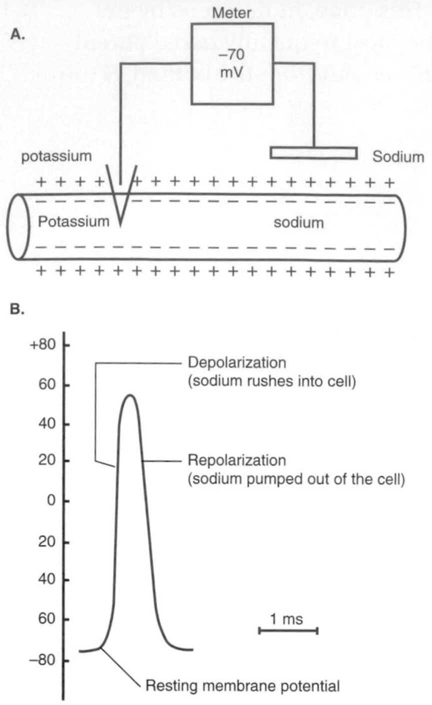

CHAPTER 18: ANXIOLYTIC AND HYPNOTIC AGENTS

FILL IN THE BLANKS

1. Anxiety
2. motivator
3. Sedatives
4. hypnotics
5. tension, fear
6. sedation
7. depress
8. Benzodiazepines

MATCHING

1. C 2. E 3. A 4. B 5. G 6. H 7. D 8. F 9. J 10. I

WEB EXERCISE: Log on to: http://www.adaa.org. Select consumer resources, then select self-help groups from the menu. Select your state and locate support groups in your area. Go back to the home page and select "About Anxiety Disorders" and print out information about the specific anxiety diagnosis related to this patient.

CHAPTER 19: ANTIDEPRESSANT AGENTS

MULTIPLE CHOICE

1. a 2. b 3. b 4. c 5. c

WORD SEARCH

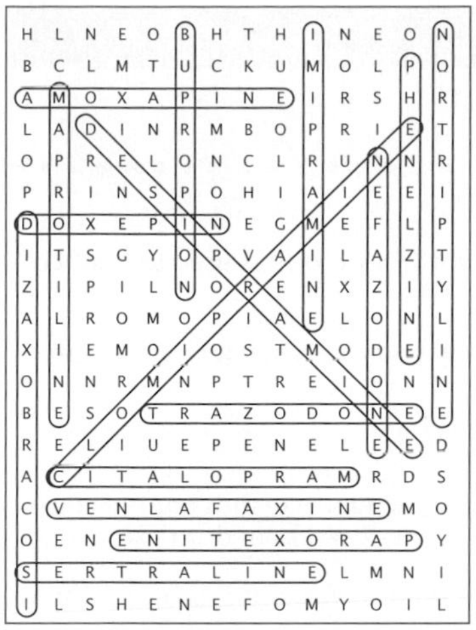

WORD SCRAMBLE

1. bupropion 2. fluoxetine 3. clomipramine 4. venlafaxine
5. phenelzine 6. paroxetine 7. imipramine 8. Nefazodone

CROSSWORD PUZZLE

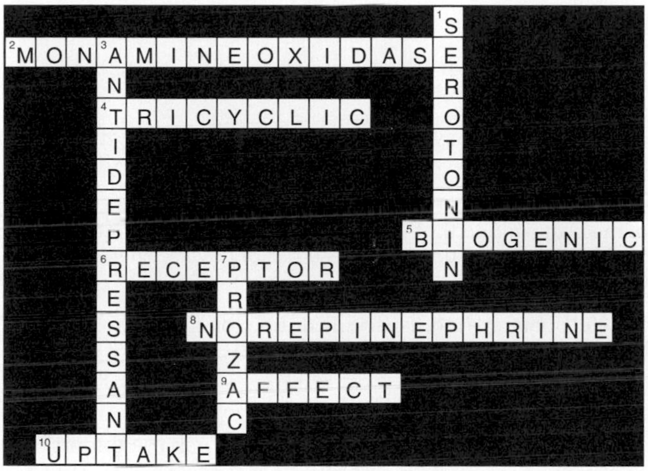

CHAPTER 20: PSYCHOTHERAPEUTIC AGENTS

MATCHING

1. F 2. C 3. B 4. G 5. D 6. A 7. E

PATIENT TEACHING CHECKLIST

PATIENT TEACHING CHECKLIST

Chlorpromazine

An antipsychotic or neuroleptic drug affects the activities of certain chemicals in your brain and is used to treat certain mental disorders.

The drug should be taken exactly as prescribed. Because this drug also affects many body systems, it is important that you have regular medical evaluation.

Common effects of these drugs include:

- Dizziness, drowsiness, fainting—Avoid driving or performing hazardous tasks or delicate tasks that require concentration if these occur. Change position slowly. The dizziness usually passes after 1–2 weeks of drug use.
- Pink or reddish urine—Do not be alarmed by this change; it does not mean that your urine contains blood. The drug causes some people's urine to change to this color.
- Sensitivity to light—Bright light might hurt your eyes and sunlight might burn your skin more easily. Wear sunglasses and protective clothing when you must be out in the sun.
- Constipation—Consult with your health care provider if this becomes a problem.

Report any of the following to your health care provider: sore throat, fever, rash; tremors, weakness; vision changes.

Tell any doctor, nurse or other health care provider that you are taking this drug.

Keep this drug, and all medications, out of the reach of children.

Avoid the use of alcohol or other depressants while you are on this drug. You also may want to limit your use of caffeine if you have increased tension or insomnia.

Avoid the use of over-the-counter drugs while you are on this drug. Many of them contain ingredients that could interfere with the effectiveness of your drug. If you feel that you need one of these preparations, consult with your health care provider about the most appropriate choice.

Take this drug exactly as prescribed. If you run out of medicine or find that you cannot take your drug for any reason, consult your health care provider. After being used for a period of time, there is a risk of adverse effects if the drug is suddenly stopped. This drug will need to be tapered over time.

Specifics related to your situation: You must be very careful about driving, especially during the first few weeks of treatment. Use sunscreen and protective clothing whenever you are outside and use sun glasses.

WEB EXERCISE: Log on to http://www.mhsource.com/ Click on the Disorders button. Select the "ask the expert" button for consumers (you may want to select "ask the expert—professionals" for additional information). Select SAD—treatment options to learn about herbal and alternative therapies; or SAD—lights to learn about the latest in light therapy, including insurance backing of the purchase of lights.

CHAPTER 21: ANTIEPILEPTIC AGENTS

FILL IN THE BLANKS

1. Epilepsy
2. seizure
3. convulsion
4. antiepileptics
5. grand mal seizure
6. absence seizure
7. myoclonic seizures
8. febrile seizures
9. status epilepticus
10. focal

NURSING CARE GUIDE

NURSING CARE GUIDE
Hydantoin

Assessment	Nursing Diagnoses	Implementation	Evaluation
HISTORY Allergies to any of these drugs; hypotension; arrhythmias, bone marrow depression, coma, psychoses, pregnancy and lactation, hepatic or renal dysfunction	Potential alteration in comfort related to GI, CNS, GU effects Potential for injury related to CNS effects Potential alteration in thought processes related to CNS effects Knowledge deficit regarding-drug therapy Alteration in skin integrity related to dermatological effects	Discontinue drug at first sign of liver dysfunction, skin rash. Provide comfort and safety measures: - positioning - give with meals - safety measures - barrier contraceptives - skin care. Provide support and reassurance to deal with diagnosis and drug effects. Provide patient teaching regarding drug, dosage, drug effects, things to report, need to wear medical alert information.	Evaluate drug effects: decrease in incidence and frequency of seizures. Monitor for adverse effects: - CNS effects - multiple - bone marrow depression - rash, skin changes - GI effects- nausea, anorexia - arrhythmias Monitor for drug-drug interactions: Increased depression with CNS depressant, alcohol; varies with individual drug Evaluate effectiveness of patient teaching program. Evaluate effectiveness of comfort and safety measures
PHYSICAL EXAMINATION CV: BP, P, peripheral perfusion CNS: orientation, affect, reflexes, strength, EEG Skin: color, lesions, texture, temperature GI: abdominal exam, bowel sounds Resp: R, adventitious sounds Other: renal and liver function tests			

CROSSWORD PUZZLE

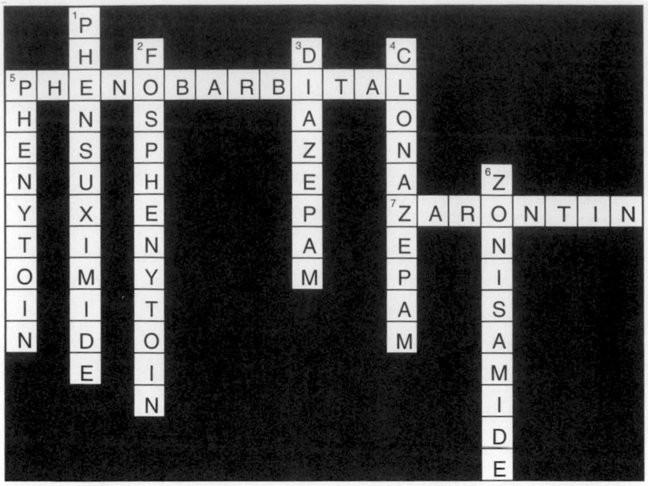

CHAPTER 22: ANTIPARKINSONISM AGENTS

FILL IN THE BLANKS

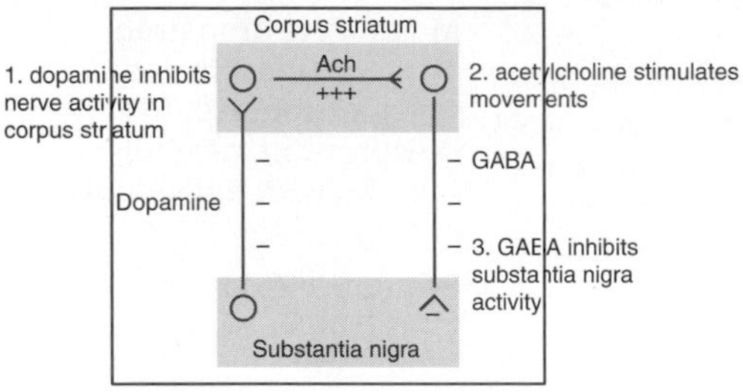

WORD SCRAMBLE

1. levodopa	2. procyclidine	3. pergolide	4. biperiden
5. amantadine	6. ropinorole	7. benzotropine	8. bromocriptine

WEB EXERCISE: Log on to http://www.ninds.nih.gov/. Select the Health Information button; on the Health Information page, select "Guide to Parkinson's disease" by clicking on Parksinson's disease. From the menu presented, select topics that would be of interest to this family—research, surgery, support groups, etc.

CHAPTER 23: MUSCLE RELAXANTS

MATCHING

1. C 2. E 3. H 4. F 5. A 6. B 7. G 8. D

FILL IN THE BLANKS

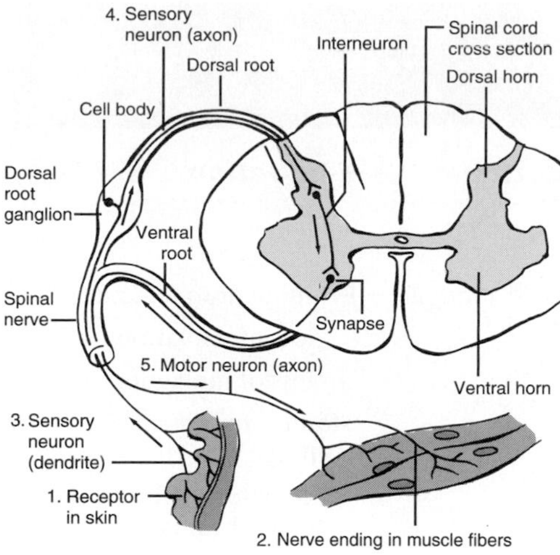

TRUE OR FALSE

1. F 2. T 3. F 4. F 5. T 6. F 7. T 8. F 9. T 10. T

CHAPTER 24: NARCOTICS AND ANTIMIGRAINE AGENTS

WORD SEARCH

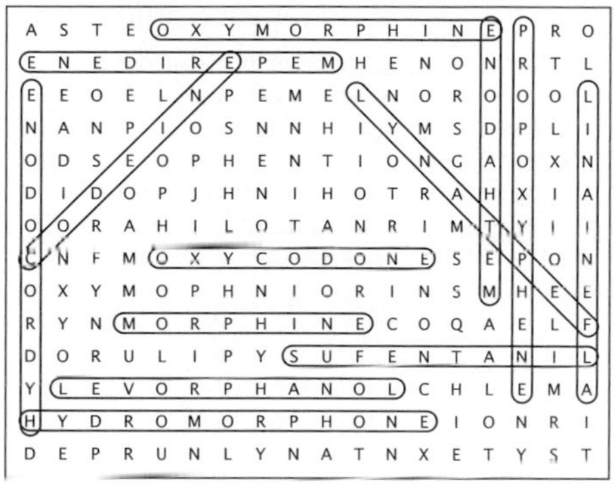

MATCHING

1. G 2. F 3. D 4. H 5. J 6. C 7. B 8. I 9. E 10. A

MULTIPLE CHOICE

1. a 2. b 3. b 4. c 5. a

CHAPTER 25: GENERAL AND LOCAL ANESTHETIC AGENTS

FILL IN THE BLANKS

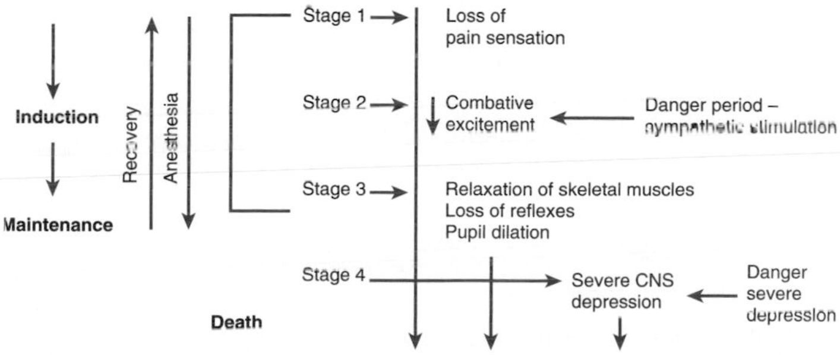

NURSING CARE GUIDE

NURSING CARE GUIDE

Local Anesthetic

Assessment	***Nursing Diagnoses***	***Implementation***	***Evaluation***
HISTORY Allergies to any of these drugs, parabens; cardiac disorders; vascular problems; hepatic dysfunction	Sensory-perceptual alteration related to anesthesia Potential for injury related to loss of sensation, mobility Potential alteration in skin integrity related to immobility Knowledge deficit regarding-drug therapy	Ensure administration of drug under strict supervision. Provide comfort and safety measures: - positioning - skin care - side rails - pain medication as needed - maintain airway - ventilate patient - antidotes on standby. Provide support and reassurance to deal with loss of sensation and mobility. Provide patient teaching regarding procedure being performed and what to expect. Provide life support as needed.	Evaluate drug effects: - loss of sensation - loss of movement. Monitor for adverse effects: - CV effects- BP changes, arrhythmias - respiratory depression - GI upset - CNS alterations - skin breakdown - anxiety, fear Monitor for drug-drug interactions as indicated for each drug. Evaluate effectiveness of patient teaching program. Evaluate effectiveness of comfort and safety measures. Constantly monitor vital signs and return to normal muscular function and sensation.
PHYSICAL EXAMINATION CV: BP, P, peripheral perfusion, ECG CNS: orientation, affect, reflexes, vision Skin: color, lesions, texture, sweating Resp: R, adventitious sounds Liver function tests, plasma esterases			

FILL IN THE BLANKS

1. pain relief, analgesia, amnesia, unconsciousness
2. loss of sensation, death
3. Induction of anesthesia
4. Balanced anesthesia
5. depolarization of nerve membrane
6. central nervous system depression
7. sensation, mobility, and the ability to communicate
8. skin breakdown, self-injury, biting oneself

CHAPTER 26: NEUROMUSCULAR JUNCTION BLOCKING AGENTS

FILL IN THE BLANKS

BOX 23-1 SUMMARY OF MUSCLE CONTRACTION AND RELAXATION

Stimulus from nerve axon to myoneural junction

Acetycholine release in synaptic gutter

Increased permeability of muscles cell membrane to sodium

Rise in membrane potential (action potential generation)

Transmission of action potential through T tubules

Release of calcium from sarcoplasmic reticulum

Binding of calcium with troponin–tropomyosin

Sliding of actin on myosin with shortening of sarcomere unit

Contraction of the muscle fiber

Calcium pump moves calcium back to sarcoplasmic reticulum

Unbinding of troponin–tropomyosin

Inhibition of actin and myosin

Lengthening of sarcomere unit

Relaxation of muscle fiber

CROSSWORD PUZZLE

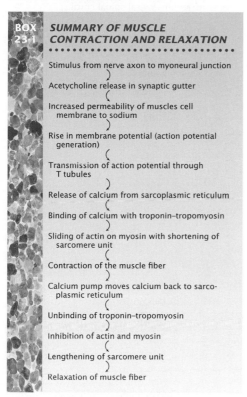

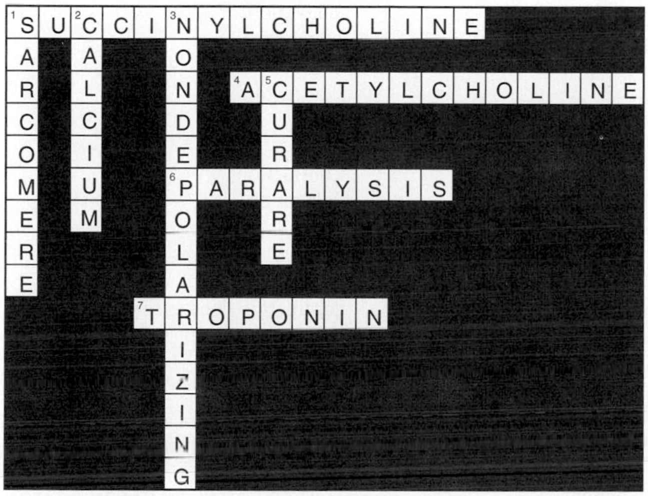

WEB EXERCISE: Log on to patient http://www.anesthesia.wisc.edu/Topics/Physiology/pseudocholin.html. Look up the definition and presenting symptoms of cholinesterase deficiency, then look up which patients are at risk. If you think this patient might be at risk, look up treatments and assessment factors and prepare a nursing alert that should be placed on the patient's chart when she goes to surgery.

CHAPTER 27: INTRODUCTION TO THE AUTONOMIC NERVOUS SYSTEM

SYMPATHETIC/PARASYMPATHETIC COMPARISON

TABLE 27-1

COMPARISON OF THE SYMPATHETIC AND PARASYMPATHETIC NERVOUS SYSTEMS

Characteristic	Sympathetic	Parasympathetic
CNS nerve origin	Thoracic, Lumbar spinal cord	Cranium, Sacral spinal cord
Preganglionic neuron	Short axon	Long axon
Preganglionic neurotransmitter	Acetylcholine	Acetylcholine
Ganglia location	Next to spinal cord	Within or near effector organs
Postganglionic neuron	Long axon	Short axon
Postganglionic neurotransmitter	Norephinephrine	Acetylcholine
Neurotransmitter terminator	Monoamine oxidase (MAO); Catechol-D-methyltransferase (COMT)	Acetylcholinesterase
General response	Fight or flight	Rest and digest

MATCHING

1. K 2. C 3. F 4. B 5. I 6. G 7. H 8. A 9. J 10. E 11. L 12. D

FILL IN THE CHART

TABLE 27-2

EFFECTS OF AUTONOMIC STIMULATION

Effector Site	Sympathetic Reaction	Receptor	Parasympathetic Reaction
Heart	↑ rate, contractility ↑ A-V conduction	$beta_1$	↓ Rate, ↓ A-V conduction
Blood vessels			
Skin, mucous membranes	Constriction	$alpha_1$	——
Skeletal muscle	Dilation	$beta_2$	——
Bronchial muscle	Relaxation (dilation)	$beta_2$	Constriction
GI system			
Muscle motility and tone	↓ activity	$beta_2$	↑ Activity
Sphincters	Contraction	$alpha_1$	Relaxation
Secretions	↓ secretions	$beta_2$	↑ Activity
Salivary glands	Thick secretions	$alpha_1$	Copious, watery secretions
Gallbladder	Relaxation	?	Contraction
Liver	Glyconeogenesis	$beta_2$	
Urinary bladder			
Detrusor muscle	Relaxation	$beta_2$	Contraction
Trigone muscle and sphincter	Contraction	$alpha_1$	Relaxation
Eye structures			
Iris radial muscle	Contraction (pupil dilates)	$alpha_1$	——
Iris sphincter muscle	——		Contraction (pupil constricts)
Ciliary muscle	——		contraction (lens accommodates for near vision)
Lacrimal glands	——		↑ secretions
Skin structures			
Sweat glands	↑ In sweating	Sympathetic cholinergic	——
Piloerector muscles	Contracted (goosebumps)	$alpha_1$	——
Sex organs			
Male	emission	$alpha_1$	Erection (vascular dilation)
Female	uterine relaxation	$beta_2$	——

(—— means no reaction or response)

CHAPTER 28: ADRENERGIC AGENTS

MULTIPLE CHOICE

1. b 2. a 3. c 4. a 5. b

WORD SCRAMBLE

1. ephedrine
2. clonidine
3. dopamine
4. ritodrine
5. dobutamine
6. norepinephrine
7. metaraminol
8. phenylephrine
9. epinephrine
10. Isoproterenol

FILL IN THE BLANKS

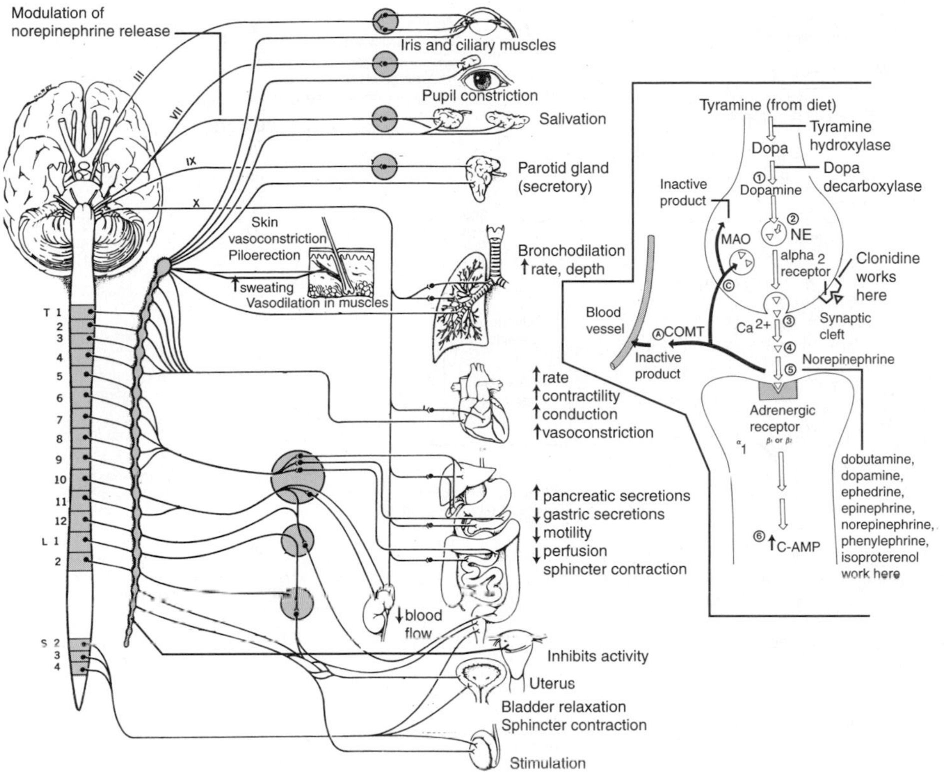

CHAPTER 29: ADRENERGIC BLOCKING AGENTS

WORD SEARCH

L	K	U	I	N	O	Z	A	S	O	N	A	C	E	T	A	C
I	O	B	M	O	R	T	X	I	T	E	C	A	M	H	A	D
B	I	B	P	I	N	D	O	L	O	L	H	R	E	E	T	H
L	P	M	E	N	I	O	Z	I	L	L	E	T	S	O	E	P
C	P	H	E	N	O	X	Y	B	E	N	Z	A	M	I	N	E
H	X	Y	S	A	Z	O	S	I	N	I	O	S	O	L	O	X
O	X	Y	P	R	A	Z	O	S	I	N	N	H	L	Y	L	G
Z	A	S	I	N	O	O	X	C	A	R	T	E	O	L	O	L
T	E	R	A	Z	O	S	I	N	M	L	Y	L	L	I	L	Z
M	I	R	R	O	B	I	S	O	P	R	O	L	O	L	I	E
U	S	G	U	A	N	A	D	R	E	L	L	L	Y	X	Z	B
T	H	H	R	A	S	N	I	N	A	D	O	L	O	L	A	F
H	I	R	O	L	A	B	E	T	A	L	O	L	X	M	Y	W
U	M	E	T	O	P	R	O	L	O	L	K	L	Y	S	I	O
P	P	T	O	P	H	S	L	L	M	Y	Y	O	Z	A	S	T

WEB EXERCISE: Log on to http://www.amhrt.org/, the American Heart Association web site. Look up risk factors, support groups, diet, exercise, and the latest research on hypertension and other cardiovascular diseases. Print out information that is pertinent to the patient's concerns.

TRUE OR FALSE

1. F 2. T 3. F 4. T 5. T 6. F 7. T 8. T

CHAPTER 30: CHOLINERGIC AGENTS

FILL IN THE BLANKS

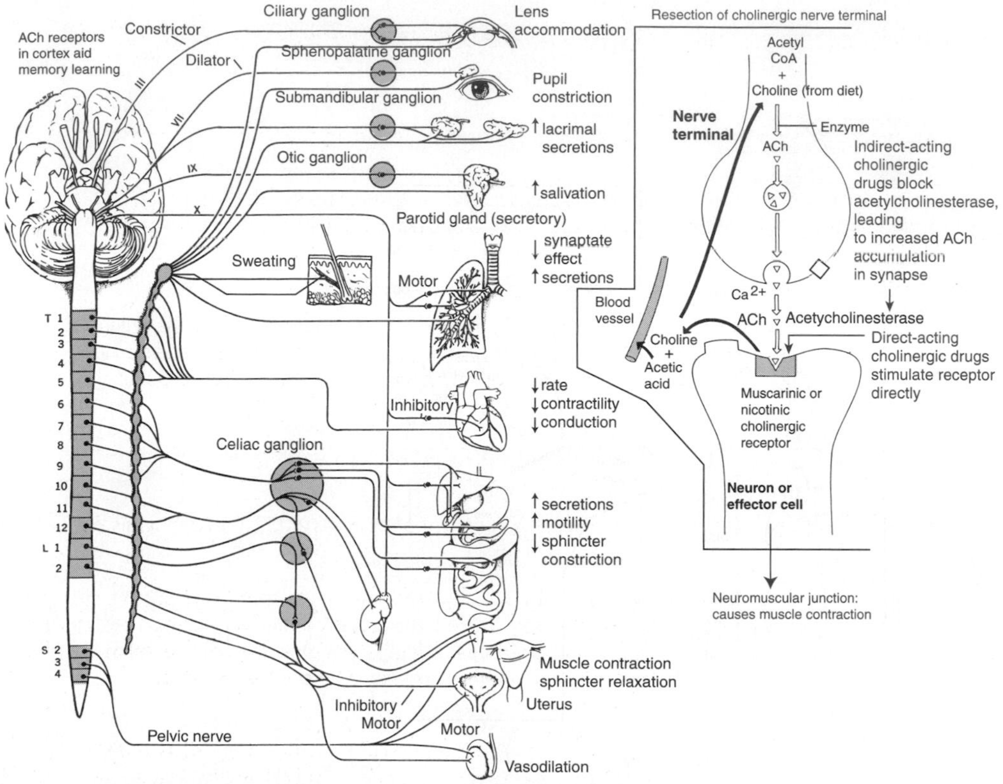

CROSSWORD PUZZLE

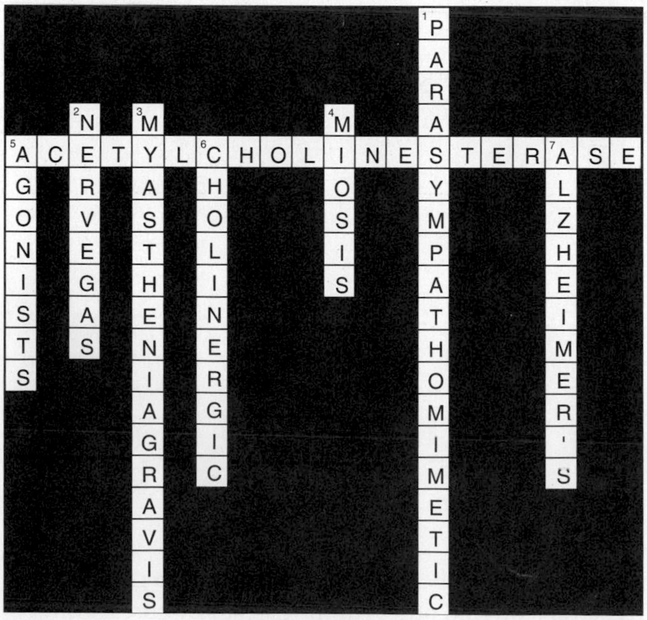

MATCHING

1. D 2. E 3. A and C 4. B 5. B 6. A and C 7. D 8. E

CHAPTER 31: ANTICHOLINERGIC AGENTS

FILL IN THE CHART

TABLE 31-1

EFFECTS OF PARASYMPATHETIC BLOCKADE AND ASSOCIATED THERAPEUTIC USES

Physiological Effect	Therapeutic Use
GI TRACT	
Smooth muscle: blocks spasm, blocks peristalsis Secretory glands: decreases acid and digestive enzyme production	Decreases motility and secretory activity in peptic ulcer, gastritis, cardiospasm, pylorospasm, enteritis, diarrhea, hypertonic constipation
URINARY TRACT	
Decreases tone and motility in the ureters and fundus of the bladder; increases tone in the bladder sphincter	Increases bladder capacity in children with enuresis, spastic paraplegics; decreases urinary urgency and frequency in cystitis; antispasmodic in renal colic and to counteract bladder spasm caused by morphine
BILIARY TRACT	
Relaxes smooth muscle, antispasmodic	Relief of biliary colic; counteracts spasms caused by narcotics
BRONCHIAL MUSCLE	
Weakly relaxes smooth muscle	Aerosol form may be used in asthma; may counteract bronchoconstriction caused by drugs
CARDIOVASCULAR SYSTEM	
Increases heart rate (may decrease heart rate at very low doses); causes local vasodilation and flushing	Counteracts bradycardia caused by vagal stimulation, carotid sinus syndrome, surgical procedures; used to overcome heart blocks following MI; used to counteract hypotension caused by cholinergic drugs
OCULAR EFFECTS	
Pupil dilation, cyclopegia	Allows ophthalmological examination of the retina, optic disk; relaxes ocular muscles and decreases irritation in iridocyclitis, choroiditis
SECRETIONS	
Reduces sweating, salivation, respiratory tract secretions	Preoperatively before inhalation anesthesia; reduces nasal secretions in rhinitis, hay fever; may be used to reduce excessive sweating in hyperhidrosis
CNS	
Decreases extrapyramidal motor activity Atropine may cause excessive stimulation, psychosis, delirium, disorientation Scopolamine causes depression, drowsiness	Decreases tremor in parkinsonism; helps to prevent motion sickness; scopolamine may be in OTC sleep aids

PATIENT TEACHING CHECKLIST

PATIENT TEACHING CHECKLIST

Dicyclomine

Parasympathetic blockers or anticholinergics block or stop the actions of a group of nerves that are part of the sympathetic nervous system. This drug may decrease the activity of your GI tract, dilate your pupils or speed up your heart.

Common effects of these drugs include:

- Dry mouth, difficulty swallowing—Frequent mouth care will help to remove dried secretions and keep the mouth fresh; sucking on sugarless candies will help to keep the mouth moist; taking lots of fluids with meals (unless you are on a fluid restriction) will help aid swallowing.
- Blurring vision, sensitivity to light—If your vision is blurred, avoid driving, operating hazardous machinery or doing close work that requires attention to details until vision returns to normal; dark glasses will help to protect your eyes from the light.
- Retention of urine—Taking the drug just after you have emptied your bladder will help; moderate your fluid intake while the drug's effects are the highest; if possible, take the drug before bed when this effect will not be a problem.
- Constipation—Include fluid and roughage in your diet; follow any bowel regimen that you may have; monitor your bowel movements so that appropriate laxatives can be taken if necessary.
- Flushing, intolerance to heat, decreased sweating—This drug blocks sweating, which is your body's way of cooling off; avoid extremes of temperature; dress coolly; on very warm days, avoid exercise as much as possible.

Report any of the following to your health care provider: eye pain, skin rash, fever, rapid heart beat, chest pain, difficulty breathing, agitation or mood changes, impotence (a dosage adjustment may help alleviate this problem).

Avoid the use of OTC medications, especially for sleep and nasal congestion; avoid antihistamines, diet pills, cold capsules. These drugs may contain similar drugs which could cause a severe reaction. Consult with your health care provider if you feel that you need medication for symptomatic relief.

Tell any doctor, nurse, or other health care provider that you are taking these drugs.

Keep this drug, and all medications, out of the reach of children. Do not share these drugs with other people.

Specific information to keep in mind with this anticholinergic drug:

- Make sure you empty your bladder before taking the drug.
- Return for your follow-up visit in 4 weeks for evaluation for increasing the dosage.

FILL IN THE BLANKS

1. acetylcholine
2. parasympatholytic
3. increase, decrease
4. sweating
5. Cyclopegia
6. mydriatic
7. Atropine
8. dry mouth, difficulty swallowing

CHAPTER 32: INTRODUCTION TO THE ENDOCRINE SYSTEM

FILL IN THE BLANKS

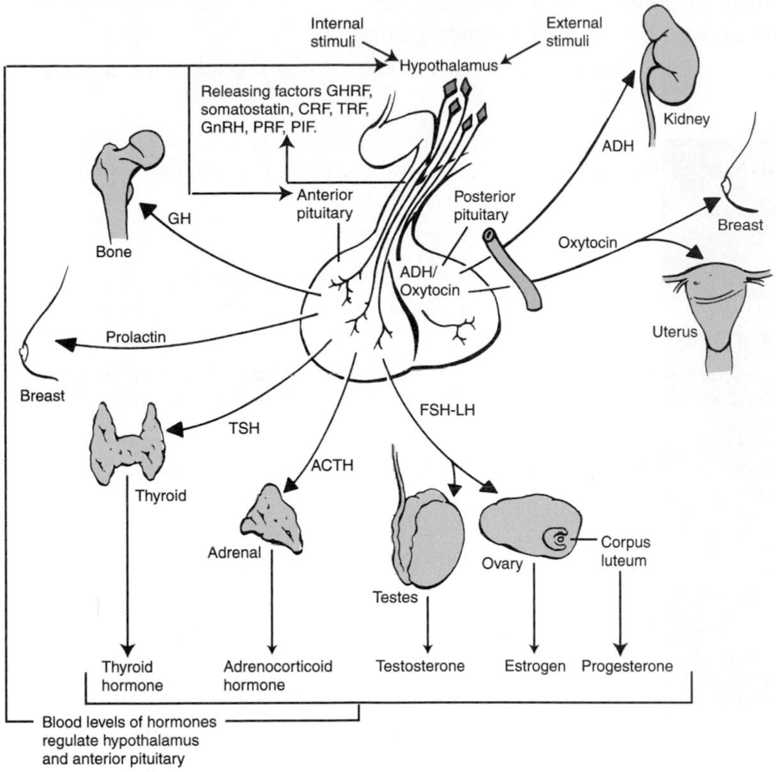

LIST ALL HORMONES:

- are produced in very small amounts
- are secreted directly into the bloodstream
- travel through the blood to specific receptor sites throughout the body
- act to increase or decrease the normal metabolic processes of cells when they react with their specific receptor sites.
- are immediately broken down.

MATCHING

1. D 2. H 3. F 4. A 5. G 6. C 7. E 8. B

CHAPTER 33: HYPOTHALAMIC AND PITUITARY AGENTS

MATCHING

1. F 2. G 3. B 4. A 5. D 6. E 7. C

WEB EXERCISE: Go to http://ourworld.compuserv.com/homepages/penspage/penspage/htm, the Pediatric Endocrinology Nursing Society home page. Check on research, new developments, and guidelines for the use of growth hormone. Print out appropriate pages to prepare handouts or a poster for your presentation.

MATCHING

1. C 2. E 3. G 4. A 5. D 6. H 7. B 8. F

CHAPTER 34: ADRENOCORTICAL AGENTS

WORD SCRAMBLE

1. prednisone
2. triamcinolone
3. betamethasone
4. hydrocortisone
5. budenoside
6. flunisolide
7. cortisone
8. dexamethasone

CROSSWORD PUZZLE

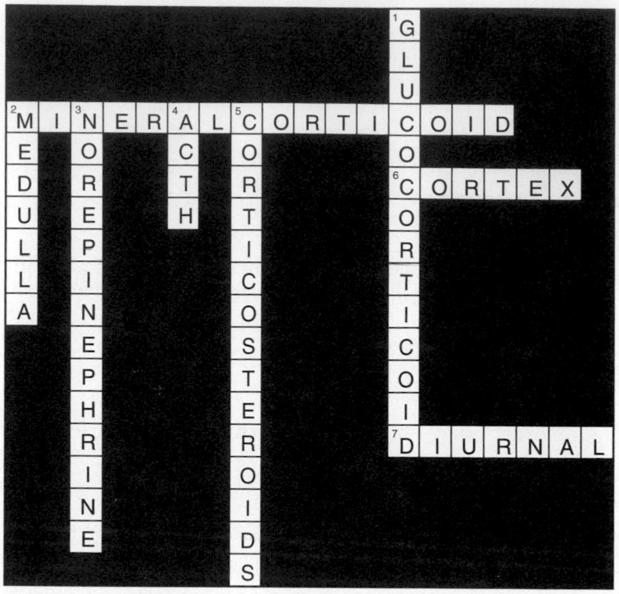

TRUE OR FALSE

1. F 2. F 3. F 4. T 5. T 6. F 7. F 8. T 9. T 10. T

CHAPTER 35: THYROID AND PARATHYROID AGENTS

PATIENT TEACHING CHECKLIST

PATIENT TEACHING CHECKLIST

Thyroid Hormone

A hormone is designed to replace the thyroid hormone that your body is not able to produce. The thyroid hormone is responsible for regulating your body's metabolism, or the speed with which your body's cells burn energy. Because of this action of the thyroid hormone, it affects many body systems. It is very important that you take this medication only as prescribed.

Never stop taking this drug without consulting with your health care provider. The drug is used to replace a very important hormone and will probably have to be taken for life. Stopping the medication can lead to serious problems.

This drug usually causes no adverse effects. You may notice a slight skin rash or hair loss in the first few months of therapy. You should notice that the signs and symptoms of your thyroid deficiency will disappear and you will feel "back to normal."

Report any of the following to your health care provider: chest pain, difficulty breathing, sore throat, fever, chills, weight gain, sleeplessness, nervousness, unusual sweating, or intolerance to heat.

Avoid the use of any over-the-counter medication without first checking with your health care provider. Several of these medications can interfere with the effectiveness of this drug.

Tell any doctor, nurse, or other health care provider that you are taking this drug. You may want to wear or carry a medical alert tag showing that you are on this medication. This would alert any medical personnel taking care of you in an emergency to the fact that you are taking this drug.

While you are taking this drug, it is important to have regular medical follow-up, including blood tests to check the activity of your thyroid gland, to evaluate your response to the drug and any possible underlying problems.

Keep this drug, and all medications, out of the reach of children. Do not give this medication to anyone else or take any similar medication that has not been prescribed for you.

Specific information that relates to your situation:

You should start feeling like your old self again soon. Your energy should return and you should regain interest in things. The dosage of your thyroid hormone may need to be adjusted. It is very important that you keep return appointments, which will include blood tests, so that the appropriate dosage can be determined. If you have any questions, please feel free to call the office at 555-5555 and ask to speak to Nurse Jones.

MULTIPLE CHOICE

1. a 2. c 3. c 4. d 5. b 6. d

MATCHING

1. E 2. A 3. F 4. B 5. J 6. C 7. H 8. D 9. G 10. I

CHAPTER 36: ANTIDIABETIC AGENTS

WORD SEARCH

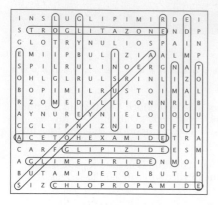

I	N	S	L	U	G	L	I	P	I	M	I	R	D	E	I
S	T	R	O	G	L	I	T	A	Z	O	N	E	N	D	P
G	L	O	T	R	Y	N	U	L	I	O	S	P	A	I	N
E	M	I	I	P	B	U	L	I	Z	I	A	A	L	M	P
S	P	I	L	R	U	L	I	N	O	E	R	G	N	A	T
O	H	L	G	L	R	U	L	S	R	I	N	L	I	Z	O
B	O	P	I	M	I	L	R	U	S	T	O	I	M	A	L
R	Z	O	M	E	D	I	L	L	I	O	N	N	R	L	B
A	Y	N	U	R	E	Y	N	I	E	L	O	I	O	O	U
C	G	L	I	P	N	I	Z	N	I	D	E	D	F	T	T
A	C	E	T	O	H	E	X	A	M	I	D	E	T	R	A
C	A	R	F	G	L	I	P	I	Z	I	D	E	E	S	M
A	G	L	I	M	E	P	I	R	I	D	E	N	M	O	I
B	U	T	A	M	I	D	E	T	O	L	B	U	T	L	D
S	I	Z	C	H	L	O	P	R	O	P	A	M	I	D	E

WEB EXERCISE: Log on to http://www.diabetes.org the American Diabetes Association web site. Click onto "diabetes" to get information about the disease. Click onto "drugs" to get information about the specific drugs that J. L. might be taking. Click onto "diet" to get a printout of the ADA diet as well as recipes that J. L. or his wife might like to check. If they seem interested in support groups, select the area and city in which they live and find the local ADA chapter and pertinent support. Print out anything that would be useful in preparing a teaching program for this patient.

NURSING CARE PLAN

NURSING CARE GUIDE

Insulin

Assessment	Nursing Diagnoses	Implementation	Evaluation
HISTORY			
Allergies to any insulins	Alteration in nutrition related to metabolic effects Sensory-perceptual alteration related to effects on glucose levels Potential for infection related to injections and disease process Potential ineffectual coping related to diagnosis and injections Knowledge deficit regarding drug therapy	Administer SC and rotate sites. Store in cool place away from light. Use caution when mixing types. Monitor blood glucose to adjust dosage as needed. Monitor during times of stress and trauma and adjust dosage. Provide support and reassurance to deal with drug injections and life-time need. Provide patient teaching regarding drug name, dosage, adverse effects, precautions, warning signs to report, and proper administration technique.	Evaluate drug effects: return of glucose levels to normal. Monitor for adverse effects: hypoglycemia injection site reaction Monitor for drug-drug interactions: delayed recovery from hypoglycemic episodes with propranolol (*Inderal*) Evaluate effectiveness of patient teaching program. Evaluate effectiveness of comfort and safety measures.
PHYSICAL EXAMINATION			
Neurological: orientation, reflexes Skin: color, lesions CV: P, cardiac auscultation, BP Respiratory: R, adventitious sounds Lab tests: urinalysis, blood glucose			

CHAPTER 37: INTRODUCTION TO THE REPRODUCTIVE SYSTEMS

FILL IN THE BLANKS

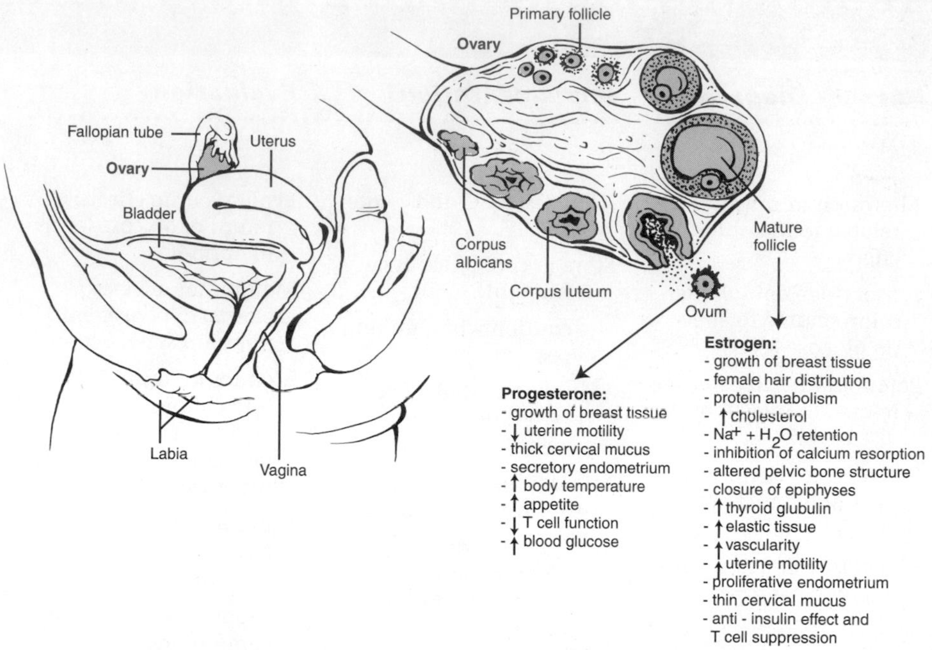

FILL IN THE BLANKS

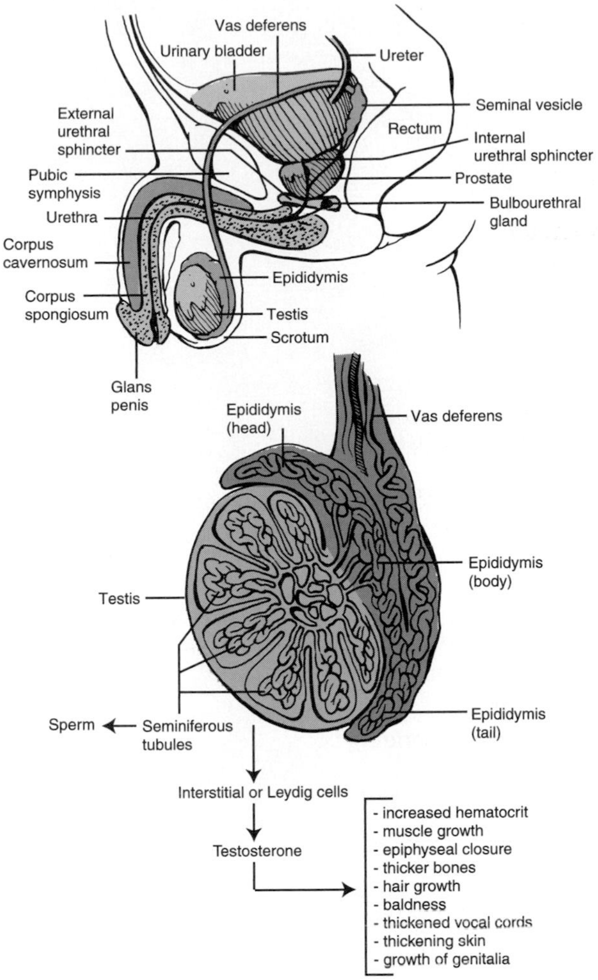

COMPLETE THE CYCLE

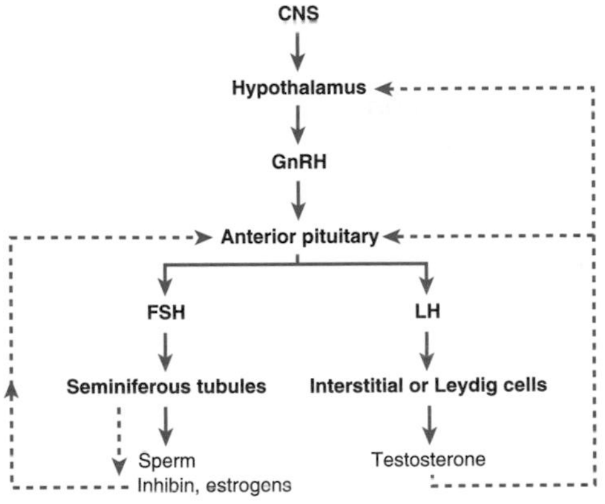

CHAPTER 38: DRUGS AFFECTING THE FEMALE REPRODUCTIVE SYSTEM

CROSSWORD PUZZLE

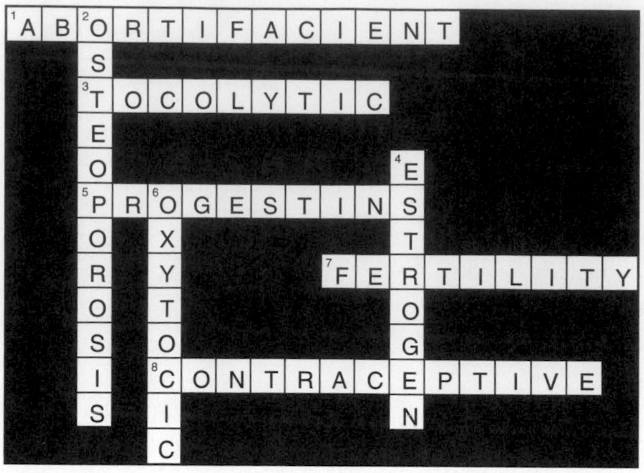

MULTIPLE CHOICE

1. d 2. a 3. b 4. b 5. b 6. c

WORD SCRAMBLE

1. toremifene 2. estradiol 3. estrone 4. raloxifene
5. dienestrol 6. estropipate 7. diethylstilbestrol 8. chlorotrianisene

CHAPTER 39: DRUGS AFFECTING THE MALE REPRODUCTIVE SYSTEM

TRUE OR FALSE

1. T 2. F 3. T 4. T 5. F 6. F 7. T 8. T 9. F 10. F

MATCHING

1. D 2. E 3. A 4. G 5. C 6. H 7. B 8. F

FILL IN THE BLANKS

1. Androgenic
2. Anabolic
3. Testosterone
4. anemias
5. Erectile penile dysfunction
6. prostaglandin, injected
7. Sildenafil
8. sexual stimulation

CHAPTER 40: INTRODUCTION TO THE CARDIOVASCULAR SYSTEM

FILL IN THE BLANKS

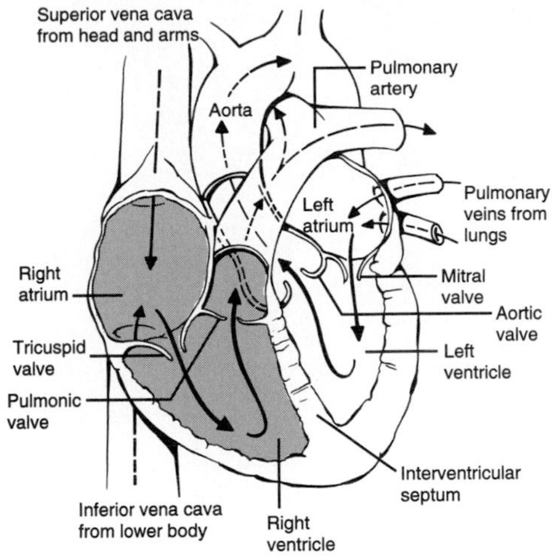

DEFINITIONS

1. troponin—chemical in heart muscle that prevents actin and myosin from reacting, leading to muscle relaxation; inactivated by calcium during muscle stimulation to allow actin and myosin to react, causing muscle contraction
2. actin—thin filament that makes up a sarcomere or muscle unit
3. myosin—thick filament with projections that makes up a sarcomere or muscle unit
4. arrhythmia—a disruption in cardiac rate or rhythm
5. Starling's law of the heart—addresses the contractile properties of the heart; the more the muscle is stretched, the stronger it will react until stretched to a point at which it will not react at all
6. fibrillation—rapid, irregular stimulation of the cardiac muscle resulting in lack of pumping activity
7. capillary—small vessel made up of loosely connected endothelial cells that connect arteries to veins
8. resistance system—the arteries; the muscles of the arteries provide resistance to the flow of blood, leading to control of blood pressure

MATCHING

1. H 2. C 3. F 4. E 5. D 6. L 7. J 8. A 9. K 10. G 11. I 12. B

CHAPTER 41: DRUGS AFFECTING BLOOD PRESSURE

MATCHING

1. B 2. A 3. E 4. B 5. D 6. D 7. A 8. B 9. C 10. D 11. A 12. C

WORD SEARCH

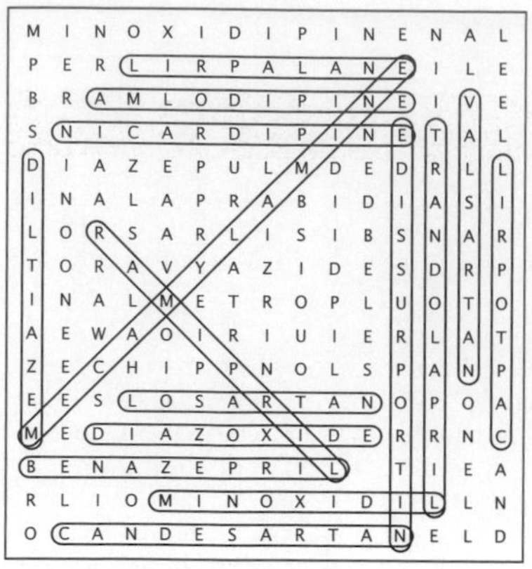

TRUE OR FALSE

1. F 2. T 3. F 4. F 5. T 6. F 7. T 8. T 9. F 10. T

CHAPTER 42: CARDIOTONIC AGENTS

PATIENT TEACHING CHECKLIST

PATIENT TEACHING CHECKLIST

Digoxin

Digoxin is a digitalis preparation. Digitalis has many helpful effects on the heart. It helps it to beat more slowly and efficiently. These effects lead to better circulation and should help to reduce the swelling in your ankles or legs and should increase the amount of urine that you produce every day. Digoxin is a very powerful drug and must be taken *exactly* as prescribed. It is important to have regular medical checkups to make sure that the dosage of the drug is correct for you and th be sure that it is having the desired effect on your heart.

Do not stop taking this drug without consulting your health care provider. Never skip doses and never try to "catch up" any missed doses; serious adverse effects could occur.

You should learn to take your own pulse. You should take your pulse each morning before engaging in any activity. Your normal pulse rate is: 82.

You should monitor your weight fairly closely. Weigh yourself every other day, at the same time of the day and in the same amount of clothing. Record your weight on your calendar for easy reference. If you gain or lose three or more pounds in one day, it may indicate a problem with your drug. Consult your health care provider. Your weight today is 148 pounds, fully clothed with shoes.

Common effects of these drugs include:

- Dizziness, drowsiness, headache—Avoid driving or performing hazardous tasks or delicate tasks that require concentration if these occur. Consult your health care provider for an appropriate analgesic if the headache is a problem.
- Nausea, GI upset, loss of appetite—Small, frequent meals may help, monitor your weight loss and if it becomes severe, consult your health care provider.
- Vision changes, "yellow" halos around objects—These effects may pass with time. Take extra care in your activities for the first few days. If these reactions do not go away after 3–4 days, consult with your health care provider.

Report any of the following to your health care provider: unusually slow or irregular pulse; rapid weight gain; "yellow vision"; unusual tiredness or weakness; skin rash or hives; swelling of the ankles, legs or fingers; difficulty breathing.

Tell any doctor, nurse, dentist, for other health care provider that you are taking this drug.

Keep this drug, and all medications, out of the reach of children.

Avoid the use of OTC medications while you are on this drug. If you feel that you need one of these, consult with your health care provider for the best choice. Many of these drugs may contain ingredients that could interfere with your digoxin.

It might be helpful to wear or carry a Medic-Alert tag to alert any medical personnel who might take care of you in an emergency that you are taking this drug.

Regular medical follow-up is important to evaluate the actions of the drug and to adjust the dosage if necessary.

Specifics related to your situation:

- Be very careful the first few days in Florida. The change in temperatures may tend to make you light headed and dizzy.
- Contact your health care provider in Florida as soon as possible to alert him to your new prescription.

CROSSWORD PUZZLE

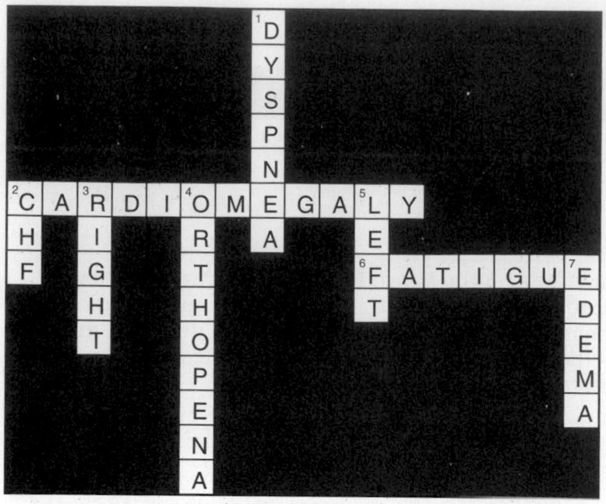

WEB EXERCISE: Log on to the Internet and go to the American Heart Association home page at http://www.amhrt.org/. Select "Your Heart." Now select "Conditions and Diseases." Then select "Congestive Heart Failure." Print out pertinent information that might be useful for J.D. Return to the home page and select "Your local AHA." Locate your area on the map and print out information on support groups and help in your specific area.

CHAPTER 43: ANTIARRHYTHMIC AGENTS

IDENTIFY THE STRUCTURES

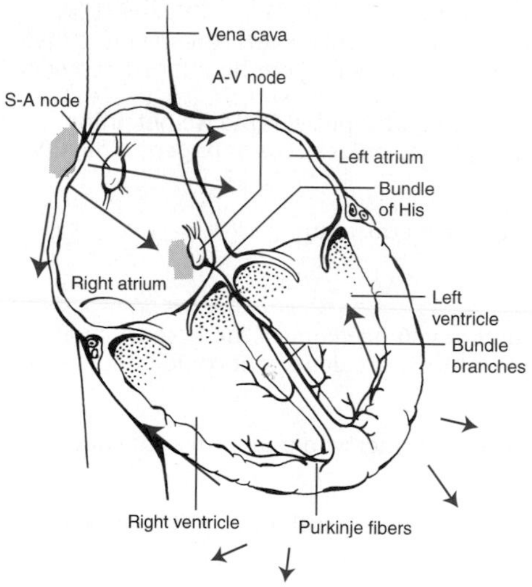

MATCHING

1. B, D 2. A, F 3. C, E

WORD SCRAMBLE

1. AMIODARONE 2. ESMOLOL 3. BRETYLIUM 4. VERAPAMIL
5. PROCAINAMIDE 6. PROPRANOLOL 7. FLECAINIDE 8. DIGOXIN

CHAPTER 44: ANTIANGINAL AGENTS

MATCHING

1. C 2. F 3. E 4. G 5. A 6. B 7. D 8. H

TRUE OR FALSE

1. F 2. T 3. F 4. T 5. F 6. F 7. T 8. T

CROSSWORD PUZZLE

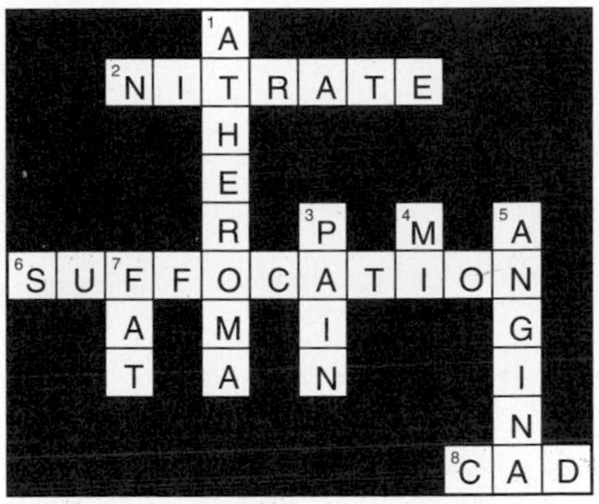

CHAPTER 45: LIPID LOWERING AGENTS

WEB EXERCISE: Go to the American Heart Association home page at http://www.amhrt.org/. Click on "What's Your Risk" for a survey of risk factors. Return to the homepage. Click on "Your Heart," then on "Heart Disease," then "Patient Information." Print out any pertinent information. Click on "Cholesterol reduction" for diet and drug guidelines and print out useful material.

LIST

1. Genetic predispositions
2. Age
3. Gender
4. Gout - T
5. Cigarette smoking - T
6. Sedentary lifestyle- T
7. High stress levels - T
8. Hypertension- T
9. Obesity- T
10. Diabetes - T

IDENTIFY

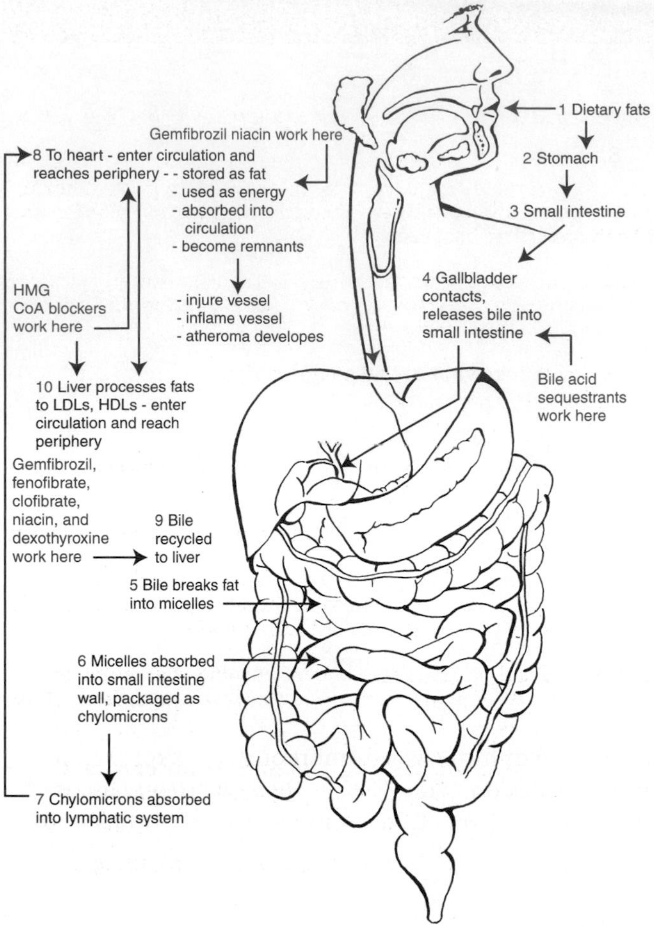
1 Dietary fats
2 Stomach
3 Small intestine
4 Gallbladder contacts, releases bile into small intestine
Bile acid sequestrants work here
5 Bile breaks fat into micelles
6 Micelles absorbed into small intestine wall, packaged as chylomicrons
7 Chylomicrons absorbed into lymphatic system
8 To heart - enter circulation and reaches periphery - - stored as fat
- used as energy
- absorbed into circulation
- become remnants
Gemfibrozil niacin work here
- injure vessel
- inflame vessel
- atheroma developes
HMG CoA blockers work here
10 Liver processes fats to LDLs, HDLs - enter circulation and reach periphery
Gemfibrozil, fenofibrate, clofibrate, niacin, and dexothyroxine work here
9 Bile recycled to liver

CHAPTER 46: DRUGS AFFECTING BLOOD COAGULATION

TRUE OR FALSE

1. T 2. F 3. T 4. F 5. T 6. F 7. T 8. F 9. F 10. T

FILL IN THE BLANKS

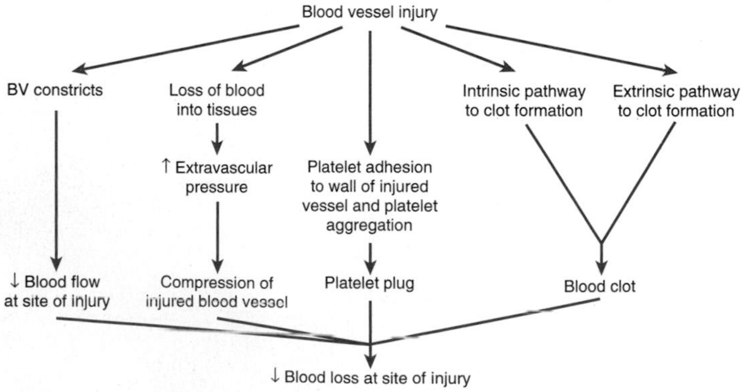
Blood vessel injury
BV constricts
Loss of blood into tissues
↑ Extravascular pressure
Platelet adhesion to wall of injured vessel and platelet aggregation
Intrinsic pathway to clot formation
Extrinsic pathway to clot formation
↓ Blood flow at site of injury
Compression of injured blood vessel
Platelet plug
Blood clot
↓ Blood loss at site of injury

PATIENT TEACHING CHECKLIST

Coumadin

An anticoagulant works to slow the normal blood clotting processes in the body. In this way, it can prevent harmful blood clots from forming. This type of drug is often called a "blood thinner." It cannot dissolve any blood clots that have already formed. Your anticoagulant has been prescribed because ________________.

Never change any medication that you are taking—adding or stopping another drug—without consulting with your health care provider. Many other drugs affect the way that your anticoagulant works; starting or stopping another drug can cause excessive bleeding or interfere with the desired effects of the drug.

Your drug should be taken once a day. The best time of day to take your drug is in the morning.

Common effects of these drugs include:

- Stomach bloating, cramps—This often passes with time; consult your health care provider if this persists or becomes too uncomfortable.
- Loss of hair, skin rash—This can be very frustrating. You may wish to discuss this with your health care provider.
- Orange-yellow discoloration of the urine—This can be frightening, but may just be an effect of the drug. If you are concerned that this might be blood, simply add vinegar to your urine. The color should disappear. If the color does not disappear, it may be caused by blood and you should contact your health care provider.

Report any of the following to your health care provider: unusual bleeding (e.g., when brushing your teeth); excessive bleeding from an injury; excessive bruising; black or tarry stools; cloudy or dark urine; sore throat, fever, chills; severe headache or dizziness.

Tell any doctor, nurse, or other health care provider that you are taking this drug. You should carry or wear a Medic-Alert tag stating that you are on this drug. This will alert emergency medical personnel that you are at increased risk for bleeding.

It is important to avoid situations in which you could be easily injured—for example, contact sports, using a straight razor.

Keep this drug, and all medications, out of the reach of children.

Avoid the use of OTC medications while you are on this drug. If you feel that you need one of these, consult with your health care provider for the best choice. Many of these drugs may interfere with your anticoagulant.

You will need to have regular, periodic blood tests while you are on this drug. This is very important for monitoring the effects of the drug on your body and adjusting your dosage as needed.

Specifics related to your situation:

- Use extra care to prevent injury when playing with the children.
- If you change your diet or cannot take your medication, consult with your health care provider.

CHAPTER 47: DRUGS USED TO TREAT ANEMIAS

FILL IN THE BLANKS

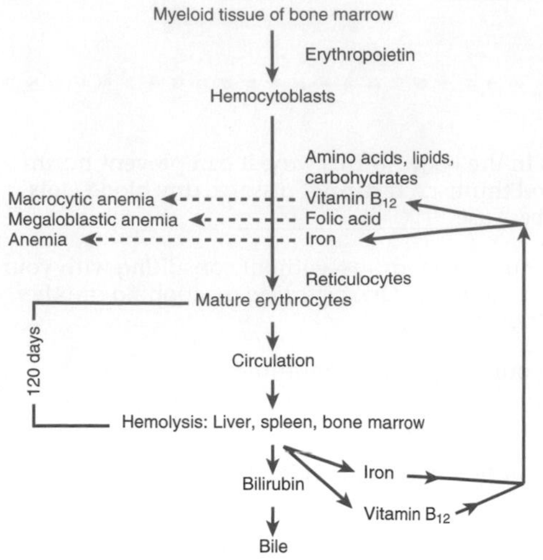

MULTIPLE CHOICE

1. a 2. c 3. b 4. d 5. a 6. c

CROSSWORD PUZZLE

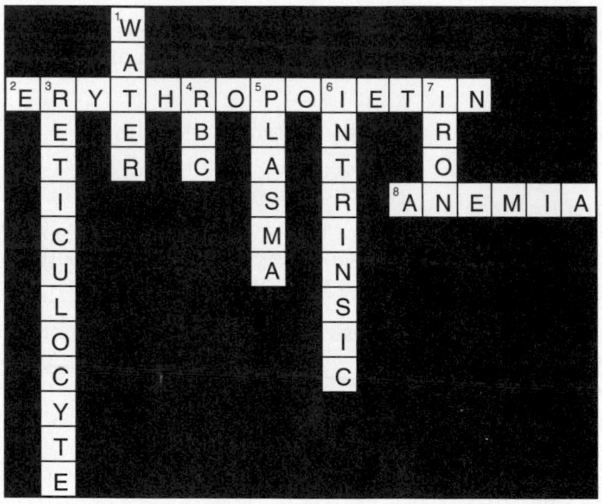

CHAPTER 48: INTRODUCTION TO THE KIDNEY AND THE URINARY TRACT

FILL IN THE BLANKS

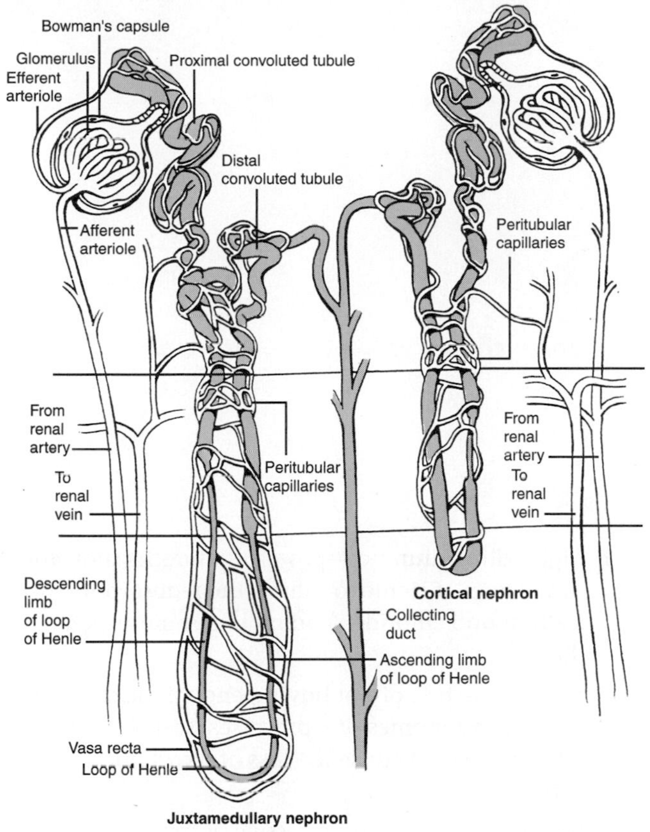

WORD SCRAMBLE

1. glomerulus
2. filtration
3. secretion
4. aldosterone
5. reabsorption
6. tubule
7. renin
8. prostate

FILL IN THE BLANKS

1. 25%
2. nephron, Bowman's capsule, loop of Henle, collecting duct
3. glomerular filtration, tubular secretion, tubular reabsorption
4. aldosterone
5. concentration, dilution
6. aldosterone
7. Vitamin D
8. renin

CHAPTER 49: DIURETIC AGENTS

WORD SEARCH

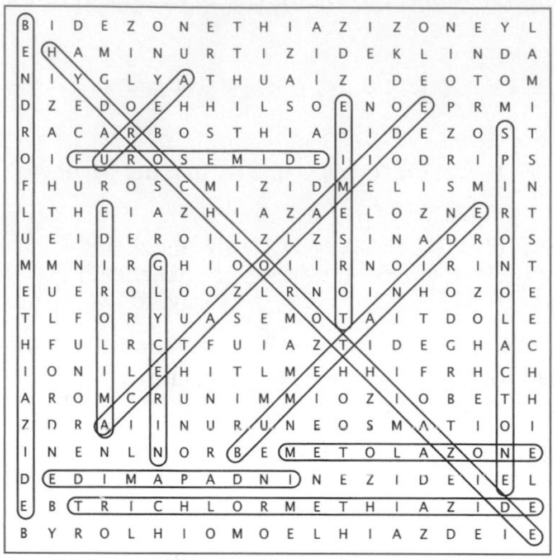

DEFINITIONS

1. edema—movement of fluid into the interstitial spaces; occurs when the balance between osmotic pull (from plasma proteins) and hydrostatic push (from blood pressure) is upset
2. fluid rebound—reflex reaction of the body to the loss of fluid or sodium; hypothalamus causes the release of ADH, which retains water, and stress related to fluid loss combines with decreased blood flow to the kidneys to activate the renin-angiotensin system, leading to further water and sodium retention
3. thiazide—a type of diuretic acting in the renal tubule to block the chloride pump, which prevents the reabsorption of sodium and chloride, leading to a loss of sodium and water in the urine
4. hypokalemia—low potassium in the blood; often occurs following diuretic use; characterized by weakness, muscle cramps, trembling, nausea, vomiting, diarrhea, and cardiac arrhythmias
5. high ceiling diuretics—powerful diuretics that work in the loop of Henle to inhibit the reabsorption of sodium and chloride, leading to a sodium-rich diuresis
6. alkalosis—state of not having enough acid to maintain normal homestatic processes; seen with loop diuretics, which cause the loss of bicarbonate in the urine
7. hyperaldosteronism—excessive output of aldosterone from the adrenal gland, leading to increased sodium and water retention and loss of potassium
8. osmotic pull—drawing force of large molecules on water, pulling it into the tubule or capillary; essential for maintaining normal fluid balance within the body; used to draw out excess fluid into the vascular system or the renal tubule

MATCHING

1. A 2. E 3. C 4. B 5. B 6. A 7. D 8. B 9. D 10. C

CHAPTER 50: DRUGS AFFECTING THE URINARY TRACT AND BLADDER

WEB EXERCISE: Using your web browser, go to http://www.pslgroup.com/ENLARGPROST.HTM. On the home page, click on "Enlarged Prostate Information," then click on "The Prostate Gland" to get information about the location and function of the gland and problems that occur. Print this information, if appropriate. Go back to "Enlarged Prostate Information," click on "Treatment," then select pertinent facts. Finally, return to the home page and scan the other buttons you can click for additional material (e.g., PSA levels, use of the TUNA approach) that might be helpful to your patient.

PATIENT TEACHING CHECKLIST

PATIENT TEACHING CHECKLIST

Urinary Tract Anti-Infectives

A urinary tract anti-infective works to treat urinary tract infections by destroying bacteria and by helping produce an environment that is not conducive to bacteria growth.

If this drug causes stomach upset, it can be taken with food. It is important to avoid foods that alkalinize the urine—for example, citrus fruits and milk—because they decrease the effectiveness of the drug. Cranberry juice is one juice that can be used. Fluids should be pushed as much as possible (8—10 glasses of water a day) to help treat the infection.

Avoid the use of any over-the-counter medication that might contain sodium bicarbonate (*e*.g antacids, baking soda, etc.). If you question the use of any OTC drug, check with your health care provider.

Take the full course of your prescription. Do not use this drug to self-treat any other infection.

Common effects of this drug that you should be aware of include:

- Stomach upset, nausea—Taking the drug with food may help; small, frequent meals may also help.
- Painful urination—If this occurs, report it to your health care provider. A dosage adjustment may be needed.

There are several other activities that could help to decrease urinary tract infections and should be considered while you are taking this drug as well as at other times:

- Avoid bubble baths
- Women should always wipe from front to back, never from back to front.
- Void whenever you feel the urge; try not to wait.
- Always try to void after sexual intercourse to flush the urethra.

Report any of the following to your health care provider: skin rash or itching, severe GI upset, GI upset that prevents adequate fluid intake, very painful urination, pregnancy.

Tell any doctor, nurse or other health care provider that you are taking this drug.

Keep this drug, and all medications, out of the reach of children.

TRUE OR FALSE

1. T 2. F 3. F 4. T 5. F 6. T 7. F 8. T

CHAPTER 51: INTRODUCTION TO THE RESPIRATORY SYSTEM

FILL IN THE BLANKS

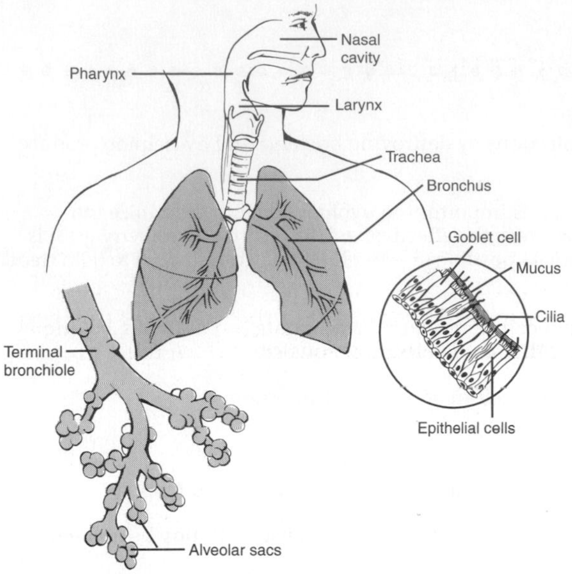

MATCHING

1. K 2. D 3. B 4. J 5. E 6. A 7. C 8. G 9. L 10. F 11. I 12. H

MULTIPLE CHOICE

1. a 2. c 3. d 4. c 5. d 6. b 7. a 8. b

CHAPTER 52: DRUGS ACTING ON THE UPPER RESPIRATORY TRACT

CROSSWORD PUZZLE

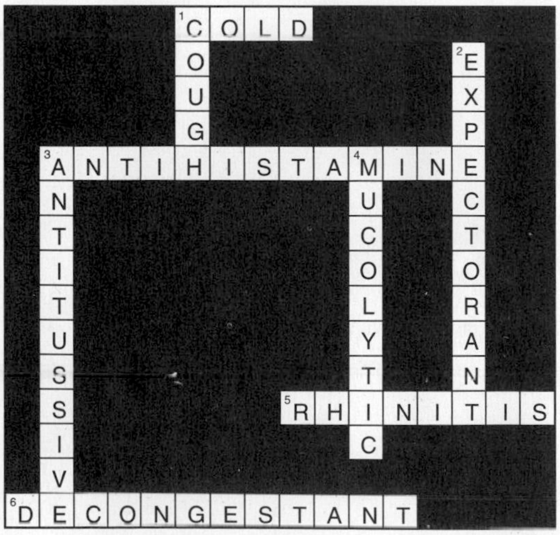

WEB EXERCISE: Using your web browser, go to: http://www.allergy.pair.com/ Select Allergies. Review the disease, symptoms, and treatment. Return to the home page. Select "Links" then go to "AllerDays" where you can select support groups, learning to live with asthma or rhinitis, and other information that may be of interest. Print out pertinent pages to prepare a teaching program for R. W.

WORD SCRAMBLE

1. clemastine
2. dextromethorphan
3. ephedrine
4. tetrahydrozoline
5. pseudoephedrine
6. budenoside
7. fluticasone
8. astemizole

CHAPTER 53: DRUGS FOR TREATING OBSTRUCTIVE PULMONARY DISORDERS

TRUE OR FALSE

1. F 2. T 3. T 4. F 5. F 6. F 7. T 8. T

WEB EXERCISE: Using your web browser, go to *http://www.lungsusa.org/index/html.* Select "Diseases A to Z" from the column on the left, then go to "Tuberculosis." Scroll down through the disease, symptoms, risks, diagnosis and treatments. Return to the home page. Select "research." Return to the home page. At the bottom of the page you can select "find your association" by scrolling down to your state and selecting your area from the map.

WORD SEARCH

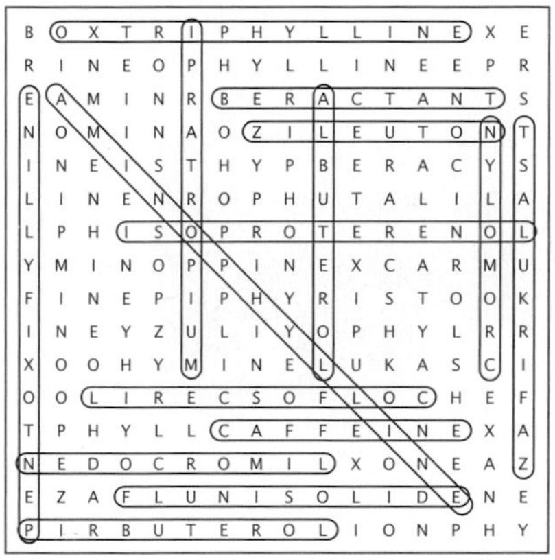

CHAPTER 54: INTRODUCTION TO THE GASTROINTESTINAL SYSTEM

IDENTIFY

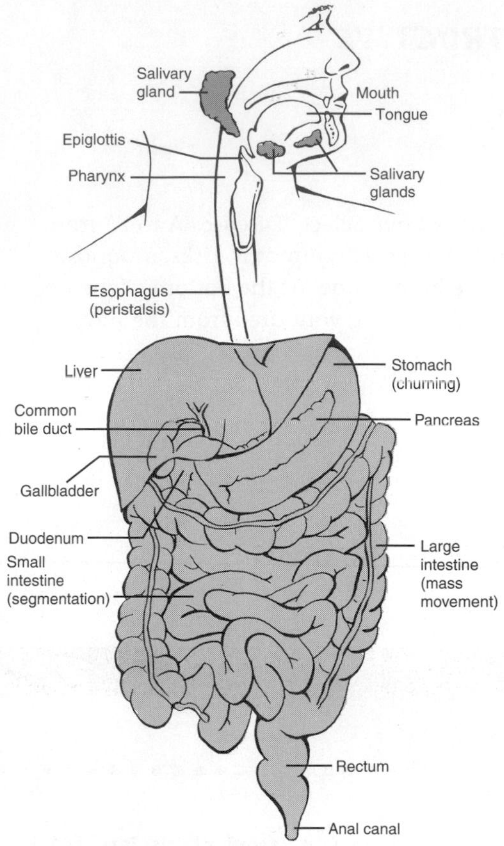

MATCHING

1. F 2. C 3. G 4. H 5. B 6. A 7. E 8. D 9. J 10. I

FILL IN THE BLANKS

1. digestion, absorption
2. acid, mucous
3. nerve plexus
4. sympathetic, parasympathetic
5. local reflexes
6. constipation, diarrhea
7. medulla
8. chemoreceptor trigger zone (CTZ)

CHAPTER 55: DRUGS AFFECTING GASTROINTESTINAL SECRETIONS

WEB EXERCISE: Using your web browser, go to http://www.healthanswers.com. Under the topics section, scroll down to digestive system and select that area. The digestive system section will present a wide variety of GI complaints on the left of the page. Select several different complaints and using the information presented for each one, prepare a teaching session including the following elements: causes, life style changes, decrease occurrence, treatment, and medical follow-up.

CROSSWORD PUZZLE

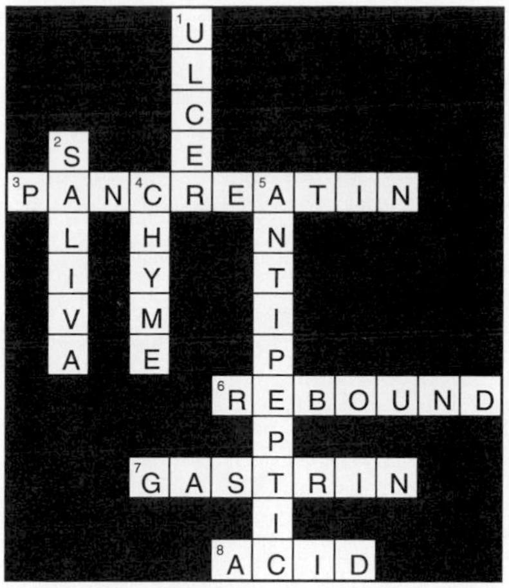

MATCHING

1. E 2. C 3. D 4. A 5. F 6. B 7. B 8. F 9. C 10. A

CHAPTER 56: LAXATIVES AND ANTIDIARRHEAL AGENTS

PATIENT TEACHING CHECKLIST

PATIENT TEACHING CHECKLIST

Laxatives

A laxative works to prevent constipation and to help keep the GI tract functioning on a regular basis. It is used when straining could be dangerous or when a situation arises that constipation might occur.

Common effects of this drug include:

- Diarrhea—Have ready access to bathroom facilities. Consult with your health care provider if this becomes a problem.
- Dizziness, weakness—Change positions slowly, if you feel drowsy avoid driving or dangerous activities and driving.

Report any of the following to your health care provider: sweating, flushing, dizziness, muscle cramps, excessive thirst

Increase your intake of dietary fiber and fluid; try to maintain daily exercise to encourage bowel regularity.

Tell any doctor, nurse, or other health care provider that you are taking this drug.

Keep this drug, and all medications, out of the reach of children.

Special information regarding your situation:

- Take the capsule at bedtime and allow yourself time in the morning for it to work.
- Do not strain or push. If this dose does not work and you are still constipated or feel the need to strain, call the office.

WORD SCRAMBLE

1. cascara 2. loperamide 3. cisapride 4. psyllium
5. senna 6. metoclopramide 7. opium 8. docusate

TRUE OR FALSE

1. F 2. T 3. T 4. F 5. T 6. F 7. F 8. T

CHAPTER 57: EMETIC AND ANTIEMETIC AGENTS

LIST

1. Ingestion of caustic or corrosive mineral acid
2. Ingestion of a volatile petroleum distillate
3. Comatose or semicomatose patient
4. Signs of convulsions

CROSSWORD PUZZLE

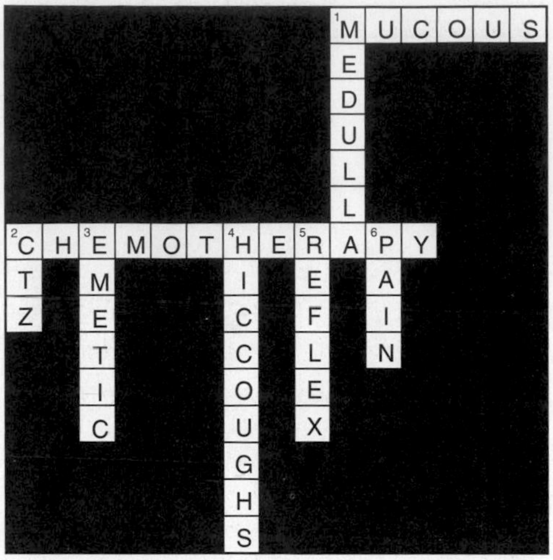

FILL IN THE BLANKS

1. vomiting
2. Ipecac syrup
3. Antiemetics
4. vomiting reflex
5. CTZ, medulla
6. pain, chemicals, uterine stretch
7. CNS depression
8. Photosensitivity

CHAPTER 58: GALLSTONE SOLUBILIZERS

NURSING CARE GUIDE

NURSING CARE GUIDE
Gallstone Solubilizer

Assessment	Nursing Diagnoses	Implementation	Evaluation
HISTORY Allergies to any of these drugs, hepatic dysfunction, bile duct abnormalities, pregnancy (Category X) and lactation	Alteration in comfort related to GI, hepatic effects Alteration in bowel function, related to diarrhea Knowledge deficit regarding drug therapy	Administer twice a day, morning and night. Provide comfort and safety measures: - small, frequent meals - access to bathroom Arrange for regular monitoring of blood tests, radiological exams. Monitor bowel function; consult with prescriber to decrease dose if diarrhea occurs. Provide support and reassurance to deal with drug effects, cost, and long-term therapy. Provide patient teaching regarding drug name, dosage, adverse effects, precautions, and warning signs to report.	Evaluate drug effects: dissolution of gallstones. Monitor for adverse effects: - GI alterations - hepatic dysfunction - elevated cholesterol Evaluate effectiveness of patient teaching program. Evaluate effectiveness of comfort and safety measures.
PHYSICAL EXAMINATION GI: abdominal evaluation Hematological: liver function tests, serum lipids, WBC, serum cholesterol, Tests: hepatic and biliary radiological studies			

WEB EXERCISE: Using your web browser, go to *http://www.mesomorphosis.com/columns/niddk/nih943677.htm.* Print out the information that would be most useful, or copy it to your own system and customize it so that it will be understandable for a nonmedical professional.

TRUE OR FALSE

1. T 2. F 3. T 4. F 5. T 6. F 7. T 8. T